AF527747

SUREŚVARA'S VĀRTIKA ON KHILA KĀṆḌA WITH HALF-VERSE INDEX

ADVAITA TRADITION SERIES

VOL. 9

BOOK ONE

Sureśvara's Vārtika on Khila Kāṇḍa with Half-Verse Index

Edited, Translated and Annotated by

K. P. Jog
Shoun Hino

MOTILAL BANARSIDASS PUBLISHERS PRIVATE LIMITED • DELHI

First Edition: Delhi 1998

ISBN: 81-208-1504-1

MOTILAL BANARSIDASS

41 U.A. Bungalow Road, Jawahar Nagar, Delhi 110 007
8, Mahalaxmi Chamber, Warden Road, Mumbai 400 026
120 Royapettah High Road, Mylapore, Chennai 600 004
Sanas Plaza, Subhash Nagar, Pune 411 002
16 St. Mark's Road, Bangalore 560 001
8 Camac Street, Calcutta 700 017
Ashok Rajpath, Patna 800 004
Chowk, Varanasi 221 001

PRINTED IN INDIA
BY JAINENDRA PRAKASH JAIN AT SHRI JAINENDRA PRESS,
A-45 NARAINA, PHASE I, NEW DELHI 110 028
AND PUBLISHED BY NARENDRA PRAKASH JAIN FOR
MOTILAL BANARSIDASS PUBLISHERS PRIVATE LIMITED,
BUNGALOW ROAD, DELHI 110 007

To

Our Fellow-travellers

in the field of Kevalādvaita Vedānta

श्रीमुखम्

भवन्तः भवदीयबृहदारण्यकोपनिषद्भाष्यवार्तिकांग्लानुवादैकदेशं श्रीजगद्गुरुचरणानां सन्निधौ समार्पयन् ।

शुक्लयजुश्शाखीयायां बृहदारण्यकोपनिषदि आत्मतत्त्वप्रतिपादनं विस्तृततया विहितं वर्तते । ब्रह्मविदामग्रणीः भगवान् याज्ञवल्क्यः विशिष्टया रीत्या अस्यामुपनिषदि तत्त्वं बोधयन् समुपलभ्यते । त्र्य्यन्तसिद्धान्तप्रचारणचणाः श्रीमच्छंकरभगवत्पादाचार्याः अस्या उपनिषदः अनवद्यं भाष्यमरीरचन् । तेषाम् अन्तेवासिषु विद्यया वयसा च ज्येष्ठाः श्रीसुरेश्वराचार्याः तस्य भाष्यस्य हृद्यं वार्तिकं व्यलिखन् । वार्तिकस्यास्य सम्यक्परिशीलनेन वेदान्तसिद्धान्तः असन्देहम् अवगन्तुं पार्यत इति निश्चप्रचं समेषाम् । अत एव अस्य वार्तिकस्य भावं लोकान् अवबुबोधयिषन्तो भवन्त आंग्लानुवादं व्यधासिषुः ।

भवदीयोऽयमुद्यमः प्रशंसनीयो वर्तते । ग्रन्थोऽयम् अपरिचितसुरगिरामपि लोकानां वार्तिकतात्पर्यावबोधनक्षमो भवतु, भवन्तश्च श्रेयःपरम्पराभिः समेधन्ताम् इत्याशासते श्रीचरणाः ।

Private Secretary
To His Holiness Sri Jagadguru Shankaracharya
Dakshinamnaya Srisharada Peetham
Sringeri

FOREWORD

The *Bṛhadāraṇyaka* is the biggest and most important one among principal Upaniṣads and contains numerous discussions of teachers, pupils, questioners and others. It is marked by philosophical speculations not opposed to but in conformity with a vigorous performance of rituals. The *Bṛhadāraṇyaka* reveals to us the towering personality of the great Upaniṣadic thinker Yājñavalkya who affirmed *neti neti*, i.e. indescribability of the Brahman, the ultimate Truth. It is on this basis that Śaṅkara built up his theory of Non-dualistic Vedānta.

Consequently, the Bhāṣya of Śaṅkara on this Upaniṣad has assumed a very great significance in Vedāntic literature. Next to his Bhāṣya on the *Brahmasūtra*– nay almost on a par with it–his Bhāṣya on this Upaniṣad is a vivid picture of the (almost aggressively) vigorous philosophical acumen of the great philosopher. And this is more pronouncingly felt in his references to and the refutations of the arguments of the followers of other systems of Indian philosophy, for they were unavoidable for him while he clarified (in his way—on the non-dualistic way) the thought of the Upaniṣad from which he was distant at least by a period of about 1000 years and since there had intervened between him and the Upaniṣad a number of thinkers of various systems. Yet, since he had set himself to the task of commenting on the Upaniṣad, he inevitably became somewhat brief, leaving quite a lot of disputations unclear (for his contemporaries).

This gave his pupil Sureśvara a scope for clarifying his Guru's thought in its fullness and he wrote the *Bṛhadāraṇyakopaniṣad-bhāṣyavārtika*. The last member of the compound-name, *vārtika*, refers to Sureśvara's discussion of *ukta*, *anukta* and *durukta* portions in Śaṅkara's writing. Sureśvara has underlined every small detail in the varied arguments in the Bhāṣya on the Upaniṣad and clarified the same with characteristic skill. It is noticed that Sureśvara is familiar with minute details of different philosophical systems—Nyāya and Mīmāṃsā, in particular—and therefore he has in a way shaped the Ṭīkā of Ānandagiri, the most read commentator of Śaṅkara's works, thus throwing abundant light on the vigorous philosophical activity of the times which preceded his teacher Śaṅkara and himself.

A special mention has to be made here of Sureśvara's detailed discussions of the views of Bhartṛprapañca, a predecessor or a senior contemporary of Śaṅkara. It may become possible for us, now, to set up a somewhat understandable scheme of Bhartṛprapañca's philosophy on the basis of these. Another significant contribution of Sureśvara deserves special notice. His discussions about the interpretation of Vedāntic passage (implying Mīmāṃsā) and various means of understanding/knowledge (implying Pramāṇavyavahāra or Nyāya) in relation to the Vedāntic logic indeed deserve in-depth studies for purposes of clarifying the method of Non-dualistic Vedānta.

The Vārtika of Sureśvara on the *Bṛhadāraṇyakopaniṣad* is truly his *magnum opus* and needed to be translated in full. I feel happy that Prof. K. P. Jog and his worthy pupil Dr. Shoun Hino have undertaken this important task. I have gone through the earlier parts of this work and find that they have well attempted to secure a satisfactory translation. This translation, I cannot forget to add, is accompanied by some brief annotation on the same. For this work Dr. Hino was awarded the 1991 Eastern Study Prize by the Eastern Institute, Inc. at the Indian Embassy in Tokyo.

Hajime Nakamura

PREFACE

While we present the translations of BU chapters 5 and 6, we should invite the readers' attention to two things. First, we have included here the translations of BU 5.15 and 6.1 even if these were presented in our earlier volumes (of course, for convenient references in the relevant portions. Those translations, we should state, were apparently tentative and had to be sufficiently revised. Therefore, they are not mere repetitions. Besides, they serve their purpose in the contexts in which they find their proper place. Secondly, the readers would feel puzzled to find that, BU chapter 5 has only 15 Brāhmaṇas 'sections' whereas BUBV has 17. This is because Sureśvara has divided the contents of BU 5 into three different Brāhmaṇas:

BUBV 5.5 corresponds to BU 5.5.1,
BUBV 5.6 corresponds to BU 5.5.2, and
BUBV 5.7 corresponds to BU 5.5.3-4.

In all he makes three Brāhmaṇas of one and consequently 17 Brāhmaṇas of 15.

Our friends and colleagues in the Deccan College, Pune have as usual helped us in tracing citations in BUBV and its commentaries to their sources. We acknowledge their help gratefully. Our special thanks go to Prof. K. Macida (ILCAA), Prof. J. Takashima (ILCAA) and Mr. N. Okaguchi. Prof. Macida is a developer of Devanāgarī printing software, called Catur, which has been used in preparing our books, and Mr. Okaguchi is a Devanāgarī font designer.

Our other volumes will soon follow at regular intervals.

Seki (Japan)
Rāma Navamī, Śake 1918

K. P. Jog
Shoun Hino

TABLE OF CONTENTS

Pages

BOOK 1

ŚRĪMUKHAM by Sri Jagadguru Shankaracharya — vii

FOREWORD by Prof. Hajime Nakamura — ix

PREFACE — xi

ABBREVIATIONS — xv

INTRODUCTION — xvii

TRANSLATION AND ANNOTATION

5TH ADHYĀYA — 1

6TH ADHYĀYA — 112

SELECT GLOSSARY — 239

BIBLIOGRAPHY — 243

BOOK 2

HALF-VERSE INDEX OF BUBV — 1

ABBREVIATIONS

AnSS	Ānandāśrama Sanskrit Series
BS	*Brahmasūtra*
BSB	*Brahmasūtrabhāṣya* by Śaṅkara
CU	*Chāndogyopaniṣad*
BU	*Bṛhadāraṇyakopaniṣad*
BUB	*Bṛhadāraṇyakopaniṣadbhāṣya* by Śaṅkara
BUBV	*Bṛhadāraṇyakopaniṣadbhāṣyavārtika* by Sureśvara
SV	*Saṃbandhavārtika* by Sureśvara
NKL	*Nyāyakalpalatikā*
SP	*Śāstraprakāśikā* by Ānandagiri
TUBV	*Taittirīyopaniṣadbhāṣyavārtika* by Sureśvara
Naiṣ	*Naiṣkarmyasiddhi* by Sureśvara

INTRODUCTION

We repeat here the purpose of the Khila Kāṇḍa, i.e. chapters 5 and 6 of the *Bṛhadāraṇyakopaniṣad* as is very succinctly brought out by Śaṅkarācārya thus:

Introducing chapter 5 he writes:

अध्यायचतुष्टयेन यदेव साक्षादपरोक्षाच्च ब्रह्म य आत्मा सर्वान्तरो निरुपाधिकोऽशनायाद्यतीतो नेति नेतीति व्यपदेश्यो निर्धारितो यद्विज्ञानं केवलममृतत्वसाधनमधुना तस्यैवात्मनः सोपाधिकस्य शब्दार्थादिव्यवहारापन्नस्य पुरस्तादनुक्तान्युपासनानि कर्मभिरविरुद्धानि प्रकृष्टाभ्युदयसाधनानि क्रममुक्तिभाञ्जि च तानि वक्तव्यानीति परः संदर्भः सर्वोपासनशेषत्वेनोङ्कारो दमं दानं दयामित्येतानि च विधित्सितानि । ...

'The foregoing four chapters have declared that the Brahman which alone is immediately and directly perceptible, which is the inner self within all (beings), which is not affected by any delimiting adjuncts, which is beyond hunger etc. and which can be described (merely) as 'Not this, not this.'; (viz. that Brahman) the knowledge of which is a means to attaining immortality. Now are to be considered (or, described) the so-far-not-mentioned modes of worship of that very Ātman (viz. the Brahman) which is delimited by adjuncts, which has been within the (worldly) dealings involving words and (their) senses (or, objects signified), which are not opposed (in nature) to (ritual) activities, which are excellent means of achieving (worldly) prosperity, and which (can) achieve (for an individual) gradual liberation. This is the purpose of the ensuing (portion of the Upaniṣad). (As such) the Śruti intends to prescribe (the worship) of

Om as an ancillary part of all of them (i.e. modes of worship), the control (in one's conduct), making of gifts and having (i.e. showing) compassion (for others). ......'

Introducing chapter 6 he writes:

न ... पूर्वशेषता। विवक्षितं तु खिलत्वादस्य काण्डस्य पूर्वत्र यदनुक्तं विशिष्टफलं प्राणविषयमुपासनं तद् वक्तव्यम् ... ।

'This chapter does not form a remainder of its preceding. But, as this Kāṇḍa has the nature of a supplementary (of the main part of the Upaniṣad),[1] it is to be stated here what has not been described before, what has specific results (to yield), viz. the worship of (or, better, meditation on) Prāṇa 'the vital force (in the body)'.'

It is evident from this extract from BUB that the contents of these two chapters are hardly philosophical in nature. They are purely descriptive of various modes of the worship of the Brahman, or various meditations related to those things which are not the Brahman and have yet to be looked upon as the Brahman. These worships can be considered as leading basically to worldly prosperity and indirectly to liberation.

In chapter 5, the objects of worship (or, meditation) are mainly the different parts or organs of the body, viz. the heart (sometimes called as *satya*), *manas*, *vāc*, the fire in the stomach (*vaiśvānarāgni*); then *vidyut* 'lightning', *tapas* 'heat', food, Prāṇa 'the principal wind in the body'; *uktha*, *yajus*, *sāman*, *kṣatra*—these four have to be looked upon as Prāṇa, the (well-known) Gāyatrī (Mantra) and thus, representing the combination of knowledge and action, these culminate into the worship of Āditya. that is, principally Agni.

In chapter 6 is taken up the meditation on Prāṇa abiding in the eye, ear etc. It is reaffirmed that among all of the organs etc. Prāṇa is the most shining, i.e. most important. It is then related to the *pañcāgnividyā* 'the lore of five fires', as becoming the origin (or, source) of a human body (*retas*) and, for emphasising this, a narrative of Śvetaketu Gautama is introduced. Also, in connection with *retas* becoming waters in the fifth *āhuti* of the *pañcāgni* worship, there is a description of the Devayāna and Pitryāna paths. As a trail of this comes a very brief statement about the funeral of a dead man, whether he knows or not the significance of the *pañcāgnividyā*. Then follows (as *retas* is already mentioned) the description of the Mantha rite for begetting a son and also, as a matter of course, a man's uniting with his wife, according to the dictates of Dharma as well as an incidental *abhicāra karman*.

In the end, there is a statement of the line of teachers related to the whole the Khila Kāṇḍa.

Now, a few general observations have to be made in relation to the various Brāhmaṇas of these two chapters. In other chapters, most of the sections bear each a name for it, but the sections in the 5th and 6th chapters do not bear each any name—apparently, there was no significance in any name.

Also, since there have been descriptions of such modes of worship as are connected with the non-Brahman (or, mundane) objects, there is a clear tendency to be traced from the Upaniṣadic times (particularly, the time of BU) and also, consequently, in Śaṅkarācārya and his followers to assimilate what are called popular notions of deities and rites offered to them with the staunch Vedāntic theory (or, *dogmas*).[2]

In almost the concluding part of the 6th chapter are noticed some aspects of the laterly known Gṛhya- and Dharma-sūtras in relation to a man's pursuit of *kāma* 'sex-desire and act', a beginning (also) of the thought in the *Kāmasūtra*, and man's attitude towards women; the notions of black magic (*abhicāra*) connected with the same also cannot be overlooked.

It has to be observed that, though he has almost closely followed Śaṅkarācārya, Sureśvara has occasionally dropped a few of his thoughts, that are expressed in BUB at great length. We have left it for the readers to see this for themselves, inasmuch as Sureśvara has not missed the spirit of the original.

In the end, we have to add a word about the Half-Verse Index of BUBV appended to the translation of these chapters of BUBV. Sureśvara is often noticed to have written verses of one line and/or three lines in addition to the normal verses of two lines. These lines, by themselves, form at times complete units of thought. Of course, in the third line of a three-line verse also, an independent thought has found expression. Therefore, the Half-Verse Index has to be preferred to Verse Index (viz. *pratīka* Index). This renders it more suitable to trace Sureśvara's thoughts *inter alia*.

Notes

[1]Hume has observed that the supplementary nature of this (Kāṇḍa) is in accordance with the heterogeneous nature of its contents. (*The Thirteen Principal Upaniṣads.* p.7)

[2]This may be assumed, to some extent, to justify that Śaṅkarācārya wrote Stotras addressed to various deities of popular worship.

****

BOOK 1

BṚHADĀRAṆYAKOPANIṢAD-BHĀṢYA-VĀRTIKA

5.1

समाप्तं याज्ञवल्कीयं काण्डमैकात्म्यनिष्ठितम् ।
खिलकाण्डमथेदानीं यथावदुपवर्ण्यते ॥१॥

The Kāṇḍa of Yājñavalkya which dealt with the singleness of the Ātman is concluded. Now then is explained (lit. described) the Khila Kāṇḍa 'Kāṇḍa of the remainder'. [1]

संभावितं न यत्पूर्वं कर्मविज्ञानकाण्डयोः ।
तदत्र भण्यते सर्वं खिलकाण्डत्वहेतुतः ॥२॥

Whatever was not treated earlier in the two Kāṇḍas pertaining to activity and knowledge is now all (of it) stated here, since this forms the remainder (of the same). [2]

अपास्तनिखिलध्वान्ततज्जं ब्रह्मोपवर्णितम् ।
पूर्वैश्चतुर्भिरध्यायैर्यद्धीः कैवल्यसिद्धये ॥३॥

The earlier four Adhyāyas dealt with (lit. described) the Brahman from which all ignorance about and the product of it (viz. ignorance) were far removed (lit. thrown away)—(that Brahman) whose knowledge results into the achievement of liberation. [3]

सोपाधिकस्य तस्यैव व्यवहारानुपातिनः ।
उपासनानि वाच्यानि यान्यनुक्तान्यतः परम् ॥४॥
प्रकृष्टाभ्युदयार्थानि क्रममुक्तिकराणि च ।
क्रियाभिश्चाविरुद्धानि वाच्यानीति परा श्रुतिः ॥५॥

Hereafter are stated those (modes of) worship of that same

(Brahman), which is delimited by adjuncts and which is subjected to worldly dealings and then such (modes of) worship as were not stated (earlier). [4]
The subsequent portion of the Upaniṣad (begins with the purpose) to state (those modes of worship) which are for the sake of excellent worldly prosperity, which cause gradual liberation and which are not opposed to (ritual) activities. [5]

This is in brief the statement of the contents of the Khila Kāṇḍa.

तथोंकारं दमं दानं दयामित्यादिकानि च ।
सर्वोपास्त्यङ्गभूतानि वक्तव्यानीति यत्यते ॥६॥

So then (*tathā*) an effort is made to state *om*, *dama* 'restraint' *dāna* 'gift-making' and *dayā* 'compassion' etc.[1] which have been the ancillaries of all modes of worship. [6]

[1]By the word etc. are understood the future (i.e. after-departure) movement of one, the oneness of the Ātman and the results attained.

कार्यकारणसंबन्धव्याजमाश्रित्य तत्परम् ।
व्याख्यातं यत्नतः पूर्वमात्मज्ञानप्रसिद्धये ॥७॥

Earlier, that highest (reality) was explained with care, by resorting to the false relation between causes and effects,[1] in order that one should acquire the knowledge of the Ātman. [7]

[1]This refers to the basic falsity (*mithyātva*) of the discussion on *kāryakāraṇasaṃbandha* among worldly objects.

चरितार्थत्वतस्तस्य कार्यकारणवस्तुनः ।
निषेधायेयमुक्तिः स्यात्पूर्णमित्येवमादिना ॥८॥

This statement in the words *pūrṇam* ... is[1] for rejecting (the existence) of the thing(s) comprising effects and causes, because that (or, they) has (or, have already) fulfilled the purpose. [8]

[1]*asti* is for *syāt*.

न व्यावृत्तमिदं सर्वं पराक्प्रत्ययमानगम् ।
नानुवृत्तं तथैवैतन्नाप्यभावैकनिष्ठितम् ॥९॥

All this world is (really) not distinguished (from it[1]), (because) it is understood by the means of knowing (which are) outside (the inner self). Similarly, this is not comparable (to it[1]) and also it is not based on (or, supported in) only non-existence.[2] [9]

[1]This refers to the Brahman which obtains everywhere (among all worldly things).
[2]One cannot ignore this world of objects, since it fulfils one's desires.

In verses 10-27 Sureśvara gave the meaning of pūrṇam adaḥ ... in the tradition known to him.

अव्यावृत्ताननुगतमात्मप्रत्ययमीरितम् ।
यस्मात्पूर्णमिदं साक्षात्तादात्म्यं तेन वर्ण्यते ॥१०॥

Since this *pūrṇa* is stated to be neither distinguished from nor similar to (any other thing) and is experienced in one's own self, therefore there is described here its oneness[1] with the Ātman. [10]

[1]It literally means: 'being of the same nature of the Ātman-Brahman'. This verse refers to the inner self which experiences the world of objects.

अज्ञातमिथ्याविज्ञाततत्त्वमात्रैकनिष्ठितम् ।
सम्यग्ज्ञानं यतस्तस्मात्पूर्णं तज्ज्ञेयमुच्यते ॥११॥

Since right knowledge rests on only the truth (lit. being that Brahman) which is either not known or falsely known, therefore that *pūrṇa* is stated as what is to be known. [11]

These two verses give the purport of the sentence beginning with the words *pūrṇam adaḥ*, viz. the Brahman within every being.

गोत्ववन्नानुवृत्तं यन्न व्यावृत्तं च खण्डवत् ।
अनन्यमानमानन्दं पूर्णं तदभिधीयते ॥१२॥

That *pūrṇa* is described as what is not (continuously) existent (in many) like cowness and what is not distinguished (from any other) like (some cow called) Khaṇḍa. It is described as not having any means of knowing (it), other than itself, bliss and (only) full. [12]

The second line is the reason for *atyantaparokṣatva* (of the Brahman).

अदः परोक्षमत्यन्तं सर्वकार्यस्य कारणम् ।
कार्यानुमेयं तद्विद्यात्पूर्णमात्रसतत्त्वकम् ॥१३॥

(The pronominal form) *adaḥ* refers to what is entirely (*atyantam*) beyond perception, the cause of all effects and one should understand that as what can be inferred from the effect(s) (it is merely *pūrṇa* in nature). [13]

इदं यज्जनिमत्किंचिन्नामरूपक्रियात्मकम् ।
प्रत्यक्षाद्यवसेयं यत्पूर्णं तदपि पूर्ववत् ॥१४॥

In the same way as before (i.e. in the preceding statements), that also is *pūrṇa* which is this, viz. whatever has origin, whatever is of the nature of name, form and activity and whatever is to be grasped (*avaseya*) by (the means) such as direct perception. [14]

This is the meaning of *pūrṇam idam*. SP adds that the two words *adaḥ* and *idam* refer to what are expressed and indicated by the usually known word *tvam*. So also the mention together of the four words *pūrṇam adaḥ pūrṇam idam* purports to establish the oneness of both which are conveyed by *adaḥ* and *idam*.

कार्यकारणयोश्चेष्टा पूर्णात्पूर्णमितीर्यते ।
वस्तुवृत्तमिदं तावत्प्रागपि ज्ञानसंगतेः ॥१५॥

In the statement *pūrṇāt pūrṇam* is conveyed the activity (*ceṣṭā*) of the cause(s) and the effect(s). This refers just to the function of the (worldly) things,[1] but that is (to be known as occurring even) before the acquisition of the right knowledge (of the same). [15]

[1]Two explanations can be offered in this respect. The 'thing' can refer (i) to the worldly thing, for one understands the same while one is only under the influence of ignorance (*avidyā*), (ii) to the Brahman, which is in reality the cause of all the apparent relations of causes and effects.

अथ हेतुफलावेशनिषेधाय परं वचः ।
पूर्णस्य पूर्णमादाय पूर्णमेवावशिष्यते ॥१६॥

Then, the subsequent statement (*vacaḥ*), viz. *pūrṇasya pūrṇam ādāya pūrṇam evāvaśiṣyate*, serves the purpose of rejecting the introduction of the idea of the result and the cause. [16]

ब्रह्म वा इदमित्यादि मधुकाण्डे यदीरितम् ।
तदेव पूर्णमित्यादिवाक्येनेहोपसंहृतम् ॥१७॥

What was stated (earlier) in the Madhu Kāṇḍa, viz. *brahma*

vā idam etc., is itself finally concluded here[1] by the statement beginning with *pūrṇam*. [17]

[1]This refers to the Khila Kāṇḍa.

अपीताखिलकार्यं सत्तमोमात्रावशेषगम् ।
भास्वत्स्वार्थं चिदेकस्थमदः पूर्णमिहोच्यते ॥१८॥

In the sentence *adaḥ pūrṇam* is stated that the sentience, the existent which has withdrawn (in itself) all (the so-called) effects, which rest in only the remainder, i.e. darkness,[1] which reveals itself (only in) brightness and which resides only in one. [18]

What was explained as the Brahman in BU first Adhyāya is explained here in the sentence *pūrṇam adaḥ*.
[1]This refers to existence of worldly objects.

तमोन्वितं च यत्कार्यं साक्षिणः साक्ष्यतां गतम् ।
प्रत्यक्षमागमापायि विद्यात्पूर्णमिदं तथा ॥१९॥

So also should one understand *pūrṇam idam* (to be referring to) whatever is effect, associated with darkness and which has become perceived by the perceiver (viz. the sentience within), which is directly perceptible, and which comes into existence and (also) to an end. [19]

Verses 18 and 19 form a pair to describe reality succinctly.

ईशक्षेत्रज्ञयोरेवं तमस्तज्जाभिसंस्थयोः ।
सामानाधिकरण्यादेर्वाक्यादैकात्म्यमुच्यते ॥२०॥

Thus is conveyed the oneness of the Lord and the knower of the field[1] who rest on[2] darkness and its effects by putting the two in *samānādhikaraṇa* in the sentence. [20]

SP adds that this verse implies the meaning of *pūrṇasya pūrṇam ādāya* ... to be the same as of *tasmāt tat sarvam abhavat*.

[1]These refer to the Ātman or Parātman and Jīva 'the inner self'.

[2]Literally, are related to.

क्षेत्रज्ञेश्वरभेदेन ह्यभिन्नं वस्त्वविद्यया ।
भिन्नं बोधात्तमोध्वस्तौ नेतीत्यात्मावशिष्यते ॥२१॥

One and the same thing (*abhinnam*), is (understood) through ignorance as the knower of the field and the Lord, viz. as two distinct objects; and owing to the knowledge (of their real nature) from the sentence *neti neti* there results the removal of darkness and (consequently) there remains only the Ātman. [21]

न भेदो न च संसर्गो नाप्यभावोऽवसीयते ।
तन्मूलाज्ञानविध्वस्तेर्यथोक्तागममानतः ॥२२॥

Neither distinction nor contact (of the two distinct ones) nor even their non-existence is concluded (from the sentence *pūrṇam* etc.), since there has occurred the destruction of the basic ignorance (about the nature of) the two, as already stated by the scripture which is other means of knowing (reality). [22]

स्रगज्ञानमनादाय तदुत्थैः संगतिः स्रजः ।
नैव संभाव्यते यद्वत्तथेहात्मनि वीक्ष्यताम् ॥२३॥

As unless one has ignorance about a wreathe there cannot be any connection of the wreathe with the (notions) that have arisen from it (viz. ignorance); so also, should it be understood about ignorance etc. with respect to the Ātman. [23]

कार्यकारणयोर्ध्वस्तावपूर्वाद्युक्तिबोधतः ।
आत्मप्रत्ययमागम्यः स्वार्थं आत्मावशिष्यते ॥२४॥

From the understanding of the statement, viz. *apūrvam* ..., (when there results) the removal of (the notion of) cause and effect, (there follows) only one meaning, viz. the Ātman, which is understood from the means of knowing, viz. the awareness of the Ātman. [24]

In the word *ātmapratyaya-mā-gamya* in the third quarter, *mā* is to be understood as *māna*.

यादृगस्य द्वये रूपमात्मनैवावगम्यते ।
तावदेव हतान्ध्यस्य तदन्यानवशेषतः ॥२५॥

What is understood by one by oneself (*ātmanā*) as a form of this (Ātman) while (there exists) duality,[1] only that much (i.e. the same) is really (the form) of it from which darkness[2] has been removed; for there does not remain anything else than that. [25]

[1]It literally means: a pair of the Ātman and the *jagat*.
[2]This stands for ignorance.

यदेवेहेति च तथा मन्त्रोऽप्युच्चैर्जगाद नः ।
अन्यदेवेति च श्रुतिः कार्येतरनिषेधिनी ॥२६॥

So also, the Mantra *yad eva* ...[1] has here[2] emphatically (lit. loudly) declared and also there is a Śruti, viz. *anyad eva*,[3] which rejects anything else than the effect.[4] [26]

[1]*Kaṭhopaniṣad* 4.10.
[2]This implies words *tad amutra*, *yad amutra*, *tad anv iha* from the Upaniṣad quoted in the preceding note.
[3]*Īśopaniṣad* 10, 13; *Kenopaniṣad* 1.4.
[4]This refers to *kāraṇa* and hereby is *kāraṇakāryabhāva* rejected.

आत्मेतिदृष्टेर्मेयत्वं स्वार्थावगतितोऽपरम् ।

नान्यदुत्सहते वोढुमिति पूर्वमवादिषम् ॥२७॥

Since there is a knowledge[1] (that all this is) the Ātman, nothing else than that can have the character of an object to be known—so have I said earlier.[1] [27]

[1]This refers to a passage *ātmani jñāte sarvaṃ jñātaṃ bhavati.*

In verses 28-63c states Bhartṛprapañca's view on pūrṇam adaḥ....

एवं यथोदिते तावत्प्रमाणार्थेऽप्यवस्थिते ।
अन्यथेदं वचः केचिद्व्याचख्युरतिनैपुणात् ॥२८॥
पूर्णमित्यादिवाक्यस्य षष्ठान्त्यवचसा सह ।
वक्तुकामो हि संबन्धमेवं यत्नादचीक्लृपत् ॥२९॥

When such has been the meaning (understood from) the authoritative means (viz. Śruti),[1] as stated (herebefore), others[2] have explained this statement (*vacaḥ*) in another way (and) with great skill. [28]
Because he, wishing to point out (i.e. see) the connection of the statement *pūrṇam* ... with the last statement of the sixth Adhyāya,[3] has presented (lit. imagined) with effort (his opinion) thus: (i.e. in what follows).[4] [29]

[1]As stated in the preceding verses.
[2]The reference is to Bhartṛprapañca—here in the plural; in the next verse, in the singular.
[3]This refers to BU 4.5.15, *yatra hi* ... Sureśvara numbers that Adhyāya as 6, according to the tradition known to him.
[4]This is made clear in verses 30ff.

द्वैताद्वैतात्मकं ब्रह्म मैत्रेय्यै वर्णितं किल ।
यत्र हि द्वैतमित्युक्त्या यत्र त्वस्येति चादरात् ॥३०॥

Indeed (*kila*) the Brahman which is of the nature of duality and non-duality is explained to Maitreyī in the statement *yatra hi dvaitam* ... and also in *yatra tv asya* ... with great regard (for the Śruti).[1] [30]

[1] Cf. BU 4.5.15.

यद्यद्वैतं परं ब्रह्म तत्र स्यात्परमार्थतः ।
कल्पितं प्रसजेद्द्वैतं तोयबुद्धिरिवोषरे ॥३१॥

If there (i.e. in the statement) was (mentioned) in reality the highest Brahman, viz. the non-dual (Brahman), there would contingently follow duality as merely what is imagined, in the same way as the apprehending of water in a barren place. [31]

मृषात्वाद्भेदजातस्य सर्गस्थित्याद्यसंभवात् ।
सर्गस्थितिलयानां स्यादन्वाख्यानं मृषैव तु ॥३२॥

Since it is impossible that there is origin, sustenance etc.[1] of the (world of) discrete objects, for the reason that they are false, a restatement of their origin, sustenance and merger would only be meaningless (lit. false). [32]

[1] This includes merger (which is later specifically mentioned).

श्रवणप्रतिपत्ती च व्यर्थे स्यातां तथाद्वये ।
अथ स्वेनैव रूपेण द्वैतमस्तीति भण्यते ॥३३॥
अन्वाख्यानं सतामेव सर्गादीनां तथा भवेत् ।

And so also in respect of the non-dual (reality, i.e. Ātman) there will be meaningless hearing, and pondering over (the same).[1] Then again (if it is said that) there is duality as a state of reality— [33]
then there would be restatement of what are (already existent objects) in respect of origin etc. [34ab]

This verse would imply the authoritativeness of the Upaniṣad which states *śrotavyo mantavyo nididhyāsitavyaḥ.*

[1]This is *śravaṇa* and *pratipatti* to which is to be added *nididhyāsa*.

तथाप्यद्वैतसंदृष्टेर्मृषात्वं स्याद्विरोधतः ॥३४॥
परिकल्पिततादोष एवमत्र प्रसज्यते ।
तद्दोषापनुनुत्सायै पूर्णमित्यादिका श्रुतिः ॥३५॥

But in that case also, there would follow from the acceptance of non-duality faslehood as opposed to it. [34cd]
Thus, there would follow the fault, viz. only imagining notions and, therefore, out of a desire for the removal of that fault, there is a Śruti beginning with *pūrṇam*. [35]

न कश्चिदपि दोषोऽत्र यथा तदभिधीयते ।
स्वानुभूत्यनुसारेण सर्वं सुस्थं भवेदतः ॥३६॥

Now is explained as to how there is not in this statement any fault, so that, in accordance with one's own experience, all would be well-stated (lit. put) in order. [36]

अदः परोक्षमत्यन्तं कारणं पूर्णमुच्यते ।
व्योमवद्व्यापि सद्ब्रह्म सर्वतोऽनवखण्डितम् ॥३७॥

adaḥ is what is entirely beyond perception and *pūrṇa* is stated to be the cause, viz. that existent Brahman, the all-pervasive like the sky, and everywhere as not consisting of parts (lit. not divided). [37]

ब्रह्मणो याद्वयावस्था सैव तावदिहोदिता ।
एवं चेदद्वयं ब्रह्म द्वैतावस्था न सिध्यति ॥३८॥

So far is stated the state of the Brahman, viz. of non-duality alone. Now, if this is so, i.e. the Brahman is non-dual, then there would not result the state of duality. [38]

इति दोषनिषेधार्थमिदं पूर्णमितीर्यते ।
यथोक्तावस्थयोर्मा भून्मृषात्वं ब्रह्मणः सदा ॥३९॥

Therefore, for avoiding (i.e. rejecting) that fault is stated *pūrṇam idam*; this (with the idea that) there would not ever be falsehood regarding the Brahman with respect to the two states that are already mentioned. [39]

पूर्णब्रह्मपरिज्ञानाव्यतिरेकत्वहेततः ।
अदोवत्कार्यमप्येतत्पूर्णमेवावसीयताम् ॥४०॥

(Therefore) for (the reason that) the effect has no distinction from (the cause, viz.) the *pūrṇa* Brahman consisting in all-sided knowledge (*parijñāna*) this *kārya* also is to be finally considered as *pūrṇa* like that (Brahman).[1] [40]

[1] *adah* refers to what is *parokṣa* 'not perceptible', in contrast with what is perceptible (*idam*).

पूर्णेनाभेदतः कार्यं पूर्णं स्यान्न मृषा श्रुतेः ।
यद्यतो नातिरेकेण तत्तदेवेति निश्चितिः ॥४१॥

The effect also would be *pūrṇa* on account of its non-distinction from *pūrṇa* (cause)—this would not give falsehood to the Śruti; for, the decision (in this regard) is: that which[1] is not in addition to (i.e. beside) what[2] it has come from (viz. the cause) is only that. [41]

Both NKL and SP only refer to *ghaṭa* and *śarāva* as examples. This needs some explanation. *ghaṭa* and *śarāva* are products of clay and are at the same time not different from it. That implies that the effect in the form of the wind is not different from its cause in the form of the Ātman.

[1] This refers to effect.

[2] This refers to cause.

एवं तर्ह्येकरूपेऽस्मिंस्तत्त्वे सत्ये समर्थिते ।
ततः सर्गाद्यभावः स्यादेकरूपतया स्थितेः ॥४२॥

(It is argued against Bhartṛprapañca:) If this is so, viz. that the truth if justifiably held to be this reality, which is only oneness; then there would follow the non-existence of the origin etc. since the reality has existed only in one form. [42]

This is an argument of the followers of Śaṅkara against Bhartṛprapañca.

नैवं यतः श्रुतिः प्राह पूर्णात्पूर्णमुदच्यते ।
पूर्णात्कारणतः पूर्णं द्वैतमेतदुदच्यते ॥४३॥

(Bhartṛprapañca's answer would be:) This is not so, since Śruti (itself) has declared *'pūrṇa* has come out of *pūrṇa'* i.e. from the *pūrṇakāraṇa* has the *pūrṇa*, viz. duality originated. [43]

The thought in verse 42 is related only to cause-effect relation between things (which are essentially one). Yet this verse specifies the Śruti *'pūrṇa* has come out of *pūrṇa'* as a specifier of the real distinction between the cause and the effect, according to Bhartṛprapañca.

यस्मादुद्रिच्यमानं हि द्वैतं नैवातिरिच्यते ।
तदेवोद्रेचनं चेत्स्याद्द्वैतस्येति मतं यदि ॥४४॥

If it is argued:[1] Duality does not exist beside (i.e. in addition to) what it has originated from—that is the (real nature of) the origin of duality. [44]

[1]This verse is yet another argument against Bhartṛprapañca.

नैतदेवं कुतो यस्माद्दृष्टहानं प्रसज्यते ।
प्रत्यक्षतो हि दृष्टोऽयं द्वैताख्यो विषयः स्फुटः ॥४५॥
तथा दर्शनतः सिद्धो विधितश्चावसीयते ।

प्रामाण्योच्छेद एव स्याच्छ्रुतेरेवं समर्थने ॥४६॥

(The argument is answered thus:) This is not so. Why? Since there follows as contingent the rejection of what is actually seen—indeed this world of objects is clearly perceived directly. [45]

(The world of objects) is established thus by direct perception and also by injunction(s). And there would be, in your justifying (the unreal nature of that world) with the help of the Śruti, (complete) discarding (lit. destroying) the authoritativeness (of the Śruti). [46]

This verse explains the *dṛṣṭatva* and *śrutatva* of this world (*idam*).

पारमार्थ्यं क्वचिच्छास्त्रं क्वचिच्चाप्यनृतात्मताम् ।
विदधन्मानतां जह्यात्परस्परविरोधतः ॥४७॥

(Thus), stating (lit. prescribing) at some place(s) the character of the ultimate reality and at some other(s) that of falsehood (i.e. unreality) of the same, the Śāstra[1] (i.e. Śruti) would give up its reliability as an authoritative means owing to mutual contradiction (in its own statements). [47]

This clarifies the thought of verse 46cd above.

[1]The definition given by Ānandagiri on BUB 5.1.1:
pravṛttir vā nivṛttir vā nityena kṛtakena vā /
puṃsāṃ yenopadiśyeta tac chāstram abhidhīyate //

पूर्णत्वेनाजहद्वृत्त्या त्रिष्वप्यध्वसु वर्तते ।
द्वैताद्वैतात्मकं ब्रह्म पूर्णत्वेनाविभागतः ॥४८॥

The Brahman, having the nature of duality and non-duality, exists as *pūrṇa*, by its not giving up its nature[1] of the three *adhvans*,[2] viz. as the *pūrṇa* Brahman without having any division in itself. [48]

[1]This is the meaning of *vṛtti*, viz. its usual existence.
[2]They are the three periods of time as noted in verse 55 below.

कुतोऽविभागो मानाच्चेदुभयोरप्यवस्थयोः ।
पूर्णादित्यादिवचनान्महाप्रलय आत्मनि ॥४९॥

(A question is asked:) 'Why is this absence of division?' The answer is: On the basis of Śruti in respect of both the states and also from the statement *pūrṇāt* ..., they have final merger in the Ātman. [49]

This is Bhartṛprapañca's explanation of the undivided nature of the Brahman as stated in the preceding verse; he refers to the state of duality at the time of *mahāpralaya* 'final merger'.

इदं च द्वैतमस्त्येव तथादोऽद्वैतमेव च ।
पूर्णत्वाख्याजहद्वृत्त्या समुद्रोर्मिवदीक्ष्यताम् ॥५०॥

And thus duality does exist and so also (does exist) that, viz. the non-duality, therefore, from the description (of the Brahman) as *pūrṇa* by its not giving up the (natural) existence (viz. the state of being undivided), let this be seen (i.e. understood) as in the case of the ripples on the ocean. [50]

The ripples on the ocean are seen at times and at other times they again merge in the water; in both these states the water and the ripples of the ocean are but one and real. This is the example for *pūrṇa* Brahman consisting in duality and non-duality.

अग्रे चलत्वमूर्मीणां मध्य ईषच्चलात्मता ।
निष्कम्पत्वं तथा मूले समुद्रः सर्वरूपभृत् ॥५१॥

In the beginning, there is undulating of the ripples and later (lit. in the course of their existence) there is a very gentle undulating, and the absence of undulating in its initial states—only the ocean has assumed all (these different) forms. [51]

This verse explains *samudrormivat* in the preceding verse.

यथैता यौगपद्येन वृत्तीरूर्मिभिरात्मनः ।
अनुभूयन्त एकत्र देवदत्तादिके तथा ॥५२॥

As these are simultaneously the different functioning forms of the ripples (of the ocean), so also (various functions) are noticed (lit. experienced or seen) in only one and the same Devadatta and others[1] [52]

[1]This refers to various knowers known as Caitra and Maitra. This is clarified fully in the two following verses.

निष्कम्पा देवदत्तस्य वृत्तिः स्यात्परमात्मना ।
ईषत्प्रचलिता प्राणभावेनेत्यवगम्यते ॥५३॥
विराड्भावेनातितरां चण्डप्रचलितोर्मिवत् ।
ऊर्म्यग्रवत्पिण्डभावे नामरूपक्रियात्मना ॥५४॥

There would be a flutterless function of Devadatta, who is (in the state of) the highest Ātman;[1] the same is seen as slight fluttering on his becoming the Prāṇa (identical with the individual self)—so is this understood. [53]

And in his being Virāj, it is like the exceedingly agitating ripples(s)—thus, in the nature of name, form and activity, (the Ātman) has become embodied (*piṇḍa*) like the upsurging ripples. [54]

[1]This is to be understood in the sense of the Sūtrātman.

जनिस्थितिलयेष्वेवं त्रिषु कालेषु पूर्णता ।
कार्यकारणयोर्ज्ञेया द्वैताद्वैतस्वभावयोः ॥५५॥

Thus, in the three states of origin, sustenance and merger and in the three periods of time, there is to be understood the character of *pūrṇa* in the cause(s) and effect(s) which are by nature duality and non-duality. [55]

सा चैकैवाविभागत्वात्कार्यकारणभेदतः ।
भेदेन व्यपदेशार्हा सर्वमेवं समञ्जसम् ॥५६॥

And that[1] is just one, on account of being undivided and is to be described as existing in distinct things on account of the differences, viz. cause(s) and effect(s); all this is thus reasonable. [56]

[1]This is *pūrṇatā* in verse 54.

आविर्भावतिरोभावैः कार्यकारणरूपिभिः ।
समुद्रवन्नृत्यति च प्रत्यवस्थं विभुः स्थितः ॥५७॥

The all-pervading (Ātman) has, in each of its states, continued to exist through its appearance and disappearance in the form of the causes and the effects, dancing (as it were) like the ocean. [57]

एवं द्वैतस्य सत्यत्वे कर्मकाण्डस्य मानता ।
अनन्तपुरुषार्थाप्तिरिष्यते कर्मकाण्डतः ॥५८॥

Thus, in (accepting) the reality abiding in duality, (there follows) the authoritativeness of (what is called) the Karmakāṇḍa; and from the Karmakāṇḍa is expected (to be realised) the accomplishment of the infinite end of human life. [58]

This expresses the result from accepting duality.

यदा तु कल्पितं द्वैतमद्वैतं परमार्थतः ।
उच्छिन्नं कर्मकाण्डस्य प्रामाण्यं विषयादृते ॥५९॥

When, however, duality is taken as the product of imagination and non-duality as the ultimate truth, then the authoritativeness of the Karmakāṇḍa is entirely to be given up (lit. destroyed), owing to the absence of the object (to be accomplished). [59]

एकदेशस्य चामात्वे वेदस्याप्यप्रमाणता ।
सर्वनाशो भवेदेवं सर्वाप्रामाण्यहेतुतः ॥६०॥

Further, in accepting one part of Vedas as unauthoritative, there follows the unauthoritativeness of the Veda[1] and thus there would follow the loss of everything in life for the reason that the whole has become unauthoritative. [60]

Already Bhartṛprapañca holds the Karmakāṇḍa as authoritative, but if that part of the Veda is held as unauthoritative, the Veda, in its entirety, cannot be accepted as authoritative—this is a complete loss!

[1]This is for the Vedānta texts, according to NKL.

अतो विरोधनुत्त्यर्थं सत्यत्वप्रतिपत्तये ।
कार्यकारणयोः शास्त्रं पूर्णमित्यादिनावदत् ॥६१॥

Therefore, in order to ward away the opposition (between the effect(s) and the cause(s)), the scripture has stated *pūrṇam* ... so the truth of the Śāstra is established. [61]

प्रत्यक्षादीनि मानानि भेदग्राहीणि सर्वदा ।
तेषां चाप्यप्रमाणत्वं प्रापदद्वैतवादिनः ॥६२॥

(Indeed) the means of knowing, viz. direct perception etc., ever accept objects which are distinct; therefore, there would result for the propounder of the non-dual (Ātman), unauthoritativeness of them[1] (also). [62]

[1]These are the accepted means of knowing.

इति वेदविदः केचिद्भिन्नाभिन्नसतत्त्वकम् ।
सर्वं वस्त्वभिवाञ्छन्ति

Thus do some knowers of the Vedas (i.e. Vedānta) hold (lit. wish) that all the things (in the universe) are of the nature of discrete and non-discrete objects.[1] [63abc]

[1] That is, being different in being non-different also.

Now in verses 63d-94 follows the refutation of Bhartṛprapañca's view.

तत्तु युक्त्या न युज्यते ॥६३॥

But that (view) is not supported with reasoning. [63d]

न युक्तिमदिदं गीतं ह्यपवादविकल्पनम् ।
न्यायासंभवतः स्पष्टं स च न्यायो विभाव्यते ॥६४॥

Indeed this division (of the Vedic statement into the general rule and) its exception is not favoured by reason (i.e. *tarka* or *nyāya*); this is clear from the want (lit. impossibility) of (proper) reasoning. And that reasoning is now examined (lit. considered). [64]

अहिंसन्सर्वभूतानीत्यहिंसा सर्वभूतगा ।
शास्त्रेणोत्सर्गतः प्राप्ता तीर्थे सापोद्यते यथा ॥६५॥

(Now) non-violence pertaining to all beings is known from the scripture in the general rule *ahiṃsan sarvabhūtāni* ... and that (*ahiṃsā*) is accepted (by the scripture) in (relation to) a sacrifice.[1] [65]

This verse points out the *utsargāpavāda* notion of the Karmakāṇḍa.

[1] Namely, the Agniṣomīya rite.

न तथेहाद्वयावस्था श्रुत्योत्सर्गेण यत्नतः ।
प्रापिता तद्विशेषेऽसौ निर्भागत्वान्निषेधभाक् ॥६६॥
विकल्पानुपपत्तेश्च षोडशिग्रहणादिवत् ।
वस्तुतन्त्रं हि नो मानं कर्तृतन्त्रं विकल्पते ॥६७॥

Not in that way[1] has the Śruti presented to us[2] the non-duality here[3] in the form of a general rule, in such a way as to offer possibilities of option;[4] nor also does it purport to reject some specific part of it,[5] since it is devoid of any parts, [66]
and because there cannot be (here)[3] any reason for (stating) an option as in the case of taking up of the *ṣoḍaśi-graha*.[6] Our authoritative means of knowing is dependent only on the (real) thing[7] and what is dependent[7] on the agent (of activity) can leave scope for option. [67]

The Advaita Vedānta distinguishes between the means of knowing as *vastutantra* and *kartṛtantra*. The first does not leave for a knower any option of understanding about the nature of the object to be known, viz. the Brahman. The second, however, depends on a knower's wish to undertake the performance of a ritual (which is conveyed by some injunction) or not to do so; as, for example, the taking up of a cup called Ṣoḍaśin—the sacrificer may or may not take it up. The *vastutantra* leads only to one end, viz. liberation. [More details of Mīmāṃsā can be overlooked.]

[1] As in the preceding verse.

[2] That is, informed us of ....

[3] That is, in respect of the Brahman.

[4] 'In such ... option' is based on SP's observation: *yatnas tu prāptau niṣedhe cobhayatra sambadhyate*.

[5] That is, partless non-duality, i.e. the Brahman.

[6] Ṣoḍaśi is the proper name of a cup to be drunk at the Atirātra sacrifice, optionally. The general note above clarifies this point.

[7]The two terms *vastutantra* and *kartṛtantra* (or, *puruṣatantra*) distinguish between the Vedānta and Pūrva-Mīmāṃsā notions regarding the authoritative means of knowing. For the Vedānta, the Brahman is all: *jñātṛ*, *jñeya* and *jñāna* (instrument of knowing). As such, knowledge about the Brahman depends only on the thing, viz. Brahman, itself. In Pūrva-Mīmāṃsā, however, the *jñātṛ* etc. are all different. As a consequence, the performance of the rituals (which is the purport of the Karmakāṇḍa) depends entirely on the performer (*kartṛ*) who is the knower; this leaves scope for his performing or not performing the ritual activity—that is, there is scope for option.

यत्कर्तुं वाप्यकर्तुं वाप्यन्यथा कर्तुमेव वा ।
कारकैः शक्यते लोके तद्विकल्पस्य गोचरः ॥६८॥

In the world that is the subject of option which is possible (for the performer) (i) to do, or (ii) not to do, or (iii) to do otherwise. [68]

Thus Sureśvara states his idea of the province of *vikalpa.*

परस्परविरोधाच्च नैकदैकत्र संभवः ।
द्वयोरवस्थयोर्यद्वत्प्रकाशतमसोरिह ॥६९॥

And, therefore, here, in respect of these two states (of non-duality and duality), there is no possibility of their existence in one and the same thing and at one and the same period of time, owing to their mutual opposition, as in the case of light and darkness. [69]

ekadā, *ekatra* refer to the three *adhvan*s already mentioned in verses 48 and 55 above.

श्रुतिन्यायविरोधाच्च कल्पनेयमशोभना ।
अपूर्वानपरानन्तप्रज्ञानैकरसाद्वयम् ॥७०॥
अपूर्वानपराबाह्यं भेदसंसर्गवर्जितम् ।

अस्थूलं नेति नेतीति यथोक्तार्थे वचांसि हि ॥७१॥

And (thus), owing to the opposition to Śruti and to reasoning (both), this view is not proper. (And) *apūrvānaparānanta-prajñānaikarasādvayam*;[1] [70]
apūrvānaparābāhyaṃ bhedasaṃsargavarjitam,[2] *asthūlam*[3] (and) *neti neti*[4] are (the Śruti) statements pointing to the matter as stated (by us). [71]

[1]BU 2.5.19.
[2]BU (Mādhyandina) 3.8.8.
[3]BU 3.8.8.
[4]BU 3.9.25; 4.2.4; 4.4.22; 4.5.15.

अमात्वाशङ्कासद्भावाद्यथोक्तार्थविनिश्चितौ ।
अब्धौ क्षिप्तानि तानि स्युरन्यार्थासंभवत्वतः ॥७२॥

And those statements would be thrown into the ocean, if there is a decision regarding the already stated object (i.e. the single Ātman) to be otherwise, owing to the possible fear of the unauthoritativeness (of them)—this is so, since there is no possibility of the existence of any (other) object. [72]

anyārthāsambhavatvataḥ is for *-sambhavāt*.

तथा न्यायविरोधोऽपि क्रियाकारकरूपिणः ।
जडाध्रुवानात्मनो हि त्वत्कृता कल्पनेष्यते ॥७३॥
न तु चिन्मात्ररूपस्य ध्रुवानंशात्मनः स्वतः ।
नित्यत्वं चात्मनः सिद्धं प्रत्यभिज्ञादिमानतः ॥७४॥
प्रसजेत्तद्विरोधश्च भिन्नाभिन्नत्ववादिनः ।
कल्पनायाश्च वैफल्यमनित्यत्वे परात्मनः ॥७५॥

So also, your view is entertained here in respect of what is of the nature of activity and agent and in respect of the non-Ātmans that are insentient and not imperennial—and thus there is opposition to reasoning. [73]

And there is not established from (your) means of knowing (the character of the agent etc.) in the case of the Ātman, which exists in its own right (*svataḥ*) as only sentient in nature, perennially partless and eternal. [74]
Then there would follow contingently opposition to that by the view of one who holds difference in non-difference and, consequently, there would be fruitlessness resulting from the highest Ātman being taken as imperennial. [75]

अकृताभ्यागमः प्राप्तः कृतनाशश्च सत्वरः ।
कर्मकाण्डस्य वैफल्यमेवं कल्पयतो भवेत् ॥७६॥

(Thus) there follows the acceptance of what is not done and also immediately (i.e. close on its heels) the destruction of what is performed. Thus, for one who has thus entertained this view (of difference in non-difference) there would result the meaninglessness (lit. fruitlessness) of the Karmakāṇḍa. [76]

मकरी ननु दृष्टान्तो भिन्नाभिन्नत्वसिद्धिकृत् ।
ब्रह्मणः प्रागुपन्यस्तोऽसाध्वीयं कल्पना कथम् ॥७७॥

(The objector puts forth one argument yet:) 'Indeed, we have earlier stated the illustration of the sea [1] to prove the duality and the non-duality of the Brahman; how then is this theory improper?' [77]

[1]That is, having crocodiles in it. The word *makarī* stands ordinarily for a female crocodile, but here it refers to the sea.

अतोऽन्यविषयत्वात्सोऽविरोधः प्रागुदीरितः ।
न तु चिन्मात्ररूपस्य ह्यत्रावोचं विरुद्धताम् ॥७८॥

(This is an answer to it:) That (illustration), which you have earlier stated, is unopposed (to our theory), since it has some other thing [1] for its subject matter (*viṣaya*), but not for what has only sentience as its form. And here, in this respect,[2]

I have said that there occurs opposition (to your illustration). [78]

[1]Here, there is reference to the Sūtra and the following embodied state of the Brahman which are accepted by the Vedāntin.
[2]This refers to *cinmātra*. Cp. verses 73-75 above.

नाध्येयत्वाच्च शास्त्रार्थकल्पनेयं त्वया कृता ।
षड्भावविक्रियं वस्तु ध्येयं वक्ति न हि श्रुतिः ॥७९॥
स्वतस्तस्य च संप्राप्तेर्विनाप्यागमशासनम् ।
ध्येयत्वेनेह सर्वेषां खरोष्ट्रादेरपीक्षणात् ॥८०॥

[In verse 80, the Siddhāntin states how various objects of meditation are not the subject matter taught in the scripture.]

And this opinion regarding the object of scriptures[1] is not to be studied, because the Śruti does not state as the object of meditation any entity which undergoes six modifications. [79]

And also because that[2] is obtained by itself,[3] without (even) an injunction in the scripture (and also because) there are noticed among all the objects to be thought of (such objects as) a mule, a camel etc. [80]

Verse 80 refers to what is called the Advaita view of Vedānta, the *vyavahārabhūmi* 'the world of various objects known' through the adoption of *pramāṇa-prameya* relation among them.
[1]This refers to what is thought by Bhartṛprapañca in the scripture.
[2]This refers to the variety of objects as objects of meditation.
[3]This is referring to actual experience.

एकधैवानुविज्ञेयमिति च श्रुतिशासनम् ।
भेददृष्ट्यपवादाच्च मृत्योरिति विनिन्दनात् ॥८१॥

Further, there is an instruction in the Śruti, viz. that (reality) is to be known as but one;[1] and this is because there is exception taken to seeing variety of things and since there is censure of the same in the words *mṛtyoḥ* ....[2] [81]

[1]Cf. BU 4.4.20: *ekadhā* ....

[2]Cf. *Kaṭhopaiṣad* 4.10-11; BU 4.4.19: *mṛtyoḥ* ....

यत्तूक्तं वेदभागत्वाद्भिन्नवस्त्ववबोधिनः ।
नामात्वं कर्मकाण्डस्येत्यत्र प्रतिविधीयते ॥८२॥

As to what is stated, viz. 'The Karmakāṇda, which informs us about discrete things, being a portion of the Veda is not authoritative', there now follows an answer (to it): [82]

न हि जात्यादिसंभेदसंसिद्धौ मानता श्रुतेः ।
प्रत्यक्षाद्यनवष्टब्धे तस्यामात्वं यतः स्थितम् ॥८३॥

Indeed the Śruti is not authoritative in respect of establishing variety such as *jāti*.[1] And this is so, since the unauthoritativeness of that (variety) is established for the reason that reality is not dependent on (the means) such as direct perception. [83]

Verse 82 has referred to the variety of objects. Therefore, that raises two questions: whether the Karmakāṇḍa refers to that variety as what is to be accepted in reality or that is to be taken as unreality. The first line answers the first question, whereas the second line answers the second one.

[1]This refers to various classes of society.

भेदग्राहि न नो मानं लौकिकं वैदिकं च यत् ।
अविचारितसंसिद्धिस्तस्माद्भेदोऽवसीयताम् ॥८४॥

For us, it cannot be a means of knowing, which accepts discreteness of objects; be it popularly (accepted) or the Vedic. Therefore, let it be concluded that the variety (of the objects of knowing) is established (even) without any thought(-activity). [84]

While commenting (only too briefly) on this verse, SP states about the means thus: *pratyakṣādīni śāstrāṇi bhedagrāhīṇi anyonyāśrayatvāt*. This is made clear in the following verses.

न स्वतः परतो वायं भेदो वस्तुन ईक्ष्यते ।
सर्वस्यैव स्वतोऽभित्तेस्तदन्यस्याप्यभेदतः ॥८५॥

Indeed this discreteness among all the things[1] is not established on account of itself or any other thing/means. (This is so) because (in the first instance) all (that variety) is itself non-different from itself[2] (and secondly) any other (distinct thing, if it is granted to be existent) also cannot be shown as distinctly existent.[3] [85]

[1]*vastunaḥ* (singular) signifies *vastūnām* (plural).
[2]The first part of the second line sets aside a possible idea that all different things cannot be said to be distinct from themselves—if it is so said, that would result into stating that there are no things in existence. Read SP: *sarvaṃ vastu svasmād abhinnam anyathā vastvabhāvaprasaṅgāt*.
[3]The second part of the second line affirms that there cannot be shown anything as distinct from all the things (itself being included among them). Here also, read SP: *parato 'pi (vastuno) bhedo na prāmāṇiko 'sti ... vastuno 'nyatveneṣṭasyāpi na sattvam (bhedasyādyāpy asiddheḥ)*.

वस्तु वस्त्वन्तरं भिन्द्याद्योगाद्यद्वा विभागतः ।
योगे नातिशयैकत्वात्तयोश्चाप्येकरूपतः ॥८६॥

A thing can distinguish another thing (from itself) by either its union (with it) or its separation from the same. In case (it is accepted that) there is a union of them, (then such distinguishing is) not (possible), because there exists some common (lit. one excellence) in them and (consequent) oneness of them. [86]

विभागेऽपि न भेदः स्यात्तयोरेकात्मना स्थितेः ।
अन्यदीयोऽपि नान्यस्य भेदः स्यात्कल्पनां विना ॥८७॥

Further, in respect of their differentiation, there is no (possibility of) variety (of differences) since both of them remain as having only one nature. And there cannot exist the difference of the other thing unless there is a notion that there exists another thing. [87]

This refers to an actual separation obtaining between two things. *yoga* refers to 'union' of two things.

In connection with this verse, SP points to a variant reading: *yoge 'natiśayaikatvāt* and remarks on the same: *bhedo 'tiśayas tasmād anyas tatprayojakasambandho 'natiśayas tasyaikyān na bhedaḥ syāt*.

मेययाथात्म्यसंलेहि मानं मानत्वमश्नुते ।
भेदं न लभते मेये मेयादन्यत्र न प्रमा ॥८८॥

A means of knowing becomes an (authoritative) means, if it touches (i.e. brings out) the true nature of the object to be known. It does not exist in the object to be known as a distinct (object). Right knowledge cannot obtain elsewhere than in the object to be known. [88]

The argument is: Since difference from the thing itself cannot naturally exist, there is doubt about its property as existing apart from it—but that is impossible.

सतो न व्यतिरेकेण भेदो नापि सदन्वयात् ।
यथैवं नासतोऽप्येवं भेदो नैवावसीयते ॥८९॥

A distinct object (does not exist) in addition to (or besides) the existent (viz. reality): nor (does it exist) as associated with (it[2] as a part of) the existent (reality). As this is so, so also there cannot exist beside the non-existent any (other) distinct object—such is the conclusion. [89]

सर्वं सदेव यस्येष्टमथवासदिदं जगत् ।
भेदः किमाश्रयस्तस्य विरोधान्न द्वयाश्रयः ॥९०॥

For him, who has accepted (lit. desired) all this as the existent alone or this as non-existent, what could be the substratum of the distinction among objects? Because it is opposed to (distinct, that distinction objects) there cannot have any duality as its substratum. [90]

SP states that the Sāṃkhyas, the Buddhists and the Jains are meant here to have the opinion expressed in the verse.

अन्यापेक्षं पृथक्त्वं चेत्स्वत एवापृथग्घटः ।
बलीयानन्तरङ्गत्वाद्बहिरङ्गं प्रबाधते ॥९१॥

If it is held that distinction depends on something other than itself, then (it has to be said that) the pot is distinct from itself. The external aspect of a thing, being stronger than the internal property, stultifies it. [91]

This is to disprove the existence of distinction among objects with reference to the views of the Tārkikas.

द्रव्याद्भिन्नं पृथक्त्वं चेदनवस्थैति सत्वरा ।
द्रव्यमेव पृथक्त्वं चेदपृथक्स्यादिदं जगत् ॥९२॥

If the distinction of some substance is considered to be different from the substance itself, then there quickly follows *infinite regress*. If again substance itself is the distinction (of itself), then this world (also) will be non-distinct. [92]

स्वतश्चेद्वस्तुनो भेदो वस्तु शून्यं प्रसज्यते ।
आपेक्षिकोऽपि क्लृप्तत्वान्न भेदो रज्जुसर्पवत् ॥९३॥

(Again) if the distinction of something comes from itself, the thing will be only void (*śūnya*). The distinction also, being imagined, would (really) be non-difference as between a rope and a serpent (imagined in its place). [93]

Verses 94-100 are related to the discussion on the Karma Kāṇḍa being unauthoritative.

इत्येवमादि बहुशो भिन्नाभिन्नत्वदूषणम् ।
प्रागप्युक्तं तदत्रापि संधेयं वस्तुसिद्धये ॥९४॥

This and such other manifold fault (in the view regarding) difference in non-difference has been explained (by us) on a number of occasions (even) before; that has to be remembered (lit. brought into this discussion) even here so that (the nature of) the thing (viz. the reality for Brahman) is established. [94]

अपि वेदैकदेशस्य प्रामाण्यं यदि नेष्यते ।
कर्मकाण्डस्य सर्वस्य वेदस्यापि प्रसज्यते ॥९५॥

And this could be said (*api vā*);[1] if it is not desired that one part of the Veda, viz. the Karmakāṇḍa, is not authoritative, then (that) unauthoritativeness follows contingently in respect of the whole of the Veda. [95]

[1]In *api vā* for introducing an alternative, Sureśvara follows Yāska, the author of the *Nirukta*.

इति यत्प्रागुपन्यस्तं तस्य दूषणमुच्यते ।
साध्यसाधनसंबन्धे तस्यापीष्टा प्रमाणता ॥९६॥

(Now) is stated a fault with respect to what has been thus

stated. (For,) that also has to be accepted as an authoritative means, when there is reference to the relation between what is to be accomplished and what accomplishes it. [96]

भेदः प्रमान्तरैः सिद्धो न त्वागमसमाश्रयात् ।
पशवोऽपि हि जानन्ति भेदमक्षादिमानतः ॥९७॥

Distinction (among different objects) is established by different cognitions and not by resorting to the Āgama (i.e. Veda). Even animals do know such differences with (the help of) the means called direct perception etc. [97]

[1]This refers to different results from different contacts of different sense-organs with different objects.

न च मिथ्यात्वधीर्भेदे जन्मनैवेह कस्यचित् ।
अप्युत्थापितबुद्धीनां भेदेऽसंभावना न च ॥९८॥

Further, the awareness of falsehood in respect of distinction among objects does not find in anyone right from their origin. So also, there cannot be impossibility of the awareness of distinction in the case of those whose intellect has been awakened (by someone). [98]

According to SP, the second line seems to refer to the followers of the Buddha and such others who do not hold the falsehood of distinct object. So also, it should apply in the case of those who do not accept the authority of the Veda.

क्रियाकारकसंभित्तौ वस्तुतत्त्वेन मा श्रुतिः ।
साध्यसाधनसंबन्धमात्रैकविषयत्वतः ॥९९॥

Let not the Śruti be considered as the means of (determining) the distinctions such as actions and their means since (it relates to) the true nature of the thing (called reality) whereas the distinctions have for their subject matter only the relation (among those distinct objects) as the ends and the means. [99]

The aim of the verse is to affirm the real silence of the Śruti in respect of the imaginary world of differences.

लोकसिद्धमतो भेदमादायेष्टार्थसिद्धये ।
इदं कार्यमिदं नेति वेदशास्त्रं प्रवर्तते ॥१००॥

Therefore, (only) having accepted what is popularly established as the distinct objects, the Śruti proceeds to establish what can be desired by men, viz. this should be done and not this. [100]

सर्वतस्तु विरक्तो यः कर्मभिः शुद्धधीर्नरः ।
कामयानः पूर्णफलमुत्पत्त्यादिविलक्षणम् ॥१०१॥
तमोमात्रान्तरायत्वात्प्रतीचः पूर्णरूपिणः ।
स्वतःसिद्धत्वतस्तस्य व्यञ्जकं नान्यदीक्ष्यते ॥१०२॥

As for a person of purified intellect, (who has become) averse to all (the worldly things) and is desirous of the result of fullness[1] that is different from origination etc.[2] [101]
does not expect any (thing else) that reveals the inner self, which has merely ignorance as the cover of obscurity, which is of the nature of the full and of the self-established. [102]

However AnSS reads: *vyañjakānnānyad īkṣyate*.
[1]*pūrṇaphalam* is for *pūrṇatvaphalam*.
[2]The word etc. refers to *āpyatā*, *saṃskāryatā* and *vikāryatā*.

स्वतः प्राप्तस्य संप्राप्तौ वाक्यान्मोहप्रहाणतः ।
मानापेक्षा न भूयः स्यात्फलाप्तेस्तत्कृतार्थतः ॥१०३॥

(In the case of that) which has come into existence, on its own, and caused by the (scriptural) sentence after there is destruction of the ignorance (about its own nature), there is not any more an expectation of a means (towards obtaining that), since the result is already obtained and its own end is (already) achieved. [103]

साध्ये हि साधनापेक्षा सिद्धेऽसौ विनिवर्तते ।
किम्वसाध्ये समस्तस्य पूर्णत्वेन समाप्तितः ॥१०४॥

Indeed, in the case of what is to be achieved there is need of some means (towards the achievement) and that (*sādhanāpekṣā*) ceases to be there when (the end) is (already) achieved. What then could one say in the case of that which is complete in itself and already obtained, since it is *pūrṇa* and therefore is not an end to be achieved? [104]

द्वैताद्वैतात्मकं ब्रह्म यदाण्वभ्युपगम्यते ।
तदापि न विरोधोऽयं केनचिद्विनिवार्यते ॥१०५॥

(And) when the Brahman, which might be even very minute (in form), is accepted as of the nature of the dual and non-dual (of the world), even then there will not be any opposition to this argument and that (argument) cannot be set aside by anyone. [105]

समस्तव्यस्तभूतस्य ब्रह्मण्यवसितात्मनः ।
ब्रूत कर्मणि को हेतुः सर्वानन्यत्वदर्शिनः ॥१०६॥

Say what reason is there for the activity of the one which has culminated into the Brahman, which has the nature of totality and also severality and which hs fully grasped that all are not anything else (than the Brahman). [106]

सर्वजात्यादिमत्त्वे च परस्परविरोधतः ।
व्याघातान्न प्रवृत्तिः स्यान्निषेधेऽथ विधौ तथा ॥१०७॥

(An objection is raised:) And in the case (that the Brahman) has all the castes etc.[1] (within itself), there will occur mutual opposition (among the duties of those castes etc.) and thus there would arise obstruction and there will be no activity since that would amount to prohibition (*niṣedha*) regarding (every) injunction.[2] [107]

[1]The word etc. refers to the various religious duties assigned to them.

[2]The case would be that an injunction would require the performance of some duty as a Brāhmaṇa and that performance will be prohibited for the same person being a Kṣatriya etc. This would result into non-performance of all the ritual that is prescribed by the Śāstra.

न चावच्छेदमानित्वं विदुषोऽस्त्यासुरत्वतः ।
विदुषोऽप्यासुरत्वे स्यान्निष्फलं ब्रह्मदर्शनम् ॥१०८॥

(The answer is:) And indeed there is not on the part of the knower (of the nature of the Ātman) any awareness of the limiting adjuncts (on it) owing to that being of demoniac nature. And in case there is this demoniac nature on the part of the knower then the knowing (lit. seeing) the Brahman would be only meaningless (lit. fruitless). [108]

तस्मादसदिदं गीतं भिन्नाभिन्नत्वसिद्धये ।
श्रुतिन्यायविरुद्धत्वात्प्रकृतं त्वधुनोच्यते ॥१०९॥

Therefore, (all) this which is stated (lit. sung) for establishing the nature of dual and non-dual (Brahman) is opposed to (both) the Śruti and reasoning. There is now stated what is begun (relevant in the Upaniṣad). [109]

Now follows the explanation of oṃ khaṃ brahma.

ओं खं ब्रह्मेति मन्त्रोऽयं श्रुत्येह ध्यानकर्मणि ।
नियुज्यते फलप्राप्तौ यथा तदभिधीयते ॥११०॥

Now as to how this Mantra, viz. *oṃ kham brahma*, it is enjoined here by the Śruti in respect of (i.e. in the context of) the activity of meditation. As to how it leads to attaining the result is now explained. [110]

परस्य ब्रह्मणः साक्षाद्याथात्म्याधिगमो यथा ।
पूर्वैश्चतुर्भिरध्यायैस्तथा श्रुत्योदितोऽञ्जसा ॥१११॥
अस्यैव प्रतिपत्त्यर्थमुपासनमथोच्यते ।
ओं खं ब्रह्मेति वचसा पुंसां श्रेयोऽभिवाञ्छताम् ॥११२॥

As regards the aquisition of the direct awareness of the oneness (of the individual self) and the highest Brahman there has been clearly stated in the four preceding Adhyāys as of the Śruti, [111]
Now a mode of worship[1] for acquiring this (desired result) is stated in the words *oṃ kham brahma*; this is for men who wish for bliss. [112]

[1]Here *upāsanam* means *dhyānam* 'meditation'.

ब्रह्मेतीह विशेष्यार्थः खमित्यपि विशेषणम् ।
सामानाधिकरण्योक्तेस्तद्वृत्तिः कृष्णसर्पवत् ॥११३॥

In this (sentence), the word Brahman signifies the object to be qualified and (*api*) the word *kham* is the attribute (qualifying it); (this is understood from) the occurrence of these two words) in *samānādhikaraṇa*[1] and this is so as in the case of (the statement:) a black sepent. [113]

[1]*samānādhikaraṇa* refers to their occurring in the substratum and grammatically in the same case relation. In the case of a black serpent, blackness and serpentness coexist, similarly Brahmanness and *kha*ness coexist. SP adds the example of *nīlam utpalam*.

प्रवृत्तिर्ब्रह्मशब्दस्य बृहद्वस्त्वेकगोचरा ।

खेन तद्विशिनष्टयत्र सामान्यांशैकपातिना ॥११४॥

The currency (lit. function) of the word *brahman* belongs to the greatest[1] thing (i.e. Brahman) only; (Brahman) the Śruti qualifies it by the *kha* which occurs as a part in that which is generality. [114]

[1]Literally, biggest.

अनाकाशस्वभावेभ्यः खेन ब्रह्म निवर्त्यते ।
तथाब्रह्मस्वभावेभ्यः सामर्थ्याद्ब्रह्मणा च खम् ॥११५॥

(As) the Brahman is set away by the word *kha* from all that have the nature of *ākāśa*; so also is *kha* set away from what do not have the nature of the Brahman, on account of the strength of the Brahman. [115]

सामान्यमात्रवाचित्वात्खशब्दस्य विशेषणम् ।
पुराणमिति निर्वक्ति कारणप्रतिपत्तये ॥११६॥

Because the word *kha* is expressive of (the sky) in a general way, therefore the Śruti has used[1] the word *purāṇa* 'the ancient one' with a view to conveying the cause of) the varied objects.[2] [116]

[1]Literally said in the word *nirvakti*; there is no purpose served by the proposition *nis* ordinarily *nis* before the verb root *vac* 'to derive, to occur'. Generally, it is used for signifying the function of etymologising a word.

[2]This is for avoiding any *tanmātra*s and gross elements.

यत्तद्ब्रह्म खमित्युक्तं तदोंशब्दाभिधानकम् ।
चिन्तयेत्सततं धीमानोमालम्बनमेव वा ॥११७॥

That Brahman which is mentioned as *kha* has for its name the word *om*. Thus should an intelligent man ever think, or (he should consider it) as a prop (or symbol of meditation). [117]

एतदालम्बनं श्रेष्ठमिति च श्रुतिशासनम् ।
एतेनैवाक्षरेणेति ह्यथर्वाणोऽप्यधीयते ॥११८॥

And there is an instruction of the Śruti *etad ālambanaṃ śresṭham* ....[1] And the followers of the *Atharvaveda* recite in their tradition *etenaiva akṣareṇa* ....[2] [118]

[1]This refers to *Kathopaniṣad* 2.17.
[2]This refers to *Praśnopaniṣad* 5.5.

अतीन्द्रियत्वात्तस्यापि कथं स्यात्तदुपासनम् ।
वायुरं खमिति प्राह तदालम्बनसिद्धये ॥११९॥

(A question is asked:) 'Since that also is beyond the sense-organs,[1] how could there be a meditation on it?' (The answer is:) The Śruti has said *vāyuraṃ kham*,[2] in order that that can be established as an object of meditation. [119]

[1]This is to indicate that it cannot be an effect or a cause.
[2]This means it is the support of wind, therefore perceptible and, as such, it can serve as an object of meditation.
Compare *madhura* or *dhīra*, derived by adding of suffix to the word *madhu*, *dhī*; therefore, *vāyura* is that which has the support of *vāyu*. The word is used only here—so Vadekar/Limaye have pointed out.

Now follow in the next three verses an objection raised by one born from Kauravyāyāṇi.

खं पुराणं न विज्ञेयं मन्त्रेऽस्मिन्निति मन्यते ।
कौरव्यायणिजो धीमान्वायुरेतिप्रसिद्धितः ॥१२०॥

The intelligent son of Kauravyāyaṇi thinks that *kham* in this

Mantra should not be taken as the ancient sky (*kha*), because the word *vāyuṛa* comes from what is well-known (from perception). [120]

रूढ्या वृत्तिः खशब्दस्य वायुरे व्योम्नि लक्ष्यते ।
बहुशश्च प्रयोगोऽतो वायुरं खं प्रतीयताम् ॥१२१॥

The word *kha* is by usage seen to refer to the sky, which is *vāyura*. So also, there is the usage (or employment of it in language); therefore, let it be understood that there is in the word *kham* reference to the sky. [121]

पुराणं यदि तद्व्योम यदि वा वायुरं भवेत् ।
ध्येयं तदोमिति सदा पक्षयोरुभयोरपि ॥१२२॥

[This verse answers two questions: (i) is there a reference to *kha* as the causal Brahman? and (ii) is there a reference to the elemental sky?; which is better?]

Whether the sky be the ancient one or whether it be the support of wind, that has to be ever meditated on as *om*—this is held true in respect of both these views. [122]

आलम्बनतयोंकार उपास्तिविषयो भवेत् ।
चतुर्भुजाङ्कितं दारु विष्णोरिव निगच्छति ॥१२३॥

The word *om* becomes[1] the object of meditation as a prop in the same way as people understand[2] a piece of wood which is marked by four hands as Viṣṇu[3] having them. [123]

[1]*bhavet* for *bhavati*.

[2]This is singular use in the form of *nigacchati* for referring to the entire mass of men.

[3]This indicates Sureśvara's reference to common practice of Viṣṇu worship at his time. In the example, a piece of wood etc., the four hands are taken as a prop (or symbol) of Viṣṇu.

नेदीयो ब्रह्मणः स्थानमोमितीदं प्रतीयताम् ।
शालग्रामो हरेर्यद्वत्सर्वानर्थापहारिणः ॥१२४॥

Let this (letter) *om* be uderstood as the nearmost expression (lit. *sthānam* 'place') of the Brahman; for, a black stone called *śālagrāma* would be a symbol of Viṣṇu who removes all the undesirable situations or things (in a man's life). [124]

यद्वाभिधानमों विद्यात्तस्यैव परमात्मनः ।
तस्मिन्निविष्टचित्तस्य तद्ब्रह्माशु प्रसीदति ॥१२५॥

One should know that *om* is the name of the highest Lord, in the case of a person who has fixed his mind on that (viz. highest Ātman), the Brahman would quickly be pleased with him. [125]

SP clarifies here under this verse that *om* as standing for the four states in the life of a human being are comparable to those described in the *Māṇḍūkyopniṣad*.

ओंकारो वेद एवेति ब्राह्मणास्तु प्रचक्षते ।
वेदैनेन यतो वेद्यं ब्रह्म वेदस्ततो मतः ॥१२६॥

And the Brāhmaṇas say that the word *om* is but the Veda, since by this one knows the knowable Brahman. Therefore, (the word *om*) is accepted as Brahman. [126]

अभिधानतयैवैनमोंकारं विदुरञ्जसा ।
ब्राह्मणास्तदभिध्यानाद्विदन्ति ब्रह्म निर्भयम् ॥१२७॥

Thus, the Brāhmaṇas have understood very smoothly the word *om* as a name (of the highest Ātman). By meditation on it do they attain to that Brahman, which is (the state of) fearlessness. [127]

वेदोऽयमिति चोक्तिः स्याद्यथोक्तोपासनं प्रति ।
स्तुतित्वादर्थवादोऽयं नातोऽन्योऽर्थोऽवसीयते ॥१२८॥

So also the statement 'This is Veda' is with reference to the meditation. This is a statement of praise and, therefore, not any other object is to be decided by it. [128]

उद्गीथादिप्रभेदेन यं वा संविद्रते द्विजाः ।
वेदोऽसाविति विज्ञेयस्त्रय्यास्तत्र समाप्तितः ॥१२९॥

The one, which the twice-born have known[1] as differentiated in the Udgītha etc.,[2] is to be known as this Veda, for there is included in that the three Vedas (*trayī*). [129]

[1]The word *saṃvidrate* is rather unusual in later Sanskrit; only in *Ṛgveda* do we find a form *vidre*. So, the variant in AnSS *da* for *dra* should have been preferred. Yet, of course, it is difficult to set aside the principle of textual criticism that the more difficult or unusual form is likely to be original!

[2]The word etc. refers to the Prastāva and the Pratihāra parts in the Udgītha chant.

तस्मिन्प्रयुज्यमानेऽतः सर्वो वेदः ससंग्रहः ।
प्रयुक्तः स्यादतो वेद ओंकार इति गम्यताम् ॥१३०॥

Therefore, that being used, the entire Veda, with its ancillaries, would become recited; as such, let *om* be understood as the Veda. [130]

इति श्रीबृहदारण्यकोपनिषद्भाष्यवार्तिके पञ्चमाध्यायस्य
प्रथमं ब्राह्मणम् ॥१॥

BṚHADĀRAṆYAKOPANIṢAD-BHĀṢYA-VĀRTIKA
5.2

उक्तमाभ्यन्तरं तावद्ब्रह्मोपासनसाधनम् ।
ओंकारोऽथ दमादीनां साधनत्वं विधीयते ॥१॥

Earlier there is stated the opinion about the worship of the Brahman within one. And now is explained (here) the nature of restraint (*dama*) etc. as the means to it (viz. Upāsanā). [1]

दान्तो दाता दयालुश्च सबाह्याभ्यन्तरः शुचिः ।
एवंविधोऽधिकारी स्यात्सर्वासूपास्तिभूमिषु ॥२॥

Thus, a person should be considered as eligible in respect of all the modes of worship: (he should be) one having his sense-organs subdued, a giver, having compassion (for others), and pure, both outside and inside (one's self). [2]

दमादिविधिशेषोऽयमर्थवादोऽभ्युपेयताम् ।
त्रया इत्यादिको ग्रन्थः स्पष्टार्थोऽतो न यत्यते ॥३॥

Let this be understood as an Arthavāda, i.e. ancillary to the injunction regarding restraint (*dama*) etc.[1] The section beginning with (the word) *trayā* has a very clear meaning and there is therefore no effort made (by me) in clarifying it. [3]

[1]The word etc. refers to *dāna* and *dayā*.

इति श्रीबृहदारण्यकोपनिषद्भाष्यवार्तिके पञ्चमाध्यायस्य
द्वितीयं ब्राह्मणम् ॥२॥

BṚHADĀRAṆYAKOPANIṢAD-BHĀṢYA-VĀRTIKA
5.3

ब्रह्मानुपाधि पूर्वत्र व्याख्यातं यत्नतोऽधुना ।
सोपाधिकस्य तस्यैव ह्युपास्तिर्वक्ष्यते स्फुटा ॥१॥

Earlier (i.e. on BUBV 5.1-2) the Brahman without any limiting adjuncts has been carefully explained. Now is stated in clear terms (*sphuṭa*) the worship of that very (Brahman) that has limiting adjuncts. [1]

In BUBV 5.1-2 there was discussion about *oṃkāra*, *dama*, *dāna* and *dayā* as ancillary to the worship of the Brahman.

श्रुतः प्रजापतिः पूर्वं कोऽसाविति न गम्यते ।
सामान्योक्तेर्विशेषार्थमेष इत्यादि भण्यते ॥२॥

(In) earlier (Brāhmaṇas, viz. BUBV 5.1-2), there was heard (the mention of) Prajāpati, (but) who he is is not understooed; therefore, the words *eṣa* ... explain (lit. state) the specific meaning of that which was stated only (in a) general (way). [2]

SP points out: Prajāpati is in a general way understood as the instructor of the gods and, therefore, this might refer to Dakṣa and others. Therefore, in order to distinguish Prajāpati in this context, there is here the use of the word *viśeṣārtha*.

हृद्गिरा मांसपेश्युक्ता तात्स्थ्याद्बुद्धिस्तु लक्ष्यते ।
हृदि नामादिसंहारं यत्र शाकल्य ऊचिवान् ॥३॥

By the word *hṛd* is to be understood (lit. stated) a lump of flesh (in the body). Yet, thereby (i.e. by that word) is indicated intellect (*buddhi*) owing to its abiding in it (*tātsthyāt*),[1] in the *hṛdaya* there is collection of name etc., as Śākalya has stated (as the secondary sense of the word).[2] [3]

[1]This is the meaning of the word *hṛdaya* that was used earlier in the Śākalya Brāhmaṇa; i.e. BU 3.9.11, 14, 16, 20-24; cf. BUB on it: *hṛdayaṃ loko hṛdayena buddhyā paśyati*. (At one place in BUB 3.9.20, however, Śaṅkara has said that the word *hṛdaya* is to be taken for the combination of *hṛdaya* and *manas*— this is to point to them as the internal organ.)
[2]This is relevant to the fifth Adhyāya.

सर्वभूतसमुत्पत्तेस्तथा सर्वेश्वरत्वतः ।
प्रजापतिरिति ज्ञेयं हृदयं तेन हेतुना ॥४॥

hṛdaya should be known as Prajāpati because there is the origin of all beings from it for the same reason.[1] [4]

[1]Cf. SP: *śākalyabrāhmaṇoktena tryannādhikāroktena hetunā tayor ekalakṣaṇatvād aikyam ity arthaḥ*.

सर्वज्ञेयस्य तद्व्याप्तेर्ब्रह्मापि हृदयं भवेत् ।
यत एवमतो यत्नादुपास्यं हृदयं सदा ।
हृदयाख्याक्षराणां च श्रुत्योपासनमुच्यते ॥५॥

Because what is to be known by all is pervaded by it, the Brahman also is *hṛdaya*. Since this is so; therefore, *hṛdaya* has to be worshipped with proper attention.[1] And, the Śruti states the worship of three *akṣara*s occurring in the word *hṛdaya*. [5]

[1]SP clarifies *yatnāt* as *ādara-nairantarya-dīrghakālarūpa*(*tayā*) 'at length time and place'.

इति श्रीबृहदारण्यकोपनिषद्भाष्यवार्तिके पञ्चमाध्यायस्य
तृतीयं ब्राह्मणम् ॥३॥

BṚHADĀRAṆYAKOPANIṢAD-BHĀṢYA-VĀRTIKA

5.4

तस्यैव हृदयाख्यस्य ब्रह्मणोऽन्यदुपासनम् ।
सत्योपाधिविशिष्टस्य तद्वै तदिति भण्यते ॥१॥

Now is stated in the words *tad vai tat* another mode of worship of that very Brahman which is called *hṛdaya* and which is modified by the limiting adjunct *satya*. [1]

तच्छब्देन परामर्शो वैशब्दः स्मरणाय च ।
प्रकारान्तरनिर्देशे तदासेति च तद्वचः ॥२॥

The word *tat* refers to what is earlier stated, the word *vai* is for reminding (one of the earlier context). When (now) there is a mention of another mode (of worship of the Brahman) there is the statement of that in the words *tad āsa*. [2]

सत्यमेव तदासेति यदुक्तं हृदयात्मना ।
मूर्तामूर्तात्मकं सत्यं ब्रह्म पूर्वं प्रपञ्चितम् ॥३॥

What is stated in the words *tad āsa* is the nature of *hṛdaya* is *satya* itself. The *satya* Brahman, having the nature of *mūrta* and *amūrta*, has been already explained fully (in BUBV 2.3). [3]

महत्तत्परिमाणेन यक्षं पूज्यतमत्वतः ।
अग्रजः प्रथमोद्भूतेस्तदन्यत्कार्यजन्मनः ॥४॥

That is called *mahat* with reference to its (great) measure, *yakṣa* for having the nature of what is to be most worshipped and *agraja* because of having its origin first (among all the things) and also because of the production of the effects other than itself. [4]

Sureśvara is very brief in his description of this Brahman as Virāj.

यः कश्चिदेतं व्याख्यातं वेदोपास्ते दिवानिशम् ।
लोकाञ्जयति स सर्वाञ्शत्रुश्चास्य जितो भवेत् ॥५॥

Whosoever knows this one (i.e. Prajāpati) thus explained and worships him day and night conquers all the worlds and his enemy becomes conquered. [5]

इति श्रीबृहदारण्यकोपनिषद्भाष्यवार्तिके पञ्चमाध्यायस्य
चतुर्थं ब्राह्मणम् ॥४॥

BRHADĀRAṆYAKOPANIṢAD-BHĀṢYA-VĀRTIKA
5.5

उक्तं प्रथमजं सत्यं कथं तदिति भण्यते ।
आप एवेदमित्युक्त्या यथोक्तार्थस्तवाय तु ॥१॥

We have already explained that *satya*, which was the first born, (and how it is[1] so is now stated). Further, the statement *āpa evedam* ... is only for praising the already stated thing.[2] [1]

[1]Namely, how it has that nature. Also the word here refers to the worship of it (*satyabrahmopāsti*).

[2]The thing already stated is the Brahman, which is described as *satya*.

पयःसोमादिका आपो ह्यग्निहोत्रादिकर्मसु ।
सर्वाहुतिषु संसृष्टा बाहुल्यादप्परिग्रहः ॥२॥

In the ritual acts Agnihotra etc., water,[1] Soma and others[2] are waters; since (waters) are mixed as an ingredient of *āhuti*s in profuse quantity. Therefore there is (here) a (specific)[3] reference to waters (in this text). [2]

This verse explains the significance of the word *āpaḥ* (accusative plural).

[1]Water may be primarily meant here, (though milk cannot be ruled out).

[2]The word 'others' refers to various sacrificial materials such as barley grains, sesame etc.

[3]This explains away the non-mention of elements other than water. This is fully clarified in the following verse.

सत्स्वप्यन्येषु भूतेषु भूयस्त्वादाप एव तु ।
प्राधान्याच्चैव गृह्यन्ते न त्वन्यद्विनिवार्यते ॥३॥

Even while there are other elements (involved in a sacrifice) only waters are mentioned because of their profuseness (in quantity) and of their (having a) principal role in the same; but (let it not be supposed that) others [1] are (wholly) excluded. [3]

[1] Actually, the verse uses the word *anyat* in singular; it means (any) other of the elements. Yet we have translated *anyat* as 'others' purposely.

प्रक्षेपोत्तरकालं ताः सर्वमानातिवर्तिना ।
तस्थुः सूक्ष्मेण रूपेण क्रियामाश्रित्य सर्वतः ॥४॥

(Those waters) have ever remained,[1] in their subtle form which surpasses all the means of perception,[2] being a part of (lit. having resorted to) the (ritual) activity, in its entirety, even after their first pouring (into the fire). [4]

[1] It means 'continued to be in existence'.
[2] The subtle form of waters could not be easily perceived after their first pouring; that is to say, in any later sacrificial activity the actual pouring of waters meant only some redundance. This is the special characteristic of waters in the sacrifice.

यावत्किंचिज्जगत्यस्मिन्नाहुत्येह व्यपेक्ष्यते ।
अन्तर्भूतं तदप्स्विति ह्याप एवेदमित्यतः ॥५॥

Since whatever here in this world is expected to be in an *āhuti* 'offering' is already included in waters, therefore, is made the statement *āpa evedam* ....[1] [5]

[1] This refers to waters which form the first thing of origin

(*mūlakāraṇa*) giving rise to the later objects in creation.

अग्रे प्रथमतः सृष्टेरग्रजस्य प्रजापतेः ।
सत्यं ब्रह्मासृजन्नापः कारणत्वादपां ततः ॥६॥
तदिदं हिरण्यगर्भस्य व्यक्तीभावो महेश्वरात् ।
आदित्यस्येह वाक्येन वर्ण्यतेऽग्रजसिद्धये ॥७॥

In the beginning (*agre*), i.e. before creating the first-born (or, the eldest-born) Prajāpati, waters created that *satya* Brahman; therefore, waters have the nature of the cause (of creation). [6]

This is then the origin, i.e. the manifestation of Hiraṇyagarbha, i.e. of Āditya, from the great Lord, thus described in this sentence,[1] for establishing 'that he was the first-born' [7]

The meaning of the statement is *tanmātram sūtrotpatteḥ pūrvaṃ jagad āsīt*.

[1]The sentence under reference is *tā āpaḥ satyam asṛjanta*. Also, it aims at pointing out how so *vyākṛta* 'manifest' came from *avyākṛta* 'unmanifest'.

भूतादिव्यक्तितो व्यक्तिरग्रजस्यापि नान्यथा ।
ताः सत्यमिति तेनाह सत्यं ब्रह्मातिविस्तृतेः ॥८॥

The origin of the first-born proceeded from the (earlier) manifestation of the elements etc.[1] and not otherwise; therefore, the Śruti has stated *tāḥ satyam*, i.e. *satyam brahma*, on account of its manifesting itself in large number (of things). [8]

Earlier, i.e. in BUBV 5.4.1, it was stated that the *satya* Brahman was *upādhiviśiṣṭa* 'modified by the limiting adjunct'. This is restated in the sentence *tāḥ satyam*.

[1]This refers to the *tanmātras*.

सूर्यादिकरणं देवं ब्रह्मास्राक्षीज्जगद्गुरुम् ।
देवान्विराडपि ब्रह्मा ससर्जेत्यनुषज्यते ॥९॥

It follows that the divine Brahman, the maker of sun etc. (first) created the teacher of the world[1] and that Virāj Brahman, on its part, created the gods.[2] [9]

[1]This is for god Prajāpati who is none other than first manifest sacrificer, the Sūtra or Āditya etc.

[2]This refers to the deities superintending over (or, associated with) the *prāṇa*s 'sense-organs'.

एवं सत्याद्यतो जातं क्रमेण ब्रह्मणो जगत् ।
महत्सत्यमतो ब्रह्म यक्षत्वं तूपवर्ण्यते ॥१०॥

Thus, since the world became gradually manifested (lit. produced) from the *satya* Brahman, therefore the Brahman is described as *mahat* 'the great one' and its being worship-deserving[1] is now explained. [10]

[1]*yakṣatva* is being *yakṣa* 'worship-deserving'.

अतीत्य पितरं देवाः पितामहमुपासते ।
यतोऽतो ब्रह्म यक्षं च सत्यं प्रथमजं विदुः ॥११॥

Since the gods, overlooking (lit. going beyond) the father,[1] worship the grandfather, therefore they have known the *satya* Brahman as worship-deserving and the first born. [11]

[1]The father refers to Virāj. The line is this: *satya* Brahman → Virāj → gods.

तस्यापि ब्रह्मणो नाम त्र्यक्षरं सत्यमुच्यते ।
प्रथमोत्तमे त्वमृतमक्षरे सस्वरत्वतः ॥१२॥

And the name of the Brahman also[1] is stated as the three-letter-word; viz. *satya*,[2] further, the first and the third letters of the two are immortal (*amṛta*) on account of their having a vowel. [12]

This is the meaning of the Śruti, *tad etad* ...
[1]This refers to *hṛdaya* Brahman.
[2]This is thus: *sa* is one letter, *t* is another and *ya* is the third.

निरच्कं मध्यतो मृत्युर्निर्जीवं देहवत्स्थितम् ।
भूयोऽमृतेन तद्ग्रस्तं मृतं चापि स्वतो यतः ॥१३॥

Between (the two letters) there is (the letter) *t* which does not have a vowel associated with it. That is *mṛtyu* and has remained like a lifeless body. And, though dead in itself,[1] it is encircled (lit. swallowed) by the immortal (pair of letters *sa* and *ya*). [13]

This is the meaning of *madhyataḥ* ...
[1]In the note above, the middle letter is shown as *t* which is without any vowel and, therefore, considered dead.

इत्येवं पर्युपासीनो नामाभिज्ञो नरः सदा ।
सत्यभूयं भवेदेव नैनमित्यादियुक्तिगीः ॥१४॥

A knowing man, ever worshipping (the Brahman) thus and conversant with the proper name (of the Brahman) which has become *satya*, would himself become *satya*— certainly thus there is a statement of the reason in the words *na enam* ... [14]

इति श्रीबृहदारण्यकोपनिषद्भाष्यवार्तिके पञ्चमाध्यायस्य
पञ्चमं ब्राह्मणम् ॥५॥

BṚHADĀRAṆYAKOPANIṢAD-BHĀṢYA-VĀRTIKA

5.6

संस्थानवदथेदानीमध्यात्मे चाधिदैवते ।
रूपं प्रकल्प्य सत्यस्य भण्यते तदुपासनम् ॥१॥

After conceiving the form of *satya* in relation to the body and also in relation to the sphere of deities, there is now explained (lit. stated) the (two modes of) worship of the same which are related to the various parts of the body.[1] [1]

[1]This is *samsthānavat*, a qualifier of *upāsana*.

अक्ष्यादित्याख्यनीडस्थौ स्थानमात्रप्रभेदतः ।
भिन्नाविव समीक्ष्येते देवतैकैव सा सती ॥२॥

(The two deities) which reside in the coteries called the Ādityas in the (two) eyes are yet considered to be different, as it were, only on account of the difference of the places (they reside in), even while there is just one and the same deity. [2]

उपकार्योपकारित्वसंबन्धेनेतरेतरम् ।
प्रतिष्ठितौ तावध्यात्मे चक्षुष्यादित्य एव च ॥३॥

They are both steady in each other through their relation as the benefactor and the beneficiary; and in relation to the body it is Āditya in the eye.

[1]It is suggested that, in the sphere of gods, there is another Āditya.

प्रतिष्ठितौ तावन्योऽन्यं कथमित्युच्यते यथा ।
अक्षिण रश्मिभिरादित्यः प्राणैस्तस्मिंश्च चाक्षुषः ॥४॥

(Now) is told how both of them are steady in each other: in the eye, Āditya has become steady by its rays and so also has the Āditya in the eye become steady in (i.e. through) the sense-organs (*prāṇa*s). [4]

It follows from the preceding verse that Āditya in the eye illuminates the objects to be seen and Āditya in the sphere of gods, the whole world.

अरिष्टदर्शनं चात्र प्रासङ्गिकमथोच्यते ।
ज्ञातारिष्टः कथं नाम कुर्यादात्महितं पुमान् ॥५॥

And now is told here the sight of some undesirable element which arises as a matter of course. (For, otherwise) 'how could a man, who has known the (imminent) undesirable element, bring about his own good? [5]

उत्क्रमिष्यन्यदा भोक्ता भवतीहायुषः क्षये ।
चन्द्रमण्डलवच्छुद्धं वीक्षते रविमण्डलम् ॥६॥

When the enjoyer is, at the end of his life, about to leave the (body) he sees the pure orb of the sun look like the orb of the moon. [6]

रश्मयो न समायान्ति विज्ञानपुरुषं प्रति ।
भोगेन प्रक्षयाद्भोक्तुस्तद्वशीकारिकर्मणः ॥७॥

The rays do not come to the *vijñānapuruṣa* (i.e. the individual self) proper, because they get exhausted through the enjoyment by the person who does his activities (*karman*) which have brought them (i.e. the rays) under (their) control. [7]

इति श्रीबृहदारण्यकोपनिषद्भाष्यवार्तिके पञ्चमाध्यायस्य
षष्ठं ब्राह्मणम् ॥६॥

BṚHADĀRAṆYAKOPANIṢAD-BHĀṢYA-VĀRTIKA
5.7

शरीरं व्याहृतिमयं कल्प्यतेऽक्षिरविस्थयोः ।
तस्यैव सत्यनाम्नोऽथ तदुपासाप्रसिद्धये ॥१॥

Now is explained (the nature of) the body of (the Brahman), named *satya*, which is made up of the *vyāhṛtis*, in order to clarify (the nature of) the worship of the two, Āditya in the eye and Āditya among the gods, in that form.[1] [1]

In the initial verse of the seventh Brāhmaṇa, Sureśvara gives the purport of the preceding Brāhmaṇa.

[1]That is, in the form of the three *vyāhṛtis*. These *vyāhṛtis*, it must be pointed out, are not the usually known *vyāhṛtis*— these are to be understood as *sa*, *t* and *ya* which form *satya* which is the name of the Brahman.

तस्यैव नामोपनिषद्ब्रह्मणो भण्यते द्वयोः ।
स्थितस्य स्थानयोः साक्षाद्यद्ग्रहात्तत्प्रसीदति ॥२॥

Now is stated the secret name[1] of that very Brahman which is residing in the two places[1] by the direct grasping of which that[3] becomes favourable. [2]

[1]These are two, viz. *ahan* and *aham*— these are related to the three *vyāhṛtis*.

[2]The eye and the sky (i.e. heaven) are meant.

[3]This is *satya* Brahman.

हन्तेर्वेदं जहातेर्वाहरित्येतदिहेष्यते ।
पाप्मानं हन्ति तेनातो जहाति च न संशयः ॥३॥

In the context, the word *ahan* or *aham* is accepted as derived from the root *han* (together with the preposition *ā*) or from the root *hā*;[1] and then it[2] certainly strikes down the sin or it abandons it. [3]

It should be noted that the various worships in the Khila Kāṇḍa are ancillary or additional and not basically philosophical. This Brahman explains the significance of worship of *satya* Brahman by each of the two names. This is based on the Brahmaṇical etymology of the words *ahan* and *aham*.

[1] *ā-han* means 'to strike down' and *ā-hā* 'to give up'. The preposition is shortened, in each case.

[2] That is, *ahan* or *aham*.

इति श्रीबृहदारण्यकोपनिषद्भाष्यवार्तिके पञ्चमाध्यायस्य
सप्तमं ब्राह्मणम् ॥७॥

BṚHADĀRAṆYAKOPANIṢAD-BHĀṢYA-VĀRTIKA
5.8

मनोमयोऽयमिति च तस्यैव ब्रह्मणोऽपरम् ।
स्वान्तोपाधिविशिष्टस्य ह्युपासनमथोच्यते ॥१॥

Now, in the words *manomayo 'yam*, there is stated yet another worship of that very Brahman, which is limited (lit. modified) by the adjuncts within. [1]

We should remember that the Khila Kāṇḍa pertains to various modes of worships of the Brahman, affected by the limiting adjuncts (*sopādhika*), as noted under verse 3 of the preceding Brāhmaṇa.

मनोभिमानतोऽज्ञानात्पुरुषोऽयं मनोमयः ।
यदि वा मनसि व्यक्तेर्मनसा वोपलभ्यते ॥२॥
भाः प्रकाशोऽमलं ज्योतिः सा सत्यमविनाशतः ।
तस्मिन्नित्यादिवचनं पूर्वोक्तस्थानसिद्धये ॥३॥

The word *manas* is based on its function called *abhimāna*;[1] it is on account of *ajñāna* 'ignorance'[2] that this Puruṣa 'the inner self' is taken as made up of *manas*; or because that becomes known owing to his manifestation in *manas*. [2]
The word *bhās* means light or spotless flame; that (=*bhās*) is *satya* for it does not (ever) perish. The words *tasmin* ... are to specify the two places (of Āditya) already stated. [3]

Here, the word *manomaya* is explained in two ways: (i) with reference to the property of *manas*, *abhimāna*, and (ii) from the substratum wherein the inner self is manifest.

[1]*abhimāna* is for *abhimanana*—*manana* which is the function

of *manas*; cf. *Sāṃkhyakārikā*. This refers to *aham ity abhimānaḥ*.
[2]*manas* is insentient (*jaḍa*), therefore there is ignorance or darkness.

बुद्ध्युपाधिव्यवच्छेदाद्व्रीह्यादिपरिमाणता ।
स्वतोऽनन्तत्वतो मानात्सर्वेशानादिरूपता ॥४॥

It has, on account of the limiting adjunct, viz. intellect, the magnitude of rice etc. (and) also the nature of the ruler of all, owing to its being known by itself and on account of its infiniteness.[1] [4]

This is to explain how the ruler of all can have even a small magnitude.

SP, in typical commentarial style, reads an alternative *ananta-tvato 'mānāt* .... Therefore the alternative translation could be: 'on account of not being known by any known means'.

[1]Cf. *satyaṃ jñānam anantam brahma* (*Taittirīyopaniṣad* 2.1).

इति श्रीबृहदारण्यकोपनिषद्भाष्यवार्तिके पञ्चमाध्यायस्य
अष्टमं ब्राह्मणम् ॥८॥

BṚHADĀRAṆYAKOPANIṢAD-BHĀṢYA-VĀRTIKA

5.9

विद्युद्देहस्य तस्यैव ब्रह्मणोऽन्यदुपासनम् ।
अशेषपाप्मविध्वस्त्यै श्रुत्याथ प्रतिपाद्यते ॥१॥

Now is prescribed by the Śruti yet another (mode of) worship of that very Brahman, which is in the form of lightning, in order that there is removal (lit. destruction) of the entire sins. [1]

This verse states the purport of the ninth Brāhmaṇa.

विद्युद्ब्रह्मेति युक्तं तद्विद्युद्धि स्याद्विदानतः ।
द्यतेरेतद्यतो रूपमवखण्डनकर्मणः ॥२॥

It is (only) proper (to look on) lightning as the Brahman. Indeed, (the word) *vidyut* is derived from its act of tearing away (*vidāna*), since this form (of the word *vidyut*) is based on the root *do* 'to tear away or asunder' in the sense of the act of cutting to pieces (or *khaṇḍana*). [2]

The root *do* in the sense of *khaṇḍana* has connection with the object, the sin.

This verse gives only the verbal meaning of the word *vidyut*.

तमोऽन्धकारमखिलमवखण्डयति क्षणात् ।
विद्युद्यथा तथास्मत्तः पाप्मानं तदुपासितुः ॥३॥

Lightning destroys *tamas* [1] 'darkness', in its entirety, within a moment; therefore, (that which is superimposed on the Brahman) cuts sin away from us, i.e. its worshippers.[2] [3]

This verse is the statement of the result, viz. destruction of sin consisting in having ignorance about the nature of the Brahman.

[1]*tamas* can be taken as darkness by the clouds and therefore can be distinguished from darkness standing for ignorance; alternatively *tamas* stands for darkening sin—this explanation is offered by SP. For bringing out that the use of both *tamaḥ* and *andhakāram* does not involve repetiton.

[2]*asmattaḥ* ... *upāsituḥ* is translated here only in the plural as that is warranted by the form *asmattaḥ*— this is despite the singular form *upāsituḥ*.

इति श्रीबृहदारण्यकोपनिषद्भाष्यवार्तिके पञ्चमाध्यायस्य
नवमं ब्राह्मणम् ॥९॥

BṚHADĀRAṆYAKOPANIṢAD-BHĀṢYA-VĀRTIKA
5.10

तस्यैव ब्रह्मणोऽथान्यदुपासनमिहोच्यते ।
वाग्धेनूपाधियोगेन फलाय महतेऽधुना ॥१॥

Now is stated here (in this Brāhmaṇa) yet another (mode of) worship of that very Brahman, in accordance with its limiting adjuncts, viz. the cow in the form of speech, since that yields great result (lit. fruit). [1]

In this Brāhmaṇa the metaphor *vāgdhenu* is fully worked out.

वागित्यत्र त्रयी ग्राह्या न स्थानकरणादयः ।
स्वाहाकारादि नान्यत्र त्रय्याः संभाव्यते क्वचित् ॥२॥

Here (i.e. in this context) the word *vāc* should be understood as the Vedic triad, not the place of articulation and the functioning organ which acts etc.[1] (This is so because) *svāhākāra* etc.[2] are not to be found anywhere else[3] than in the Vedic triad. [2]

This refers to the *sthāna* of *vāc*. The functioning organ which acts is mentioned as *karaṇa* 'sense-organs'.

[1]The word etc. stands for the deity that superintends over the place of articulation and the functioning organ which acts.

[2]This word etc. stands for *vaṣaṭkāra*, *hantakāra* and *svadhākāra*. The utterance of *svāhākāra* and *vaṣaṭkāra* accompanies the offerings to gods. The utterance of *hantakāra* indicates invitation to a priest for the ritual act which the sacrificer undertakes. The utterance of *svadhākāra* is to accompany the offering to the Pitṛs 'manes'.

[3]The words 'anywhere else' refer to the place of articulation, the organ (itself) and its superintending deity.

त्रयीयं धयते सर्वं स्वाहाकारादिभिः स्तनैः ।
धेनुमित्येव तां तेन सदोपासीत भारतीम् ॥३॥

This Vedic triad suckles all (human beings) by its udders in the form of *svāhākāra* etc.;[1] therefore, one should ever worship Vāc (i.e. Bhārati).[2] [3]

Cp. a later classical verse, i.e. *Uttararāmacarita* 5.31:
kāmān dugdhe viprakarṣaty alakṣmīm kīrtiṃ sūte duṣkṛtan yā hinasti /
tāṃ capy etām mātaram maṅgalānām dhenuṃ dhīrāḥ sūnṛtām vācam āhuḥ //

[1]Cf. note 3 on the preceding verse.
[2]This refers to the Vedic triad, not Vāc.

केभ्यः क्षरति सा धेनुरित्येतदधुनोच्यते ।
तस्यै द्वौ स्तनावित्युक्त्या कथ्यन्ते च स्तनास्तथा ॥४॥

Now is stated here as to wherefrom that cow trickles drops of milk: and to explain that are mentioned the four udders[1] in the statement *tasyai dvau stanau*.[2] [4]

[1]The plural refers to the four udders.
[2]This Vedic use of the dative for the genitive.

ऋषभोऽस्यास्तथा ज्ञेयः प्राणस्तस्मात्प्रसूयते ।
अप्राणस्य न वागस्ति वागप्युच्चार्यते बलात् ॥५॥

Then (*tathā*) for this one (viz. *vāc*, i.e. cow) is to be known the bull in (the form of) Prāṇa 'sentience'. From that (Prāṇa) it produces (offspring). (Indeed), in the case of one without Prāṇa, there does not exist *vāc*, and *vāc* also is enabled to utter through strength (of the Prāṇa). [5]

वाक्प्रस्रवणहेतुत्वाद्धेन्वा वत्सो मनो भवेत् ।
यद्यद्ध्यायति मनसा तत्तद्वाचा प्रभाषते ॥६॥

manas is then the calf (of that cow), since it is the cause of the trickling (i.e. activity) of *vāc*;[1] whatever one ponders over with one's *manas* is what one speaks through *vāc*.[2] [6]

[1]This is for *vāgdhenu*.
[2]This is usual *vāc* 'the organ of speech'.

यथोक्तोपासनफलमुक्तब्रह्मात्मरूपता ।
तं यथा यथा इत्युक्तेरनिर्देशेऽपि गम्यते ॥७॥

The result of the worship thus stated is (now stated as an individual's) becoming of nature (lit. form) of the Brahman. (In this case), this (viz. result) is to be understood even while there is no mention of the result, in the words *taṃ yathā yathā*. [7]

इति श्रीबृहदारण्यकोपनिषद्भाष्यवार्तिके पञ्चमाध्यायस्य
दशमं ब्राह्मणम् ॥१०॥

BṚHADĀRAṆYAKOPANIṢAD-BHĀṢYA-VĀRTIKA 5.11

उपास्त्यन्तरमस्यैव कौक्षेयाग्नेर्वपुर्भृतः ।
अयमग्निरिति श्रुत्या यत्नेनाथ विधीयते ॥१॥

Now is carefully (*yatnena*)[1] prescribed yet another (mode of) worship of this very (Brahman) which possesses a body, viz. what is fire in the stomach of beings (i.e. Vaiśvānarāgni), in the Śruti *ayam agniḥ ....*[2] [1]

Cf. *Gītā* 15.14ab: *aham vaiśvānaro bhūtvā prāṇināṃ deham āśritaḥ.*

[1]Cf. SP: *upāsyārthasya sākṣāttvakathanaṃ yatnaḥ.*

[2]This refers to BU 2.9.1.

वैश्वानरगिरास्याग्नेः सामान्येनाभिधानतः ।
योऽयमन्तरितीत्युक्त्या तद्विशेषणमुच्यते ॥२॥

After there is a general mention of this Agni in the words *vaiśvānarāgni*, there is then stated specification (of the same) in the statement *yo 'yam antāḥ....*[1] [2]

[1]This also refers to BU 2.9.1.

तस्याग्नेरेष घोषः स्यात्कर्णौ प्रोर्णूय यच्छ्रुतिः ।
उपास्यार्थस्य साक्षात्त्वं घोषरूपेण वर्ण्यते ॥३॥

This is the loud noise (*ghoṣa*) or 'roaring' of that fire, which is heard by one after one has closed (or covered) one's ears; the direct perceptibility of the object of worship (viz. Vaiśvānarāgni) is explained as that which has a form of *ghoṣa*.[1] [3]

[1]SP states *haukṣeyam hi jyotir iha spaṣṭayitavyam brahmaṇas tadupādhikasyopāsyatvāt*.

अरिष्टदर्शनं चात्र प्रासङ्गिकमथोच्यते ।
नैनं घोषं शृणोतीति प्रत्यासन्नमृतिर्नरः ॥४॥

And now, as a matter of course, is stated in the words, 'he does not hear this *ghoṣa*' that there is the possibility of some danger, i.e. the man's death is imminent. [4]

This is similar to the statement at BUBV 5.6.5 above.

इति श्रीबृहदारण्यकोपनिषद्भाष्यवार्तिके पञ्चमाध्यायस्य
एकादशं ब्राह्मणम् ॥११॥

BṚHADĀRAṆYAKOPANIṢAD-BHĀṢYA-VĀRTIKA
5.12

गतिः फलं च वक्तव्यं पर्वत्र तदनुक्तितः ।
उपासनानां सर्वेषामित्यर्थः पर आगमः ॥१॥

(Now) is to be told the aim and the result of all the Upāsanās as there has been no mention of them in the earlier (portion of the Upaniṣad), therefore there follows the subsequent (portion of) the scripture. [1]

This is the general purport of this Brāhmaṇa.

उत्क्रामति यदा विद्वाञ्शरीरादायुषः क्षयात् ।
आश्वेव वायुं दुर्भेद्यं स आगच्छति वेगवान् ॥२॥

When, at the expiration (of the length) of life, the knower (of the Brahman) moves upwards (*ut-*) from the body, then he, possessed of speed, quickly[1] reaches Vāyu which is impregnable. [2]

There are explanations of different words occurring in this Brāhmaṇa.

[1]This refers to CU 8.6.5: *sa yāvat kṣipyen manas tāvad ādityaṃ gacchati* ....

प्राप्ताय लोकभोगार्थं वायुस्तस्मै विगच्छति ।
कियच्छिद्रं मरुद्दद्याद्रथचक्रखमानगीः ॥३॥

As he arrives there for the enjoyment of the region, Vāyu gives way to him. (At this, in answer to a question:) 'Of what size does Vāyu offer him a hole (i.e. the way for him)?', there is (an answer in) the statement of the magnitude of the hole in the chariot. [3]

द्विकाष्ठसंतताघातमाडम्बरमिहोच्यते ।
भेरीं च दुन्दुभिं विद्यात्तेनोर्ध्वं यात्युपासकः ॥४॥

Here is stated the *āḍambara* which means continuous beating (of a drum) by two sticks. One should know *dundubhi* in the sense of a *bherī* 'drum'. The worshipper goes upwards through that (viz. the hole in the drum). [4]

लोकं प्रजापतिं ब्रह्म प्रैत्यसौ भावनाबलात् ।
अशोकमहिमं चेति दुःखतद्धेतुवर्जितम् ॥५॥

(Then) he reaches the region, viz. (of) Prajāpati, (then) the Brahman, on account of the strength of his devotion. The region is described as devoid of sorrow[1] and pain because it is free from any misery and its cause. [5]

[1]*aśoka* refers to physical (*śārīra*) pain and *ahimam* refers to mental pain.

शाश्वतीश्च समा नित्या अस्मिंल्लोके वसत्यसौ ।
पूर्वत्रानुक्तकार्याणामुपास्तीनामिदं फलम् ॥६॥

Then he stays there in this region for ever-lasting years (*śāśvatīḥ samāḥ*). This is the result of the (modes of) worship whose results (or effects) were not stated. [6]

SP points out that, since the results of the modes of worship of *hṛdaya*, *satya* etc. have been already stated, this verse refers to various other modes of worship whose effects have not been stated.

इति श्रीबृहदारण्यकोपनिषद्भाष्यवार्तिके पञ्चमाध्यायस्य
द्वादशं ब्राह्मणम् ॥१२॥

BṚHADĀRAṆYAKOPANIṢAD-
BHĀṢYA-VĀRTIKA
5.13

ज्वरादिव्याधिना तप्तो व्याधितस्तप्यते तु यत् ।
परमं तत्तपश्चिन्त्यं परमं लोकमीप्सता ॥१॥

That one is pained (or, tormented) by the diseases like fever etc. and that one is pained (i.e. tormented), be considered as the highest penance (*tapas*) done by one who desires for the highest region (viz. the Brahman). [1]

In the earlier Brāhmaṇas, there have been stated some modes of worship, together with their results, and now there is a discussion of some modes of worship not related to the Brahman proper.

व्याधिग्रहग्रहाविष्टोऽसह्यं दुःखं समश्नुते ।
तपोऽतः परमं हि स्यात्तच्चिकित्सामकुर्वतः ॥२॥

A person experiences unbearable pain as he is afflicted by the goblins in the form of the attacks of (i.e. seizure by) diseases. Therefore, penances are indeed the highest (pain for a person), who does not censure it.[2] [2]

[1]The word *graha* is used twice. The first *graha* with *vyādhi* stands for the attack of some disease and the second *graha* is metaphorically understood as goblins.

[2]This is the meaning of the words *cikitsām akurvat*. Normally *cikitsā* refers to treating of some disease, i.e. ascertaining the nature of the disease and determining the medicine for it. In *tapas* there is no scope for anybody's becoming sorry for it. In other words, *cikitsām akurvat* means 'One who does not fret

over it' (*anindā* is *aviṣāda*).

निर्हरन्त्यृत्विजोऽरण्यमन्ये वा मां मृतं गृहात् ।
परमं तदपि ध्येयं वानप्रस्थ्येन संमितम् ॥३॥

(A person should think thus:) 'That either the *ṛtvik*s or others take me out of my house, when I shall be dead is also to be considered as the highest penance).' This is on par with the state of a person's taking to the stay in the forest. [3]

This is the meaning of *etad vai paramaṃ tapo yaṃ pretam* ....

अभ्यादधति यच्चाग्नौ प्रेतं मां ज्ञातयोऽथ तत् ।
परमं तदपि ध्येयमग्न्यावेशसमत्वतः ॥४॥

(Also he should think:) 'And that the relations put me into the fire when I am dead is also to be considered as the highest (penance), since that is similar to entering into the fire.' [4]

उचितं यस्य यद्यत्स्यात्तत्तल्लोकगिरोच्यते ।
तपसस्तापसस्यैवमग्न्यावेशस्य यत्फलम् ॥५॥

In the words of *loka*[1] is stated the result, viz. that whichever is proper in the case of each of *tapas*, *tāpasa* and putting (the dead body) into fire. [5]

Ordinarily, there is (but) one statement about the result of (any) *upāsanā*, viz. *paramaṃ haiva lokaṃ jayati*. But, here are meant different Upāsanās and different results.

[1]Here the word *loka* stands for the results achieved by different modes of worship or various kinds of the *upāsanā*s.

इति श्रीबृहदारण्यकोपनिषद्भाष्यवार्तिके पञ्चमाध्यायस्य
त्रयोदशं ब्राह्मणम् ॥१३॥

BṚHADĀRAṆYAKOPANIṢAD-BHĀṢYA-VĀRTIKA
5.14

अन्नं ब्रह्मेति निर्वक्ति पुरेवान्यदुपासनम् ।
उदारफलसिद्ध्यर्थं तस्य न्यायेन निर्णयः ॥१॥

The words (of the Śruti) *annam brahma* state,[1] as before, another mode of worship (viz. other than that of the Brahman). In order that there follows more profuse result, there is now a decision (about that) with proper reason. [1]

In the three previous Brāhmaṇas, the Śruti has discussed (those modes of) worship which were not related to the Brahman. But, here, (in this Brāhmaṇa), is discussed the worship of the Brahman proper. This is the purport of this Brāhmaṇa.

In the case of other modes of worship like those of *anna* and *prāṇa*, which involved the view of the Brahman in some things other than the Brahman, there do follow some results but actually viewing the non-Brahman as the Brahman meant greater result followed them. That is discussed here (in verses that follow) with proper reason so as to establish the same.

[1]*nirvakti* here is only *vakti*.

अन्नमेव परं ब्रह्मेत्येक आहुर्विपश्चितः ।
तत्तथा नावगन्तव्यं क्लिद्यत्यन्नमसुं विना ॥२॥

Some wise men have declared that *anna* alone is the highest Brahman.[1] But that should not be so accepted, (because) *anna*, which is without Prāṇa, becomes putrid. [2]

Regarding the Brahman (i.e. Ātman), it is said in the *Gītā*

2.24ab: *acchedyo 'yam adāhyo 'yam akledyo 'śoṣya eva ca*. The verb root *klid* means 'to get wet, to become putrid or rotten'.

[1]Cf. BU 5.12.1.

प्राणो ब्रह्मेति चाप्यन्ये तच्च ग्राह्यं पुरेव न ।
अन्नादृते यतः प्राणः शोषमाशु निगच्छति ॥३॥

And also, some others (have declared), 'Prāṇa is the Brahman'.[1] And that also is not to be accepted, as before;[2] (this is so) owing to that, without food, Prāṇa quickly withers up. [3]

Sureśvara considers that the words *anna* and *prāṇa* without each other would not be properly having the characteristics of the Brahman. He bases his argument probably on the statement in the *Gītā* as noted under the preceding verse.

[1]BU 4.1.3; CU 4.10.4; *Kauṣītakyupaniṣad* 2.1; *Taittirīyopaniṣad* 3.3.

[2]It is as in the case of *annam brahma* as mentioned above.

ब्रह्मत्वं नानयोर्यस्मादेकैकस्य न युक्तिमत् ।
संभूय देवते तस्माद्ब्रह्मत्वं संनिगच्छतः ॥४॥

Since (each of) these two,[1] taken singly, does not reasonably have the nature of the Brahman; therefore, the two deities of those, joining together, obtain the nature of the Brahman. [4]

[1]It refers to *anna* and *prāṇa*.

तदेतत्संप्रधार्याह प्रातृदः पितरं किल ।
किंस्विदित्यादि संहृष्टस्तद्दोषस्यासमीक्षणात् ॥५॥

Having well considered this (in mind), (i.e. ascertaining, a person called) Prātṛda is reported to have said to his father, *kiṃsvit* ... 'Should I indeed ... ', surprised as he was by the worshippers' not seing a fault (in worshipping what was other than the Brahman).[2] [5]

[1]This has reference to the sentence in BU 5.12.1.
[2]Read SP: *guṇahīnoktabrahmaṇopāstau doṣasyeti.*

किंस्विदेवंविदे साधु कृत्स्नसाध्वाप्तिहेततः ।
कुर्यामसाधु वा तस्मै सर्वासाधुनिराकृतेः ॥६॥

(He meant) 'Could I do (any) good to the person, who knows thus,[1] for the reason that he has obtained all good (or, everything),[2] or could I do him any evil owing to his having discarded all that is not good?'[3] [6]

This explains the meaning of the sentence *kiṃ svit* ....
SP points out the purport of the sentence thus: the worshipper of the Brahman, in the form of *anna* or *prāṇa*, has his desires fulfilled, and, therefore, does not have anything to obtain or to discard.
[1]That is, who knows *anna* and *prāṇa* as the Brahman.
[2]Namely, since, by his worship, he has obtained all his desires.
[3]His proper worship has avoided all untouched happenings.

पाणिना मैवमित्युक्त्या तं पिता प्रत्यषेधयत् ।
संभूय परमत्वं कः स्वतोऽशक्तिरवाप्नुयात् ॥७॥

With the words 'Do not (think or, say) like this', the father prohibited him by the (wave of his) hand. He asked, 'The state of being the highest (can be obtained by these two) being together. Who, himself without ability, could obtain (that)? [7]

The meaning of the question in the second line is: A worshipper of only *anna* or only of *prāṇa* would become one with the objects of his worship and would not have ability to attain the highest status, viz. the nature of the Brahman.

स्वतोऽशक्तिमतोर्लोके शक्तिर्योगेऽपि नेक्ष्यते ।
जात्यन्धयोर्न योगेऽपि शक्ती रूपवदीक्षणे ॥८॥

Nowhere in this world is seen ability of (any) two (individuals), each one of whom has, on his own, no ability, even when they are in union; there is no ability for seeing objects that have forms in the case of two persons who are (both) born blind. [8]

This verse points out that the union of any two persons each of whom has no ability of his own, is also ineffective. This is made clear by the illustration in the second line. Read SP (at the beginning of the comment on the next verse): *aśaktānām mitho yoge 'pi na śaktiḥ.*

तस्माच्छक्तिमतोरेव ग्रासांशानां यथा तथा ।
तृप्तिशक्तिरिहापि स्यात्प्राणान्नाद्यात्मनोर्युतौ ॥९॥

Therefore, as (there is capacity of bringing about satisfaction) in the case of two of the morsels of eatables, which alone are (then) capable (for that purpose), in the union of Prāṇa and (eatable) food, so also is here the capacity of (effecting the union with the Brahman) in the union of *prāṇa* and *anna*. [9]

न चेत्परमतां यातः कथं परमतोच्यताम् ।
प्रत्येकं शक्तिमत्त्वोक्तिर्वीत्यादिवचसोच्यते ॥१०॥

Let it be said: If a person does not attain the status of the highest (by worshipping *anna* and *prāṇa* together), how could there be (for him) the nature of the highest achieved? The answer is given in the words *vi* ... by the statement of each (of *anna* and *prāṇa*) as having the capacity. [10]

The second line of this verse is fully explained in the following verses.

व्याख्यानाय तु वीत्यस्य त्वन्नं वै वीति भण्यते ।
अन्ने विष्टानि सन्त्येव भूतत्वं यान्ति येन हि ॥११॥
अन्नविष्टानि सर्वाणि भूतानीत्यन्नमुच्यते ।
वीति तेन सदा प्राणो रमित्येवमिहोच्यते ॥१२॥
प्राणे सति रमन्ते हि लोके दृष्टानि सर्वदा ।
भूतानि रमिति प्रोक्तस्तस्मात्प्राणोऽपि सूरिभिः ॥१३॥

Just (*tu*) for explaining *vi* ..., it is said (in the Śruti) *annaṃ vai vi*, (which means), since only on having entered into food, (the elements) they come to have the nature of the elements, [11]
therefore, food is called all the elements that have entered into (i.e. supported in) food. Therefore, they are ever (called) *vi* .... Similarly, *prāṇa* is called here *ram*. [12]
In the world are seen the elements enjoying happiness while Prāṇa is there among them. Therefore Prāṇa also is called by the wise ones as *ram*. [13]

These are two instances of the symbolic references to *anna* and Prāṇa (viz. *vi* and *ram*), and also their Brāhmaṇical etymologies: *vi* stands for *viṣṭa*, which seems to be an abbreviation from root *viṣ*, so also *ram* from root *ram*.

स्वतो गुणवतोरेवमन्नप्राणात्मनोर्भवेत् ।
संभूय परमत्वं हि फलोक्तिः सैव योदिता ॥१४॥

Thus, there would be (the attainment of) the highest status for the two which are of the nature of *anna* and Prāṇa and which are (in their own nature) possessed of capacities, when they have continued together. (This is to say:) 'That is the statement of the result which is (thus) described'. [14]

This refers to the Śruti: *sarvāṇi ha vā asmin* ... and it is taken as the statement of the result for a person who worships *anna* and Prāṇa together as the Brahman.

विशन्ति सर्वभूतानि ह्यन्नभूते प्रजापतौ ।
रमन्ते प्राणभूते च फलमेतदुपासितुः ॥१५॥

Indeed, all the elements enter into Prajāpati, who has become *anna* and feel delight (in him) who has become the Prāṇa. This is the result for him, who worships this (union of *anna* and Prāṇa). [15]

इति श्रीबृहदारण्यकोपनिषद्भाष्यवार्तिके पञ्चमाध्यायस्य
चतुर्दशं ब्राह्मणम् ॥१४॥

BṚHADĀRAṆYAKOPANIṢAD-BHĀṢYA-VĀRTIKA
5.15

उक्थादिगुणपूगेन विशिष्टस्यानरूपिणः ।
उपासनमथेदानीं ब्रह्मणो भण्यते परम् ॥१॥

Now hereafter is stated the worship of the Brahman in the form of *ana* (i.e. Prāṇa) which is characterized by the multitude of qualities beginning with *uktha*.[1] [1]

[1]The word *ādi* in *ukthādi* refers to *yajus*, *sāman* and *kṣatra*. And *uktha* stands for the *ṛc*.

उक्थं प्राणः कुतो यस्मात्प्राणे सति चराचरम् ।
उत्थापयति कर्मेदं कर्ता वा नान्यथा ततः ॥२॥

uktha[1] is Prāṇa. Why? (It is so) because while there exists Prāṇa (in a body), an agent can raise (i.e. perform) movable and/or immovable[2] to an (i.e. any) activity—is not possible in any way other than that. [2]

[1]The word *uktha* stands for what is known in Vedic ritual as *śastra*; this latter is derived from the verb root *śaṃs* 'to praise, to recite'. Therefore, it means a praise comprising one verse (*ṛc*) or more. Actually, *uktha* is derived from the verb root *vac* 'to speak, to utter' and therefore means 'prayer'. See [Vol.4;1991] Introduction, where we have pointed out the relation between *uktha* and the Ṛgvedic Upaniṣads. Yet Sureśvara derives this word in a different way (of course, following the Upaniṣad which retains the Brāhmaṇa style of etymologising)—cf. *Jaiminīya Brāhmaṇa* 2.24: *tān ukthair utthāpayati tad ukthānām ukthatvam*; and *Śatapatha Brāhmaṇa* 10.4.1.4: *eṣa u eva ukthasyaitad annaṃ*

thaṃ tad uktham, and also Śaṅkara who follows suit!). Obviously, *uktha* is derived here from verb root *ut-sthā* (in causal) 'to raise' and means 'what raises'. This *uktha* is Prāṇa, as declared in this verse, and also identical with the Brahman—cf. *brahman* which is *anarūpin* in verse 1 above.

[2]The words 'movable and immovable' refer to *punyā-* and *apuṇya-karman*s (SP).

वीरश्चोक्थात्मवित्पुत्र उपासीनस्य जायते ।
दृष्टं फलमदृष्टं तु ह्युक्थस्यैकात्म्यमश्नुते ॥३॥

To him, who is the worshipper (of *uktha*), is born a son who is brave and also a knower of the nature of *uktha*. (There is a) seen result (or reward of this) *uktha*[1] and (*tu*) also an unseen result in that he (i.e. the worshipper) attains oneness with the Ātman. [3]

[1]This refers to *śastra* in Vedic ritual, as mentioned above, yielding (at times) some worldly (known) results also.

यजुश्च प्राण एवेति सदोपासीत यत्नतः ।
कुतो यजुष्ट्वं तस्येति युक्तिलेशोऽभिधीयते ॥४॥
युज्यन्ते सर्वभूतानि संहन्यन्ते परस्परम् ।
प्राणे सति यजुस्तस्मात्फलोक्तिः पूर्ववत्तथा ॥५॥

yajus also (*ca*) is but Prāṇa; if one should worship with attention/care.[1] Why is there the character of *yajus* in that (viz. Prāṇa)? With regard to that, (here) is stated some (*leśa*) reason. [4]

Because *yajyante sarvabhūtāni*[2] means 'They get mixed with one another', when there exists Prāṇa (in them),[3] therefore, it is *yajus*;[4] (and) the result (which follows) is also like the one (stated) before. [5]

This is to explain *prāṇe hīmani*... (BU 5.15.2).

[1]SP paraphrases *yatna* as *ādara* 'respect' and alternatively as

nairantarya 'continuity'.

[2]This indicates the derivation of *yajus* from verb root *yuj* 'to unite, to get mixed (with another)'!

[3]Cf. verse 2 above.

[4]The word *yajus* is usually derived from verb root *yaj* 'to worship, to offer'. Also cf. *Jaiminīya Upaniṣad* 1.40: *vāg eva yajuḥ, vācā hi yajur anuvartate*. This indicates the recitation of a prose formula for offering.

सामापि प्राण एवेति कथं तदिति भण्यते ।
सम्यञ्चि सर्वभूतानि प्राणे सति यतस्ततः ॥६॥

sāman also is Prāṇa. How is it (so)? It is stated (thus): Because all the beings assemble (*añc*) together, (only) when Prāṇa exists there (in them); therefore (it is so). [6]

क्षत्रं च प्राण एवेति चिन्तयेत्सततं हृदा ।
त्रायते हेति युक्त्युक्तिः क्षत्रत्वस्य प्रसिद्धये ॥७॥

kṣatra also is but Prāṇa: (thus) should one entertain (lit. meditate) in mind (lit. heart). 'Because it protects' is the statement of the reason (adduced) for establishing the character (of Prāṇa as *kṣatra*). [7]

क्षणितोर्हि क्षतात्प्राणस्त्रायते न तु तं विना ।
क्षत्रं प्राणस्ततो ज्ञेयो यथोक्तन्यायगौरवात् ॥८॥

Because Prāṇa protects (one) from an injury (caused) by an injuring (person/thing)[1]; and (*tu*) there is none other than that (for protection). Therefore should it be known that Prāṇa is *kṣatra*, out of regard for the reason[2] stated. [8]

[1]Cf. *Raghuvaṃśa* 2.53: *kṣatāt kila trāyata ity udagraḥ kṣatrasya śabdo bhuvaneṣu rūḍhaḥ*.

[2]Note Sureśvara's use of *nyāya* in the sense of reason, viz. cause.

प्राप्नोत्यत्रमसौ क्षत्रमत्रातृकमनीश्वरम् ।
स एव त्राता सर्वस्य ह्यत्रं क्षत्रमतो भवेत् ॥९॥

He[1] attains here[2] the character of an eater (of all food), viz. *kṣatra*, which does not have a lord (or ruler) over (it). He himself (becomes) the protector of all, the eater (of all food) and *kṣatra*.[3] [9]

[1]This refers to the worshipper of Prāṇa.
[2]That is, in/by the worship of Prāṇa.
[3]This indicates the worshipper's union/oneness with Prāṇa.

इति श्रीबृहदारण्यकोपनिषद्भाष्यवार्तिके पञ्चमाध्यायस्य
पञ्चदशं ब्राह्मणम् ॥१५॥

BṚHADĀRAṆYAKOPANIṢAD-BHĀṢYA-VĀRTIKA
5.16

हृदयं सत्यमित्यादिबहूपाधिसमाश्रयम् ।
उपासनमतिक्रान्तं ब्रह्मणः फलवद्बहु ॥१॥

So far has been described (in the Brāhmaṇa) beginning with *hṛdayaṃ satyam* the worship (of various kinds) in relation to many limiting adjuncts (of the Brahman), which is profusely fruitful. [1]

SP states the connection of this Brāhmaṇa with its immediately preceding Brāhmaṇa (viz. BU 5.15). This is, according to him, the reference in this verse. Yet the words *hṛdayaṃ satyam* refer to the third Brāhmaṇa onwards (viz. BU 5.3-15) and this is according to Śaṅkara—Sureśvara follows him.

सर्वोपाध्युपसंहारिगायत्र्युपाधिकं प्रभोः ।
अधुनोपासनं वाच्यमित्यर्थः पर आगमः ॥२॥

Now is to be discussed (lit. stated) the worship of the All-pervader (*prabhoḥ*), who has the limiting adjuncts of Gāyatrī that concludes (the sphere of) all the limiting adjuncts. For this purpose, there follows the subsequent text of the Śruti. [2]

sarvopādhyupāsaṃhāri refers to the purport of the Gāyatrī Brāhmaṇa (viz. BU 5.16) which now begins.

उदारफलसंप्राप्तावैश्वर्यं तत्र तत्र हि ।
श्रुतं श्रुतौ हि गायत्र्यास्तदुपास्तिर्वरा ततः ॥३॥

Since,[1] in the different portions (lit. here and there in the

Śruti) is heard great richness (*aiśvarya*) in the obtainment of profuse fruit through (lit. from) Gāyatrī (the deity of the metre) indeed;[2] therefore, the worship of that is superior to them (all).[3] [3]

[1]This refers to the first *hi* in the verse.
[2]This refers to the second *hi* in the verse.
[3]That is, the other modes of worship.

उदारफलसंबन्धो ब्राह्मणस्यैव नान्यतः ।
ब्राह्मणस्य च गायत्री कारणं तेन सा वरा ॥४॥

Enjoying (lit. connection with) profuse fruit is only in the case of a Brāhmaṇa and not of anybody else, and Gāyatrī is the origin[1] of a Brāhmaṇa; therefore, that one is considered as superior. [4]

[1]This is for *utpattikāraṇa*; cf. Śruti: *brāhmaṇo vyutthāya* ... (BU 3.6.1) and also *gāyatryā brāhmaṇam asṛjata. anyataḥ* (untraced) is for *anyasya*.

BU 5.16.1 is under reference.

भूमिरित्यादिवाक्येन त्रिलोकयष्टाक्षरोच्यते ।
अष्टाक्षरं पदं सिद्धं गायत्र्याः प्रथमं च यत् ॥५॥

In the sentence beginning with the word *bhūmiḥ*, there is mentioned (the collection of) the three worlds (whose names together) comprise eight letters; thereby is established that foot[1] of Gāyatrī which is its first. [5]

This verse refers to *bhūmi* (two letters), *antarikṣa* (four letters) and *dyaus* (two letters)—this refers to the Vedic practice of accepting the word *dyaus* as bi-syllabic, viz. diaus. This is an instance of the known mystical Brāhmaṇical equations.
[1]*pada* stands for 'a foot of a metre'.

अष्टाक्षरत्वसामान्याद्गायत्र्याः प्रथमं पदम् ।
तच्चेदं चैकतामेति संख्यासामान्यहेतुतः ॥६॥

On account of the similarity in having eight letters, the first foot of Gāyatrī and that, viz. this (triad of worlds), become one, the reason being the equality of numbers.[1] [6]

Because there are eight letters in *bhūmiḥ* ... and also in the foot of Gāyatrī, therefore they are equal. So also, because the number three is common, therefore Gāyatrī is equated to the three worlds. Thus, there are two levels considered; the level of words and the level of mystic oneness. This is explained in the following verse.

[1]The verse in Gāyatrī metre has three feet and there are three worlds, *bhūmi*, *antarikṣa* and *dyaus*.

त्रैलोक्याभिहितिरियमष्टाक्षरसमत्वतः ।
गायत्र्याद्यपादसमतो विराजात्मैक्यमश्नुते ॥७॥

This mentioning of (the collection of) the three worlds is owing to the equality in respect of eight letters. Because of the equality with the first foot of Gāyatrī, (a worshipper) attains oneness with Virāj. [7]

The three worlds together are Virāj and, therefore, the knowledge of the first foot of Gāyatrī as having the nature of the three worlds together means that one attains the nature of Virāj.

एवं पदं त्रयो लोका अभिधानाभिसंगतेः ।
अत्यन्तमभिधेयस्य विराजैक्यं प्रपद्यते ॥८॥

Thus, by construing together the expressions, viz. the foot (of Gāyatrī) and the three worlds, a worshipper acquires oneness with Virāj, which is the ultimate end (*atyantam*) of (this) expression.[1] [8]

[1]Possibly, what is to be said, viz. equality (of them). This is clarified in the following verse.

उक्ताभिधानद्वारेण संपन्नो यस्त्रिलोकताम् ।
यथोक्तोपासनाभ्यासाद्विराडेव भवेदसौ ॥९॥

He, who has thus obtained the nature of (the collection of) the three worlds through the already stated expression himself becomes Virāj, by the repetition of the worship thus stated. [9]

The worship consists in meditating on the first line of Gāyatrī as identical with the three worlds together.

त्रिषु लोकेषु यावत्स्यात्पुंभोगायेह साधनम् ।
तावत्सर्वं जयत्याशु प्रथमोपास्तितः फलम् ॥१०॥

Whichever is in the three words the means of/for the enjoyment of a man, all that he easily (lit. quickly) wins; this is the result from (i.e. of) the worship of first foot (of Gāyatrī). [10]

In the previous verse, there was a mention made of the Śrauta result of the worship under reference and in this verse there is now a mention of a non-Śrauta result (of the same).

रूपराशिरशेषेण भूम्याद्युक्त्योपसंहृतः ।

(Thus), by the mention of *bhūmi* etc. is stated together the entire mass of what has forms (viz. the mass of different things). [11ab]

BU 5.16.2 is under reference.

ऋच इत्यादिना ज्ञेया नामराश्युपसंहृतिः ॥११॥

By the words *ṛcaḥ* etc.[1] is to be understood (the collection of) what are names.[2] [11cd]

[1]The word etc. stands for *yajūṃṣi* and *sāmāni*.
[2]This refers to the form of the second foot of Gāyatrī.

अभिधेयाभिधानाख्यराशी नित्यौ व्यवस्थितौ ।
परस्पराभिसंबन्धौ गायत्रीवर्त्मनोदितौ ॥१२॥

The two collections of what is to be named and what is name arc thus clearly enumerated (*vyavasthitau*); (the two) having close (*abhi*) mutual relationship are expressed in the way of (the mention of the first two feet) of Gāyatrī. [12]

ऋगादेरभिधानस्य यावती व्याप्तिरिष्यते ।
तावत्सर्वमवाप्नोति यथोक्तोपासनान्नरः ॥१३॥

Whatever is extent of that (which is conveyed by the) name *ṛc* (i.e. Ṛgveda etc.) is all that a man attains through the worship already stated. [13]

व्याख्या तुल्यैव पूर्वेण वाक्येनोत्तरवाक्ययोः ।
अक्षराणामिह ज्ञेया नातो व्याख्यायते पुनः ॥१४॥

The explanation of the two subsequent statements is the same as that of the previous (i.e. first) sentence, i.e. in respect of (the number of) letters here. Therefore, it is not stated again. [14]

BU 5.16.3 is under reference.

कर्मराशिरथेदानीं प्राण इत्यादिनोच्यते ।
विधृतिः पूर्वयोः प्राणो मधुकाण्डे यथोदितः ॥१५॥

Now, in the words beginning with *prāṇa* is mentioned the mass of ritual actions. That *prāṇa* is the supporter of the two former collections[1] is stated in the Madhu Kāṇḍa.[2] [15]

[1]Supply: of names and forms in the earlier portion of Brāhmaṇa.
[1]This refers to BU 1.5, i.e. Saptānna Brāhmaṇa.

प्राणात्मानं यथोक्तेन पादेनापाद्य यत्नतः ।
प्राणात्मैव भवत्याशु सदा तद्भावभावितः ॥१६॥

Having carefully understood the nature of Prāṇa as consisting in (the third) foot of Gāyatrī, as stated (before), (the worshipper), having ever devoted himself to become that (Prāṇa), soon becomes (possessed) of the nature of Prāṇa. [16]

SP adds that the worship of the second foot of Gāyatrī has also a similar result. This is very likely to be becoming equal in status to the Trayī, or all that is nameable.

अभिधेयोपसंहारस्त्रिलोकीवचसोदितः ।
ऋच इत्यादिना तद्वदभिधानोपसंहृतिः ॥१७॥

In the statement of (the collection of) the three worlds, there is expressed the collection of all that is to be expressed. And, (in the statement) beginning with the word *ṛcaḥ*, there is similarly (a statement of) (the collection of) all the names. [17]

कर्मणोऽप्युपसंहारः प्राण इत्यादिना तथा ।
एतावद्वस्तु जगति गायत्रीपादसंश्रयम् ॥१८॥

In the same way, in the words beginning with *prāṇa*, there is (a statement of) the collection of (the content in ritual) activity. So far, (there has been a statement made about) the collection of things in the worlds as what rests on (the three) feet of Gāyatrī. [18]

अभिधेयस्य गायत्री यस्येयं त्रिपदा मता ।
तस्याभिधित्सयेदानीं प्रारब्धैषोत्तरा श्रुतिः ॥१९॥

Now the subsequent portion of Śruti begins with the intention of stating that which(ever) is to be named or expressed, viz. consisting in which is taken Gāyatrī having three feet. [19]

SP points out that this refers to the explanation of Hiraṇyagarbha which is of the nature of Āditya.
[1] Alternatively, expressive of which.

व्याचष्टे स्वयमेवार्थं तुर्यादिपदसंहतेः ।
यद्वै चतुर्थमित्यादिवचसा यत्नतः श्रुतिः ॥२०॥

The Śruti itself carefully (or regardfully) explains the meaning of the unit of words beginning with *turya* in the statement beginning with the wrods *yad vai caturtham.* [20]

रागो रज इति ज्ञेयः प्रवृत्तेः कारणं तु यत् ।
रञ्जनं काम आसङ्गः सर्वानर्थकृदात्मनः ॥२१॥

It is colour (*rāga*) that is to be taken (or known) as *rajas* and the cause of this usage of it is (the act of) colouring, viz. desire (or) close attachment (to the objects) which causes all undesirable (effects) on the individual self. [21]

The verse uses the word *ātman* in the sense of Jīva. SP justifies it with *Gītā* 2.62c: *saṃgāt saṃjāyate kāmaḥ*

तं क्रमित्वोपरि स्थित्वा तपतीति क्रियापदम् ।
भूतानि वा रजोवाचा भण्यन्तेऽत्राखिलानि तु ॥२२॥

The verb *tapati* means (i.e. refers to) transgressing (from verb root *kram*) that and remaining above (the same). And (*tu*) here (in the BU sentence) are expressed all the *bhūtas* 'elements' by the expression *rajaḥ*. [22]

उपर्युपरि तान्येष तपत्युल्बणरश्मिवान् ।
श्रीयशोभ्यां यथैवायं तपत्येवमुपासकः ॥२३॥
गुणैः सर्वानतिक्रम्य स्थित्वोपरि श्रिया ज्वलन् ।
यशसा च सुदीप्तेन विद्वांस्तपति विद्विषः ॥२४॥

As this one (i.e. Āditya), of very powerful rays, shines over and above (*upary-upari*) them, so also the worshipper (who is) thus (devoted to Gāyatrī) shines with glory and fame. [23]
A knower (of the nature of Gāyatrī) causes torment to his haters by his brilliantly shining fame, after having overcome all of them by his excellences, and thus, having stood over and above (them), with exceedingly shining (lit. burning) fame. [24]

These two verses explain the contents of verse 22 above.

कामितार्थस्य लब्धत्वात्सर्वग्रहणमात्रतः ।
उपर्युपरीति वीप्सा किमर्थमिति भण्यते ॥२५॥

(An objection is raised:) 'Since, by the very mention of the word *sarva*, all the desired objects are understood (lit. grasped), for what purpose is there then a repetition mentioned (in the words) *uparyupari*?' [25]

नैव दोषो यतो येषां सूर्यः स्यादुपरि स्थितः ।
लोकानां सर्वशब्देन तेषामेव ग्रहो भवेत् ॥२६॥
पराञ्चो ये रवेर्लोकास्तेषामपि परिग्रहः ।
कथं नु नाम सिद्धः स्यादतो वीप्सा प्रयुज्यते ॥२७॥

(The answer is given:) This[1] is not at all a fault, because there would be grasping (i.e. understanding) from the word

sarva of only those regions above which the sun is shining (lit. standing). [26]
(For) there is grasping of even those regions, which are beyond (the light of) the sun, (and since there would be a difficulty) as to how that (understanding) would be possible (lit. established), there is therefore repetition employed, (in the words *uparyupari*). [27]

[1]This refers to the so-called repetition.

BU 5.16.4 is under reference.

व्याख्याता या पुरा यत्नाद्गायत्री जगदात्मिका ।
मूर्तामूर्तरसे भानौ त्रिपादेषा प्रतिष्ठिता ॥२८॥

That Gāyatrī, which has been so far explained as having the nature of the entire world (*jagat*), is, with its three feet, supported in the sun which is (the very) essence of *mūrtāmūrta*. [28]

This is the meaning of *saiṣā* ... (BU 5.14.4).

तदपीदं पदं तुर्यं सत्येऽध्यात्मे प्रतिष्ठितम् ।
अक्ष्णि प्रकाशरूपे हि सर्वं रूपं प्रतिष्ठितम् ॥२९॥

And that, viz. this fourth foot (of Gāyatrī), in relation to the body also is supported in truth (*satya*); indeed in the eye, which is of the nature of light, is all (that has) form is supported. [29]

This explains the meaning of *tad vai tat satye pratiṣṭhitam*.

किं पुनस्तत्सत्यमिति सत्यं चक्षुरितीर्यते ।
चक्षुषः सत्यता कस्मादिति चेदुच्यते तथा ॥३०॥

(The question is:) 'What again is (that) *satya*?' Therefore (in answer) it is stated (*iti*) the nature of the truth (*satyatā*) abiding in the eye. Again, if (the question is): 'Why?', it is likewise (*tathā*) answered (now): [1] [30]

[1] That is, in the following two verses.

तस्मादित्यादिवाक्येन सत्यताक्ष्णो विभाव्यते ।
दृष्टं मृषापि श्रवणं न तु दृष्टिर्मृषेक्ष्यते ।
तस्या विशेषनिष्ठत्वान्मृषात्वं नोपपद्यते ॥३१॥

In the statement *tasmāt* ..., there is expressed (clearly seen) the nature of truth (*satyatā*) abiding in the eye. Also what is heard (*śravaṇam*) is found (lit. seen) to be false, but the act of seeing (*dṛṣṭi*) is not found (lit. seen) to be (grasping what is) false (i.e. what does not have the nature of truth). Since that (viz. seeing) is rooted in some particular (form), the idea of untruth in it cannot stand to reason. [31]

एवं तुरीयमेतस्मिन्सत्ये चक्षुषि सर्वदा ।
प्रकाशैकस्वभावे हि साक्षादेव प्रतिष्ठितम् ॥३२॥

Thus this fourth (foot of Gāyatrī), is ever perceptibly supported in the eye (viz. this truth) which has the nature of only illuminating objects. [32]

The purpose of this verse is to point out the similarity in the nature of the eye and Āditya as *ādheya-ādhāra*.

अक्ष्णि प्रकाशरूपेऽस्मिन्सर्वं रूपं प्रतिष्ठितम् ।
बले प्राणे प्रतिष्ठा च चक्षुषोऽपि प्रदश्यते ॥३३॥

In this eye, which is of the nature of light, all (that is) form is supported and the support of the eye also is shown (i.e. stated) (in the Śruti) to be in strength, viz. the Prāṇa. [33]

This is the explanation of *tad vai tad* ....

इन्द्राग्नी ताविमौ सिद्धावग्निस्तत्र प्रकाशकः ।
इन्द्रो विधरणः प्राणः पूर्वयोर्नामरूपयोः ॥३४॥

These two (viz. Indra and Agni) are thus established (as supported) [1] and, between the two, Agni is the illuminator whereas Indra the sustainer, and (further) Prāṇa (is the supporter) of the first two (viz. name and form). [2] [34]

[1] In Āditya and the eye.
[2] Prāṇa is the same as Indra and Agni (wich is itself Āditya). This is in relation to the world.

यावान्प्रकाशो जगति स सर्वोऽग्निरिहोच्यते ।
परिस्पन्दश्च सर्वत्र प्राण इन्द्रस्तथोच्यते ॥३५॥

Whatever light there is in this world is the whole of it called here Agni, (and whatever) movement (lit. throbbing) obtains everywhere is, in the same way, [1] called Prāṇa (viz. Indra). [35]

Prāṇa is known as the deity of strength and therefore is to be worshipped as being Indra, i.e. *bala*.
[1] As in the case of Agni earlier.

त्रिलोकी च त्रिवेदी च प्राणादित्रयमेव च ।
प्रतिष्ठितमिहाध्यात्म एवमुक्तेन वर्त्मना ॥३६॥

(The collection of) the three worlds, and that of the three Vedas and also the triad beginning with Prāṇa, [1] is here [2] supported in relation to the body (*adhyātme*), in the way described. [36]

This is the purport of *prāṇo vai balam*.
[1] This refers to *prāṇa*, *apāna*, *vyāna*.
[2] In the metre Gāyatrī.

प्राणादित्यौ हि गायत्रीसक्तावुक्तेन वर्त्मना ।
संजीवनं तदन्येषां प्राणानां भवतीश्वरात् ॥३७॥
सा हैषेति श्रुतिरतो यथोक्तार्थावबुद्धये ।
प्राणान्गयान्यतस्तत्रे गायत्रीयमतो मता ॥३८॥

(Thus), in the way stated (earlier), Prāṇa and Āditya are supported (*sakta*) in the Gāyatrī and that[1] becomes the life of all other *prāṇas*, i.e. through (the strength of) the overlord.[2] [37]

Therefore (follows) the Śruti *sā haiṣā* for making one know what is already stated. Since it protected the *prāṇas*, the *gayas*,[3] it is called (or known) as Gāyatrī. [38]

This is the explanation of *evam v eṣā gāyatry adhyāmam pratiṣṭhitā sā haiṣā gayāṃs tatre*.

The word Gāyatrī is here derived from *gaya* connected with a root *trai* 'to protect'.

[1]This refers to their being so supported in the Gāyatrī.

[2]This stands for the powerful Gāyatrī.

[3]Śaṅkara (in BUB p.736) derives the word *gaya* (for *prāṇa* 'organ') from the verb root *gai* 'to produce sound' (*śabdakaraṇāt*). Read Ānandagiri on BUB: *gāyantīti gayā vāgupalakṣitāś cakṣurādayaḥ*— here the expressed vocal organ stands for all organs.

उपनीतौ स आचार्यः पच्छश्चार्धर्चशस्तथा ।
सावित्रीं याममं प्राह बटवे मन्त्रलक्षणाम् ॥३९॥
साप्येषैव च विज्ञेया व्याख्याता या प्रयत्नतः ।
यस्मै प्राह स आचार्यस्तस्य प्राणानवत्यसौ ॥४०॥

This Sāvitrī[1] (*ṛc*) which the preceptor recited to a pupil, foot by foot, or (also) by half-verse by half-verse, at the time of the thread ceremony (*upanītau*), viz. that (verse) which has the nature of a Mantra, [39]

that also is to be known as this very verse,[2] the one which is carefully explained. It protects the *prāṇas*[3] (of that pupil) to whom the preceptor has recited (this Mantra). [40]

This is the meaning of *sa yām evāmūṃ sāvitrīm anvāha* ....

[1]The word Savitṛ refers to a *ṛc* in Gāyatrī metre which is addressed to the deity Savitṛ. Cf. *Ṛgveda* 3.62.10.

[2]Namely, the Gāyatrī *ṛc*.

[3]This is the explanation why the Gāyatrī and the Sāvitrī are identical.

एवंवित्सन्स आचार्यो यस्मा अन्वाह सादरः ।
त्रायते तस्य गायत्री बटोः प्राणान्न संशयः ॥४१॥

Undoubtedly, Gāyatrī protects the *prāṇas* of that pupil to whom the preceptor, being conversant with (the matter) thus (stated), carefully recited the *ṛc*. [41]

This explains the meaning of the preceding verse more clearly.

BU 5.16.5 is under reference.

माणवकस्योपनयनसमये वेदवादिनाम् ।
छन्दः प्रति विवादोऽयं तन्निर्णीतौ परा श्रुतिः ॥४२॥

Among those, who recited the Veda, this is a dispute on *Chandas* 'metre' of this verse, (recited) at the time of the thread ceremony of a young boy; (therefore), in order to give a decision on that, there follows the subsequent Śruti (statement). [42]

This is the purport of *tām etām* ....

तां हैतामिति वाक्येन सावित्रीं प्रतिदर्श्यताम् ।
अनुष्टुप्छन्दसं ब्रूयात्पूर्वपक्षप्रसिद्धये ॥४३॥
तामेतामेक आचार्या उपनीताय यत्नतः ।
अनुष्टुप्छन्दसं प्राहुः सावित्रीं न्यायसंश्रयात् ॥४४॥

By the sentence *tām haitām* (one should express the opinion) regarding the Sāvitrī as having the metre Anuṣṭup, so that the *prima facie* view is established. [43]

Some preceptors have carefully recited to the initiated pupil this verse, viz. Sāvitrī *ṛc*, in the metre Anuṣṭup—this (they did) by resorting to some reason.[1] [44]

[1]This is explained in the following verse.

वागनुष्टुब्यतः साक्षाद्वाक्च साक्षात्सरस्वती ।
उपनीताय सैवातो वक्तव्या न ततोऽपरा ॥४५॥

Since Vāc is itself the Anuṣṭup[1] and Vāc is the Sarasvatī (also), the same (i.e. only that) is therefore to be taught to the one who is initiated, not any[2] other (*ṛc*). [45]

[1]For Vāc as Anuṣṭup, cf. the Śruti: *vāg vā anuṣṭup*.
[2]SP points out the purport of this Sāvitrī Mantra in the words *tathā ca tat satitur vṛṇīmahe vayaṃ devasya bhojanam, śreṣṭhaṃ sarvadhātaraṃ turam bhagasya dhīmahīy anuṣṭupchandaska-sāvitryarpaṇe sarasvaty evārpitā syād ity arthaḥ.*

यथैतदुक्तमाचार्यैः कुर्याद्विद्वान्न तत्तथा ।
गायत्रीमेव सावित्रीं ब्रूयात्सर्वफलाप्तितः ॥४६॥

A learned man should do as he has been taught by the preceptors, not in that way as said before by other preceptors: He should recite the Gāyatrī itself as Sāvitrī, since (thereby) (for him) (i.e. all the results accrue to him). [46]

This verse states the Siddhāntin's view *na ... phalāptitaḥ*.

SP points out that, by the mention of only Anuṣṭup, the result that accrues to the worshipper is (the favour of) Sarasvatī; but, by the mention of Gāyatrī, the result is the acquisition of everything. Therefore, there is emphasis on recitation of only Gāyatrī.

This would mean that a verse addressed to Savitṛ can be in Anuṣṭup metre, but that is set aside in favour the one (to Savitṛ) in Gāyatrī metre.

यथोक्तायां हि गायत्र्यां कृत्स्नं जगदुपाहितम् ।
तदुक्तौ सर्वमुक्तं स्याद्यत्पुमर्थाय साधनम् ॥४७॥

Indeed, the entire world is placed in the Gāyatrī, as has been already explained; in reciting that, there occurs the statement of all that which is the means to (the acquisition of) the end of human life. [47]

विज्ञानपुरुषस्येदं स्वभावादेव सर्वदा ।
आत्मैव हि जगत्कृत्स्नं साधारणविशेषवत् ॥४८॥

This entire world is ever the Ātman owing to the very nature of the *vijñānapuruṣa*, 'the individual self', which comprises the common and the uncommon[1] (things in it). [48]

This verse explains the purport of *yadi ha ....*

[1] Cf. next verse where *viśeṣa* is paraphrased as *asādhāraṇa*.

साधारणानि वस्तूनि तथासाधारणान्यपि ।
नानुपादाय कृत्स्नानि जन्तोः काचित्क्रियेष्यते ॥४९॥

Without taking up the common things and also the uncommon things, there is never done (lit. desired) any action of whosoever was born. [49]

SP states that the thought of this verse has been fully clarified in the Madhu Brāhmaṇa.

अभिव्यक्तेः पुराप्येतद्रूपमासीत्स्वभावतः ।
अभिव्यक्तौ तु तत्साक्षात्समष्टिव्यष्टिलक्षणम् ॥५०॥

Before the manifestaion (of an individual self), there was this form (of its cause), by its very nature, and, after the manifestaion (of an individual), the same became characterized by collective (world) and particulars in it. [50]

एवं सिद्धे महिम्न्यस्मिन्यथोक्तेनैव वर्त्मना ।
कनीयस्ता विवृद्धिर्वा नैव संभाव्यते मितेः ॥५१॥

Thus, when the greatness (of Gāyatrī) is thus established here, in the way stated, there is not possible any decrease (i.e. becoming less) or increase of the knowledge.[1] [51]

[1]Sureśvara uses the word *miti* for *mātṛ*, i.e. the knower, viz. one who knows the Ātman.

ऊरीकृत्येममेवार्थं स य इत्यादिनोच्यते ।
महाप्रतिग्रहेणापि नैवंविद्दोषमृच्छति ॥५२॥

Having accepted this as the very purport, the Śruti has stated in words *sa yaḥ* ... that the person, who knows thus, does not come to have any blemish, even though he has obtained (varied) great advantage.[1] [52]

This verse marks the statement of the particular result acquired from the knowledge of the nature or the purposefulness of the Gāyatrī.

[1]Add: (as are hinted at) in the preceding verse (SP).

दर्शनस्य स्तुतिरियं स य इत्यादिनोच्यते ।
तादृक्प्रतिग्रहस्येह न क्वचित्संभवो यतः ॥५३॥

In the words (of the Śruti) *sa yaḥ* ..., there is a praise of (this view), because there is no possibility here, any similar advantage. [53]

प्रतिग्रहस्य निन्दा वा विद्वन्मानात्प्रसक्तितः ।

निःशेषपुण्यमोषित्वान्निषेधार्थाय कुत्स्यते ॥५४॥

Or rather, there is here censure of accepting gifts since there is a contingency of a person's being proud of being a knower [1]—such a person is found fault with,[2] because (his pride) has the nature of wiping away [3] all his merit—(thus is this censure) for prohibiting.[4] [54]

This is another way of stating the purport of what is mentioned earlier.

[1]That is to say: he may have greater pride than what he might legitimately have as the feeling of a knower. Or he might be proud, even if he would not be a knower—A knower of the significance of Gāyatrī is meant.

[2]Or, 'is spoken ill of'; alternatively, 'made a butt of ridicule'.

[3]Literally, steals away, i.e. destroys.

[4]Supply: acceptance of gifts.

BU 5.16.6 is under reference.

उक्तपादेष्वपि ज्ञानं नैवालमपबाधितुम् ।
गायत्रीवेदिनो जन्तोरपि भूयान्प्रतिग्रहः ॥५५॥

Even knowledge in relation to the feet (of the Gāyatrī, i.e. Sāvitrī *ṛc*) which are stated is not effective (lit. capable) in warding away (that censure); for, in the case of a knower of the Gāyatrī [1] also, there can be greater acceptance of gifts. [55]

[1]This refers to its significance.

नैवं दाता जगत्यस्मिन्न च तादृक्प्रतिग्रहः ।
ग्रहीता वेह नैवेति कुत इत्यादिनोच्यते ॥५६॥

In the words of the Śruti *kutaḥ* ...,[1] the purport is: there is not in this world a giver of gifts like this one, there is not a similar acceptance of gifts, and there is not any one who (has the capacity) to secure them. [56]

[1]Cf. BU 5.14.6.

अप्यभ्युपगमे चैषां नैव दोषस्य संभवः ।
विदुषोऽस्तीत्यतः प्राह स य इत्यादिना श्रुतिः ॥५७॥

When all these[1] are accepted, there is no blemish to follow in the case of a knower of the Gāyatrī—to say this,[2] the Śruti has begun with (the words) *sa yaḥ* .... [57]

[1]What we mentioned in preceding verse, viz. rich gifts.
[2]That is, to answer the question implied in this statement.

स यः कश्चिदिमाँल्लोकान्पूर्णान्पुंभोगसाधनैः ।
विद्वान्संप्रतिगृह्णीयात्कथंचित्कामसंप्लुतेः ॥५८॥
आद्यपादपरिज्ञानमात्रस्यैव प्रतिग्रहः ।
क्षयायालं न शेषस्य गायत्रीदर्शनस्य सः ॥५९॥

He whosoever, a knower (of the Gāyatrī), would accept these worlds, abounding in (various) means of enjoyment for human beings (and) somehow, on account of being overpowered by desires, [58]
(would have received only what can come as) the result from the complete (*pari*) knowledge of (just) the first foot (of the Gāyatrī); that is not powerful enough to destroy (i.e. exhaust) (the result of) the knowledge of the remaining feet of the Gāyatrī. [59]

These verses answer the question implied in the preceding verse in a very cryptic style.

यावतीयं त्रयी विद्या तावन्तमपि गृह्णतः ।
द्वितीयपदविज्ञानक्षतिरेव न सर्वतः ॥६०॥

In the case of the one who accepts only that much (the reward) as a result of his knowledge of the three Vedas, there is destruction, a loss only in respect of his knowledge of the second foot, (but) not the destruction of all (that he has known from the Gāyatrī). [60]

असंभवेऽपि कल्प्येत यदि तादृक्प्रतिग्रहः ।
त्रैविद्यलक्षणः सोऽपि तृतीयं नाप्नुयात्पदम् ॥६१॥

If a result of that is magnitude imagined, (for a person) even while there is no possibility of it, then he, though possessed of the knowledge of (all) the three Vedas will not obtain (the result of) the third foot (of the Gāyatrī). [61]

अन्तरण्डविभक्तस्य यथोक्तैः स्यात्प्रतिग्रहैः ।
क्षयो नानन्तरूपस्य स्यात्समष्टिवपुर्भृतः ॥६२॥

By the acceptance of the gifts (thus) described, there would not be destruction of the one (viz. the inner self of a person, i.e. the Ātman) which has divided itself (as it were) in the universe[1] and has infinite (number of) forms (and yet, in reality) bearing the form of collection (of all beings together).[2] [62]

[1]Literally, the egg (form of the Brahman); cf. the commonly used word *brahmāṇḍa*.
[2]This refers to the result of a person's knowledge of the fourth foot of the Gāyatrī, viz. the whole of the Gāyatrī.

परिच्छिन्नेन सर्वत्र प्रतिमानं जगत्यपि ।
अन्तवद्विषयं दृष्टं न त्वनन्तस्य कुत्रचित् ॥६३॥

And there is seen in the world 'an example for what is limited (in magnitude) and is, therefore, having an end, but there is not seen anywhere that (viz. example) one for what is limitless. [63]

The purport of the verse is to bring out the result of the worship of the fourth foot of Gāyatrī which is imperishable, as against that of any of the other three feet. This is to strengthen further what is said in the end of the preceding verse.

अयं चानन्तमात्मानमक्षिसूर्यव्यवस्थितम् ।
अगादुपासनात्प्राणमात्मत्वेन दिवानिशम् ॥६४॥

For, this one, i.e. the worshipper, has reached the infinite Ātman, through worshipping it, day and night as the Prāṇa, viz. the Ātman that has been abiding in the eye as the sun. [64]

संभाव्यते क्षयस्तस्य न कुतश्चिदनन्ततः ।
अन्तवान्क्षीयते लोके न त्वनन्तः कुतश्चन ॥६५॥

There can never be conceived the destruction (lit. loss) of this one, since it has infiniteness.[1] In this world, that which has an end is seen to come to destruction but not, on any account, that which is limitless. [65]

[1]*anantataḥ* stands for *anantavattvataḥ*.

आवृत्तिः क्षयशब्देन दुःखप्रायासु भूमिषु ।
कैवल्यावसितेर्नासौ स्यात्समष्टिवपुर्भृतः ॥६६॥

By the word *kṣaya* (is) indicated rebirth (lit. repeated existence of one) at various levels which are mostly full of grief/sorrow, whereas that (rebirth) is not to be conceived in the case of one who has assumed the form of collection (of all beings, i.e. the Ātman) on account of having achieved liberation (lit. the state of singleness). [66]

BU 5.16.7 is under reference.

उपस्थानं यथोक्ताया गायत्र्याः श्रद्धयान्वितः ।
गायत्र्यसीतिमन्त्रेण कुर्यादुक्तार्थवित्सदा ॥६७॥
एकद्वित्रिपद्यसीति पर्वान्पादान्विचिन्तयेत् ।
चतुष्पात्त्वं च तुर्येण यथोक्तेन विचिन्तयेत् ॥६८॥
अपदसीत्यपि गिरा तस्या आनन्त्यमुच्यते ।
अव्यया चाक्षयासीति न ह्यन्तस्तेऽधिगम्यते ॥६९॥
नमस्तेऽस्तु तुरीयायेत्युक्त्या तुर्यप्रधानताम् ।
गुणभावं यथोक्तस्य विद्यात्पादत्रयस्य तु ॥७०॥
शत्रुनामगृहीत्यर्थमसावितिपदं त्विह ।
फलोक्तिरद इत्येतदुपासितुरहं तथा ॥७१॥

A person, who has known the significance (of Gāyatrī) which is already explained, should ever with faith offer the worship[1] to Gāyatrī which is described before, with the Mantra *gāyatry asi* .... [67]

He should ponder (think to himself) over the first three feet, (reciting the Mantras) *ekapadī asi*, *dvīpadī asi*, and *tripadī asi*.[2] And he should ponder over the nature (of the Gāyatrī) as being four-footed (reciting the whole Mantra of Gāyatrī, viz.) *turya* (the fourth one which is laready stated). [68]

Also in the words *apad asi* there is stated the infiniteness of that (Gāyatrī) and (in the words) *avyayā cākṣayāsi* is understood (the meaning) 'there is indeed no end of you (O Gāyatrī)'. [69]

One should know from the statement *namas te 'stu turīyāya* ... that the *turya* has prominence (with reference to the three feet) and also the subordinateness of those three feet that are (already) described. [70]

And, in this context (of the Brāhmaṇa), the word *asau* is for uttering (in its place) the name of the enemy and the word *adaḥ* and *aham* as well are used as the statements of the result for the worshipper. [71]

[1]This is meant by the word *upasthāna*; verse 73 also uses

it in the same sense.

[2]Sureśvara uses the compound of *eka*, *dvi* and *tri* with *padī*. Also, as a consequence, the verb *asi* is used only once. Translation indicates this, by separating one sentence into three sentences.

शत्रुणा कामितो योऽर्थो मा प्रापत्तमसाविति ।
मा समृद्ध्यथवा सोऽस्मै तं वाहं प्राप्नुयामिति ॥७२॥

'Let that thing which is desired by my enemy not come to him.' Or, let it not prosper for him. Or, may I obtain that. [72]

This explains Mantras *asāv ado mā prapat kāmo 'smai mā samṛddhy aham adaḥ prāpam.*

अभिचारार्थमेतस्मिन्नुपस्थाने यथोदिते ।
अभिधानैकदेशोक्त्या विकल्पः फलगोचरः ॥७३॥

In this worship, which is thus described in this (statement),[1] is for conveying black magic (*abhicāra*) (and) in this statement (of one of the three names of the Gāyatrī as said before) there is option pertaining to the result. [73]

[1]Namely, what is said under verse 72: *asāv ado ....*

स्वार्थे त्वहमद इति ह्युपस्थाने फलं भवेत् ।
अदः प्रयोजनं देवि प्राप्नुयां त्वत्प्रसादतः ॥७४॥

And with reference to the purpose for himself the result (of the worship) is (as expressed in the words) *aham adaḥ*. (The thought in worshipper's mind is:) 'O goddess (Gāyatrī), may I obtain that purpose through your favour'. [74]

BU 5.16.8 is under reference.

एतावदेव किं ज्ञेयं किं वान्यदपि शिष्यते ।

अस्त्यन्यदपि विज्ञेयं तद्विनाकृत्स्नता यतः ॥७५॥

(A question could be asked:) 'Only this much is to be known, or, is there anything else which remained to be stated?' (In answer it is said:) 'Yes, another thing is also to be known, since without that there is incompleteness (in respect of the knowledge about the Gāyatrī). [75]

कात्स्न्येन विद्या स्वभ्यस्ता फलायालमुपासितुः ।
विपर्ययेणानर्थाय तदेतत्प्रतिपाद्यते ॥७६॥

The lore (of the Gāyatrī) which is well-studied[1] in its completeness, results into (good) effect thereof for the worshipper; as against this, that is alternatively, it results into undesirable (result for him). It is this that is put forth, (in the subsequent portion of the text). [76]

[1]That is, Gāyatrī is repeatedly recited.

In the following, Sureśvara has referred only to the significant part of a small bit of narrative that is told in BU—he omits a few details thereof. This marks the cryptic character of his treatment of the whole Brāhmaṇa.

सर्वात्मकत्वाद्गायत्र्या अग्नेरपि परिग्रहः ।
तन्मुखत्वेनासंसिद्धेस्तादर्थ्येनोत्तरा श्रुतिः ॥७७॥

Since the Gāyatrī is of the nature of all (objects in the world), therefore, there is understood even Agni. Thus since (Agni has been) established as the mouth of the Gāyatrī, the subsequent (portion of the) Śruti is for (stating) its purpose. [77]

मुखविज्ञानविरहादनर्थफलकीर्तनम् ।
अग्निरेव मुखं तस्या इत्युक्त्या कृत्स्नतोच्यते ॥७८॥

There is (in the narrative in the Brāhmaṇa) the statement about the undesirable result arising from the absence of the knowledge (of the Gāyatrī) of the mouth. (As such), by the statement *agnir eva mukhaṃ tasyāḥ* there is stated the fullness of the worship. [78]

गायत्रीदर्शनस्येह फलकात्स्न्यं तथैव च ।
यथोक्ताग्निमुखज्ञानाद्यदीत्यादिगिराधुना ॥७९॥

There is thus stated here[1] the fullness of the result (arising) from viewing the Gāyatrī (in this way) and also from knowing that Agni is its face, as said (before)—now in this statement *yadi* ....[2] [79]

[1] That is, in the Brāhmaṇa.
[2] Read: *yadi ha vā api bahv ivāgnāv abhyādadhati sarvam eva tat saṃdahati*.

यो वेदाग्निमुखामेतां गायत्रीमग्निरेव सः ।
अग्निरिन्धनवत्सर्वं दहेद्विद्वान्प्रतिग्रहम् ॥८०॥

He, who has known this Gāyatrī as having Agni as its face, himself is Agni. The learned man, (who has thus become) Agni, burns the mass of all advantages,[1] just as a fire (burns) the fire-wood. [80]

[1] Add: which he has received by accepting the gifts as fees.

दाहकस्य न बह्वस्ति दाह्ययोगाभिवृद्धितः ।
क्षयश्चाशेषदाह्यस्य यस्मात्तस्मादिवेतिगीः ॥८१॥

For the one that burns,[1] there does not exist (too) much (to burn), (even) when there is increase in what is to be burnt[2] and there is destruction of what is to be burnt, in its entirety—since (this is so), therefore there is (in the text) the word *iva*. [81]

This is an explanation of the use of *iva* in BU, and SP points to the connection of *iva* with the *dārṣṭāntika* also.

[1]This refers to the worshipper of the Gāyatrī.

[2]The sins of the worshipper are meant.

एवंविदेवमेव स्यात्पापं वह्निवदिन्धनम् ।
सर्वं संभक्ष्य तत्पापं शुद्धः पापवियोगतः ॥८२॥

One, who has known this, would become just this one (viz. Prajāpati), his sin would be the fuel associated with fire.[1] That knower will have eaten up that sin and would become pure, owing to his separation from the sin. [82]

[1]That is to say: It will get burnt.

पूतोऽसंसर्गिधर्मत्वादजरोऽपरिणामवान् ।
अमृतोऽस्थूलदेहत्वात्प्राणमात्रस्वभावतः ॥८३॥

He is pure because he has not any contact with various Dharmas (implied by ritual), he would never be aging because he will not have any modifications (in him by the ritual). He would be immortal because his body will not have grossness and because he has the nature of only Prāṇa. [83]

इति श्रीबृहदारण्यकोपनिषद्भाष्यवार्तिके पञ्चमाध्यायस्य
षोडशं ब्राह्मणम् ॥१६॥

BṚHADĀRAṆYAKOPANIṢAD-BHĀṢYA-VĀRTIKA
5.17

यथोक्तोपासनाभ्यासभावितस्य क्रियाकृतः ।
उपस्थानं प्रवक्तव्यमित्यर्थः पर आगमः ॥१॥

(Now) there is to be prescribed some mode of worship for the performer of religious acts, (for him) who has known and repeatedly devoted himself to the (already prescribed modes of worship). For this purpose, there now follows the subsequent Āgama (i.e. Brāhmaṇa). [1]

In the beginning, Sureśvara does intend to include *jñāna-karmasamuccaya* even in respect of the worship of Gāyatrī, of course, following Śaṅkara.

तुरीयं पदमादित्यो लोकद्वारं च येन सः ।
संभाव्यते प्रसङ्गोऽत आदित्योपस्थितेरिह ॥२॥

The fourth foot (of the Gāyatrī) is Āditya and, because that (Āditya) is the entrance [1] to the *loka* (of the Brahman), therefore, there necessarily follows (*prasaṅga*) here the occasion for (prescribing) the worship of Āditya. [2]

In the earlier Brāhmaṇa, a special mode of worship of Āditya was not discussed, but here it is discussed for one in whom there is *jñānakarmasamuccaya*; cf. note under verse 1 above.

[1] Āditya is extraodinarily so called, because, in the case of one who attains liberation, one has always to come to Āditya and then proceed onwards.

हिरण्यं ज्योतिरमृतं मण्डलेन तदात्मना ।

सत्यस्य परमार्थस्य द्वारमाच्छादितं रवेः ॥३॥

Hiraṇya means flame, immortality. And by the orb of Āditya, which has that (flame) as its nature, is closed the door to Āditya, the highest reality, viz. *satya*. [3]

त्वद्दर्शनार्थिने मह्यं पूषन्द्वारमपावृणु ।
जगत्पुष्णाति वृष्ट्याद्यैः पूषादित्यस्ततः स्मृतः ॥४॥

'O God, Pūṣan, open that door for me, who am desirous of seeing you.'[1] Since he nourishes the world by showers etc.,[2] therefore, Pūṣan is known as Āditya. [4]

This explains *tattvam* ....
The Vedic god Pūṣan is identified with Āditya. And also, there is a derivation of the name Pūṣan attempted.
[1]This is a gist of a verse from *Vājasaneyi Saṃhitā* 40.17 (also in BU of Kāṇva recension). This gist continues in the next verse also.
[2]The word etc. refers to nourishing plants and beings by giving them suitable heat, protecting the human beings from the fear of the dark, and showing them the proper paths (as will be clarified later in verses 6ff. and also verse 19 below).

सत्या अवितथा धर्मा यस्य मानव्यपाश्रयात् ।
तस्मै मे सत्यधर्माय दृष्टयै द्वारमपावृणु ॥५॥

'Open the door for me, who have *satya* as religious duty,[1] so that I can see (Reality)'[2]—for me, whose religious duties are never false, on account of (my) resorting to the (authoritative) means (of knowing the same). [5]

This explains *satyadharmāya* ....
[1]This is *dharma* which can be a law (for one's conducting oneself) also.
[2]This is clear from verse 3 above.

हिमघर्माम्बुदानेन पुष्णातीदं यतो जगत् ।
तस्मात्पूषा यतश्चैको गच्छत्येकर्षिता ततः ॥६॥
संयमात्सर्वयाम्यानां यमोऽसि परमेश्वरः ।
स्वीरणाच्छीततोयादेः सूर्यस्तेनासि घर्मदः ॥७॥
प्रजापतिः परं ब्रह्म कारणं तदपत्यतः ।
प्राजापत्योऽसि तेन त्वं गीयसे विपुलश्रुतैः ॥८॥

Since he nourishes this world by giving cool, heat and waters, he is called Pūṣan and, since he is the only one that acts (lit. goes), therefore, he is the only Ṛṣi 'seer'.[1] [6]
By controlling all those, who need to be controlled, you are Yama, the Great Lord. And by a proper (lit. good, *su*) urging of cool water etc.[2] you are Sūrya and, therefore, the source (lit. giver) of heat.[3] [7]
Prajāpati is the highest Brahman, the cause (viz. origin) (and therefore), being an offspring of his, you are described as Prājāpatya—and, therefore, praised (lit. sung) by those who have much learning.[4] [8]

Sureśvara explains the different words in the prayer to Pūṣan.
[1] In the original Mantra there is an epithet of Pūṣan, *ekarṣi*.
[2] The word etc. refers to *gharma* 'heat'.
[3] This gives the derivation of the names Yama from verb root *yam* and Sūrya from verb root *īr* with *su* prefixed to it.
[4] That is, who have studied the Vedas extensively.

रश्मीनपनुदाशेषांस्तेजः संयच्छ संहर ।
कल्याणं ते यदत्यर्थं रूपं यच्च तवैव तत् ॥९॥
सदा त्वाहं प्रपश्यामि सत्यधर्मान्वयाद्यथा ।
भगवन्सत्यरूपेण मद्धर्मोऽपि भवांस्तथा ॥१०॥

Drive far and wide (your) rays, well control the lustre, i.e. well-organize (it) most, that form (of yours) which is the most blissful and is only yours. [9]
And as I ever see you on account of your association with

the *dharma*s 'laws'[1] and *satya* 'truth', O Bhagavan, let my *dharma* also be of the nature of *satya* and may you look upon me to be so.[2] [10]

Now follows the meaning of *vyūha* ....

[1]Or, 'duties'; in the Vedic notions of religion, the gods also follow certain laws (there, the word is *vrata*). Cf. *dhṛtavrata* of Varuṇa, *śucivratā* of the two Aśvins.

[2]That is, I also am *satyadharmānvayin*.

योऽसावादित्यगो देवः सोऽहमस्मीतिबुद्धिगः ।
स्थानमात्राच्च तौ भिन्नौ वस्तुतो नावयोर्भिदा ॥११॥

That god, which resides in Āditya, and that, which abides in (my) intellect in the form of the awareness 'I am that' are distinct only on account of the (difference in their) abodes. In reality, however, there is no difference (whatsoever) between us two. [11]

This explains *yo 'sāvasau puruṣaḥ so 'ham asmi* in BU 5.15.1.

देवतामनिलं यातु वायुर्योऽयं शरीरगः ।
शरीरं भस्मसाद्यातु मर्त्यत्वं ह्येतदाश्रितम् ॥१२॥

May this wind (Vāyu), which is existing in my body, go to the divine Vāyu. (And) may (this) body which is rendered to ashes go (to the earth), since this one, has related[1] to mortality. [12]

This explains *vāyuḥ* ... *śarīram* in BU 5.15.1.

[1]That is, is beset with; however, lit. resorted.

भस्मान्तमिति लिङ्गाच्च कर्मिणः स्यादुपस्थितिः ।
न तु संन्यासिनो न्याय्या दाहासंभवहेतुतः ॥१३॥

And, there, the notion understood about a performer of rituals on the basis of the indicative word *bhasmāntam* 'ending into ashes', does not, however, reasonably pertain to an ascetic, because there is no possibility of the burning (of the body) of that one. [13]

This explains the significance of the word *bhasmāntam*.

वायुरित्यादिकं ग्राह्यमुपलक्षणमेव तु ।
शिष्टानां देवतांशानां यथास्वं प्रतिपत्तये ॥१४॥

The words, beginning with *vāyuḥ*, are to be taken only as an indicator of the deities (who superintend over different parts of the body), so that it becomes what was its own source.[1] [14]

This explains *tathānyadevatāḥ svām* ... in BUB.
[1]Each of these deities merges into its own origin.

अग्निं स्वात्ममनःसंस्थामधुना देवतां गृही ।
प्रार्थयत्योमिति गिरा मुमूर्षुस्तत्परीप्सया ॥१५॥

Now, a householder, who is about to die, offers a prayer to Agni, (who is the deity) residing in his own body and *manas*, uttering the word *om*, with a desire to obtain (oneness) with the same. [15]

One remembers here *Gītā* 8.6:
yaṃ yaṃ vāpi smaran bhāvaṃ tyajaty ante kalevaram /
taṃ tam evaiti kaunteya sadā tadbhāvabhāvitaḥ //
[1]Here, the word *ātman* refers to the body.

सर्वस्याप्यवनादोमं स्यादवतेरों यतस्ततः ।
क्रतुर्मनोमयत्वाच्च सा हि संकल्परूपिणी ॥१६॥

Since Om is derived from the root *ava*, this one (Agni) is Om on account of his offering protection to all. And *kratu* is because it originates in *manas*; that (deity) [1] is of the nature of a design (of what is to be done). [16]

[1]The verse uses the word *sā* (a feminine form) and therefore it should be taken to refer to the *devatā* (feminine) of *kratu* (masculine).

ओं क्रतो इति संबोध्य स्मरेत्यत्र नियुज्यते ।
प्रकृष्टफलसंप्राप्तेः स्मृतिमात्रैकहेतुतः ॥१७॥
स्मर्तव्यं स्मर तेनाद्य मरणे प्रत्यपस्थिते ।
आदरार्थं स्मरेत्यस्य पुनः पुनरुदीरणम् ॥१८॥

Having addressed (the deity) with the words *Oṃ krato* ...— that (address) is connected with the word *smara*, because we obtain excellent fruit only by remembrance (of the deity). [17] Therefore (it is meant to say) remember what is to be remembered, now when (my) death is imminent. The repetition of the word *smara* again and again is only to express regard (for the deity). [18]

This is anakoluthic construction that was at times noticed only in Vedic Saṃhitās.

सुपथा नय नो वह्ने सुपथेति विशेषणात् ।
उदङ्मार्गग्रहो न्याय्यः शिष्टानां पुनरागतेः ॥१९॥

From the specification by the adjective *supatha* in 'O fire, lead us by a good path', it is only reasonable to accept the (movement of a departed Jīva by) the northern path; (this is so) because the others (who are not included in us in the prayer) do come back (to the mortal world) again. [19]

राये कर्मफलायेति रयिः कर्मफलं यतः ।
प्रज्ञानानि च सर्वाणि देव विद्वान्क्रियास्तथा ॥२०॥

The word *rāye* means *karmaphalāya* 'for securing the result of the (ritual) activity', since it (viz. *rayi*) is the result of *karman* 'ritual activity'. (So also it is said) 'O god ...' (for) he is a knower—there is here a reference to all the inner thoughts[1] (of the worshippers) as also to (ritual) actions. [20]

[1]These are *prajñānāni*, a paraphrase of the word *vayunāni* in the Vedic Mantra. Since the phrase *kriyās tathā* stands baside *prajñānāni*, we have to refer it to the inner thoughts.

कुटिलं च तथा पापमस्मत्तस्त्वं वियोजय ।
वयं तु कृतकृत्यत्वादशक्ताश्च मुमूर्षवः ॥२१॥
नमउक्तिमतो भक्त्या तुभ्यं बहुतमां धिया ।
आयुषोऽन्ते विधेमाद्य क्षम देव प्रसीद मे ॥२२॥

And similarly remove from us our sin, i.e. evil, (O God). As for ourselves, we are now weak after having done our religious duties and are about to die. [21]
Therefore, at the end of our life, we offer to you with devotion a respectful prayer (which is) the most potent in thought (*bahutamā dhiyā*).
Therefore we offer you at the end of our life a prayer in (full) respect, with devotion, and the most potent in thought (*bahutamā*). Forgive me, O God, and be favourable also. [22]

Here, in these verses, there is a change from *vayam* understood from 'us' to *aham* (viz. me). This is because Sureśvara is trying to explain the intention in the Vedic verse, viz. the offering of a prayer by one which meant the offering by all.

मस्करीन्द्रप्रणीतस्य भवनामभृतो यतेः ।
भाष्यस्य वार्तिकोक्त्यैवमध्यायः सप्तमो गतः ॥२३॥

Thus ends the seventh Adhyāya of my statement in the Vārtika on the Bhāṣya composed by the best of the ascetics who bears the name of Bhava (i.e. Lord Śiva). [23]

इति श्रीबृहदारण्यकोपनिषद्भाष्यवार्तिके पञ्चमाध्यायस्य
सप्तदशं ब्राह्मणम् ॥१७॥

इति श्रीमत्परमहंसपरिव्राजकाचार्यभगवत्पूज्यपादशिष्य-
श्रीसुरेश्वराचार्यविरचिते बृहदारण्यकोपनिषद्भाष्यवार्तिके
पञ्चमोऽध्यायः ॥५॥

****

BṚHADĀRAṆYAKOPANIṢAD-BHĀṢYA-VĀRTIKA

6.1

समाप्तः सप्तमोऽध्यायः प्राप्तावसर उच्यते ।
अष्टमः खिलकाण्डेऽस्मिन्पूर्वकाण्डेष्वनुक्तितः ॥१॥

The seventh[1] Adhyāya has been discussed conclusively. Now will be explained the eighth Adhyāya, which has an occasion (i.e. proper scope) in this Kāṇḍa, the Khila Kāṇḍa 'book pertaining to what is to be appended',[2] owing to the absence of the discussion (lit. statement) about it in the former Kāṇḍas.[3] [1]

[1]Sureśvara refers to the traditional method of numbering the Adhyāyas of BU. Therefore Adhyāyas 1, 2 ... 6 are mentioned by him as Adhyāyas 3, 4 ... 8. Cf. note at the beginning of our Udgītha Brāhmaṇa [Vol.4,1991], i.e. BUBV 3.1.1.

[2]BU Adhyāyas 1-2 are named Madhu Kāṇḍa, Adhyāyas 3-4, Yājñavalkya Kāṇḍa (cf. 3.1.1 above) or Muni Kāṇḍa and Adhyāyas 5-6 comprise Khila Kāṇḍa.

[3]This indicates the matter in this Adhyāya, viz. what is non-Brahman (SP).

गायत्र्याः प्राणभावोक्तिः कस्माद्धेतोः पुरोदिता ।
न तु वागादिभावोऽस्यास्तत्र हेतुरिहोच्यते ॥२॥

There was statement earlier of the reason as to why the Gāyatrī[1] became Prāṇa; but it was not stated as to why it did not become Vāc and others. (Now) is stated here the reason for that (viz. not so happening). [2]

[1]Refer to BU 5.14.

ज्येष्ठः श्रेष्ठो यतः प्राणो न तु वागादयस्ततः ।
प्राणात्मभाव एवोक्त आनन्तर्यार्थमेव तु ॥३॥

Since Prāṇa is the eldest and the greatest, and (*tu*) Vāc and others are not (so); therefore, there it was stated that Gāyatrī became (only) Prāṇa. And (this subsequent Brāhmaṇa is) only for stating (what) follows (*prāṇopāsanā* in the preceding Brāhmaṇa). [3]

This verse rejects the view that the reference to the *jyeṣṭhatva* ... of Prāṇa would indicate this section to form an ancillary of *ukthopāsanā*.

उपास्त्यन्तरमेवैतत्फलवत्तु विवक्षितम् ।
न तूक्तशेषतैतस्या भिन्नोपास्तित्वकारणात् ॥४॥

(One would say:) 'This is another worship [1] and has a result also; it is intended to state this'. (The Vedāntin answers:) 'This is not for conveying any ancillary (or a subordinate) to what is mentioned (earlier); [2] since there is a different reason for another worship'. [4]

[1] One connected with Mantha 'offering of a stream of clarified butter'.
[2] This refers to the Mantha offering at BU 6.3.1.

मन्थकर्मणि ये मन्त्राः पञ्च ज्येष्ठादयः श्रुताः ।
प्राणात्मवेदिनस्तेषां प्रयोगोऽत्रोपवर्ण्यते ॥५॥

Here is described the mode (of the performance of the recitation) of the five Mantras, [1] viz. *jyeṣṭha* etc., in the ritual of the Mantha by one who knows the nature of Prāṇa. [5]

[1] These are discussed in BU 6.3 and this Brāhmaṇa is then ancillary to the Mantha worship and is thus useful.

पृथग्वा फलनिर्देशाद्यो ह वा इति पञ्चधा ।
प्राणविद्या पृथङ्मन्थान्मन्थस्तु महिमार्थिनः ॥६॥

Or rather, on account of the distinct mention of the fivefold result in (the words) *yo ha vā* (BU 6.1.2-6),[1] the worship of Prāṇa is different from the Mantha (offering) and (*tu*) the Mantha is (prescribed) for one who seeks for (or, desires) greatness.[2] [6]

[1]This is to reaffirm the distinction between the worship in BU and that in CU; in this latter, the Prāṇavidyā is described to be fivefold. The reason for the distinction is the reference to the Mantha worship.

[2]The ritual of the Mantha aims at achieving worldly prosperity and, as against this, the worship of Prāṇa aims at oneness with it.

फलेऽन्यस्मिन्ननिर्दिष्टे वाक्यशेषगतं फलम् ।
तस्मिन्सति हि सद्भावाद्वागादीनां न तं विना ॥७॥

If the result (of the worship of Prāṇa) were not mentioned as distinct, then it could belong to what was ancillary to (that mentioned in) the statement (of the Mantha worship). (But, only) that[1] being there, there would ensue (a result).[2] (And, the result) of speech and others could not (realise) without that.[1] [7]

[1]Namely, Prāṇa.

[2]That is, becoming one with Prāṇa.

शास्त्रेणोक्ता शरीरेऽस्मिन्वृत्तिः प्राणस्य जीवनम् ।
पूर्वमाविशति प्राणो देहं पश्चाच्च मुञ्चति ॥८॥

The (distinct) function[1] (of each of Vāc and others) in a body is described by the scripture as the existence[2] of Prāṇa (in it). (Thus:) Prāṇa first enters into a body and leaves it later (i.e. in the end). [8]

[1]This is *vṛtti*.
[2]This is also *vṛtti* (=*astitva*).

ज्येष्ठः श्रेष्ठश्च सर्वेषां प्राणानामाश्रयो हि सः ।
श्रेष्ठता वक्ष्यमाणेन ग्रन्थेनास्य विभाव्यते ॥९॥

And that (Prāṇa is) the eldest and the greatest, because it is the support[1] of *prāṇas*.[2] The greatness of this (Prāṇa) is explained by the text which will be stated.[3] [9]

This explains *yo ha vai jyeṣṭham...* (BU 6.1.1).
[1]That is, abode (during the span of an individual's life).
[2]It means: organs and/or the winds in a body.
[3]This refers to BU 6.1.7ff.

अस्मिंल्लोके परस्मिंश्च वागेव न विहन्यते ।
देहान्तरस्थान्प्राणांश्च नियुङ्क्ते सा ततोऽधिका ॥१०॥

Only Vāc is not destroyed in this world and in that beyond; it enjoins the *prāṇas* abiding in various bodies.[1] Therefore, it is greater (than them).[2] [10]

[1]Like Prāṇa, Vāc remains in both the worlds; even though it exists in different bodies.
[2]Read SP: *sarvapravṛtter vāgadhīnatvād atas tebhyo 'dhikā*. It adds: *sopāsyā* 'that Vāc is to be worshipped'.

श्रुतान्मतात्तथोक्ताद्वा प्रमाणं दृष्टिरात्मनः ।
चक्षुः प्रतिष्ठा ज्ञानानामात्मा तत्र प्रतिष्ठितः ॥११॥

Knowledge (lit. seeing) of the Ātman[1] is considered (by some) a (greater) means of knowing than what is heard,[2] thought or as stated by;[3] (therefore,) *cakṣus* is the support of all kinds of knowledge, for the Ātman is steady there (in *cakṣus*). [11]

This explains *yo ha vai pratiṣṭhām* ... (BU 6.1.3).
[1]That is, the nature of it.
[2]Or alternatively, accepted/upheld by the elites.
[3]Three alternatives are understood thus: *śruta*, *mata* or *ukta*.

वाग्घि संपद्यते श्रोत्रादश्रुतं न हि भाषते ।
स्ववृत्तेः परवृत्तेश्च संपच्छ्रोत्रे प्रतिष्ठिता ॥१२॥

Since Vāc is enriched on account of ear and does not 'indeed' speak what is not heard; (therefore) the richness from the function of itself (i.e. ear) or of others is steadied[1] in the ear. [12]

This explains *yo ha vai sampadam* ... (BU 6.1.4); *sampad* here is 'riches'.
[1]Or alternatively, firmly established.

मन आयतनं तत्र वागादीनां हि वृत्तयः ।
स्थितास्तत्पूर्विकाश्चैव ध्यायतः साधनं हि तत् ॥१३॥

manas is the abode and therein, indeed, (are performed) the functions of Vāc and the others and they are steadied[1] only (when) preceded by it,[2] (for) that is the means for one who meditates. [13]

This explains *yo ha vā āyatanam* ... (BU 6.1.5).
[1]In other words, they continue to be performed.
[2]Namely, the function of *manas*.

उपस्थेन्द्रियं प्रजातिः स्यात्तस्य जन्मैकहेतुतः ।
न हि रेतो विना जन्म प्राणिनोऽत्र समीक्ष्यते ॥१४॥

prajāti[1] is the generative organ, because it is the cause of the origin (of beings); nowhere is here[2] noticed the birth of any being without a seed. [14]

This explains *yo ha vai prajātim* ... (BU 6.1.6).
[1]That which has the attribute of generation.
[2]Namely, in this world.

वृत्तीनां प्राणपूर्वत्वाद्व्यपदेशाच्च तत्कृतात् ।
प्राणानां प्रथमः प्राणः स ह्यत्तान्नं हि तस्य तत् ॥१५॥

Since the (various) functions (of the organs in the body) are preceded by Prāṇa[1] and mention is made of them[2] by that,[3] therefore, Prāṇa is the first[4] of *prāṇas*. It is indeed[5] the eater and that food is for it.[6] [15]

This states the purport of the six worships mentioned earlier in BU 6.1.1-6.
[1]Cf. verse 8 above.
[2]That is, the organs.
[3]Namely, by the word *prāṇa*.
[4]Possibly both the eldest and the greatest.
[5]Read SP: *prathamo hiśabdo mukhyaprāṇasya jīvābhedenāttṛtopapādako dvitīyo vāgāder bhogyāntarbhāvena tathātvāvedakaḥ*.
[6]The words 'for it' can be expressed as 'belonged to it'. 'That food' refers to the enjoyment through various organs.

Now follows the exposition of the narrative of the dispute among prāṇas over the greatness of only one (BU 6.1.7ff.). This occurs also at CU 5.1.6-12; 5.2.2; (in brief at) Kauṣītakyupaniṣad 2.14, 3.3; Praśnopaniṣad 2.1.2-4.

ते प्राणाः स्वगुणैरुक्तैर्वसिष्ठत्वादिलक्षणैः ।
श्रेयानस्म्यहमेवेति विवदन्तः परस्परम् ॥१६॥

Those *prāṇas* (which are thus) characterized by their own properties, beginning with the word *vasiṣṭha*[1] as stated (before in BU 6.1.2ff.) were disputing with one another (over their relative greatness in words) 'I am greater'.[2] [16]

[1]The best helper or the one who covers/protects best.
[2]SP comments: *nirdhārayituṃ na pārayanti sma.*

निर्णयार्थाय ते ब्रह्म जग्मुरिन्द्रं प्रजापतिम् ।
को नो वसिष्ठ इति तं पप्रच्छुर्निर्णयार्थिनः ॥१७॥

For obtaining a decision (regarding that matter), they[1] approached the Brahman,[2] viz. Indra[3] Prajāpati. They,[1] seeking decision, asked him, 'Who amongst us is *vasiṣṭha* 'most shining'?' [17]

[1]This refers to Prāṇa.
[2]Or Prajāpati denoted by the word Brahman. That is also Indra because of his connection with, or superintending over, the *prāṇa*s.
[3]Indra, possibly because of his connection with *indriya*?

यस्मिन्व इति वाक्येन वसिष्ठत्वस्य लक्षणम् ।
प्राणेभ्यः प्राब्रवीद्ब्रह्म पक्षपातभयात्किल ॥१८॥

The Brahman declared to the *prāṇa*s the description[1] of being *vasiṣṭha* in the sentence *yasmin vaḥ ...*,[2] lest he might be taken to have shown partiality, (as it were). [18]

[1]Literally, indication.
[2]Cf. BU 6.1.7.

जानन्नपि वसिष्ठादिगुणवत्त्वं यथार्थतः ।
तथापि नावदद्ब्रह्म स्वानुभूत्यवबुद्धये ॥१९॥

Knowing though full well[1] about the (character of Prāṇa as) being possessed of the qualities of *vasiṣṭha*[2] etc., the Brahman did not declare (the same yet), with the intention that (they[3] should have) their own (i.e. direct) experience. [19]

[1]Or alternatively, though he (Indra Prajāpati), in reality, knew full well.
[2]These are: being *vasiṣṭha*, *pratiṣṭhā*, *sampad*, *āyatana* and *prajāti* mentioned in BU 6.1.2-6.
[3]This refers to the *prāṇas*.

उत्क्रान्तेऽन्यतमे यस्मिन्प्रत्येकमपसर्पणे ।
पापीयो मन्यते लोको वसिष्ठो वः समीक्ष्यताम् ॥२०॥

'Let that one amongst you be known as *vasiṣṭha* who having departed from (the body), i.e. gone away (from it), the people would consider the body as more wretched.[1] [20]

[1]Already, it is held, the body is wretched (lit. full of sin or impurity), but it would now be more wretched. SP paraphrases *pāpa* as *aspṛśya* 'not worth touching'.

अन्वयव्यतिरेकाभ्यां वसिष्ठत्वावबुद्धये ।
उपास्यार्थपरीक्षायै प्रवृत्तैषा परा श्रुतिः ॥२१॥

Now proceeds this subsequent (Śruti) text to examine (the nature of) the object (worthy) to be worshipped by Anvaya and Vyatireka, with a view to ascertaining the character of *vasiṣṭha* etc. [21]

This refers to *vāg ghoccakrama* ... (BU 6.1.8ff.).

संहतानां क्रियासिद्धेः करणानां पृथक्पृथक् ।
नैकैकस्य क्रियासिद्धिः शिबिकोद्वाहवत्ततः ॥२२॥

(This is so) since the activity of the organs can be secured (only if they function) as jointly,[1] there cannot be therefore the performance of the function by (any) one of them, by itself, as in the case of carrying a palanquin (by its bearers jointly and not severally).[2] [22]

[1]The words 'jointly' and 'by itself (i.e. severally)' are emphasised with a view to ignoring the period of a year (which is not of much significance) in the context.

[2]This is an instance of Sureśvara's cryptic expression of a simile; that is, some relevant corresponding details are omitted.

प्राणप्राधान्यसिद्ध्यर्थं श्रुत्याख्यायिकच्छद्मना ।
अन्वयव्यतिरेकाभ्यां न्यायो लौकिक उच्यते ॥२३॥

(Here) is stated in the Śruti a well-known instance in the worldly happenings, under the pretext of a narrative, yet by employing (the method of) Anvaya and Vyatireka, with a view to establishing the superiority of Prāṇa (to the *prāṇas*). [23]

The word *-khyāyika-* is adopted for *-khyāyikā-*.

This states the purport of *yathākalāḥ yathāsandhāḥ yathā badhirāḥ yathā mugdhāḥ* and *yathā klībāḥ* in BU 6.1.8-12.

यथा मूका विना वाचा यथान्धाश्चक्षुषा विना ।
इत्यादिवचसा प्राणे सति जीवनमुच्यते ॥२४॥

By the statement 'as they are dumb, when without Vāc', (and) 'as they are blind, when without *cakṣus*' etc. it is asserted that there is activity (or capacity for any function) (in a body) when there is Prāṇa in it.[1] [24]

[1]SP adds *tasmāt prāṇāḥ śreṣṭha iti śeṣaḥ.*

उत्क्रान्तौ च प्रवेशे च ह्यलं देहः स्वकर्मणे ।
वागादीनां न पातोऽस्य नापि चोत्थानमीक्ष्यते ॥२५॥

Since a body is capable of activity even while Vāc and others leave it and/or enter into it, the fall or rise of Vāc and others (by themselves) is not (anywhere) seen. [25]

उत्क्रान्ते प्राण एवास्माच्छरीरं पततति ध्रुवम् ।
उत्तिष्ठति प्रविष्टे च प्राणः श्रेयांस्ततोऽन्यतः ॥२६॥

A body certainly falls when only Prāṇa has departed from it[1] and it rises when (Prāṇa) has entered (into it); therefore Prāṇa is greater (than others and not for any other reason.[2] [26]

[1]Literally, this one.
[2]That is to say: No other reason needs be adduced to prove its superiority.

मामृते जीवितुं यूयं यद्यशक्ताः स्थ सर्वदा ।
प्रधानं तर्हि मां वित्त भवन्तश्चापराधिनः ॥२७॥

'If you are, at all times, unable to live[1] without me; then know me (as) the principal (one) and you (who have denied this earlier) are offenders.'[2] [27]

This is the purport of *te hocur* ... (BU 6.1.13).
[1]That is to say: to perform your function.
[2]This is the intended/imaginary remark by the Brahman (Prajāpati Indra) which concludes the controversy among the *prāṇa*s. They are offenders in not recognising the greatness of Prāṇa.

करं बलिं प्रधानाय दत्त वागादयोऽचिरात् ।
इत्युक्तास्ते तथेत्यूचुः सर्वस्वं ददते प्रभोः ॥२८॥

'Therefore, O Vāc and others, quickly[1] give tribute, i.e. offering of oblation, to the principal one', (said the Brahman). Thus told, they said, 'So (be it)' and they gave all that was their own to the lord.[2] [28]

[1]That is, without hesitation or delay.

[2]That is, Prāṇa, their overlord.

त्वद्वसिष्ठतयैवाहं वाग्वसिष्ठेत्युदाहरत् ।
इत्युक्त्वान्येऽपि सर्वस्वं ददुर्वागादयः सुराः ॥२९॥

Vāc said, 'I am *vasiṣṭha* only through your being *vasiṣṭha*'. Thus saying,[1] the other deities,[2] also (addressed Prāṇa) Vāc and others gave (to Prāṇa) all that was their own. [29]

[1]It means: in these words.
[2]That is to point out that the deities of the organs, viz. Agni etc., accepted the superiority of Prāṇa.

किमन्नं मे बुभुक्षोः स्याद्वासो वा मे किमीर्यताम् ।
इति प्राणवचः श्रुत्वा प्रत्यूचुः करणानि तम् ॥३०॥
आ श्वभ्यो यदिदं किंचिदा कृमिभ्यश्च लक्ष्यते ।
अन्नं तद्भवतः सर्वं वयं त्वच्छेषभोगिनः ॥३१॥

Then having heard the words of Prāṇa, 'What is the food for me, who am hungry (lit. desirous of eating), and (*vā*) what garment for me? Tell me', said the organs to it, [30]
'Whatever food is noticed (to be) for (the beings, viz.) from the dogs and up to the insects, (all of it) is (only) for you and we are partakers of what remains (from it).' [31]

जीवः प्राणोऽत्र संसारी भोक्तेन्द्रियमनःपरः ।
प्राणो ह्येतानि सर्वाणि भवतीति च लिङ्गतः ॥३२॥

In this context, Prāṇa is the individual being (which is) transmigratory, the enjoyer, and dependent on organs and *manas*. That Prāṇa, indeed, becomes all of these (known) from the indication (in the Śruti).[1] [32]

Verse 32 averts the idea that sentience in an individual is different from Prāṇa, which can be devoid of a body.
[1]Cf. *ātmendriyamanoyuktam* ... (*Kaṭhopaniṣad* 3.4).

तन्मया हीतरे प्राणास्तन्मूलास्तन्निबन्धना: ॥३३॥

Indeed, the other *prāṇa*s are made up of that;[1] they have it as their origin and they have dependence on it.[2] [33]

[1]That is, Prāṇa, called *jīva* when in a transmigratory body.
[2]The origin, the sustenance and also the merger into it are understood from this. Cf. BS 1.1.2: *janmādy asya yataḥ*. Also cf. *sa eva teṣāṃ svāmī tam utkrāmantam iti śruteḥ* (SP).

एवंविदे हि नानन्नं किंचिदस्तीति दर्शनात् ।
फलं स्यात्प्राणसायुज्यं सर्वं तस्य हि भोजनम् ॥३४॥

In the case of the one, who knows thus, there is not anything which is not food—this is so, because of (thus) seeing (by the Śruti). Therefore, the result will be one's union (i.e. oneness) with Prāṇa, because all the food is (only) for it.[1] [34]

[1]Cf. verses 30 and 31 above; (only) is used to indicate the force of *hi*.

भक्तृत्वता स सर्वस्य नान्नं भवति कस्यचित् ।
केवलेऽवस्थितेऽत्तृत्वे मृत्युनापि न गीर्यते ॥३५॥

And (Prāṇa) is the eater of all; food cannot be for anyone (else). Thus is established as the character (of Prāṇa) as the (one) eater, without a second, it is not swallowed even by Death. [35]

अद्भि: परिदधत्येनमशिष्यन्त इति श्रुते: ।
विदधाति ह्यपां पानमपूर्वं शास्त्रलक्षणम् ॥३६॥

(It is understood) from the Śruti (statement) *adbhiḥ paridadhaty enam aśiṣyantaḥ*. ['They encircle this one with water, when they are proceeding to eat.'] (Here) the scriptural injunction[1] lays down sipping of water which was not (known) before.[2] [36]

[1]Cf. *bhokṣyamāṇam bhuktavantaṃ ca prāṇam adbhiḥ paridadhati* (not traced).

[2]SP tells that sipping of water is different from that prescribed by a Smṛti.

शास्त्रं मुख्यार्थमेव स्याद्विध्यर्थं यदि कल्प्यते ।
युक्तः फलानुषङ्गोऽस्य वासोलाभो विधिर्यदि ॥३७॥

Śāstra would (generally) be[1] conveying the primary sense,[2] if[3] it is taken for an injunction.[4] (And) it is only proper that it (viz. this injunction)[5] has association with a result, viz. if[6] (it is accepted as) an injunction for acquiring garments.[7] [37]

[1]The words 'would be' mean 'is'.

[2]That is, that which is expressed by the verbs in the Present Indicative sense.

[3]This 'if' is for 'because'.

[4]Cf *dadhnā juhoti* (a *vidhi* 'injunction' means '*dadhnā juhuyāt*').

[5]This injunction has reference to sipping of water which is mentioned earlier.

[6]The word 'if' means 'when'.

[7]Cf. SP: *nāphalānuṣaṅgo yukto vidheḥ.*

एके च शाखिनो व्यक्तं विधिरूपमधीयते ।
मन्त्रेण प्राशनं चापामेकेषां शाखिनां मतम् ॥३८॥

But (*ca*) some followers of another branch (of the Veda) read (in this context) a clear form of the injunction[1] and the opinion of the followers of yet another branch (of the Veda) is that there is 'sipping of water with (the recitation of) a Mantra'.[2] [38]

[1]These are the followers of CU. The injunction is *aśiṣyann ācāmed aśitvā cācāmet* (cp. BU 6.1.14). SP refers to *sarva-vedāntapratyayanyāya*, i.e. BS 3.3.1; cf. note under BUBV 3.1.3 above.

[2]*amṛtopastaraṇam asy amṛtāpidhānam asi* (*Taittirīya Āraṇyaka* 10.32.1; *Hiraṇyakeśī Gṛhya Sūtra* 1.13). This implies that sipping of water, which is mentioned earlier, is without any recitation.

अन्नदर्शनवच्चैके वासोदृष्टिं प्रचक्षते ।
प्रायत्यार्थमपां पाने दृष्टेः प्रकरणादिह ।
सर्वाभक्ष्यप्रसक्तिः स्याद्यदि कर्म विधित्स्यते ॥३९॥

Some say that this looking upon (water) is accepting it as a garment, because, here, through the force of the context (*prakaraṇa*), looking upon water has the meaning of not being naked.[1] If a ritual were (actually) prescribed, then there would be the contingency of eating all forbidden food. [39]

[1]See Śaṅkara's paraphrase of *prāyatyārtham* (CU 5.2.2) as *anagnatārtham* 'for not remaining naked'.

इति श्रीबृहदारण्यकोपनिषद्भाष्यवार्तिके षष्ठाध्यायस्य
प्रथमम् ब्राह्मणम् ॥१॥

BṚHADĀRAṆYAKOPANIṢAD-BHĀṢYA-VĀRTIKA
6.2

Introductory.

यन्न संभावितं पूर्वं वस्तुप्राधान्यहेतुतः ।
वक्तुं तदत्र वक्तव्यं खिलकाण्डाधिकारतः ॥१॥

What was not considered earlier for saying, on account of the fact that there was prominence (given to) the thing (i.e. Ātman) is (to be stated) here, since there is the scope [1] for it in this (portion of the) Khila Kāṇḍa. [1]

[1]This refers to *adhikāra*, viz. the topic which is begun in BU fifth Adhyāya.

सप्तमावसितावुक्तं मार्गप्रार्थनमग्नितः ।
सुपथेति श्रुतं तत्र श्रुत्या मार्गविशेषणम् ॥२॥

In the end of the fifth Adhyāya is stated a request to Agni (for showing) the way; there, in the words *supathā* ...[1] of the Śruti, is heard a qualifying attribute of the path. [2]

This verse states what is not said in the end of BUBV 5.17.
[1]This is reference to BUBV 5.17.19; the *ṛc* in view is *Ṛgveda* 1.189.1.

[2]Sureśvara uses *supathā* as an adjective of *mārga*; but, the *ṛc* has *supathā*, (in the instrumental case) which means 'by good path'. Sureśvara clarified his thought in the following verse.

संभवे व्यभिचारे च विशेषणविशेष्ययोः ।
दृष्टं विशेषणं लोके यथेहापि तथेक्ष्यताम् ॥३॥

And as, about the rule of the concomitance of an adjective and a substantive (in common parlance), there is a possibility of deviation from it, viz. (only) the adjective is noticed (or, used); so also should this[1] be understood (lit. seen) here. [3]

[1]Sureśvara seems to take *supathā* as only an adjective of *mārgeṇa* which is to be supplied. His idea is: the word *loke* 'in common parlance (lit. the world)' refers, as SP points out, to the use of *nīlam* (*ānaya*) for *nīlaṃ kamalam* (*ānaya*); the use of the adjective alone becomes meaningful. NKL (ms p.822) writes *raktakambalaḥ ityādau viśeṣaṇaviśeṣyayor vyabhicāre viśeṣaṇaṃ dṛṣṭam ity arthaḥ*! Also, it adds: *vimatānām pathāṃ kathanāyottarabrāhmaṇam iti*.

सुपथेति ततो युक्तं संभवे भूयसां पथाम् ।
विशेषणमतो वाच्याः पन्थानः कर्महेतवः ॥४॥

Therefore, the adjective *supathā* would be proper, since there is a possibility that there are many paths (available). And, as such, the paths of ritual action, as their cause, have to be stated. [4]

This is according to NKL (ms pp.822-823) the result following from the preceding verse (*phalitam āha*). Sureśvara appears to take *supatha* only as an adjective and implies the substantive *mārgeṇa* (in the plural sense). But that appears to be tautologous like *gavāṃ gopatim*. In the Vedic word *supathā*, *su* qualifies *pathin* and therefore it is there only a noun and that precludes the need of any other substantive.

दक्षिणोदगधोमार्गा विहितप्रतिषिद्धयोः ।
विपाकाः कर्मणोर्वाच्यास्तद्वैराग्यप्रसिद्धये ॥५॥

They are the paths to the south, to the north and towards (the world) below; they are the results of actions, either prescribed or prohibited. They are to be stated so that one comes to have aversion to that.[1] [5]

Read with profit NKL (ms p. 823) *ke mārgāḥ kimartham vā kathyante (ity) āha.*

[1]This refers to ritual action implied by *vihitapratiṣiddha.*

नाविरक्तस्य निःशेषसांसारिकपुमर्थतः ।
प्रवृत्तिर्मुक्तये तस्माच्छ्रुत्या यत्नात्तदुच्यते ॥६॥

There is here not (seen) any tendency (lit. activity) of one who is not averse to the entire group of the ends of human activity; therefore, that[1] is stated by the Śruti with special care. [6]

SP introduces this verse with *vairāgyoktir akiñcitkareti cen nety āha.*

[1]This is referring to ritual activity which should be, according to the author, the cause for one's aversion to the same.

शक्नुवन्ति न कर्माणि सर्वकामसमापनम् ।
निषेद्धुं वाखिलानर्थांस्तत्फलस्यातिफल्गुतः ॥७॥

Ritual activities are not sufficient for (i.e. capable of) accomplishing all the desires (of a man), or for warding off all the undesirable results, because the result (lit. fruit) of them is[1] entirely insignificant. [7]

[1]The singular implies all results— *jātāv ekavacanam.*

न कर्म कारणं मुक्तेर्नाग्निर्दाहज्वरापनुत् ।
कर्मभ्यो जन्म नियतं जन्म चेन्निर्वृतिः कुतः ॥८॥

Ritual activity is not the cause for (effecting) liberation, (in the same way as) fire is not a remover of burning fever. From (the performance of) rituals, it is certain that there is birth (of an individual for a second time). So also, if there is a birth (again), how could there be the highest delight (i.e. liberation)? [8]

This verse argues, with examples, that rituals do not lead to the attainment of liberation.

न कर्मणा कनीयस्ता महत्त्वं चान्तरात्मनः ।
इति बाहुमिवोद्धृत्य वेदान्तैर्घोषणा कृता ॥९॥

There is neither inferiority nor superiority of the inner self by (one's doing the performances) of ritual activity—the Vedānta (texts) have loudly declared this, raising the hand upwards, as it were![1] [9]

Here is cited an argument for proving what is said in the preceding verse.

[1]This indicates the sense: with full force.

न तत्र दक्षिणा यन्ति विद्ययैव तदाप्यते ।
इति श्रीयाज्ञवल्क्येन मुक्तकण्ठमुदाहृतम् ॥१०॥

There *dakṣiṇā*s do not approach,[1] that is obtained only through knowledge—the revered Yājñavalkya has uttered this, giving full vent to his throat. [10]

[1]*Śatapatha Brāhmaṇa* 10.5.4.16.

अतो मुक्ति परीच्छद्भिरुत्पत्त्यादिविरोधिनीम् ।
त्यक्त्वा कर्माण्यथैकात्म्यज्ञानं सर्वात्मनाश्रयेत् ॥११॥

Therefore, those, who aspire[1] for liberation which is opposed to origin etc. (should abandon ritual activities). Then (one should), after having abandoned (all) activities, whole-heartedly (*sarvātmanā*) turn to (securing) the knowledge of (one's own) oneness with the Ātman. [11]

SP quotes in support of the last part of the verse the Śruti statement *brahmasaṃstho 'mṛtatvam eti* (CU 2.23.1).

[1]*parīcchadbhiḥ* is derived from *iṣ* with the preposition *pari*.

तमोन्तरायतो मुक्तेर्नान्तरायोऽपरोऽस्ति हि ।
तमोहतिर्न कर्मभ्यो ज्ञानात्सा व्यञ्जकत्वतः ॥१२॥

Since liberation has only darkness (i.e. ignorance) as its impediment and that there is, therefore, no other impediment, there is no destruction of darkness through rituals. It is (effected) by knowledge, because that has the capacity to reveal (the true nature of the Brahman). [12]

Thus, in the first twelve verses of this Brāhmaṇa, Sureśvara has stated the twofold connection of it with what is foregone: (i) something remained to be stated regarding rituals, viz. regarding many paths as indicated by the word *supathā*, and (ii) there is liberation resulting only from knowledge and ritual actions are connected with it as causes of bondage.

न तु त्वमेतयोर्वेत्थेत्युत्क्रान्त्यादिस्वलक्षणम् ।
षड्विधं परिणामार्थमग्निहोत्राहुतीहयोः ॥१३॥
इति प्रश्नप्रतिवचस्ते वा इत्यादिकं जगौ ।
लोकं प्रत्युत्थितं यावदग्निहोत्राहुतीहयोः ॥१४॥

'Have you indeed not known of these two?'—this, as indicative of the upward movement etc.,[1] viz. the sixfold things which result from the two, viz. Agnihotra-offering and desire; [13]
these are the question and the answer, thus has the Śruti stated (lit. sung) in (the words) *te vai* ... and up to the words *lokam pratyutthitam* ... which have resulted from Agnihotra and desire. [14]

[1]The word etc. refers to *gati*, *pratiṣṭhā*, *tṛpti*, *punarāvṛtti* and *loka*.

Now, Sureśvara refers to what was said in the context of the Agnihotra.

अपूर्वपरिणामोऽयमग्निहोत्राख्यकर्मणः ।
उत्क्रान्त्यादिगिरेहोक्त आलोकोत्थानवाक्यतः ॥१५॥

Here is stated the result[1] of *apūrva*[2] coming from the ritual activity called Agnihotra, beginning with the word *utkrānti* (and up to) rising unto a *loka*.[3] [15]

[1]SP refers this to the sixfold character of worldly existence.
[2]*apūrva* is a term used by the Mīmāṃsakas for referring to the subtle form of a ritual performance which has the potency to produce its effects (even at a later day, though not necessarily immediately).
[3]See note 1 on the preceding verse.

आहुत्योरग्निहोत्रस्य ह्यन्तरिक्षादिभेदतः ।
आ लोकोत्थानतः श्रुत्या उक्तापूर्वस्य विक्रिया ॥१६॥

The Śruti has declared (i.e. explained) the modification of *apūrva* in the words up to rising unto *loka*, viz. as divided into the sky etc. (as the result of) the two[1] *āhuti*s of Agnihotra. [16]

[1]Cf. SP: *agnihotrasya dve sāyaṃ prātarāhuti tayor apūrvasyāntarikṣadvyādilakṣaṇaṃ lokaṃ pratyutthānād ā ṣaḍvidhā jagadātmikā vikriyā.*

BU 6.2.1 is under reference.

तदेवोक्तमिहालम्ब्य तदग्नीक्षणसिद्धये ।
श्वेतकेतुरिति ग्रन्थः पर आरभ्यतेऽधुना ॥१७॥

Having stuck to that very statement here, this subsequent part of the Śruti, which begins with the word *śvetaketuḥ*, is now taken up for establishing the viewing of Agni (in the manifold world). [17]

पञ्चाग्निविद्या यत्नेन वृद्धेनाब्राह्मणादपि ।
हित्वा धनं च मानं च लब्धेत्युक्तिः स्तुतिर्धियः ॥१८॥

The statement, viz. an elderly person gave up wealth and respect and obtained with effort the lore of five fires, even from one whois not a Brāhmaṇa, is a statement of praise of the knowledge (of the Ātman). [18]

Cf. BU 6.3.1-15.

परिणामो हि पाकेन पाकश्च न विनाग्निना ।
दर्शनात्परिणामस्य पक्ता सर्वत्र पावकः ॥१९॥

Ripeness (can be effected) only by heating and there cannot be heating without fire; therefore, since there is sight of ripeness, one should see everywhere the fire as the heater. [19]

This is the purport of the narrative (*ākhyāyikā*). It occurs at BU 6.3.1-15 (cp. CU 5.3.1-5.10.2). Read NKL (ms p.823): *pariṇāmasya pākakāryatvāt pākasyāgnikāryatvāt dyulokādipañca-padārthānāṃ dehapariṇāmahetutvād agniśabdatvam ity arthaḥ*. (This is clearer than SP.)

The narrative is given in the following verses.

समाप्ताशेषविद्यं हि समावर्त्य पिता सुतम् ।
समाप्ताशेषविद्योऽसीत्येवमाहोत्ससर्ज च ॥२०॥

The father (saw) the son, who returned (from his preceptor's house), after he had acquired fully[1] all the lores (to be learned), and said to him 'Now, you have fully obtained all the lores' and sent him away. [20]

[1]SP states that the word *aśeṣa* refers to the knowledge of the Veda, together with the Purāṇas and Nyāyaśāstra.

निकषोपलसंस्थेषु वेदवित्सु परीक्ष्यताम् ।
विद्येयं यत्नतो वत्स द्रढिम्ने मच्छ्रुतस्य च ॥२१॥

(He said to him:) My child, let this learning (of yours) be tested among the knowers of Veda who stand as touch-stone (of knowledge); this (for) confirming that (learning) and also (that) which you have received from me. [21]

This explains the father's purpose in sending the son away.

प्रसिद्धातीव विद्वत्ता पञ्चालब्राह्मणेषु हि ।
तामेव परिषदं तस्मादाजगाम त्वरान्वितः ॥२२॥

Since the excellence of knowledge of the Brāhmaṇas of the Pañcāla country had been known; therefore, he went to the assembly of them, hastening (or, with haste). [22]

पञ्चालब्राह्मणाञ्जित्वा विद्योत्कर्षैकहेतुतः ।
राजानमपि जेष्यामीत्याजगाम नृपं ततः ॥२३॥

Then, with an intention, 'after having conquered the Brāhmaṇas of the Pañcāla country by the excellence of (my) learning, I shall conquer the king also', he came to the king. [23]

तं जिगीषुं समायान्तमुन्मार्गे संस्थितं द्विजम् ।
सन्मार्गप्रतिपत्त्यर्थं राजोवाच स्वशास्त्रतः ॥२४॥

Having seen him, a Brāhmaṇa, who was desirous of winning (others) and thus going on a wrong way, the king said to him with the purpose that he learnt (about) a good path, in accordance with the scriptural injunction for himself.[1] [24]

[1]Cf. SP: *unmārgagā prajā sanmārge saṃkramaṇīyeti rājakṛtyam* and NKL: *unmārgasthaḥ sanmārge netavyo rājñeti dharmaśāstrād ity arthaḥ.*

आमन्त्रयामास च तं कुमारा३ इति बालवत् ।
प्रतिशुश्राव सोऽप्युक्तो भो३ इत्युक्त्या गुरुं यथा ॥२५॥

And he addressed him as unto a young lad 'O, boy'; he, on his part, answered 'Yes, Sir' as unto a teacher. [25]

These two ways of addressing are unusual according to the custom of the day. The boy was a Brāhmaṇa, and the king a Kṣatriya and, therefore, these ways of addressing were not considered as having propriety in them. But, that way was adopted by the king purposefully.

दर्पोत्सेकसमावेशान्नानुशिष्टोऽयमादरात् ।
पित्रेति जातसंदेहः पर्यपृच्छद्दतो नृपः ॥२६॥

Then, on account of excessive pride (in Śvetaketu), the king entertained a thought (lit. doubt in his mind), 'This one was not instructed by his father carefully[1]' and asked (him) a question. [26]

[1]Literally, with respect for the method of instruction.

अनुशिष्टोऽसि किं पित्रा उताहो नेति भण्यताम् ।
नानुशिष्टस्य जगति वृत्तमीदृक्समीक्ष्यते ॥२७॥

'Have you been instructed by your father?[1] or not? Tell me this.' (This he did) since such a behaviour (as Śvetaketu's) is not seen in this world, on the part of one who is instructed. [27]

[1]This (viz. *pitrā utāho*— not joined in Saṃdhi) is in accordance with SP: *kalpadvayaspaṣṭatāyai visaṃdhikaraṇam.*

बाढं पित्रानुशिष्टोऽस्मि किं न पश्यसि मज्जयम् ।
त्वत्पण्डितेषु सर्वेषु पृच्छ मां यदि शङ्कसे ॥२८॥

'Yes, I have been instructed by my father. Why! do you not see my victory (in debate) among all your learned men (i.e. Paṇḍits)? Ask them, if you have any doubt (about my instruction).' [28]

This is the meaning of *om* in BU.

एवं राज्ञो यथोक्तोक्त्या ह्यभ्युपेतेऽनुशासने ।
श्वेतकेतुमथाप्राक्षीत्पञ्च प्रश्नान्क्रमान्नृपः ॥२९॥

Thus, at the words of the king that are stated (before), when (Śvetaketu) admitted[1] (that he had received) instruction from the father, the king asked him five (following) questions in order. [29]

[1] Add, in his answer '*om*'.

BU 6.2.2 is under reference.

अनुशिष्टोऽसि चेद्ब्रूहि तुल्येऽपि मरणे प्रजाः ।
यथा विप्रतिपद्यन्ते भिन्नवर्त्मप्रभेदतः ॥३०॥

(i) 'Tell me, now that (lit. if) you have been instructed, how all people, (who) have a common death, proceed variously along different ways.' [30]

येन कर्मविशेषेण समानायां मृतौ प्रजाः ।
अन्या अन्येन संयान्ति यथान्येनापरास्तथा ॥३१॥

(ii) 'By what specific action do the people, who have a common death, proceed, some of them by one way and some others, by another?' [31]

त्वयोक्तं न विवेदाहं नानुशिष्टिरिहास्ति मे ।
वेत्थेह ता यथा भूय आवर्तन्ते प्रजा इति ॥३२॥

(Śvetaketu answered:) 'I do not know what you have asked (lit. said); there has been no instruction imparted unto me, in this respect.' (iii) 'Have you known as to how the people once again come to this world?', (the king asked). [32]

यथा येन मृताः सत्यो हेतुनानेन च प्रजाः ।
तं वेत्थ स्विन्न वेत्युक्तो नेति होवाच तं पुनः ॥३३॥

'(And) as to how, after having died, the people (return to life) and by such and such a cause, have you or have you not known that?', thus asked, Śvetaketu answered him again, 'No, (I do not know)'. [33]

प्रयद्भिरसकृद्भूतैर्महद्भिर्बहुभिः सदा ।
नैवासौ पूर्यते लोको यथा वेत्थ तथात्र किम् ॥३४॥

(iv) 'Also, have you known how the world does not get fully filled when the ever large number of beings are moving (unto it) again and again?' [34]

नेति होवाच पृष्टः सन्राजा पप्रच्छ तं पुनः ।
हुतायामाहुतौ वेत्थ यतिथ्यां पुरुषाभिधाः ॥३५॥
आप एव समुत्थाय पुरुषाकृतयो हुताः ।
प्रवदन्ति यथा वेत्थ तथाशु प्रतिपद्यताम् ॥३६॥

(Thus) asked, (Śvetaketu) answered, 'No, (I do not know)'. Then the king asked him again (v) 'Have you known as to what is the number of the offering, in order, in which waters are called men, [35]
rise in the form of men and begin to speak?, tell me quickly, if you know this.' [36]

राजानं नेति होवाच नाहं वेद्मि त्वयोदितम् ।
पर्यपृच्छदतो राजा शान्तदर्पं द्विजं पुनः ॥३७॥
पथस्त्वं देवयानस्य पितृयाणस्य वाञ्जसा ।
वेत्थ प्रतिपदं किंवा न वेत्सीत्यभिधीयताम् ॥३८॥

To the king he said (in answer): 'No, I do not know what you have said'. Then the king again asked the Brāhmaṇa, whose pride was subdued; [37]
'Have you known well about the path Devayāna and/or Pitṛyāṇa? or, have you known or not known the means to the access (to it)? Tell me.' [38]

This verse explains the meaning of the word *pratipad* 'action towards securing (Devayāna etc.)' i.e. what becomes useful as a means. Read also BU *yat kṛtvā* (*devayānaṃ vā panthānam*) *pratipadyante*; cf. the following verse.

प्रतिपद्वचनस्यार्थं यत्कृत्वेत्यादराच्छ्रुतिः ।
व्याचष्टे देवयानादिप्रतिपत्तौ क्रियैव सा ॥३९॥

In the words *yat kṛtvā* ... 'i.e. by doing which' the Śruti has respectfully explained the meaning of the word *pratipad*: it is just an action for securing the Devayāna etc. [39]

स्वाभ्यूह इति मा शङ्कीर्यतो मार्गद्वयेऽपि नः ।
ऋषेर्मन्त्रस्य श्रवणमस्ति तच्च विभाव्यते ॥४०॥

'Do not think that this is my construct (or, imagination), since, in respect of the two paths also, we have heard a Mantra from a seer and that is being revealed (i.e. explained) to you.' [40]

द्वे सृती अश्रृणवं साक्षात्संबन्धिन्यौ दिवौकसाम् ।
पितृणां चापि मर्त्यानां मार्गौ तावधिकारतः ॥४१॥

'I have heard (i.e. known about) two paths which are related directly to the dwellers of the heaven (i.e. gods) and also of the manes; and these two are for men according to their eligibility.' [41]

This is *Ṛgveda* 10.88.15.

ताभ्यां सर्वमिदं गच्छद्यथाकर्म यथाश्रुतम् ।
समेति मध्ये भोगाय रोदस्योः कर्मणो जगत् ॥४२॥

Going by those two paths, all this world attains (to them): between the two worlds,[1] in accordance with its actions or knowledge, for experiencing the result[2] of the action. [42]

[1]This refers to the heaven and the earth.
[2]Singular form implies plural (*jātāv ekavacanam*).

त्वदुक्तात्प्रश्नगणतो न वेद्म्येकमपीरितम् ।
प्रश्नं मा मामतः प्राक्षीरित्युक्त्वावाक्शिरा ह्यभूत् ॥४३॥

(Śvetaketu) said: 'From the number (lit. group) of questions I have not known any one question, which you have asked me; therefore, do not ask me (any more)'. Having said this, he stood with his head lowered down. [43]

This explains *athainam* ... (BU 6.2.3).

BU 6.2.3 is under reference.

निर्धूताशेषकलुषं शान्तदर्पं समीक्ष्य तम् ।
वसत्यामन्त्रयांचक्र उष्यतामिति पार्थिवः ॥४४॥

Having seen him with all his blemish washed away (and) with his pride subdued, the king invited him to stay[1] (with himself), saying, 'Stay with me'. [44]

[1]*vasatyā* is for *vasatyartham* as paraphrased in the next verse.

ह्रीतो रोषाच्च तद्वाक्यं वसत्यर्थमुदीरितम् ।
अनादृत्य प्रदुद्राव यत्रास्ते गौतमः पिता ॥४५॥

Disregarding his words, for invitation to stay, (Śvetaketu), on account of shame and anger, rushed away (*pra*) to where his father Gautama stayed. [45]

This explains *anādṛtya* in BU text.

प्राप्याथ पितरं रोषात्साभ्यसूयं निराह सः ।
इति वावेति वचनं पूर्वोत्तरविरोधतः ॥४६॥

Having approached his father he said to him, with anguish (lit. anger) with exasperation, '(Have you not) thus (declared to me) "Thus indeed (you have been fully instructed)."?' (The words) contradict (what was said) earlier and (what the situation is now) later. [46]

This explains *taṃ hovāca* in BU.

इतीत्युक्तपरामर्शो वाकोवाक्यं नृपेरितम् ।
अप्रात्यक्ष्यात्किलेत्युक्तिरनुमानाद्धि तद्गतिः ॥४७॥

The word *iti* (in BU 6.2.3) refers to what was said (viz.) the series of questions asked by the king; the word (lit. utterance) *kila* is owing to the indirectness (in it); it is understood by inference.[1] [47]

The falsehood in the father's words, 'You have been fully instructed' is inferred from the son's ignorance about what the king asked. This is 'clarified' in the following verses: The word *vākovākya* in the verse primarily means Tarka (as also *praśnavacanasamūha*– NKL) and therefore the use of the words *anumānād dhi tadgatiḥ* becomes imperative.

नृपोक्त्यभिभवाल्लिङ्गाद्वञ्चितोऽस्मीति लिङ्ग्यते ।
यथावदनुशिष्टस्य नाभिभूतिर्यतोऽन्यतः ॥४८॥

From the indication, viz. the insult inflicted (on the son) by the words of the king, is conveyed (lit. indicated), 'I have been deceived (by you)', since there would not have come any insult from (another person) to one (i.e. me, here) who was properly instructed (by you, as told by you then)'. [48]

तं मामननुशिष्यैव किमित्युक्तं त्वया पुरा ।
अनुशिष्टोऽसि पुत्रेति वञ्चितोऽस्मीत्यतो मतिः ॥४९॥

'(Thus) having not (fully) instructed me, why did you tell me thus earlier: 'O son, you are (now fully) instructed'? Therefore, I feel that I have been deceived', said the son. [49]

कथं त्वं नानुशिष्टोऽसि ब्रूहि तत्कारणं मम ।
पञ्च मामित्यतोऽवोचद्यथा ह्यननुशासनम् ॥५०॥

'(Now) how do you say, you were not fully instructed (by me)? Tell me the reason (for your saying this)', (said the father). Then (Śvetaketu said in answer), '(The king) asked me five questions and then spoke to me in a way (that indicated:) (I have) not received (full) instruction.' [50]

प्रश्नास्ते कतमे वत्स यांस्त्वं न ज्ञातवानसि ।
प्रश्नप्रतीकानवदत्पृष्टः पित्रा समासतः ॥५१॥

(The father asked him), 'What are those (five) questions, my son, which (i.e. whose answers) you did not (know)?' (Śvetaketu), thus asked, told him the initial words of the questions,[1] in brief. [51]

[1]This is the meaning of *ima iti ha* ... in BU 6.2.3.

BU 6.2.4 is under reference.

ब्राह्मणज्ञानतोऽन्यत्र विद्यां पप्रच्छ भूमिपः ।
न हि ब्राह्मणविज्ञाने किंचिदस्ति त्वयागतम् ॥५२॥

(The father said:) 'The king has asked you about the lore (which exists) elsewhere than in the knowledge of the Brāhmaṇas; indeed, there is nothing of what is in the knowledge of a Brāhmaṇa, viz. that which is not known to you. [52]

This is the meaning of *sa hocāca* ... in BU.

इत्येतद्धृदये कृत्वा तथा न इति सोऽवदत ।
मा शङ्किष्ठास्ततो मां त्वं नोक्तं सर्वं ममेति हि ॥५३॥

Thinking about it to himself, the father said to him: 'It is not so'.[1] Do not therefore disbelieve in me. (Do not think) indeed, "All is not told to me"'. [53]

This explains *tathā naḥ* in BU.
He meant: 'Also, know that I have told you all that a Brāhmaṇa should be taught. You should not doubt about the instruction you have received.'

[1]Note the absence of Samdhi in (*tathā*) *na iti*.

प्रेहि तत्र गमिष्यावस्तद्विद्यालब्धिसिद्धये ।
ब्रह्मचर्यं च वत्स्याव आवां तत्र नृपे गतौ ॥५४॥

'Go quickly (*pra*) (with me), let us go there[1] for securing that (or, his) lore; let us, on going, accept studentship under the king.' [54]

[1]This means unto the king or, to his (capital) city (SP).

यातु तत्र भवानेव नाहं तं गन्तुमुत्सहे ।
इत्युक्तः सूनुना ह्रीतः स्वयमेव जगाम तम् ॥५५॥
ससंभ्रमः स चोत्थाय तस्मा आसनमाहरत् ।

अप आहारयांचक्र अर्घ्यपाद्यार्थसिद्धये ॥५६॥
सत्कृत्य च यथाशास्त्रं राजाथ तमुवाच ह ।
वरं कामं प्रयच्छामो यः कामो वाञ्छितस्त्वया ॥५७॥
ऋषिराहाथ राजानं कामितार्थस्य सिद्धये ।
प्रतिज्ञातो वरस्तावद्भवताप्रार्थितोऽपि सन् ॥५८॥

'May you go there yourself, I do not feel like going to him', thus told by the son, out (of his sense) of shame, (the father) himself went to him. [55]

He (i.e. the king), on his part (*ca*), rose up hastily in respect for him, and brought to him a seat (and) also caused water to be brought for effecting worship of him and washing of his feet. [56]

Having received him respectfully, according to the custom, the king then said to him, 'We wish to give you a boon, according to your choice, viz. that which you desire'. [57]

For securing what he wished, the sage (i.e. Gautama) said to the king, 'You have promised the boon for the fulfilment of my desire,[1] even if that boon was not asked for by me'.[2] [58]

This explains *bhavān eva* ... in BU 6.2.4.

[1]*kāmitārthasya* is paraphrased as *vidyālābhāya* (NKL ms p. 802)!

[2]Cf. SP and NKL: *brāhmaṇaṃ svayam āhūya yācamānam akiñcanam ityādinyāyas te mā bhūd iti* (*sūcitam*). (*Mahābhārata* iii.App.I.321.35), cf. *Mahābhārata* iii. App. I. 32(35).

अस्तु सत्यप्रतिज्ञोऽत्र प्रतिज्ञातं त्वयेह यत् ।
देहि प्रश्नात्मिकां वाचं यां मत्सूनोरभाषथाः ॥५९॥

'May you be truthful in this your promise, the promise which you have given me here (i.e. in this assembly).[1] Give me those words, in the form of questions, which you had spoken to my son.'[2] [59]

[1]These insistent words of the father imply the king's possible reply, 'My promise ever stands'.

[2]This implies 'the answers to them'.

BU 6.2.5 is under reference.

राजापि तमुवाचाथ दैवेष्विति परं वचः ।
दैवेष्वयं वरः सिद्धो मानुषाणां वरं वृणु ॥६०॥

And then the king said to him in the words *daiveṣu* ....:[1] 'This boon is known (lit. established) as one among the gifts by the gods (to men), therefore, choose a boon of men'. [60]

[1]This refers to the word *daiveṣu* in BU 6.2.6.

BU 6.2.6 is under reference.

न हि मानुषतो दैवः प्रार्थनीयो विजानता ।
मानुषस्तूचितो दातुमादातुं मानुषाद्वरः ॥६१॥

'Indeed a person, who is learned (*vijānat*), should not ask of a human being for a boon of a divine gift. It is only proper to give what is a human boon and also to receive (that) from a human being.' [61]

BU 6.2.7 is under reference.

ममाप्यस्त्येव तत्सर्वं यद्दित्ससि मानुषम् ।
विज्ञायते मयैवादौ भवतापि प्रमान्तरात् ॥६२॥

(Gautama said), I have indeed all that, viz. whichever human gift you wish to give me (and) it is already known by me; (this is known) to (lit. by) you also from other means of knowing.[1] [62]

[1]This is for *pramāntara* which is paraphrased by SP as *āptavākyādi*. In all probability, *pramā* stands for *pramāṇa*.

न च तत्प्रार्थनीयं मे भूरि यद्विद्यते मम ।
तस्माद्दैवो वरो मह्यं दीयतां नास्त्यसौ मम ॥६३॥

'I do not have to ask for that which I have in plenty. Therefore, may that divine boon be given to me, since I do not have it. [63]

बहोरनन्तापर्यन्तदैववित्तस्य लोभतः ।
मा भूरभ्यवदान्यस्त्वं दाता भूत्वेह नः प्रति ॥६४॥

'Do not be a misery giver owing to attachment (*lobhataḥ*) to that ample, endless, immeasurable divine wealth after you have been a (liberal) giver.' [64]

दैवं वरं न संदातुं प्रत्याख्यातुं च तं द्विजम् ।
इति दुःखित्वमापन्नस्तीर्थेनेच्छेत्युवाच तम् ॥६५॥

(The king) became grief-stricken (as he was) unable to grant to the Brāhmaṇa the boon of a divine gift and also to displease (lit. discard) him; nevertheless (he said) to him, 'Wish (for this boon) in a proper way.[1]' [65]

[1]*tīrtha* means according to the customary mode regarding one's approach to a preceptor.

तीर्थेन विद्या देयेति नातीर्थेनेति चागमः ।
यतोऽतस्तीर्थसृत्यैव मत्तो विद्यां त्वमाप्नुहि ॥६६॥

Since the tradition[1] is that a lore is to be taught (lit. given) by one who is a preceptor[2] and not by one who is not a preceptor; therefore, you should obtain this lore from me, in the customary way. [66]

[1]So it is heard from old.

[2]This is for *tīrtha*. Refer to *Yājñavalkyasmṛti* 1.28 where six types of teachers are stated.

BU 6.2.8 is under reference.

शास्त्रार्थं स्मारितः सोऽथ राज्ञोपैमीत्यथोचिवान् ।
वाचैव ह्यवरान्पूर्व उपयन्ति यतस्ततः ॥६७॥

(Gautama), thus reminded by the king of the Śāstra, said to him: 'I am approaching you, (O preceptor)'. (Thus he did) since the higher born approached the lower born only uttering (i.e. with) these or such words.[1] [67]

[1]The higher and the lower refer to the higher and the lower castes. 'Only uttering (i.e. with these (or such) words)' in this case means the Brāhmaṇa sage should not take in his hands sacrificial fuel etc. as was customary. (Cf. *Taittirīya Āraṇyaka* 2.11)

स होपायनकीर्त्यैव ब्रह्मचर्यमुवास ह ।
उपैमीति हि संकीर्तेर्नान्यत्किंचिच्चकार सः ॥६८॥

By merely stating about (his) approach (*upāyanakīrtyaiva*), he stayed (with the king) as (his) student. He did not do anything else than saying; 'I approach (you)'. [68]

सापराधं स्वमात्मानं राजा परिहरन्नथ ।
क्षमयामास तमृषिं तथा न इतिवाक्यतः ॥६९॥

Then the king, wishing himself not to have any blemish,[1] requested him (for forgiving), in the words 'Do not do so ...'. [69]

[1]It literally means an offence. An alternative translation could be: "... king, avoiding himself (to be) one who has committed

an offence...."

मा नोऽपराधिनो मंस्थास्तव पूर्वे पितामहाः ।
नामन्यन्त यथा तद्वद्भवानप्यपराधिनः ॥७०॥

'Please do not consider me as offending, since your elders (or forefathers) did not consider (themselves) as offending (towards my elders). So also do you (not consider yourselves as offending me.)' [70]

त्वत्संप्रदानतः पूर्वं विद्येयं हि कदाचन ।
नोवास ब्राह्मणे साध्वी साक्षादपि बृहस्पतौ ॥७१॥

(He continued to say:) 'Before my imparting (lit. giving this) to you, this excellent[1] lore did not (ever) abide in any Brāhmaṇa; yes, not even in Bṛhaspati himself (*sākṣāt*)'. [71]

[1]This is for *sādhvī*, though it may merely mean 'good'.

एवं गुप्तामपि तु तां वक्ष्याम्येवाहमञ्जसा ।
प्रत्याख्यातुं समर्थः को ब्रुवन्तं ब्राह्मणं नृपः ॥७२॥

'I shall impart this unto you, without any hitch (*añjasā*), the one which was kept (*gupta*) from (the Brāhmaṇas);[1] who can stop him who is imparting this instruction to a Brāhmaṇa'? [72]

[1]Cf. verse 71 above.

BU 6.2.9 is under reference.

असाविति क्रमोऽभेदि कस्माद्धेतोरितीर्यताम् ।
प्रश्नस्येह चतुर्थस्य प्राधान्याद्भिद्यते क्रमः ॥७३॥

(Now) let it be said as to why the order (of the answers to the king's questions) has been set aside (lit. broken) in the words *asau* ...;[1] (the answer is:) 'The order is set aside, since there is prominence of (the answer to) the fourth question'.[1] [73]

This refers to verse 35 above and also to the discussion on this point occurring in BUB at the beginning of this Brāhmaṇa.

[1]BU 6.2.9: *asau vai loko'gninā* ....

उत्पत्तेस्तदधीनत्वाज्जन्मायत्ता स्थितिस्तथा ।
स्थित्यपाये प्रयाणं च श्रुत्याभेदि क्रमस्ततः ॥७४॥

The order of the (answers to the questions) has been set aside by the Śruti, since origination depends on that (viz. what is said in the fourth question), so also sustenance depends on origination and merger (lit. departure) on sustenance. [74]

This supplies the reason for *bhidyate kramaḥ* in the preceding verse.

दूरतोऽमुष्य लोकस्य स्यादसाविति गीरियम् ।
समिद्धूमादिभी रूपैर्लोक्यते लोकगीरपि ॥७५॥

The word *asau* is for that world (*dyauḥ*), (for it is) in the distance; so also the word *loka* (is used) since it is seen (from the verb root *lok* 'to see') by means of sacrificial fuel, smoke etc.[1]. [75]

Now follows the discussion of the answers in BU.

[1]This refers to cinders, sparks etc.

वैशब्दः स्मरणाय स्यादग्निस्तत्परिणामतः ।
यत आहवनीयोऽग्निर्द्युलोकात्मतया स्थितः ॥७६॥

The word *vai* is for the remembrance (of what is commonly known) and the word *agni*, for its result (*pariṇāma*);[1] since *āhavanīya*[2] Agni has stayed (in this world) as the form of heavenly fire. [76]

[1]*pariṇāmataḥ* is used for *pariṇāmatvataḥ*.
[2]This is the principal fire in a sacrifice, this is Agni's earthly existence.

अपूर्वपरिणामोऽयमग्निहोत्राख्यकर्मणः ।
द्युलोकोपक्रमो ज्ञेयो यावत्पुरुषसंभवः ॥७७॥

This is the result of *apūrva*,[1] pertaining to the ritual called Agnihotra. This introductory reference in BU to the heavenly world is to be understood in relation to the origin of a man. [77]

[1]For *apūrva*, refer to note 2 on verse 15 above. SP understands *utkrānti* etc. by *dyulokopakrama*.

आहुत्योरग्निहोत्रस्य या विभूतिः पुरोदिता ।
सैवेह दृष्टिविध्यर्थं श्रुत्या व्याख्यायतेऽञ्जसा ॥७८॥

That (particular) appearance of the two *āhuti*s of Agnihotra[1] ritual which was stated formerly is now explained here by the Śruti so as to prescribe (that) viewing[2] without difficulty.[3] [78]

[1]Cf. SP: *karmāpūrvapariṇāmo jagat ity āhutyoḥ stutyatvena uktam* (*pūrvatra* i.e. *agnihotrādhikāre*).
[2]This points out the significance of *asau*, viz. *tad eva jagat* (*iti dṛṣṭiḥ*). This justifies the *āhavanīya* etc. as Agnikārya; i.e. *apūrvapariṇāma* as understood in the preceding verse.
[3]That is, smoothly (*añjasā*).

अध्यात्मे चाधियज्ञे च ह्यधिलोकाधिदैवयोः ।
श्रुतिराहवनीयादेर्व्याचष्टे विस्तृतिं स्फुटाम् ॥७९॥

The Śruti has clearly stated extensively about *āhavanīya* etc.

in the spheres of the body, of the sacrifice, of the world and of the gods.[1] [79]

[1]God here means one who superintends over the subtle form of organs and bodies.

लोक आहवनीयोऽग्निरसाविति विचिन्तयेत् ।
आदित्यादिष्वपि तथा समिदादिसमीक्षणम ॥८०॥
समिन्धनात्समिद्भानू रश्मयो धूम इत्यपि ।
समिन्निर्गमसामान्यादर्चिरहस्तथैव च ॥८१॥

One should think that the *āhavanīya* fire of this world is that[1] Agni; so also in the case of Āditya and others should one hold that they are the sacrificial fuel etc.[1] [80]
(The word) *samidh* is (based) on the act of enkindling, so also are the words *bhānu*, *raśmi* and *dhūma* coming from the *samidh*;[2] in the same way, *arcis* also is from *ahan*.[1] [81]

[1]In the entire verse, the different effects of one cause are identified with it.
[2]All these words refer to act of enkindling. This is how the Brāhmaṇa relates these words to the meaning at the base.

शान्तत्वाच्च दिशोऽङ्गाराः समिद्धि परिणामतः ।
अर्चिरङ्गारभावस्य यथैवं भानुहेतुकाः ।
रश्मयश्च दिशश्चैता आदित्यसमिदाश्रयाः ॥८२॥

Further, owing to their coolness, the (cardinal) quarters are cinders; indeed they are the *samidh* itself, since they are the effects (of the same). As the flame (is the cause of) the (becoming) of cinders, so do the rays have *bhānu* as their cause, and these quarters are dependent on[1] the *samidh* (in the form of) Āditya. [82]

Verses 81-82 explain why one has to understand fire and the things related to the fire to be, in reality, Āditya.

As in verse 81 we understand *dhūma* etc. to be the effects (*pariṇāmas*) of *samidh*, so should we understand here *raśmi* etc. to be the *pariṇāma* of Āditya.

[1]That is, caused by. Read SP: *raśmyādīnām ādityavikāratvāt tadāśrayatvāt teṣu dhūmādidṛṣṭiḥ kāryā.*

अवान्तरदिशस्तद्वद्विक्षिप्तत्वैकहेततः ।
विस्फुलिङ्गा इति ज्ञेयास्तस्मिन्नग्नौ यथोदिते ॥८३॥

In the same way, the subordinate quarters are to be known as small sparks, for the reason that they are scattered variously. Into that fire described above (do gods make their offerings).[1] [83]

[1]SP states *devā juhuvatīti śeṣaḥ*.

त्रयस्त्रिंशच्च ये देवाः स्युस्तेऽध्यात्मादिभूमिगाः ।
होतारस्तत्र तत्र स्युः कर्मज्ञानानुरोधतः ॥८४॥

And those gods, thirty-three [1] in number, who belong to the various levels, viz. those related to the body etc., are to be known as the Hotṛ priests at different (levels), in accordance with the knowledge about their activities. [84]

[1]These are eight Vasus, eleven Rudras, twelve Ādityas, Indra and Prajāpati. These are subdivided as supported in *adhyātma*, *adhibhūta* and (*adhidaivika* cf. verse 79 above) and they become the Hotṛs in the body of a sacrificer in accordance with his different actions in the sacrifice and thus they represent his *prāṇas*, viz. *vāc* and other sense-organs.

ऋत्विग्रूपेण ते ह्यासन्यथा प्राकृतकर्मणि ।
होतारः परिणामेषु तथैवोत्तरभूमिषु ॥८५॥

As they were in the form of different Hotṛs in the initial (ritual) act, so are they in the later levels (i.e. subsequent ritual actions), which are their outcome (or modifications). [85]

*uttarabhūmi*s refer to the initial sacrificer's subsequent lives which are the effects of the acts in every later life.

आहुत्योः परिणामोऽयमूर्ग्रसोऽपूर्वमित्यपि ।
तस्य श्रद्धैकहेतुत्वाच्छ्रद्धा नामेति कीर्त्यते ॥८६॥

The effects of two *āhuti*s is this energy, the essence, and also the *apūrva* and, that (viz. effect), has only Śraddhā as its cause, (that is why) it is named as Śraddhā. [86]

तस्याश्चाप्याहुतेः सोमो राजा संभवतीति च ।
तस्याभिवृद्धिः संभूतिर्न त्वभूतजनिर्यतः ॥८७॥

And also (it is said in the Śruti) that Soma is the king of that offering, because it (i.e. Soma) has growth but not an origin,[1] for it was never born (of anything else). [87]

[1]The reason for this statement is that Soma is already in existence as the cause of the growth of one's body after it reaches the heaven, in the lunar orb.

द्यौरग्निः समिदादित्यः श्रद्धा तस्मिन्हि हूयते ।
सूर्ये समिधि दीप्तायां श्रद्धां जुह्वति देवताः ॥८८॥

The heaven (is) the fire, Āditya (is) the sacrificial fuel, and Śraddhā is offered into that; (indeed) gods make their offerings (of Śraddhā) when the sun, the sacrificial fuel, is blazing. [88]

In verses 80-88, there was the discussion of the first way of metaphorically looking at the Agnihotra in its elaborate form. Now, there will be the discussion of the second metaphorical explanation of Agnihotra from verse 97cd. Verses between 89 and 97ab are some general observations regarding the metaphorical explanations.

श्रयतेः श्रद्दधातेर्वा श्रद्धेत्याहुर्विपश्चितः ॥८९॥
श्रयणाद्धारणाच्चापः श्रद्धाह्वाः कारणात्मिकाः ।
भूत्वाप इति लिङ्गाच्च आपः श्रद्धाभिधास्ततः ॥९०॥

The wise ones have used the word *śraddhā* on the basis of (its derivation) from the verb root *śri* 'to resort to, or, the verb root *śrat-dhā* 'to support'.[1] [89]
Waters are called Śraddhā,[1] since they are resorted to and they lend support, and (thus) they are (also) of the nature of the cause—on the basis of the indication by the words *bhūtvāpaḥ* and therefore waters are known by the name Śraddhā. [90]

Verses 89-90 are Brāhmaṇical explanations of the name Śraddhā for waters.
[1]Cf. *Taittirīya Saṃhitā* 1.4.8.1. The verb root *śrat-dhā* has the sense of *dhāraṇa*.

आकृष्टं रश्मिभिस्तोयमादित्ये प्रतितिष्ठति ।
तस्मादादित्यगः सोमः क्षीण आप्यायते पुनः ॥९१॥

Waters, pulled (lit. attracted, i.e. drawn) by the rays, become steady in Āditya. Therefore, Soma which abides in the Sun, has waxed again[1] though it has waned. [91]

[1]This waxing of Soma, who had waned, is called its birth from *āhuti*.

परिणामो ह्यपां सोमः शीतांशुस्तेन सोऽम्मयः ।
श्रद्धाहुतेर्हि सोमस्य संभवः शास्त्र उच्यते ॥९२॥

Since Soma is the effect (lit. modification) of waters, therefore, it (i.e. Soma) is of cool rays,[1] it is described as full of waters; indeed, in the scriptures, the birth of Soma is said to be from the offering with Śraddhā.[2] [92]

This is to refute the opinion that Soma is born (only) of Tejas. And this offers the reason for the argument in the preceding verse (NKL ms p.826).

[1]This points to the direct perceptibility of Soma.

[2]Sureśvara does not oppose the origin of Soma from Tejas also, for *śraddhāhuti* indicates that.

अङ्गाराश्चन्द्रमास्तस्मिन्हुतेऽग्नौ सोमसंभवः ।
सोमचन्द्रमसोरेवं भेदः शास्त्रेण दर्शितः ॥९३॥

The cinders (of the above-said fire) are the moon and, after the offering is made into that fire,[1] there is the origin of Soma; thus is the difference between Soma and the moon explained by the scripture. [93]

In common parlance, Soma and Candramas are understood as synonymous, but there is a basic difference between them, as scripture has shown.

Also, the argument proceeds against those who stand on the Śruti *candramā aṅgārāḥ*. The argument is according to SP: *kārakabhūtaś candramā phalabhūtaḥ somaḥ*.

[1]This refers to the heavenly fire.

चन्द्रमा मण्डलं स्वच्छं चन्द्रकेण मितो हि सः ।
सोमस्तु मण्डले श्वेतो वर्धते ह्रसते च यः ॥९४॥

The moon is the brilliant orb and it is compared with mica; but, the moon is white in the orb[1] and it waxes and wanes also. [94]

SP notes that Soma is comparable to a creeper which also grows and withers (i.e. it wanes.) Also, it is meant that the Śruti statement *evam enāns tatra bhakṣayanti* does not refer to the moon's orb, since only the *tanmātra* is not *bhogya* 'an object of enjoyment' (in contrast with the Soma plant, cf. BUBV 2.1.57).

[1]This has, according to SP, reference to the Puruṣa in the moon.

चन्द्रमाः पर आदित्यादर्वाक्सोमः श्रुतेर्मतः ।
आदित्याच्चन्द्रमित्याह नैते संवत्सरं तथा ॥९५॥
सोमचन्द्रमसोस्तस्माद्भेदः समवगम्यते ।
देशाभेदादभिन्नौ तावेष सोम इति श्रुतः ॥९६॥
भिन्नौ च धर्मभेदेन तस्माद्द्वयथा श्रुतिः ।

The Śruti has held that Candramas 'moon' is beyond Āditya 'the sun' and Soma is below (not beyond Āditya); therefore, the Śruti said in the words *ādiyāt candram* and also *naite saṃvatsaram.* [95]

Therefrom is understood the difference between Soma and Candramas; but, considering them as belonging to the same region, they are held as identical and the Śruti has said *eṣa somaḥ.* [96]

And (yet), in respect of their properties, they are different; therefore, the Śruti has expressed itself in two ways.[1] [97ab]

Verse 95 points out the difference between Soma and Candramas on the basis of the Śruti, viz. CU 5.10.2: (referring to Devayāna) *māsebhyaḥ saṃvatsaram. saṃvatsārād ādityam ādityāc candramasam* and 4: (referring to Pitṛyāna) *māsebhyaḥ pitṛlokam. pitṛlokād ākāśam. ākāśāc candramasam. eṣa somo rājā.* The first points out that the Jīvas who go by the Devayāna path proceed thus: Saṃvatsara → Āditya → Candra. As against this, those who go by the Pitṛyāna proceed thus: (They do not go to Saṃvatsara) Months → Pitṛyāna → Candra → Soma, the king. This leads to the difference: Candra is beyond Āditya whereas Soma is below the same.

SP has supplied the Śruti passages which are cited in the note under the preceding verse. This justifies the non-difference between Soma and Candramas that are already described as different. Read SP: *svarūpabhede saty eva deśābhedena pitṛlokāc candram eṣa somo rājety abhedaśrutiḥ somasya maṇḍalasthatvād deśāntarābhāvād ity arthaḥ.*

[1]The two passages quoted above are meant.

BU 6.2.10 is under reference.

पर्जन्योऽग्निरिति ज्ञेयः समित्संवत्सरः स्मृतः ॥९७॥
संवत्सरे समिद्धे हि पर्जन्यस्य समेधनात् ।
धूमोऽभ्राणीति सादृश्याद्विद्युदर्चिस्तथैव च ॥९८॥
शान्तिवर्तुलतोऽङ्गाराः पर्जन्यशिखिनोऽशनिः ।
विक्षिप्तत्वैकसामान्यात्स्फुलिङ्गाः स्तनयित्नवः ॥९९॥
सोमं जुह्वति तत्राग्नौ देवाश्चात्रोदिताः पुरा ।
वृष्टेश्च संभवस्तस्माल्लोकेऽस्मिन्सापि हूयते ॥१००॥

Parjanya is to be known as Agni and Saṃvatsara is known as the sacrificial fuel,[1] [97cd]
because Parjanya is active (lit. enkindled) when the Saṃvatsara is enkindled. Smoke is the clouds on account of their similarity in appearance; in the same way, lightning is the flame. [98]
Lightning is cinders of the fire in the form of Parjanya, since (both) become cool (or extinguished) and are round in shape.[2] Thunders are sparks owing only to their similarity in respect of being scatterd. [99]
In that fire do the gods, who are mentioned above,[3] make their offering of Soma and from that[4] is the origin of showers. Therefore, that[5] also is poured into that fire. [100]

[1]In *samit saṃvatsaraḥ*, there is *kramabheda*.

[2]*śāntivartulataḥ* is for *śāntitaḥ vartulatvataś ca*; cf. *śāntatva-vartulatvābhyām* in verse 103 below.

[3]Cf. verse 88 above.

[4]The gods' act of pouring Soma into fire.

[5]Namely, *vṛṣṭi*.

BU 6.2.11 is under reference.

लोकोऽयमग्निर्विज्ञेयः पृथिवी समिदुच्यते ।
पृथिव्या हि समिद्धोऽयं समित्तेन क्षितिर्मता ॥१०१॥

This world is to be known as fire. (And) the earth is called the sacrificial fuel; the earth is understood as the sacrificial fuel, since this fire is enkindled by the earth. [101]

This is yet another way of considering *loka* and *pṛthivī* as Agni and *samidh*.

अग्निर्धूमस्तदुत्थानाद्रात्रिरर्चिस्तथैव च ।
रात्रिमाहुः क्षितिच्छायामङ्गाराश्चन्द्रमास्तथा ॥१०२॥
शान्तत्ववर्तुलत्वाभ्यां विस्फुलिङ्गसमत्वतः ।
नक्षत्राणि स्फुलिङ्गाः स्युस्तस्मिन्नित्यादि पूर्ववत् ॥१०३॥

Smoke is Agni, since it rises from that; in the same way is the night the flame (of that). They have called night the shadow of the earth and similarly the moon is cinders, [102]
because of its coolness (or, extinction) and roundness (of shape) and owing to its similarity with sparks. The constellations (also) are [1] sparks. (The statement) *tasmin* ... is (to be understood) as before.[2] [103]

[1] *syuḥ* is for *santi*.
[2] That is, as in the instances considered before.

अन्नस्य संभवस्तस्मात्पुमग्नौ तच्च हूयते ।

The origin of food is from that [1] and that (food) is offered in the fire in the form of man. [104ab]

BU 6.2.12 is under reference.

पुरुषोऽग्निरिति ध्येयो व्यात्तं तस्य समित्स्मृता ॥१०४॥

Puruṣa is to be considered (lit. worshipped) as Agni and his open mouth is taken (lit. known) as the sacrificial fuel. [104cd]

व्यात्ते मुखे हि तद्दीप्तिर्धमः प्राणो मुखोत्थितेः ।
पुंदीप्तेर्वाङ्निमित्तत्वादर्चिर्वाक्तेन भण्यते ॥१०५॥

Since in (his) open mouth there is his lustre,[1] his vital breath is smoke for it rises from his mouth. And because the lustre of man is caused by Vāc 'power of speech',[2] therefore Vāc is called the flame. [105]

[1]This refers to his being famed by his speech and learning.
[2]That is, it manifests the same.

स्थितेरङ्गारवच्चक्षुरङ्गाराः श्रोत्रमेव च ।
विस्फुलिङ्गा इति ज्ञेयं तस्य विक्षेपसंस्थितेः ॥१०६॥
अन्नं जुह्वति तत्राग्नौ संभवो रेतसस्ततः ।

The eyes[1] are cinders, since they exist like cinders[2] and the ears[2] are to be known as sparks, since they are in the state of being scattered. [106]
In that fire, they (the gods) pour food; from (that) fire, there is the origin of semen. [107ab]

[1]The word eyes is for eye in the singular.
[2]This refers to the cooling down and being the substratum of lustre (i.e. fame).
[3]The word ears is for ear in the singular.

BU 6.2.13 is under reference.

योषिदग्निरिति ज्ञेया उपस्थश्च समित्तथा ॥१०७॥
तदुपस्थेन संदीप्तेर्धमो लोमानि साम्यतः ।
अर्चिर्वर्णसमानत्वाद्योनिरर्चिर्भवेत्ततः ॥१०८॥

A woman is to be known as fire and also her sexual organ (is to be known as) sacrificial fuel, [107cd]
since there is enkindling (of the fire) through her sexual organ. The hair (on her sexual organ) are smoke; her sexual organ is the flame owing to its similarity of colour. [108]

अन्तः करोति यत्कामी तेऽङ्गारास्तत्समानतः ।
विस्फुलिङ्गाः सुखलवाः क्षणिकत्वैकहेतुतः ॥१०९॥

And, that a man, full of desire, puts (semen drops) into (the sexual organ) they are cinders, because they are similar.[1] The moments of happiness are sparks, since they have momentariness. [109]

[1]In that they culminate into extinction (or, cool down).

रेतो जुह्वति तत्राग्नौ देवाश्चेन्द्रियरूपिणः ।
पञ्चम्या आहुतेस्तस्याः पुरुषः संभवत्ययम् ॥११०॥

There, in that fire, do the gods, who have the form of the organs, pour semen; and from that fifth offering (i.e. pouring) is this Puruṣa born. [110]

Verses 101-110 describe the cohabitation of a man and a woman as similar to Agni's union with the sacrificial fuel, which is the act of sacrifice. Thus, based on religious union, that of man and woman and the consequent begetting of a son are looked upon as a holy act.

Also this is the answer to the fourth question that was asked by the king.

यथोक्तवर्त्मना ह्यापः प्राप्ताः पुंस्परिणामताम् ।
पाकजः परिणामोऽयमेवं पञ्चभिरग्निभिः ॥१११॥

Waters have thus, in the way described, attained the nature of modification, viz. manhood. This modificaton (or manifestation) is produced thus by the heating by the five fires (mentioned so far). [111]

तस्मादापः सूक्ष्मभावाः स्थूलतां यान्ति पाकतः ।
अग्निभिः पञ्चभिः पक्वाः पुरुषाख्या भवन्ति हि ॥११२॥

Therefore waters, having (earlier) a subtle form, attain to grossness through heating; thus, (being) cooked by five fires, they become known by the name Puruṣa. [112]

BU 6.2.14 is under reference.

तस्मान्मृतं प्रियं बन्धुं हरन्त्यग्नय ऋत्विजः ॥११३॥

Therefore, do *ṛtvik*s, take him, the dear relation (lit. brother), who is dead, for the fire.[1] [113]

This refers to the funeral of the worldly sacrificer. It is explained in the following verses.

[1]That is, to be offered into the fire, i.e. *agnaye* should stand for (*śmaśāne*) *agnau* (*hotum*) *dagdhum*.

यथैवाहवनीयाग्नेः प्रसिद्धं समिदादिकम् ।
श्मशानाग्नेस्तथैवैतत्सर्वं ज्ञेयं न कल्प्यते ॥११४॥

As the sacrificial fuel etc. of the *āhavanīya* fire is known, so also, all this is to be known in the case of the usual fire, that is used in the cremation ground; (a new fire)[1] is not imagined. [114]

[1]This is on the basis of BUB. There is not any idea of *dṛṣṭi* as in the previous portion of the Brāhmaṇa.

अन्त्यसंस्कारसिद्ध्यर्थं तस्मिन्नग्नौ यथोदिते ।
ऋत्विजो जुह्वति नरमन्त्याहुत्यै विधानतः ।

आहुतेर्जायते तस्याः पुमान्भास्वररूपभृत् ॥११५॥

For completing the final Saṃskāra (of the deceased sacrificer), the *ṛtvik*s offer the man into that fire (which is enkindled) according to the procedure prescribed (in the Pitṛmedha section of the Gṛhyasūtra); from that offering (of his body) is (then) born a human being with a brilliant form.[1] [115]

[1]This is the result of the Sāttvika portion in the dead sacrificer's body. It is the *sattva* that makes the form brilliant (*bhāsvara*).

राजसं तामसं रूपमितो ह्यन्यत्र वक्ष्यते ॥११६॥

The Rājasa and the Sāttvika forms (of the sacrificer's body) are described elsewhere. [116]

This is to point out specifically the brilliant form mentioned in the preceding verse.

इतोऽग्निभ्योऽग्निमेवायं स्वां योनिं प्रतिपत्स्यते ।
इति लोके समाचारादग्निभ्यः संभवस्ततः ॥११७॥

From here, i.e. from that fire,[1] this one (the deceased sacrificer) assumes the form of his own origin[2]—such is the supposition (among the people of) this world that (i.e. after the burning in the funeral fire, there is then this) origin (of the body) from fires. [117]

[1]This refers to the funeral fire.
[2]This refers to the subtle form from which the sacrificer's gross (i.e. worldly) body had originated.

पञ्चम्यामाहुतावेवं पुंनाम्नो जन्म कीर्तितम् ।
गतिस्तस्याथ वक्तव्या उदग्दक्षिणभेदतः ॥११८॥

Thus is told (i.e. described) the origin (lit. birth) of one, called Puruṣa, when the fifth offering is offered and now is to be described his movement in the different directions, with reference to north and the south. [118]

BU 6.2.15 is under reference.

ते य एतद्यथाजातं ज्ञानं पञ्चाग्निसंश्रयम् ।
विदुरर्चिः समायान्ति बहूक्तेश्च द्विजातयः ॥११९॥

They (i.e. the learned), who have known this, viz. the thus produced (i.e. originated) *jñāna* [1] pertaining to five fires, reach [2] thc flame; because there is a mention of many (persons), [3] only the twice-born (i.e. the first three castes) [4] are meant. [119]

[1] This refers to the knowledge of the five fires which are discussed earlier.

[2] This refers to the *arcirādi mārga*, i.e. *udanmārga*— cf. verse 118 above.

[3] That is, the use of *te*, a form in the plural.

[4] *dvijātayaḥ* is a plural form, it shows that it does not refer only to the Brāhmanas.

उत्पत्तिसंस्थितिलया यथोक्ताग्न्येकहेतवः ।
इत्थं ये विदुरर्चिस्ते संभवन्त्यात्मभाविताः ॥१२०॥

The origin, the sustenance and the final merger of a man are caused only by the fires mentioned earlier (i.e. the five fires). Those who have known thus become the flame, [1] being devoted to the Ātman. [2] [120]

[1] That is, attain to the flame etc. and finally to (oneness with) the Brahman.

[2] This refers to those sacrificers who have ever thought that, by worshipping the five fires, thcy would attain the nature of

(i.e. oneness with) the Ātman.

इष्टापूर्तकृतो ये वै ग्रामस्थेभ्यश्च ये परे ।
अरण्य इति गृह्यन्त इतरेषां पृथग्ग्रहात् ॥१२१॥
यज्ञदानतपांसीह गृहस्थ इव तापसे ।
गृहस्थाचार्यवासाच्च न ग्रहो ब्रह्मचारिणाम् ॥१२२॥
नारण्यस्था न च ग्राम्या अपेक्षन्तेऽत्र विद्यया ।
सामान्यवचसोपात्तेर्न विशेषपरिग्रहः ॥१२३॥
सश्रद्धस्यापि सत्यस्य यद्यप्यन्यत्र संभवः ।
तथापि यतयो ग्राह्या अरण्येन विशेषणात् ॥१२४॥
ते य एवं विदुरिति यदि वा गृहिणां ग्रहः ।
अग्निसंबन्धतो न्याय्यो वनस्थस्यापि संभवात् ॥१२५॥

They, who had done (in their life) sacrificial and charitable acts [1] and also those who are other than the inhabitants of villages (and towns) and those, mentioned as (dwelling in the) forest—(but the celebates are not meant) since there is a separate mention of them— [121]
here (in this context), sacrificial performances, making gifts and performing penances are to be understood in the case of a mendicant [2] in the same way as in the case of a householder; but (*ca*) there is no inclusion of the celebates, because of their stay with (i.e dependence on) householders and/or preceptors. [122]
Here,[3] in respect of this lore,[4] the forest-dwellers and the villagers are not to be reckoned; since there is only a statement (of *dvijāti*s in general), there should not be included any particular (or, specific) individuals.[5] [123]
Where, however, there is a possibility that there can be elsewhere (i.e. among the householders) one who has faith (in the worship of) truth and is himself truthful, the mendicants also are to be included, because there is a mention of them by the specifying word *aranya*. [124]
Or, in the words *te ya evam viduḥ*, there is mention made

of (only) the householders; (even then) the (inclusion) of a dweller in a forest is reasonably possible on account of their relation to the fire. [125]

These verses refer to those who are intended as eligible to secure the knowledge of the five fires and through that oneness with the Brahman.

[1]Cf. Kullūka on *Manusmṛti* 4.126: *iṣṭam antarvedi yajñādikarma pūrtaṃ tato 'nyat puskariṇīkūpa prapārāmādi (nirmāṇam).*

[2]This is a reference to the *vānaprasthas* 'those who have taken to a forester's life', i.e. 'who stay away from human dwellings'.

[3]This refers to the topic of five fires, so far discussed.

[4]That is, the lore regarding worship of five fires.

[5]That means: this refers only to householders.

न चाग्निहोत्रशेषत्वमुक्तदृष्टेरिहेष्यते ।
सामान्येन ग्रहात्तस्याः पञ्चाग्निरितिलिङ्गतः ॥१२६॥

And here it is not accepted that (the connection with Agnihotra) is only, in the case of such a knower,[1] because this seeing (viz. possessing the knowledge of five fires) is mentioned in a general way and understood from the word *pañcāgni* by indication. [126]

[1]This refers to the wise ones mentioned above.

त्रिलोकीसाधनत्यागान्नापि संन्यासिनो ग्रहः ।
दैवी विद्या हि वित्तं स्याद्वित्ताच्च व्युत्थितिर्यतः ॥१२७॥
प्रजया किं करिष्याम आक्षेपो ब्रह्मवेदनात् ॥१२८॥

On account of his abandoning the various means (for the attainment of) the three worlds, there is no inclusion of a Saṃnyāsin[1] also, because this lore pertains to the gods (i.e. godly gifts of) wealth and because they have risen above that wealth. [127]

This is so, because they ask a question, 'What shall we do

with offspring?' [128]

Why they abandon the three worlds, i.e. the pleasures in them, is explained in verse 128.

[1]Non-performance of a ritual is prescribed for a person.

पञ्चाग्निज्ञानवद्गाव्या गतिरप्यत्र सर्वदा ।
यतोऽतो गतिरप्युक्ता नान्यथा तदुदीरणम् ॥१२९॥

Here, (we should understand) everywhere that the movement is to be in conformity with the knowledge of the five fires, since the movement is also mentioned from this,[1] and the statement is not to be taken in another sense. [129]

[1]Cf. *Viṣṇupurāṇa* 2.8.92abc and 94d:
aṣṭāśitisahasrāṇām ṛṣīṇām ūrdhvaretasām /
uttareṇāryamṇaḥ panthās te 'mṛtatvaṃ hi bhejire //
[The text quoted here is from BUB. But *Viṣṇupurāṇa* reads *munīnām* for *ṛṣīṇām* and *udakpanthānam aryamṇaḥ* for *uttareṇāryamṇaḥ*.]

देवतोपासनस्येह प्रकृतत्वात्तथा गतेः ।
अर्चिःशब्देन तेनेह देवतैवात्र गृह्यते ॥१३०॥

Since there is here under reference worship of the god and so also the movement (or, the departure), the word *arcis* is to be understood here in the sense only of a god. [130]

अर्चिर्देवतयैकत्वं प्राप्याहर्देवतैकताम् ।
संभवन्तीति सर्वत्र संबन्धोऽत्रानुषज्यते ॥१३१॥
गृह्यते देवता नो चेदर्चिरादिगिरा तदा ।
असंभवोऽन्यत्र मृतेरित्यपार्था गतिश्रुतिः ॥१३२॥
यत्तूदगयनापेक्षा भीष्मस्य श्रूयते स्मृतौ ।
सत्यवादित्वसिद्ध्यर्थं शंतनोस्तदपीक्ष्यताम् ॥१३३॥
अन्यथा कृतनाशः स्यादकृताभ्यागमस्तथा ।

देवताग्रहणात्तस्माद्देवतैवार्चिरुच्यते ॥१३४॥

Later after having obtained oneness with the god of the flame (*arcis*), the householders (etc.) become one with the god of the day—thus this relation continues everywhere in the relevant text. [131]

If a god is not understood here by the words *arcis* etc., it is that the Śruti statement *anyatra mṛteḥ* about the movement (of the departed) would be without any meaning. [132]

(And) what is heard in the Smṛti as the desire of Bhīṣma (to die) when there is the movement (of the sun) towards the north is (only) for establishing his truthfulness in speech; (in the case) of Śantanu[1] also, it should be thus understood (lit. seen). [133]

Otherwise,[2] there would result the loss of what has been done[3] and the acceptance of (a result) of what is not done. Therefore, accepting (the sense of a) god (i.e. as the becoming the god of *arcis* etc.) means that *arcis* is but the god. [134]

[1] This refers to Śantanu's boon to his son Bhīṣma that he would die only at his own will.

[2] It means: if *arcis* etc. were not accepted as gods.

[3] This refers to the performance of sacrificial rituals.

तस्मादेवंविदो धीरा अर्चिराद्यभिमानिनीम् ।
क्रमेण देवतां यात्वा वैरिञ्चं यान्ति तत्पदम् ॥१३५॥

Therefore, the wise ones[1] who know thus, becoming (lit. going to) (each) god of *arcis* etc., attain to that status of Viriñca.[2] [135]

[1] They are sacrificers who have knowledge about rituals.

[2] That is, they become one with the god Viriñca.

श्रद्दधानास्तपस्यन्तः सत्यं ब्रह्म समाहिताः ।
उपासते बहिर्ग्रामादर्चिरते संभवन्त्यतः ॥१३६॥

Therefore, those, who have faith (in this), performing penances and, with their mind well-composed, worship the truth, the Brahman (even) outside the village (etc.), become (one with) the flame (etc.). [136]

ब्रह्मणः स्थानमायान्ति यद्वा स्वाश्रमकर्मभिः ।
संन्यासादब्रह्मणः स्थानं तथा च स्मृतिशासनम् ॥१३७॥

Or, they attain to the abode of the Brahman[1] by the performances of their (own) duties in keeping with the orders of their life (*āśrama*); so also do they attain to the abode of the Brahman—thus is the instruction in the Smṛti.[2] [137]

[1]This refers to what is mentioned as the truth, the Brahman, in the preceding verse and is the same as the Sūtrātman.
[2]*Manusmṛti* 6.96.

ततोऽहर्देवतां यान्ति शुक्लपक्षं ततः क्रमात् ।
षण्मासांश्च ततो यान्ति ह्युत्तरायणलक्षणान् ॥१३८॥
देवतां च ततो यान्ति देवलोकाभिमानिनीम् ।
तत आदित्यमायान्ति वैद्युतं चापि भास्करात् ॥१३९॥
ब्रह्मणा मनसा सृष्टो मानसः पुरुषस्ततः ।
ब्रह्मलोकान्स नयति सोऽप्यभ्येत्याथ वैद्युतान् ॥१४०॥
ते तेषु ब्रह्मलोकेषु दीप्यमानाः पराः समाः ।
ब्राह्ममानाः समा ग्राह्या ब्रह्मलोकेषु तच्छ्रुतेः ॥१४१॥

Thence they attain to the godhead of *ahan*, then, in sequential order, the half of a month, and then the two half-years (lit. six months together) which are characterized by the northward movement (of the sun); [138]
thence to such a god as has the awareness of belonging to the region of gods, then to Āditya-(loka) and from (that *loka* of) Āditya to that of lightning— [139]
Then is created by the Brahman a man from his mind. He

(i.e. that man) having approached from the region of the Brahman takes (the departed one) to the regions[1] of the Brahman and later to the worlds of lightning. [140]

Then those[2] (many men, i.e. departed sacrificers), looking brilliant in the worlds of the Brahman, (stay there) for years; here the years are to be taken to have the magnitude of the days of the Brahman; this is, on the basis of a Śruti about the same. [141]

[1]The plural indicates the wideness of them.
[2]This refers to the many departed men, who are thus brought by the man born from the mind of the Brahman.

सार्ष्टिसालोक्यसायुज्यव्यपेक्षा बहुगीरियम् ।
समष्टिव्यष्टिभेदं वा व्यपेक्ष्य बहुवागियम् ॥१४२॥

(This use of) the word *bahu* is in view of (the three states,) viz. similarity in appearance, sameness of the abode and being just one; or, this word *bahu* is owing to the difference between collected form and severality of forms (*samaṣṭivyaṣṭi*). [142]

There are offered two alternative explanations of the preceding verse.

आवृत्तिर्न पुनस्तेषां यावदाभूतसंप्लवम् ।
आभूतसंप्लवस्थानममृतत्वं हि भाष्यते ॥१४३॥

There is no return (or, rebirth) of them till when there is a complete merger (of them) into elements. Indeed the state of complete merger into elements is spoken of as immortality. [143]

ऐकात्म्यधीसमुत्पत्तेर्यदि वा ब्रह्मलोकतः ।
मुच्यन्ते न निवर्तन्ते यथा धूमादिमार्गगाः ॥१४४॥

Or, since there has arisen (in them) the knowledge of their

oneness with the Ātman, they do not return (to this world) from the world of the Brahman,[1] as those who go by the path beginning with smoke (do). [144]

[1]This refers to Hiraṇyagarbha, Virāj.

इमं मानवमावर्तमित्याद्यस्य विशेषणात् ।
अत्रैव कल्पेऽनावृत्तिर्न त्वन्येष्वनिवारणात् ॥१४५॥
देवयानः समासेन पन्था यत्नात्प्रपञ्चितः ।

Since there is a specification in the words *imam mānavam āvartam* ...; therefore, they (i.e. the sacrificers' Jīvas) do not return in (i.e. during) the period of this creation (*kalpa*)[1]; but (this is not so) in other (i.e. subsequent) creations, since there is no prohibiting statement (regarding their return in them). [145]
(So far), the path called Devayāna is thus briefly and carefully (*yatna*) explained.[2] [146ab]

[1]This explains the sentence *teṣām* ... where there is stress on the word *imam* (*kalpam*).
[2]This refers to the BU proposition: *atha ye yajñena* ....

BU 6.2.16 is under reference.

व्याख्याथ पितृयाणस्य सम्यगारभ्यतेऽधुना ॥१४६॥

Now there begins properly the explanation of the path called Pitṛyāṇa. [146cd]

This is the purport of the following verses.

देवादिज्ञानहीनेन येऽथ यज्ञेन सदद्विजाः ।
लोकाञ्जयन्ति दानेन सद्देशादिमता तथा ॥१४७॥
निःशेषकल्मषध्वंसितपसा वाविपश्चितः ।
मृतास्ते धूममायान्ति धूमाद्रात्रिं तमस्विनः ॥१४८॥

रात्रेरपरपक्षं च दक्षिणायनदेवताम् ।
मासेभ्यः पितृलोकं हि पितरो यत्र शेरते ।
पितृलोकाच्च ते चन्द्रं यान्त्यन्नं तद्दिवौकसाम् ॥१४९॥

Now those good twice-borns,[1] who win the worlds by the performance(s) of sacrifice(s) wherein their knowing about (the real nature of) gods etc.[2] is lacking and who, by making gifts
such as (that of) a good land etc., win different *lokas*; [147]
or, the ignorant ones, who have by penances washed off (their) entire sins,[3] go to smoke, when they are dead, from smoke,
which is full of darkness,[4] they go to the night; [148]
from the night to the second half of the month (and thence) to the god of the period of the movement of the sun to the south;[5] from those months to the world of the manes, where indeed the manes rest (lit. sleep); and from the world of the
manes they move to the moon as the food of the gods.[6] [149]

[1]This refers to three castes as already understood in verse 119 above.

[2]This refers to their ignorance about reality or the Brahman.

[3]Cf. a Smṛti statement: *tapasā kalmaṣaṃ hanti*, cp. *Manusmṛti* 12.104 where *kilbiṣam* is read for *kalmaṣam*.

[4]Or alternatively: *tamasvinaḥ* is further in addition to *avipaścitaḥ* and hence the translation: ... are dead and, from smoke they, full of ignorance (lit. darkness), go to the night;

[5]This refers to the months which are the period for the sun's movement to the south.

[6]This whole, viz. verses 147-149, is the description of the *dhūmādhimārga* mentioned in verse 144 above.

चन्द्रं प्राप्यान्नभावं च ते यतस्तत्र संस्थिताः ।
असकृद्भक्षयन्त्येतानाप्याय्याप्याय्य सोमवत् ॥१५०॥

Since, after having attained to the moon, i.e. to the status of food, they stay there, (the gods in the region of the moon) eat them again and again, repeatedly fattening them just as (the *ṛtvik*s in the sacrifice fatten) the Soma.[1] [150]

This explains *te candram* ....

[1]This refers to sacrificial practice of *somāpyāyana* 'fattening the juice of Soma with milk and water'; the *ṛtvik*s partake of this fattened Soma. So also do the gods in the moon eat the well-fed and thereby fattened sacrificers who have attained to the moon.

पक्षे शुक्ले तमाप्याय्य कृष्णे तं भक्षयन्त्यथ ॥१५१॥
भोगसाधनभावश्च भक्षयन्तीति भण्यते ।
न त्वभ्यवहृतिर्न्याय्या वेदवर्त्मनि तिष्ठताम् ॥१५२॥

Or (*atha*), they (i.e. the Jīvas), after having fattened it (i.e. the moon) in the bright (half of the month), eat it in the dark (half of the month); [151]
in the word *bhakṣayanti* is stated the Jīvas' becoming the means of enjoyment (for the gods); indeed, it is not reasonable (to accept) the eating up of those who have followed the path of the Vedic (ritual). [152]

This is another explanation of *te candram*...

यदा तपचितं कर्म पर्यवस्यति भोगतः ।
तेषामथैतमध्वानमावर्तन्ते यथागतम् ॥१५३॥
आकाशमनुनिष्पद्य वायुमायान्त्यभोगिनः ।
वायोर्वृष्टिमवाप्याथ वृष्टेश्च पृथिवीं ततः ।
अन्नभावं पृथिव्यातस्ते समायान्ति भूमिगाः ॥१५४॥

And when the *karman* (i.e. the *apūrva* caused by it), which is collected (by them in the worldly life), gets exhausted through their enjoyment,[1] they return to this path by which they have come. [153]
Having fallen to the sky, they, not having enjoyment (any more), come to Vāyu, from Vāyu to rain, then from rain to the earth and then, together with the earth,[2] to the state of food—they

who thus come to the earth. [154]

[1]See verses 151 and 152 above.

[2]The instrumental form of *pṛthivī* is explained by SP as *sahārthe tṛtīyā*. Therefore, they become food along with (i.e. as) the earth becomes it.

घटीयन्त्रवदश्रान्ता एवमेव पुनः पुनः ।
परिवर्तन्ति संसारे कर्मवायुसमीरिताः ॥१५५॥

In this very way, like a *ghaṭīyantra* 'a mechanical device of raising water from a well', they keep on rotating,[1] without becoming tired (as it were), rotate[1] in this world, impelled by the wind in the form of the ritual activity. [155]

[1]The Parasmaipada is for the Ātmanepada form.

दक्षिणस्य पथो व्याख्या यथावदनुवर्णिता ॥१५६॥

Thus is described the path to the south, as given in scriptures (*yathāvat*). [156]

यथोक्तलक्षणौ ये तु पन्थानावुत्तरेतरौ ।
न विदुस्ते भवन्तीह कीटाद्या दुःखभोगिनः ॥१५७॥

And (*tu*) those, who do not know these two paths, viz. one to the north and the other (to the south), which are thus described, become here (i.e. in this world) insects etc., experiencing miseries. [157]

नाद्रियन्त इदं ज्ञानमुदङमार्गाप्तिसाधनम् ।
कर्म वा पितृयाणाप्तौ ते कीटाद्यामियुर्गतिम् ॥१५८॥

Those, who disregard this knowledge, which is the means to attaining to the path to the north, or (follow that which leads) to the Pitṛyāṇa, attain to the state of insects etc. [158]

गोमयाद्युद्भवाः कीटाः पतङ्गाः शलभास्तथा ।
दंशाश्च मशकाश्चैव दन्दशूकाः सपन्नगाः ॥१५९॥

(The insects etc. means) the insects born from cow-dung, flying insects, locusts and biting insects, mosquitoes, as also biting insects and the serpents. [159]

यतिथ्यामिति यः प्रश्नः स पुंजन्मोक्तितो गतः ।
तदनन्तरमेवोक्ता व्यावृत्तिश्च पथोर्द्वयोः ॥१६०॥

The question in the words 'In what is the number of ...' is (thus) answered by the statement about the birth of man;[1] then immediately thereafter is stated the difference between the two paths. [160]

[1]This is reference to the *mānasa puruṣa* mentioned in verse 140 above.

आकाशाद्यभिसंभूत्या पुनरावर्तनं गतम् ।
देवयानं च यत्कृत्वा पितृयाणं च लभ्यते ॥१६१॥
साधनं तदपीहोक्तं ज्ञानकर्मस्वलक्षणम् ।
लोकस्यापूरणे हेतुः समाप्तावुदितः स्फुटः ॥१६२॥
कीटादीनामगमनाद्गतानां चागतेस्तथा ।
एवं पञ्चापि निर्णीताः प्रश्ना ये प्राक्प्रचोदिताः ॥१६३॥

By (the statement about) becoming the sky etc. (of the deceased worshippers) is explained their return (and also that means) by adopting which, they attain to the Devayāna and/or the Pitṛyāṇa. [161]
Also, there is stated the means of each, viz. having the nature of knowledge and of ritual. And also there is clearly stated why the world does not get filled. [162]
And (there are explanations about) the Jīvas not going to or going to the states of insects etc. Thus, all the five questions,

which were first put forth, have been answered. [163]

इति श्रीबृहदारण्यकोपनिषद्भाष्यवार्तिके षष्ठाध्यायस्य
द्वितीयं ब्राह्मणम् ॥२॥

BṚHADĀRAṆYAKOPANIṢAD-BHĀṢYA-VĀRTIKA 6.3

वित्तं विना न सिद्धिः स्याद्दृष्टादृष्टार्थकर्मणः ।
यतोऽतः कर्म मन्थाख्यं तादर्थ्येनाभिधीयते ॥१॥

Since there cannot be accomplishment of the (ritual) action intended for securing the seen and/or the unseen results, unless one has the wealth (necessary for the performances); therefore, a ritual act that is called Mantha is now prescribed (lit. stated) for that purpose. [1]

This introduces the relation between this Brāhmaṇa and the earlier ones. The earlier discussed effects, viz. the movement of the departed ones, relate to their *jñāna* (of BU 6.1) and *karman* (of BU 6.2). Now follows the subsequent portion which is allied to it.

पितुर्लोक्यो यथा पुत्रः कर्मणेहोपजायते ।
तादृक्पुत्रार्थिनः कर्म त्वेषामित्यादिनोच्यते ॥२॥

In the words *eṣām* ...[1] there is prescribed (lit. stated) a (ritual) action for one desiring to have a son, in a way that through that action becomes born to a father a son who is conducive to (his achievement of) the *loka*. [2]

[1]Cf. BU 6.4.1.

यः स्यात्कामग्रहग्रस्तो वित्तापत्योद्भवं प्रति ।
तं प्रत्येवेति विज्ञेयं कर्मेदं न त्वकामिनम् ॥३॥

It should be known that this (ritual act) is (intended) for

him who is possessed by a strong desire (*kāmagraha*) for getting (lit. for the rise of) wealth and offspring and not for one who has no (such) desire. [3]

Thus, every householder, who desires for an excellent after-life, should perform the Mantha ritual.

प्राप्नुयां सुमहद्वित्तमिति यः कामयेत ह ।
इत्युक्त्यावाप्तवित्तस्य नेदं कर्मेति गम्यते ॥४॥
महत्त्वमात्मनोऽत्यर्थं यो वा कामयते गृही ।
महत्ता न विना वित्तं कर्मातो वित्तसिद्धये ॥५॥

It is implied that this (ritual) act is not for one who has (already) obtained wealth, as it is understood from the statement: he who desires, 'May I obtain very great wealth'; [4]

or a householder, who desires to obtain for himself exceeding importance; (as) indeed (such) greatness cannot be (obtained) without wealth, therefore is this (ritual) act meant for acquring wealth. [5]

In the two verses the word *mahat* is understood in two ways: (i) in verse 4, *mahat* is adjective of wealth, (ii) in verse 5, *mahat* means importance among people or *aisvarya* 'fame etc.' for which wealth is implied as the essential part.

The following is the explanation of BU sentence sa yaḥ udagayane ....

कालो विधीयते चास्य मन्थाख्यस्येह कर्मणः ।
श्रुत्योदगयनाद्युक्त्या कर्मसिद्ध्यै प्रयत्नतः ॥६॥

The time for the performance of this rite called Mantha is prescribed here, since the Śruti has specifically stated in the words beginning with *udagayane* for the accomplishing of the (ritual) act. [6]

This explains the meaning of the BU sentence *udagayane* '(at the time of the movement of the sun) ... northward ...',

SP points out: This is according to the accepted belief *kāle karma vidhīyate nākāle* (not traced).

प्रार्थनीयः पुरा कालो विशुद्धिश्चात्मनस्ततः ।
द्रव्याण्योषधयश्चैव देशश्च तदनन्तरम् ॥७॥

First, the time (for the ritual act) has to be properly desired (i.e. decided by the householder), then also his own purification, various materials (for example, utensils and grains (lit. herbs) (have to be acquired), and then (a suitable) place for the performance (is to be fixed). [7]

कालादीनां गुणानां च कर्मण्यस्मिन्समुच्चयः ।
न विकल्पः समृद्धिः स्यात्कर्मणोऽस्य समुच्चितौ ॥८॥

And, in this (ritual) action, there is a combination of time etc.[1] and also of excellences;[2] there is no alternative (for the same prescribed here), because only in (such a) combination (is ascertained) the richness of the (ritual) action. [8]

[1]This refers to the material and the place.
[2]This is called *guṇa*s, not qualities, viz. purified body and mind and faith etc.

कर्मणश्चास्य निष्पत्तौ विद्वत्तापि समाश्रिता ।
यतोऽतः सूत्रितं नेदं सूत्रकृद्भिर्यथोदितम् ॥९॥

Since again, in (successfully) completing this (ritual) action, the state of (the worshipper's) being possessed of the knowledge (about the action) is also expected; therefore, this (ritual act), which is mentioned (above), is not prescribed in their (Gṛhya-)sūtra by the composers[1] of the same. [9]

[1]The plural here marks the respect for the composer of the Gṛhyasūtra, or for indicating more than one Gṛhyasūtra related to the Saṃhitā of the relevant Vedic school.

यो ह वै ज्येष्ठमित्युक्त्या विद्वत्ता या पुरोदिता ।
तस्यां सत्यामिदं कर्म ज्येष्ठायेत्यादिलिङ्गतः ॥१०॥

This (ritual) act is (to be performed) by a worshipper, in case he is possessed of the knowledge (about the ritual action), this (lit. which) was stated before in the words *yo ha vai jyeṣṭham* ... (BU 6.1). This (is understood) from the indicatory (words) *jyeṣṭhāya* etc. [10]

भूमिशय्या पयःपानं ब्रह्मचर्यं च वाग्यमः ।
उपसद्व्रतमेतत्स्यादमावास्येति लिङ्गतः ॥११॥

Also (there is to be understood) from the indicatory (word) *amāvāsyā* that this is the vow called *upasad* wherein a worshipper has to observe sleeping on bare earth, subsist (only) on (lit. drink) milk, (observing) abstinence from sex act and restraint on speech. [11]

अग्निमित्येकवचनात्तथैवोल्लेखनादितः ।
न मुख्योपसदामत्र संभवोऽस्तीति गम्यते ॥१२॥

Also it is understood from the use of the singular form *agnim* and also from the reference to drawing (of lines) etc. (on the place of the ritual) that there is no acceptance (lit. possibility) of the principally known *upasads*.[1] [12]

[1]These refer to those vows prescribed in relation to a Jyotiṣṭoma sacrifice. They are more elaborate and those under reference are comparatively simpler. *ullekhana* etc. are prescribed for various domestic rituals.

ताम्रं नौदुम्बरं ग्राह्यमिध्मैस्तस्य विरोधतः ।
वानस्पत्यमतो ग्राह्यं कर्मण्यौदुम्बरं श्रुतौ ॥१३॥

And an Audumbara (vessel) made of copper is not to be used in this (ritual) act, because that is opposed by the *idhmas* 'sacrificial fuel sticks'.[1] Therefore, one should use in this (ritual) act an Audumbara (vessel) made of wood. [13]

This verse rejects a view that the Audumbara vessel, made of copper, is to be used in this (ritual) act; because there is the scriptural statement *audumbara idhmaḥ* (BU 6.3.13).

ग्राम्याणि दश धान्यानि फलपुष्पाणि सर्वतः ।
अप्रमादकराणीह भक्ष्यमेध्यानि यानि च ॥१४॥

(One should use during the performance of the ritual) ten types of grains produced from land, as also fruits and flowers which do not cause intoxication and such eatables as are suitable (for the performance of the rituals).[1] [14]

[1]This is to avoid the eating of garlic etc.

दशेति नियमार्थं स्यान्न ततोऽन्यनिषेधने ।
भूरिदोषोपदुष्टत्वात्परिसंख्याविधेरिति ॥१५॥

The word *daśa* is mentioned (here) for restricting (the nature of the kinds of grains to be offered in the Mantha rite) though not for prohibiting other grains, because the injunction called Parisaṃkhyā[1] (is not to be accepted) as it suffers from many defects (or, faults).[2] [15]

[1]*niyama* refers to what is adopted among/between alternatives that are enjoined in an injunction (*pakṣe 'prāptasya prāpako vidhiḥ*) and *parisaṃkhyā* refers to what is excluded from alternatives that obtain simultaneously (*ubhayoś ca yugapatprāptāv itaravyāvṛttiparaḥ parisaṃkhyāvidhiḥ*). (*Arthasaṃgraha*. ed. S.S.

Sukthankar, Bombay: 1931, pp. 78-79).

[2]Read SP: *śrautasarvaviśeṣaṇatyāgo 'śrutānyanivṛttisvīkāraḥ ... ityādismṛtivirodhaś ca.*

कंसाद्याकारसिद्ध्यर्थं कंसाद्युक्तिरिहोच्यते ।
तण्डुलान्फलपुष्पाणि पिष्ट्वा पात्रे निधापयेत् ॥१६॥
दध्ना च मधुना पिष्टं सम्यगालोड्य पात्रगम् ।
स्थापयेत्कृतरक्षं सच्छुचौ देशे प्रयत्नतः ॥१७॥

Here is a statement made about bronze etc.[1] in order to get effected the vessel of a material called bronze. The performer of this rite should first paste (together) rice grains, fruits and flowers and then place them in that vessel. [16] Then, having softened the paste with curds and honey by vigorously stirring these in the pot together, he should place them carefully in a purified region, properly protected.[2] [17]

[1]That refers to the material from which the Audumbara vessel is made.

[2]Cf. BUB pp. 786-787.

परीत्यादिगिरा चात्र देशसंस्कार उच्यते ।
संस्कृते भूप्रदेशेऽथ ह्यग्निं संस्थापयेद्गृही ॥१८॥

And by the mention of *pari-*[1] etc., here is expressed the purification of the place (for the performance), then, on this (purified) place, the householder should establish the fire. [18]

[1]This refers to the three acts *parisamūhana* 'sprinkling water (in some particular way) around the fire(-place)', *parilepana* 'smearing with cowdung the altar,' and *paristaraṇa* 'strewing or spreading (*darbhas*) around (the fire)'.

लेपनादि च कर्तव्यं कृतपर्वेऽपि तद्विधेः ।
इति कातीयवचनमदृष्टार्थत्वकारणात् ॥१९॥

Smearing (that place) etc. has to be done, even if (that has been already) performed, since it has been so prescribed in a statement of Kātyāyana[1] for (effecting) some unseen purpose. [19]

[1]Read SP: *dṛṣṭārthatayā kṛtaśodhane 'pi deśe lepanādi kartavyam* (*Kātyāyana Gṛhyasūtra*; and also SP: *parisamuhyopalipyollikhyoddhṛtyābhyukṣyeti*.

पाकयज्ञविधानेन संस्कृत्याज्यं यथाविधि ।
पुंसा हस्तादिनक्षेण मन्थमानीय सिद्धये ॥२०॥
खजकेनैकधीकृत्य मन्थद्रव्यमतः परम् ।
आवापस्थान आज्यस्य हुत्वा नित्याहुतीस्ततः ॥२१॥
यावन्त इत्युपक्रम्य मन्त्रैराज्यं यथाक्रमम् ।
हुत्वा हुत्वा च मन्थेऽथ संस्रवं प्रक्षिपेन्मुहुः ॥२२॥

(The performer of the rite) should, in keeping with the prescription of simple offering(s), (viz. *pākayajñas*), first purify the clarified butter according to the procedure and then, bringing the Mantha for accomplishment (of the rite), at the time of the constellation of Hasta etc. (which bears) a male (name), [20]
mixing together the material for Mantha, by means of a churning stick and then making usual offerings of clarified butter, in the place of the offerings, [21]
he should begin with Mantras *yāvantaḥ* ...– Then, making the offerings, one after another, he should later in the Mantha rite, offer (into the fire) the remainder of the (clarified butter). [22]

Now, BU 6.3.2 is under reference.

स्वाहाकारावसानाः स्युर्मन्त्राः सर्वे यथोदिताः ॥२३॥

All the Mantras, as stated, should end with the utterance *svāhā*.

[23]

मन्त्रद्वयेन ज्येष्ठादौ होमः कार्यो विजानता ।
अग्न्यादावेकशः कार्यो यावन्मन्थावमर्शनम् ॥२४॥

A knower (of the ritual) should perform the *homa* (i.e. make the offerings) under the constellations Jyeṣṭhā etc., with the recitation of the two Mantras *agni* ... till there is the completion of the Mantras. [24]

SP states: *uktaṃ ca bhāṣye retasa ityādyārabhyaikaikām āhutiṃ hutvā ityādi* (possibly from Bhartṛprapañca on BU).

अथ स्विष्टकृदन्तेऽस्मिन्होमानन्तरमेव तत् ।
द्वितीयेन मथालोड्य ह्यथाभिमृशति पाणिना ॥२५॥
भ्रमसीत्यादिना मन्थं स्मरंस्तद्देवतां हृदा ।
भ्रमसि प्राणभूतस्त्वं न ह्येकत्रावतिष्ठसे ॥२६॥
ज्वलज्जाज्वल्यमानस्त्वं जठरस्थान्नपाककृत् ।
पूर्णं च सर्वतोऽव्यापि सर्वत्रानवखण्डितम् ॥२७॥
प्रस्तब्धोऽसि स्थिरत्वाच्च वियद्वन्न विकम्पसे ॥२८॥
सर्वतोऽपरिपन्थित्वात्सर्वैश्चाप्यनुकूलतः ।
त्वगेकशाफगित्युक्तं शाफैका या त्वदात्मिका ॥२९॥

Then, after the *sviṣṭavṛt* [1] offering is made in the rite–which is immediately after that offering [2]–he should mix together that material of the Mantha offering for a second time. Then he touches (the Mantha) by his hand, [25]
remembering the deity of the Mantha and reciting the Mantra *bhramasi* ...; (the Mantra means:) You have now become Prāṇa and you do not stay just at one place (in the body).[3] [26]
The Mantra *jvalat* ...– means: 'You are shining brilliantly and the author of the digestion of food that is in (viz. has reached) the stomach. And you are (the Brahman), *pūrṇa* and pervading on all sides, and nowhere obstructed'. [27]
'(And) you are, on account of steadiness, steady (in the body)

and, (even) like the sky, you do not shake. [28]
Since from all sides you do not have any opposition and because all are agreeable[4] (or helpful) to you, therefore it is said 'you have (only) one hoof'. What is a single hoof is only yourself in nature.[5] [29]

[1]This is an offering to Agni, made from all the remnants of the materials for the *homa* put together. It marks an unimpeded completion of an offering (*su* 'well'). (Incidentally Agni—specially the Āhavanīya in the Śrauta ritual—is also called *sviṣṭakṛt*).

[2]This is explained by *homānantaram eva tat* where *tat* is the *manthadravya* 'material for the Mantha rite'.

[3]That is to say: the deity of the Mantha, being Prāṇa, moves everywhere in the body. Now follows the explanation of *jvalat* ....

[4]*anukūlataḥ* is to be understood as *anukūlaiḥ*, qualifying *sarvaiḥ*. To paraphrase this: *sarveṣām anukūlatvāt*.

[5]Read SP here: *yā khalv ekā śaphā jagadātmikā nikhilam api jagat tava pādabhāgatvena vartate na tu pādatve 'pi paryāptam ato 'navacchinnas tvam ity arthaḥ*.

उद्गात्रा हिंकृतं पूर्वं स्तोत्रमुद्गायता स्फुटम् ।
यज्ञारम्भे तदा मध्ये गीयमानेऽथ सामनि ॥३०॥
अपि हिंक्रियमाणोऽसि तथोद्गीथे विनिर्दिशेत् ।
श्रावितोऽध्वर्युणा च त्वमग्नीधा च तथोत्तरम् ॥३१॥

(You are) what was produced by the Udgātṛ as *hum* sound while he was singing in clear voice, at the beginning of the sacrifice and in the middle of it and also while the Sāman was being sung.[1] [30]
You are also the one who are addressed with *hiṃkāra* and so he (i.e. the performer of the Mantha rite) should mention in the Udgītha song. You have been sung by the Adhvaryu and later by the priest Agnīdh also. [31]

[1]The words *hiṃkṛta*, *hiṃkriyamāṇa* refer to different points of time, yet the *hiṃkāra*, being only one, belongs to all points of time and does not involve any contradiction.

आर्द्रे मेघोदरे विद्युत्संदीप्तोऽसीति कथ्यते ।
विविधं त्वमेव भवसि यतोऽतो विभुरुच्यते ॥३२॥
सोमो वृष्ट्यादिभावेन प्रभुः प्रभवसीत्यतः ।
आदित्यः प्राणभावेन ह्यन्नभावेन सोमता ॥३३॥

It is said that you are resplendent in lightning in the wet interior of a cloud. Since you yourself become varied (in form), therefore, you are called *vibhu* 'all-becoming'.[1] [32]
You are Soma by becoming rain etc. and the Lord because you prevail; also Āditya by becoming Prāṇa and you have the nature of Soma[2] by becoming food. [33]

[1]This is from *vi* in the sense of *vividha* 'various' with the verb root *bhu*— not the usual explanation: 'all-pervading'.
[2]Possibly this refers to the Soma plant which has been identified with Soma earlier, (see under BUBV 2.1.57).

अन्नान्नादद्वयं सर्वं त्वमेव तदपि प्रभो ।
निधनं कारणत्वात्त्वं कारणे कार्यसंलयः ॥३४॥

You are yourself the pair, viz. food and the eater of food, O Lord and you are the end, because you are the cause (of all) (in that) all effects merge into the cause. [34]

This is like a pot, which is made of clay and finally merges into clay itself.

वागग्न्याद्यात्मसम्पातात्संवर्गोऽसीति भण्यते ।
इति मन्त्रः समाप्तोऽयमभिमर्शनकर्मणि ॥३५॥

It is said (in the Mantra), 'You are the *saṃvarga*[1] (of all), since Vāc, Agni and others end themselves (into you)'. Thus is this Mantra adopted (lit. obtained or accepted) while there is the action of touching the Mantha. [35]

This is the meaning of *saṃvargo 'si* in BU; where *saṃvarga* can be translated alternatively as 'collection or collective form'.

[1]*saṃvarga* refers to what stands for a collection of some things belonging to one class; e.g. *vāyu* is called the *saṃvarga* of all winds in the body.

Now, BU 6.3.5 is under reference.

अथैनं मन्त्रपूतं सदुद्यच्छति यथोदितम् ।
आमंसीत्यादिमन्त्रेण तदर्थाविष्कृतिस्त्वियम् ॥३६॥

Now that this one is purified by the Mantras as prescribed, he lifts it up, reciting the Mantra *ā maṃsi* .... The explanation of its meaning is thus: [36]

आमंसीति भवेद्रूपं ज्ञानार्थस्यैव मन्यतेः ।
लेटयाङ्पूर्वस्य संसिद्धं शब्लुकीत्यवधारणात् ॥३७॥

The form *āmaṃsi* is derived from the verb root *man* conveying the meaning 'to know', with the prefix *ā*, in the *let* 'subjunctive mood' and determined[1] by the dropping of the conjugational sign *śap*. [37]

[1]This is in accordance with the grammatical rule regarding the dropping of it.

आसमन्ताद्विजानासि सूक्ष्मादि जगति स्थितम् ।
ज्ञेयं यावज्जगत्किंचिदामंसीति ततः सदा ॥३८॥

You know everything around, viz. what is existing in the world beginning with the subtle (and) whatever is to be known; therefore, (it is said) 'You ever know all the world'. [38]

This explains the meaning of *āmaṃsi* which is in BU and also in BUB as *āmaṃhi*.

यथास्मांस्त्वं विजानासि तथैव त्वां वयं सदा ।
मन्यामहे वरीयांसं गुणवद्भ्यो गुणाधिकम् ॥३९॥

As you know us all, so do we ever think about you, who are better (than all others) and having more excellent qualities than those who are possessed of (those) qualities. [39]

महि महत्त्वं जानीम आमोऽसि त्वं तथा प्रभो ।
न त्वं पाकसमायोगात्फलवन्नाशमृच्छसि ॥४०॥
आमोऽपक्वं त्वयि गतं महत्त्वमपि भण्यते ।

We know your *mahi*, i.e. *mahattva* 'greatness'. So also you are, O Lord, unbaked or uncooked, i.e. you never meet destruction like a fruit (which meets destruction) after coming into contact with heat or cooking. [40]
āma means unbaked; thus the greatness in you is described (lit. expressed). [41ab]

यस्माद्राजास्य सर्वस्य मां च देवः स सर्वदा ॥४१॥
राजानं च तथेशानं करोत्वधिपतिं च माम् ।
उद्यम्यानेन मन्त्रेण भक्षयत्यथ भागशः ॥४२॥

And since you (are) the king of all this, therefore, may you, the god, ever (rule or protect) me. [41cd]
May (his Mantha) make me a king, a ruler, (and) the lord.[1]
Reciting this Mantra, he first lifts up (the Manthagraha) and then partakes of it, part by part. [42]

[1]That is, May that grant me power/excellence similar to yours.

Now, BU 6.3.6 is under reference.

गायत्र्या मधुमत्या च व्याहृत्या चेति पादशः ।

ग्रासमश्नाति मन्थस्य ह्युत्तरेषु तथैव च ॥४३॥

He partakes of the Mantha, bit by bit, each with one line of the Gāyatrī Mantra, and a verse containing (the word) *madhu* in it and also a Vyāhṛti[1] (one after another). [43]

The elaborate procedure is this: the first line of the Gāyatrī Mantra and a verse containing (the word) *madhu* in it and the *vyāhṛti bhūḥ*; then the second line etc. with the *vyāhṛti bhvaḥ*; and then the third line, etc. with the *vyāhṛti svaḥ*.

[1]This refers to the sacred utterances *bhūḥ*, *bhvaḥ* and *svāhā*. This is clear from BU.

सवितुस्तद्वरेण्यं स्याद्भर्गमन्नं महात्मनः ।
ऋतायन्ते तथा वाता मधुवत्सुखकारिणः ॥४४॥

The words *savituḥ tat ...*, *vareṇya* is *bharga*[1] referring to the food of the great one. So also *ṛtāyante vātāḥ* (which should be) 'causing pleasure' like *madhu*. [44]

Sureśvara paraphrases the words in the original verses and supplies only some words in their paraphrase for clarifying the ideas in the same.

[1]This is for the Vedic form *bhargaḥ*. Of course, it is possible that the Vedic word *bhargas* could also have another alternative form *bharga*. But the meaning *annam*, as suggested by Sureśvara is not meant in the well-known Gāyatrī Mantra—it means there 'lustre'.

अनुद्वेगकरा हृद्या ऋतायन्ते वहन्ति च ।
अमृतं मधु नद्योऽपि मदर्थं सर्वदा शुभम् ॥४५॥

(The verses convey the following thoughts): (The winds) which do not cause any pain (and) which are delightful to the heart, follow the *ṛta*, and thus (may) they flow (pleasantly). So also do the rivers (bring) *amṛta*, viz. sweet,[1] for my sake and (also) bliss, forever, [45]

[1]*madhu* refers to harmony in every walk of life; here it is called 'sweet' only metaphorically.

तृप्ता मोदामहे येन क्षरन्तीति क्रियापदम् ।
अत्यर्थं मधुररसाः सन्तु ह्योषधयश्च नः ॥४६॥

so that we do feel delight, satisfied that we are. The word *kṣaranti* '(they) trickle' is a verb (conveying the idea:) may they indeed be for us exceedingly sweet in their juice; and so also may the herbs (flow sweet) for us. [46]

त्रिकमुच्चार्य भूः स्वाहेत्याहुतिं प्रक्षिपेन्मुखे ।
त्रिकं त्रिकं तथोच्चार्य ह्युत्तरेष्वपि योजयेत् ॥४७॥

Having recited the three (*vyāhṛtis*) together, he puts into (his own) mouth the offering (i.e. mouthful) with the utterance; so also he recites, the group of the three one by one, while taking the subsequent mouthfuls.[1] [47]

[1]The elaborate procedure is clearly explained in the following verses up to verse 55.

देवस्य द्योतनवतो हृद्यं यच्चिन्तयेमहि ।
मधु नक्तमथो रात्रिर्मधुरा दुःखहानिकृत् ॥४८॥
उषसो दिवसस्यापि माधुर्यं नोऽस्तु सर्वदा ।
पार्थिवं च रजो लोको ह्लादकृन्मधुमांस्तथा ॥४९॥
द्युलोकः पितृलोकोऽथ पिता हि द्यौर्यतो मतः ।
भुवः स्वाहेति मन्थस्य द्वितीयामाहुतिं क्षिपेत् ॥५०॥

(The *bharga*[1]) of the resplendent god, which is pleasant to the heart (and) sweet[2]—and (*atho*) *naktam* is night[3]—let (night) be (sweet and) ever a remover of misery. [48]
Also may there be for us the sweetness of Uṣas, and of the

day also. And may the earthly region, viz. this world, be for us the cause of delight and full of sweetness as well. [49]
So also may the heavenly region and the region of the Pitṛs be pleasant (for us), for the heaven is known as the father indeed. Then, let him, reciting (the *vyāhṛti*) *bhuvaḥ* and (the word) *svāhā*, make the second offering of the Mantha (into his own mouth). [50]

[1]This is taken from verse 44 above (where *bharga-* is for the Ṛgvedic *bhargas-* as already pointed out there).
[2]That is, agreeable.
[3]This is parenthetic.

धियः प्रचोदयेद्यो न उद्यन्प्रज्ञेन्द्रियाणि च ।
प्रचोदयतु नो देवः श्रेयसे सर्वदात्मनः ॥५१॥

dhiyaḥ pracodayet yo naḥ means 'May that god, rising, ever incite our intellect and sense-organs, may (he be) for the well-being of the Ātman (the inner self). [51]

वनस्पतिस्तथा चन्द्रः सूर्यस्तु मधुरोऽस्तु नः ।
गावो दीधितयः सन्तु मधुमत्यो दिशोऽथवा ॥५२॥

In the same way, may the herb, also the moon, and (*tu*) the sun be for us sweet; may the cows, the rays, be for us full of sweet, or, may the quarters (be sweet).[1] [52]

[1]*diśo 'thavā* is possibly added as an explanation of *dīdhitayaḥ*, because they, in the sense of the rays (of the sun). Yet this might be taken as a repetition after the mention of *sūrya*. This leaves *gāvaḥ* 'cows' as an independent source of delight.
Possibly Sureśvara refers *gāvaḥ* to rays and *dīdhitayaḥ* to the quarters; so SP.

स्वः स्वाहेत्याहुतिक्षेपः समस्तां व्याहरेत्ततः ।
सावित्रीं मधुमतीश्चैव तिस्त्रोऽपि व्याहृतीस्तथा ॥५३॥

चतुर्थीं प्रक्षिपेदेवमाहुतिं पर्ववन्मुखे ।
अहमेव जगत्सर्वं भूयासमिति निर्ब्रुवन् ॥५४॥

Let there be the (third) offering with (the utterance of the *vyāhṛti*) *svaḥ* (and the word) *svāhā*. Then he should recite the full Sāvitrī (i.e. Gāyatrī) verse and all those verses which contain the word *madhu* in them, together with all of the three *vyāhṛtis* [53]

and thus he should make the fourth offering into (his own) mouth, (even) as before, saying 'May I be the entire world'. [54]

स्मार्तमाचमनं त्वन्ते प्रायत्यार्थमिहोच्यते ।
अग्नेः पश्चिमतोऽथान्ते प्राक्शिराः संविशेत्ततः ॥५५॥

Then there is prescribed here, in the end, the sipping of water, according to the Smṛti, for *prāyatya*.[1] Then may he sleep to the west of the fire, with his head towards the west. [55]

[1]This is for securing purity. SP refers to *Manusmṛti* 2.222 for clarifying *prāyatya*:
ācamya prayato nityam ubhe saṃdhye samāhitaḥ /
śucau deśe japej japyam upāsīta yathāvidhi //

प्रत्यूषसि ततो भक्त्या ह्यादित्यमुपतिष्ठते ।
वक्ष्यमाणेन मन्त्रेण ह्युपासीत रविं सदा ॥५६॥

Then, in the morning, he indeed, worships the sun, with devotion; let him indeed[1] ever worship the sun with the verse which is being stated hereafter. [56]

[1]SP states that the use of the word *hi* is to point out the well-known prescription of the worship.

एकपुण्डरीकमिति प्रधानत्वं विवक्षितम् ।
एकशब्देन नो संख्या यथैकः श्वेतवाहनः ॥५७॥

The use of the word *ekapuṇḍarīka* intends to convey the prominence (of the object of worship); the word *eka* does not signify the number; (It is like in the phrase *ekaḥ śvetavāhanaḥ*,[1] viz. the only one, who has white horses.) [57]

This verse gives the meaning of the Mantra which is referred to in the preceding verse.

[1]This refers to Arjuna. He alone is known by the name Śvetavāhana.

दिशां यद्वत्प्रधानस्त्वं मनुष्याणां तथा ह्यहम् ।
भवेयं त्वत्प्रसादाद्भोः स्फीतः पुंभोगसाधनैः ॥५८॥

As you are prominent among all the quarters, so also may I be among men, O Lord, through your favour, enriched with many means of men's enjoyments. [58]

Now, BU 6.3.7 is under reference.

यथेतमेत्याथासीनः पश्चादग्नेः समाहितः ।
तं हैतमिति यत्नेन वंशं जपति भक्तितः ॥५९॥

Then, going (back by the way which) he has come, he seats himself by the side of the fire, and with his mind (well) composed, he recites, with full attention and with devotion the words *taṃ ha etam* ..., he mentions (lit. utters) the line of his teachers (*vaṃśam*). [59]

Now, BU 6.3.8 is under reference.

तं हैतं मन्थं यत्नोक्तमुद्दालतनयः सुधीः ।
उक्त्वाथ याज्ञवल्क्याय तं प्रोवाचाथ विस्मितः ॥६०॥
मन्थं शुष्केऽपि यः स्थाणौ निषिञ्चेदुक्तसंस्कृतम् ।
जायेरन्नेव तच्छाखाः प्ररोहेयुर्दलानि च ॥६१॥

Then, having told with an attentive mind, (about) this Mantha

(rite) to Yājñavalkya, the intelligent son of Uddālaka[1] (again) said, with a smile: [60]
'Whosoever would offer this Mantha, which is thus sanctified, even on a dry (i.e. withered) tree, (would find that) its branches become full of life and also would put forth young leaves.' [61]

This asserts the potency of the Mantha.

Now, BU 6.3.9-12 are under reference.

यादृगर्थोऽस्य वचस उत्तरेष्वपि तादृशः ।

The meaning of the words even in the subsequent sentences is similar to what it is of this statement (viz. BU 6.3.8). [62ab]

Now, BU 6.3.13 is under reference.

चतुरौदुम्बरोक्त्यर्थो व्याख्यातः पूर्वमेव तु ।
सुखावबोधतश्चैव स्वयमेव प्रतीयताम् ॥६२॥

The meaning of the statement in the words *caturaudumbara* ... is already explained;[1] may one know it with ease for understanding. [62c-f]

[1]That is, as in the case of Audumbara vessel made of bronze in verses 13ff. above.

इति श्रीबृहदारण्यकोपनिषद्भाष्यवार्तिके षष्ठाध्यायस्य
तृतीयं ब्राह्मणम् ॥३॥

BṚHADĀRAṆYAKOPANIṢAD-BHĀṢYA-VĀRTIKA
6.4

In some of these verses Sureśvara often refers to the actual words of the Mantras in BU and supplies together with them his paraphrases of the same. Therefore, our translation had to appear as bits of phases!
BU 6.4.1-2 are under reference.

एषामिति नृबीजस्य स्तुतिरुक्त्या विवक्ष्यते ।
प्रतिष्ठां कल्पयानीति यस्यां पुंस्त्वं प्रपद्यते ॥१॥

In the words *eṣām* ..., the statement (in the Śruti) intends to express the praise of the seed of man. And, the words *pratiṣṭhāṃ kalpayāni* (signify that) in which the nature (lit. birth) of a male is secured. [1]

In this verse, Sureśvara summarizes the introductory arguments of BU 6.4.1-2 by citing only a few words from it.

Now, only BU 6.4.2 is under reference.

शुक्रं निषिक्तं यत्रेदं पुरुषत्वं निगच्छति ।
प्रतिष्ठां तादृशीमीशः प्रजापतिरचीक्लृपत् ॥२॥

Prajāpati, the ruler (or, Lord), thought of such a firm abode in which the semen planted (lit. poured) gets the (potential) quality of a male. [2]

This explains the thought of the second half of the preceding verse.

स्त्रियं ससर्ज तद्योग्यां मधुकाण्डे यथोदिताम् ।

सृष्ट्वाथाधः प्रदेशे तामुपास्ते ग्राम्यधर्मतः ॥३॥

Then he created a woman who is suitable for that,[1] as mentioned in the Madhu Kāṇḍa.[2] Then, after creating her, he attended to her in her lower part (of the body), as in common life.[3] [3]

This explains *sa striyaṃ sasṛje* in BU.

[1]That is, for being an abode for the seed.

[2]Cf. *tataḥ patiś ca patnī cābhavatām* (BU 1.4.3).

[3]This is, *grāmya dharma*, that is to say it is not the sign of the religious elite. This indicates that Sureśvara's expression is the precurser of Ānandagiri's expression *paśukarma* and that it conforms to the *Kāmaśāstra*. The lower part here means a woman's sexual organ.

अपत्योत्पत्तये स्त्रीणामधोदेशं प्रजापतिः ।
प्रागुपासितवान्यत्नादुपास्यं तेन तत्ततः ॥४॥

(Since) Prajāpati had, in earlier time, attended to the lower part of the body of the woman,[1] for producing a son (lit. a child),[2] therefore, one should attend to that with special care (*yatna*). [4]

This is to explain *tasmāt striyam adha upāsīta* in BU.

[1]It is possible to understand that Sureśvara uses the word *strīṇām* (plural) to express the idea of the class-word *striyam*.

[2]In such a context, the word *apatya* is to be taken as a synonym of *putra*.

सोमाभिषवरूपत्वक्लृप्तयेऽथाधुनोच्यते ।
एतं ग्रावाणवच्छिश्नमुदपारयदात्मनः ॥५॥

Now is stated hereafter to establish the form of the Soma-pressing in the placing of the seed in a woman. In the words *etam*,[1] (the Śruti states) that he made his generative organ penetrate (into the woman's sexual organ), like the stone (for Soma-pressing). [5]

This and the following two verses explain *sa etam ... abhyasrjata* in BU.

[1]This refers to the generative organ because of its hardness at the time of intercourse. SP refers to the similarity between human intercourse and the preparation of the Soma drink, i.e. Vājapeya 'strong drink' -sacrifice.

प्राञ्चं कृत्वाथ तं शिश्नं यथैवाभिषवोपलम् ।
एकीभावेन तं नार्यां यत्नात्समुपवेशयेत् ॥६॥

Then he makes his penis hard like the Soma-pressing stone and becoming one (in mind with the woman) he enters it into the woman[1] with (proper) attention (*yatna*). [6]

SP states *nārīśabdas tadīyendriyaviṣayaḥ*.

तथाभूतेन ग्राव्णैतां स्त्रियमभ्यसृजन्मुहुः ।
आत्मनः पुरुषार्थाय यथोक्तोपासनं भवेत् ॥७॥

By that (which has become as hard as the Soma-pressing) stone,[1] he united with the woman again (and again) for securing his own aim of life—so that the attendance on the woman, as prescribed would be effected. [7]

This points out the significance of *tenainām abhyasrjata*.

Now, BU 6.4.3 is under reference.

यस्यां प्रजननं पुंसा स्त्रियामभ्यन्तरीकृतम् ।
तस्या वेदिरुपस्थः स्यादूर्वोरुपरि दर्शनम् ॥८॥

The (sexual organ of that woman) in which the man has entered his own generative organ is the alter; and it is seen between (lit. above) her laps—so is to be understood.[1] [8]

[1]This is a metaphorical identity (*dṛṣṭi*).

बर्हिस्तज्जानि लोमानि चर्माधिषवणे तथा ।
चर्मेहानडुहं पश्येत्सोमाभिषवसिद्धये ॥९॥

The hair grown there are the *barhis* (grass) and the lips (of the vulva) are the stones for pressing (Soma, *adhiṣavaṇe*) and the skin of hers is the bull's skin—so should he see (it, viz. the skin) for securing *abhiṣava* 'sprinkling of Soma'[1] [9]

[1]It means: planting the seed in the woman.

फलके चाधिषवणे यथासंख्येन निर्दिशेत् ॥१०॥
यो योन्यन्तर्गतो देशः समिद्धश्चर्म निर्दिशेत् ।
तद्देशमभितस्तौ यौ मुष्कौ तौ वृषणाविति ॥११॥

And he should refer to the stones for Soma-pressing thus in order: [10]
That part which is within her vulva is (to be taken as) what is enkindled (viz. Agni). And he should consider (lit. refer to) the part around the region (of the vulva) as the (bull's) skin and those two fleshy parts as the testicles. [11]

लोकः स्याद्वाजपेयेन यजमानस्य मानतः ।
तावन्तं लोकमाप्नोति यावन्तं वाजपेयतः ॥१२॥

By the authoritative means (i.e. by the text of the Śruti); a sacrificer of the Vājapeya (sacrifice) would get the world; the householder also (by his act under reference) secures as extensive a world as from (the performance of) a Vājapeya (sacrifice). [12]

अन्नानि संभ्रियन्ते हि दश सप्त च भागशः ।
वाजपेये कृतावन्नकामस्य स विधीयते ॥१३॥

Since, in a Vājapeya sacrifice, ten and seven foods are brought (lit. collected together)—in (two) portions; therefore, that (viz. a Vājapeya) is enjoined on one who is desirous of food. [13]

The purport of this verse is not fully/clearly understood by us. However, read SP: *paśukarmāṅgeṣu vājapeyāṅgādhyāse 'pi katham tatra tadadhyāsaḥ sāmyābhāvād ity āśaṅkya sāmyārtham vājapeyasyānnatvaṃ sādhayati.*

रेतसोऽन्नरसस्यैव यत्रान्नाहुतिरीक्ष्यते ।
वाजपेयाभिसंपत्स्यान्मैथुनाख्यक्रतोरतः ।
सामान्यादिति विज्ञेयं वाजपेयफलार्थिनाम् ॥१४॥

Therefore, where (the planting of) the seed by man is seen as the very offering of the essence of food, there would result from the ritual of intercourse the rich result of a Vājapeya rite[1]; this should be known from the similarity by those who desire for the results of the Vājapeya.[2] [14]

[1] Alternatively: SP quotes a Śruti: *yasmin puruṣe 'nnāhutir iṣṭā tasminn etasminn agnau devā annaṃ juhuvati* and adds *iti tasya puṃso reto bhuktānnarasas tasyaiva yasmin karmaṇi hūyamānatvam tasya pūrvavad annatvāt tasmin vājapeyadṛṣṭiḥ.*

[2] That means: the result would follow, even without the actual performance of a Vājapeya rite.

स्त्रीणां च सुकृतं वृङ्क्ते सर्वमावर्जयेच्छुभम् ।
अधोपहासं यो विद्वान्यथोक्तमुपसेवते ॥१५॥

He, who, knowing this, attends to the lower part of the woman,[1] as prescribed (by the scripture), secures (for himself) the woman's merits and all bliss. [15]

[1] That is, unites with her in intercourse.

अनेवंविदुषः पुण्यं सुकृतं वृञ्जते स्त्रियः ।
मैथुनोपनिषत्तत्त्वमेतद्ध स्माह भावितः ॥१६॥

In the case of him, who is not knowing this, women[1] take away his merit, and his good deed(s). This is the secret doctrine of intercourse. Thus has he (Āruṇi), knowing well,[2] stated. [16]

[1]The plural is somewhat strange!
[2]Or, having devotion (properly determining it).

Now, BU 6.4.4 is under reference.

सर्वदैवाहुतीर्विद्वाञ्जुहोत्यश्ननन्नपः पिबन् ।
उपगच्छन्स्त्रियं तद्वदारुणिर्गोत्रतः किल ॥१७॥

A knower (of the Vājasaneya sacrifice) makes all the offerings to gods, eating, and (drinking water); (so) also uniting with (his) woman; (just) in the same way (as in a Vājapeya sacrifice, secures his desired result)—so, it is reported (*kila*), did Āruṇi (know) in family tradition (*gotrataḥ*)[1] [17]

[1]SP adds: and spoke about it.

ब्राह्मणा जातिमात्रेण स्त्रीभिर्हृतशुभागमाः ।
उक्तं विधिमजानन्तो म्रियन्ते मैथुने रताः ॥१८॥

Those, who are Brāhmaṇas only by birth, not knowing the prescribed mode of intercourse (and) whose excellences (i.e. merits collected) are taken away by women, die (if only) addicted to (or, engaged in) intercourse. [18]

It signifies censure on those given to intercourse just for deriving delight from it.

बह्वेतदिति विज्ञेयं प्रयोजनबहुत्वतः ।

रेतः स्कन्दति यत्सुप्तौ जाग्रतो वापि कामिनः ॥१९॥

Since it has many purposes, it (i.e. semen) has to be known as (having) manifold (effects), viz. that man's semen sometimes spills while (he is) in sleep, or even while (he is) awake; (of that man) who is (only) sensuous (i.e. full of desire). [19]

Now, BU 6.4.5 is under reference.

हस्तेनालभ्य तद्रेतः पश्चाच्चाप्यनुमन्त्रयेत् ॥२०॥
यदद्य मेऽपतद्रेत ओषधीरसरच्च यत् ।
अपोऽगच्छत्स्वयोनिं च तदहं भूय आददे ॥२१॥

He should touch that semen and later recite the Mantra (*yan me* ....) [1] [20]

May that semen of mine, which has spilt (lit. fallen) and has moved to the herbs, gone to its origin, viz. the waters, so that I take it up again.[2] [21]

[1]This is given in the text of BU; also paraphrased in the following verse.

[2]Ānandagiri in his commentary on BUB explains: *mamādyāprāptakāle yad retaḥ pṛthivīm ... rāgātirekeṇa skannam āsīt ... svayonim gatam abhūt tad idaṃ retaḥ sampraty ādade 'ham* (*ity ādānamantrārthaḥ*).

अभिमर्शनस्य यो मन्त्रो ग्रहणस्य स एव तु ।
पुनर्मामैतु तद्रेतो विज्ञानं तेज उच्यते ॥२२॥

The Mantra, which is recited (at the time) of *abhimarśana* 'touching', is the same in taking it up, viz. 'May that semen, that lustre (*vijñāna*), come back to me, (for) that is called *tejas*. [22]

This and the following three verses have reference to verses 20 and 21 above.

सौभाग्यं पुनरग्निः स्युः परिशिष्टाश्च देवताः ॥२३॥

'May that fortune (once again come back to me); and let Agni and the other gods (be for me).'[1] [23]

[1]The protectors of various organs, which they superintend over, are meant. The idea is that those gods once assume again the nature of that semen.

प्रकाशकत्वात्सर्वासां धिष्ण्याश्चाप्यग्नयो मताः ।
गमयन्तु यथास्थानं देवा अग्न्यादयो मम ॥२४॥

And fires are understood as the *dhiṣṇyas*, since they are the illuminators of all. Also, those other gods are fircs, let them make my (dropped) semen go back to the places (over which they superintend). [24]

अङ्गुष्ठानामिकाभ्यां तद्रेत आदाय चात्मनः ।
स्तनौ भ्रुवौ वा निमृजेन्मध्ये च स्तनयोस्तदा ॥२५॥

And, taking up that semen by his thumb and the ring finger, he should smear with it his breast and brows. Also (he smears it) between the breasts. [25]

Now, BU 6.4.6 is under reference.

रेतःस्वयोनावुदक आत्मानं चेत्प्रमादतः ।
पश्येन्मन्त्रेण तत्तोयमनेनैवानुमन्त्रयेत् ॥२६॥

If, by mistake, he sees himself[1] in the waters, viz. the origin of (his) own semen, he should look at them, reciting this (same) Mantra. [26]

[1]That is, his own reflection. Here, waters are understood as the *yoni* 'origin' of semen.

मयि तेजोऽस्तु विज्ञानमिति रेतोऽभिधीयते ।
विशिष्टापत्यहेतुत्वाज्जपेदेवं तथोत्तरे ॥२७॥

(In the Mantra) *mayi tejo 'stu ...*;[1] semen is called *vijñāna*.[2] Thus he should recite it later also, because that semen is the cause of the desired son (lit. child). [27]

[1]The Mantra stated in BU is: *mayi teja indriyam yaśo dravinam sukṛtam* where *indriyam* is for *vijñānam* as is *specifically* so mentioned in verse 22 above.

[2]See verse 22 above.

उद्गतं मलवद्वासश्चतुर्थेऽहनि यत्स्त्रियाः ।
तां मलोद्वाससं पत्नीमाहुस्तत्कर्मकारिणः ॥२८॥

When, on the fourth day (of her period), a woman's soiled garment has been given up, the wise ones, who wish to enter on sexual act, consider this wife as one who has given up wearing a soiled garment. [28]

This is to prohibit a sex act during a woman's period.

गुणाढ्यापत्यफलवत्पुष्पभृतत्वकारणात् ।
मलवद्वाससं प्राहुः श्रियं श्रीहेतुतः स्त्रियम् ॥२९॥

They have known a woman, who wore (during her period) a soiled garment, as glory, since she had become (the bearer of) a flower that fructifies in (the form of) a son that is rich in qualities, thus (verily) a cause of (future) glory. [29]

This brings out the purport of *śrīr ha vā eṣā strīṇām* ... in BU.

चतुर्थे दिवसे स्नातां गत्वा तामुपमन्त्रयेत् ।
आत्मनोऽभिमुखीभावे वाग्यत्नोऽत्रोपमन्त्रणम् ॥३०॥

On the fourth day, when she has taken a bath (after her period), may he approach and invite her (for sexual union). This invitation here[1] is his (careful) attempt in words to make her inclined towards himself (for the union). [30]

[1]That is, to the proposed sex act.

Now, BU 6.4.7 is under reference.

प्रेम्णोपमन्त्रिताप्यस्मै पत्ये दद्यान्न चेदसौ ।
वस्त्राभरणभोगाद्यैरात्मनो वशमानयेत् ॥३१॥

If she does not give him that consent for the sex act, though invited with love, then he should bring her to willingness (lit. under his control) by (offering to her) garments, ornaments and enjoyments etc.[1] [31]

This explains *sā ca* ... in BU.
[1]The word etc. is for other unsaid means for effecting her willingness (SP).

तथाप्युक्ता न चेद्दद्याद्बलात्तां वशमानयेत् ।
उपेयात्तामतिक्रम्य शापदानाय रोषितः ॥३२॥
इन्द्रियेण त इत्यादिमन्त्रेणाथ शपेद्रुषा ।
पतिशापादपुत्रा सा वशमाशु भवेत्तदा ॥३३॥

So addressed also, if she does not give her (consent), then he should bring her under his control with force; he should unite with her, over-riding (her disagreement) (and) being full of anger, be bent on pronouncing a curse on her. [32]
He should then curse her with anger, reciting the Mantra *indriyeṇa te* ....[1] Then she would be under his control, (for fear that) she should be without a child (or, a son), on account of her husband's curse. [33]

[1]This Mantra is given in BU thus: *indriyeṇa yaśasā te yaśa*

ādade.

शप्स्यामि त्वामिति ह्युक्त्वा वशं तामानयेत्पतिः ।
दद्याच्छापभयात्सा चेदनुलोमं तदाचरेत् ॥३४॥

May the husband bring her under (his) control (only) [1] saying 'I shall curse you' and she also, owing to the fear of the curse, would behave in an agreeable way. [34]

[1]The word (only) is added to point out that such a curse would result into misery for her and for himself also. Therefore, he should, as far as possible, avoid cursing her.

Now, BU 6.4.8 is under reference.

अथ शापभयाद्दद्यात्पत्ये कामितमादरात् ।
तदा निवर्तयेच्छापं मन्त्रेणानेन सत्पतिः ॥३५॥

If, however, she gave to her husband what he has desired, owing to the fear of the curse, the good husband should then withdraw the curse with the Mantra *anena* .... [1] [35]

[1]This Mantra is *anenendriyeṇa te yaśasā yaśa ādadhāmi*.

Now, BU 6.4.9 is under reference.

पुरुषद्वेषिणीं भार्यां पतिश्चेदभिकामयेत् ।
मामियं कामयेतेति कुर्यात्तस्या इमं विधिम् ॥३६॥

If (again) a husband would have a longing (for a union with) a wife, who hates the man (i.e. union with the husband), then he should perform this (i.e. the following) rite, [1] with a desire 'Let her long for me'. [36]

This explains *sa yām* ... in BU.

[1]This refers to the (Putra)mantha rite already described—cf.

the next verse.

उक्तमन्थविधानेन चरितव्रत एव सन् ।
उत्तरेष्वपि कार्येषु सर्वं तदनुवर्तयेत् ॥३७॥

Certainly, being one who has followed the procedure of the already prescribed (Putra)mantha rite, he should do all that (which is prescribed there) in later actions of his (as well).[1] [37]

[1]Cf. verses 3ff. above.

स्त्रीलक्षणे प्रवेश्यान्तरात्मीयं पुंस्त्वलक्षणम् ।
वक्त्रं वक्त्रेण संधाय स्पृष्ट्वोपस्थं जपेदथ ॥३८॥
अङ्गादङ्गात्संभवसि जग्धान्नपरिणामतः ।
रसाच्छोणितमित्यादिक्रमाच्छुक्रतया मम ॥३९॥

Having entered his generative organ into the sexual organ of (his) woman and, putting his mouth to her mouth, he should touch her sexual organ, (and) then rccite the Mantra: [38]
aṅgād aṅgāt sambhavasi ... to mean 'You are produced from each of my limbs', in the form of my semen as the result of the food (I have eaten); beginning with, my blood is from the *rasa* of the food etc.[1] [39]

This explains *hṛdayād* ... in BU.
[1]The word etc. refers to the flesh.

शुक्रप्रवहया नाड्या हृदयाच्चाभिजायसे ।
स त्वमङ्गकषायोऽसि दिग्धविद्धां मृगीमिव ।
स्नेहोपरोधादेवैतां पत्नीं मे वशमानय ॥४०॥

(Flowing) by the vein which carries the semen, you are produced from the heart. You are thus the essence of my limbs and, thereby, bring this my wife under my control, with a bent of love, even like a female deer who is affected by (an arrow) smeared (with herbs). [40]

This explains *atha yām* ... in BU.

Now, BU 6.4.10 is under reference.

मा बिभर्गर्भमित्येवमथ यां कामयेत सः ।
रूपभ्रंशो हि भवति यतो गर्भस्य धारणे ॥४१॥
तथा यौवनहानिश्च तस्मादेवं स कामयेत् ।
तस्यां स्वमर्थं निष्ठाय मुखेनेत्यादि पूर्ववत् ॥४२॥

Now, if (he would think about a woman) whom he longs for that she should not bear a foetus—for a woman's beauty is lost (or diminishes) in case she bears a foetus[1]— [41]
so also is there a loss of youth—he should thus desire, having placed verse,[2] (putting his mouth) with her mouth (he should unite with her). [42]

[1]This is parenthetic.
[2]That is, reciting the Mantra: *indriyeṇa te retasā reta ādade*; cf. verse 38ef above.

प्राण्यादौ रेचकं कृत्वापानयेत्तदनन्तरम् ॥४३॥
निषिक्तमपि तद्रेतः प्राणवृत्त्या यथाविधि ।
अपानवृत्त्या तद्ध्वस्तमित्येतत्कर्मणः फलम् ॥४४॥

Having first inhaled breath and then having held his breath within, he should exhale later. [43]
Then that semen of his, though planted in her, with the function of *prāṇa(-vāyu)*, according to prescription, would become destroyed—this is the result of this act. [44]

इन्द्रियेण त इत्यादिमन्त्रोक्त्या तां परामृशेत् ॥४५॥
इन्द्रियेणैव त्वद्रेतो रेतसा आददे स्वयम् ।
अरेता एव सा स्त्री स्यादेवं पत्याभिमन्त्रिता ॥४६॥

He should approach (i.e. touch, or unite with) her, reciting the Mantra *indriyeṇa te* .... [45]
Through my sexual organ (*indriya*), the semen, do I myself take away[1] the semen from you; thus addressed by her husband, that woman would then be without the seed. [46]

This explains *atha yām* ... in BU.
[1]In *retasā ādate* there is the absence of *saṃdhi*, in occasional Vedic way (SP).

Now, BU 6.4.11 is under reference.

दधीत गर्भमित्येवं यामिच्छेत्पतिरङ्गनाम् ।
तामपान्य प्रयत्नेन प्राण्यान्मन्त्रेण कारयेत् ।
इन्द्रियेण त इत्युक्त्या आदधामीति सत्पतिः ॥४७॥

The husband, who wishes the wife (*aṅganā*) to bear for him a foetus, should first carefully (*prayatnena*) make her exhale, and then, himself inhaling, induce (lit. make) her do (what he desires)[1]—the good husband, reciting (at that time) the Mantra (which begins with) *indriyeṇa te* (and ends with) *ādadhāmi*. [47]

[1]That is, his wish that she joins him in the sex act.

Now, BU 6.4.12 is under reference.

अथाभिचारिकं कर्म प्रसङ्गादभिधीयते ।
उपायत्वेन विज्ञप्त्यै श्येनवन्न विधीयते ॥४८॥

Now is described some act of black-magic (*abhicāra*) that the occasion has demanded. This is (only) to inform one about it as some remedy[1] and, therefore, is not prescribed as the rite of Śyena.[2] [48]

[1]SP points out: *na hiṃsyād iti śrutivirodhān na hiṃsārtho*

vidhir ity āśaṅkya ... (upāyatvena).

[2]Śyena is a ritual not prescribed, since it involves violence (*hiṃsā*).

अथ यस्य गृहस्थस्य पत्न्या जारो भवेत्क्वचित् ।
तं चेद्द्विष्याद्रुषैवैनामारभेत तदा क्रियाम् ॥४९॥

Now, in case a householder's wife has some lover, and if he should hate him, he should, in utter[1] anger, begin the performance of the act (which is now prescribed). [49]

[1]This is the force of *eva*.

न ह्यद्विष्टमनस्कस्य कर्मैतत्सिद्धिमश्नुते ।
अतोऽधिकारिविज्ञप्त्यै द्विष्यादिति विशेषणम् ॥५०॥

Indeed, this act would not be successful (in yielding the result), if a man is not having anger in his mind; therefore, in order to convey his eligibility for that act, there is this specification by the words *dviṣyāt* .... [50]

आमपात्रेऽग्निमित्युक्त्या ह्यभिचाराख्यकर्मणः ।
योग्यतैवामपात्रस्य भिदुरत्वसमन्वयात् ॥५१॥

In the statement *āmapātre 'gnim* ... is stated the suitability of that pot for the rite of black-magic, because a raw pot (of clay (*āmapātra*)) is invariably associated with breakability. [51]

यथामं भिदुरं पात्रमप्सु सद्यो विलीयते ।
प्राप्तजारोऽपि मे शत्रुस्तथैवाशु विदीर्यताम् ॥५२॥

As a raw pot which is breakable melts away at once when (put) into waters, so '(my wife's) lover should get destroyed into pieces quickly'[1], (should he recite). [52]

[1]This is the significance of the comparison with *āmapātra*.

अग्निमित्येकवचनादुल्लिख्यादेश्च लिङ्गतः ।
आवसथ्याग्निनिर्देशो न तु त्रेताग्निसंग्रहः ॥५३॥

From the word *agni* in the singular and by the use of the word *ullikhya* etc.,[1] which serves as indication, there is here the mention of the domestic fire and not of the three fires.[2] [53]

[1]The word etc. refers to *āmapātra*, *śarabarhis* etc.; cf. BU text. Also the word *ullikhya* implies *parisamūhana*, *parilepana* etc. as mentioned earlier (cf. BUBV 6.3.18-19 above).
[2]This refers to the three sacred fires, viz. *āhavanīya*, *gārhapatya* and *tretā*.

प्रतिलोममवस्तीर्य कर्मणः प्रतिलोमतः ।
शरबर्हिः प्रयत्नेन विद्वान्रोषसमन्वितः ॥५४॥
तस्मिन्नग्नौ शरेषीका घृताक्ता जुहुयादथ ।
जारस्य दोषं प्रख्याप्य मन्त्रेणानेन सत्वरः ॥५५॥

Then he, the knower, full of anger, should with effort strew (the *barhis* grass) against the usual procedure[1]—since this act is contrary to the normal act— [54]
then offer into that fire the spearlike *śara* grass, smear the same with ghee, (and) having quickly (i.e. at the same time) spoken aloud the blemish of the lover with this Mantra. [55]

[1]That is, the procedure of *paristaraṇa* in a domestic rite.

मम स्वभूते योषाग्नौ समिद्धे यौवनादिना ।
शुक्राहुतिं यतोऽहौषीरेष तेऽत्र व्यतिक्रमः ॥५६॥
आददेऽतोऽपराधात्ते प्राणापानौ जिजीविषोः ।
फट्कारेणैव जुहुयाच्छरभृष्टीर्यथोदिताः ॥५७॥

'Since you have offered the oblation of your semen into the

fire in the form of (my) woman that has been enkindled (with desire for you) by her youth etc., let this (lit. this my offering) be your dishonour (*vyatikrama*).[1] [56]
Hereby, have I taken (away), on account of your offence, Prāṇa and Apāna, from you, who are wishing to live.' Let him offer the spear-like *śara* grass,[2] which is mentioned earlier producing the sound *phaṭ*. [57]

[1] Or rather, let this be my revenge on you.
[2] Refer to verse 55 above.

तथा पुत्रान्पशूंश्चैव आददे तेऽद्य कामुक ।
श्रौतमिष्टं विजानीयात्स्मार्तं सुकृतमित्यपि ॥५८॥

Also,[1] (let him say) 'so also do I take away now (lit. today) your sons and cattle, O voluptuous one!'. In this act, one should understand that which is approved by the Śruti as *iṣṭi* and also *sukṛta* in (the prescription(s) of) Smṛti(s). [58]

[1] SP adds: 'he should announce the blame of that clandestine lover'.

श्रौतं स्मार्तं च यत्किंचित्पुण्यं कर्म त्वया कृतम् ।
तत्सर्वं त आददेऽहमाहुतिं प्रक्षिपेद्रुषा ॥५९॥

With the words, 'I am taking away all of yours, viz. whatever meritorious work as prescribed by the Śruti and also thc by Smṛti which you have done', let him make the offering in anger. [59]

प्रार्थनाशेति विज्ञेया पराकाशा प्रतीक्षणम् ।
आदानान्तो भवेन्मन्त्रः सर्वत्रैवं विनिर्दिशेत् ॥६०॥
वाङ्मात्रेण प्रतिज्ञातं कर्मणा नोपपादितम् ।
तत्प्रतीक्षणमाकाङ्क्षा पराकाशेति भण्यते ॥६१॥

By the word *āśā* one should know desire and by *parākāśā*,[1] hope for the result; the Mantra should have *ādāna* (i.e. *aham ādade*) at its end. This he should mention everywhere (i.e. at the end of every offering). [60]

parākāśā is that which is announced (as what will be undertaken) in mere words but not actuated in action and what is mentioned as what is longed for. [61]

These two verses explain the words *āśā* and *parākāśā*.

[1]Sureśvara has used the feminine *parākāśā* for masculine *parākāśa* in BU.

स वा इत्यादिनाथास्य फलमुक्तस्य कर्मणः ।
भण्यते वचसोक्तस्य निरिन्द्रियपुरःसरम् ॥६२॥

Then in the words beginning with *sa vā* is stated the result of the act that is described,[1] viz. what is stated in the words beginning with *nirindriya*. [62]

[1]Namely, of the *abhicārakarman* 'act of black-magic'.

निःशेषपुरुषार्थाप्तिलोपकृत्कर्म वर्णितम् ।
जायया मैथुनाख्यं यच्छ्रोत्रियस्य विपश्चितः ॥६३॥

Thus is described the act of one's intercourse with the wife by a learned, *śrotriya*,[1] which is the destroyer of the entire achievement of the ends of human life. [63]

[1]Cf. the oft-quoted verse:
janmanā brāhmaṇo jñeyaḥ saṃskārair dvija ucyate /
vidyayā yāti vipratvaṃ tribhiḥ śrotriya ucyate //

उपहासमतो नेच्छेत्सार्धं श्रोत्रियजायया ।
मैथुनं तु विशेषेण ह्युक्तानर्थजिहासया ॥६४॥

Therefore, one should not wish even to play jokes with the wife of a *śrotriya* and (*tu*), in particular, a sex act, so that (one fulfils one's) desire to avoid any untoward result that is mentioned. [64]

Now, BU 6.4.13 is under reference.

कर्माभिचारिकं प्रोक्तं प्रसङ्गान्न प्रधानतः ।
यदर्थस्तु प्रयासोऽयं तत्कर्माथ प्रपञ्च्यते ॥६५॥

The act of black-magic is mentioned here, for it was so occasioned and not with (the idea of giving) it as of principal significance. And now is explained that ritual act[1] for whose result all this effort (is undertaken). [65]

[1]The text of the AnSS edition has a misreading *tatkamārtha*.

यस्य मन्थविधिज्ञस्य जाया चेदार्तवं व्रजेत् ।
तिस्रो रात्रीर्न कांस्येन पानं कुर्यात्तथाशनम् ॥६६॥

If the wife of the knower of the procedure of the Mantha (rite) comes to have her period, she should not drink (water) with a metal (lit. bronze) cup for three nights, nor should she take food in a similar way. [66]

The construction of this verse is a little awkward. Yet SP laudably avoided the awkwardness by observing (at the end) *tadā tasya sā jāyeti śeṣaḥ*.

तथैवाहतवासाः स्यादहःस्वेतेषु शुद्धधीः ।
वृषलो वृषली वैनां नोपहन्यात्कदाचन ॥६७॥

Similarly, in these three days, she, of pure mind, should have put on an uncut garment; so also, no Śūdra man or Śūdra woman should even (or ever) touch[1] her. [67]

[1]The verb *upahan* is used in some peculiar sense. The verb root *han* with *upa* means 'to touch' also 'to approach' [already

so in BU], but 'to strike' is not the usual sense.

अन्यो वा पापकृत्कश्चित्स्पर्शसंभाषणादिभिः ।
व्रतस्थां नोपहन्यात्तामभीप्सितफलाप्तये ॥६८॥

Nor should any other man contact[1] her, who is in her vow, by touch or conversation, for securing what he longed for. [68]

[1]*sparśa* with *upahanyāt* would demand this translation; that avoids tautology.

सा त्रिरात्रान्त आप्लुत्याहतवासाः शुचिः सती ।
श्रपणाय चरोर्भर्ता व्रीहींस्तामवघातयेत् ॥६९॥

That woman wears an uncut garment when she has bathed at the end of the third night and become purified.[1] The husband makes her pound rice grains for preparing (lit. cooking) the *caru* 'ball of cooked rice'. [69]

[1]We take the first line as a complete sentence. The construction in the text is awkward, or anakoluthic.

From this verse onwards, Sureśvara occasionally gives us, almost in a parenthetic way, his paraphrases of (some) words in the Mantras of BU. It has been difficult, therefore, to translate his Vārtika in a well connected form. As such, our translation will appear to the readers disconnected bits of sentences. We regret our helplessness!
Now, BU 6.4.14-16 are under reference.

शुक्लो गौरोऽत्र विज्ञेयः शुक्लो वा बलदेववत् ।
सुव्याख्येयत्वतः शेषः स्वयमेवावगम्यताम् ॥७०॥

The word *śukla* should be understood in the sense of fair (lit. white) or fair like Baladeva.[1] The remaining portion (of the Śruti) is to be understood by oneself, because of its easy explanation. [70]

[1]It refers to Kṛṣṇa's elder brother.

क्षीरौदनं तयैवाथ पाचयित्वा स्वयं पतिः ॥७१॥

Then, after the husband has made the wife herself cook rice in milk— [71]

दंपती घृतवन्तं तमश्नीयातामथौदनम् ।
स्वतन्त्रावीश्वरौ स्यातां सत्पुत्रप्रसवाय तौ ॥७२॥

The couple should eat that rice cooked in ghee, and then they would be able, i.e. eligible [1] for begetting a good son. [72]

[1]Read SP *īśvaraśabdārtham āha svatantrāv iti.*

यथोक्तपुत्रप्रसवे यदि वा क्षिप्रकारिणौ ।
यथोक्तकर्मणैतेन स्यातां तावेव दंपती ॥७३॥

Or if that very couple are in a haste to beget a son of already given description, (they would be able to do so) [1] by performing the rite described earlier. [2] [73]

[1]This is suggested by *svatantrāvīśvarau* in the preceding verse.
[2]Possibly it refers to Mantha ritual.

Now, BU 6.4.17 is under reference.

दुहिता पण्डितेत्यत्र स्त्रीणामुचितकर्मसु ।
तत्पाण्डित्यमिह ज्ञेयं न तु वेदार्थगोचरम् ॥७४॥

In the words *duhitā paṇḍitā* should be understood the daughter's being learned in the duties proper for women, not in respect of Vedic matters. [74]

This may indicate the commonly held belief of the people in Sureśvara's times that learned women meant those who were capable of discharging all the household duties of a woman but not eligible for Vedic studies and rituals!

Now, BU 6.4.18 is under reference.

विजिगीतो जगत्यस्मिन्नत्यर्थं यो विशब्दितः ।
विद्वत्सभा च समितिस्तद्योग्यः समितिंगमः ।।७५।।

The word *vijigīta* means one who is in the world exceedingly praised, i.e. praised in many (or, various) words. The word *samiti* means the assembly of the learned; therefore, *samitiṅgama* means one who is fit (or, eligible) to sit in (that) assembly. [75]

This explains *vijigīta* ... in BU.

प्रकृतायां त्रिसंख्यायां सर्वशब्दप्रयोगतः ।
प्रतीयाच्चतुरो वेदान्सर्वशब्दार्थवित्तये ।।७६।।

Ordinarily, the number three is used (in the context of the Vedas), yet there has been used the word *sarva* and therefrom one should understand that (there are meant) four Vedas, in order that the meaning of all words become understood. [76]

This is to explain that the usual sense of three Vedas as understood from the word *sarva* should not be accepted.

तण्डुलान्मांससंमिश्रान्पक्त्वा मांसौदनं विदुः ।
उक्षा सेचनशक्तो गौः स एव ऋषभो महान् ।।७७।।

They have understood by meat-rice that which one has cooked

with rice grains mixed with meat. *ukṣan* means a bull which has become capable of sprinkling seed and the same, when well (or fully) grown up, is *ṛṣabha*. [77]

The second line specifies two phases in the growth of a bull and thus explains away the doubted repetition in *aukṣeṇa vārṣabheṇa vā* in BU (SP).

प्रसिद्ध्यसंभवात्त्वद्य ह्युक्तं मांसौदनं प्रति ।
मांसं कृष्णमृगच्छागविषयं त्वद्य कुर्वते ॥७८॥

This is so said here since, with reference to this meat-rice, there is no acceptance of it[1] today.[2] As such, they take that meat to be referring to that of a black deer or a goat. [78]

[1]Either *aukṣa māṃsa* or *ārṣabha māṃsa*.

[2]This is in keeping with the popular avoidance of beef, in Sureśvara's times. Cf. *Vimalodayamālā of Jayantasvāmin*. (ed. K.P. Jog, Poona: University of Poona, p.96): *tato gor ālambhaḥ prāptaḥ gor ālambhasya loke duṣṭatvād goḥ pratinidhitvena cchāga ālabhyate*. Possibly, Jayantasvāmin was a (senior) contemporary of Sureśvara.

यत्नेनोपार्जितं तच्चेत्क्रीत्वा वा मांसमाहरेत् ।
हिंसायाः प्रतिषिद्धत्वात्पशून्हन्यान्न तु स्वयम् ॥७९॥

If that were to be obtained with (great) effort, then he should buy that meat and bring (it to the ritual), because killing has been prohibited; (any way), he should not kill animals. [79]

Now, BU 6.4.19 is under reference.

अथशब्दो विकल्पार्थो यथोक्तानां यथारुचि ।
काम्यानां ह्यन्यतमं पक्षमाश्रित्य भण्यते ॥८०॥

The word *atha* has the sense of an option[1] (among meats)

mentioned or (that which is) according to one's choice. This is said with any one (of the desired meats) in view. [80]

[1]This explanation of *atha* is occasioned by its repeated use in BU (SP).

आरभ्योद्गमने भानोः सर्वं स्नानाद्यशेषतः ।
निर्वर्त्य संस्कारमथ यत्नात्प्राग्य उदाहृतः ॥८१॥

Having begun at the sunrise, all Saṃskāras, viz. a bath etc., he should perform the rite (of Mantha), which has been described before.[1] [81]

[1]Cf. BUBV 6.3.3ff.

स्थालीपाके क्रिया या सा चावृदित्यभिधीयते ।
स्थालीपाकविधानेन संस्कृत्याज्यं तथैव तु ॥८२॥

And that (series of actions) which is prescribed in the context of a *sthālīpāka* is called here by the name *āvṛt*; therefore, having purified (*saṃskṛtya*) the clarified butter just in the same way as is prescribed for the *sthālīpāka* (he makes his offering).[1] [82]

The procedure of the *sthālīpāka* rite is well-known among the Vedists and, therefore, no details of the same are given with any particular attention.

[1]The word *juhoti* is understood.

उपलक्षणमन्येषामाज्यस्य ग्रहणं भवेत् ।
आदिशब्दस्य वा लोपादाज्यादिमिति गम्यताम् ॥८३॥

The mention of taking up *ājya* 'clarified butter' is indicative of other (details of the rite),[1] or the word to be understood is *ājyādi* with the suppresion (*lopa*) of the word *ādi* in it. [83]

This verse averts a possible doubt that could arise from the words *saṃskṛtyājyam* in the preceding verse and restricting that the performance should be with *ājya* alone.

[1]This refers to other materials of the *sthālīpāka* ritual.

उपहत्योपहत्याथ स्थालीपाकस्य मन्त्रतः ।
नित्यास्तत्राहुतीर्हुत्वा आवापस्थान आदरात् ॥८४॥

Then, having repeatedly pounded (the rice grains), he should (utter) the Mantra(s) of the *sthālīpāka* ritual and he should respectfully offer the usual *āhuti*s, in the place where *āhuti*s are poured. [84]

This is the meaning of *sthālīpākasya* ... in BU.

प्रधानाहुतयस्तिस्त्रो याः स्युरग्न्यादिपूर्विकाः ।
हुत्वा स्विष्टकृदन्तं तत्समापय्य यथोदितम् ॥८५॥
कर्मेदं तत उद्धृत्य चरुं स्थाल्याः समाहितः ।
सर्पिष्मन्तमथाश्नीयात्कामितार्थानुरोधतः ॥८६॥

Having offered those three principal *āhuti*s 'offerings' which begin with those for Agni, he should have completed up to the end of the *sviṣṭakṛt*, as mentioned (in the ritual text), [85]
this rite; then he should have lifted up the *caru* from the plate which was kept (aside). He should then eat it having ghee in it, intending it (to effect) his desired end. [86]

This specifies the number of offerings.

चरुं प्राश्य स्वयं शेषं भार्यायै संप्रयच्छति ।
उच्छिष्टमेव भार्यायै चरुं भर्ता प्रयच्छति ॥८७॥

Having eaten of that *caru*, he should give the rest of it to his wife. A husband (always) gives to the wife only what is left over (after he has eaten).[1] [87]

This explains *prāśya* ... in BU.

[1]The second line is to specify that *śeṣam bhāryāyai prayacchati* does not refer to the remains of the *caru* from the plate.

पाणी प्रक्षाल्य यत्नेन सामर्थ्यादेव गम्यते ।
स्मार्तमाचमनं शुद्धयै पाणिप्रक्षालनोक्तितः ॥८८॥

(The instruction) 'Having washed his hands with care'[1] is understood from the force (i.e. power) of the words. Here is meant the sipping of waters, as prescribed by the Smṛti, since there is a mention of the washing of hands. [88]

This explains *prakṣālya* ... in BU.

[1]With care (*yatnena*) is clarified by SP thus: *malatyāgārtham bahujalam ānīya paunaḥpunyena kṣālanaṃ yatnaḥ*.

उदपात्रमथादाय तदद्भिस्त्रिः सुताप्तये ।
वक्ष्यमाणेन मन्त्रेण जायामभ्युक्षयेन्मुहुः ॥८९॥

Having then taken up (in his hand) that pot containing water, he should repeatedly sprinkle water over his wife three times; reciting the Mantra which is stated (just below). [89]

This is the meaning of *udapātram* ... in BU.

अतोऽस्मदीयदारेभ्य उत्थायान्यत आव्रज ।
विश्वावस्वभिधानेन गन्धर्वोऽत्र प्रबोध्यते ॥९०॥

'Leaving (lit. rising away) from my wife, do you go elsewhere', (this is the meaning of the Mantra.) Here (i.e. in the Mantra), the mention 'O Viśvāvasu' refers to the Gandharva of that name. [90]

This is the content of Mantra.

प्रपूर्व्यामिति नार्यत्र भण्यते तरुणी किल ।
प्रपूर्वीं पीवरीमन्यां याहि विश्वावसो द्रुतम् ॥९१॥

In the text *prapūrvyām*, the word *prapūryā* conveys (the sense of) a young woman.[1] (Therefore, the meaning of the verse is:) 'You, O Viśvāvasu, quickly go away to another *prapūrvī*, i.e. plump[1] woman. [91]

This explains *anyām iccha*.
[1]The line *prapūrvyām ... kila* is to be taken parenthetically.

प्रपूर्व्यामिति लिङ्गाच्च तरुण्यां सत्पतिः सदा ।
यथोदितं कर्म सत्यां कुर्यात्सत्पुत्रजन्मने ॥९२॥

From the indicative word *prapūrvyām* (one should understand that) a good householder (lit. husband) should ever[1] perform the said ritual only with a young and chaste wife,[2] so that there is born a good son. [92]

[1]SP states that the word *sadā* 'ever' stands for the time after the woman's period.
[2]SP elaborates thus: *prapūrvyām iti tāruṇyadyotakaśabdavaśāt ... taruṇyāṃ satyām iti sambandhaḥ.*

अहं तु स्वामिमां जायां समुपैमीति संगतिः ।
एवं प्रस्थाप्य गन्धर्वमथैनामभिपद्यते ॥९३॥

As for myself, I am uniting with this my wife—this is the construe of the sentence (in BU).[1] Having thus sent away that Gandharva,[1] he approaches (i.e. unites with) her. [93]

This explains *jāyām patyā saha* in BU.
[1]Ānandagiri on BUB (also in his comment on this verse, SP, with some difference) makes this cryptic verse clear, thus: *pīvarīm anyāṃ yāhi* means: *viśvāvaso gandharva tvam uttiṣṭhānyāṃ*

ca jāyām prapūrvyām taruṇīm patyā saha saṃkrīḍamānām ichhāham punaḥ svām imāṃ jāyāṃ samupaimi.

Now, BU 6.4.20 is under reference.

अभीष्टगर्भाधानाय जायामालिङ्गते पतिः ।
अमोऽहमितिमन्त्रोक्त्या तावावां देवतात्मकौ ॥९४॥
कर्मारभावहै देवि सत्सुतोत्पत्तिसिद्धये ।
त्वं चाहं चैव संभूय योनौ रेतो दधावहै ॥९५॥

The husband embraces (i.e. unites with) the wife for placing in her the desired foetus, reciting the Mantra *amo 'ham ....*[1]
'Now both of us, of the nature of gods, [94]
let us begin our act (of union), O my dear, for begetting a good son; let us, you and I, having joined together, place the seed in the womb'. [95]

This is the meaning of *abhipadyate* in verse 93 above.

[1]BU gives the full Mantra thus: *amo 'ham asmi sā tvam asy amo 'ham sāmāham asmi ṛk tvam dyaur aham pṛthivi tvam tāv ehi saṃ rabhāvahai saha reto dadhāvahai puṃse putrāya vittaye dyotake.*

रेतःक्षेपफलं चाह पुंसे पुत्राय लब्धये ।
मन्त्रोक्त्यनन्तरं तस्या विजिहीथामितीरयेत् ॥९६॥

(The Śruti) has mentioned the result of the placing of the seed (in the words) *puṃse putrāya labdhaye.*[1] After the Mantra is recited, he should say, 'May you separate (your thighs), [96]

[1]*labdhaye* is Sureśvara's word for the original Vedic word *vittaye*.

विहापयति मन्त्रेण ऊरू पत्न्याः प्रयत्नतः ।
ऊर्वोरामन्त्रणं चैतद्विजिहीथामितीक्ष्यताम् ॥९७॥

thus, reciting the Mantra,[1] he carefully makes apart the thighs of his wife. The invocation[2] to the thighs is to be seen in the word *vijihīthām*. [97]

[1]*mantreṇa ūrū* is an instance of the absence of Saṃdhi in Vedic style.

[2]This is for *āmantraṇa* in the sense of 'address (i.e. invocation) to'. An unusual sense! Already, Sureśvara used in verse 30 *upamantraṇam* and in 31 *upamantrita*.

विजिहीतेरिदं रूपं ण्यन्तस्य गतिकर्मणः ॥९८॥

This is a form of the verb root *hi* with *vi* (as prefix), referring to the activity or movement, with its causal ending (suppressed).[1] [98]

[1]*vijihīthām* is to be understood as *vijihāpayethāḥ*.

मन्त्रतः पाणिनाथैनां त्रीन्वाराननुलोमतः ।
अनुमार्ष्टयथ तां जायां मन्त्रं विष्णुरितीरयन् ॥९९॥

Reciting the Mantra *viṣṇuḥ* .... he caresses his wife's limbs[1] with his hand three times, in an agreeable manner, (and) then[2] (unites with her). [99]

SP on this verse does not appear to be quite satisfying!

[1]SP explains *anulomataḥ* thus: *mūrdhānam ārabhya pādāntam iti yāvat*.

[2]Cf. SP: *paśukarmānantaryārtho 'thaśabdaḥ*. Thus Ānandagiri suggests the sense of *anumārṣṭi* as 'he unites with her in sex act'.

Now, BU 6.4.21 is under reference.

समर्थनं कल्पनार्थस्त्वष्टावयवशस्तथा ।

निर्वर्तयतु रूपाणि शोभनानि सुतस्य मे ॥१००॥

The meaning of *kalpana* (from the verb root *klp*) is enabling.[1] (The Mantra continues:) So also, may god Tvaṣṭṛ create in all your limbs beautiful appearance[2] and (also in those) of my son.[2] [100]

[1]This refers to the word *kalpayatu* in the Mantra *viṣṇuḥ* ... etc. cited in the end of the preceding verse. SP states: *putra-janmani śaktatvāpādanam iti yāvat.*

[2]BU and Ānandagiri on BUB seem to take the creation of the beautiful appearance in the limbs of the wife who has delivered a son—cf. Ānanagiri: *tvaṣṭā savitā tava rūpāṇi piṃśatu vibhāgena darśanayogyāni karotu*. But, Sureśvara adds *sutasya me*, he does not specifically mention the wife. Yet, see on this SP: *ātmano bhāryāyāś ca rūpāṇi nirvartitāni kim tvaṣṭrety āśaṅkyāha sutasyeti.*

दर्शाहर्देवता चेह सिनीवालीति भण्यते ।
पृथुष्टुकेति सैवोक्ता पृथुस्तुतिरसौ यतः ॥१०१॥

Here, the goddess of the new moon night is called Sinīvālī; that very goddess is stated by the name Pṛthuṣṭuka, since she has profuse praise offered to her. [101]

गर्भं ते सम्यगाधत्तामश्विनौ पुष्करस्त्रजौ ।
सूर्याचन्द्रमसावेव विज्ञेयावश्विनाविह ॥१०२॥
स्वरश्मिस्रग्विणौ तौ हि प्रसिद्धौ जगति यतः ॥१०३॥

May the two Aśvins, who wear lotus garlands, properly place you foetus; the two Aśvins are to be known here as the sun and the moon; [102]
they are indeed known as wearing (or, having) the wreathes in the form of their own rays. [103]

Now, BU 6.4.22 is under reference.

हिरण्यं ज्योतिरमृतं तन्मय्यावरणी शुभे ।
निरमन्थतां याभ्यां तावश्विनावमृतं पुरा ॥१०४॥

The word *hiraṇya* means the immortal flame and the two coverings, which are made up of that (*hiraṇya*, for the flame) are resplendent (lit. beautiful) wherewith those two Aśvins have formerly produced (lit. churned) immortality. [104]

अश्विनौ यादृशं गर्भं प्रयत्नान्निरमन्थताम् ।
आदधावस्तथा रूपं दशमे मासि सूतये ॥१०५॥

Let us two place (in our son), to be born in the tenth month, such (beautiful) form as will be similar to what the two Aśvins have carefully produced (lit. churned) as the foetus.[1] [105]

[1]This refers to the beauty and immortality as implied by *amṛtam* and *rūpam* in verses 104 and 105.

यथाग्निगर्भा पृथिवी द्यौरिन्द्रेणेव भानुना ।
वायुर्दिशां यथा गर्भो दृष्टः श्लथनकर्मकृत् ॥१०६॥

Just like the earth which has Agni in the womb, like Dyaus by Indra,[1] (who is possessed of) bright lustre; so also like Vāyu, the foetus of the quarters, that (foetus in you) is seen as the agent of loosening.[2] [106]

The verse is very awkwardly expressive of the meaning of the BU passage.

[1]*indreṇa bhānunā* is taken here a substantive (noun) followed by an attribute (noun). SP states that *bhānu* is the meaning of Indra. Yet, here it is not so specifically understandable as in Ānandagiri's comment on BUB, viz. *indreṇa sūryeṇeti yāvat*.
[2]Cf. verse 109 below.

आत्मनाम समुच्चार्य तथा गर्भं दधामि ते ।

तस्या वा नाम गृह्णीयान्मन्त्रमुच्चारयन्पतिः ॥१०७॥

Then, uttering his own name, this householder says, 'I place the foetus in you', after that, he should utter her name; all this, while he is reciting the Mantra.[1] [107]

[1]This refers to *garbhaṃ dadhāmi te* stated in the second line.

Now, BU 6.4.23 is under reference.

मन्त्रेणाथैष सोष्यन्तीमद्भिरभ्युक्षयेच्छनैः ।
वायुः पुष्करिणीं यद्वत्समिङ्गयति चालयेत् ॥१०८॥
यथा पुष्करिणीं वायुश्चालयन्नपि सर्वतः ।
न करोति क्षतिं तद्वद्गर्भ एजतु ते सुखम् ॥१०९॥

Then, when she is about to deliver, he should gently sprinkle her with water, reciting the Mantra,[1] that is to say, 'in the same way as Vāyu makes the lotus-lake stir[2]'; so does he activate her. [108]

(This is to mean:) As Vāyu, while making the lotus-lake stir everywhere, does not cause any harm to it, so (also) should this foetus stir in a way that causes your happiness. [109]

Verse 108 is the meaning of *sosyantīm* ....

[1]This is *yathā vāyuḥ puṣkariṇīm* ....

[2]AnSS reads *samiñjayati* which should be corrected as shown above.

गर्भस्त्वां सुखयन्नेत सहोल्बेण जरायुणा ।
व्रजो मार्गो हि गर्भस्य सार्गलोऽयं कृतः पुरा ॥११०॥

May your foetus move, causing you happiness, wrapped as it is by the chorion; indeed the way, this path of the foetus was earlier barred by the bolt (of Indra). [110]

This explains the meaning of (*garbhah*) ... *sahāvaitu jarāyuṇā* ... in BU.

जरायुरर्गलस्तं त्वमिन्द्र निर्जहि सत्वरः ।
गर्भे विनिःसृते पश्चाद्या निर्गच्छति योनितः ॥१११॥
मांसपेशी समा तन्वी सावरेति निगद्यते ।
प्राणश्चेन्द्रोऽत्र विज्ञेयः स एव प्रार्थ्यते ततः ॥११२॥

The word *jarāyu* 'chorion' refers to the bar. 'O Indra, do you strike it down, being quick.' Then, that which moves out of the genital organ (of the woman) after (the foetus has moved out), [111]
a lump of flesh, which is slender and straight(?) is called *avarā* chorion, (i.e. the outer membrane of a foetus). And here Prāṇa should be understood as Indra, as he is addressed in the prayer. [112]

Now, BU 6.4.24 is under reference.

जाते कुमारेऽथ पतिरङ्कमारोप्य तं पिता ।
अग्निं ह्युपसमाधाय प्रसिद्धार्थमथापरम् ॥११३॥

After the son was born, the husband, viz. the father now,[1] having first placed the son on his lap and, having enkindled the fire (which is known),[2] (offers oblation to it). [113]

This refers to the Jātakarman rite (*saṃskāra*).

[1]The words 'After ... now' for *atha* indicate that the rite of the Jātakarman is over.

[2]This is *āvasathya* 'domestic fire'.

घृतं दधि च संमिश्रं पृषदाज्यमितीर्यते ।
एकीकृत्याथ संनीय पृषदाज्यस्य मन्त्रतः ॥११४॥
उपघातं जुहोतीति णमुल्वाभीक्ष्ण्य इष्यते ।
उपहत्योपहत्येति पृषदाज्याहुतीः क्षिपेत् ॥११५॥

Ghee and curds, which are mixed together, is known as *pṛṣadājya*.[1] Then, having mixed them together and brought from the *pṛṣadājya*, with the recitation of the Mantra,[2] [114] he makes an offering, pounding (the rice grains) again and again; the suffix *ṇamul* (in the word-form *upaghātam*) is desired to convey the repetition of the action conveyed in the words *upahatyopahatya*; thus he pours the offerings of *pṛṣadājya*. [115]

[1]It is the mixture of clarified butter, curds (and according to some honey etc. also). This is offered in rituals.
[2]This is mentioned in verse 116 below.

पुष्यासं स्वे गृहेऽत्राहं मनुष्याणां प्रकामतः ।
सहस्रसंख्यया शश्वद्बहोर्नाम सहस्रगीः ॥११६॥

'May I nourish, in my house here, men, thousand in number, to their hearts' content; the word *sahasra* is a word signifier of many. [116]

एवं त्वं वर्धमानोऽत्र मन्वीथाः पुत्र संततिम् ।
संततावुपसन्द्यां त्वं पश्वादेर्मे करिष्यसि ॥११७॥

'Thus, growing here (i.e. in my home), O my son, may you think of continuity'—the word *upasandyām* means 'in respect of continuity' (*saṃtatau*)— (to mean) 'you will multiply the cattle etc. which belong to me'. [117]

नैव व्यपेक्षते व्याख्यां स्पष्टार्थत्वेन हेतुना ।
मयि प्राणानिति ग्रन्थः स्वयमेवावगम्यताम् ॥११८॥

The portion, beginning with the words *mayi prāṇān*, being very clear in meaning, does not expect any explanation; therefore, may you understand it yourself.[1] [118]

[1]This is Sureśvara's address to his readers.

Now, BU 6.4.25 is under reference.

अथास्य स्वमुखे कर्णं दक्षिणं प्रणिधाय तु ।

वाग्वागिति हि त्रिर्ब्रूयात्त्रयी वागिति भण्यते ॥११९॥

Then, having placed the right ear of the son near unto (lit. into) his own mouth,[1] he should utter the word *vāc* three times; (because, indeed,) the three Vedas are called Vāc. [119]

[1]That is, having placed his mouth near unto the son's ear.

Now, without referring to BU 6.4.26, Sureśvara turns to BU 6.4.27.

त्रयी वाक्त्वां श्रोत्रमार्गेण श्रेयसे प्रविशत्वियम् ।
यस्ते स्तन इति गिरा शस्यतेऽत्र सरस्वती ॥१२०॥

May the three Vedas, viz. Vāc, enter you through your ear for your bliss. In the words *yas te stanaḥ* here (in this context)[1] is praised Sarasvatī. [120]

[1]This refers to the child's sucking the mother's breast.

उदारगुणसंपत्तिः सुतस्यास्त्विवति भण्यते ।
शशयः सशयो ज्ञेयः शयश्च फलमुच्यते ॥१२१॥

What is said is: May there be for the son profuse excellence of qualities. The word *śaśaya* is to be known as *saśaya* 'which is accompanied by a result',[1] (wherein) *śaya* means the result. [121]

[1]That is, which shall yield a result.

गुहा शयो वा शशयः श्रुत्यैव प्रतिपादितः ।
मयोभूरन्नभूतोऽयं सर्वप्राणिभृदच्यते ॥१२२॥
रत्नस्य पयसोऽत्यर्थं रत्नाधारश्च यः स्तनः ।
वसुनो धनस्य लब्धा च तस्य वृष्ट्यादिहेतुनः ॥१२३॥

The word *guhā* means *śaya*[1] or *śaśaya*; and the Śruti itself has stated thus: this one is the source (or, cause) of well-being.

It has become the food and nourishment (i.e. sustainer) of all living beings. [122]
The word *ratnasya* means *payasaḥ* 'of milk' and the breast is what is the substratum of *ratna*. It is the procurer of *vasu* 'wealth', the cause of showering (profuse milk) etc.[2] [123]

[1]The word *guhā* means the base of the heart and *śaya* refers to the result that would be produced.
[2]We have followed the reading in the AnSS edition which is to be taken as an adjective of *dhanasya* (in neuter).

भूरिकल्याणदातृत्वात्सुदत्र इति भण्यते ।
येन पुष्यसि वार्याणि सर्वाणीह सरस्वति ॥१२४॥
देवादीनि वराणि त्वं सर्वैर्भोगैः प्रपुष्यसि ॥१२५॥

Being a giver of extensive well-being, it is described here (i.e. in this sentence by the word) *sudatra* 'liberal donor'. Since you nourish, O Sarasvatī all the choice gifts here (i.e. of this world), [124]
(this is to say:) you increase[1] the excellent gifts (*varāṇi*), viz. (those from) the gods[1] etc., by all (kinds of) enjoyments'. [125]

Sureśvara begins a new sentence in 124cd and completes it in 125 which is a verse of one line.
[1]*prapuṣyasi* literally means 'nourish', yet 'increase' can go well with both the gifts and gods etc. The word etc. refers to the elements, semi-divine and human beings. It can be argued that 'increase' indicates 'growth' 'nourishment' as well.
[2]*devādīni* qualifies *varāṇi* (used for *vāryāṇi*— a Vedic word).

पानाय मम पुत्रस्य स्त्रीस्तने संनिवेशय ।
यथोक्तगुणकं देवि स्वस्तनं सर्वकामदम् ॥१२६॥

O Goddess, place into the breast of my wife your own breast about whose excellences I have just (spoken) and which grants all the desires (of beings), so that my son may drink. [126]

Now, BU 6.4.28 is under reference.

इलासीत्यथ मन्त्रेण सूनोर्मातरमादरात् ।
अभिमन्त्रयते साधुकर्मावाप्त्यै स्वयं पतिः ॥१२७॥

Then, reciting the Mantra *ilāsi*, he lovingly (lit. respectfully) praises the mother of the son, so that (he,) the husband himself, should be able to complete well (i.e. successfully) his ritual performances. [127]

इति श्रीबृहदारण्यकोपनिषद्भाष्यवार्तिके षष्ठाध्यायस्य
चतुर्थं ब्राह्मणम् ॥४॥

BṚHADĀRAṆYAKOPANIṢAD-BHĀṢYA-VĀRTIKA
6.5

संभावितं न यत्पूर्वं कृत्स्नेऽस्मिन्ब्राह्मणेऽपि तत् ।
खिलकाण्डे तदखिलं पुत्रमन्थान्तमीरितम् ॥१॥

Whatever was not considered (i.e. discussed) in the whole of this Brāhmaṇa [1] earlier, is all of it considered in the Khila Kāṇḍa (so far) up to the end of (the discussion on) the Putramantha ritual. [1]

This refers to what has been discussed up to the end of the preceding Brāhmaṇa (viz. BU 6.4); cf. SP *vṛttaṃ saṃkīrtayati.*

[1]This is for BU itself.

पूर्वकाण्डैकदेशत्वात्खिलकाण्डं न वंशभाक् ।
पूर्वत्र विद्यासंभेदाद्भिन्नौ वंशाविहोदितौ ॥२॥

The Khila Kāṇḍa, being a (complementary) part of the earlier Kāṇḍas, (it does not have a separate) line of teachers. In the earlier Kāṇḍas (i.e. in their two groups) there were two distinct lines (of teachers), therefore, they (viz. the two lines) were stated here [1] with reference to the distinction of the lores in them. [2] [2]

In this verse and the preceding, it is pointed out as to why there is no mention of any line of teachers in relation to the Khila Kāṇḍa.

[1]The word here refers to the two Kāṇḍas, viz. Madhu Kāṇḍa and Muni Kāṇḍa.

[2]One could have objected that the two Kāṇḍas (Madhu- and Yājñavalkya-) pertained to only one lore, i.e. *brahmavidyā.*

Therefore, it would not be right to say: *pūrvatra vidyāsambhedaḥ*. This objection is answered away by the present verse.

पूर्वैश्चतुर्भिरध्यायैस्त्वाष्ट्रं कक्ष्यं च यन्मधु ।
व्याख्यातं तदशेषेण वंशस्तत्र तदर्थभाक् ॥३॥

In the first four Adhyāyas (of the Upaniṣad) was fully explained that Madhu, which belonged to Tvaṣṭṛ and was hidden, and, therefore, (for those Adhyāyas) the line (of teachers) related to the contents of the same. [3]

मधुकाण्डागमार्थस्य यथावत्प्रतिपत्तये ।
काण्डं स्याद्याज्ञवल्कीयं वंशस्तद्विषयस्तथा ॥४॥

In order that one should well understand the meaning of the tradition relating to the Madhu Kāṇḍa, there followed (or better, was presented) the Kāṇḍa of Yājñavalkya and also the line (of the teachers) relating to the same.[1] [4]

[1] *yathāvatpratipatti* makes this verse significant. In the earlier Kāṇḍa, there was refutation of varying views, whereas, in the latter Kāṇḍa, the thought (though the same) was presented with suitable reasoning in support of it. This clarifies what is meant by *vidyāsambheda*.

अयं तु वंशो विज्ञेयः कृत्स्नप्रवचनाश्रयः ।
समाप्तौ ब्राह्मणस्योक्तेरयमर्थोऽवसीयते ॥५॥

As for (*tu*) this line (of teachers), it has been related to the entire discussion in the Upaniṣad. Therefore, at the end of (the entire) Brāhmaṇa,[1] this (line of teachers is to be for the whole of it); this is to be concluded from the statement. [5]

उक्तवेदार्थविज्ञानसाकल्यप्रतिपत्तये ।
जपो वंशस्य येनातः श्रुत्या वंश इहोदितः ॥६॥

Since, in order that one attains completeness in one's knowledge about the meaning of the Veda that is taught, there is the recitation of the line (of teachers of the same). As such, this Śruti (also) has stated here the line (of teachers). [6]

सर्वज्ञानां यतो वंशास्त्रयोऽप्येते यथोदिताः ।
अतस्तत्स्मृतितः सम्यग्ज्ञानभानुदयो भवेत् ॥७॥

Since all these three lines of the all-knowing teachers have been stated (here in the Upaniṣad), therefore, by the remembrance of them (all), there would certainly (lit. well) arise the sun in the form of knowledge. [7]

पुत्रमन्थेन संस्कारः स्त्रीणामेवेह वर्णितः ।
यतोऽतः स्त्रीप्रधानोऽयं पुत्राणां वंश उच्यते ॥८॥

Since, in (the prescription of) the Putramantha there was described here (i.e. in this Upaniṣad) a Saṃskāra for women, therefore, this line of the sons (who are teachers) is stated, prominence (being given) to women (who were their mothers). [8]

अन्यतोऽन्यत एवायं संप्रदायो यथाभवत् ।
न तथा ब्रह्मणस्तस्मात्तत्स्वयंभ्विति शब्द्यते ॥९॥

As this tradition followed (i.e. came into being) from one to another, so it did not happen in the case of the Brahman; therefore, it is mentioned as self-born. [9]

This explains why the word *svayambhu* is used with *brahman*.

अन्येषां वेदतो ज्ञानं भूरिसाधनसंश्रयात् ।
स्वतो वेदात्मनस्तस्मात्सर्वज्ञानमयो हि सः ॥१०॥

In the case of others, there occurs the knowledge from (the

study of) the Veda, by using many means (towards acquiring the same); but, in the case of the Ātman of the Veda, (its) knowledge (occurs of itself). Therefore, that (viz. the Vedātman) is (said to be) 'possessed of all knowledge'. [10]

सर्वस्यैष वशीत्यादि तथापि प्रागवादिषम् ।
परैव देवता वेदो यच्च किंचिच्चराचरम् ॥११॥

(As regards) *sarvasyaiṣa vaśī* etc. also *api* [1] I have said earlier: [2] the Veda (or the Vedātman) is the highest deity itself and also (it is) whatever exists, movable and immovable. [11]

[1]The force of 'also' evokes reference to *yaḥ sarvajñaḥ sarvavid* ... (*Muṇḍakopaniṣad* 2.2.7).
[2]Cf. BUBV 3.8.29.

प्रतिपाद्यात्मनात्मानं नामरूपादिसाधनः ।
एति पूर्णात्मतां साक्षाद्धियां वाचामगोचरम् ॥१२॥

(Therefore), one, possessed of the means, viz. name, form etc., knows one's own self by oneself and becomes complete in nature, directly perceptible to oneself, not (becoming) a subject of one's own intellect and words. [12]

त्रय्यैव ब्राह्मणो विद्वानात्मनैवाद्वयं परम् ।
विदित्वा निर्वृतिं याति कार्यकारणयोः पराम् ॥१३॥

A Brāhmaṇa becomes a knower only through (the study of) the *trayī* and by himself (becoming) the knower of the non-dual highest (Vedātman) and then, having known (his own true nature), attains the highest bliss which is beyond the cause and effect relations. [13]

वेदोऽसीत्यत एवास्य नाम जातस्य कुर्वते ।
वेदात्मना कथं नाम परं ब्रह्म प्रपत्स्यते ॥१४॥

For this very reason do they name the newly born (son) in the words *vedo 'si*. How can he, being himself the Veda, understand the highest Brahman? [14]

This brings out the purpose of naming the new-born son as Veda. Being Veda, i.e. the Ātman, he is considered to be a natural knower of his own self.

वाजिशाखासु सर्वासु ह्यासुरायणपर्वकाः ।
समाना वंशर्षयोऽमी ह्या समाप्तेरितीक्ष्यताम् ॥१५॥

In all the branches of Vājasaneyins, the lines of seers are the same, as beginning with Āsurāyaṇa. Let this be understood up to the end (of this last Brāhmaṇa). [15]

आदित्येन हि प्रोक्तानि यजूंष्येतानि यानि तु ।
आदित्यानीत्यतस्तानि सम्यगाचक्षते बुधाः ॥१६॥

Since all these Yajuṣ Mantras are declared by Āditya, therefore, the wise ones have well described them as coming from Āditya. [16]

वेदात्मनो रवेरेवं संप्रदायोऽयमागतः ।
परमेष्ठ्यादिकान्सर्वान्पारंपर्येण मानुषान् ॥१७॥

This entire tradition has thus come from the sun, the Ātman of the Veda, up to all men, beginning with Parameṣṭhin in a successive line. [17]

असंसृष्टं परं ब्रह्म सर्वदोषविवर्जितम् ।
एतदादित्यगं भाति तद्वेदानां परं वपुः ॥१८॥

The highest Brahman is unaffected by (lit. mixed with) anything else, and is devoid of any fault. This one, existing in the sun, shines forth as the highest form of the Veda. [18]

उत्सन्नमपि यद्ब्रह्म तदादित्ये न नश्यति ।
तदार्षेणैव विन्दन्ति तपस्तप्त्वा महर्षयः ॥१९॥

And that Brahman, even though destroyed,[1] does not (really) perish.[2] The great seers come to know it after performing penances in the seers' tradition.[3] [19]

[1]This refers to *tasmād yajñāt sarvahutaḥ*, conveying thereby that the Vedas, comprising composition of words, get destroyed at the time of the deluge (*pralaya*).
[2]This is because Āditya, identified with the Brahman, does not perish even in the deluge.
[3]SP clarifies this tradition by a verse, viz. *Mahābhārata*:
yugānte 'ntarhitān vedān setihāsān maharṣayaḥ /
lebhire tapasā pūrvam anujñātāḥ svayambhuvā // (12.203.17)

वेदब्रह्मण आरभ्य सर्वेषामपि शाखिनाम् ।
सांजीवीसूनुपर्यन्तो वंश एको न भिद्यते ॥२०॥

In the case of the followers of all the branches (of this Veda), this one line of teachers, which begins with Vedabrahman and up to (the mention of) the son of Sāñjīvī, does not differ. [20]

सांजीवीपुत्रतस्त्ववार्क्प्रतिशाखं पृथकपृथक् ।
आचार्यभेदाद्भिद्यन्ते वंशा वाजसनेयिनाम् ॥२१॥

And, from the son of Sāñjīvī, the later lines of the teachers of the Vājasaneya Brāhmaṇas differ from one another in relation to different teachers. [21]

इत्युक्तैकात्म्यवाक्यप्रविकचकमला प्राज्यसन्न्यायगन्धा
काण्डैश्चित्रा षडर्धैर्मधुमुनिखिलकैर्मस्करीन्द्रालिजुष्टा ।
श्लोकग्रन्थिप्रबद्धाविषर्यमितिफला प्रेमसत्सत्रसूत्रा
माला गङ्गेव शंभु पदममलमजं वैष्णवं सानुयाता ॥२२॥

Thus, this wreathe of fully blown lotuses in the form of sentences (relating to) the singleness of the Ātman (which is propounded in the Śruti), having the profuse fragrance (in the form) of good reasoning, variegated in its three (lit. half of six) sections (called) Madhu, Muni and Khila, enjoyed by the bee (in the form of) the pre-eminent (or the chief) ascetic, tied up by knots (in the form of) Ślokas, bearing fruit (in the form of) knowledge of what cannot be the object (of knowing) and stringing (together) the bliss(-giving) existent Sūtra (i.e. Hiraṇyagarbha), has followed the step of the all-pervading (lit. Viṣṇu) which is the most pure (or faultless) and unborn, in the same way as Gaṅgā (followed the head of) the source of well-being (lit. Śambhu, i.e. Śiva). [22]

This is a very ornate verse, deliberately worked out by Sureśvara. He compares his composition in verses to a wreathe of lotuses, many minute details of the composition and the different components of the wreathe being shown as similar; these are explained in their fullness in SP. The words Śambhu and Vaiṣṇava *pada* are purposely used by Sureśvara because (it appears) he wants to show his great regard for, or devotion to, the bliss-bringing Śaṅkara, who could be compared to the commonly accepted gods of his times—Śiva and Viṣṇu.

यत्प्रज्ञोदधियुक्तिशब्दनखजश्रद्धैकसन्नेत्रक-
स्थैर्यस्तम्भमुमुक्षुदुःखितकृपायत्नोत्थबोधामृतम् ।
पीत्वा जन्ममृतिप्रवाहविधुरा मोक्षं ययुर्मोक्षिणस्
तं वन्देऽत्रिकुलप्रसूतममलं वेधोभिधं मद्गुरुम् ॥२३॥

I bow down to my Guru, who is born in the family of Atri, called Vedhas[1] and (the purest among the) pure, from whose nectar(-like) instruction/teaching, that came from his efforts out of compassion for the sorrow-stricken seekers of liberation, as the steadying pillar for the churning rod in the form of the reasonful preaching words and the churning rod in the form of faith which helps churning the ocean-like intelligence, and drinking which the seekers of liberation attained liberation, being freed from (lit. becoming bereft of) the stream of births and deaths. [23]

SP offers an elaborate explanation of the first two lines which can be read with profit.

यामस्मद्गुरुरेव वेदशिरसामैकात्म्यतात्पर्यतो
वृत्तिं सज्जनशंकरीं सुविमलां नानानयोद्द्योतिताम् ।
चक्रे काण्वसमाश्रितोपनिषदो दुस्तर्कदोषापहां
श्रद्धामात्रबलेन वार्तिकमिदं तस्याः समासात्कृतम् ॥२४॥

With the strength of my faith (in my Guru) alone have I composed in brief this Vārtika on that Vṛtti on the Upaniṣad belonging to the Kāṇvas' recension which my Guru himself has written as the purport (of all the Upaniṣads), viz. the singleness of the Ātman (conveyed as) the head (i.e. most important) of all the Vedas, illuminated by varied reasoning, extremely clear and causing happiness to the wise (lit. good) men. [24]

Thus Sureśvara emphatically asserts the extreme clarity and faultlessness of Śaṅkara's Vṛtti on BU of Kāṇva recension.

आ शैलादुदयात्तथास्तगिरितो भास्वद्यशोरश्मिभिर
व्याप्तं विश्वमनन्धकारमभवद्यस्य स्म शिष्यैरिदम् ।
आराज्ज्ञानगभस्तिभिः प्रतिहतश्चन्द्रायते भास्करस्-
तस्मै शंकरभानवे तनुमनोवाग्भिर्नमस्तात्सदा ॥२५॥

May this be my obeisance, with my body, mind and speech, to the Sun in the form of Śaṅkara, whose disciples have pervaded this universe from the rising mountain up to the setting mountain [1] by the brilliant rays of their fame and, (as a consequence), it (viz. the universe) has become free from darkness, and by the rays of whose knowledge, the Sun is vanquished, (even) from afar and (he then) appears like the moon. [25]

Once again, Sureśvara works out the sustained metaphor here as in verse 22 above.

[1]Actually the mountain from behind which the sun rises and that beyond which it sets.

इति श्रीबृहदारण्यकोपनिषद्भाष्यवार्तिके षष्ठाध्यायस्य पञ्चमं ब्राह्मणम् ॥५॥

इति श्रीमत्परमहंसपरिव्राजकाचार्यश्रीमच्छंकरभगवत्-
पूज्यपादशिष्यश्रीमत्सुरेश्वराचार्यकृतौ
बृहदारण्यकोपनिषद्भाष्यवार्तिकप्रस्थाने
षष्ठोऽध्यायः ॥६॥

****

SELECT GLOSSARY

(1) Below are given mostly such words [or, almost all of them] in the text under consideration as Sureśvara used in their peculiar senses.

(2) Figures after the specified meanings are the numbers of Adhyāya, Brāhmaṇa and Verses in the text, e.g. 5.2.2 stands for 5th Adhyāya 2nd Brāhmaṇa 2nd Verse.

aṇḍa — universe (5.16.62)

adhiṣavaṇa — a stone on which Soma is pressed (6.4.9)

adhvans — origin, sustenance and merger (5.1.48)

apūrva — subtle form of a ritual performance (6.2.15, 77)

abhāva — non-existence (5.1.22)

ahima — mental pain (5.12.5)

ātman — body (5.17.15)

ātmabhāvitā — devoted to the Ātman (6.2.120)

ābhūtasaṃplava — complete merger into elements (6.2.143)

āmantraṇa — address (6.4.97)

āvasathyāgni — domestic fire (6.4.53)

āvṛtti — rebirth (lit. repeated existence) (5.16.66)

āhavanīya — the principal fire in a sacrifice (6.2.76)

audumbara — a vessel of that name (6.3.13, 17)

iṣṭāpūrtakṛt — one who has done sacrificial and charitable acts (6.2.121)

uktha — *śastra* (5.14.2)

ukṣan — bull (6.4.77)

utkrāntādi — sixfold result of performing the Agnihotra which begins with *utkrānti* (6.2.14, 15)

upaniṣad — secret name (5.7.2)

upasad — vows prescribed (in Jyotiṣṭoma sacrifice

	(6.3.12)
upahan	to touch (6.4.67)
ṛṣabha	grown up bull (6.4.77)
kartṛtantra	[the performance of rituals] which depends on a performer or an agent (5.1.67); cf. *vastutantra* below
kṛdātman	all undesirable (effects) on the individual self (5.16.21)
kṣaya	destruction (5.16.65, 66)
gaya	*prāṇa* 'organ' (5.16.38)
gāyatrī	Gāyatrī Mantra (the word is derived from *gaya* '*prāṇa*' connected with a root *trai* (5.16.38)
guṇa	excellence (6.3.8)
graha	attack of a disease, goblin (5.13.2)
ghatīyantra	a mechanical device of raising water from a well (6.2.155)
cikitsā	censure (5.13.2)
tīrtha	sacrifice (5.1.65)
	a customary mode regarding one's approach to a preceptor (6.2.65)
	a preceptor, a king, or an elderly person (6.2.66)
tryakṣara	comprising three letters, three-letter-word, viz. *satya*, (=Brahman) (5.5.11)
dṛṣṭi	deliberate or purposeful view of a thing taken as another (6.2.78)
	acceptance of metaphorical identity (6.4.8)
deśasaṃskāra	purification of the region/place on which some ritual is performed (6.3.18)
niyama	restrictive rule (one kind of the injunctions) (6.3.15)
nyāya	reason (=*tarka*) (5.1.65, 5.15.8)
	proper reasoning (5.1.64)
parākāśā	intention which is announced (6.4.61)

pariṇāma	ripeness (6.2.19)
	result (6.2.76)
pūrṇa	[the Brahman] beyond cause(s) and effect(s) (5.1.8, 40)
	all-sided knowledge (5.1.43)
pṛṣadājya	mixture of clarified butter, curds (and honey) (6.4.114)
pratipad	means for securing a desired result (6.2.38, 39)
prapūrvā	young woman (6.4.91)
prāyatya	being naked (6.1.39; 6.3.55)
buddhi	intellect (5.3.3)
bheda	(i) distinct objects, (ii) distinction between distinct objects (5.1.97)
makarī	the sea (5.1.77)
mahat	having great dimension (5.4.4)
	great (adjective of wealth) (6.3.4)
	importance or fame (6.3.5)
māṃsapeśi	lump of flesh (5.3.3)
yakṣa	of the nature of what is to be worshipped or, worship-deserving (5.4.4)
yakṣatva	nature of what is worship-deserving (5.5.10)
yatnataḥ	at length of time and place (5.3.5)
	(=*yatnāt*) with special care (6.2.6; 6.4.4)
	(*yatna*) attention (6.4.6)
ra	verb root *ram* (5.14.13)
loka	result achieved by different modes of worship (5.13.5)
vasiṣṭha	best helper (6.1.16, 17, 18)
vastutantra	[the knowledge of Brahman] which depends on only knowledge (5.1.67)
vākovākya	series of questions (6.2.47)
vāgdhenu	cow in the form of speech (5.10.1)
vāyura	that which has the support of *vāyu* or, as Śaṅkara explains 'containing *vāyu*

	in it (5.1.119, 121)
vi	*viṣṭa* (5.14.12)
vijñāna	lustre (6.4.22, 27)
vibhu	all-becoming (6.3.32)
vibhūti	of extense of something (6.2.78); =*vistṛti* (6.2.79)
vṛtti	nature (5.1.48)
vyāhṛtis	three *vyāhṛtis*—*sa*, *t* and *ya*, which form *satya*, the name of the Brahman (5.7.1)
	sacred utterances *bhūḥ*, *bhvaḥ* and *svāhā* (6.3.43)
śāstra	a text teaching people what activity they should enter upon and what, they should avoid/abandon, be it compulsory or optional <given by Ānandagiri> (5.1.47)
śraddhā	deviated from verb roots *śri* 'to resort to' or *śrat-dhā* 'to support' and (6.2.89)
saṃvarga	collection of some things belonging to one class (6.3.35)
saṃsrava	remainder of the clarified butter, sacrificial material (6.3.22)
samānādhikaraṇa	(i) occurring in the same substratum, (ii) (grammatically) in the same case relation (5.1.113)
sārṣṭisālokyasāyujya	similarity in appearance, sameness of the abode and being just one (6.2.142)
sthālīpāka	the basic ritual (or, a series of actions) for other rituals (6.4.82)
sviṣṭakṛt	the final offering for well-being (6.3.29; 6.4.85)
hṛdaya	Prajāpati (5.3.4) and Brahman (5.3.5)

****

BIBLIOGRAPHY

TEXTS

Brahmasūtraśāṅkarabhāṣya with the Commentaries Bhāmatī, Kalpataru and Parimala. Bombay: Nirnayasagar Press, 1917.

Bṛhadāraṇyakopaniṣad with Śaṅkara's Commentary. AnSS 15, Poona: 1891.

Bṛhadāraṇyakopaniṣadbhāṣyavārtika with Ānandagiri's Commentary Śāstraprakāśikā. 3 vols., AnSS 16, Poona: 1892-94.

Bṛhadāraṇyakavārtikasāra of Vidyāraṇya. Chowkhamba Sanskrit Series Nos. 205-208, 243-244, 257-258, 271-272, Benares: 1915-19.

Bṛhadāraṇyakavārttikavyākhyā-Nyāyakalpalatikā. GOML Ref. No. 5283, vol. 2.

Taittirīyopaniṣadbhāṣyavārtika with Ānandagiri's Commentary. AnSS 13, Poona: 1977.

Naiṣkarmyasiddhi. (revised ed.) M. Hiriyanna, Poona: Bhandarkar Inst., 1925.

Manusmṛti with Kullūka's Commentary Manvarthamuktāvali. Bombay: Nirnayasagar Press, 1946.

BOOKS

Jog, K. P. and S. Hino, *Advaita Tradition Series*. 12 vols., Delhi: Motilal Banarsidass.

vol. 1 (1982): Hino, *Sureśvara's Vārtika on Yājñavalkya-Maitreyī Dialogue*.

vol. 2 (1988): Jog and Hino, *Sureśvara's Vārtika on Madhu Brāhmaṇa*.

vol. 3 (1990): Hino and Jog, *Sureśvara's Vārtika on Aśva and Aśvamedha Brāhmaṇa*.

vol. 4 (1991): Jog and Hino, *Sureśvara's Vārtika on Udgītha*

Brāhmaṇa.

vol. 5 (1993): Jog and Hino, *Sureśvara's Vārtika on Puruṣavidha Brāhmaṇa.*

vol. 6 (1995): Hino and Jog, *Sureśvara's Vārtika on Saptānna Brāhmaṇa.*

vol. 7 (1996): Jog and Hino, *Sureśvara's Vārtika on Śiśu and Mūrtāmūrta Brāhmaṇa.*

vol. 8 (1997): Jog and Hino, *Sureśvara's Vārtika on Ajātaśatru Brāhmaṇa.*

Limaye, V.P. and R.D. Vadekar, *Eighteen Principal Upaniṣads.* vol. 1, Poona: Vaidika Samshodana Mandala, 1958.

Madhavananda, S., (tr.) *The Bṛhadāraṇyaka Upaniṣad.* Calcutta: Advaita Ashrama, 1975.

Mahadevan, T.M.P. (ed. and tr.) *The Saṃbandha-Vārtika of Sureśvarācārya.* Madras: University of Madras, 1972.

Röer, E., (tr.) *The Twelve Principal Upaniṣads.* vol. 2, Madras: Theosophical Publishing House, 1931.

Hume, R.E., (tr.) *The Thirteen Principal Upaniṣads.* first Indian paperback edition, Delhi: Oxford University Press, 1983.

SUREŚVARA'S VĀRTIKA ON KHILA KĀṆḌA WITH HALF-VERSE INDEX

ADVAITA TRADITION SERIES

VOL. 9

BOOK TWO

Sureśvara's Vārtika on Khila Kāṇḍa with Half-Verse Index

Edited, Translated and Annotated by

K. P. Jog
Shoun Hino

MOTILAL BANARSIDASS PUBLISHERS PRIVATE LIMITED • DELHI

First Edition: Delhi 1998

ISBN: 81-208-1504-1

MOTILAL BANARSIDASS

41 U.A. Bungalow Road, Jawahar Nagar, Delhi 110 007
8, Mahalaxmi Chamber, Warden Road, Mumbai 400 026
120 Royapettah High Road, Mylapore, Chennai 600 004
Sanas Plaza, Subhash Nagar, Pune 411 002
16 St. Mark's Road, Bangalore 560 001
8 Camac Street, Calcutta 700 017
Ashok Rajpath, Patna 800 004
Chowk, Varanasi 221 001

PRINTED IN INDIA

BY JAINENDRA PRAKASH JAIN AT SHRI JAINENDRA PRESS,
A-45 NARAINA, PHASE I, NEW DELHI 110 028
AND PUBLISHED BY NARENDRA PRAKASH JAIN FOR
MOTILAL BANARSIDASS PUBLISHERS PRIVATE LIMITED,
BUNGALOW ROAD, DELHI 110 007

BOOK 2

HALF-VERSE INDEX OF BUBV

अंशं निदधति स्वं स्वं कर्मभोगप्रसिद्धये 3.2.127cd
अंशत्रयमतो युक्तमपूर्वविधिरेव तु 1.4.787cd
अंशांशित्वविवक्षायां न प्रायोक्ष्यत्तदेदृशम् 2.1.526cd
अंशांशित्वादि चेत्साक्षाद्ब्रह्मज्ञाने विवक्षितम् 2.1.524ab
अंशांशित्वेऽपि नैव स्यात्पूर्वोक्तादेव कारणात् 4.3.661ab
अंशांशिसंगतेरात्माप्यहंबुद्ध्यानुभूयते 4.4.926ab
अंशिसंसारिभावत्वं न्यायेनाप्युपपद्यते 2.1.528cd
अकर्ताप्यश्वमेधस्य ब्राह्मणश्चेह बुद्धिमान् 1.1.6ab
अकर्तुरपि कर्तृत्वं स्वात्माज्ञानैकहेतुतः 4.3.923ab
अकर्तृकं चेत्कार्यं स्यात्कारणं कार्यतां व्रजेत् 1.4.197cd
अकर्तृत्वात्मयाथात्म्यसम्यग्ज्ञानाग्निना यतः 4.4.1287ab
अकर्तृत्वात्मविज्ञानाद्ध्वस्तात्माज्ञानहेतुतः 4.4.1283ab
अकर्तृत्वान्न संबन्धो विदुषोऽस्तीह पाप्मभिः 4.4.1290cd
अकर्त्रात्मपरिज्ञानाद्ध्वस्ताविद्यस्य सर्वतः 3.2.27ab
अकर्मकत्वादस्यादेर्न तावत्कर्म विद्यते SV 702ab
अकल्पितस्य चैकत्वान्नितरां न प्रसिध्यति 2.1.166cd
अकस्माद्भवतः सक्तेर्मुक्तावप्यनिषेधतः SV 52ab
अकामतः क्रिया काचिद्दृश्यते नेह कस्यचित् 1.4.1816ab
अकामतः क्रिया काचिद्दृश्यते नेह कस्यचित् 2.1.578ab
अकामप्रमुखैर्योगैस्तथा कामादियोगतः 4.4.191cd
अकाममित्यतो ध्वस्तसमस्तव्यस्तरूपकम् 4.3.1343cd
अकामस्य क्रिया काचिद्दृश्यते नेह कस्यचित् 4.4.223ab
अकामस्य क्रिया यस्मान्निष्फलैव समीक्ष्यते 4.3.1017ab
अकामहतताहेतोर्वृद्धौ ह्लादो विवर्धते 4.3.1866cd
अकामहततैवातः पूर्वाभ्यां साधनं परम् 4.3.1868cd
अकामहततैवात्र तारतम्यात्मकत्वतः 4.3.1873ab
अकामहतधीगम्य आनन्दः प्रत्यगात्मनि 4.3.1882ab

अकामोऽपि क इत्येवं पृष्टे निष्काम उच्यते 4.4.267ab
अकारकक्रियाकार्यं रूपं प्राक्प्रतिबोधतः 2.1.207ab
अकारकफलत्वेन तेन प्रायार्थतेष्यते 2.1.188cd
अकारकस्य कौटस्थ्याद्विरोधो नात्मदर्शने 1.4.1309cd
अकारकस्वभावत्वाददृष्टेत्यभिधीयते 4.3.1804cd
अकारकस्वभावत्वान्नैवं वृत्तं ममात्मनः 4.3.1476ab
अकारकस्वभावस्य परमार्थात्मवस्तुनः 4.3.391ab
अकारकात्मकं ज्योतिरद्वयं प्रत्यगात्मकम् 4.3.1489cd
अकारकात्मकान्येव पुंसः कारकरूपिणः 4.3.63ab
अकारकात्मना तस्थौ प्रत्यग्दृष्टिरसंगतः 3.4.83cd
अकारकात्मनोऽदृष्टिर्द्रष्टव्यार्थाप्रयुक्तितः 4.3.1479ab
अकारकात्मबोधस्य जन्मनैव तमोह्नुतिः 4.4.853cd
अकारकाद्वयत्वाभ्यां द्रष्टृत्वं नाक्षरात्मनः 3.8.175cd
अकारकैकात्म्यमात्रं मेयं वस्त्विष्यते यतः 2.4.149ab
अकारणं सत्कार्यं चेड्डिम्भकैरपि हस्यते 1.4.427cd
अकारणं सदज्ञानात्कारणत्वं यथैत्यजम् 1.2.128ab
अकारणमकार्यं सत्कार्यकारणतामगात् 1.2.130ab
अकात्स्न्र्यदोषहानाय प्रतीचः कृत्स्नतोच्यते 1.4.941cd
अकार्यं कारकमिति सुप्तोन्मत्तप्रभाषितम् 1.4.326cd
अकार्यकरणोऽप्यात्मा बुद्धिप्राणादिहेतुगः 4.3.406ab
अकार्यकारणं प्रत्यग्ज्योतिः संमुह्यते कुतः 4.4.10cd
अकार्यकारणं साक्षादित्यादिगुणलक्षणम् 3.8.123ab
अकार्यकारणस्त्वात्मा तमपह्नुत्य तिष्ठति 2.4.347ab
अकार्यकारणात्मत्वात्कैवल्येऽनुगतिः कुतः 2.4.206cd
अकार्यकारणात्मैतद्वास्तवं रूपमात्मनः 3.4.84ab
अकार्यकारणे व्याप्तिः कथं स्यात्प्रत्यगात्मनि 4.4.689cd
अकार्यत्वात्त्वविद्यायास्त्वदुक्तं तुषकण्डनम् 1.4.1220cd
अकार्यत्वास्वभावत्वादविनाभावमात्रतः 4.3.761ab
अकार्यश्चास्वभावश्च नालिङ्गं कृत्तिकोदयः 4.3.759cd
अकार्याकारणात्मैव कार्यकारणवस्तुनः 4.4.647ab
अकार्येऽपि हि मेर्वादावस्ति मेरुरिति श्रुतेः 1.3.81ab
अकालकुसुमानीव नैव प्रीतिकरं सताम् 1.4.99cd

अकुर्वतः प्रसक्तिः स्यादकुर्वत्त्वाविशेषतः 1.4.325cd
अकुर्वत्कारकं तस्मात्कुर्वतोऽतिशयः कुतः 4.3.1443cd
अकुर्वत्कारणं चेत्स्यात्तद्वत्कार्यं सदा भवेत् 1.4.324ab
अकृतस्य क्रिया त्वत्र विधिर्नैवोपपद्यते 2.4.198cd
अकृताभ्यागमः प्राप्तः कृतनाशश्च सत्वरः 5.1.76ab
अकृताभ्यागमो दोषः कृतनाशश्च ते भवेत् 4.3.688ab
अकृताभ्यागमो यस्मात्कृतनाश्च नेष्यते 1.4.1787cd
अकृत्स्न एव तावत्स्यात्तदन्यो यावदीक्ष्यते 1.4.1057cd
अकृत्स्नज्ञानतो नापि पुरुषार्थोऽवगम्यते 1.4.1093ab
अकृत्स्नत्वान्निषेधश्च न त्वात्मोपासनस्य सः 1.4.938ab
अकृत्स्नदृष्टिविषयो निषेधोऽपि न युज्यते 3.5.23ab
अकृत्स्नब्रह्मवेदित्वाददृप्तोऽसावल्पकस्ततः 2.1.17ab
अकृत्स्नभोगतो युक्तं वागादिषु विशेषणम् 1.3.172ab
अकृत्स्नवचसा तद्वत्प्रमाभासोऽप्यपोदितः 1.4.1056cd
अकृत्स्नव्यपदेशेन मिथ्याज्ञानत्वमुच्यते 1.4.672cd
अकृत्स्नस्तावदस्मीति जडः संभावयत्ययम् 1.4.1838cd
अकृत्स्नस्य च ब्रह्मत्वं विरुद्धं भानुशैत्यवत् 1.4.1095ab
अकृत्स्नानात्मनः सर्वान्कृत्स्नांश्चानात्मनस्तथा 1.4.1349ab
अकृत्स्नो हीति हेतूक्तिः सापि चैवं समर्थ्यते 1.4.660cd
अक्रत त्वां यतो विप्राः संदंशं मयि पावके 3.9.62cd
अक्रियाकर्तृसंबन्धे ननु षष्ठी प्रसज्जते SV 526ab
अक्रियाकारकं ज्ञात्वा निःशेषपुरुषार्थदम् SV 133cd
अक्रियाकारकं वस्तु न तावद्वेद तत्त्वतः 1.4.710cd
अक्रियाकारकं वस्तु पारोक्ष्यान्नैव लभ्यते 1.4.180ef
अक्रियाकारकफलं यतो ब्रह्माद्वयं ततः 4.4.446ab
अक्रियात्वान्नियोगस्य द्वितीया चेद्रवेत्तथा SV 529cd
अक्रियेऽपि यथा व्योम्नि ह्युत्पत्तिस्थितिहानिभिः 1.4.988ab
अक्रियेऽपि यथा व्योम्नि ह्युद्भूतिस्थितिहानिभिः 4.3.1742ab
अक्षण्येव यतः पूर्वं व्याख्यातो देवतागणः 2.2.25ab
अक्षमा भवतः कैयं साधकत्वप्रकल्पने 1.4.1279ab
अक्षरं यदि न स्थूलमणु तर्हि तदिष्यताम् 3.8.71ab
अक्षरं येन रूपेण स्थूलं वस्तु निषेधति 3.8.101ab

अक्षरं यो विदित्वास्माल्लोकाद्गार्गि प्रमीयते 3.8.168ab
अक्षरं स्वात्मसंमोहात्कारणत्वं निगच्छति 3.8.178ab
अक्षरस्य श्रुतिः साक्षात्तद्वा इत्येवमादिना 3.8.171cd
अक्षराज्ञानतः पुंसां कार्पण्येनावियुक्तताम् 3.8.167cd
अक्षराणां न तत्रास्ति वस्तु किंचित्तिरोहितम् 1.4.1799cd
अक्षराणामतात्पर्याद्युक्तितश्चाप्यसंभवात् 1.4.951ab
अक्षराणामिह ज्ञेया नातो व्याख्यायते पुनः 5.16.14cd
अक्षरात्मनि नास्तित्वे तस्माद्वेतूक्तिरिष्यते 3.8.126cd
अक्षरात्मावसानानां पूर्वपूर्वप्रहाणतः 3.6.13cd
अक्षरानन्वयात्त्याज्या व्याख्येयं साध्वपीदृशी 2.5.74cd
अक्षरानुगतोऽप्यर्थो यदि संशय्यते तदा 1.4.1625ab
अक्षरान्तेषु तत्त्वेषु नाव्याकृतवचो यतः 3.8.27cd
अक्षरे तदसंभाव्यममात्रं तद्यतस्ततः 3.8.106cd
अक्षसूत्रवदन्योऽन्यं सामर्थ्यस्याप्रहाणतः 2.3.33ab
अक्षाणि भौतिकान्येव नातः शक्तय आत्मनः 4.4.29cd
अक्षादि तत्तमोबाधान्न मानं रज्जुसर्पवत् 1.4.1358cd
अक्षादिभिश्च नैकात्म्यं बाधितत्वात्प्रमाणवत् SV 911cd
अक्षादिमेयासारूप्यादैकात्म्यं स्यान्न तत्प्रमम् 2.4.176ab
अक्षादीनां स्वतःसिद्धो यत्र तेषां प्रमाणता SV 1002cd
अक्षादेरकृतार्थत्वात्कथं स्यात्तेन बाधनम् SV 916cd
अक्षादेरपि मानत्वं यथोक्तादेव कारणात् 2.4.326cd
अक्षाद्यगोचरो यद्वच्छास्त्रादध्यवसीयते 2.1.443ab
अक्षाद्यविषयं प्रत्यक्स्वतः सिद्धेरसाधनम् 2.4.154ab
अक्षाद्यविषया ये तु गुणा आगमतो मताः 1.3.47ab
अक्षितित्वं कथं पुंस इत्येतच्चाधुनोच्यते 1.5.84ef
अक्षीणं क्षीणकर्माणं तं देवा ब्राह्मणं विदुः 4.4.594cd
अक्षीणा इति ता ज्ञात्वा नान्नक्षयमुपाश्नुते 2.2.23cd
अक्षीणैः कर्मसंतानैस्तथैव जनयत्यपि 3.2.66cd
अक्षिण प्रकाशरूपेऽस्मिन्सर्वं रूपं प्रतिष्ठितम् 5.16.33ab
अक्षिण प्रकाशरूपे हि सर्वं रूपं प्रतिष्ठितम् 5.16.29cd
अक्षिण रश्मिभिरादित्यः प्राणैस्तस्मिंश्च चाक्षुषः 5.6.4cd
अक्षण्युपनिषदो वाच्यास्तमेता इत्यतः श्रुतिः 2.2.22cd

अक्ष्यादित्याख्यनीडस्थौ स्थानमात्रप्रभेदतः 5.6.2ab
अगत्वरं सद्विज्ञानं भूतार्थं ढौकते कथम् 1.4.457cd
अगादुपासनात्प्राणमात्मत्वेन दिवानिशम् 5.16.64cd
अगाद्वयं यतोऽतोऽभूदरतिस्तस्य कामिनः 1.4.95cd
अगृहीत्वैव संबन्धमभिधानाभिधेययोः 1.4.861ab
अगृहीत्वैव संबन्धमभिधानाभिधेययोः 4.4.697ab
अगृह्यमाणं सत्तत्त्वं विपरीतमिवेक्ष्यते 3.5.40ab
अगृह्याद्यात्मतां यातः स्वमहिम्नि व्यवस्थितः 4.4.1159cd
अगौणाव्यवधानादिविशेषणविशेष्यता 3.5.21ab
अग्नयोऽर्काश्चिता आसन्षट् च त्रिंशत्सहस्रशः 1.3.277cd
अग्निं न ढौकते शैत्यमग्निवस्तुस्वभावतः 1.5.361ab
अग्निं स्वात्ममनःसंस्थामधुना देवतां गृही 5.17.15ab
अग्निं ह्युपसमाधाय प्रसिद्धार्थमथापरम् 6.4.113cd
अग्निः शीतस्तथोष्णश्चेत्येवमाद्युक्तितो ननु 2.1.557ab
अग्निः सूर्यो मरुद्यद्वत्प्रविष्टो भुवनं तथा 1.4.622ab
अग्निदाहादिवत्साक्षाद्वेदान्तज्ञानजं फलम् 2.1.548ab
अग्निप्राणौ पुरैवोक्तावथ संवत्सरोद्भवः 1.2.171cd
अग्निब्राह्मणयोर्यस्माद्ब्रह्म साक्षादभूत्पुरा 1.4.1658ab
अग्निब्राह्मणयोर्विष्णोस्तावन्मात्रसमाप्तितः 1.4.1660cd
अग्निब्राह्मणयोर्हेतुः प्राधान्ये भण्यते स्फुटः 1.4.1657ab
अग्निब्राह्मणरूपेण ब्रह्म साक्षाद्व्यवस्थितम् 1.4.1663ab
अग्निभिः पञ्चभिः पक्वाः पुरुषाख्या भवन्ति हि 6.2.112cd
अग्निमित्येकवचनात्तथैवोल्लेखनादितः 6.3.12ab
अग्निमित्येकवचनादुल्लिख्यादेश्च लिङ्गतः 6.4.53ab
अग्निरिन्धनवत्सर्वं दहेद्विद्वान्प्रतिग्रहम् 5.16.80cd
अग्निरेव न धूमादिभेदः कश्चन लक्ष्यते 2.4.298cd
अग्निरेव मुखं तस्या इत्युक्त्या कृत्स्नतोच्यते 5.16.78cd
अग्निरेव यतः सर्वप्रकाशो जगतीष्यते 1.5.184ab
अग्निरेष यतस्तस्मादुपास्योऽयं प्रयत्नतः 1.2.161cd
अग्निर्धर्मस्तदुत्थानाद्रात्रिरर्चिस्तथैव च 6.2.102ab
अग्निर्मूर्धेति च तथा मन्त्रेणापि प्रकाशितः 1.4.35ab
अग्निर्हिमस्य भेषजमिति चातोऽन्यथा भवेत् 4.3.1748cd

अग्निर्हिरण्यगर्भो वा ह्यापस्तत्कारणं मताः 3.2.18ab
अग्निवत्फलभोक्तृत्वान्नो चेदाकाशकल्पता SV 142ab
अग्निसंबन्धतो न्याय्यो वनस्थस्यापि संभवात् 6.2.125cd
अग्निस्तु सात्त्विकं रूपमाधेयत्वेन स क्षितौ 1.5.172ab
अग्निहोत्राग्निसंस्कारं यतो नावाप शापतः 3.9.130cd
अग्निहोत्राभिसंबन्धात्स्यातां वा श्रुतिचोदिते 1.5.42cd
अग्निहोत्राहुतेः साक्षाच्छ्रुतावेव समीरितम् 1.5.59cd
अग्नीषोमात्मना श्रुत्या ध्यानार्थमिह भण्यते 4.2.45cd
अग्नेः पश्चिमतोऽथान्ते प्राक्शिराः संविशेत्ततः 6.3.55cd
अग्नेः प्रकाशरूपस्य साधारत्वेन संस्थिता 1.5.171cd
अग्नेरन्यस्य पुंसोऽग्निज्वलनादिनिमित्ततः 4.4.314ab
अग्नेरर्चिर्यथा भास्वत्सत्त्वोत्कर्षात्तथा मनः 2.3.165ab
अग्नेरात्यन्तिको नाशो भवतापि न मृष्यते 4.3.1587ab
अग्नेर्धूमाच्च धूमस्य कार्यत्वस्य समीक्षणात् 4.3.749ab
अग्नेश्चाव्यभिचारित्वात्कार्यस्यापि स्वभावता 4.3.755ab
अग्नौ प्रास्ताहुतिः सम्यगादित्यमुपतिष्ठते 1.5.60ab
अग्न्यम्बुभिश्च शमनं तथाग्नेरेव दृश्यते 4.3.235cd
अग्न्यादयस्तथा लोका अमृताद्याश्च देवताः 3.9.108cd
अग्न्यादावेकशः कार्यो यावन्मन्थावमर्शनम् 6.3.24cd
अग्न्यादिदृष्टिभिश्चास्य देहः प्राक्प्रतिपादितः 3.1.40cd
अग्न्यादिदेवतांशा ये भोगार्थं कर्मणार्जिताः 3.2.125ab
अग्न्यादिदेवताः सोऽयमुपसंहार उच्यते 3.2.126cd
अग्न्यादिदेवतानां च व्याप्तिरेतावती मता 3.3.145cd
अग्न्यादिभेदभिन्नानां देवतानामशेषतः 1.2.227ab
अग्न्यादिषु परिस्पन्दो वायोरेवेति निश्चयः 1.5.372cd
अग्न्यादिषु यतः षट्सु यथोक्ताः सर्वदेवताः 3.9.20ab
अग्न्यादीनां तु सांशत्वाद्बलवद्भिस्तदिन्धनैः SV 144cd
अग्न्यादीनामिव तत आत्मानेकत्वमापतेत् 2.1.603cd
अग्न्यादौ विप्रकृष्टेऽर्थे निश्चिता जायते मतिः 4.3.732cd
अग्न्याद्यौष्ण्यादिवच्चेन्न द्रष्टुरस्याविनाशतः 4.3.1551cd
अग्न्युष्णवच्चाशक्योऽतः कर्मोत्थ इति भाषितुम् 4.4.310cd
अग्रजः प्रथमोद्भूतेस्तदन्यत्कार्यजन्मनः 5.4.4cd

अग्रहासंभवान्नैवं सर्वज्ञा देवता यतः 2.1.122cd
अग्रात्प्रभृति वंशोऽयमावेदब्रह्ममूलतः 2.6.4ab
अग्रे चलत्वमूर्मीणां मध्य ईषच्चलात्मता 5.1.51ab
अग्रे प्रथमतः सृष्टेरग्रजस्य प्रजापतेः 5.5.6ab
अघटादिव्युदासेन न घटाद्यर्थसंगतिः 4.3.1663ab
अघटार्थव्युदासाच्च घटार्थस्यावबोधनम् 4.3.1665cd
अङ्कुरादि मतं कार्यं नोभयत्रापि युज्यते 1.2.38cd
अङ्कुराद्यभिनिष्पत्तौ मुख्यतैवं हि तेजसः 2.3.43cd
अङ्कुराद्यात्मना तद्वद्बीजमेव तु कारणम् 2.4.323cd
अङ्गं वा वीर्यवद्दृष्टं पुंसां प्रायेण दक्षिणम् 4.2.38ab
अङ्गप्रधानवद्येन कल्पेतात्रैकवाक्यता SV 832cd
अङ्गस्य कृष्णसारस्य चक्षुषः करणस्य च 4.3.1941ab
अङ्गादङ्गात्संभवसि जग्धान्नपरिणामतः 6.4.39ab
अङ्गानां करणानां च रसः सारो यतस्ततः 1.3.207ab
अङ्गाराङ्कितमुत्पाते वारिराशेरिवोदकम् 3.5.45cd
अङ्गारावक्षयणोक्त्या विद्वान्कि ब्रह्म श्रेयसः 3.9.66ab
अङ्गाराश्चन्द्रमास्तस्मिन्हुतेऽग्नौ सोमसंभवः 6.2.93ab
अङ्गीकर्तव्यमेतच्च भवद्भिरविशङ्कितैः 1.2.78ab
अङ्गीकृत्य प्रदृश्यन्ते प्रवृत्ताः सर्व एव हि 1.4.1488cd
अङ्गुल्याद्यभिधानोक्तौ न हि तद्वान्प्रबुध्यते 2.1.124ab
अङ्गुष्ठानामिकाभ्यां तद्रेत आदाय चात्मनः 6.4.25ab
अचित्कत्वात्प्रधानादि पुंसो न स्थानमिष्यते 3.2.142ab
अचिन्त्या चाप्रतर्क्या च प्राणभावेन च स्थिता 3.6.27ab
अचेतनत्वानित्यत्वदोषदुष्टं पुरोदितम् 3.2.147cd
अचेतनांशप्राधान्यात्कार्यकारणतोच्यते 2.5.23ab
अचेतने जगत्यस्मिन्साक्ष्येवैकोऽत्र चेतनः 2.4.481ab
अचेतनेषु लोकेऽस्मिन्न दृष्टा पुरुषाभिधा 2.3.66ab
अचेतनैकनीडत्वं मयापीह प्रसाध्यते 4.4.477ab
अचेतनोऽपि बुद्ध्यादिश्चेतनावानिवेक्ष्यते 4.3.344ab
अचेतनो यथा जाल ऊर्णनाभेः सचेतनात् 2.1.392ab
अचैतन्यात्तथोक्तस्य कुतो भोक्तृत्वसंभवः 2.1.134ab
अजत्वादेव निःशेषविकाराणामपाक्रिया 4.4.702cd

अजमेकं स्वतःसिद्धं प्रत्यग्रूपमनन्यदृक्	1.2.26ab
अजागलस्तनस्येव प्रमाणाद्बन्धमोक्षयोः	4.4.457cd
अजातशत्रुः काश्योऽतो गार्ग्यबुद्धिविरुद्धधीः	2.1.31cd
अजातशत्रुजनकसुलभादिनिदर्शनात्	1.4.1645ab
अजातशत्रुरैकात्म्याद्गार्ग्याचार्यः प्रकल्पते	2.1.18cd
अजातशत्र्वभिप्रेतब्रह्मणः प्राक्प्रमाणतः	2.1.115cd
अजातिब्रह्मतत्त्वं मां योऽयं जात्यात्मनेक्षते	2.4.252cd
अजोऽजरश्च तेनोक्तोऽमरश्चैष ततः स्मृतः	4.4.1332cd
अजो न जायते नेति ध्यायतीवेति चागमैः	4.4.356ab
अजो न जायते यस्मान्महान्सर्वमहत्तरः	4.4.736cd
अज्ञः कामाङ्कुशाकृष्टो जायते म्रियतेऽसकृत्	4.4.250cd
अज्ञस्तु श्रावितोऽप्यस्माद्विना नाप्नोति तत्फलम्	SV 785cd
अज्ञात आत्मा जगतः कारणं न गुणत्रयम्	1.4.480cd
अज्ञात एव यद्यत्र ज्ञाते तस्मिन्न तद्भवेत्	1.4.441ab
अज्ञात एव सर्वत्र मानानां मेय उच्यते	4.4.893ab
अज्ञात एष एवात्मा तावन्मात्रसतत्त्वतः	4.4.1005ab
अज्ञातं जगदज्ञाते ज्ञाते ज्ञातं च यत्र तत्	1.4.952ab
अज्ञातं ज्ञायते यस्य तथाजातं च जायते	1.2.64ab
अज्ञातं न यथा मानान्मिथ्याधीसंशयौ तथा	1.4.257ab
अज्ञातं यदि वा ज्ञातं वस्तु नानात्वभाङ्न हि	4.4.659cd
अज्ञातं वस्तु चोद्दिश्य तत्तत्त्वप्रतिपत्तये	4.4.217ab
अज्ञातं संशयज्ञातं मिथ्याज्ञातमिदं जगत्	2.5.137ab
अज्ञातः पुरुषो यस्मात्कार्यकारणशब्दभाक्	2.3.65ab
अज्ञातः संशयज्ञातो मिथ्याज्ञातो न भित्तये	4.4.660cd
अज्ञातचितिवत्तस्मादज्ञातोऽनुभवः स्मृतः	4.4.900cd
अज्ञातज्ञाततोऽन्यत्वान्निर्देश्यं न तदक्षरम्	3.8.53ab
अज्ञातज्ञापकं शास्त्रमेवंस्वाभाव्यतो मितेः	2.1.493ab
अज्ञातज्ञापनं चातो विधिरत्राभिधीयते	2.4.115ab
अज्ञातज्ञापनं तस्माद्विधिरत्रोपपद्यते	2.4.198ab
अज्ञातज्ञापनं मुक्त्वा न चेहास्त्यपरो विधिः	4.4.924ab
अज्ञातज्ञापनादन्यच्छास्त्रान्नेति पुरोदितम्	SV 852cd
अज्ञाततत्त्वः स परो न भुनक्ति ह्यतद्विदम्	1.4.1676ab

अज्ञातत्वं न मानेभ्यो ज्ञातत्वं तत्कृतं यतः 1.4.295ab
अज्ञातत्वं विना मानं नाहंप्रत्यय आत्मनः SV 1074ab
अज्ञातत्वक्षतिं कुर्वन्मानं मानत्वमश्नुते SV 989ab
अज्ञातत्वमतो वाच्यमात्मनोऽत्र घटादिवत् SV 1074cd
अज्ञातत्वस्य माव्याप्तेः पूर्वमेव प्रसिद्धितः SV 686ab
अज्ञातत्वान्यथाज्ञातसिद्धेरात्मैकसाक्षितः 4.4.359ab
अज्ञातत्वापनुन्मानात्किमन्यदिति कथ्यताम् 1.4.248cd
अज्ञातत्वापमार्ष्ट्यर्थमुपादित्सन्ति मानिनः 1.2.101ab
अज्ञातत्वाविशेषेऽपि मानानां यदि मानता SV 689ab
अज्ञातब्रह्मतत्त्वस्य दुःसंभाव्यमिदं वचः 2.1.90ab
अज्ञातमिथ्याविज्ञाततत्त्वमात्रावलम्बिना 1.4.1457ab
अज्ञातमिथ्याविज्ञाततत्त्वमात्रैकनिष्ठितम् 5.1.11ab
अज्ञातमिथ्याविज्ञानरूपत्वान्न तु तत्त्वतः 2.3.65cd
अज्ञातमेव च ज्ञातं नातश्चोद्यस्य संभवः 4.3.1483cd
अज्ञातरज्जुतत्त्वो हि रज्जुं सर्पधियेक्षते 1.3.65ab
अज्ञातवस्तुतत्त्वस्य दुष्करं नास्ति किं चन 1.4.499ab
अज्ञातवस्तुना योगो मानस्येह यतस्ततः 4.4.684ab
अज्ञातवस्तुहेत्वेव यस्मान्नाना ततोऽवदत् 4.4.669ab
अज्ञातस्य प्रमेयस्य युक्तः स्वध्वान्तसाक्षिणः 3.4.88cd
अज्ञातात्मातिरेकेण ब्रुवतः कारणं तथा 1.4.238ab
अज्ञातात्मावबोधित्वात्तथा पूर्वमवादिषम् 1.4.413cd
अज्ञातात्मा ह्यविद्योत्थसंघातो देहलिङ्गवान् 1.4.1783ab
अज्ञातात्मैकसंसिद्धबीजावस्थमिदं जगत् 1.4.191ab
अज्ञातात्मैकसाक्षित्वादज्ञानोत्थं न वस्तुगम् 1.4.724cd
अज्ञातात्मैकहेतूनां मिथोपेक्षात्मनां श्रुतौ 1.4.400ab
अज्ञातादात्मनः साक्षादभिव्यक्तिः पुरोदिता 1.6.7ab
अज्ञाताधिगमं कुर्वन्मानं स्यात्सर्ववादिनाम् 1.2.24ab
अज्ञातायां यथा रज्ज्वां तदध्यस्तैकरूपिणाम् 1.4.673ab
अज्ञातायां यथा शुक्तौ रजताद्यर्थनिश्चितिः 4.4.901ab
अज्ञातार्थाधिगतौ तु ज्ञानं मानमितीर्यते 4.4.747cd
अज्ञातार्थाधिगमनं त्वदुक्ते तन्न युज्यते 4.3.158cd
अज्ञातावगमे यद्वत्प्रमातर्यर्पितं फलम् SV 1077ab

अज्ञाते च तथाज्ञातमेतदेव तदुच्यते 2.4.392cd
अज्ञाते जगदज्ञातं ज्ञाते ज्ञातं च यत्र तत् 2.1.87ab
अज्ञाते न विरोधोऽस्ति ज्ञाते चान्यानपेक्षतः 1.4.1296cd
अज्ञातैकात्म्यकार्यं तद्यदेतदभिशब्दितम् 1.6.2ab
अज्ञातैकात्म्ययाथात्म्यो यदा त्विह विवक्ष्यते 2.1.26ab
अज्ञातोऽर्थः प्रमेयः स्याज्ज्ञाते कोऽतिशयो मितेः 1.4.1296ab
अज्ञातोऽर्थोऽन्यतो यस्मान्नैवैकात्म्यात्प्रसिध्यति 4.4.894ab
अज्ञातोऽलुप्तदृष्टिर्यः स आत्मा ज्योतिरुच्यते 4.3.332cd
अज्ञात्वैव परं तत्त्वमेवं प्राप्ते परा श्रुतिः 1.4.1665cd
अज्ञात्वैव परं देवमागमापायरूपिणः 1.4.1675ab
अज्ञानं कारणं तत्र कार्यत्वं परिशिष्टयोः 1.4.1368cd
अज्ञानं च तदुत्थं च ह्यात्मैवाज्ञाततत्त्वकः 2.1.174ab
अज्ञानं चेच्चिदाकारं संशयादिषु का कथा 1.4.1502ab
अज्ञानं तदुपाश्रित्य ब्रह्म कारणमुच्यते 1.4.371cd
अज्ञानं संशयज्ञानं मिथ्याज्ञानमिति त्रिकम् 1.4.1368ab
अज्ञानं संशयत्वान्नो मिथ्याज्ञानात्तथैव च 1.4.440ab
अज्ञानकामजन्यत्वं वाङ्मनःकायकर्मणाम् 3.5.120ab
अज्ञानकालेऽप्यस्तीह किमुताज्ञाननिह्नुतौ 4.4.519cd
अज्ञानध्वंसकारित्वान्मोक्षो ज्ञानस्य भण्यते 3.3.90ab
अज्ञानध्वंसि विज्ञानं न च कारकरूपताम् 4.4.942ab
अज्ञानभूमिगं वस्तु मानसंगतिमाप्नुवत् 3.4.117ab
अज्ञानमनभिव्यक्तिर्बोधोऽभिव्यक्तिरात्मनः 3.3.95ab
अज्ञानमनिराकुर्वज्ज्ञानमेव न सिध्यति 3.3.69ab
अज्ञानमन्यथाज्ञानमतो नास्त्यात्मसाक्षिणः 4.4.359cd
अज्ञानमागमज्ञानं सांगत्यं नास्त्यतोऽनयोः 3.3.71cd
अज्ञानमात्रव्यवधेर्ब्रह्मैकात्म्यफलस्य च 2.5.82ab
अज्ञानमात्रव्यवधौ वस्तुनि व्यापृतिर्मितेः 3.3.21ab
अज्ञानमात्रहेतौ तु सर्वमेतत्समञ्जसम् 1.4.379ab
अज्ञानमात्रोपाधित्वादविद्यामुषितात्मभिः 1.4.372ab
अज्ञानमिथ्याविज्ञातप्रत्यक्त्वादात्मवस्तुनः 4.3.380cd
अज्ञानमिथ्याविज्ञानसंस्थस्यास्यात्मनः क्व नु 4.3.1410ab
अज्ञानमिथ्यासंशीतिव्यतिरेकेण नापरम् 4.4.787ab

अज्ञानमेव बाध्यं नो मानस्येह यतस्ततः 1.4.419ab
अज्ञानमेव मिथ्याधीः प्रमेयानभिसंगतेः 1.4.1217ab
अज्ञानलक्षणं शास्त्राज्ज्ञानं हन्ति समुत्पतत् SV 903cd
अज्ञानसंगतिं मुक्त्वा न स्यात्तज्जेन संगतिः 2.1.308cd
अज्ञानस्यापि तेनैव सत्यत्वं केन वार्यते 1.4.442cd
अज्ञानहानं नो मुक्तिस्तस्याः कर्म न साधनम् 3.3.37ab
अज्ञानहेतोरन्यादृक्स च ज्ञानान्निवर्तते 1.4.1018cd
अज्ञानहेत्वनर्थार्थकारिता गम्यते मितेः 1.3.90cd
अज्ञानात्संसरत्यत्र वर्ण्यते तत्समासतः 4.4.168cd
अज्ञानादभिमानोऽयं बुद्ध्यादौ विषयावधौ 2.4.353cd
अज्ञानादात्मनस्तद्वत्तेजोबन्नादिविक्रिया 4.4.178cd
अज्ञानादि तथा कृत्स्नमात्मनोऽन्यत्र वेदने 4.4.871cd
अज्ञानादित्रयं तस्मात्स्वतोबोधैकसंश्रयम् 4.4.898cd
अज्ञानादित्रयं प्रत्यगाभासं यद्यपीष्यते 3.3.41ab
अज्ञानादित्रयं बाध्यं मेययाथात्म्यसंश्रयात् 4.4.788ab
अज्ञानादि पुनः कर्तुं शक्यतेऽकारकत्वतः SV 136cd
अज्ञानादेश्च चिद्रूपं तद्याथात्म्यान्न वार्यते 4.4.652cd
अज्ञानाद्यनिरासेन नास्ति लोके प्रबोधकम् 4.4.786cd
अज्ञानाद्यात्मिका सिद्धा द्वैविध्यं स्यात्तदा कुतः 4.4.892cd
अज्ञानानुपमर्देन व्याकृतिर्यास्य जायते 1.2.132ab
अज्ञानान्तरितत्वेन संप्राप्तत्यक्तयोः पुनः SV 888ab
अज्ञानान्नान्यदस्तित्वं सर्वस्यानात्मनो यथा 4.3.1521ab
अज्ञानान्यार्थविज्ञानप्रसक्तावेव युज्यते 3.9.197ab
अज्ञानान्यार्थविज्ञानप्रसङ्गाङ्गीकृतावपि 3.9.198ab
अज्ञानिनः स्यान्मरणं संसर्गः कारणात्मनि 1.4.1673ab
अज्ञाने सति संसारो वद केन निवार्यते 4.4.769cd
अज्ञानोच्छित्तये ज्ञानं स्वतन्त्रं तेन भण्यते SV 373cd
अज्ञानोत्थमनूद्यातो मिथ्याक्लृप्तमशेषतः 2.4.239ab
अज्ञानोत्थमिदं जाग्रज्जडरूपसमन्वयात् 4.3.1073ab
अज्ञायमानो मात्रादिर्न यस्मादनुभूयते 4.4.900ab
अणिमादावविद्योत्थे पराक्चित्ततया रताः 4.4.602cd
अणिमानमणोर्भावं कार्श्यं देहो यदैत्ययम् 4.3.1927ab

अणुमात्रं न तद्ग्राह्यं वस्तु यन्निष्प्रमाणकम्	3.3.80cd
अणुरात्मैकयाथात्म्यज्ञानं पन्थाः पुरातनः	4.4.546cd
अणुस्थूलादिनिःशेषविकल्पातिक्रमादयम्	4.4.546ab
अणून्प्रत्येकशः सर्वान्स गृह्णीयादयत्नतः	3.2.108ab
अण्डस्यान्तस्त्विमे लोकाः सप्तद्वीपा च मेदिनी	3.7.40cd
अण्डाद्बहिः पुराणे तु विरोधे स्मृतिबाधनम्	3.3.149cd
अण्डान्तमेव व्याख्यातं किमन्यदवशिष्यते	3.6.19cd
अण्डारम्भकभूतानां ब्रह्मलोकाभिधेष्यते	3.6.18cd
अण्वन्तानिति शब्दोऽयं न स्यात्पशुविशेषणम्	4.1.8ab
अण्वाद्यवयवं मूर्तं पीनं संस्थानवद्दृढम्	2.3.23ab
अत आपेषणाद्योऽसावुत्थितः करणैः सह	2.1.154ab
अत आहाविनाशित्वाद्द्रष्टुर्दृष्टिकृतः सदा	4.3.1552ab
अत इत्यादिकं तस्मादाजगामोत्तरं वचः	4.4.1168cd
अत ऊर्ध्वं विमोक्षायेत्युक्तं प्राग्यत्पुनः पुनः	4.3.1813ab
अत ऊर्ध्वमिति गिरा निरुणद्ध्येव मां नृपः	4.3.1892cd
अत एव च रागादिसंसृष्टोऽपि विविच्यते	SV 492ab
अत एव मनुष्यत्वहेतवोऽप्यसुराः समम्	1.3.177ab
अत एव श्रुतिर्यत्नाच्छमादीनेव वक्ष्यति	4.4.1025ab
अत एव सभागत्वं वाक्यवाक्यार्थयोर्मतम्	SV 868ab
अत ऐकात्म्ययाथात्म्यज्ञानादज्ञानहानतः	SV 397ab
अतः कर्त्रादितन्त्रत्वात्सर्वकामादिवस्तुनः	4.4.451ab
अतः कामयमानत्वं कर्तृतन्त्रमबोधतः	4.4.261cd
अतः कामाशयवशात्सृज्यतेऽन्नं मुहुर्मुहुः	3.2.69cd
अतः कृताधिकारोऽपि यो विद्यादकृतार्थताम्	SV 539ab
अतः क्रियातिरेकेण नास्त्यन्यन्मुक्तिसाधनम्	SV 191cd
अतः परं परावस्था निरविद्या प्रदर्श्यते	4.3.1295cd
अतः परं प्रयत्नेन श्रुत्या व्याख्यायते स्फुटम्	3.1.1cd
अतः परमनन्तत्वाद्गणितं विनिवर्तते	4.3.1876ab
अतः प्रजापतौ तत्त्वं कृमौ वा न विशिष्यते	SV 354ab
अतः प्रमाणतोऽशक्याविद्यास्येति निरीक्षितुम्	SV 184ab
अतः प्रैषादितुल्योऽयं क्रियाफलनिबन्धनः	SV 518ab
अतः प्रैषादिसंसृष्टोऽप्यर्थः सिद्धो विवेकतः	SV 501cd

अतः श्रुतिवचो न्याय्यं तस्मादेषामितीरितम् 1.4.1803ab
अतः संन्यस्य कर्माणि सर्वाण्यात्मावबोधतः SV 219ab
अतः समीहितोपायतया वस्त्ववबोधयन् SV 637ab
अतः सर्वं कृतं ज्ञानं नातोऽन्यदवशिष्यते 4.3.1302cd
अतः सर्वविकल्पानामविद्यामात्रहेततः 4.3.402ab
अतः सर्वानपेक्षं यत्स्वमहिम्नैव सिध्यति 4.3.1328ab
अतः सर्वोऽपि वेदोऽयं प्रमाणत्वैकहेतुतः SV 556ab
अतः सामान्यतो दृष्टं क्रियात्वादित्यदूषणम् SV 641cd
अतः सामान्यवृत्त्यात्मा प्राविशद्देहमीश्वरः 1.4.635cd
अतत्त्वज्ञस्य तमसो रज्ज्वज्ञानोरगादिवत् 1.3.314ab
अतत्त्वज्ञोऽधिकार्यत्र विद्याया उपवर्ण्यते 1.5.273cd
अतथ्यान्यपि तथ्यानि दर्शयन्तीह वादिनः 1.4.1628ab
अतद्धर्मक आभान्ति ह्यागमापायसाक्षिणि 1.4.668cd
अतद्वद्बोध एवैतत्सिध्यतीव न तु स्वः 3.8.125cd
अतद्वानपि संमोहाद्यथोक्तात्मकतामगात् 2.4.429cd
अतद्विकारतो जन्म प्रलयश्च तथात्मनः 2.1.453ab
अतस्तत्तत्त्वसंबोधात्तां जग्ध्वामृतमश्नुते 1.5.165cd
अतस्तत्त्वमसीत्युक्त्या तादात्म्यं प्रतिपाद्यते 3.9.153cd
अतस्तत्प्रतिषेधार्थं भूयोऽकाममितीरणम् 4.3.1345cd
अतस्तत्फलनिष्पत्तेः संप्रत्तिः संविधीयते 1.5.282cd
अतस्तत्स्मृतितः सम्यग्ज्ञानभानूदयो भवेत् 6.5.7cd
अतस्तदर्थमाहेयमेवम्विति पुनः श्रुतिः 1.3.159ab
अतस्तद्विषया तावत्कर्तृतेहोच्यते प्रभोः 1.4.674cd
अतस्तद्व्यभिचारेण नामरूपक्रियात्मनाम् 1.4.672ab
अतस्तस्यां निवृत्तायां कृत्स्नो भेदो निवर्तते 4.3.1792cd
अतस्मिंस्तदग्रहात्सर्वं मिथ्या स्यात्सविकल्पकम् 4.3.486ab
अतादात्म्यान्न हि घटं जनयन्तीह तन्तवः 3.2.88cd
अतिकारकहेतुश्च यथात्मायं सुषुप्तगः 4.3.1908ab
अतिक्रमो जयार्थश्चेत्सामर्थ्यादेव सिद्धितः 1.5.242ab
अतिक्रान्तं यतश्छन्दमतिच्छन्दमिदं ततः 4.3.1297cd
अतिक्रामति तान्यात्मा जाग्रत्स्थानाश्रयाण्यतः 4.3.459ab
अतिक्रामेदिमं लोकं नोभयत्रापि युज्यते 1.5.245cd

अतिग्रहाः स निष्कामो विद्वद्भिरभिधीयते 4.4.268cd
अतिच्छन्दा इति वचः कामाधारत्व आत्मनः 4.4.441ab
अतिच्छन्दा इति शुभं कामशोकनिषेधकृत् 4.4.454cd
अतिच्छन्दोक्तिबाधः स्याद्वस्तुतन्त्रत्वहेतुतः 4.4.451cd
अतिनिर्बन्धतो वापि निषेध्योऽयं प्रमादवान् 3.9.60ab
अतिनिर्मथनादग्निश्चन्दनादपि जायते 3.9.63cd
अतिप्रमाणविषयं ब्रह्म सर्वत्र विश्रुतम् 3.9.172cd
अतिभक्तितया मां त्वं मोक्षेऽपि न जिहाससि 2.4.67cd
अतिमानाभिधानस्य प्रत्यङ्मात्राद्वयात्मनः 2.3.174cd
अतिमोक्षाः स्युः सर्वत्र यथोक्तादेव लक्षणात् 3.1.46cd
अतिमोक्षातिदेशोक्तेस्तद्विशेषोऽथ भण्यते 3.2.9cd
अतिरोहितरूपं यज्जगत्यव्याकृते तथा 1.4.715ab
अतिरोहितसंवित्कं सदानस्तमितोदितम् 1.4.212ab
अतिरोहितसंवित्को व्यपास्ताशेषविक्रियः 2.3.225ab
अतिलङ्घ्यासुरं भावं देवतात्मानमाप्नुमः 1.3.32cd
अतिवर्तत आत्मायं वस्तुवृत्तानुरोधतः 4.3.1353cd
अतिशीतेरसद्भावान्न च बाधोऽस्य माश्रयात् 4.4.895cd
अतिशीतोऽग्निरित्यत्र दृष्टान्तानां शतैरपि 2.1.496ab
अतिष्ठा इति नामास्य तेनादित्यात्मनोऽभवत् 2.1.51ab
अतिसूक्ष्मशरीरा हि पुत्तिका प्लुषिरुच्यते 1.3.305ab
अतिसूक्ष्मस्वभावत्वादपि लोहसमुद्रगम् 4.4.86cd
अतिसूक्ष्माभिरेताभिर्जग्धमन्नं समास्रवत् 4.2.56ab
अतिसृष्टिरतः प्रोक्ता सातिसाध्वीति निश्चिता 1.4.163cd
अतिसृष्टिरनुग्राह्यसृष्टेः सा स्यात्प्रजापतेः 1.4.161cd
अतिस्नेहापकृष्टोमा देहार्धं शूलिनः श्रिता 2.4.69ab
अतीतत्वाच्च तद्वान्यै नालमात्मावबोधनम् 1.4.1530cd
अतीतानागतज्ञानं मिथ्येशस्य प्रसज्यते 1.2.109cd
अतीतानागतत्वादिभेदः स्यात्किंनिबन्धनः 2.1.406cd
अतीतानागतयोस्तु कालयोर्जगदात्मनः 3.8.12ab
अतीतानागताद्यर्थज्ञानोत्पत्तौ च हेतुताम् 1.4.87ab
अतीतानागतानां च मिथः कालासमागमात् 4.3.632cd
अतीतानागतेहत्यजन्मनाशादिहेतुनुत् 2.4.399ab

अतीतैष्यद्घटज्ञानं सद्घटालम्बनं भवेत् 1.2.108ab
अतीतैष्यन्मितघटप्रतिषेधस्तथाविधः 1.2.113cd
अतीतोऽनागतोऽर्थोऽसन्यदि वाभ्युपगम्यते 1.2.109ab
अतीत्य दुःखहेतून्या हन्ति दुःखान्यशेषतः 2.1.350ab
अतीत्य पितरं देवाः पितामहमुपासते 5.5.11ab
अतीत्य वस्तुवृत्तेन स्वमहिम्नि व्यवस्थितः 3.5.55cd
अतीत्य सर्वभूतानि प्राधान्येन स्थितो यतः 2.1.50ab
अतीन्द्रियत्वात्तद्व्यापि व्यापित्वाच्चामृतं ततः 2.3.31cd
अतीन्द्रियत्वात्तस्यापि कथं स्यात्तदुपासनम् 5.1.119ab
अतीन्द्रियार्थबोधित्वं समानं चोदनोक्तिभिः 2.4.165cd
अतीन्द्रिये तदन्येन ज्ञातुं शक्यं न तद्यतः 2.4.155cd
अतीन्द्रियो लिङ्गाद्यर्थः सिद्धिश्चास्य कथं भवेत् SV 625cd
अतीव कठिनं ज्ञानं त्वचातोऽस्य समागमात् 2.4.344ab
अतीव कामवशगः स्त्रीगुणोपेतया स्त्रिया 4.3.1312ab
अतीव जायते ह्लादो दृष्टान्तः स विवक्षितः 2.1.351cd
अतीव भास्वरास्माकं चक्षुर्मुट्सकृदुद्गता 2.3.166cd
अतृणाद इति तृणं नाद्याप्यत्ति मनागपि 1.5.53cd
अतोऽकृत्स्ना वयं मोहात्कृत्स्नात्मानोऽपि वस्तुतः 1.4.1083ab
अतोऽक्षरं प्रवक्तव्यं निरुपाध्यात्मनि स्थितम् 3.8.1cd
अतोऽज्ञस्यैव निःशेषमुमुक्षुप्रजिहासितः SV 138ab
अतोऽतिदृप्तोऽविज्ञातदर्पकारणघस्मरः 2.1.29ef
अतोऽत्र कर्मसामान्यं गृह्यते देहसंश्रितम् 1.6.27cd
अतोऽत्र विध्यभावोऽयं न कथं चन दूषणम् SV 238ab
अतोऽधिकारिविज्ञप्त्यै ब्रूष्यादिति विशेषणम् 6.4.50cd
अतोऽधिक्रियते प्रत्यग्ज्ञानोत्पत्तौ न रागवान् 2.4.94cd
अतोऽनधिगतावेशात्सर्वेषां संप्लवः कुतः SV 1078ab
अतोऽनपेक्षता युक्ता सर्वदैवाभिधाश्रुतेः 2.4.182ab
अतोऽनभ्युपगच्छद्भिर्मुक्तौ कर्त्रादिरात्मनः SV 148ab
अतोऽनवगतैकात्म्यकर्माधिकृतिहेतुतः SV 122cd
अतोऽनुज्ञार्थमेवाह मैत्रेयीमृषिरात्मनः 2.4.39cd
अतोऽनुपेतमेव त्वां करविन्यस्तबिल्ववत् 2.1.95ab
अतोऽनुभव एवैको विषयोऽज्ञातलक्षणः SV 1002ab

अतोऽनुभवतो लब्धमज्ञातं ज्ञापयत्सदा SV 990ab
अतोऽनुभवमुल्लङ्घ्य न भेदो नाप्यभिन्नता SV 986ab
अतोऽनुमीयतेऽस्त्यन्यद्यस्मिन्नसति नेक्षते 1.5.105ab
अतोऽनुमीयते पित्रा तेभ्यः प्रत्तं पयः पुरा 1.5.49cd
अतोऽनुविन्देदित्याह लाभार्थेनैव तत्फले 1.4.1019cd
अतोऽन्वय यथासिद्धमन्वयव्यतिरेकतः 2.1.169ab
अतोऽनेनैव रूपेण य उपास्ते दिवानिशम् 2.3.168ab
अतोऽन्यदार्तं तद्वच्चाप्येकमेवेति च श्रुतिः 1.3.186cd
अतोऽन्यमाक्रमं देहं प्राप्य भावनयाञ्जितः 4.4.136cd
अतोऽन्यविषयत्वात्सोऽविरोधः प्रागुदीरितः 5.1.78ab
अतोऽपि देवतैवेह वाक्शब्देनाभिधीयते 1.3.132ab
अतोऽपुरुषतन्त्रत्वान्नात्मज्ञाने विधिर्भवेत् 2.4.121ab
अतोऽभावत्वसिद्ध्यर्थमभावेनाप्यपेक्ष्यते 1.2.20ab
अतोऽभ्युपेयोऽज्ञातोऽर्थः प्रमाणत्वप्रसिद्धये 4.3.546cd
अतोऽर्थवादाद्धि विधिर्लिङ्गादत्रानुमीयते 1.3.39cd
अतोऽलमात्मने कामानागातुं स्वामिने तथा 1.3.367ab
अतोऽवगतिरेवात्र गतित्वेन विवक्ष्यते 4.2.35ab
अतोऽवगत्यभावोऽपि न स्वतोऽवगतिं विना 3.8.120ab
अतोऽवगम्यते ननं न कर्म सहतेऽखिलम् 4.5.27ab
अतोऽवधारणार्थाय तत्रैवग्रहणं कृतम् 2.3.34cd
अतोऽवबोधकत्वेन दुष्टकारणवर्जनात् SV 882ab
अतोऽविद्यामहानिद्रासंवीतमनसामसौ 1.4.1327ab
अतोऽविद्यासमुच्छित्तावियं संज्ञा निवर्तते 2.4.468cd
अतोऽविद्यासमुच्छित्तौ तद्धेतूनामशेषतः 4.4.383ab
अतोऽविद्यासमुच्छित्तौ मुक्तिः स्यात्परमात्मनः 4.3.1151cd
अतोऽविद्यासमुच्छित्तौ यथावस्त्ववबोधतः 4.4.166ab
अतोऽव्याकृतयाथात्म्यं व्याकृतेनोपदिश्यते 2.3.251ab
अतोऽशुद्धिनिषेधोक्तिस्तदविद्यानिषेधतः 1.4.486cd
अतोऽशेषमहानर्थहेतोर्मोहस्य हानये 4.3.1824ab
अतोऽशेषमहानर्थहेत्वात्माज्ञानहानिकृत् SV 1135ab
अतोऽसाधारणं वाच्यं रूपं संतानवस्तुनः 4.3.643ab
अतोऽस्मदीयदारेभ्य उत्थायान्यत आव्रज 6.4.90ab

अतोऽस्मि लोके वेदे च प्रथितः पुरुषोत्तमः 2.4.246cd
अतोऽस्यानभिसंबन्धः सर्वप्रत्यक्त्वहेतुतः 4.3.413cd
अतोऽहमित्यनेनैव ह्यात्मनात्मानमभ्यधात् 1.4.43cd
अतो गवादेर्भेदेऽपि सन्मात्रमवसीयते SV 965cd
अतो जिता हृता गावो याताः सर्वे यथायथम् 3.9.147cd
अतो दुःस्थितसिद्ध्येतत्पराग्वस्त्वन्तरात्मनि 1.4.975ab
अतो न जायत इति तद्विकारनिषेधतः 4.4.36cd
अतो नान्येन काम्यत्वं कर्मणः स्यात्कथं चन 1.3.95cd
अतो नान्योऽभिसंबन्धः कर्मविज्ञानकाण्डयोः SV 325cd
अतो नाभावनिष्ठः स्यादभावस्यापि निह्नवात् 2.3.198cd
अतो निमित्तादत्यर्थमहं पापमकारिषम् 4.4.1169ab
अतो नियत एवात्र व्यापारः फलवान्भवेत् 1.2.107cd
अतो निर्विषयत्वादि ब्रह्मैकत्वाद्यदीरितम् 2.1.581ab
अतो निषिद्धकाम्यादिवर्जनान्नात्ममुक्तता SV 50cd
अतो ब्राह्मण्यतोऽन्यद्यत्क्रियाकारकलक्षणम् 3.5.214ab
अतो भयादिमां विद्यां युवाभ्यां न ब्रवीम्यहम् 2.5.100ab
अतो भोक्ता स्वयंसिद्धो यथोक्तेनैव हेतुना 4.3.1133ab
अतो मात्रादिसंभेदो यत्र यत्र निवर्तते 2.3.228ab
अतो मात्राद्यभावेऽपि योऽज्ञातत्वस्य सिद्धये 4.4.897ab
अतो मानोत्थविज्ञानध्वस्ता साप्येत्यथात्मताम् SV 177cd
अतो मुक्तिं परीच्छद्भिरुत्पत्त्यादिविरोधिनीम् 6.2.11ab
अतो मृषात्वसिद्ध्यर्थं तनुनाडीपरिग्रहः 4.3.1213cd
अतो यथोक्तादेतस्मात्साध्यसाधनलक्षणात् 3.2.6ab
अतो यदेव साध्यार्थसाधनत्वेन गम्यते SV 632ab
अतो लोकहितार्थं तं पुत्रमाहुर्मनीषिणः 1.5.299cd
अतो विरोधनुत्त्यर्थं सत्यत्वप्रतिपत्तये 5.1.61ab
अतो विवेको भूतानां यः परोऽतीव शुद्धितः 4.4.35ab
अतो विशेषकार्येण विशेष्यन्ते हृदैव ते 4.4.402cd
अतो विशेष्यते श्रुत्या द्विषन्भ्रातृव्यरूपया 1.3.190cd
अत्तारोऽतोऽन्नविरहान्नालं स्थानाय संहताः 1.4.154cd
अत्तृसर्गोऽथवोक्तः प्रागन्नसर्गोऽधुनोच्यते 1.2.170ab
अत्यक्रामदिति त्वस्य निर्बीजावस्थतोच्यते 2.4.386cd

अत्यन्तं क्षेममाप्नोतीत्यापस्तम्बोऽप्यभाषत 4.4.1067cd
अत्यन्ततनुतो ह्यन्तर्विन्ध्यादेरीक्षणं कुतः 4.3.1212cd
अत्यन्तभेदो विज्ञेयः संसारीश्वरयोरतः 1.4.1240cd
अत्यन्तमपि शूराणां स्वस्वभावैकहेतुतः 1.2.187ab
अत्यन्तमभिधेयस्य विराजैक्यं प्रपद्यते 5.16.8cd
अत्यन्तसंनिकृष्टानामपि भिन्नात्मनां मितेः 2.1.353ab
अत्यन्ताननुभूतेषु हिमवत्पृष्ठवस्तुषु SV 995ab
अत्यन्तापूर्वदृष्टेऽर्थे प्राङ्नाद्राक्षमिमं नगम् 1.4.270ab
अत्यन्ताप्राप्तमर्थं हि विधयो बोधयन्ति नः SV 413ab
अत्ययश्चेदभिप्रेतः पुत्रोत्पत्त्यादिभिस्त्रिभिः 1.5.259ab
अत्यर्थं मधुररसाः सन्तु ह्योषधयश्च नः 6.3.46cd
अत्यर्थं व्यापृता दृष्टा वाचमूचुस्ततः सुराः 1.3.128cd
अत्यल्पं भवताभाणि सर्वमात्मैव नो यतः 2.3.62cd
अत्यवादीस्त्वमज्ञः सन्का विद्या फलिनी तव 3.9.66cd
अत्येति वस्तुवृत्तेन स साक्षादिति गृह्यताम् 3.5.56cd
अत्येतीति तु ये पाठं कुर्वते तेऽविपश्चितः 3.3.132ab
अत्र चोपनिषच्छब्दो ब्रह्मविद्यैकगोचरः SV 3ab
अत्र ज्ञाते यतः सर्व ऐकात्म्यं यान्त्यशेषतः 1.4.750ab
अत्र यत्प्रतिवक्तव्यं तदुक्तमसकृत्पुरा 3.2.45ab
अत्र विप्रतिपद्यन्ते तदन्यात्मनिषेधिनः 1.4.143ab
अत्रात्मत्वादुपेयस्य का शङ्का मानतां प्रति SV 901cd
अत्रापि युगपज्ज्ञानमुक्तयोः पक्षयोर्यथा 4.3.1128ab
अत्राप्यनर्थकं कर्म तत्फलासंभवत्वतः SV 263ab
अत्रायमित्यनेनात्र पूर्वपक्षनिराक्रिया 4.3.962ab
अत्रास्थूलादिवाक्यानामुपास्यार्थसमर्पणे 1.4.791ab
अत्राह यदि विज्ञानजन्ममात्रात्प्रसिध्यति 4.3.737ab
अत्रैव कल्पेऽनावृत्तिर्न त्वन्येष्वनिवारणात् 6.2.145cd
अत्रैव च क्रियायोगे तद्रूपाह्वः स इष्यते 1.4.677cd
अत्रैव संनिमज्जन्ति प्राणाः सर्वे स्वकारणे 1.4.1755ab
अत्रैवेति फलं चोक्त्वा प्रथमायाः समुच्चितेः 1.4.1757ab
अत्रोच्यतेऽन्यदेवेदं विज्ञानान्तरमात्मगम् 1.4.802ab
अत्रोच्यते ह्यभिप्रेतं गम्यमानं प्रमाणतः SV 201ab

अथ कः संशयो येन स तेनैवं नियुज्यते 4.2.15ef
अथ काममयत्वेऽस्य संसारोऽपि न वार्यते 4.4.455cd
अथ कारणसंसर्गो नाशशब्देन भण्यते 1.4.1750ab
अथ कार्यान्तराभावेऽप्यस्य कार्यत्वमिष्यते SV 613cd
अथ कुर्वदभीष्टं तत्तत्कार्यं तर्हि भण्यताम् 1.4.326ab
अथ केन क्रमेणायं सुषुप्तं प्रतिपद्यते 2.1.319ab
अथ क्रियैव प्राक्कार्योत्सिद्धं नो यत्समीहितम् SV 610cd
अथ गार्हस्थ्य एवायं कर्मकाले विभिन्नधीः 1.4.1725ab
अथ चेन्मोक्ष्यते सोऽत्र यस्य संपत्स्यते तथा SV 72cd
अथ ज्ञानात्तदभवत्कृत्स्नं ब्रह्मेति चेन्मतम् 1.4.1116ab
अथ तद्विपरीतेन संगतिर्ज्योतिषेक्ष्यते 4.3.25cd
अथ तन्मान्तरायोग्यं विध्यभावेऽपि तत्तथा SV 676cd
अथ तस्यावदत्पूर्वं योषिदालिङ्गने यथा 4.4.253ab
अथ द्वितीयोऽभिमतो न तथाप्युपपद्यते 1.4.1715cd
अथ नाशोऽपि नैवास्ति तं विना सदिदं जगत् 1.2.48cd
अथ निश्चयसिद्ध्यर्थमुत्पन्नेऽपि प्रवर्त्यते SV 664ab
अथ नैतदमानत्वं काममस्तु न वार्यते 1.4.909ab
अथ प्रकल्प्य संबन्धं घटस्येत्यभिधीयते 1.2.119ab
अथ प्रजात्मना तस्यां जायेय स्थास्नुकर्मणे 1.4.1825ab
अथ प्रसिद्धोऽसावात्मा तद्दृष्टिः किं विधीयते 2.4.139cd
अथ प्रस्पन्दतेऽत्यर्थं सा क्रिया प्राण उच्यते 1.4.1845cd
अथ ब्रवीषि भेदोऽत्र स्याद्द्वयोर्धर्मधर्मिणोः 4.3.1697ab
अथ ब्राह्मण इत्युक्त्या फलावस्थास्य भण्यते 3.5.190ab
अथ भेदस्तयोरिष्टो व्यवधानं प्रसज्यते 4.4.335ab
अथ मन्तव्य इत्यस्य प्रपञ्चः पर उच्यते 2.4.263cd
अथ मर्त्योऽमृतः प्राज्ञो भवतीत्येष निश्चयः 4.4.403cd
अथ मर्त्योऽमृतो भवत्यत्र ब्रह्म समश्नुते SV 355cd
अथ मानान्तरापेक्षं तन्मानं मेयबोधकम् SV 683ab
अथ मुक्तौ तदन्वेति कारणेन सहान्वियात् 4.4.769ab
अथ मूर्तरसोक्त्यापि चेतनस्यैव चेद्ग्रहः 2.3.62ab
अथ मेयप्रभेदेऽपि प्रमाणैकत्वमिष्यते SV 822ab
अथ यत्रात्ममोहोत्थं घ्नन्तीवैनमितीक्षणम् 4.3.1248ab

अथ यत्रेति चाल्पस्य प्राणान्तस्य च लक्षणम् 2.4.99cd
अथ यस्य गृहस्थस्य पत्न्या जारो भवेत्क्वचित् 6.4.49ab
अथ यानीतराणीति ह्युद्गातान्नाद्यमात्मने 1.3.365ab
अथ ये शतमित्यादिवाक्यैरेतत्प्रपञ्चितम् SV 1020ab
अथ योऽन्यामिति गिरा प्राहाविद्यां तथा फलम् 4.4.413cd
अथ योऽन्यामिति ग्रन्थादारभ्योरुप्रयत्नतः 1.5.1ab
अथ योऽन्यामिति तथा भेददृष्टिनिराकृतेः 2.5.81ab
अथ योऽन्यामिति तथाविद्यां चानूद्य नश्वरीम् 2.1.10ab
अथ यो वेदेति तथा ज्ञातृसाक्षित्वमात्मनः 2.1.314ab
अथर्वाङ्गिरसस्तद्वन्मन्त्राः स्युर्ब्राह्मणोद्धृताः 2.4.313cd
अथ वस्तुनि तन्मानं न लये स्यान्न च द्वये SV 393cd
अथ वस्तु पृथक्त्वेन विशिष्टं गम्यते तदा SV 961ab
अथ वस्त्वन्तरज्ञानं नितरां तस्य वस्तुता SV 978ab
अथवा पुरुषार्थत्वात्प्रज्ञायाः करणं नृणाम् 4.4.866ab
अथवा लक्षणोक्तिः स्याद्यथोक्तब्रह्मवेदिनः 3.5.207ab
अथ विज्ञातसंबन्धं सिद्धार्थं स्याद्विधायकम् SV 731cd
अथ व्यावर्तते तेभ्यो गोत्वं ते खण्डवद्भवेत् 1.6.56cd
अथ शक्त्यन्तराच्छक्तिरनवस्था प्रसज्यते 2.1.404cd
अथशब्दोऽत्र हेत्वर्थ उक्तस्य तदपेक्षतः 4.4.255ab
अथशब्दो विकल्पार्थो यथोक्तानां यथारुचि 6.4.80ab
अथ शापभयाद्बद्ध्यात्पत्ये कामितमादरात् 6.4.35ab
अथ शास्त्रप्रमाणत्वाददृष्टाप्यभ्युपेयते SV 648ab
अथ श्रवणभावार्थविषयं कार्यमिष्यते SV 804ab
अथ सत्यपि संमोहे संघातश्चेद्विशीर्यते 1.4.1751cd
अथ संभूय सर्वाणि मुक्तिं कर्माणि कुर्वते 3.3.48cd
अथ सावयवत्वेऽपि नित्यं स्यात्कुलिशादिवत् 1.4.595ab
अथ सोमादिसंबद्धे यागादौ विषये मतः SV 609ab
अथ स्वप्रक्रियाक्लृप्तं स्वभावादि परीक्ष्यते 4.3.768cd
अथ स्वभावसंत्यागे को हेतुरिति भण्यताम् 4.3.1788cd
अथ स्वस्य स्वभावश्चेदात्मीयोऽर्थो विवक्षितः 4.3.766ab
अथ स्विष्टकृदन्तेऽस्मिन्होमानन्तरमेव तत् 6.3.25ab
अथ स्वेनैव रूपेण द्वैतमस्तीति भण्यते 5.1.33cd

अथ हेतुफलावेशनिषेधाय परं वचः 5.1.16ab
अथाकाशो ह वै नाम सता सोम्येति च श्रुतिः 2.1.243ab
अथाग्निवच्चेत्तद्ब्रह्म सिद्धं मानान्तरान्मतम् 1.4.1111ab
अथाग्नेरुच्यते जन्म हयमेधोपयोगिनः 1.2.1ab
अथाज्ञातानि नश्यन्ति जायमानानि वेति चेत् 4.3.596ab
अथात इति वाक्येन ह्यहमेवेति निश्चितेः 2.4.100ab
अथातो धर्म इत्युक्तेश्चोदनालक्षणोक्तितः SV 242ab
अथातो ब्रह्मजिज्ञासा इत्याद्युक्तं नयान्वितम् SV 245cd
अथात्माविद्याऽव्यक्तादिरूपेण प्रथते तदा 1.3.188ab
अथाधिभूतविषये विभागस्तस्य कीर्त्यते 1.5.155cd
अथाधुना निगमनस्थानीयमिदमुच्यते 4.5.3ab
अथाधुना यथोक्तस्य तस्यैव करणात्मनः 2.3.84ab
अथानधिगताभावादुत्तरस्याप्रमाणता SV 684ab
अथानन्तरमेवोक्तात्कर्मोपासनचेष्टितात् 1.5.282ab
अथानन्दः श्रुतः साक्षान्मानेनाविषयीकृतः SV 348ab
अथानुभवतोऽस्तीति पृथक्त्वं भवतो मतम् 4.3.1675ab
अथानुष्ठेयमपि संस्तुत्यर्थं भवतेष्यते 4.4.1140ab
अथान्यतस्तदज्ञातं किंरूपं वस्त्वतीर्यताम् 1.4.250ab
अथान्यदपि तन्मानं भवताभ्युपगम्यते 1.4.898ab
अथान्यापोहवद्वस्तु गम्यं गमकमेव च 4.3.779ab
अथापकृष्यमाणायाः कार्यतः कार्यमुच्यते 4.3.1270cd
अथापि कार्यविरहात्सिद्धार्थमनुवादकम् SV 674ab
अथापि क्षणिकानीति मत्वर्थोऽत्र विवक्ष्यते 4.3.587ab
अथाप्यवगमो मेये तथापि स्यान्न संप्लवः SV 1079ab
अथाब्रह्मात्मकं वस्तु जग्ध्वा चेद्ब्रह्म तद्भवेत् 2.4.15ab
अथाभावोऽपि तद्ग्राह्य इति चेदभिधीयते 4.3.250ab
अथाभावोऽपि वस्त्वेव नास्तीति मितिजन्मतः SV 928ab
अथाभिचारिकं कर्म प्रसङ्गादभिधीयते 6.4.48ab
अथाभिन्नं तदैकत्वात्कार्यकारणता कुतः 2.1.400ab
अथाभिन्नं मतं ताभ्यां द्रव्यस्यापह्नवस्ततः 1.6.82ab
अथाभेदस्तयोरिष्टः कार्यध्वस्तौ प्रसज्यते SV 62cd
अथाभ्युपगमाद्युक्तं वेदाभ्युपगतिस्तथा 4.3.255cd

अथाभ्युपेयतेऽज्ञातः प्रमेयाव्यतिरेकतः 1.4.247ab
अथायास्याङ्गिरोदूर्भिर्विशिष्टमसुकर्मकम् 1.3.194ab
अथारूपज्ञतामेति यः प्राग्रूपादिवेद्यभृत् 4.4.65cd
अथावगमवैयर्थ्यं भवता परिचोद्यते 1.4.1231ab
अथावधारणं कस्मादनेनैवेति भण्यते 1.3.242ab
अथावस्थित एवायं किमर्थं हेतुमार्गणम् SV 49cd
अथावाच्यं तदन्यत्व इतरत्रास्तु वाच्यता 4.3.638cd
अथावाच्यत्वमेवास्य रूपमित्यभिधीयते 4.3.643cd
अथाविद्यावतोऽविद्याहान्यहानिकृतो भवेत् 4.4.353ab
अथाविद्योत्थाकृत्स्नत्वनिवृत्तिं चेदिहेच्छसि 1.4.1204ab
अथाविशेषणोऽभावो भवद्भिरभिधीयते SV 943ab
अथासंवेदनविधिर्मुमूर्षोरुच्यते यथा 4.4.54cd
अथासंसारिणो नाम न्यायतोऽध्यवसीयते 2.1.429ab
अथासंसारितैतस्य कथंचिदुपपद्यते 2.1.467ab
अथासाधारणज्ञानपरिच्छेद्यत्वमिष्यते SV 715ab
अथास्त्वयुतसिद्धानां नासतोऽयुतसिद्धता 1.2.121cd
अथास्य स्वमुखे कर्णं दक्षिणं प्रणिधाय तु 6.4.119ab
अथेत्यनन्तरोक्तिः स्यात्तथाभिनयवृत्तये 1.3.165ab
अथैकात्म्यार्थनिष्ठं सच्छास्त्रं स्यात्प्रतिपादकम् SV 842ab
अथैतदुच्यते स्पष्टं तद्यथावत्प्रतीयताम् 4.3.847ab
अथैतयोरिति तथा चोदनार्थातिलङ्घिनाम् SV 81ab
अथैतस्मिन्नन्नरसपरिणामे यथोदिते 4.3.1241ab
अथैतस्य यथोक्तस्य साध्यसाधनरूपिणः 1.4.167ab
अथैतस्याप्रमाणत्वं मानत्वं क्वेति भण्यताम् 1.4.910ab
अथैनं पार्श्वगाः प्राहुर्बन्धवोऽस्य मुमूर्षतः 4.4.66ab
अथैनं मन्त्रपूतं सदुद्यच्छति यथोदितम् 6.3.36ab
अथैनमुच्चिक्रमिषुं विज्ञानात्मानमीश्वरम् 4.4.16ab
अथैवं कृशतापन्ने देहेऽन्तरुपजायते 4.3.1930ab
अथैवं ज्ञस्वभावोऽपि कस्मात्प्राज्ञे न पश्यति 4.3.1539cd
अथैवं देवतात्यक्ते लिङ्गे देहाद्बहिर्गते 4.4.108ab
अथैवं सत्यरूपज्ञो देवताकरणच्युतः 4.4.61ab
अथैष एव इति च तथोदर्के प्रवक्ष्यते 3.9.168cd

अथैष एव परमो यो वै भूमेतिशास्त्रतः 3.9.154cd
अथैष यो वै भूमेतिश्रुतिमानानुभूतितः SV 1096cd
अथैष यो वै भूमेति श्रुत्यैव प्रतिपाद्यते 1.4.189cd
अथैषाज्याहुतिर्यज्ञे यद्धविः सर्वरूपकम् 1.5.57ab
अथो इत्यादिना धर्मविशिष्टत्वावबुद्धये 1.4.1618cd
अथो खल्वत्र पूर्वोक्ते प्राहुरुच्चैर्विपश्चितः 4.4.210ab
अथो खल्वाहुरित्यादिग्रन्थं पश्येत्तथा क्रमात् 4.3.955cd
अथोत्पत्तिक्षणे नाशो भवताभ्युपगम्यते 4.3.593ab
अथोत्पन्नस्य नाशोऽयं द्वितीये स्यात्क्षणे यदि 4.3.599ab
अथोपचारतो देशो लिङ्गमेवात्मनो मतः 2.3.128ab
अथोपचारतो मोक्षः कार्यं स्यान्नित्यकर्मणः 3.3.89ab
अथोपचारात्कार्यत्वमविद्[illegible]षयत्वतः 1.4.1221ab
अथोपच्छन्दनार्थानि स[illegible]ादीनि विमुक्तये SV 403ab
अथोपसंहृताशेषकरणस्यात्मनो यथा 4.4.73ab
अथोभयात्मकं कार्यं सिद्धासिद्धस्वभावकम् SV 1032ab
अथोभयात्मतादृष्टा तदापि स्यादनिश्चितिः 4.3.26cd
अदः परोक्षमत्यन्तं कारणं पूर्णमुच्यते 5.1.37ab
अदः परोक्षमत्यन्तं सर्वकार्यस्य कारणम् 5.1.13ab
अदः प्रयोजनं देवि प्राप्नुयां त्वत्प्रसादतः 5.16.74cd
अदाहकानां दग्धृत्वं यथा दाहकसंगतेः 2.1.182ab
अदाहकोऽपि वह्निः सन्दाहाद्द्रव्यसमाश्रयात् 3.7.35ab
अदीर्घमित्यतो द्रव्यं न स्यादक्षरमव्ययम् 3.8.93ef
अदुःखिनोऽपि दृश्यन्ते सुखप्राप्तीच्छया यतः SV 1012ab
अदुष्टकारणत्वं चेत्सिद्धं वेदे नृवर्जनात् SV 849cd
अदृष्टफलता वापि कल्प्याग्निष्टोमवद्भवेत् SV 838ab
अदृष्टफलसंप्रेप्सोर्दृष्टकर्मफलत्यजः 3.9.158ab
अदृष्टमपि दृष्ट्वास्ति बोधो नाज्ञासिषं त्विति SV 996cd
अदृष्टशतभागोऽपि न कल्प्यो निष्प्रमाणकः 2.5.76cd
अदृष्टशतभागोऽपि न कल्प्यो निष्प्रमाणकः 4.4.461cd
अदृष्टात्मतत्त्वमपि तच्च नैवोपपद्यते 1.4.1667cd
अदृष्टार्थ्रा हि दृष्टार्थ्रा रागाद्युत्थाः प्रवृत्तयः SV 415ab
अदृष्टोऽश्रुत इत्युक्त्या क्रियते ज्ञानशुद्धये 3.7.48cd

अदेहतोऽजरोऽमृत्युरस्वान्तोऽमोहशोकवान् 1.4.1379ab
अदोमयत्वं लिङ्गं स्याल्लिङ्गेनेदंमयात्मना 4.4.193ab
अदोवत्कार्यमप्येतत्पूर्णमेवावसीयताम् 5.1.40cd
अदोषो विस्फुलिङ्गादिदृष्टान्तादिति चेन्मतम् 2.1.492ab
अद्भिः काष्ठैश्चोपकारः पावकस्यैव वीक्ष्यते 4.3.235ab
अद्भिः परिदधत्येनमशिष्यन्त इति श्रुतेः 6.1.36ab
अद्भिरन्तर्बहिश्चेयं व्याप्तैवेह समीक्ष्यते 3.6.7cd
अद्भिश्चेयं क्षितिर्व्याप्ता तस्मात्तासामपीष्यते 3.6.10ab
अद्यते चेत्सदैवान्नं जन्यते न तु तत्ततः 1.5.78ab
अद्यमानान्यथान्नानि यथोक्तान्यत्तृभिः सदा 1.5.76ab
अद्यापि क्रियते तैस्तत्कर्तारश्चापि तत्सुराः 1.5.383ab
अद्यैव मरणं श्रेयो मम दुःखार्दितात्मनः 1.4.1034cd
अद्रव्ये चासजातीये चैतन्ये वासना कुतः 2.3.106cd
अद्वितीयत्ववतश्चास्य नोत्पत्त्यादि प्रसिध्यति 4.3.1598cd
अद्वितीयपदार्थस्य तथा नैवात्मनोऽन्यतः 3.5.182ab
अद्वितीयार्थतैवातो द्वितीयार्थनिषेधतः 4.3.1802cd
अद्वितीयार्थनिष्ठत्वमात्मप्रत्ययशब्दयोः 3.5.171ab
अद्वैतदर्शनार्थाय शास्त्रारम्भोऽत एव च 3.2.49ab
अद्वैतदर्शनेनातो नास्ति किंचित्प्रयोजनम् 3.2.48cd
अद्वैतदर्शनेनास्य द्वैतदृष्ट्यपनुत्तये 3.2.44ab
अद्वैतपक्षो भवता मदीयोऽयं प्रसाध्यते 4.3.1701cd
अद्वैतविधिनाक्षिप्ता वेदान्ता नेति का मितिः SV 568cd
अद्वैतविषयं चेदमेकं ब्रह्मेति भण्यते 1.4.1183ab
अद्वैतविषयैवेयं द्वौ त्रयश्चेति या मतिः 4.3.1682ab
अद्वैतात्परमार्थाद्वा मायाद्वैतमपीष्यते 2.4.462ab
अद्वैतानभिसंबन्धो नाशो वा मलशुद्धिवत् 3.2.99cd
अधरेष्वपि वाक्येषु श्रोत्रियादि विवक्षितम् 4.3.1854cd
अधर्मधर्मयोरात्मा दुःखानन्दान्प्रपश्यति 4.3.850cd
अधर्मादिप्रकर्षोत्थं गर्तादिपतनादिकम् 4.3.1250ab
अधर्मादिभयाभावाद्धन्युरेनमशङ्किताः 2.1.147ab
अधिकारः स्वसिद्ध्यर्थमतः कामस्य साध्यताम् SV 536ab
अधिकारपरिच्छेदे सर्वं यस्मात्समाप्यते 1.5.198ab

अधिकारपरीक्षायां तथा प्राक्प्रतिपादितम् SV 796cd
अधिकारप्रवेशित्वं नात्मज्ञानस्य युज्यते SV 759ab
अधिकारविचारो हि नृतन्त्रे वस्तुनीष्यते SV 229ab
अधिकारविनिश्चित्यै मनुष्या इति गीरियम् 1.4.1084ab
अधिकारविभागस्य प्रसिद्धेरेव कारणात् SV 312cd
अधिकारविशेषेण पृथिवीत्यादिनाधुना 3.9.33cd
अधिकारस्य सौलभ्यप्रतिपत्त्यर्थमीरणम् SV 1023ab
अधिकारिविशेषस्य ज्ञानाय ब्राह्मणग्रहः 3.5.88ab
अधिकारोऽपि तस्यां च सिद्धोऽशेषक्रियात्यजः SV 282ab
अधिकारोऽविशेषेण ह्याश्रमाणां यथायुति 4.4.1026cd
अधिकारो द्वयोरत्र प्रकृतः पाङ्क्तकर्मणः 1.5.203ab
अधिकारो यतस्तासामात्मनो देहसंगतौ 4.3.1143cd
अधिकालं तु योऽस्यात्मा सोऽयं चन्द्रमसोच्यते 1.5.208ab
अधिकृताधिकारित्वान्नान्योऽधिक्रियते यतः SV 380cd
अधिक्रियन्ते येनैते बृहस्पतिसवादिषु SV 122ab
अधित्यकादौ देशे तु यावत्साक्षान्न दर्शनम् 4.3.727cd
अधित्यकादौ देशे तु ह्युपलब्धेरसंभवात् 4.3.725ab
अधिदैवं च विभ्वीयं द्वैतैकत्वेन विष्ठिता 4.2.73ab
अधिदैवं तथादित्यश्चक्षुषो देवता मता 1.5.183cd
अधिदैवं तथाध्यात्मं तथापीयान्न गृह्यते 2.3.72cd
अधिदैवतमप्येवं वायोरग्न्यादिसंभवः 1.5.379ab
अधिदैवविवक्षायां तस्या वाच इदं वपुः 1.5.169cd
अधिदैवात्मना तेषां दृष्टयः साधनात्मनाम् 3.1.46ab
अधिदैवात्मना वेत्ति स होतैवंविधो भवेत् 3.1.23cd
अधिदैवादिदेहस्य रसहेतुः स्थितिर्यतः 4.3.1229ab
अधिदैवेऽपि तद्वाच्यमित्यर्थः पर आगमः 1.5.179cd
अधिदैवे त्रयं तूक्तं मनोवाक्प्राणलक्षणम् 1.5.205ab
अधिभूत इह प्रोक्ता विज्ञातं यच्च सा च वाक् 1.5.156cd
अधिभूतं तथास्यैव वायुमय्यः समन्तगाः 4.2.74ab
अधिभूतात्मनैवायं नाडीलक्षणवर्त्मना 4.2.75ab
अधिभूताधियज्ञादिपरिच्छेदफलात्मकः 3.2.3ab
अधिभूते यतोऽशक्या वक्तुं वागादिविस्तृतिः 1.5.161ab

अधिष्ठातृवियुक्तानि न्यस्तदात्रोपमानि हि 3.2.129ab
अधिष्ठायात्मकार्यत्वादुत्पत्तिस्थितिहानिषु 4.4.992ab
अधिष्ठेयेन्द्रियाणां हि स्वप्नभूमावसंभवात् 4.3.1132ab
अधीतवेदवेदार्थोऽप्यत एव न मुच्यते SV 295ab
अधीयतेऽत्र यत्नेन संप्रदायविदः स्वयम् 4.4.886cd
अधुनोपासनं वाच्यमित्यर्थः पर आगमः 5.16.2cd
अधोपहासं यो विद्वान्यथोक्तमुपसेवते 6.4.15cd
अधोभावस्त्वधर्मात्स्याद्द्वाभ्यां मानुष्यसंभवः 1.3.114cd
अधोलोकफलेष्वेव प्राकृतज्ञानकर्मसु 1.3.116ab
अध्यस्तदिङ्निषेधश्च व्योम्न्येकस्मिन्यथा तथा 3.8.78ab
अध्यस्यात्मनि देहादीन्मूढस्तद्वद्विचेष्टते 3.3.65cd
अध्यात्मं चक्षुरध्वर्युरधियज्ञं द्वयं रविः 3.1.33ab
अध्यात्मं चक्षुषि रवेश्चक्षुर्व्यापारसिद्धिकृत् 4.4.55cd
अध्यात्मं चाधिदैवं वा नामरूपविभागतः 2.3.91cd
अध्यात्मं दैहिके शब्दे बुद्धौ चेति विनिर्दिशेत् 2.1.74cd
अध्यात्मं पिण्डकृद्यच्च सोऽयं धर्माभिधोदितः 2.5.49cd
अध्यात्मं प्राण एव स्यादुद्गाता योऽधियज्ञगः 3.1.42ab
अध्यात्मं मन एवात्मा तदायत्तत्वकारणात् 1.4.1843ab
अध्यात्मं यश्च शारीरः पार्थिवांशसमाश्रयः 2.5.30ab
अध्यात्मदेवताः सर्वा हृदि नीत्वात्मनस्ततः 4.2.80ab
अध्यात्ममधिदैवं च देवताकरणाश्रयम् 2.2.4cd
अध्यात्ममधिदैवं च प्राणवायुतयोदितः 1.4.350cd
अध्यात्ममधिभूतं च तथा चैवाधिदैवतम् 1.4.1337ab
अध्यात्ममधिभूतं च तथा चैवाधिदैवतम् 1.5.194ab
अध्यात्ममधिभूतं च तथा चैवाधिदैवतम् 2.1.11ab
अध्यात्ममधिभूतं च तेनास्थास्न्वात्मसाक्षिकम् 4.3.292cd
अध्यात्ममधिभूतं च प्रजा गीर्मनसोर्यथा 1.5.179ab
अध्यात्ममधिभूतं च यस्या रूपं पुरोदितम् 1.5.169ab
अध्यात्ममधिभूतं च वागेकैवाधिदैविकी 1.5.173ab
अध्यात्ममधिभूतं च व्याख्याता यात्र वाक्पुरा 1.5.170ab
अध्यात्मादिपदार्थेभ्यो विविक्तं स्वात्मनि स्थितम् 4.3.951ab
अध्यात्मादिपरिच्छिन्ना या वाक्सा तावती मता 1.5.175cd

अध्यात्मादिपरिच्छेद आसुरत्वान्न गृह्यते 1.3.24cd
अध्यात्मादिपरिच्छेदाद्यथोक्तोपासनाश्रयात् 4.2.30ab
अध्यात्मादिप्रपञ्चो हि शुक्तिकारजतादिवत् 4.3.1233cd
अध्यात्मादिविभागेन मात्रा जागरिते यथा 4.3.866ab
अध्यात्मादिविभागेन सर्वा वास्यात्मनो यतः 4.3.864ab
अध्यात्मादिविभागे स्यादात्मात्मीयादिभेदधीः 1.4.25ab
अध्यात्मादिविभागोऽयं न स्वतः प्रत्यगात्मनः 4.3.1223ab
अध्यात्मादिव्यवच्छेदान्मुच्यमान उपासनैः 4.2.8ab
अध्यात्मादिषु कार्त्स्न्येन तेषु तेष्ववतिष्ठते 3.9.32cd
अध्यात्माद्यखिलं विश्वं संव्याप्य समवस्थितः 2.1.117ab
अध्यात्माद्यधिभूताधिदैवतं सर्वदाखिलम् 1.3.274ab
अध्यात्माद्यधियज्ञादेराधिदैवतरूपता 3.5.81ab
अध्यात्माद्यर्थविरहे यतः स्वप्नान्प्रपश्यति 4.3.963cd
अध्यात्मेऽथाधिदैवे च तस्यैव प्रकृतत्वतः 2.3.149cd
अध्यात्मे चाधियज्ञे च ह्यधिलोकाधिदैवयोः 6.2.79ab
अध्यात्मोक्त्यवधिज्ञप्त्या अधिदैवतकीर्तनम् 2.3.68ab
अध्यायस्यात्र चाविद्वान्वर्णाद्यात्माभिमानवान् 1.5.2ab
अध्यायो वा समस्तोऽयमध्यायद्वयमेव वा 1.4.1064cd
अध्यासश्च विना हेतुं न लोक उपपद्यते 1.4.478cd
अध्येतव्यार्थनिष्पत्तिस्त्वनिष्पत्त्या मया कृता 1.5.292cd
अध्रियन्त यममुर्हि तस्मिन्काले पराजिताः 1.5.383cd
अध्वर्युरहमेवेति साक्षात्कृत्वा विमुच्यते 3.1.34cd
अध्वस्तप्रत्यगज्ञानो विरिञ्चः पर उच्यते 1.3.262cd
अन इत्यविशिष्टस्य वायोर्ग्रहणमिष्यते 1.5.144ab
अनग्निरनिकेतः स्यादशर्माशरणो मुनिः 4.4.1260cd
अनधीत्य द्विजो वेदानित्यादिवचनान्मनोः 1.5.261cd
अननुक्रमसंन्यासे न संप्रत्तिक्रियेष्यते 1.5.265ab
अननुशिष्टहेतूक्त्या मती राज्ञस्तदाभवत् 4.2.1cd
अननुष्ठेयरूपत्वात्तत्सिद्धिश्चात्मबोधतः 1.4.850ab
अनन्तकल्पोपचयाद्वासनानामुदाहृतिः 2.3.169cd
अनन्तदेहहेतोश्च विप्रघातस्य संभवात् SV 94cd
अनन्तपुरुषार्थाप्तिरिष्यते कर्मकाण्डतः 5.1.58cd

अनन्तभिन्नकार्येषु समाप्तिर्देवतात्मनः	4.2.77cd
अनन्तभेदभिन्नस्य पुनरप्यष्टधोच्यते	3.9.34ab
अनन्तभेदभिन्नो वा एक एवान उच्यते	1.3.267ab
अनन्तमेव तेनासौ सम्यग्ज्ञानेन विन्दति	3.1.56ab
अनन्तरं प्रवृत्तिः स्याद्विषये तस्य सिद्धये	SV 586cd
अनन्तरमपूर्वस्य कार्यं निर्दिश्यतेऽधुना	3.3.160cd
अनन्तरमिति तयोरन्ध्रस्य प्रतिषेधनम्	2.5.140ab
अनन्तराग्निसंबन्धप्रसङ्गविनिवृत्तये	1.2.175ab
अनन्तरेण संबन्धसामर्थ्ये सत्यमानतः	1.4.1127ab
अनन्तविग्रहः सोऽग्निर्होता मृत्योर्यथोदितात्	3.1.24ab
अनन्तवित्तो हि भवानन्तवद्दीयते कुतः	2.4.63ab
अनन्ताः सर्व एवैते वाङ्मनःप्राणलक्षणाः	4.4.129cd
अनन्ताकाशदेशत्वान्नाञ्जसान्तो दिशां यतः	1.3.219cd
अनन्ताग्न्यादिभावेन यो नः सञ्जितवानसुः	1.3.199ab
अनन्तात्मैकमेयत्वाद्विततश्चातिविस्तृतः	4.4.547ab
अनन्तानर्थसंप्राप्तिस्तथापि तदबोधतः	4.4.573cd
अनन्तापार आत्मैव स्वमहिम्नि व्यवस्थितः	2.5.61cd
अनन्तेऽन्तवतां यत्र तद्ब्रह्मेत्यवसीयताम्	2.3.188cd
अनन्तैकोर्ध्वगा नाडी तया गच्छन्विमुच्यते	2.1.324cd
अनन्दा इति वाक्येन तद्दोषोऽथाभिधीयते	4.4.606cd
अनन्यज्ञातृकत्वाच्च प्रत्यग्ज्ञानस्य सर्वदा	1.4.1522cd
अनन्यत्वं प्रविष्टैः स्यान्नानात्वमिति दुर्भणम्	1.4.552ab
अनन्यपक्षेऽहं ब्रह्मेत्युक्तेर्ब्रह्म प्रपत्स्यते	2.1.471cd
अनन्यबोधप्रत्यक्षो य एष इति भण्यते	2.1.233ab
अनन्यबोधमानत्वादयमित्युच्यते ततः	4.4.153cd
अनन्यभूतं तेनातः साक्षात्तत्त्वं प्रगीयते	4.5.10cd
अनन्यममषष्ठ्यर्थं वैशब्दस्तत्प्रसिद्धये	3.8.59cd
अनन्यमातृमानादिर्दृष्टिमात्रात्मकत्वतः	2.3.225cd
अनन्यमातृमानोऽतः प्रत्यगात्मा तमोपनुत्	2.4.238cd
अनन्यमानमानन्दं पूर्णं तदभिधीयते	5.1.12cd
अनन्यमानमेयेऽर्थे न भेदः प्रत्यगात्मनि	2.1.598ab
अनन्यमेयतन्मानमातृ वस्त्वविभागवत्	1.4.699ab

अनन्यवृत्तितो नात्मा संसर्गं प्रैत्यनात्मभिः 1.4.1406cd
अनन्यसाक्षिकः प्रत्यङ्ङासीन्नामादिजन्मतः 1.4.611cd
अनन्यसाधनं तस्मात्स्वात्मस्थं परमं सुखम् 4.3.1851cd
अनन्यहेतुकं तावत् त्रयमेतद्यथोदितम् 3.4.92ab
अनन्यानुभवं साक्षाद्ददर्शैकात्म्यमात्मनि 1.4.61cd
अनन्यानुभवः प्रत्यङ्न प्रमात्रादिगोचरः 4.3.186ab
अनन्यानुभवात्प्रत्यक्संविदव्यभिचारिणी 4.3.1737cd
अनन्यानुभवात्माभं तत्प्रमाणं सदादृशेः 3.4.126cd
अनन्यानुभवादेव सिद्धिस्तद्ध्वंससाक्षितः 4.3.1419cd
अनन्यानुभवेनैव भावाभावात्मभूमिषु 2.3.227ab
अनन्यापेक्षतो ज्ञेया प्रत्यग्बुद्धेः स्वतन्त्रता 4.4.843cd
अनन्यापेक्षसंसिद्धेर्देशादेस्तदपेक्षतः 1.4.1331cd
अनन्यापेक्षसंसिद्धेर्देशादेस्तदपेक्षतः 3.4.133cd
अनन्यापेक्षि प्रत्यक्त्वमहंरूपेण लक्ष्यते 1.4.1428ab
अनन्यायत्तमैकात्म्यं यदा साक्षाद्व्यवस्थितम् 2.3.211ab
अनन्यायत्तविज्ञाने श्रवणादेरुपायतः 2.4.221ab
अनन्यायत्तसंसिद्धेर्निरविद्यात्मवस्तुनः SV 237ab
अनन्यायत्तसंसिद्धेर्मेयत्वं किंनिबन्धनम् 1.4.228cd
अनन्योऽपि स्वतो यत्र मोहादन्य इवेक्ष्यते 4.3.1790cd
अनन्योऽप्यात्मनो भिन्नामुपास्ते देवतां नरः 1.4.1567cd
अनन्वागत इत्यस्य हेतुत्वं हिगिरोच्यते 4.3.1003cd
अनन्वागतगीः कुप्येत्स्वप्नेऽन्वेत्येव तत्कृतम् 4.3.1047cd
अनन्वागतवचनात्तथासङ्गश्रुतेरपि 4.4.432cd
अनन्वागतवाक्येन विवेकः कर्मणः कृतः 4.3.1015ab
अनन्वितपदज्ञानगोपिण्डैकावसायिनी 1.4.995cd
अनन्वितार्थसिद्ध्यर्थं दृष्टान्तोऽयं तथा सति 1.4.994cd
अनपास्ततमस्कोऽपि भेदं नात्मनि पश्यति 4.3.1331cd
अनपेक्षितमात्रादि तदविद्यासमन्वयात् 2.3.13cd
अनप्रतिष्ठा देहोऽतः श्रुत्येह प्रतिपाद्यते 1.3.343cd
अनभीष्टफलानां च दुरितत्वात्क्षयो भवेत् SV 84ab
अनया गीयते यस्माद्गीथा वाक्तेन भण्यते 1.3.320ab
अनयैव दिशा शास्त्रं संसृष्टार्थाभिधाय्यपि SV 780cd

अनयोरैक्यसंमोहात्पारोक्ष्यद्वयकल्पने 4.3.1823ab
अनरोक्तौ तु तात्पर्यं युक्तेरर्थो न युक्तितः 3.1.9cd
अनर्थकः कल्पितोऽपि तस्येहानुपयोगतः SV 235cd
अनर्थको भवेदेवं विधिर्निर्विषयत्वतः SV 726cd
अनर्थको विधिस्तमात्सर्वो निःश्रेयसं प्रति SV 270ab
अनर्थपरिपाकत्वमपि जानन्प्रवर्तते 1.4.1811ab
अनर्थहेतुदाहित्वाद्यथोक्तात्मस्मृतेरतः 1.4.847ab
अनर्थहेतुरज्ञानं तदुत्थं चाखिलं जगत् 2.1.3ab
अनर्थाभावमात्रत्वान्न चाभावः फलं क्वचित् SV 747cd
अनवच्छिन्नयाथात्म्यब्रह्मैकात्म्यादविद्यया 2.4.186ab
अनवच्छिन्नरूपायाः प्रीतेराप्तौ कृतार्थता SV 307ef
अनवच्छिन्नवपुषः पिण्डावच्छेदहेतुतः 1.2.155ab
अनवस्था च दुर्वारा ह्यविश्वासश्च जायते 1.2.65ab
अनवस्थाप्रसक्तिश्च तत्र तत्र प्रसङ्गतः 1.4.829ab
अनवस्थेति दुर्वारा नैष दोषः कुतो यतः 4.3.519cd
अनवस्थेति योऽप्युक्तः सोऽपि दोषो निराकृतः 4.3.260ab
अनवाप्तस्वरूपं सद्वस्तु स्याच्छशशृङ्गवत् 4.3.1661cd
अनसस्तदङ्गताच्चार्थाद्विलक्षणवपुर्भृता 4.3.1913cd
अनस्थिकगिरा स्थूलदेहस्येह निवारणम् 4.4.520ab
अनाकाशस्वभावेभ्यः खेन ब्रह्म निवर्त्यते 5.1.115ab
अनात्मतत्त्वमन्वेति ह्यात्मासङ्गोऽगुणोऽद्वयः 1.4.945ab
अनात्मतत्त्वमन्वेति ह्यात्मासङ्गोऽगुणोऽद्वयः 1.4.1364ab
अनात्मत्वप्रसक्तिः स्याद्द्रष्टृदृश्यप्रभेदतः 3.2.104cd
अनात्मत्वप्रसिद्धिः स्याल्लिङ्गपिण्डात्मनोरतः 3.4.71cd
अनात्मत्वमतः सिद्धं प्राणादेः करणोक्तितः 3.4.70ab
अनात्मधर्मोऽविद्येति वदन्तश्चोषरादिवत् 2.3.124ab
अनात्मनस्तु या सिद्धिः सा सर्वाव्यतिरेकतः 4.3.388ab
अनात्मनि च तद्दृष्टं तेन मृत्युरिदं जगत् 4.3.457cd
अनात्मनि प्रमेयेऽर्थे या फलत्वेन संमता SV 230ab
अनात्मनिश्चितिस्तद्वदज्ञातेऽनुभवात्मनि 4.4.901cd
अनात्मनीव नेच्छेयं कथंचित्स्यादिहात्मनि SV 250cd
अनात्मनोऽत आत्मानमन्वयव्यतिरेकतः 2.4.114ab

अनात्मनोऽपि चानन्त्यं न स्वतः सिद्धमात्मवत् 4.4.132cd

अनात्मनोऽस्य सर्वस्य व्याकृताव्याकृतात्मनः 1.4.979ab

अनात्मनो यतोऽशेषान्कल्पितत्वादकल्पितः 2.1.192ab

अनात्मनो यदात्मानं प्रत्यगज्ञानकल्पितात् 4.4.864ab

अनात्मप्रत्ययः सोऽहमुत्पत्त्यैवास्मि केवलः 4.4.844cd

अनात्मप्रत्ययोऽतोऽहं स्वत एकोऽस्मि केवलः 2.3.14cd

अनात्मप्रत्ययोऽतोऽहं स्वत एवास्मि केवलः 4.3.78cd

अनात्मप्रत्ययोत्पत्तिरहंप्रत्ययपूर्विका 1.4.917cd

अनात्मबुद्धिविषयं यतो यत्नान्निषेधति 2.4.241cd

अनात्मबोधवत्सिद्धाविद्यातः प्रत्यगात्मनि 4.4.655cd

अनात्मभूत एतस्मिन्कार्यकारणलक्षणे 4.4.150ab

अनात्ममानमेयोऽर्थो यतोऽतः केवलात्मता 3.5.188cd

अनात्ममेयभाज्ज्येव विज्ञेयानीति निश्चितिः 4.4.905cd

अनात्मवत्तदप्यात्मविशेषणतया भवेत् 2.4.283cd

अनात्मवस्तुनः प्रत्यक्प्रत्यक्त्वान्नातिरिच्यते 2.4.274ab

अनात्मवस्तुनः प्रत्यङ्ङात्मा ह्यात्मीयतो भवेत् 1.4.729cd

अनात्मवस्तुना नात्माकारकत्वाद्विना तमः 4.4.944ab

अनात्मवस्तुमानानां प्रागनात्माभिसंगतेः 4.3.1290ab

अनात्मवस्तु यत्किंचित्तद्ब्रह्मानवबोधतः 1.4.1280ab

अनात्मवस्तु सकलं प्रत्यगज्ञानहेतुजम् 1.3.316ab

अनात्मवस्तूत्प्रेक्ष्यं स्याद्यथा संविदियं स्वतः 1.4.985cd

अनात्मसिद्धिवन्न स्यादात्मसिद्धिरनात्मनः 1.4.725ab

अनात्मसु तथा चात्मा संहतेष्वप्यसंहतः 1.4.1002cd

अनात्माकारमानेषु ह्यन्योऽन्यव्यभिचारिषु 4.3.305ab

अनात्माज्ञात एव स्याच्छुक्तिकारूप्यबोधवत् 1.4.976cd

अनात्मानं तथा दुःखं पुमर्थत्वेन संमतः SV 1016cd

अनात्मानं विजानाति तज्जज्ञात्राद्यनन्वयात् 1.4.1384cd

अनात्मा नात्मरूपेण प्रत्यक्त्वात्सिद्धिमर्हति 1.4.658ab

अनात्मापि विनात्मानं नैवानात्मायते यतः 4.3.1292ab

अनात्माब्रह्मताहेतौ प्रत्यग्ध्वान्ते निवर्तिते 1.4.1430ab

अनात्माभिजना ह्येषा व्यावृत्तिर्यात्मनो भवेत् 4.3.1654cd

अनात्मार्थनिषेधेन यो नेतीति पुरोदितः 3.9.132ab

अनात्मार्थप्रधानोऽयं यावदात्मा समीक्ष्यते 4.4.863ab
अनात्मार्थविशिष्टस्य ह्यधिकारित्वहेतुतः SV 108cd
अनात्मार्थापनुत्त्यर्थमात्मानमिति शब्द्यते 1.4.940ab
अनात्मार्थे तु विज्ञाते स्वाध्यस्ताहिप्रबोधवत् 1.4.972ab
अनात्मा हि स्वतोऽसिध्यन्स्वतःसिद्धमपेक्षते 4.4.645ab
अनात्मिकात्मवत्यत्र येनासौ किमपेक्षते 1.4.872cd
अनात्मैव फलं तत्र देवानामीशता भवेत् 1.4.1508ab
अनात्मोपासनप्राप्तौ ध्यायेदात्मानमित्यतः 1.4.926ab
अनात्मोपासनमिदमितिशब्दप्रयोगतः 1.4.933ab
अनात्मोपास्तेः सामर्थ्यान्निवृत्तिर्न तु शब्दतः 1.4.926cd
अनात्यन्तिकरूपत्वादत्ययोऽसौ न गृह्यते 3.5.69cd
अनादिकालमज्ञानं ज्ञानेनादिमता क्षणात् SV 1089ab
अनादित्वान्निर्गुणत्वात्परमात्मायमव्ययः 4.3.1079ab
अनादिमत्परं ब्रह्म न सत्तन्नासदुच्यते 2.4.245cd
अनादिमद्व्यवहृतेः संबन्धस्य च सिद्धितः 4.3.785cd
अनादिवृद्धव्यवहृद्व्युत्पत्त्यैव च तत्स्थितेः SV 874ab
अनादृत्य प्रदुद्राव यत्रास्ते गौतमः पिता 6.2.45cd
अनादृत्य यथोक्तार्थं नियोगार्थैकरागतः SV 477ab
अनादृत्यान्यथा प्राहुरहो विद्या महीयसी 4.3.1809cd
अनादेरपि बाधश्चेत्तमसो नाभ्युपेयते 1.4.1306ab
अनादेर्नाप्यनुच्छित्तिः सर्वत्रोच्छित्तिदर्शनात् 4.4.921ab
अनाद्यज्ञातमेयेषु ह्यज्ञानस्य प्रहाणतः 4.4.921cd
अनाद्यज्ञानवन्मेयमूरीकृत्येह सर्वतः 4.4.922ab
अनाद्यविद्यायोगोऽस्य तत्कार्यैरादिमान्मतः 4.3.1409cd
अनानन्दाभिधा लोकास्तीव्रदोषसमन्विताः 4.4.607ab
अनापन्नादिमध्यान्तं ब्राह्मण्यं लभते तदा 4.4.1295cd
अनापन्नादिमध्यान्तं सदेव तदितीष्यते SV 936cd
अनाप्तकामं तत्सर्वमपेक्ष्येदमिहोच्यते 4.3.1335cd
अनाप्तकाममस्योक्तमात्माविद्यैकहेतुकम् 4.3.1296ab
अनाप्तपुरुषार्थोऽयं निःशेषानर्थसंकुलः 1.4.1814ab
अनामरूपकाः सन्तः सत्यसंयोगहेतुतः 2.3.94ab
अनारब्धफलं कर्म न त्वारब्धफलं यदि 1.4.1532ab

अनारब्धफलं हन्तीत्यत्रापि स्यान्न निश्चितिः	1.4.1533cd
अनारब्धफलेहानां गम्यते संस्थितिस्ततः	SV 95cd
अनारब्धेषु नितरां पुंसोऽपि स्याद्यथेष्टता	1.4.1534cd
अनारभ्यत्ववचनं तद्धेतुप्रतिपत्तये	3.3.16cd
अनारभ्या त्वियं मुक्तिस्तत्सिद्धेर्ज्ञानहेतुतः	3.3.17cd
अनारभ्योक्तितश्चापि नेह प्रकरणग्रहः	SV 338ab
अनारम्भश्च शून्येऽपि यथायमुपलभ्यते	3.2.154ab
अनालिङ्गितबाह्यार्था बुद्धावेव स्मृतिर्यतः	1.4.454cd
अनावरणता चेत्स्यात्कपालादेर्घटात्मनि	1.2.95ab
अनावृत्तिश्च कर्मभ्यो न क्वचिच्छ्रूयते स्फुटम्	SV 374ab
अनाशकं चानशनं कामानशनलक्षणम्	4.4.1057ab
अनाश्रितविभागार्थमथवास्तु विशेषणम्	4.4.437ab
अनिङ्गनमनाभासं निष्पन्नं ब्रह्म तत्तदा	4.4.888cd
अनिच्छतापि विध्यर्थमत्र प्रतिविधीयते	SV 126cd
अनित्यं दर्शनं ज्ञेयं नित्यस्यापि परात्मनः	1.4.1156ab
अनित्यत्वं क्वचिन्नास्ति यथान्येषां प्रवादिनाम्	1.4.592ab
अनित्यत्वप्रसङ्गाच्च न सती संततिर्भवेत्	4.3.647ab
अनित्यत्वस्य धर्मस्य घटादेर्धर्मिणस्तयोः	SV 925ab
अनित्यत्वस्य सर्वस्य प्रत्यग्दृष्ट्येकसाक्षितः	4.3.1472cd
अनित्यदुःखशून्यत्वं पदार्थानां ब्रुवन्स्फुटम्	1.4.410ab
अनित्यदुःखशून्यादेः पृथुबुध्नादिरूपवत्	4.3.699cd
अनित्यमितरत्सर्वं यदविद्याविजृम्भितम्	1.4.1155cd
अनित्यहेतुतोऽनित्यं तेन कर्त्रादि लक्ष्यते	1.4.670ab
अनिमित्तं स्वतस्तस्य सर्वदाव्यभिचारतः	2.1.206cd
अनिमित्तोऽपवर्गोऽपि शास्त्रं चैवमनर्थकम्	SV 399ef
अनिर्ज्ञातात्मतत्त्वं सदब्रह्मैवावभाति तत्	1.4.1314cd
अनिर्ज्ञातात्मतत्त्वः सन्कामबन्धनबन्धनः	4.4.248ab
अनिर्ज्ञातात्मयाथात्म्यैर्यत्तु कैश्चिदिहोच्यते	3.3.14ab
अनिर्णीतं किमुद्दिश्य नृपोऽप्राक्षीन्मुनिं पुनः	4.3.1897cd
अनिर्देश्यस्य निर्देश्या ये भेदाः कार्यलक्षणाः	2.3.245ab
अनिर्मोक्षप्रसक्तिः स्यात्तस्य चासङ्गरूपतः	3.5.67cd
अनिर्मोक्षप्रसक्तिः स्याद्यद्यविद्या परात्मनः	2.3.131ab

अनिर्मोक्षप्रसक्तित्वाच्छ्रुत्यनारम्भसक्तितः 4.4.499cd
अनिर्मोक्षप्रसक्तिर्वस्तथा सति समापतेत् SV 52cd
अनिर्मोक्षप्रसक्तिश्च क्षेत्रज्ञपरमात्मनोः 3.5.22cd
अनिर्मोक्षप्रसक्तिश्च विकारश्चेत्परात्मनः 4.3.320ab
अनिवृत्ते सती भूयोऽविद्यां जनयितुं क्षमे 3.2.60cd
अनिश्चयात्मिका वृत्तिर्विचिकित्सेत्युदाहृता 1.5.111ab
अनिश्चिता यथा रज्जुरन्धकारे विकल्पिता 2.1.2ab
अनिश्चिता यथा रज्जुरिति न्यायोपबृंहितम् 1.4.389ab
अनिषेधाद्द्वयोरेका प्रतिष्ठेहावसीयताम् 1.3.342cd
अनिष्ठितं न कर्मापि फलायालं भवेत् क्वचित् 3.2.152ab
अनिष्ठितक्रियारम्भोऽविव्यत्सन्निति भण्यते 1.3.173cd
अनीक्षमाणास्ते शर्म संभूयोचुः परस्परम् 1.3.31ab
अनीप्सितानिवृत्तिः स्यात्समाहारेऽविवक्षिते 1.3.224cd
अनीलाभावपृष्टेन नापि नीलस्य वेदनम् SV 950cd
अनुक्तदेवतानाम्नां सामर्थ्यात्तद्ग्रहोऽथवा 2.1.111cd
अनुक्तविषयाशङ्का सर्वस्याप्रतिषेधतः 2.3.204ab
अनुक्रमेण संचरन्मत्स्योऽन्यः कूलतो मतः 4.3.1084cd
अनुक्रमेणाविद्यावान्सदा संचरतीश्वरः 4.3.403cd
अनुगृह्णाति कर्मोत्थां प्रत्यगज्ञानकारणात् 4.3.86cd
अनुगृह्णाति कूटस्थः स्वात्माविद्यानुरोधतः 4.3.89cd
अनुग्रहनियन्तृत्वे ब्राह्मणस्याग्नितो यतः 1.4.1640cd
अनुग्रहव्यपेक्षायां मनसश्चन्द्रमा भवेत् 1.5.183ab
अनुग्रहीत्रीर्वक्ष्यामीत्यतः प्रववृते श्रुतिः 1.4.125cd
अनुग्राहकदेवानां या सृष्टिरुदिता पुरा 1.4.161ab
अनुग्राहकदेवानां सर्गोऽयं प्रस्तुतो महान् 1.4.127ab
अनुग्राह्यसजातीयं न च प्रत्यक्षमानिनः 4.3.224ab
अनुग्राह्यसजातीयं यच्च ज्योतिरिहेष्यते 4.3.107ab
अनुग्राह्याभिसंबन्ध एकजातिसमन्वयात् 4.3.90ab
अनुग्राह्येण पुंसेह सर्वदानुग्रहं मुहुः 4.3.62cd
अनुच्छित्तिगिरा नाशो वार्यते यो निरन्वयः 4.5.13cd
अनुच्छित्तिश्च भोगेन स्पष्टं श्रुतिवचः श्रुतम् 1.5.251ab
अनुज्ञातोऽथ तामाह हन्तेत्यादि परं वचः 2.4.42ab

अनुत्पन्नागमोत्थत्वात्पुराणश्चेति शब्द्यते 4.4.547cd
अनुत्पन्ने च नितरां प्रवृत्तेर्हेत्वसंभवात् SV 663cd
अनुत्पन्नोत्पित्सूत्पन्नोऽनष्टो नाशादिकृत्तथा 1.2.69ab
अनुद्वेगकरा हृद्या ऋतायन्ते वहन्ति च 6.3.45ab
अनुन्मृदितकामो हि पूर्वावस्थाविशेषतः SV 535ab
अनुपश्यति साक्षात्तमीश्वरं भूतभव्ययोः 4.4.630cd
अनुपाख्यतनुः सोऽयं व्यवहारप्रसिद्धये 1.2.163ab
अनुपात्तप्रमाणं सदित्यर्थप्रतिपत्तये 1.4.484cd
अनुपात्तान्यधर्मः सन्न तु पाषाणसर्पवत् 1.4.536cd
अनुपादीयमानश्च न च ज्ञाताङ्गभावकः SV 452ab
अनुपास्यं भवेत्तादृक्प्राणादिवदसंशयम् 1.4.1090cd
अनुप्रविश्य भोक्तारं रञ्जयित्वावतिष्ठते 4.3.1096cd
अनुप्रवेशः कल्प्येत येन कार्यान्तरं प्रति SV 409cd
अनुबन्धाभिसंबन्धात्फलं चेत्स्याद्व्यवस्थया SV 651ab
अनुभूतिस्तदज्ञानहेतत्थानात्मजन्मना 1.4.335cd
अनुभूतेः प्रसिद्धत्वान्नैवं स्यादिति चेन्मतम् 4.3.1467cd
अनुभूतेः सुषुप्त्यादेर्न चाप्यनुभवत्वतः 4.4.908cd
अनुभूतेः स्वतः सिद्धेः कापेक्षा ह्यात्मसिद्धये SV 189cd
अनुभूतेस्तदज्ञातं सिद्धं ब्रह्म पुरा मितेः 1.4.1307ab
अनुभूत्यैव संधत्ते नान्तरातोऽस्य लुप्तता SV 997cd
अनुभूयन्त एकत्र देवदत्तादिके तथा 5.1.52cd
अनुमाकुशला यूयं क इत्येतद्विभाष्यताम् 2.1.599ab
अनुमानत्वतो लिङ्गाद्दूषणानुमितिर्यथा 4.3.247cd
अनुमानप्रयोगेऽस्मिन्प्रतिज्ञार्थः सुदुर्लभः 4.3.579ab
अनुमानबलेनैव देहादिव्यतिरेकतः 4.3.145ab
अनुमानविरोधस्य वचसोऽस्य प्रसज्यते 4.3.1576ab
अनुमानविरोधाच्च न नित्यात्मादिसंभवः 4.3.479ab
अनुमानश्रुतिस्तस्मादागात्तस्यैव सिद्धये 3.8.129ab
अनुमानाच्च सत्सर्वं यथा तदधुनोच्यते 1.2.30cd
अनुमानादनेकत्वमात्मनो ये प्रचक्षते 2.1.611ab
अनुमानादृते तेषां संसिद्धिर्नेष्यते यतः 4.3.241cd
अनुमानाप्रमाणत्वं न प्रत्यक्षेण साध्यते 4.3.244ab

अनुमानेन तादृक्षं वस्तु प्राक्प्रतिपादितम् 4.3.716ab
अनुमानैकसिद्धत्वाद्भिन्नाभिन्नात्मवस्तुनः 1.6.52ab
अनुमापि क्रिया साक्षाद्भवतैवाभ्युपेयते 2.1.604ab
अनुमाष्टर्य्यथ तां जायां मन्त्रं विष्णुरितीरयन् 6.4.99cd
अनुमावर्त्मना ज्योतिः साक्षान्नः प्रत्यपीपदत् 4.3.32cd
अनुमास्यामहे ज्योतिस्तादृगेव तदा वयम् 4.3.25ab
अनुमीयात्मनात्मानं कृत्स्नात्मानं प्रपश्यति 1.4.1350cd
अनुमेयं च सत्पूर्वं कारणं कार्यमेव च 1.2.31ab
अनुरक्तां प्रियां साध्वीं बद्ध्वा वित्तेन मां कथम् 2.4.58ab
अनुवादत्वमेव स्यात्स्याच्च शास्त्रादभिन्नता SV 817cd
अनुवादविसंवादात्तेषामुक्तेरमानता SV 484cd
अनुवादाद्विधिर्ज्यायाननुवादे वृथा श्रमः 1.3.195ab
अनुवादे यथोक्तानां प्रक्रान्ते दर्शनादिषु 2.4.232ab
अनुवादो न तु विधिरेवंविदमितीर्यते 4.3.1969ab
अनुशाधि यथातत्त्वमित्येवंवादिनं नृपः 2.1.92cd
अनुशिष्टमतो लोक्यं पुत्रमाहुर्विपश्चितः 1.5.300cd
अनुशिष्टेन पुत्रेण लोक्यः स्यामिति यत्नतः 1.5.301cd
अनुशिष्टोऽथ नृपतिर्विद्यानिष्क्रयहेतुतः 4.4.1303ab
अनुशिष्टोऽसि किं पित्रा उताहो नेति भण्यताम् 6.2.27ab
अनुशिष्टोऽसि चेद्ब्रूहि तुल्येऽपि मरणे प्रजाः 6.2.30ab
अनुशिष्टोऽसि पुत्रेति वञ्चितोऽस्मीत्यतो मतिः 6.2.49cd
अनुशिष्टो यतः पुत्रः पित्रैवैति समर्थताम् 1.5.300ab
अनुशिष्यापि स नृपं यदा नैच्छद्धनं नृपात् 4.2.1ab
अनुष्टुप्छन्दसं प्राहुः सावित्रीं न्यायसंश्रयात् 5.16.44cd
अनुष्टुप्छन्दसं ब्रूयात्पूर्वपक्षप्रसिद्धये 5.16.43cd
अनुष्ठेयतया श्रुत्या निवृत्तिः सर्वकर्मणाम् 4.4.1228ab
अनुष्ठेयस्य दर्शादेः स्तुत्यर्थत्वं प्रसज्यते 4.4.1140cd
अनुष्ठेयोऽननुष्ठेय इति पश्चान्मतिर्भवेत् 1.3.76cd
अनुसंधानसंसिद्धौ न किंचिन्मानमिष्यते 2.1.144cd
अनुसंधेयमत्रापि वस्तुतत्त्वविशुद्धये 3.4.113cd
अनूक्तं यदधीतं स्याद्यच्चाध्येतव्यमिष्यते 1.5.291ab
अनूक्तेर्यदिदमिति सिद्धोऽर्थोऽनूद्यते यतः 1.5.28cd

अनूद्य च प्रियात्मानं स द्रष्टव्य इतीर्यते	2.1.436cd
अनूद्य निखिलं विश्वं तत्तत्त्वप्रतिपत्तये	4.4.159ab
अनूद्य ब्रह्मता वाक्यान्न प्रविष्टाद्यतः श्रुतेः	2.1.473cd
अनूद्य लोकतो दृष्टे तद्याथात्म्यं प्रबोध्यते	1.4.606cd
अनूद्यापूर्वमैकात्म्यं विधेयमुपपत्तिमत्	1.4.692cd
अनूद्यापैतदुःखेन साक्षात्संगतिमब्रवीत्	3.5.96cd
अनूद्यैव यथाप्राप्तमात्मदृष्टिर्विधीयते	3.2.112cd
अनूद्योक्त्येकदेशेन शीतोऽग्निरिति बोध्यते	2.1.558cd
अनृतन्त्रत्वसामान्यात्तथातीन्द्रियबोधतः	2.4.153cd
अनृतन्त्रे विधिर्नेष्टो वन्ध्यापुत्रोद्भवे यथा	2.4.143ab
अनेककारणं कार्यं यस्माद्दृष्टं शरादिकम्	4.3.758ab
अनेकजन्मसंसिद्धस्ततो यातीति च स्मृतेः	4.4.1059cd
अनेकजन्मोपात्तस्य पुण्यापुण्यस्य कर्मणः	SV 94ab
अनेकभेदसंभिन्नं यदेतद्व्याकृतं जगत्	1.6.10ab
अनेकवासनाचित्रं तल्लिङ्गं पटभित्तिवत्	2.3.86ab
अनेकव्यापृतिमती ह्यावृत्तिर्जगतीक्ष्यते	4.3.580ab
अनेकसाधना यस्मादभिव्यक्तिरिहेक्ष्यते	1.2.97cd
अनेकार्थाभिसंबन्धाच्छौक्ल्यस्य रजते च कः	1.4.473ab
अनेकार्थावबोधित्वे न स्याल्लक्षणवद्वचः	2.1.564cd
अनेकार्थावसायः स्यान्न त्वेवमिह युज्यते	1.5.346cd
अनेकैः संहतश्चैवं कदाचिदुपकारकः	1.4.1573cd
अनेन च यथोक्तेन पाणिपेषोत्थितस्य हि	2.1.364ab
अनेन ध्यानमार्गेण ध्यायमानस्य सर्वदा	2.5.70ab
अनेन वाचोद्गात्रा नो बलं ध्वान्तं तु देवताः	1.3.144ab
अनेन विधृतं जन्म वायुनेदं शरीरकम्	3.7.14ab
अनेन वै न उद्गात्रा वाचात्येष्यन्ति स्वं वपुः	1.3.146cd
अनेन ह्येतदित्युक्त्या तत्पूर्वमुपवर्णितम्	1.4.1007cd
अनेनातिशयवता ह्यस्मद्गोचरवर्तिना	4.3.1877ab
अनेनाप्रतिरूपेण वचसा कार्यशायिना	1.3.149ab
अनेनेति तृतीयेयमित्थंभूतार्थलक्षणा	1.4.983ab
अनेनैव यथोक्तेन ज्योतिषा सकलं जगत्	4.3.343ab
अनेनैवानुमानेन विद्याद्ब्रह्मापि तादृशम्	1.6.47cd

अनेवंविदुषः पुण्यं सुकृतं वृञ्जते स्त्रियः 6.4.16ab
अनैकान्तिकता हेतोः कार्यत्वस्येह सज्जते 4.3.749cd
अनैकान्तिकता हेतोराद्यसंततिवद्भवेत् 1.4.1518cd
अनैकान्तिकता हेतोस्तथा वः संप्रसज्यते 2.1.606cd
अनैकान्तिकता हेतोस्तद्वत्संततिवादिनः 1.4.1511ab
अनोवल्लिङ्गमेत्येतत्प्रत्यगात्मार्थसिद्धये 4.3.1916cd
अन्त आत्मेत्युपासीत तथैवोपासनश्रुतेः 1.4.776cd
अन्तःकरणचेष्टाया निवृत्तौ शान्त उच्यते 4.4.1206ab
अन्तःकरणवृत्तिर्या चक्षुरादिसमाश्रया 3.4.149ab
अन्तःकरणसंबन्धे विज्ञानमिति कर्तरि 2.1.185ab
अन्तः करोति यत्कामी तेऽङ्गारास्तत्समानतः 6.2.109ab
अन्तः संस्थाप्य नयति समष्टिव्यष्टितामसुः 3.3.156cd
अन्तरङ्गं हि विज्ञानं प्रत्यङ्मात्रैकसंश्रयात् SV 367ab
अन्तरण्डविभक्तस्य यथोक्तैः स्यात्प्रतिग्रहैः 5.16.62ab
अन्तरायनिवृत्तौ च व्यपेक्षा वः प्रसज्यते 4.4.341ab
अन्तरायो यतस्तस्मात्पदार्थज्ञानचोदना 4.4.861cd
अन्तरिक्षं यजुर्वेदः पितरश्च पिता तथा 1.5.157ab
अन्तरिक्षगतः प्राणः स एष परमेश्वरः 1.5.188cd
अन्तरिक्षमनाधारं गतौ हेतुनिषेधनम् 3.1.39cd
अन्तरित्यन्यथा मा भूत्प्रसङ्गः प्राणनिश्चितौ 1.3.202cd
अन्तरेण क्रियां तद्वत्फलं नैव प्रसिध्यति 2.4.476ab
अन्तरेण प्रमेयार्थं नापि ते साध्वसाधुनी 1.4.176ab
अन्तरेण विधिं वाक्यश्रवणायापि नेहते 1.4.828ab
अन्तरेणाधिकारं चेन्नात्मबोधस्य संभवः 1.4.1443ab
अन्तरेणापि देहादींस्तत्कार्यं चेत्करोत्ययम् 2.1.300ab
अन्तरेणापि मानानि प्रमातृत्वादिसाक्षितः 4.3.530ab
अन्तरेणापि वचनं बौद्धादेरिव सिद्धितः SV 458ab
अन्तरेणापि संबन्धं कार्यकारणवस्तुनः 4.3.1799ab
अन्तरो यः पृथिव्याः स्यात्क्षितेरभ्यन्तरो हि यः 3.7.27ab
अन्तर्णीतफलं तस्मादिह साधनमुच्यते 1.4.1832cd
अन्तर्णीताखिलानन्तदेवतः प्राणविग्रहः 2.1.14cd
अन्तर्बही रसघनः सैन्धवस्य घनो यथा 4.5.11ab

अन्तर्भवन्ति निखिला विशेषा इति केचन 1.4.947cd
अन्तर्भावः परानन्दे सुखानामाविरिञ्चतः 1.4.1691ab
अन्तर्भावश्च सामान्ये विशेषाणामथोच्यते 1.6.22ab
अन्तर्भावान्न साध्वेतद्विभक्तानां भवेद्यतः 1.2.95cd
अन्तर्भावेऽपि दृष्ट्यादौ मतिविज्ञानयोरिह 4.3.1636ab
अन्तर्भावो यतोऽमीषां श्रोत्रादीन्द्रियकर्मणाम् 1.5.385cd
अन्तर्भूतं तदप्स्वति ह्याप एवेदमित्यतः 5.5.5cd
अन्तर्मेयबलाज्ज्ञानं प्रत्यङ्मोहजसंश्रयम् 2.4.256ab
अन्तर्यामिकृता चैषा नान्यः संभाव्यते प्रभोः 1.4.368cd
अन्तर्यामी तथा साक्षी सर्वज्ञश्चेत्यविद्यया 2.3.10ab
अन्तर्यामीति सोऽत्रापि नातोऽन्योऽस्तीति भण्यते 3.7.53cd
अन्तर्यामी परः साक्षादशरीरोऽगुणोऽद्वयः 3.7.33ab
अन्तर्याम्यादिरूपेण स एव प्रथते मृषा 3.9.157cd
अन्तवद्विषयं दृष्टं न त्वनन्तस्य कुत्रचित् 5.16.63cd
अन्तवान्क्षीयते लोके न त्वनन्तः कुतश्चन 5.16.65cd
अन्तःशरीरे ज्योतिर्मयो हि शुभ्रो यं पश्यन्ति यतयः क्षीणदोषाः 4.4.1257ef
अन्तस्थातीन्द्रियत्वाभ्यां चक्षुरादीन्द्रियं यथा 4.3.143cd
अन्तस्थानि यतोऽक्षाणि प्रत्यक्षाणि न चात्मवत् 4.3.142cd
अन्ताय धावतीत्युक्तं तस्यान्तस्य विशेषणम् 4.3.1163ab
अन्ते वृत्तिमवर्थः स्यात्सर्वं प्राण इतीरणात् 1.5.151cd
अन्त्य एव तमोघाती प्रत्ययश्चेन्मतं यदि 1.4.75ab
अन्त्यं तस्मात्परिज्ञानं सर्वबाध्यस्य बाधकम् 1.4.1557cd
अन्त्यसंस्कारसिद्ध्यर्थं तस्मिन्नग्नौ यथोदिते 6.2.115ab
अन्त्या विशेषा दृष्टान्तः परपक्षेऽपि विद्यते 1.6.55ab
अन्त्योऽविद्यापनुद्बोधो रागादिप्रत्ययोत्थितेः 1.4.1509ab
अन्त्यो नाशो महांश्चेत्स्यान्नाशः सातिशयो यतः 4.3.609ab
अन्त्राद्यभेदतो द्वौ वा यदि वाध्यर्ध उच्यते 1.3.266ab
अन्धं तम इति श्रुत्या तदिहापोद्यतेऽखिलम् 4.4.598cd
अन्धं मूढं तमो यान्ति येऽविद्यां समुपासते 4.4.600ab
अन्धकारस्तमो ज्ञेयं तथा छायामयः पुमान् 3.9.54ab
अन्न एव यतो वृत्तिरत्तुरन्नाद एव च 1.2.184ab

अन्नं चराचरं कृत्स्नमन्नादः प्राण उच्यते 1.4.159cd
अन्नं जुह्वति तत्राग्नौ संभवो रेतसस्ततः 6.2.107ab
अन्नं तद्बवतः सर्वं वयं त्वच्छेषभोगिनः 6.1.31cd
अन्नं दामेति चाप्युक्तं रसादिपरिणामतः 4.3.1942ab
अन्नं दामेति यत्पूर्वं व्याख्यातं शिशुबन्धनम् 4.2.48cd
अन्नं नाड्याश्रयं सूक्ष्मं तच्छ्रुत्येहोपवर्ण्यते 4.2.59ab
अन्नं प्राणश्च देवौ द्वौ द्वयोरेष विनिर्णयः 3.9.22ab
अन्नं ब्रह्मेति निर्वक्ति पुरेवान्यदुपासनम् 5.14.1ab
अन्नत्रयं यदुत्कृष्टं तस्यायं निर्णयोऽधुना 1.5.95ab
अन्नत्रयविभागेन प्रक्रिया त्वधुनोच्यते 1.5.193cd
अन्नत्रयविभागोऽयमध्यात्म उपवर्णितः 1.5.155ab
अन्नत्रयाधिकारे हि मनआदावनात्मनि 1.3.125cd
अन्नदर्शनवच्चैके वासोदृष्टिं प्रचक्षते 6.1.39ab
अन्नपानगृहाद्यर्थान्कृत्वा राजप्रतीक्षिणः 4.3.1964cd
अन्नपानसमुत्था हि शक्तिः प्राणो बलं तथा 2.2.14ab
अन्नप्रतिष्ठमागानमेक आहुर्विपश्चितः 1.3.342ab
अन्नभावं पृथिव्यातस्ते समायान्ति भूमिगाः 6.2.154ef
अन्नमल्पं ततोऽप्यल्पात्कनीयोऽन्नं भवेदतः 1.2.190cd
अन्नमेव परं ब्रह्मेत्येक आहुर्विपश्चितः 5.14.2ab
अन्नमेव भवेदन्नं नान्नमन्नस्य कुत्रचित् 1.2.195cd
अन्नविष्टानि सर्वाणि भूतानीत्यन्नमुच्यते 5.14.12ab
अन्नस्य परिणामेऽनः स्थितो गीतित्वमेति हि 1.3.343ab
अन्नस्य प्रविवेकार्थं भोक्तुः सौक्ष्म्यार्थमेव च 4.2.51ab
अन्नस्य युक्तमेवातस्तमभिव्याददादिति 1.2.184cd
अन्नस्य संभवस्तस्मात्पुमग्नौ तच्च हूयते 6.2.104ab
अन्नाक्षयत्वहेतुत्वात्पुरुषोऽक्षितिरुच्यते 1.5.79ab
अन्नाक्षयो भवेदेवं तयोरव्यतिरेकतः 1.5.81cd
अन्नात्तृत्वनिषेधार्थं सर्वमस्येति भण्यते 2.2.31cd
अन्नात्तेजोभिरत्यर्थं देहः संदिह्यते यतः 4.4.617ab
अन्नाद इत्यतो वक्ति साफल्यप्रतिपत्तये 1.3.284cd
अन्नादवसुदानाभ्यां गुणाभ्यां यः समीक्षते 4.4.1314ab
अन्नादवसुदानाभ्यामविद्योत्थं तु भण्यते 4.4.1309cd

अन्नादृते यतः प्राणः शोषमाशु निगच्छति 5.14.3cd
अन्नादे भ्रूणहा मार्ष्टीत्यादीह वचनं स्मृतेः 1.5.31ef
अन्नाद्यागानमुद्गातुस्तज्ज्ञानं तद्वदाश्रितम् 1.3.386cd
अन्नानि कस्मादित्याह प्रश्नवाक्यविवक्षया 1.5.75cd
अन्नानि संभ्रियन्ते हि दश सप्त च भागशः 6.4.13ab
अन्नान्नादद्वयं सर्वं त्वमेव तदपि प्रभो 6.3.34ab
अन्नाभावे विवक्ष्यन्ते काण्वानां ज्योतिषा सह 4.4.640cd
अन्नार्थिनोऽतो मां सर्वेऽप्यभिसंविशताशु वै 1.3.251cd
अन्नाशितृत्वसिद्ध्यर्थं यथा व्युत्पत्तिरुच्यते 3.9.28ab
अन्नेनाश्नुत इत्येवमध्यर्धस्यापि योजना 3.9.28cd
अन्ने विष्टानि सन्त्येव भूतत्वं यान्ति येन हि 5.14.11cd
अन्नोपकारः सर्वेषामविशिष्टः समीक्ष्यते 1.3.241ab
अन्य आहुः पदार्थत्वात्प्रमाणान्तरगम्यताम् SV 440ab
अन्यकार्यमकार्यं च नान्यत्कारणमीक्ष्यते 2.4.119cd
अन्यच्छ्रेयोऽन्यदुतैव प्रेयस्ते उभे नानार्थे पुरुषं सिनीतः SV 24ab
अन्यतः संगतिः सेयमविचारितसिद्धिका 1.4.217cd
अन्यतः संगतिः सेयमविचारितसिद्धिका 1.4.1323ab
अन्यतः संगतिः सेयमविचारितसिद्धिका 4.4.646ab
अन्यतद्बुद्ध्यपेक्षत्वं तद्बुद्धेर्वः प्रसज्यते 1.2.62cd
अन्यतोऽन्यत एवायं संप्रदायो यथाभवत् 6.5.9ab
अन्यतोऽसौ स्वभावाद्वा न तु मानेन वार्यते SV 82cd
अन्यतो भवने मानं न चेदस्त्विह संशयः SV 80ab
अन्यतो मातृतो जाता अन्यतस्त्या उदाहृताः 2.1.64ab
अन्यत्र यदि नाम स्याद्धूमभावेऽग्निभावता 4.3.726cd
अन्यत्रापि विधौ कल्प्य इहैवासौ समर्थ्यताम् 4.4.1142ab
अन्यत्रापि हि मानानां नैव संप्लव इष्यते SV 1076cd
अन्यत्रावगमो न स्यात्संबन्धज्ञानवर्जनात् SV 872cd
अन्यत्रैव न चाप्यत्र वाक्यार्थो भेदलक्षणः SV 902ab
अन्यत्वमेव विज्ञेयमालोकघटयोस्ततः 4.3.500ab
अन्यत्वेऽवस्थिता बन्धहेतुत्वेन च सर्वदा 4.4.408cd
अन्यथा कल्प्यमानेऽस्मिन्नुक्तदोषपरंपरा 1.4.1123cd
अन्यथा कृतनाशः स्यादकृताभ्यागमस्तथा 1.4.1809ab

अन्यथा कृतनाशः स्यादकृताभ्यागमस्तथा 6.2.134ab
अन्यथाकृत्स्नमेव स्यादनिर्मोक्षश्च सज्यते 3.8.85cd
अन्यथातोऽनुवादः स्याच्छ्रुतेर्ज्ञातार्थबोधनात् 1.6.17cd
अन्यथानुपपत्त्या चेद्विश्वजिद्वत्प्रकल्प्यते 3.3.84ab
अन्यथाप्युपपन्नत्वादर्थापत्तेः क्षयो यतः 3.8.148cd
अन्यथाव्याकृतावस्थाल्लोकादिति वदेच्छ्रुतिः 1.4.1778ab
अन्यथेदं वचः केचिद्व्याचख्युरतिनैपुणात् 5.1.28cd
अन्यथैवाभिसंबन्धं केचिदत्र प्रचक्षते 1.5.225ab
अन्यदीयोऽपि नान्यस्य भेदः स्यात्कल्पनां विना 5.1.87cd
अन्यदीयोऽपि नान्यस्य भेदः स्यात्कल्पनां विना 4.3.1717cd
अन्यदेवेति च श्रुतिः कार्येतरनिषेधिनी 5.1.26cd
अन्यदेवेति वाक्याच्च प्रत्यक्षं नात्मगोचरम् 1.4.565cd
अन्यद्धि मुक्तिफलतः काम्यानां श्रूयते फलम् 3.3.50ab
अन्यद्वाय्वन्तरिक्षाभ्यां भूतत्रयमिहोच्यते 2.3.35cd
अन्यद्विभक्तमिति च तथा द्रष्टव्यमित्यपि 4.3.1616ab
अन्यधर्मे त्वभिन्नं स्यात्स्वतो वस्तु प्रमाश्रयम् SV 955ab
अन्यप्रमाणाविषया वाक्यादेवावगम्यते 1.3.71ab
अन्ययोगव्यवच्छेदे प्रशंसेयमसोर्भवेत् 3.3.171ab
अन्यसंसर्गभावात्तत्तुषकण्डनवद्वृथा 4.3.710cd
अन्यस्मिन्निष्यमाणे च सापेक्षत्वं प्रसज्यते SV 665cd
अन्यस्य ज्योतिषोऽभावात्स्वयंज्योतिः पुमानयम् 4.3.895cd
अन्यस्य तादृशोऽभावात्कुतो दुःखादिसंप्लुतिः 4.3.697cd
अन्यस्यान्यत्र संपत्स्याद्द्वये सा कथं भवेत् 1.4.1256cd
अन्यस्यासौ न चादेशः शक्यो वक्तुं प्रमाणतः 2.3.154ab
अन्यस्यैव हि संवित्स्यात्स्वप्नबुद्धान्तनीडतः 4.3.1123cd
अन्या अन्येन संयान्ति यथान्येनापरास्तथा 6.2.31cd
अन्यादृक्षप्रमाणस्य न च नास्त्यत्र संभवः SV 858cd
अन्यानन्यत्वयोश्चात्र वाच्यावाच्यत्वयोस्तथा 4.3.639ab
अन्यानन्यप्रमेयत्वे तथापीष्टं न सिध्यति 1.4.1116cd
अन्यानन्यप्रमेयेऽपि दोषोऽयं दुर्निवारणः 1.4.1118cd
अन्यानन्योभयात्मत्वकल्पने ह्यसदेव तत् 4.3.637cd
अन्यानपेक्षं तदभूदिति चेन्नैवमिष्यते 1.4.72ab

अन्यानपेक्षं यद्यस्य वृत्तं तत्पारमार्थिकम् 1.6.74ab
अन्यानपेक्षं सन्मानं प्रमेयार्थसमर्पकम् 3.3.81cd
अन्यापेक्षं पृथक्त्वं च स्वयमेवापृथग्घटः 4.3.1673ab
अन्यापेक्षं पृथक्त्वं चेत्स्वत एवापृथग्घटः 5.1.91ab
अन्यापेक्षं पृथक्त्वं चेत्स्वयं तर्ह्यपृथग्घटः SV 964ab
अन्यापेक्षं यतोऽन्यत्वं तेन तद्व्योमकार्ष्ण्यवत् 1.6.74cd
अन्यापेक्षाणि चेद्दद्युः कर्मैकत्वं तदा भवेत् 1.5.229ab
अन्यापोहनपक्षेऽपि शब्दव्यावृत्तिभेदतः 4.3.769ab
अन्याभावस्य भावत्वे स्यादभावः खपुष्पवत् SV 952ab
अन्यार्थानुपपत्तेश्च वेदान्तवचसां तथा SV 276ab
अन्यासाधारणं प्रश्नमप्राक्षीदिति विस्मितः 3.2.133cd
अन्यूनाधिकरूपासु त्वष्टावस्थास्विहात्मनः 1.4.1044ab
अन्येऽतो मृत्यवो गौणास्तैर्मृतौ स्यात्पुनर्जनिः 3.2.21ab
अन्येऽमृतमिदं प्राहुर्दिव्यं चान्द्रमसं पयः 3.9.47ab
अन्ये गतिविवक्षार्थं मुनेः प्रश्नं प्रचक्षते 4.2.14cd
अन्ये तु पण्डितंमन्याः संप्रदायानुसारतः 4.4.796ab
अन्ये तु मन्वते केचिद्गम्भीरन्यायवादिनः SV 378ab
अन्ये त्वत्राभिसंबन्धमेवं व्याचक्षते बुधाः 2.1.21ab
अन्ये त्वाहुर्न शक्नोति कामसंदूषिताशयः SV 343ab
अन्येन केनचिद्व्याप्तिर्व्यापकत्वाद्यथा भुवः 3.6.10cd
अन्येनान्यस्य संबन्धः कृशोऽहमितिवत्क्वचित् SV 117ef
अन्येनान्येन रूपेण विरुद्धान्हन्ति पावकः 3.8.102ab
अन्ये पुनरिमं ग्रन्थमन्यथैव यथोदितात् 4.3.1537ab
अन्ये व्याचक्षते बुद्धिविज्ञानेनेति विस्मिताः 2.1.248ab
अन्येषां वेदतो ज्ञानं भूरिसाधनसंश्रयात् 6.5.10ab
अन्यैव तु विभिन्नात्मा वस्तुनोर्मानमेययोः 4.3.552cd
अन्योऽनन्यश्च विज्ञेयः स्वाभाव्यात्सर्ववस्तुनः 2.1.470cd
अन्योऽन्यं कार्यता चैषां कारणत्वं तथैव च 2.1.222ab
अन्योऽन्यकारणत्वाच्च श्रुत्येह ज्ञानकर्मणी 4.4.122cd
अन्योऽन्यपरिहारेण स्वप्नजाग्रदवस्थयोः 4.3.1081ab
अन्योऽन्यरूपभेदेऽपि प्रेरणानुगमात्तथा SV 635cd
अन्योऽन्यव्यतिरेकित्वान्नान्योऽन्यात्मकता तयोः 1.2.14ab

अन्योऽन्यव्यभिचारित्वं प्राणादेरीक्ष्यते यतः 1.4.661cd
अन्योऽन्यव्यभिचारित्वमज्ञानेऽपि ह्यनात्मनाम् 1.4.1497ab
अन्योऽन्यव्यभिचारित्वात्स्वप्नजाग्रत्पदार्थयोः 2.1.296cd
अन्योऽन्यव्यभिचारोऽस्य वीक्ष्यतेऽनात्मवस्तुनः 2.3.222ab
अन्योऽन्यश्च प्रबन्धेन यतस्तत्रापि जायते 4.3.472cd
अन्योऽन्यानभिसंबन्धान्न विशेषस्तथेतरत् 1.6.80cd
अन्योऽन्यापेक्षतः सिद्धेर्विनान्योऽन्यं न तद्द्वयम् 1.4.363cd
अन्योऽन्यापेक्षसंसिद्धेरन्योऽन्यव्यभिचारतः 1.4.686ab
अन्योऽन्यापेक्षसिद्धित्वान्मिथ्या तदपि पूर्ववत् 1.4.477cd
अन्योऽन्याभावदृष्टेः स्यादन्योऽन्याश्रयता तव SV 959cd
अन्योऽन्यार्थव्यपेक्षित्वात्कार्यकारणवस्तुनोः 4.4.1312ab
अन्योऽन्यार्थसमाप्तित्वात्कर्मधारय एव तु 4.4.1299ab
अन्योऽन्यार्थसमाप्तित्वान्न भेदोऽत्र पदार्थयोः 1.4.1348cd
अन्योऽन्याविषयत्वे तु कुतः सादृश्यधीरियम् 1.2.70ab
अन्योऽन्याव्यतिरेकाच्च कुतो नाशादिसंभवः 1.4.198cd
अन्योऽन्याव्यतिरेकित्वादैकात्म्यं प्राप्नुयात्तयोः 1.6.84ab
अन्योऽन्याश्रयता च स्यान्न च कार्यप्रधानता SV 616ab
अन्योऽन्याश्रयतादोषः कार्यप्रामाण्यवादिनः 1.3.75ab
अन्योऽन्याश्रयतादोषः सत्येवं प्रसजेद्यतः 4.3.547cd
अन्योऽन्याश्रयता दोषः स्यादहंवृत्तिवीक्षणे 1.4.1526cd
अन्योऽन्याश्रयतैवं स्यादहंबुद्ध्यात्मनोर्ध्रुवम् SV 1060cd
अन्योऽन्याश्रयतैवं स्यादेकस्यासिद्धितोऽन्यतः SV 891cd
अन्योऽपि चेद्भवेदन्योऽविरोधो नीलवद्भवेत् SV 947cd
अन्योऽपि योऽत्र कल्प्यः स्यात्सोऽप्यस्मान्नैव भिद्यते 1.4.1399ab
अन्योऽप्यनुभवोपायो मननध्यानलक्षणः SV 761ab
अन्योऽसाविति मिथ्या धीस्तदा स्यान्मोहकारणात् 2.3.156cd
अन्योऽसाविति वाक्येन व्याख्योपासापदस्य तु 1.4.1568ab
अन्योपाये सत्यसति निरोधादेव मुक्तता SV 446cd
अन्यो वा पापकृत्कश्चित्स्पर्शसंभाषणादिभिः 6.4.68ab
अन्वक्षमेव विलयो दृश्यते सार्वलौकिकैः 3.8.142cd
अन्वयव्यतिरेकाख्यो व्यापारोऽत्र तपो मतम् 1.4.1060cd
अन्वयव्यतिरेकाख्यो व्यापारोऽत्र विधीयते 1.4.1059cd

अन्वयव्यतिरेकाख्यो व्यापारो विहितः पुरा 1.4.1345ab
अन्वयव्यतिरेकाभ्यां जाग्रत्स्वप्नसुषुप्तितः SV 441ab
अन्वयव्यतिरेकाभ्यां तथा कृत्स्नानात्मनः 1.4.1349cd
अन्वयव्यतिरेकाभ्यां न जाड्यमतिवर्तते 1.4.308cd
अन्वयव्यतिरेकाभ्यां नातो वाक्यार्थबोधनम् 4.3.401ab
अन्वयव्यतिरेकाभ्यां न्यायो लौकिक उच्यते 6.1.23cd
अन्वयव्यतिरेकाभ्यां पदार्थः स्मर्यते ध्रुवम् SV 207ab
अन्वयव्यतिरेकाभ्यां पदार्थः स्मर्यते ध्रुवम् 2.4.112ab
अन्वयव्यतिरेकाभ्यां प्राणप्राधान्यसिद्धये 1.3.19ab
अन्वयव्यतिरेकाभ्यां ब्रह्मास्मीति तदेक्षते 1.4.64cd
अन्वयव्यतिरेकाभ्यां यथोक्ताभ्यां पदार्थयोः 4.3.1281ab
अन्वयव्यतिरेकाभ्यां यथोक्तैः साधनैर्युतः 4.4.1272ab
अन्वयव्यतिरेकाभ्यां यथोक्तोऽर्थः प्रसिध्यति 1.4.251ab
अन्वयव्यतिरेकाभ्यां लौकिकत्वात्पदार्थयोः 4.4.859ab
अन्वयव्यतिरेकाभ्यां वसिष्ठत्वावबुद्धये 6.1.21ab
अन्वयव्यतिरेकाभ्यां वाक्यनीडपदार्थयोः 4.4.857ab
अन्वयव्यतिरेकाभ्यां विज्ञायात्मानमादितः 4.4.704cd
अन्वयव्यतिरेकाभ्यां स्यात्पदार्थविचक्षणः 4.4.1190cd
अन्वयव्यतिरेकाभ्यां हेतोः स्यात्तत्र निश्चयः 4.3.739cd
अन्वयव्यतिरेकाभ्यामभाववपुषाथवा 2.4.290ab
अन्वयव्यतिरेकाभ्यामात्मानात्मविवेचने 2.4.107cd
अन्वयव्यतिरेकाभ्यामुपरिष्टात्प्रवक्ष्यते 1.3.208cd
अन्वयव्यतिरेकार्था योऽयमित्यादिका श्रुतिः 4.4.977ab
अन्वयव्यतिरेकोक्तिस्तदैक्यान्नेह युज्यते 2.1.165cd
अन्वयव्यतिरेकौ तु वाक्यार्थज्ञानपूर्वकौ SV 499ab
अन्वयव्यतिरेकौ स्तो न ताभ्यामनुमेयधीः 4.3.740cd
अन्वयादिक्रिया त्वस्य तत्तन्त्रत्वाद्विधीयते 2.4.121cd
अन्वयादिनिषेधाय सर्वमात्मेति वाक्यतः 2.4.18ab
अन्वयाद्यात्मबोधार्थं तावत्तत्केन वार्यते 2.1.173cd
अन्वयुङ्क्तात ऊर्ध्वं त्वं मुक्तये ब्रूहि यत्परम् 4.3.1887cd
अन्वर्थे प्रतिशब्दोऽयं फलस्य पुरुषार्थतः 2.1.69ab
अन्ववायानि पाप्मानं प्रतिषेधातिलङ्घनात् 1.3.225cd

अन्वशात्स कथं धीमान्राजानमिति चेच्छृणु 4.3.1827cd
अन्वशात्सकलानर्थहेत्वविद्यापनुत्तये 4.3.1826cd
अन्वाख्यानं सतामेव सर्गादीनां तथा भवेत् 5.1.34ab
अन्वारभेते गच्छन्तं यथोक्ते ज्ञानकर्मणी 4.4.116ab
अप आहारयांचक्र अर्घ्यपाद्यार्थसिद्धये 6.2.56cd
अप एव ससर्जादौ तासु वीर्यमवासृजत् 1.2.178cd
अपकर्षेतरौ याभिः कार्यस्यात्मा समीक्षते 4.3.1214cd
अपकारिण्यपि जने किमु भक्तजनं प्रति 2.4.56cd
अपक्षधर्मता हेतोर्नामरूपाश्रयत्वतः 2.1.607ab
अपक्षपातपतितैर्विद्वद्भिर्वस्तुसिद्धये 4.3.1204cd
अपजुहूनुषितत्वात्तु नादोत्थस्य विकारतः 1.6.12cd
अपत्योत्पत्तये स्त्रीणामधोदेशं प्रजापतिः 6.4.4ab
अपदसीत्यपि गिरा तस्या आनन्त्यमुच्यते 5.16.69ab
अपन्यायो न युक्तोऽतो न्यायवर्त्मासमन्वयात् 3.8.154cd
अपन्यायो वृथा च स्यात्पुमर्थासंभवादिह 1.4.1209cd
अपरब्रह्मतापन्नो भोज्याद्व्यावृत्तमानसः 1.4.1199ab
अपराजिष्णुरित्येवं तस्मादेवाभिधीयते 2.1.63cd
अपराधलघुत्वं च दृष्टं पुंसोऽप्यकामतः 4.4.224cd
अपराधीनसंसिद्धौ भानाविव तमो भवेत् 1.4.686cd
अपरायत्तबोधोऽत्र निदिध्यासनमुच्यते 2.4.217ab
अपरिच्छिन्नसंव्याप्तिर्भुज्युप्रश्नेन भण्यते 3.3.136cd
अपरे पण्डितंमन्याः सम्यग्ज्ञातात्मतत्त्वकाः 3.9.123ab
अपरे लोहितं प्राहुर्जपाकुसुमसंनिभम् 4.4.564ab
अपरोक्षाद्ब्रवेत्तादृङ्नातोऽन्यादृक्कथं चन 3.4.38cd
अपरोक्षान्तमथवा ब्रह्मान्तं वोत्तरस्य तु 3.4.35cd
अपवादं श्रुतिरियं तस्य त्विति जगाद नः 1.4.1553ef
अपवादः पुरा तस्य न पश्यन्तीति वर्णितः 4.4.795cd
अपवादश्च बहुशः कर्मकार्यस्य दृश्यते 1.4.1115ab
अपवादस्य विषयो ज्ञातात्मैकसतत्त्वकः 3.8.77cd
अपविद्धद्वयोऽप्येवं तत्त्वमित्यादिना विना SV 212ab
अपविद्धयशोवीर्यं शरीरं कवियोगतः 1.2.207ab
अपविद्धातिशीत्येव तज्ज्ञानं केन हन्यते 1.2.110cd

अपव्याख्यानतस्तेषां कामा आत्माश्रया इति	4.4.501cd
अपसर्प्यस्य सर्पादेर्न च कार्यं फलं मतम्	SV 747ab
अपह्नुतिर्विभागस्य ह्यविभक्तगिरोच्यते	4.3.1615ab
अपां कतकसंपर्काद्यथात्यन्तप्रसन्नता	4.3.975ab
अपां गुणोऽत्र स्नेहः स्याच्छायादीप्तिरिहेष्यते	3.8.95ab
अपाक्येषु नियुक्तोऽपि कृष्णलाञ्श्रपयेदिति	2.4.179ab
अपाञ्चभौतिकं रूपमिह तन्निर्दिदिक्ष्यते	2.3.103ab
अपादानार्थतैवास्तु दोषस्यान्यत्र दर्शनात्	2.1.369cd
अपान एष कथितो व्यानः सांप्रतमुच्यते	1.5.146cd
अपानवृत्त्या तद्ध्वस्तमित्येतत्कर्मणः फलम्	6.4.44cd
अपानेनाहृतो गन्धो घ्राणस्यैति वशं यथा	3.2.11ab
अपामन्नं भवन्दृष्टो बह्वीनां तनुविग्रहः	3.2.17cd
अपामार्गलतेवायं विरुद्धफलदो भवः	1.4.27ab
अपारमिति कार्यस्य पारः कार्यस्य कारणम्	2.4.413cd
अपारार्थ्यान्न बोधो हि स्यादबोधनिरासतः	SV 908cd
अपास्तकार्यकरणकर्मासङ्गो न तु क्वचित्	4.3.1153ab
अपास्तदेवतात्यक्तद्रव्यं कर्मापि दुर्घटम्	1.4.1730cd
अपास्तनिखिलध्वान्ततज्जं ब्रह्मोपवर्णितम्	5.1.3ab
अपास्तरागादिमला ईक्षन्ते ज्ञं स्वमात्मनि	SV 1134cd
अपास्तर्णोऽथ स कथं कर्मस्वेष नियुज्यते	1.5.259cd
अपास्ताज्ञानतत्कार्यं तत्तु मानात्प्रसिध्यति	1.4.1307cd
अपास्तातिशयानन्दं सुखेनेहानुमीयते	4.3.1877cd
अपास्ताध्यात्मरूपाणां देवतानां समाश्रयः	1.3.259ab
अपास्तानर्थहेतुत्वं यदुक्तं प्रत्यगात्मनः	4.4.285ab
अपास्तान्यव्यपेक्षं चेदात्मदृष्ट्या समीक्षितम्	4.3.307ab
अपास्ताविद्यातज्जत्वदस्थूलाद्युक्तिगोचरः	1.4.151ab
अपास्ताशेषकरणदैवतस्यापि चात्मनः	4.3.874ab
अपास्ताशेषतमसो यत्तत्त्वं प्रत्यगात्मनः	1.4.1410ab
अपास्ताशेषनिर्देशं यदनन्यप्रमाणकम्	3.8.56cd
अपास्ताशेषबाह्यार्थस्तज्जवासनयाञ्चितः	1.3.262ab
अपास्ताशेषभेदस्य यद्रूपं भेदवद्गतम्	2.4.439ab
अपास्ताशेषसंसर्गं यया ब्रह्माधिगम्यते	4.4.804ab

अपास्ताशेषसंसारभावनस्यैवमात्मनः 4.3.975cd
अपास्ताशेषानर्थाप्तपुरुषार्थत्वतः स्वतः 3.5.137ab
अपि काम्यं कृतं सर्वं दुःखात्मकफलत्वतः SV 1108ab
अपि कूटस्थवपुषः प्रतीचः सङ्गकारकम् 4.3.349ab
अपि खे तदसंभाव्यं किमु तत्प्रत्यगात्मनि 3.8.82cd
अपि च ध्वस्तनिःशेषकार्यप्राणादिसाधनः 1.4.1753ab
अपि चाधीयतेऽत्रार्थे वेदवाक्यान्यनेकशः 1.4.808ab
अपि चाभ्यस्यमानस्य दार्ढ्यं दृष्टं जगत्यपि 4.4.830ab
अपि चेद्व्यक्त्यनिर्देश्यं कथंचिन्मोहविभ्रमात् 3.8.54ab
अपि जागरितस्थाने कामो हेतुर्यतस्तयोः 4.3.1016cd
अपि ज्ञातात्मतत्त्वानामभावाज्ज्ञानसंततेः 1.4.1508cd
अपि ज्ञानातिरेकेण बाह्योऽर्थोऽभ्युपगम्यते 4.3.541ab
अपि तत्कार्यकर्तृत्वे तदेवाभ्युपगम्यते 2.4.322cd
अपि दृष्टक्रियाधर्मसामर्थ्यमनिरस्य तु 3.8.153ab
अपि दृष्टार्थतैकात्म्ये कर्मस्विव न भिद्यते SV 669ab
अपि देवान्स संयाति तथोर्जं चोपजीवति 1.5.94ab
अपि दोषद्वयं न स्यादेकरूपे हि शङ्क्यते 4.3.240cd
अपि धानारुहो वृक्षो बीजात्तज्जन्मदर्शनात् 3.9.137ab
अपि पाशुपतास्त्रेण विद्धश्चेन्न ममार यः 1.4.833ab
अपि प्रतीचोऽसत्त्वं स्याज्ज्योतिषः स्थास्नुरूपिणः 4.3.536cd
अपि प्रत्यक्तमो नित्यं भास्वच्चैतन्यबिम्बितम् 1.4.834ab
अपि प्राङ्मानसंव्याप्तेर्यावद्व्युत्पाद्यते न ना 4.4.906cd
अपि प्राणस्य पारार्थ्यं संहतत्वाद्गृहादिवत् 2.1.157ab
अपि प्राप्तं कर्मकाण्डे तद्विरोधात्तु नाब्रवीत् 3.9.121cd
अपि ब्रह्मैव तत्कृत्स्नं तन्मोहादतथेक्ष्यते 1.4.1315cd
अपि भूरिपशोः पुंस एकस्मिन्नपि तस्करैः 1.4.1576ab
अपि भेदेन या बुद्धिः स्यात्सामान्यविशेषयोः SV 974ab
अपि मानान्तरप्राप्तं वस्तुबोधं निवर्तयेत् 1.4.893ab
अपि मानान्तराज्ज्ञाते तद्विरुद्धस्वभावके 4.4.817ab
अपि मानाभिसंबन्धो मेयार्थेनैव युक्तिमान् 1.4.262ab
अपि मिथ्याधियोऽभ्यासः सम्यग्ज्ञानस्य जन्मने 4.4.828ab
अपि वात्स्यायनादीनां शास्त्राणामुक्तहेतुतः 1.4.408ab

अपि विप्रतिषिद्धं च यत्स्वयंज्योतिरात्मकम् 4.3.1383ab
अपि वृन्दावने शून्य इति कामिवचस्तथा SV 423cd
अपि वेदैकदेशस्य प्रामाण्यं यदि नेष्यते 5.1.95ab
अपि शास्त्रं समुल्लङ्घ्य रागादिबलवत्तया 2.1.584ab
अपि शास्त्रात्प्रपन्नेऽस्मिन्पारोक्ष्यानपहारतः SV 771ab
अपि शास्त्रार्थसंबन्ध उत्तरस्याः श्रुतेरयम् 3.9.107ab
अपि सत्यामविद्यायां न संज्ञास्त्यात्मनीदृशी 2.4.479cd
अपि सम्यक्प्रमाणज्ञास्तच्च नर्ते महेश्वरम् 3.8.143cd
अपि सर्वप्रमाणानां किमु वेदान्तशासने SV 471cd
अपि सर्वप्रमाणानामज्ञातत्वादिसिद्धये 1.4.258ab
अपि सर्वप्रमाणानि स्वप्रमेयाभिसंगतेः SV 563ab
अपि सर्वाणीन्द्रियाणि मन एव यतस्ततः 1.5.124ab
अपि स्वार्थविघातं च करोत्युपनिषद्यतः 2.1.539ab
अपि हिंक्रियमाणोऽसि तथोद्गीथे विनिर्दिशेत् 6.3.31ab
अपीतकरणग्रामः पुमान्यद्वत्सुषुप्तगः 4.4.696ab
अपीतकरणग्रामः शब्दाद्यपि न वेत्ति हि 1.4.713cd
अपीताखिलकार्यं सत्तमोमात्रावशेषगम् 5.1.18ab
अपुण्यपुण्योपरमे यं पुनर्भवनिर्भयाः 1.4.1770ab
अपुण्यपुण्योपरमे यं पुनर्भवनिर्भयाः 4.4.592ab
अपुमर्थमिदं प्राप्तं न चेदात्मैव तद्भवेत् 3.4.21ab
अपुमर्थे नियोगे च तात्पर्यं स्यात्तथा सति SV 1037ab
अपुमर्थोपदेष्टृत्वात्तच्च नात्रेत्यकारणम् SV 893cd
अपूर्वं निष्प्रमाणं च दातुं शक्तिरथास्य च 3.8.157ab
अपूर्वदेवतास्वर्गपदार्थेष्वपि लोकतः SV 863ab
अपूर्वपरिणामोऽयमग्निहोत्राख्यकर्मणः 6.2.15ab
अपूर्वपरिणामोऽयमग्निहोत्राख्यकर्मणः 6.2.77ab
अपूर्वमिति कार्यत्वनिषेधायाभिधीयते 2.5.139ab
अपूर्वमिति चेदं स्याददृष्टमिति चोच्यते 4.4.233ab
अपूर्वमेव सं पश्येत्स्वप्नदृग्जाग्रतो यदि 4.3.960ab
अपूर्वादि तथा वाक्यमपि सैन्धवखिल्यवत् 2.1.525cd
अपूर्वादिवचोऽर्थे तु न प्रत्यक्षाद्यपेक्षते 2.4.164ab
अपूर्वादिश्रुतेर्ज्ञेयो ब्रह्मत्वं न ततोऽन्यथा 1.4.1169cd

अपूर्वादिषु जीवत्सु श्रुतिवाक्येषु शक्यते 3.2.103ab
अपूर्वादिस्वभावोऽयं प्रविष्टः प्रतिपादितः 4.3.2cd
अपूर्वाद्यर्थ एवैकः प्राधान्येन विवक्षितः 1.4.1265ab
अपूर्वाद्यर्थवचसा नान्वयाद्यवबोध्यते 4.4.952cd
अपूर्वाद्यात्मकं ब्रह्म निःसंसर्गं प्रपद्यते 3.4.48cd
अपूर्वाद्यात्मकं वस्तु यत्र साक्षात्प्रसिध्यति 1.4.182ab
अपूर्वाद्यात्मनात्मायमात्मन्येवावसीयताम् 2.1.237cd
अपूर्वाद्यादिभिर्वाक्यैः प्रतिज्ञार्थोपसंहृतिः 2.1.502cd
अपूर्वानपराद्युक्तेर्न ध्वस्तान्ध्यस्य युज्यते 1.4.102cd
अपूर्वानपराद्युक्तेर्नेति नेत्यादिवाक्यतः 4.4.37cd
अपूर्वानपराद्येकः पूर्णः स्वात्मन्यवस्थितः 3.9.99cd
अपूर्वानपरानन्ततत्त्वं ब्रह्मैव वाक्यतः 3.7.56cd
अपूर्वानपरानन्तप्रज्ञानैकरसाद्वयम् 5.1.70cd
अपूर्वानपरानन्तप्रत्यगात्मैव केवलः 2.4.299cd
अपूर्वानपरानन्तराबाह्यं ब्रह्मलक्षणम् 4.4.162ab
अपूर्वानपरानन्तराबाह्योक्तिश्च दुःस्थिता 1.4.962cd
अपूर्वानपराबाह्यं ब्रह्मास्मीति विजानतः 1.4.817ab
अपूर्वानपराबाह्यं भेदसंसर्गवर्जितम् 5.1.71ab
अपूर्वानपरामध्यप्रत्यग्याथात्म्यवित्तये 2.5.62ab
अपूर्वानपरेत्याद्या तथा च सति युज्यते 4.4.996cd
अपूर्वानपरोक्तेर्हि कार्यकारणतात्मनः 2.4.243ab
अपूर्वार्थपरिच्छेदात्स्मृतिर्नातो भवेदियम् 4.3.678cd
अपृथक्त्वगुणद्रव्यं पृथक्त्वं संश्रयेत्कथम् 4.3.1670ab
अपृथग्वा मिथस्ते स्युर्न तथापि भिदेक्ष्यते 4.3.1669cd
अपृष्टेनापि वक्तव्या तस्मै विद्या विपश्चिता 2.1.35cd
अपेक्षते चेत्सिद्धोऽसौ नासिद्धोऽपेक्षितुं क्षमः 1.4.232ab
अपेक्षते यतो नान्यत्किंचित्साधनमण्वपि 2.1.522cd
अपेक्षा जायते किंतु ह्यन्वयेतरमात्रतः 4.3.760cd
अपेक्षाज्ञानमात्रैकहेतुत्वथानत्वकारणात् 4.3.400ab
अपेक्षाज्ञानहेतुत्थं कार्यकारणवस्त्वतः 2.3.193ab
अपेक्षाप्यत्र लिङ्गोक्तेः कार्यादौ नैव जायते 4.3.759ab
अपेक्षामात्रतः सिद्धेर्व्योम्नि कार्ष्ण्यादिवृत्तवत् 1.6.64cd

अपेक्षावृत्तवद्वस्तु यावत्किंचिदिहेक्ष्यते 3.4.148ab

अपेक्ष्याभिधयैकात्म्यमवबोधयति श्रुतिः 2.4.181cd

अपेतकारकग्रामः प्रतीचैवानुभूयते 1.4.667cd

अपेतकारकत्वादिहेतोरज्ञानतो हते: 4.3.1300ab

अपेतकारकत्वोऽपि कर्मोत्थापितभावनः 4.3.876ab

अपेतसाधनस्यापि पश्यतः स्वप्नविभ्रमम् 4.3.1007ab

अपेताशेषसंसर्गं तयैव ब्रह्म गम्यते 4.4.808ab

अपैति नासि शबरो राजासीत्युक्तितो यथा 4.4.882cd

अपोऽगच्छत्स्वयोनिं च तदहं भूय आददे 6.4.21cd

अपोदितत्वाद्ब्रह्मादिदर्शनस्येति किं पुनः 2.4.261ab

अपौरुषेयवाक्यत्वं समानमभिधाश्रुते: 2.4.165ab

अप्क्लिन्नः पार्थिवो धातुस्तेजसा परिपच्यते 2.3.43ab

अप्पात्रोत्थापिताद्भानोर्दिवि भानुर्यथेक्ष्यते 1.4.613ab

अप्प्रतिष्ठागुणं देवमुपास्ते योऽनिशं नरः 1.2.168ab

अप्यज्ञातफलं साक्षान्मान्तरैर्विधिसंश्रयात् SV 767ab

अप्यज्ञातात्मयाथात्म्यो जिज्ञासुर्योऽत्र वस्तुनि 3.5.141ab

अप्यज्ञानादि निःशेषप्रमेयव्यवधानकृत् SV 793ab

अप्यद्वयं परं ब्रह्म द्वयवत्प्रथते मृषा 3.5.42cd

अप्यधूमनिवृत्तिश्चानग्निव्यावृत्तिरूपिण: 4.3.778ab

अप्यनर्थाय कर्म स्यात्क्रियमाणं न मुक्तये SV 261ab

अप्यन्यतस्त्वजायी स्यात्सापत्नभ्रातृमर्दनः 2.1.64cd

अप्यभावात्मकत्वेऽपि सतोऽभावात्मकत्वतः SV 935ab

अप्यभावो न लभते किमु भावोऽतिरेकताम् 3.8.21cd

अप्यभिव्यक्तिरूपेऽस्मिन्मोक्षे नैवास्ति कार्यता 4.4.315ab

अप्यभ्युपगमे चैषां नैव दोषस्य संभवः 5.16.57ab

अप्यभ्युपगमे नायं दोषोऽस्मान्प्रति ढौकते 4.4.1038ab

अप्ययश्च यथाध्यात्मं श्रेयान्प्राणस्ततोऽन्यतः 1.5.379cd

अप्यर्थे चनशब्दोऽयमभावस्यापि वारकः 2.1.318ab

अप्यसङ्गस्वभावस्य संपर्कं कुरुतो बलात् SV 53cd

अप्यात्मैवेह सर्वत्र स्वयंज्योतिः प्रतीयते 4.3.1466ab

अप्युत्थापितबुद्धीनां भेदेऽसंभावना न च 5.1.98cd

अप्युत्पन्नात्मबोधानामधिकारासमाप्तितः 1.4.103ab

अप्युपादीयमानं च सिद्धं वस्तु न कर्मणि SV 451ab
अप्येतर्हि यथान्यायं यो वेदात्मानमद्वयम् 1.4.1460ab
अप्यौपनिषदंमन्याः केचिदत्यन्तनैपुणात् 2.3.90ab
अप्रकाशप्रकाशित्वान्न तथात्मप्रकाशने 4.3.1457cd
अप्रख्यातो यथैवात्मा व्याकृते ख्यातिमेयिवान् 1.4.1020ab
अप्रज्ञातात्मतत्त्वः सन्यदि नाम दिवानिशम् 1.4.1680ab
अप्रज्ञातात्मयाथात्म्यं ब्रह्मैव तदितीक्ष्यताम् 1.4.1223cd
अप्रतर्क्यमविज्ञेयमित्येतत्स्वानुभूतितः 1.4.291cd
अप्रत्यक्षं मतं येषां ज्ञानं तान्प्रति भण्यते 1.4.450ab
अप्रत्यक्षेऽपि तस्मिंस्तत्पुंस्क्रियालिङ्गदर्शनात् 4.3.24cd
अप्रत्यक्षात्परज्ञप्तिसंगतेः स्यादनर्थिका 2.1.145cd
अप्रत्याख्येयो ह्यर्थश्च सत्यस्यावश्यरक्षणात् 4.3.1891ab
अप्रधृष्यं तथा प्राणमृत्वा नेशुः सहस्रधा 1.3.176ab
अप्रपञ्चात्मके भूम्नि प्रत्यग्बोधः प्रजायते 1.4.996cd
अप्रबुद्धात्मतत्त्वः सन्कारणात्मतया स्थितः 4.4.988cd
अप्रमत्तस्तदा भवति योगो हि प्रभवाप्ययौ 4.4.1255cd
अप्रमाणं ब्रुवाणस्तु नास्माभिर्विनिवार्यते 1.4.1768cd
अप्रमादकराणीह भक्ष्यमेध्यानि यानि च 6.3.14cd
अप्रमित्सित एकस्मिन्निष्ठां यात्यचिकीर्षिते 2.3.200cd
अप्रमेयं कथं वस्तु प्रमाणेन प्रमीयते 4.4.680ab
अप्रमेयं हि यद्वस्तु न तच्छक्यं प्रमाणतः 3.4.81ab
अप्रयत्नोत्थितो वेदो नित्यः स्याद्व्योमवत्स्वतः 2.4.305cd
अप्ररूढेन्द्रियत्वाच्च रागद्वेषाद्यसंप्लुतिः 2.1.345ab
अप्रवर्त्यक्रियावत्स्युर्व्योम्नि सर्वाः प्रवृत्तयः 2.1.62cd
अप्रविश्य प्रयोगं तद्वित्तमित्युपदिश्यते 3.5.112cd
अप्रविष्टं यतो वेश्म परिच्छिन्नेन शक्यते 1.4.530ab
अप्रविष्टस्वभावस्य दिग्देशाद्यनभिप्लुतेः 1.4.608ab
अप्रविष्टस्वभावस्य सशब्देन परिग्रहात् 1.4.104ab
अप्रविष्टस्वभावोऽपि कार्यमात्माविशज्जगत् 1.4.622cd
अप्रवृत्तप्रवृत्तिश्च तथा बुद्धार्थबोधनम् SV 756cd
अप्रवृत्तप्रवृत्तिस्तु न्यायाभावान्न युज्यते 2.4.115cd
अप्रवृत्तप्रवृत्तेश्च कारकत्वं न युज्यते SV 525ab

अप्रसिद्धघटाद्यर्थोऽघटाद्यर्थापनोदनम् 4.3.1664ab
अप्रसिद्धाभिधानोक्त्या वादिव्यामोहसिद्धये 3.3.140ab
अप्रसिद्धार्थसंज्ञाभिरुक्तेश्चेदप्रबोधनम् 2.1.131ab
अप्रसिद्धे त्वथैकात्म्ये निवृत्तिरिह चोद्यते 1.4.1233ab
अप्रसिद्धे प्रसिद्धानां निषेधाच्छून्यताग्रहः 2.3.205cd
अप्राक्षीत्परमात्मानं कहोलोऽपि न दुःखिनम् 3.5.9cd
अप्राणस्य न वागस्ति वागप्युच्चार्यते बलात् 5.10.5cd
अप्रात्यक्ष्यात्किलेत्युक्तिरनुमानाद्धि तद्गतिः 6.2.47cd
अप्राधान्यं तदन्येषां तथापि तु न कर्मणाम् 1.4.1490cd
अप्राप्तं दुःखवन्मोहान्मन्वानः सुखमुत्तमम् 4.4.258ab
अप्राप्ततत्त्वनिष्ठोऽतः पाण्डित्ये विनियुज्यते 3.5.174cd
अप्राप्तपरमार्थार्थी ज्ञानमात्रं जिघृक्षितम् 4.4.114cd
अप्राप्तांशानुपात्येव सर्वं एव विधिर्यतः 1.4.759cd
अप्राप्तांशे यतो नित्यं विधिः सर्वोऽपि चेष्यते 4.4.937cd
अप्राप्ता सर्वमात्मेति सैवातो धीर्विधीयते 2.4.96cd
अप्राप्य परमात्मानमन्तराले व्यवस्थितिः 1.4.1713cd
अप्रामाण्यं कथं तस्याः कुतोऽतो मानतान्यथा 2.1.545cd
अप्रामाण्यं पुनस्त्रेधेत्यत एतत्सुसंस्थितम् 1.4.422cd
अप्रामाण्यं श्रुतेः प्राप्तस्वार्थस्याप्रतिपादनात् 4.4.785cd
अप्रामाण्यप्रसक्तिश्च स्यादितोऽन्यार्थकल्पने SV 160ab
अप्रामाण्यप्रसक्तिश्चेन्न क्लृप्त्यन्तरसंश्रयात् 1.4.149cd
अप्रामाण्यमतस्तस्याः कर्मकाण्डस्य मानता 2.1.539cd
अप्रियं विजिहासन्ति न तु जानन्ति साधनम् SV 1015cd
अप्रियारिष्टिवाक्याभ्यामयमर्थोऽवसीयते 1.4.1473ab
अप्सु कारणभूतासु तस्मादग्निः प्रतिष्ठितः 1.2.167cd
अप्सु रेतसि बुद्धौ च पुरुषं ब्रह्म चेतनम् 2.1.67ab
अबलः सन्पतत्येष जीर्णमन्दिरवत्क्षितौ 4.3.1929cd
अबल्यं नीत्वेति तथा प्राणोत्क्रान्तिः प्रवक्ष्यते 2.2.15ab
अबाधाच्च प्रमाणत्वं वस्तुन्यक्षादिवच्छ्रुतेः SV 882cd
अबाधितं तमोऽत्रास्त इत्युक्तिर्जडवक्तृका 2.4.209cd
अबाह्याभ्यन्तरः कृत्स्नः प्रज्ञानघनमात्रभाक् 4.4.275ab
अबिभेदन्यतो हेतोर्न त्वसामर्थ्यकारणात् 4.3.1888cd

अबुद्धं प्रेरको वेदो ज्ञापना प्रेरणा मता SV 637cd
अबुद्धबोधनं मुक्त्वा नान्यत्कार्यं क्वचिद्यतः 4.3.165ab
अबुद्धिपूर्वकत्वाच्च यथावस्त्वनुरोध्यपि 2.4.306ab
अबुध्यमानः संसुप्त आपिष्यापिष्य बोधितः 2.1.153cd
अबुभुक्षोऽपिपासश्च प्राणकारणवर्जनात् 1.4.1379cd
अब्देशा पृथिवी कृत्स्ना तेजोदेशं तथा जलम् 4.2.24ab
अब्धिरेकायनं यद्वत्सर्वासां सरितां तथा 2.4.332ab
अब्धिस्थानीयमैकात्म्यं प्राप्योक्तेर्विनिवर्तते 2.4.415cd
अब्धौ क्षिप्तानि तानि स्युरन्यार्थासंभवत्वतः 5.1.72cd
अब्रवीद्भ्रान्तिमात्रत्वं मृत्तिकादिनिदर्शनैः 3.8.22cd
अब्रवीन्न तु तत्साध्यं तदुक्त्यर्थं परा श्रुतिः 1.5.221cd
अब्रह्मत्वं न तद्धानिरुपायासंभवात्क्वचित् 1.4.1210cd
अब्रह्मविषये क्लृप्ते ब्रह्मभावी पुमानिति 1.4.1235cd
अब्रह्मानात्मताहेतौ प्रत्यग्ध्वान्ते निवर्तिते 1.4.1414ab
अब्रह्मानात्मते यद्वदत्राज्ञाननिबन्धने SV 905ab
अब्रह्मानात्मविज्ञानमोहोत्थध्वंसहेतुतः 1.4.819ab
अब्रह्मानात्मविषयमोहस्येति न तत्तथा 1.4.822cd
अब्रह्मानात्मापह्नुत्यासंसर्गैकात्म्यधीर्भवेत् 3.4.46cd
अब्रह्माप्रकृतं ब्रूयात्कथं राजातिपण्डितः 2.1.449cd
अब्रह्मिष्ठत्वसिद्ध्यर्थमतोऽप्राक्षीद्रुषान्वितः 3.9.103ab
अब्रह्मेव तदाभाति मोहसंवीतचेतसः 1.4.1170cd
अब्राह्मणादिवत्तत्स्यादसदेवेति निश्चितिः 4.3.576cd
अभग्नं मृत्युना यस्मात्प्राणस्यैव व्रतं ततः 1.5.384ab
अभयं त्वामिति कथं राज्ञाशीस्तं प्रतीर्यते 4.2.99cd
अभयं त्वामिति नृपो यथोक्तज्ञानलिङ्गनम् 4.2.109cd
अभयं त्वामिति प्राह याज्ञवल्क्यं स पार्थिवः 4.2.96cd
अभयं त्वामिति वचस्तद्ध्यस्याप्राप्तमुच्यते 4.2.101cd
अभयं वेदयसीत्येतन्न चासाक्षात्कृते परे 4.2.106ab
अभयस्य प्रदातृत्वान्नन्ववाप्ताभयो गुरुः 4.2.99ab
अभावगमकं नापि संबन्धेनास्य तुल्यता SV 879cd
अभावत्वनिषेधार्थं द्रष्ट्रक्षरमिहोच्यते 3.8.174ab
अभावनिश्चयाभावात्प्रसंख्यानं फलाय नः SV 767cd

अभावनिष्ठं तच्चेत्स्यान्मुख्यं ब्रह्म न सिध्यति 2.4.11ab
अभावभावयोस्तद्वद्भावरूपेषु का भिदा SV 924cd
अभावमपि नाप्नोति कास्था भूत्यै विनात्मना 4.3.1692cd
अभावमात्रबोधित्वान्नाभावादपि भेदधीः 4.4.665ab
अभावमानक्लृप्त्यर्थो यश्चायासः कृतो महान् 1.6.90ab
अभावयोगं भावश्चेत्सहते नीलयोगवत् SV 930ab
अभावस्य च भावत्वाद्भावसिद्धेश्च दृष्टितः 4.3.1437ab
अभावस्य ततोऽन्यत्वादन्वयव्यतिरेकतः 2.4.11cd
अभावस्यापि तत्साक्ष्यात्तदभावः कुतो मितेः 3.9.152cd
अभावाच्च त्वदन्यस्य सर्वमात्मेति शासनात् 4.2.112cd
अभावात्पुरुषस्येह न तु सिद्धोऽपि वैदिकः SV 679cd
अभावात्मकतां प्राप्ता गम्यन्ते नेश्वरैरपि 4.3.1690cd
अभावादनयोरात्मा स्वात्मस्थः संप्रसीदति 4.3.1098cd
अभावादविशेषात्मज्ञानोऽयं व्यवतिष्ठते 4.3.1200cd
अभावेऽप्युपपन्नत्वात्सुषुप्ते चाप्यनीक्षणात् SV 386cd
अभावेन प्रमाणेन तेनोक्तं ते विरुध्यते SV 173cd
अभावोऽप्युपकुरुते लोकेऽस्मिन्भाववद्यतः 4.3.233ab
अभावो येन भावेन भाव्यतेऽस्ति न नास्ति सः 1.4.1374ab
अभिचारार्थमेतस्मिन्नुपस्थाने यथोदिते 5.16.73ab
अभितोऽनुभवाक्रान्ता ज्ञाताज्ञातत्वभूमिषु SV 1001ab
अभित्तौ च तयोरैक्यात्कार्यकारणता कुतः SV 258cd
अभिधाज्ञानगम्यत्वनिषेधायेतिशब्दनम् 1.4.718ab
अभिधा तत्त्वमस्यादि सरित्तीरफलोक्तिवत् 2.4.159cd
अभिधानतयैवैनमोंकारं विदुरञ्जसा 5.1.127ab
अभिधानस्य शान्तादेः प्रत्यक्षेणेह सर्वतः 4.4.1204cd
अभिधानाकृतिर्नामशब्देनेहाभिधीयते 1.4.391ab
अभिधानाभिधेयार्थज्ञानमेव व्यपेक्षते 2.4.182cd
अभिधानैकदेशोक्त्या विकल्पः फलगोचरः 5.16.73cd
अभिधा बोधयन्तीयं नान्यत्किंचिदपेक्षते 2.4.154cd
अभिधाभिधेयसंबन्धमङ्गीकृत्य यतोऽक्षरे 2.3.242ab
अभिधायाश्च सास्त्येव किमिति स्यादमानता 2.4.169cd
अभिधाश्रुतिश्चेत्तत्सिद्धौ व्यायच्छेत प्रयत्नतः 1.4.879ab

अभिधाश्रुतेः प्रमाणत्वं सुप्तोत्थापकवाक्यवत् 2.4.148cd
अभिधीयत इत्यादिवचसापि स नोच्यते SV 314ab
अभिधेयं न यद्वस्तुप्रत्ययश्च न ढौकते 1.4.892ab
अभिधेयस्य गायत्री यस्येयं त्रिपदा मता 5.16.19ab
अभिधेयाकृतिस्तद्वद्रूपमित्युपदिश्यते 1.4.391cd
अभिधेयाभिधानाख्यराशी नित्यौ व्यवस्थितौ 5.16.12ab
अभिधेयार्थजन्मापि ह्यभिधासंभवोक्तितः 2.4.315ab
अभिधेयोपसंहारस्त्रिलोकीवचसोदितः 5.16.17ab
अभिन्न एव भूतात्मा प्रतिभूतसमाप्तितः 1.4.142ab
अभिन्नं सद्विभिन्नत्वं न कथंचित्प्रपद्यते 1.6.73ab
अभिन्ननामरूपैकः प्रलयोऽयनमेकता 2.4.328cd
अभिन्नबुद्ध्याभिन्नत्वं भिन्नधीभिश्च भिन्नताम् 1.4.153ab
अभिन्नमातृमानादिरात्मैवैकोऽद्वयः स्वतः 1.4.1330cd
अभिन्नमातृमानादिरात्मैवैकोऽद्वयः स्वतः 3.4.132cd
अभिन्नवचसा भिन्नप्रतिषेधोऽभिधीयते 1.6.69ab
अभिन्नस्यात्मनो मोहाद्भेदकानीति मन्वते SV 114ab
अभिन्नोऽपि हि बुद्ध्यात्मा विपर्यासितबुद्धिभिः 4.3.476ab
अभिप्रायवतोऽभावादभिप्रायानुपातिनः SV 503ab
अभिप्रेतापि न तदा प्रवृत्तिर्यदि वेतरा SV 598ab
अभिभूतस्वरूपाणां काष्ठनिर्मथनादिना SV 145ab
अभिमन्त्रयते साधुकर्मावाप्त्यै स्वयं पतिः 6.4.127cd
अभिमर्शनस्य यो मन्त्रो ग्रहणस्य स एव तु 6.4.22ab
अभिमानश्च यत्रायं सर्वलोकस्य गम्यते SV 187ab
अभिव्यक्तं च सदिदं पुनरव्यक्ततामितम् 3.8.11ab
अभिव्यक्तस्मृतिः सोऽथ बाह्यां चेष्टां प्रपद्यते 4.3.285cd
अभिव्यक्तस्य भूयोऽपि निष्फलं मान्तरेक्षणम् SV 698cd
अभिव्यक्तिं प्रयात्यर्थः पुरा सन्नेव सर्वदा 1.2.98cd
अभिव्यक्तिः सतश्चेत्स्याद्यस्य मुक्तस्य तत्सुखम् 4.4.326cd
अभिव्यक्तिः सुखस्यास्तु कामं ज्ञानेन संगतेः 4.4.338ab
अभिव्यक्तिः स्वतोभास्वद्बोधमात्रैकरूपतः 4.4.313cd
अभिव्यक्तितिरोभूतिद्वैविध्यापेक्षयैव तु 1.2.92cd
अभिव्यक्तिर्न चेदेवं नाभिव्यक्तिः सदा तदा 4.4.343cd

अभिव्यक्तिर्मताथापि कादाचित्की न सर्वदा 4.4.340ab

अभिव्यक्तिश्च नैवास्ति सौष्ण्याद्यात्मकवस्तुन: 4.4.316ab

अभिव्यक्ते: पुराप्येतद्रूपमासीत्स्वभावत: 5.16.50ab

अभिव्यक्तोऽथ सिद्धोऽयं स्वतो वा यदि वान्यत: SV 698ab

अभिव्यक्तौ तु तत्साक्षात्समष्टिव्यष्टिलक्षणम् 5.16.50cd

अभिव्यङ्ग्यसजातीयो व्यञ्जको रूपदीपवत् 3.9.73cd

अभिव्यङ्ग्याभिसंबन्ध: स च वागित्यथावदत् 4.4.421cd

अभिव्यञ्जकतन्त्रस्तु मोक्षस्तेनाक्षयो मत: SV 300cd

अभिव्यञ्जकधर्मा वा परिस्पन्दात्मकास्तथा 4.3.435ab

अभिव्यञ्जकमेवेष्टं प्रमाणं न तु कारकम् 1.4.1211ab

अभिव्यनक्ति दीपोऽयमात्मनात्मानमस्ववत् 4.3.513cd

अभिव्यनक्ति नो ज्ञातं नातोऽस्य स्यात्प्रमेयता 4.4.685cd

अभिष्टुतं प्रयत्नेन फलं यज्ज्ञानकर्मणो: 1.4.53ab

अभिष्टुतौ कथं नाम भवेतामिति भण्यते 1.2.209cd

अभिसंधिरविव्यत्सन्नित्यभूत्सुरविद्विषाम् 1.3.173ab

अभीति चाभिमुख्येऽर्थे सं तु सामस्त्य इष्यते 4.4.17ab

अभीष्टगर्भाधानाय जायामालिङ्गते पति: 6.4.94ab

अभीष्टपुरुषार्थस्य बाधश्चैवं प्रसज्यते 1.4.1263ab

अभुक्तस्याप्युपात्तस्य ह्यविद्यापिहितात्मनाम् 1.4.1789ab

अभूतदृष्टिकर्तृत्वे द्रष्टृत्वं द्रष्टुरिष्यते 4.3.1572ab

अभूतभवनं चार्थे नित्यत्वादात्मनश्च न SV 702cd

अभूतभूतिर्नैवातो युज्यतेऽनुभवात्मनि 2.4.192cd

अभूत्प्रतीचोऽन्यत्रायमन्यस्माच्चायमागत: 2.1.210ab

अभूत्वा भवनं तस्मात्कादाचित्कं न दोषभाक् 2.1.202cd

अभून्मम मनोऽन्यत्र यतो नाद्राक्षमित्यत: 1.5.106cd

अभेद: किं तयोर्योग: किं वैकात्म्यमभिन्नता 1.6.60ab

अभेदधी: कथं तत्र विशेषणविशेष्ययो: 1.6.68cd

अभेदव्यतिरेकाभ्यां वस्त्वन्तरमिहात्मन: 2.1.381ab

अभेदेऽनित्यतासक्ति: स्थास्नुर्भेदे प्रसज्यते 4.3.634ab

अभेदे च तयोरैक्यात्कार्यकारणता कुत: SV 61cd

अभेदेनैव वर्तेत पृथक्ता यदि वस्तुषु SV 962ab

अभ्यन्तरतमं सूत्रं ब्रह्मलोकावधेरपि 3.7.8ab

अभ्यस्तेनामृतेर्यस्मात्सायुज्यादि समश्नुते 1.5.390ab
अभ्याददान इति तत्कर्तृत्वं स्यादिहात्मनः 4.4.22cd
अभ्याददान इति तु तेजोमात्राः स्वदेशतः 4.4.23cd
अभ्याददान एवायमन्ववक्रामतीश्वरः 4.4.44ab
अभ्यादधति यच्चाग्नौ प्रेतं मां ज्ञातयोऽथ तत् 5.13.4ab
अभ्यारोहजपः कर्म ज्ञानं त्विह परीक्ष्यते 1.3.33cd
अभ्यारोहजपः सोऽथ प्राप्तावसर उच्यते 1.3.345cd
अभ्यारोहजपस्येह प्राण एवास्तु देवता 1.3.18ab
अभ्यारोहत्यनेनातो ह्यभ्यारोहो जपः स्मृतः 1.3.352cd
अभ्यासस्य तदाप्राप्तेरपूर्वविधिरिष्यते 1.4.778cd
अभ्याहितमपि जगत्सहतेऽग्निर्यतस्ततः 2.1.66ab
अभ्युपेताप्यभिव्यक्तिर्नाभिव्यङ्ग्यस्य विक्रिया SV 147ab
अभ्युपेतार्थहानं च तदभ्युपगमे सति 4.3.585cd
अभ्युपेतार्थहानिः स्यात्तथापीष्टं न सिध्यति 4.3.589cd
अभ्युपेतेऽपि च विधौ न प्रवृत्तिरिहेष्यते 1.4.920ab
अभ्युपेतो मदुक्तश्चेत्सिद्धं नः स्यात्प्रयोजनम् 4.3.259cd
अभ्युपेतौ च मानादेस्तस्य कार्त्स्न्यं विहन्यते 1.4.1285ab
अभ्युपेत्यापि वक्ष्यामीत्येवमेतत्समञ्जसम् 1.4.921cd
अभ्युपेत्याप्यसिद्धत्वं तत्सिद्धत्वाभिधित्सया 2.5.9ab
अभ्युपेत्यैतदस्माभिरुच्यते संभवादिति 1.4.851ab
अभ्युपेत्यैतदुदितं न तु वाक्यविदां नयः 2.1.563ab
अभ्युपेयस्त्वयापीह यथा तदपि मे शृणु 4.3.253cd
अभ्रयानं यथाज्ञानाच्छशभृत्यध्यवस्यति 4.3.418ab
अभ्रान्तं चेन्द्रियज्ञानं तेषु चैवोपजायते 4.3.703ab
अभ्रान्तस्य हि केशादौ यदा सदृशधीस्तदा 4.3.668ab
अममापरिग्रहोक्तेर्निष्कर्मा मुनिरुच्यते 3.5.127cd
अमात्यादीन्यथादाय स्वात्मभोगप्रसिद्धये 2.1.302ab
अमात्वाशङ्कासद्भावाद्यथोक्तार्थविनिश्चितौ 5.1.72ab
अमात्वाशङ्कासद्भावान्मान्तरैश्चाविरोधतः SV 209ab
अमानकं कथं च स्यादज्ञातत्वमिहोच्यताम् SV 988ab
अमानात्कल्प्यते यादृक्तत्तथैवेति साहसम् 1.4.901cd
अमानित्वादिकं वस्तु यथेहापि तथेष्यताम् 4.4.849cd

अमितार्थानुगं ज्ञानं प्रमेयार्थानुरञ्जितम् 4.4.751ab
अमीमांसक इत्युच्चैरमीमांसक इत्यतः SV 552ab
अमुक्तावथवा मुक्तौ विशेषोऽस्ति न कश्चन 4.4.329ab
अमुमग्निममुं सोमं यजेति यजिसंश्रवात् 1.4.131cd
अमुमुक्षुत्वमाशङ्क्य भवत्यै तत्प्रदित्सितम् 2.4.65ab
अमूर्तत्वादमर्त्यं तद्यद्वद्यापि त्यदतीन्द्रियम् 2.3.31ab
अमूर्तयोरपि रसो लिङ्गात्मा गृह्यतां तथा 2.3.60ab
अमूर्तस्य परा निष्ठा कारणात्मा पुरोदितः 2.3.178ab
अमूर्तामृतयत्त्यत्तु वाय्वाकाशद्वयं स्मृतम् 2.3.28cd
अमृतं तद्विरुद्धं च ध्रुवं यन्न विपद्यते 2.3.24cd
अमृतं मधु नद्योऽपि मदर्थं सर्वदा शुभम् 6.3.45cd
अमृतं मृत्युघातित्वाच्छास्त्रीये ज्ञानकर्मणी 1.3.357cd
अमृतत्वस्य नाशापि वित्तसाध्येन कर्मणा 2.4.54cd
अमृतप्राप्तयेऽलं स्यात्साधनान्तरनिस्पृहम् 4.5.21cd
अमृतिश्चाप्यनुत्क्रान्तौ सत्सु प्राणेषु का मृतिः 3.2.25cd
अमृतोऽमृतमित्याह स्वयं विद्वानिति श्रुतिः 4.4.642cd
अमृतोऽस्थूलदेहत्वात्प्राणमात्रस्वभावतः 5.16.83cd
अमृतोक्त्याथ नाशोऽस्य वार्यते यो निरन्वयः 4.4.1333cd
अमृतो नित्य एवातो न नाशी स्थूलदेहवत् 2.5.26cd
अमेयमानमात्रेकं तदात्मेति प्रचक्षते 1.4.699cd
अमोऽहमितिमन्त्रोक्त्या तावावां देवतात्मकौ 6.4.94cd
अम्भोऽतिपाण्डरं वासो यस्माच्चन्द्राभिमानिनः 2.1.55ab
अयं गुणविधिर्ज्ञेयः प्रत्येकं तत्फलश्रुतेः 1.3.247ab
अयं चानन्तमात्मानमक्षिसूर्यव्यवस्थितम् 5.16.64ab
अयं चाप्यभिसंबन्धस्तथा चान्योऽपि वर्ण्यते 4.3.833ab
अयं चोराकुलः पन्था देशोऽयं निधिमानिति SV 590cd
अयं ज्ञेयोऽर्थ इत्युक्तौ स्याद्विवक्षितधीर्यतः SV 666cd
अयं तु तदभिन्नत्वान्न ततो गुप्तिमिच्छति 4.4.632cd
अयं तु वंशो विज्ञेयः कृत्स्नप्रवचनाश्रयः 6.5.5ab
अयं त्वसङ्गो येनातो न करोति न लिप्यते 4.3.1044cd
अयं दुःख्यहमस्मीति विषयेण तदीक्षणात् 1.4.567cd
अयं नाशो महानस्य ह्यन्यः शक्यश्चिकित्सितुम् 1.4.1802cd

अयं प्रयोजको राशिर्लिङ्गमेव किलाश्रितः 2.3.116ab
अयं भोक्ता विज्ञानात्मा तथा दैवतिकास्त्वमी 2.3.97cd
अयं मेयः प्रमाताहं मानमेतदितीक्षणे 1.4.648ab
अयंरूपेण भोग्योऽर्थो ह्यहंरूपेण भोजकः 4.3.274ab
अयं लोकश्च पुत्रेण यादृशेन च जीयते 1.5.274ab
अयथावस्तुरूपत्वात्स्वप्नमेयादिवत्तु सा 1.4.1094cd
अयथावस्तुरूपत्वादात्माज्ञानैकहेतुके 1.4.1835cd
अयथावस्तुसर्पादिज्ञानं हेतुः पलायने SV 365ab
अयथावस्त्वविद्या स्याद्विद्यैतस्या विरोधिनी 3.3.61ab
अयथावस्त्विति ज्ञानं वक्तुं शक्यं विपश्चिता 4.4.816cd
अयनं गमनं च स्यादायो धातोरिणो घञि 4.3.991cd
अयमग्निरिति श्रुत्या यत्नेनाथ विधीयते 5.11.1cd
अयमात्मेति निर्देशो विराजः प्रथमो मतः 2.5.56ab
अयमास्येऽन्तरित्येवं प्राणं दृष्ट्वा यतः पुरा 1.3.206ab
अयमास्येऽन्तरित्येवमरनाभिनिदर्शनात् 1.3.205cd
अयमित्यभिधायोग्यवहोरर्थस्य संनिधिः 4.3.308ab
अयमित्यस्य शेषः स्याद्योऽयमित्यादिकः परः 2.5.36ab
अयमित्युच्यते साक्षात्संनिकर्षाच्चतुष्टयम् 2.5.38cd
अयमेव च नोऽनर्थो यत्संसार्यात्मदर्शनम् 2.4.138cd
अयमेव तथारूपः कल्पितोऽविद्ययाद्वयः 2.5.134cd
अयमेव स इत्युक्त्वा सामानाधिकरण्यतः 2.5.34ab
अयमेवेन्द्रियत्वेन देहत्वेन च कल्पितः 2.5.133ab
अयास्यनामा सोऽगायद्वाचा प्राणप्रधानया 1.3.321cd
अयुक्तिमद्यथा चैतत्तत्पूर्वं प्रतिपादितम् 4.3.961cd
अयौगपद्यदर्शित्वमात्मास्तित्वेऽनुमेष्यते 4.3.1136ab
अयौगपद्येनोत्क्रान्तौ तल्लिङ्गं देवतात्मनाम् 4.4.68cd
अरण्य इति गृह्यन्त इतरेषां पृथग्ग्रहात् 6.2.121cd
अरण्याध्ययनाच्चैतदारण्यकमितीर्यते SV 9ab
अरत्यपनुनुत्सुः सन्स द्वितीयं यथारुचि 1.4.108ab
अरत्यादि यथा दृष्टं तथैव स्यात्प्रजापतेः 1.4.103cd
अरत्युद्भूतिलिङ्गेन ह्ययमर्थोऽवसीयते 1.4.97cd
अरनाभ्यादिदृष्टान्ताद्वायुप्राधान्यतस्तथा 2.1.137cd

अराः प्राणादयस्तद्वदोताः प्रोताः परात्मनि 2.5.66cd
अरिष्टदर्शनं चात्र प्रासङ्गिकमथोच्यते 5.6.5ab
अरिष्टदर्शनं चात्र प्रासङ्गिकमथोच्यते 5.11.4ab
अरुणः साधको दृष्टो नानपेक्षो वृथा च सः SV 645cd
अरूपज्ञत्वहेतुः क इत्याशङ्क्योत्तरं वचः 4.4.63ab
अरूपोऽपि हि सूत्रात्मा लक्ष्यते रूपवानिव 1.2.156cd
अरेता एव सा स्त्री स्यादेवं पत्याभिमन्त्रिता 6.4.46cd
अरौत्सीन्मां तथाप्येष सर्वस्वादित्सया नृपः 4.3.1895cd
अर्कनामाभिसंबन्धो नोपासनमृते यतः 1.2.148cd
अर्काभिधोऽथ संवृत्तः प्राणो मृत्युः प्रजापतिः 1.2.147cd
अर्चतो मे यतो जज्ञे कममम्भः सुखकृत्ततः 1.2.147ab
अर्चिरङ्गारभावस्य यथैवं भानुहेतुकाः 6.2.82cd
अर्चिर्देवतयैकत्वं प्राप्याहर्देवतैकताम् 6.2.131ab
अर्चिर्वर्णसमानत्वाद्योनिरर्चिर्भवेत्ततः 6.2.108cd
अर्चिःशब्देन तेनेह देवतैवात्र गृह्यते 6.2.130cd
अर्जितान्युचितं देहं भोक्तुर्भोगक्षमं तथा 4.3.1965cd
अर्थक्रमो बलीयान्स्याद्यतः पाठक्रमादिह 4.4.1203cd
अर्थक्रियां वर्तमानाः कुर्युर्ग्रामाद्यवाप्तिवत् 4.3.621cd
अर्थक्रियादिलिङ्गेन विरोधित्वाच्च नेष्यते 4.3.616ab
अर्थक्रिया न मानं वस्तेन चैव विरोधतः 4.3.617cd
अर्थक्रिया यथा नास्ति रथादेरुक्तहेतुतः 4.3.650ab
अर्थवाद च बन्धादिशास्त्रं व्याचक्षते तथा 4.4.369cd
अर्थवादस्वरूपेण हेतुः श्रुत्या प्रयत्नतः 4.4.1095cd
अर्थवादीभविष्यन्ति विरोधः स्यादितोऽन्यथा 2.1.459cd
अर्थवादेन लिङ्गेन तस्माद्विधिरयं स्फुटः 4.4.1135ab
अर्थवादोक्तितो यापि प्रतिष्ठाकामिकल्पना SV 565ab
अर्थसिद्धिश्च मासिद्धौ सिद्धैवेति न साध्यते SV 710cd
अर्थस्य ब्राह्मणोक्तस्य द्रढिम्नेऽतः परा श्रुतिः 4.4.374cd
अर्थस्य मूलं निकृतिः क्षमा च कामस्य रूपं च वयो वपुश्च 4.4.596ab
अर्थाक्षेपोऽपि योग्यस्य कर्तुर्भोक्तुश्च युज्यते SV 435ab
अर्थात्साध्याभिधानं स्यात्साधनाभिहितौ यथा 1.4.1834ab
अर्थादपि न तात्पर्यं द्रव्यार्जनविधेरिव SV 407ab

अर्थान्तरं चेद्देहादेरात्मज्योतिर्विवक्षितम् 4.3.280ab
अर्थान्तरं न संभाव्यं वाक्यवाक्यार्थवेदिना 1.4.823cd
अर्थान्तरत्वाद्युक्तीनां प्रमाणेभ्यो यतस्ततः 3.1.6cd
अर्थान्तरनिरासार्थं दूषणं चोदितं पुरा 1.4.617ab
अर्थान्तरमभावश्चेदुक्तं संस्मर्तुमर्हसि 1.2.120ab
अर्थान्तरात्स्वभावाद्वा भवन्न तु निवार्यते SV 79cd
अर्थापत्तिक्षयोऽतः स्यादन्यथाप्युपपत्तितः 3.3.116ab
अर्थापत्तेरपूर्वस्य कल्पनापि न युज्यते 3.8.148ab
अर्थापत्तेश्च तत्रैव क्षीणत्वान्मोक्षकल्पने 3.3.106ab
अर्थावबोधनं कार्यं वाचो नान्यदितोऽपरम् 1.5.132cd
अर्थाविष्करणं कुतार्किककृताशङ्कासमुच्छित्तये SV 2c
अर्थिनेऽर्थं प्रतिज्ञाय नासंपाद्य निवर्तते 2.1.199ab
अर्थैकत्वगतौ सत्यां वाक्यभेदप्रकल्पना SV 276cd
अर्थैकत्वादिति तथा वाक्यलक्षणमुच्यते 2.1.564ab
अर्थोऽयमेव निर्णीतस्तद्विरुद्धं किमुच्यते 4.3.1775cd
अर्द्यमाना न शरणं लेभिरेऽल्पत्वकारणात् 1.3.30cd
अर्धत्वं स्यात्कनीयस्त्वाद्व्याप्यस्याग्न्यादिरूपिणः 3.9.25cd
अर्पितेन विरोधश्चेदस्तु कामं न दुष्यति 1.4.1294cd
अर्वागेवाक्षराज्ज्ञेया सत्तेयं जगतो निधिः 3.8.19ab
अर्वाग्यच्च कपालात्स्यान्मध्ये यच्च कपालयोः 3.8.4cd
अर्वाग्यस्मादयं कालो विकुर्वञ्जनिमज्जगत् 4.4.636ab
अलं सर्वमतिस्तद्वत्सर्वभावफलाप्तये 1.4.1131cd
अलं स्वकार्यनिष्पत्तौ न तु प्राणैकसंश्रिताः 2.2.12cd
अलक्तकादिः सर्वत्र यथैवं ह्यात्मवस्त्वपि 4.3.1585cd
अलंकारोऽयमस्माकं यदशेषप्रवर्तन- 1.4.913ab
अलंकृतिरियं साध्वी वेदान्तेषु प्रशस्यते SV 238cd
अलब्धब्रह्मयाथात्म्यं ज्ञानं वाक्योद्भवं यतः 4.4.803ab
अलब्धात्मकमन्यत्र लब्धात्मकमिवेक्ष्यते 4.3.125cd
अलमर्थः स एवात्र मेयोऽज्ञात इहेष्यते 4.4.897cd
अलुप्तदृक्सुषुप्तेऽपि जाग्रद्बोधाविशेषतः SV 994cd
अलुप्तदृष्टिरात्मायं यथोक्तं स्वप्नबोधयोः 4.3.1907ab
अलुप्तानुदितो बोधः प्रथते प्रत्यगेकलः SV 1000cd

अलौकिकत्वाद्बोधस्य स्वतश्चावगमात्मनः 1.4.868ab
अलौकिकार्थवादित्वादात्मब्रह्माभिधानयोः SV 859ab
अल्पत्वमभिभूतेः स्यात्तयोरासुरपाप्मभिः 1.3.4cd
अल्पीयःपापहानिश्च नापि शब्दात्प्रतीयते 1.5.35ab
अल्पीयःफलसंप्राप्तिरल्पीयोज्ञानकर्मतः 1.3.4ab
अल्पीयसां वा न त्यागः कस्मादित्यभिधीयताम् 4.4.969cd
अल्पीयोऽभ्यासजा साध्वी भावनेत्यत्र का प्रमा 1.4.1538cd
अल्पीयोहःसमभ्यस्तो निरोधोऽलं विमुक्तये 1.4.1537ab
अवगत्यवसाना स्यात्प्रमातुः प्रत्यगात्मनि 4.3.297cd
अवगत्यात्मना सत्त्वं सर्वदृक्स्यादविक्रियः 1.4.989cd
अवगत्यात्मना सत्त्वमवाक्यार्थत्वमश्नुते 4.3.1743cd
अवघातस्य पाक्षिक्यां प्राप्तौ यद्वन्नियम्यते 1.4.925ab
अवघातादिवत्कामं नियमोऽस्तु तथा सति 1.4.927cd
अवच्छिन्नवदाभाति क्षेत्रज्ञो रज्जुसर्पवत् 2.4.186cd
अवतिष्ठत एवायं किं वा कर्मैव संश्रितः 3.2.131cd
अवदध्रेऽत एवेति मा भूत्स्वप्नादिवत्स्थितिः 4.4.53ab
अवदध्रे यतश्चेयं मनसैवेति च श्रुतिः 4.4.649ab
अवदानविधेः शेषो ह्यर्थवादो हि तद्वचः 1.4.1562cd
अवदानविधौ तच्च विशेषेण विचारितम् 1.4.1805ab
अवधारणाय वावेति द्वे एवेति विनिश्चितौ 2.3.16ab
अवधीकृत्यान्तत्वोक्तेर्नतु दोषो मनागपि 1.3.220cd
अवध्यर्थे तथाऽत्र यन्तीत्यस्य विशेषणम् 4.4.17cd
अवध्यवधिमद्भेदे प्रागभावोऽपि सिध्यति 1.2.118cd
अवध्रियत एवेति तमेव इति च श्रुतेः 4.3.43cd
अवनीयन्त इत्युक्त्या नाशादिभ्योऽन्यतोगतिः 4.4.292ab
अवबुद्धस्वभावोऽपि सहतेऽनवबुद्धताम् 4.3.181ab
अवबुद्धे तु शब्दार्थे पुरुषार्थानुरोधतः SV 620ab
अवबोधयतीत्येवं भण्यते दृष्टितत्त्वतः 4.4.687cd
अवभासात्मकः कुम्भः क्षणमात्रस्थितिर्यतः 4.3.472ab
अवरेष्वपि भोगेषु न चोत्तमसुखं ततः 4.3.1872cd
अवशिष्टं च यत्तच्च न प्रमाणोपपादितम् 3.8.109cd
अवशिष्टं यदप्यस्य तन्मां पृच्छतु कामतः 3.9.59ab

अवशिष्टं स्वतो बुद्धं शुद्धं मुक्तमतो भवेत् 1.4.864ab
अवश्यं चेत्प्रकल्प्यं स्यात्पुंस्प्रवृत्तिप्रयोजकम् 3.3.105ab
अवश्यमभ्युपेयोऽत्र भेदो मानप्रमेययोः 4.3.543cd
अवश्यमृणवत्कृत्यं यावज्जीवादिवाक्यतः 1.4.1804ab
अवश्यमेव भिन्नार्थौ भिन्नाभिन्नरवाविमौ 4.3.1762ab
अवस्तुत्वान्निरात्मत्वाद्वन्ध्यासूनुनृशृङ्गवत् 4.3.1292cd
अवस्तु सन्नपि ह्येष इति पूज्यैरपीरितम् 1.4.443cd
अवस्त्वपि च वस्त्वेव वस्तुरूपात्तदन्यतः 1.4.428cd
अवस्थां तैजसीं भुक्त्वा स्वापो भवति देहिनः 4.3.1065cd
अवस्थां प्रययावन्यां मायावीवात्ममायया 2.1.284ab
अवस्थात्रितयस्यास्य कुतः सिद्धिरितीर्यताम् 2.1.274cd
अवस्थान्तरसंबन्धादसंसारी भविष्यति 2.1.438ab
अवस्था यानभिव्यक्ता तस्यैव परमात्मनः 1.4.1703ab
अवस्थावदवस्थाभिः क्वचित्कार्त्स्न्यं प्रचक्षते 1.4.949ab
अवस्थितं भवेत्साक्षादेवं कृत्वेदमुच्यते 4.4.733cd
अवस्थिते हि संबन्धे वृद्धेभ्योऽसौ प्रजायते SV 877cd
अवस्थेत्यत्र दृष्टान्तः स यथेत्यभिधीयते 2.1.343cd
अवहन्यादिति तथा ह्यात्मोपास्तिर्नियम्यते 1.4.925cd
अवाक्यार्थात्मकं ब्रह्म कुतोऽज्ञायीति कथ्यताम् 1.4.897ab
अवाक्यार्थात्मकं ब्रह्म तेनादो दुष्करं मतम् 1.4.896cd
अवाक्शिरस्कमालोक्य नृपो गार्ग्यमनुत्तरम् 2.1.85ab
अवाग्वायोरपश्वासो देहस्यावाग्गतिस्तथा 1.5.146ab
अवाच्यं यद्यनन्यत्वे ह्यन्यत्वे वाच्यमेव तत् 4.3.638ab
अवाच्यमिति पक्षश्चेन्मैवं तस्याप्यसंभवात् 4.3.637ab
अवान्तरदिशस्तद्वद्विक्षिप्तत्वैकहेतुतः 6.2.83ab
अवाप्तपुरुषार्थोऽपि यामरक्षच्छचीपतिः 2.5.95ab
अवाप्तराजसूनुत्वात्तत्प्राप्तौ नापि चेष्टते 2.1.515cd
अवाप्ताग्न्यादिरूपास्ते प्राणलिङ्गनसंश्रयात् 1.3.198ab
अवाप्ताशेषकामेऽसौ भवंस्तन्मोहतो भवेत् 3.5.128cd
अविकारात्मसंपत्तिः सा च तत्त्वावबोधतः SV 257cd
अविक्षिप्तमसंसृष्टं ह्यनुभवन्किमपेक्षते 1.4.873cd
अविचारितसंसिद्धं क्रियाकारकलक्षणम् 4.3.921ab

अविचारितसंसिद्धः सोऽयं श्रुत्या निषिध्यते 1.6.16cd
अविचारितसंसिद्धप्रत्यगज्ञानकारणात् 1.4.1170ab
अविचारितसंसिद्धप्रत्यगज्ञानलक्षणम् 3.5.73ab
अविचारितसंसिद्धा संगतिः परमात्मनः 4.3.1181ab
अविचारितसंसिद्धिःप्रमात्रादिस्वलक्षणा 2.4.484ab
अविचारितसंसिद्धि तमोऽनुभवसंश्रयात् 4.3.352cd
अविचारितसंसिद्धि तमोवत्स्यात्तदुद्भवम् 1.4.1329ab
अविचारितसंसिद्धितमोवत्स्यात्तदुद्भवम् 3.4.131ab
अविचारितसंसिद्धिप्रत्यगज्ञानसंस्थितिः 3.8.31ab
अविचारितसंसिद्धिप्रत्यङ्मोहहतौ सदा 2.3.192ab
अविचारितसंसिद्धिप्रत्यङ्मोहादिलक्षण- 4.4.307ab
अविचारितसंसिद्धिमोहोपहतचेतसाम् 3.5.42ab
अविचारितसंसिद्धि यत्तु बुद्ध्यादिकारणम् 4.3.382ab
अविचारितसंसिद्धिरविद्या लिङ्गते कथम् 4.3.75cd
अविचारितसंसिद्धिरात्मविद्यैकरूपतः 2.3.224ab
अविचारितसंसिद्धि सर्वानर्थैककारणम् 1.4.1341ab
अविचारितसंसिद्धिस्तथैवानात्मधीरपि 4.3.1286ab
अविचारितसंसिद्धिस्तस्माद्भेदोऽवसीयताम् 5.1.84cd
अविचारितसिद्धित्वान्न स्वतः परतोऽपि ते 1.4.444cd
अविचारितसिद्धीनि यान्यविद्येत्यवादिषम् 2.4.422ab
अविचारितसिद्ध्येवं तमस्तज्जं च वीक्ष्यताम् 1.4.333cd
अविजानन्हि विज्ञेयं कामं कामगते कथम् 4.4.280ab
अविज्ञातं परं तत्त्वं जनिमत्कारणं श्रुतौ 1.4.15ab
अविज्ञातः प्रमाणानां विषयो वादिनां मतः SV 987ab
अविज्ञातचिदुत्सङ्गसंस्थैवेयं न वस्तुनि 1.4.1323cd
अविज्ञातपरानन्दान्प्रत्येषानुमितिर्मता 4.3.1881ab
अविज्ञातात्मतत्त्वः संस्तदध्यस्ताभिमानवान् 2.1.15ab
अविज्ञातात्मतत्त्वस्य विकारो वास्त्वदोषतः 4.4.177cd
अविज्ञातात्मयाथात्म्यं हेतुत्वेनेह शब्द्यते 1.2.125cd
अविज्ञातार्थगन्तॄणि प्रमाणानीति वादिनाम् 1.4.221ab
अविद्यमानवज्ज्ञेयो महिमाप्रतिबोधतः 4.4.1187ab
अविद्यया चिदाभासः संसारीवावभासते 4.3.406cd

अविद्यया चेद्विध्वस्ता विद्येयं कात्स्न्र्यतस्तदा 4.4.918ab
अविद्यया तथाकृत्स्नं ब्रह्म सत्रादिरूपकम् 1.4.1144cd
अविद्यया तथाभूतं तद्ध्वस्तौ किमपेक्षते 4.3.715cd
अविद्यया भयं चेह स्वप्ने तद्धेत्वसंभवात् 4.3.943cd
अविद्यया यतो बोध आत्मायमुपलक्ष्यते 4.3.1154cd
अविद्यया विद्यया तु ब्रह्मात्मैवाभवत्स्वतः 1.4.1388cd
अविद्यया विभागोऽस्य चिद्बिम्बस्योपजायते 4.3.1175cd
अविद्ययास्य स्रष्टृत्वं कूटस्थस्यापि सर्वदा 1.4.17ab
अविद्यया स्वमात्मानमशुद्धं मन्यते यदा 4.3.913ab
अविद्यां गमयित्वेति श्रुतितोऽप्यवसीयताम् 1.4.256cd
अविद्याकर्मसंस्कारास्तेजोऽप्क्ष्मासूत्रसंश्रयाः 1.4.205ab
अविद्याकल्पितांस्तस्मादन्वयव्यतिरेकतः 1.4.1180ab
अविद्याकल्पितेऽप्यस्मिन्नात्मप्रत्ययमानभाक् 2.1.168ab
अविद्याकल्पितैव स्यात्संगतिः खेऽसितादिवत् 4.3.391cd
अविद्याकल्पितो ज्ञेयो न ह्यसौ परमार्थतः SV 148cd
अविद्याकामकर्माणि निःसङ्गत्वस्वभावतः 4.3.1353ab
अविद्याकामकर्माणि सृष्टिबीजमिदं दृशेः 4.3.915cd
अविद्याकामकर्मादिप्रविविक्तमिहात्मनः 4.3.1209ab
अविद्याकामकर्मादि बिभर्तीव न तु स्वतः 4.3.1377cd
अविद्याकामकर्मादिविविक्तं यत्सुषुप्तगम् 4.3.1205cd
अविद्याकामकर्मादिसाधनैः समुपार्जितान् 2.1.285ab
अविद्याकार्यनिष्ठः सञ्श्रुत्या गार्ग्यशरीरया 2.1.26cd
अविद्याकार्यबुद्धिस्थप्रत्यगाभासरूपवत् 2.4.427ab
अविद्याकार्यमेतच्चेदविद्यावन्मृषेष्यते 4.3.1213ab
अविद्याकार्यसंस्थैव न त्वसौ प्रत्यगात्मनः 1.5.100cd
अविद्याकार्यसिद्ध्यर्थमिह त्वस्य प्रपञ्चनम् 1.4.1597cd
अविद्याकृत एवायं न यथावस्तुधीकृतः 1.4.1141ef
अविद्याकृतमेवातः संसारित्वं न तु स्वतः 4.3.1151ab
अविद्याग्रथितः सोऽयं परमात्माशरीरतः 4.3.1259ab
अविद्याघस्मरज्ञानजन्ममात्रावलम्बिनः SV 293ab
अविद्याघातिनः शब्दाद्याहं ब्रह्मेति धीर्भवेत् 1.4.863ab
अविद्या च न वस्त्वष्टं मानाघातासहिष्णुतः SV 180cd

अविद्यातज्जकार्याणां प्रत्यग्दर्शनबाधतः 4.4.1280ab
अविद्यातज्जकार्याणामात्मना संगतिस्ततः 1.4.1370ab
अविद्यातज्जकार्याभ्यामात्मान्यानवशेषतः 4.3.1177ab
अविद्यातज्जकार्याभ्यामेवमेवेति गम्यताम् 4.3.1181cd
अविद्यातज्जनिर्मुक्तं वस्त्वत्रैवेति भण्यते 4.4.291ab
अविद्यातज्जनिर्मुक्तौ ब्रह्म ब्रह्माभवत्स्वतः 1.4.1435ab
अविद्यातज्जसंबन्धात्कर्तृत्वेऽपि न दोषभाक् 1.4.1227cd
अविद्या तद्विकारश्च न युक्तस्तत्परादिवत् 1.4.1760cd
अविद्यातिमिरान्धानां ध्येयत्वमधिगच्छति 2.5.71cd
अविद्यातिमिरोच्छित्तौ नानाविष्कृतमण्वपि SV 1115ab
अविद्यातो हि संभूतिः सर्वस्य जगतो यतः 4.4.601cd
अविद्या त्वात्मविज्ञानसंश्रितैव न सान्यतः 4.3.1090cd
अविद्यादीनि भूतानि तत्रोच्यन्ते ततो ध्रुवम् 4.4.31cd
अविद्यादेरभावोक्त्या कूटस्थात्मैव भण्यते 4.3.1520ab
अविद्यादेस्तदात्मत्वादिति ब्रह्मेति बोध्यते 2.3.234cd
अविद्याद्यतिरेकेण कारणादिविधर्मकम् 2.3.231ab
अविद्याद्वारिकाप्यस्य संगतिर्नाञ्जसेष्यते 1.4.1324ab
अविद्याधिकृतावस्यां धर्माधर्म्यादिसंगतिः 1.5.100ab
अविद्याधिकृतौ तेषां सृष्टिरूर्ध्वं प्रवक्ष्यते 1.4.128ab
अविद्याध्वंसमात्रत्वात्तेनात्रास्त्वविरुद्धता 1.4.1010cd
अविद्याध्वंसमात्रेण पुमर्थस्य समाप्तितः 1.4.1450ab
अविद्याध्वंसिनो बोधात्किंचित्साधनमिष्यते 2.1.6cd
अविद्याध्वस्तिमापेक्ष्य सम्यग्धीजन्ममात्रतः 4.4.373ab
अविद्यानन्वयाद्भास्वत्प्रत्यग्ज्योतिःसतत्त्वतः 3.4.162cd
अविद्यानाभिसंबन्धो मिथ्याधीचक्रसंस्थितः 2.1.223ab
अविद्यानाशमात्रश्च मोक्ष आत्मन इष्यते 3.3.23ab
अविद्यान्वेति कार्यं स्वं न त्वात्मानमकार्यतः 4.3.1319ab
अविद्यापक्षपात्येव न तत्स्याच्चित्तवत्स्वतः 4.3.1390ab
अविद्यापटसंवीतचक्षुषामियदेव तु 1.4.165ab
अविद्यापटसंवीतचेतसां स्थास्न्ववेक्ष्यते 1.5.88cd
अविद्यापटसंवीतचेतसामागमादृते 4.4.565ab
अविद्यापटसंवीतधिषणान्कामिनो नरान् 4.4.1112ab

अविद्या पूर्ववच्चेत्स्यात्सम्यग्ज्ञातेऽपि वस्तुनि 4.4.914ab
अविद्याप्रतिपक्षाया विद्याया विषयोऽधुना 2.1.375ab
अविद्या प्रथते मौली व्यक्ताव्यक्तात्मनानिशम् 1.2.136cd
अविद्याप्रविवेकार्थमेवमेतावदुच्यते 4.3.1101cd
अविद्याप्रविवेकोऽयं वक्ष्यतेऽस्यात उत्तरम् 4.3.1094cd
अविद्याफलकारूढं तदेवंरूपकं परम् 1.4.1335ab
अविद्याभावनाकर्महेतुतो नान्यकारणात् 2.3.53cd
अविद्यामवधिं कृत्वा द्वे रूपे ब्रह्मणस्त्विमे 2.3.15cd
अविद्यामस्पृशन्नास्ते निष्क्रियोऽकारकोऽफलः 1.4.1403cd
अविद्यामात्मनो मृत्युं तस्मादाहुर्विपश्चितः 4.3.453cd
अविद्यामात्रयाथात्म्यादतस्तद्भेदमुच्यते 1.4.207cd
अविद्यामात्रविध्वंसाज्ज्ञानादेवामृतं यतः 2.4.54ab
अविद्यामात्रविध्वस्तौ यतोऽनाप्तवदाप्यते 4.2.34ab
अविद्यामात्रव्यवधिर्यतो मोक्षोऽभ्युपेयते 3.3.28ab
अविद्यामात्रशेषत्वं जगतः प्रागवादिषम् 2.4.455ab
अविद्यामात्रहेतुत्वं न त्वैकात्म्यानुसारिता 1.6.6ab
अविद्यामात्रहेतुत्वं पाणिपेषप्रबोधनात् 2.1.288cd
अविद्यामात्रहेतुत्वात्कामकर्मादिसाधनाः 4.3.1830ab
अविद्यामात्रहेतुत्वान्नामीषां विद्यते क्रमः 2.1.413cd
अविद्यामात्रहेतूत्थगोचरत्वसमाश्रयात् 4.4.354ab
अविद्यामात्रहेतूत्था ह्यात्मनोऽनर्थसंगतिः 4.4.170ab
अविद्यामात्रहेतूत्थो रज्जुसर्पादिवन्मतः 4.5.14cd
अविद्यामात्रहेतौ तु सर्वमेतत्समञ्जसम् 4.3.1450ab
अविद्यामात्रोपाध्येतद्ब्रह्म कारणमुच्यते 2.3.7ab
अविद्या यच्च तत्कार्यमात्मानं स्वात्मसिद्धये 4.3.1178ab
अविद्याया अविद्यात्व इदमेव तु लक्षणम् SV 181ab
अविद्याया इदं कार्यमन्योऽसाविति भण्यते 4.4.414cd
अविद्यायाः परा काष्ठाथेदानीमुच्यते स्फुटम् 4.3.1243ab
अविद्यायाः समाम्नाता आ समाप्तेर्विभूतयः 1.5.1cd
अविद्यायाः समुच्छित्तावलमेवमिदं वचः 4.3.1274ab
अविद्यायाः स्वभावोऽयं यदसत्करणं मृषा 2.4.456cd
अविद्याया न चोच्छित्तौ ज्ञानादन्यदपेक्ष्यते 1.3.98ab

अविद्यायामतोऽसत्यां नात्मनः कर्तृकर्मणी 4.3.1358ab
अविद्यायामवस्थानं तदुद्भूतस्य वस्तुनः 4.3.1172ab
अविद्याया यतः कार्यमध्यात्मादिविशेषणम् 4.4.382ab
अविद्याया यतो नात आसङ्गाद्याहृतिः स्वतः 4.3.1108cd
अविद्यायाश्च यत्कार्यं तच्च वाच्यमशेषतः 4.3.1210ab
अविद्यारोपितमलो विद्ययात्मा विशोध्यते 2.1.304cd
अविद्यालिङ्गते वह्निं घृतपिण्ड इवोल्बणम् 4.3.1180cd
अविद्यावत्परं ब्रह्म मूर्तामूर्तादिलक्षणैः 2.3.18ab
अविद्यावद्द्वितीयं वा नित्यदृष्टेर्विवक्ष्यते 4.3.1515ab
अविद्यावर्त्मदृष्ट्यैव ह्यविद्याकार्यवस्तुगम् 4.3.1332ab
अविद्या वाथ तत्कार्यं नाभेदान्नातिरेकतः 1.4.332ab
अविद्यावानविद्यां तां न निरूपयितुं क्षमः SV 179ab
अविद्यावान्पुरा योऽभदविद्याकार्यगश्चितिः 4.3.1175ab
अविद्यावान्पुरा योक्तो मृत्युजन्मादिसंसृतिः 4.4.1319ab
अविद्या विद्यमाना चेच्छक्तोत्पादयितुं बलात् 1.4.1749ab
अविद्याविद्ययोः कार्यं तथा च श्रुतिरब्रवीत् 2.1.211cd
अविद्याविद्ययो रूपं कार्यं चापि समासतः 4.3.1289ab
अविद्याविद्ययोर्यस्मात्तद्योग्यप्रश्नगीरतः 2.1.376cd
अविद्याविद्ययोर्यस्माद्बाध्यबाधकसंगतिम् 4.4.915ab
अविद्याविषयं तत्स्यात्तस्य कर्तृत्वकारणात् 1.4.1559cd
अविद्याविषयः साक्षादथ योऽन्यामितीर्यते 1.4.1564cd
अविद्याविषयस्तावत्संसारानर्थ ईरितः 2.1.373ab
अविद्याविषये यस्मात्तेषामधिकृतिः स्मृता 1.4.1469ab
अविद्याविषसंदष्टं तज्ज्ञानं परमात्मनः 4.3.1092ab
अविद्यान्यवधानस्य नात्मज्ञानातिरेकतः SV 1102ab
अविद्यासंगतेरस्य जायतेऽनेकरूपवान् 2.4.423cd
अविद्या सह कार्येण नासीदस्ति भविष्यति SV 183cd
अविद्यास्रोतसैवास्य क्रियाकारकतात्मनः 4.3.1029ab
अविद्याहानमात्रत्वात्कैवल्याप्तिफलात्मनः 1.4.1493ab
अविद्याहेतुकर्त्रादिसंगतिस्तत्र मोहजा 4.3.1451cd
अविद्याहेतुरागादीन्सम्यग्ज्ञानादनन्तरम् 4.4.880ab
अविद्येति मतं चेत्स्यान्नैवमप्युपपद्यते 1.4.1748cd

अविद्येति वयं ब्रूमो येह नास्ति सदात्मनि 1.4.1157cd
अविद्यैकोद्भवत्वं स्याद्यद्यपि ज्ञानकर्मणोः 3.3.38ab
अविद्यैव यतोऽमीषां प्रागभावो न तत्परम् 1.4.1149ab
अविद्यैव यतो हेतुः कर्तृत्वस्य न वस्तुतः 4.3.1357ab
अविद्यैव यतो हेतुः कार्यकारणतां प्रति 4.3.1796ab
अविद्योत्थपमर्थेभ्यो विमुखीभूतमानसः 1.6.4ab
अविद्योत्थातिरेकेण स्वत एवेति चेन्मतम् 1.4.1210ab
अविद्योत्थाधिकाराच्च लोकोक्तिर्न परात्मनि 1.4.1645cd
अविद्योत्सङ्गसंस्थैव तत्त्वज्ञानाद्विनश्यति 4.4.646cd
अविद्योद्भूतकामः सन्नथो खल्विति च श्रुतिः 1.4.1815cd
अविद्योपप्लुतस्यैव ते सर्वे स्युर्न तु स्वतः 4.4.998cd
अविद्योपहतात्मा सन्नात्मत्वेनाभिमन्यते 4.3.1227ef
अविद्वद्देवताभित्तिप्रतिषेधाय सांप्रतम् 1.4.129cd
अविद्वद्विषयैवात ऋणश्रुतिरपीष्यते 1.5.338cd
अविद्वन्मृतिसिद्ध्यर्थमस्माल्लोकादितीर्यते 1.4.1674cd
अविद्वांसो न सामान्यात्किंतु येऽत्राबुधो जनाः 4.4.608cd
अविधायित्वतस्तेषां न न्याय्यं भवतोदितम् SV 35cd
अविधिश्चार्थतः प्राप्तेस्तज्ज्ञानस्मृतिसंततेः 1.4.842ab
अविध्यन्निति योऽर्थोऽस्य तद्व्याख्यानाय यत्यते 1.3.161ab
अविनाभावसिद्ध्यर्थं नन्विदं वर्ण्यते त्रयम् 4.3.742ab
अविनाभाविता यस्मादनित्यकृतकत्वयोः 4.3.1576cd
अविनाशमतस्तानि तस्येच्छन्त्यात्मदेहवत् 1.4.1800cd
अविनाशीति चाप्यत्र विकारापह्नुतेर्वचः 4.3.1497cd
अविनाशीति मैत्रेय्यां द्विधानाशनिषेधकृत् 4.3.1498ab
अविनाशीत्यपि तथा विनाशद्वयमात्मनः 4.4.1334ab
अविनिर्भागवृत्तित्वात्सर्वदैव परस्परम् 3.2.61ab
अविभक्तं विरुद्धत्वात्तस्मादुक्तमशोभनम् 4.3.1614cd
अविभक्तोऽपि चान्यः स्याद्वैलक्षण्यात्परस्परम् 4.3.1618cd
अविभक्तो विशेषेषु भवतीति प्रदर्शितम् 4.3.1397cd
अविभागात्मतां यातं न पुनः कामकर्मवत् 4.3.1380ab
अविभागादनाख्येयं तदुद्भूत्या फलायते 4.3.1741cd
अविभागादनाख्येया तदुद्भूत्या फलायते 1.4.987cd

अविभागोऽपि तादर्थ्याद्वोक्तातः सोऽत्र गृह्यते 2.5.32cd
अविरुद्धं सुविस्पष्टं मया तुभ्यं प्रभाषितम् 2.4.447ab
अविरोधः क्रमेण स्यात्स्थितिगत्योरिवेति चेत् SV 168ab
अविरोधादभावेन न भावापह्नुतिर्भवेत् SV 930cd
अविरोधो न तन्न्याय्यं त्वदुक्तार्थविरोधतः SV 170cd
अविलुप्तार्थविज्ञानो यद्यात्माभ्युपगम्यते 1.4.458ab
अविवक्षितनुत्त्यर्थमथात्र विधिरिष्यते SV 666ab
अविवक्षितमप्येवं लिङ्गसंख्यं विवक्ष्यते SV 532ab
अविवक्षुमयं राजा कामप्रश्नबलाश्रयात् 4.3.1890ab
अविवक्षुरपि प्राह यत्पृष्टं जनकेन सः 4.3.11ab
अविशिष्टः स बाह्येन मेयेनार्थेन संगतेः 4.4.715cd
अविशिष्टश्च वाक्यार्थस्तथा लौकिकवैदिक- SV 668ab
अविशिष्टाधिकारित्वात्तेषामात्मावबोधने 4.4.1029cd
अविशिष्टाधिकारित्वान्न विज्ञानात्मनोऽपरः 1.5.15cd
अविशिष्टो भवेत्कर्ता भिन्नकालस्थयोस्तथा 1.4.535cd
अविशिष्टो मतो यस्मात्तदाभासैकवर्त्मना 4.3.315cd
अविशेषाच्च सत्तायाः सर्वतः सर्वसंभवः 1.2.83ab
अविशेषात्मिका सास्य कारणत्वात्त्वनश्वरी 1.4.1703cd
अवृक्षात्मनिवृत्त्यात्म गम्यं च स्यात्तदेव तु 4.3.781cd
अवृक्षापोहरूपं च तयोर्गमकगम्यता 4.3.780cd
अवृक्षापोहरूपस्य तयोरत्यन्तभेदतः 4.3.777cd
अवेत्स्पृष्टं जगत्स्रष्टा ह्यहं वावाखिलं जगत् 1.4.122cd
अवेदिनं तदा बालं विनष्टिर्महती व्रजेत् 4.4.625cd
अवैदिकं भवेद्वस्तु स्याच्च शास्त्रानुवादता SV 816cd
अव्यक्तं व्याकृतं विश्वं यत्र चाप्यभिधीयते 1.4.527ab
अव्यक्ताध्यक्ष एकाकी व्यक्तं यत्साक्षिकं जगत् 1.4.520cd
अव्यक्तावस्थामापाद्य सदोपास्ते परात्मना 1.4.1705ab
अव्यया चाक्षयासीति न ह्यन्तस्तेऽधिगम्यते 5.16.69cd
अव्याकृतं स एषेह तथात्मैवेति चापरः 1.4.1066ab
अव्याकृतगिरा तस्य व्याकृताव्याकृतत्वतः 3.8.28cd
अव्याकृतपदस्यातो यथोक्तोऽर्थोऽत्र युज्यते 1.4.518cd
अव्याकृतमविज्ञातं प्रमाणाविषयं मतम् 1.4.220ab

अव्याकृतमिदं ब्रह्म ह्यन्तर्यामीति चोच्यते 1.2.131cd
अव्याकृतव्याकरणं प्रत्यग्दर्शनसिद्धये 1.4.1025ab
अव्याकृतव्याकरणप्रभृतीन्यपरे विदुः 1.4.1065ab
अव्याकृतव्याकरणरूपाभ्यां छाद्यते परः 1.4.1646cd
अव्याकृतव्याकरणात्स्वाभिप्रायाच्च नेष्यते 1.4.1646ab
अव्याकृतव्याकरणे यदुक्तं सर्वमेव तत् 3.4.113ab
अव्याकृतस्य जगतो भूतकालाभिसंगतेः 1.4.192ab
अव्याकृतस्य तत्त्वस्य नामरूपक्रियात्मभिः 4.4.417ab
अव्याकृतादिपिण्डान्तं पर एव त्वविद्यया 1.4.1178ab
अव्याकृतादिभावेन खवाय्वादित्यसंज्ञितम् 4.4.492cd
अव्याकृतादिभावेन व्रीह्यादित्वाय जन्यते 3.2.64cd
अव्याकृताद्व्याकृतः स्यादेतावानेव सोऽत्र तु 2.3.92ab
अव्याकृताधिकारे च यदुक्तं प्राक्समासतः 1.4.1215ab
अव्याकृताभिधानाच्च कार्यस्य स्यात्कदा चन 1.4.202cd
अव्याकृतेऽनभिव्यक्तेर्न चेत्तत्त्वमीक्ष्यते 1.4.711ab
अव्यावृतानन्नुगतं वस्तु ब्रह्मगिरोच्यते 1.4.1076ab
अव्यावृतानन्नुगतः पूर्णः स्वात्मन्यवस्थितः 1.4.745ab
अव्यावृताननुगतात्प्रतीचोऽन्यन्न शिष्यते 1.4.1579cd
अव्यावृताननुगतो ब्रह्मशब्दार्थ इष्यते 4.4.164ab
अव्यावृत्तं विशेषेभ्यस्त्वथ सामान्यमुच्यते 1.6.58ab
अव्यावृत्तविसंवादिप्रत्यग्धीव्याप्तिकारणात् 2.4.265ab
अव्यावृत्तस्वरूपत्वात्कुम्भे तावन्न धीरियम् 4.3.1702cd
अव्यावृत्ताननुगतं अस्तु ब्रह्मेति भण्यते 3.4.20cd
अव्यावृत्ताननुगतं चैतन्यं संविदीक्ष्यताम् 3.8.58cd
अव्यावृत्ताननुगतं ततोऽप्यक्षरसंज्ञितम् 3.8.52cd
अव्यावृत्ताननुगतं तद्वैतत्प्रत्यगात्मनि 1.4.1445ab
अव्यावृत्ताननुगतं द्वितीयासंभवादजम् 2.3.12ab
अव्यावृत्ताननुगतं निःसामान्यविशेषतः 4.3.1815ab
अव्यावृत्ताननुगतं पूर्णं ब्रह्म विवक्षितम् 2.1.371ab
अव्यावृत्ताननुगतं पूर्णं वस्त्ववतिष्ठते 4.4.505cd
अव्यावृत्ताननुगतं प्रत्यग्वस्तु स्वतो मितेः 1.4.656ab
अव्यावृत्ताननुगतं प्रत्यङ्मात्रसतत्त्वकम् 4.4.447cd

अव्यावृत्ताननुगतं ब्रह्मागौणं प्रचक्षते 3.4.38ab
अव्यावृत्ताननुगतं ब्रह्मात्मानं प्रपश्यति 4.4.1280cd
अव्यावृत्ताननुगतं ब्रह्मात्मैव ततो भवेत् 3.4.41cd
अव्यावृत्ताननुगतं ब्रह्मेत्यत्राभिधीयते 4.4.1298ab
अव्यावृत्ताननुगतं वस्तु ब्रह्मत्वमश्नुते 2.4.14ab
अव्यावृत्ताननुगतः पूर्णः स्वात्मन्यवस्थितः 3.7.55ab
अव्यावृत्ताननुगतध्वस्ताविद्यातदुद्भवः 2.5.37cd
अव्यावृत्ताननुगतप्रत्यक्तत्त्वसमीक्षणात् 2.4.110cd
अव्यावृत्ताननुगतप्रत्यङ्मात्रसमाप्तितः 2.1.361ab
अव्यावृत्ताननुगतप्रत्यङ्मात्रावशेषतः 4.3.368ab
अव्यावृत्ताननुगतब्रह्मत्वप्रतिपत्तये 2.4.411ab
अव्यावृत्ताननुगतब्रह्मरूपातिरेकतः 4.4.569ab
अव्यावृत्ताननुगतब्रह्मार्थान्नापि चान्यतः 4.4.847ab
अव्यावृत्ताननुगतब्रह्मार्थोऽनात्मनोऽन्यतः 4.4.846ab
अव्यावृत्ताननुगतभास्वद्विज्ञानमात्रतः 3.9.156ab
अव्यावृत्ताननुगतमतिहेतु सदैकलम् 2.4.473ab
अव्यावृत्ताननुगतमात्मप्रत्ययमीरितम् 5.1.10ab
अव्यावृत्ताननुगतयाथात्म्यादात्मवस्तुनः 1.4.529ab
अव्यावृत्ताननुगतसंगती रज्जुसर्पवत् 1.4.730cd
अव्यावृत्ताननुगतस्वतःसिद्धात्मवस्तुनि 2.1.88ab
अव्यावृत्ताननुगतेर्महानात्मेति भण्यते 4.4.703ab
अव्यावृत्ताननुगतेर्मुख्यार्थश्च तथा सति 1.4.1272ab
अव्यावृत्ताननुगतो ब्रह्मशब्दार्थ इष्यते 2.3.240ab
अव्यावृत्तिश्च पाप्मभ्यो वैश्वदेवान्नसंग्रहे 1.5.31ab
अव्याहतमतिर्बालः सर्वातिशयवर्जिताम् 2.1.357ab
अव्युत्पन्नप्रवृत्तिश्चेत्युक्तदोषप्रसङ्गतः SV 749cd
अव्युत्पन्नेऽपि संबन्धे विध्यर्थावगमस्तथा SV 731ab
अशक्तं शक्तिमच्छक्त्या शक्तिः शक्तिमता तथा 4.3.1785ab
अशक्तैति कथं योगमन्योऽन्यं हेत्वसंभवात् 4.3.1785cd
अशक्नुवंस्तथा कर्तुं लिङ्गेन प्रतिबोधयेत् 3.4.75cd
अशक्या ब्रह्मदृष्टिश्च कर्तुं ब्रह्माप्रसिद्धितः 1.4.1110ab
अशक्ये विनियुक्तोऽपि कृष्णलाञ्श्रपयेदिति 1.4.881ab

अशनायादिकांस्तस्मात्कार्यकारणलक्षणान् 3.5.86ab
अशनायादिनिर्मुक्तं साक्षादित्यादिलक्षणम् 3.8.1ab
अशनायादिमत्त्वात्स स्वभावबलचोदितः 1.2.181cd
अशनायादिसंसारधर्मापायागमात्मकः 4.3.38cd
अशनायादिसंबन्धः सम्यग्बोधादतो ह्नुतिः 3.5.68cd
अशनायादिसंबन्धो नात्मनो वास्तवो मतः 3.5.67ab
अशनायाद्यतिक्रान्तं कथंचित्सत्त्वशुद्धितः 4.4.609cd
अशनायाद्यतिक्रान्तं ब्रह्मास्मीत्यात्मवेदिनम् 4.4.1172cd
अशनायाद्यतिक्रान्तदृष्टिद्रष्टृपदार्थयोः 3.5.172cd
अशनायाद्यतिक्रान्त्या प्रश्नार्थाविष्कृतिः कृता 3.6.3ab
अशनायाद्यतीतत्वं पर्वोक्तस्यैव वस्तुनः 3.5.28ab
अशनायापिपासादिधर्मिणं प्राहुरीश्वरम् 3.5.73cd
अशनायापिपासाभ्यां तस्मात्तत्कारणग्रहः 3.5.71ab
अशनायापिपासाभ्यां मृत्यो रूपं प्रचक्षते 1.2.141ab
अशनायापिपासे द्वे एव नात्येति केवले 3.5.60ab
अशनायापिपासे यस्तद्धेतोरत्ययात्सदा 3.5.56ab
अशनायावती योक्ता मृत्युः सर्वान्नघस्मरा 1.2.225ab
अशनायावतो यस्मान्नास्त्यन्नविरहात्स्थितिः 1.2.170cd
अशनायावदुत्पत्तेरुत्पन्नाः प्राणिनोऽखिलाः 1.4.154ab
अशनायेति हि प्राह मूलकारणसंगतिम् 1.2.175cd
अशब्दादिमयोऽप्यात्मा तन्मयत्वं निगच्छति 4.4.183cd
अशब्दाद्यात्मकं साक्षान्निचाय्यात्मानमेकलम् 1.4.839ab
अशरीरं शरीरेष्वनवस्थेष्ववस्थितम् 1.2.158ab
अशिंशपानिवृत्तिर्या कासाविह भवन्मता 4.3.790ab
अशिंशपानिवृत्तिर्वः कुतोऽज्ञायि प्रमाणतः 4.3.783ab
अशिंशपानिवृत्तिर्हि न स्वभावो भवेद्यतः 4.3.777ab
अशिंशपानिवृत्त्यात्मरूपं वस्त्वेव चेन्मतम् 4.3.780ab
अशिंशपानिवृत्त्यात्म स्वभावाद्भमकं भवेत् 4.3.781ab
अशिंशपाविविक्तं च तद्वदेवाभिधीयते 4.3.770ef
अशिंशपाविविक्ते च संकेतः शिंशपेति च 4.3.771cd
अशुच्यपि पयः प्राप्य गङ्गां याति पवित्रताम् 2.4.47cd
अशेषपाप्मविध्वस्त्यै श्रुत्याथ प्रतिपाद्यते 5.9.1cd

अशेषविषयात्मत्वं मनोबुद्ध्योर्विनिर्दिशेत् 3.9.74ab
अशेषानर्थमूलस्य प्रत्यगज्ञानरूपिणः 1.4.188ab
अशेषानर्थविच्छेदं वाञ्छतः श्रुतितः श्रुतेः SV 889ab
अशेषानर्थहेतुं तामविद्यां शास्त्रजा मतिः 4.4.352ab
अशोकमहिमं चेति दुःखतद्धेतुवर्जितम् 5.12.5cd
अशोकादपरोऽशोकोऽशोकान्तरमितीर्यते 4.3.1350cd
अशोकान्तरमिति वा श्रुत्यन्तरसमाश्रयात् 4.3.1350ab
अशोकान्तरमित्युक्तं याथात्म्यं प्रत्यगात्मनः 4.3.1386cd
अश्नुते मान्तराभावाज्ज्योतिष्टोमादिवाक्यवत् SV 675cd
अश्मनः परिणामत्वात्सर्पादेः परिपाकतः 1.4.532cd
अश्रद्धा च मुमुक्षूणां कार्यबाधोऽपि च स्थितः SV 839cd
अश्रान्तः प्राण एवातो जागर्त्यत्र दिवानिशम् 2.1.108cd
अश्रुतामनभिप्रेतां कल्पयस्यबुधो यथा SV 202cd
अश्रेयोभ्योऽनुग्राह्येभ्यः ससर्ज श्रेयसः सुरान् 1.4.162ab
अश्रोष्यत्स न चेद्बोक्ता नाश्रोष्यदुपलादिवत् 2.1.112cd
अश्वमेधकृतो यत्र पूर्वे तस्थुरितो गताः 3.3.162ab
अश्वमेधकृतो वक्ति भुज्युः पारिक्षिता इति 3.3.140cd
अश्वमेधक्रतोरेष समष्टिव्यष्टिलक्षणः 3.3.172ab
अश्वमेधक्रियापूर्वपरिणामैकवर्त्मना 1.2.221ab
अश्वमेधफलं चार्कं वेत्ति मृत्युं यथोदितम् 1.1.5cd
अश्वमेधमखापूर्वं देवताग्निरिहोच्यते 3.3.159ab
अश्वमेधमखापूर्वफलप्रकथनेन या 3.3.163ab
अश्वमेधो भवेद्भूयान्भूयोदक्षिणको हि सः 1.2.198cd
अश्वमेधो रविः साक्षादुषा इत्यादिनोदितः 1.2.221cd
अश्वलोऽप्युपरेमेऽथ स्वोक्तप्रश्नविनिर्णयात् 3.1.59cd
अश्वसंज्ञपनात्पूर्वं तथोर्ध्वं चापि हाटक- 1.1.7ab
अश्वस्य यच्छिरः साक्षात्तदुषा इति चिन्तयेत् 1.1.2ab
अश्वस्य शिरसा वां यदवोचन्मध्वसावृषिः 2.5.110ab
अश्वाश्वमेधनाम्नोऽथ कारणप्रतिपत्तये 1.2.197ab
अश्वाश्वमेधावेवं च प्राजापत्यात्मनाञ्जसा 1.2.209ab
अश्विनौ यादृशं गर्भं प्रयत्नान्निरमन्थताम् 6.4.105ab
अश्विभ्यां प्रार्थितोऽथर्वा मधुविद्यामिमां किल 2.5.99ab

अश्व्याथर्वणयोरेतत्कर्म पश्यन्नृचाब्रवीत् 2.5.107ab
अश्व्याथर्वणयोर्वृत्तं ब्रह्मविद्याप्तिकारणात् 2.5.98ab
अषष्ठ्यर्थतया तस्माद्विकल्पोऽयं न वस्तुग: SV 980cd
अष्टधात: पुनस्तस्य भेदोऽयमुपवर्ण्यते 3.9.33ab
अष्टम: खिलकाण्डेऽस्मिन्पूर्वकाण्डेष्वनुक्तित: 6.1.1cd
अष्टाक्षरं पदं सिद्धं गायत्र्या: प्रथमं च यत् 5.16.5cd
अष्टाक्षरत्वसामान्याद्गायत्र्या: प्रथमं पदम् 5.16.6ab
अष्टावस्थाप्रभेदेन मिथ्याज्ञानं प्रजायते 1.3.314cd
अष्टावायतनान्यत्र पृथिव्यादीनि निर्दिशेत् 3.9.108ab
असंविज्ञानता चोक्ता हृदये चोपसंहृति: 4.4.72cd
असंवित्केऽपि पक्षादौ दृश्यते पुरुषाभिधा 2.3.67cd
असंवित्तेरवेद्यं हि न दु:खं वैरिदु:खवत् SV 1014cd
असंवेद्यं सुखं नापि पुमर्थो न च कर्मता SV 1010ab
असंवेद्यं सुखं मोक्षे केचिन्नेति प्रचक्षते 3.9.176cd
असंसारी परोऽस्तीशो यस्य सर्वमिदं वशे 2.1.446cd
असंसृष्टं परं ब्रह्म सर्वदोषविवर्जितम् 6.5.18ab
असंसृष्टात्मबोधित्वान्नापि संसर्गधीरत: SV 703ab
असंसृष्टार्थबोध: स्याद्यथैवं सदसीत्यत: 1.4.902cd
असंस्कार्योऽक्रियाङ्गत्वान्निर्गुणत्वात्तथात्मन: 4.4.1115ab
असंहतं मिथो नालं जडं वस्तु प्रवर्तितुम् 1.4.1790cd
असंहत: संहत: सन्प्रत्यङ्मोहैकहेतुत: 1.4.665ab
असकृद्भक्षयन्त्येतानाप्याय्याप्याय्य सोमवत् 6.2.150cd
असकृन्निर्णयोऽकारि पृष्टे वस्तुन्यशेषत: 4.3.1895ab
असंकुचितचित्पद्म: प्राज्ञे स्वप्नप्रबोधवत् SV 1085ab
असंख्येया बहुत्वात्ते संक्षेपोऽतोऽत्र भण्यते 4.4.188cd
असङ्ग इति चाप्युक्तिरसकृच्छ्रूयते श्रुतौ 2.3.109cd
असङ्गत्वादकर्तेति नन्वसिद्धोऽयमुच्यते 4.3.1063ab
असङ्गत्वादसंबन्धो यथेह स्वप्नकर्मभि: 4.3.1071ab
असङ्गवचसा त्वस्य कामनिर्मोक उच्यते 4.3.1015cd
असङ्गानन्वयोक्तिभ्यां कामादेश्च मृषात्वत: 4.3.1408cd
असङ्गोऽयं स्वतो यस्मान्नात: केनचिदात्मन: 4.3.1359ab
असङ्गो मत्स्यवत्प्रत्यङ्कामकर्मादिभि: क्रमात् 4.3.1902ab

असङ्गो हीति वाक्येन तद्वतोऽसंभवादिह 4.3.1019ab
असङ्गो हीति हेतूक्तिः प्रतिज्ञार्थोऽथवा भवेत् 4.3.1001cd
असज्जाग्रदवस्थेयं जाग्रद्रूपत्वकारणात् 4.3.1072ab
असतः कीदृशं दानं सदेवातः प्रदीयताम् 2.4.63cd
असतश्च न संबन्धोऽकारकत्वात्कथं चन 1.2.116ab
असतश्च समुत्पत्तावन्ते च क्षयसंगतेः 4.3.607ab
असतश्चाप्यभिव्यक्तिर्न युक्ता खरशृङ्गवत् 4.4.332cd
असत्कारणकं कार्यं तद्विनाश्यास्य जन्मतः 1.2.34ab
असत्त्वं चेन्मृदादेः स्यान्न मानानुपपत्तितः 1.2.53cd
असत्त्वान्न द्वयं तेऽस्ति सांख्यकाणादपक्षवत् 4.3.658cd
असत्यकामनुत्त्यर्था कामोक्तिर्यापि चाष्टमी 4.4.453ab
असत्यस्याप्यसत्यत्वं परमार्थसदात्मना 1.3.51cd
असत्योपाधिभिः सोऽयं कूटस्थासङ्गविग्रहः 2.1.304ab
असत्सदतिरेकेण यदि वाव्यतिरेकतः 1.2.11ab
असत्समं भवेत्तावत्तदपूर्वात्मना स्थितम् 4.3.817cd
असत्स्वात्मानमेवाश्वं कल्पयित्वा नियोजयेत् 1.1.4cd
असदेवेदमित्युक्तेरात्मनो भानुसंभवः 1.5.380cd
असद्विषयतैवेह सर्वासामपि चेद्धियाम् 1.2.71cd
असंतोषाक्षमाहेतोश्चेतसो यानवस्थितिः 1.4.105ab
असंतोषात्कहोलोऽत उषस्तप्रश्नमेव तु 3.5.31ab
असंतोषादतोऽन्येऽत्र भूरिदोषप्रदर्शिनः 4.4.876ab
असंनिधिर्वा न्याय्योऽयं भेदेऽसौ द्रव्ययोर्यतः 4.3.511cd
असन्मृत्युस्तयोर्ज्ञेयः पूर्वयोर्मृत्युहेतुतः 1.3.357ab
असपत्नमुपासीनः ससपत्नः कुतो भवेत् 1.5.192cd
असमस्तमिदं ब्रह्म न युक्तं समुपासितुम् 4.1.15cd
असमाप्तेः पुमर्थस्य मतं नास्यानुशासनम् 4.1.32cd
असमासेन निर्देशो भिन्नकार्यत्वकारणात् 3.5.64ab
असंपृक्तस्य सम्यक्त्वं स्वरूपेणावभासते 4.3.486cd
असंबद्धः सुषुप्तस्थः कर्महेत्वनभिप्लुतेः 4.3.1364cd
असंबुद्धात्मकोद्भूतमनोबुद्ध्यादिरूपिणा 2.1.224cd
असंबोधः सति ज्ञाने कथं स्यादिति शङ्क्यते 4.3.1399ab
असंबोधात्तु तैः सर्वैः प्राणिभिर्नानुभूयते 2.5.73cd

असंभवः स्वतो यस्मात्तदबोधाच्च संभवः 4.3.407ab
असंभवात्ततोऽन्यस्य ह्युपदेशोऽफलो भवेत् 1.4.1226cd
असंभवात्तदन्यत्र ब्रह्मत्वस्य यतस्ततः 3.4.44cd
असंभवात्तदन्यस्य द्रष्टृभावः प्रसज्यते 1.4.581cd
असंभवात्प्रयत्नस्य युगपद्देवतात्मनः 4.3.1129ab
असंभवादसंप्राप्तेः कुतो विधिरिहेष्यते 1.4.768cd
असंभवाद्द्वितीयस्य स्यामपूर्वादिमानहम् 1.4.1411cd
असंभवाद्द्वितीयस्य स्यामपूर्वादिमानहम् 2.4.441cd
असंभवेऽपि कल्प्येत यदि तादृक्प्रतिग्रहः 5.16.61ab
असंभवे हि कर्माणि विधीयन्तेऽस्य सर्वतः 4.4.1090cd
असंभवोऽन्यत्र मृतेरित्यपार्था गतिश्रुतिः 6.2.132cd
असंभवो यथा मुक्तेः क्रियासाधनसंश्रयात् 3.8.163ab
असंभित्तिः पृथक्त्वस्य ततोऽन्येभ्यः प्रसज्यते 4.3.1672ab
असंभिन्नव्यवस्थाः स्युः कथं नाम यथोदिताः 4.4.1017ab
असंभिन्नस्वावयवः खिल्यः सोऽथ निगद्यते 2.4.405ab
असंभेदाय लोकानामेषामित्यभिधीयते 4.4.1016cd
असम्यग्ज्ञानयाथात्म्यो जनिमत्प्रकृतित्वतः 4.4.700ab
असर्वज्ञो भवेदात्मा तथानाप्तार्थ एव च 1.4.1015cd
असह्यदुःखफलतः स्वकार्यविनिवृत्तिकृत् SV 1107ab
असह्यानन्तदुःखौघमहाभयमुपस्थितम् 4.4.1170ab
असाक्षिकं चेच्छून्यत्वं साक्षिवत्स्यादसाक्षिकम् 3.4.119cd
असाधनत्वान्नाप्याप्यः प्रत्यङ्मात्रस्वभावतः 3.3.118cd
असाधारणकारित्वं तस्य साधारणात्मनः 1.5.36cd
असाधारणगन्धादिग्राहकत्वानुमानतः 2.4.363ab
असाधारणतन्मातृमानमेयात्मकत्वतः 1.4.1360cd
असाधारणतो न स्यात्कालदिग्देशभिन्नयोः 1.4.629ab
असाधारणतो न स्यादहं वेद्मीतिवत्तदा 4.3.201cd
असाधारणधर्मोत्थं विज्ञानं वस्तुनि प्रमा 4.2.107ab
असाधारणधर्मोत्थो न साधारणकारणः 1.4.452ab
असाधारणमज्ञानं प्रतीच्येव यतः स्थितम् 1.4.179ab
असाधारणमात्रादि प्रत्यग्वस्तु यतस्ततः 1.4.1361ab
असाधारणमेयत्वान्मानानां चक्षुरादिवत् 4.4.792cd

असाधारणरूपत्वात्प्रत्यक्चिन्मात्रवस्तुनः 4.3.1726ab
असाधारणरूपेण भेदो जगति निश्चितः 1.6.87ab
असाधारणरूपेण विभिन्नानां परस्परम् 4.3.680ab
असाधारणरूपेण व्यावर्तन्ते परस्परम् 4.3.1649ab
असाधारणरूपेषु व्यावृत्तेष्वितरेतरम् 1.2.56ab
असाधारणरूपोत्थज्ञानेनैव प्रमीयते 4.3.210ab
असाधारणसाध्यानि पुत्रादीनि यथा तथा 4.4.1081ab
असाधारणसामान्यरूपाभ्यामीक्ष्यमीक्षते 1.4.647ab
असाधारणसिद्ध्यैव सिद्धिः स्यादात्मवस्तुनः 4.4.155ab
असाधारण्यसिद्ध्यर्थमावामेवेत्यतोऽवदत् 3.2.134ab
असाध्यसाधने तस्मिन्कापेक्षा भावनां प्रति SV 799cd
असामान्यत्वमेवैति शौक्ल्यमन्यानपेक्षतः 1.4.447cd
असामान्यविशेषात्मद्रव्यवत्प्राप्नुतश्च तौ 1.6.78cd
असामान्येन तत्सिद्धेः साक्षिसाक्ष्यपदार्थयोः 4.4.360cd
असारफलसंप्राप्तिः पुमर्थो नेष्यते यतः SV 303ab
असावन्नं स्थितं यस्माद्देहं प्राणानवत्यतः 1.3.245ab
असावपि च भूतो वा भावी वा वर्ततेऽथवा SV 294cd
असाविति क्रमोऽभेदि कस्माद्धेतोरितीर्यताम् 6.2.73ab
असिद्धं शास्त्रयुक्तिभ्यामावृत्त्यापि न सिध्यति SV 857ab
असिद्धार्थस्य वा सिद्धिरनुभूत्येकमात्रतः SV 559ab
असिद्ध्यन्स स्वतःसिद्धौ सिद्धिं क्वान्यत्र लप्स्यते 1.4.1364cd
असुप्तोऽकर्महेतुत्वात्सुप्तान्प्राणान्क्रियोत्थितेः 4.3.931ab
असुप्तो भावनारूपान्सुप्तान्प्राणान्प्रपश्यति 4.3.930cd
असुबुद्धी यतो हेतू सर्वेषामिन्द्रियात्मनाम् 4.4.174cd
असृष्टाविनियोगत्वे प्राप्नुतस्तद्ग्रहे सति 1.5.33ab
अस्तं यातेषु सर्वेषु ज्योतिःषूक्तेषु वासनाः 4.3.111ab
अस्ति चायं विशेषोऽत्र यत्संस्पर्शनमात्रतः 2.1.153ab
अस्ति चेदनवस्था स्यादनिर्मोक्षो न चेद्भवेत् 3.2.14ab
अस्ति तावदयं लोको यथोक्तपरिमाणवान् 3.3.152ab
अस्तित्वमक्षरस्येह सिद्धं तावद्दृगात्मनः 3.8.114cd
अस्तित्वव्यतिरिक्तत्वे बद्धस्य च विनिश्चिते 3.5.1cd
अस्तित्वे तस्य संसिद्धे तन्मुक्त्यै यत्यते यतः 3.4.4cd

अस्ति नास्तीति वा ब्रूहि याज्ञवल्क्य यथातथम् 3.2.13cd
अस्ति भोगः सुषुप्तेऽपि तथा चानन्दभुङ्मतः 4.3.1051ab
अस्ति मानं यतो नित्यं कर्म सर्वत्र चोद्यते 3.3.75ab
अस्ति मेरुर्यथा वर्णचतुष्टयविशेषणः 1.3.80cd
अस्ति यत्राप्युपादानं साधनं वास्य जागरे 4.3.925ab
अस्ति यस्मादतोऽद्वैतं वस्तु वस्तुनि सर्वदा 4.3.1700cd
अस्ति यस्मादसुर्नित्यमासन्योऽयमतो मतः 1.3.166ab
अस्ति वेदे क्वचिद्येन शक्तेर्विध्येकदेशता SV 76cd
अस्ति शुद्धो ध्रुवश्चात्मा स चैक इति यत्स्थितम् 4.3.460ab
अस्तीशो व्यतिरिक्तश्चेत्सोऽपि केन प्रवर्तितः 2.1.397ab
अस्तु कामं तदुज्ञातुर्न तु तद्यजमानगम् 3.1.44cd
अस्तु कामं प्रमामेयसंगतिर्गम्यते कुतः 4.3.551cd
अस्तु कामं स कामादेराश्रयो न निवार्यते 4.4.497cd
अस्तु काममनिर्मोक्षो विक्रियावत्त्वतो दृशेः SV 141cd
अस्तु प्रकाशकेष्वेवं न प्रतीचीति चेन्मतम् 4.3.1464ab
अस्तु वस्त्वन्तरं चान्यत्तस्याप्यात्माभिसंगतौ 4.3.1186ab
अस्तु सङ्गात्मकं तर्हि वासनासङ्गदर्शनात् 3.8.97ab
अस्तु सत्यप्रतिज्ञोऽत्र प्रतिज्ञातं त्वयेह यत् 6.2.59ab
अस्त्यन्यदपि विज्ञेयं तद्विनाकृत्स्नता यतः 5.16.75cd
अस्त्यर्थवत्स्वमात्रेण नाभावोऽस्ति विना सता 4.3.574ab
अस्त्यर्थव्यतिरेकेण विज्ञानादि यदीष्यते 4.3.576ab
अस्त्यर्थव्यतिरेके हि न किंचिदपि सिध्यति 4.3.575ab
अस्त्यात्मा चित्स्वभावोऽत्र चक्षुश्चाविकलं तथा 1.5.104ab
अस्त्युपासिक्रियायोगो देवतातोऽन उच्यते 1.3.212cd
अस्त्येकैकमतोऽनूक्तिः प्राप्ता दृष्टिरनूद्यते 1.4.689cd
अस्त्वविद्या परे भूम्नि यथोक्तन्यायगौरवात् 1.4.1218ab
अस्त्वेवं प्रतिषेधेषु निवृत्तेरुपकारतः SV 411cd
अस्त्वेवं शङ्क्यते नो चेद्व्यभिचारः स्वगोचरे 4.3.719ab
अस्त्वेवं सर्वबुद्धीनां मृषात्वमिति चेन्मतम् 1.2.72cd
अस्त्वेषोऽवगते दोष इतोऽन्यः कीदृशो गुणः 1.4.1230cd
अस्थास्नुत्वाच्च धर्मादेः प्रयोज्यं साधिदैवतम् 4.3.292ab
अस्थितत्वादमूर्तं तदाकारव्यक्तिवर्जितम् 2.3.32ab

अस्थूलं नेति नेतीति ज्ञाताज्ञातह्नुतेस्तथा 1.6.53cd
अस्थूलं नेति नेतीति न जायत इति श्रुतिः 4.4.996ab
अस्थूलं नेति नेतीति प्रतीचोऽन्यन्निषिध्यते 4.3.1591cd
अस्थूलं नेति नेतीति यथोक्तार्थे वचांसि हि 5.1.71cd
अस्थूलत्वान्न तच्छक्यं निर्देष्टुमिति सोऽब्रवीत् 3.8.70cd
अस्थूलादिवचः साक्षाद्देहादिप्रतिषेधकृत् SV 426cd
अस्थूलाद्यक्षरोक्तेश्च तथापूर्वादिवाक्यतः 2.1.446ab
अस्थूलाद्यर्थशंसीनि द्रष्टव्यादिविधेर्यदि 1.4.824ab
अस्थूलाशब्दनेतीति सर्वमात्रादिनिह्नुतेः 4.4.567ab
अस्थूलोऽजोऽजरः शुद्धो यत्र चाप्यभिधीयते 1.4.526ab
अस्थूलोऽनणुरित्येवमक्षरात्मावधारितः 3.9.149cd
अस्थूलोक्तिसमुत्थात्मयाथात्म्यज्ञानवह्निना 3.8.80cd
अस्थौल्यादणु तत्प्राप्तं तन्नानणु यतोऽक्षरम् 3.8.93ab
अस्पर्धन्त ततोऽन्योऽन्यं दैतेया विबुधैः सह 1.3.26cd
अस्पृशन्नपि नीलं खमिति संभावयेत्तथा 4.3.419cd
अस्मज्जिगीषूनसुराञ्जित्वोद्गात्रात्मसंश्रयात् 1.3.32ab
अस्मत्पक्षे तु दोषोऽत्र मनागपि न विद्यते 4.3.1617ab
अस्मत्पक्षे हि कर्तव्यमविद्यामात्रकल्पितम् SV 1087ab
अस्मत्प्रत्ययसंभिन्नं प्रत्यक्कर्तरि वेदनम् SV 1069ab
अस्मदन्यत्र मन्वीथा यत्रेदं हृदयं क्वचित् 3.9.84cd
अस्मदादेरपि तथा प्रसङ्गः स्यान्न चेक्ष्यते 1.4.72cd
अस्मदादेर्यथा तद्वद्विद्याकर्मानुरोधतः 4.4.132ab
अस्मदादेस्तमस्वित्वान्न संभाव्येति चेन्न तत् 1.4.1458cd
अस्मदाद्यभिमानित्वे तस्यास्मद्दुःखसंगतिः 1.5.355ab
अस्मदुक्ताविरोधीति तेन नेहातियत्यते 1.5.278cd
अस्मद्भ्राद्धान्तसंसिद्धौ नान्यद्राद्धान्तसिद्धता 1.4.1367ab
अस्माकं दुःखसंप्राप्तिरनैश्वर्यकृतैव तु 1.5.356cd
अस्माकं न प्रवृत्तिः स्यात्कृतार्थत्वाच्च कारणात् 4.4.1112ef
अस्मादेवात्मविज्ञानात्तत्तत्सुखमुपाश्नुते 1.4.1689cd
अस्माद्धयेवेति लिङ्गाच्चेल्लोकोऽन्यः स्यात्परात्मनः 1.4.1774ab
अस्माद्धयेवेति वाक्येन सर्वेषां नः प्रबोध्यते 1.4.1691cd
अस्माभिर्लिङ्गकुशलैरित्येतच्च न युक्तिमत् 2.1.597cd

अस्माल्लोकादमुं लोकममुष्मादिममेव च 4.4.250ab
अस्मिन्काले तु सा प्रज्ञा निष्ठां नीता कृता भवेत् 4.4.708cd
अस्मिन्नर्थे जगादेमौ श्लोकौ यदुकुलोद्वहः 2.1.268ab
अस्मिन्नेव तु स स्वप्ने स्थाने तिष्ठन्प्रपश्यति 4.3.840ab
अस्मिन्प्रशास्तरि सति क्रियातत्फलसंगतेः 3.9.159ab
अस्मिंल्लोके परस्मिंश्च वागेव न विहन्यते 6.1.10ab
अस्मीतीहत्यनिर्देशाद्विद्याकालैव मुक्तता 1.4.1433ab
अस्मै लोकाय देहाय देहयोगश्च कर्मणे 4.4.247ab
अस्य जाग्रदवस्थायामिन्द्रियार्थादिसंभवात् 4.3.983ab
अस्य दग्धोदरस्यार्थे को न कुर्यादसांप्रतम् 1.2.183ab
अस्य द्वैतेन्द्रजालस्य यदुपादानकारणम् 1.4.371ab
अस्य प्रत्यक्पदार्थस्य ह्यां समाप्तेर्विधीयते 3.5.179ab
अस्य भोक्तृसमूहस्य साधारणमचीक्लृपत् 1.5.23ab
अस्य लोकस्य चेत्युक्तं शुक्रमित्यादि चापरम् 4.4.33ab
अस्यस्मीत्यभ्युपेतत्वान्नैवमप्युपपद्यते 1.3.80ab
अस्यस्म्याद्याख्यातपदमस्त्येवेहाभिधाश्रुतौ 2.4.161cd
अस्य हि द्वैतविषये विज्ञानं भानुरश्मिवत् 4.3.1188ab
अस्यां पृथिव्यां यश्चासौ भास्वद्विज्ञानविग्रहः 2.5.26ab
अस्याकामहतत्वेन सुखोत्कृष्टिरिहोच्यते 4.3.1865cd
अस्यातिलङ्घने दोषः संसारानर्थसंगतिः 2.5.147ab
अस्यात्यन्तमसंबन्धादात्मलोकस्य कर्मभिः 4.4.1156cd
अस्याप्यन्तर्गतः प्राणो विज्ञानात्मेति यं विदुः 1.6.40ab
अस्यामविद्याधिकृतौ सप्तान्नाविष्कृताविह 4.4.416ab
अस्यायमिति षष्ठ्यर्थः प्रत्यक्षादवगम्यते 4.3.1704ab
अस्यार्थस्य प्रसिद्ध्यर्थं स यदित्यादि भण्यते 1.4.1794cd
अस्येति लोकशब्देन तदेतदभिधीयते 4.3.861cd
अस्येति शैषिकी षष्ठी कृत्स्नसंगत्यपेक्षया 1.4.973ab
अस्यैकस्य स्वतः सिद्धेर्न वृद्धिः पुण्यकर्मभिः 4.4.1183ab
अस्यैव तद्विजानीयादतः सर्वकृदुच्यते 1.4.348cd
अस्यैव प्रतिपत्त्यर्थमुपासनमथोच्यते 5.1.112ab
अस्यैवार्थस्य दार्ढ्यार्थं पूर्वपक्ष उदीर्यते 4.3.460cd
अस्यैवार्थस्य दृष्टान्तो यथा हेत्यभिधीयते 1.4.1575ab

अस्यैवार्थस्य सिद्ध्यर्थमग्निसर्गादनन्तरम् 1.4.1595ab
अस्वभूताद्देहलोकान्म्रियते योऽवशो नरः 1.4.1675cd
अस्वातन्त्र्यं तु येषु स्यात्कर्तुः कर्मसु सर्वदा 4.4.1246ab
अस्वैः पिण्डादिभिर्योग आ विरिञ्चादविद्यया 1.4.1672ab
अहं कृत्स्नस्य जगतः प्रभवः प्रलयस्तथा 1.4.236cd
अहं तु स्वामिमां जायां समुपैमीति संगतिः 6.4.93ab
अहं ब्रह्मेति तद्ध्वंसात्पूर्णमेवाभवत्स्वतः 1.4.1187cd
अहं ब्रह्मेति पितरं पूर्वमेवोपशिक्षितः 1.5.289ab
अहं ब्रह्मेति यज्ज्ञानं स्वार्थमेव तदिष्यते 1.4.1162ab
अहं ब्रह्मेतिवाक्योत्थविज्ञानात्प्रत्यगात्मनः 4.4.1324ab
अहं ब्रह्मेत्यतः साक्षाद्यथोक्तेनैव वर्त्मना 4.4.1337ab
अहं ब्रह्मेत्यतोऽयुक्तं ब्रह्म प्रत्यक्तयाञ्जसा 2.1.457ab
अहं ब्रह्मेत्यवसितुं युक्तमेव भवेदतः 2.1.465cd
अहं मनुष्य इत्यादि तत्र प्रतिविधीयते 4.3.200cd
अहं मनुष्य इत्येवं सामानाधिकरण्यतः 4.3.118ab
अहं ममेत्यवच्छेदो नात्माविद्यामृते यतः 4.3.1265cd
अहं ममेत्यविद्याधीः सहेतुर्नाशिता यदा 4.2.113ab
अहंरूपेण योऽन्वेति स प्रमाता परो मतः 3.4.106cd
अहं वाव जगत्सृष्टं यतोऽसृक्ष्यहमेव तत् 1.4.123ab
अहः क्षपायां च कुतः संहताक्षस्य चेक्षणम् 2.1.297ab
अहंदृष्ट्यधिगम्यत्वमपि द्रष्टुरिहेष्यते 3.4.185ab
अहंधीरात्मनः कार्यं कारणेनाप्यते सदा SV 1061ab
अहंधीविषयत्वाच्चेत्तेषां स्यादर्थवादता 1.4.1525ab
अहंनामाभवत्तस्माद्विराडेष प्रजापतिः 1.4.44cd
अहमर्थो विशेष्योऽत्र तत्प्राधान्यप्रसिद्धितः 1.4.1417cd
अहमस्मि पृथिव्येका बिभर्मि जगदव्ययम् 3.7.29cd
अहमासं मनुरिति विद्यायाः फलमुच्यते 1.4.1447cd
अहमित्यभ्यधादग्रे यस्मादात्मानमात्मना 1.4.44ab
अहमित्यादिबुद्धीनां व्यवहाराय कल्पते 4.3.126cd
अहमेव जगत्सर्वं भूयासमिति निर्ब्रुवन् 6.3.54cd
अहमेव परं ब्रह्मेत्यस्यार्थस्याप्रबुद्धता 1.4.1157ab
अहमेवेति चिन्मात्रमात्मनोऽत्रावधार्यते 4.3.1273ab

अहमेवेति न स्वप्नः साक्षादत्रात्मवस्तुनः 4.3.1278ab
अहमेवेदमस्मीति दर्शनं यत्सुभावितम् 1.4.39ab
अहंप्रत्ययगम्यत्वमेकत्वादात्मनो न च 4.3.660cd
अहंप्रत्ययगम्यत्वे ह्यभ्युपेतेऽपि चात्मनः 1.4.917ab
अहंबुद्ध्येक्ष्यते प्रत्यक्प्रतीचा चाप्यहंमतिः 1.4.1526ab
अहंब्रह्मश्रुतेः साक्षात्तादात्म्यमिह गम्यते 1.4.1431cd
अहंममेतिविज्ञानं विद्यया ध्वंसितं यदा 1.4.29ab
अहल्लिकेति वचसा नाधारान्तरमुच्यते 3.9.82ab
अहिंसन्सर्वभूतानीत्यहिंसा सर्वभूतगा 5.1.65ab
अहिदेहवियोगोऽत्र मृतशब्देन भण्यते 4.4.507ab
अहिनिर्मोकदृष्टान्तदार्ष्टान्तिकमितीरितम् 4.4.512ab
अहिनिर्मोकयोरत्र संगतिः पूर्ववन्मिथः 4.4.513ab
अहिनिर्मोकविषयो व्यापारस्तावदीरितः 4.4.508ab
अहिनिर्ल्वयनीवाचा सर्पनिर्मोक उच्यते 4.4.506ab
अहीनो हीयते योऽसौ तथानागत एति यः 1.4.1380ab
अहेतुफलतासक्तेर्न चैतदुपपद्यते 4.3.652cd
अहेतुफलरूपत्वाच्छोकान्तरमतो मतम् 4.3.1348cd
अहेतुफलरूपस्य नामरूपक्रियात्मभिः 1.6.7cd
अहेतुफलरूपेण प्रतीचा तद्विलक्षणम् 2.4.440ab
अहो कष्टं न पश्यन्ति कं याम शरणं वयम् 4.3.953cd
अहोरात्रविभागोऽयं भानौ तद्रहिते यथा 1.4.723cd
अहोरात्राणि तावच्च शतसंवत्सरायुषः 1.3.276cd
अहोरात्रे ततो मृत्युस्ताभ्यां मुक्तिः कुतो भवेत् 3.1.32cd
आकारतद्वतोर्भेदो यदि नामाभ्युपेयते 4.3.551ab
आकारो जायतेऽनित्यो दुःखशब्दादिलक्षणः 3.4.152cd
आकारो जायते बुद्धेरागमापायधर्मवान् 3.4.153cd
आ कार्यावसितेः स्थाने सिद्धान्तस्ते विनश्यति 4.3.625cd
आकाश एव किं वा स्यादित्येवं पर्वशेषता 3.8.47cd
आकाशमनुनिष्पद्य वायुमायान्त्यभोगिनः 6.2.154ab
आकाशमात्रताशेषो यथैवेह तथात्मनि 4.4.984cd
आकाशवचसा चोक्तः परोऽज्ञातो जगद्गुरुः 4.4.987ab
आकाशवचसात्मैव ज्ञेयो नान्योऽत्र कश्चन 3.8.23ab

आकाशशब्दवाच्यो यः सर्वकारणकारणः 2.3.77ab
आकाशस्तस्य सर्वस्य तत्त्वमत्र विवक्षितम् 3.8.15cd
आकाशस्य च नित्यत्वं नेष्टमागमवादिभिः 1.4.590ab
आकाशात्स परो ज्ञेयस्तस्यापूर्वादिरूपतः 4.4.701cd
आकाशादिजगत्कार्यमात्मनश्चेतनात्तथा 2.1.392cd
आकाशादेस्ततो जन्म यस्माच्छ्रुत्याभिधीयते 4.3.1787cd
आकाशाद्यभिसंभूत्या पुनरावर्तनं गतम् 6.2.161ab
आकाशे तदविज्ञातं सत्तामात्रेण विद्यते 3.8.14cd
आकाशो वा इति तथा ब्रह्मैव श्रुतिरब्रवीत् 3.8.24ab
आकाशो ह वै नामेति ब्रह्मैवानामरूपकम् 2.1.451ab
आकूतानुविधायीनि जायन्ते करणान्यथ 4.4.21cd
आकृत्यर्थाभिसंबन्धादभिधानस्य न श्रुतेः 1.3.332ab
आकृष्टं रश्मिभिस्तोयमादित्ये प्रतितिष्ठति 6.2.91ab
आकृष्टं रूपिणो रूपं न पृथग्व्यवतिष्ठते 2.3.184ab
आक्रमः स यथा यस्य सोऽयमात्मा यथाक्रमः 4.3.848cd
आक्रामद्धृदयं लिङ्गमन्ववक्रामतीव सः 4.4.48cd
आक्षिपन्ति यदज्ञानात्तच्छान्त्या उत्तरं वचः SV 552cd
आक्षिप्तसाध्यं साध्यत्वादितरत्कर्मसाधनम् 1.4.1830cd
आक्षिप्यतेऽत इच्छेह किमिच्छन्नितिवाक्यतः 4.4.611cd
आक्षिप्यते वा संबन्धः संबन्धो नाभिधीयते SV 316ab
आक्षेप्तृत्वं न शब्दोत्थं न च मानान्तरात्तथा SV 749ab
आख्यातपदहेतुत्वात्सर्वत्र पदसंहतेः 2.4.160cd
आख्यानप्रचुरा यस्मात्त्रय्यन्ता इह लक्षिताः SV 196cd
आख्यायिकार्थं मन्त्राभ्यां व्याचष्टे श्रुतिरादरात् 2.5.94ab
आख्यायिकेयं स्तुत्यर्था प्रवृत्त्यङ्गतया परा 2.5.93cd
आगच्छति गुरौ तूष्णीमासीनस्तद्वदत्र च 4.4.1225ab
आगते न त्वविद्याया भवतैवैतदुच्यते 3.2.89cd
आगन्तुकी स्याद्विषये नैसर्गिक्यात्मनीष्यते 4.4.881cd
आगन्तु चेदिहाज्ञानमनिर्मोक्षः प्रसज्यते 1.4.361ab
आगन्तोरधिकारः स्यान्न प्रवृत्तौ कथं चन SV 254cd
आगन्त्वनात्मरूपं तत्स्वसंवित्त्यैव गम्यताम् SV 110ab
आगमस्य प्रवृत्तिस्तु मेयवृत्तव्यपेक्षया 3.1.11cd

आगमादन्यतः साक्षान्न तु पापादिदर्शनम् 4.3.851cd
आगमादन्यतो मानाद्भिन्नाभिन्नत्वमात्मनः 4.3.1746ab
आगमादेवमात्मानं प्रतिपाद्याथ तर्कतः 4.3.3ab
आगमाज्ज्ञौतमोऽप्राक्षीद्याज्ञवल्क्यमुदारधीः 3.7.2cd
आगमाद्दर्शनं पूर्वमागमाचार्यतो मतिः 2.4.219ab
आगमाद्वेद चेद्ब्रह्म ब्रह्मैव भवतीति हि 1.4.1540ab
आगमापायसाक्षित्वादात्मा सोऽनुभवाश्रयात् 1.4.1381cd
आगमापायिज्योतिर्भिर्धर्माधर्मनिबन्धना 4.3.60ab
आगमापायितासिद्धिर्बुद्ध्यादेर्यत्समाश्रयात् 4.3.333ab
आगमापायिनो द्रष्टुर्दृष्टिस्तत्साक्षिणी तु या 4.3.1426ab
आगमापायिरूपेषु स्थितोऽनेकेषु चैकलः 4.3.91cd
आगमापायिसाक्षित्वं नित्यमेवानिमित्ततः 2.1.201cd
आगमार्थं विनिश्चित्य मनसाथ प्रवर्तते 1.4.1846ab
आगमार्थविनिश्चित्यै मन्तव्य इति भण्यते 2.4.214cd
आगमार्थविशुद्ध्यर्थं युक्तीरत्र प्रवक्ष्यति 3.1.5cd
आगमार्थे यथैवं स्याद्युक्त्यर्थे नागमेक्षणम् 3.1.10cd
आगमेनात्र किं कार्यं लिङ्गसिद्धानुवादिना 1.6.52cd
आगमैकप्रधानत्वं कथं तस्येति भण्यते 3.1.12cd
आगमैकप्रमाणत्वात्कथं धर्माद्युदाहृतिः 4.3.255ab
आगमैकप्रमाणत्वान्न पदार्थत्वमिष्यते 1.3.79cd
आगमैकप्रमाणत्वे वदन्तीत्यभिशब्दनम् 3.8.66cd
आगमैस्तु निषिद्धत्वात्कुतस्तस्येह संभवः 1.4.100cd
आगमोक्तिप्रधानत्वं मधुकाण्डस्य वर्णितम् 3.1.5ab
आगानमवशिष्टेषु स्तोत्रेषूद्गातुरुच्यते 1.3.237cd
आगायेद्वचनात्कर्तुः कामयोगोऽपि गम्यते 1.3.365cd
आग्नेयो ब्राह्मणश्चातस्तत्संबन्धाच्छ्रुतौ श्रुतः 1.4.1640ab
आग्रजस्थाणुपर्यन्तशरीरग्रहणान्यतः 1.3.115ab
आचक्षते तथा चात्र केचिदाख्यायिकां शुभाम् 2.1.506ab
आचक्षाणा श्रुतिः पुंसो नान्यार्थं वक्ति कंचन 2.1.575cd
आचक्ष्वैतद्द्वयं गार्ग्य स्थितावागमनेऽवधिम् 2.1.209cd
आचष्टे कारणे वृत्तं कार्यगेणासुरात्मना 1.3.150cd
आचारस्य स्मृतेर्वापि बौद्धाद्याचारवद्ध्रुवम् 4.4.1149cd

आचार्यभेदाद्भिद्यन्ते वंशा वाजसनेयिनाम् 6.5.21cd
आचिच्छेषादतो नासौ मृषा स्याद्धर्मकार्यवत् 1.4.1319cd
आच्छादिकातः सा युक्ता समस्तव्यस्तरूपिणः 3.2.84cd
आजग्मतुश्च तौ सुप्तं नरं कार्यविवक्षया 2.1.96cd
आजानदेवानन्देन समं तस्य च यत्सुखम् 4.3.1865ab
आजानदेवानन्दोऽतः पूर्वेभ्यः स्याच्छताधिकः 4.3.1862cd
आजानदेवावधिककामानुपहताशयः 4.3.1864ab
आजानदेवास्तेऽत्र स्युः पूर्वेभ्यः सूक्ष्ममूर्तयः 4.3.1860cd
आज्ञापितार्थनिष्पत्तौ कृतिमत्त्वेक्षणात्प्रभोः SV 488ab
आज्ञार्थमात्रसिद्ध्यर्थं न कश्चित्स्ववशो नरः SV 1040ab
आज्ञोक्तेरेव न तदा कश्चिज्जगति चेष्टते SV 1039cd
आज्याभिघारसंस्कारात्सर्वमेव पयो हविः 1.5.58ab
आतिवाहिकदेहेन किं वा देहान्तरं प्रति 4.4.127ab
आत्मकर्मप्रयुक्तैव धर्मादिफलभुक्तये 4.3.872ab
आत्मकामोक्तिमानाच्च प्रागप्येतद्विनिश्चितम् 4.4.405ab
आत्मकारणवादोऽयमेवं सत्युपपद्यते 4.4.40ab
आत्मक्रीड आत्मरतिः क्रियावानिति चागमः 1.4.101ab
आत्मचैतन्यबिम्बेन बिम्बिता धीर्यथा तथा 4.3.1258ab
आत्मचैतन्यवत्तस्मात्प्रायश्चित्तं तदुद्भवम् 4.3.1013cd
आत्मच्छायं पयोऽशेषं यथा मारकतो मणिः 4.3.346ab
आत्मजायाप्रजावित्तविद्याभिः पञ्चभिः कृतम् 1.4.1840ab
आत्मज्ञानं तु नैवं स्यान्न तत्प्रकरणे श्रुतम् SV 432cd
आत्मज्ञानं यतोऽत्याक्षीत्सम्यग्ज्ञानोऽपि तन्मुनिः 4.5.27cd
आत्मज्ञानं विकृत्यास्तेऽविद्येत्येतच्च दुर्भणम् 4.3.1110cd
आत्मज्ञानं ससंन्यासं मोक्षायेत्यागमाद्यथा 4.5.6ab
आत्मज्ञानप्रमेयाच्च नान्यस्तज्ज्ञानकृद्यतः 2.4.238ab
आत्मज्ञानविधिस्तद्वदात्मबोधेऽवतिष्ठताम् SV 755cd
आत्मज्ञानस्य सामर्थ्यान्न नाम विधिसंश्रयात् SV 107cd
आत्मज्ञानाधिकारस्य यदि तावदिदं मतम् SV 410cd
आत्मज्ञानाधिकारानुप्रवेशित्वं भविष्यति SV 400ef
आत्मज्ञानाधिकारार्था निःशेषा विधयः स्थिताः SV 383cd
आत्मज्ञानावतारार्थः सर्वशास्त्रसमुद्यमः 1.4.405cd

आत्मज्ञाने तु निःशेषफलान्तर्भावकारणात् 4.4.1102cd
आत्मज्ञानेन तद्बाधात्कर्मापेक्षा कुतो भवेत् 1.3.100cd
आत्मज्ञानोदयायैव याज्ञवल्क्योऽप्यतोऽवदत् 4.1.35ab
आत्मज्योतिः सुविस्पष्टं राजानं योऽयमित्यतः 4.3.283cd
आत्मज्योतिरभावेऽतो नाभावमपि विन्दति 4.3.59cd
आत्मज्योतिस्तथैवेदं सदानस्तमितोदितम् 4.3.65ab
आत्मतत्त्वविजिज्ञासुस्तद्व्यावृत्तो भवेन्नरः 1.6.4cd
आत्मतत्त्वानभिव्यक्तेर्नाभिव्यक्तं तदुच्यते SV 1114cd
आत्मता ब्रह्मणो लाभो ब्रह्मताप्यात्मनः फलम् 1.4.1012ab
आत्मताब्रह्मते नैवमन्यस्मादित्यतः स्वतः SV 905cd
आत्मत्वमात्मनः सिध्येन्नान्यशेषमनात्मवत् 4.4.154cd
आत्मत्वरूपतस्तस्य ह्यात्मा चाभेदसंगतेः 1.4.551cd
आत्मत्वाच्च तथा वाचो नात्मीयोऽन्योऽवशिष्यते 1.6.15ab
आत्मत्वादपृथक्त्वे च मानं नाशे च नेक्ष्यते 4.4.948ab
आत्मत्वादाप्ततत्त्वोऽयं न देशाद्यन्तरायवान् 4.2.91ab
आत्मत्वादेव चावाप्तः सर्वसाधननिःस्पृहः 4.4.1101ab
आत्मत्वान्न विभागोऽत्र ज्ञातृज्ञानादिलक्षणः 4.3.1331ab
आत्मत्वान्न हि दीपस्य कुम्भादेरिव संनिधिः 4.3.511ab
आत्मत्वावगमाद्वापि जडस्यैवेह वस्तुनः 4.4.476ab
आत्मदृष्टिरतो ग्राह्या प्रत्यङ्मात्रानुरोधिनी 4.3.1476cd
आत्मदृष्टिस्त्वियं नित्या जन्मनाशादिवर्जिता 3.4.150cd
आत्मदृष्ट्या तथेक्ष्यन्ते नानात्मानो विरोधतः 3.2.110cd
आत्मधीमात्रगम्यार्थाद्यस्तदन्योऽवभासते 2.4.240ab
आत्मधीमानमात्रत्वात्प्रत्यगात्मैकवस्तुनः 4.4.348ab
आत्मधीरात्मसंबन्धो नातोऽनात्मन ईक्ष्यते 4.3.422cd
आत्मधीविषयं नैति तदज्ञानैककारणः 3.5.188ab
आत्मनः कर्त्रवस्थापि भोक्त्रर्थमिति निश्चयः SV 475ab
आत्मनः कर्मशेषत्वात्तद्धियः कर्मशेषता SV 45ab
आत्मनः कामनीडत्वे न च मानान्तरं क्वचित् 4.4.442ab
आत्मनः कारणत्वादेः प्रयोजकमिहेष्यते 4.3.355cd
आत्मनः परलोकाय यत्स्याद्गमनकारणम् 4.4.109ab
आत्मनः पुरुषार्थाय यथोक्तोपासनं भवेत् 6.4.7cd

आत्मनः प्रतिपाद्याथ लोक ।ऽपि विभाव्यते 4.3.945cd
आत्मनः प्रोषितत्वात्तु भोग।ऽस्मै न प्रयुज्यते 2.1.105ab
आत्मनः सद्वितीयत्वं ब्रह्मणोऽपि तथा मम 4.4.165cd
आत्मनः स्यादिदं विश्वमन्धकारप्रनृत्तवत् 4.3.98cd
आत्मनश्चापि निःशेषविकारप्रतिषेधतः 4.3.319ab
आत्मनस्तत्त्वमेतच्च सिद्धं चैतन्यवद्यतः SV 1096ab
आत्मनस्तत्त्वविज्ञानं तद्वन्नाङ्गं क्रियाविधौ 3.3.67cd
आत्मनस्तत्स्वभावत्वात्सर्ववेदेति विनिश्चयः 4.4.328cd
आत्मनस्तदविद्योत्थं निरविद्ये निषेधतः 1.3.124cd
आत्मनस्तु स्वतः सिद्धिरात्मसिद्धेरनन्यतः 1.4.727cd
आत्मनस्तु स्वतः सिद्धेर्नापेक्षानात्मसंश्रयात् 4.4.645cd
आत्मनस्तूपचारात्स्यान्न तु साक्षाद्गुणो भवेत् 4.3.1033ef
आत्मनानन्यभूतः सञ्जलपात्रार्कवद्बहिः 4.4.93ab
आत्मनाम समुच्चार्य तथा गर्भं दधामि ते 6.4.107ab
आत्मनीति श्रुतेर्वाक्यमप्रमाणं प्रसज्यते 3.2.105cd
आत्मनैवं तमोयोगो नात्मवृत्तानुरोधतः 1.4.1322cd
आत्मनैव तदा चेष्टां ज्योतिषा संप्रपद्यते 4.3.84cd
आत्मनैव स्वभावेन वस्त्वात्मानं बिभर्ति हि 1.4.435ab
आत्मनैवात्मविज्ञानं ज्ञेयज्ञात्रादिवर्जितम् 1.4.1401ab
आत्मनैवायमिति च ध्यायतीवेति च श्रुतेः 4.3.1077ab
आत्मनोऽकारकत्वं च प्राधान्येन विवक्षितम् 4.3.894cd
आत्मनोऽकारकस्यैव भोग इत्यभिधीयते 4.3.450cd
आत्मनोऽद्वयतत्त्वस्य द्वितीयं यदविद्यया 4.3.1509ab
आत्मनोऽनवशेषेण तदन्यार्थस्य संगतेः 3.4.58ab
आत्मनोऽनवशेषेण संबन्धोऽनात्मवस्तुना 1.4.942ab
आत्मनोऽनात्मना योगो वास्तवो नोपपद्यते 2.1.305cd
आत्मनोऽनात्मना योगो वास्तवो नोपपद्यते 4.3.1179cd
आत्मनोऽनात्मसिद्धिश्च नैव स्यादात्मसिद्धिवत् 1.4.725cd
आत्मनोऽन्यत्प्रियमिति यो ब्रूते मोहसंप्लुतः 1.4.1047ab
आत्मनोऽन्यद्यतः सर्वं पञ्चभूतात्मकं विदुः 3.6.14cd
आत्मनोऽन्वेषणं साक्षादापस्तम्बोऽब्रवीन्मुनिः SV 221cd
आत्मनोऽपि परोक्षत्वं ब्रह्मणोऽपि तमोन्वयात् 3.4.47cd

आत्मनोऽपि परोक्षत्वं ब्रह्मणोऽविद्यया यथा 4.4.165ab
आत्मनोऽभिमुखीभावे वाग्यत्नोऽत्रोपमन्त्रणम् 6.4.30cd
आत्मनोऽभ्युपगम्येत तेषां तत्प्रतिषेधतः 4.4.481cd
आत्मनोऽविक्रियस्यैव लिङ्गे स्वाभासवर्त्मना 4.3.1232ab
आत्मनोऽव्यतिरेकेण यतोऽनात्मा प्रसिध्यति 4.4.156cd
आत्मनोऽव्यभिचारित्वं सर्वत्रात्मैकसाक्षिकम् 4.3.1456ab
आत्मनोऽस्तित्वकर्तृत्वभोक्तृत्वप्रतिपत्तये 2.1.23ab
आत्मनोऽस्याभयं रूपं सदानस्तमितोदितम् 4.3.1301cd
आत्मनोऽहंधियः सिद्धिरात्मसिद्धिरहंमतेः SV 1060ab
आत्मनो द्रव्यभूतस्य यदेतद्भासनात्मकम् 2.3.88ab
आत्मनो नागमात्सिद्धिर्व्रीह्याद्यन्यपदार्थवत् SV 440cd
आत्मनो ब्रह्मता यत्र ब्रह्मणोऽप्यात्मता स्वतः 1.4.818ab
आत्मनो ब्रह्मता यस्माद् ब्रह्मणोऽप्यात्मता स्वतः 2.4.436ab
आत्मनो ब्रह्मता साक्षाद्ब्रह्मणोऽप्यात्मता स्वतः 4.3.1115ab
आत्मनो ब्रह्मतेहोक्ता न त्वनात्मन ईरिता 3.5.213ab
आत्मनो भोक्तृतासिद्धिर्ज्ञातृत्वं च प्रसिध्यति 4.3.1134ab
आत्मनो मरणेनापि सत्यं रक्ष्यं प्रयत्नतः 2.5.112cd
आत्मनो मोहकर्तृत्वमकर्तृत्वं यदीष्यते 4.4.355ab
आत्मनो यदविद्योत्थं रूपं संसारभूमिगम् 4.3.1335ab
आत्मनो विषयस्तद्वदात्मशब्देन गृह्यते 1.6.25cd
आत्मनो व्यतिरेकेण नैःस्वाभाव्यादनात्मनः 1.4.726ab
आत्मन्यध्यासरूपोऽयं संसारः प्रतिपादितः 1.4.478ab
आत्मन्यवगते साक्षात्प्रमाणार्थसमाप्तितः 1.4.840ab
आत्मन्येतत्समध्यस्तमात्माविद्यैकहेतुतः 4.3.911cd
आत्मन्येवं प्रबुद्धेऽस्मिञ्ज्योतिषि ध्वान्तनाशतः 4.3.364ab
आत्मन्येव च संतुष्टस्तस्य कार्यं न विद्यते 1.4.133cd
आत्मन्येव तमात्मानं निष्कृष्यानात्मराशितः 4.4.1273ab
आत्मन्येव यदात्मानं विभज्यानात्मनोऽखिलात् 4.4.1278ab
आत्मन्येव यदात्मानं व्युत्थाप्यानात्मनो नरः 4.4.865ab
आत्मन्येष यतः सर्वस्तदविद्यैकहेतुकः 4.3.1233ab
आत्मन्वीति च वश्यात्मा प्रजा चापि शमान्विता 2.1.80cd
आत्मन्वी स्यामिति तथा साकूतः सृष्टिकारणः 1.2.144cd

आत्मप्रत्यय आत्मैको द्वितीयः पुनरात्मनः 4.3.78ab
आत्मप्रत्यय आत्मैको द्वितीयः पुनरात्मनः 4.4.844ab
आत्मप्रत्यय एकात्मा सर्वदेहेषु सर्वदा 2.1.610ab
आत्मप्रत्यय एकार्थस्तथा श्रुतिवचांस्यपि 3.5.18cd
आत्मप्रत्ययगम्येऽर्थे निष्क्रियेऽकारकेऽफले 4.3.420ab
आत्मप्रत्ययनिर्ग्राह्यं केवलं प्रागभूदिदम् 1.4.1821ab
आत्मप्रत्ययमागम्यः स्वार्थ आत्मावशिष्यते 5.1.24cd
आत्मप्रत्ययमागम्यमात्मानं देवमञ्जसा SV 134ab
आत्मप्रत्ययमामेयः सर्वेषामपि देहिनाम् 4.3.113ab
आत्मप्रत्ययमामेयो लक्षितो यो नञाञ्जसा 2.3.234ab
आत्मप्रत्ययमैकात्म्यं द्वितीयस्त्वात्मनो भवेत् 2.3.14ab
आत्मप्रमातृमानादेरनेकस्येह संभवात् 3.4.51ab
आत्मबुद्धिमनश्चक्षुरालोकार्थादिलक्षणम् 4.3.903ab
आत्मबुद्धिमनश्चक्षुर्विषयालोकसंकरात् 4.3.375ab
आत्मबुद्धिरियं तावत्सर्वेषां जायते स्वतः 2.4.96ab
आत्मबुद्धिरियं पुंसां लक्ष्यतेऽव्यभिचारिणी 2.1.235ab
आत्मब्रह्मपदार्थैकरूपेणैव ह्नुतिर्यतः 4.4.854cd
आत्मब्रह्मानुलोम्येन ह्येषणात्याग इष्यते 4.4.1106ab
आत्मभूता इति ज्ञेयास्तद्भेदेनोपलम्भनात् 2.1.293cd
आत्ममात्रं समुत्सृज्य सत्यत्वं नान्यतो यतः 4.3.1339ab
आत्ममात्रावसायित्वान्नानात्मार्थस्पृगीक्ष्यते 4.3.422ab
आत्ममात्रैकयाथात्म्यान्न मुक्तौ स्याद्गतिस्ततः 4.2.25cd
आत्मयाजीति मनुना स एवेहाभिधीयते 3.3.129cd
आत्मयाथात्म्यविज्ञाननिष्ठता तद्वदीक्ष्यताम् 1.3.89ab
आत्मयाथात्म्यविज्ञानसर्वाविद्योपमर्दिना 4.4.1077ab
आत्मयाथात्म्यविज्ञानात्कर्मणोऽतः क्षयो भवेत् 1.4.1789cd
आत्मयाथात्म्यविज्ञानाद्यदन्यत्साधनान्तरम् 1.4.1439ab
आत्मयाथात्म्यवित्सोऽयं विपापो विरजाः स्वतः 4.4.1293ab
आत्मलाभे न शास्त्रं च नित्यत्वात्कार्यमीक्षते SV 834ab
आत्मलोकपरीप्सायां तस्मात्साधनमुत्तमम् 4.4.1088ab
आत्मलोकस्य युक्ता स्यान्नापि तज्ज्ञानसंस्तुतिः 4.4.1139cd
आत्मलोकाभिधानाभ्यां देहान्तोऽत्राभिधीयते 1.4.1783cd

आत्मलोकार्थिनां पुंसामिति पृष्टेऽर्थ उच्यते 4.4.1094cd
आत्मवन्तो निरात्मानः प्राणाद्याः प्रत्यगात्मना 2.3.248cd
आत्मवन्तो यथा रज्ज्वा रज्जुसर्पादयस्तथा 2.3.248ab
आत्मवस्त्वतिरेकेण नान्यद्वस्त्वस्ति मानतः 4.3.1185ab
आत्मवस्त्वतिरेकेण नास्ति वस्त्वन्तरं यदि 4.3.1105ab
आत्मविद्याधिकारेऽस्मिंस्तदुपासाविधानतः 1.3.192cd
आत्मविद्योपकारित्वं तस्माद्वाक्याच्च गम्यते 1.3.193ab
आत्मशब्दप्रयोगोऽयं तदा लोके समञ्जसः 1.4.1777cd
आत्मशब्दश्च लोकेऽस्मिन्प्रसिद्धोऽनेकवस्तुषु 4.3.281ab
आत्मशब्दाभिधेयेऽर्थे प्रत्यक्सामान्यरूपके 1.4.947ab
आत्मशुद्धेर्विवक्षेह न त्वशुद्धेः कथं चन 4.4.433ab
आत्मसंस्कृतये कर्म यः करोति यथाविधि 3.3.129ab
आत्मसामान्यसंभूतिलयहेतुसमाश्रयात् 2.4.396ab
आत्मसाम्यग्रहेऽप्यात्मभेदमात्रगृहीतितः 1.4.961ab
आत्मस्तुतिरसौ तस्मात्त्वन्मनोरथकल्पितम् SV 200cd
आत्मस्मृतेः स्वतः प्राप्तिरितरस्यास्तु बाध्यता 1.4.847cd
आत्मस्वभावतो नाप्तिस्तथाप्यज्ञानहेतुतः SV 1101cd
आत्मस्वभावोऽविद्येयं न वेत्येतद्विचार्यते 4.3.1208cd
आत्मस्वभावो मोक्षश्चेद्विद्यच्छिद्रत्ववत्सदा 4.4.310ab
आत्मस्वरूपान्नान्यत्र संभाव्या सा हि मानतः SV 572cd
आत्माकर्तापि कर्तृत्वमेति तासां समुद्भवे 4.4.180cd
आत्मा कर्त्रादिरूपश्चेन्मा काङ्क्षीस्तर्हि मुक्तताम् SV 55cd
आत्माकृतिरतो नित्या तद्धेतोः संभवात्सदा 4.4.652ab
आत्मा चेदिष्यते लोकः कर्माण्येव न किं नराः 4.4.1155ab
आत्मा चेन्नास्य शेषत्वं विधिं प्रत्युपपद्यते SV 452cd
आत्मा जानन्यथा शत्रोरात्मनोऽतो न युज्यते SV 155cd
आत्माज्ञानं सकार्यं स्यात्तस्य बाध्यत्वकारणात् 1.4.1556cd
आत्माज्ञाननिमित्तस्य ह्यन्यत्वानुपपत्तितः SV 255ab
आत्माज्ञानमतः प्रत्यक्चैतन्याभासवत्सदा 4.3.355ab
आत्माज्ञानमनादाय तद्वन्नानात्मवीक्षणम् 1.4.506cd
आत्माज्ञानमनादाय न तथानात्मवीक्षणम् 4.3.1454cd
आत्माज्ञानाविरोधित्वात्साक्षान्न त्वात्मबोधवत् SV 1133cd

आत्माज्ञानैकहेतुत्वाद्वाङ्मनःकायकर्मणाम् 1.3.100ab
आत्मा ज्योतिरिति ह्येकः समान इति चापरः 4.3.831ab
आत्मा तत्त्वं विभक्तस्य प्रमात्रादेरनात्मनः 2.4.237ab
आत्मा तस्मात्स्वतो मुक्तः कूटस्थज्ञप्तिमात्रतः 2.1.309cd
आत्मात्मवत्त्वरूपा स्यान्न तु सोभयकर्मजा 1.4.1370cd
आत्मात्मवत्त्वसंबन्ध आत्मात्माज्ञानयोर्मतः 1.4.381ab
आत्मात्मानं पराज्ञासीद्वाक्यार्थज्ञानजन्मतः 2.4.113cd
आत्मात्मानं विजानाति यत्र वाक्यादिमानतः 2.4.225ab
आत्मात्मानं सदोपास्ते तत्प्रत्ययसमन्वयात् 1.4.918ab
आत्मात्मानमलं द्रष्टुं रूपं श्रोत्रधिया यथा 1.4.1385cd
आत्मात्मीयत्वतस्तस्माच्चित्स्वभावमिदं जगत् 4.4.928cd
आत्मात्येतीति संबन्धो योऽशनायादिलक्षणान् 3.5.58ab
आत्मा त्वनात्मप्रत्यक्त्वाद्व्यतिरेकं न सोऽर्हति 4.4.157ab
आत्मादीनां क्रियास्तित्वात्प्रत्येकं कारकत्वतः 2.1.603ab
आत्माद्यतीन्द्रियं वस्तु वस्तुत्वादिति गम्यताम् 4.3.1644cd
आत्माद्यर्थे च संवादाभावाद्वाक्यस्य नेष्यते 4.3.478ab
आत्मा द्रष्टव्य इत्यादावयमेव विधीयते 4.4.860ab
आत्मा द्रष्टव्य इत्युक्त्या ह्येषोऽर्थोऽत्राभिधीयते 2.4.211cd
आत्माधाराणि यस्यापि ज्ञानादीनीह वादिनः 4.4.934ab
आत्माध्यानसमुच्छित्तौ तज्जस्य न हि वस्तुनः 4.3.365ab
आत्मान एते तस्यापि त्रयो लोका यथोदिताः 1.2.223cd
आत्मानं चेद्विजानीयात्सर्वधीवृत्तिसाक्षिणम् 4.4.609ab
आत्मानं प्रियमित्येतद्वाक्यशेषेऽवगम्यते 1.4.937ab
आत्मानं यो यथा वेत्ति सम्यग्वा यदि वान्यथा 2.4.259ab
आत्मानं रथिनं विद्धीत्यपि श्रुत्यन्तरे वचः 4.3.1920cd
आत्मानं लभते तद्वद्व्यावृत्तिं न पटादितः SV 981cd
आत्मानं लभते सत्यः सोऽध्यक्षोऽत्राभ्युपेयताम् SV 1084cd
आत्मानं विरहय्यान्यो नालमात्मावबुद्धये 1.4.1360ab
आत्मानं वेद भोक्तारं वेद सर्वं जगत्तथा 3.7.6cd
आत्मानं व्यभजत्स्थूलैस्त्रिधा वाय्वग्निभानुभिः 1.2.163cd
आत्मानं स मुनिः पृष्टो यतस्तं पर्यपृच्छत 3.9.69cd
आत्मानं स्थितिजन्मादिकल्पनोपायमात्रतः 4.4.1342cd

आत्मानमनुपास्येह नानात्मानं जनोऽपि हि 1.4.916ab
आत्मानमभिसंयान्ति वागादीनि यथा स्फुटम् 4.4.19cd
आत्मानमश्वं संकल्प्य काललोकादिधर्मिणम् 1.2.213ab
आत्मानमात्मनैवात्मा साक्षाद्वेत्ति सुषुप्तवत् 4.4.304cd
आत्मानमितिकर्मोक्तेर्वैलक्षण्यमतिस्फुटम् 1.4.935ab
आत्मानमिति निर्वक्ति श्रुतिः परिहृतिं पराम् 1.4.1683cd
आत्मानमित्यतो वाक्यात्कर्मेदृक्चेत्प्रसेत्स्यति 1.4.1733ab
आत्मानमेव तदवेन्निष्ठां कात्स्न्र्यात्मनः पराम् 1.4.1340cd
आत्मानमेव तद्ब्रह्म ब्रह्मैवात्मेत्यवेच्छ्रुतेः 1.4.1413ef
आत्मानमेवेति तथा चात्मशब्दो विशेषणम् 1.4.1772ab
आत्मानमेवेत्यत्रैव न भूयोऽत्राभिधीयते 3.2.120cd
आत्मानात्मत्वमात्रं हि लिङ्गाद्वस्तुषु गम्यते 2.4.227ab
आत्मानात्मद्वयार्थैव विवक्षा तत्र गम्यते 1.4.527cd
आत्मानात्मन आप्नोति तेनात्मेत्यभिधीयते 1.4.740cd
आत्मानात्मनिमित्तेऽपि व्यपदेशोऽपि दुर्घटः 1.4.1275ab
आत्मानात्मपदार्थेषु विज्ञानोत्पत्तिसाधनम् 4.4.650ab
आत्मानात्मपरिज्ञाने यस्य साधारणं मतम् 4.4.927ab
आत्मानात्मप्रधानत्वाद्ब्रह्मरूपेण नेक्ष्यते 4.4.1275ab
आत्मानात्मविभागोऽपि नायमात्मस्पृगीक्ष्यते 1.4.724ab
आत्मानात्मा च तत्कर्म तदन्यस्याप्रसिद्धितः 1.4.923cd
आत्मानात्मात्मकं विश्वं प्रत्यक्षादिप्रमाणकम् 1.4.1340ab
आत्मानात्मानमाप्नोति यतः प्रत्यक्तयाखिलम् 1.4.657ab
आत्मानात्मार्थसंदृष्ट्योः स्फुटं नः प्रत्यपीपदत् 3.2.111cd
आत्मानात्मावबोधाय यतो धीरेव कारणम् 4.3.313ab
आत्मानुभवपूर्वत्वात्प्रत्यक्षत्वस्य न स्वतः SV 190ab
आत्मानुभवमाश्रित्य प्रत्यक्षादि प्रसिध्यति SV 189ab
आत्मान्तेनास्य वाक्येन स्वतस्तत्त्वमिहोच्यते 4.4.1309ab
आत्मान्वितेः स्वतः सिद्धेर्न कार्या तस्य चात्मधीः 4.4.925cd
आत्मापि ब्रह्मणोऽन्यत्र नैव संभाव्यते यतः 3.4.45ab
आत्मापि सदिदं ब्रह्म मोहात्पारोक्ष्यदूषितम् SV 909ab
आत्मापि साक्षात्तद्ब्रह्म परोक्षं तदबोधतः 1.4.1391ab
आत्मा प्रत्यक्प्रसिद्धेः स्यात्तत्रैवात्मानुभूतितः 2.4.95ab

आत्मा बुद्ध्यादितस्तस्माद्व्यतिरिक्तोऽवसीयताम् 4.3.430cd
आत्मा ब्रह्मेति पारोक्ष्यसद्वितीयत्वबाधनात् SV 910ab
आत्मा ब्रह्मेति वाक्येभ्यस्तथा चेदं प्रतीयते 4.3.115ab
आत्मा ब्रह्मेति विज्ञानं विधिं नैव व्यपेक्षते SV 660ab
आत्मा ब्रह्मेत्येवमादौ सामानाधिकरण्यगीः 1.4.1256ab
आत्मा ब्रह्मैव सन्नेष धर्मैर्यावद्भिरन्वितः 4.4.168ab
आत्मा ब्रह्मैव सन्नेष ब्रह्माप्येति स्वतोऽद्वयम् 4.4.166cd
आत्मा ब्रह्मैव सन्साक्षाद्ब्रह्माप्येतीति भण्यते 4.4.373cd
आत्माभासैकसंसिद्धेस्तदज्ञानसमुद्भवम् 1.4.23ab
आत्माभासोऽपि योऽज्ञाने तत्कार्ये चावभासते 4.3.1320ab
आत्माभिन्नो भवत्येष यथोक्तोपासनाद्बुधः 1.2.227cd
आत्माभिमानधीः पुंसां जायते नियता ततः 4.3.362cd
आत्मामीषां तदा ब्रह्म देवादीनां भवेद्वशी 1.4.1507ab
आत्मा मेयस्तथा मानमात्मप्रत्यय एव तु 1.4.1353cd
आत्मायं कारणं यस्मात्कार्यमित्यखिलं ततः 4.4.1310cd
आत्मायं संगतिं याति तन्मोहाध्यस्तरूपिणा 2.4.236cd
आत्मार्थान्नाद्यसंगीतेर्विद्धो नासुरपाप्मभिः 1.3.243ef
आत्मार्थेनैव सत्यत्वं कृत्स्नात्मीयस्य वस्तुनः 1.5.123ab
आत्मार्थोपासनविधिदेशे तद्विनियोज्यते 1.4.790cd
आत्मावयव एवायं सूर्यश्चक्षुर्ममांशुमान् 3.1.34ab
आत्मा वा अर इत्युक्तौ नैवानात्मेक्षणे विधिः 3.2.112ab
आत्माविद्याग्रहग्रस्तः संहतस्तज्जवस्तुभिः 1.4.1570ab
आत्माविद्या तदुत्थो वा बाध्यत्वाद्रज्जुसर्पवत् 4.3.80cd
आत्माविद्यापनुत्त्यर्थं प्रारब्धोपनिषत्परा 1.4.1055ab
आत्माविद्याप्रसिद्ध्यैव ह्यविद्याप्यात्मनो यतः 4.3.1109ab
आत्माविद्यामनाश्रित्य कारकत्वं न लभ्यते 2.4.475ab
आत्माविद्या यथोक्तात्मविद्याभ्यासेन यत्नतः 4.4.885cd
आत्माविद्यासमुत्थानामात्मयाथात्म्यमात्रतः 1.4.1436ab
आत्माविद्यासमुत्थाभ्यामेव व्याक्रियते परः 1.4.395cd
आत्माविद्याहतेर्बोधात्तत्कैवल्यमवाप्यते SV 28cd
आत्माविद्यैव नः शक्तिः सर्वशक्यस्य सर्जने 4.3.1784ab
आत्माविद्यैव निर्दिष्टा सामानाधिकरण्यतः 4.4.627cd

आत्माविद्यैव मृत्युः स्यान्नित्यस्यापि मृतेस्ततः 4.3.452ab
आत्माविद्यैव संबन्धस्तस्मादात्मन इष्यते 4.3.390cd
आत्माविद्यैव सर्वत्र प्रथते स्वात्मसाक्षिका 1.4.309cd
आत्माविशेषणोऽतः स्यात्स्रगाभरणवस्त्रवत् 4.3.825cd
आत्माश्रयत्वं कामानां केचिद्ब्रूयाचक्षतेऽबुधाः 4.3.1345ab
आत्माश्रयत्वं कामानां न युक्त्या नापि शास्त्रतः 4.4.501ab
आत्माश्रयत्वं कामानां निष्प्रमाणकमुच्यते 4.4.427cd
आत्माश्रयाणां कामानां विनिवृत्तिः फलं हि तत् 4.4.399cd
आत्माश्रयातिरेकेण तच्चावोचं पुराप्यहम् 4.4.484cd
आत्माश्रितास्तु ये त्वस्य प्रमुच्यन्ते न ते सदा 4.4.394cd
आत्मा संसारितां यातो यथा कार्ष्ण्यं वियत्तथा 2.4.435cd
आत्मा सक्त इदं लिङ्गं कर्मणा सह तत्सदा 4.4.235cd
आत्मासाधारणात्मोत्थभास्वच्चैतन्यरूपिणा 4.3.304ab
आत्मासाधारणार्थोत्थरूपमात्रसमाश्रयात् 1.4.317ab
आत्मासामान्यचैतन्यरूपोत्थेनात्मगं तमः 3.5.75ab
आत्मासामान्यरूपोत्थं ज्ञानमज्ञानमात्मनि 2.4.208ab
आत्मासामान्यरूपोत्थं न चाभूत्वोपजायते 2.4.191ab
आत्मासावन्य इति च नानुन्मत्तस्य गीरियम् 1.4.982cd
आत्मा स्वकर्मणोपात्तं प्रद्योतेन यथोचितम् 4.4.82ab
आत्मा स्वतस्तु भास्वच्चिन्मात्रः पूर्णो निरञ्जनः 3.9.112cd
आत्मा स्वाभाससचिवो धियमिच्छादिरूपिणीम् 4.3.86ab
आत्मा ह्यात्मानमैकात्म्यादात्मना वेत्त्यकारकः 1.4.297cd
आत्मा ह्येषामितीत्याह तद्धेतुप्रतिपत्तये 1.4.1466cd
आत्मीयः शिखिनो धूमस्तस्यापि स्यात्स्वभावता 4.3.766cd
आत्मेति च प्रमात्रादेरागमापायसाक्ष्यपि 3.4.53cd
आत्मेतिदृष्टेर्मेयत्वं स्वार्थावगतितोऽपरम् 5.1.27ab
आत्मेति प्राणपिण्डादितदंशसमुदायतः 4.3.101ab
आत्मेति मेयनिर्देशो वैशब्दस्तत्स्मृताविह 2.4.130ab
आत्मेति वेत्तुरन्यश्चेन्न ब्रह्माहमिति श्रुतेः 1.4.1270ab
आत्मेत्यनेन कृत्स्नात्मदर्शनाय नियुज्यते 1.4.1347ef
आत्मेत्यनेन वाक्येन ब्रह्मविद्योपासूत्रिता 1.4.1063ab
आत्मेत्युपक्रमं यच्च तत्सूत्रं प्रागुदाहृतम् 1.4.1055cd

आत्मेत्येकमिदं सूत्रं कण्डिकाद्वयमेव वा 1.4.1064ab
आत्मेत्येवं श्रुतिर्वक्ति कारणादिनिषेधकृत् 2.4.244cd
आत्मेत्येवेति नो वक्ति चोद्यहेतुनिवृत्तये 1.4.714cd
आत्मेत्येवेति विद्यायाः सूत्रमित्युदितं पुरा 2.1.7ab
आत्मेत्येवेति विद्याया विषयः प्रागुदाहृतः 2.1.372cd
आत्मेत्येवेति विधिना पराक्प्रत्यग्विवेककृत् 1.4.1345cd
आत्मेत्येवेति सूत्रस्य व्याख्या प्रस्तूयते स्फुटा 2.1.19cd
आत्मेत्येवेति सूत्रस्य व्याख्येयं प्रस्तुता स्फुटा 2.4.1ab
आत्मेत्येवेति सूत्रस्य व्याख्येयं सम्यगात्मनः 2.5.91ab
आत्मेत्येवोपासीतेति महान्यत्नः श्रुतेरिह 1.4.969cd
आत्मेत्येवोपासीतेति हेतुरत्रोपदिश्यते 1.4.941ab
आत्मैकगम्यमैकात्म्यं वेदान्तेष्ववगम्यते SV 190cd
आत्मैकगुणवत्त्वेन न त्वत्रात्मैव चिन्त्यते 1.4.934ab
आत्मैकविषयं सौख्यमिति चेन्मन्यसे न हि 1.4.570cd
आत्मैकसाक्षिकं तच्च ह्युक्तार्थापत्तिसंश्रयात् 1.5.103cd
आत्मैकस्मिन्नपि तनौ म्रियमाणस्तथैव सः 4.3.809cd
आत्मैको ब्रह्मविद्याया विषयः श्रुतितो मतः 2.1.9cd
आत्मैव कामा अस्येति न भिन्ना हार्दकामवत् 4.4.405cd
आत्मैव कामा निःशेषा नात्मरूपप्रभेदतः 4.3.1342ab
आत्मैव कारणं यस्य सर्वज्ञानस्य कार्यतः 4.4.925ab
आत्मैव चेद्विशेषाः स्युर्धर्मिणो धर्मलक्षणाः 4.3.1653ab
आत्मैव ज्ञेय एष्टव्यो ध्रुवमैकात्म्यवादिना 4.4.893cd
आत्मैव ज्योतिरथवा रविसोमाग्न्युपाधिगम् 4.3.43ab
आत्मैव त्वस्य कर्मेति तथैवाभिहितं पुरा 1.6.27ab
आत्मैव प्राणशब्दः स्यात्प्राणबन्धनवाक्यतः 1.5.380ab
आत्मैव प्रिय इत्यत्र हेतुः स्पष्टोऽभिधीयते 1.4.1040ab
आत्मैव प्रिय इत्येवं प्रतिज्ञां प्रत्यभाषत 1.4.1049cd
आत्मैव ब्रह्म चात्मापि ब्रह्मैव स्याद्यतः स्वतः 4.4.553ab
आत्मैव ब्रह्म विज्ञेयं ब्रह्मैवात्मेति संभवात् 1.4.1389cd
आत्मैव भण्यते मोहात्तदात्माव्यतिरेकतः 1.4.23cd
आत्मैवमुक्तानुक्तेषु योज्यं प्राणेष्वशेषतः 4.4.61cd
आत्मैव स इति ज्ञेयस्तदबोधप्रसूतितः 2.5.35cd

आत्मैव सर्वमित्येवं द्रष्टुं शक्यमिहाञ्जसा 2.4.264cd
आत्मैव सर्वमित्येवं बुद्धावस्याप्तकामता 4.4.274ab
आत्मैव सर्वमित्येष प्रतिज्ञार्थः समर्थितः 2.4.396cd
आत्मैव हि जगत्कृत्स्नं साधारणविशेषवत् 5.16.48cd
आत्मैवाकाशशब्देन श्रुत्येह प्रतिपाद्यते 4.4.700cd
आत्मैवात्मीयभूतस्य या दृष्टिरविनश्वरी 4.3.1425ab
आत्मैवानन्दयाथात्म्यं नातो ज्ञानादिसाधनम् 3.9.208cd
आत्मैवास्य तदा ज्योतिर्भवतीत्यभ्यधादृषिः 4.3.84ab
आत्मैवास्येति जनकं याज्ञवल्क्योऽप्युवाच ह 4.3.77cd
आत्मैवास्येति वचनात्पूर्वोत्तरविरोधतः 4.3.279ab
आत्मैवास्येत्युपश्रुत्य पूर्वोत्तरविरुद्धताम् 4.3.276ab
आत्मैवेति श्रुतं यस्मान्नातोऽन्यत्किंचिदिष्यते 4.4.159cd
आत्मैवेत्यब्रवीत्साक्षात्कुतो भेदस्य संभवः 4.3.1660cd
आत्मैवेत्यादिवाक्येन पूर्णब्रह्मावबोधिना 2.4.101ab
आत्मैवेत्यादिशास्त्रेण सृष्ट्यादौ कर्तृतोच्यते 1.4.1cd
आत्मैवेदं जगत्सर्वं सत्यापूर्वादिलक्षणम् 2.1.271ab
आत्मैवेदं सर्वमिति प्रत्यङ्मात्रावशेषतः 4.3.1342cd
आत्मैवेदमिति गिरा श्रुत्यैतत्प्रागपीरितम् 4.4.225cd
आत्मैवैकः पुमानासीन्नासीत्पुत्रादि किं चन 1.4.1820cd
आत्मैवैकोऽत्र द्रष्टव्यः कृत्स्नत्वान्नात्मनोऽपरः 1.4.1057ab
आत्मोपपादितः साक्षाद्वचस्येकत्र यत्नतः 4.3.1153cd
आत्मोपास्तिनिषेधाच्च न पश्यन्तीति वाक्यतः 1.4.935cd
आत्मोपास्यत्ववाक्याच्च वैलक्षण्यं श्रुतेर्भवेत् 1.4.934cd
आत्यन्तिकसुखानर्थप्राप्तिविच्छेदकाङ्क्षिणः SV 298ab
आत्यन्तिकसुखेच्छायां यदि रागित्वमुच्यते SV 1019ab
आत्यन्तिकी समुच्छित्तिः स्याच्चेन्मोहस्य कारणे 3.2.93ab
आदत्तेऽनात्मनः प्राज्ञे ततश्चात्मेति तं विदुः 1.4.741cd
आददाना यतो यन्ति तेनादित्या अमी स्मृताः 3.9.17cd
आददाना यतो यन्ति मर्त्यानां स्थितिकारणम् 3.9.16ab
आददीत समुद्राम्भस्तं जिघृक्षुर्यतो यतः 2.4.403ab
आददीताप्तिसिद्ध्यर्थं गन्तव्यस्य तथैव च 4.2.5cd
आददेऽतोऽपराधात्ते प्राणापानौ जिजीविषोः 6.4.57ab

आदद्युश्च बलाद्वित्तमेतद्व्युत्पत्तितः फलम् 2.1.147cd
आदधावस्तथा रूपं दशमे मासि सूतये 6.4.105cd
आदरं कुरुते शास्त्रमुपास्यत्वाय देहिनाम् 1.3.296cd
आदरार्थं स्मरेत्यस्य पुनः पुनरुदीरणम् 5.17.18cd
आदानान्तो भवेन्मन्त्रः सर्वत्रैवं विनिर्दिशेत् 6.4.60cd
आदाय कर्मशास्त्रं तन्निषेधविधिबोधकृत् 1.4.184cd
आदाय भावनाबुद्ध्या शेते ज्ञो हृदयाम्बरे 2.1.253cd
आदाय वासनामात्रां स्वप्नमायां तनोत्ययम् 4.3.865cd
आदाय वास्तवं वृत्तं ज्ञानमज्ञाननाशकृत् 2.4.197ab
आदायाकाशशब्दाभ्यामैकात्म्यं प्रतिपाद्यते 2.1.238ab
आदायेति च क्त्वान्तोक्तेः पूर्वकालैककर्मणः 2.1.275ab
आदावभिहितं सर्वं बन्धनं सप्रयोजकम् 3.5.1ab
आदावव्याकृतं तत्त्वं नामरूपक्रियात्मना 1.4.397ab
आदावेवाधिकारी स पुनः कर्म न वीक्षते SV 89cd
आदिकर्ता स भूतानां ब्रह्मा ऽग्रे समवर्तत 1.4.21cd
आदिकर्ता स भूतानां ब्रह्माग्रे समवर्तत 1.2.162cd
आदित्यः प्राणभावेन ह्यन्नभावेन सोमता 6.3.33cd
आदित्यचक्षुर्बुद्धिस्थश्चेतनः सर्वगो ध्रुवः 2.1.44ab
आदित्यरश्मिवद्ग्राह्या दृष्टिरप्यविनाशिनी 4.3.1556cd
आदित्यलोकसंप्राप्तौ चक्षुष्टोऽयं निगच्छति 4.4.84ab
आदित्यवर्णवचनादस्तु तद्रोहितात्मकम् 3.8.94ab
आदित्यविषयं त्वाष्ट्रं मध्वचोचदथर्वणः 2.5.113ab
आदित्यस्येह वाक्येन वर्ण्यतेऽग्रजसिद्धये 5.5.7cd
आदित्याच्चन्द्रमित्याह नैते संवत्सरं तथा 6.2.95cd
आदित्याज्जायते वृष्टिर्वृष्टेरन्नं ततः प्रजाः 1.5.60cd
आदित्यात्परमेवेति नादित्यस्यावधारणे 4.3.40ab
आदित्यादिगतिश्चेत्स्यात्कालोऽव्यक्तसमुत्थितौ 2.1.407ab
आदित्यादित्रयं ज्ञेयं ज्योतिषामुपलक्षणम् 4.3.49ab
आदित्यादिलयेनेह भौतिकं त्वेव तद्भवेत् 4.3.136cd
आदित्यादिष्वपि तथा समिदादिसमीक्षणम् 6.2.80cd
आदित्यादिसजातीयमात्मज्योतिरतीन्द्रियम् 4.3.143ab
आदित्यादीनि तेजांसि तथाध्यात्माधिभूतयोः 4.4.42ab

आदित्यादेरिहावाप्तिरात्मनोऽज्ञानवर्त्मना 4.3.90cd
आदित्यादेर्विलीनत्वान्न तदा तत्क्रियेष्यते 2.1.407cd
आदित्याद्यसजातीयः पूर्वोक्तादनुमानतः 4.3.261cd
आदित्यानीत्यतस्तानि सम्यगाचक्षते बुधाः 6.5.16cd
आदित्यान्तर्गतः साक्षात्करणात्माभिधीयते 2.3.46ab
आदित्यान्तर्गतो देवो व्याख्यातायतनादिकः 4.2.36cd
आदित्यावधृतिश्चेत्स्यान्नेन्द्रादेः स्यादनुग्रहः 4.3.41ab
आदित्येन सदैवास्ते यात्यायाति करोति च 4.3.39cd
आदित्येन हि प्रोक्तानि यजूंष्येतानि यानि तु 6.5.16ab
आदित्येनैव चेत्पुंसोऽनुग्रहो भवतोच्यते 4.3.47ab
आदित्येनैव संधत्ते मनश्चन्द्रमसा न तु 1.5.181cd
आदिदिक्षितमेतस्य तत्त्वं यद्ब्रह्मणः परम् 2.3.238ab
आदिमत्त्वादिदुष्टत्वात्पुमर्थत्वेन वर्ण्यते SV 846cd
आदिमध्यान्तभागत्वे निरंशत्वं च दुर्घटम् 4.3.606ab
आदिमध्यान्तहेतूत्थविकल्परहितोऽपि वा 4.3.601cd
आदिशब्दस्य वा लोपादाज्यादिमिति गम्यताम् 6.4.83cd
आदिष्टिरथवादेशो नेति नेत्यद्वयात्मनः 2.3.175cd
आदीयमानं विज्ञानं सामर्थ्यं विषयोन्मुखम् 2.1.226ab
आदेश इत्युपक्रम्य प्रतिषेधोऽयमुच्यते 2.3.206ab
आदेशं प्रत्ययतिमहानथात इति संभ्रमः 2.3.236ab
आदेशोऽतोऽयमेवात्र ब्रह्मण्यादेश इष्यते 2.3.237cd
आदेशोऽनन्तरं तस्य क्रियतेऽनन्यमानिनः 2.3.172cd
आदेशो नेति नेत्येव तेनेह घटतेऽञ्जसा 2.3.243ab
आदेशो ब्रह्मणोऽतोऽयं निरादेशस्य भण्यते 2.3.174ab
आदौ संन्याससंसिद्धेर्ऋणानीति ह्यपस्मृतिः SV 436cd
आद्यन्तयोरभावाच्च स्वप्नपुत्रादिलाभवत् 1.4.1017cd
आद्यन्तयोर्यतो बीजं प्रत्यक्षेणावसीयते 2.4.324ab
आद्यन्तवत्त्वस्वाभाव्याद्दुःखहेतव एव ते 4.3.1837cd
आद्यन्तवत्त्वात्तद्दुःखं दुःखसंस्कारजं तथा 3.9.155cd
आद्यपादपरिज्ञानमात्रस्यैव प्रतिग्रहः 5.16.59ab
आद्यमित्युच्यते तस्य विशेषणतया वचः 1.3.238cd
आद्यात्मबुद्धिवद्धेतोरनैकान्तिकतेक्ष्यते 1.4.1510cd

आद्युदात्तत्वलिङ्गेन ह्यभिधानं विदग्धवत् 3.9.82cd
आद्योऽन्त्यः संततो वासौ बोधो मुक्तिफलः स्मृतः 1.4.1527cd
आधाराधेययोगेषु घटोऽत्रेति यथा मतिः SV 926ab
आधाराधेययोरैक्यात्पृथिव्यग्न्यादिषु त्रिषु 3.9.21ab
आधाराधेययोर्भित्तौ तयोः कारकतेष्यते 2.1.377cd
आधाराधेयसंबन्धस्तत्राश्मोरगयोः स्फुटः 1.4.547cd
आधारेषु निरंशेषु यद्याधेयस्तथाविधः 2.1.409ab
आधिभौतिकभूतानां तथैवाध्यात्मरूपिणाम् 1.4.513ab
आधिस्वभावजेनेति कर्तादानस्य भण्यते 2.1.225ab
आध्यात्मिकं परिच्छेदमुक्तदर्शनवर्त्मना 4.2.78ab
आध्यात्मिकपरिच्छेदव्यावृत्तिर्यत्समाश्रयात् 1.3.2ab
आध्यात्मिकस्य नेत्रादेर्बाह्यज्योतिरसंगतौ 4.3.81ab
आध्यात्मिकस्य सर्वस्य कार्यस्य करणस्य च 3.9.38ab
आध्यात्मिकस्येव पुंसः कृत्स्नाध्यात्माधिभूतयोः 4.2.77ab
आध्यात्मिकादिलेपानां विशुद्धिरिह भण्यते 2.1.291cd
आध्यात्मिकाधिभूताधिदैविकार्थातिसंकरात् 4.4.618ab
आध्यात्मिकेन देहेन न्यूनकार्यसमाप्तये 1.5.318ab
आध्यायावसितेः कार्यं तस्या व्याख्यातमञ्जसा 2.1.10cd
आध्यायावसितेस्तस्मादविद्याया विभूतयः 1.4.1594ab
आनखाग्रेभ्य इत्युक्त्या मर्यादातोऽस्य भण्यते 1.4.634cd
आनन्तर्ये क्रियाद्वित्वादथशब्दे भवेद्ध्रुवम् 1.3.229cd
आनन्त्यं नित्यतैवास्य नाम्नो न व्यक्तिभूरिता 3.2.39cd
आनन्त्यं बहुशब्देन देवानां प्राब्रवीन्मुनिः 3.9.9cd
आनन्त्यं ब्रह्मता चास्य दुर्घटा स्यात्तथा सति 3.2.109cd
आनन्द एष परमो मनुष्याणामिहोच्यते 4.3.1848cd
आनन्दं ब्रह्मणो विद्वान्न बिभेतीति शास्त्रगीः 4.4.633cd
आनन्दं ब्रह्म विज्ञानं साक्षादित्यादिलक्षणम् 4.1.1ab
आनन्दः परमोऽस्यैष इत्युक्तार्थप्रसिद्धये 4.3.1839ab
आनन्दः परमोऽस्यैष सुखोत्कर्षसमाप्तितः 4.3.1836ab
आनन्दः स्वयमेवात्मा भेदसंसर्गवर्जितः 2.1.362ab
आनन्दज्ञानविषया कल्पनेयं वृथा श्रमः 3.9.196cd
आनन्दनिर्णयान्तं तु संप्रसादवचो यदा 4.3.1906ab

आनन्दब्रह्मविज्ञानपदार्थैकत्वहेतुतः 3.9.205ab
आनन्दभुक्तथा प्राज्ञ इति चागमशासनम् 1.4.744cd
आनन्दवद्वाशङ्क्योक्तिर्योऽशनायेतिपूर्विका 3.5.84cd
आनन्दस्य परां काष्ठामतिघ्नीमेत्य निर्वृतः 2.1.347cd
आनन्दस्य परां निष्ठामतिघ्नीं प्रतिपद्यते 2.1.357cd
आनन्दस्य परा निष्ठा तेनातिघ्नीति भण्यते 2.1.350cd
आनन्दाद्यन्नपर्यन्तान्कारणेतररूपिणः 1.4.33ab
आनन्दानतिशेतेऽन्यान्सर्वानस्यैव कृत्स्नतः 4.3.1841cd
आनन्दान्पाप्मनश्चित्रान्स्वप्न आत्मा प्रपश्यति 4.3.852cd
आनन्दैकस्वभावत्वाद्वेद्यता तत्र नार्थ्यते SV 1022ab
आनन्दैकस्वभावत्वान्नात्मनः सुखकामिता 3.5.129ab
आनन्दैकस्वभावोऽस्य सुषुप्तेऽध्यवसीयते 3.9.210ab
आनन्दो ब्रह्मेति तथा तैत्तिरीयश्रुतौ श्रुतम् 3.9.168ab
आनयामासुरीर्भूमीरिति दैतेयनिश्चितिः 1.3.28cd
आनर्थक्यं ब्रह्मधियो न च युक्तं कथं चन 1.4.1752cd
आनर्थक्यभयादेव श्रुतादन्यत्र कल्प्यते SV 580ab
आ नाभितस्तथा कण्ठाद्धृदयं मध्यतः स्थितम् 2.1.320ab
आनुलोम्यं सुषुप्ताप्तिरेवमुक्तेन वर्त्मना 4.3.989ab
आनुषङ्गिफलोक्त्या वा तदुपासा विमुक्तये 1.3.192ab
आन्तरं मेयमाश्रित्य स्वतःसिद्धमनन्यमम् 1.4.273ab
आन्तरप्रलयाद्या तु विराजोऽधीयमुच्यते 1.4.20cd
आन्त्यात्कार्यात्तदेव स्यात्सर्वकार्यविशेषणम् 1.4.15cd
आप एव समुत्थाय पुरुषाकृतयो हुताः 6.2.36ab
आप एवेदमित्युक्त्या यथोक्तार्थस्तवाय तु 5.5.1cd
आ परात्मावबोधात्स्यात्तत्र सर्वसमाप्तितः SV 162cd
आपरोक्ष्यात्तदा कार्यं व्यर्थं पारोक्ष्यहानिकृत् SV 842cd
आपादयन्ति यत्नेन तेभ्योऽन्यः कोऽधिको धिया 2.1.441cd
आपाद्य गमयामास तत्र प्राणैकरूपिणः 3.3.161cd
आपाद्य विषयं सम्यक्स्वयमेव प्रलीयते 4.4.724ef
आपीतकरणग्रामे पुंसि स्वात्मन्यवस्थिते 2.4.382ab
आपीताशेषसंसारं शुद्धसंस्कारसंश्रयम् 1.2.131ab
आ पुमर्थावधेः शास्त्रमप्रामाण्यभयात्स्फुटम् SV 776cd

आपूर्येदं जगत्सर्वं स्थित आध्यात्मिकः पुमान् 4.2.75cd
आपेक्षिकं तु यद्रूपं तन्मिथ्येत्युपपादितम् 4.3.1327ab
आपेक्षिकत्वान्मृत्युः स्याच्छास्त्रीये ज्ञानकर्मणी 1.3.360ab
आपेक्षिकोऽपि क्लृप्तत्वान्न भेदो रज्जुसर्पवत् 5.1.93cd
आपेक्ष्य नवमादानं तत्कार्यं नवमुच्यते 4.4.142ab
आपेदे कारणात्मत्वं नामरूपादिसर्जने 1.4.492cd
आपेषणेन बुबुधे यः प्राणादिविलक्षणः 2.1.184ab
आपेषणे विशेषस्य दृष्टत्वाद्देहसंहतिः 2.1.148ab
आपेषाल्लीनबुद्ध्यादिसमुत्पत्तौ परात्मनः 2.1.180ab
आपेषोद्भूतसंक्षोभस्ततोऽसौ प्रत्यबुध्यत 2.1.178cd
आपोऽजायन्त इति च सर्वभूतोपलक्षणम् 1.2.145cd
आपो वा अर्क इति तु चित्यनामार्थमेव तत् 1.2.149cd
आपो ह वा इति तथा ह्ययमेव क्रमः श्रुतौ 1.2.180ab
आपो ह्यणुतराः सत्यमसृजन्तेति हि श्रुतिः 1.2.138ab
आप्तं बोधात्तथाप्तव्यं वर्जनीयं च वर्जितम् 4.4.531cd
आप्तकामतया तद्वन्निष्कामत्वं समश्नुते 4.4.282ab
आप्तकामात्मकामत्ववचसैव निराकृताः 4.3.1344ab
आप्तकामादिकं सर्वं वस्तुवृत्तव्यपेक्षया 4.3.1336ab
आप्तकामादिवचसा यथावस्त्ववबोधिना 4.4.270cd
आप्तशेषपुमर्थोऽपि प्रत्यग्याथात्म्यमोहतः 1.4.1015ab
आप्ताः सर्वे स्वतोऽप्यस्य कामा ये बाह्यसाधनाः 4.4.271ab
आप्ताप्तव्यादिहीनत्वादानन्दैकात्म्यवस्तुनः 4.3.1336cd
आप्ताशेषक्रियाकार्यो मुक्तौ स विनियुज्यते 1.4.1053cd
आप्ताशेषपुमर्थत्वात्त्यक्तानर्थस्य च स्वतः SV 250ab
आप्ताशेषपुमर्थत्वान्नापेक्षा साधनं प्रति 3.5.139ab
आप्ताशेषपुमर्थस्य त्यक्ताशेषासुखस्य च 4.4.1108cd
आप्ताशेषपुमर्थस्य प्रत्यग्याथात्म्यबोधिनः 4.4.1107ab
आप्ताशेषपुमर्थोऽथ सोऽमन्यत ततो विराट् 1.4.62cd
आप्ताशेषपुमर्थोऽयं सर्वसाधननिस्पृहः 4.3.1337cd
आप्ताशेषसुखापास्तदुःखत्वादात्मवस्तुनः 4.4.214cd
आप्ते कर्मफले नात आरम्भः कर्मणामिह 4.4.1163cd
आप्त्युत्पत्त्यादिकं शक्यमनारोप्यस्वभावतः SV 626cd

आबद्धात्माभिमानोऽयं गार्ग्योऽविद्यासमन्वितः 1.6.43cd
आबाधितधियाभ्यस्तो गार्ग्यस्यानुक्तिकारणात् 2.1.47cd
आ ब्रह्मणोऽस्मात्संसाराच्छुद्धधीर्न विरज्यते 2.4.71ab
आ ब्रह्मणोऽस्य ये सिद्धा अविद्याकर्महेतुतः 4.4.1181ab
आब्रह्मस्थाणुभेदोऽयं नामरूपक्रियात्मकः 1.4.1141cd
आब्रह्मास्थाणु चाजस्रं यः संसरति मूढधीः 3.4.2cd
आब्रह्मास्थाणु चान्वक्षं सर्वेषु व्यभिचारिषु 1.4.1397ab
आब्रह्मास्थाण्वयं योनीर्बम्भ्रमीत्यनिशं परः 2.1.223cd
आभवादर्जितानां तु सर्वेषामपि कर्मणाम् 3.2.82ab
आभाजयस्व क्षुधितांश्छान्दसत्वाण्णिचोऽश्रवः 1.3.250cd
आभाति बहुधैवेयं तदविद्योत्थहेतुभिः 3.7.60cd
आभाति बहुरूपेव तत्पराधीनचेतसाम् 1.4.1633cd
आभासते मृषैवातो यथाभूतात्मविद्यया SV 269ab
आभासादिप्रमाणान्तं तद्विशिष्टफलोत्थितेः 3.4.142cd
आभिमानिक एवास्य येन येन विशेष्यते 4.3.825ab
आभूतसंप्लवस्थानममृतत्वं हि भाष्यते 6.2.143cd
आभूतसंप्लवस्थानमानन्त्यं चेह गृह्यते 1.5.200ab
आभ्यां संभूय सिद्धोऽर्थ एवं सति भवेद्यतः 4.3.1506cd
आमंसीति भवेद्रूपं ज्ञानार्थस्यैव मन्यतेः 6.3.37ab
आमंसीत्यादिमन्त्रेण तदर्थाविष्कृतिस्त्वियम् 6.3.36cd
आमगोऽपीममात्मानं तत्तमोध्वस्तिवर्त्मना 4.4.687ab
आमन्त्रयां तदा चक्रे बृहन्नित्येवमादिभिः 2.1.98cd
आमन्त्रयामास च तं कुमारा३ इति बालवत् 6.2.25ab
आमपात्रेऽग्निमित्युक्त्या ह्यभिचाराख्यकर्मणः 6.4.51ab
आ मैत्रेय्याः परब्रह्मसत्यस्य प्रतिपत्तये 2.2.2cd
आमोऽपक्वं त्वयि गतं महत्त्वमपि भण्यते 6.3.41ab
आम्नायस्य क्रियार्थत्वादित्यत्राप्यभिधीयते SV 270ef
आम्नायस्य क्रियार्थत्वाद्विधिनेति च सूत्रणात् SV 36ab
आम्रं यथा रसादाढ्यें स्वस्माद्वृन्तात्प्रमुच्यते 4.3.1931ab
आम्रेडनं हि शब्दार्थः सर्वत्रोपासनश्रुतेः 1.4.771cd
आम्रे निमित्त इत्यादि ह्यापस्तम्बस्मृतेर्वचः SV 97ab
आयातस्तर्ह्यनाश्वासस्त्वदभ्युपगतावपि SV 389cd

आयुर्वीर्यं स्मृतिं प्रज्ञां सौकुमार्यं वपुःश्रियम् 3.9.17ab
आयुषोऽन्ते विधेमाद्य क्षम देव प्रसीद मे 5.17.22cd
आरब्धकार्यभूतानां गृहीतौ न च संभवः 2.3.74ab
आरब्धफलशेषैकहेतुत्वाद्देहसंस्थितेः 1.4.1529ab
आरब्धेयं प्रयत्नेन वेदान्तोपनिषत्परा SV 1135ef
आरभ्यत्वाभ्युपगमे मुक्तेस्तत्स्याद्यथोदितम् 3.3.17ab
आरभ्यमाणता मुक्तेः प्रत्यज्ञायि त्वयैव सा 3.3.87ab
आरभ्य सर्वं वेदेति ज्ञानार्थेनोपसंहृतिम् 1.4.1019ab
आरभ्येऽर्थेऽफलं ज्ञानं व्यञ्जकत्वात्प्रदीपवत् 3.3.21cd
आरभ्ये कारकत्वे न बलात्प्रामाण्यमापतेत् SV 1030ab
आरभ्योद्गमने भानोः सर्वं स्नानाद्यशेषतः 6.4.81ab
आरम्भकत्वं जगति तस्या नैवोपपद्यते 3.3.20cd
आरम्भकबहुत्वाच्च बहूक्तिरिह गृह्यते 3.6.14ab
आरम्भकाणां विज्ञानप्रमुखाणामिहात्मनः 4.4.205cd
आरम्भवादे त्विच्छादेः कार्यत्वादसदात्मता 4.4.332ab
आरम्भेऽवसितौ शास्त्रं परस्परविरोधतः 1.4.1268ab
आराज्ज्ञानगभस्तिभिः प्रतिहतश्चन्द्रायते भास्करः 6.5.25c
आरादेवोपकुर्वन्ति नित्यान्यात्मविशुद्धितः SV 1133ab
आराध्य परमोत्कर्षं तत्प्रसादात्समश्नुते 2.1.458cd
आराममेव मायोत्थं स्वप्ननिर्माणलक्षणम् 4.3.944ab
आरुरुक्षोर्मुनेर्योगं कर्म कारणमुच्यते 3.5.124ab
आरुरुक्षोर्मुनेर्योगं कर्म कारणमुच्यते 4.4.1093ab
आरुह्याप्यथवा दूरं विसंवादपराङ्मुखः SV 837ab
आरोप्यात्मशरीरेऽस्मिंस्तत्साधर्म्येण संततम् 1.5.219cd
आर्जिता एव विज्ञेयास्तन्निमित्तफलेक्षणात् 1.4.1786cd
आर्तं विनाशि तज्ज्ञेयं ब्रह्मानार्तं यतस्ततः 3.5.214cd
आर्तं विनाशि तत्तुच्छं शुक्तिकारजतादिवत् 3.4.187cd
आर्तभागो मुनिर्विद्वान्स च नेति तमब्रवीत् 3.2.26cd
आर्तश्रुतेश्च प्राणादि वाचारम्भणशास्त्रतः 1.5.332ab
आर्द्रे मेघोदरे विद्युत्संदीप्तोऽसीति कथ्यते 6.3.32ab
आलभन्ते यतस्तस्माद्यथाव्याख्याततत्त्ववित् 1.2.218ab
आलम्बनतयोंकार उपास्तिविषयो भवेत् 5.1.123ab

आ लोकोत्थानतः श्रुत्या उक्तापूर्वस्य विक्रिया 6.2.16cd
आलोचयन्यथातत्त्वमपास्तध्वान्ततद्भवम् 1.4.61ab
आलोचयेद्यथातत्त्वं भीध्वस्तौ तद्वदीश्वरः 1.4.60cd
आलोच्यालोचकयोर्हि योगो मिथुनमुच्यते 1.2.174ab
आवयोरेव विज्ञानं यथेदं प्रागभूदितः 3.2.135ab
आवसथ्याग्निनिर्देशो न तु त्रेताग्निसंग्रहः 6.4.53cd
आवापस्थान आज्यस्य हुत्वा नित्याहुतीस्ततः 6.3.21cd
आवामेव तथैवोर्ध्वं वेदिष्यावो यथोदितम् 3.2.135cd
आविद्वदङ्गनाबालं देहादौ घटवन्मतिः 4.3.208ab
आविद्वदङ्गनाबालं विश्वसित्यनपेक्षतः 1.4.1400cd
आ विरिञ्चात्तथास्थाणोः सर्वं कर्मात उच्यते 4.3.814cd
आ विरिञ्चात्पुमर्थानामकृत्स्नत्वादिदोषतः 1.4.1073ab
आविरिञ्चादितो भूप यास्यसि क्वेति भण्यताम् 4.2.8cd
आविरिञ्चाद्विरक्तश्चेत्कुम्भीपाकादिवेह यः 1.4.1053ab
आविरिञ्चाद्विरक्तस्य तद्विविक्तात्मकामिनः 1.3.96ab
आविरिञ्चाद्विरक्तो हि संसारान्निविवृत्सति 1.4.10ab
आविरिञ्च्यात्स्वकार्येभ्यः स्यादेव विनिवृत्तये SV 1108cd
आविर्भावतिरोभावैः कारणात्मनि वर्तते 1.3.260cd
आविर्भावतिरोभावैः कार्यकारणरूपिभिः 5.1.57ab
आविर्भावतिरोभावौ स्वतःसिद्धेश्च कारणात् SV 146cd
आविर्भूतस्वकार्यस्य संसर्गः कारणात्मना 2.1.230ab
आविश्चिकीर्षितं तत्त्वं तदेतदधुनोच्यते 2.3.4cd
आविश्चिकीर्षुः साक्षादिममर्थं च श्रुतिः परा 4.3.904ab
आविश्चिकीर्षुः साक्षान्नस्तद्यथेति परा श्रुतिः 2.5.65cd
आविश्चिकीर्षुभिस्तस्माद्वेदान्तार्थं महात्मभिः 2.3.148ab
आविष्करिष्यन्हेत्वर्थमकृत्स्नत्वप्रसिद्धये 1.4.663ab
आविष्करोमि तत्कर्म युवयोरद्य हे नरौ 2.5.108ab
आविष्कृतिस्तन्निषेधादन्यदेवेति च श्रुतेः 1.4.1647ab
आवृतं ज्ञप्तिमात्रेण सर्वमात्मीकृतं जगत् 2.5.124ab
आवृतत्वमथ मतं भङ्ग एव प्रसज्यते 1.2.96ab
आवृत्तिः क्षयशब्देन दुःखप्रायासु भूमिषु 5.16.66ab
आवृत्तिर्न पुनस्तेषां यावदाभूतसंप्लवम् 6.2.143ab

आवृत्तिर्हि प्रसंख्यानं शब्दयुक्त्योरिति स्थितम् SV 803cd
आवृत्तिवीप्सासद्भावात्क्षणिकोक्तेः प्रमाणतः 4.3.579cd
आवृत्तिश्च प्रसंख्यानं कुर्यात्सातिशयं कथम् SV 818ab
आशंसते बलीयांसमबलीयानपि स्वयम् 1.4.1619ab
आशङ्कितनिवृत्त्यर्थमथेत्यत्र प्रयुज्यते 1.4.1670ab
आशङ्क्य जनकोऽप्राक्षीदात्मायं कतमो न्विति 4.3.276cd
आशङ्क्य हेत्वसिद्धत्वं मधुब्राह्मणमुच्यते 2.5.5ab
आशङ्क्येत तदैवैतद्यदेतद्भवतोदितम् SV 205ef
आ शाकल्यात्परो ग्रन्थ इतो व्याख्यायतेऽधुना 3.6.1cd
आ शैलादुदयात्तथास्तगिरितो भास्वद्यशोरश्मिभिः 6.5.25a
आश्रयं क्वेति पुंसोऽसावप्राक्षीन्मुनिसत्तमम् 3.2.130cd
आश्रयादेव जन्मैवं कामानां हृदयाश्रयात् 4.4.401cd
आश्रयाश्रयिभावेन नामरूपक्रियात्मनाम् 1.6.33ab
आश्रयाश्रयिसंबन्धे हेतुरन्नरसो भवेत् 4.3.1941cd
आश्रितं स्थितमत्र स्याद्गत्वाव्याप्य च तिष्ठति 2.3.25ab
आश्रिताश्रयसंबन्धः कार्यकारणयोः स्मृतः 1.4.459ab
आ श्वभ्यो यदिदं किंचिदा कृमिभ्यश्च लक्ष्यते 6.1.31ab
आश्वेव वायुं दुर्भेद्यं स आगच्छति वेगवान् 5.12.2cd
आ संसारात्स्थितः स्थास्नुः परिणामात्मकः सदा 1.6.40cd
आसङ्ग आत्मनश्चेत्स्यात्साक्षाच्चैतन्यवद्गुणः 4.3.1040ab
आसङ्ग एव भूतानामुपादानमिहेष्यते 3.2.51cd
आसङ्गकार्यमुच्छिन्नं द्वैतदृष्ट्यात्मनो यतः 3.2.51ab
आसङ्गपाप्मभिर्विद्धा यस्माद्रागादयोऽसुरैः 1.3.163ab
आसङ्गपूर्वकः कामो नासङ्गविरहादसौ 4.4.226cd
आसङ्गप्रविवेकार्थं स वा इत्यादि भण्यते 4.3.969ab
आसङ्गश्च तथैवास्ते ते एते सङ्गकर्मणी 3.2.60ab
आसङ्गस्यागतिरतो विषयेन्द्रियवर्त्मना 4.3.1107ab
आसङ्गाविद्ययोरेवमन्योऽन्याश्रयतोदिता 4.3.1098ab
आसनादिक्रियाकारी पीठक्षेत्रादि कर्म च 4.3.21cd
आसन्दीस्थमुपास्ते त्वं राजन्ब्रह्मेति संभ्रमात् 1.4.1604cd
आसन्प्राणविदप्येवं प्राणात्मोपासनाद्भवेत् 1.5.370cd
आसन्यत्वादयोऽन्यस्य न च योषाग्निवद्यतः 1.3.46ab

आसमन्ताद्विजानासि सूक्ष्मादि जगति स्थितम् 6.3.38ab
आ समाप्तेस्तृतीयस्य प्रत्यगज्ञानहेतुकम् 4.4.415ab
आसादयति शुद्धात्मा मोक्षं वै प्रथमाश्रमे 1.4.1587cd
आसादयति शुद्धात्मा मोक्षं वै प्रथमाश्रमे 2.4.33cd
आसादयति शुद्धात्मा मोक्षं वै प्रथमाश्रमे 4.4.1060cd
आसामेवात्मभिः साकं तद्दुःखमुपयुज्यते 1.5.358cd
आसीदिति च निर्देशस्तस्मिन्नपि न युज्यते 1.4.1193ab
आसीदित्यपि यः शब्दः स तन्मोहाद्यपेक्षया 1.4.1301ab
आसीदिदं तमोभूतमप्रज्ञातमलक्षणम् 1.4.291ab
आसुरज्ञानकर्मभ्यां मां व्युत्थाप्याथ तज्जितेः 1.3.358ab
आसुरात्कर्मणो मृत्योरतिमुक्तिरिहोदिता 3.1.27ab
आसुरात्साधनाद्दैवप्राप्तिर्मुक्तिरिहोच्यते 3.1.25ab
आसुरी तु यदा सेना कामक्रोधपुरःसरा 1.3.120ab
आसुरेणावरुद्धांस्तान्वागादीन्हतपाप्मनः 1.3.228ab
आसुरेभ्योऽधिकारेभ्यो व्युत्थाप्येह प्रजापतिम् 1.3.27ab
आस्त इत्यादि सुबहु श्रुत्योपन्यस्तमादरात् 4.3.45cd
आस्तां तावत्प्रवेशोऽयं न्याय्योऽन्याय्यो यथा तथा 1.4.555ab
आस्तां वेदान्तमानत्वं त्यक्तं तत्कामतस्तव SV 1048ab
आस्तिक्यबुद्धिः श्रद्धा स्यादश्रद्धा तद्विरोधिनी 1.5.111cd
आस्ते पल्ययते कर्म कृत्वा भूयो निवर्तते 4.3.35cd
आस्त्र्यादिविषयोद्भूतवासनावासितं दृशेः 2.3.161cd
आस्यपर्यन्तशायीनि त्वगादीनि न मध्यतः 1.3.204ab
आस्वभावात्मविज्ञानादुपास्ते यः स तं व्रजेत् 1.3.236cd
आस्वेवोपनिषत्स्वेनं यतो व्याचक्षते बुधाः 3.9.116ab
आह मानान्तरेणासौ किल नार्थोऽवगम्यते SV 496ab
आहुतिः पय एव स्यादाज्यं वा पय एव वा 1.5.56ab
आहुतेर्जायते तस्याः पुमान्भास्वररूपभृत् 6.2.115ef
आहुत्योः परिणामोऽयमूर्ध्वसोऽपूर्वमित्यपि 6.2.86ab
आहुत्योरग्निहोत्रस्य या विभूतिः पुरोदिता 6.2.78ab
आहुत्योरग्निहोत्रस्य ह्यन्तरिक्षादिभेदतः 6.2.16ab
आहुरेवं द्विजाः केचिद्विरक्ताः पूर्वभूमितः 1.4.1129ab
आह्लादाः स्युरिहानन्दा हर्षाश्चात्र मुदस्तथा 4.3.918ab

इक्ष्वाक्वादिरभूत्पूर्वः क्षत्रियस्तद्वदुत्तरः 1.4.1641cd
इच्छन्नपि यतो नातो भूयो विन्देदतोऽधिकम् 1.4.1837ab
इच्छन्नपेक्षते योग्यमुपायमपि तत्परः SV 884cd
इच्छातत्साधनानां च स्यादानन्त्यं तथा सति 3.3.112cd
इच्छातश्चापि भाव्यत्वात्तदपि स्यान्न निर्वृतिः 1.4.1728cd
इच्छादिधर्मवत्साक्षाद्यः सदा वीक्षते मनः 4.4.471ab
इच्छादीनां स्वहेतुत्वेऽनर्थं कुर्यात्कथं स्वयम् SV 155ab
इच्छादेश्चित्तधर्मत्वात्कर्मस्थत्वं सुनिश्चितम् 4.4.470cd
इच्छाद्वेषादिमानात्मा यतस्तैरभ्युपेयते 1.4.573cd
इच्छाद्वेषादिरप्येवं नात्मनो धर्म इष्यताम् SV 153ab
इच्छामात्रमरत्युत्थं पुंस्यलब्धस्थिति स्त्रियम् 1.4.111ab
इच्छाम्युभयमप्येतदित्येवं ह्यन्यथा वदेत् 4.1.9cd
इच्छाम्येवार्थवादत्वं वचसोऽन्यपरत्वतः SV 127ab
इच्छाविशेषास्ताभ्यां च जज्ञिरेऽन्ये सहस्रशः 3.5.57cd
इच्छेदेष्टव्यमित्येवं तत्रापि प्रत्ययो यतः SV 514cd
इज्येते स्वर्गलोकाय दर्शादर्शौ यथा तथा SV 128ab
इत आरभ्य संसार आत्मनो वर्ण्यतेऽधुना 4.3.1910ab
इत उक्तात्मसंबोधमोहोच्छित्तेरनन्तरम् 4.4.557ab
इत एव तु विज्ञानात्तेषां तत्फलकीर्तनम् SV 1118cd
इतं बहुत्वमेकं सद्द्वियद्यद्वद्घटादिषु 1.2.127cd
इतः परं वस्तुतत्त्वपरीक्षणकृतक्षणा 1.4.185ab
इतः प्रवसतो देहाद्देहिनः कर्मसंक्षयात् 4.3.1973cd
इतरत्रापि विज्ञेयं तत्र वस्त्वसमीक्षणात् 4.3.1061cd
इतरस्यापि सामत्वं प्राणनिर्वर्त्यतो मतम् 1.3.303ab
इतश्च प्रत्यगात्मस्थो नान्यत्रागादयं पुमान् 2.1.247ab
इतश्च व्याहृतिः स्पष्टा ब्रह्मविद्या विरुध्यते 1.4.1721ab
इतश्चाभ्युपगन्तव्यमेतत्तुल्येऽपि वस्तुनि SV 599ab
इतिकर्तव्यता चात्र ह्यर्थवादप्रशंसनम् 1.4.785cd
इतिकर्तव्यता त्यागब्रह्मचर्यादिसाधनम् 1.4.788cd
इतिकर्तव्यतादानं करणादानमेव च SV 249ab
इति काण्डद्वयोक्तोऽर्थः संहृत्य सफलोऽखिलः 4.4.1345ab
इति कातीयवचनमदृष्टार्थत्वकारणात् 6.3.19cd

इति कामप्रधानत्वसिद्धान्तस्योपसंहृतिः 4.4.244ab
इति कामप्रधानस्य संसारानर्थसंगतिम् 4.4.251ab
इति क्रमविधानार्थं हिता नामेति भण्यते 2.1.319cd
इति क्षरार्थसंबन्धज्ञानेऽस्मिंल्लोकचक्षुषा 2.1.279ab
इति चाहेश्वरो वाक्यमुक्तार्थप्रतिपत्तये 4.4.1316cd
इति चेतसि संधाय याज्ञवल्क्यमपृच्छत 3.8.55ab
इति चेतसि संधाय याज्ञवल्क्योऽभ्यभाषत 3.9.59cd
इति चेतसि संधाय संबन्धं नोक्तवान्गुरुः SV 319cd
इति चेतसि संधाय सर्वयोगेश्वरेश्वरः 3.5.47cd
इति चेतसि संधाय ह्याक्षिपन्ति प्रजादिकम् 4.4.1104ab
इति चेद्वीक्षसे तर्हि मूढमज्ञं च कुम्भवत् 4.4.362cd
इति चेन्नात्मनो ध्रौव्याद्विक्रियानुपपत्तितः SV 142cd
इति चेन्नैतदेवं स्याच्छ्रुतेः प्रामाण्यकारणात् 4.4.538ab
इति चेन्नैतदेवं स्यात्सादृश्यासंभवात्तव 4.3.664cd
इति चेन्नैतदेवं स्यादचित्केष्वपि दर्शनात् 2.3.66cd
इति चेन्नैतदेवं स्यादागमोक्तिविरोधतः 1.4.538cd
इति चेन्नैतदेवं स्यादाद्येऽनैकान्तिकत्वतः 1.4.1509cd
इति चेन्नैतदेवं स्यादेवं वेदेति तद्विधेः 1.3.34cd
इति चेन्नैतदेवं स्याद्यतोऽधिपतिरुच्यते 4.4.991cd
इति चोद्यं समाशङ्क्य परिहारं प्रचक्षते 1.5.138ab
इति ज्ञात्वा ह्यभिद्रुत्य स्वैरासङ्गशरोर्मिभिः 1.3.147ab
इति दुःखित्वमापन्नस्तीर्थेनेच्छेत्युवाच तम् 6.2.65cd
इति दृष्टान्तवचसा निर्णयोऽस्योपवर्ण्यते 4.4.139ab
इति दोषनिषेधार्थमिदं पूर्णमितीर्यते 5.1.39ab
इति दोषापनुत्त्यर्थं यं न वेदेति भण्यते 3.7.28cd
इति द्वयं प्रतीच्येव संभाव्यं ब्रह्मणीरितम् 3.4.27cd
इति धूमोपलम्भत्वाद्भ्राष्ट्रधूमोपलम्भवत् 4.3.728cd
इति नावक्ष्यद्यद्येतदुभयं नाभवत्पुरा 1.2.7cd
इति निर्युक्तिकं कैश्चिद्व्याख्यानं यत्नतः कृतम् 1.5.239cd
इति निश्चित्य निःसङ्गाः प्रव्रजन्त्येव सर्वतः 4.4.1109cd
इति निःशेषतन्मोहकार्यध्वंसो विवक्षितः 2.1.380cd
इति नेदं प्रवृत्त्यर्थं वचो नापि निवृत्तये SV 576cd

इति न्याय्यं श्रुतेर्वाक्यं कस्मान्नाद्रियतेऽञ्जसा 1.5.269cd
इति पूर्वाश्रमे वासो ध्वस्तर्णस्य निषिध्यते 1.5.260cd
इति पृष्टोऽनुमानेनाविरुद्धं प्रत्यपीपदत् 4.3.283ab
इति पृष्टोऽब्रवीद्गार्गि मातिप्राक्षीः कथं चन 3.6.21cd
इति पृष्टोऽब्रवीद्वित्तसाधनस्य प्रयोजनम् 2.4.52cd
इति प्रकाशरूपत्वं करणानां श्रुतिर्जगौ 4.4.27cd
इति प्रतिवचः कष्टं मत्वैनं पर्यपृच्छत 3.2.14cd
इति प्रबोधस्वप्नाभ्यां विविक्तं स्थानमुच्यते 4.3.1170cd
इति प्रमाणमत्रार्थे वचनं भाल्लविश्रुतौ 2.4.26ab
इति प्रमेयनिर्देशो द्रष्टव्य इति तत्प्रमा 2.4.95cd
इति प्रश्नप्रतिवचस्ते वा इत्यादिकं जगौ 6.2.14ab
इति प्रश्नप्रतिवचो याज्ञवल्क्योऽप्युवाच तम् 3.1.21cd
इति प्राणवचः श्रुत्वा प्रत्यचुः करणानि तम् 6.1.30cd
इति बाहुमिवोद्धृत्य वेदान्तैर्घोषणा कृता 4.3.1835cd
इति बाहुमिवोद्धृत्य वेदान्तैर्घोषणा कृता 6.2.9cd
इति बुद्धात्मतत्त्वस्य गीरियं न तमस्विनः 1.4.311cd
इति ब्रह्म तमित्यादेः संक्षेपार्थः समीरितः 2.4.260ab
इति ब्रह्मविदोपेत्य प्रष्टव्या भेदवादिनः 2.1.592cd
इति ब्रुवाणं प्रब्रूयादनिष्टं श्रूयते कुतः 1.4.828cd
इति ब्रुवाणो लोकेऽस्मिन्हस्यते बालकैरपि 2.3.110cd
इति भाल्लविशाखायां श्रुतिवाक्यमधीयते SV 220ab
इति भाल्लविश्रुतिवचः सम्यग्ज्ञानस्य जन्मने 3.5.146ab
इति भूतार्थसंबोधज्ञानोन्मीलितचक्षुषाम् 2.1.276ab
इति भूरिविकल्पायां भूमौ सिद्धान्त उच्यते 4.4.129ab
इति भेदविवक्षायां व्याख्या कार्या पदद्वये 1.3.226ab
इति मत्वाथवाप्राक्षीत्पृष्टमर्थं पुनर्ऋषिम् 3.5.29cd
इति मन्त्रः समाप्तोऽयमभिमर्शनकर्मणि 6.3.35cd
इति मन्त्रसमाम्नायस्तथा च ब्राह्मणान्यपि 2.1.463ab
इति मन्त्रोऽपि चानन्त्यमैकात्म्यस्यावदत्स्वयम् 4.4.1178cd
इति मन्त्रोक्त एवार्थो ब्राह्मणेनापि वर्ण्यते 4.4.1193cd
इति यत्प्रागुपन्यस्तं तस्य दूषणमुच्यते 5.1.96ab
इति यद्वत्तथोक्तिस्ते प्रत्यक्षेण विरुध्यते 2.1.547cd

इति लोकप्रसिद्धत्वात्तस्मिंल्लोकोऽनुशास्ति तत् 4.3.947cd
इति लोके समाचारादग्निभ्यः संभवस्ततः 6.2.117cd
इति वस्तु स्वतो बुद्धमज्ञानं चानुभूतितः 4.4.294ab
इति वावेति वचनं पर्वोत्तरविरोधतः 6.2.46cd
इति विप्रतिषिद्धं यत्तदैकात्म्यान्न दुष्यति 4.3.1411cd
इति वेदविदः केचिद्भिन्नाभिन्नसतत्त्वकम् 5.1.63ab
इति वेदविदाप्युक्तं तदप्रामाण्यकारणम् 3.5.159cd
इति वेदशिरःसूक्तिस्तथा चोद्घृष्यते स्फुटा 1.4.382ef
इति वेदात्मनः साक्षाद्वचनं श्रुतिसंमतम् 2.4.248ab
इति वैषम्यतो वर्णो धातुसाम्येऽतिलोहितः 4.3.1239cd
इति व्याख्या न साध्वीयं द्रष्टव्यासंभवे यतः 4.3.1607ab
इति व्याचक्षते केचित्प्रश्नावेतौ यथोदितौ 3.5.15ab
इति व्याचक्षते केचिद्ग्रन्थमेतं महाधियः 4.2.19ab
इति व्याचक्षते केचिद्विज्ञायेति वचः स्फुटम् 4.4.891ab
इति व्याचक्षते केचिन्नियोगार्थैकरागिणः SV 454cd
इति व्याचक्षते केचिन्महामत्स्यादिकां श्रुतिम् 4.3.1104ab
इति व्याचक्षते ये तु तेषां वेदान्तमात्रकम् 4.4.1032cd
इति व्यासस्मृतौ वाक्यं प्रत्यक्षश्रुतिबन्धनम् 3.5.153ab
इति शब्दोपदिष्टानां निषेधोऽनुभवात्मनि 2.3.188ab
इतिशब्दो यथोक्तार्थपरामर्शनकर्मणे 4.3.1825ab
इति श्रीमत्सुरेशस्य वाक्यमेवं समञ्जसम् 1.4.327cd
इति श्रीमन्महाभर्तृप्रपञ्चस्य महीयसः 4.4.412ab
इति श्रीयाज्ञवल्क्येन मुक्तकण्ठमुदाहृतम् 6.2.10cd
इति श्रुतिर्जगादार्थं यथैवेह प्रपञ्च्यते 1.2.151cd
इति श्रुत्या पुराप्युक्तं तस्मान्नात्मा विनश्यति 4.3.1405cd
इति श्रुत्युक्तितस्तेषां प्रतिप्राणि यथामति 4.4.130cd
इति श्रुत्यैव निर्दिष्टं नोपास्यं ब्रह्म तेन नः 1.5.255cd
इति श्रौतं वचो ज्ञेयमागमैकप्रमाणतः 3.2.165cd
इति संजातपरमवैराग्यो नित्यकर्मणः 4.4.1216ab
इति संदेहहेतुश्च विचारस्य प्रयोजकः 2.1.432ab
इति सर्वपदार्थेषु पुंसोऽशक्यं विधित्सितम् 1.4.957cd
इति स्पर्शविशेषं ना मनसैव प्रपद्यते 1.5.125cd

इति स्पष्टं वचो मानं कुतो हेतोरुपेक्ष्यते 4.3.1731cd
इति स्पष्टं श्रुतेर्वाक्यं कस्मान्नाद्रियते त्वया 3.3.56cd
इति स्यादर्थवत्त्वाय समाधिर्ज्ञानकर्मणोः 1.4.1701cd
इति स्ववचसैवैतद्विरुद्धमभिधीयते 4.3.1573cd
इति स्वोक्तमविस्मृत्य वासनाभेदगीः कथम् 2.3.111cd
इतिहासपुराणादेर्वेदमूलत्वकारणात् 2.4.319ab
इतिहासपुराणादेस्तदन्यस्येह कार्यतः 2.4.321cd
इतिहासपुराणाभ्यां वेदं समुपबृंहयेत् 2.4.318ab
इतिहासादिसंभेदभिन्नं ब्राह्मणमेव तु 2.4.314ab
इति हेतूपदेशाय स यदित्यादि भण्यते 1.4.46cd
इति हेतूपदेशार्थमुभे इति परं वचः 4.4.1174cd
इतीत्युक्तपरामर्शो न्विति खेदानुकम्पयोः 4.4.249ab
इतीत्युक्तपरामर्शो वाकोवाक्यं नृपेरितम् 6.2.47ab
इतीत्युक्तपरामर्शो वेदाज्ञा चानुशासनम् 2.5.146ab
इतीत्युक्तपरामर्शो ह्यतिदेशार्थ उच्यते 3.1.45ab
इतीमं पक्षमाश्रित्य श्रुत्या दृष्टान्त उच्यते 4.4.133ab
इतीममर्थं भार्यायै याज्ञवल्क्योऽभ्यभाषत 2.4.451ab
इतोऽग्निभ्योऽग्निमेवायं स्वां योनिं प्रतिपत्स्यते 6.2.117ab
इतोऽधिकारबन्धान्माभूनजत्पालयेदिति 1.5.297cd
इतोऽन्यत्रातिमोक्षा ये तेऽप्येवमिति वीक्ष्यताम् 3.1.45cd
इतोऽन्यत्रापि तद्भाष्यं गमयेदेवमेव तु 1.4.1164cd
इतोऽन्यथा कल्पनायां न प्रागाणं सामीक्ष्यते 4.4.344ab
इतोऽन्यथा कल्पनायां यतो दोषेण संगतिः 2.1.472cd
इतोऽन्यथा कल्प्यमाने सर्वं स्यादसमञ्जसम् SV 733ab
इतोऽन्यथा चेद्व्याख्यानं क्रियते बुद्धिलाघवात् 4.4.591ab
इतोऽन्यथा चेन्मोक्षः स्यादारम्भोऽनर्थकः श्रुतेः 4.4.308ab
इतोऽन्यथा तत्सत्यत्वं निष्फलं न च लभ्यते 1.4.432cd
इतोऽन्यथा तु यद्रूपं जाग्रत्स्वप्नस्वलक्षणम् 4.3.1206ab
इतोऽन्यथाभिसंबन्धे न किंचिन्मानमीक्ष्यते SV 331cd
इतोऽन्यथावबोधस्य प्रतीचोऽनुपलब्धितः 4.3.1461cd
इतोऽन्या गतयः सर्वाः क्षयिसाधनसंश्रयात् 4.3.1829ab
इतोऽपरे तु ये लोकास्तेऽस्याविद्याप्रकल्पिताः 4.3.1275cd

इतो जिगमिषुं विद्याकर्मणी ये पुरार्जिते 4.4.111ab
इतो मुक्तस्य रूपाणि त्वग्न्यादीनि पुराब्रवम् 3.2.4ab
इतो विरुद्धमानत्वं स्वतोऽपास्तद्वयात्मनः 1.4.490ab
इत्थं न चेदहं कुर्यां प्रतिषेधश्रुतीरितम् 1.3.225ab
इत्थं ये विदुरर्चिस्ते संभवन्त्यात्मभाविताः 6.2.120cd
इत्थंसतत्त्व इत्युक्त्या कथं द्रष्टृक्रियोच्यते 4.3.1570cd
इत्थंसतत्त्वकस्तावद्द्रष्टव्यः श्रुतियुक्तिभिः 4.3.1542ab
इत्थंभूते तृतीयातः स्वेन भासेति गृह्यते 4.3.893cd
इत्यकामयतानाप्तान्पुमर्थान्साधनैर्जडः 1.4.1814cd
इत्यत्र किंनिमित्तेयमाशङ्केत्यभिधीयते 1.4.1470cd
इत्यत्र चोदयित्वैके परिहारं प्रचक्षते 4.4.1229ab
इत्यनात्यन्तिकलयो भयोजन्मकृतक्षणः 2.4.398cd
इत्यनुक्रमसंन्यासे संप्रत्तिरुपदिश्यते 1.5.263cd
इत्यन्तर्याम्यवस्थायां स्थित्वैकां प्राणदेवताम् 3.9.5ab
इत्यर्थं कोपकृद्वाक्यं शाकल्यो मुनिरब्रवीत् 3.9.65cd
इत्यर्थं तेज एवेति श्रुतिः संसर्गवारिणी 4.4.526cd
इत्यर्थप्रतिपत्त्यर्थं दृष्टान्तोऽत्राभिधीयते 4.3.1911ab
इत्यर्थप्रतिपत्त्यर्थमाजगामोत्तरं वचः 4.4.147cd
इत्यर्थप्रतिपत्त्यर्थमीदृग्दृष्टान्त उच्यते 1.3.174cd
इत्यर्थमपि दृष्टान्तः पर्ववद्वण्यते पुनः 4.3.1973ab
इत्यर्थस्य कुतः सिद्धिरिति चेदुच्यते यतः 1.3.252cd
इत्यर्थस्यावबोधार्थं परो ग्रन्थोऽवतार्यते 2.1.311ab
इत्यर्थे लोकसंसिद्धां प्रसिद्धिं श्रुतिरब्रवीत् 3.7.18cd
इत्यर्थोऽत्र विधेयः स्यादन्वयव्यतिरेकतः 3.5.181cd
इत्यलं शुष्कतर्कोत्थवाङ्मात्राक्षेपदूषणैः 4.3.275ab
इत्यविद्याव्यवस्थेयं विद्यायास्तद्विपर्ययः 2.1.378cd
इत्यविप्रतिपत्तिर्हि व्याख्यातृणामशेषतः 2.1.503cd
इत्यस्मिन्नपि सिद्धान्ते प्रसङ्गो न निवर्तते 4.3.690ab
इत्यस्य परिहाराय स इत्यादि परं वचः 4.4.98ab
इत्यस्य परिहारार्थं दृष्टान्तोऽत्राभिधीयते 4.3.1956ab
इत्यस्य परिहारार्थं निःश्वासोदाहृतिस्त्वयम् 2.4.305ab
इत्यस्य परिहारार्थं परो ग्रन्थोऽवतार्यते 4.3.1385ab

इत्यस्य परिहारार्थं स वा इत्यादिकं वचः 4.3.1064ab
इत्यस्य परिहारार्थमसङ्गो हीति भण्यते 4.3.1017ef
इत्यस्य परिहारोक्तिं केचिदाचक्षते बुधाः 4.2.100ab
इत्यस्य प्रतिपत्त्यर्थं परो ग्रन्थोऽवतार्यते 4.3.1924cd
इत्यस्य प्रतिपत्त्यर्थं परो ग्रन्थोऽवतार्यते 4.4.170cd
इत्यस्य प्रतिपत्त्यर्थं स एष इति भण्यते 1.2.165cd
इत्यस्य हेतुसिद्ध्यर्थं न हि द्रष्टुरितीरणम् 4.3.1418cd
इत्यस्यार्थस्य विज्ञप्त्यै दृष्टान्तोऽत्राभिधीयते 4.3.1124ab
इत्याचक्षत इत्युक्त्यानुमादोषोऽपनुद्यते 3.8.7cd
इत्यादिकल्पनाः प्रत्यगैकात्म्याज्ञानहेतुजाः 4.3.494ab
इत्यादिगुणविध्यर्थं परो ग्रन्थोऽवतार्यते 1.3.246ef
इत्यादिदूषणान्यत्र वक्तव्यानि सहस्रशः 4.3.659ab
इत्यादिदोषदुष्टत्वान्न च नोऽनुमितिः प्रमा 4.3.144cd
इत्यादिनापि विज्ञानं नादृष्टार्थमितीरितम् SV 297ab
इत्यादिनामव्युत्पत्तिच्छद्मना प्रकृतोचितम् SV 10ab
इत्यादि पूर्वपक्षोक्तिदूषणेष्वभिधास्यते 3.2.62ab
इत्यादि पूर्वमुक्तं यदनुसंधेयमत्र तत् 1.4.1005cd
इत्यादि पूर्वमेवोक्तं दूषणं दूषितात्मनाम् 3.2.120ab
इत्यादिबहुदोषत्वाद्दुःसंभाव्यं प्रमाणतः 1.4.1122ab
इत्यादि भवतैवोक्तं वासनोक्तिप्रसङ्गतः 4.4.495ab
इत्यादिमनुनाप्युक्तं कथं तत्त्यागमर्हति 2.4.318cd
इत्यादि मनुनाप्युक्तं तद्विरुद्धं च भण्यते 1.5.310cd
इत्यादिवचसा प्राणे सति जीवनमुच्यते 6.1.24cd
इत्यादिवर्त्मना शास्त्रं साक्षाद्वस्तु प्रसाधयत् SV 779ab
इत्यादिशतशो वाक्यैः श्रुतिस्मृत्युदितैरमी 2.1.485ab
इत्यादिश्रुतिवाक्यानि स्मृतिभिः सह कोटिशः SV 226ab
इत्यादि सुविरुद्धं स्यान्न चापीहापरा मितिः 3.2.106cd
इत्यादिस्थानभेदोऽपि वेदान्तोक्तौ विनिश्चितः 1.4.615cd
इत्यादि हृदये कृत्वा न्यायं श्रुतिरुदाहरत् 1.5.357ab
इत्यादेः पूर्वमुक्तत्वान्नेह भूयोऽपि यत्यते 4.3.1594cd
इत्यादेः प्रतिषेधेन प्रत्यङ्मात्रावलम्बिना 2.3.182cd
इत्यादेर्न्यायबाह्यत्वं यथा तदभिधीयते 4.3.496cd

इत्याविष्कृतिसिद्ध्यर्थं परो ग्रन्थोऽवतार्यते 4.3.1210cd
इत्याशङ्कापनुत्त्यर्थं परो ग्रन्थोऽवतारितः 4.3.1540ab
इत्याशङ्कापनुत्त्यर्थं परो ग्रन्थोऽवतार्यते 1.4.1468ab
इत्याशङ्क्य नृपो दोषं याज्ञवल्क्यमपृच्छत 4.3.965cd
इत्याशङ्क्योत्तरो ग्रन्थस्तस्य वा इति भण्यते 4.3.830ab
इत्याह भगवान्व्यासः सर्वज्ञोऽपि महामतिः 3.8.151cd
इत्याहुः श्रुतयः सर्वाः स्मृतयश्चाप्यनेकशः 3.3.10cd
इत्युक्तं किंनिमित्तं चेत्तत्र प्रतिविधीयते 1.4.1558cd
इत्युक्तः पूर्ववाक्येन समुदायार्थ ईदृशः 4.3.1152ab
इत्युक्तः सूनुना ह्रीतः स्वयमेव जगाम तम् 6.2.55cd
इत्युक्तन्यायहेतुत्वान्न विरोधोऽत्र कश्चन 1.4.498cd
इत्युक्तपरिफल्गुत्वप्रबोधायाभिधीयते 4.3.1646ab
इत्युक्तपरिहारार्थं नैतत्सम्यगितीर्यते 3.3.16ab
इत्युक्तप्रतिपत्त्यर्थं हेतुरेषोऽभिधीयते 1.4.501ab
इत्युक्तप्रतिपत्त्यर्थमाजगामोत्तरं वचः SV 1109ab
इत्युक्तमभिसंधाय दृष्टादिवचनं जगौ SV 1047ab
इत्युक्तवन्तं प्रत्याह तद्वक्ष्यामि तवाधुना 4.2.33ab
इत्युक्तार्थपरिज्ञानदार्ढ्यार्थं सर्वसाधनम् 4.5.24ab
इत्युक्तार्थप्रसिद्ध्यर्थमित्युदाहरणत्रयम् 2.4.289cd
इत्युक्तावतिसंव्याप्तिप्रसक्तावुत्तरं वचः 3.7.26cd
इत्युक्तावसकृत्पूर्वं परिहारोऽपि वर्णितः 4.4.370ab
इत्युक्तास्ते तथेत्यूचुः सर्वस्वं ददते प्रभोः 6.1.28cd
इत्युक्तिर्वो विरुध्येत पूर्वोत्तरविघाततः 1.4.1730ab
इत्युक्ते तमृषिं भूयः स प्रतिष्ठामपृच्छत 3.9.71cd
इत्युक्तेन प्रकारेण मुमुक्षुं जनकं मुनिः 4.3.1826ab
इत्युक्तेन प्रकारेण संतानासंभवो ध्रुवः 4.3.647cd
इत्युक्ते परिहाराय शृणु यद्भण्यतेऽधुना SV 724ab
इत्युक्तैकात्म्यवाक्यप्रविकचकमला प्राज्यसन्न्यायगन्धा 6.5.22a
इत्युक्तोऽहल्लिकेत्येवं संबोध्योत्तरमब्रवीत् 3.9.81cd
इत्युक्त्यर्थोपरोधेन व्याचक्षीत परायणम् 3.9.164cd
इत्युक्त्यावाप्तवित्तस्य नेदं कर्मेति गम्यते 6.3.4cd
इत्युक्त्वा तमथो पाणौ गृहीत्वोत्थितवान्नृपः 2.1.96ab

इत्युक्त्वान्येऽपि सर्वस्वं ददुर्वागादयः सुराः 6.1.29cd
इत्युक्त्वा सांख्यत्वभयात्कल्पयन्ति ततोऽन्यथा 2.3.116cd
इत्युपासीत यः सोऽथ कलात्मानं प्रपद्यते 1.5.218cd
इत्येतज्जगतो वृत्तं ब्रह्मैवाकार्यकारणम् 4.4.447ab
इत्येतत्कर्मरागोक्तं निष्प्रमाणं न गृह्यते 1.5.302cd
इत्येतत्प्रतिपत्त्यर्थं तद्वा एतदिति श्रुतिः 3.8.173ab
इत्येतत्प्रतिपत्त्यर्थं परो ग्रन्थोऽवतार्यते 1.5.101ab
इत्येतत्प्रतिपत्त्यर्थं विराट्स्थानस्य कृत्स्नम् 1.4.57cd
इत्येतत्प्रतिसंधानं न भिन्नद्रष्टृकं भवेत् 4.3.269cd
इत्येतत्सर्ववेदान्तसर्वस्वं ब्राह्मणोदितम् 4.4.374ab
इत्येतदधुनाचष्टे रत्वेत्यादिगिरा श्रुतिः 4.3.980cd
इत्येतदभिसंधाय पप्रच्छ जनको मुनिम् 4.3.27ab
इत्येतदविरुद्धं स्यात्प्रसादाज्जातवेदसः 3.2.98cd
इत्येतदाह विस्पष्टं भाल्लविब्राह्मणं वचः 4.4.1253cd
इत्येतदुररीकृत्य विज्ञायेत्युक्तमादरात् 4.4.709ab
इत्येतद्गम्यतेऽविद्याभयारत्यादिमत्त्वतः 1.4.89cd
इत्येतद्धृदये कृत्वा कारुण्यात्तमथाब्रवीत् 3.9.60cd
इत्येतद्धृदये कृत्वा तथा न इति सोऽवदत् 6.2.53ab
इत्येतद्धृदये कृत्वा याज्ञवल्क्यो निराह तम् 3.4.67ab
इत्येतद्बहुशोऽश्रावि पूर्वग्रन्थेषु चागमैः 1.3.6cd
इत्येतद्ब्राह्मणेनेह प्रयत्नेन विधीयते 4.4.1202cd
इत्येतन्न्यायतः सिद्धं यत्तु प्रावचोदितं त्वया SV 270cd
इत्येतस्माद्भयाद्राजा श्लोकशुश्रूषयेरितः 4.4.537ab
इत्येतस्येह चोद्यस्य परिहाराय चोत्तरम् 1.4.999cd
इत्येते विचिकित्से द्वे सर्वस्य भवतो मृतौ 4.4.1171cd
इत्येवं केचिदिच्छन्ति तत्तु युक्त्या न युज्यते 1.5.28ab
इत्येवं केचिदिच्छन्ति तथान्यादृगपीष्यते 1.5.174ab
इत्येवं चेन्न तद्युक्तं क्षणिकत्वस्य हानितः 4.3.695ab
इत्येवं चोदितेऽथात्र परिहारोऽभिधीयते 4.3.1140ab
इत्येवं चोदिते केचित्परिहारं प्रचक्षते 4.3.1049ab
इत्येवं चोदिते कैश्चिदत्र प्रतिविधीयते 4.3.1121ab
इत्येवं धर्मकाराणामपि वाक्यानि कोटिशः 3.3.7cd

इत्येवं ध्वस्तनिःशेषकल्मषः पूर्वसाधनैः 4.4.1198ab
इत्येवं नरतन्त्रेऽर्थे ज्ञेया द्वादशलक्षणी SV 243cd
इत्येवं न्यायवद्वाक्यमाहुर्वेदप्रमाणकाः 4.4.1150cd
इत्येवं पण्डितंमन्या अनुमानबलादिह 4.3.1645ab
इत्येवं पर्युपासीनो नामाभिज्ञो नरः सदा 5.5.14ab
इत्येवं पूर्वसिद्धेऽर्थे निगमार्थं पुनर्वचः 4.3.1909ab
इत्येवं भगवद्व्यासवचांस्यत्र सहस्रशः 1.4.1589ab
इत्येवं मनुनाप्युक्तः श्रौतोऽयं सर्गविस्तरः 1.2.179cd
इत्येवं यस्य वेदान्तवाक्योत्थं ज्ञानमात्मनि 4.4.275cd
इत्येवं याज्ञवल्क्यस्तं नृपमुक्तेन वर्त्मना 4.4.1302ab
इत्येवं वर्धमानः सन्क्रतुत्वं प्रतिपद्यते 4.4.230ab
इत्येवं शतशः सन्ति यथोक्तार्थप्रसिद्धये 4.4.1050ab
इत्येवं श्येनदृष्टान्तः कैश्चिद्व्याख्यायि सादरैः 4.3.1203ab
इत्येवं सांख्यसिद्धान्तमनुवर्तन्ति संभ्रमात् 2.3.124cd
इत्येवं स्मृतयः सन्ति श्रुतयश्च सहस्रशः 4.4.583ab
इत्येवं स्मृतिशास्त्राणि सर्वत्यागपुरःसरम् 4.4.597ab
इत्येवंदृष्टयो धीरा यदाहुरसदेव तत् 1.5.69cd
इत्येवमपराधोत्थकोपाविष्टेव बालिशम् 2.4.251cd
इत्येवमपरिश्रान्तो बंभ्रमीति पुनः पुनः 4.4.247cd
इत्येवमभिमाना या नान्तर्यामीति सोच्यते 3.7.29ef
इत्येवमभिसंधिः सन्विद्वान्प्राणव्रतं चरेत् 1.5.389ab
इत्येवमभिसंबन्धः कर्मकाण्डस्य युज्यते SV 331ab
इत्येवमभिसंबन्धो वक्तुर्भाष्यकृतः स्फुटः 1.5.278ab
इत्येवमयथावस्तुदर्शिनः फलमीरितम् 4.4.1315ab
इत्येवमसतामेव स्रष्टात्मा स्वात्ममायया 4.3.919cd
इत्येवमात्मकामत्वादाप्तकामोऽत्र यो भवेत् 4.4.281ab
इत्येवमादयोऽनन्ताः संबन्धा मोहहेतवः 4.3.1367ab
इत्येवमादयोऽनेके कोशाः स्युर्भावनामयाः 4.4.188ab
इत्येवमादि चोद्यानां पुंस्वभावानुरोधतः 2.1.390ab
इत्येवमादिचोद्यानि परिहाराश्च वर्णिताः 2.1.534ab
इत्येवमादि बहुधा परिणामं प्रचक्षते 4.3.1240ab
इत्येवमादि बहुशो भिन्नाभिन्नत्वदूषणम् 5.1.94ab

इत्येवमादिभाष्यार्थः क्रमेणैकात्म्यवस्तुनि SV 573ab
इत्येवमादि यच्चोक्तं पूर्वमेवातिविस्तरात् 2.4.210ab
इत्येवमादि वक्तव्यमित्यर्थः पर आगमः 2.3.2cd
इत्येवमादिवाक्यानि गम्भीरन्यायवेदिनः 4.4.810ab
इत्येवमादिवाक्यानि यथोक्तार्थसमर्थने 3.4.165ab
इत्येवमादिवाक्यानि श्रौतान्युक्तार्थसिद्धये 4.4.1043cd
इत्येवमादि व्याख्येयं व्याख्यातं पूर्वमेव तु 4.4.1132ab
इत्येवमादि सौलभ्यं दृष्टान्तानामिहेष्यते 4.3.561cd
इत्येवमायुर्वेदज्ञाः करणानि प्रचक्षते 4.4.26cd
इत्येवमाहुः केचित्तु न तु तद्युक्तिमद्वचः 4.3.961ab
इत्येष घोरसंकल्पो हिक्किकावशवर्तिनः 4.4.1170cd
इत्येष तावत्संबन्धस्तथान्योऽप्यभिधीयते 4.3.830cd
इत्येष भयहेतुः स्याद्याज्ञवल्क्यस्य नान्यतः 4.3.1894ab
इत्येष मानव्यापारो यथावदनुवर्णितः 4.4.754cd
इत्येषोऽर्थो विधेयोऽत्र येनेति वचसा श्रुतेः 3.5.199ab
इत्यौत्सर्गिकमाचारं यथा ब्रह्मा प्रबाधते 4.4.1224cd
इदं कार्यमिदं नेति कर्मकाण्डश्रुतेर्गतिः SV 323cd
इदं कार्यमिदं नेति वेदशास्त्रं प्रवर्तते 5.1.100cd
इदं क्षणिकमित्येतत्क्षणिकत्वे न सिध्यति 1.2.63ab
इदं च द्वैतमस्त्येव तथादोऽद्वैतमेव च 5.1.50ab
इदं च हेतुवचनं प्रतिज्ञातस्य वस्तुनः 4.4.381ab
इदं जगदुपादानं सर्वशक्त्यजमव्ययम् 1.2.126ab
इदं जगन्नियन्त्रादिविभिन्नानेकरूपवत् 1.4.519ab
इदं जन्म परं चैव स्वप्नस्तन्मध्यगस्तथा 4.3.834cd
इदं ज्ञानं च ध्यानं च शेषोऽन्यो ग्रन्थविस्तरः 4.4.890cd
इदं तत्तदिदं चेति त्रिषु कालेषु नित्यताम् 3.2.74ab
इदं तत्सर्ववेदेषु यथाभूतार्थवित्तये 1.4.375ab
इदं तावद्वदत्वत्र लिङ्गलक्षणतत्त्ववित् 4.3.729ab
इदं दृष्टमदोऽद्राक्षमिति नैवोपपद्यते 4.3.682ab
इदं धीनामगम्यं यच्चित्रं सत् प्रथते हिरुक् 1.4.30ab
इदं ब्रह्मेति वचसा सर्वमात्मेति नोऽवदत् 2.4.239cd
इदं मानुषमित्येवं व्याख्या तस्यास्तु पूर्ववत् 2.5.53cd

इदं मिथ्येति चैतस्मान्मिथ्यात्वस्य कथं ग्रहः 4.3.489ab
इदं मेऽङ्गमनेनेति पुंसंस्कारश्रुतेस्तथा 4.4.1042ab
इदं यज्जनिमत्किंचिन्नामरूपक्रियात्मकम् 5.1.14ab
इदं रजतमित्येतज्ज्ञानं शुक्तौ कुतोऽन्वभूत् 1.4.450cd
इदं रजतमित्येवंरूपं वस्तु न कुत्रचित् 1.4.275ab
इदंरूपं समापेदे रशनेवाहिरूपताम् 1.4.1334cd
इदं वै तन्मधु प्रोक्तं यत्तत्प्रकरणान्तरे 2.5.105ab
इदंशब्दाभिधानेन ह्येकाधिकरणश्रवात् 1.4.518ab
इदंशब्देन चाविद्याकार्यमत्र विवक्षितम् 4.3.1273cd
इदंक्षणिकताबुद्ध्योर्भिन्नाधिकरणत्वतः 1.2.63cd
इदंधीशब्दगम्यं यद्ब्रह्मरूपाद्विशिष्यते 1.4.1176ab
इदंधीशब्दगम्यस्य प्रत्यङ्मात्रसतत्त्वतः 1.4.983cd
इदमत्र विचिन्त्यं स्याज्ज्ञानकर्मसमुच्चयात् 1.3.378ab
इदमित्युच्यते ब्रह्म तदुपाधिस्वभावकम् 1.4.1313ef
इदमित्येव यत्साक्षात्किंचित्कर्मोपलक्ष्यते 4.4.189ab
इदमेव ततो ग्राह्यं न तु यद्दोषवन्मतम् 1.5.281cd
इदमेव तदेवेदमित्येषोऽनुभवो दृढः 4.3.671ab
इदमेवमिदं नैवमिति बुद्धिर्विभागभाक् 1.4.872ab
इदमेव यतो वृत्तं कारणापेक्षिणां सताम् 2.1.202ab
इदंमयेन लिङ्गेन संबन्धोऽदोमयात्मनः 4.4.190ab
इध्यतेऽहर्निशं यस्मादिन्धनामा ततः पुमान् 4.2.37ab
इन्द्रगोपोऽतिरक्तश्च भृशं रक्तं मनस्तथा 2.3.162cd
इन्द्रगोपोपमानेन कौसुम्भस्य गतत्वतः 2.3.160cd
इन्द्रमित्यादिमन्त्रोक्तिरेष ब्रह्मेति च श्रुतिः 1.4.145cd
इन्द्रश्च देवता ज्ञेया मेघनादाभिमानिनी 3.9.18ab
इन्द्राग्नी ताविमावुक्तौ प्राण इन्द्रस्तयोर्मतः 1.3.265ab
इन्द्राग्नी ताविमौ सिद्धावग्निस्तत्र प्रकाशकः 5.16.34ab
इन्द्रादयोऽपि नैवालं कैवल्याप्तिनिवारणे 1.4.1463cd
इन्द्रादिसर्गः प्राङ्नोक्तो मोहकार्यविवक्षया 1.4.1595cd
इन्द्रादिसर्गस्तत्रैव तच्छेषत्वात्समीक्ष्यताम् 1.4.1597ab
इन्द्रियाणीन्द्रियार्थाश्च न विकारः परात्मनः 4.4.36ab
इन्द्रियाण्यपि सर्वाणि स्वान्तस्यैव तु वृत्तयः 1.5.115cd

इन्द्रियाण्युपसंहृत्य शेते नाडीभिरात्मनि 2.1.331cd
इन्द्रियाण्येव हरयो हरणाद्विषयान्प्रति 2.5.131ab
इन्द्रियालोचितार्थस्य स्यात्संकल्पोऽवधारणम् 1.5.110cd
इन्द्रियेण त इत्यादिमन्त्रेणाथ शपेद्रुषा 6.4.33ab
इन्द्रियेण त इत्यादिमन्त्रोक्त्या तां परामृशेत् 6.4.45ab
इन्द्रियेण त इत्युक्त्या आदधामीति सत्पतिः 6.4.47ef
इन्द्रियेणैव त्वद्रेतो रेतसा आददे स्वयम् 6.4.46ab
इन्द्रियेभ्यः प्रियः प्राण आत्मा प्रियतमस्ततः 1.4.1031cd
इन्द्रोऽसपत्नोऽब्देहश्च नामरूपसमावृतः 2.1.116cd
इन्द्रो लोकेश्वरश्चात्र वरुणाद्यात्मना तथा 4.4.1011cd
इन्द्रो विधरणः प्राणः पर्वयोर्नामरूपयोः 5.16.34cd
इन्धं सन्तं तमात्मानमिन्द्रनाम्ना प्रचक्षते 4.2.39cd
इन्धतैजससौषुप्ततुरीयाण्येव सांप्रतम् 4.3.5ab
इन्धो नामैष पुरुषो दक्षिणेऽक्षणि यः स्थितः 4.2.36ab
इमं देशं यतः प्राप्तानादित्याद्युक्तवर्त्मना 3.3.157cd
इमं देहस्थमात्मानं विज्ञायोक्तेन वर्त्मना 4.4.874ab
इमं मानवमावर्तमित्याद्यस्य विशेषणात् 6.2.145ab
इमं लोकमिदं जन्म स्वप्नो भूत्वातिवर्तते 4.3.449ab
इममर्थं श्रुतिर्वक्ति दृष्टान्तेन प्रयत्नतः 1.5.351cd
इममर्थं श्रुतिर्वक्ति सर्वकर्मानपेक्षिणी 2.4.30ab
इममित्यप्रसिद्धत्वात्प्राणस्येह त्वगादिवत् 1.3.165cd
इममेव तु वाक्यार्थं व्याचक्षीताविचारयन् 2.5.42cd
इममेवेत्यवधृतेर्न विराजो द्विधाभिधा 1.4.114ab
इमामवस्थां संप्राप्य सर्वो ब्राह्मण उच्यते 3.5.191ab
इमामवस्थामापन्नो मुख्यो ब्राह्मण उच्यते 4.4.1296ab
इमावेवेति च तथा फलवत्स्यादुपासनम् 2.2.30cd
इमौ द्वावेव पन्थानौ कर्मतत्त्यागलक्षणौ 3.5.201ab
इयं तावत्पदार्थोक्तिः संबन्धोक्तिरथाधुना 2.1.194ab
इयं तु न तथा स्थूला यां त्वं पृच्छसि देवताम् 3.6.26cd
इयं सा ब्रह्मविद्योक्ता मधुकाण्डे पुरोदिता 4.4.1282ab
इयता यदि पाण्डित्यं लभ्यते वेद तर्हि तम् 3.9.40ab
इयत्ता कारकावस्था परिच्छिज्ज्ञानमेव तु 3.2.54cd

इयदेव जगत्यस्मिन्पुंसां कर्म समीक्ष्यते 4.4.1208cd
इयन्त एव पक्षाः स्युर्विकारे परमात्मनः 2.1.477cd
इयमाख्यायिका चक्षुर्नान्यथोपास्यनिश्चितिः 1.3.170cd
इयमेवात्मनो ज्ञेया कर्माधिकृतिकारणम् SV 121cd
इयानेव तु देशोऽयं प्राणिनां भोगसिद्धिकृत् 3.3.145ab
इलासीत्यथ मन्त्रेण सूनोर्मातरमादरात् 6.4.127ab
इवेत्यनर्थकं केचिदेवार्थेन विरोधतः 4.2.65ab
इषे त्वादिषु दृष्टत्वान्न न्याय्यैकार्थकल्पना SV 277cd
इष्टं विकारवद्वस्तु यथा कापिलशासने 4.4.38cd
इष्टमेव सदा मे स्यान्मा भूच्चानिष्टमण्वपि 2.1.574cd
इष्टस्यार्थस्य बाधः स्यान्न च ध्वान्तनिराकृतिः 1.4.1267cd
इष्टानिष्टफलानीति साधनानि प्रकाशयेत् 2.1.583ab
इष्टापूर्तकृतो ये वै ग्रामस्थेभ्यश्च ये परे 6.2.121ab
इष्टापूर्तादिहेतूनामानन्त्यात्स्वर्गसिद्धये SV 92ab
इष्ट्वेति च तथा क्त्वान्तश्रवणात्पूर्वकालता 1.5.262ab
इष्यते कर्मवन्नातस्तदर्थं विधिकल्पना SV 672cd
इह केचिन्महात्मानः प्रत्यङ्मोहच्छिदा सह 4.4.586ab
इह चोपरतश्रुत्या तिष्ठत्यादिवदुच्यते 4.4.1227ab
इह जन्मन्यसंभाव्यं स्वप्ने यस्मात्प्रपश्यति 4.3.853ab
इह तत्फलतां यातो भूयोवाग्युज्यते ततः 1.2.201cd
इह त्वक्षितिरेवोक्ता भवता ज्ञानकर्मणोः 1.4.1714ab
इह त्वज्ञात आत्मैव मिथ्याज्ञातस्तथैव च 4.4.911ab
इह त्वन्नत्रयस्यैव सर्वात्मत्वं विवक्षितम् 1.5.134cd
इह त्वीशातिरेकेण नान्यत्किंचित्प्रकल्प्यते 3.8.158ab
इह त्वेवेति निःशेषा लिङ्गस्यास्योपसंहृतिः 4.4.52ab
इह त्वैकात्म्यधीयोगः काम्ययाज्येष्टिवन्न हि SV 340ab
इह त्वैकात्म्यवाक्येषु तत्त्वमात्रावबोधतः SV 587ab
इह पुनर्न शक्यन्ते विशेषाः प्रसमीक्षितुम् 4.3.1398ab
इह प्रदर्शितो वाक्ये तत्समाप्तिविवक्षया 4.4.1345cd
इह प्रविष्ट इत्युक्तिः पुरस्ताद्ब्राह्मणोदिता 2.1.463cd
इह यच्च विजिज्ञास्यं तन्मनोऽत्राधिभौतिकम् 1.5.157cd
इह यद्दूषणं वाच्यं तदुक्तमिति नोच्यते 4.3.1628ab

इह वागादयः शब्दा देवतार्थाभिधायकाः 1.3.23ab
इह वामुत्र वा ज्ञानं जायते मोक्षकृद्ध्रुवम् 3.3.130cd
इह व्याचक्षते केचिदुक्ताद्व्याख्यानतोऽन्यथा 4.4.706ab
इह व्याचक्षते केचिन्नानात्वैकत्वरूपता 4.3.1639ab
इहापि कारणोपाधिः केवलोऽप्यविवेकतः 1.4.619ab
इहापि चानवस्थेति नानुमातोऽत्र युज्यते 1.4.264ab
इहापि नेति वाक्येन प्रतीचोऽतत्स्वभावकम् 2.4.104ab
इहापि सपरीवारं श्रुतिन्यायोपपत्तिमत् 4.4.297ab
इहापि हेतुसंसिद्ध्यै तत्स्पष्टमभिधीयते 1.4.1505cd
इहाभिधीयतेऽन्यस्तु न कश्चित्सप्रयोजनः 1.3.14cd
इहाभिधीयते ज्योतिरन्यत्र तु विभागवत् 4.3.1492cd
इहैव कृतकृत्यत्वात्सन्तः स्याम परं यदि 4.4.624ab
इहैव देवभूतत्वादाशङ्का किंनिबन्धना 1.3.372ab
इहैव लोकभूतत्वादप्राप्तेऽर्थे हि शङ्क्यते 1.3.376cd
इहैवासुरभावस्य प्राणोऽस्मीत्यभिमानतः 1.3.377ab
इहोक्तेस्तद्विरुद्धत्वात्परस्परविरुद्धता 4.4.495cd
इहोच्चिक्रमिषा यास्य विज्ञानात्मैकसंश्रया 4.4.90ab
ईक्षतेऽत्राधिकं नान्यदभावादि यदुच्यते SV 982cd
ईक्षते योगयुक्तात्मा सर्वत्र समदर्शनः 4.4.582cd
ईक्ष्यन्ते चाप्यकृपणास्तच्च सत्येव यन्तरि 3.8.166cd
ईदृगेव फलं चात्र मानमेयादिकं तथा 3.4.128ab
ईदृगैकात्म्यसंबोधो निदिध्यासनमुच्यते 2.5.16cd
ईदृङ्न लोके वेदेऽपि प्रसिद्धं कर्म कुत्रचित् 1.4.1732cd
ईदृशी कल्पनायुक्ता कर्तुं परहितार्थिभिः 2.3.148cd
ईर्यसुंस्तमबर्थे स्यात्पुत्रादीनां बहुत्वतः 1.4.1030ab
ईशक्षेत्रज्ञयोरेवं तमस्तज्जाभिसंस्थयोः 5.1.20ab
ईशादिविषयान्तं यत्तदविद्याविजृम्भितम् 1.4.382ab
ईशादेर्विषयान्तस्य कल्पितत्वमतो भवेत् 4.4.1005cd
ईशितव्यत्वसंक्रान्तेर्न ततो विजुगुप्सते 4.4.631cd
ईशितव्यापनुत्तौ च तदपेक्षैकसंश्रयात् 4.4.983ab
ईशितव्यार्थसंबन्धादन्तर्याम्येतदक्षरम् 3.8.128ab
ईशित्वमपि निःशेषं प्रतीचो विनिवर्तते 4.4.983cd

ईशेशितव्यसंबन्धः प्रत्यगज्ञानहेतुजः 1.4.1465ab
ईश्वरं स यथादृष्टि फलमाप्नोति मानवः 4.4.1314cd
ईश्वरत्वाच्च तस्यास्मद्दुःखैर्न स्यात्समागमः 1.5.356ab
ईश्वरप्रत्यगात्माप्तेस्तदा तद्भेदनाशतः 4.4.631ab
ईश्वराणां न च न्याय्यो भोगः प्रत्यवरस्तथा 4.3.432ab
ईश्वराणामनैश्वर्यं कस्माद्ब्रह्मविदीति चेत् 1.4.1466ab
ईश्वरात्कारणाद्यस्माल्लिङ्गं तेन रसस्तयोः 2.3.47cd
ईश्वरादिविकल्पानां प्रत्यग्वस्त्वविकल्पितम् 1.3.61ab
ईश्वराव्याकृतप्राणविराड्भूतेन्द्रियादिकम् 1.4.487ab
ईषत्पाण्डु यथोर्णादि तद्वल्लिङ्गं प्रकाशते 2.3.162ab
ईषत्प्रचलिता प्राणभावेनेत्यवगम्यते 5.1.53cd
ईषत्संस्पृष्टमात्रस्य बलाच्चापेषणात्तथा 2.1.150ab
उक्तं च न्यायमापेक्ष्य नियमोऽत्यन्तदुर्लभः 1.4.931ab
उक्तं च वक्ष्यमाणं समस्तव्यस्ततां प्रति 1.4.702ab
उक्तं तर्हि त्वया रूपं संततेर्घटरूपवत् 4.3.644ab
उक्तं प्रथमजं सत्यं कथं तदिति भण्यते 5.5.1ab
उक्तं प्राग्व्यतिरेकेण स्वयंज्योतिष्ट्वमात्मनः 4.3.1388cd
उक्तं मधुत्वं येनातस्तत्सामस्त्यमथोच्यते 2.5.55cd
उक्तं यदपनुत्त्यर्थं तत्र प्रतिविधीयते 1.4.1492cd
उक्तं यदपि वेदेऽस्मिन्कस्यचिद्विलयः क्वचित् SV 424ab
उक्तं विधिमजानन्तो म्रियन्ते मैथुने रताः 6.4.18cd
उक्तं विमोक्षणं तावत्करणानां स्वदेशतः 4.4.72ab
उक्तं समासतस्तावदेकत्वं नामरूपयोः 1.6.24ab
उक्तं हृदय एवेति नीडं नात्मा परो मतः 4.4.425cd
उक्तकार्यातिरेकेण विषदध्यादिवन्मितिः 3.3.33ab
उक्तज्ञानप्रवृत्त्यर्थमर्थवादोऽयमिष्यते 1.4.1022cd
उक्तत्वात्परिहारस्य नैवमेतद्भवेदिह 1.4.1253ab
उक्तदोषद्वयासक्तिर्न च वस्त्वीदृशं क्वचित् SV 1032cd
उक्तदोषापनुत्तिः स्यात्कथमस्येति चोदिते 1.4.1683ab
उक्तदोषापनुत्त्यर्थं प्रत्युक्तिर्गौरवी त्वियम् 1.4.1351ab
उक्तद्वयनिषेधेन तस्य चोपक्षयाद्भवेत् 2.3.203cd
उक्तपादेष्वपि ज्ञानं नैवालमपबाधितुम् 5.16.55ab

उक्तप्रज्ञाप्रसिद्ध्यर्थं येषु स्वातन्त्र्यमिष्यते 4.4.961cd
उक्तब्रह्मविदो मोक्ष इत्यर्थे ब्राह्मणोदिते 4.4.545ab
उक्तब्राह्मणसादृश्यं सर्वकर्मनिरासतः 3.5.198ab
उक्तमन्थविधानेन चरितव्रत एव सन् 6.4.37ab
उक्तमप्युत्तरत्रैतदसंतोषात्प्रवक्ष्यते 1.4.1006cd
उक्तमभ्युदयार्थं यद्वागादीनामथाधुना 1.3.237ab
उक्तमाभ्यन्तरं तावद्ब्रह्मोपासनसाधनम् 5.2.1ab
उक्तमेव तु संशीतावियं त्वत्र विनिश्चितिः SV 98ab
उक्तयोरात्मनोरन्तर्यद्रूपं भावनामयम् 4.4.185ab
उक्तयोर्मध्यवर्त्येव कार्यकारणयोरसौ 2.3.179cd
उक्तवद्धृदि संभाव्य वक्ष्यमाणान्यपि श्रुतिः 1.5.75ab
उक्तवत्मीतिरेकेण नात्मवस्तु घटादिवत् 3.4.79ab
उक्तवस्त्वतिरेकेण नामीषां सत्यता यतः 2.3.247ab
उक्तविध्यर्थविषयाद्याः क्रिया विषयान्तरे 4.4.1243ab
उक्तवेदार्थविज्ञानसाकल्यप्रतिपत्तये 6.5.6ab
उक्तव्याख्यानतोऽन्यस्य व्याख्यानस्य यथोदित- 4.4.965ab
उक्तश्च तस्य सूत्रस्य संबन्धः सप्रयोजनः 1.4.1590cd
उक्तस्वप्नो भवेदन्यो यथा पूर्वगतस्तथा 4.3.960cd
उक्तहेतुबलात्तस्माद्विदित्वात्मानमात्मना 4.4.1118ab
उक्तहेत्वर्थदीप्येतद्धीति तस्य निपाततः 2.4.457ab
उक्ताक्षरात्मावसितेर्न किंचिदवशिष्यते 3.8.180cd
उक्तात्मच्युतदृष्टीनां तदबोधैकहेतुतः 1.4.1141ab
उक्तात्मवस्तुनो रूपं कामाविद्यादिवर्जितम् 4.3.1329cd
उक्तात्मवस्तुस्वाभाव्यादात्मा ब्रह्मेत्यतो वचः 4.4.162cd
उक्ताधिकारविषयप्रतिपत्त्यर्थमीरितम् SV 15ab
उक्तानि तावद्भूयांसि दूषणानि विभागशः 1.4.1235ab
उक्तानुवचने तस्य विज्ञानेनेतिनिर्णयात् 1.4.899cd
उक्तान्वयादिनोत्पन्नविवेकः सन्नबुध्यत 1.4.1387cd
उक्ता परिहृतिस्तत्र न भूयोऽपि व्यपेक्ष्यते 1.4.1515cd
उक्ता पाङ्क्तानुरोधेन वाङ्मनःप्राणसंश्रया 1.5.193ab
उक्ता प्रमेयसंसिद्धिः स्वमहिम्नैव नश्रुतेः 2.3.233ab
उक्ताभिधानद्वारेण संपन्नो यस्त्रिलोकताम् 5.16.9ab

उक्ता यथावत्तत्रैव श्रोतव्यः श्रुतिवाक्यतः 2.5.3cd
उक्तार्थवाचिनौ तस्मात्स्वशब्दौ समुदाहृतौ 4.3.880cd
उक्तार्थस्य प्रकाशार्थमुत्तरार्धेन भण्यते 4.4.628ab
उक्तार्थस्यैव संक्षेपस्त्रयं वा इत्यथोच्यते 1.6.1cd
उक्तार्थापरिहारेण तदज्ञानजभूमिषु 3.4.130ab
उक्ता वागादयः सर्वे समा एवेति गृह्यताम् 1.5.194cd
उक्तासुरपराभूतौ नान्योऽरिरवशिष्यते 1.3.191ab
उक्तेऽर्थे संशयश्चेत्स्यात्प्रत्यग्दृष्ट्या समीक्ष्यताम् 4.3.421cd
उक्ते दार्ष्टान्तिकेऽर्थेऽस्मिन्प्रश्नार्थस्य समाप्तितः 4.3.1901ab
उक्तेन वचसा तावत्स्वाराज्यं विदुषोऽवदत् 1.4.1780ab
उक्तेर्नातोऽविनाशित्वं द्रष्टुर्दृष्टेरिहेष्यते 4.3.1431cd
उक्तोऽत्र परिहारः प्रागूर्ध्वं चापि प्रवक्ष्यते SV 199ab
उक्तो निरन्वयोऽभावो न बौद्धादिसमाश्रयात् 3.8.121ab
उक्तो न्यायः प्रहीयेत फलं चाकस्मिकं भवेत् SV 420cd
उक्तोपनिषदर्थस्य सम्यगाविष्कृदुत्तरम् 2.1.425ab
उक्तोपायातिरेकेण पृच्छ्यते साधनान्तरम् 3.5.192cd
उक्तोपासाफलं नातो गन्तव्यं वेद्मि किं चन 4.2.32cd
उक्तो मनस एकस्मिन्प्रत्ययो मानसो यतः 4.4.731cd
उक्तौ युक्तिबलादत्र नान्यस्येति विनिश्चितिः 1.5.37cd
उक्त्याविष्क्रियते साक्षात्करविन्यस्तबिल्ववत् 2.5.136cd
उक्त्योर्मिथोविरुद्धत्वादात्मा मोमुह्यते मम 2.4.446cd
उक्त्वा तदुपसंहारमितीतिवचसाकरोत् 4.4.251cd
उक्त्वात्मनोऽद्वयत्वं च सुषुप्ते चाधुनोच्यते 2.1.312cd
उक्त्वाथ याज्ञवल्क्याय तं प्रोवाचाथ विस्मितः 6.3.60cd
उक्त्वा सलिलवत्तस्मादेक इत्यब्रवीच्छ्रुतिः 4.3.1800cd
उक्त्वैवं वस्तुनो वृत्तं तद्याथात्म्याप्रबोधजम् 4.4.448ab
उक्थं प्राणः कुतो यस्मात्प्राणे सति चराचरम् 5.15.2ab
उक्थादिगुणपूगेन विशिष्टस्यानरूपिणः 5.15.1ab
उक्षा सेचनशक्तो गौः स एव ऋषभो महान् 6.4.77cd
उग्रास्तेऽत्राभिधीयन्ते जातितो वाभिधा भवेत् 4.3.1961cd
उग्रे कर्मणि ये राज्ञा नियुक्ताः पापकारिषु 4.3.1961ab
उचितं यस्य यद्यत्स्यात्तत्तल्लोकगिरोच्यते 5.13.5ab

उचिता दक्षिणैषैव योक्तेहाभयलक्षणा 4.2.97ab
उचितोऽस्या भवेत्प्रश्नो देवता येन पृच्छ्यते 3.6.23ab
उच्चैरनूद्य तत्तत्वं वेदान्ताः प्रत्यपीपदन् 1.2.129cd
उच्च गीथा च तद्योगादुद्गीथ इति शब्द्यते 1.3.320cd
उच्चनीचादिभेदेषु मिथः स व्यभिचारिषु 2.4.276ab
उच्चावचानि वस्तूनि भावनातः करोति सः 4.3.1068cd
उच्चावचान्बहूनर्थान्सोऽसृजत्सृजतेऽनृतान् 2.1.284cd
उच्छिन्दन्ति प्रमाणानि ह्यज्ञातत्वं प्रमेयगम् 4.4.922cd
उच्छिन्नं कर्मकाण्डस्य प्रामाण्यं विषयादृते 5.1.59cd
उच्छिन्नकामकर्मासौ कृत्स्नतत्फलभोगतः 3.2.43ab
उच्छिन्नाशेषबुद्ध्यादिस्तत्कारणपरिक्षयात् 3.2.43cd
उच्छिष्टमेव भार्यायै चरुं भर्ता प्रयच्छति 6.4.87cd
उच्छ्वासादिक्रियं केचिद्वायुं स्थूणां प्रचक्षते 2.2.15cd
उच्यते पूर्वपक्षोऽयं तस्य सिद्धान्तरूपिणः 4.3.954cd
उच्यते लोकतः सिद्धं भेदमाश्रित्य चोदना SV 917ab
उच्यते वचसा बुद्धौ वस्तुमात्रं समर्प्यते 4.4.707ab
उच्यते विधिशब्दो हि मान्तराज्ञातगोचरः SV 729ab
उच्यमानं यथा तत्त्वं सम्यक्त्वं श्रोतुमर्हसि 2.1.213cd
उज्ज्वलत्वादिसामान्याद्देवलोकादिसंपदः 3.1.53ab
उताविद्वानिति तथा प्रश्नपूर्वं स्वयं श्रुतिः 1.4.316ab
उतेवेत्यादिना स्पष्टमैकात्म्यप्रतिपत्तये 2.1.286cd
उतैकस्यैव धर्मस्य तदबोधोत्थभेदतः 4.3.1638ab
उत्कर्षहेतुर्देहे तु वृत्तिः सोदानसंज्ञिता 1.5.148cd
उत्कर्षातिशयः संपद्विभूतिश्चेति भण्यते 4.3.1831cd
उत्कर्षो मानुषादूर्ध्वं पुंसः केवलधर्मतः 1.3.114ab
उत्कृष्टव्यो यथाशक्ति विबुधानां चिकीर्षितम् 1.3.117cd
उत्क्रमिष्यन्यदा भोक्ता भवतीहायुषः क्षये 5.6.6ab
उत्क्रान्तिकाले प्राणानां स्वस्थानादार्ढ्यहेतुका 4.4.12ab
उत्क्रान्तिस्वप्नकालेषु ताः प्रयान्ति यथागतम् 4.3.431cd
उत्क्रान्तेऽन्यतमे यस्मिन्प्रत्येकमपसर्पणे 6.1.20ab
उत्क्रान्ते प्राण एवास्माच्छरीरं पतति ध्रुवम् 6.1.26ab
उत्क्रान्तौ च प्रवेशे च ह्यलं देहः स्वकर्मणे 6.1.25ab

उत्क्रान्तौ स्यादनिर्मोक्षो जन्मार्थं मरणं यतः 3.2.25ab
उत्क्रान्त्यादिगिरेहोक्त आलोकोत्थानवाक्यतः 6.2.15cd
उत्क्रान्त्यादेश्च कृत्स्नस्य सर्वमात्मेतिशास्त्रतः 4.4.293cd
उत्क्रामति यदा विद्वाञ्शरीरादायुषः क्षयात् 5.12.2ab
उत्क्रामन्तं तमात्मानं यथोक्तेनेह वर्त्मना 4.4.87ab
उत्क्रामन्ति न चेत्प्राणा नायं तर्हि मृतो भवेत् 3.2.32ab
उत्खातचक्षुषां चापि दृष्टिः स्वप्नेऽनुभूयते 4.3.1470ab
उत्खातदन्तोरगवदविद्या किं करिष्यति 1.4.1746ab
उत्खातनयनश्चायमनुत्खाताक्षवद्धटम् 4.3.265ab
उत्खातविधिको लोके तोयबुद्धिरिवोषरे SV 723cd
उत्तब्धं विधृतं यस्मात्प्राणेन जगदित्वरम् 1.3.319ab
उत्तमः परमात्माख्यो राशिरत्राभिधीयते 2.3.113ab
उत्तमाभिजनोपेतं भूर्युदारगुणं द्विजम् 1.4.1613ab
उत्तरक्षणविध्वस्तौ न हि पूर्वो नियुज्यते 4.3.605ab
उत्तरत्र स्वशब्देन लोकस्य च विशेषणात् 1.4.1648ab
उत्तरानभिसंबन्धाद्व्यपदेष्टुः कुतो भवेत् 4.3.683cd
उत्तरेष्वपि कार्येषु सर्वं तदनुवर्तयेत् 6.4.37cd
उत्तरेष्वपि वाक्येषु कर्तव्या पण्डितैरतः 4.3.1622cd
उत्तरेष्वपि वाक्येषु यथोक्तमुपपादयेत् 3.9.48ab
उत्तरेष्वपि वाक्येषु यथोक्तमुपपादयेत् 4.3.1536ab
उत्तरेष्वपि वाक्येषु यथोक्तमुपपादयेत् 4.3.1858ab
उत्तरेष्वपि वाक्येषु यथोक्तेनैव वर्त्मना 2.5.42ab
उत्तरेष्वपि वाक्येषु योजनेयं यथोदिता 2.4.467ab
उत्तरेष्वपि वाक्येषु समाना योजनेक्ष्यताम् 1.4.1799ab
उत्तरोत्तरकार्याणां श्रुत्या स्रष्टृतयोच्यते 1.4.349cd
उत्तरोत्तरभूयांसि नामादीनि यथाक्रमम् 2.4.98ab
उत्तरोत्तरवृद्ध्यात आनन्दान्मानुषादधि 4.3.1844ab
उत्तरोत्तरवृद्ध्यातो दुःखहेतुक्षयाच्छ्रुतौ 2.1.360ab
उत्तिष्ठत जाग्रत प्राप्य वरान्निबोधत 4.4.1257ab
उत्तिष्ठति प्रविष्टे च प्राणः श्रेयांस्ततोऽन्यतः 6.1.26cd
उत्थानं चाप्यविद्यायाः परस्मादात्मनः स्वतः 2.3.130ab
उत्थापयति कर्मेदं कर्ता वा नान्यथा ततः 5.15.2cd

उत्थितस्य पुनर्भावादनुच्छेदोऽथ शङ्क्यते SV 389ab
उत्पत्तिभोगयोरेवं भावना कर्मणः सदा 4.3.1256ab
उत्पत्तिराप्तिः संस्कारो विकारश्च विधेः फलम् SV 236ab
उत्पत्तिसंस्थितिलया यथोक्ताग्न्येकहेतवः 6.2.120ab
उत्पत्तिस्थितिनाशेषु कारणं नातिवर्तते 1.4.347ab
उत्पत्तिस्थितिभङ्गानां न वेद्मीति च साक्षितः 4.3.351cd
उत्पत्तिस्थितिविध्वंसाः कार्याणां स्युः कुतो न्विति 1.4.1059ab
उत्पत्तेस्तदधीनत्वाज्जन्मायत्ता स्थितिस्तथा 6.2.74ab
उत्पत्तौ भोगकाले च कर्मादायैव भावनाम् 4.3.1034ab
उत्पत्त्यादावशक्तत्वात्कौटस्थ्यादात्मवस्तुनः 4.3.1598ab
उत्पत्त्यादिक्रियाकार्यं तस्माच्चेह न शङ्क्यते 1.4.1081cd
उत्पत्त्यादिप्रकाराणामनित्यत्वसमन्वयात् 3.3.27cd
उत्पत्त्यादिफलोद्भूतौ मुक्तिरस्तु ततः फलम् 3.3.76cd
उत्पत्त्यादिविकल्पोऽयमस्यैव प्रतिपत्तये 4.4.1338cd
उत्पत्त्यादिविरुद्धत्वान्मुक्तेर्नान्यव्यपेक्षिता 1.4.812cd
उत्पत्त्यादिविरुद्धत्वान्मोक्षरूपस्य नित्यतः 3.3.117ab
उत्पत्त्यादिविरुद्धोऽयं लोको येषामकर्मजः 2.4.31ab
उत्पत्त्यादि स्वतश्चेत्स्यात्किं मुक्तौ कर्मणा वद 1.4.813cd
उत्पत्त्यादि स्वतो नो चेत्किं मुक्तौ कर्मणः फलम् 1.4.813ab
उत्पत्त्यादि स्वतो यस्य यस्य चात्यन्तमेव न 2.4.117ab
उत्पत्त्यादेरन्यतमो न च मोक्ष इहेष्यते 3.3.116cd
उत्पत्त्यादौ तु यच्छक्तं शक्तिमात्रात्मना स्थितम् 4.3.1597ab
उत्पत्त्यादौ तु यच्छक्तं हेतुमात्रमपेक्षते 1.4.814ab
उत्पत्त्यादौ तु यच्छक्तं हेतुमात्रमपेक्षते 2.4.118ab
उत्पत्त्यादौ समर्थं यद्धेतुमात्रमपेक्षते 4.4.1117ab
उत्पत्त्यादौ हि साध्येऽर्थे पुंव्यापृतिरपेक्ष्यते 1.4.812ab
उत्पत्त्याद्यतिरेकेण संसारविनिवृत्तये 3.3.74ab
उत्पत्त्याद्यन्तरायं सत्कारकोपात्तिपूर्वकम् 1.4.1016cd
उत्पत्त्याद्यन्वयात्तस्मादनित्यं स्याद्घटादिवत् 3.2.5cd
उत्पत्त्याद्यर्थनिष्ठानां सर्वेषामपि कर्मणाम् SV 1099ab
उत्पत्त्याद्यात्मकं कार्यं साध्यं सर्वस्य कर्मणः 4.1.28ab
उत्पत्त्याप्तिविकारा हि संस्कारश्च क्रियाफलम् 3.3.26ab

उत्पद्यते निर्विषया विषयाशयहानतः 1.4.1542cd
उत्पन्न एव ज्ञानेऽतस्तत्संदेहनिवृत्तये 4.3.740ab
उत्पन्नः क्षत्रियायां यः शूद्रेणैव स उच्यते 4.3.1363ab
उत्पन्नत्वात्तदुत्पन्नं नानुत्पन्नं कथं चन 4.3.733cd
उत्पन्ननिखिलानर्थैतित्यक्षा दोषदर्शनात् 4.4.1078cd
उत्पन्नमपि सज्ज्ञानं प्रमातृत्वाद्युपग्रहात् 2.4.127ab
उत्पन्नमेव विज्ञानं तदा प्रागपि मन्यते 2.4.128cd
उत्पन्नसंभोगफलः पुमान्मैथुनकर्मणि 4.3.1314ab
उत्पन्नसम्यग्ज्ञानस्य संन्यासो लक्षणं यतः 3.5.3ab
उत्पन्नस्यापि चोत्पत्तिः कूपाकाशादिवत्ततः 4.4.656ab
उत्पन्नात्मधियः पश्चाज्ज्ञानमेव हि तत्तथा 4.4.544cd
उत्पन्नात्मप्रबोधानामात्माविद्यातदुद्भवम् 3.5.51ab
उत्पन्नात्मबुभुत्सुः संस्त्यक्तसर्वपरिग्रहः 4.4.1198cd
उत्पन्नात्मबुभुत्सुः सन्वेदानुवचनादिभिः 4.4.1195ab
उत्पन्नेऽपि कृतार्थत्वान्न स्याद्वाक्यार्थबोधने 4.4.858cd
उत्पन्नेन च तन्नाश उत्पन्नत्वादनर्थकः 1.2.39cd
उत्पन्नैकात्म्ययाथात्म्यभास्वद्विज्ञानभास्कर- 1.4.134ab
उत्पाद्य त्रीण्यथान्नानि मेधया तपसा पिता 1.5.98ab
उत्पाद्यमाप्यं संस्कार्यं विकार्यं च क्रियावशात् 1.4.1150cd
उत्पाद्यमाप्यं संस्कार्यं विकार्यं चैषणाफलम् 4.4.1105ab
उत्पाद्यापि मितिं शास्त्रं यदि युक्त्याद्यपेक्षते SV 828ab
उत्पित्सूत्पद्यमानाभ्यामसत्त्वात्तद्वदेव न 4.3.623cd
उत्पित्स्वजातं सज्जातमनष्टं वाभ्युपेयते 4.3.620ab
उत्पित्स्वनागतं कृत्स्नं ज्ञानं हन्ति तदेव नः 1.4.1531cd
उत्प्राणोऽतः प्रसिद्धस्तु गुणादुद्गीथ उच्यते 1.3.319cd
उत्सन्नमपि यद्ब्रह्म तदादित्ये न नश्यति 6.5.19ab
उत्सर्गस्यास्ति विषयो योऽनिर्ज्ञातात्मतत्त्वकः 3.8.77ab
उत्सर्गाद्रूपनिर्माणे प्राधान्यं तेजसो यतः 2.3.42ab
उत्सर्गानवकाशत्वाच्छून्यतैवात आपतेत् 1.6.71cd
उत्सर्गापवादविधिनिषेधा एकलात्मनि 3.8.78cd
उत्सर्गो मुखनासाभ्यां पिण्डस्य प्रणतिस्तथा 1.5.145ab
उत्सर्जद्याति लिङ्गं तदिति प्रत्यक्षगोचरः 4.3.1923ab

उत्सार्यानात्मनः सर्वानन्वयव्यतिरेकतः 1.4.1386ab
उत्सृज्यमानः कर्मत्वं विज्ञानात्मन एति सः 1.4.666cd
उदक्रामद्यशो वीर्यं विराजः श्रमकर्शितात् 1.2.204ab
उदगायत्तदा सोमो भक्ष्यमाणः शिरो मम 1.3.329ab
उदङ्मार्गग्रहो न्याय्यः शिष्टानां पुनरागतेः 5.17.19cd
उदपात्रमथादाय तदद्भिस्त्रिः सुताप्तये 6.4.89ab
उदपात्रार्कगतिवदगतेर्गतिरात्मनः 4.4.237ab
उदपादि च यच्छब्दैर्ज्ञानमाकारवद्धियः 1.4.858ab
उदयः कार्तिको लिङ्गं प्रत्यासत्तेर्भवेद्ध्रुवम् 4.3.761cd
उदर्क इममेवार्थं नातोऽन्यत्कारणं ततः 1.4.481cd
उदर्के च शमादीनि साधनानि प्रवक्ष्यति 4.4.961ab
उदानवायौ प्रबले यत्रैतत्स्यान्मुमूर्षतः 4.3.1925ab
उदारगुणसंपत्तिः सुतस्यास्त्विति भण्यते 6.4.121ab
उदारधिषणः प्राह भाष्यकृन्न्यायवद्वचः 1.4.607cd
उदारफलदायीनि बहुशोऽनुष्ठितान्यपि 3.8.164ab
उदारफलवद्यस्मादपि ज्ञानमिह श्रुतम् 1.3.37ab
उदारफलसंप्राप्तावैश्वर्यं तत्र तत्र हि 5.16.3ab
उदारफलसंबन्धो ब्राह्मणस्यैव नान्यतः 5.16.4ab
उदारफलसिद्ध्यर्थं तस्य न्यायेन निर्णयः 5.14.1cd
उदारफलसिद्ध्यर्थं सा वा एषेत्यतः श्रुतिः 1.3.209cd
उदारातेऽखिलाः सुप्ते देवताः करणैः सह 2.1.105cd
उदासीनस्य तस्य स्याद्वशित्वमिति चेन्मतम् 4.4.989cd
उदितैकात्म्ययाथात्म्यसम्यग्ज्ञानदिवाकरे 2.4.482cd
उदीची दिगुदञ्चश्च सर्वे सार्वा दिशस्तथा 4.2.87cd
उद्गच्छति यतस्तस्माद्धृद्विशेषे लयं विदुः 2.1.252cd
उद्गतं मलवद्वासश्चतुर्थेऽहनि यत्स्त्रियाः 6.4.28ab
उद्गाता नैमिषीयाणां मदभ्युपगताद्यदि 1.3.328ab
उद्गाता नैमिषीयाणामयास्योपासनादभूत् 1.3.321ab
उद्गातुरपि तत्तुल्यं नोद्गातर्ते क्रियां यतः 1.3.385cd
उद्गातुरपि विज्ञानं दृष्टार्थत्वाच्च कारणात् 1.3.336cd
उद्गातुर्विदुषो नापि परकीयेन कर्मणा 1.3.382ab
उद्गात्रा हिंकृतं पूर्वं स्तोत्रमुद्गायता स्फुटम् 6.3.30ab

उद्गीथ इति चोद्गानं कर्मैवेहाभिधीयते 1.3.129cd
उद्गीथं समुपाश्रित्य ज्योतिष्टोमक्रताविह 1.3.123ab
उद्गीथदेवता प्राण इत्यभूत्सुरनिश्चयः 1.3.167cd
उद्गीथदेवतामेवं परीक्ष्याथाधुना श्रुतिः 1.3.333ab
उद्गीथदेवतावाप्तिर्ज्ञानकर्मसमुच्चयात् 1.3.33ab
उद्गीथदेवतावाप्त्यै प्रारब्धेहोत्तरा श्रुतिः 1.3.7cd
उद्गीथदेवतेहास्तु सविता वा मनःश्रितः 1.3.323cd
उद्गीथप्रमुखा येऽर्था मधुकाण्डे पुरोदिताः 3.1.16ab
उद्गीथब्राह्मणे पूर्वमश्वलब्राह्मणे तथा 3.2.4cd
उद्गीथलिङ्गसंयोगाज्ज्ञानमात्रेऽस्य शक्तितः 1.3.348ab
उद्गीथविधिशेषश्चेदुद्गीथप्रकृतौ श्रवात् 1.3.35ab
उद्गीथादिप्रभेदेन यं वा संविद्रते द्विजाः 5.1.129ab
उद्गीथोपास्तिसंबन्धादद्वया हेत्यादिकस्य च 1.3.17ab
उद्बिभावयिषुः साक्षात्प्रवृत्तैषा परा श्रुतिः 1.4.1700cd
उद्भूषति यो द्वेषात्स्वेषु प्राणविदं प्रति 1.3.288ab
उद्भासयन्ति संहृष्टा ब्रह्मैकत्वप्रदूषकाः 2.1.591cd
उद्भूततज्जिहासः संस्तद्धाने साधनस्पृहः 2.4.4ab
उद्भूतस्पर्शविज्ञानस्त्वचा तस्य समागमात् 2.4.342ab
उद्भूताकूतविज्ञानो मृतिं प्रति यदा तदा 4.4.21ab
उद्भूतिः कर्मणोऽत्यर्थं ज्ञानस्य च निगद्यताम् 1.3.5cd
उद्भूतिस्थितिनाशाः स्युर्जगतोऽतः प्रतिक्षणम् 2.1.413ab
उद्भूतिस्थितिहानीनां न क्वचित् संभवो यथा 1.4.403ab
उद्यम्यानेन मन्त्रेण भक्षयत्यथ भागशः 6.3.42cd
उद्यास्यन्वा अरे स्थानादस्माज्ज्ञार्हस्थ्यलक्षणात् 2.4.40ab
उद्विजेताथवा ज्ञानात्सर्वपुंभोगघस्मरात् SV 423ab
उन्मुक्तबन्धनस्तैः सन्नापितसेज्ज्ञानमात्मनः 1.4.1582cd
उपकाराद्यपेक्षं तद्वक्तृकर्त्रोः प्रसिध्यति SV 1038cd
उपकारापकारत्वे पूर्वोक्तेनैव वर्त्मना 4.3.236cd
उपकारि सजातीयमुपकार्यस्य वस्तुनः 4.3.137ab
उपकारो जगत्यस्मिन्नादित्याद्यैर्यथा तथा 4.3.139cd
उपकारो नियोगस्य कथं न घटतुल्यता SV 1036cd
उपकार्योपकारित्वभिन्नं यज्जगदीक्ष्यते 2.5.11ab

उपकार्योपकारित्वसंबन्धेनेतरेतरम् 5.6.3ab
उपकार्योपकारित्वात्तत्स्यादेकात्मतत्त्वकम् 2.5.11cd
उपकुर्वन्ति नः सर्वान्स धर्म इति संज्ञितः 2.5.44cd
उपक्रमोपसंहाराद्यथोक्तोऽर्थो विवक्षितः 2.1.501ab
उपक्षयकरौ व्याधेर्दस्रौ स्यातामतोऽश्विनौ 2.5.114ab
उपगच्छन्स्त्रियं तद्वदारुणिर्गोत्रतः किल 6.4.17cd
उपग्वादिर्हि पित्रादिः प्रकृत्यर्थो विशेषणम् SV 118ab
उपघातं जुहोतीति णमुल्वाभीक्ष्ण्य इष्यते 6.4.115ab
उपचारात्कार्यमिति तदसत्त्वान्न कर्मणः 3.3.90cd
उपचारात्क्रिया सास्य यः प्रकाश्यस्य संनिधिः 4.3.892cd
उपचारात्क्रिया सास्य यः प्रकाश्यस्य संनिधिः 4.3.1460cd
उपचारार्थतः शास्त्रं सावकाशं जपेऽथवा SV 916ab
उपजीवन्ति भूतानि ब्रह्मानन्दस्य विप्लुषम् 4.3.1840cd
उपतापान्वितो वा सन्यथोक्तं प्रतिपद्यते 4.3.1926cd
उपदेशशतेनापि ब्रह्मत्वं न कथं चन 3.4.9ab
उपदेशस्य विषयः प्रश्नप्रत्युक्तिवाक्ययोः 3.5.26ab
उपदेशादिसंबन्ध इत्येतदिह भण्यते 4.3.1410cd
उपदेशानपेक्षत्वाद्ब्रह्मत्वस्य परात्मनः 1.4.1226ab
उपनिश्रयति ब्रह्म गुणभावेन पूर्ववत् 1.4.1608cd
उपनीताय सैवातो वक्तव्या न ततोऽपरा 5.16.45cd
उपनीतौ स आचार्यः पच्छश्चार्धर्चशस्तथा 5.16.39ab
उपनीयेममात्मानं ब्रह्मापास्तद्वयं यतः SV 5ab
उपन्यस्यात्मयाथात्म्यं तत्तत्वं प्राब्रवीच्छ्रुतिः 2.4.98cd
उपन्यासो द्वयोरत्र विज्ञानात्मपरात्मनोः 3.5.14ab
उपपत्तिप्रधानेऽपि सैव मोक्षेऽवसीयते 4.5.5cd
उपपत्तिशतैरीशः साध्यते वादिभिः पृथक् 1.4.1239cd
उपपन्नस्तदारम्भो मिथःकार्यपृथक्त्वतः 3.2.50ab
उपप्रदर्शकोऽशेषनामादेरितिरिष्यते 2.3.183ab
उपमर्दोऽपि कार्यत्वात्किं न हन्यात्स्वकारणम् 1.2.41ab
उपमार्थ इवेत्येतद्भवतीति क्रियापदम् 2.4.458ab
उपमार्थमिवेत्येतत्पदमत्र प्रयुज्यते 4.2.66cd
उपमृद्नाति चेत्कार्यमथासिद्धं स्वकारणम् 1.2.40ab

उपमृद्योपमृद्यास्य नित्योपात्तं किमिष्यते 4.4.138ab
उपमृद्योपमृद्यैषां रचनां प्राक्तनीं पुनः 4.4.144ab
उपमेयोपमाभावो दिग्धीरिव विहायसि 2.4.460cd
उपयन्नपयन्वेह लोके दृष्टः प्रमाणतः 1.4.588cd
उपयुक्तं विशेषत्वादितरस्याप्यनन्वयात् 1.6.63ab
उपयोगः फलं मोक्षस्तमसो वस्त्वपह्नुतिः 1.4.791cd
उपयोगो यतस्तस्मान्नात्मज्ञानोदयात्परः 4.4.1070cd
उपर्युपरि तान्येष तपत्युल्बणरश्मिवान् 5.16.23ab
उपर्युपरीति वीप्सा किमर्थमिति भण्यते 5.16.25cd
उपलक्षणं वा तद्ग्राह्यं ब्राह्मणग्रहणं श्रुतौ 1.4.1653ab
उपलक्षणकृज्ज्ञेयः परिव्राट्तापसग्रहः 4.3.1366cd
उपलक्षणमन्येषामाज्यस्य ग्रहणं भवेत् 6.4.83ab
उपलप्स्यामहे शब्दादेवैनामिति चेन्मतम् 4.3.785ab
उपलब्धोऽस्ति सन्कुम्भो लम्बोष्ठो देशकालवान् 1.4.986ab
उपलब्धोऽस्ति सन्कुम्भो लम्बोष्ठो देशकालवान् 2.4.281ab
उपलब्धोऽस्ति सन्कुम्भो लम्बोष्ठो देशकालवान् 4.3.1740ab
उपलब्धौ तयोरुक्ते कारणे श्रोत्रचक्षुषी 1.4.705cd
उपलब्ध्यभावं मुक्त्वेह नान्यादृक्चित्तमीक्ष्यते 4.3.800ab
उपलब्ध्यभावतो नैवं यथा तदभिधीयते 4.3.792ab
उपलब्ध्या विनाभावाद्यद्यभावः प्रसिध्यति 4.3.798ab
उपलब्ध्येकनीडत्वे व्यवधानस्य कल्पना 4.4.342ab
उपवादिनेह विदुषो न भाव्यं कस्यचित्क्वचित् 3.9.127ab
उपसद्य गुरुं न्यायादाहुः केचिन्मुमुक्षवः 1.4.1070cd
उपसद्व्रतमेतत्स्यादमावास्येति लिङ्गतः 6.3.11cd
उपसर्ग उदित्येष स चात्यन्तक्रियाश्रितः 1.3.318ab
उपसर्गः समित्येष एकीभावप्रसिद्धये 4.3.1944ab
उपसीदन्ति तत्रैव ब्राह्मणाः क्षत्रियान्सदा 4.1.6cd
उपस्थानं प्रवक्तव्यमित्यर्थः पर आगमः 5.17.1cd
उपस्थानं यथैन्द्र्या स्यान्नापि लिङ्गेन संगतिः SV 333cd
उपस्थानं यथोक्ताया गायत्र्याः श्रद्धयान्वितः 5.16.67ab
उपस्थापयतः कर्म तथा क्षपयतो यतः 3.1.32ab
उपस्थिते च मनसि तस्य योषिदभूत्क्रतोः 1.4.112ab

उपस्थेन्द्रियं प्रजातिः स्यात्तस्य जन्मैकहेतुतः 6.1.14ab
उपहत्योपहत्याथ स्थालीपाकस्य मन्त्रतः 6.4.84ab
उपहत्योपहत्येति पृषदाज्याहुतीः क्षिपेत् 6.4.115cd
उपहासमतो नेच्छेत्सार्धं श्रोत्रियजायया 6.4.64ab
उपात्तं तदभुक्त्वा तु कैवल्यं लभते न चेत् 1.4.1467cd
उपात्तद्रव्यकाण्येव विशिंषन्त्युत्पलादिकम् 1.4.1421ab
उपात्तमेयरूपत्वं मानानां सत्यतोच्यते 1.4.429ab
उपात्तस्वविशेष्याणि साक्षादित्यादिकानि हि 3.4.32ab
उपात्तान्योऽन्यरूपाणां विशेषणविशेष्यता 1.4.1420cd
उपात्ताशेषभूतोऽयं यथोक्तोपात्तदेवतः 1.6.42ab
उपादानं हि बुद्ध्यादेरात्माविद्येति भण्यते 4.3.338ab
उपादानमतः श्रौती स्याद्वाणी भावनात्मनः 1.5.329cd
उपादानाय वालं स्युर्नापि हानाय तद्विदः SV 589cd
उपादित्सन्ति मानानि ह्यज्ञातार्थोपलब्धये 4.3.546ab
उपादित्सा जिहासा च तत्कृतैवानुपाल्यताम् 2.4.91cd
उपाधिभूतया दृष्ट्या हानोपादानरूपया 3.4.154ab
उपायः सोऽवताराय तथा तज्ज्ञैश्च सूत्रितम् 1.2.27cd
उपायः सोऽवताराय नास्ति भेदः कथं चन 2.1.387cd
उपायतां यथा सर्वो वेदोऽयं प्रतिपद्यते 4.4.1019ab
उपायत्वेन काम्यानां रागाद्याक्षिप्तहेतुतः SV 418cd
उपायत्वेन विज्ञप्त्यै श्येनवन्न विधीयते 6.4.48cd
उपायमात्मविज्ञाने श्रुतिरेवाब्रवीत्स्वयम् SV 216cd
उपायमात्रभेदोऽत्र न तूपेयः प्रभिद्यते 4.5.15cd
उपायसत्यतां मुक्त्वा नान्यादृगुपयुज्यते 1.4.993ab
उपायाङ्गतया कुर्यात्तच्छास्त्रस्यार्थवादताम् SV 783cd
उपायानात्मयाथात्म्यविज्ञानाय यमात्मकान् 4.4.1025cd
उपायानीत्युवाचेमं परब्रह्मावबुद्धये 2.1.91cd
उपायैरीश्वरं साक्षादपेताशेषकल्पनम् 4.4.1020cd
उपायो न्यास एवातः प्रत्यग्ज्ञानस्य जन्मने 4.4.1086ab
उपास इत्यभिहिते काश्यः प्रत्याह पूर्ववत् 2.1.71cd
उपास एतमित्युक्तः काश्यः प्रत्याह पूर्ववत् 2.1.67cd
उपासतेऽक्षणि प्राणं रुद्राद्याः सप्त देवताः 2.2.23ab

उपासते बहिर्ग्रामादर्चिस्ते संभवन्त्यतः 6.2.136cd
उपासनं च कर्मैव युक्तमुक्तमिदं ततः 4.1.28cd
उपासनं च तात्पर्यमिह श्रुत्याभिधीयते 1.5.26ab
उपासनं च यत्किंचिद्विद्याप्रकरणे श्रुतम् SV 329ab
उपासनं च वेद्म्यस्य गुणं तत्फलमेव च 2.1.49cd
उपासनं विकल्पेन वागन्नाख्यप्रतिष्ठयोः 1.3.344ab
उपासनं विधास्यामीत्यारब्धैषोत्तरा श्रुतिः 1.3.194cd
उपासनमतिक्रान्तं ब्रह्मणः फलवद्वह 5.16.1cd
उपासनमतोऽनस्य विधित्सितमितीक्ष्यताम् 1.3.40cd
उपासनमतोऽस्यापि नाग्नेरेवेति निश्चितिः 1.2.148ab
उपासनमथेदानीं ब्रह्मणो भण्यते परम् 5.15.1cd
उपासनमसोः काममस्तु सूक्तोपपत्तितः 1.3.41ab
उपासनादिसिद्ध्यर्थमात्मानं व्यभजत्स्वयम् 1.2.164cd
उपासनानां सर्वेषामित्यर्थः पर आगमः 5.12.1cd
उपासनानां सर्वेषामैकात्म्यज्ञाननिष्ठता 4.2.3ab
उपासनानि वाच्यानि यान्यनुक्तान्यतः परम् 5.1.4cd
उपासनानि सर्वाणि परविद्याधिकारतः 4.2.13ab
उपासनान्यशेषाणि तथा कर्माण्यशेषतः 4.1.35cd
उपासनार्थं नामास्य तस्योपनिषदित्यतः 1.4.43ab
उपासनार्थं यद्गुह्यं नामोपनिषदुच्यते 2.1.420ab
उपासने विकल्पेन प्राप्ते मीमांस्यते व्रतम् 1.5.362cd
उपासांचक्रिरे देवा एषैवोद्गीथदेवता 1.3.136cd
उपासाविधिशेषत्वादर्थवादोऽत ईक्ष्यताम् 1.3.43cd
उपासाविध्यपेक्षस्य प्रक्रियापतितस्य च 1.4.790ab
उपासिक्रियया योगो देवताया इहेष्यते 1.3.131cd
उपासिक्रियया व्याप्तिरब्रह्मत्वस्य लक्षणम् 1.5.255ab
उपासिक्रियया व्याप्तिरब्रह्मत्वस्य लक्षणम् 2.5.84ab
उपासीत स्वमात्मानमिति साक्षाद्वचःश्रवात् SV 453ab
उपासीतेति च तथा मुक्तावपि समीक्ष्यते SV 22cd
उपासीनस्य तं प्राणं कृत्स्नो नश्येत्तथासुरः 1.3.189cd
उपास्त इति जानाति न स्वभावादुपासनम् 1.4.688cd
उपास्तिक्रमसिद्ध्यर्थं क्रमभङ्गोऽयमिष्यते 1.3.210ab

उपासितफलमेवास्य पितुर्यद्वदिहोच्यते 1.5.311ab
उपास्तेऽन्तवतो यस्तु सोऽन्तवन्तमवाप्नुते 1.5.202ab
उपास्ते तेन तत्प्राप्तिर्नित्यैवेत्यभिधीयते 1.4.916cd
उपास्तेरपि कर्मत्वादश्वमेधक्रतोरिव SV 1121ab
उपास्त्यन्तरमस्यैव कौक्षेयाग्नेर्वपुर्भृतः 5.11.1ab
उपास्त्यन्तरमेवैतत्फलवत्तु विवक्षितम् 6.1.4ab
उपास्यत्वैकदोषेण नियोगोऽतोऽत्र नेष्यते 1.4.886cd
उपास्यार्थपरीक्षायै प्रवृत्तैषा परा श्रुतिः 6.1.21cd
उपास्यार्थविशुद्ध्यर्था प्रवृत्ताख्यायिका ततः 1.3.17cd
उपास्यार्थस्य साक्षात्त्वं घोषरूपेण वर्ण्यते 5.11.3cd
उपास्यार्थातिरेकेण न चोपासनकृद्विरुक् 1.4.930ab
उपास्योपासनविधिर्न सम्यगिति मे गतिः 2.5.81cd
उपेति सामीप्यवचस्तन्निष्ठा प्रत्यगात्मनि 1.4.720ab
उपेत्य कूटस्थमजमासीतापरिणामवान् 1.4.722cd
उपेयप्रतिपत्त्यैव प्रमाणानां प्रमाणता 1.2.134ab
उपेयबोधनं मुक्त्वा मितेर्नान्यास्ति सत्यता SV 896ab
उपेयात्तामतिक्रम्य शापदानाय रोषितः 6.4.32cd
उपेयाप्तौ कृतार्थत्वादुपायं प्रत्यनीक्षणात् SV 894cd
उपैमीति हि संकीर्तेर्नान्यत्किंचिच्चकार सः 6.2.68cd
उपोद्घातस्तथा तस्य प्रागुक्तः सप्रयोजनः 2.1.7cd
उपोद्घातोक्तदोषाणां परिहाराय यत्यते 1.4.1166cd
उपोपसर्गः सामीप्ये तत्प्रतीचि समाप्यते SV 4ab
उभयं त्वितरतः शेषादद्वयं पृष्टमतो भवेत् 4.1.8cd
उभयं विदधद्वाक्यं भिद्येतैव न संशयः 1.4.1734cd
उभयं संविदायत्तं दर्शनं प्राक्प्रमागमात् 4.3.1294cd
उभयत्रापि युगपद्भोगः स्यान्न तु दृश्यते 4.3.429ab
उभयोः सिद्धयोर्योगान्नेष्टा कारणकार्यता 4.4.333cd
उभयोरन्तरालस्था मिथः संकीर्णलक्षणाः 2.3.78cd
उभयोरपि दृष्टोऽन्तस्त्वनयोस्तत्त्वदर्शिभिः 1.4.234cd
उभयोरप्यसंभेदः कथं भिन्द्याद्विरोधिनम् 4.3.1718cd
उभयोर्देवतैकत्वादुपास्यं तेन तद्द्वयम् 2.1.57cd
उभाभ्यां पुण्यपापाभ्यां कुतस्तदपि चेन्मतम् 4.3.1371cd

उभे एते तरत्येष विद्वांस्तद्धेतुबाधनात् 4.4.1175ab
उभे न तरतोऽतस्तमुभे न तपतश्च तम् 4.4.1175cd
उभे न व्याप्नुतोऽज्ञोऽत्थे नेति नेत्यात्मनि स्थितम् 4.4.1167cd
उभे सत्यानृते त्यक्त्वा येन त्यजसि तं त्यज 3.5.162cd
उभे सत्यानृते त्यक्त्वा येन त्यजसि तं त्यज 4.4.593cd
उभे सत्यानृते त्यक्त्वा येन त्यजसि तं त्यज 4.4.1261cd
उरगादेः स्रजीवास्य ब्रह्मणोऽकारणत्वतः 4.4.923cd
उर्व्यामुत्पादितायां तु श्रमात्तापात्प्रजापतेः 1.2.160ab
उलूकचक्षुषोऽरूपाद्रसादिग्रहणं क्वचित् 3.3.122cd
उल्लिखज्जायते साक्षादतीतेऽहन्यधर्मकम् 4.3.670cd
उषसो दिवसस्यापि माधुर्यं नोऽस्तु सर्वदा 6.3.49ab
उषस्तप्रश्न एवायं कहोलेनापि पृच्छ्यते 3.5.5ab
उषस्तोक्तो विशेष्योऽत्र कहोलोक्तो विशेषणम् 3.5.98ab
उष्णप्रकाशयोर्व्यक्तिर्व्यवधानस्य संभवात् 4.4.314cd
ऊरीकृत्येममेवार्थं स य इत्यादिनोच्यते 5.16.52ab
ऊर्ग्रसो लोहितस्यात्र पिण्डो यः सोऽन्नमेतयोः 4.2.48ab
ऊर्णनाभिः स्वयं कर्ता प्रयुङ्क्ते कर्म चात्मना 2.1.391ab
ऊर्णनाभ्यग्निदृष्टान्ते न निमित्तादि गम्यते 2.1.368cd
ऊर्ध्वं दारादिसंबन्धात्पुत्रपौत्रादिसंयुतेः 1.4.1818cd
ऊर्ध्वं दिवः कपालाद्यदधो यच्चाधरात्पुटात् 3.8.5ab
ऊर्ध्वं प्राणा उत्क्रामन्ति यूनः स्थविर आयति 4.4.1223cd
ऊर्ध्वं व्यक्तेः पुरा चैव तदेवातो नियामकम् 1.4.344cd
ऊर्ध्वमूल इति तथा मन्त्रवर्णोऽपि विद्यते 1.4.187ab
ऊर्ध्वोच्छ्वासी पुमांस्तत्र यथोक्तं जायते मृतौ 4.3.1925cd
ऊर्म्यग्रवत्पिण्डभावे नामरूपक्रियात्मना 5.1.54cd
ऊर्वोरामन्त्रणं चैतद्विजिहीथामितीक्ष्यताम् 6.4.97cd
ऊषरादिवदित्यादिकल्पना नोपपद्यते 2.3.130cd
ऋगादेरभिधानस्य यावती व्याप्तिरिष्यते 5.16.13ab
ऋग्यजुःसामनिर्देशः क्रमेणेति प्रतीयते 1.3.300cd
ऋग्वेदादिगिरा तस्मान्मन्त्रब्राह्मणयोर्ग्रहः 2.4.316cd
ऋग्वेदादिगिरोच्यन्ते ऋग्यजुःसामलक्षणाः 2.4.313ab
ऋच इत्यादिना ज्ञेया नामराश्युपसंहृतिः 5.16.11cd

ऋच इत्यादिना तद्वदभिधानोपसंहृतिः 5.16.17cd
ऋणं हेत्यर्थवादेषु तस्मात्कुर्याद्यथोदितम् 1.4.1805cd
ऋणानि चानपाकृत्य कर्म त्यक्तुं न लभ्यते 1.4.1697cd
ऋणानि त्रीण्यपाकृत्य मनो मोक्षे निवेशयेत् 1.5.260ab
ऋणानि त्रीण्यपाकृत्येत्येवं च स्मृतिशासनम् 1.4.1698ab
ऋणिनोऽप्यस्य देवाद्या नेशते ब्रह्मवेदिनः 1.4.1558ab
ऋतायन्ते तथा वाता मधुवत्सुखकारिणः 6.3.44cd
ऋतायन्सत्यमात्मानं कर्तुमिच्छन्नसावृषिः 2.5.111cd
ऋतेऽपि ब्रह्मविज्ञानात्सर्वे स्युर्मुक्तबन्धनाः 2.4.17cd
ऋत्विग्रूपेण ते ह्यासन्यथा प्राकृतकर्मणि 6.2.85ab
ऋत्विङ्नामाभिसंबन्धान्न त्वसौ यजमानगा 1.3.335cd
ऋत्विजो जुह्वति नरमन्त्याहुत्यै विधानतः 6.2.115cd
ऋद्धिं प्रापद्यतः सर्वं वायौ सति चराचरम् 3.9.26ab
ऋषभोऽस्यास्तथा ज्ञेयः प्राणस्तस्मात्प्रसूयते 5.10.5ab
ऋषयश्च यशश्चेति प्राणा उक्तेन हेतुना 2.2.27cd
ऋषिरार्षेयदृष्ट्यैव तदेतदभिधीयते 2.5.107cd
ऋषिराहाथ राजानं कामितार्थस्य सिद्धये 6.2.58ab
ऋषीणां तेन लोकोऽयं गृहस्थो भोज्य उच्यते 1.4.1798cd
ऋषेर्मन्त्रस्य श्रवणमस्ति तच्च विभाव्यते 6.2.40cd
ऋष्यादिवचसा चापि ब्रह्मविद्याविशेषतः 1.4.1196ab
एक आत्मेति तद्वद्धीः स्वप्नजाग्रदवस्थयोः 4.3.1285ab
एक आत्मेति विज्ञाने दोषोऽप्यप्रतिबन्धकः 1.4.1500ab
एक एव ततः प्रश्नो न प्रश्नद्वयमिष्यते 3.5.25ab
एक एव तु विश्वात्मा मायया मोहयञ्जगत् 1.4.141ab
एक एवाहमस्मीह द्वितीयाद्धि भयोत्थितिः 1.4.93ab
एकं चेद्भिन्नता नास्ति भेदश्चेदेकता कुतः SV 975ab
एकं तावदिदं रूपं ब्रह्मणो मोहहेतुजम् 2.3.11ab
एकं ब्रह्म सदा बुद्धं यथा मानानुभूतितः 1.4.1303ab
एकं सदेकरूपं च यदि नामोक्तलक्षणम् 3.4.19ab
एकः पन्था हि मोक्षस्येत्यपि व्यासोऽपि चावदत् 4.4.1083cd
एकः सन्नेष आत्मापि त्रयमेतत्प्रपद्यते 1.6.34ab
एकः साक्षात्कृतब्रह्मा मृतेरूर्ध्वं च तल्लयः 4.2.102cd

एककारणसाक्षित्वकर्तृदुःखित्वरूपतः 3.4.121cd
एककाले विरुद्धत्वात्सर्वलोको विरुध्यते 4.3.595cd
एककालौ मतौ यच्च नाशोत्पादौ तुलान्तवत् 4.3.652ab
एकजातिनिमित्तातः प्रत्यभिज्ञेयमिष्यते 4.3.669cd
एकजातौ हि भिन्नानां शब्दानां शब्द एव तु 2.4.300ab
एकजात्यभिसंबन्धादेकत्वं गुणतो यतः 2.1.478cd
एकतां बहुतामेति कुम्भवन्मणिसंश्रयात् 1.4.141cd
एकत्र च न संभाव्यावात्मानौ द्वौ शरीरके 3.5.18ab
एकत्र समवायः स्यात्समस्तव्यस्तधर्मयोः 3.2.102cd
एकत्रापि प्रमाणत्वप्रसिद्ध्यर्थं क्षणात्मनि 1.4.247cd
एकत्वधीव्यवस्थापि मानस्येवेति गम्यताम् 4.4.732ab
एकत्वमेव तेनात्र भेदादर्शनकारणम् 4.3.1310ab
एकत्वात्पवमानस्य तदाहुरिति चोदना 3.9.23cd
एकत्वात्समुदायस्य न प्रमातो भिदां प्रति 4.3.1682cd
एकत्वादात्मनश्चैवं विषयीकरणे सति 1.4.581ab
एकत्वादात्मनो भेदो द्वयाभावान्न चेष्यते 1.4.1407cd
एकत्वासंभवोऽत्यन्तं क्षेत्रज्ञपरमात्मनोः 2.3.127cd
एकदा निर्विभागेन कात्स्न्र्यसंगतिकारणात् 1.4.1423ab
एकदेश उपन्यासादैकार्थ्यमवसीयते 3.5.10ab
एकदेशस्य चामात्वे वेदस्याप्यप्रमाणता 5.1.60ab
एकदेशानवस्थानान्न समुच्चयता तयोः 3.3.59cd
एकदेशो विकारो वा संसारी त्वात्मनो यदा SV 253ab
एकदैकत्र न स्यातां प्रकाशतमसी यथा 3.5.33cd
एकद्वित्रिपद्यसीति पूर्वान्पादान्विचिन्तयेत् 5.16.68ab
एकधा चेत्परं ब्रह्म द्रष्टव्यं कथमुच्यते 4.4.679ab
एकधानेकधा मूढैः कल्प्यते रज्जुसर्पवत् 2.1.84cd
एकधा बहुधा चैव दृश्यते जलचन्द्रवत् 1.4.142cd
एकधैव यतस्तत्त्वं सर्वस्य जगतस्ततः 4.4.677ab
एकधैवात आत्मायं द्रष्टव्यः श्रुतिवर्त्मगैः 4.4.673cd
एकधैवानुविज्ञेयमिति च श्रुतिशासनम् 5.1.81ab
एकनीडत्वहेतुत्था साक्षिणः साक्ष्यसंगतिः 4.3.414ab
एकपुण्डरीकमिति प्रधानत्वं विवक्षितम् 6.3.57ab

एकप्रत्ययगम्यत्वं स्यात्तदा कृष्णसर्पवत् 4.3.207cd
एकप्रत्ययनिर्ग्राह्यमेकं वस्त्विति भण्यते 4.3.1712ab
एकप्रभृतिसंख्येयं रेखासंकेतवर्त्मना 4.4.1339ab
एकबुद्ध्यधिगम्यत्वं विशेषणविशेष्ययोः 4.4.473ab
एकमन्नं पिता सृष्ट्वा तच्चेदं यदिहाद्यते 1.5.23cd
एकमात्रादिके त्वस्मिन्कः किं कस्मादपेक्षते 2.4.223cd
एकमानानधिगतेर्न सुखग्राहिणात्मनः 1.4.580ab
एकमेव जगद्बीजमीशाभिप्रायहेतुतः 1.3.312ab
एकमेव त्वभेदे स्यादसामान्यविशेषवत् 4.3.1768cd
एकमेव भवत्येतत्त्रयं सद्देहमात्रकम् 1.6.28cd
एकमेव यदा वाक्यं कृत्स्नो वेदोऽभ्युपेयते 2.1.565ab
एकमेव व्रतं प्राणं चरेदा मरणात्सदा 1.5.384cd
एकमेव व्रतमिति संन्यासिन्येव युक्तिमत् 1.5.271cd
एकमेव हि सद्वस्तु यद्वेदान्तप्रमाणकम् 1.4.1371ab
एकमेवाद्वितीयं सद्द्वितीयं तदबोधतः 4.4.321ab
एकमेवेत्यवधृतेर्युक्तं प्राणव्रतं पितुः 1.5.312ab
एकमेवैकरूपं सद्वस्त्वज्ञातं निरञ्जनम् 4.4.566ab
एकयैव स आहुत्या जगदात्मानमश्नुते 1.5.70cd
एकयैव स आहुत्या देवेभ्योऽन्नं ह्यशेषतः 1.5.73ab
एकरूपं च विज्ञानमेकरूपात्ममेयतः SV 375ab
एकरूपं परं ज्योतिरेकं सद्वीक्षते धियः 4.3.1774cd
एकरूपं यतो मानं विरुद्धानेकरूपिणाम् 1.3.77ab
एकरूपमतस्तत्त्वं सर्वत्रैव विवक्षितम् 4.5.18cd
एकरूपस्य मोक्षस्य भिन्नरूपं न साधनम् SV 376ab
एकरूपस्य मोक्षस्य ह्येकरूपं हि साधनम् SV 376cd
एकवस्त्ववसायित्वादन्योन्यार्थानुरोधतः 3.4.31ab
एकवाक्यत्वतो तद्वा ऐकात्म्यज्ञानजन्मने 1.4.412ab
एकवाक्यत्वतो यद्वा सर्वोऽपीत्यादि भण्यते SV 557ab
एकवाक्यत्वमेतस्माद्द्वैताद्वैतार्थवाक्ययोः 3.2.58ab
एकवाक्यत्वमेवं च वेदस्य स्यादसंशयम् SV 1109cd
एकवाक्यावशीभावात्साध्यैक्यायोगतस्तथा SV 358ab
एकवाक्योपसंहारे न पुञ्जीकृत्य दर्शितम् 4.3.1157cd

एकशब्देन नो संख्या यथैकः श्वेतवाहनः 6.3.57cd
एकशब्दो न संख्यार्थः संख्येयासंभवादिह 4.3.1802ab
एकसंख्यैव नान्यास्ति द्विसंख्याया यतस्ततः 3.9.24ab
एकस्मात्कारणात्तस्मात्पिण्डाभावे घटोद्भवः 1.2.52cd
एकस्मिन्देवदत्तादौ सा च बौद्धस्य नेष्यते 4.3.580cd
एकस्मिन्नपि चेन्मानमेयत्वादिप्रकल्पना 4.3.555ab
एकस्य हानधीस्तस्मिन्नुपादित्सा परस्य च SV 599cd
एकस्यानेकतापत्तिर्द्रव्यस्यापि प्रसज्यते 1.6.79cd
एकस्यामनुभूतौ चेद्भेदो नात्मन इष्यते 4.3.1677ab
एकस्यामपि सत्तायां सर्वाक्षाणां प्रमाणता SV 691ab
एकस्यैव हि देवस्य विभागः स्थानभेदतः 4.2.45ab
एकस्योभयरूपत्वं पण्डितैः सुनिराकृतम् 4.3.483cd
एकहंस इति प्रोक्तः पुराणज्ञैस्ततः प्रभुः 4.3.934cd
एकाकारा हि संवित्तिः सद्द्रव्यं सन्गुणस्तथा SV 968cd
एकाकिनो विराजो वाविद्यासंवीतचेतसः 1.4.91ab
एकाकिन्या न तत्साध्यं विद्ययैवेति निश्चितिः 1.5.233cd
एकाकी तेन तत्सृष्टावेको न रमते नरः 1.4.106cd
एकाक्यसमीतिविज्ञानात्त्रैलोक्यात्मैकगोचरात् 1.4.95ab
एकाग्निव्यक्तेर्न यथा दाह्यदग्धृत्वसंगतिः 4.3.512ab
एका चानेकरूपा च ह्यध्यात्मादिविभागतः 1.3.278cd
एका तावदियं व्याख्या यथोक्तैषोपवर्णिता 4.3.1014ab
एकात्मकाः सर्वदेहा विवादो येषु वर्तते 3.5.19ab
एकादिदक्षिणास्वेतं विकल्पस्तुल्य इष्यते 3.3.44cd
एकाधिकरणज्ञानात्खण्डाद्यैस्तद्विभिन्नता 1.6.65cd
एकाधिकारितां वाच्यं मानं तैर्ज्ञानसंगतौ SV 427cd
एकापर्वप्रयुक्तत्वात्समस्तव्यस्तरूपिणाम् 1.3.273ab
एकार्थत्वेऽपि च सति नैवास्य पुनरुक्तता 3.1.4ab
एकार्थप्रश्नवाक्यस्य ह्येका प्रत्युक्तिरिष्यते 3.5.6cd
एकार्थयोगाद्वाक्यस्य नैकोक्तौ स्याद्द्वयार्थता 3.4.179cd
एकार्थवृत्तिता यस्मात्तेनैकवचनं कृतम् 1.3.302ab
एकार्थसिद्धयेऽलं स्यान्नान्यथेदं त्रिदण्डवत् 4.4.589cd
एकार्थानां सतां तेषां संहतिः स्याच्छरीरके 1.6.33cd

एकार्थोपनिपातित्वात्सापेक्षत्वं यदीष्यते SV 690ab
एकार्थोल्लेखिवृत्तीनामातादात्म्याभिमानतः 1.4.771ab
एका लोकैषणैवेयं त्रिधातो व्यपदिश्यते 3.5.135cd
एकाश्रयत्वतः स्थास्न्वी संसृष्टेवोपजायते 3.4.154cd
एकीकृत्य स्वमात्मानमक्षरे परमात्मनि 2.5.68ab
एकीकृत्याथ संनीय पृषदाज्यस्य मन्त्रतः 6.4.114cd
एकीभवति सावित्रः सवित्रांशस्तथैव च 4.4.64ab
एकीभावेन तं नार्यां यत्नात्समुपवेशयेत् 6.4.6cd
एके च शाखिनो व्यक्तं विधिरूपमधीयते 6.1.38ab
एकेनैव कृतार्थत्वान्नानुतिष्ठेत्ततोऽपरम् 3.3.47cd
एकेनैव प्रकारेण भास्वच्चिन्मात्ररूपिणा 4.4.674ab
एकैकं भेदतो वस्तु निःसंसर्गं परस्परम् 4.3.1768ab
एकैकं मुक्तिकृच्चेत्स्याद्यवव्रीह्यादिहोमवत् 3.3.47ab
एकैकक्रियया लोक एकैकस्वामिकः पशुः 1.4.1573ab
एकैकत्राधिकारेऽग्निः स एव व्यवतिष्ठते 1.5.177ab
एकैकमपि जायादेर्यावन्नाप्नोति पूरुषः 1.4.1838ab
एकैकरूपासंसर्गबोधमात्रस्वभावतः 1.4.1426ab
एकैकरूपैकात्म्यार्थधियो दार्ढ्यप्रसिद्धये 2.1.527ab
एकैकश्येन नीत्वाथ निष्ठां पाण्डित्यलक्षणाम् 3.5.170ab
एकैकस्मिन्परिस्पन्द एवं सर्वापि देवता 1.3.278ab
एकैकस्याः पुनर्नाड्याः सूक्ष्मभेदाः प्रकीर्तिताः 2.1.325ab
एकैकस्यात्मनः कृत्स्नं भोग्यत्वेनावतिष्ठते 2.5.28cd
एकैकस्यामवस्थायां जाग्रत्स्वप्नसुषुप्तिभिः 4.3.1167ab
एकैकस्येन्द्रियस्येह मनोबुद्ध्योर्यथा तथा 2.4.365cd
एकैकस्वामिको लोके गवादिः पशुरिष्यते 1.4.1572ab
एकैकेन जगत्कृत्स्नमुपात्तं भोगसिद्धये 1.5.11cd
एकैकेनोपकारित्वात्तस्माज्जगदुपार्जितम् 1.5.6cd
एकैकोऽनन्ततां याति पुनरेकात्मतामतः 1.3.268cd
एकैको निखिलं विश्वं बिभर्त्यज्ञो दिवानिशम् 1.4.1574cd
एकैव गोता गोपिण्डे सास्नाद्यर्थानुसारिणी 4.3.1641ab
एकैव देवता तस्मान्नामरूपाद्युपाधिभिः 1.4.1633ab
एकैवेयमतो दृष्टिर्जन्महानादिवर्जिता 4.3.1631ab

एकोत्तरं नाडिशतं विष्वक्ताभ्यो विनिर्गतम् 2.1.322cd
एको देवः सर्वभूतेषु गूढः सर्वव्यापी सर्वभूतान्तरात्मा SV 356ab
एको देवो बहुधेतिमन्त्रब्राह्मणयुक्तितः 1.4.554ab
एतं ग्रावाणवच्छिश्नमुदपारयदात्मनः 6.4.5cd
एतं तमिति वाक्येन दृष्ट्यादेः साक्षिणं श्रुतिः 3.5.96ab
एतं विविदिषन्त्युक्तं वेदानुवचनादिभिः 4.4.1020ab
एतच्च दुर्लभं तस्य द्वितीये सति लक्षणम् 2.4.14cd
एतच्च दृष्टं लोकेऽपि यैर्भावैः संप्रयुज्यते 4.4.727ab
एतच्च भण्यते श्रुत्या पुंसो वैराग्यसिद्धये 1.5.89ab
एतच्च श्रुतितः सिद्धं विश्वमाहुतिकारणम् 1.5.61cd
एतच्चानुपपन्नं स्यादुपचारपरिग्रहात् 4.3.584cd
एतच्चानुभवादेव भवताप्यभ्युपेयते 1.4.323ab
एतत्कर्तृत्वमापेक्ष्य श्रुत्यैवमभिधीयते 4.4.23ab
एतत्तमोऽभिसंबन्धात्साक्षित्वं प्रतिपद्यते 3.4.85ab
एतत्त्वदीयं व्याख्यानं तद्विरुद्धमिदं वचः 1.4.1759ab
एतत्प्रमेयमेवातः प्रमाणं नान्यदिष्यते 1.4.179cd
एतत्सर्वं मनो ज्ञेयमिति तादात्म्यमुच्यते 1.5.114cd
एतत्साराणि हि त्रीणि भूतान्याहुर्विपश्चितः 2.3.44cd
एतत्स्थितं परिच्छिन्नमेतत्सत्सविशेषणम् 2.3.36cd
एतदप्रमयं ब्रह्म मृत्युहेतोर्निषेधनात् 4.4.676ab
एतदस्य प्रशास्तृत्वं स्वमोहाभासहेतुकम् 3.8.172ab
एतदस्य विरोधित्वं कार्यकारणवस्तुभिः 3.8.104cd
एतदस्य स्वतो रूपं यदत्रोपप्रदर्शितम् 4.3.1205ab
एतदादित्यगं भाति तद्वेदानां परं वपुः 6.5.18cd
एतदालम्बनं श्रेष्ठमिति च श्रुतिशासनम् 5.1.118ab
एतदुक्तं भवत्यत्र पूर्वोपात्तस्य कर्मणः 4.3.1254ab
एतदुक्तं भवत्यत्र योऽयमित्यादिनोदितः 4.4.980ab
एतदेवंविधं सूत्रमागमज्ञाः प्रचक्षते 3.8.8ab
एतदेव तु विज्ञाय व्युत्तिष्ठन्त्येषणात्रयात् 3.8.69ab
एतदेवमनार्तं स्यात्स्वतःसिद्धत्वकारणात् 3.4.188ab
एतदेवमभिप्रेत्य तदुक्तं नेह किं चन 4.4.730ab
एतदेव यतो ज्यायो रूपं धर्मेत्युदाहृतम् 1.4.1622ab

एतद्ध स्मेति वचसा पारिव्राज्येऽभिधीयते 4.4.1095ab
एतद्बलेन संन्यास एषणाभ्योऽवसीयते 4.4.1127ab
एतद्याथात्म्यतो ज्ञात्वा तदेवाप्नोत्यशेषतः 1.4.1853cd
एतद्वस्तु स्वतःसिद्धं प्रमात्राद्यनपेक्षतः 2.3.232ab
एतद्वाक्यानुरोधेन व्याख्येयं तदपि स्फुटम् 4.3.1338cd
एतद्विरुद्धबुद्धीनामेवमेव हि शक्यते 2.4.265cd
एतद्विषयमेवैतद्वेदशास्त्रमधीयते 4.4.202cd
एतद्वै तदिति प्राह प्रत्यक्साक्षिकमक्षरम् 3.8.56ab
एतन्निदानमधुना मिथ्याज्ञानं निरूप्यते 1.4.385ab
एतन्मयोऽयमात्मेति तथा पूर्वं प्रपञ्चितम् 1.6.35ab
एतन्मोहसमुत्थत्वात्प्रमात्रादेर्मनागपि 3.4.166ab
एतमेके वदन्त्यग्निं योऽसावितिस्मृतेरपि 1.4.146ab
एतमेव तमात्मानं विदित्वोक्तेन वर्त्मना 3.5.87cd
एतमेव विदित्वाथ मुनिः स्यात्प्राग्यथोदितः 4.4.1068cd
एतमेव विदित्वेति पारिव्राज्यं च वक्ष्यति 4.4.1065cd
एतमेव सदोपासे ब्रह्मेति रविमध्यगम् 2.1.44cd
एतमेव समुद्दिश्य मन्त्रो नारायणस्तथा 3.7.42ab
एतमेवेति च तथा प्रत्यग्याथात्म्यवित्तये SV 13ab
एतमेवेत्यवधृतेरस्यैवैकस्य वस्तुनः 4.4.1074ab
एतमेवेत्यवधृतेर्न लोकत्रयकामिनाम् 4.4.1080ab
एतया संपदा पूर्वं यजमानेन तद्विदा 1.3.277ab
एतर्ह्यपि तु तद्ब्रह्म यो यः साक्षादबुध्यत 1.4.1459ab
एतस्माज्जायते प्राणो मनः सर्वेन्द्रियाणि च 1.2.142ab
एतस्माज्जायते प्राणो मनः सर्वेन्द्रियाणि च 1.4.356ab
एतस्मादेव निःसृत्य शरीरात्सर्वतो गताः 4.2.74cd
एतस्मादेव विज्ञेयो वाक्यान्नान्यप्रमाणतः 3.5.100cd
एतस्मादेव हेतोस्तां तर्कशास्त्रेषु तार्किकाः 3.6.28ab
एतस्मिन्नक्षरे गार्गि स्रजि क्लृप्तफणीन्द्रवत् 3.8.177ab
एतस्मिन्ननृतोपाधौ शक्यो दर्शयितुं परः 4.3.899ab
एतस्मिन्मण्डले योऽन्तर्विज्ञानात्मत्वमागतः 2.3.53ab
एतस्य पुरुषस्येति रूपं निर्दिश्यतेऽधुना 2.3.101ab
एतस्य वा अक्षरस्य प्रशासनविधौ सति 3.8.130ab

एतस्या एव पूजायै देवताया निषेधनम् 1.5.215ab
एतस्यां सम्यगुक्तायां नानुक्तमवशिष्यते 3.3.6cd
एतस्यैव यथोक्तस्य सर्वानन्दातिवर्तिनः 4.3.1840ab
एतस्यैवेति वचसा समर्थो हेतुरुच्यते 4.3.1839cd
एतानीति च निर्देशाद्यजूंषीत्यवगम्यते 1.3.350ab
एताभिरित्यतो यावच्छारीरादिति चोदना 4.2.59cd
एताभिर्वा इति तथा तेनैता इति च श्रुतिः 4.3.1229cd
एताभ्यामेव रूपाभ्यां यतो ब्रह्माभवत्स्वयम् 1.4.1657cd
एतामवस्थामापन्नो ध्यातृत्वाद्विनिवर्तते 2.5.71ab
एतावतापि पक्षस्ते प्रतिबद्धो न सिध्यति SV 80cd
एतावतैव पर्याप्तमस्मद्राद्धान्तसिद्धये 1.4.1366cd
एतावदर इत्यन्त उपसंहारदर्शनात् 1.4.1266ab
एतावदर एवैतदमृतत्वस्य सिद्धये 4.5.23ab
एतावदिति तं प्राह शेषाशङ्कानिवृत्तये 2.1.85cd
एतावदेव कर्तव्यं गृहिणेहाधिकारिणा 1.5.296ab
एतावदेव किं ज्ञेयं किं वान्यदपि शिष्यते 5.16.75ab
एतावदेव चेदत्र भवतैवं विवक्षितम् SV 1122ab
एतावदेव प्रत्यक्षं सर्वयाथात्म्यवेदिनाम् 3.8.67ab
एतावद्वस्तु जगति गायत्रीपादसंश्रयम् 5.16.18cd
एतावद्वास्तवं वृत्तं मोहोत्थं भण्यतेऽधुना 1.4.31ab
एतावद्व्याकृतं सर्वं यदेतत्संहतं त्रिभिः 1.6.35cd
एतावन्मात्रमेवेति यत्र भ्रान्ता निरागमाः 2.3.87ab
एतावन्मात्रयाथात्म्यं सर्वस्य जगतस्ततः 3.9.22cd
एतावन्मात्रयाथात्म्यात्कार्यकारणवस्तुनः 3.4.41ab
एतावन्मात्रयाथात्म्यात्कार्यकारणवस्तुनः 3.9.153ab
एतावन्मात्रसंव्याप्तेरज्ञानादेः पुरा मितेः 1.4.293cd
एतावानुपदेशः स्याद्वेदे श्रेयोऽर्थिनां नृणाम् 4.5.30ab
एतावानेव कामोऽस्य नातोऽन्योऽर्थोऽवशिष्यते 1.4.1827ab
एतावानेव शास्त्रार्थः कर्त्रधीनः सुखाप्तये 4.4.106cd
एतावानेव संघातो देहः प्राणादिरूपकः 1.5.153ab
एति चित्स्वतमोहेतोर्न किंचिदपि दुःस्थितम् 1.4.153cd
एति पूर्णतमतां साक्षाद्धियां वाचामगोचरम् 6.5.12cd

एते एव विभोः स्थाने द्वे एवेत्यवधारणात् 4.3.835cd
एते न तरतोऽज्ञोत्थे तद्वेत्त्वज्ञानघस्मरम् 4.4.1172ab
एतेनैव विजानातीत्यपि च श्रुतिशासनम् 4.3.1771cd
एतेनैवाक्षारेणेति ह्यथर्वणोऽप्यधीयते 5.1.118cd
एतेभ्योऽविद्याभूतेभ्यः कार्यकारणतामगात् 2.4.419cd
एतेभ्योऽसौ समुत्थाय स्वाभासानात्मजन्मना 1.2.137ab
एतेभ्यो हेतुभूतेभ्यो भूतेभ्योऽकार्यकारणः 2.4.422cd
एन एनः प्रति तथा नियुक्ता ये नराधिपैः 4.3.1962ab
एनं भूतानि सर्वाणीत्युपासनफलाभिधा 4.1.22cd
एनांस्यौषध्यतोऽग्रेऽतः संवृत्तः पुरुषाभिधः 1.4.48cd
एनेन संवदिष्येऽहमिति व्याख्यायते यदा 4.3.12ab
एभ्योऽङ्गेभ्य इति गिरा तदेतदभिधीयते 4.3.1943cd
एमं लोकं परं चात्मा कर्मज्ञानादिसंस्कृतः 4.3.840cd
एवं काण्डद्वयेनेयं सफलानवशेषतः 4.5.29ab
एवं कामयमानोऽयं स्वप्नबुद्धान्तवन्नरः 4.4.252ab
एवं कार्यमुखेनैव ज्योतिष्टोमादिवाक्यवत् SV 445ab
एवं कृत्वेदमत्राह श्रुतिः कामं न कंचन 4.3.1202ab
एवं केचिद्व्यवस्थाप्य प्रसंख्यानविधिं पुनः SV 769ab
एवं क्रमेण निःशेषं जगद्बुद्ध्युपसंहृतम् 3.9.78cd
एवं गुप्तामपि तु तां वक्ष्याम्येवाहमञ्जसा 6.2.72ab
एवं चतुर्भिरध्यायैर्यथाव्याख्यातवर्त्मना 4.4.1161ab
एवं च लोकतः सिद्धो वाक्यार्थः स्याच्छ्रुतावपि SV 870ab
एवं च सति तत्पूर्णं ब्रह्म कृत्स्नं च युज्यते 3.8.85ab
एवं च सति दीपादेर्भिन्नजातीयचेतन- 4.3.505ab
एवं च सति दृष्टान्तो भवतो नोपपद्यते 4.3.474ab
एवं च सति यद्यस्मात्कार्यमाविरभूत्पुरा 2.4.372ab
एवं च सति यावत्यो नाड्यो हृदयबन्धनाः 4.2.71ab
एवं च सति विज्ञानव्यतिरेकेण कुम्भवत् 4.3.536ab
एवं च सति वेदान्तवाक्यार्थप्रत्ययो भ्रमः SV 723ab
एवं च सति वेदान्ता यदि मानमलौकिकम् SV 709ab
एवं च सति संबन्धो न भावाभावयोर्मिथः 1.2.115ab
एवं च सत्यनिर्दिष्टाशङ्कापि विनिवर्तते 2.3.202cd

एवं च सत्यभिव्यक्तिः सर्वदा सुखबोधयोः 4.4.343ab
एवं चाज्ञातपारार्थ्ये नार्थवादः फलश्रुतिः SV 434ab
एवं चावस्थिते पक्षे श्रुत्याकारि समञ्जसम् 4.3.1041ab
एवं चिदन्वयात्सर्वस्तदध्यस्तः समीक्ष्यते 2.4.282ab
एवं चेत्कोऽनयोर्भेदः कार्यकारणयोर्मितेः 1.4.308ab
एवं चेत्साधनोद्भूतं यावत्किंचित्सुखं मतम् 2.4.86ab
एवं चेत्स्यादभिप्रायः किमर्थं निष्प्रयोजनम् 1.4.1208ab
एवं चेदक्षरं तादृक्कथमस्तीति गम्यते 3.8.110ab
एवं चेदद्वयं ब्रह्म द्वैतावस्था न सिध्यति 5.1.38cd
एवं चेदनपेक्षत्वं विधेः किमिति भण्यते 2.4.180ab
एवं चेदप्रमाणत्वं किमिवेहाभिधाश्रुतेः 2.4.168ab
एवं चेद्ब्राह्मणोक्तिः स्याद्ध्वस्ताविद्यगृहीतये 3.5.92ab
एवं चेन्न सतो नाशो नोत्पत्तिरसतस्तथा 1.4.202ab
एवं चेन्मानतो मेयो विज्ञात इति का प्रमा 1.4.226cd
एवं चैकत्वमनयोरिह व्याख्येयमादृतैः 3.5.134cd
एवं जागरिते तावदादित्याद्युक्तलक्षणम् 4.3.68ab
एवं जिगमिषुं देवमनुगच्छन्ति के तु तम् 4.3.1972ab
एवं ज्ञातपदार्थः सन्यथा पूर्वमवादिषम् 2.4.109ab
एवं ज्ञानक्रियाशक्तिविक्षेपाज्जगदात्मनः 2.4.371ab
एवं तदवबोधान्ना ख्यातिमेत्यविनश्वरीम् 1.4.1020cd
एवं तद्देवतोत्क्रान्तावेकीभावेन संगतेः 4.4.71ab
एवं तमस्यपि ज्ञेयं क्षेत्रज्ञश्चात्मसंज्ञितः 3.7.46cd
एवं तर्हि न कर्माङ्गं कर्तुश्चेष्टैकहेतुतः SV 106ab
एवं तर्ह्येकरूपेऽस्मिंस्तत्त्वे सत्ये समर्थिते 5.1.42ab
एवं ताः संप्रधार्योचुरुद्गीथं साधनं परम् 1.3.127ab
एवं तावत्समासेन षष्ठाध्यायोक्तमादरात् 4.4.1018ab
एवं तावत्स्थितं पूर्वं पश्यन्निति यदीरितम् 4.3.1558ab
एवं तावदयं पक्षो न्यायतः प्रतिपादितः 2.1.444ab
एवं तावदविद्यैकनीडानामुदितो विधिः 4.3.1247ab
एवं तावदुपोद्घातो व्याख्यातोऽत्र समासतः 1.4.1124ab
एवं तुरीयमेतस्मिन्सत्ये चक्षुषि सर्वदा 5.16.32ab
एवं ते कर्मकाण्डेऽपि कार्यं तावन्न युज्यते SV 653ab

एवं तौ संप्रधार्यैतदुक्तदोषानभिप्लुतम् 3.2.159ab
एवं त्वं वर्धमानोऽत्र मन्वीथाः पुत्र संततिम् 6.4.117ab
एवं त्वगादिवाच्यासु स्पर्शादीनां यथायथम् 2.4.375ab
एवं दुःखादिषु ज्ञेयमुक्तं प्रत्यक्षसंश्रयात् 4.4.470ab
एवं दृष्टं यतस्तस्माद्गार्गी पप्रच्छ लिङ्गतः 3.6.8ab
एवं द्वाभ्यां प्रकाराभ्यामीशो व्याकृतजन्मनाम् 1.4.392ab
एवं द्वैतस्य सत्यत्वे कर्मकाण्डस्य मानता 5.1.58ab
एवं ध्वस्तात्ममोहस्य कुतोऽविद्योत्थवस्तुभिः 3.5.77ab
एवं न कर्मतो मोक्षः कर्मणः क्षयवत्त्वतः 1.4.1699ab
एवं न पुनरुक्तत्वं द्रष्टव्यादेः प्रसज्यते 4.3.1619cd
एवं नित्यानि कर्माणि कुर्वतः शुद्धचेतसः 4.4.1214ab
एवं निराशाः पूर्वासु देवतास्वसुरार्दनात् 1.3.164ab
एवं निर्दुःखमात्मानमक्रियं प्रतिपद्यते SV 207cd
एवं निर्दुःखमात्मानमक्रियं प्रतिपद्यते 2.4.112cd
एवं निःशेषसंसारप्रत्याख्यानेन निर्वृतिम् 1.4.1339ab
एवं निषिद्धवाक्येषु यथोक्तं न्यायमादिशेत् SV 93ab
एवं नृत्यज्जगन्नित्यमतद्वृत्त्यात्मनि स्थितम् 1.4.1485cd
एवं पञ्चापि निर्णीताः प्रश्ना ये प्राक्प्रचोदिताः 6.2.163cd
एवं पदं त्रयो लोका अभिधानाभिसंगतेः 5.16.8ab
एवं पदात्परिज्ञाते पदार्थे लोकमानतः SV 862ab
एवं परिजिहीर्षन्ति न तु न्यायोक्तिरीदृशी 4.2.103ab
एवं परिहृतेऽप्याहुर्यथेच्छं दूषणं परे 1.4.371ab
एवं पारिक्षितान्सर्वानग्निरिन्द्रो वियत्पथा 3.3.158ab
एवं पूर्वोक्तमन्त्रार्थज्ञानतत्फलवित्सुधीः 4.4.1201ab
एवं प्रचोदिते केचित्परिहारं प्रचक्षते 2.1.468ab
एवं प्रत्यक्ष एतस्मिञ्छुक्तिकोदरवर्तिनि 1.4.449ab
एवं प्रत्यक्षतस्तावद्देहादिव्यतिरेकतः 4.3.199ab
एवं प्रबन्धरूपेण साध्यसाधनलक्षणम् 1.5.88ab
एवं प्रमेयसिद्ध्यर्थं प्रवृत्तैषोत्तरा श्रुतिः 1.4.180ab
एवं प्रवृत्तं सर्वत्र शास्त्रं दृष्टान्तपूर्वकम् 2.1.495ab
एवं प्रस्थाप्य गन्धर्वमथैनामभिपद्यते 6.4.93cd
एवं प्रागात्मसंबोधाददृयैकात्म्यनिह्नुतिः 1.4.312cd

एवं बहिरविद्येयं निष्क्रामत्यात्मनः पृथक् 4.3.1093cd
एवं बुद्धेः परं बुद्ध्वा संस्तभ्यात्मानमात्मना 4.4.387ab
एवं भयाभिभूतः स ईक्षांचक्रेऽथ लोकवत् 1.4.59ab
एवं मनुवसिष्ठादिधर्मेष्वपि सहस्रशः 4.4.1266ab
एवं मन्तव्य आत्मायं तर्कतः प्राग्यथोदितः 2.4.395ab
एवं मोक्षार्थतां तेषां पुत्रादीनां प्रचक्षते 1.5.336ab
एवं यतोऽभ्युपगतौ लिङ्गं स्यांच्छब्द एव तु 4.3.787ab
एवं यथोदिते तावत्प्रमाणार्थेऽप्यवस्थिते 5.1.28ab
एवं यस्मात्स्वतः शुद्धो द्वितीयासंगतेरयम् 2.1.309ab
एवं रागादिहेतूत्थप्रवृत्तिलयवर्त्मना SV 383ab
एवं राज्ञो यथोक्तोक्त्या ह्यभ्युपेतेऽनुशासने 6.2.29ab
एवं लक्षणतः पञ्च भूतान्येतानि निर्दिशेत् 2.4.335ab
एवंलक्षणहेतूक्तिमौर्ख्यलिङ्गं भवेदतः 2.1.605cd
एवं लौकिकतादात्म्यतदुत्पत्ती प्रतीरितम् 4.3.768ab
एवं वा अर इत्यस्य कार्यकारणरूपतः 2.4.410ab
एवं वागादयः शब्दा देवतार्थाभिधायिनः 1.3.135ab
एवं वाङ्मनसे सम्यग्व्याख्याय प्रविभागशः 1.5.143ab
एवंवित्त्वविरोधित्वाद्दूरं पाप्मा भवेदतः 1.3.213cd
एवंवित्सन्स आचार्यो यस्मा अन्वाह सादरः 5.16.41ab
एवंविदपि सञ्शत्रुरुपवादादभूद्यतः 3.9.127cd
एवंविदादरात्तस्मात्प्रत्यक्प्रवणधीर्नरः 4.4.1194cd
एवंविदेवमेव स्यात्पापं वह्निवदिन्धनम् 5.16.82ab
एवंविदे हि नानन्नं किंचिदस्तीति दर्शनात् 6.1.34ab
एवं विद्वत्प्रयोज्यत्वादत एव न सूत्रितम् 1.3.347ab
एवं विद्वानवाप्नोति पुत्रामात्यादिसंहतिम् 1.4.1022ab
एवंविधस्य कर्मत्वमुपास्तिं चात्मनस्तथा 1.4.1734ab
एवं विधिमिहेच्छन्ति विध्ययोग्येऽपि वस्तुनि SV 757ab
एवंविधोऽधिकारी स्यात्सर्वासूपास्तिभूमिषु 5.2.2cd
एवं विप्रतिपन्नेषु नानावादिषु निश्चितः 1.3.325ab
एवं विरुद्धधर्मत्वे न च दोषोऽस्ति कश्चन 3.5.38ab
एवं वृन्दारकः पूज्य आढ्यो मानुषवित्तवान् 4.2.6cd
एवं व्यवस्थितौ सत्यां युक्तिलेशोऽभिधीयते 1.4.1046ab

एवं व्यष्टिसमष्ट्यात्मा वैराजं देहमात्मनः 1.2.152ab
एवं व्याक्रियताज्ञानहेतुमात्रव्यपाश्रयात् 1.4.390cd
एवं व्याचक्षते केचिद्गम्भीरन्यायवादिनः 1.4.1202cd
एवं श्रुतिरियं कैश्चिद्व्याख्यातातिप्रयत्नतः 2.1.255ab
एवं श्रोतव्य आत्मायं समाप्तः श्रवणे विधिः 2.4.263ab
एवं संसरतस्तावत्परं ब्रह्म परायणम् 3.9.160ab
एवं संसारविध्वस्तिस्तद्धेतोर्ज्ञानहानितः 3.5.98cd
एवंसतत्त्व एवायमिति हेतुरिहोदितः 4.3.1568cd
एवं सति कुतो मे भीरिति विद्वांस्त्रपायते 1.4.67cd
एवं सति प्रबोधे यद्भुक्तं प्राक्कर्मणः फलम् 4.3.1257ab
एवं सति प्रमाणत्वमपूर्वार्थावबोधनात् 1.6.17ab
एवं सति प्रमामातृफलमेयात्मनां तव 4.3.197ab
एवं सति भवेत्सिद्धं यथा पूर्वं प्रपञ्चितम् 2.5.29cd
एवं सति विधिः कस्मान्नानर्थक इतीर्यताम् SV 728ab
एवं सति समर्थः स्यात्सर्वाश्रमसमुच्चयः 3.5.150cd
एवं सतीह योऽनन्तानुपास्ते सततोद्यतः 1.5.201ab
एवं सत्यनुकूलार्थं तत्त्वमित्यादिकं वचः SV 246cd
एवं सत्यप्रमाणत्वं मितेश्चापि प्रसज्यते 1.4.1544cd
एवं सत्ययमात्मेति संहतो जगदात्मना 1.4.1793ab
एवं सत्यर्थवत्सर्वमन्यथा तदनर्थकम् 1.4.939cd
एवं सत्यर्थवान्त्रः स्यादन्यथा स्यादनर्थकः 1.5.334cd
एवं सत्यस्य बाधः स्यात्परमार्थात्मसंश्रयात् 4.3.1182ab
एवं सत्याद्यतो जातं क्रमेण ब्रह्मणो जगत् 5.5.10ab
एवं समर्थ्यमानेऽपि न मुक्तिः कर्मणो भवेत् 1.4.1724ab
एवं समवनीतेषु प्राणेष्वात्मनि तद्विदः 4.4.502ab
एवं समादधानस्य कामितोऽर्थो न सिध्यति 1.4.1726ab
एवं समाने संक्षेपो विकासोऽनन्तदेवताः 3.9.110cd
एवं सर्वात्मकत्वेन स्तुवन्प्राणं प्रयत्नतः 1.3.296ab
एवं स शिशुसंरावसंलब्धालोचनक्षणः 1.2.188ab
एवं सिद्धेऽप्यनुभवे स्वमहिम्ना पुरा मितेः 4.3.180ab
एवं सिद्धे महिम्न्यस्मिन्यथोक्तेनैव वर्त्मना 5.16.51ab
एवंस्वभावमप्येतदविज्ञातं स्वभावतः 1.4.214ab

एवं स्वात्मनि विज्ञाते निष्क्रियेऽकारकेऽफले 4.4.954ab
एवंक्रमप्रयुक्ताङ्गा तथा चैवंफला क्रिया 1.3.70cd
एवमज्ञः कामवशाद्भूयो योनीः प्रपद्यते 4.4.249cd
एवमत्रैकवाक्यत्वं नानुष्ठेयसमाप्तितः SV 302ab
एवमन्योऽपि यो वेद सृष्टिकृत्स्यादसावपि 1.4.124cd
एवमप्यविरोधः स्यादस्य मानान्तरैरपि 2.1.560cd
एवमर्थमुपोद्घातमेवं स कृतवान्मुनिः 4.2.16cd
एवमष्टक्षणावस्थो भावोऽवश्यं त्वयेष्यते 1.2.69cd
एवमस्त्वित्यनुज्ञाते छित्वा तस्याथ तच्छिरः 2.5.102ab
एवमस्मिन्परे तत्त्वे भाव्यमाने मुमुक्षुणा 4.4.728ab
एवमागमतः सिद्ध ऐकात्म्येऽनुभवाश्रयात् 4.3.806ab
एवमात्मपरिज्ञानाद्ध्वस्ताविद्यो भवेद्यदा 4.4.1295ab
एवमात्मा सविज्ञानो गन्तव्यं यत्पुरार्जितम् 4.4.103ab
एवमाभासयत्यात्मा कृत्स्नं कार्यं सकारणम् 4.3.361cd
एवमुक्ते विरक्तोऽस्मान्मुमुक्षुः श्रद्धयान्वितः 1.6.3ab
एवमेव जगद्योनिरेकैकः कर्मकृन्नरः 1.5.3cd
एवमेव महामोहसंवीतधिषणः पुमान् 1.4.1172ab
एवमेवैष विज्ञेयो मेयमानान्तरेष्वपि 4.4.752cd
एवमेष समानान्तः शाकल्यप्रश्ननिर्णयः 3.9.91cd
एवमैकात्म्यतात्पर्ये शास्त्रस्येष्टेऽपि युक्तिभिः SV 790ab
एवंप्रकारं प्रत्यक्षं स्वसंवेद्यं न बाध्यते 4.3.704cd
एवंभूतात्मसिद्ध्यर्थं कारणादि प्रसाध्यते 1.2.27ab
एवंभूतोऽपि चाज्ञातः कार्यकारणरूपताम् 4.4.764ab
एवंभूतोऽप्ययं प्रत्यक्स्वात्मानुभवसंश्रयात् SV 1090ab
एवंभूतोऽप्यसंबुद्धस्वात्मतत्त्वो महेश्वरः 1.4.492ab
एवंमहिममप्येतत्संसारं नात्यवर्तत 1.4.53cd
एवम्वित्युक्तशेषाणां पाप्मविद्धत्वसिद्धये 1.3.160cd
एवार्थस्योपमामन्य इवार्थे चावधारणम् 4.2.65cd
एवेत्ययोगावच्छित्तौ नान्ययोगव्यपेक्षया 1.5.241cd
एवेत्यवधृतावेतत्संसर्गप्रतिषेधकृत् 2.5.36cd
एवेत्यवधृतावेतदात्मवृत्तव्यपेक्षया 1.4.395ab
एवेत्यवधृतावेतदात्मीयार्थनिषेधकृत् 1.4.24ab

एवेत्यवधृतिर्ज्ञेया ज्ञानादेव ततो भवेत् 1.4.1438cd
एवेत्यवधृतिर्ज्ञेया प्रत्यङ्मात्रेक्षणाय तु 1.4.1684cd
एवेत्यवधृतिश्चात्र स्वप्नप्राज्ञनिवृत्तये 4.4.49cd
एवेत्यवधृतेर्यद्वा पूर्वप्रश्नार्थशेषता 3.8.46ab
एवेत्यवधृतौ ज्ञेयं ब्रह्मात्मार्थविशेषणम् 1.4.1389ab
एवेत्याहान्यदेवेति तथा चोच्चैः श्रुतीरणम् 1.4.719cd
एष आत्मा स्वयंज्योती रविसोमाग्निवाक्षु यः 4.3.112ab
एष आत्मेति प्रत्युक्तिर्यः प्राणेनेति चापरा 3.5.32ab
एष इत्यात्मनिर्देशो यत्साक्षादिति च श्रुतिः 4.3.1814cd
एष इत्यादिवचसा सर्वेशस्यात्मनः स्फुटः 4.4.1006cd
एष इत्यादिवाक्योक्तिः सम्यग्दर्शनजन्मने 4.3.1824cd
एष एवं यथातत्त्वमश्वमेधं विवेद यः 1.2.212ab
एष एवंविदुज्ञातेत्यमुतो लिङ्गतो भवेत् 1.3.336ab
एष एवंविधो यस्मादानन्दः परमस्ततः 4.3.1841ab
एष एव क्रमो ज्ञेयः प्राधान्यगुणभावयोः 4.2.70cd
एष एवानवगतः स्वतोऽवगततत्त्वकः 1.4.293ab
एष एवानुसंधेयो न्यायो योऽयमिहोदितः 3.9.75ab
एष एवैकलो द्रष्टा कारकादिविवर्जितः 3.7.58ab
एष एवैकलो नित्यो बाह्यसाधननिस्पृहः 4.4.1182ab
एषणाः सकला एताः कस्मादित्यभिधीयते 4.4.1098cd
एषणा कामपर्यायः कामश्चात्रागगोचरः 3.5.128ab
एषणात्रितयस्यापि किमित्याक्षेप उच्यते 4.4.1099cd
एषणास्त्यजतां तेषामभिप्रायमिमं शृणु 4.4.1099ab
एषणे एव चाप्येते साध्यसाधनकल्पिते 1.4.1828ab
एषणैकैव तेनेयमुत्तरत्राभिधास्यते 1.4.1833ab
एष नित्यो महिमेति श्रुतिवाक्यं विहन्यते 4.4.309ab
एष प्रजापतेरुक्तो महिमा तद्वदेव तु 1.3.280ab
एष मार्ग उपन्यस्त ऐकात्म्यज्ञानजन्मने 4.2.90ab
एष योऽभिहितः पूर्वं तं साक्षाद्दृष्टवानृषिः 4.4.1180ab
एष वा इति यत्नेन ह्याजगामोत्तरा श्रुतिः 1.2.219cd
एष सर्वेश्वर इति पुनरुक्तं किमुच्यते 4.4.1004ab
एष सर्वेश्वर इति स्वातन्त्र्यं श्रूयतेऽसकृत् 1.4.543cd

एष सर्वेश्वरोक्त्या च यथोक्तस्यैव संस्तुतिः 4.4.979cd
एष सर्वेश्वरो देव ईशितव्यव्यपेक्षया 4.4.1003cd
एष साधारणस्तावत्प्रलयोऽबुद्धिपूर्वकः 2.4.330cd
एष स्वकार्यं संश्रित्य नानाभेदान्प्रपद्यते 1.4.354ab
एष ह्येवेति च व्यक्तं तैत्तिरीयश्रुतावपि SV 1020cd
एषां नामविकाराणामुक्थं नादस्तदुत्थितेः 1.6.13ab
एषामिति नृबीजस्य स्तुतिरुक्त्या विवक्ष्यते 6.4.1ab
एषा हि नेति केचित्तु नेयं दीपादिवन्मता 1.5.138cd
एषा हि नेत्यतो वक्ति वागिन्द्रियनिवृत्तये 1.5.136cd
एषैका देवता विभ्वी प्रत्येकार्थावसायिनी 2.1.58ab
एषोऽन्तर्याम्येष योनिः सर्वस्य प्रभवाप्ययौ 3.8.26ab
एषोऽभ्युपायः सर्वत्र वेदान्तेषु विधीयते 4.4.1248ab
एषोऽर्थो वचसस्तस्य न तूपासाविधिर्भवेत् 2.5.88ab
एषोऽस्य परमः पूर्णः कृत्स्नो लोकस्तु विद्यया 4.3.1275ab
एषोऽस्य परमो लोको यः सर्वोऽस्मीति दर्शितः 4.3.1295ab
एषोऽस्य परमो लोको लोकास्त्वन्ये क्षयिष्णवः 4.3.1832ab
एषोऽस्यानुग्रहः श्रुत्या प्रतीचोऽत्र विवक्षितः 4.3.100ab
एषोऽस्येति प्रतिज्ञात आनन्दः सोऽनुमानतः 4.3.1880ab
एष्यद्घटनिषेधे च विरोधोऽपि प्रसज्यते 1.2.112ab
ऐककर्म्यं ध्रुवं प्रापत्सर्वेषामपि कर्मणाम् 3.3.49ab
ऐकात्म्यं न तयोर्युक्तं प्रकाशतमसोरिव 2.1.456cd
ऐकात्म्यं वीक्ष्यते तेन त्यक्त्वा सर्वाननात्मनः 1.4.1346ab
ऐकात्म्यं सर्वभावानां भिन्ननामादिमत्स्वतः 4.3.1696cd
ऐकात्म्यं सर्वभूतेषु प्रतीचोऽसौ ददर्श ह 1.4.1446cd
ऐकात्म्यं सर्वभूतेषु प्रात्यक्ष्याच्चात्मनस्तथा 2.1.609cd
ऐकात्म्यज्ञानतश्चेत्स्याद्व्यर्था कर्मप्रधानता SV 86ab
ऐकात्म्यज्ञानतात्पर्यं कर्मणामिति निश्चितम् SV 87cd
ऐकात्म्यज्ञानतात्पर्यं तस्यापीच्छन्ति युक्तिभिः SV 769cd
ऐकात्म्यज्ञाननिष्ठायास्त्यागोऽतीव हि साहसम् SV 310cd
ऐकात्म्यज्ञानमन्वेति तपोमुषितकल्मषः SV 88cd
ऐकात्म्यज्ञानमन्वेति स्वातन्त्र्येऽप्यर्थवत्त्वतः SV 336cd
ऐकात्म्यतत्त्वासंबोधः सुषुप्तः प्राज्ञ उच्यते 4.3.1059cd

ऐकात्म्यतो हिरुग्रूपं न वस्तूत्प्रेक्ष्यतेऽण्वपि 4.3.1326cd
ऐकात्म्यदर्शनादुक्ताद्यदन्यद्दर्शनान्तरम् 4.4.598ab
ऐकात्म्यदर्शनाद्विद्वान्यत्र त्वस्येतिशास्त्रतः 4.4.634cd
ऐकात्म्यधीसमुत्पत्तेर्यदि वा ब्रह्मलोकतः 6.2.144ab
ऐकात्म्यपरतैवातः सृष्ट्यादिवचसां भवेत् 2.1.505cd
ऐकात्म्यप्रतिपत्तेः प्राङ्न मिथ्या हेत्वभावतः SV 895ab
ऐकात्म्यप्रतिपत्त्यर्थं क्षेत्रज्ञपरमात्मनोः 2.1.239cd
ऐकात्म्यप्रतिपत्त्यर्थस्तस्मादत्र विवक्षितः 2.1.500cd
ऐकात्म्यबुद्धेस्तद्बुद्धिद्वारं नैव निरीक्ष्यते SV 332cd
ऐकात्म्यबोधमात्रेण निषेधस्याप्यपह्नवात् 1.2.28cd
ऐकात्म्यमात्रकूटस्थप्रबोधावसितेः कुतः 4.4.279ab
ऐकात्म्यमात्रवस्तुत्वादविद्यैकैव युज्यते 2.4.199cd
ऐकात्म्यमात्रावसितेर्न वेदान्तर्बहिस्तथा 4.3.1323cd
ऐकात्म्यमात्रे जगति समाप्तपुरुषार्थके 2.1.532ab
ऐकात्म्यमेव नो ज्ञातं सर्वत्रैव पुरा मितेः 4.3.1483ab
ऐकात्म्यमेव मानानां सर्वेषां मेयमिष्यते 1.3.55ab
ऐकात्म्यलक्षणं साक्षाच्छेत इत्यभिधीयते 2.1.352cd
ऐकात्म्यवन्तो देहाः स्युर्विवादो येषु वर्तते 2.1.608ab
ऐकात्म्यवस्तुतात्पर्यं हेत्वादिच्छद्मनोच्यते 2.5.7ab
ऐकात्म्यवस्तुनः साक्षाद्व्युत्पत्तिरविचालिनी SV 1091cd
ऐकात्म्यवस्तुनिष्ठस्य तथा पूर्वमवादिषम् 1.4.755cd
ऐकात्म्यवस्तुनिष्ठे तु यथोक्तन्यायवर्त्मना SV 1045ab
ऐकात्म्यवस्तुबोधित्वादुपान्त्यप्रत्ययो यथा 1.4.76cd
ऐकात्म्यवस्तुयाथात्म्यप्रकाशनपटीयसः SV 719ab
ऐकात्म्यवस्तुयाथात्म्यप्रकाशनपरत्वतः 4.4.463cd
ऐकात्म्यवस्तुयाथात्म्यबोधे जात्यादिबाधनात् SV 364ab
ऐकात्म्यवस्तुयाथात्म्यमभिप्रेत्यात उत्तरः 3.5.52ab
ऐकात्म्यवस्तुविज्ञानं कर्मभिर्हि विरुध्यते 3.9.122cd
ऐकात्म्यवादिनावश्यमेको मेयोऽर्थ इष्यते 4.3.1485ab
ऐकात्म्यविज्ञानफलं प्राप्तमेव हि तत्त्वतः 2.4.235cd
ऐकात्म्यविषयान्नान्यो वेदान्तवचसां यतः SV 16ab
ऐकात्म्यव्यक्तितोऽन्यत्र तस्मादेवेति गीरियम् 1.4.208cd

ऐकात्म्यसिद्धौ दोषः स्यात्तत्सिद्धिश्च न वास्तवी 2.1.171ab
ऐकात्म्यसिद्धौ यत्नेन तथात्र प्रतिपाद्यते SV 797cd
ऐकात्म्यस्य स्वतः सिद्धेः साध्यत्वाद्रूपवस्तुनः SV 657cd
ऐकात्म्यस्य स्वतः सिद्धेर्न क्रियापेक्ष्यते यतः 2.4.157ab
ऐकात्म्यस्य स्वतो मुक्तेरज्ञानात्तस्य बद्धता SV 798ab
ऐकात्म्यस्यागमार्थत्वाच्छ्रुतेश्चान्यानपेक्षतः 4.4.482ab
ऐकात्म्यस्यैव मेयत्वं तस्यैवाप्रतिबोधतः SV 172cd
ऐकात्म्याज्ञानविध्वंसव्यतिरेकेण नेष्यते 2.4.235ab
ऐकात्म्याद्द्वैतविषये यथाग्नीन्धनयोस्तथा 4.3.1555cd
ऐकात्म्यानवबोधस्य कार्यमुक्तमशेषतः 3.4.1ab
ऐकात्म्यानुभवो नो चेद्विसंवादादमानता SV 835cd
ऐकात्म्यानुभवो हि स्यात्कथमक्षादिबाधनात् SV 850cd
ऐकात्म्याबोधबाधेन सिद्धा तूपायसत्यता SV 899cd
ऐकात्म्याविद्यया सर्वं प्रतीचि परिकल्पितम् 2.1.164ab
ऐकात्म्येऽपि विरोधश्चेन्नाशो नाशेऽपि शङ्क्यते 1.2.49cd
ऐकात्म्ये तन्निवृत्तिश्चेदसंभाव्येति चोद्यते 1.4.1232ab
ऐकात्म्ये तु यथा नास्ति विशेषेणोच्यते तथा SV 653cd
ऐकात्म्ये वर्तमानस्य ब्रह्मात्मास्य परायणम् 3.9.162cd
ऐकात्म्ये वाक्यहेतूत्थबोधस्योद्भूतिकारणात् 4.4.799cd
ऐकात्म्ये सर्वमेवेदं कार्यकारणलक्षणम् 3.9.106ab
ऐकात्म्योक्तौ विधिर्व्यर्थ इति द्वैतप्रकल्पनम् SV 847cd
ऐकार्थ्यमेतयोर्न्याय्यं मिथोऽर्थावसितेस्तथा 3.4.43cd
ऐकार्थ्यमेव चेदिष्टं भिन्नाभिन्नाभिधानयोः 4.3.1763ab
ऐकार्थ्यात्प्रश्नवाक्यस्य नात्मानौ द्वौ विवक्षितौ 3.5.20cd
ऐकार्थ्याद्वचसोऽशक्या विरुद्धद्व्यर्थकल्पना SV 566cd
ऐकार्थ्यान्नेह संसर्गस्तद्विरुद्धार्थयोरिव 3.5.172ab
ऐकार्थ्ये चैकवाक्यत्वात्कर्मविज्ञानकाण्डयोः SV 317cd
ऐकार्थ्ये न विरोधोऽस्ति द्व्यर्थत्वेऽपि न माश्रयात् 2.1.562ab
ऐक्यं सुखस्य विच्छेदो दुःखं वा किं न कल्प्यते SV 1011cd
ऐक्यमुक्तमतः प्राणो बोध्यते चन्द्रनामभिः 2.1.110cd
ऐक्यादनुपलब्धिश्चेदनैकान्तिकता तथा 4.3.1384ab
ऐक्षतेह न कामार्तः कश्चिदालोचने क्षमः 1.2.188cd

ऐतिह्यार्थं च ह स्मेति वैशब्दः स्मरणाय च 4.4.1096cd
ऐतिह्यार्थस्तथा हेति सम्राडित्यभिमन्त्रणम् 4.3.1825cd
ऐदंपर्यमिदं तावत्पदार्थोऽथाधुनोच्यते 4.4.986ab
ऐश्वरो वात्र भोगोऽस्ति सर्वस्थानाभिमानतः 4.3.1051cd
ऐश्वर्यं कारणत्वं च साक्षित्वमपि चात्मनः 4.3.354ab
ऐश्वर्यं चैव धर्मश्च सहसिद्धमिति स्मृतिः 1.4.79cd
ऐश्वर्यं न प्रमाणस्य सत्त्वं वस्तुबलाद्यतः 1.2.87cd
ऐश्वर्यं पारतन्त्र्यं च नापि संभाव्यते मितेः 2.1.398ab
ऐश्वर्याच्च प्रयत्नोत्थकार्येष्वस्यात्मनो न तु 4.3.1131cd
ओं क्रतो इति संबोध्य स्मरेत्यत्र नियुज्यते 5.17.17ab
ओं खं ब्रह्मेति मन्त्रोऽयं श्रुत्येह ध्यानकर्मणि 5.1.110ab
ओं खं ब्रह्मेति वचसा पुंसां श्रेयोऽभिवाञ्छताम् 5.1.112cd
ओंकारोऽथ दमादीनां साधनत्वं विधीयते 5.2.1cd
ओंकारो वेद एवेति ब्राह्मणास्तु प्रचक्षते 5.1.126ab
ओतं प्रोतं च तत्कस्मिन्निति पृष्टो ब्रवीहि मे 3.8.8cd
ओतं प्रोतं च यत्रेदं तदक्षरमथोच्यते 3.9.93cd
ओतं प्रोतं जगद्यस्मिन्नरनाभिनिदर्शनात् 2.1.117cd
ओतः प्रोतश्च निःशेष आकाशोऽकारणात्मनि 3.8.177cd
ओतप्रोतं जगत्सर्वं प्राण एवोपदिश्यते 1.4.351cd
ओतप्रोतकतां वायोर्जगतोऽसौ प्रयत्नतः 3.8.13cd
ओतप्रोतगिराशेषदृश्यवस्तुनिराकृतेः 3.8.175ab
ओतप्रोतात्मतां गार्गी तयोरेवान्वपृच्छत 3.8.3cd
ओतप्रोतात्मना कार्यं येन येन समाप्लुतम् 3.6.9ab
ओतप्रोतात्मना तस्थुरर्वाग्या भूमयोऽक्षरात् 1.4.638ab
ओतप्रोतात्मना तस्थौ विराट्सूत्रादिवस्तुषु 1.4.138cd
ओतप्रोतानि तत्त्वानि तेन पूर्वाणि सर्वशः 3.6.17cd
ओताः प्रोताश्च कस्मिन्नु ब्रह्मलोका इतीर्यताम् 3.6.21ab
ओदनं पचतीत्यादि तथेहापि भविष्यति 1.4.1201cd
ओमित्येवं सदा ध्यायेदन्या वाचो विमुञ्चथ 4.4.966ab
ओषतीत्यादिकं ज्ञेयं वेदोपासीत यः सदा 1.4.50cd
ओषतीत्युक्तितः साक्षाद्गुणोपास्तिफलश्रवात् 1.4.52cd
औत्सर्गिकत्यागविधिं नित्यकर्मविधिर्बलात् 4.4.1225cd

औदासिन्यं निवृत्तिर्हि स्वरूपालम्बनं च तत् SV 892cd

औदासीन्यान्निषेधेषु न लभ्येत प्रमाणता SV 892ab

औद्गात्रमेव चोद्गीथो भक्तिर्वा काचिदिष्यताम् 1.3.317ab

औपगवो नृपहयस्तथा श्येनचिदादयः SV 117ab

औपाधिकश्च मिथ्या स्यात्साध्यसाधनलक्षणः SV 652ab

औषत्स्वान्पाप्मनः पूर्वं ज्ञानाद्यतिशयाग्निना 1.4.49ab

औष्ण्यं शैत्यं यथात्येति वस्तुवृत्तेन सर्वदा 3.5.59ab

औष्ण्यस्वभावो दृष्टोऽग्निस्तस्यान्यत्रापि दर्शनात् 4.3.744ab

क एतत्साधयेद्धीमान्कि वा रूपमितीर्यताम् SV 621cd

कं विशेषं समाश्रित्य ह्यात्मान्तरतमो मतः 1.4.1044cd

कं विशेषमपेक्ष्यैका चेष्टा मुक्त्यनुरोधिनी SV 419cd

कंसाद्याकारसिद्ध्यर्थं कंसाद्युक्तिरिहोच्यते 6.3.16ab

कः प्रमाता प्रमाणं वा यमेवेति तथा श्रुतिः 4.4.692cd

कंचिद्विशेषमापेक्ष्य पृष्टो भूयोऽपि पृच्छ्यते 3.5.25cd

कठवल्लीषु चाप्युक्तं विमुक्तश्च विमुच्यते 4.4.296cd

कठिनोदकविध्वंसमनु खिल्यो विलीयते 2.4.407cd

कठिनोदकविलयमनु खिल्यो विलीयते 2.4.401ab

कणभुग्जैमिनीयैर्य आत्मधर्मा इतीरिताः 4.4.419ab

कणभुङ्न्यायसिद्धा चेत्कामाद्याश्रयतात्मनः 4.4.464ab

कण्टकादिसमायोगे शरीरे विक्रिया यदा 2.4.347cd

कतम इति पृष्टोऽथ वस्वादीन्प्रत्यपद्यत 3.9.11ab

कतमो भवतात्मेति ज्योतिष्ट्वेन विवक्षितः 4.3.282cd

कतमो याज्ञवल्क्येति स तं प्रत्याह शुद्धधीः 3.5.54cd

कथं कर्मणि सर्वज्ञो मनो दध्याद्वसन्नपि SV 135cd

कथं केन क्रमेणात्र प्रत्यगात्मा प्रसीदति 4.3.980ab

कथं च तस्य कर्तृत्वं व्यापित्वान्निष्क्रियत्वतः SV 1053ab

कथं चेदुच्यमानं तच्छृणवेकाग्रमना यथा 2.1.567cd

कथं चैवंस्वभावस्य तदज्ञानजभूमिषु 4.3.377ab

कथं तदिति चेदत्र मानव्यापार उच्यते 4.4.711cd

कथं तदिति चेदत्र युक्तिलेशोऽभिधीयते 1.4.610cd

कथं तदिति दृष्टान्त ऊर्णनाभ्यादिरुच्यते 2.1.383ab

कथं तद्द्वारकस्तेषामुपकार इतीर्यते 1.3.243ab

कथं तद्विषयः शब्दो वागित्यत्राभिधीयते 1.5.133cd
कथं तमभिजानीयादित्युक्त इदमुच्यते 4.4.610ab
कथं तमभिसंयान्तीत्युक्ते श्रुत्याभिधीयते 4.4.19ab
कथं ते व्याप्नुतोऽविद्याहेतूत्थे ब्रह्मवेदिनम् 4.4.1172ef
कथं तेषाममानत्वं तदा स्यादाप्तवाक्यवत् SV 710ab
कथं त्वं नानुशिष्टोऽसि ब्रूहि तत्कारणं मम 6.2.50ab
कथं नाम मतिस्तस्य ब्रह्मास्मीति भवेदिह 4.3.1968ab
कथं नित्यं भवेत्तन्नो यदि स्यात्कर्मणः फलम् SV 38ab
कथं नु नाम सिद्धः स्यादतो वीप्सा प्रयुज्यते 5.16.27cd
कथं नूपकरोत्यज्ञो देवतादीनिति भण्यते 1.4.1780cd
कथं पश्यंस्तमात्मानं साक्षाद्वेदेति चोदिते 1.4.714ab
कथं पुनरबोधोत्थक्लृप्तोपायेन तत्परम् 1.4.991ab
कथं यतस्त्वमी सर्वे प्राणाः क्षेत्रज्ञलक्षणाः 2.3.93cd
कथं वा तद्विना मानं विषयासंभवाद्भवेत् SV 988cd
कथं विपरिलोपोऽस्याः क्रियात्वे सति वार्यते 4.3.1571cd
कथं वेत्यादिकोऽत्रार्थो विस्तरेणोपवर्ण्यते 4.4.5cd
कथंचित्साधयेत्कार्यं तच्च नास्तीत्यसाधकः SV 646cd
कथमाङ्गिरसः प्राण इत्यस्य प्रतिपत्तये 1.3.208ab
कथमात्मचितौ तत्स्यात्तद्विरुद्धार्थसिद्धये 4.3.214cd
कथमित्युच्यते तेषां बुद्धिसंशुद्धिहेतुतः 4.4.1041cd
कथमेतद्विजानीम इत्येतदभिधीयते 1.5.50cd
कथमेति स कैवल्यमक्षितौ कामकर्मणोः 1.4.1720ab
कथमेवंविधं गार्गि नास्तीत्यक्षरमुच्यते 3.8.165cd
कदम्बकुसुमोद्भूतकेसरा इव रार्वतः 2.1.326ab
कदम्बपुष्पवत्सैषा देवता हृदयाश्रया 4.2.67ab
कनीयस्ता विवृद्धिर्वा नैव संभाव्यते मितेः 5.16.51cd
कनीयान्नापि पापेन तदकर्तृत्वहेतुतः 4.4.999cd
कपालसंधिगं व्योम सामर्थ्यात्परिमाणतः 3.3.155ab
कया मर्यादया कार्यं मायावी माययाविशत् 1.4.634ab
करं बलिं प्रधानाय दत्त वागादयोऽचिरात् 6.1.28ab
करणं कर्म कर्ता च कर्मैतत्कारकात्मकम् 4.3.910ab
करणं कर्म कर्ता च नातो ध्यात्रादिसाक्षिणि 4.3.411cd

करणं कर्मशक्तिर्वा चरणं प्रत्ययात्मकम् 4.4.195cd
करणं नियतं चैव ततोऽन्यच्चरणं तथा 4.4.195ab
करणं बुद्धिरेवेह न तं प्रत्यपि चोदना 4.4.927cd
करणत्वं विहायेह केवलाज्ञानमात्रकम् 4.3.1375ab
करणद्वारिका नापि ग्राहकद्वारिका तथा 4.3.526cd
करणव्यापृतिं चर्ते मनुष्योऽस्मीति धीर्भवेत् 4.3.203ab
करणस्य तु नैवोक्तस्ततत्कस्मादिति भण्यते 2.4.393cd
करणस्यैव तत्स्थत्वाद्विज्ञानात्मा हि लिङ्गगः 2.3.64cd
करणांशो विधिज्ञानं किमंशः पुंस्प्रवर्तनम् 1.4.785ab
करणात्प्रत्यवायस्य हतेर्भोगेन च क्षयात् SV 41cd
करणात्मन एवातस्तस्य हेति ग्रहो भवेत् 2.3.158ab
करणाद्यनपेक्षस्य न च विज्ञानसंभवः 3.9.187ab
करणानां समुत्क्रान्तिर्गमनं च तयोः समम् 4.4.2ab
करणानामभोक्तृत्वं देहांशानामिवेष्यते 2.1.133cd
करणानामिदं सर्वं ज्ञानकर्मादिहेतुकम् 4.4.131cd
करणानि च देहश्च पुरुषोऽत्र विवक्षितः 4.3.21ab
करणानि व्यपेक्ष्यन्ते न त्वकारकवीक्षणे 4.3.1415cd
करणानुग्रहीतॄणि भूतानि च मुमूर्षतः 4.3.1971ab
करणान्तरव्यपेक्षायामनवस्था प्रसज्यते 4.3.522cd
करणान्यनपाश्रित्य नालं स्वाधिकृतिं प्रति 4.3.1142ab
करणान्यन्तरेणेह जात्यन्धादिर्न वीक्षते 4.3.1414cd
करणायतनं स्थूलं वैराजं यत्प्रचक्षते 1.6.39cd
करणायतनत्वाय देहाविर्भूतिरात्मनः 2.4.371cd
करणायतनान्देवान्स्वप्रतिष्ठान्व्रजेत्तु सः 4.1.11ab
करणे देवता यस्मिन्पूर्वं मुञ्चत्यनुग्रहम् 4.4.67ab
करणेष्वेषु सर्वेषु तथा कार्यात्मकेषु च 3.9.32ab
करणैः संहतिं चर्ते परिहारः कुतो दृशेः SV 157ab
करोति भूतसंघातः स्वप्ने बालयुवादिवत् 4.3.130cd
करोत्यनामरूपस्य मणेरास्तरणं यथा 4.4.494cd
करोत्येष रथाद्यर्थं स्वप्नभोगप्रसिद्धये 4.3.909cd
करोम्यन्धो द्विजो बालो दग्धश्छिन्नोऽहमित्यपि SV 120cd
कर्तव्यं कार्यमित्येवं ततोऽपि व्यतिरिच्यते SV 630cd

कर्तव्यः कट इत्यत्र तथैव स्यान्न चेक्ष्यते SV 512cd
कर्तव्यः कट इत्यादावव्यापारेऽपि कार्यता SV 509ab
कर्तव्यः कारकापेक्षो विधेयः स न संशयः 1.4.888cd
कर्तव्यता न च ज्ञाता पारिव्राज्यस्य कुत्रचित् 4.4.1141ab
कर्तव्यता न साध्यस्य विज्ञातत्वाद्विधीयते 4.4.939ab
कर्तव्यता निवृत्तेस्तु न प्राप्तेति विधीयते 4.4.1220cd
कर्तव्यताविवक्षैव नृवाक्येभ्योऽपि गम्यते SV 500ab
कर्तव्यत्वादभीष्टत्वसिद्धौ कर्मार्थलाभतः SV 513ab
कर्तव्यत्वेन न ज्ञातं वृक्षाद्यारोहणं यथा 4.4.1145ab
कर्तव्यमात्मविज्ञानमित्यत्रैव निराकृतः 4.4.938ab
कर्तव्यमेतद्विज्ञानमिति वेदानुशासनम् 2.5.146cd
कर्तव्याभावतस्त्वेवं विकारेऽपि न कर्मणि SV 256ab
कर्तव्योऽतो विचारोऽत्र युक्तिमार्गेण यत्नतः 3.9.177ab
कर्तव्यो यत्नमास्थाय कृते यस्मिन्कृतार्थता 4.4.1306ab
कर्तव्यो याग इत्येवं यागाद्भिन्ना यथेक्ष्यते SV 630ab
कर्तान्यत्रापि सद्भावान्नाक्षेप्ता व्यभिचारतः SV 337cd
कर्ताप्यत्यन्तमेव स्यादन्योऽन्याव्यतिरेकतः 1.5.87cd
कर्ता भोक्तेव चाभाति स्वप्नजाग्रदवस्थयोः 4.3.1259cd
कर्तारमश्वमग्निं च चित्यं सर्वं प्रजापतिम् 1.1.5ab
कर्तुं विवेकोऽतो यातः सुप्तं पुरुषमादरात् 2.1.103cd
कर्तुः प्रमेयता न स्यादहंबुद्ध्या कथं चन SV 1062cd
कर्तुर्ज्ञातुर्हि या दृष्टिः साविद्योत्थार्थलेहिनी 1.4.1432ab
कर्तृकार्यादिवद्भाति कूटस्थोऽप्यात्ममोहतः 4.3.1630cd
कर्तृकार्यैरसंबन्धो द्रष्टुर्दृष्टेरितीर्यते 4.3.1429ab
कर्तृकार्यावभासित्वाज्जाग्रत्कालेऽपि चात्मनः 4.3.1028ab
कर्तृकार्यावभासित्वात्कर्तृकार्यादिसाक्ष्ययम् 4.3.1630ab
कर्तृकार्यावभासित्वात्कर्तृकार्याभिधायिभिः 3.4.156ab
कर्तृक्रियादिसादृश्यात्सान्यत्वेऽपीति चेन्मतम् 4.3.583cd
कर्तृता भोक्तृता चैषां षष्ठ्यन्तेनाभिधीयते 2.5.22cd
कर्तृत्वं करणत्वं च कर्मत्वं चात्मसाक्षितः 3.4.110ab
कर्तृत्वं चास्याविद्यातो न स्वतः कर्तृतात्मनः 1.4.1788ab
कर्तृत्वं न स्वतः स्वप्ने किमु वक्तव्यमिष्यते 4.3.1028cd

कर्तृत्वकञ्चुको यद्वदात्मानात्मानमीक्षते 2.4.284ab
कर्तृत्वप्रतिषेधार्थं द्रष्टुर्दृष्टेरितिश्रुतिः 1.4.735ab
कर्तृत्वमात्मनः सिद्धं यतोऽन्यत्रापि यागतः SV 103ab
कर्तृत्वमात्मनो बोध उपचाराद्यतस्ततः 4.3.1076cd
कर्तृत्वमात्मनो युक्तं चित्प्राधान्याच्च भोक्तृता 3.4.112cd
कर्तृत्वादिसमुच्छेदिज्ञानस्येहाश्रितत्ववतः 4.3.1870cd
कर्तृत्वादीह यत्सिद्धं वागादिद्वारमीक्ष्यते 1.3.124ab
कर्तृत्वाद्यन्यथाज्ञानहेतुत्वादात्मरूपिणः 1.4.379cd
कर्तृत्वाद्यभिमानित्वान्नेशस्य तदसंभवात् 4.4.1000cd
कर्तृत्वे सति कर्माणि नान्यथाकर्तुरात्मनः 4.3.1357cd
कर्तृभिः क्रियते तस्माद्भावनाज्ञानकर्मभिः 1.5.333ab
कर्तृभोक्तृस्वरूपेऽतो ह्यभ्युपेतेऽन्तरात्मनि SV 100ab
कर्तृभोक्त्रादिरूपत्वं प्रत्यगज्ञानतोऽन्यतः SV 111ab
कर्तृस्थभावकं स्थास्नु चलं कर्मस्थभावकम् 1.4.509cd
कर्तृस्थेन हि स्वर्गादिकामदोषेण काम्यता 1.3.95ab
कर्तृस्वामित्वविरहान्नेशस्य फलसंगतिः 4.4.994cd
कर्तेव भोक्ताप्यज्ञः स्याद्विद्यायां द्वयमप्यसत् 1.4.1788cd
कर्तेवानुभवेनैव प्रतीचा गम्यतेऽञ्जसा 4.3.185cd
कर्त्रात्मनः पुरा सिद्धेर्बुद्ध्याद्यव्यतिरेकतः 3.4.6ab
कर्त्रादिकारकं नो चेत्सुषुप्ते विद्यते कथम् 4.3.1441ab
कर्त्रादिकारकस्थाने नातोऽन्वेत्यक्रियात्मनः 4.3.1005cd
कर्त्रादिकारकाण्यस्मिन्नसाधारणरूपतः 1.4.668ab
कर्त्रादिकारकापेक्षं क्रियावृत्तमभाषत 4.4.448cd
कर्त्रादिकारकापेक्षं विरिञ्चान्तफलप्रदम् 1.4.166ab
कर्त्रादि चात्ममोहोत्थं वस्तु सिद्धं स्वतोऽद्वयम् 3.4.136cd
कर्त्रादि चात्ममोहोत्थं स्वतोऽकारकतात्मनः 3.3.62cd
कर्त्रादि तु तमोन्तस्य रूपं धर्माद्यपेक्षया 1.4.669cd
कर्त्रादिव्यापृतेः पूर्वं संवित्संवित्तिमात्रतः 4.3.1741ab
कर्त्रादिव्यापृतेः पूर्वं संवित्स्वात्मन्यवस्थितेः 1.4.987ab
कर्त्रादिव्यापृतेः पूर्वमसंकीर्णमुपाधिभिः 1.4.873ab
कर्त्रादिश्चेत्स्वभावः स्यात्प्रत्यक्षाकर्तृरूपिणः SV 140cd
कर्त्रादिसाक्षिणोऽस्याभूत्कर्तृत्वं यत्पुरात्मनः 4.3.1030ab

कर्त्रादिहेतूच्छित्तेश्च प्रवृत्तेर्नास्ति संभवः 4.4.941ab
कर्त्रादेरिह साक्ष्यात्मा दृष्टेर्द्रष्टोच्यतेऽधुना 3.4.6cd
कर्त्राद्यनात्मधर्मस्य कर्माधिकृतिरात्मनः SV 138cd
कर्त्राद्यात्मस्वभावस्य प्रात्यक्ष्यान्न तदात्मनि SV 149ab
कर्त्राश्रितं स्वं विज्ञेयं माधुर्यादीह सामनि 1.3.337ab
कर्त्रेह यत्कृतं कार्यं तद्भोगायावकल्पते 1.4.1787ab
कर्त्र्यो भोक्त्र्यश्च देहेऽस्मिन्देवता एव नापरः 2.1.22cd
कर्मकर्त्रुक्तितोऽकस्मात्कथं कर्ताभिधीयते 1.4.515cd
कर्मकाण्डप्रमाणत्वविरोधध्वस्तये किल 2.1.531ab
कर्मकाण्डप्रमाणत्वे प्रामाण्यं चेद्द्वयोरपि 2.1.537ab
कर्मकाण्डस्य वैफल्यमेवं कल्पयतो भवेत् 5.1.76cd
कर्मकाण्डस्य सर्वस्य वेदस्यापि प्रसज्यते 5.1.95cd
कर्मकाण्डादपच्छिद्य तेनात्रैवैष भण्यते 3.9.121ab
कर्मकाण्डेऽधिकार्यस्मिन्यादृक्संभाव्यतेऽञ्जसा SV 1051ab
कर्मकाण्डे यथा मानं तथैवोपनिषत्स्वपि 2.4.147ab
कर्मकाण्डे विरोधित्वान्नैवैनं व्याचचक्षिरे 3.9.116cd
कर्मकाण्डोपनिषदोर्निष्प्रामाण्यं द्वयोरपि 2.1.535cd
कर्मकार्यनिवृत्त्यर्थमर्थवत्स्याद्विशेषणम् 1.4.1650cd
कर्मकार्यश्च लोकोऽत्र ज्ञेयोऽग्न्यादिसमाश्रयात् 1.4.1644ab
कर्मकार्यसजातित्वात्पारिशेष्यनयः कुतः 3.3.115cd
कर्मकार्यस्य हि सतो मुख्यानन्त्यं न युक्तिमत् 1.5.200cd
कर्मकार्यान्तरं नित्यं विषदध्यादिवद्ध्रुवम् 3.3.125ab
कर्मकार्योऽथ हृदयान्निष्क्रामति यथासुखम् 4.4.80cd
कर्म कुर्यां यथाप्राप्तं दृष्टादृष्टार्थसिद्धये 1.4.1826cd
कर्म कृत्वाथ तच्छान्तौ कर्म ब्रह्मेति वेत्स्यति 1.4.1725cd
कर्म कृत्वा परं यत्नादन्यस्यार्थयते फलम् 2.4.74cd
कर्म कृत्स्नं समाप्यापि तत्त्वज्ञानाद्बहिष्कृतः 1.4.1671ab
कर्मकृद्धिषणान्तो यः कामाविद्यासमन्विताः 4.3.905ab
कर्मक्षयात्तथा बुद्धिः कारणत्वेन तिष्ठति 2.4.330ab
कर्मगोचरतैवात्र विज्ञानस्यापि चेन्मतम् SV 1119ab
कर्मच्छिद्रेषु कुर्वन्ति येऽपि सम्यग्धियं बलात् 1.4.1521ab
कर्मजान्येव तान्यस्य न तु चैतन्यवत्स्वतः 1.4.685cd

कर्मज्ञानादिहेतुत्वान्नियमस्य यथा तव 1.4.471ab
कर्मज्ञानाधिकारः स्यात्संग्रामस्तद्विरोधतः 1.3.113ef
कर्मज्ञानानुरूपेण रूपमुच्चावचं मुहुः 4.3.942ab
कर्मज्ञानान्तराणां स्यान्नाश्वमेधगृहीतये 1.3.3cd
कर्मज्ञाने सुतस्तस्य साधनत्वं व्रजेत्कथम् 1.5.277cd
कर्मणः क्रियमाणस्य संस्कारो यो हृदि श्रितः 4.4.118ab
कर्मणः फलभोगान्ते देहो यस्मात्पतत्ययम् 4.3.872cd
कर्मणः फलसंप्राप्तिरप्राप्तिश्चेह येक्ष्यते 1.4.1491ab
कर्मणः साधनत्वेन नामरूपे व्यवस्थिते 1.6.29cd
कर्मणः स्यात्प्रशंसैवं तत्प्राधान्योपपत्तितः 3.2.161cd
कर्मणश्चास्य निष्पत्तौ विद्वत्तापि समाश्रिता 6.3.9ab
कर्मणां चात्मविद्यायां चरितार्थत्वकारणात् 4.4.1160ab
कर्मणां फलमेवात्र लोकशब्देन भण्यते 1.4.1648cd
कर्मणानार्जितो यस्मान्न कश्चिदुपकारकृत् 1.4.1785ab
कर्मणा निर्मितं लोकमात्मा पश्यत्यविद्यया 4.3.1095ab
कर्मणा पितृलोकादि नित्यानामेव तत्फलम् SV 1128cd
कर्मणा पितृलोकाप्तिर्नाश्रुतेरन्यसाधना 1.5.252ab
कर्मणा पौरुषेणैवं रसभूतेन संभवः 2.3.56ab
कर्मणा सगुणः साक्षाद्भवतीति प्रचक्षते 2.3.119cd
कर्मणे नैव पर्याप्तं ब्रह्माभूत्पूर्ववत्ततः 1.4.1614cd
कर्मणैव स्वसिद्ध्यर्थं तेषां क्रोडीकृतत्वतः 1.4.1480ab
कर्मणैवास्य विज्ञानं तादात्म्यमुपनीयते 4.4.77ab
कर्मणोऽचिन्त्यशक्तित्वान्नैवमप्युपपद्यते 1.4.1679cd
कर्मणोऽदृष्टसामर्थ्यं यद्यज्ञानापनुन्मतम् 3.3.97ab
कर्मणोऽन्तं फलं प्राप्य भुक्त्वा निरवशेषतः 4.4.244cd
कर्मणोऽपि तथात्यन्तं प्रयोगैकसमाश्रयात् 4.3.1035ab
कर्मणोऽपि तथा मानं न किंचिदुपपद्यते 3.3.74cd
कर्मणोऽपि तथैकत्वमधुना प्रतिपाद्यते 1.6.24cd
कर्मणोऽप्युपसंहारः प्राण इत्यादिना तथा 5.16.18ab
कर्मणोऽवसरश्चेत्स्यात्त्वद्दीक्षावसरो यथा 1.3.103ab
कर्मणो गमनस्येह साधनाभावहेतुना 4.3.916ab
कर्मणोद्भावितः सोऽयं स्मृतिरूपेण जायते 4.3.85cd

कर्मणोद्भाविता यत्र वासना कामरूपिणी 4.3.941ab
कर्मणो भुज्यमानस्य परिशेषो हि भावना 4.4.124ab
कर्मण्यनुचिते तेषां प्रहीणमनसां तदा 1.3.145cd
कर्मण्यप्रक्रियास्थं सज्जुहूपर्णमयीत्ववत् SV 334cd
कर्मण्यस्तमिते तद्वत्प्रत्यङ्ङास्ते स्वभावतः 4.3.1201cd
कर्मण्यादेशशब्दोऽयं यदि वा करणे भवेत् 2.3.175ab
कर्मण्यानि भवन्त्यस्य न तु तानि तथा यतः 3.7.22cd
कर्मण्यग्नात्रपेक्षावज्ज्ञानेऽपीति मतं यदि 1.3.385ab
कर्मण्येव तु विज्ञेया नासावर्थान्तरे यतः 3.4.169cd
कर्मतः कालतो मृत्योर्मुक्तोऽयं स्वर्गमेष्यति 3.1.38ab
कर्म तत्फलभोगश्च बाह्यानि करणानि च SV 111cd
कर्म तस्यास्तमेवेति विज्ञायेत्यनुवादतः 4.4.872cd
कर्म दर्शयितव्यं स्याद्दृष्ट्या द्रष्टा न दृश्यते 3.4.174cd
कर्मधारय एवातः समासोऽत्रोपपद्यते 4.3.1817ab
कर्म ध्यानादिकं यत्नाच्छ्रेयोऽर्थिभिरनुष्ठितम् 1.4.8cd
कर्म नारभते यावद्दुःखादिफलमात्मनः 4.3.817ab
कर्म निर्वर्त्यते तेन स हि कर्तेति भण्यते 4.3.926cd
कर्म निस्पन्दमेवास्ते भावनापि च शाम्यति 4.3.1198cd
कर्म पाङ्क्तं भवेदेवं पाङ्क्तेन च्छन्दसा मितम् 1.4.1840cd
कर्मप्रकरणाकाङ्क्षि ज्ञानं कर्मगुणो भवेत् 4.4.1125ab
कर्मप्रकरणे नायं श्रुतः पूर्वं कदा चन 3.9.120ab
कर्म प्रधानमिच्छन्ति यतः कर्म प्रयोजकम् 4.4.206cd
कर्म प्रधानमित्येवं साक्षाच्छ्रुत्योपसंहृतम् 4.4.209ab
कर्मप्रधानाः पुंसः स्यादाश्रयोऽयमनुत्तमः 3.2.149cd
कर्मप्रयुक्तो भोगश्च ततः संस्कारसंभवः 2.1.220cd
कर्मप्रयोजकान्कामांस्तस्मात्सुस्थं यथोदितम् 4.3.1372cd
कर्मप्राधान्यमेवातः स्वयमेवाब्रवीच्छ्रुतिः 3.2.156ab
कर्म ब्रह्मेति संपश्यन्मृतश्चेद्ब्रह्मसाद्भवेत् 1.4.1727cd
कर्मभिः शुद्धसत्त्वस्य सम्यग्ज्ञानस्य जन्मनि 4.4.583cd
कर्मभिर्नापनीतोऽतः प्रत्यङ्मोहोऽप्रमाणतः SV 1104ab
कर्मभिश्चाविरुद्धं यद्देवताद्रव्यतत्त्वगम् 3.3.101ab
कर्मभिस्तदसिद्धेर्हि वेदान्तज्ञानसिद्धितः 4.4.555cd

कर्मभ्य इव च ज्ञानात्फलप्राप्तिं सुनिश्चिताम् 1.4.1087ab
कर्मभ्य एव तत्सिध्येच्छ्रुतत्वात्कर्मणः श्रुतौ SV 32cd
कर्मभ्यः प्रव्रजिष्यन्वा प्रैष्यन्नित्यभिधीयते 1.5.288ab
कर्मभ्यः फलमिच्छद्भिरदृष्टं दृष्टमेव वा SV 1052ab
कर्मभ्योऽपि न मुक्तिः स्यात्कर्मापि न हि वस्तुनुत् 1.4.239ab
कर्मभ्यो जन्म नियतं जन्म चेन्निर्वृतिः कुतः 2.4.55ef
कर्मभ्यो जन्म नियतं जन्म चेन्निर्वृतिः कुतः 6.2.8cd
कर्मभ्यो निर्वृतिर्नास्तीत्यादिवाक्यैः प्रदर्शितम् SV 308cd
कर्ममन्त्रौषधितपःकालादीनां च विद्यते 1.4.1476ab
कर्मराशिगिरात्मापि यदि तत्र विवक्षितः 4.4.496ab
कर्मराशिरथेदानीं प्राण इत्यादिनोच्यते 5.16.15ab
कर्मवत्काङ्क्षते ज्ञानं विशिष्टं नाधिकारिणम् 1.4.1436cd
कर्म वा पितृयाणाप्तौ ते कीटाद्यामियुर्गतिम् 6.2.158cd
कर्मण्यध्वेषु कुर्वन्ति यथावस्त्वात्मबोधनम् 3.9.123cd
कर्मण्यध्वोपरोधेन ह्यन्यथात्वं प्रपद्यते 3.9.124cd
कर्मशब्देन विद्या च भावना कर्म चोच्यते 3.2.157cd
कर्मशास्त्रं व्यनक्तीति न तु वस्त्ववबोधकृत् SV 324cd
कर्मश्रुतानुरोधेन ह्यन्येभ्यो वा यथायथम् 4.4.85ab
कर्मसाधनरूपत्वाज्जायादेर्न पुमर्थता 1.4.1829ab
कर्म साध्वेव कर्तव्यमिच्छताभ्युदयं चिरम् 4.4.204ab
कर्म सिध्यद्यतो दृष्टं प्रधानं कर्म तेन तत् 3.2.162cd
कर्मस्वनियतो दृष्टो नान्यथा चोपपद्यते 1.4.1484cd
कर्मस्वरूपबोधे हि व्यापारो नेष्यते विधेः SV 758ab
कर्मस्वेव नियच्छन्ति देवताश्च न मुक्तिदाः 1.4.1693cd
कर्महीनेऽपि विदुषि स्यान्न वेत्यतिशङ्क्यते 1.3.371ab
कर्महेतुत्वतः कर्ताकर्ताप्यात्माभिधीयते 4.3.922cd
कर्महेतुविरुद्धं तु न वित्तं ज्ञानमिष्यते 4.4.1124ab
कर्महेतुविरुद्धत्वात्सम्यग्ज्ञानस्य कर्मणा 4.5.28ab
कर्माकर्मैव पुंसोऽस्य ह्यनुष्ठेयतयामृतेः 4.4.1227cd
कर्माङ्गता वा कल्प्या स्यादुद्गीथविधिवत्तदा SV 838cd
कर्माणि कर्मसंत्यागसामर्थ्यार्थं दिवानिशम् 4.4.1092ab
कर्माणि चापनुद्याशु प्रवव्राजाविचारयन् 4.5.24cd

कर्माणि मानवस्त्यक्तुं स करोतु यथाविधि 4.4.1091cd
कर्माण्यतो विधीयन्तेऽविद्यावन्तं नरं प्रति SV 164ab
कर्मातः कारणं मुक्तेर्न कथं चन युज्यते 3.3.42ab
कर्मातस्तेषु सर्वेषु प्रधानमिति भण्यते 3.2.163cd
कर्मातोऽनर्थकं मुक्तावेकदेशविकारयोः SV 260cd
कर्मादिपरतन्त्रत्वात्स्वाश्रयो नायमिष्यते 3.2.141ab
कर्मादिषु जगत्यस्मिंस्तानपेक्ष्यात उच्यते 4.4.440cd
कर्मादिहेतुजं रूपमतत्त्वं तदनन्वयात् 2.1.206ab
कर्मादिहेतुसाध्येषु गौणी लोकार्थता भवेत् 4.3.1834cd
कर्माधिकारवच्चात्र प्रवृत्तिरपि सेत्स्यति SV 756ab
कर्माधिकारविच्छेदि ज्ञानं चेदभ्युपेयते 3.5.90ab
कर्माधिकारहेतुर्मे जाया स्यात्कर्मसाधनम् 1.4.1824ab
कर्माधिकारहेतूनि स्वतोऽस्यानधिकारिणः SV 113cd
कर्माधिकृतिसंबन्धप्रतिपत्त्यर्थमेव तु 1.4.128cd
कर्माधिकृतिहेतुत्वादग्न्यादेर्देवतात्मनः 1.4.1694ab
कर्माध्यक्षः सर्वभूताधिवासः साक्षी चेता केवलो निर्गुणश्च SV 356cd
कर्मानपेक्षसंसिद्धेः कथं ते भवतो वद 4.4.1184cd
कर्मानाक्षिप्य नात्मानं तच्चापि लभते स्वतः 1.4.1831cd
कर्मानित्यं पृथग्रूपं नित्यं चानित्यबाधकम् SV 370cd
कर्मापेक्षा हि साध्येऽर्थे सिद्धेऽर्थे तदनर्थकम् SV 90cd
कर्मापेक्षितकर्त्रादिरूपविध्वंसकृन्न तु SV 336ab
कर्माभिचारिकं प्रोक्तं प्रसङ्गान्न प्रधानतः 6.4.65ab
कर्मारभावहै देवि सत्सुतोत्पत्तिसिद्धये 6.4.95ab
कर्मारभेत तेनैतन्मुक्तौ कर्म निरर्थकम् SV 261ef
कर्मारम्भे विकर्त्रैव स्वाश्रयस्य सदेष्यते 3.2.54ab
कर्मार्थद्योतिका वेह विद्यात्राप्यभिधीयते 4.4.604ab
कर्मालं सिद्धये लोके शिबिकोद्वहनं यथा 1.4.1600cd
कर्माविद्याविनिर्मुक्त एतस्मिन्नेव लक्ष्यते 4.3.1103ab
कर्माश्रयत्वतो लिङ्गादविद्वानिह गृह्यते 3.2.123ab
कर्मासनादि कुरुते तस्माच्च फलसंगतिः 4.3.19cd
कर्मिणः कर्मशेषत्वं स्वाराज्यं ब्रह्मवेदने 1.4.1696ab
कर्मिणोऽपि हि देवाप्तिर्ज्ञानादेव न कर्मणः 1.3.374ab

कर्मेतं कर्म तेनेदृग्विद्येतं न कथं चन 3.3.35ab
कर्मेदं तत उद्धृत्य चरुं स्थाल्याः समाहितः 6.4.86ab
कर्मेन्द्रियाणां सर्वेषां तत्सामान्येषु पञ्चसु 2.4.378cd
कर्मेन्द्रियाणां सर्वेषां वागेवात्रोपलक्षणम् 1.3.155ab
कर्मेन्द्रियाणां सार्थानां प्राणः कारणमुच्यते 4.4.175ab
कर्मेन्द्रियाणि सर्वाणि तथा बुद्धीन्द्रियाण्यपि 2.4.381cd
कर्मेप्सिततमं रूपं दृष्टेः कार्यत्वहेतुतः 3.4.171ab
कर्मेव ज्ञानमप्यत्र फलाभावादनर्थकम् SV 263cd
कर्मैतदेव कुर्वाणः काले चात्रैव भण्यते 1.4.677ab
कर्मैव कारणं केचित्फलप्राप्तौ प्रचक्षते 1.4.1487ab
कर्मैव वेदशास्त्रेऽस्मिन्प्रधानं निश्चितं यतः 4.4.203ab
कर्मैवाग्नेर्नियन्तृ स्यात्कर्मणो देवता तथा 1.4.1666cd
कर्मैवावधृतं यद्वत्कर्मान्तानां प्रयोजकः 4.4.212ab
कर्मैवैतत्त्रयं तच्च नात्मानं लभते यतः 3.8.32ab
कर्मैवोक्तेषु सर्वेषु प्रशशंसतुरादरात् 3.2.160cd
कर्मैवोपास्तिरूपं यत्तद्विद्येत्यत्र भण्यते 1.5.252cd
कर्मोत्थं न यतः किंचिद्ध्रुवं जगति वीक्ष्यते SV 38cd
कर्मोत्थत्वात्प्रमात्रादेस्तत्क्षये क्षयवत्त्वतः 2.1.317ab
कर्मोत्थफलबिम्बेन बिम्बितेयं मतिः सदा 4.3.1258cd
कर्मोत्था भावना याश्च रूपं ता अपि लिङ्गवत् 4.3.1224cd
कर्मोद्भावितसंस्कारस्तत्र स्वप्नरिरंसया 2.1.283cd
कर्मोपभोगसिद्ध्यर्थं परिच्छिन्नः स्वचक्षुषा 4.4.56ab
कर्मोपभोगसिद्ध्यर्थं वर्ण्यन्ते भूमयोऽधुना 4.3.834ab
कर्मोपसंहृतं श्रुत्या यथोक्तेनैव हेतुना 4.4.208cd
कर्मोपात्तानि भूतानि तत्प्रयुक्तानि देहिनः 4.3.1958ab
कर्मोपासनमुक्त्वाथ तत्फलोपदिदिक्षया 1.2.219ab
कर्षन्ति नासिकाग्रेण कर्णमूलं सुखेन ते 4.3.1184cd
कलञ्जभक्षणस्येव ननु न श्रौतकर्मणः 1.3.90ab
कलञ्जभक्षणेनातस्तन्निवृत्तौ निवर्तते 1.3.91cd
कलाकाष्ठालवाद्यात्मा विश्वं विपरिणामयन् 1.5.209cd
कलाभिरस्तः कृत्ताभिः कृकलास इति स्मृतः 1.5.212ab
कलावृद्धिक्षयाभ्यां तु पक्षयोरुभयोस्तथा 3.1.35ab

कलिङ्गारम्भसिद्ध्यर्थं वाय्वाकाशसमुद्भवः 2.3.47ab
कलुषत्वमिवापन्नं भेदरूपं प्रकाशते 3.5.44cd
कल्पं बुद्ध्वाथ तमृषिराजगाम महीपतिम् 4.1.3cd
कल्पकोटिसहस्राणि कुर्यात्कर्म महच्छुभम् 1.4.1680cd
कल्पनाधिक्यतश्चैतदपूर्वं नोपपद्यते 3.8.155ab
कल्पना नापि गौण्यत्र मुख्यार्थे सति युज्यते 1.4.1091ab
कल्पनाबीजविरहात्कल्पना न हि लभ्यते 4.3.1455ab
कल्पनामात्रनिष्पत्तेर्नापेक्षाज्ञानभूमिषु 1.4.500cd
कल्पनायाश्च वैफल्यमनित्यत्वे परात्मनः 5.1.75cd
कल्पनाहेत्वसद्भावे निराकाङ्क्षे तथा श्रुते 4.3.1818cd
कल्पनेतरतः सर्वं सम्यङ्मिथ्येति मानतः 4.3.481ab
कल्पनेयं वृथैव स्याद्ब्रह्मभावीति या कृता 1.4.1204cd
कल्पयित्वा निदिध्यासेत्तद्भावाविष्टधीः सदा 2.5.69cd
कल्पितं प्रसजेद्द्वैतं तोयबुद्धिरिवोषरे 5.1.31cd
कल्पितत्वादनेकत्वाद्रज्जुसर्पद्विचन्द्रवत् 4.3.1687cd
कल्पिताकल्पितं सर्वं यदात्मैवाभ्युपेयते 2.1.165ab
कल्पितेनाभिसंबन्धो न ह्यकल्पितवस्तुनः 4.4.519ab
कल्पितोपाधिहेतुश्चेदंशिसंसारिकल्पना 2.1.529ab
कल्प्य ईशोऽथवापूर्वं किं कल्प्यमुपपद्यते 3.8.155cd
कल्प्यते तद्वदेवेह प्रत्यक्षेणावबोधतः 3.3.99cd
कल्प्याविद्यैव मत्पक्षे सा चानुभवसंश्रया SV 182cd
कल्प्ये चादृष्टसामर्थ्ये नित्यानां कर्मणां त्वया 3.3.102ab
कल्याणं ते यदत्यर्थं रूपं यच्च तवैव तत् 5.17.9cd
कल्याणवदनोत्थं यत्कृत्स्नं देवेभ्य एव तत् 1.3.142ab
कल्याणादिति दृष्टान्तो यथा तद्वदिहापि च 4.4.141cd
कल्याणासङ्गसंबन्धाद्रागाद्यधर्मकारणम् 1.3.233ab
कल्याणेतररूपेण परिशिष्टेष्वपीक्ष्यते 1.3.158ab
कश्चिदप्यधिकार्यस्ति कृत्स्नेऽपि जगतीदृशः 1.6.92cd
कश्चिदर्थोऽत्र दृष्टोऽतो वस्तुनि स्यान्न मानतः SV 481cd
कश्चिदेति जगत्यस्मिन्नन्यत्रेश्वरहेतुतः 2.1.439cd
कश्चिद्बिभेत्यबिभेच्च तेनाविद्वान्प्रजापतिः 1.4.56cd
कषायं पाचयित्वा च श्रेणीस्थानेषु च त्रिषु 3.5.152ab

कषायं पाचयित्वा तु श्रेणीस्थानेषु च त्रिषु 1.4.1586ab
कषायपक्तिमापेक्ष्य विकल्पोऽयं त्रिधोदितः 3.5.155cd
कस्तर्हि क्रमहेतुः स्याद्देवताहेतुकोऽस्तु सः 4.3.1127ab
कस्मात्क्षयं न संयान्ति यवपूर्णकुसूलवत् 1.5.76cd
कस्मात्पुनरिदं त्यक्त्वा दृष्टादृष्टार्थसाधनम् 1.4.969ab
कस्मात्पुरुष इति चेत्पुरुषार्थं श्रुतिः स्वयम् 2.5.119ab
कस्मादविकलस्यैव दृष्ट्यादिर्न तथेक्ष्यते 4.3.148cd
कस्मादात्मन आगायेदिति हेतुरिहोच्यते 1.3.366ab
कस्मादिति च हेतूक्तिर्भीत्याचिक्षिप्सया परम् 1.4.66cd
कस्मादेतन्न तत्सर्वं यतोऽप्राणं तदक्षरम् 3.8.99cd
कस्माद्भयभेष्यदिति च पूर्वोक्तार्थसमर्थनम् 1.4.70ab
कस्माद्रागादयो नेति तत्परीक्षात ईर्यते 1.3.18cd
कस्मान्न गम्यते साक्षाज्जीवद्देहगतं यथा 4.3.127cd
कस्मान्न शब्दबोधोऽपि ह्यनुमानपुरःसरः SV 737cd
कस्मिंश्चित्करणे वृत्तिनिरोधः पर्वमीक्ष्यते 4.4.68ab
कस्मिन्काल इदं जन्तोः किंनिमित्तं च जायते 4.3.1924ab
कस्मिन्विषय ऐश्वर्यं तेषां स्यात्सोऽधुनोच्यते 1.4.1563cd
कस्य कर्मण इत्युक्ते यत्किंचेहेति तद्वचः 4.4.245ab
कस्य कामाय वा चातोऽप्यनात्माक्षिप्यतेऽखिलः 4.4.612cd
कस्यचिन्मुक्तयेऽलं स्यात्कस्यचित् त्र्यन्नवित्तये 1.5.344ab
कस्य दुःखनिवृत्त्यर्थं प्रारब्धोपनिषत्त्वया 1.4.598cd
कहोलब्राह्मणे नातस्तद्व्याख्यानाय यत्यते 4.4.1132cd
कहोलोषस्तवक्त्रोक्तौ प्रश्नाविति विनिर्णयः 3.5.8cd
काकोलूकनिशेवायं संसारोऽज्ञातमवेदिनोः 1.4.313ab
काठिन्यकारणध्वस्तौ खिल्यस्येह महोदधौ 2.4.407ab
काणकुण्ठादिविषये यत्तु कैश्चित्प्रकल्प्यते 4.4.1144ab
काणकुब्जादिविषया न्यासक्लृप्तिरतोऽशुभा 3.5.164cd
काण्डं विचारभूयिष्ठमधुनारभ्यते परम् 3.1.2cd
काण्डं स्याद्याज्ञवल्कीयं वंशस्तद्विषयस्तथा 6.5.4cd
काण्डद्वयसमाख्या हि तत्प्रमेयानुरोधतः SV 554cd
काण्डद्वयस्य वा योऽर्थः स संक्षिप्याभिधीयते 4.4.1318ab
काण्डद्वयेऽपि नैतस्मादन्योऽर्थः कश्चिदीक्ष्यते 1.4.1265cd

काण्डैश्चित्रा षडर्धैर्मधुमुनिखिलकैर्मस्करीन्द्रालिजुष्टा 6.5.22b
कातिशीतिरजातस्य विनाशागमने सति 4.3.597ab
कात्यायन्या सपत्न्या ते विभागं करवाण्यहम् 2.4.42cd
कादाचित्कोऽवबोधोऽस्य कुत इत्युच्यतां यथा 2.1.196cd
कानेषोऽवति पशुवत्कर्मभिः कैश्च सर्वदा 1.4.1781cd
काम एवेति तत्स्पष्टं स यथेति विभाव्यते 4.4.212cd
काम एष क्रोध एष इत्यादिवचनं स्मृतेः 1.4.1817ab
कामं क्रोधं तथा धर्मं तद्विरुद्धं च मोहतः 4.4.186ab
कामं घटाद्यभावोऽयं प्रत्यक्षादवसीयताम् 4.3.1695ab
कामं प्रवर्ततां कर्म न च दोषोऽत्र कश्चन 4.3.1032ab
कामं ह्युपनिषद्व्याख्या भवतु ब्राह्मणद्वयम् 2.1.426ab
कामः स एव बाह्येऽस्य विज्ञानात्मन इष्यते 4.3.1194cd
कामः संकल्प इत्याद्या मनसो धर्मिणः श्रुताः 2.3.134ab
कामः संकल्प इत्येवं तथा च प्राक्श्रुतीरणम् 4.4.380cd
कामः संकल्प इत्येवं मनोधर्मत्वसंश्रयात् SV 153cd
कामकर्मक्षये यस्मादमृतत्वं फलं श्रुतम् 1.4.1719ab
कामकर्मतमोभावादमरोऽमृत एव च 4.4.1335ab
कामकर्ममहामोहरहितं रूपमात्मनः 4.3.1304ab
कामकर्मात्मकासङ्गविविक्तत्वमिहोदितम् 4.3.1081cd
कामकर्मादिनिर्मुक्तं सुषुप्ते रूपमात्मनः 4.3.1202cd
कामकर्मादियन्नेदं मृत्योर्धर्मो भवेदतः 4.3.1330ab
कामकर्मादिविध्वस्तौ नाविद्यानर्थभुक्तये 1.4.1747ab
कामकर्मादिहानेऽपि यद्यविद्यावशिष्यते 3.2.95ab
कामकर्माद्यसद्भावात्पूर्ण आत्मावतिष्ठते 4.4.284ab
कामकामिप्रभेदेन प्रतीचोऽस्याप्तकामता 4.3.1341ab
कामकाम्यादि तस्यास्तु दृष्टिमात्रात्मनो न तु 4.4.476cd
कामक्लृप्तिरतो नेह प्रत्यगात्मनि युज्यते 4.4.460ab
कामक्रोधादिपूर्वैव कर्तृता पुण्यपापयोः 4.4.201ab
कामक्रोधादिभूयिष्ठः पुमानुग्रेण कर्मणा 4.4.197cd
कामक्षयप्रकर्षोऽत्र ह्युत्कृष्टाह्लादसाधनम् 4.3.1869cd
कामद्वेषादिसंभूतिर्मिथ्याज्ञानत्वकारणात् 4.4.216cd
कामप्रधानता चैवं प्रकृतार्थानुरोधिनी 4.4.238cd

कामप्रयुक्तो हि नरः संचिनोति शुभाशुभे 4.4.225ab
कामप्रविलयायातस्तद्विपक्षार्थभावनम् SV 349ab
कामप्रश्नः समाप्तोऽतो निराकाङ्क्षोऽभवन्नृपः 4.4.532ab
कामप्रश्नाङ्कुशेनैव मां वशीकृत्य मद्गतम् 4.3.1893ab
काममस्तु न तादृक्षु धीराणां सत्यधीर्भवेत् 2.1.529cd
कामयानः पूर्णफलमुत्पत्त्यादिविलक्षणम् 5.1.101cd
कामश्च वासनाः सर्वा माहारजनपूर्विकाः 3.2.52cd
कामस्य च प्रधानत्वात्तत्प्राधान्यानपायतः SV 524ab
कामस्यातः प्रधानत्वं तत्प्रयुक्तात्मसंसृतेः 4.4.241cd
कामहेतौ हि विध्वस्ते न कश्चिदवशिष्यते 4.4.379ab
कामाः पुनरिहोच्यन्ते य उक्ता वासनात्मकाः 4.4.396ab
कामाः सर्वेऽकाममिति तथापि पुनरुच्यते 4.3.1344cd
कामादयः स्वभावोऽस्य मृत्यवोऽथ न वा भवेत् 4.3.965ab
कामादयो यतो धर्माः स्वान्तस्यैवेह कीर्तिताः 4.4.239ab
कामादिधर्मसिद्ध्यर्थं काम इत्याद्यथोच्यते 1.5.108cd
कामादिप्रविवेके हि मोक्षयोग्यत्वमात्मनः 4.3.969cd
कामादिमयतोक्त्येह तदिदानीं विभाव्यते 4.4.185cd
कामादिविषयासक्तेर्न किंचिद्विविनक्ति यत् 4.3.1056ab
कामादिहेतुकः शोकः कामाद्यज्ञानहेतुकम् 4.3.1346ab
कामादीनामनर्थानां प्रतीचि शतशः श्रुतौ 4.4.459ab
कामादेरात्मनोऽन्यत्वे तच्चापि स्यात्प्रबाधितम् 4.4.480cd
कामाद्यशेषबीजात्माप्रज्ञातात्मैकतत्त्वकः 1.4.1822ab
कामाद्यशेषोपाधीनां निवृत्तौ न निवर्तते 4.3.1755ab
कामाद्यात्मगुणश्चेत्स्यादनिर्मोक्षः प्रसज्यते 4.3.970ab
कामाद्याश्रयतोक्त्यार्थात्सा त्वया बाधिता भवेत् 4.4.479cd
कामानशनबोधार्थं वेदव्यासोऽपि यत्नतः 4.4.1058ab
कामानामपि नाशः स्याद्ग्रहातिग्रहरूपिणाम् 4.4.383cd
कामापहतबुद्धीनामेवमाद्या विकल्पनाः 4.4.565cd
कामाभावे च तद्धानिं योऽकामश्चेति चावदत् 1.4.174cd
कामा यस्य न विद्यन्ते दृष्टानुश्रविका बहिः 4.4.265ab
कामा येऽस्य हृदीत्यादि तीर्णो हीति तथा वचः 2.3.135cd
कामास्तेऽस्य प्रमुच्यन्त इत्येतत्प्रागपीरितम् 4.4.410cd

कामास्ते कतम इति तद्विशेषणमुच्यते 4.4.393cd
कामिकामप्रभेदस्य प्रसक्ताविदमुच्यते 4.4.273ab
कामितादि्वषयान्नान्यस्तदा तस्येह रोचते 4.4.229ab
कामितार्थस्य लब्धत्वात्सर्वग्रहणमात्रतः 5.16.25ab
कामितार्थस्य संसिद्धिः कर्मिणां कामिनामिह 1.4.1643ab
कामितार्थस्य संसिद्धेर्लौकिकादेव मानतः SV 455cd
कामिनं दुःखिनं मूढं योऽविलुप्ताक्ष ईक्षते 4.4.469ab
कामिनाप्यग्निहोत्रादि शूद्रेणानधिकारिणा SV 292ab
कामेहाभावनाज्ञानपदार्थानां यथाक्रमम् 4.3.1196ab
कामैकक्षयतन्त्रैव यस्मात्पुंसः सुखोन्नतिः 4.3.1868ab
कामैकपाशाकृष्टः सन्निच्छयैव प्रवर्तते SV 592ab
कामो गर्धोऽभिलाषश्च तृष्णेत्येकार्थवाचकाः 4.4.226ab
कामोच्छित्तिमकृत्वा च संन्यसन्ति भवद्विधाः 2.4.58cd
कामोपायत्वमेवाथ नेष्टं यदि च कर्मणाम् SV 420ab
कामो विवर्धते पुंसस्तावत्तावत्सुखं हृदि 4.3.1867cd
काम्यकर्मफलानां हि तथा तत्साधनस्य च 3.3.110cd
काम्यकर्मफलैर्नित्यफलस्येत्यभिधीयताम् 3.3.120cd
काम्यकर्मापि नैवेह मुमुक्षोः संभवत्यतः 4.4.1210cd
काम्यमेवाखिलं पाङ्क्तं कर्मेत्येवं प्रकृत्य तु 1.5.337ab
काम्याग्निहोत्रवन्नित्यं काम्यं चापि प्रसज्यते 3.3.85ab
काम्यात्स्वर्गादिकं मा भूदक्रियायां तदुद्भवम् SV 79ab
काम्यादिकर्मवत्तेषां मनोव्याक्षेपहेतुतः 4.4.1230ab
काम्यादिवर्जनं त्वेतत्स्वमतिप्रभवं यतः SV 77ab
काम्यादिवर्जनादिभ्यस्तस्याः सिद्धिश्च वर्ण्यते SV 47cd
काम्यानां ह्यन्यतमं पक्षमाश्रित्य भण्यते 6.4.80cd
काम्यानामिह निर्देशस्तज्जिहासाप्रसिद्धये 4.4.1051cd
काम्येऽपि शुद्धिरस्त्येव भोगसिद्ध्यर्थमेव सा SV 1130ab
काम्येव हि यतोऽजस्रं संसरत्यविचक्षणः 4.4.255cd
काम्यैर्दक्षिणमन्वेति ज्ञानयुक्तैस्तथोत्तरम् SV 1111ab
काम्यैर्वा यदि वा नित्यैः सर्वैर्वा मुक्तिरिष्यते 3.3.45ab
कायस्यापि न चैतन्यमेवमेव विशेषणम् 4.3.205ab
कारकं चानपाश्रित्य न क्रियेह प्रसिद्ध्यति 2.4.475cd

कारकं ज्ञापकं शास्त्रं तयोः स्यादेकता कथम् SV 823cd
कारकं नाप्यसिद्धत्वान्नाप्यन्यदनिरूपणात् SV 623cd
कारकं वा क्रियान्यद्वा कारणं कार्यमेव च 2.3.180cd
कारकं वा क्रिया वा स्याद्यदि वा स्यात्क्रियाफलम् SV 1044ab
कारकं वापि कार्यत्वं लभते न स्वतन्त्रतः SV 515cd
कारकं सत्तथैकात्म्यं न कथं चन वीक्षते 3.4.162ab
कारकत्वं न संभाव्यं तन्मोहविरहात्क्वचित् 1.4.817cd
कारकत्वमविद्योत्थं स्वतश्चाकारकात्मता 1.4.762cd
कारकत्वमृतेऽविद्यां कूटस्थस्यात्मनः कुतः 3.4.161cd
कारकत्वेऽप्यकार्यत्वाद्दुःसंभाव्यं त्वयोदितम् 3.9.184cd
कारकव्यवहारे हि शुद्धं वस्तु न वीक्ष्यते SV 166ab
कारकव्यवहारोऽयमविद्याविषयः सदा 2.1.377ab
कारकव्यापृतिस्तत्र निपुणेनापि नेक्ष्यते 1.4.323cd
कारकाकारकधियोर्नैकदैकत्र वस्तुनि SV 167ab
कारकाणां क्रियापेक्षा नोभयापेक्षितात्मनि 1.4.815cd
कारकाणां स्वभावोऽयं यदकृत्वा प्रवर्तनम् 4.3.1589ab
कारकाणां हि सत्यत्वं स्वकार्यापेक्षयेष्यते 1.4.432ab
कारकाणि विनोत्पत्तौ प्रयोगमनुरुध्यते 3.8.32cd
कारकाण्युपमृद्नाति विद्या बीजमिवोषरम् 3.4.137ab
कारकाण्युपमृद्नाति विद्या बीजमिवोषरम् 4.4.262ab
कारकाण्युपमृद्नाति विद्या बुद्धिमिवोषरे 1.4.762ab
कारकादिर्यथा भ्रान्तिस्तथा पूर्वमवादिषम् 2.1.412ab
कारकादिवशाद्यावत्किंचिद्वस्तूपलभ्यते 3.4.135ab
कारकादिविधर्मापि प्रत्यगज्ञानहेतुजैः 4.3.1629ab
कारकादिविभागस्य वस्तु पूर्णं स्वतो यतः 4.3.714cd
कारकादेरसद्भावात्सुषुप्ते परमार्थतः 4.3.1628cd
कारकाद्यन्यतो मोहान्नात्मानं प्रति ढौकते 2.1.306cd
कारकाद्यभ्युपगतौ मुक्तौ ब्रह्मणि केवले 3.9.195cd
कारकाद्यात्मना सेयमविद्यैव प्रकाशते 2.4.476cd
कारकैः शक्यते लोके तद्विकल्पस्य गोचरः 5.1.68cd
कारणं च तमस्व्यात्मा नातः स्वप्ने मनस्थितिः 4.3.896cd
कारणं चात्मनो नान्यत्रय्यन्तेषूपलभ्यते 3.8.24cd

कारणं जगतः साक्षी नियन्तेति च भण्यते 3.4.86cd
कारणं तर्हि बुद्ध्यादेरात्मेत्यत्र प्रसज्यते 4.3.335ab
कारणं त्वन्यदेवातो यतः श्रुतिरभाषत 4.3.1889cd
कारणं न विहायेह कार्यमन्यत्र वर्तते 1.4.139cd
कारणं प्रत्यगज्ञानं कार्यं संसार उच्यते 3.5.95ab
कारणं रसशब्देन यस्मादत्राभिधीयते 2.3.49cd
कारणं सत्स्वकार्येषु नियन्तृत्वं प्रपद्यते 3.9.3cd
कारणत्रितयेनाथ एकैकस्य प्रसिध्यति 1.2.86ab
कारणत्वं न कौटस्थ्यात्तन्मोहविरहाद्भवेत् 3.4.87ab
कारणत्वं प्रमाणेन यस्य साक्षाद्विनिश्चितम् 2.4.322ab
कारणत्वं सुविस्पष्टं श्रुतौ हि बहुशः श्रुतम् 1.4.237cd
कारणत्वनिषेधाय तथानपरगीरियम् 2.5.139cd
कारणत्वनिषेधेन ब्रह्मात्मानं प्रपद्यते 3.4.40cd
कारणत्वसमानत्वस्वात्मलाभत्वहेतुभिः 1.6.9ab
कारणत्वात्सदन्यस्य कार्यत्वाच्च सततस्तथा 1.4.198ab
कारणत्वाद्धि तत्स्थं तत्तदृते कारणं कथम् 1.2.89cd
कारणत्वाविशेषेऽपि किं प्रधानमितीक्षणे 3.2.161ab
कारणप्रतिषेधेन कृत्स्नकार्यनिषेधतः 3.8.100ab
कारणप्रवणं सर्वं कार्यं दृष्टं जगत्यपि 1.2.202ab
कारणस्य तथा कार्यमन्तोऽनादेः प्रसिद्धितः 2.4.414ab
कारणस्य त्वनुत्पत्तेरनिषेधस्तथा सति 1.2.3cd
कारणस्य न नास्तित्वमुक्तहेत्वोरसंभवात् 1.2.4cd
कारणस्य निषेधोऽतो भयकार्यनिषेधतः 4.4.1335ef
कारणस्य निषेधोक्तिरनन्तमिति यद्वचः 2.4.413ab
कारणस्य स्वकार्यैश्च तदबोधसमन्वयात् 4.3.385cd
कारणस्यापि नास्तित्वं कार्यासत्त्वे प्रसज्यते 1.2.80ab
कारणस्याप्यपह्नुत्यै नेतीत्यात्मानमब्रवीत् 4.4.426cd
कारणस्याप्यविद्याया वस्तुबोधाद्विनाशतः SV 391ab
कारणस्यास्तिता तस्मात्सिद्धा कार्योद्भवात्पुरा 1.2.73cd
कारणात्मनि संसिद्धे सर्वं सिद्धं भवेद्यतः 3.8.129cd
कारणात्मनि संसृष्टं नान्यथातोऽस्य संस्थितिः 3.8.33cd
कारणात्मा जगत्कृत्स्नं श्रौतदर्शनसाधनः 1.3.272ab

कारणात्मा यतस्तस्माज्जाग्रत्स्वप्नाख्यकार्यकृत् 4.3.979cd
कारणात्मा यतोऽभावः कार्याख्यस्येह वस्तुनः 4.3.1520cd
कारणात्मा हि संवर्त्य कार्यात्मत्वं प्रपद्यते 4.3.399cd
कारणात्मैव जगतः समानोक्त्याभिधीयते 2.4.389ab
कारणादक्षरादन्नं पुरुषेणेह कर्मणा 3.2.64ab
कारणादल्पमेव स्यात्तद्व्याप्तेरदितिर्यतः 1.2.190ab
कारणादिधियः पूर्वं प्रतीचि ब्रह्मधीस्ततः 2.4.438cd
कारणादिनिषेधेन न चाद्वैतमभीप्सितम् 1.2.28ab
कारणाद्यखिलं विश्वं देवतावधि भण्यते 4.1.21cd
कारणाद्या निषिध्यन्ते क्रमेण प्राप्त्यपेक्षया 3.8.72cd
कारणानन्तरत्वाच्च तथा स्वच्छस्वभावतः 4.3.358ab
कारणानां यथोक्तानां यच्च तौ प्रशशंसतुः 3.2.160ab
कारणानामिदं वृत्तं यन्निमित्तान्तराश्रयात् 2.1.179ab
कारणानुविधायित्वात्फलमप्यस्तु चेत्तथा 3.3.119cd
कारणान्तस्य जगत ओतप्रोतौक्तिततस्तथा 1.4.965cd
कारणान्नान्यतः कार्यं तथा कार्याच्च कारणम् 1.4.498ab
कारणान्यसमर्थानि यथा देहमृते मृतौ 4.3.1141ab
कारणान्वयवद्बुद्धेश्चिदाभासोऽपि सर्वदा 4.3.93ab
कारणेऽनुपयुक्तं यत्कार्यं तन्नेह विद्यते 4.4.1311ab
कारणेतररूपेण तयोरव्यभिचारतः 1.4.386cd
कारणेन हि पाल्यन्ते कार्याणीह यतस्ततः 4.4.1010ab
कारणे पाप्मवेधोऽभूद्यो वाचि प्राक्प्रजापतेः 1.3.151cd
कारणैकत्वसंपत्तेः स्वतःसिद्धत्वहेतुतः SV 256cd
कात्स्न्र्यात्तदन्ययाथात्म्यात्पश्यन्नपि न पश्यति 4.3.1493cd
कात्स्न्र्यात्सर्वो भवेदेष चिन्मात्रत्वात्तथानुभूः 2.5.145cd
कात्स्न्र्येन तस्य चोक्तत्वादतस्तदभिधीयते 1.3.346cd
कात्स्न्र्येन यत्र वृत्तिः स्याद्व्याप्यव्यापकवस्तुनोः 3.4.97ab
कात्स्न्र्येन वा परिणमेत्क्षीरद्रव्यादिवत्परः 2.1.477ab
कात्स्न्र्येन विद्या स्वभ्यस्ता फलायालमुपासितुः 5.16.76ab
कात्स्न्र्येनावसितिर्भोक्तुः शेत इत्यभिधीयते 2.1.244cd
कात्स्न्र्येनैवाभिसंबन्धादात्मीयस्येह वस्तुनः 1.6.15cd
कार्पासबीजसंस्थैव योक्ता रक्तादिवासना 4.3.693ab

कार्य ऐक्ये यतोऽमीषां व्यवहारो न सिध्यति 4.3.545cd
कार्यं कारणतन्त्रं स्यात्ततस्तस्यात्मलाभतः 2.4.119ab
कार्यं कारणवत्तस्मादुपचारात्समीरितम् 4.3.986cd
कार्यं चाक्रियमाणं सन्न कार्यत्वं समश्नुते 1.4.197ab
कार्यं चान्यपरं चेति द्वयमेतद्विरुध्यते SV 801ab
कार्यं चैतन्यबिम्बेन प्रविष्टं जलचन्द्रवत् 1.4.1312cd
कार्यं तदपि विषयमीक्षेतासाध्यरूपतः SV 615ab
कार्यं नाक्रियमाणं सन्नाकुर्वत्कारणं तथा 4.3.1600ab
कार्यं प्रयोजनार्था च प्रवृत्तिरिति युज्यते SV 519cd
कार्यं यन्नापि भावार्थात्तदावृत्तिगुणात्कथम् SV 808cd
कार्यं येऽनुभवं प्राहुर्वाच्यं तैः कार्यसाधनम् 1.4.320cd
कार्यं विना नाधिकारी नापीज्याफलसंगमः SV 20cd
कार्यं सर्वं यतो दृष्टं प्रागभावपुरःसरम् 1.4.338ab
कार्यं सर्वं यथा लोके तथेहाप्यवसीयताम् 1.4.347cd
कार्यं स्वकारणस्थं च न त्वात्मस्थमकारणात् 4.3.1319cd
कार्यं स्वेनात्मना सिद्धं पुमर्थं साधयेद्यदि SV 627ab
कार्यकरणयोः सिद्धिरन्योऽन्याव्यतिरेकतः SV 99cd
कार्यकर्तव्यता कार्येत्येवमेवातिरिच्यते SV 631ab
कार्यकारणगे तत्त्वे नाम लब्धास्पदं यतः 2.3.253ab
कार्यकारणगो भेदः प्राप्तो लोके य ईक्ष्यते 1.6.16ab
कार्यकारणतां यात आत्माप्येवं तमोवशात् 2.4.425ab
कार्यकारणता न स्यात्स्वतो भेदेन सिद्धयोः SV 61ab
कार्यकारणताभेदस्तयोः स्याद्भिन्नकालतः 4.3.653cd
कार्यकारणतारूपस्तमप्येषोऽतिवर्तते 4.3.1320cd
कार्यकारणताहीना तस्मात्संविर्प्रतीयताग् 3.4.118cd
कार्यकारणनाशेऽपि स्वतःसिद्धमनन्यगम् 2.4.452ab
कार्यकारणनिर्मुक्तमक्षरं वक्ष्यते यतः 3.8.19cd
कार्यकारणपक्षेऽपि कार्यं नान्यत्र कारणात् SV 353ab
कार्यकारणबुद्धौ ताविष्येते विश्वतैजसौ 1.4.712ab
कार्यकारणभावश्च न च वः स्यादभीप्सितः 4.3.634cd
कार्यकारणभावोऽयं यस्मिन्नुक्ते समाप्यते 3.7.25cd
कार्यकारणभूताभ्यां प्रत्यङ्नेदीय ईक्ष्यते 1.4.720cd

कार्यकारणभेदेन तदविद्यैव संस्थिता 4.4.995cd
कार्यकारणभेदेन प्रपञ्चो यः पुरोदितः 1.4.206ab
कार्यकारणभेदोऽयं ब्रह्मास्मीतिप्रबोधतः 2.4.420cd
कार्यकारणयोः शास्त्रं पूर्णमित्यादिनावदत् 5.1.61cd
कार्यकारणयोः स्पष्टं मृत्युनैवेति सादरा 1.2.6cd
कार्यकारणयोरेवं निषेधान्नेतिवाक्यतः 4.4.427ab
कार्यकारणयोरेवं भिन्नाभिन्नविकल्पतः 1.4.631ab
कार्यकारणयोर्ज्ञेया द्वैताद्वैतस्वभावयोः 5.1.55cd
कार्यकारणयोर्ध्वस्तावपूर्वाद्युक्तिबोधतः 5.1.24ab
कार्यकारणयोर्नित्यमभेदोऽध्यवसीयते 1.4.194cd
कार्यकारणयोर्बाह्यमबाह्यमिति वार्यते 2.5.140cd
कार्यकारणयोर्भित्तौ कार्यकारणता कुतः SV 258ab
कार्यकारणयोश्चेष्टा पूर्णात्पूर्णमितीर्यते 5.1.15ab
कार्यकारणयोस्तत्त्वं प्रत्यगात्मा चितिर्यतः 3.4.151ab
कार्यकारणयोस्तत्त्वं यस्मादात्मैव निर्द्वयः 4.4.641ab
कार्यकारणयोस्तत्त्वमुभयोरविलक्षणम् 2.4.302cd
कार्यकारणरूपः संस्तद्विरुद्धैकरूपिणा 4.3.1317ab
कार्यकारणरूपस्य तदेवालम्बनं मतम् 3.4.144cd
कार्यकारणरूपस्य निष्ठानन्दः परो मतः 3.9.206cd
कार्यकारणरूपस्य संसारस्य मृषात्मनः 3.7.56ab
कार्यकारणरूपाभ्यामतद्वत्तत्त्विका ततः 1.4.309ab
कार्यकारणरूपेण कर्मैतत्प्रथते जगत् 4.3.911ab
कार्यकारणरूपेण क्वचिद्व्याचक्षते तथा 1.4.949cd
कार्यकारणरूपेण तस्या एषोपसंहृतिः 1.5.163cd
कार्यकारणरूपेण द्वयोरव्यतिरेकतः 1.4.362ab
कार्यकारणरूपेण भोज्यभोक्तृतयोदितम् 2.5.31ab
कार्यकारणरूपेण मिथोपेक्षाश्रयं तमः 2.4.424cd
कार्यकारणरूपेण यदेतद्वेददर्शनम् 4.4.414ab
कार्यकारणरूपोऽयं मोहवृत्तानुरोधतः 4.4.299cd
कार्यकारणवज्जग्ध्वा द्रष्टैवैकोऽवशिष्यते 2.4.440cd
कार्यकारणवत्पीत्वा स्वात्मनैवावतिष्ठते 2.4.308cd
कार्यकारणवद्रूपं समुत्थायेति शब्द्यते 2.4.423ab

कार्यकारणवद्वस्तु क्षरमत्र निषिध्यते 3.8.63cd
कार्यकारणवद्वस्तु नानपास्तं तमोऽप्यतः SV 1115cd
कार्यकारणविध्वस्तौ ब्रह्मैकात्म्यप्रबोधतः 2.4.416ab
कार्यकारणसंबन्धः साविद्यस्यैव युक्तिमान् 1.4.102ab
कार्यकारणसंबन्धव्याजमाश्रित्य तत्परम् 5.1.7ab
कार्यकारणसंबन्धान्मुक्तिस्तत्र सुदुर्लभा 4.4.767cd
कार्यकारणसंबन्धे चिदाभासस्य संगतेः 3.4.90cd
कार्यज्ञेयसमाप्तिः स्यात्प्रत्यग्याथात्म्यबोधतः 2.4.102cd
कार्यताकार्यता वात्र मेयायत्ता न मानतः SV 716cd
कार्यता वा कुतोऽस्य स्यान्न चेत्कारणतन्त्रता SV 70ab
कार्यतोऽपि न भेदः स्याद्वस्त्वभेदव्यवस्थितेः SV 957cd
कार्यत्वात्कारणं मुक्त्वा न हि तत्कार्यसंभवः 1.3.183cd
कार्यत्वाद्द्वयमप्येतद्यतो न स्वाश्रयं ततः 3.9.89ab
कार्यत्वान्नेन्द्रियेष्वेव विषयप्रलयो भवेत् 2.4.355cd
कार्यत्वान्नैव धूमादिरेति निश्चयहेतुताम् 4.3.757ab
कार्यत्वेऽपि च धूमादेर्न सोंऽशोऽनुमितौ मतः 4.3.756ab
कार्यत्वे चानवस्था स्यात्कुर्वच्चापि सुदुर्लभम् 4.3.1448cd
कार्यधर्माननतीत्यैतांस्तद्धेतोरप्यतिक्रमात् 3.9.99ab
कार्यबुद्धिव्यपेक्षातो नानुभूत्यात्मवस्तुनः SV 468cd
कार्यबुद्ध्यैव संव्याप्तिः प्रवृत्तेर्न च गम्यते SV 745ab
कार्यभूमिगतो ह्यात्मा सुषुप्तं प्रसमीक्ष्यते 4.3.1052ab
कार्यमारभते शक्तिर्यत्किंचेह व्यवस्थिता SV 98cd
कार्यमुक्त्योः क्वचिद्दृष्टं स्वतःप्रामाण्यबाधनात् SV 848cd
कार्यमुत्पत्तिमत्त्वाच्चेत्प्रागुत्पत्तेर्निषिध्यते 1.2.3ab
कार्यमेतदविद्यायाः प्रोद्भूतायाः प्रदर्शितम् 4.3.1270ab
कार्यमेतदविद्यायाः श्रुत्या व्याख्यायतेऽखिलम् 4.4.418cd
कार्यमेव तु पिण्डादि तस्य कार्येष्वनन्वयात् 1.2.51cd
कार्यरूपाभिधाभेदादतीतानागतेष्विव 4.3.1696ab
कार्यलिङ्गसमुच्छित्तिः फलं नाद्यसमुच्चितेः 1.4.1738ab
कार्यलिङ्गाद्धि शक्तीनामस्तित्वं कारणत्वतः 4.3.1781ab
कार्यश्चेत्कारणोच्छेदे कार्योच्छेदः स्वतो न हि SV 387cd
कार्यसिद्ध्या फलावाप्तावशेषफलसंभवः SV 650ab

कार्यस्य कारणव्याप्तेर्न सुषुप्तपरोक्षता 4.3.1052cd
कार्यस्य रूपभूतस्य कर्मणः करणस्य च 1.3.295ab
कार्यस्य शक्तितन्त्रत्वे सर्वदा कारणस्थितेः SV 67ab
कार्यस्यान्तर्यतो दृष्टं सर्वत्रैव च कारणम् 4.3.335cd
कार्यस्यापि च नित्यत्वं वचनाच्चेत्प्रसिध्यति 4.3.1574ab
कार्यस्यापि च बुद्ध्यादेस्तद्धेतोरविभागतः 4.3.1524ab
कार्यस्यापि यथास्तित्वं तथेदानीं प्रपञ्च्यते 1.2.74ab
कार्यस्यापि स्वभावत्वं भवेदात्मीयवाचके 4.3.763cd
कार्यस्यैव न कार्यत्वमकार्ये कार्यतेष्यते SV 617cd
कार्यांशाद्यभिसंबन्धान्मानमेयत्वसंगतिः 4.3.552ab
कार्याकार्यादि यत्साक्षात्प्रमाणात्प्रसमीक्षते 4.3.1055ab
कार्याणां कारणं मुक्त्वा नान्यत्रास्त्यप्ययो यतः 4.2.84ab
कार्याणां कारणे वृत्तिर्नान्यत्र जगतीक्ष्यते 4.4.376ef
कार्याणां मारणान्मृत्युः कारणं प्रथितं भुवि 3.2.18cd
कार्यात्मकं मनोऽवादि कार्यत्वात्कटकुम्भवत् 1.2.32cd
कार्यात्मना यतस्तस्मादात्माज इति भण्यते 4.4.1325cd
कार्यात्मा कारणात्मा च द्वावात्मानौ परात्मनः 2.4.242ab
कार्यात्मा कारणात्मा च यदर्थौ भवतः सदा 2.5.57ab
कार्यात्मापचयं गच्छन्यत्र निष्ठां निगच्छति 2.4.418ab
कार्याद्यदि तु मानत्वं मानत्वात्कार्यनिष्ठता SV 891ab
कार्यानुमेयं तद्विद्यात्पूर्णमात्रसतत्त्वकम् 5.1.13cd
कार्यान्तरं न संभाव्यं नितरां वस्त्वपाक्रिया 1.4.424cd
कार्यान्तरं न संभाव्यं व्यर्थं चापि भवेद्वचः 2.1.523cd
कार्यान्तरं भवेद्वङ्गात्तेनाप्यावृतता घटे 1.2.106cd
कार्यान्तरसमुत्पत्तौ कर्मणोऽपि न विद्यते 3.3.33cd
कार्यान्तरस्य चाभावात्कार्यार्थैकाभिधायिनः SV 606ab
कार्यान्तरेण संस्थानान्मृदादेर्नोपलभ्यते 1.2.91ab
कार्यान्वयित्वे सर्वेषामपि चेह परस्परम् SV 607ab
कार्याभावादयुक्तं चेन्नोक्तिबुद्धेस्तथार्थतः 1.3.73ab
कार्यार्थता ततश्चेष्टा हीयेतानुष्ठितिं विना SV 613ab
कार्येऽपि कार्यतैवं च भवेद्विषयहेतुका SV 615cd
कार्येऽप्यनुपयुक्तं यन्न तत्कारणमुच्यते 4.4.1311cd

कार्ये कार्यान्तराभावात्कार्यबुद्धिः कुतो भवेत् SV 612ab
कार्येतरानवसितिः संभूतौ युगपत्तयोः 1.4.324cd
कार्ये प्रविष्टः स्रष्टैव पुमान्वेश्मेव तत्कृतम् 1.4.534cd
कार्ये यथा प्रमाणत्वमैकात्म्येऽप्येवमिष्यताम् SV 890cd
कार्येष्वपि च सर्वेषु कर्तृत्वं यत्समीक्ष्यते 1.4.348ab
कार्यैकनीडमेवास्य चिदाभासैकहेतुतः 4.3.405ab
कार्यैकमात्रनिष्ठत्वात्प्रमाणस्यागमात्मनः SV 478ab
कार्यैकविषयैवेयं वाक्यस्यातः प्रमाणतः SV 483cd
कार्यैकव्यतिषङ्गे च वाक्याद्भूतानुवादकात् SV 605ab
कार्यैर्मान्तरगम्यैः सा न कथंचिद्विशिष्यते SV 713cd
कार्योऽत्र वचसा बाधः केवलो नान्य इष्यते 4.4.529cd
कार्योत्पत्तिः सदैव स्यान्निदाघे घर्मवद्यतः SV 67cd
कार्योत्पत्तिस्थितिलयाः प्राप्नुयुर्युगपत्सदा 1.2.82cd
कार्योत्पत्तौ स्वतन्त्रत्वं कारणस्यैव निश्चितम् 4.4.829ab
कार्त्स्न्येन हृदय एव पिण्डीभावं व्रजत्यतः 4.4.53ef
कार्श्यं प्रापय्य पूर्वोक्तैर्जरारोगादिहेतुभिः 4.4.7cd
कार्श्यसंमोहरूपा या प्रसिद्धा जगतीदृशी 4.4.14cd
कार्श्यसंमोहसंबन्धो यतो नास्य स्वतस्ततः 4.4.11ab
कार्ष्ण्येनेव वियद्योगः खवृत्तापेक्षया त्वसन् 1.4.1322ab
कालदैवेश्वरादिभ्यः कालादेस्तत्प्रयुक्तितः 3.2.156cd
कालभागैर्भवेद्योग इति नः सिद्धसाध्यता 4.3.588cd
कालमन्त्रौषधादीनामचिन्त्या शक्तिरिष्यते 1.4.1475cd
काललोकादिवपुषस्त्वश्वस्याग्नेश्च सांप्रतम् 1.2.210ab
कालश्च द्विविधः प्रोक्त एकोऽहोरात्रलक्षणः 3.1.31ab
कालस्य जरणादात्मा श्रुतौ कालंजरो मतः 4.4.637cd
कालात्कर्मातिरेकेण मृत्योर्मुक्तिरिहोच्यते 3.1.27cd
कालात्मना ह्यवच्छेदान्नायं कालंजरत्वतः 4.4.1328ab
कालादावमखाङ्गत्वान्नाश्वदृष्टिर्विधित्स्यते 1.1.3cd
कालादिप्रविभक्तं सद्यद्ब्रह्माभूदविद्यया 1.4.1413ab
कालादिविषयं ज्ञानं ध्वंसिनः कर्मणः कुतः 3.2.148cd
कालादीनां गुणानां च कर्मण्यस्मिन्समुच्चयः 6.3.8ab
काला देवादयस्तस्यां ध्वस्तायां तद्विनाशतः 1.4.1504ab

कालादौ तदभावोऽतो न ज्ञानस्यापवादकृत् 2.4.257cd
कालाद्यन्तरितं यत्स्यात्प्राप्त्युत्पत्त्यादिलक्षणम् 1.4.1507cd
कालाद्यव्यवधानत्वान्न ह्यात्मस्थमतीतभाक् 1.4.300cd
कालोपबन्धः किंत्वत्र कार्यबुद्धिविघातकृत् SV 508ab
कालो विधीयते चास्य मन्थाख्यस्येह कर्मणः 6.3.6ab
का वा कार्येऽस्ति ते युक्तिः शास्त्रं चेदुभयोः समम् SV 852ab
का वा युक्तिः प्रदीपस्य सर्पाद्याकम्पनाशनम् SV 830ab
का विद्या सफला साक्षात्तवेतिप्रश्नवादिनम् 3.9.68ab
काश्याभिप्रायतोऽनस्य भोज्यतैव न भोक्तृता 2.1.102cd
किं कारणं पुमान्यस्माद्यथाकारी भवत्ययम् 4.4.194ab
किं कारणात्मतामेति किं वा केनचिदात्मना 3.2.131ab
किं ग्राह्यज्ञानगम्यत्वं किं वा ग्राहकगम्यता 4.3.516cd
किं च सिद्धत्वसंबन्धादैकात्म्ये मान्तरानुमा SV 711ab
किं चातो यदि नामैवं प्रकृतार्थोपयोगि यत् 2.1.544ab
किं चाध्यस्ताहिदृष्टस्य तद्विषव्याप्तचेतसः SV 584ab
किं तदाप्युक्तमार्गेण मुक्तिः किं वा क्रियाश्रयात् SV 253cd
किं तद्ब्रह्मानुगं सर्वं किं वा तस्माद्विविच्यते 2.4.10ab
किं तत्पन्नस्य सापेक्ष्यादधिकारेण संगतिः SV 758cd
किं तेन न कृतं पापं चोरेणात्मापहारिणा 2.4.253ab
किं न पश्यसि संसारं तत्रैवाज्ञानकल्पितम् 1.4.1279cd
किं न्वेतदिति जिज्ञासोर्निषिद्धेऽप्यन्यथाग्रहे 1.4.466ab
किं पुनः स्यात्समानत्वमात्मबुद्ध्यादिवस्तुनोः 4.3.389ab
किं पुनस्तत्सत्यमिति सत्यं चक्षुरितीर्यते 5.16.30ab
किं प्रमाणमहंरूपमुतात्मैवेति कथ्यताम् SV 1071ab
किं बलं समुपाश्रित्य शुद्ध्यादेरर्थवादता 1.3.44cd
किं भावात्कार्यता भिन्ना लडादिर्यां न भाषते SV 508cd
किं भोः शब्दादिभेदेन खस्यैकत्वं विरुध्यते 2.1.593ab
किं भोः सदपि मानेन वस्तु साक्षान्निरस्यते 1.4.423ab
किं मानसंगतेरर्थे जातेयमवबुद्धता 4.3.169ab
किं मूलं भिन्नदृष्टेः स्यादिति श्रुत्या तदुच्यते 1.4.1569ab
किंलक्षणेन ग्रस्तोऽयं मृत्युनेति प्रचोदिते 3.2.2ab
किं वाक्यस्यानुवादत्वं सिद्धेऽर्थे मान्तरेण वा SV 677ab

किं वा तद्विपरीतेन ज्योतिषेत्यभिधीयताम् 4.3.23ab
किं वा नेति परीक्षेयं जातत्वात्स्यादपार्थिका 4.3.734cd
किं वा प्रागपि संबन्धाद्बुद्धोऽर्थोऽभून्न मानतः 4.3.169cd
किं वाभिन्नेति मे ब्रूहि प्रज्ञोपनिषदं स्फुटम् 4.1.18cd
किं वा संभूय सर्वाणि कर्माणि घ्नन्ति संसृतिम् 3.3.43cd
किं वा सर्वगतानां स्यात्करणानामिहात्मनि 4.4.128ab
किं वोत्पत्त्यादिमत्किंचित्सामर्थ्यं यत्र कर्मणः 3.3.104ab
किं समाशङ्क्यते येन तदाशीः संप्रयुज्यते 4.2.108cd
किंसाधनो ब्राह्मणः स्यादिति साधनमुच्यताम् 3.5.196cd
किं साध्यं साधनं चेह निश्चयो नोपपद्यते 4.3.1449cd
किं स्वार्थमात्रनिष्ठत्वमुत कार्यैकनिष्ठता SV 602ab
किं स्वावयवसंघातभिन्नजात्यतिरेकिणा 4.3.22ab
किंस्विदित्यादि संहृष्टस्तद्दोषस्यासमीक्षणात् 5.14.5cd
किंस्विदेवंविदे साधु कृत्स्नसाध्वाप्तिहेतुतः 5.14.6ab
किं च ज्ञानमदृष्टार्थमग्निहोत्रादिवद्यदि SV 291ab
किं च भुक्त्वाथवाभुक्त्वा ज्योतिष्टोमफलं नरः 1.5.245ab
किं च मानादविज्ञाता विमुक्तिः काम्यते न च SV 289ab
किं च सर्वाणि भूतानि तमवन्ति यथाबलम् 1.5.351ab
किं च हेतुमतो जन्म सर्वत्र स्यात्पुनः पुनः 4.4.919ab
किं चातो यदि नामैवं शृण्वतो यत्प्रसिध्यति 4.3.23cd
किं चानुभूयमानस्य ह्यर्थस्य पुरुषार्थता SV 449ab
किं चापि तदवेदन्यद्यज्ज्ञानात्कृत्स्नतामगात् 1.4.1089cd
किं चाप्यव्यभिचारेण स्वभावत्वं विवक्षतः 4.3.752ab
किंचिज्जिज्ञास्यते ज्ञात्रा प्रत्यक्षादिप्रमाणतः SV 597cd
किंचित्तत्रोपलभ्येत ह्यनवद्यं भवेद्वचः 4.3.734cd
किंचित्साधनमित्येवं भण्यते लोकवेदयोः 2.4.188cd
किंचित्सामान्यमाश्रित्य जामित्वं प्रतिपद्यते 2.1.292ab
किंचिदप्यस्ति तत्सिद्धिरतः स्यान्निष्प्रमाणिका 4.3.462cd
किं चैतमेवमात्मानं सर्वानर्थैककारणम् 4.4.1076ab
किं चोपलब्धितः सर्वसिद्धिमाप्नोति नान्यथा 4.3.800cd
किं चोपलब्ध्यभावेन सा सिद्धा किं ततोऽन्यतः 4.3.794cd
किं चोपायेऽप्रवृत्तः सन्पुरुषोऽयं प्रवर्त्यते SV 581ab

किंज्योतिरयमित्येवं प्रत्यग्ज्योतिर्बुभुत्सया 4.3.20cd
किंज्योतिरिति मे ब्रूहि पुंव्यापारानुभूतितः 4.3.72cd
किंज्योतिरित्युपक्रम्य यत्नेन महतादरात् 4.3.1775ab
किंज्योतिरित्युपक्रम्य स एवार्थः प्रपञ्च्यते 4.4.429cd
किंज्योतिरित्येवमादिमप्राक्षीन्मां पुनः पुनः 4.3.1890cd
किंतु चैतन्यमप्यस्य कामकर्मादिवद्भवेत् 4.3.1752ab
किंतु पाङ्क्तक्रियापेक्षं प्राणजन्माभिधीयते 1.5.187cd
किंतु बुद्ध्याद्युपाधौ तदात्मच्छायैककर्मकम् 1.4.566ab
किंतु मानार्पितत्वात्सा यथाभूतार्थतेष्यते 1.3.73ef
किंतु साधनसाध्यत्वादनित्यं कर्मजं सुखम् SV 300ab
किंत्वमानत्वहेतूनां वेदवाक्येष्वसंभवात् 2.4.325cd
किमंश आत्मा विज्ञेयः करणांशस्तथा मनः 1.4.788ab
किमत्र विधिना कार्यमनृतन्त्रत्वहेतुतः SV 30ab
किमनेकत्र लीनिः स्यात्सूत्रस्यापि क्षितेरिव 3.8.47ab
किमन्नं मे बुभुक्षोः स्याद्वासो वा मे किमीर्यताम् 6.1.30ab
किमन्यत्सुखमिष्टं स्याद्यस्याप्तेः पुरुषार्थता SV 1008cd
किमन्यत्स्मृतिसंतानात्प्रार्थ्यते निष्प्रमाणकम् 1.4.840cd
किमपेक्ष्य व्यपेतत्वं कालोऽयं वार्तमानिकः 2.1.405ab
किमयं दृष्टिकारित्वात्पुमान्द्रष्टेति भण्यते 4.3.1580ab
किमर्थं देवताशङ्का क्रियते हिरुगात्मनः 4.3.1147cd
किमर्थं सेतुरित्येवमाकाङ्क्षायां परं वचः 4.4.1016ab
किमर्थमिति चेत्तत्र लोकः कारणमीक्षते 4.3.946cd
किमर्था तर्हि तत्रैषां कल्प्यते भवता स्थितिः 4.4.456cd
किमवेदिति यः प्रश्नः स किं स्यात्कर्तृकर्मणोः 1.4.1133ab
किमात्मैव स्वशब्देन किं वेहात्मीय उच्यते 4.3.764ab
किमाप्यमधिकं शास्त्राद्येन युक्त्याद्यपेक्षते SV 829cd
किमाहुरित्यपेक्षायामिदं तदभिधीयते 1.4.1075ab
किमिक्षो रसमाप्नोति यत्नान्निष्पीडयन्न ना 2.4.75ab
किमिच्छन्कस्य वार्थाय शरीरं संज्वरेत्तदा 4.4.610ef
किमिवेहान्यमानेषु तवापेक्षाभिधाश्रुतेः 1.4.869cd
किमु तद्ब्रह्म यद्वेद्यं यज्ज्ञानात्सर्वताप्यते 1.4.1089ab
किमुतैकस्य वक्तव्यं पर्यपृच्छदतो नृपः 4.3.30cd

किमुत्क्रामन्त्यतः प्राणा उताहो नेति भण्यताम् 3.2.24cd
किमु निःशेषभिन्नार्थव्यापिन्यात्मन्यसौ मयि 1.4.137cd
किमु प्रध्वस्तनिःशेषभेदहेताविहात्मनि 2.1.354ab
किमु भावो जगत्यस्मिन्साक्षी चानन्यसिद्धिकः 3.4.123cd
किमु विध्वस्तनिःशेषघनाज्ञानेऽन्तरात्मनि 1.4.1497cd
किमु विध्वस्तनिःशेषद्वैतहेतौ सुषुप्तगे 4.3.1512cd
किमु वेद्मीति बुद्धिः स्याच्चिदतोऽव्यभिचारिणी 2.4.129cd
किमु सर्वस्वहरणे वक्तव्यं दुःखकारणम् 1.4.1576ef
किमेकविषयत्वेन किं वा विषयभेदतः 2.1.553ab
किमेतद्भौतिकं ज्ञानं भूतेभ्योऽन्यस्य चात्मनः 4.3.1117cd
किमेनं न जहातीति पृष्टो नामेत्यथाब्रवीत् 3.2.37ab
किमेवं भवतः सिद्धं यदि नाम तमोहनुतैः 1.2.100ab
किंभूतं ते तदा चित्तमभावप्रसमीक्षणे 4.3.799cd
किंमानपूर्वकोऽस्यार्थसंबन्ध इति नोच्यते 4.3.786ab
किम्वसाध्ये समस्तस्य पूर्णत्वेन समाप्तितः 5.1.104cd
कियच्छिद्रं मरुद्दद्याद्रथचक्रखमानगीः 5.12.3cd
कियती कर्मणस्तस्य व्याप्तिः स्यादिति भण्यते 3.3.3cd
कियांस्ते वयसा वत्स इत्याचष्टे वयो यथा 1.5.53ab
कीटादीनामगमनाद्गतानां चागतेस्तथा 6.2.163ab
कीदृग्व्यापारसंयुक्तः सोऽस्राक्षीदिति भण्यते 1.2.169cd
कीदृशी वा कुतो वासावनुभूत्येकरूपतः SV 184cd
कीर्तिं चैकात्म्यविज्ञानं श्लोकं चैकात्म्यसंगतिम् 1.4.1024ab
कुक्षिस्थक्रिमिदुःखैर्नो न मनागपि संगतिः 1.5.354cd
कुक्षिस्थस्यापि हि सतो वामदेवस्य तद्यथा SV 232cd
कुटिलं च तथा पापमस्मत्तस्त्वं वियोजय 5.17.21ab
कुड्याद्यावरणं दृष्टं भिन्नदेशं सदावृतात् 1.2.93ab
कुत आगादिति त्वस्य प्रश्नार्थाविविचिकीर्षया 2.1.365ab
कुत एकाधिकारत्वमपेक्षाभावतो वद SV 398cd
कुत ऐकात्म्यनिष्ठत्वं त्वया यदुदितं पुरा SV 478cd
कुतः कात्स्न्र्यं यतः सर्वं मानादेव प्रसिध्यति 1.4.1284cd
कुतः क्रियाभ्यः सिद्धिश्चेच्छृणु तद्भण्यते यतः SV 40cd
कुतः पुनरिदं ज्ञानं धीसमानाश्रयत्वतः 4.3.445ab

कुतः पुनरिदं सिद्धं विशेषज्ञानसंक्षये 4.3.1387cd
कुतः प्रज्ञात्वसंसिद्धिर्वाच इत्येतदुच्यते 4.1.19cd
कुतः प्रत्यक्षतासिद्धिर्यदि नात्माभ्युपेयते 4.3.197cd
कुतः प्रमाणात्संभाव्या कार्यकारणघस्मरे 2.4.243cd
कुतः प्राप्तं फलमिति प्रत्यक्षं ह्यात्मधीफलम् SV 129ab
कुतः सुषुप्तौ तानि स्युर्यत्र तद्वासनापि न 4.3.1416cd
कुतश्चिदागमाज्ज्ञात्वा तमुपेत्याप्रतारकः 2.1.512ab
कुतस्तज्ज्ञानमिति चेत्तद्धि बन्धपरिक्षयात् SV 294ab
कुतस्तत्प्राप्तिरिति चेद्यथा प्राप्तिस्तथोच्यते 4.4.1207cd
कुतस्तदिति चेदाह स वा इति परा श्रुतिः 4.3.808cd
कुतस्तदिति चेन्मत्तः शृणु सर्वं यथोच्यते 4.3.1130cd
कुतस्तस्याभिभूतस्य रागाद्यासुरपाप्मभिः 1.3.5ab
कुतूहलवतां तद्वन्निर्वृत्ताख्यानमात्रतः SV 588ab
कुतोऽकामयमानः स्यादित्येवमभिचोदिते 4.4.264ab
कुतोऽकारकवस्त्वत्र प्रमाणादभिधीयते 4.3.1482cd
कुतोऽकारणकार्येऽस्मिञ्शुक्लादेः संभवः परे 4.4.567cd
कुतोऽज्ञायि विना मानान्मानं नाज्ञाततां विना 1.4.1302cd
कुतोऽदो लभतेऽसत्त्वं यत्सदात्मनि निष्ठितम् 1.2.13cd
कुतोऽधिकारनियमो व्युत्थाने क्रियते बलात् 3.5.90cd
कुतोऽभयत्वसंसिद्धिः प्रतीच इति शङ्किते 4.4.1336ab
कुतोऽमृतत्वसंप्राप्तिर्ज्ञानमात्रैकहेतुना 2.4.55ab
कुतोऽविभागो मानाच्चेदुभयोरप्यवस्थयोः 5.1.49ab
कुतोऽविशेष इति चेदत आह यथा तथा 1.4.781ab
कुतोऽसंन्यासिनस्तत्स्यान्मुनित्वं निष्प्रमाणकम् 4.4.1071cd
कुतोऽसिद्धत्वमिति चेच्छृणु तद्गदतो मम 2.5.5cd
कुतोऽस्य बहुरूपत्वमिति हेतुरिहोच्यते 2.5.129ab
कुतो भेदावकाशः स्याददृयैकप्रमात्मनि 3.4.128cd
कुतो भेदावकाशः स्याद्भेदेऽसति कुतो युतिः SV 935cd
कुतो यजुष्ट्वं तस्येति युक्तिलेशोऽभिधीयते 5.15.4cd
कुतो वेदान्तविद्यायां तस्य प्राप्तिर्मनागपि 4.4.1209cd
कुतो हेतुफलत्वं स्यात्सव्येतरविषाणवत् 4.3.654cd
कुप्येरञ्श्रुतयः सर्वा नान्यदन्यद्धवेद्यतः 2.1.430cd

कुमारनृपवत्तत्स्यादीशानत्वं परात्मनः 4.4.991ab
कुमारवक्त्रोद्गतया वाचर्गादीन्ससर्ज सः 1.2.192ab
कुमारोत्थरवत्रस्तः स्वभावं चिच्छिदे भयात् 1.2.186cd
कुम्भ आरोप्यते यद्वत्प्रकाशो भानुसंगतेः 3.8.118ab
कुम्भवत्प्रतिनिर्देष्टुं यथा तदभिधीयते 3.4.81cd
कुम्भवद्वीक्ष्यते यस्मान्नात आत्मा मनोऽपि नः 4.3.271cd
कुम्भस्य वियता यद्वन्निर्हेतुः संगतिः सदा 4.3.61ab
कुम्भाकारेण कुम्भार्थो यथा प्रत्यक्ष ईक्ष्यते 4.3.302ab
कुम्भादेः कर्मयोग्यत्वं स्यादेवं धिषणादिसु 4.3.96cd
कुम्भाद्यभिन्नदेशस्थं पिण्डाद्यावरणं कथम् 1.2.93cd
कुरुते तादृशं कर्म वाङ्मनःकायसाधनैः 4.4.231cd
कुर्यादेवं यथोक्तार्थं मृत्युत्वप्रतिपित्सया 1.2.218cd
कुर्यान्मेरावणुधियमणौ मेरुधियं तथा 1.3.313ab
कुर्यामसाधु वा तस्मै सर्वासाधुनिराकृतेः 5.14.6cd
कुर्वतश्च महाल्लाँभ आत्मनः कृतकृत्यता 2.5.147cd
कुर्वती स्वर्गकामेन गच्छतः सह मानताम् SV 788cd
कुर्वत्यौ मानतां यातः प्रसंख्यानेन नान्यथा SV 789cd
कुर्वन्ति बहुरूपत्वं मणेरास्तरणं यथा 2.3.159cd
कुर्वन्त्येव प्रमां यत्र तदसंभावना कुतः 1.4.874cd
कुर्वन्त्येव प्रमां यत्र तदसंभावना कुतः 2.1.552cd
कुर्वाण एव चेत्कर्म कर्म ब्रह्मेति पश्यति 1.4.1729ab
कुर्वाण एव स्वप्नेऽपि प्राण आस्ते प्रबोधवत् 2.1.118cd
कुर्वाणमभिवीक्ष्याज्ञः कुरुते कारणानुमाम् SV 1026cd
कुर्वाणमुपकारं तं ददृशुः प्राग्विवादरात् 1.3.200cd
कुर्वाणस्तुमुलं शब्दं स्वव्यापारमशेषतः 2.1.118ab
कुर्वीत क्रतुमित्यादिर्विधिरभ्युदये यथा SV 22ab
कुर्वीत स क्रतुं कर्ता ह्यकार्यत्वेऽपि वस्तुनः 4.4.449cd
कुशलोऽपि कुलालः सन्नघटादिस्वभावकम् SV 54cd
कुसुमापगमेऽप्येवं लिङ्गस्था वासनात्मनि 2.3.117cd
कुसूलवन्न भिद्येते सांशत्वात्पततोऽपि न 3.8.135ab
कूटस्थ एव साक्ष्यत्र स्वमोहाभासहेतुतः 4.3.352ab
कूटस्थं तत्स्वतःसिद्धेस्तत्कस्माद्विनिवर्तते 2.4.450cd

कूटस्थज्ञानमात्रत्वान्न तमोऽस्य स्वभावतः 1.4.1369ab
कूटस्थज्योतिषैवास्ते स्वप्नस्थानेऽक्रियोऽद्वयः 4.3.906ab
कूटस्थदृष्टावेकस्मिन्नविभक्ते सहस्रधा 4.3.1518ab
कूटस्थदृष्टितन्मोहौ दृष्ट्याभासश्च तत् त्रयम् 3.4.86ab
कूटस्थदृष्टिमात्रत्वात्तथा स्वप्नप्रबोधयोः 4.3.1908cd
कूटस्थदृष्टिमात्रत्वान्न तथात्मानमीक्षते 2.4.284cd
कूटस्थदृष्टिमात्रत्वान्न तु द्रष्टृत्वमुच्यते 3.8.174cd
कूटस्थदृष्टिरात्मैको निषेद्धुं शक्यते परः 4.3.562cd
कूटस्थदृष्टिस्वाभाव्यात्स्वप्न आत्मा प्रपश्यति 4.3.931cd
कूटस्थदृष्टेः साक्षित्वं जडस्येव न युज्यते 3.4.89ab
कूटस्थदृष्टेरस्तित्वं प्रागपि प्रतिपादितम् 4.3.530cd
कूटस्थबोधतन्मोहचिदाभासैकमात्रया 1.3.261ab
कूटस्थबोधपूर्णत्वं प्रत्यक्त्वं वस्तुनः स्वतः 3.8.104ab
कूटस्थमक्षरं ध्वान्तध्वस्तौ स्यान्नो निरन्वयम् 3.8.123cd
कूटस्थमेकं चैतन्यं सिद्धं श्रुत्यनुसारतः 3.8.176ef
कूटस्थवादसक्तिः स्यान्मिथ्यासंगतितस्तयोः 4.3.608cd
कूटस्थसंविन्मात्रैकं ब्रह्मास्मीतिस्वभावकम् 1.4.211cd
कूटस्थसाक्षिसंबन्धो बोद्धृकर्त्रोस्तथैव च 4.3.412cd
कूटस्थस्य द्वितीयेन संबन्धोऽबोधकारितः 3.8.43cd
कूटस्थस्य न साक्षित्वं द्वितीयासंगतेर्भवेत् 1.4.378ab
कूटस्थस्यापि साक्षित्वमागमापायिनं प्रति 1.4.380cd
कूटस्थात्कथमुत्पत्तिरचित्कं चेतनात्कथम् 2.1.388cd
कूटस्थात्मचिदाभेऽस्य प्रत्यग्ध्वान्ते हि तद्भवैः 4.3.392ab
कूटस्थात्मस्वभावत्वात्सर्वसाधननिस्पृहः 4.3.1838ab
कूटस्थात्मातिरेकेण रूपमन्यन्न लक्ष्यते 1.3.126cd
कूटस्थात्मानुरोधित्वात्तावन्मात्रात्मकत्वतः 4.3.1321ab
कूटस्थात्मैकचैतन्यबिम्बितं सत्स्वदोषतः 4.3.382cd
कूटस्थात्मैकहेतूत्थचिद्बिम्बो मोहगस्तु यः 4.3.415ab
कूटस्थादत्तानुज्ञं सत्प्रत्याख्यातं सहान्वयम् 2.1.306ab
कूटस्थादितमोन्तेन नित्यमव्यतिरेकतः 1.4.1326ab
कूटस्थानित्ययोर्भासोर्मध्यवर्ती पुमानयम् 4.3.58ab
कूटस्थे विक्रिया नास्ति तस्मादज्ञानतो जनिः 1.4.626cd

कूटस्थे विक्रिया नास्ति तस्मादज्ञानतो जनिः 2.1.384cd
कूटस्थोऽपि स्वतः प्रत्यङ्ङनात्मवृत्त्यपेक्षया 1.4.319cd
कूटस्थोऽस्यावबोधश्चेत्कादाचित्कं कुतो भवेत् 2.1.200ab
कूटस्थो वासनाः स्वप्ने चिदाभासाः करोत्ययम् 4.3.887cd
कूर्चादुत्थाय विधिना तं राजोपससाद ह 4.2.4ab
कूर्मलोमादिवच्चेत्स्यादबुद्धत्वं तथापि वः 1.4.240ab
कूर्मलोमादिवत्तद्वन्नापि तत्स्याद्विनश्यता 4.3.624ab
कूलाभ्यां क्रमसंबन्धाद्व्यतिरेकाच्च कूलतः 4.3.1085ab
कृकलासे प्रसिद्धा या हिंसा प्राणभृतां स्वतः 1.5.214ab
कृतं चिकीर्षितं सर्वं बुद्धं यच्च बुभुत्सितम् 4.4.531ab
कृतं चिकीर्षितं सर्वं बुद्धं यच्च बुभुत्सितम् 4.4.782ab
कृतं तन्नित्यसंप्राप्तिहेतूक्त्यानवशेषतः 1.4.914cd
कृतं फलप्रदानेन प्रत्यवायेन चाकृतम् 4.4.1176ab
कृतकृत्यत्वतो हेतोर्लोकोऽयं तस्य लोकिनः 4.4.621cd
कृतकृत्यस्य मुक्तस्य विधिरेष कथं भवेत् 4.4.1146cd
कृतकृत्यो भवेत्क्षिप्रमेतज्ज्ञात्वानुशासनम् 4.5.30cd
कृतकृत्यो भवेत्सर्वो विशेषज्ञानसंगतिः 4.4.101ab
कृतत्वात्तर्हि प्रज्ञाया निष्फलोऽयं पुनर्विधिः 4.4.818cd
कृतनाशस्तथा च स्यादकृताभ्यागमस्तथा 1.5.359cd
कृतनाशाकृतप्राप्ती प्राप्नुतो नुस्तथा सति 3.2.143cd
कृतमप्यफलं तेन यत्नात्तत्र निरूप्यते SV 292cd
कृतसंप्रत्तिकं दैवाः प्राण वागादयः समम् 1.5.325ab
कृतस्य हि क्षयोऽवश्यमकृतस्याक्षयात्मता 1.4.1682ab
कृतायाः करणं कीदृक्प्रज्ञाया इति चोदिते 4.4.706cd
कृतार्थता तथा च स्यादन्यथा नोपपद्यते 2.3.212cd
कृतार्थत्वान्नरस्यापि रागादेव प्रवृत्तितः SV 591cd
कृतार्थस्याकृतार्थस्य तस्य नैवाश्रमान्तरम् 3.5.195cd
कृता विवक्षितं त्वत्र सर्वमप्येतदीरितम् 1.4.3cd
कृतोपकारं स्मृत्वोचुः प्राणा वागादयस्तदा 1.3.198cd
कृत्तिकात्वादिति ह्युक्तेनैव कार्यस्वभावयोः 4.3.760ab
कृत्यानां युक्तितोऽपि स्यान्नैव कर्माभिधायिता SV 511cd
कृत्वा तत्प्राप्तितः पूर्वं यथा सूतादयो नृपम् 4.3.1966ab

कृत्वा देहं प्रतीक्षन्ते नृपस्येव गृहं नराः 4.3.1971cd
कृत्वा देहान्तरं योग्यं तस्थू राज्ञोऽग्रगा इव 4.3.1958cd
कृत्स्न आत्मेत्यतो वाक्यात्तथारूपं दिदृक्षति 1.4.1348ab
कृत्स्नं जगत्स्वभोगार्थं पुंसोपात्तं स्वकर्मणा 4.3.1956cd
कृत्स्नं जगदतो मोहध्वस्तौ ध्वस्तं भवेच्चितिः 1.4.1329cd
कृत्स्नं जगदतो मोहध्वस्तौ ध्वस्तं भवेच्चितिः 3.4.131cd
कृत्स्नं जगदनादाय नैकस्यापीष्यते क्रिया 1.3.156ab
कृत्स्नं जगदुपादाय क्रियैकैकस्य सिध्यति 4.3.863ab
कृत्स्नं तदात्मनो लोकात्सिद्धमस्येति नूयते 1.4.1775cd
कृत्स्नं पश्येदिति ततो वाक्यं वस्तुनि वर्तते 1.4.1347ab
कृत्स्नं वा यदि वाकृत्स्नं यथेच्छसि तथास्तु तत् 1.4.1103ab
कृत्स्नकारणतत्कार्यवृत्त्युपाधिसमाश्रयात् 1.4.636cd
कृत्स्नचोदितकारित्वात्सर्वपापविवर्जितः 4.3.1863cd
कृत्स्नज्ञेयसमाप्तत्वान्न किंचिदवशिष्यते 4.4.1281cd
कृत्स्नत्वार्थमतोऽप्राक्षीत्काश्यं प्रज्ञासमन्वितम् 2.1.34cd
कृत्स्नदेहाभिमान्येवं नैकदेहाभिमानभुक् 2.1.124cd
कृत्स्नपुंविक्रियोत्सारि वाक्यं कस्मादुपेक्ष्यते 1.4.321cd
कृत्स्नप्रकरणार्थस्य ज्योतिष्टोमादिगामिनः 1.4.789ab
कृत्स्नप्रपञ्चविलयः कर्तुं शक्यो न केनचित् SV 388ab
कृत्स्नप्रयोजनावाप्तेः पूर्वोक्तैरेव कर्मभिः SV 1093cd
कृत्स्नप्राप्त्या क्षये मानं न तथा किंचिदिष्यते 3.2.83cd
कृत्स्नप्राप्त्या क्षयो नातो विद्यते कामकर्मणोः 3.2.76ab
कृत्स्नमात्राद्युपादानतमोबाधस्तु बोधतः SV 1006ab
कृत्स्नमेवं परं ब्रह्म सदोपासीत यत्नतः 1.4.948cd
कृत्स्नमेव यतः प्रोक्तं वस्तु यत्पारमार्थिकम् 1.4.1079ab
कृत्स्नमेव यतो वस्तु तदन्यत्तदबोधजम् 1.4.1346cd
कृत्स्नवेदग्रहादाद्यव्याख्याने दोष एव न 4.4.1038cd
कृत्स्नसंसारधर्मार्थं देहेष्विति च भण्यते 1.4.502cd
कृत्स्नसंसारमान्येष सर्वोऽस्मीति व्यवस्थितः 1.6.44ab
कृत्स्नसाधनसंपन्नः समृद्धोऽत्राभिधीयते 4.3.1846ab
कृत्स्नस्य ब्रह्मणो रूपे मूर्तामूर्ते विवक्षिते 2.3.73ab
कृत्स्नाध्यात्माधिदैवादावात्मज्योतिरनुग्रहः 4.3.290cd

कृत्स्नानन्दस्य चानाप्तिरवाप्तिरसुखस्य च 4.4.260ab
कृत्स्नानात्मानुवादेन प्रत्यग्दृष्टिर्विधीयते 3.2.113cd
कृत्स्नाविद्योत्थमानी च प्रत्यगज्ञानकारणात् 1.6.42cd
कृत्स्नेन जगता यद्वत्कर्मकृत्समुपार्जितः 1.5.4ab
कृत्स्नेष्टार्थस्य संप्राप्तिः कृत्स्नानर्थहनुतिस्तथा SV 572ab
कृत्स्नोऽपि चैष आनन्दस्तदविद्यैकहेतुजः 4.3.1842ab
कृत्स्नोऽस्मीति तदात्मानं संभावयति मानवः 1.4.1839cd
कृष्णद्वैपायनो व्यासो वेदात्मा ध्वान्तहानिकृत् 3.7.39ab
कृष्णशक्तिरविद्यापि परस्मादेव सोत्थिता 2.3.122ab
कृष्णसारं यथा स्थानं चक्षुषः करणात्मनः 2.3.41ab
कृष्णसारादिदेशेषु स्वान्तस्यानुग्रहस्ततः 4.3.284cd
कृष्यादि वान्यदकृतं कर्म नालं फलाय च 1.4.1678cd
क्लृप्तं सत्कल्प्यते कस्माद्विमुक्तिर्नित्यकर्मणः 3.3.82cd
क्लृप्तसर्पादिभिर्यद्वदज्ञातायाः स्रजः सदा 2.3.21ab
क्लृप्तसर्पाद्यभावोऽयं न स्रक्तत्त्वात्पृथङ्मितः 4.4.949ab
क्लृप्तस्यैव ह्यभावस्य व्यपदेशः प्रसज्यते 1.2.119cd
क्लृप्तानामपि रज्ज्वादौ कल्पितान्तरसंश्रयात् 2.1.175ab
क्लृप्तान्तरापनुत्तिः स्याद्यथा तद्वदिहात्मनि 2.1.175cd
केचित्कार्यमपीच्छन्ति तदर्थं तन्न युज्यते SV 790cd
केचित्कार्यैकनिष्ठत्वं वेदान्तानां प्रचक्षते SV 477cd
केचित्तु पण्डितंमन्या विरोधीनि परस्परम् 2.1.588ab
केचिद्व्याचक्षतेऽपूर्वं विधिमेतं महाधियः 1.4.751ab
केचिद्व्याचक्षते धीराः प्रसादाज्जातवेदसः 3.4.167cd
केचिद्व्याचक्षते यत्नादत्र प्रतिविधीयते 4.4.810cd
के ते उभे न तरत इत्युक्तार्थविवक्षया 4.4.1168ab
केन चोक्तं क्रिया मुक्तेः साधनत्वं न गच्छति SV 192ab
केन यागादिनिर्वृत्त्येत्येतच्छास्त्रात्प्रतीयते SV 533cd
केनाथ ब्राह्मणः स स्यादिति प्रश्नमपृच्छत 3.5.192ab
केनायं यजमानोऽतो मृत्योराप्तेर्विमुच्यते 3.1.19cd
केनेति च व्यपेक्षायां विज्ञानेनेति गम्यते 4.4.805ab
केनेति यदि वाक्षेप उत्पत्त्यादेरसंभवात् 3.5.205ab
केनैक इत्यपेक्षायां हृदयेनेति भण्यते 4.3.381ab

केभ्यः क्षरति सा धेनुरित्येतदधुनोच्यते 5.10.4ab
केवलं कर्म याम्यायां प्रतीच्यां पुत्रजन्म च 3.9.77ab
केवलं तत्तमोमात्रव्यवधानैकहेतुतः 1.4.1206ab
केवलज्ञानमात्रेण मा भूत् त्र्यन्नात्मकं फलम् 1.5.217ab
केवलस्तु परिस्पन्दः कर्मशक्तिषु निष्प्रभः 2.4.379cd
केवलस्मृत्यभावाच्च न व्याधत्वं जहात्यसौ 2.1.511cd
केवलाज्ञानमात्राधिरिह प्रत्यङ् व्यवस्थितः 4.3.979ab
केवलाज्ञानमात्रेण व्यवधानं परात्मनः 1.4.1713ab
केवलालोचनाल्लिङ्गात्तथा बुद्धेश्च देवताम् 4.4.70cd
केवलेऽवस्थितेऽत्तृत्वे मृत्युनापि न गीर्यते 6.1.35cd
केवलोऽनात्मनोऽदृष्टेः प्रतीचोऽन्यस्य वस्तुनः 2.4.228cd
केवलोक्तिश्रवोद्भूतज्ञानादर्थान्तरं स्फुटम् 1.4.831cd
केवलो मतिसंवादो भवदुक्तेर्ममाभवत् 2.1.45cd
केशादिजातेरेकत्वाद्धीरियं तन्निबन्धना 4.3.666cd
कैवल्यफलदानेन प्रत्यगात्मापि सन्परः 1.4.1676cd
कैवल्यात्तं पराकुर्याद्द्विप्रजातिः पराङ्मुखम् 2.4.252ab
कैवल्याभूत्या उद्युक्ता ईश्वरा अपि नेशते 1.4.1464cd
कैवल्यावसितेर्नासौ स्यात्समष्टिवपुर्भृतः 5.16.66cd
कैवल्यावाप्तिविघ्नाय नालं देवा अपीश्वराः 1.4.1468cd
कैवल्यावाप्तौ च कथं तयोरक्षितिरुच्यते 1.4.1720cd
कैवल्याश्रममादाय ब्राह्मण्यस्य समाप्तितः 3.5.194cd
कैवल्याश्रममास्थाय प्राप तद्वैष्णवं पदम् 2.4.22cd
कैवल्येऽपि च तत्सक्तेरनिर्मोक्षः प्रसज्यते SV 50ab
कैवल्ये न तु सापेक्षा सर्वसाधननिःस्पृहा 3.9.208ab
कोऽभावानुपलब्ध्योर्वा भेदः स्यादिति कथ्यताम् 4.3.792cd
कोऽभिप्रायोऽखिलं कर्म त्यजतां साधनैः सह 4.4.1094ab
कोऽर्थस्तेनेह पुंसः स्यादकृतेन कृतेन वा 4.4.1215cd
कोऽसौ स्वाभाविकः पाप्मा तस्योद्भूतिस्तथा कुतः 1.3.10ab
कोऽहं कस्य कुतो वेति कः कथं वा भवेदिति 1.4.1058ab
कोऽहं कस्य कुतो वेति कः कथं वा भवेदिति 4.4.1263ab
को द्वेषोऽस्मासु भवतो येनोपालम्भ ईर्यते SV 497cd
को नो वसिष्ठ इति तं पप्रच्छुर्निर्णयार्थिनः 6.1.17cd

को न्वेषु ब्राह्मण इति चोदिते स्यात्परा श्रुतिः 1.4.1636cd
कोशपञ्चकतां यातः प्रत्यगज्ञानतो यतः 1.4.31cd
को हेतुरक्षयत्वे स्यादिति पृष्टमथाधुना 1.5.84ab
को हेतुरिति वक्तव्यं नाविद्याकारकत्वतः 4.3.1186cd
कौटस्थ्यं यदि वा पुंसोऽसङ्गशब्देन भण्यते 4.3.1026ab
कौटस्थ्यसिद्धौ हेतूंश्च प्रागवोचमनेकशः 4.3.1581cd
कौटस्थ्याच्च ध्रुवो ज्ञेयो विकारोच्छित्त्यसंभवात् 4.4.703cd
कौटस्थ्यात्त्वात्मनः सृष्टिर्न कथं चन युज्यते 2.1.385cd
कौटस्थ्यादमृतं ज्योतिर्मृत्युभूम्यतिलङ्घनात् 4.4.637ab
कौटस्थ्यादविकार्योऽयं वद स्यात्कर्मणा हि किम् 4.4.1115cd
कौटस्थ्याद्ध्रुवमक्षय्यं प्रत्यगात्मन्यवस्थितम् 4.4.735ab
कौटस्थ्याद्विक्रियाभावान्निश्चित्कत्वाद्विकारिणः 4.3.98ab
कौटस्थ्यान्नास्य कर्तृत्वमकार्याकारणत्वतः 4.4.995ab
कौटस्थ्यान्निर्द्वयोऽप्यात्मा साक्षीत्यध्यस्यते जडैः 1.4.372cd
कौटस्थ्यासंगतो नास्य मोहतत्कार्यसंगतिः 1.4.1321ab
कौटस्थ्यैकत्वहेतुभ्यां प्रत्यग्याथात्म्यवस्तुनः 3.2.29cd
कौरव्यायणिजो धीमान्वायुरेतिप्रसिद्धितः 5.1.120cd
कौषीतकिश्रुतौ तद्वद्गृहस्थस्यैव जीवतः 1.5.309ab
कौष्ठ्याग्निप्रेरितो वायुर्नानास्थानसमाहतः 1.3.299ab
क्त्वायोगात्पूर्वकालत्वमविद्यायाः प्रतीयते 1.4.1765ab
क्रतुकालेव ब्रह्माप्तिः क्षत्रस्येत्यवसीयते 1.4.1609cd
क्रतुतत्साधनात्मानावादित्याग्नी यथोदितौ 1.2.224ab
क्रतुना यादृशेनायं यत्क्रतुः स्यात्पुमानिह 4.4.231ab
क्रतुर्मनोमयत्वाच्च सा हि संकल्परूपिणी 5.17.16cd
क्रत्वङ्गिजर्तधियो यद्वत्स्वात्मदेहस्य साक्षिता 1.5.316ab
क्रत्वङ्गिजतैस्तदा प्राणैः सह पुत्रं विशत्ययम् 1.5.313cd
क्रत्वात्मा मृत्युरस्मीति तादात्म्यं सोऽधिगच्छति 1.1.6cd
क्रत्वात्मेत्यभिमानेद्धः पर्वजन्मन्यभूत्प्रभुः 1.2.199cd
क्रत्वात्मैवाभिसंपन्नो द्वैतैकत्वात्मकः प्रभुः 1.2.201ab
क्रममुक्तिफलानीति क्व गमिष्यसिगीरतः 4.2.13cd
क्रमवृत्तेस्तु बोधस्य न बोधो भौतिकस्ततः 4.3.1123ab
क्रमशोऽक्रमशो वापि शक्यः कर्तुं कदा चन 1.4.954cd

क्रमसंचारिणस्तस्य जाग्रत्स्वप्नसुषुप्तिषु 4.3.1114ab
क्रमेण ज्ञातृसंबन्धस्तद्वत्स्वप्नप्रबोधयोः 4.3.1125cd
क्रमेण देवतां यात्वा वैरिञ्चं यान्ति तत्पदम् 6.2.135cd
क्रमेण युगपद्वातः सेवासांग्रहणीहयोः SV 416cd
क्रमेण वृत्तिस्तासां स्यादधिष्ठातृत्वकारणात् 4.3.1127cd
क्रमेण संचरन्नद्यां महामत्स्यो यथा बली 4.3.1124cd
क्रमेणासेदुरासन्यं प्राणं पाप्मपराभवात् 1.3.169cd
क्रियतामविचारेण हन्तेत्यनुमतौ पदम् 1.3.31cd
क्रियतेऽध्याययोरेवं मधुकाण्डं समाप्यते 2.5.116ab
क्रियतेऽलौकिकोऽप्यर्थः पदार्थान्वयरूपतः 1.4.896ab
क्रियते कल्पना येन सर्वन्यायविरोधिनी 2.3.138cd
क्रियते कामकर्मादिविवेकस्य विवक्षया 4.3.1220cd
क्रियते न स्वतस्तस्य जन्माद्यैः संगतिर्यतः 4.3.810cd
क्रियमाणानि कर्माणि यथा स्युः फलसिद्धये 3.5.160ab
क्रियमाणो यथा कामः क्रत्वादीनि प्रसूयते 4.4.266ab
क्रिययोर्हि प्रभेदे तत्किं पूर्वमिति चोद्यते 4.4.695cd
क्रियां प्रत्यगुणीभूतं नेश्वराद्यपि सिध्यति 3.2.163ab
क्रियां मोहनिमित्तत्वादपेक्षा कर्त्रपह्नवे 1.4.764cd
क्रियां विना न संसर्गः पदार्थानामथोच्यते SV 700ab
क्रियाकर्तृत्वमेवास्य हेतुर्बुद्ध्यादिसंगतौ 4.3.928ab
क्रियाकारककर्मभ्यो व्युत्थाप्यात्मानमेकलम् 4.4.430ab
क्रियाकारकभेदाद्या लोकतः शेमुषी त्वभूत् 2.1.379ab
क्रियाकारकभेदेन नामरूपक्रियात्मकः 2.1.373cd
क्रियाकारकभेदे हि गतिः सर्वत्र दृश्यते 4.2.27ab
क्रियाकारकभेदोऽयं प्रत्यगज्ञानहेतुजः 4.4.572ab
क्रियाकारकभेदोऽयमज्ञातैकात्म्यवस्तुनः 2.4.194ab
क्रियाकारकयोगे च द्वितीयादिर्लडादि तु SV 527ab
क्रियाकारकयो रूपमितरेतरहेतुकम् 4.3.1592cd
क्रियाकारकरूपस्य तस्माच्छ्रुत्याभिधीयते 4.3.407cd
क्रियाकारकरूपस्य प्रत्यङ्मात्रसतत्त्वतः 4.3.1582ab
क्रियाकारकरूपस्य मिथ्यात्वं प्रत्यगात्मनि 4.3.408ab
क्रियाकारकरूपाणां नित्यानित्यमतिः कुतः 1.4.671cd

क्रियाकारकरूपाभ्य एषणाभ्यः प्रबोधतः 4.4.1131ab
क्रियाकारकरूपेऽस्मिन्व्यवहारे तमोन्वयात् 1.4.180cd
क्रियाकारकरूपेयमक्रियाकारकात्मना 3.4.96ab
क्रियाकारकवद्बुद्धिं तथा तत्साक्षिणीक्षते 4.3.418cd
क्रियाकारकवद्वस्तु किंचिदीक्षामहेऽमितेः 4.3.1325cd
क्रियाकारकवद्वस्तु संभावयति तज्जडः 4.3.420cd
क्रियाकारकसंज्ञाया विषयोऽयं समीरितः 2.4.468ab
क्रियाकारकसंबन्धो वाक्यार्थो यैरपीष्यते SV 484ab
क्रियाकारकसंभित्तौ वस्तुतत्त्वेन मा श्रुतिः 5.1.99ab
क्रियाकारकसंभेदधीर्मृषेत्यवधार्यताम् 4.4.677cd
क्रियाकारकसंभेदहेतौ सत्यसतीदृशम् 4.3.1324ab
क्रियाकारकसिद्ध्यर्थं भावनैवास्य कारणम् 4.3.874cd
क्रियाकाले गुणीभावात्क्रियासिद्धावसंभवात् SV 1062ab
क्रिया चापेक्ष्यमाणापि न या काचिदपेक्ष्यते SV 701ab
क्रियातः फलमित्येवं शास्त्रमेतावति प्रमा SV 416ab
क्रियातः स्तुतिनिन्दादेः सुखदुःखादिलक्षणम् 4.3.254ab
क्रियातत्फलयोर्भेदान्न भेदः क्रिययोरतः 1.4.866ab
क्रियातत्फलयोश्चापि पौर्वापर्यप्रसिद्धितः 4.3.1449ab
क्रियातो ज्ञानतो वा तद्यदि वोभयसंश्रयात् 1.4.1113cd
क्रियात्मकं च यत्किंचिन्मानतो जगतीक्ष्यते 4.4.422ab
क्रियात्मकत्वाद्दानादे राजसेवाफलाप्तिवत् 3.8.150cd
क्रियाद्वारोपकारीणि यतोऽतः पृच्छ्यते क्रिया 2.4.50cd
क्रियाधीफलभूतस्य स्वातन्त्र्यमुपवर्ण्यते 1.4.2cd
क्रियानपेक्षसिद्धत्वात्स्वतःसिद्धं तदुच्यते 2.4.117cd
क्रिया निर्वर्त्यते सा च सुखादिफलदात्मनः 4.3.983cd
क्रियानिवृत्तिविषये प्रयोगो जगतीक्ष्यते 4.4.1204ab
क्रियान्तरप्रसक्तेश्च तत्कार्यत्वेऽनवस्थितिः 1.4.196cd
क्रियान्तरस्य निर्वृत्तौ द्रष्टा तत्रापि पूरुषः 4.3.1547ab
क्रियाप्यस्ति फलं चास्ति तद्वद्वस्त्वन्तरं च सत् 1.2.48ab
क्रियाप्रकरणस्थानां विधिशेषात्मनां सताम् SV 272ab
क्रियाप्रभेदविरहाज्ज्ञानं वा निखिलं तमः 1.4.865ab
क्रियाप्रयोक्त्री नाप्येषा तस्माद्विषममुच्यते 1.3.108cd

क्रियाफलं तद्विज्ञेयमनपेक्षिततत्त्वकम् 3.4.135cd
क्रियाफलाभिसंबन्धो देहेष्वेवेति नात्मनि 1.4.503cd
क्रियाफलाश्रयाण्येष तस्माच्छुद्धो ध्रुवश्च सः 4.3.459cd
क्रियाफलोपभोगार्थं सर्वैरेव स्वकर्मभिः 2.5.18ab
क्रियाबुद्धिप्रबन्धेन यतो भोक्ताप्यहर्निशम् 1.5.80ab
क्रियाभावोऽवगन्तृस्थो विज्ञानात्मैककर्तृकः 4.3.1548ab
क्रियाभिश्चाविरुद्धानि वाच्यानीति परा श्रुतिः 5.1.5cd
क्रियाभेदे न च न्याय्यं ध्वान्तनाशः क्रियाफलम् 1.2.102cd
क्रियायां गुणभूतोऽर्थो देवतेत्युपदिश्यते 1.3.212ab
क्रियायां स्याद्विकल्पोऽयं न तु वस्तुन्यसंभवात् 3.9.175cd
क्रियायाः फलरूपेण ध्वस्तिर्नावस्थितेर्भवेत् 1.4.200ab
क्रियायाश्चाप्यकार्यत्वे कारकं न प्रसिध्यति 4.3.1448ab
क्रियायै कारकं किंचित्तस्मात्सर्वात्मनेहते 1.3.271cd
क्रियायोगाच्च तन्नाम्नो ज्ञानाभ्यासोऽपि दुर्लभः 1.3.380ab
क्रियार्थैरविशिष्टत्वाद्विद्यार्थोक्तेः परात्मनि 1.3.69cd
क्रियार्थोऽत्येतिशब्दश्चेन्न क्रियार्थो विवक्षितः 3.5.58cd
क्रियावद्भिर्हि कौन्तेय देवलोकः समावृतः 1.4.1581ab
क्रिया वा कारकं वेह सदसद्वेह यन्मतम् 1.4.1223ab
क्रिया वा तत्फलं वा स्यात्कारकं वा न किं चन 1.4.199ab
क्रिया वा तत्फलं वा स्यादभावो नात्महेतुहा 1.2.17ab
क्रिया वा तत्फलं वा स्याद्वस्त्वन्तरमथापि वा 1.2.47ab
क्रियाविज्ञानशक्तित्वात्प्रकृतस्य प्रजापतेः 1.2.154cd
क्रियाविज्ञानशक्त्यात्मा सोऽपि ब्रह्मासृजत्परः 1.2.138cd
क्रियाविधिपरत्वेन प्रामाण्यं वचसः स्थितम् SV 454ab
क्रियाविरोधः प्राप्नोति द्रष्टुः स्वात्मसमीक्षणे 2.4.137ab
क्रियाविरोधः प्राप्नोति यद्यनन्यस्य मेयता 1.4.1117ab
क्रियाशक्तिविकाशेषु ह्यन्योऽन्यव्यभिचारिषु 1.4.683cd
क्रियाशक्त्युद्भवानां च कारणं तत्त्रिकालदृक् 1.4.708cd
क्रियाशून्यं च यद्वस्तु तच्चाकारकमिष्यते 2.1.401cd
क्रियाश्लेषमृते यस्मान्नाध्यक्षफलसंगतिः 4.3.1026cd
क्रियासमुच्चयोऽतोऽयं न तु विद्यासमुच्चयः 3.3.35cd
क्रियासाध्ये फले स स्याल्लिङर्थस्त्वक्रियात्मकः SV 537cd

क्रियासिद्ध्युत्तरे काले फलं कस्यापि वेष्यते 3.4.173cd
क्रियैव ननु सर्वत्र तत्र तत्र विधीयते 1.4.795ab
क्रियैवापेक्ष्यतां तर्हि किं न सिद्धं विधिं विना SV 700cd
क्रियैवावसरापेक्षा तस्याः कारकतन्त्रतः 1.3.104cd
क्रोधहर्षभयोद्वेगज्ञानधर्मैर्विशेषयन् 2.1.156ab
क्लैद्यमापद्यमानोऽथ पाककाल उपस्थिते 4.3.1934ab
क्वचिच्चोभयथा कार्यं द्रव्यादीक्षणचित्रतः 1.5.10cd
क्वचिज्ज्ञातेषु दूरादिकारणे संशयोऽपि च SV 880ab
क्वचित्प्रमातृवित्साक्षी क्वचित्प्रत्ययवित्परः 2.1.315ab
क्वचित्साधारणात्मैव तथासाधारणं क्वचित् 1.5.10ab
क्वचिदात्मैव निर्देश्योऽनात्मैव क्वचिदुच्यते 1.4.524ab
क्वचिदेकप्रधानत्वं कस्मिंश्चिद्विषये द्वयोः 2.3.164ab
क्वचिद्बाह्यार्थविच्चात्मा तत्कर्तृत्वं निषिध्यते 2.1.315cd
क्व चेष्टमस्य मानत्वं न यागादौ स्वशब्दमे SV 751ab
क्व नु प्रतीयमानस्य पुमर्थत्वं समीक्षितम् SV 469ab
क्व न्वसौ वर्तते ह्यात्मा योऽस्मच्छत्रुविनाशकृत् 1.3.199cd
क्व सिद्ध इति वक्तव्यं यथोक्तार्थप्रसिद्धये 4.3.856cd
क्वान्यत्र फलवत्तत्स्यान्नातोऽन्यत्स्यान्मितेः फलम् 1.4.1229cd
क्वाभूदयं पुरा बोधात्कुतश्चागतवान्पुमान् 2.1.184cd
क्वाभूदेष पुरा बोधात्कुतश्चायमुपागतः 2.1.209ab
क्षणत्रयस्य संव्याप्तेः शृङ्खलाकटकादिवत् 4.3.695cd
क्षणद्वये यथा स्थायी तद्वदस्तु क्षणान्तरे 4.3.600cd
क्षणप्रध्वंसिनी चेयं तद्धेतोर्भङ्गुरत्वतः 3.4.95ab
क्षणभङ्गि घटाभासं क्लृप्तानेकविशेषणम् 4.3.473cd
क्षणभङ्गे च भावानां प्रत्यभिज्ञाद्यसंभवः 4.3.661cd
क्षणवादे विनष्टानां कस्य किं केन गृह्यते 4.3.490cd
क्षणस्य संततौ चापि सिद्धसाध्यत्वमुच्यते 4.3.606cd
क्षणस्यान्तर्बहिर्वेति न तथाप्युपपद्यते 4.3.603cd
क्षणानां क्षणिकानां वः सादृश्यं केन हेतुना 4.3.680cd
क्षणान्तरं बहिर्यस्मात्क्षणमध्ये ध्रुवत्वतः 4.3.611cd
क्षणान्तरेऽपि नाशोऽयं पूर्वाभावान्न युज्यते 4.3.604cd
क्षणान्तरे क्षणादृष्टेरसत्त्वं वः प्रसज्यते 4.3.570cd

क्षणान्तरश्चेद्भवेन्नाशः क्षणिकत्वं विहन्यते 4.3.604ab
क्षणिकं चेदिदं सर्वं प्रत्यभिज्ञाप्रमाणकम् 1.2.62ab
क्षणिकत्वं न भावानां कथंचिदपि युज्यते 4.3.618ab
क्षणिकत्वं न भावानां स्वभावः स्यात्तथा सति 4.3.746cd
क्षणिकत्वं यथा नास्ति रथादेर्येन हेतुना 4.3.651ab
क्षणिकत्वं यदैकस्य तदासाधारणात्मता 4.3.748ab
क्षणिकत्वस्य हानिः स्यात्किं नश्छिन्नं तथा सति 4.3.615cd
क्षणिकत्वादसंबन्धात्संतानान्तरबुद्धिवत् 4.3.687cd
क्षणिकत्वाद्धियां नापि स्थायिधर्मः क्रमो भवेत् SV 950ab
क्षणिकत्वे च भावानां प्रत्यभिज्ञाद्यसंभवः 1.2.61ab
क्षणिकत्वे न सा युक्ता तद्धेतुविरहात्सदा 4.3.622cd
क्षणिकाः सर्वभावाः स्युरिति यत्प्राक्समीरितम् 4.3.616cd
क्षणिकाः सर्वसंस्कारा इत्यादिवचनैरियम् 4.3.586cd
क्षणिकाः सर्वसंस्कारा इत्याद्यभ्युपगम्यते 4.3.586ab
क्षणिकार्थैस्तिरोभाव इति चेदभिधीयते 4.3.589ab
क्षणितोर्हि क्षतात्प्राणस्त्रायते न तु तं विना 5.15.8ab
क्षत्रं च प्राण एवेति चिन्तयेत्सततं हृदा 5.15.7ab
क्षत्रं प्राणस्ततो ज्ञेयो यथोक्तन्यायगौरवात् 5.15.8cd
क्षत्रस्य योनिर्ब्रह्मेदं क्षत्रं ह्याविरभूत्ततः 1.4.1606cd
क्षत्रस्यापि यतो धर्मः साक्षादधिपतिस्ततः 1.4.1617ab
क्षत्रादाविव तुल्याग्निविप्रयोर्विकृतिर्दृशेः 1.4.1662ab
क्षत्रादिनियमाशक्तेस्तस्याचैतन्यरूपतः 1.4.1630cd
क्षत्रादीनां पुरोक्तत्वादनुक्तेर्ब्राह्मणस्य च 1.4.1636ab
क्षत्रियं ब्राह्मणो जात्या यदुपेयादनापदि 2.1.93ab
क्षत्रियादौ समापेदे तेनाग्निर्ब्राह्मणाश्रयात् 1.4.1642cd
क्षपयन्वर्ततेऽजस्रं सर्वं तत्कर्मसाधनम् 3.1.29cd
क्षपाहान्यपि तावन्ति संख्ययेह भवन्ति हि 1.5.65ab
क्षमयामास तमृषिं तथा न इतिवाक्यतः 6.2.69cd
क्षय आरब्धकार्याणां ज्ञानिनोऽपि न बोधतः 3.2.81cd
क्षयः कर्मफलस्योक्तः कृतकत्वसमन्वयात् 1.4.1686ab
क्षयवृद्धिप्रबन्धेन मात्राः स्युर्वासनात्मिकाः 4.3.867cd
क्षयश्चाशेषदाह्यस्य यस्मात्तस्मादिवेतिगीः 5.16.81cd

क्षयातिशययोगित्वात्तथा व्यासोऽप्यभाषत 4.4.1173cd
क्षयान्ता निचयाः सर्वे पतनान्ताः समुच्छ्रयाः 2.4.84ab
क्षयायालं न शेषस्य गायत्रीदर्शनस्य सः 5.16.59cd
क्षयिण्योऽतो हि परमा गतिरेषैव नापरा 4.3.1829cd
क्षयिष्णु पुण्यं चैतस्माद्धेतोरकरवं पुरा 4.4.1171ab
क्षयिष्णुफलवन्त्येव कर्माणि यदबोधतः 3.8.164cd
क्षयिष्णुसाधनाधीनं जीवितं स्याद्यथा नृणाम् 2.4.53ab
क्षयिष्णुसाधनोत्पत्तेर्न त्वेषोऽसाधनाश्रयात् 4.3.1832cd
क्षयी कर्मार्जितो लोकः स्वराड्ब्रह्मावबोधतः SV 371ab
क्षयी कर्मार्जितो लोको नित्यो ज्ञानजितस्तु यः 3.3.56ab
क्षयोऽनारब्धकार्याणां सम्यग्ज्ञानप्रसूतितः 3.2.82cd
क्षयो नानन्तरूपस्य स्यात्समष्टिवपुर्भृतः 5.16.62cd
क्षराद्विरुद्धधर्मत्वादक्षरं ब्रह्म भण्यते 3.8.63ab
क्षामवत्यादिवन्नित्यं कस्मान्न स्यात्सलक्षणम् 3.3.121cd
क्षितितोयाग्निमरुतां दृष्टा स्पर्शस्वभावता 4.3.744cd
क्षितिदेशे घटाभावो घटवन्न प्रमीयते SV 933ab
क्षितिदेहोऽग्निनयनो मनःसंकल्पसाधनः 3.9.37ab
क्षितिर्जलं तथा वह्निरित्येतन्मूर्तमुच्यते 2.3.27ab
क्षितौ करणवत्यां किमन्योऽपि करणादिमान् 3.7.31ab
क्षित्यादिवियदन्तं स्यान्मूर्तामूर्तस्य लक्षणम् 2.3.80cd
क्षित्यादिसूत्रपर्यन्तं नियम्यापेक्षयोच्यते 3.8.37ab
क्षित्यादेर्वियदन्तस्य नातः प्रश्नार्थनिर्णयः 3.6.5cd
क्षित्यादेर्वियदन्तस्य यावन्नैकात्म्यमुच्यते 3.6.4ab
क्षित्यादौ वियदन्तेऽस्मिन्स्थूलादेः संभवो ननु 3.8.81ab
क्षिप्रः श्येनः सुपर्णस्तु बलवानल्पविग्रहः 4.3.1160cd
क्षीणस्वप्नोत्थसंभोगो जाग्रद्भोगाश्रयं पुनः 4.3.933ab
क्षीयन्तेऽन्याश्च भोगेन चीयन्तेऽन्याश्च कर्मणा 3.2.70ab
क्षीयन्ते चास्य कर्माणि तस्मिन्दृष्टे परावरे SV 296cd
क्षीयन्ते चास्य कर्माणि तस्मिन्दृष्टे परावरे 3.2.80cd
क्षीरौदनं तयैवाथ पाचयित्वा स्वयं पतिः 6.4.71ab
क्षुत्पिपासापरिम्लानचेतस्त्वान्नितरां न सा 1.4.1516ab
क्षुधादिदोषहेत्वेव त्वस्मद्भुज्यादि नो मतम् 1.3.106ab

क्षुरधानाद्विभज्यन्ते तथात्मा नाडिभेदतः 1.4.637cd
क्षुरविश्वंभरौ श्रुत्या दृष्टान्तौ प्रतिपादितौ 1.6.54cd
क्षेत्रं क्षेत्री तथा कृत्स्नं प्रकाशयति भारत 4.4.366cd
क्षेत्रं क्षेत्री तथा कृत्स्नं व्यनक्तीति तथा स्मृतिः 4.3.87cd
क्षेत्रं क्षेत्री तथा कृत्स्नं व्यनक्तीति स्मृतेर्चवः 4.3.345cd
क्षेत्रक्षेत्रज्ञभेदेन ह्या स्थाणोरुत्थितिर्दृशेः 2.4.430cd
क्षेत्रक्षेत्रज्ञयोरेष स्वभावः प्राक्समीरितः 4.4.988ab
क्षेत्रज्ञः करणात्मैव तस्मादिह विवक्षितः 2.3.151cd
क्षेत्रज्ञः कारणं कस्मादित्यत्र न्याय उच्यते 2.3.52cd
क्षेत्रज्ञद्वारतायाः स्यादसत्तस्माद्विकल्पितम 2.3.145cd
क्षेत्रज्ञपरमात्मानौ नात्रात्मानौ विवक्षितौ 3.5.16cd
क्षेत्रज्ञपरमात्मानौ नापि प्रश्ने विवक्षितौ 3.4.179ab
क्षेत्रज्ञस्तदुपाधित्वात्सत्य इत्यभिधीयते 2.3.244cd
क्षेत्रज्ञस्य च संभित्तौ परस्मादात्मनः स्वतः 2.3.127ab
क्षेत्रज्ञस्य तु नैवैते वासनामात्ररूपितः 2.3.143cd
क्षेत्रज्ञस्य सतो यद्वत्पुण्यपापाभिसंगतिः 4.4.1000ab
क्षेत्रज्ञस्यार्थवद्भाति शेते हृदीत्यतो वचः 2.1.254cd
क्षेत्रज्ञाकाशयोरेवं कार्यकारणसंगतिः 2.4.415ab
क्षेत्रज्ञात्मानमप्राक्षीदुषस्तो न परं पदम् 3.5.9ab
क्षेत्रज्ञानां विशेषोऽत्र यतो नैवोपपद्यते 2.3.100cd
क्षेत्रज्ञार्थात्पराङेव पर्यावर्तत आत्मनि 4.4.57cd
क्षेत्रज्ञेश्वरभेदेन संज्ञा नैवेह विद्यते 2.4.444ab
क्षेत्रज्ञेश्वरभेदेन ह्यभिन्नं वस्त्वविद्यया 5.1.21ab
क्षेत्रज्ञेश्वरयोः साक्षाच्छ्रुत्येहाज्ञानहानतः 2.1.238cd
क्षेत्रज्ञेश्वरयोरुक्तेर्मृगव्याधादिभेदवत् 1.4.1241cd
क्षेत्रज्ञेश्वरसंभेदशङ्कानुत्त्यर्थमुच्यते 3.4.10cd
क्षेपीयस्त्वाच्च कालस्य दुर्ज्ञेयो मतिविभ्रमात् 1.4.1486cd
क्षोण्युपक्रममाकाशात्षष्ठ्यन्तेनाभिधीयते 3.4.53ab
क्ष्माकार्यकरणेनैव कार्यवान्करणी च यः 3.7.32ab
क्ष्माद्येतत्सूत्रपर्यन्तं नाशादूर्ध्वं जनेः पुरा 3.8.14ab
क्ष्माबग्निवायुभिः साक्षान्नातो नियम इष्यते 4.3.231cd
क्ष्मैकदेशं विकृत्यास्तेऽविद्या तद्वत्परात्मनः 2.3.123cd

खं पुराणं न विज्ञेयं मन्त्रेऽस्मिन्निति मन्यते 5.1.120ab
खं वायुर्ज्योतिरापश्च पृथ्वी विश्वस्य धारिणी 1.2.142cd
खकार्ष्ण्यवदतस्तत्स्यादविचारितसिद्धिकम् 4.4.668cd
खजकेनैकधीकृत्य मन्थद्रव्यमतः परम् 6.3.21ab
खण्डमुण्डादिवन्मत्तो नानात्मा लभते भिदाम् 4.4.950cd
खण्डवत्स्याद्विशेषादौ यत्सामान्यमितीरितम् 2.4.270cd
खण्डशो न यथा मूर्तं खं पूर्णं चाप्रवर्तनात् 2.1.62ab
खण्डादौ गोत्ववद्यस्मात्प्रत्यग्दृष्ट्यान्तरात्मनि 1.4.980ab
खद्योतस्यानुमानेन न हेत्वन्तरकल्पनम् 4.3.150cd
खद्योतादिप्रकाशस्य यच्चानित्यत्वमुच्यते 4.3.248ab
खपुष्पे त्वनुपायत्वान्निश्चयोऽस्ति विपर्यये SV 768cd
खपूर्ण एव रान्कुम्भो द्रव्यैर्नानाविधैर्युतिम् 1.4.837ab
खस्थस्य कर्मणस्तस्य मरुत्प्रस्पन्दरूपिणः 2.3.54cd
खस्य कुम्भादिनेवासोर्निरवर्तत शब्दनम् 1.2.155cd
खिलकाण्डमथेदानीं यथावदुपवर्ण्यते 5.1.1cd
खिलकाण्डे तदखिलं पुत्रमन्थान्तमीरितम् 6.5.1cd
खिल्यदृष्टान्तवचसा विज्ञानात्मा प्रवेशितः 2.5.58cd
खेन तद्विशिनष्टयत्र सामान्यांशैकपातिना 5.1.114cd
खे लीनास्त्वस्तितामात्रा अव्यक्ताख्याः सहात्मना 1.4.205cd
गङ्गावतारवन्नापि बहूपासितृकर्मता 1.4.956ab
गच्छतः पठतो भोक्तृन्नानाकर्मकृतो रविः 4.3.1773ab
गच्छतोऽतोऽनुशब्दोऽत्र पश्चादर्थे प्रयुज्यते 4.4.116ef
गच्छन्तं पुरुषं यस्मादन्वेते स्वस्वभावतः 4.4.116cd
गच्छन्तः कस्य गत्या वा स्वातन्त्र्येणात्मनोऽथवा 4.3.1972cd
गच्छन्तमनु यः शब्दो बहिर्वच्छ्रूयतेऽध्वनि 2.1.74ab
गच्छेत्याद्येकदेशोक्तौ लोभादेव प्रवर्तते SV 493cd
गतः प्रत्यागतश्चेति सावृत्तिः स्यात्सुदुर्लभा 4.3.581cd
गतयोऽपरमाः सर्वा माया स्वप्नगतिर्यथा 4.3.1830cd
गतिः फलं च वक्तव्यं पूर्वत्र तदनुक्तितः 5.12.1ab
गतिगन्तव्यगन्त्रादेरोतप्रोतात्मवर्त्मना 4.2.23ab
गतिर्न विदिता तस्य तां स तस्मै विवक्षति 4.2.16ab
गतिर्विकाशसंकोचौ भिन्नकुम्भस्थदीपवत् 4.4.127cd

गतिविज्ञानवैकल्यात्परमात्मविदप्यसौ 4.2.18ab
गतिसाधनवत्त्वाच्च गन्तव्यमनुमीयते 4.2.7cd
गतिस्तस्याथ वक्तव्या उदग्दक्षिणभेदतः 6.2.118cd
गतौ प्राणवियोगः स्याद्यथाकालस्य चेक्षणम् 4.3.1069ab
गतौ सत्यां तदप्यत्र नान्यत्रेवोपलभ्यते SV 644cd
गतौ सत्यामनूज्वीयं नापि विद्यास्तुतिर्मता 4.4.540cd
गत्यर्थो नापि च प्रश्नः क्व गमिष्यसिलक्षणः 4.2.21ab
गत्यादिसाधनानां च देह एव स्थितेः कुतः 2.1.204ab
गन्तव्य आत्मनि कुतः क्रियाकारकसंभवः 4.2.27cd
गन्तव्यं पृच्छ्यते यस्मान्न पिपृच्छिषिता गतिः 4.2.21cd
गन्तव्यदेशाभावाच्च गतिर्नैवोपपद्यते 1.4.1243cd
गन्तव्यमुपमानोक्तिः क्रियते तस्य सांप्रतम् 3.3.154cd
गन्तृगन्तव्ययोर्भेदे विरुध्येत न संशयः 4.2.26cd
गन्धः पुष्पाश्रयो यद्वत्पुटमाश्रित्य तिष्ठति 2.3.117ab
गन्धर्वं तत्र काले तमथाब्रूम क्व तेऽभवन् 3.3.139cd
गन्धर्वाः पितरो देवा रक्षोभिश्च सहासुराः 4.4.639ab
गन्धशब्देन कृत्स्नापि पृथिवी परिगृह्यते 2.4.357cd
गन्धादिविषया धीस्थाः कर्मसंबोधिता यतः 3.2.12ab
गन्धादिषु तथा योज्यो भेदोऽयं गुणभेदतः 2.4.338ab
गन्धादिसंहतिः पृथ्वी रसान्तानां तथा जलम् 2.4.334ab
गन्धो गुरुः क्षितिप्रायो ह्लादी शीतोऽप्प्रधानतः 2.4.358cd
गमनादिविधौ पुंसः साधनत्वं निगच्छतः 4.4.117ab
गमयते सत्यमित्यस्य परिहृत्यै परं वचः 1.4.991cd
गमयत्यस्तसंभेदमतो वोपनिषद्भवेत् SV 6cd
गमयन्तु यथास्थानं देवा अग्न्यादयो मम 6.4.24cd
गमयाशु ततो दैवे शास्त्रीये ज्ञानकर्मणी 1.3.358cd
गमयित्वा तथाविद्यां जाड्यं निःसंज्ञतामिदम् 4.4.136ab
गमिक्रियां साधयति तथैकत्रापि चात्मनि 2.1.391ef
गमिष्यसीत्यतो वक्ति स्वास्थ्यं यातो यथा तथा 4.2.34cd
गम्यतेऽसंहतस्तद्वदात्मा प्रत्यग्धियात्मना 2.4.285cd
गम्यते तदुपायानां विधानाद्यत्नतः श्रुतौ 4.4.1021cd
गम्यते न विशेषोऽतः कर्मैवेति न गम्यते SV 224cd

गम्यते पुरुरूपोऽज्ञैरेकोऽपि जलसूर्यवत् 2.5.127cd
गम्यते भिन्नवाक्यत्वं नैकत्र विनियोगगीः 4.4.1022cd
गम्यते लक्षणं तादृङ्न चासौ ब्रह्मविन्मतः 3.5.212cd
गर्तादेरिव वित्तत्वं तस्य ज्ञानस्य कर्मसु 4.4.1123cd
गर्ताद्यत्ययवत्त्वत्र न मानादुपपद्यते 3.5.59cd
गर्भं ते सम्यगाधत्तामश्विनौ पुष्करस्त्रजौ 6.4.102ab
गर्भस्त्वां सुखयन्नेतु सहोल्बेण जरायुणा 6.4.110ab
गर्भे विनिःसृते पश्चाद्या निर्गच्छति योनितः 6.4.111cd
गवादिखुरबिम्बो वा पदमित्युपदिश्यते 1.4.994ab
गवादिबोधनिर्वृत्तिः पदतज्ज्ञानहेतुतः 1.4.995ab
गानप्रतिष्ठाहेतुत्वाद्धीति हेतुवचस्तथा 1.3.341cd
गायत्रीदर्शनस्येह फलकात्स्न्र्यं तथैव च 5.16.79ab
गायत्रीमेव सावित्रीं ब्रूयात्सर्वफलाप्तितः 5.16.46cd
गायत्रीवेदिनो जन्तोरपि भूयान्प्रतिग्रहः 5.16.55cd
गायत्र्यसीतिमन्त्रेण कुर्यादुक्तार्थवित्सदा 5.16.67cd
गायत्र्याः प्राणभावोक्तिः कस्माद्धेतोः पुरोदिता 6.1.2ab
गायत्र्याद्यपादसमतो विराजात्मैक्यमश्नुते 5.16.7cd
गायत्र्या मधुमत्या च व्याहृत्या चेति पादशः 6.3.43ab
गार्ग्यं काश्यो यदप्राक्षीत्क्वाभूदेष तदेति तत् 2.1.363ab
गार्ग्यकाश्येतिहासेन वक्ष्यते तस्य निर्णयः 2.1.22ab
गार्ग्यक्षरमनिर्देश्यं तां चासावब्रवीदिदम् 3.8.55cd
गार्ग्योऽनुमाय राज्ञोऽथ प्रावीण्यं ब्रह्मवेदने 2.1.91ab
गार्ग्योक्तब्रह्माभोक्तृत्वं तथामीषामनात्मताम् 2.1.97ab
गार्ग्यो ब्रह्मान्तरं राज्ञे प्रवक्तुमुपचक्रमे 2.1.53cd
गार्भैर्होमैर्जातकर्मचूडामौञ्जीनिबन्धनैः 4.4.580ab
गार्भैर्होमैर्जातकर्मचूडामौञ्जीनिबन्धनैः 4.4.1048ab
गावो दीधितयः सन्तु मधुमत्यो दिशोऽथवा 6.3.52cd
गीतयस्त्वधियज्ञं ता अध्यात्मं कास्तु ता इति 3.1.58ab
गीतास्वपि तथैवैतदूर्ध्वमूलमितीरणम् 1.4.187cd
गीर्मनोगम्यधर्माणां सर्वेषामात्मनि ह्नुतेः 1.4.539cd
गुणक्रियाणां सर्वासां कर्तृमात्रव्यपाश्रयात् 2.1.606ab
गुणतन्त्रं यदा द्रव्यं प्रसिद्धेर्बाधनं तदा 1.6.79ab

गुणत्वं लभते लोके गुणः कश्चिद्गुणी यथा 4.3.1671cd
गुणत्वं व्रजति ज्ञाने प्रमेयोऽर्थः प्रमातरि 4.4.750cd
गुणत्वाच्छोकशब्दस्य मतुपो लुप्तता भवेत् 4.3.1347cd
गुणप्रधानभावश्च देवकालेश्वरादिषु 1.4.1484ab
गुणप्रधानभावश्च पदार्थानामनन्ततः 1.4.1486ab
गुणप्रधानभावेन गहनोऽयं ततो मतः 4.4.618cd
गुणप्रधानभावेन साधारणविशेषतः 1.5.8ab
गुणप्रधानभावो हि विना नैवैकवाक्यताम् SV 831ab
गुणप्रधानरूपेण कार्यकारणगीरियम् 1.4.362cd
गुणप्रवेशवद्द्रव्य इति चेन्नानपाश्रयात् 1.4.542ab
गुणभावं तदा यान्ति सर्वास्तां प्रति देवताः 4.2.69cd
गुणभावं यथोक्तस्य विद्यात्पादत्रयस्य तु 5.16.70cd
गुणवत्ताप्यसोरस्तु यथास्योपासनं तथा 1.3.42ab
गुणवद्दोषवत्त्वं च तथैव च समुच्चयः 1.4.85ab
गुणवद्दोषवद्रूपविकल्पितसमुच्चितम् 1.4.83ab
गुणवृत्त्यान्यथा वा तद्व्याख्येयं सुविपश्चिता 4.4.833cd
गुणाढ्यापत्यफलवत्पुष्पभृतत्वकारणात् 6.4.29ab
गुणानां केशकृष्णत्वं व्येति केशेषु सत्स्वपि 4.3.1586cd
गुणान्तराधिकारोऽपि न च भानदये मतः 1.4.1038cd
गुणान्वा यदि वेशानं कालं वा दैवमेव वा 3.2.132ab
गुणिस्थित्यनुरोधित्वं न च सर्वत्र वीक्ष्यते 4.3.1586ab
गुणिस्थित्यनुरोधित्वमस्तु नाम गुणात्मनः 4.3.1588ab
गुणिस्थित्यनुरोधित्वाद्गुणानामग्निदाहवत् 4.3.1549cd
गुणैः सर्वानतिक्रम्य स्थित्वोपरि श्रिया ज्वलन् 5.16.24ab
गुणोत्पत्तिक्रियारूपस्तुतिनामाद्युपाधिभिः 1.4.130ab
गुणोपास्तिफलोक्त्यर्थमेवं हेति श्रुतिः परा 1.3.281ab
गुणो यत्र हि यः पुंसो नाम्ना संभाव्यतेऽत्र तु 2.1.60ab
गुणो यत्रापि दध्यादिः कार्यावच्छेदको मतः SV 806ab
गुप्तिमिच्छति सर्वोऽपि यत ईशाद्भयातुरः 4.4.632ab
गुरुत्वाद्बन्धनाद्भ्रन्ताद्रसाद्वाथ प्रमुच्यते 4.3.1935ab
गुरुत्वाल्लोहवत्पृथ्वी द्यौरपीत्यतिविस्मयः 3.8.135cd
गुरुद्वारैव विद्येह श्रेयःप्राप्तौ क्षमा यतः 1.4.1074cd

गुरुराह वचः स्पष्टं दृढन्यायोपबृंहितम् SV 553cd
गुर्वी स्यान्नन्ु कैवल्यं फलं नित्यमिहेष्यते SV 37cd
गुहा शयो वा शशयः श्रुत्यैव प्रतिपादितः 6.4.122ab
गृहस्थाचार्यवासाच्च न ग्रहो ब्रह्मचारिणाम् 6.2.122cd
गृहस्थो भार्यां विन्देत शास्त्रे चापि समीक्ष्यते 1.4.1202ab
गृहाच्च प्रव्रजेत्तद्वत्प्रव्रजेच्च वनात्तथा 3.5.154cd
गृहाश्रमं समाप्याथ वानप्रस्थं समापयेत् 3.5.149cd
गृहीतास्तद्विशेषाः स्युस्तेषां तादात्म्यकारणात् 2.4.279cd
गृहीतिरभिषिक्तानामिन्द्रादीनां श्रुतौ श्रुता 1.4.1601ab
गृहीत्वा परिपप्रच्छ शाकल्यमभिमानिनम् 3.9.101ab
गृहीत्वेह तमो हन्ति द्वैधीभावेऽसिवत्क्वचित् 4.4.942cd
गृही देवादिभिस्तस्मादार्जितोऽभूत्स्वकर्मभिः 1.4.1785cd
गृह्यतेऽविद्ययाभिन्नो मणिर्यद्वदुपाश्रयैः 3.4.155cd
गृह्यतेऽविद्यया मूढैर्मणिः शुद्धो यथाश्रयैः 4.3.1756cd
गृह्यते देवता नो चेदर्चिरादिगिरा तदा 6.2.132ab
गृह्यमाणेऽनुमानेन न तच्छक्यं प्रबाधितुम् 4.3.146cd
गृह्यमाणो घटो नासन्निति यद्वद्धिरुध्यते 1.2.113ab
गोत्ववन्नानुवृत्तं यन्न व्यावृत्तं च खण्डवत् 5.1.12ab
गोत्वसत्त्वप्रमेयत्ववस्तुत्वादीनि भिन्नवत् 1.6.75ab
गोत्वादिमेयपक्षेऽपि सद्रूपस्यानपायतः SV 966ab
गोदोहनादिवद्विद्यादेवं सर्वमुपासनम् 2.1.422ab
गोदोहनेनेत्यत्रापि विलयोऽन्याधिकारिणः SV 380ab
गोध्नाद्यभिमान्येवं धनी गोमानितीर्यते 2.3.9cd
गोभिधानाभिधेयार्थाद्यथेहाश्वगिरोच्यते 4.3.1765ab
गोमयाद्युद्भवाः कीटाः पतङ्गाः शलभास्तथा 6.2.159ab
गोसहस्रं ददाम्यद्य विनाप्यैकात्म्यनिर्णयात् 2.1.40cd
गोसहस्रप्रदानस्य निमित्तं श्रुतिरभ्यधात् 2.1.41ab
गौडाचार्यैरिदं वस्तु यथास्माभिः प्रपञ्चितम् 2.1.386cd
गौणं ब्रह्म यथा गौणो वह्निर्मुख्याग्निपर्वकः 1.3.67cd
गौणस्य मुख्यापेक्षत्वान्मुख्यं ब्रह्म विना न सत् 1.3.67ab
गौतमेन पुरा पृष्टे सूत्रान्तर्यामिवस्तुनी 3.8.3ab
ग्रन्थभूयस्त्वसंत्रासान्नेह कृत्स्नोऽभिधीयते 3.2.62cd

ग्रन्थार्थधारणाशक्तिर्मेधा यद्यपि भण्यते 1.5.17ab
ग्रन्थे नानन्तरे यस्मादात्मज्ञानं समीरितम् 4.2.20cd
ग्रन्थेनाविष्कृतिः साक्षादात्मनोऽस्योपपद्यते 4.4.1033cd
ग्रस्तमत्र मनः कामि वासनामात्रशेषतः 4.3.1019cd
ग्रहणं ब्राह्मणस्येति तस्यैवेहात्मवस्तुनः 4.4.1185cd
ग्रहणं यज्ञदानादिवाचकस्यैव संश्रयात् 4.4.1035cd
ग्रहणादेश्च यो भिन्नः स आत्मेत्यवगम्यताम् 4.3.518cd
ग्रहस्तस्य गृहीतौ तु नास्यान्तःपातिता तथा 1.5.32cd
ग्रहा घ्राणादयो ज्ञेया गन्धाद्यास्तदतिग्रहाः 3.2.10ab
ग्रहातिग्रहबन्धेन तथापि सितमेव तत् 3.2.7cd
ग्रहातिग्रहरूपं तत्प्रयुक्तं केन बन्धनम् 3.2.122ab
ग्रहातिग्रहरूपस्य मृत्योः कर्मेति निश्चितम् 3.3.3ab
ग्रहातिग्रहरूपाणां नातो मुक्तः प्रजापतिः 3.2.8cd
ग्रहातिग्रहरूपेण ग्रस्तोऽयमिति कथ्यते 3.2.2cd
ग्रहीता वेह नैवेति कुत इत्यादिनोच्यते 5.16.56cd
ग्रहीतुं दुःखिनोऽन्यत्वाद्दोषभाक्स्यादतोऽन्यथा 2.1.457cd
ग्रहीतुं सुधिया शक्यो वैश्वानरवरादृते 1.4.1779cd
ग्रहीतुर्ग्राह्यता लोके न न्यायेनोपपद्यते 4.3.212cd
ग्रहीतृग्रहणग्राह्यं वस्तु द्रष्टव्यमुच्यते 4.3.1490ab
ग्रहीत्रेव हि चैतन्यमात्मनोऽनात्मनस्तथा 4.3.212ab
ग्रहैर्गन्धादयो ग्रस्ता ग्रहाश्चात्मा च गोचरैः 3.2.10cd
ग्रामण्यो ग्रामनेतारः सेनाधिपतयो मताः 4.3.1963cd
ग्रामशब्देन लोकेऽस्मिंस्तथेहापि जगद्गिरा 1.4.523cd
ग्रामादि किंचिदप्राप्तं प्राप्तुमिष्टमिहेच्छति SV 885ab
ग्रामाप्तिर्नगरप्राप्तिस्तदाप्यर्थान्न मानतः SV 406cd
ग्रामोपायेन सेवायाः सांग्रहण्याविरुद्धता SV 415cd
ग्राम्याणि दश धान्यानि फलपुष्पाणि सर्वतः 6.3.14ab
ग्राम्यारण्यान्पशून्प्रादादन्याभ्यः स प्रजापतिः 1.2.216cd
ग्रासमश्नाति मन्थस्य ह्युत्तरेषु तथैव च 6.3.43cd
ग्राहकग्रहणग्राह्यभावाभावप्रसिद्धता 4.4.358ab
ग्राहकग्रहणग्राह्यभावाभावविभागवित् 4.3.242ab
ग्राहकग्रहणग्राह्यभावाभावविभागवित् 4.3.518ab

ग्राहकग्रहणग्राह्यभावाभावाद्यपह्नुतेः 4.3.1609cd
ग्राहकग्रहणग्राह्यरूपैरात्मेक्ष्यते तथा 4.3.1629cd
ग्राहकग्रहणग्राह्यरूपोऽनात्मा प्रवाहवान् 4.3.331ab
ग्राहकग्रहणग्राह्यहीनं रूपं यदात्मनः 4.3.1480ab
ग्राहकस्थश्च कामादिः स कथं ग्राह्यतां व्रजेत् 4.4.474cd
ग्राहकादि जगत्सर्वं येन कूटस्थसाक्षिणा 2.4.480ab
ग्राहकादिर्न तत्रापि साक्षिसिद्धावपेक्ष्यते 2.4.481cd
ग्राहकादिविभागोऽत्र नास्ति तद्धेत्वसंभवात् 2.4.474ab
ग्राहकाद्यतिरिक्तश्चित्सिद्धस्तत्साक्ष्यतः परः 4.3.528cd
ग्राहकाद्यतिरेकेण तद्विरुद्धात्मवस्तुनः 4.3.527ab
ग्राहकाद्यन्तरापेक्षा नैव स्यादविशेषतः 4.3.520cd
ग्राहकेऽसति तद्भिन्ने बुद्धीनां चैकरूपतः 1.2.67cd
ग्राह्यग्राहकतैतेन विज्ञानस्याप्यपोदिता 1.4.584cd
ग्राह्यग्राहकभेदेन या विद्यामात्रकारणा 4.4.603ab
ग्राह्यग्राहकमित्येवं नैव तत्प्रथते यतः 4.3.485ab
ग्राह्यग्राहकयोर्भेदो ननु भेदानुभूतितः 4.3.482ab
ग्राह्यग्राहकरूपेण यच्चापि मलकल्पनम् 4.3.710ab
ग्राह्यग्राहकसंवित्तिभेदवानिव लक्ष्यते 4.3.476cd
ग्राह्यग्राहकसंबन्धः सर्वभेदापनोदिनि 2.1.354cd
ग्राह्यग्राहकसंबन्धस्तत्साक्षी न च वीक्ष्यते 3.7.50cd
ग्राह्यग्राहकसंबन्धे नियमो न हि वीक्ष्यते 4.3.523cd
ग्राह्यग्राहकसंभिन्नं दीपवत्करणान्तरम् 4.3.524ab
ग्राह्यत्वं शरणं सङ्गो भयं चाज्ञानकारणम् 3.9.97ab
ग्राह्यभूतप्रधानत्वं घ्राणादिष्वपि निर्दिशेत् 2.4.363cd
ग्राह्यमत्र प्रसिद्धस्तु नेतिहासादिरिष्यते 2.4.314cd
ग्राह्यादिभेदवद्रूपं प्रत्यक्षं लिङ्गसंमतम् 4.3.483ab
ग्लानौ तस्यास्तदर्थेऽस्य मनोऽस्मिन्नाधिवर्तते 4.4.739ab
घट एव घटस्येति व्यपदेशो न युज्यते 1.2.117cd
घटकार्ययजत्यादि स्वस्वभावतया स्थितम् SV 618cd
घटज्ञानत्वतः साक्षादिहत्यघटबोधवत् 1.2.108cd
घटते कालसंबन्धो विरिञ्चे तूपपद्यते 1.4.1191cd
घटदुःखादिरूपत्वं धियां धर्मादिहेतुतः SV 544ab

घटप्रदीपयोस्तावद्व्यङ्ग्यव्यञ्जकसंगतिः 4.3.503ab
घटबोधप्रयुक्तेयमघटस्य ह्यपाक्रिया 4.3.1665ab
घटवच्चाघटस्यापि तदन्यापाक्रियां विना 4.3.1666ab
घटवत्तदहंबुद्धेः प्रत्यग्वृत्तेर्न गोचरः SV 1068cd
घटवन्नात्मनात्मानं प्रकाशयति दीपकः 4.3.502cd
घटशब्दादघटे मा भूत्कालास्पर्शेन कार्यता SV 624cd
घटसत्त्वे पुरोत्पत्तेरनुमा च प्रदर्शिता 1.2.111ab
घटस्तम्भादिवन्नापि मृद्वत्परिणमेत्स्वयम् 4.3.657cd
घटस्य दर्शनं तावत्प्रदीपादिपुरःसरम् 4.3.525ab
घटाकाशवदुत्पत्तिर्नाञ्जसैव सदा दृशेः 2.1.180cd
घटाकाशो महाकाश इत्युक्तेः केवलं वियत् 3.5.99ab
घटाकाशो महाकाश इत्युक्ते कुम्भखह्नुतौ 4.4.984ab
घटाकाशो महाकाश इत्युक्तौ खैकधीर्यथा 2.1.240ab
घटाकाशो महाकाश एवमाद्युक्तितोऽपि नः 1.4.902ab
घटादयः प्रमासिद्धा मुञ्चन्त्यज्ञातताां न तु SV 1004ab
घटादिजन्मना तद्वत्तन्नाशे म्रियतेऽमरः 4.3.812cd
घटादिज्ञानवज्ज्ञानं भिन्नहेत्वनपेक्षतः 2.4.191cd
घटादिज्ञानविषयः स कथं नेष्यते त्वया 4.3.567cd
घटादिनानपेक्षत्वान्न समासः प्रसिध्यति SV 945cd
घटादिमेयविषयात्पूर्वोत्पन्नक्रियात्मनः 4.3.1546cd
घटादिमेयसाधर्म्ये निषेधोऽपि श्रुतीरितः 1.4.1310ab
घटादिवत्क्षितेरस्य ह्येकदेशस्य विक्रिया 2.1.476ab
घटादिवद्यतो दृष्टमतोऽदुःखित्वमात्मनः 1.4.597cd
घटादेः कारणं पिण्ड इति नाभ्युपगम्यते 1.2.44ab
घटाद्यभाव इत्युक्तिर्न सम्यगिति मे मतिः SV 944ab
घटाद्यर्थाभिसंबन्धो धर्माधर्मादिकारणः 3.4.93cd
घटाद्यर्थाविशिष्टैव यत्त्वेतदभिधीयते 4.3.508cd
घटाद्याकारसंविद्वच्छुद्धायामपि संविदि SV 1064ab
घटाद्याभासवत्तस्मान्नात्माभासो विनश्वरः 3.4.101cd
घटाद्याभासवत्तस्मान्मोहादेरभ्युपेयताम् 4.3.99ab
घटाद्युत्पद्यमानं तु कार्यं दृष्टमतो ध्रुवम् 1.2.50cd
घटाभावं घटो यद्वद्धटाभावत्वकारणात् 4.3.795ab

घटाभावः पटे किं न कुतो वास्य घटेऽस्तिता 4.3.1704cd
घटाभावे घटः सिध्येत्पटाभावे पटस्तथा SV 959ab
घटाभावो विरोधित्वान्न घटेऽर्थान्तरेऽपि न SV 980ab
घटार्थोऽव्यभिचारित्वात्तयोर्मानप्रमेययोः 4.3.303cd
घटासामान्यरूपोत्थप्रत्यक्षैकप्रमाणकः 4.3.303ab
घटीभूतमिदं सर्वं द्वैतं ते किंप्रमं मतम् 4.3.1709cd
घटीयन्त्रवदश्रान्ता एवमेव पुनः पुनः 6.2.155ab
घटीयन्त्रवदश्रान्तो बंभ्रमीत्यनिशं नरः 4.4.248cd
घटे पटो निषिद्धोऽपि घटादन्यत्र तिष्ठति 2.3.185ab
घटोऽत्रास्तीति वाक्येऽस्मिन्को न्वर्थः संप्रतीयते 4.3.1735ab
घटोऽन्यो ह्यनुभतेः सन्नास्तीति कथमुच्यते 4.3.569cd
घटोऽयमिति संवित्तेर्घटो मेयः प्रतीयते SV 979ab
घटोऽवगत इत्येतत्ततः संपद्यते फलम् 1.2.105cd
घटो घटं रविर्वेन्दुं नानुगृह्णाति कुत्रचित् 4.3.230cd
घटो नास्तीति कोऽन्वस्मान्मानादर्थः प्रतीयते 1.4.984ab
घटो नास्तीति चान्यद्वा संगतिर्नानयोर्मितेः 4.3.1739cd
घटो भावात्मनाप्नोति त्वत्साध्यं चेदशेषतः 4.3.1709ab
घटो हि संविदं कुर्वन्नात्माकारविशेषणम् SV 981ab
घृतं दधि च संमिश्रं पृषदाज्यमितीर्यते 6.4.114ab
घ्नन्तीवाविद्यया यद्वन्मन्यते स्वप्नभूमिगः 4.3.1277ab
घ्राणं चक्षुस्तथा श्रोत्रं मनश्चैवमनुक्रमात् 1.3.154ab
घ्राणपादादयः सर्वे सर्वोपादानकारणात् 1.5.349cd
घ्रातृघ्रेयाभिसंबन्धाद्घ्राणाद्याहृतिरिष्यते 2.4.466ab
घ्रातेतरः सन्नितरं गन्धं घ्राणेन जिघ्रति 2.4.465cd
चक्रक्लृप्तिरतोऽसाध्वी श्रुत्यादिमितिबाह्यतः 2.5.89ab
चक्रनाभिवदात्मानं कल्पयित्वा विचक्षणः 2.5.68cd
चक्रनाभौ यथा प्रोताश्चक्रनेमौ च बाह्यतः 2.5.66ab
चक्रिरे दध्रिरे धर्मं धारणं प्रकृतं यतः 1.5.382cd
चक्रे काण्वसमाश्रितोपनिषदो दुस्तर्कदोषापहाम् 6.5.24c
चक्षुः प्रतिष्ठा ज्ञानानामात्मा तत्र प्रतिष्ठितः 6.1.11cd
चक्षुः श्रोत्रं मनस्तद्वज्जायते तत एव च 1.5.378cd
चक्षुः स्यान्मानुषं वित्तं यथायुर्घृतमुच्यते 1.4.1848cd

चक्षुरन्यत्प्रपश्यामो यद्बलात्स्यादयं मृषा 1.3.45cd
चक्षुरादिग्रहास्तद्वत्प्राणादिसचिवैरिह 3.2.11cd
चक्षुरादिपरिच्छेदः प्राकृतज्ञानहेतुतः 1.3.215ab
चक्षुरादीन्द्रियाणां च न च स्वप्नेऽस्ति संभवः 4.3.193ab
चक्षुराद्यनुगृह्येत स्फुटा व्यवहृतिस्तदा 4.3.67cd
चक्षुरालोचनायैव संशयं कुरुते मनः 1.4.682ab
चक्षुरुद्दीप्तिमत्वाच्च राजेत्येषोऽभिधीयते 2.1.51cd
चक्षुर्दृष्टेन चक्षुस्थं कृष्णत्वाद्येति दृश्यताम् 4.4.475ab
चक्षुर्द्रष्ट्रापि बाह्यं हि न प्रकाशं विनार्थदृक् SV 876ab
चक्षुर्मनो वा बुद्धिर्वा कर्तुः करणमिष्यते 3.4.171cd
चक्षुर्वदाततं व्योम्नि व्याचष्टे प्रत्यगात्मनि 1.4.746cd
चक्षुःश्रोत्रे धीन्द्रियाणां मनो बुद्धेस्तथैव च 1.3.155cd
चक्षुषः सत्यता कस्मादिति चेदुच्यते तथा 5.16.30cd
चक्षुषश्चक्षुरप्येवं यथा चक्षुर्मयस्तथा 4.4.181ab
चक्षुषो विषयश्चक्षुःशब्देनेहाभिधीयते 1.6.18ab
चक्षुष्टो वाथ मूर्ध्नो वा यं यं लोकं प्रपत्स्यते 4.4.83ab
चक्षू रसस्त्रयाणां स्याद्विशेषेणात्र निष्ठितम् 2.3.70ab
चक्षूरूपाभिसंबन्धसमकाला यथेष्यते 1.4.1494ab
चतुरौदुम्बरोक्त्यर्थो व्याख्यातः पूर्वमेव तु 6.3.62cd
चतुर्णां कतमेनेति न तु प्रश्नोऽत्र युज्यते 3.5.194ab
चतुर्णामन्वयो हीति हेतुनात्र विभाव्यते 2.3.40ab
चतुर्णामाश्रमाणां वा वेदानुवचनादिना 4.4.1063ab
चतुर्णामाश्रमाणां स्यान्नोपेक्षातोऽनुमानतः 4.4.1148cd
चतुर्थीं प्रक्षिपेदेवमाहुतिं पूर्ववन्मुखे 6.3.54ab
चतुर्थे दिवसे स्नातां गत्वा तामुपमन्त्रयेत् 6.4.30ab
चतुर्थे नाड्युपन्यासो विज्ञानात्मविशुद्धये 4.3.1218cd
चतुर्धा प्रविभज्यैनं सात्वताः पर्युपासते 3.7.38ab
चतुर्भिः कारणैरेतैर्याथातथ्यं न विन्दति 4.4.826cd
चतुर्भिराश्रमैरेभिर्यथाशास्त्रमनुष्ठितैः 4.4.1067ab
चतुर्भुजाङ्कितं दारु विष्णोरिव निगच्छति 5.1.123cd
चतुर्भूतात्मको देह इत्येतत्कथमुच्यते 4.3.232cd
चतुर्विशेषणस्यास्य क्षित्यबग्न्यात्मकस्य हि 2.3.37ab

चतुष्टयं पृथिव्यादि तस्य तत्त्वमथोच्यते 2.5.31cd
चतुष्टयं हि मूर्तादि मण्डले गृह्यते यतः 2.3.39cd
चतुष्टयरसत्वार्थं पुनरुच्चारणं कृतम् 2.3.37cd
चतुष्टयविभागेन स्वार्थोऽप्यात्मा विभज्यते 2.5.32ab
चतुष्टयान्वयादेष भूतत्रयरसः स्मृतः 2.3.38cd
चतुष्पदोऽथ पशवः पुरश्चक्रे स्वमायया 2.5.117cd
चतुष्पात्त्वं च तुर्येण यथोक्तेन विचिन्तयेत् 5.16.68cd
चतुष्पान्मानिरासेन साक्षाज्ज्ञानफलं ततः SV 210ab
चत्वारिंशत्तथाष्टौ च संस्कारा इति च स्मृतिः 4.4.1046ab
चन्दनादिसुखोपायसंपन्नाः सुखिनोऽप्यलम् SV 1013ab
चन्द्रं प्राप्यान्नभावं च ते यतस्तत्र संस्थिताः 6.2.150ab
चन्द्रः कर्तेह तत्प्राप्त्या पक्षाभ्यां विप्रमुच्यते 3.1.35cd
चन्द्रमण्डलवच्छुद्धं वीक्षते रविमण्डलम् 5.6.6cd
चन्द्रमा एव पुंसोऽस्य तदा ज्योतिरनुग्रहे 4.3.48ab
चन्द्रमाः पर आदित्यादर्वाक्सोमः श्रुतेर्मतः 6.2.95ab
चन्द्रमा मण्डलं स्वच्छं चन्द्रकेण मितो हि सः 6.2.94ab
चन्द्रलोकादिसंप्राप्तिः श्रूयते कर्मणः फलम् 1.5.249ab
चन्द्रेण मनसा लोकमवष्टम्भेन यास्यति 3.1.41cd
चन्द्रे मनसि बुद्धौ च ब्रह्मोपासेऽहमद्वयम् 2.1.54ab
चरन्त्यग्रसपूर्णासु भोगार्थं पुरुषस्य तु 4.2.57cd
चरितार्थत्वतस्तस्य कार्यकारणवस्तुनः 5.1.8ab
चरितार्थत्वतोऽमीषां नापेक्षा सिद्धवस्तुनः 3.5.140cd
चरित्वा च विहृत्यात्मा वासनामात्रसाधनः 4.3.981cd
चरुं प्राश्य स्वयं शेषं भार्यायै संप्रयच्छति 6.4.87ab
चर्मेहानडुहं पश्येत्सोमाभिषवसिद्धये 6.4.9cd
चलनात्मा मरुन्नित्यं दाहकोऽग्निरितीरिते 4.4.486ab
चाक्षुषे पुरुषे तस्मिन्नावृत्ते कर्मणः क्षयात् 4.4.60ab
चाक्षुषोऽतः स विज्ञेयः सामान्यात्मापि भास्करः 4.4.56cd
चातुर्वर्ण्यप्रसाध्यं सन्नैकजातिप्रसाधनम् 1.4.1600ab
चापलान्यपि कर्माणि नातः सन्त्यस्य कानिचित् 4.4.1211cd
चिकित्सयेव संप्राप्यं स्वास्थ्यं रोगार्दितस्य तु SV 28ab
चिकित्साशास्त्रतत्त्वज्ञा जग्धस्यान्नस्य नाडिगम् 4.3.1240cd

चिकीर्षवे मे संन्यासमनुज्ञां दातुमर्हसि 2.4.40cd
चितिवन्नश्यतां यद्वा कायोऽयं हेतुनाशतः 4.3.219cd
चितेरकारकत्वाच्च सर्वान्तरतमत्वतः 4.3.1493ab
चितेरव्यभिचारित्वात्तथापीष्टं प्रसिध्यति 4.3.221cd
चितेर्यथाविनाशश्च स्वप्नजाग्रदवस्थयोः 4.3.1495ab
चितेस्तद्भावभावित्वाद्वायुरेवास्तु चेतनः 4.3.218cd
चित्तत्वं सदविद्यावत्कारणत्वं निगच्छति 2.5.8ab
चित्तसंमोहमात्रेऽस्मिंल्लोकोऽयं परिखिद्यते 2.1.267ab
चित्यात्मात्र सुपर्णः स्यादादित्यात्माथवोच्यते 3.3.157ab
चित्राग्निष्टोमयागादेः पश्वादिफलसंकरः SV 306ab
चित्रेऽपि विषये चित्रमेकं वस्त्वेकमानतः SV 953cd
चित्रेऽप्यनुगमाभावान्न सामान्यविशेषता SV 975cd
चित्संबन्धोपलब्ध्यर्थं तज्ज्ञाता कः प्रकल्प्यते 2.1.140cd
चित्सामान्यचिदुत्पत्तिचिदेकप्रलयात्मभिः 2.5.4cd
चित्सामान्याद्यतः सिद्धं प्रागप्येतत्प्रसाधितम् 2.5.8cd
चित्स्वभावं सदा तत्स्यादन्यहेत्वनपेक्षणात् 4.4.929ab
चित्स्वभावातिरेकेण नाविद्यादेः प्रसिध्यति 4.3.1235ab
चिदज्ञानैकहेतुत्वाद्धातव्यानां चिदात्मनि 3.5.187ab
चिदन्यस्य च भोग्यत्वात्कम्बलौदनतोयवत् 2.1.139cd
चिदन्यस्य च भोज्यत्वान्नान्यस्यातोऽस्ति भोक्तृता 2.1.134cd
चिदन्वयो हि सर्वत्र तत्कार्येषु समीक्ष्यते 2.1.170ab
चिदाभं वासनामात्रं प्रथतेऽतोऽविकारिणः 4.3.984cd
चिदाभकारकोद्भूतवासनाकर्महेतुकः 4.3.920ab
चिदाभया वासनया तत्साक्षित्वं प्रकल्पते 4.3.906cd
चिदाभा वासनाश्चैवं संगतिर्न तयोर्मिथः 4.3.889cd
चिदाभाविद्ययैवात्मा कूटस्थोऽप्येति साक्षिताम् 4.3.91ab
चिदाभासं तमो ज्ञेयं नाज्ञासिषमितीक्षणात् 1.4.341ab
चिदाभासं स्वमज्ञानं संनिपत्य तदक्षरम् 3.9.3ab
चिदाभासस्वमोहोत्थकार्यैस्तद्वानिवेक्ष्यते 3.7.37cd
चिदाभासातिरेकेण बुद्धेः परिणतिर्वृथा 4.3.93cd
चिदाभासाश्रयाज्ञानात्कार्यसंगतिहेतुतः 4.3.416ab
चिदाभासैकमात्रेण तमःसिद्धिर्न मातृतः 3.4.105ab

चिदाभासोऽथ मनसि बुद्ध्यानन्तर्यकारणात् 4.3.360ab
चिदाभासोऽपि सर्वत्र न वेद्मीत्यनुभूतितः 4.3.99cd
चिदुत्पत्तिलयासिद्धिः सांख्यादीन्प्रति वादिनः 2.5.6cd
चिद्ग्राह्याकृतिसंबन्धे कर्मणेऽलं भवेन्मतिः 4.3.97ab
चिद्बिम्बस्यापि संहारो जलार्कप्रविलापवत् 4.3.1174cd
चिद्बिम्बितावधिश्चान्यश्चतुर्थो नेति नेति यः 4.3.286cd
चिद्रूपैरेव तैः सद्भिरनात्मार्थोऽपि शक्यते 4.3.1291ab
चिद्व्यङ्ग्यत्वे च बोधस्य साक्षादवधृते सति 4.3.516ab
चिन्तयेत्सततं धीमानोमालम्बनमेव वा 5.1.117cd
चिन्मात्रतैव तेनास्य कार्यकारणवस्तुनः 4.3.1236ab
चिन्मात्रस्य स्वतः सिद्धेर्विज्ञानघनगीरतः 2.4.474cd
चीयमानादितो देहाद्रसाद्यन्नेन भौतिकात् 4.2.61ab
चेतनाचेतनाभास आत्मानात्मत्वलक्षणः 2.4.424ab
चेतनावत्स्वतन्त्रत्वाद्देवतात्मत्वकारणात् 3.8.136ab
चेतनावदधिष्ठानात्करणादेर्जडात्मनः 4.4.62ab
चेतस्याधाय वाक्यार्थमिममाह पिता सुतम् 1.5.298ab
चेतोनुरागसिद्ध्यर्थं प्रिययेति विशेषणम् 4.3.1311ab
चेतोवत्यक्षसंवेद्ये कष्टकल्पनयानया 4.3.155ef
चेत्यते साक्षिणा यस्मान्नातः क्षेत्रज्ञरूपिता 2.3.152cd
चेष्टातः पूर्ववत्तस्य ज्योतिस्तत्रानुमीयते 4.3.55cd
चेष्टितं नामरूपाभ्यां देहेऽमुष्योपलभ्यते 1.4.646cd
चैतन्यं कायधर्मश्चेन्मनुष्योऽसाविति प्रमा 4.3.201ab
चैतन्यं देहधर्मश्चेन्मृतावविकलस्य तत् 4.3.127ab
चैतन्यं प्रत्यगात्मैव यस्मादुक्तेन हेतुना 4.3.1330cd
चैतन्यं भूतकार्यं चेत्कायवत्तिष्ठतां चितिः 4.3.219ab
चैतन्यं स्वप्नगं स्वार्थं शरीरद्वयवर्जनात् 4.3.1145cd
चैतन्यमपि नैव स्यादात्मनः कामकर्मवत् 4.3.1378ab
चैतन्यमात्मनस्तत्त्वं कूटस्थं न तु कामवत् 4.3.1409ab
चैतन्यमात्ररूपं सत्प्रथतेऽज्ञानमात्मनि 1.4.306ab
चैतन्यमात्ररूपोऽयं सदानस्तमितोदितः 1.4.1403ab
चैतन्याकारमेवैतत्प्रथते सर्वमेव तत् 2.4.124cd
चैतन्यात्मतया ज्ञेया तदबोधात्तु भिन्नता 4.3.1222cd

चैतन्यात्मस्वभावोऽपि तच्चापि शृणु सांप्रतम् 4.3.1407cd
चैतन्याभासपर्यन्तं साक्षिणः परमात्मनः 4.3.442ab
चैतन्याभासमोहाख्यवर्त्मनैव न तु स्वतः 3.8.128cd
चैतन्याभासवत्प्रत्यङ्मोहान्तात्प्रत्यगात्मनः 4.3.356ab
चैतन्याभासवत्प्राणस्तां वृत्तिं व्याप्य तिष्ठति 2.4.346cd
चैतन्याभासवत्येषा धीः पूर्वमभिजायते 4.3.358cd
चैतन्याभासवपुषा कूटस्थैकत्वमिष्यते 4.3.385ab
चैतन्याभाससंमोहं भावनेयं समाश्रिता 4.3.1263ab
चोदनाप्रतिषेधौ वः स्यातां निर्विषयौ तदा 2.1.532cd
चोदनाभिर्नियुक्तोऽहं तथा ब्रह्माहमित्यपि SV 239ab
चोदना मानकं चेत्तत्कथं कार्यं तदुच्यताम् SV 1033cd
चोदनालक्षणत्वादि धर्मं प्रत्येव गृह्यताम् SV 241ab
चोदितार्थानुवादोऽयं परिहारविवक्षया 4.3.1412ab
चोद्यपूर्वक एतस्मिन्नन्यचोद्यस्य संभवात् 4.4.1234cd
चोद्यमेतत्समानं स्यादुभयोरपि पक्षयोः 1.4.417cd
चोद्यस्यासंभवोऽस्यात्र श्रुत्यैव विहितत्वतः 4.4.1231cd
चोद्यैकमलां प्रश्नोक्तिं केचिद्व्याचक्षतेऽपरे 2.1.195ab
चोरोऽसौ मामभिप्रैतीत्येवं चोरविशेषणम् SV 115cd
छन्दः कामोऽधिकारात्स्यात्साहचर्याच्च पाप्मना 4.3.1297ab
छन्दः प्रति विवादोऽयं तन्निर्णीतौ परा श्रुतिः 5.16.42cd
छान्दसत्वात्प्रियतमस्तथात्मा संभवत्यपि 1.4.1030cd
छान्दोग्योपनिषद्वाक्यं तथा च सति युक्तिमत् 4.3.1793ab
छायामये तथाज्ञाने बुद्धौ चैकैव देवता 2.1.79ab
छित्त्वा तवाश्व्यं संधाय शिरः श्रोष्यावहे ततः 2.5.101ab
जक्षत्क्रीडन्रममाण इत्यादिश्रुतिवाक्यतः 3.9.178cd
जक्षदित्यादि यच्चोक्तं तच्चापि न विरुध्यते 3.9.200ab
जगच्चाप्यनभिव्यक्तमाविर्भवति सांप्रतम् 3.8.10ab
जगज्जनिस्थितिध्वंसनृत्तसाक्ष्यतिरेकतः 1.4.521ab
जगज्जनिस्थितिध्वंसप्रवेशानां प्रयोजनम् 1.4.623cd
जगज्जनिस्थितिध्वंसहेतुरात्मविशेषणम् 4.4.987cd
जगज्जनिस्थितिध्वंसहेतुरेष सदेश्वरः 1.4.376cd
जगज्जनिस्थितिध्वंसहेतुरेष सदेश्वरः 3.7.44cd

जगज्जनिस्थितिध्वंसा यस्मात्सिध्यन्ति तत्परम् 2.2.1ab
जगज्जनिस्थितिध्वस्तिनियमाद्यर्थकार्यपि 3.8.25ab
जगज्जनिस्थितिलया एवंभूते परात्मनि 1.4.341cd
जगज्जन्मादिसामर्थ्यं सामग्र्यादि च दुःखिनः 2.1.454ab
जगतः प्रक्रियाबीजं यदवैषीत्पुरा गृही 1.2.176ab
जगतश्चाप्युपादानं स्वात्मविद्यासमन्वयात् 3.9.160cd
जगतोऽतो न नाशः स्यादात्मदृष्टेः कुतश् चन 4.3.1427cd
जगतो व्याकृतस्याभूद्बीजावस्थाविनश्वरी 1.4.167cd
जगत्कारणरूपिण्य आपो रेतोभिधा इह 1.4.156ab
जगत्पुष्णाति वृष्ट्याद्यैः पूषादित्यस्ततः स्मृतः 5.17.4cd
जगत्प्रसूतेस्तच्चेह प्रयोगेण प्रदर्श्यते 1.2.31cd
जगत्प्रसूतौ को हेतुस्तदन्याव्यतिरेकतः 2.1.396cd
जगत्यकल्पितमपि किमु मोहादिकल्पितम् 2.3.184cd
जगत्यर्थो हि यः कश्चिज्ज्ञात एव स बुद्धिवत् 1.4.224ab
जगत्यस्मिन्यतो दृष्टमादित्यश्चक्षुषोर्यथा 4.3.137cd
जगत्सृष्ट्वात्मनः साक्षाज्ज्ञानकर्मादिसाधनः 1.4.122ab
जगदात्मनि निर्माय साधिभूताधिदैवतम् 4.3.1242ab
जगदात्मैव कृत्स्नं स्यान्न ह्यज्ञातोऽवशिष्यते 4.3.307cd
जगदुत्पत्तिसंहारस्थित्यादौ जगदात्मनः 1.4.2ab
जगदुत्पत्तिसंहारास्तद्वदात्मनि कल्पिताः 2.1.411ab
जगदुत्पत्तिसंहारैः क्रीडन्निव विचेष्टते 1.5.348cd
जगदेतद्यथा तद्वन्नाविद्याविलये भवेत् 2.4.478cd
जगद्धेतुत्वमन्याय्यमिति चेन्न श्रुतेर्बलात् 2.1.442cd
जगद्ब्रह्मात्मसंसिद्धेर्नातो मुक्तिः क्रियोद्भवा 3.3.18cd
जगद्वैचित्र्यदृष्टेश्च स्वभावे तदसंभवात् 1.4.1478cd
जगन्ननर्ति मय्येवं सदसद्विश्वरूपभृत् 1.4.988cd
जगन्नर्नर्ति मय्येवं कार्यकारणवस्त्वदम् 4.3.1742cd
जगन्निर्मिनुयादेतत्स्वतश्चेत्सर्वदा न किम् 2.1.397cd
जग्धनिःशेषबीजस्य तत्फलं नाप्यतेऽण्वपि 1.2.191cd
जग्धमन्नं यतो देहलिङ्गभावेन याति नः 1.3.248ab
जग्धाशेषजगन्मूर्तेरव्यक्ताद्व्याकृतिर्मुहुः 1.4.388cd
जग्धाशेषमहाविद्यातज्जानर्थाय विष्णवे 2.5.1cd

जग्धे कार्ये च निःशेषे कारणे चात्मविद्यया 2.1.237ab
जग्ध्वा नित्यात्मना विद्वान्पूर्णदृष्ट्यावशिष्यते 4.2.89cd
जग्ध्वा मानेन निःशेषं प्रत्यङ्पूर्णोऽवशिष्यते 3.5.75cd
जज्ञाते तेजसो भूते जलं च पृथिवी तथा 2.3.55cd
जडत्वात्तत्र मेयस्य फलं मातरि चेन्मतम् SV 1066ab
जडत्वादिति पूर्वोक्तो दोषोऽत्रापि च विद्यते 3.2.144ef
जडस्वभावकं नित्यमवभासयति स्वयम् 4.3.347cd
जडस्वभावतश्चापि कार्ष्ण्यादेर्धर्मतेष्यते 4.3.121ab
जडस्वभावतो नान्यद्रूपं कार्येषु गम्यते 1.4.307cd
जडाध्रुवानात्मनो हि त्वत्कृता कल्पनेष्यते 5.1.73cd
जडेष्वेकमनेकेषु कूटस्थं क्षणभङ्गिषु 1.4.1002ab
जनकव्यापृतेः पश्चाज्जन्यो निष्पद्यतेऽङ्कुरः 4.3.653ab
जनकस्यैव शिष्यत्वे ग्रन्थच्छायोपलक्ष्यते 4.1.7cd
जनको जनक इति नामाभ्यासोक्तितः स्फुटम् 2.1.41cd
जनित्वा म्रियते सर्वो मृत्वा भूयश्च जायते 3.9.145cd
जनिमत्कारणादात्मा योऽस्थूलादिविशेषणः 4.4.701ab
जनिमत्सर्वभूतानां प्राणेऽन्तर्भावहेतुतः 3.9.29ab
जनिमत्सर्वमेवेदमविद्यायाः समुत्थितम् 2.1.11ef
जनिस्थितिलयेष्वेवं त्रिषु कालेषु पूर्णता 5.1.55ab
जनो विशिष्टो देशेन देशो जनविशेषितः 1.3.223ab
जन्तुभिः पृथिवी सृष्टा मधु तेषां ततो मही 2.5.18cd
जन्मनाशादिहीनेयमतो दृष्टिः परात्मनः 4.3.1438cd
जन्मनैव तु तत्सिद्धेर्नोपदेशव्यपेक्षता 1.4.1197ab
जन्मनैवाखिलं ज्ञानं फलवत्किमपेक्षते 1.4.835cd
जन्मनैवाप्तमाप्नोति स्वतोऽमेयं वचःश्रवात् 3.4.33ef
जन्मनैवास्य तत्सिद्धेर्न युक्ता ब्रह्मगीरियम् 1.4.1192cd
जन्मस्थितिलयान्यान्ति समुद्रस्तेन विश्वकृत् 1.2.124cd
जन्मादिविक्रियाधर्मप्रसक्तेरात्मवस्तुनः 1.4.544cd
जन्मादिविक्रियाषट्कं साक्षान्न परमात्मनः 4.4.37ab
जन्मादिविक्रियाषट्कं स्वप्नदर्शनविभ्रमः 1.4.1327cd
जन्मादिविक्रियाषट्कसंगतिः स्यात्परात्मनः 4.4.39cd
जन्मादिविक्रियाषट्कसंगतिस्तस्य नेष्यते 4.4.635cd

जन्मादिहेतुध्वंसेन नेतीति ब्रह्म गम्यते 4.4.1344cd
जन्माद्यसंभवात्तस्माद्ब्रह्मबोधातिरेकतः 2.1.523ab
जन्मानन्तरमेवैतदनादितमसाखिलम् 4.4.879ab
जन्मान्तरसमभ्यस्तविद्याकर्मादिहेतुतः 1.2.185ab
जन्मेदं च परं चैव संसरत्येष न स्वतः 4.3.427cd
जन्यकर्मप्रयुक्तः सञ्शिशुर्भाणित्यथाकरोत् 1.2.185cd
जन्यकारणसंबन्धात्कार्यकारणसंगतेः 4.3.1356ab
जन्यते यत्फलं तादृक्कल्प्यतां नित्यकर्मणः 3.3.103cd
जन्यहेत्वतिवृत्तत्वात्पिताप्यत्रापिता ततः 4.3.1356cd
जन्यादयो विकारा ये संबन्धाश्चापि ये मताः 4.4.998ab
जपकर्मानबोधाभ्यां लोकप्राप्तौ हि शङ्क्यते 1.3.372cd
जपकर्माभिधा चेयमभ्यारोह इतीष्यते 1.3.351ab
जपमन्त्राभिधेयेयं वागित्येवं विनिश्चिताः 1.3.136ab
जपमन्त्राभिधेयोऽत्र पारिशेष्यात्प्रतीयताम् 1.3.167ab
जपस्य चाप्यनित्यत्वात्स्यादेवंवित्प्रयोज्यता 1.3.36cd
जपोऽयं ब्रह्मविज्ञानजन्मने चोद्यते श्रुतौ 2.6.1cd
जपो वंशस्य येनातः श्रुत्या वंश इहोदितः 6.5.6cd
जयतीमं पिता लोकमेवंभूतेन सूनुना 1.5.323cd
जयत्येव पुनर्मृत्युं न भूयो मृतिभाग्भवेत् 1.5.63cd
जयो भूरादिलोकानां संख्यादित्वादिसाम्यतः 3.1.59ab
जय्य एव सुतेनायं लोक इत्यवधार्यते 1.5.240ab
जरया रोगतो वास्य जायते विषमाग्निता 4.3.1928ab
जरया रोगहेतोर्वा ऊर्ध्वोच्छ्वासी तदा भवेत् 4.3.1927cd
जराजन्मनिषेधेन सर्वोऽतोऽत्र निषिध्यते 4.4.1329cd
जरादिधर्मवांस्तस्माद्ब्रह्मणैव विशेष्यते 4.4.1322cd
जरादिहेतुपाके तु पतत्याम्रादिवद्द्रुतम् 4.3.1943ab
जरामरणजन्मानि देहाधिकरणानि च SV 112cd
जरामृत्यू तु देहस्य धर्माविति विनिश्चयः 3.5.66cd
जरामृत्यू विराजश्च सर्वकार्योपसंहृतिः 3.5.80cd
जरायुजादिसंभेदभिन्ना लोकाः पृथग्विधा 2.1.415ab
जरायुरर्गलस्तं त्वमिन्द्र निर्जहि सत्वरः 6.4.111ab
जरेति परिणामः स्याद्वलीपलितलक्षणः 3.5.65ab

जलार्कवदकृत्स्नत्वमापेदेऽविद्यया परः 4.3.1cd
जलार्कस्येव संक्रान्तिः स्वाभासभ्रमकारणात् 1.5.315ab
जलूकावद्गतिरियमात्मनः प्रतिपादिता 4.4.137ab
जले जलं यथा तस्मिन्संसार्यप्येकतां गतः 3.9.189ab
जल्पन्यायेन तत्पूर्वं पञ्चमे प्रतिपादितम् 4.5.2ab
जल्पे वाद्यतिरेकेण नान्यो वक्ति यतस्ततः 3.2.137cd
जहत्यपि प्रियान्प्राणाञ्शक्यत्वादेव नान्यतः 1.4.880cd
जहाति मृत्यो रूपाणि मृतिस्वप्नादिभूमिषु 4.3.820ab
जहि शत्रुं महाबाहो कामरूपं दुरासदम् 4.4.387cd
जाग्रच्छरीरवच्चेत्स्यात्स्वप्नकायोऽपि भूततः 4.3.220ab
जाग्रज्जागरितं तादृक्तत्स्वप्नो यन्मृषेक्षणम् 4.3.1055cd
जाग्रतोऽनुभवोऽप्येवं सुषुप्तान्न विशिष्यते SV 995cd
जाग्रतो यदुपात्तं प्राग्भावनालक्षणं स्वयम् 4.3.877ab
जाग्रत्कर्मक्षयादात्मा बाह्यदेहाभिमानतः 4.3.860ab
जाग्रत्कर्मक्षये यान्ति स्वप्नकर्मोद्भवे सति 4.3.908cd
जाग्रत्कर्मक्षये सोऽयमादायाशेषभावनाः 2.1.224ab
जाग्रत्कर्मण्युपक्षीणे स्वप्नभोग उपस्थिते 2.1.282cd
जाग्रत्कामनिषेधोऽतस्तत्र कामादिसंभवात् 4.3.1166cd
जाग्रत्कालं परित्यज्य सुप्तं किमिति जग्मतुः 2.1.100ab
जाग्रत्काले ततो ज्ञोऽयमभिव्यक्तविशेषधीः 2.1.336ab
जाग्रत्काले नरस्यास्य भान्वादिज्योतिषा यदा 4.3.67ab
जाग्रत्काले विशेषेण स्थित्वा हृदयसद्मनि 1.3.263ab
जाग्रत्कुम्भादिकं वस्तु जाग्रज्ज्ञानातिरेकतः 4.3.535ab
जाग्रत्फलप्रयोगस्य यदा कर्म प्रहीयते 2.1.219ab
जाग्रत्यपि न कर्तायमेतस्मादेव कारणात् 4.3.1071cd
जाग्रत्समीक्षणं यासु पुंसो नाडीषु तास्विदम् 4.3.957ab
जाग्रत्सुषुप्तं तादृक्स्यान्निर्विवेकस्वभावतः 4.3.1056cd
जाग्रत्स्थं स्वप्नकर्मैवं स्वप्ने समधिगच्छति 4.3.1048cd
जाग्रत्स्थानात्ततः पूर्वं स्वप्नमात्मा प्रवेशितः 4.3.1905ab
जाग्रत्स्वप्नकुलायाभ्यां क्रमसंबन्धतस्तथा 4.3.1086ab
जाग्रत्स्वप्नक्रियोद्भूतान्भुक्त्वा भोगानशेषतः 2.1.331ab
जाग्रत्स्वप्नक्षये कामाः प्रमुच्यन्तेऽखिला नृणाम् 4.4.378ab

जाग्रत्स्वप्नप्रपञ्चेऽस्मिन्नात्माविद्यैकहेतुके	4.3.1790ab
जाग्रत्स्वप्नप्रहाणेऽपि प्रत्यङ्मात्रं न हीयते	4.3.1453ab
जाग्रत्स्वप्नविवेकोऽतो वाक्यार्थप्रतिपत्तये	4.3.1112ab
जाग्रत्स्वप्नसुषुप्तानां जाग्रत्स्वप्नसुषुप्ततः	4.3.1054cd
जाग्रत्स्वप्नसुषुप्तानां त्रैविध्यप्रतिपादकम्	4.3.1168cd
जाग्रत्स्वप्नसुषुप्तानि तदैतानि प्रपद्यते	4.3.913cd
जाग्रत्स्वप्नसुषुप्ते च तस्मादात्मा स एव सः	4.3.1404cd
जाग्रत्स्वप्नसुषुप्तेभ्यो यदि नामातिरेकतः	SV 856ab
जाग्रत्स्वप्नसुषुप्तेषु घटोऽयमिति संविदः	1.4.871ab
जाग्रत्स्वप्नसुषुप्तेषु त्वात्माविद्या मृषा सति	4.3.1293ab
जाग्रत्स्वप्नसुषुप्तेषु शुक्तिकारजतादिवत्	1.4.1377cd
जाग्रत्स्वप्नसुषुप्तेषु संचारोऽयं प्रमान्तरात्	4.3.1113ab
जाग्रत्स्वप्नात्मकौ पक्षौ वितत्यात्मात्ममोहवान्	4.3.1171ab
जाग्रत्स्वप्नादिकं वस्तु तन्मिथ्येति निषिध्यते	4.3.539cd
जाग्रत्स्वप्नावतः सिद्धौ स्वार्थं प्रत्येव न स्वतः	2.1.273cd
जाग्रत्स्वप्नावयं पीत्वा ह्यास्ते प्राणात्मना प्रभुः	1.3.261cd
जाग्रदेव न तु स्वप्नो भावनामात्रशेषतः	4.3.903cd
जाग्रद्दृष्टं मृषा स्वप्ने स्वप्ने सज्जागरे मृषा	2.1.296ab
जाग्रद्देशाप्तये ज्ञेया नाडी स्वप्नाख्यभूमितः	4.2.50cd
जाग्रद्बन्धुपुरामपग्रश्वारामादिलक्षणान्	4.3.959ab
जाग्रद्भूमावथ स्वप्ने जायते सैव भावना	4.3.1271cd
जाग्रद्भूमावपि मतं किमु स्वप्नैकनीडगम्	4.3.921cd
जाग्रद्भूमिं स नेतव्यो दार्ष्टान्तिकविवक्षया	4.3.1905cd
जाग्रद्भूमिष्वतस्तस्य जाग्रत्स्थप्रतिवादिवत्	4.3.560cd
जाग्रद्भूमौ न तच्छक्यं ज्योतिर्दर्शयितुं ततः	4.3.375cd
जाग्रद्भूमौ प्रसिद्धोऽस्य लोके स्वप्ने यथा तथा	4.3.1234cd
जाग्रद्योगप्रयुक्तस्य कर्मणः प्रक्षयात्तदा	2.1.106ab
जाग्रद्वद्वीक्षते स्वप्ने दृष्टपूर्वं यतो नरः	4.3.263cd
जाग्रद्वद्वेत्ति तेनास्य चैतन्यं कामकर्मवत्	4.3.1306cd
जाग्रद्वन्न यतः शब्दं सुषुप्ते वेत्ति कश्चन	1.4.862ab
जाग्रद्वस्तूनि सर्वाणि भावनामात्ररूपताम्	4.3.908ab
जाग्रद्विषय एवायं यदैक्षिष्ट पुराप्यसत्	4.3.1252ab

जाग्रद्व्यपेक्षया स्वप्ने किंचिच्छ्लेषः प्रसीदति 4.3.978ab
जाग्रल्लोकं यतो हित्वा स्वप्नलोकं प्रपद्यते 4.3.451ab
जाठराग्न्यभिसंबन्धाज्जग्धमन्नं त्रिधा क्रमात् 2.2.16ab
जाड्यं चात्मन इच्छन्ति कणभुङ्मतजीविनः 4.3.336ab
जाड्यं जन्मादिबद्धत्वं ब्रह्मणः प्राप्नुयाद्ध्रुवम् 3.9.198cd
जाड्यपारार्थ्यहेतुभ्यां शक्तिर्नास्ति मनागपि 3.7.49cd
जाड्यात्सापेक्षतः सातो मृषासिद्धिरुदाहृता 4.3.388cd
जाड्यात्स्यान्नापि कायस्य चिदभावश्चितेः कुतः 4.3.216cd
जाड्यान्वयाच्च बुद्ध्यादेर्युक्ता तत्कारणानुमा 3.4.87cd
जात एवेत्यतोऽसाधु यदुक्तं पूर्वपक्षिणा 3.9.145ab
जातं किमविनाभावसंबन्धेनेदमीदृशम् 4.3.734ab
जातकादिपरिज्ञानाज्ज्ञातुं कालोऽपि शक्यते 1.5.286cd
जातदेहाभिषङ्गः संस्तादात्म्यप्रतिपित्सया 1.2.206ab
जातरूपव्यवहितं लेहयन्ति घृतं जनाः 1.5.51cd
जातरूप्यस्मृतेर्लोके मिथ्याज्ञानं प्रसिध्यति 1.4.415cd
जाता कर्मण एवेयं भावनास्यान्तरात्मनः 4.3.1189cd
जातिक्रियागुणादीनां निषेधादात्मवस्तुनः 4.3.1591ab
जातितो बधिरस्येह व्यक्तिः स्याद्रूपमात्रजा 1.4.399ab
जातिरूपेण सा स्थित्वा जातिमेव नियच्छति 1.4.1639cd
जातिर्गुणः क्रिया द्रव्यं संबन्धो भाव एव च 2.3.181ab
जातिस्मरणदृष्टान्तादात्मा नित्यो मतो यदि 4.3.132ab
जाते कुमारेऽथ पतिरङ्कमारोप्य तं पिता 6.4.113ab
जाते नापेक्षते किंचित्प्रतीचोऽनुभवात्परम् 2.4.221cd
जातौ ब्राह्मणशब्दोऽयं मा प्रापदिति तं श्रुतिः 4.4.1297ab
जात्यन्तरनिषेधाय विज्ञानघनगीरपि 2.4.414cd
जात्यन्धगजदृष्ट्येव कोटिशः कल्प्यते मृषा 4.4.566cd
जात्यन्धयोर्न योगेऽपि शक्ती रूपवदीक्षणे 5.14.8cd
जात्यन्धवन्न चादृष्ट्वा कश्चिद्व्यपदिशेदिह 4.3.685ab
जात्यन्धादेश्च नाम्नैव तथा चोभयथाप्यसौ 1.4.399cd
जानन्नपि वसिष्ठादिगुणवत्त्वं यथार्थतः 6.1.19ab
जानीयात्तमनात्मानं जाग्रत्स्वप्नसुषुप्तिषु 1.4.1380cd
जानीयात्सर्वमात्मेति नेति नेत्युपलक्षणम् 2.5.41cd

जाने पुत्रायुतं जातं जाने पितरमागतम् 4.3.1023ab
जायतेऽतोऽभिमानोऽस्यां जायते महतामपि 4.3.357cd
जायतेऽनन्तरं शब्दः स्वव्यापारक्रमादथ 4.4.746cd
जायते नश्यतीत्येवं तत्साक्ष्यप्यभिधीयते 3.4.157cd
जायते यदि विज्ञानं प्रामाण्यं केन वार्यते 1.4.908cd
जायते यद्यपि ज्ञानं कृत्स्नैकात्म्यसमाश्रयम् 4.4.878cd
जायते सर्वभूतानामपि सर्वविदामिह 4.3.359cd
जायते ह्यजयस्तेषामसुराणां जयस्तु सः 1.3.120cd
जायया मैथुनाख्यं यच्छ्रोत्रियस्य विपश्चितः 6.4.63cd
जायादिः स्यात्प्रियो भक्त्या बन्धक्याः कामुको यथा 2.4.82cd
जायादिरप्रियः सर्वः स्वत आद्यन्तदुःखकृत् 2.4.80ab
जाया मानुषवित्तं च कर्मैकार्थत्वकारणात् 1.5.276cd
जायेरन्नेव तच्छाखाः प्ररोहेयुर्दलानि च 6.3.61cd
जारस्य दोषं प्रख्याप्य मन्त्रेणानेन सत्वरः 6.4.55cd
जिघृक्षत्यायसं तप्तं शास्त्राचार्यात्मनिश्चयात् 4.4.286ab
जिघ्रतीत्यपि निर्देशः क्रियातत्फलयोर्भवेत् 2.4.466cd
जिघ्रन्ती भवति घ्राणं पश्यन्ती चक्षुरुच्यते 1.5.118ab
जिघ्राणीममहं गन्धमिति यो वेत्त्यविक्रियः 1.4.616ab
जिघ्राणीममहं गन्धमिति यो वेत्त्यविक्रियः 1.4.717ab
जिघ्रेदैकात्म्यमात्रेण सर्वस्यास्यात्ममात्रतः 2.4.471ef
जिज्ञासुरपि चैतस्य यथोक्तस्यात्मवस्तुनः 3.5.122ab
जिज्ञासोरेव कर्तुस्तु न सिषाधयिषोः सदा SV 282cd
जिज्ञासोरेव चैकात्म्यं श्रूयन्तेष्वधिकारिता SV 12cd
जितलोकास्त उच्यन्ते पितरो दिव्यभोगिनः 4.3.1856cd
जित्वा देया द्विजान्गाव इत्यर्थं चोत्तरा श्रुतिः 3.9.133cd
जिनन्तीवैनमिति च मृषैवमभिमन्यते 4.3.1248cd
जिष्णुः स्याज्जयशीलत्वाज्जीयते न परैर्यतः 2.1.63ab
जिष्णुरिन्द्रगुणोपास्तेर्वैकुण्ठगुणतः परः 2.1.65ab
जिहासति तथानर्थानविद्वानात्मनि श्रितान् 1.4.1815ab
जिहासितस्यानर्थस्य हेतुः स्यात्सशरीरता 1.4.169cd
जिहासितुः स्वभावोऽसावित्युक्तिः शिशुवक्तृका SV 140ab
जिह्रेमि बहुशोऽत्रोक्तौ तस्मादेवोपरम्यते 2.4.312cd

जिह्मेम्यत्र पुनर्वक्तुं पुनरुक्तगिरा भृशम् 3.2.45cd
जिह्वामूलीयकादीनि ह्यष्टौ स्थानानि वागिह 1.3.341ab
जीर्णकूपादिवत्कर्तुर्यदप्यस्मरणं न तत् SV 879ab
जीवः प्राणोऽत्र संसारी भोक्तेन्द्रियमनःपरः 6.1.32ab
जीवग्रहोऽत्र नन्वस्तु प्रकृतत्वाविशेषतः 2.3.150ab
जीवता किं व्रतं धार्यमिति मीमांस्यतेऽधुना 1.5.363cd
जीवतो देवभूतस्य भावनोपचयात्कुतः 1.3.373ab
जीवत्येव शरीरेऽस्मिंस्तत्स्थ एव कथं पुनः 4.3.1370ab
जीवापेतमिति ह्युक्तेर्जन्मादेश्च निषेधतः 3.2.33ab
जीवाविष्ट उपास्योऽत्र देवताविग्रहः सदा 1.3.181ab
जुहोत्यादिक्रियाद्वारा यस्मात्सर्वमवत्ययम् 4.3.862ab
जुहोत्यादिर्जगद्धेतुः सर्वावानुच्यते ततः 4.3.863cd
जुह्वाद्यव्यभिचारित्वकर्मसंगतिकारणात् SV 431ab
जुह्वाद्यव्यभिचारित्वात्प्रत्युपस्थापयेत्क्रतुम् SV 337ab
जुह्वाद्याकृतिसंपत्तिव्यपेक्षापूरणक्षमम् SV 335ab
जेतुमाशंसते तस्माद्धर्मः स्याद्बलवत्तमः 1.4.1620cd
जेतुमुत्सहते भूपं धर्मात्मकबलाश्रयात् 1.4.1621cd
ज्ञातं ध्रुवमनेनैतद्यज्ज्ञोकर्मकमीक्ष्यते SV 1027ab
ज्ञातं ब्रह्म यथावच्च न चापागात्ततस्तमः 3.2.98ab
ज्ञातः सोऽर्थो मयेत्यत्र नाप्तवाक्यं विहन्यते SV 707ab
ज्ञातत्वकार्यतश्चातः सिद्धं तत्फलतोऽथवा 1.4.286cd
ज्ञातत्वात्तदभावोऽपि प्रात्यक्ष्यान्नेष्यते स्मृतिः 1.4.274cd
ज्ञातयः पुरुषं प्रेतमाहुः कार्यं मृतेरिदम् 3.7.20cd
ज्ञातयोऽभिविशन्त्येवं तद्विदं जीवनार्थिनः 1.3.282cd
ज्ञातरूपातिरेकेण नान्यद्रूपं समीक्ष्यते 1.4.226ab
ज्ञातस्य चाप्रमेयत्वान्नापेक्षा मानसंगतौ 4.4.684cd
ज्ञातस्याज्ञाततोऽन्यत्वात्तत्र स्यात्किं न मानता SV 689cd
ज्ञातस्याव्यतिरेकित्वादज्ञातस्याप्यमानतः 1.4.223cd
ज्ञाताज्ञातं निषिध्याथ सदा दृष्टौ प्रतिष्ठति 2.3.207cd
ज्ञाताज्ञातविभागोऽतः स्वतःसिद्धात्ममातृकः 1.4.285ab
ज्ञाताज्ञातापनिह्नुत्या ज्ञातृभावादिसाक्षिणः 1.4.887ab
ज्ञाताज्ञाते प्रति त्वस्य न व्यापारोऽप्रमाणतः SV 992cd

ज्ञातात्मतत्त्वो जानाति त्रिकालं तदसंभवम् 1.4.217ab
ज्ञातायां स्रजि तन्मोहकल्पितानां यथैकता 1.4.946ab
ज्ञातायां स्वात्मरूपत्वात्सुतरां नास्ति कामना SV 289cd
ज्ञातारिष्टः कथं नाम कुर्यादात्महितं पुमान् 5.6.5cd
ज्ञातार्थव्यतिरेकेण मानानां मानता यतः 1.4.242ab
ज्ञातार्थसंगतिः शब्दो वाक्यार्थावगमक्षमः SV 860ab
ज्ञातुर्ज्ञानाभिनिष्पत्तिर्निष्पन्नं मेयमेति तत् 1.2.103ab
ज्ञातृज्ञेयप्रभेदः स्यात्तत्र प्रत्यगनात्मनोः 4.4.691cd
ज्ञातृज्ञेयादिकं भेदं तमोध्वस्तौ न सोऽस्त्यतः 4.4.277cd
ज्ञातृतत्साक्षिणौ चैवं नाज्ञाने साक्षिणोऽपरम् 1.4.294cd
ज्ञातृत्वसिद्धये ज्ञानं ज्ञातृत्वं तत्कृतं यतः 3.4.146cd
ज्ञाते ज्ञातं च कृत्स्नोऽसौ तावत्त्वात्सर्ववस्तुनः 1.4.943cd
ज्ञाते ज्ञातं च तत्कात्स्न्र्यात्तावत्त्वात्सर्ववस्तुनः 1.4.1362cd
ज्ञातोऽनर्थेन संबन्ध आत्मनो न तु वास्तवः SV 456cd
ज्ञातोऽपि तद्वदेवास्मान्नात्मनो विद्यते परः 1.4.978ab
ज्ञातोऽयमर्थोऽज्ञातो वा धीरियं कर्तृसंश्रया 1.4.283ab
ज्ञातोपायत्वतो यद्वा विधिनोपेयसिद्धये SV 581cd
ज्ञातो वार्थोऽथवाज्ञात उभयं वा न चोभयम् 1.4.222ab
ज्ञात्राद्यसंभवं वक्ति कूटस्थैकत्वकारणात् 3.9.194cd
ज्ञात्वात्मानं तमेवेति तन्मोहोत्थादनात्मनः 4.4.862ab
ज्ञात्वानुष्ठानवचनाद्विद्वान्यजत इत्यपि SV 198cd
ज्ञात्वैव विषयाँल्लोके सर्वः कामयते यतः 4.4.280cd
ज्ञानं घटो दीप इति शब्दार्थज्ञानभित्तये 4.3.543ab
ज्ञानं जगति रांसिद्धं सा चैकात्म्येऽतिदुर्लभा 1.4.416cd
ज्ञानं तदविनाभूतः परः साक्षीति भण्यते 1.4.374cd
ज्ञानं न च द्वयं भेदादभेदेऽनुभवः स्वतः SV 1070cd
ज्ञानं प्रत्यभिजानाति ध्वंसित्वान्नापि चापरम् 4.3.676ab
ज्ञानं मुक्त्वा ततः प्राप्तौ नान्यत्किंचिदपेक्षते 4.2.91cd
ज्ञानं सप्रतिघं यद्वत्कार्यं वास्मासु दृश्यते 1.5.350ab
ज्ञानं हन्ति तमोऽशेषं न तु कर्म तमोन्वयात् 3.3.40cd
ज्ञानं हि वस्तुतन्त्रं स्यान्न तु तत्कारकाश्रितम् 3.3.34cd
ज्ञानकर्तव्यतायां तन्नियोज्य पुरुषं प्रति 1.4.876cd

ज्ञानकर्मफलं चैतत्कर्मकाण्डप्रचोदितम् 1.4.1ab
ज्ञानकर्मफलं दिव्यं यदि नाम पुरोदितम् 3.2.7ab
ज्ञानकर्मादितन्त्रं सत्सूत्रं जज्ञे ततो विभोः 1.4.18ab
ज्ञानकर्मादिबीजस्य गर्भ एवं प्रजापतेः 1.2.180cd
ज्ञानकर्मोपदेशो हि नरं प्रत्येव सर्वथा 1.3.15ab
ज्ञानकाण्डार्थशेषत्वं कर्मकाण्डस्य यत्पुनः SV 278ab
ज्ञानकाण्डे प्रवेशो वा तेषां नार्थान्तरं ततः SV 301cd
ज्ञानकार्यवदित्येवं मतं चेन्नैवमिष्यते 3.3.89cd
ज्ञानक्रिया प्रमातृस्था न यथावस्तुबोधकृत् 2.4.183ab
ज्ञानक्रियाभ्यां व्याप्योऽयमित्याकाङ्क्षा निवर्तते 2.3.200ab
ज्ञानक्रियाशक्तिमद्यद्यत्रेदं जगदाहितम् 1.4.18cd
ज्ञानजन्माभिदधति तथा श्रुतिवचांसि च 4.4.597cd
ज्ञानज्ञात्रतिरेकेण तमस्यपि न विद्यते 1.4.281ab
ज्ञानतुल्याममन्वानो दक्षिणां गुरवे नृपः 4.2.96ab
ज्ञानतोऽज्ञानहानिः स्याद्देवत्वं भावनाबलात् 1.3.229ab
ज्ञानप्रधानतामेति स्वार्थसंकेतवर्त्मना 4.4.746ef
ज्ञानप्रसादेन विशुद्धसत्त्वस्ततस्तु तं पश्यते निष्कलं ध्यायमानः
4.4.1258cd
ज्ञानबोधेन नैवात्मा मितो नाप्यात्मसंविदा SV 1070ab
ज्ञानमप्रतिघं यस्य वैराग्यं च जगत्पतेः 1.4.79ab
ज्ञानमप्रतिघं यस्य वैराग्यं चेति च स्मृतेः 1.4.1197cd
ज्ञानमाकारवल्लोके सर्वाकारप्रसक्तितः 1.4.475cd
ज्ञानमात्मनि महति तद्यच्छेच्छान्त आत्मनि 4.4.1256cd
ज्ञानमात्रमिदं सर्वं न ज्ञेयं विद्यते पृथक् 4.3.700ab
ज्ञानमात्रसतत्त्वं यद्ब्रह्माज्ञातसतत्त्वकम् 1.2.9ab
ज्ञानमात्रस्वभावत्वाद्भवता नाभ्युपेयते 4.3.701cd
ज्ञानमुत्पद्यते पुंसां क्षयात्पापस्य कर्मणः 4.4.579ab
ज्ञानमुत्पद्यते पुंसां क्षयात्पापस्य कर्मणः 4.4.1044ab
ज्ञानमूर्तेर्न चाज्ञानमागन्तु सहजं तथा 1.4.1105ab
ज्ञानमेयप्रभेदोऽपि मानस्य स्वार्थरूपिणः 1.4.244ab
ज्ञानमेवात्मनात्मानमुपासीनोऽमृतो भवेत् 2.4.25ef
ज्ञानयुक्तमुदीच्यां च कर्मैवमुपसंहृतम् 3.9.77cd

ज्ञानयोगेन सांख्यानां कर्मयोगेन योगिनाम् 3.5.200cd
ज्ञानरूपं यथा शुद्धं क्षणं चैवावभासते 4.3.488ab
ज्ञानलक्षणसंप्राप्तावथवाप्यविशेषतः 4.3.722cd
ज्ञानलाभार्थयोर्यस्मादेकार्थत्वं विवक्षितम् 1.4.1010ab
ज्ञानवज्ज्ञानसंभूतेर्नैव प्रागभ्युपेयते 3.3.41cd
ज्ञानव्यक्तौ तु किं मानं यतोऽभिव्यक्तिवागियम् 4.4.338cd
ज्ञानव्याप्तिर्हि शब्दादौ स्यादेकप्रकृतित्वतः 4.4.689ab
ज्ञानशक्तिक्रियाशक्तिविभुत्वात्परमक्षरम् 2.4.385ab
ज्ञानशक्तिविकाशानां मनः साधारणं मतम् 1.4.708ab
ज्ञानसंततिनिष्पत्तौ तमोमात्रसमाप्तितः 1.4.1520cd
ज्ञानसंततिरन्त्या नः सेत्स्यतीत्यत्र का प्रमा 1.4.1519cd
ज्ञानस्य च विशुद्धस्य स्वसंविन्मात्ररूपिणः 4.3.697ab
ज्ञानस्य प्राप्तिर्नित्या वेत्यस्त्वपूर्वो विधिः स्फुटः 1.4.770cd
ज्ञानस्य यदुपन्यस्तं विशेषस्तत्र नेक्ष्यते SV 1069cd
ज्ञानस्य वस्तुतन्त्रत्वान्न कर्त्रनुविधायिता 1.4.1514ab
ज्ञानस्य वस्तुतन्त्रत्वान्नोपासनसमुत्थितिः 1.4.882ab
ज्ञानस्यैवार्थरूपं तद्बोधवच्चेत्प्रकल्प्यते 4.3.565ab
ज्ञानस्वभावाद्व्युत्थानं ज्ञेयवस्तूपरोधतः 3.5.104ab
ज्ञानाग्निः सर्वकर्माणि भस्मसात्कुरुते तथा 1.4.1548cd
ज्ञानाग्निः सर्वकर्माणि भस्मसात्कुरुते तथा 4.4.1289cd
ज्ञानाच्च मुक्तिः संसारात्कथं नास्ति प्रशास्तृ तत् 3.8.160cd
ज्ञानाज्ञाने ततोऽपेक्ष्य व्यवहारोऽयमात्मनि 3.5.50ab
ज्ञानात्कार्यान्तराभावान्नैतत्साध्वभिधीयते 1.4.809cd
ज्ञानात्पुरापि ब्रह्मैव गातो ज्ञानफलं भवेत् 2.5.138cd
ज्ञानात्पृथगसंसिद्धे रजतादेरमेयता 4.4.902ab
ज्ञानादतिशयो यद्वन्नास्तीतीह तथैव सन् 4.3.569ab
ज्ञानादन्या गतिश्चेत्स्यात्प्राप्स्यसीत्येव तं वदेत् 4.2.95cd
ज्ञानादेव तु कैवल्यमज्ञानादेव नास्ति तत् 1.4.1669cd
ज्ञानादेव त्वनावृत्तिः श्रूयते बहुशः श्रुतौ SV 374cd
ज्ञानादेव पुमर्थाप्तेर्निष्फले सुतकर्मणी 1.5.225cd
ज्ञानादेव भवेन्नेति तद्वैतदिति हि श्रुतिः 1.3.372ef
ज्ञानाद्ध्वस्ते हि तमसि ध्वस्ते द्वैते सहेतुके 4.3.1283ab

ज्ञानाद्ध्वान्तनिवृत्तिस्तु मरणं स्याद्विपश्चिताम् 1.4.1673cd
ज्ञानानुरूपामेवातो दक्षिणां दित्सुरब्रवीत् 4.2.109ab
ज्ञानानुरोधिनी यद्वत्प्रवृत्तिः प्राणिनामिह 3.5.110ab
ज्ञानाभावादसिद्धौ च क्व न्वभ्यासव्यपेक्षणम् 2.4.207cd
ज्ञानाभावान्न विज्ञानान्नोभाभ्यां तदसंभवात् 1.4.1699cd
ज्ञानाभावोऽथवा सर्वमविद्यैवेति निश्चितिः 1.4.1439cd
ज्ञानाभिव्यक्तिरित्येवं स्वसिद्धान्तसमाश्रयात् 4.4.324cd
ज्ञानाभेदात्तु तत्सिद्धिस्तदध्यासात्तथा परम् 4.3.484ab
ज्ञानाय विदधत्युच्चैः संन्यासं सर्वकर्मणाम् SV 226cd
ज्ञानार्थे प्रकृते कस्माल्लाभार्थेनोपसंहृतिः 1.4.1009cd
ज्ञानेऽधिकारिणोऽभावात्प्रामाण्यं क्षिप्यते स्वतः SV 288cd
ज्ञानेऽपि स्यादनाश्वासस्तस्यानुभवसिद्धितः 4.3.568cd
ज्ञानेन किं न विज्ञातं वद किं वा न बाधितम् 1.4.1457cd
ज्ञानेन गम्यते साक्षात्तावन्मात्रानुरोधिना 1.4.1412cd
ज्ञानेन गम्यते साक्षात्तावन्मात्रानुरोधिना 2.4.442cd
ज्ञानेन ज्ञायते तादृक्कृत्स्नं कथमिहोच्यते 1.4.958cd
ज्ञानेन तमसो दाहात्कुतो विध्यर्थसंभवः 1.4.761cd
ज्ञानेन भित्त्वा संमोहं सर्वानर्थैकसंश्रयम् 4.4.1251cd
ज्ञानेनाज्ञानविध्वस्तेः प्रात्यक्ष्यात्तदसद्वचः 3.3.97cd
ज्ञानेनाप्रतिघेनासौ वेदोक्तां सृष्टिपद्धतिम् 1.2.173ab
ज्ञानोत्पत्तावतो ध्वस्तिः सर्वेषामपि कर्मणाम् 1.4.1547cd
ज्ञानोत्पत्तौ क्षये मानं कर्मणां विद्यते यथा 3.2.83ab
ज्ञानोत्पत्तौ तु तद्बाधान्नानेवेति प्रयुज्यते 4.4.672cd
ज्ञानोत्पत्तौ न चैवान्यच्छमादिभ्यो ह्यपेक्ष्यते 1.3.98cd
ज्ञानोत्पत्तौ न संज्ञास्तीत्यास्तां तावदिहात्मनः 2.4.479ab
ज्ञानोत्पत्त्यादिकालिलिङ्गाद्यतस्तद्धेतुमात्रकम् SV 224ab
ज्ञानोपबृंहितस्यापि क्रतुराजस्य कर्मणः 3.3.12ab
ज्ञापकत्वात्प्रमाणस्य प्रेरयन्कारको भवेत् SV 486cd
ज्ञापकानि हि शास्त्राणि कारकाणि न कुत्रचित् 1.4.1262cd
ज्ञेय आत्मैव नानात्मा पदनीयत्वकारणात् 1.4.981ab
ज्ञेयं यत्तत्प्रवक्ष्यामि यज्ज्ञात्वामृतमश्नुते 1.4.235ab
ज्ञेयं यत्तत्प्रवक्ष्यामि यज्ज्ञात्वामृतमश्नुते 2.4.245ab

ज्ञेयं यावज्जगत्किंचिदामंसीति ततः सदा 6.3.38cd
ज्ञेयकार्यसमाप्तत्वान्न किंचिदवशिष्यते 4.4.1162cd
ज्ञेयत्वसिद्धये प्राह यथोक्तेश्वरवर्त्मना 3.8.171ab
ज्ञेयव्याप्त्यतिरेकेण न विज्ञानात्फलान्तरम् SV 672ab
ज्ञेयाज्ज्ञाता परो नास्ति प्रत्यग्ज्ञाने यतस्ततः 4.4.550cd
ज्ञेयोऽर्थः पुरुषार्थो वा पदनीयमतो भवेत् 1.4.971cd
ज्येष्ठः श्रेष्ठश्च सर्वेषां प्राणानामाश्रयो हि सः 6.1.9ab
ज्येष्ठः श्रेष्ठो यतः प्राणो न तु वागादयस्ततः 6.1.3ab
ज्योतिः प्रत्यक्स्वयं दृष्टमासनाद्याः प्रकाशयेत् 4.3.111cd
ज्योतिः संविच्चितिः प्रत्यङ्ङात्मेति व्यपदिश्यते 4.3.340ab
ज्योतिः साधयितुं युक्तमनुमानद्विषः सतः 4.3.224cd
ज्योतिरात्मा जडाद्देहात्तस्याचैतन्यरूपतः 4.3.309cd
ज्योतिरित्यस्य बुद्ध्यादेरागमापायसिद्धिदः 4.3.342ab
ज्योतिरेकात्मकं नित्यमसाधारणमानगम् 4.3.102cd
ज्योतिर्जागरिते यद्वद्रवीन्द्वादि समीक्ष्यते 4.3.70ab
ज्योतिर्दर्शयितुं शक्यं स समान इतीर्यते 4.3.376cd
ज्योतिर्भ्यो देहतो लिङ्गाद्बुद्ध्यन्ताच्चातिरेकतः 4.3.378ab
ज्योतिर्मात्रतया स्थानं दृशेः प्राज्ञे जगौ सुधीः 4.3.1538cd
ज्योतिर्मात्रतयैवात्मा सुषुप्ते व्यवतिष्ठते 4.3.1387ab
ज्योतिषाकारकेणात्मा वर्ततेऽसंस्पृशन्परम् 4.3.889ab
ज्योतिषानात्मना पूर्वं लिङ्गेन प्रतिपादितः 4.3.278cd
ज्योतिषापि स चेज्जेयो जीयतां न निषिध्यते 1.5.240cd
ज्योतिषामपि तज्ज्योतिः स्वयंज्योतिःश्रुतेस्तथा 4.4.367ab
ज्योतिषामपि तज्ज्योतिरसद्धीपरिमोषणात् 1.4.373ab
ज्योतिषामपि तज्ज्योतिरस्मद्धीपरिमोषणात् 4.3.1471ab
ज्योतिषामपि तज्ज्योतिरायुर्देवा उपासते 4.4.636ef
ज्योतिषामपि तज्ज्योतिस्तमेवेति च शास्त्रतः 4.3.1466cd
ज्योतिषा व्यवहार्येषोऽसंहतेन पुमानिति 4.3.22cd
ज्योतिषा स्वेन निर्जित्य यास्यन्त्यग्न्यादिरूपताम् 1.3.144cd
ज्योतिषेत्यत्र संचोद्य परिहारं प्रचक्षते 1.5.234cd
ज्योतिषोऽत्यन्तवैधर्म्यप्रसिद्ध्यर्थं विशेषणम् 4.3.45ab
ज्योतिष्टोमादिका यद्वद्विशिष्टानेकसाधना 1.3.70ab

ज्योतिष्टोमादिवाक्यस्य ब्रह्मास्मीत्यत्र तन्न तु 1.4.911cd
ज्योतिष्टोमेन संप्राप्तिर्भोगायैव तु तत्कृतः 1.5.237ab
ज्योतीरूपमिदं तत्त्वं सुषुप्ते व्यवतिष्ठते 4.3.1388ab
ज्योती रूपमिदं भास्वत्प्रत्यङ्मात्रसतत्त्वकम् 4.3.339cd
ज्योत्स्नया राजतेऽत्यर्थं सोमो ब्राह्मणराजतः 2.1.56ab
ज्वरादिव्याधिना तप्तो व्याधितस्तप्यते तु यत् 5.13.1ab
ज्वलज्जाज्वल्यमानस्त्वं जठरस्थान्नपाककृत् 6.3.27ab
ज्वलनव्यापृतेरग्नेः प्रकाशौष्ण्यादि चेत्फलम् 4.4.311ab
ज्वलनव्यापृतेर्वह्नेः प्रकाशौष्ण्यादिजन्मनः 4.4.312ab
ज्वलन्नपि यथा वह्निर्नानभ्याहितमिन्धनम् 4.3.1565ab
ज्वलन्निव समुत्तस्थौ यः स भोक्तेति गम्यताम् 2.1.155cd
ज्वालानुग्रहतो वह्नेस्तत्प्रकाशादिदर्शनात् 4.4.317ab
डतमच्प्रत्ययस्तस्माद्बह्वर्थस्यात्र संभवात् 4.3.282ab
त एतान्सप्त पुरुषानित्यादिश्रुतिवाक्यतः 2.3.67ab
त एवामी इति मतिः कस्यचिद्व्यक्तिहेतुजा 4.3.667cd
त एवामी इति मतिर्जायते न तु कस्यचित् 4.3.669ab
तं क्रमित्वोपरि स्थित्वा तपतीति क्रियापदम् 5.16.22ab
तं चेत्कुर्वन्ति वेदान्ताः कुतस्तेषाममानता 2.1.550cd
तं चेदद्विष्याद्द्रुषैवैनामारभेत तदा क्रियाम् 6.4.49cd
तं जिगीषुं समायान्तमुन्मार्गे संस्थितं द्विजम् 6.2.24ab
तं तमेवैति कौन्तेय सदा तद्भावभावितः 4.4.102cd
तं त्वा पृच्छामि शाकल्य तं मह्यं ब्रूहि तत्त्वतः 3.9.117cd
तं त्वौपनिषदं देवं साक्षादित्यादिलक्षणम् 3.9.115cd
तं त्वौपनिषदं धीरा ब्रह्मात्मानं प्रचक्षते 3.9.117ab
तं त्वौपनिषदमिति नियमार्थे सतीष्यते 4.4.1034ab
तं दृष्ट्यादिदृशं साक्षादात्मानं कल्पितात्मनाम् 3.5.97ab
तं न पश्यत्यहो कष्टं दौर्भाग्यं दुष्टचेतसाम् 4.3.951cd
तं पण्डितमिति प्राहुः सोऽत्र श्रुत्या नियुज्यते 3.5.173cd
तं परादादिति तथा प्रतीच्यज्ञानकल्पितम् 1.4.697ab
तं प्रत्याहामृतमिति याज्ञवल्क्योऽपि देवताम् 3.9.43cd
तं प्रत्येवेति विज्ञेयं कर्मेदं न त्वकामिनम् 6.3.3cd
तं प्रयास्यति केनायमाक्रमेणेति पृच्छ्यते 3.1.38cd

तं बोधयद्भवेन्मानं न तु तत्कुर्वदिष्यते 4.3.164cd
तं मामननुशिष्यैव किमित्युक्तं त्वया पुरा 6.2.49ab
तं यथा यथा इत्युक्तेरनिर्देशोऽपि गम्यते 5.10.7cd
तं वन्देऽत्रिकुलप्रसूतममलं वेधोऽभिधं मद्गुरुम् 6.5.23d
तं वर्णं देवतादेहो यथोक्तमनुरुध्यते 4.3.1231cd
तं वायुं तच्च कर्मेह य उपेत्य व्यवस्थितः 3.7.12ab
तं विदित्वेत्यतः प्राह फलं वाक्यार्थबोधतः 4.4.1192ab
तं विदित्वैतमेवेति कर्मकर्तृविभागतः 1.4.1241ab
तं वेत्थ स्विन्न वेत्युक्तो नेति होवाच तं पुनः 6.2.33cd
तं समन्वारभेते ते या चाभूत्पूर्ववासना 4.4.111cd
तं समुद्रं समुत्तीर्य यदन्यत्परतस्ततः 3.3.154ab
तं सर्गमुक्तवत्सर्वमपेक्ष्येहोपसंहृतिः 1.4.129ab
तं हैतं मन्थं यत्नोक्तमुद्दालतनयः सुधीः 6.3.60ab
तं हैतमिति यत्नेन वंशं जपति भक्तितः 6.3.59cd
तक्रकौण्डिन्यवन्न्यायो न चेहाप्यवसीयते 1.6.71ab
तच्चक्षुरादिकरणग्राह्यं दृष्टं घटादिवत् 4.3.107cd
तच्च सर्वपदार्थानां न दण्डैर्विनिवार्यते SV 715cd
तच्चापहस्तितं चोद्यं वक्ष्यते च निराकृतिः SV 194cd
तच्चापि पञ्चभूतोत्थं विद्यात्पाङ्क्तमशेषतः 1.4.1852cd
तच्चाप्यसत्त्वयाभाणि धर्मित्वेन परिग्रहात् 4.3.237cd
तच्चाविद्यानिरास्येव व्याधभावनयाञ्जितः SV 233ab
तच्चेज्ज्ञानादपध्वस्तं समाप्तं यच्चिकीर्षितम् 4.4.781cd
तच्चेत्ततो न विश्वासो जातावप्येकबुद्धितः SV 969cd
तच्चेदं चैकतामेति संख्यासामान्यहेतुतः 5.16.6cd
तच्चेष्टां कुरुतेऽकुर्वन्नयस्कान्तो मणिर्यथा 3.4.72cd
तच्चोद्यपरिहारोऽतः क्रियते नाफलत्वतः 1.4.419cd
तच्छक्तेरपि विध्वंसस्तयोरव्यतिरेकतः SV 63ab
तच्छक्त्युपाधिहेतुत्वाज्जायमानेव चिद्ध्रुवा 1.4.328cd
तच्छब्देन परामर्शो वैशब्दः स्मरणाय च 5.4.2ab
तच्छायापाश्रयाद्यस्मात्प्रत्यक्षस्यापि मानता 1.4.577cd
तच्छास्त्रं विधिनिष्ठत्वान्न स्वरूपेऽर्थवादतः SV 770cd
तच्छीलरूपकर्मभ्यो व्यावृत्तधिषणः स्वतः 2.1.511ab

तज्जं वा तत्तमोऽपेक्ष्य ह्यव्याकृतगिरोच्यते 1.4.340cd
तज्जन्मनः पुरेवार्थो न तेन ज्ञायतेऽञ्जसा 1.4.1355cd
तज्जन्मनाशसाक्षित्वादजोऽनाशी स्वयंप्रभः 3.4.157ab
तज्जातिकर्मसंबन्धतत्त्ववित्तत्पितुः सखा 2.1.512cd
तज्जात्याकृतिसंबन्धगुणकर्मविलक्षणः 4.3.101cd
तज्जालकमिवाभाति बहुच्छिद्रत्वसाम्यतः 4.2.49cd
तज्जेष्वपि स एव स्यान्मरुद्बुद्ध्यादिरूपिषु 1.4.508cd
तज्ज्ञातयोऽपि फलिनो यथा वागादयस्तथा 1.3.286cd
तज्ज्ञानं चेत्प्रमाणं तत्तच्च शास्त्रान्न कार्यतः SV 825cd
तज्ज्ञानजन्मकालत्वादग्निजन्मोत्थकार्यवत् 1.4.841cd
तज्ज्ञानजन्मनो नोर्ध्वं मुनिता तत्फलत्वतः 4.4.1073cd
तज्ज्ञानजन्ममात्राच्च पुरुषार्थोऽपि नेष्यते 1.4.779cd
तज्ज्ञानमात्रमेवोक्त्वा प्राप्तोऽसीति यतोऽवदत् 4.2.104ab
तज्ज्ञानात्किं तमोऽध्वस्तं किं वाज्ञानं वदात्मनः 2.4.231cd
तज्ज्ञानेऽसावसंभाव्यस्तद्धेतूच्छित्तिकारणात् 2.4.194cd
तज्ज्ञानेनैव तज्ज्ञातं तदन्यानवशेषतः 2.4.439cd
तज्ज्ञानोत्पत्तिविघ्नापध्वस्तिकृज्ज्ञानलब्धये 1.3.7ab
तज्ञानं यस्य संजातं जातमेवास्य नान्यथा SV 232ab
तटस्थनरवद्यस्माद्ध्यानकम्पादिधर्मिकाम् 4.3.439ab
तटस्थनरवन्नावो नौस्थो नैवेक्षते गतिम् 4.3.437ab
तण्डुलान्फलपुष्पाणि पिष्ट्वा पात्रे निधापयेत् 6.3.16cd
तण्डुलान्मांससंमिश्रान्पक्त्वा मांसौदनं विदुः 6.4.77ab
तत आदित्यमायान्ति वैद्युतं चापि भास्करात् 6.2.139cd
तत उक्तेन मार्गेण कर्तृसंस्कारकारिणाम् SV 87ab
तत एव च मानत्वं संविदर्ते न तत्रयम् 1.4.287cd
तत एव न कार्यत्स्यात्तदा तद्भावभावतः SV 651cd
तत एव विराडैक्यविज्ञानादेव तद्द्वयम् 1.4.94ab
तत एवाभयः प्रत्यङ्भयं हि तदबोधतः 4.4.1335cd
तत एवेति वचनं तदेवं स्यात्समञ्जसम् 1.4.69cd
तत एवैकलाद्यस्मात्संसाराद्विप्रमुच्यते 4.4.1253ab
ततः कर्त्रादिसंसिद्धिः प्रमाकर्मफलं ततः 4.3.57cd
ततः क्षेत्रज्ञरूपस्य सर्वभोज्यातिलङ्घिनः 1.4.1712cd

ततः परस्ताच्छाकल्यं याज्ञवल्क्योऽप्यपृच्छत 3.9.105cd
ततः परेण लोकादेरपि याथात्म्यमुच्यते 2.2.4ab
ततः परेषु भोगेषु जाततृष्णश्च यः पुमान् 4.3.1864cd
ततः पश्येद्विभक्तं सन्न त्वेवमिह विद्यते 4.3.1563cd
ततः प्रत्यक्षबाधः स्यात्तद्भेदो हि तदाश्रयः 1.6.84cd
ततः शब्दस्य सामर्थ्यं प्रतीतेरवधार्यते SV 483ab
ततः शेषेण वचनात्तथा तद्य इहेत्यतः SV 95ab
ततः संवत्सरादूर्ध्वं तं चाप्यालभतात्मने 1.2.215cd
ततः स याज्ञवल्क्योत्थशापवाक्याख्यवह्निना 3.9.119ab
ततः सर्गाद्यभावः स्यादेकरूपतया स्थितेः 5.1.42cd
ततश्च कर्ता भोक्ता च बध्यते मुच्यते तथा 2.3.120ab
ततश्च कार्यनिष्ठत्वं मुधैव परिवर्जितम् SV 845ab
ततश्च कार्यानुत्पत्तिर्यदि वा सर्वदास्तिता 4.3.594ab
ततश्च जामितासक्तिर्नीतः स्यात्पारिशेष्यगीः 2.3.216cd
ततश्च नैतत्संसिध्येदज्ञानादि प्रमाणतः 4.3.175cd
ततश्च प्रतिभामात्रं शब्दादिति न मानतः SV 450ab
ततश्च प्रातिलोम्येन कार्यं स्याच्छास्त्रबाधनात् SV 839ab
ततश्च ब्रह्मतासिद्धिर्द्वितीये सति वस्तुनि 2.3.219ab
ततश्च भवदुक्तस्य चोद्यस्येह न संभवः SV 286cd
ततश्च भावनाभावो भावनायाः क्रियाश्रयात् 2.4.157cd
ततश्च भोग्यरूपस्य भोक्तृत्वं नोपपद्यते 2.1.157cd
ततश्च मानतः सिद्धिर्नाज्ञातत्वस्य कुत्रचित् SV 686cd
ततश्च वेदसिद्धान्तसंत्यागः कारणादृते 1.4.243ab
ततश्च स्वर्गकामो यः स्वनियोगं स साधयेत् SV 533ab
ततश्चापरिलोपोऽस्याः कार्यत्वान्नोपपद्यते 4.3.1429cd
ततश्चारोग्यकामस्य पथ्यभोजनवाक्यवत् SV 517ab
ततश्चावाच्यमिति ते प्राप्ता स्वोक्तिविरुद्धता 4.3.645ab
ततश्चैतद्भवेत्सिद्धं यः स्वप्ने कुम्भमीक्षते 4.3.266ab
ततश्चैवं समूहस्य वाचकत्वमवस्थितम् SV 869ab
ततस्तदर्थग्रहणमनुष्ठानं ततः परम् 1.4.1551ab
ततस्तदेतदिति च ब्रह्मात्मपदवाच्ययोः 2.4.37ab
ततस्तवस्तल्लवणं वेत्ति खिल्यं न कुत्रचित् 2.4.403cd

ततस्तु या सुखोद्भूतिर्विज्ञानात्मन एव सा 1.3.256cd
ततस्ते कर्मसूद्युक्ताः प्रावर्तन्त दिवानिशम् 4.4.1250cd
ततस्ते कर्मसूद्युक्ताः प्रावर्तन्ताविचक्षणाः SV 218cd
ततस्ते कर्मसूद्युक्ताः प्रावर्तन्ताविपश्चितः 2.4.24cd
ततोऽधिकारिचिन्ता स्यात्कृतेऽप्यफलशङ्कया SV 291cd
ततोऽन्यत्रमना आसं नातोऽद्राक्षं त्वदीरितम् 1.5.102cd
ततोऽन्यद्ग्रहणं नास्ति विभक्तं ग्राह्यमेव च 4.3.1511cd
ततोऽन्येनाभिसंबन्ध आत्मनोऽज्ञानहेतुकः SV 109cd
ततोऽपि कालसंकोचं स वा इत्यादिनावदत् 1.3.349ab
ततोऽपि दुर्लभतरमुपायाल्लभ्यते कुतः 4.4.1023cd
ततोऽपि पापात्पापीयान्स स्याद्ब्रह्मापवादतः 1.4.1612cd
ततोऽपि बाह्यो देहश्च जातिस्तत्समवायिनी SV 112ab
ततोऽपि मुक्तिर्वक्तव्येत्यत आरभ्यते परः 3.1.30cd
ततोऽपि सूक्ष्मं विज्ञानं बुद्धिसंयोगजं भवेत् 2.4.345ab
ततोऽप्यतिशयः पुंसां सर्वलोकोपकारिता 1.4.1572cd
ततोऽप्यपरितुष्टस्त्वमन्यथैव बुभुत्ससे 3.4.78cd
ततोऽप्यूर्ध्वं फलोक्तिश्चेत्तच्छब्देनोच्यते कथम् 1.4.1126cd
ततोऽभावात्तथा सिद्धोऽवृक्षाभावोऽपि सर्वदा 4.3.791cd
ततोऽवबोधयिष्यामि यथोपात्तविशेषणम् 3.4.66cd
ततोऽहंप्रत्ययात्सिद्धिमीक्षतेऽनुभवः कथम् SV 1058cd
ततोऽहर्देवतां यान्ति शुक्लपक्षं ततः क्रमात् 6.2.138ab
ततो दर्शननिष्ठत्वं न तयोरुपपद्यते SV 564cd
ततो बुद्धिसमुत्पत्तौ विज्ञानोऽस्मीतिभावतः 4.4.173ab
ततो भूयस्तमो यान्ति ये विद्यायां रता जनाः 4.4.602ab
ततो लब्धात्मलाभायाः प्रथमा जन्महेतुतः 1.5.328cd
ततो लोकाद्विनिष्क्रम्य द्विगुणा पृथिवी स्थिता 3.3.153ab
ततो वायावपक्रान्ते चैतन्यमपि नश्यति 4.3.128cd
तत्कर्मज्ञानजत्वाच्च तत्प्राणाः शुद्ध्यशुद्धिजाः 1.3.16ab
तत्कर्मफलभोगार्थं कृत्वा देहं प्रतीक्षते 4.3.1957ab
तत्कर्मा तदहंकारः कालेन महताभवत् 2.1.509ab
तत्कल्पितनिवृत्तिः स्यादष्टावस्थस्य बोधतः 1.3.315cd
तत्कारणं कथं तत्स्यान्न चेत्तस्मात्प्रजायते 1.2.40cd

तत्कारणत्वात्कार्याणां न तु कार्यान्तरे लयः 2.4.373cd
तत्कारणत्वात्तद्बुद्धेर्मृत्स्नेव घटजन्मनः 4.3.1679cd
तत्कारणत्वात्सर्वस्य हेतूक्तिस्तत्र दुर्घटा 1.4.1659cd
तत्कारणनिषेधो यः स्वमहिम्नैव वस्तुनः 3.5.70ab
तत्कारणविनाशाय तत्सूतेः प्राक्क्व ईर्यताम् 1.2.35cd
तत्कारणोपमर्दित्वाज्जन्मनैव न कारकम् 3.4.137cd
तत्कारणोपमर्दित्वाज्जन्मनैव न कारकम् 4.4.262cd
तत्कात्स्न्यील्लभ्यते तत्र व्यवहारो न मोहजः 1.4.182cd
तत्कार्यगेण लिङ्गेन ज्ञापयन्कारणाभिधाम् 1.4.45ab
तत्कार्यतारतम्येन साविद्या भिद्यते यतः 4.3.1243cd
तत्कार्यत्वाच्च भूतानां भूतपालत्वमात्मनः 4.4.1010cd
तत्कार्यत्वाच्च सर्वस्य न किंचिदसमञ्जसम् 4.3.1450cd
तत्कार्यत्वात्पशुः पाङ्क्तो यच्च किंचिच्चराचरम् 1.4.1852ab
तत्कार्यश्रवणान्नापि दृष्टान्तोऽस्ति ततोऽपरः 1.4.590cd
तत्कार्यस्येह प्रात्यक्ष्यात्तदभेदोपचारतः 2.5.46ab
तत्काले भिन्नकाले वा प्राणादन्यस्य भोज्यतः 2.1.119cd
तत्किमर्थं पुनः प्रश्नः स एव कृतनिर्णयः 3.5.5cd
तत्कृत्स्नमनुसंधेयं सर्वाविकारहानिकृत् 2.4.210cd
तत्केन कमिति श्रुत्या भेददृष्टिर्निषिध्यते 4.3.1309cd
तत्केन कमितीत्यादि साक्षेपं वचनं स्वयम् 4.4.278cd
तत्कैवल्यमतः साध्यमुपचारात्प्रचक्षते SV 27cd
तत्क्षये स निरासङ्गः स्वात्मन्येव प्रसीदति 4.3.977cd
तत्तत्त्वबोधात्तद्बाधः सर्परज्ज्वादिबाधवत् 2.1.174cd
तत्तत्त्वमात्रगं तत्स्थध्वान्तनुन्मानमुच्यते 1.4.360cd
तत्तत्त्वानुविधाय्येव प्रमात्रादिर्भवन्भवेत् 4.3.1726cd
तत्तत्सृजत इत्युक्त्योः पूर्वोत्तरविरुद्धता 1.4.1718cd
तत्तथा नावगन्तव्यं क्लिद्यत्यन्नमसुं विना 5.14.2cd
तत्तद्भूमिपरिच्छेदात्क्षेत्रज्ञः पर एव सन् 1.4.638cd
तत्तद्रूपमिति ज्ञेयं तैजसत्वाविशेषतः 1.6.19cd
तत्तद्वस्तु समुद्दिश्य दुःखित्वं तत्र मानिनः 2.4.353ab
तत्तन्नामाप्युपादत्ते स्वप्नो भूत्वेत्यतो वचः 4.3.447cd
तत्तमोध्वस्तितः कार्यं नान्यदस्तीति लिङ्ग्यते 4.2.98cd

तत्तमोमात्रविध्वंसान्न तु प्राणादिराप्यते 1.3.183ab
तत्तमोहतितः कार्यं किमन्यत्तत्प्रमाणजम् SV 794cd
तत्तस्य गुणभूतं स्यान्न प्रधानाद्गुणो यतः 3.3.68cd
तत्तु तत्रैव विलयं कार्यमेति स्वकारणे 2.4.372cd
तत्तु द्वितीयं नेहास्ति तमोऽनर्थस्य कारणम् 4.3.1519ab
तत्तु द्वितीयं नेहास्ति द्रष्टव्यं यत्समाश्रयात् 4.3.1561ab
तत्तु नैवं यतः सत्त्वं मोहादित्रयकृद्धियः 1.4.1037ab
तत्तु नैवेह वस्त्वस्ति द्वितीयं मोहहेतुजम् 4.3.1522ab
तत्तूपलक्षणं विद्याद्देहव्याप्तिविवक्षया 2.1.328cd
तत्तेज ऐक्षत इति तेजोदेहं सदेव तु 1.4.349ab
तत्तोयतत्त्ववित्कश्चिन्न हि धावति मूढवत् 4.4.1110cd
तत्त्वं चतुष्टयस्यास्य प्रत्यगात्मैव केवलः 2.5.37ab
तत्त्वं नान्यद्यतस्तस्मात्तन्मात्रेणैव तद्गतिः 4.4.839cd
तत्त्वज्ञानात्तमोध्वस्तौ नेतीत्यात्मावशिष्यते 2.5.144cd
तत्त्वप्रबोधनं मुक्त्वा कार्यकारणवस्तुनः 4.4.952ab
तत्त्वबोधातिरेकेण न नाशोऽन्यो यथा तथा 1.4.203ab
तत्त्वबोधान्न नाशः स्याद्व्यतिरेकान्वयौ न च 4.4.766ab
तत्त्वमस्यादितस्तस्मादागमादेव नान्यतः SV 1091ab
तत्त्वमस्यादिवाक्यस्य विरोधोऽतो न केनचित् SV 571ab
तत्त्वमस्यादिवाक्यस्य विषयोऽयमिहोदितः 4.3.1115cd
तत्त्वमस्यादिवाक्यानां तावन्मात्रावबोधनात् 1.4.823ab
तत्त्वमस्यादिवाक्यानां नानुष्ठानं मनागपि 1.3.89cd
तत्त्वमस्यादिवाक्यानां सोऽरोदीदितिवाक्यवत् 1.4.904cd
तत्त्वमस्यादिवाक्यार्थज्ञानोत्पत्त्यर्थमादरात् 4.4.1248cd
तत्त्वमस्यादिवाक्यार्थश्रवणानन्तरं न किम् 1.4.906cd
तत्त्वमस्यादिवाक्येन गुरुः संबोधयेन्नरम् 2.1.520cd
तत्त्वमस्यादिवाक्येभ्यः श्रवणात्समनन्तरम् 2.4.167cd
तत्त्वमस्यादिवाक्येभ्यः सर्वज्ञानप्रसूतितः 4.4.912ab
तत्त्वमस्यादिवाक्येभ्यस्तद्वदेवेति निश्चयः 1.3.86cd
तत्त्वमस्यादिवाक्योक्तौ शब्दमात्रावलोकनम् 4.4.712ab
तत्त्वमस्यादिवाक्योत्थज्ञानबाध्यं च यद्विदुः 4.3.349cd
तत्त्वमस्यादिवाक्योत्थबोधाच्चेत्किमितीहते 1.4.818cd

तत्त्वमस्यादिवाक्योत्थविज्ञानविरहात्क्वचित् 3.8.121cd

तत्त्वमस्यादिवाक्योत्थविज्ञानेन यथोदितम् 4.4.797ab

तत्त्वमस्यादिवाक्योत्थसम्यग्धीजन्ममात्रतः SV 183ab

तत्त्वमस्यादिवाक्योत्थात्पर्णैकात्म्यस्वलक्षणात् SV 1006cd

तत्त्वमात्मैव सर्वस्य कार्यकारणवस्तुनः 4.4.868ab

तत्त्वमाध्यात्मिकं दृष्ट्वा तत्त्वं दृष्ट्वा तु बाह्यतः 4.4.887ab

तत्त्वमुक्तं पृथिव्यादेर्नभोन्तस्याक्षरं परम् 4.4.647cd

तत्त्ववित्स्यान्महिम्नोऽस्येत्येष मन्त्रो विधित्सितः 4.4.1189ab

तत्त्वस्माभिर्यथाभाणि मनसैवेति दर्शनम् 4.4.744ab

तत्त्वीभूतस्तदारामस्तत्त्वादप्रच्युतो भवेत् 4.4.887cd

तत्पक्षस्य निषेधोऽयं यत्र हीत्यादिनोच्यते 2.4.464cd

तत्परिच्छेदि विज्ञानमविद्यैवावशिष्यते 3.2.53cd

तत्परीक्षां प्रयत्नेन चक्रुः संभूय देवताः 1.3.127cd

तत्पर्जन्यादिना जातं दार्ढ्यकृत्क्षितिदेहयोः 3.9.47cd

तत्पश्यन्नित्यनेनात्र ब्रह्मविद्या प्रदर्श्यते 1.4.1447ab

तत्पाण्डित्यमिह ज्ञेयं न तु वेदार्थगोचरम् 6.4.74cd

तत्पारार्थ्यजडत्वाभ्यां मित्यभावस्तथा समः 3.8.115cd

तत्पूरणात्पितुस्त्राणात्पुत्र इत्यधिधीयते 1.5.320cd

तत्पूर्वको मनुष्येषु विभागस्त्वधुनोच्यते 1.4.1637cd

तत्पृष्टं जगतो मूलं न विदुर्ब्राह्मणा यतः 3.9.147ab

तत्पृष्ठेन नु गानानि विरोधः किंसमाश्रयः SV 986cd

तत्प्रक्रियानुसारेणाप्यत्र नैवास्ति भेदधीः 4.3.1668cd

तत्प्रतिष्ठामथाप्राक्षीच्छाकल्यो निर्णयेच्छया 3.9.89cd

तत्प्रति स्यात्प्रमाणत्वं शुक्तिकारजते यथा 4.3.168cd

तत्प्रतीक्षणमाकाङ्क्षा पराकाशेति भण्यते 6.4.61cd

तत्प्रत्यक्तत्त्वसंबोधाद्ध्वस्ते ध्वान्तेऽन्तरात्मनि 1.4.1413cd

तत्प्रत्यगात्मदृष्टिस्तु विज्ञेया पारमार्थिकी 3.4.99cd

तत्प्रत्यगात्मदृष्ट्या तां प्रत्याख्यायाश्नुतेऽद्वयम् 1.4.1432cd

तत्प्रत्यगात्मयाथात्म्यभास्वज्ज्ञानोदयात्तमः 3.5.74ab

तत्प्रत्यगात्मा तद्धीनः कूटस्थोऽनन्यमानगः 3.8.64cd

तत्प्रत्यपादि निखिलं पूर्वं श्रुत्यैव यत्नतः 2.1.374cd

तत्प्रत्याख्यानश्रुत्यैव तद्याथात्म्यावबोधनात् SV 462cd

तत्प्रबोधविशेषोऽयं युक्त एव भवेत्तदा 2.1.152cd
तत्प्रमाणविशुद्ध्यर्थं चोदयन्ति मुमुक्षवः 1.4.1079cd
तत्प्रमाणार्पितो मेयो ग्रहीतुं शक्यतेऽञ्जसा 2.4.266cd
तत्प्रमेयमिति न्याय्यं न तु वस्त्वद्वयं स्वतः 3.8.107cd
तत्प्रयोक्तृक्रियाभावाद्बुद्ध्यादिज्योतिषामिह 4.3.907ab
तत्प्रयोगावसाने च सर्वं तदपवृज्यते 3.1.28cd
तत्प्रवृत्त्यङ्गतायै च तत्फलस्य प्रकीर्तनम् 1.4.1125cd
तत्प्रवेशाद्यतोऽतोऽयमश्वमेधोऽभवत्प्रभुः 1.2.208cd
तत्प्रसङ्गनिवृत्त्यर्थमपरोक्षादितीर्यते 3.4.15cd
तत्प्राप्तमपि किं कुर्यात्स्वात्मायोग्यासु भूमिषु 2.4.175cd
तत्प्राप्तेर्ज्ञानकालत्वान्नालं विघ्नाय देवताः 1.4.1493cd
तत्प्राप्तौ तत्तमोमात्रं व्यवधानमतो भवेत् 1.4.1080cd
तत्प्राप्तौ हेतुताग्न्यादेरिति निर्ह्रीकवागियम् 1.4.1663cd
तत्प्राप्त्यर्थं प्रयत्नेन कुर्वन्तीह दिवानिशम् 4.4.1155cd
तत्फलं यत्तदन्वीक्ष्य नात्मनोऽन्यद्ददर्श सः 1.4.39cd
तत्फलं वर्तते यत्र मानं तत्र न वर्तते 4.3.196cd
तत्फलस्य च भुक्तस्य पूर्वप्रज्ञेति सोच्यते 4.4.118cd
तत्फलस्य तु या प्राप्तिः सा सकृत्करणादपि 4.4.200cd
तत्फलस्य समाप्तत्वादपेक्षा निष्फला यतः 2.1.172cd
तत्याज कर्म त्वरया वाङ्मनःकायसाधनम् 4.5.26cd
तत्र कर्मप्रसूतोऽयं कामः सर्वप्रवृत्तिकृत् 4.3.1189ab
तत्र को मोह इत्येवं मन्त्रवर्णोऽपि नो जगौ 1.4.820ab
तत्र चेत्तदसत्सत्स्यात्कथमन्यत्र निष्प्रमम् 1.4.733cd
तत्र चेत्स्याद्विसंवादः केनान्येन चिकित्स्यते 1.4.1398cd
तत्र तत्र विधिः स्थाने प्रहितस्य फलेच्छया SV 249cd
तत्र तत्रैकलः प्रत्यक्स्वमहिम्नैव सिध्यति 2.3.228cd
तत्र तत्रैव ता धत्ते मात्राः स्वात्मांशुभिः सह 4.3.996cd
तत्र त्रयाणां स्थानानां जाग्रत्स्वप्ननिषेधनम् 4.3.1169ab
तत्र देहान्तरारम्भ उपादानं किमात्मनः 4.4.137cd
तत्र भावनयैवात्मा कामान्कामयते तथा 4.3.1197ab
तत्र मात्रादिसंभेदे न मनागपि लभ्यते 2.4.225cd
तत्र मिथ्याग्रहग्रस्तो द्रष्टृदृश्यादिभेदधीः 2.4.453cd

तत्र युक्तमयुक्तं वा श्रुतिवाक्यानुसारतः 4.3.1203cd
तत्र ये त्वात्मनोऽभिन्नास्तेभ्योऽनन्यत्वकारणात् 4.4.406ab
तत्र रत्वा यथाकामं कंचित्कालं यदृच्छया 4.3.1067ab
तत्र लब्धविशेषः संस्तामेवायं नियच्छति 3.7.34cd
तत्र लब्धात्मकस्तस्य दग्धा दाह्यस्य न स्वतः 3.7.35cd
तत्र विद्या न वक्तव्या शुभं बीजमिवोषरे 2.1.36cd
तत्र संदिह्यमानेऽर्थे यथालोकं विनिश्चितिः 4.3.517ab
तत्र स्पर्शग्रहेणैव वायोरंशोऽत्र गृह्यते 2.4.336cd
तत्र स्वप्नविधौ तिष्ठन्पश्यतीह समीक्षते 4.3.998cd
तत्र हेत्वभिधानार्थं वरदानं श्रुतिर्जगौ 4.3.11cd
तत्रागन्तु यदज्ञानं तत्सकृज्ज्ञानजन्मना 4.4.882ab
तत्राग्नेरुदितोत्पत्तिर्न त्विन्द्रादेरिहोच्यते 1.4.127cd
तत्राङ्गभाव इति चेन्मत्पन्थानं भवानितः SV 453cd
तत्रात्मा किं स्वरूपे प्राङ्न स्थितो येन तत्स्थितौ SV 48ab
तत्रात्मा लब्धाविद्वान्स्याल्लब्धव्यं च क्रियाफलम् 1.4.1016ab
तत्राधिदैवमुक्तानि त्रीण्यन्नानि विभागशः 1.5.204ab
तत्रानात्मैव वाच्योऽर्थः प्रत्यगात्मोपसर्जनः 1.4.525cd
तत्रानुवादि शास्त्रं स्यान्निवृत्तावेव तन्मितिः 1.4.407cd
तत्रान्यः कारको द्रष्टा तथान्येनैव चक्षुषा 4.3.1791ab
तत्रापि च धियो वृत्तेर्ग्राह्यग्राहकरूपतः 4.3.1546ab
तत्रापि च समं पश्यन्नात्मयाजी भवत्ययम् 3.3.128cd
तत्रापि चानवगमध्वस्तिः प्रतिवचो भवेत् 1.4.1231cd
तत्रापि तुल्यचोद्यत्वादनवस्था प्रसज्यते 4.3.1786cd
तत्रापि नैव शब्दस्य व्यापारः सिद्धवेदनात् SV 591ab
तत्रापि भिन्नमेयत्वान्नैव संभयमानता SV 819cd
तत्रापुरुषतन्त्रत्वान्न कश्चिद्विधिरिष्यते 4.4.756cd
तत्राप्यात्मचिदाभासमनोबुद्ध्यादिकारकैः 4.3.925cd
तत्राम्नायाभिधानस्य ह्याम्नायांशाभिधानतः SV 271ab
तत्रार्थप्रत्ययो योऽसौ प्रमातुर्मानसो भवेत् 4.4.715ab
तत्राविद्योत्थबुद्ध्यादिगुणभृतात्मविन्नरः 2.4.454cd
तत्राविद्योद्भवं कार्यं यावत्किंचिद्विवक्षितम् 2.1.374ab
तत्रावृक्षविविक्तेऽर्थे संकेतो वृक्षसंज्ञया 4.3.771ab

तत्राव्युत्पन्नता हेतुः शब्दानां न त्वशक्तितता SV 875cd
तत्राश्वविषयं तावदादौ दर्शनमुच्यते 1.1.1ab
तत्रेन्द्रियाणि सर्वाणि बुद्धितन्त्राणि सर्वदा 2.1.333cd
तत्रेह तावन्नोपाये पुत्रजन्मादिलक्षणे SV 582ab
तत्रैकस्या यदा कार्यं दृष्ट्यादि स्यादुपस्थितम् 4.2.69ab
तत्रैतच्छङ्क्यते चोद्यं ब्रह्मत्वासिद्धिदोषकृत् 2.4.9ab
तत्रैतच्छङ्क्यते ज्ञानेऽसंबोधः कथमात्मनः 4.3.1396ab
तत्रैतस्मिन्यथोक्तेऽर्थे दृष्टान्तोऽप्यभिधीयते 4.3.1959ab
तत्रैतस्यामवस्थायां विभागो विनिवर्तते 2.3.97ab
तत्रैवं सति को मूढो द्राघीयांसं प्रतीक्षते 1.5.71ab
तत्रैवं सति तं दृष्टेर्द्रष्टारं कर्मभूतया 3.4.175ab
तत्रैवं सति यत्र स्यान्मूर्ताद्युक्तं चतुष्टयम् 2.3.76ab
तत्रैवं सति यद्येतदद्येतैव हि केवलम् 3.2.65ab
तत्रैवं सति योऽकात्स्न्यीमित्वा ब्रह्माप्रबोधतः 1.4.1159ab
तत्रैवं सति योऽप्यस्य देवताविषयो भवेत् 4.4.717cd
तत्रैवं सति यो द्रष्टा प्राणनादिक्रियं परम् 1.4.688ab
तत्रैवं सति यो मूढः कार्यकारणदर्शनः 2.4.249ab
तत्रैवं सति लोकेऽस्मिन्द्वैताद्वैतात्मसंस्थितौ 1.4.1704ab
तत्रैवं सति वाग्रूपे एवंव्याख्यातरूपके 1.5.174cd
तत्रैवं सति संसारी यद्यन्यो ब्रह्मणो भवेत् 1.4.1267ab
तत्रैवं सति सासङ्गाः प्रायेण प्राणिनो यतः 3.2.69ab
तत्रैवं संभवत्यर्थे सर्वमानाविरोधिनि 4.4.875ab
तत्रैव चास्य सद्भावादभिधार्थस्य तत्कुतः SV 3cd
तत्रैव निरधार्येतद्यत्र नान्यदिति श्रुतेः 4.3.1339cd
तत्रैव निष्ठां यातः सन्मन्त्रमेतमुदीरयेत् 4.4.1180cd
तत्रैव मान्तरापेक्षा न तु विध्वस्तभेदके SV 720cd
तत्रैव वर्तमानस्य यथैवं प्रत्यगात्मनः 4.4.510cd
तत्रैवात्मेति धीरेषा नागमापायिवस्तुषु 4.4.468cd
तत्रैवाविद्यावस्थायां संज्ञेयं युज्यते मृषा 2.4.458cd
तत्संयोगवियोगाभ्यां स्रग्वस्त्राभरणादिवत् 4.3.823cd
तत्संहतः स्वयं त्वात्मासंहतो निर्गुणः शुचिः 4.3.912cd
तत्सतत्त्वं तदात्मत्वादज्ञानाद्यवभासयत् 4.3.102ab

तत्सतत्त्वमविद्यैव यतोऽतः सैव कारणम् 1.4.1145cd
तत्सद्भावात्तु पूर्वस्य ज्ञानस्यास्तु प्रमाणता SV 684cd
तत्सद्भावे न नो मानं प्रत्यक्षानुमयोर्यतः 4.3.462ab
तत्संनिधौ चिदाभत्वं कार्यकारणवस्तुनः 4.3.888ab
तत्संन्यासो विरक्तत्वात्स्वत एव न शास्त्रतः 2.4.6cd
तत्समुच्चयसिद्ध्यर्थमित्येतच्चोक्तयुक्तितः 1.4.1737cd
तत्समुद्रं परं ब्रह्म संविन्मात्रसतत्त्वकम् 1.2.125ab
तत्संप्रमोक्षणं कस्मिन्पुंसः कालेऽभिजायते 4.4.5ab
तत्सर्वं त आददेऽहमाहुतिं प्रक्षिपेद्रुषा 6.4.59cd
तत्सर्वं परिहृतं ज्ञेयं यथोक्तेनैव वर्त्मना 2.1.581cd
तत्सर्वं प्राण एवेति संजहार श्रुतिः स्वयम् 4.4.422cd
तत्सर्वं श्रुतिराचख्यावस्मत्प्रियचिकीर्षया 3.2.140cd
तत्साक्षात्करणान्नान्यस्तल्लयो वात इष्यते 4.2.104cd
तत्साक्षात्करणायैव प्रसंख्यानं विधीयते SV 771cd
तत्साक्षित्वाच्च तद्व्यक्तौ यदक्षैर्व्यज्यते न च 1.4.715cd
तत्साक्ष्यत्वाच्च निद्राया विध्वस्तं मोहहानतः 4.4.698cd
तत्साधनत्वाच्छ्रोत्रस्य श्रोत्रमाध्यात्मिकं धनम् 1.4.1849cd
तत्साधनस्य संत्यागे श्रद्धावित्तगिरात्र किम् 4.4.1267cd
तत्साधनेन चावश्यं भवितव्यमतो भवेत् SV 39ab
तत्साधनेष्वममताविधानार्थं वचो यतः 4.4.1268cd
तत्सामर्थ्यश्रवाभावात्फले नातो मितिश्च नः 3.3.79cd
तत्सामर्थ्यात्प्रणोद्यत्वात्सर्वेषां सर्वकर्मसु 1.4.1483cd
तत्सिद्ध्येऽनुमायत्नः क्रियतेऽतः परोक्तिभिः 3.8.127cd
तत्सिद्धावस्य संसिद्धिर्न कथंचिन्निवार्यते 1.4.1367cd
तत्सिद्धावेव तौ स्यातां स च ताभ्यामिति श्रयः SV 787cd
तत्सृष्ट्वेति तथा वाक्यं तैत्तिरीयश्रुतौ श्रुतम् 2.1.464ab
तत्सेवातोऽतिवृद्धिः स्यान्निवृत्तिर्दोषदर्शनात् SV 345cd
तत्स्थचैतन्यबिम्बेन भुङ्क्तेऽसौ कर्मणः फलम् 4.3.1029cd
तत्स्थास्नुत्वाभ्युपगतौ क्षणिकत्वं विनश्यति 4.3.684cd
तत्स्थितौ च फलेऽभीष्टे नित्ये साधनवर्जिते SV 134cd
तत्स्थोऽपि तदसंबद्ध ईश्वराद्यात्मतां गतः 1.3.53cd
तत्स्वकार्ये स्वतन्त्रत्वादुच्यते कारणं बुधैः 1.4.462cd

तत्स्वरूपावधृतये प्रारब्धैषोत्तरा श्रुतिः 3.2.40cd
तत्स्वाभाव्याविशेषः स्यात्तत्कार्यत्वाद्घटादिवत् 1.4.507cd
तथा कार्यत्वमप्येतन्निरवद्यं तदेकलम् 3.8.178cd
तथा कालानवच्छिन्नत्तेरासीदिति न तत्प्रति 1.4.1191ab
तथा किं प्रजयेत्यादिः पन्थाः कर्मत्यजां श्रुतः 3.5.202cd
तथा कूटस्थसंवित्के नितरां नैतदिष्यते 4.3.353cd
तथाक्षपादकाणादतर्कशास्त्रेषु यत्नतः 1.4.1239ab
तथा क्षयश्रुतेस्तस्य यद्वैतदितिवाक्यतः 1.5.342ab
तथा गन्धादिशब्देन घ्राणादिविषयो मतः 2.4.333cd
तथागमविरोधं च ग्रामकामादिभेदतः 2.1.591ab
तथागमविरोधश्च बहुत्वं चेत्परात्मनः 1.4.553cd
तथा गुणगुणित्वेन ह्यक्षलिङ्गाधिगम्ययोः 1.4.585ab
तथा च करणात्मानो बाह्यगोचररञ्जिताः 2.1.216cd
तथा च ज्ञानसाध्यत्वं ब्रह्मणः संप्रसज्यते 1.4.1118ab
तथा च तन्नियन्तारं जगज्जन्मादिकारणम् 3.7.2ab
तथा च पक्षहेत्वादेरनन्यत्वं प्रसज्यते 4.3.765ef
तथा च प्रतिवेदान्तं सृष्टिर्नानाविधेक्ष्यते 1.2.146cd
तथा च प्राह भगवान्व्यासः सत्यवतीसुतः 4.4.824ab
तथा च भगवान्व्यास इममर्थमुवाच ह 4.4.1164ab
तथा च भगवान्व्यासः सर्ववेदार्थतत्त्ववित् 4.3.1883ab
तथा च मन्त्रवर्णोऽत्र ह्यग्निर्मूर्धेति दृश्यते 1.4.512ab
तथा च यत्परिज्ञानात्कृत्स्नकार्पण्यनिःसृतिः 3.8.165ab
तथा च यदि नाम स्याद्यथोक्तज्ञानपूर्वकम् 4.4.574ab
तथा च युक्तिमद्यत्नान्महद्भिरपि भाषितम् 1.4.422ab
तथा च वक्ष्यते स्पष्टमतो मुक्तिर्न कर्मतः SV 437cd
तथा च वस्तुयाथात्म्यज्ञापनेन प्रमाणता SV 638ab
तथा च सति दृष्टान्तो भवतो नोपपद्यते 2.1.289ab
तथा च सति सिद्धान्तहानिर्वः संप्रसज्यते 2.1.479ab
तथा च सर्वमानानां सापेक्षत्वं प्रसज्यते SV 690cd
तथा चाक्रियमाणं सत्कथं कार्यमिहोच्यते 2.1.401ab
तथा चात्मैकनिष्ठत्वमद्वितीयस्य मानतः 3.5.171cd
तथा चानुपलब्धेश्च कार्यस्यैवास्तु नास्तिता 1.2.4ab

तथा चाव्रणवाक्येन विरोधोऽपि प्रसज्यते 2.1.489ab
तथा चाहरहः शास्त्रं पर आत्मनि चेति यत् 2.1.452ab
तथा चेवगिरा युक्तान्स्वप्नान्व्याचक्षते जनाः 4.3.1023cd
तथा चेहागमवचः पराञ्चीति विरुद्धताम् 3.2.111ab
तथा ज्ञेयस्य सर्वस्य ज्ञाताज्ञातविभागिनः 3.8.180ab
तथात ऊर्ध्वं प्रब्रूहि भगवन्मे विमुक्तये 4.3.972cd
तथा तत्साधनानां च काम्येष्टार्थप्रयुक्तितः 3.3.111cd
तथा तदभिधेयानामादेशोऽयं मतः परः 2.3.241cd
तथा तद्व्यतिरिक्तत्वे जाग्रत्स्वप्नकुलायतः 4.3.1136cd
तथा तयोरमानत्वे संबन्धोक्तिर्न युज्यते SV 318ab
तथात्मनस्तु कामाय तस्मान्नान्यत्सुखं भवेत् SV 1017cd
तथात्मनि च विज्ञाते सर्वं ज्ञातं भवेदिति 1.4.960ab
तथात्ममिथुन इति यस्त्वात्मरतिरित्यपि 1.4.101cd
तथा दर्शनतः सिद्धो विधितश्चावसीयते 5.1.46ab
तथा दिग्भेदभिन्नानां नामरूपक्रियात्मनाम् 4.4.425ab
तथा दुःख्यहमित्यादौ प्रत्यक्षमुपचारतः 1.4.566cd
तथा दृष्टविरोधो वः प्राप्नुवन्न निवार्यते 1.4.1233cd
तथादृष्टेऽपि दृष्टः स्यादकृत्स्नस्तादृगुच्यते 1.4.662cd
तथा देवतया सूत्रं नियन्तापि वियद्गिरा 4.1.21ab
तथा देहादिसंबन्धं दुःखजात्यादिमद्भवेत् 2.3.9ab
तथा द्रष्टृगृहीत्यैव कामितार्थरामाप्तितः 3.4.182ab
तथाधिदेवतात्मानो देवाः स्युर्बहुभेदकाः 2.1.415cd
तथाधिपतिरन्येषां नृणामेवेह यो भवेत् 4.3.1847ab
तथाधिपतिशब्देन स्वातन्त्र्यमभिधीयते 2.5.64ab
तथा न जायत इति विध्वस्ताशेषकल्पनम् 1.4.235cd
तथानतिशयत्वात्स्यान्न पुमन्तरगोचरः 4.3.103cd
तथानधिकृतानां च संन्यासस्य विधानतः 3.5.164ab
तथानपेक्षतस्तेषां संगतिः स्यात्कदा चन 2.3.19cd
तथानर्थपरिप्राप्तावुपायानां निषेधनम् 4.4.106ab
तथानुभवतः साक्षादात्मायं प्रतिपादितः 4.3.199cd
तथान्यान्यपि विद्यन्ते वाक्यान्यत्र सहस्रशः 3.5.153cd
तथा न्यायविरोधोऽपि क्रियाकारकरूपिणः 5.1.73ab

तथान्योऽपि गुणोऽनस्य दूरिति प्रतिपाद्यते 1.3.209ab
तथा पदतदर्थांश्च लिङ्गप्रत्यक्षगोचरान् 2.1.498ab
तथा परनिमित्तत्वेऽनर्थस्यापरिहारतः SV 156ab
तथा परिहृताशेषदुःखहेतुः स्वतोऽपि सन् 4.4.259ab
तथा परोऽपि संबन्धः कैश्चिदत्राभिधीयते 4.3.1386ab
तथापि कर्मग्रहणं सप्तान्नोद्भूतिहेतुतः 1.5.19cd
तथापि क्षतसंप्राप्तिरव्रणस्य प्रसज्यते 2.1.487cd
तथापि गतिरेवेयमुत्तरत्र स्फुटं हि तत् 4.2.17cd
तथापि चोदितोऽत्रार्थ उपास्यो नागतोऽर्थतः 1.3.157cd
तथापि ज्ञानमेवेह साधनत्वाद्विवक्षितम् 1.5.17cd
तथापि तज्जागरिते शक्यं दर्शयितुं न तु 4.3.374cd
तथापि ताञ्श्रुतिर्यत्नाज्जरादीन्प्रतिषेधति 4.4.1327ab
तथापि तान्प्रशंसन्ति दुःखार्जितधनत्यजः 3.8.143ab
तथापि दोषवद्ब्रह्म यथा तदधुनोच्यते 1.4.1102cd
तथापि नापराधो नस्तदन्यासंभवादिह 1.4.1221cd
तथापि नावदद्ब्रह्म स्वानुभूत्यवबुद्धये 6.1.19cd
तथापि नासजातीयं व्यञ्जकत्वात्प्रदीपवत् 4.3.140cd
तथापि निह्नुते शास्त्रं न लिप्यत इतीरणात् 1.4.190cd
तथापि बाध्यते ज्ञानमविद्याकार्यदर्शनात् 4.4.879cd
तथापि यतयो ग्राह्या अरण्येन विशेषणात् 6.2.124cd
तथा पुत्रान्पशूंश्चैव आददे तेऽद्य कामुक 6.4.58ab
तथापेक्षात्मकत्वाच्च मृगतृष्णोदकादिवत् 4.3.1073cd
तथाप्यद्वैतसंदृष्टेर्मृषात्वं स्याद्विरोधतः 5.1.34cd
तथाप्यनुभवादेव प्रत्यक्तत्त्वानभिज्ञता 4.4.655ab
तथाप्यब्रह्मवित्तेन न कैवल्यं पथैति तत् 4.4.575ab
तथाप्यसन्प्रतिज्ञार्थो न ह्यभावस्य नाशिता 4.3.596cd
तथाप्यसौ न तद्ग्राह्या ताभ्यामेवात्मबोधनात् SV 193cd
तथाप्यागामिदोषेष्वाशङ्का पूर्ववदुद्भवेत् SV 83cd
तथाप्युक्ता न चेद्दद्याद्बलात्तां वशमानयेत् 6.4.32ab
तथा प्रकर्षसिद्ध्यर्थं प्रोपसर्गः प्रयुज्यते 4.3.1944cd
तथा प्रफुल्लबोधाब्जः प्राज्ञवत्स्वप्नबोधयोः SV 1085cd
तथा प्राणाग्नयः शुद्धा जाग्रतीति श्रुतेर्वचः 2.4.382cd

Half-verse	Reference
तथाब्रह्मस्वभावेभ्यः सामर्थ्याद्ब्रह्मणा च खम्	5.1.115cd
तथा ब्रुवाणं तं गार्ग्यं काश्यो मा मेत्यथोचिवान्	2.1.45ab
तथाभूतं तदा ज्योतिरनुमास्यामहे वयम्	4.3.26ab
तथाभूतेन ग्राव्णैतां स्त्रियमभ्यसृजन्मुहुः	6.4.7ab
तथाभ्युदयकैवल्यसाधनानां विधानतः	1.4.1244ab
तथाभ्युपगतार्थस्य हानिः स्याद्वो न संशयः	4.3.592cd
तथाभ्युपगमे तस्य नापनुत्तिः कुतश् चन	1.4.253cd
तथा यत्नात्समीक्षन्ते स्वरसंपत्समन्वितम्	1.3.338cd
तथा यस्तमुपासीत यथोक्ताख्यानवर्त्मना	1.3.180ab
तथा यौवनहानिश्च तस्मादेवं स कामयेत्	6.4.42ab
तथा रूपं रूपमिति मन्त्रवर्णोऽपि चात्मनः	1.4.627ab
तथारूपः स्वकार्यस्थः प्रात्यक्ष्यादेष उच्यते	1.4.496cd
तथा रूपविशेषाणां रूपमात्रात्मकत्वतः	1.6.23cd
तथार्थान्तरसंबन्धे प्रत्यक्षे देहनिष्ठिते	2.1.144ab
तथा लोकगिरा ब्रह्मतत्त्वमात्मोपलक्ष्यते	4.3.1821ab
तथा लोकयतेर्धातोर्दर्शनार्थत्वहेतुतः	4.3.1816ab
तथावगतिसंबन्धे नापेक्षावगतेः स्वतः	3.8.119cd
तथाविद्योत्थकर्त्रादिधर्मशून्यमविक्रियम्	SV 133ab
तथाविधशरीरः सन्सर्वलोकपितामहः	1.2.213cd
तथा विधिमुखेनापि द्विरेफोदरवत्तमः	3.8.39cd
तथा विप्रतिपत्तिः स्यादनुक्तौ च पराजितः	3.8.54cd
तथा विषयरूपेण सैवैका प्रथते द्विधा	4.3.468cd
तथा शतसहस्रादिसंख्याभेदेन चाप्ययम्	2.5.133cd
तथाशरीरशब्देन सूक्ष्मो देहो निषिध्यते	4.4.520cd
तथा संवर्गविद्यायां प्राणवाय्वात्मना श्रुतिः	2.1.228ab
तथा संवर्गविद्यायामप्राणः प्राणतां गतः	1.4.350ab
तथा संशयमिथ्यात्वबुद्ध्योरेष यथोदितः	SV 688ab
तथासकृत्पुराप्युक्तमधुनाप्यभिधीयते	4.3.1567cd
तथा सति मृषाज्ञानं सर्वत्रैव प्रसज्यते	1.4.461ab
तथा सति शरीरादेरुपादानमनर्थकम्	3.9.187cd
तथा सतीति संप्राप्तावत्र प्रतिविधीयते	2.1.460cd
तथा सत्यप्रयत्नेन मुक्तिः स्यात्सर्वदेहिनाम्	4.4.821cd

तथा सत्यविरोधः स्याद्भिन्नाधिकरणत्वतः 1.4.1107cd
तथा संतानविच्छिन्नकल्पनापि न युज्यते 4.3.645cd
तथा संत्यज्यमानोऽपि नैष्कर्म्येणावतिष्ठते 4.4.266cd
तथा संदेह एकस्मादन्यस्माद्धि विनिश्चयः SV 1080cd
तथा स ब्रह्मणः केन स्याद्येनेति प्रदर्शितम् SV 297cd
तथा सर्वविकाराणां प्रत्यङ्मात्रैकसाक्षिता 4.3.1499cd
तथा सर्वान्तरत्वस्य भेदवृत्तिविरोधतः 3.4.28ab
तथा सामान्यतो वाचो विशेषाणां तदात्मता 1.6.14ab
तथासिद्धः स्वतः सिद्धं नात्यन्ताभावरूपतः 1.4.231cd
तथाहमेव जानामि माता नान्य इतीदृशाः SV 984ab
तथाहंप्रत्ययात्साक्षादात्मयाथात्म्यनिश्चितेः 1.4.768ab
तथा हि क्षितितोयाग्निमरुतां योगजं मतम् 4.3.117ab
तथा हिरण्यगर्भत्वं बुद्ध्युपाधिः स एव तु 1.4.152ab
तथा हिरण्यगर्भस्य मण्डलं करणात्मनः 2.3.41cd
तथा हृदयशब्देन तत्स्था धीरभिधीयते 4.4.49ab
तथा हैरण्यगर्भीयास्तथा पाशुपतादयः 3.7.38cd
तथा हैरण्यगर्भेण लिङ्गात्मा सम एव तु 1.3.306cd
तथा ह्यकारकः कामी स्वर्गकामपदार्पितः SV 523ab
तथेदममलं ब्रह्म निर्विकारमविद्यया 3.5.44ab
तथेन्द्रियमनोबुद्धिविषयेष्वपि योजयेत् 2.1.609ab
तथेप्सितं च संप्राप्तमित्येवं कृतकृत्यता 4.4.783ab
तथेयं श्रुतिरप्याह यो वा इत्यादिवाक्यतः 3.8.163cd
तथेश्वरोऽपि नो विघ्नं कुर्वन्केन निषिध्यते 1.4.1475ab
तथेहान्नरसग्लानौ लिङ्गं देहात्प्रमुच्यते 4.3.1931cd
तथेहापि कथं नाम प्रत्यग्धीः स्यादितीर्यते 2.1.240cd
तथेहापि श्रुतिर्वक्ति प्रत्यग्याथात्म्यवेदिनाम् 3.5.110cd
तथैकत्वविरोधान्न संवेद्यानन्दकं परम् 3.9.187ef
तथैकात्म्ये विशेषाद्वा पुमर्थातिशयत्वतः SV 883cd
तथैतत्सर्वं वेदेति यत्र यत्र श्रुतिर्भवेत् 1.4.778ab
तथैव कामकर्मभ्यामत्यन्तं स्याद्विलक्षणः 4.3.1150ab
तथैव तदभावोऽपि सिद्धोऽनुभवमात्रतः 3.4.91cd
तथैव तव वित्तेन जीवितं नामृतात्मता 2.4.53cd

तथैव नाग्रहीत्सूक्तं शाकल्यः कालचोदितः 3.9.64cd
तथैव पृथगर्थत्वगतौ भिन्नवचस्त्वतः SV 277ab
तथैव ब्रह्मरूपेण प्रतीचोऽप्यद्वयात्मता 1.4.1428cd
तथैव योऽशनायेति परमात्मापि शब्दितः 3.5.180ab
तथैव वचसोक्तिः स्याद्देवो भूत्वेति संभवात् 4.1.25ab
तथैव वस्तुस्वाभाव्याच्चिच्छक्तिर्भूतनिष्ठिता 4.3.126ab
तथैव शक्त्यतन्त्रत्वेऽप्येष दोषो यतो भवेत् SV 68ab
तथैव शास्त्रतद्युक्ती स्वाभिधेयार्थपालनम् SV 789ab
तथैव संप्रसादेऽस्मिन्नुक्तहेतुसमन्वयात् 4.3.1495cd
तथैवाकाशशब्देन तत्र तत्रैष एव तु 1.4.352ab
तथैवाचाररूपेण प्रत्यक्षेण यदीक्ष्यते 2.5.50ab
तथैवाज्ञानभूतेभ्यः परः क्षेत्रज्ञतां ययौ 2.4.417cd
तथैवात्मनि दृष्टे च सर्वं दृष्टं भवेदिति 4.4.480ab
तथैवात्मापि तद्ब्रह्म तदविद्यैकहेतुतः 4.4.851ab
तथैवाधीतवेदश्च युक्तः साधनसंपदा 4.2.7ab
तथैवानभिसंबन्ध आश्रमाख्यैश्च कर्मभिः 4.3.1365ab
तथैवान्यपदार्थेषु तद्द्वयोरपि काण्डयोः 3.1.17cd
तथैवाव्यतिरेकेण रज्जुसर्पखपुष्पवत् 1.4.726cd
तथैवाव्यभिचारेण स्वभावत्वं विवक्षतः 4.3.754ab
तथैवाहतवासाः स्यादहःस्वेतेषु शुद्धधीः 6.4.67ab
तथैवैतद्ग्रहीतव्यं स्वप्नजाग्रदवस्थयोः 4.3.1494cd
तथैवैवंविदं भोगैः सर्वभूतानि सर्वदा 1.5.352cd
तथैष ह्रीति विस्पष्टं संसार्येवाभिधीयते 1.4.1238ab
तथोक्तत्वात्पुरा नेह भूयो वक्तव्यमिष्यते 3.8.162cd
तथोंकारं दमं दानं दयामित्यादिकानि च 5.1.6ab
तथोच्यतेऽनयेत्यस्मात्करणं वागुदाहृता 1.4.680cd
तथोत्पत्त्यादिकाध्यासवर्त्मना तद्विलक्षणम् 4.4.1344ab
तथोदर्के प्रवक्ष्यामः सर्वं भद्रं ततोऽस्त्विदम् 3.2.116cd
तथोदर्के प्रवक्ष्यामि नातो मानविरोधिता 2.1.595cd
तथोपास्यस्य ब्रह्मत्वे श्रुत्या साक्षान्निराकृते 1.4.964ab
तथोभयनिमित्तत्वे नैकान्तिकफलोदयः SV 157cd
तथोभयविवक्षापि व्याकृताव्याकृतोक्तितः 1.4.524cd

तदकर्तृत्वतो ब्रह्म विरजोऽकारणत्वतः 4.4.699cd
तदकर्तृत्वतो हेतोर्ब्रह्मवित्तु सकारणम् 4.4.1292ab
तदकारणतः कर्तुं मृत्स्नेभाश्वादिकं यथा 3.2.90cd
तदकृत्स्नत्वसंसिद्ध्यै प्राणन्नेवेत्युदीरणम् 1.4.661ab
तदक्रियोक्ता श्रुत्येह तथात्मज्ञानजन्मने 3.5.160cd
तदक्षरं प्रवक्तव्यमित्यर्थैषोत्तरा श्रुतिः 3.8.2cd
तदग्न्याद्यभिमान्यत्र ब्रह्मेति व्यपदिश्यते 1.4.1598cd
तदज्ञानं तदुत्थं च जगत्कृत्स्नं तदात्मकम् 1.3.54ab
तदज्ञानैकहेतुत्वात्तेनैव परमात्मना 1.4.1140ab
तदज्ञानैकहेतुत्वात्सर्वस्यानात्मवस्तुनः 4.4.1074cd
तदण्डमभवद्धैमं सहस्रांशुसमप्रभम् 1.2.179ab
तदत्ययाद्द्वयान्तानि न सन्ति प्रत्यगात्मनि 3.9.97cd
तदत्र न परिग्राह्यं सर्वापत्कारणापनुत् 4.4.113cd
तदत्र निखिलं सत्यं श्रुत्या संशोधितं स्फुटम् 2.3.95cd
तदत्र भण्यते सर्वं खिलकाण्डत्वहेतुतः 5.1.2cd
तदत्र स्वप्नेऽसंभाव्यं मन्यतेऽविद्ययैव सः 4.3.1252cd
तदधःपातहेतुत्वान्मन्त्रेऽसदिति भण्यते 1.3.355cd
तदध्यारोपगत्यैव तथापि प्रतिपत्तये 4.4.1341cd
तदनन्तरतो वाचो व्याख्या प्रस्तूयतेऽधुना 1.5.128cd
तदनन्तरमेवोक्ता व्यावृत्तिश्च पथोर्द्वयोः 6.2.160cd
तदनन्यत्वतः प्रापन्महेशस्याप्यनेकता 1.4.550cd
तदनन्यमिति व्याप्तेः प्रत्यक्त्वाद्दिनकृद्यथा 4.3.108cd
तदनुक्तौ यतः पूर्वं सर्वं स्यात्तुषकण्डनम् 3.9.107cd
तदनुत्पन्नवद्भाति तद्व्युत्पत्तेः पुरा नृणाम् 2.4.127cd
तदन्तरतमोऽनस्य प्रतिष्ठागुण उच्यते 1.3.340cd
तदन्तरायबाहुल्यात्सुषुप्तादौ च नेष्यते 1.4.1513ab
तदन्तरायसद्भावादव्यक्तिः स्यात्सदा ध्रुवम् 4.4.340cd
तदन्तरायस्तत्सक्तिस्तन्निवृत्तौ परा श्रुतिः 1.4.1025cd
तदन्तरायासद्भावाद्वास्तवी न तु मोहजा 4.4.316cd
तदन्तर्गतमात्मानं ब्रूह्यन्तर्यामिणं मम 3.7.24cd
तदन्नं जनयत्येव तस्मादन्नं न हीयते 1.5.80cd
तदन्यकारणासत्त्वाद्द्वैविध्यं तमसः कुतः 2.4.201cd

तदन्यकालासंदृष्टेरिति चेदसदुच्यते 4.3.570ab
तदन्यत्र द्वयाभावात्साक्ष्यादावपि नेष्यते 1.4.276ab
तदन्यत्रापि सद्भावादनिषिद्धस्य धर्मिणः 2.3.185cd
तदन्यत्वादिमां त्वाहुरनतिप्रश्न्यनामिकाम् 3.6.24cd
तदन्यदीपयोगे तु नियमेनावभासते 4.3.498cd
तदन्यद्यत्तदाभासं तन्नञा प्रतिषिध्यते 2.3.191cd
तदन्यधीगृहीतौ स्याद्यतोऽनात्मत्वमात्मनः 4.3.306cd
तदन्यभावासंसिद्धेरार्तत्वं हेतुमद्भवेत् 3.4.189cd
तदन्यवस्तुसद्भावे तद्ब्रह्मत्वं विहन्यते 1.4.1097cd
तदन्यविषयज्ञाने न किंचिद्वेत्ति तत्त्वतः 4.4.869ab
तदन्यव्यवधाने हि प्रमाणं नोपपद्यते 3.3.28cd
तदन्यस्य जडत्वाच्च नान्यप्रत्यक्षमिष्यते 4.3.103ab
तदन्यस्य तदात्मत्वाद्ब्रह्मणि स्यात्कथं गतिः 4.2.22cd
तदन्यस्य त्वकृत्स्नत्वाज्जिहासाविषयत्वतः 1.4.1186cd
तदन्यस्य यतो मानाद्व्यतिरेको न लभ्यते 2.4.149cd
तदन्यस्याप्रसिद्धेश्च कथं स्यात्तत्समीक्षणम् 2.4.139ab
तदन्यस्येह कार्यत्वात्कर्तात्मैव तमोवधिः 4.3.923cd
तदन्यात्मस्वनित्योऽसौ मोहसंवीतबुद्धिषु 1.4.1158cd
तदन्यात्मैकनिर्ग्राह्या प्रत्यक्षेणानुभूयते 4.3.503cd
तदन्यानवशिष्टत्वादकृत्स्नः स्यादतोऽन्यथा 1.4.657cd
तदन्यान्यात्मवन्ति स्युः सर्पादीनि स्रजा यथा 1.4.1140cd
तदन्येषु पदार्थेषु प्रत्यक्षादिप्रमाणतः 3.2.114cd
तदपह्नवमानस्य तवात्यन्तमसंभवात् 4.3.736cd
तदपीदं पदं तुर्यं सत्येऽध्यात्मे प्रतिष्ठितम् 5.16.29ab
तदपेक्ष्य पुनःशब्दः श्रुत्यैवेहाभिधीयते 4.3.1947cd
तदप्यन्यत्पुराज्ञासीदनवस्था प्रसज्यते 1.4.1119cd
तदप्यशेषतश्चोद्यमूर्ध्वमुन्मूलयिष्यते SV 31cd
तदप्यस्त्विति चेन्मैवं धर्मादेरप्रसिद्धितः 4.3.154ab
तदप्यस्य तथाभूतमन्तवत्त्वात्प्रतिक्षणम् 1.4.1681ab
तदप्यात्मन आगामि शङ्क्यते कामकर्मवत् 4.3.1305cd
तदप्यैकात्म्यविज्ञानयोग्यत्वायैव कल्प्यते SV 329cd
तदप्रबोधताबाधात्तस्याश्चाशुक्तिकात्मनः 4.4.904cd

तदबोधप्रसूतानामाकाङ्क्षाणां निषेधतः 2.3.243cd
तदबोधप्रहाणेन प्रतीमो जगदात्मनः 4.4.951cd
तदबोधमृते तत्र कुतः पिण्डादिदर्शनम् 1.4.696cd
तदबोधसमुच्छित्तावववाक्यार्थोऽवशिष्यते 4.4.985cd
तदबोधात्तदन्यत्तद्बोधाद्ब्रह्मैव तत्त्वतः 1.4.1153cd
तदबोधैकहेतुत्वादप्राप्तैकात्म्यवस्तुकः 4.3.1223cd
तदभावं सुषुप्ते च स आत्मेत्यभ्युपेयताम् 4.3.192cd
तदभावश्च तत्सर्वं नेतीति प्रतिषिध्यते 2.3.197cd
तदभावात्क्रियाभावस्तामृते कार्यता कुतः 1.4.322cd
तदभावादथैकात्म्यं शोकान्तरमितीर्यते 4.3.1346cd
तदभावाददुष्टत्वात्प्रवेशो मुखबिम्बवत् 1.4.617cd
तदभावादनुष्ठेयो विषयोऽपि न ते भवेत् SV 612cd
तदभावाद्विकुर्वन्ति चेतो न विषयाः सदा 2.1.344cd
तदभावान्न संसारो भूतो भावी न वर्तते SV 1087cd
तदभावेऽनभिव्यक्तं वस्तु नास्तीति दुर्वचः 3.8.113cd
तदभावे च माभावात्कुतस्तत्स्यात्प्रमां विना 1.4.266cd
तदभावे तु पूर्वेषामुत्तरस्यैव मानता SV 821cd
तदभावे पुमानेष किंज्योतिरिति कथ्यताम् 4.3.83cd
तदभिव्यक्तये नालं स्वतःसिद्धस्य वस्तुनः SV 1103cd
तदभ्यासवशादेवमत्राप्यध्यवसीयताम् 4.4.830cd
तदभ्युपगमे वः स्यादनवस्थानिवारणा 3.4.181ab
तदभ्युपेतौ ब्रह्मत्वं व्यावृत्तेर्न प्रसिध्यति 1.4.1101cd
तदयुक्तं पुमर्थस्य तदुक्त्यैव समाप्ततः 2.4.310ab
तदयुक्तं यथान्यायस्तथायमभिधीयते 2.3.104cd
तदयोगव्यवच्छित्त्यै नान्ययोगव्यपेक्षया 4.3.838ab
तदर्थं यत्नसाफल्यं शास्त्रारम्भोऽपि चार्थवान् 4.4.350cd
तदलं क्षितितोयाग्निमरुतां परिणामजे 4.3.155cd
तदवच्छित्तये नालं प्रत्यग्बोधादृतेऽन्यधीः 1.4.1410cd
तदवच्छेदविध्वस्तौ न साधनमपेक्षते 2.4.185cd
तदवद्योतको हेति निपातोऽत्र प्रयुज्यते 1.3.13cd
तदवष्टम्भतः सिद्धेर्व्यभिचारस्य सर्वदा 4.4.152cd
तदवस्थस्य तस्यैकदेशः संसारितामगात् 2.1.480ab

तदविज्ञातयाथात्म्यमेतत्कारणमुच्यते 2.4.391cd
तदविद्यादिविध्वंसात्रिवृः शपथयाम्यहम् 4.4.303cd
तदविद्यानिरासेन मुक्तिर्नातोऽन्यसाधनात् 4.3.1833cd
तदविद्यापनुत्त्यर्थं गार्ग्यकाश्यादिच्छद्मना 4.3.2ab
तदविद्यैव निःशेषविशेषाणां प्रसूतिकृत् 4.4.351cd
तदविद्योत्थदेहादिसंतत्युच्छेदहेतुतः 4.4.372cd
तदसत्प्रतिपत्तव्यं यतोऽभिन्नैव देवता 1.4.136cd
तदसंप्राप्तिविच्छेदक्षयेष्वसुखकृद्यतः 2.4.85cd
तदसंभावनायाश्च को हेतुरिति भण्यते 4.4.1158ab
तदसंभाव्यदेशादौ दर्शनात्तन्मृषात्मता 4.3.1069cd
तदसूतेरिह त्वात्मन्यादिमध्यान्तबाधधीः 1.4.1498cd
तदस्य परं गुह्यं तेनोपासीत तत्त्वतः 2.1.420cd
तदस्य परतो ज्ञेयमात्माज्ञानैकहेतुकम् 4.3.1206cd
तदस्राक्षीन्मनुः सर्वं स्त्रीपुंद्वन्द्वप्रयोगतः 1.4.120cd
तदाकूतानुगुण्यं स्यात्प्राणादेः कथमुच्यते 4.4.94cd
तदाख्यायिकया हेतुस्तयोः संवाद इष्यते 4.3.12cd
तदा चैकपदार्थस्य नियोगः साध्यतामियात् SV 608cd
तदा तीर्णो भवत्येष शोकान्न्दयसंश्रितान् 4.4.410ef
तदात्मज्योतिषेद्धं सन्नित्यमेवावतिष्ठते 4.3.351ab
तदात्मत्वं समापेदे न त्वसौ परमार्थतः 1.4.1178cd
तदात्मत्वाभिमानित्वाद्विज्ञानमयतात्मनः 2.1.187cd
तदात्मभावविज्ञानस्तदेवातो निगच्छति 4.4.103cd
तदात्ममानिनोऽतः स्युरात्मनस्ते न तु स्वतः 4.4.239cd
तदात्मविद्याविध्यर्थं नोपासनविधायकम् 2.5.85cd
तदाद्वये दृशौ दृष्टे न भयादि तमोहतेः 1.4.29cd
तदा द्वयोरसंसिद्धेर्विरोधाच्चाप्यसंगतिः 4.3.1714cd
तदाधर्मादितो दुःखं विक्रियातोऽभिजायते 2.4.348ab
तदाधेयोपसंहृत्यै यश्चायमिति शब्द्यते 2.5.25cd
तदानन्त्याच्च तद्बोधो नेश्वरेणापि कात्स्न्र्यतः 1.4.954ab
तदानन्दात्मकब्रह्मविज्ञानाय मनागपि 3.9.190ab
तदा न शक्यते वक्तुं वैलक्षण्यं तयोरिति SV 696cd
तदा नश्यन्ति भूतानि येभ्यः क्षेत्रज्ञतां गतः 2.4.431cd

तदा निगमनार्थं तत्प्रतिज्ञातार्थगोचरम् 4.3.1906cd
तदा निवर्तयेच्छापं मन्त्रेणानेन सत्पतिः 6.4.35cd
तदापत्तिश्रुतेश्चेयं संपन्नेहोपपद्यते 1.4.1258ab
तदापि जीवद्वारेण विक्रियां व्रजतो विभोः 2.3.144ab
तदापि न विरोधोऽत्र विभिन्नार्थावबोधिनोः 2.1.566cd
तदापि न विरोधोऽयं केनचिद्विनिवार्यते 5.1.105cd
तदापि वस्तुपरता नागमस्य विहन्यते SV 705cd
तदापि विकृतेर्नाशो मुक्तिरित्यभिधीयते SV 262cd
तदाप्यविद्याविध्वस्तावधिकारो न कर्मणि SV 255cd
तदाभासानुविद्धेन प्रमात्राहंवपुर्भृता 4.3.296ab
तदा भ्राष्ट्राद्यदूरस्थे साध्याभावादि सज्जते 4.3.723cd
तदार्षेणैव विन्दन्ति तपस्तप्त्वा महर्षयः 6.5.19cd
तदा विविच्य रूपाणि क्रमशो यो धियः शुभम् 4.4.721cd
तदाविष्करणे ग्रन्थः क्रमेणारभ्यते परः 4.3.1544ab
तदाविष्क्रियते तस्मात्करविन्यस्तबिल्ववत् 4.3.1334cd
तदाशङ्कानिवृत्त्यर्थं प्रारब्धैषोत्तरा श्रुतिः 3.3.11ef
तदा शङ्कानिवृत्त्यर्थं मानादन्यत्किमिष्यताम् 4.4.814cd
तदाशङ्कानिवृत्त्यर्थमतः कार्यं प्रयत्नतः 4.3.721ab
तदाशङ्कापनुत्त्यर्थं तद्धैतदिति हि श्रुतिः 1.3.371cd
तदा श्रवणमेव स्याद्विशिष्टो विषयस्तव SV 804cd
तदा स एव विज्ञेयस्तज्ज्ञानादेव मुक्तता 2.1.427cd
तदा स्यात्सर्वकर्माणि यदि संन्यस्य तिष्ठति 1.5.307cd
तदा हि कल्पनाः सर्वा विकारावयवादिकाः SV 267cd
तदाहुरिति वाक्येन ब्रह्मविद्याप्रयोजनम् 2.5.90ab
तदाहुरिति विस्पष्टं श्रूयते श्रुतिवाक्यतः 3.3.127cd
तदित्यनेनाभ्यधायि परोक्षार्थाभिधायिना 1.4.191cd
तदिदं नामरूपाभ्यामनामकमरूपकम् 1.4.390ab
तदिदं भण्यते श्रुत्या पुंसां वैराग्यजन्मने 4.3.1923cd
तदिदं हिरण्यगर्भस्य व्यक्तीभावो महेश्वरात् 5.5.7ab
तदुक्तौ सर्वमुक्तं स्याद्यत्पुमर्थाय साधनम् 5.16.47cd
तदुच्छित्तावतः प्रत्यग्याथात्म्यज्ञानमुच्यते 4.4.270ab
तदुच्छित्तौ न हेतुः स्याद्विरोधस्य प्रमाश्रयात् 4.4.793cd

तदुत्पत्तौ ससंवित्को मोहो मूढप्रधानकः 3.8.41cd
तदुत्पत्त्यादिमत्स्वेव युक्तं कल्पयितुं फलम् 3.3.105cd
तदुपस्थेन संदीप्तेर्धूमो लोमानि साम्यतः 6.2.108ab
तदुपात्तविशेषं सच्छुक्लकृष्णादिनोच्यते 1.4.394cd
तदुपादानमात्राः स्युर्देवताः स्वाभिमानजाः 1.4.512cd
तदुपाधिर्नियन्तैष परः प्रोक्तो न तु स्वतः 3.7.43cd
तदुपाये प्रवर्तन्तस्तदभेदे न युज्यते SV 1012cd
तदुपासां न वेद्मीति मा च शङ्कां कृथा यतः 2.1.49ab
तदेकदेशाभिहितेर्विज्ञानात्मानमेष्यति 3.5.11cd
तदेतत्कल्पितं सर्वं सहेतु फलवज्जगत् 2.5.135ab
तदेतत्कारणं स्पष्टं पारिव्राज्येऽभिधीयते 4.4.1096ab
तदेतत्खलु वैराजं नामरूपक्रियात्मकम् 1.6.36ab
तदेतत्प्रेय इत्यादिवाक्येभ्योऽनेकधा श्रुतम् SV 1017ab
तदेतत्सत्यमिति च सबीजः पर उच्यते 1.4.352cd
तदेतत्संप्रधार्याह प्रातृदः पितरं किल 5.14.5ab
तदेतत्सृष्टं धर्माख्यं क्षत्रस्याधिपतेरपि 1.4.1616ab
तदेतदात्मतत्त्वं हि पदनीयमितीरणात् 1.4.6cd
तदेतदिति च स्पष्टं श्रुतिरैकात्म्यमब्रवीत् 4.3.803cd
तदेतदिति मानेन तत्त्वमस्यादिना तथा 4.3.1733ab
तदेतदितिवाक्यार्थो ग्राह्योऽतः संभवान्मितेः 2.5.89cd
तदेतदिति वाक्येन प्रतीचोऽन्यैव वार्यते 2.5.80cd
तदेतदितिशास्त्रेण भण्यते तद्बुभुत्सवे 1.4.1027cd
तदेतदित्यनद्वैतत्तत्त्वमवबोध्यते 2.5.137cd
तदेतदुच्यते श्रुत्या नैनं पाप्मेति यत्नतः 4.4.1291ab
तदेतद्ब्रह्मविद्याया आरम्भे फलमुच्यते 1.4.1125ab
तदेतन्नित्यमज्ञानं तज्जकालाद्यनाप्लुतेः 1.4.358ab
तदेतन्मथ्यमानं सदैक्यदर्शनलक्षणम् 4.3.1393ab
तदेतरत्तदर्थमित्येवं चैतत्समञ्जसम् SV 611ab
तदेतल्लोकनिर्माणमोतप्रोतात्मनोदितम् 3.6.19ab
तदेव ज्ञातृतामेति बुद्ध्युपाधिसमाश्रयात् 2.3.7cd
तदेव तदपेक्षं स्यान्न तु देशादिसिद्धिदम् 1.4.1332cd
तदेव तदपेक्षं स्यान्न तु देशादिसिद्धिदम् 3.4.134cd

तदेव दुःखकृद्भूरि तद्धेत्वोरनवस्थितेः 2.4.77cd
तदेव परमार्थं स्याद्वस्त्वैकात्म्यस्वलक्षणम् 4.3.1328cd
तदेव पूर्णमित्यादिवाक्येनेहोपसंहृतम् 5.1.17cd
तदेव ब्रह्म पूर्णत्वान्न त्वदुक्तमकृत्स्नतः 2.1.87cd
तदेव ब्रह्मविज्ञानं कथं नेह विरुध्यते 1.4.1722cd
तदेव ब्रह्म विद्धि त्वं न त्विदं यदुपासते 2.5.83cd
तदेव विद्धि ब्रह्मेति न त्विदं यदुपासते 1.5.254cd
तदेव हेत्वपेक्षं सदुत्पत्त्यादि प्रपद्यते 4.3.1597cd
तदेवानुप्रविश्येति तत्त्वं यत्पारमार्थिकम् 1.4.445ab
तदेवेदमिति मतौ वियन्नकुलयोरिव 4.3.679cd
तदेवैकं प्रमाणं नः सर्ववाद्यविरोधि यत् 1.4.1376cd
तदेवैति पुमानस्य सक्तं यत्र मनो भवेत् 4.4.235ab
तदेवैतीति यदि वा गन्तव्यमभिधीयते 4.4.238ab
तदेवोक्तमिहालम्ब्य तदग्नीक्षणसिद्धये 6.2.17ab
तदेवोत्तरकार्येषु न कार्यं कारणं मितेः 1.2.45cd
तदेवोद्रेचनं चेत्स्याद्द्वैतस्येति मतं यदि 5.1.44cd
तदेषामिति षष्ठीयं श्रुत्या तस्मात्प्रयुज्यते 2.1.215cd
तदोतप्रोतवाक्येन तच्च सर्वं निराकृतम् 3.8.81cd
तदोत्क्रान्तां विजानीयान्मनसो देवतामितः 4.4.70ab
तदोपदेशानर्थक्यं तमृतेऽप्यस्य मुक्ततः 2.1.467cd
तदोपलब्ध्यभावोऽसौ यो भावो भवतोच्यते 4.3.798cd
तद्गुणस्मरणाभ्यासादिच्छा पुंसोऽभिवर्धते 4.4.228cd
तद्गृहीत्यै सशब्दोऽयं तत्स्मृत्यर्थं तथा च वै 4.4.149cd
तद्गोचरातिवर्तित्वं विद्याकाले तमोहतेः 1.4.1506cd
तद्गोचरैकसंद्रष्टृविज्ञात्रर्थं समीक्ष्य हि 2.1.162ab
तद्ग्राहीणि च मानानि व्यावृत्तिः केन गम्यते SV 953ab
तद्दर्शननिषेधार्थं ब्रह्मेत्याह परा श्रुतिः 2.4.240cd
तद्दर्शनविधित्सायै स्तुत्यर्थोत्पत्तिरिष्यते 1.2.1cd
तद्दर्शनात्समस्तस्य पुरुषार्थस्य सिद्धितः 1.4.653cd
तद्दर्शनादृषिः साक्षात्पश्यन्सर्वं प्रपन्नवान् 1.4.1445cd
तद्दृष्टावखिलं दृष्टं रज्जुसर्पादिवद्भवेत् 1.4.748cd
तद्दृष्टावेव निःशेषपुरुषार्थसमाप्तितः 1.4.1112ab

तद्दृष्टिमात्रतः सिद्धेर्नान्यतस्तदवाप्यते 1.4.1677ab
तद्दृष्टिरिति वचसा साक्षान्नः प्रतिपाद्यते 4.3.1480cd
तद्दृष्टेः पुरुषार्थत्वश्रवणादसकृच्छ्रुतौ 1.4.624ab
तद्दृष्टेर्नित्यसंप्राप्तेर्विध्यानर्थक्यसंगतिः 2.4.137cd
तद्दृष्ट्यैवेह तं दृष्ट्वा ब्रह्मवद्यं यदीक्षसे 3.4.80cd
तद्देशमभितस्तौ यौ मुष्कौ तौ वृषणाविति 6.4.11cd
तद्दोषापनुनुत्सायै पूर्णमित्यादिका श्रुतिः 5.1.35cd
तद्द्रव्यसंक्षये यस्मात्पूर्ववत्सहजेक्षणम् 4.3.709cd
तद्द्वारेण प्रकाशोऽयं न मनस्युपजायते 4.3.81cd
तद्द्वारेण भवेन्नापि संदिग्धे स्यात्प्रवर्तनम् SV 836cd
तद्द्वारेणैव निष्क्रामन्न क्वचित्प्रतिहन्यते 4.4.83cd
तद्द्वारेद्धमनाः स्मृत्वा बाह्यां चेष्टां प्रपद्यते 4.3.288cd
तद्धानेरात्मसाक्षित्वात्प्रत्यङ्जन्मादिवर्जितः 4.3.1453cd
तद्धेतुनाशात्प्रकृतिं स्वामेव प्रतिपद्यते 4.5.12cd
तद्धेतुप्रतिषेधेन वाक्यमेतन्निषेधति 4.4.524cd
तद्धेतुहेतुमत्त्वस्य प्रसिद्धयर्थमथावदत् 4.1.9ab
तद्धेतोरात्मनः प्रीतेर्जायादिः प्रिय उच्यते 2.4.80cd
तद्धेतौ तमसि ध्वस्ते कुतः संज्ञानिमित्ततः 2.4.444cd
तद्धेत्वतिक्रमादात्मा सर्वशोकातिगस्ततः 4.4.436cd
तद्धेदमिति चात्रापि जगदेवाभिधीयते 3.8.28ab
तद्धेदमिति चानन्दो नैवेहेति तथोच्यते 1.4.34cd
तद्धेदमित्यनेनास्याः प्रमेयोऽर्थो निरूपितः 1.4.1056ab
तद्धेदमित्यनेनोक्तिव्याकृताव्याकृतात्मनोः 1.4.219ab
तद्धेदमित्यविज्ञातप्रत्यक्तत्त्वादिदं जगत् 2.1.1ab
तद्धेदमित्यविद्याया उक्तं कार्यमशेषतः 1.6.1ab
तद्धैतत्प्राणविज्ञानं यथाव्याख्यातरूपकम् 1.3.375ab
तद्धैतदिति सिद्धत्वादुद्गातृयजमानयोः 1.3.388cd
तद्धैतदित्यतो ज्ञानं फलवत्त्वाद्विधित्सितम् 1.3.37cd
तद्ध्यदृष्टं सदज्ञानकार्यं स्रगिव पन्नगम् 1.4.181ab
तद्ध्वंसादेव निःशेषपुमर्थाप्तिरतो भवेत् 1.4.169ab
तद्ध्वस्तये चिकित्सेयं तदा फलवती भवेत् 1.4.186cd
तद्ध्वस्तावात्मनस्तस्मात्पुरुषार्थः समाप्यते 4.4.169cd

तद्ध्वस्तेर्वस्तुवृत्तत्वान्मृदि लोष्टादिनाशवत् 2.4.196cd

तद्बलेनैव मेयस्थं घ्नन्ति मोहादि नान्यतः 1.4.429cd

तद्बाधे नाप्यपेक्षास्ति मिथ्याधीबाधनं प्रति 1.4.437cd

तद्बुद्धेः पृथगर्थत्वमुक्तमेवातिविस्तरात् SV 275cd

तद्ब्रह्मात्मानमेवावेद्यदनात्मेत्यभूत्पुरा 1.4.1388ab

तद्ब्रह्मात्मानमेवावेन्मेयं मानं च भण्यते 1.4.1353ab

तद्ब्रह्मैवंविधिं कृत्स्नं न गोवृक्षादिवन्मतम् 1.4.952cd

तद्भावभावतस्तस्मादन्यज्ज्योतिरितीक्ष्यताम् 4.3.429cd

तद्भावभावतस्तस्य तद्ध्वस्तौ ध्वंसतस्तथा 2.4.409cd

तद्भावभावतो लिङ्गाद्भासनैकसमाश्रयात् SV 456ab

तद्भावभावहेतुत्वात्कारकत्वस्य कारणम् 1.4.173ab

तद्भावभाविहेतुत्वादतोऽकामो विमुच्यते 4.4.256ab

तद्भावभाव्यपः सृष्ट्वा रेतोबीजेन स प्रभुः 1.2.177cd

तद्भावमचिरेणैति स्थैर्यं चात्रैव गच्छति 4.4.728cd

तद्भावाभावयोरात्मा न कार्यं नापि कारणम् 4.2.88cd

तद्भावाभावसाक्ष्यात्मा ह्येतच्च श्रुतिमस्तके 1.4.616cd

तद्भूतानां क्रियार्थेन ह्याम्नायस्य क्रियार्थतः SV 242cd

तद्भूतेः पुरुषार्थत्वाद्देवता हीश्वरा परा 1.3.132cd

तद्भूतौ तदभिव्यक्तेस्तत्स्वापेऽव्याकृतात्मता 1.4.364cd

तद्भेदस्योपलब्धत्वात्तद्योगात्प्राक्प्रमाणतः 4.3.467cd

तद्भेदाभेदतासिद्धौ न च मानमिहास्ति वः 4.4.335cd

तद्यथा बोधयेद्वाक्यं तत्तथैवेति गृह्यताम् 4.4.812cd

तद्यथावस्तुसंबोधान्मूलनाशात्प्रणश्यति 1.4.1207cd

तद्यथा श्येन इत्यस्माद्यावत्स्त्रीब्राह्मणादिति 4.3.1101ab

तद्यथा श्येन इत्युक्त्या तद्दृष्टान्तप्रदर्शनात् 4.3.1158ab

तद्यया वेद्यते बुद्ध्या तदसाधारणात्मना 1.4.1077ab

तद्याथात्म्यप्रसिद्ध्यर्थं ब्रह्मार्थस्तु विशेषणम् 1.4.1418ab

तद्याथात्म्यात्प्रतीचोऽतः सम्यग्दृष्ट्या न वीक्ष्यते 4.3.79cd

तद्याथात्म्यात्महेतुभ्यामनात्मार्थसमागमे 1.4.730ab

तद्याथात्म्यापरिज्ञानात्तद्विपर्ययधीरियम् 4.4.553cd

तद्याथात्म्याप्रबोधात्तु तयोरेष विपर्ययः 1.4.1390cd

तद्यावत्कठिनं देहे तावल्लिङ्गं स्थिरं भवेत् 4.3.1942cd

तद्रूपं चेदवाच्यत्वं भवताभ्युपगम्यते 4.3.642ab
तद्रूपो मध्यमो वायुः श्रमास्तमयवर्जितः 1.5.368ab
तद्वत्कर्मोपभोगार्थं वागाद्याः कर्मशक्तयः 2.4.368cd
तद्वत्पुत्रादिदेहेषु मोहान्नानात्मविभ्रमः 1.5.316cd
तद्वत्प्राणमयं कर्म देहस्यास्यैष संग्रहः 1.5.154cd
तद्वत्संसारिकारित्वं जगतो गम्यतां श्रुतेः 2.1.443cd
तद्वत्सकारणोऽनात्मा नाभूदस्ति भविष्यति 2.3.209cd
तद्वत्सुषुप्सोरुत्क्रम्य देवताः स्वाधिकारतः 4.3.1139ab
तद्वदद्वयतत्त्वोऽपि तदसंबोधहेतुतः 2.4.435ab
तद्वदव्यतिरेकेण घटाभावाद्यसंभवात् 1.4.329cd
तद्वदात्मातिरेकेण नात्मीयार्थो मनागपि 2.4.268ab
तद्वद्गच्छति यो यस्माद्भेदे सत्येव याति सः 2.1.378ab
तद्वद्बाधोऽप्यबोधस्य बोधेनाभ्युपगम्यते 1.4.1366ab
तद्वद्रूपस्य सामान्यं रूपमित्युपदिश्यते 1.4.394ab
तद्वद्वागाश्रयत्वं च तयोः स्याद्रूपकर्मणोः 1.6.32ab
तद्वन्न व्यतिरेकेण ब्रह्मणो द्वे स्वतः सदा 2.3.22ab
तद्वन्मृतस्य वक्तव्यं न तु पुत्रप्रपौत्रवत् 3.9.141cd
तद्वर्जनस्य संसिद्धेः प्रसिद्धोपायसंश्रयात् SV 159ab
तद्वशान्न तु शब्दार्थः स हि पूर्वं प्रतीयते SV 501ab
तद्वा अस्यैतदिति तच्छ्रुत्या निर्वर्ण्यतेऽधुना 4.3.1333cd
तद्वा अस्यैतदित्यत्र यथोक्तं रूपमात्मनः 4.3.1156ab
तद्वा अस्यैतदित्यादेः प्राज्ञस्यान्तररूपतः 4.4.490ab
तद्वा अस्यैतदित्युक्त्या नातः कामादयोऽत्र ते 4.4.489cd
तद्वा अस्यैतदित्येवं प्राक्श्रुत्या प्रतिपादितम् 4.4.254ab
तद्वानसमकालं तु प्राणनादिक्रियोत्थितेः 1.4.678ab
तद्वासनानिरोधेऽतः पुमाञ्श्रुत्या नियुज्यते SV 442cd
तद्विज्ञानस्य नित्यत्वाज्जानीयान्नित्यमेव तत् 3.9.188cd
तद्विज्ञानार्थं स गुरुमेवाभिगच्छेत्समित्पाणिः श्रोत्रियं ब्रह्मनिष्ठम् SV 25cd
तद्वित्तिसाधनाभावात्कथं तदवगम्यते 1.4.210cd
तद्विदः फलसिद्ध्यर्थं भूयः प्रश्नोऽयमुच्यते 1.5.84cd
तद्विदश्च भवेन्मृत्युर्दूरमित्युपदिश्यते 1.3.218cd
तद्विदस्तिष्ठमानस्य समाप्तिः स्यात्परायणम् 3.9.161cd

तद्विदस्तिष्ठमानस्येत्यस्य चेहोपसंहृतिः 4.4.1308cd
तद्विदो ब्रह्मणश्चेह भेदहेतोरसंभवात् 3.9.163ab
तद्विद्या ब्रह्मविद्येति प्रतिपद्यामहे तदा 2.1.428cd
तद्विध्येकोक्तियोगस्य ह्यक्लेशात्संभवे सति 2.1.504ab
तद्विना व्यवहाराच्च सिद्धा संबन्धनित्यता SV 878cd
तद्विनाशेऽपि तत्साक्ष्याद्विनश्यन्तीव लक्ष्यते 1.4.336ab
तद्विनाशेऽपि तत्साक्ष्याद्विनश्यन्तीव लक्ष्यते 3.4.116ab
तद्विपक्षः सुखं तावदल्पं तत्संक्षये क्षयः 2.4.76cd
तद्विपक्षस्तु यो बालो बलादेव मुमुक्षति 1.4.1583ab
तद्विपर्ययतो मिथ्या सर्वं मोहादि भण्यते 1.4.430ab
तद्विमुक्तेः समाप्तत्वादेष इत्यभ्यधान्मुनिः 4.3.1813cd
तद्वियोगादतो दैवा आविशन्ति यथोदिताः 1.5.327ab
तद्वियोगाद्विशुद्धं तदिति वः कल्पना कथम् 4.3.705cd
तद्विरुद्धं कथं पश्येद्दृष्ट्या तत्कर्मभतया 3.4.159cd
तद्विरुद्धं तथा यत्स्यादेत्येव न तु तिष्ठति 2.3.25cd
तद्विरुद्धं स्मृतेर्वाक्यं नापेक्ष्यं दुर्बलत्वतः 3.5.158cd
तद्विरुद्धतनुर्मोहः कुतो ब्रह्मणि चेन्मतम् 1.4.1213cd
तद्विरुद्धफले बाह्यसाधनेऽनेककारके SV 135ab
तद्विरुद्धमथैकात्म्यं प्रत्यपद्यत मायया 1.4.604cd
तद्विरुद्धमभूज्ज्ञानं रजताभमबोधजम् 1.4.449cd
तद्विरुद्धममर्तं स्यान्निरंशं देशवन्न च 2.3.23cd
तद्विरुद्धरवीन्द्वादिज्योतिषोर्मोहहेतुकः 4.3.37cd
तद्विरुद्धात्मकः प्रत्यङ्ब्रह्मापर्वादिवाक्यतः 3.5.95cd
तद्विरुद्धात्मकान्मत्तो मय्येवासौ प्रसिध्यति 2.3.226cd
तद्विरुद्धात्मकेनैव ज्योतिषोद्दीपितेक्षणः 4.3.39ab
तद्विरुद्धात्मविज्ञानादध्वंसित्वात्मैकलो भवेत् 3.5.86cd
तद्विरुद्धेह या दृष्टिर्मिथ्यारूपा न सान्यथा 1.4.656cd
तद्विरोधादभिन्नत्वं कथं मानात्प्रतीयते 1.6.72cd
तद्विरोधाविरोधाभ्यां ध्रुवं प्राप्नोत्यनीप्सितम् 4.3.594cd
तद्विवेकापरिज्ञानाद्युक्तं तच्चाभ्युपेयते 4.3.465cd
तद्विशेषेऽङ्गभूयस्त्वात्फलभूयस्त्वमित्यतः SV 361ab
तद्विशेषैकनिष्ठत्वान्न वः संबन्धधीभवेत् SV 734ab

तद्विष्णोरिति मन्त्रोऽपि विष्णोस्तत्परमं पदम् 1.4.746ab
तद्वृत्त्युपाधिसंस्थं सत्तज्ज्ञानमिति भण्यते 2.3.8ab
तद्व्यक्तेरग्निकार्यत्वान्न सा कार्यं भवेदतः 4.3.778ef
तद्व्याख्यानं यथावच्च ह्यक्षराणां विभाव्यते 4.3.1540cd
तद्व्याख्यानाय भूयोऽपि तस्य चेहानुवादतः 4.4.986ab
तद्व्याख्यानाय यत्नोऽतो न भूयः क्रियतेऽधुना 4.5.7cd
तद्व्यापारात्पुरा मेयः स्यात्स्वतोऽधिगतात्मकः 4.3.172cd
तद्व्याप्तौ चापि संव्याप्तिरापादतलमस्तकम् 4.4.46ab
तद्व्युत्थानं प्रातिलोम्यं स्वप्नादिस्थानसंचरः 4.3.989cd
तद्व्युत्पत्तेः पुरा साक्षाद्बोधो व्युत्पत्तिमात्रतः SV 547cd
तनुते देहजातानि भूरिरूपाण्यविद्यया 4.4.146cd
तन्तुवीरणमृद्दारुसाधनानां पृथक्त्वतः 1.5.230ab
तन्तून्स्वतः प्रसिद्धेन करणेन च तन्तुना 2.1.391cd
तन्त्रान्तरेषु तस्यापि कार्यत्वेन श्रुतत्वतः 1.4.848cd
तन्न पश्यतिशब्देन कारकत्वं निषिध्यते 4.3.1477cd
तन्न प्रत्यक्षवचनाद्देहादिलयसिद्धितः SV 425cd
तन्नातत्परतस्तूक्तेर्न देहादिलयस्ततः SV 424cd
तन्नातिच्छन्दवचसा विरोधान्नास्य मानता 4.4.443ab
तन्नाम्ना नामवत्येवं देवतान्तरयोजना 1.4.1632cd
तन्नाशमनु नाशः स्याद्यतो दुःखात्मनस्ततः 4.4.30cd
तन्नास्ति कारणं कार्यं यन्नानेनात्मना हृनुतम् 2.5.125cd
तन्नास्ति कारणं कार्यं यन्नानेनात्मसात्कृतम् 2.5.125ab
तन्नास्ति तदद्वितीयं च विभक्तं नात ईक्षते 4.3.1514cd
तन्नारितत्वेऽपि च तथा तयोस्तस्मात्प्रसिद्धितः 3.8.124cd
तन्नास्ति विषयोल्लेखिदर्शनस्येह कारणम् 4.3.1526cd
तन्नित्यकर्मवत्कस्माच्छ्रुत्येह न निषिध्यते 4.4.1236cd
तन्निर्णयादशेषोऽर्थोऽनिर्णीतः स्यात्कथं न्विति 4.4.148ef
तन्निर्णयार्थमारम्भो न कार्यो जामिदोषतः 2.1.367cd
तन्निर्दिदिक्षया यत्नात्प्रवृत्तैषा परा श्रुतिः 1.4.167ef
तन्निर्धार्यानया श्रुत्या पदमाप्नोत्युपासनात् 1.3.12cd
तन्निवृत्तौ निवर्तेते इतिकर्तव्यसाधने SV 250ef
तन्निवृत्तौ निवृत्तिः स्यान्निवृत्तिः केवलात्मता 1.3.188cd

तन्निवृत्त्येकसाक्षित्वात्कामाद्यस्तित्वसाक्षिवत् 4.3.1755cd
तन्निःशेषं परित्यज्य सुखमात्यन्तिकं श्रयेत् 2.4.86cd
तन्निषेधश्रुतेश्चापि नापेक्ष्यं तद्विरोधतः 4.4.465ab
तन्निषेधात्तु या सिद्धिर्न सा कार्यप्रसादतः SV 851ab
तन्निषेधानुवादेन प्रतीचि ब्रह्म बोध्यते 3.8.86cd
तन्निषेधाय यत्नोऽतः काण्वश्रुत्या न भण्यते 4.4.521cd
तन्निषेधेन चाद्वैतं प्रत्यग्वस्त्वभिधीयते 4.3.1807cd
तन्निषेधेन तत्सिद्धेः कथं स्यात्तदभिन्नता 1.6.81cd
तन्निषेधोऽमरोक्त्यात्र नित्यस्यात्मन उच्यते 4.4.1331cd
तन्निष्ठं च भवेद्वाक्यं व्यर्थता च विधेस्तदा SV 658cd
तन्निष्ठा चेह विज्ञेया यथोक्तन्यायवर्त्मना SV 281cd
तन्न्याय्यमथवान्याय्यं यत्नान्न्यायैः परीक्ष्यताम् 4.3.1104cd
तन्मदान्ध्यनिषेधार्थं महाब्राह्मण उच्यते 2.1.349cd
तन्मनोऽथ परे तत्त्वे लब्धलक्ष्यं स्व आत्मनि 4.4.722ab
तन्मयत्वं तथैवैतिक्रमेणैव स मानवः 4.4.718cd
तन्मया हीतरे प्राणास्तन्मलास्तन्निबन्धनाः 6.1.33ab
तन्मात्रावर्त्मनैवैनं बुबोधयिषुरादरात् 4.3.1843ab
तन्मानमपि मानत्वं लभते न तु केवलम् 1.4.317cd
तन्मानमिति चेन्मैवं यतस्तत्प्राक्प्रबोधतः 4.3.1185cd
तन्मानानवगम्यत्वादादित्यादेश्च तद्ग्रहात् 4.3.106cd
तन्मा शङ्कीर्यतः प्राज्ञे पश्यन्नात्मात्र वर्तते 4.3.1541cd
तन्मिथ्याप्रतिपत्त्यर्थमिवेति व्यपदिश्यते 4.3.417cd
तन्मुखत्वेनासंसिद्धेस्तादर्थ्येनोत्तरा श्रुतिः 5.16.77cd
तन्मुमुक्षुत्वमायातं कुतो हेतोरितीर्यताम् 2.4.142cd
तन्मुमुक्षुरतो मुक्त्यै त्यजेत्सर्वैषणा यतिः 1.5.224cd
तन्मूलध्वस्तयेऽथोर्ध्वं परो ग्रन्थोऽवतार्यते 3.4.1cd
तन्मूला च स्मृतिः साक्षाद्वेदानित्यादिका स्फुटा 1.4.14cd
तन्मूलाज्ञानघातित्वाज्ज्ञानस्येह प्रसिद्धितः SV 124ab
तन्मूलाज्ञानविध्वस्तेर्यथोक्तागममानतः 5.1.22cd
तन्मूलानि तथान्यानि स्मृतिवाक्यानि कोटिशः 4.4.1259cd
तन्मेयप्रथने मानं न किंचिदनुभूतितः 1.3.48cd
तन्मोहजानां सर्वेषां स तत्त्वं परमार्थतः 1.4.1139cd

तन्मोहमात्रजे तस्मादेषणे प्रत्यगात्मनि 3.5.137cd
तन्मोहमात्रविध्वंसादित्यपि श्रुतिशासनम् 1.3.185cd
तपःशब्देन कृच्छ्रादि यदि नामाभिधीयते 1.5.19ab
तपसस्तापसस्यैवमग्न्यावेशस्य यत्फलम् 5.13.5cd
तपसा कल्मषं हन्ति विद्ययामृतमश्नुते 1.4.1767cd
तपसा कल्मषं हन्ति विद्ययामृतमश्नुते 3.2.118cd
तपसा कल्मषं हन्तीत्यपि च स्मृतिशासनम् 4.4.1055cd
तपसा तत्परं ब्रह्म विद्धीति वचनादतः 1.4.1060ab
तपसा तापसस्यैव यज्ञेन गृहिणस्तथा 4.4.1064cd
तपोऽतः परमं हि स्यात्तच्चिकित्सामकुर्वतः 5.13.2cd
तपोऽप्सु तप्यमानासु ह्यण्डं जज्ञे हिरण्मयम् 1.2.151ab
तपो विद्या च विप्रस्य निःश्रेयसकरं परम् 3.2.118ab
तप्तलोहवदेकत्वं भवत्यावृत्तिदुर्लभम् 2.5.70cd
तप्तलोहादिवद्व्याप्य शेते प्राणात्मतां गतः 4.4.51cd
तप्तायोवच्छरीरं स्वं व्याप्य शेते स्व आत्मनि 2.1.339cd
तम एवेति चेन्नैवं स्वयंज्योतिष्ट्वमात्मनः 4.3.1399cd
तमःप्रकाशवत्कर्म नाज्ञानेन विरुध्यते 3.3.93cd
तमःप्रधानः क्षेत्राणां चित्प्रधानश्चिदात्मनाम् 1.4.342ab
तमः सूर्योदयेनेव ज्ञानेनोत्कृत्य नाश्यते SV 1088cd
तमत्ययं मोक्षविधौ तद्विद्वांसः प्रचक्षते 3.5.70cd
तमप्यपह्नुतेऽविद्या नाज्ञानस्यास्ति दुष्करम् 4.3.74cd
तमवस्थान्तरं नीत्वा स्वप्नदर्शनवर्तिना 2.1.435ab
तमसा बीजभूतं तद्व्यज्यते संस्कृतेः पुनः 1.4.343cd
तमसैव यथा सर्पं स्रक्प्रविष्टा न तु स्वतः 1.4.633ab
तमसो ज्ञानविध्वस्तावब्रह्मानात्मताहतेः 3.4.48ab
तमस्तदुत्थकार्याणामत्यन्तासंभवादतः 2.5.59cd
तमस्यवस्थितः कुम्भः स्वात्मना नावभासते 4.3.498ab
तमस्यवस्थितोऽपश्यञ्ज्ञातृज्ञानतमांसि हि 4.3.1608ab
तमस्युत्सार्यमाणे तु वाचोज्ज्ञात्रा सुरद्विषाम् 1.3.143ab
तमस्विनः प्रलीनत्वान्नाविद्याकार्यमीक्षते 4.3.1534cd
तमस्विनि निवृत्तेऽस्मिन्देहान्ते प्रत्यगात्मनि 4.3.1318ab
तमस्विनोऽथ द्वे रूपे तदन्याव्यतिरेकतः 2.3.20cd

तमःसंवृतदृष्टीनां षड्विकारादिवीक्षणम् 1.4.404cd
तमःसत्त्वरजोयोगाद्याति क्षेत्रज्ञतामजः 1.4.152cd
तमासाद्य तु मुक्तस्य दृष्टार्थस्य विपश्चितः 1.4.1588ab
तमासाद्य तु मुक्तस्य दृष्टार्थस्य विपश्चितः 2.4.34ab
तमश्चतुः परैवावामिन्द्रश्चछेदनतः शिरः 2.5.100cd
तमेकं सर्वभूतेषु ज्ञानकर्मफलाश्रयम् 1.3.236ab
तमेकमन्तरात्मानमप्रत्यक्षं प्रपश्य भोः 4.3.191cd
तमेतमिति च तथा सर्वेषामपि कर्मणाम् 3.2.79ab
तमेतमिति च स्पष्टं श्रौतानि च वचांसि नः 4.4.584cd
तमेतमिति नाश्रौषीः संस्कारा इति च स्मृतिम् SV 192cd
तमेतमिति वाक्यात्तु यागादेः प्रत्युताङ्गता SV 342ab
तमेतमिति वाक्येन तदेतदभिधीयते 4.4.1019cd
तमेतमिति वाक्येन नित्यानां वक्ष्यते विधिः SV 321cd
तमेतमिति वाक्येन संयोगस्य पृथक्त्वतः SV 322cd
तमेतमिति वाक्येन संयोगस्य पृथक्त्वतः 4.4.1052cd
तमेतमिति विज्ञाय यथाव्याख्यातलक्षणम् 3.5.97cd
तमेतमित्यतश्चोच्चैर्वेदानुवचनादिना SV 1132ab
तमेवंलक्षणं मह्यं यथावद्वक्तुमर्हसि 3.4.42cd
तमेवंविधमात्मानं ज्ञात्वा कुर्यान्मतिं दृढाम् 4.4.737ab
तमेव कारणात्मानं विद्वान्मन्येऽमृतोऽमृतम् 4.4.640cf
तमेव युक्तिभिः सार्धं वदन्ती स्वार्थमीक्षते SV 853cd
तमेवासृत्य निर्गम्य बाह्यतो व्यवतिष्ठते 4.3.1097cd
तमेवेति च वाक्यस्य विध्यसंभवमब्रुवम् 1.4.915ab
तमोऽन्धकारमखिलमवखण्डयति क्षणात् 5.9.3ab
तमोऽन्वितत्वाद्बुद्ध्यन्ते न प्राज्ञेऽनन्वयात्तमः 4.3.1517cd
तमोऽप्यनुभवादेव प्राक्तद्व्युत्पत्तिजन्मनः 1.4.1357cd
तमोंशत्वं यथा भानोः सतश्चाप्यसदंशता 4.3.1812ab
तमोजस्यापि कार्यस्य न प्रतीच्यस्त्यकारणात् 1.4.1318cd
तमोध्वन्यैव ततो ब्रह्म प्राप्यते ब्रह्मविद्यया 1.4.1142ab
तमोध्वंसातिरेकेण सम्यग्ज्ञानस्य नापरम् 1.4.1261ab
तमोध्वस्तौ निवृत्तिः स्यात्तथात्मज्ञानतोऽपि नः 1.3.87cd
तमो ध्वान्तमिति ज्ञेयमतमोऽक्षरमुच्यते 3.8.95cd

तमो नियामकं यस्मात्स्वकार्याणां तदन्वयात् 1.4.344ab
तमोन्तः कारणं बुद्धेर्दृष्टान्तःकरणावधिः 4.3.1528ab
तमोन्तरायतो मुक्तेर्नान्तरायोऽपरोऽस्ति हि 6.2.12ab
तमोन्तात्कारणात्तद्धि द्वितीयं कार्यरूपतः 4.3.1511ab
तमोन्वयस्तमःकार्ये बुद्ध्यादावेव युज्यते 4.3.1530ab
तमोन्वयाप्रमेयत्वात्तदभावेऽपि नेक्ष्यते 1.4.997cd
तमोन्वितं च यत्कार्यं साक्षिणः साक्ष्यतां गतम् 5.1.19ab
तमोमात्रातिरेकेण व्यवधानान्तरं न च 4.2.29ab
तमोमात्रान्तरायत्वात्तद्ध्वस्तावेव साप्यते 2.4.436cd
तमोमात्रान्तरायत्वात्प्रतीचः पूर्णरूपिणः 5.1.102ab
तमोमात्रान्तरायत्वादाप्तमप्याप्यते न तत् 1.4.1260ab
तमोमात्रान्तरायत्वादैकात्म्याख्यस्य वस्तुनः SV 799ab
तमोमात्राभिजनतो नातोऽविद्यां निहन्ति तत् 3.3.39cd
तमोमात्रावसायित्वान्न यथावस्तु तत्ततः 1.4.1356ab
तमोमात्रैकहेतुश्च मोहसंगतिरात्मनः 3.4.85cd
तमोमोहादिभेदेन तमोऽनेकस्वलक्षणम् 4.4.599ab
तमोरजोभ्यां मुक्ता धीर्यदा स्यादुक्तसाधनात् 4.4.758ab
तमोरूपमिवाभाति भानुर्नक्तंदृशामिव 1.4.373cd
तमोरूपमिवाभाति भानुर्नक्तंदृशामिव 4.3.1471cd
तमोविनाशनायैव प्रदीपोऽपीति चेन्मतम् 1.2.99ab
तमोवृत्तमपेक्ष्यैतन्न तु यद्वास्तवं स्वतः 1.4.214cd
तमोव्यवहितैकात्म्यस्तथाविद्योत्थकार्यग. 4.3.1316ab
तमोहतिर्न कर्मभ्यो ज्ञानात्सा व्यञ्जकत्वतः 6.2.12cd
तमोहेतु समुत्थानं न वेद्मीत्यग्रहात्मकम् 2.4.426ab
तया तस्य कथं व्याप्तिरव्याप्तौ मेयता कथम् SV 1061cd
तयानुरञ्जित इव ह्यात्मा कामान्परीप्सति 4.3.1191ab
तया प्रयुक्तः प्राणोऽयं प्राणानादाय चेतरान् 4.4.92cd
तया विनैव स्वप्ने तदात्मा पूर्ववदीक्षते 4.3.264cd
तयासाधनया दृष्ट्यापरिणामस्वभावया 4.3.1473ab
तयोः पर्वोक्तरूपेण ज्योतिषानुग्रहो यदि 4.3.24ab
तयोः श्रेय आददानस्य साधु भवति हीयतेऽर्थाद्य उ प्रेयो वृणीते SV 24cd
तयोः संचरतोर्मार्गौ यैषोर्ध्वा हृदयाद्गता 4.2.50ab

तयोः समागमश्चास्मिन्हृद्यन्तस्थे सुषौ मिथः 4.2.47ab
तयोरव्यतिरेकत्वात्स एवायात्यनीप्सितः SV 64ab
तयोरिहार्थवत्त्वाय त्रयो वावेति भण्यते 1.5.227ab
तयोरुद्दिष्टयोर्मूर्तं प्रथमं तावदुच्यते 2.3.35ab
तयोरुपासनं नो चेत्प्राणवत्स्याद्विवक्षितम् 1.5.366cd
तयोरैकात्म्यतो युक्ता नापि तन्नाश इष्यते 3.2.101ab
तयोर्गीर्मनसोरेवं प्रकाशप्रसवात्मनोः 1.5.185ab
तयोर्भिन्नाश्रयत्वे तु दुःख्यस्मीति न सिध्यति 4.3.97cd
तयोर्मिथो विरोधित्वात्सम्यग्ज्ञानं तमोपनुत् 2.4.258cd
तयोर्विधरणः प्राणस्त्वनिरुक्तोऽथ भण्यते 1.5.143cd
तयोर्विवेकादुभयोः स्वाभाव्यं प्रतिपद्यते 4.3.1095cd
तयोश्च युगपद्भावे न स्यात्कारणनिश्चितिः 1.4.196ab
तयोस्तत्त्वविवक्षायामज्ञानं तत्त्वमुच्यते 1.4.440cd
तयोस्तु सावशेषेण प्रतीचा संगतिस्त्वयम् 4.3.386cd
तरन्त्यनेन विस्पष्टं संसारानर्थसागरम् 4.4.548ab
तरावेव च्छिदा यद्वद्द्वैधीभावे तु नेष्यते 4.4.686ab
तर्कतो यदि वा वाक्यादत एवेदमेव तु 4.5.20ab
तर्कशास्त्रैस्तथा लोकन्यायैरप्यविरुद्धता 2.1.460ab
तर्कादागमतश्चापि तद्यो य इति हीदृशात् SV 354cd
तर्हीति ह्यनभिव्यक्तमव्याकृतगिरोच्यते 1.4.204cd
तल्लिङ्गं वासनानीडं सूक्ष्मं स्वच्छस्वभावकम् 4.3.1245ab
तवात्मेत्यपि निर्णीतौ नैव स्यात्प्रश्ननिर्णयः 3.4.61cd
तवैव न स्याद्दृष्टान्तः सर्वस्यैकस्वरूपतः 4.3.1763cd
तस्थावसंव्याप्य यथा क्षुरधानं क्षुरस्तथा 1.4.641cd
तस्थुः सूक्ष्मेण रूपेण क्रियामाश्रित्य सर्वतः 5.5.4cd
तस्माच्च ब्राह्मणोऽध्यस्ताद्राजसूये महाक्रतौ 1.4.1604ab
तस्माच्चाकाशशब्देन ब्रह्मैवात्राभिधीयते 2.1.242cd
तस्माच्छक्तिमतोरेव ग्रासांशानां यथा तथा 5.14.9ab
तस्माच्छ्रेयोऽर्थिनः पुंसः प्रेरकोऽनिष्टकर्मणि 1.4.1812ab
तस्माज्ज्ञानं पुरस्कृत्य संन्यसेदिह बुद्धिमान् SV 217cd
तस्माज्ज्ञानं पुरस्कृत्य संन्यसेदिह बुद्धिमान् 2.4.32cd
तस्माज्ज्ञानं पुरस्कृत्य संन्यसेदिह बुद्धिमान् 3.5.4cd

तस्मात्कर्तव्यतावेशात्क्रिया वा यदि वा फलम् SV 515ab
तस्मात्कर्मगुणस्यैव कर्मस्थस्यैव सर्वदा 4.3.1039ab
तस्मात्कर्मफलं नाना नानाकर्मसमुद्भवम् SV 377ab
तस्मात्कर्मातिरेकेण कालो मृत्युः प्रतीयताम् 3.1.30ab
तस्मात्कर्माभिसंबन्धो नैवैकात्म्यधियोऽमितेः SV 340cd
तस्मात्कर्मैव विद्यायाः पिपृच्छिषितमत्र तु 1.4.1135ab
तस्मात्कारणसंप्राप्त्या यायान्नेतीत्यकारणम् 4.2.84cd
तस्मात्कृतकदृष्टान्तमुपादायात्मनोऽञ्जसा 2.1.291ab
तस्मात्केशविभागोऽयं नाडीसौक्ष्म्यार्थमुच्यते 4.2.53cd
तस्मात्तत्कार्यभूतासु प्रजास्वद्यापि दृश्यते 1.3.239cd
तस्मात्तत्कार्यभूतोऽज्ञ एकाक्यद्य बिभेति ना 1.4.58cd
तस्मात्तदिति विद्यायाः पूर्णता फलमुच्यते 1.4.1186ab
तस्मात्तन्मध्यकार्येषु बीजमेवास्तु कारणम् 2.4.324cd
तस्मात्तन्मोहविध्वस्तौ ध्वस्तिः स्यान्मोहजस्य च 1.3.59cd
तस्मात्तमस्विनो ब्रह्म भेदेनैव परायणम् 3.9.165ab
तस्मात्तिसृष्ववस्थासु ह्यागमापायिनीष्वजः 1.4.304ab
तस्मात्तेषु वरं कामं यजमानो यथारुचि 1.3.368ab
तस्मात्त्रितयमप्येतत्कर्मशब्देन भण्यते 3.2.158cd
तस्मात्त्वगादयः शब्दास्त्वगाद्यारम्भकाभिधाः 2.4.356cd
तस्मात्परतरं तत्त्वं दुर्वचोऽपि बृहस्पतेः 3.8.50cd
तस्मात्परस्य साक्षित्वं स्वमोहाभासवर्त्मना 3.4.90ab
तस्मात्पाण्डरवासाः स्यात्सोमः सौम्यत्वकारणात् 2.1.55cd
तस्मात्पिण्डादिवैधर्म्यमेवेतीहावधार्यते 4.3.41cd
तस्मात्पूषा यतश्चैको गच्छत्येकर्षिता ततः 5.17.6cd
तस्मात्प्रज्ञां प्रकुर्वीत साक्षाद्ब्रह्मैकगोचराम् 4.4.803cd
तस्मात्प्रत्यक्षवर्तिकंचिद्व्यभिचारकृदञ्जसा 4.3.735cd
तस्मात्प्रमाप्रमाभासाप्रमाणानामशेषतः 1.4.272ab
तस्मात्प्रवसितप्राणो मृतोऽयं नात्र संशयः 3.7.23ab
तस्मात्संसारसंबन्धनिदानस्य प्रसिद्धितः SV 457ab
तस्मात्संघातविध्वंसो निर्युक्तिक इहोच्यते 1.4.1751ab
तस्मात्सदेव कार्यं स्यात्प्रागुत्पत्तेरपि ध्रुवम् 1.2.111cd
तस्मात्समुच्चयाशेह कार्या नाक्षरसंश्रयात् 1.4.1768ab

तस्मात्संप्रत्तिकर्मेह वक्तव्यं तत्फलार्थिने 1.5.283cd
तस्मात्संभावनामात्रः संसारः प्रत्यगात्मनि 4.3.421ab
तस्मात्सर्वपदार्थानामाकाङ्क्षायोग्यसंनिधेः SV 754ab
तस्मात्सर्वप्रवृत्तीनां हानिः स्यादात्मबोधतः 4.4.1113cd
तस्मात्सलिलवच्छुद्धः कार्यकारणहानतः 4.3.1798cd
तस्मात्सामर्थ्यतः सिद्ध उत्तरप्रश्ननिर्णयः 2.1.367ab
तस्मात्सिद्धोऽत्र वाक्यार्थो लोके वेदे प्रमाणवान् SV 881cd
तस्मात्सिद्धोऽधिकारोऽत्र ब्रह्मरूपं विवक्षताम् SV 313ab
तस्मात्सोमान्नसृष्ट्यर्थं परो ग्रन्थोऽवतार्यते 1.4.155ab
तस्मात्स्याद्देवतावाप्तिर्ज्ञानकर्मसमुच्चयात् 1.3.370ab
तस्मादकारकः कामी स्वनियोगप्रसिद्धये SV 530ab
तस्मादकृत्स्नं ब्रह्मेति न मानेनोपपद्यते 1.4.1095cd
तस्मादजायमानैव जायमानेव लक्ष्यते 1.4.335ab
तस्मादजायमानैव जायमानेव लक्ष्यते 3.4.115ab
तस्मादज्ञात आत्मैव कामादेः स्यात्प्रयोजकः 4.4.220ab
तस्मादज्ञात आत्मैव शक्तिरित्यभिधीयते 4.3.1787ab
तस्मादध्यर्ध इत्येवं वायुमाचक्षते बुधाः 3.9.26cd
तस्मादपीति वक्त्येतां प्रसिद्धिं लोकसाक्षिकीम् 1.4.45cd
तस्मादप्रतिबोधेन प्राणोऽभोक्तेति गम्यताम् 2.1.181ab
तस्मादर्थान्तरासूतेरेकपिण्डात्ममात्रतः 1.4.40ab
तस्मादवश्यं बोद्धव्यं बोध्यं साक्षादुपस्थितम् 2.1.120ab
तस्मादविद्याभूमिष्ठः कृत्स्न एतावता भवेत् 1.4.1837cd
तस्मादविद्यासंभूतं नानात्वं प्रत्यगात्मनि 1.4.436ab
तस्मादविपरीतार्थज्ञानाच्छ्रेयो ह्यवाप्यते 1.3.58ab
तस्मादव्यभिचारेण कार्यमप्येति हेतुताम् 4.3.758cd
तस्मादसङ्गोऽकर्ता च स्वयंज्योतिरितीक्ष्यताम् 4.3.451cd
तस्मादसदिदं गीतं भिन्नाभिन्नत्वसिद्धये 5.1.109ab
तस्मादसदिदं गीतमात्मानमिति यद्वचः 1.4.1737ab
तस्मादाकाशशब्देन प्रत्यगात्माभिधीयते 2.1.241cd
तस्मादाङ्गिरसः प्राणो ज्ञेय आत्मेति पण्डितैः 1.3.294cd
तस्मादाचक्षते नाम पारोक्ष्येणैव मानवाः 4.2.41cd
तस्मादात्मनि विज्ञाते कामहेतोरसंभवात् 4.4.283cd

तस्मादात्मपरिज्ञानात्कार्यज्ञेयसमाप्तितः 4.3.1852ab
तस्मादात्माभिमानो हि बुद्धौ जनिमतां सदा 4.3.359ab
तस्मादात्मैवोपास्यः स्यान्नानात्मोपास्य इष्यते 1.4.937cd
तस्मादादित्यगः सोमः क्षीण आप्यायते पुनः 6.2.91cd
तस्मादापः सूक्ष्मभावाः स्थूलतां यान्ति पाकतः 6.2.112ab
तस्मादावृत्तिपक्षेऽपि स्वतस्तत्सिद्धितो विधिः 1.4.838ab
तस्मादासङ्गवैशेष्यादन्यस्य प्रक्रिया पुनः 3.2.68cd
तस्मादितरतुल्यत्वान्न विध्यर्थनिबन्धनः SV 753ab
तस्मादिति श्रुतिर्वक्ति ह्युत्पत्त्यादिनिवृत्तये 1.4.1434cd
तस्मादित्यात्मनश्चेति सामानाधिकरण्यतः 2.1.447cd
तस्मादित्यादिकं वाक्यं श्रुतेरिति च निर्दिशेत् 3.3.165ab
तस्मादित्यादिका योज्या न्यासहेतुत्वसिद्धये 3.5.107cd
तस्मादित्यादिवाक्येन सत्यताक्ष्णो विभाव्यते 5.16.31ab
तस्मादेवंविदित्यत्र श्रुतिः स्पष्टं यथोदितम् 3.5.142ab
तस्मादेवंविदित्येवं तथा चोर्ध्वं प्रवक्ष्यति 3.5.108ab
तस्मादेवंविदो धीरा अर्चिराद्यभिमानिनीम् 6.2.135ab
तस्मादेवाविनाशित्वादिति हेतुरिहोदितः 4.3.1601cd
तस्मादैकात्म्यतात्पर्ये प्रसंख्यानादि सुस्थितम् SV 775cd
तस्माद्देहोऽप्यनर्थः स्याद्देहो नाशाच्च सर्वदा 4.4.1285cd
तस्माद्दैवोऽप्यनर्थः स्याद्देहो नाशाच्च सर्वदा 4.3.816cd
तस्माद्दैवो वरो मह्यं दीयतां नास्त्यसौ मम 6.2.63cd
तस्माद्द्रव्यनिषेधोऽयं परिमाणनिषेधतः 3.8.89cd
तस्माद्धेतूपदेशाय यः कारणमितीर्यते 1.4.479ab
तस्माद्बुध्यस्व शाकल्य महद्भयमुपस्थितम् 3.9.63ab
तस्माद्भाष्याक्षरैरेव शेषोऽर्थोऽत्र प्रतीयताम् 3.2.121cd
तस्माद्यः कर्मणां कर्ता स भुङ्क्ते कर्मणः फलम् 4.3.688cd
तस्माद्यद्यपि सांनिध्यं प्राणादीनां प्रजागरे 2.1.104ab
तस्माद्याथात्म्यविज्ञानसमुत्पत्तेः पुरैव तु 1.4.1556ab
तस्माद्रजतसंस्कारसंस्कृतात्स्वान्ततः स्मृतिः 1.4.279cd
तस्माद्रसत्वनिर्देशः क्रियते मण्डलात्मनि 2.3.42cd
तस्माद्वस्त्वेकनिष्ठत्वान्न भेदोऽक्षादिगोचरः SV 978ef
तस्माद्वस्त्वेकनिष्ठस्य प्रामाण्यं वचसो ध्रुवम् 1.3.111ab

तस्माद्वाक्योत्थविज्ञानसाधनाभ्यासतोऽनिशम् 4.4.807ab
तस्माद्विचारः कर्तव्य उक्तसंदेहहानिकृत् 2.1.432cd
तस्माद्विज्ञातसंबन्धं पदं सर्वत्र बोधकम् SV 732cd
तस्माद्विज्ञानमित्यादि यथावस्थितवस्तुनः 3.9.199ab
तस्माद्विद्याफलावाप्तौ विघ्नं कुर्वन्ति देवताः 1.4.1473cd
तस्माद्विधेः प्रमाणत्वं साध्यसाधनबोधने 2.4.155ab
तस्माद्विलक्षणस्तद्वदीश्वरोऽप्यभिधीयते 1.4.1238cd
तस्माद्विषयसामान्यं चक्षुःशब्देन भण्यते 1.6.20cd
तस्माद्व्युत्थाय कर्मभ्यः प्रत्यक्प्रवणबुद्धयः 1.4.1769ab
तस्मान्न कश्चिदप्यत्र कार्त्स्न्यात्मावगमे भवेत् 1.4.1311ab
तस्मान्न काचिदाशङ्का कर्मिणं प्रति विद्यते 1.3.370cd
तस्मान्न चिन्तयेदेतान्किंतु यैकत्ववाचिनी 4.4.740ab
तस्मान्न जीवतो वाच्यं गौणं विशरणं त्वया 1.4.1756cd
तस्मान्न देशकालादिभेदो वस्त्वाश्रयो मितेः 2.1.410ab
तस्मान्न वस्तुधर्मोऽयं शब्दादेव प्रकर्षतः SV 631cd
तस्मान्न वास्तवं रूपं तद्ध्वान्ताद्यपनोदकृत् 1.4.314ab
तस्मान्न साधिवदं सर्वं भावनासंचयार्थिभिः 4.4.779ab
तस्मान्न सिद्ध इत्येव संभाव्येत प्रमान्तरम् SV 699ab
तस्मान्नानात्मनोऽस्त्यात्मा नाप्यनात्मात्मनः स्वतः 1.4.727ab
तस्मान्नासङ्गगन्धोऽपि स्वप्ने पुंसोऽस्य विद्यते 4.3.1070cd
तस्मान्नित्यश्चिदाभासो बुद्धौ तत्प्रत्ययेषु च 3.4.151cd
तस्मान्निवृत्तिः केन स्यात्कथं वेत्येतदुच्यते 1.3.10cd
तस्मान्निषेधशास्त्रस्य यथा भूतार्थनिष्ठता 1.3.88ab
तस्मान्नृहस्तिदेहादौ जाग्रत्स्वप्नादिभूमिषु 4.3.222ab
तस्मान्नैवानवस्थेह कथंचिदपि शङ्क्यते 4.3.526ab
तस्मान्नैवानुमा नाम मानं युक्तिमदिष्यते 4.3.731ab
तस्मान्नैवोपवादी स्याद्याज्ञवल्क्योऽपि शत्रुताम् 3.9.129ab
तस्मान्मुमुक्षुर्देवादीन्सम्यगाराध्य कर्मभिः 1.4.1582ab
तस्मान्मृतं प्रियं बन्धुं हरन्त्यग्नय ऋत्विजः 6.2.113ab
तस्माल्लोकादिमं लोकं पुनरैति स कर्मणे 4.4.246cd
तस्मिंश्च प्राणने वायोर्व्यापारः करणात्मना 1.4.666ab
तस्मिंस्तु शास्त्राद्विज्ञाते शक्यते कर्तुमञ्जसा 1.4.1250ab

तस्मिञ्जाग्रति जागर्ति सुप्ते स्वपिति तद्वशात् 2.1.129cd
तस्मिञ्ज्ञातेऽखिलं ज्ञातं सर्वाज्ञाननिराकृतेः 1.4.1687cd
तस्मिन्दृष्टेऽथ सर्वस्य तावन्मात्रैकतत्त्वतः 4.4.759ab
तस्मिन्ध्वस्तेऽथ संबोधात्केवलैकात्म्यशेषतः 2.4.421ab
तस्मिन्नग्नौ शरेषीका घृताक्ता जुहुयादथ 6.4.55ab
तस्मिन्नपहतध्वान्तेऽप्यविद्या स्वानुभूतितः 1.4.216ab
तस्मिन्नपि निषिद्धेऽथ तूष्णीं गार्ग्यो बभूव ह 2.1.83cd
तस्मिन्नसति सा न स्यादपेक्षाविरहाद्विभोः 1.4.25cd
तस्मिन्नस्तंगते पुंस आसनादि कुतो भवेत् 4.3.47cd
तस्मिन्नात्माभिमानो यः सा संपत्तिरविद्यया 4.3.818cd
तस्मिन्नित्यादिवचनं पूर्वोक्तस्थानसिद्धये 5.8.3cd
तस्मिन्निरस्ते किं शेषं यस्मिन्मानस्य मानता 1.4.423cd
तस्मिन्निविष्टचित्तस्य तद्ब्रह्माशु प्रसीदति 5.1.125cd
तस्मिन्नेवंविधे कः स्यात्संतोषो विदुषामपि 4.4.1105cd
तस्मिन्नेव स विज्ञान आत्मरूपे स्थितो भवेत् 4.4.720cd
तस्मिन्प्रयुज्यमानेऽतः सर्वो वेदः ससंग्रहः 5.1.130ab
तस्मिन्भवंस्तैजसः स्यात्प्रत्यक्प्रवणधीर्नरः 4.4.578cd
तस्मिन्सति कुतः कर्म का वापेक्षास्य गोचरे SV 362cd
तस्मिन्सति वृथा कस्माज्जनोऽयं परिखिद्यते 3.5.166cd
तस्मिन्सति समुच्छित्तिरविद्यायाः कथं भवेत् 3.2.92cd
तस्मिन्सति स्वयंज्योतिः कथमात्माभिधीयते 4.3.897cd
तस्मिन्सति हि सद्भावाद्रागादीनां न तं विना 6.1.7cd
तस्मिन्सत्यप्रमाणत्वं किमिवेहोच्यते त्वया 1.4.907cd
तस्मिन्सत्येव मोहादि व्युत्पत्तेः प्रागभूद्यतः 1.4.314cd
तस्मिन्संध्य इतीदं च तथा सति समञ्जसम् 4.3.838cd
तस्मिन्सर्वमिति ह्यस्य दर्शनस्य विधित्सया 1.5.62cd
तस्मिन्साक्षी च मूढश्चेत्यतीवैतद्विरुध्यते 4.4.361ab
तस्मै तस्मै फलायालं सेतुरीशो भवेत्ततः 4.4.1017cd
तस्मै नमोऽस्तु देवाय निर्गुणाय गुणात्मने 3.7.41ab
तस्मै मे सत्यधर्माय दृष्टयै द्वारमपावृणु 5.17.5cd
तस्मै शंकरभानवे तनुमनोवाग्भिर्नमस्तात्सदा 6.5.25d
तस्मै हिरण्यगर्भाय ब्रूयाद्विद्यां तमस्विने 1.4.1338cd

तस्य कर्मण्यपेक्षा स्यान्नान्यथा तदपेक्षते 1.4.814cd
तस्य का देवतेत्येनमप्राक्षीत्क्षोभितो रुषा 3.9.43ab
तस्य कार्यं द्विधेहोक्तं सामान्यात्मविशेषतः 2.5.45ab
तस्य कृत्स्नाभिमानित्वान्नास्मन्मात्राभिमानता 1.5.355cd
तस्य क्रत्वात्मनश्चित्यो योऽङ्गभूतः पुरोदितः 1.2.222cd
तस्य चैकत्वनाशित्वात्संतानो नोपपद्यते 4.3.628ab
तस्य जीवनमात्रैकहेतुत्वाद्बाधते ध्रुवम् 4.4.1225ef
तस्य ज्ञातात्मतत्त्वस्य प्रध्वस्ततमसो यतेः 1.4.1463ab
तस्य तन्मात्रयाथात्म्यादिति पूर्वमवादिषम् 1.5.123cd
तस्य तस्य तथैवेति सानवस्था प्रसज्यते 1.2.86cd
तस्य तस्यान्यसंव्याप्तिर्दृष्टा लोके क्षितेर्यथा 3.6.9cd
तस्य तेनाभिसंव्याप्तेर्न कथंचिदपह्नुतिः 1.2.16cd
तस्य त्वेवंविदः पुंसस्तावदेव चिरं भवेत् 1.4.1554ab
तस्य दार्ष्टान्तिको योऽर्थो यावत्साक्षान्न कथ्यते 4.3.1899ab
तस्य निष्ठाविधानार्थं बाल्येनेति परं वचः 3.5.180cd
तस्य निष्पन्नरूपत्वान्नाप्युपेये सुखे तथा SV 582cd
तस्य प्रकाशकस्तद्वत्सर्वः शब्दो विवक्ष्यते 1.5.135cd
तस्य प्रकाशिकैवेयं न प्रकाश्या प्रदीपवत् 1.5.139cd
तस्य प्रथमजस्याग्नेर्विराजोऽर्कस्य वाजिवत् 1.2.166ab
तस्य प्रमाणसंबन्धात्सर्वाज्ञानप्रहाणतः 4.4.911cd
तस्य ब्रह्मतमोहेतोस्तन्निवृत्तौ निवर्तते 1.4.1472cd
तस्य ब्रह्मत्वबोधाय नेति ब्रह्मेतिनोच्यते 2.3.233cd
तस्य भागस्य भागोऽसौ निमित्तं स्यान्न तु प्रमा SV 867cd
तस्य भावस्य सद्भावो वद केन निवार्यते 1.4.1374cd
तस्य भावार्थनिष्ठत्वाद्वस्तुन्यनुपपत्तितः SV 654cd
तस्य मेयैकनिष्ठत्वात्फलं तु स्यात्प्रमातरि 4.3.195cd
तस्य मेयैकहेतुत्वान्नैव स्यान्मातृतन्त्रता 2.4.152cd
तस्य यत्कर्मरूपं तद्वियद्वायुप्रयोजकम् 2.3.54ab
तस्य योऽतिशयः प्रोक्तो व्याकृताव्याकृतात्मकः 1.4.1313cd
तस्य लौकिकमासिद्धेर्लौकिकत्वं प्रसज्यते SV 1044cd
तस्य वस्त्वनुरोधित्वादभेदादविरोधिता 1.4.1297cd
तस्य विध्यन्तरात्सिद्धेर्वेदान्तस्यानुवादता 1.4.797cd

तस्य वृत्तफलत्वान्नो ज्ञानं स्यात्तन्निवृत्तिकृत् 1.4.1530ab
तस्य वृद्धिर्मितेर्वृद्धावित्यन्योऽन्यसमाश्रयः SV 827cd
तस्य शक्त्यभिसंबन्धान्न त्वकारण आत्मनि 4.4.498cd
तस्य शास्त्रानभिज्ञत्वान्नाधिकारोऽत्र वैदिके SV 539cd
तस्य श्रद्धैकहेतुत्वाच्छ्रद्धा नामेति कीर्त्यते 6.2.86cd
तस्य संवत्सर आत्मा तस्यादित्यैकहेतुतः 1.2.222ab
तस्य संसिद्धिविषयमैकात्म्यमधुनोच्यते 2.4.19cd
तस्य सद्वस्तुमेयत्वादभावस्याप्यसंभवात् 4.3.1694cd
तस्य संप्रतिपत्त्यर्थमन्तर्हृदयकीर्तनम् 2.1.233cd
तस्य साक्षादयं लोको योऽहं ब्रह्मेतिबोधितः 4.4.623ab
तस्य साक्षादयं श्रुत्या निर्देशः क्रियतेऽधुना 3.9.150cd
तस्य सावयवस्य स्यादेकदेशस्य विक्रिया 2.1.475ab
तस्य स्थानवरिष्ठस्य सर्वे निरयसंज्ञिताः 4.4.1173ef
तस्य हैतस्य संबन्धमेवं केचित्प्रचक्षते 2.3.104ab
तस्या अपि त्वदुक्त्यैवं शब्दार्थत्वं प्रसज्यते SV 596cd
तस्यां तस्यामधिकृतौ तत्तद्रूपं प्रपद्यते 1.4.140cd
तस्यां सत्यामिदं कर्म ज्येष्ठायेत्यादिलिङ्गतः 6.3.10cd
तस्यां स्वमर्थं निष्ठाय मुखेनेत्यादि पूर्ववत् 6.4.42cd
तस्याः सर्वाप्तिहेतुत्वान्नैतदेवं पृथक्त्वतः 1.5.232cd
तस्याकृत्स्नापवादेन कृत्स्नैकात्म्यावबुद्धये 1.4.1344ab
तस्याक्षरे कः प्रसङ्गो यतस्तत्प्रतिषिध्यते 3.8.82ab
तस्याग्नेरेष घोषः स्यात्कर्णौ प्रोर्णय यच्छ्रुतिः 5.11.3ab
तस्यात्मनि निषिद्धत्वादात्माद्वैतो भवेत्ततः 4.3.1808cd
तस्यादित्येन संबन्धः कस्मादत्राभिधीयते 1.5.180cd
तस्या दृष्टेः क्रियाया हि द्रष्टृधर्मत्वतः सदा 4.3.1548cd
तस्याधिदेवता चन्द्र इति माध्यंदिनश्रुतिः 3.1.37cd
तस्याधिलोकमात्मोक्तो योऽयमन्नत्रयात्मकः 1.5.207cd
तस्यानाधेयरूपत्वान्न कदाचित्फलं भवेत् SV 628cd
तस्यानित्यफलोत्पत्तौ प्रभविष्णुत्वकारणात् 1.4.239cd
तस्यानु तदभावे वा पाययन्ति स्तनं शिशुम् 1.5.52ab
तस्यानुभवतत्त्वस्य कुतः सापेक्षतोच्यते SV 467cd
तस्यानुमित्यनङ्गत्वात्प्राप्तं तत्तुषकण्डनम् 4.3.741cd

तस्यानुवासना धीस्था भावनेत्यभिधीयते 4.3.1257cd
तस्यानेकार्थशायित्वादहेतुत्वं प्रसज्यते 4.3.747ab
तस्यान्तरतम इति दुर्घटं वचनं भवेत् 1.4.1043cd
तस्या न्यायसमाश्रितेन वचसा प्रक्रम्यते लेशतः SV 2d
तस्यापसर्पणेऽङ्गानि नालं स्युः कर्मणे मृतौ 3.7.18ab
तस्यापि चान्तःपातित्वात्सर्वोद्यस्यैव युक्तिमान् 1.5.32ab
तस्यापि दूषणं ज्ञेयं यथोक्तन्यायवर्त्मना 1.4.1761cd
तस्यापि नात्मधीः कार्या नित्यप्राप्तत्वकारणात् 4.4.934cd
तस्यापि नित्यसंबन्धान्न विधेयात्मधीरियम् 4.4.926cd
तस्यापि बुद्धिसंशुद्धिहेतुत्वं शास्त्रतो मतम् 4.4.1054cd
तस्यापि ब्रह्मणो नाम त्र्यक्षरं सत्यमुच्यते 5.5.12ab
तस्यापि मृत्युर्विज्ञेयो यत आविरभूदसौ 4.4.670cd
तस्यापि शब्दपूर्वत्वादिति चेल्लिङ्गपूर्वतः SV 737ab
तस्यापि शुद्धरूपस्य शान्तिमन्ये प्रचक्षते 4.3.477ab
तस्यापि संवित्साक्षित्वात्प्रागभावो न संविदः 1.4.338cd
तस्यापि संविन्मात्रेण पूर्णतैवोच्यते सतः 1.2.29cd
तस्यापि सदपेक्षत्वात् किमन्यत्स्यात्सता विना 1.4.330cd
तस्याप्यनुभवात्सिद्धिर्यद्युच्येत घटादिवत् SV 1075ab
तस्याप्यनुमितेरेव शब्दार्थप्रत्ययो भवेत् SV 738cd
तस्याप्यविद्यारूपत्वाज्जडोऽनात्मेति हीष्यते 4.4.896cd
तस्याप्यविषयत्वात्तद्धिज्ञानान्तरगोचरः 1.4.806cd
तस्याप्यसंभवः स्पष्ट उपरिष्टात्प्रवक्ष्यते 1.4.932cd
तस्याप्यस्तमयात्प्राज्ञे समिति स्याद्विशेषणम् 4.3.978cd
तस्याप्यस्तमयेऽग्निः स्यादासनादिप्रवृत्तये 4.3.48cd
तस्याप्येतत्परं सत्यं यन्नेतीत्यवधारितम् 2.3.246cd
तस्याभिधित्सयेदानीं प्रारब्धैषोत्तरा श्रुतिः 5.16.19cd
तस्याभिवृद्धिः संभूतिर्न त्वभूतजनिर्यतः 6.2.87cd
तस्याभिव्यक्तिधर्मत्वादन्यथा स्यान्नृशृङ्गवत् 1.2.74ef
तस्यामभिरता ये स्युर्वेदान्तार्थानपेक्षिणः 4.4.604cd
तस्यामविद्यावस्थायां स्वप्नावस्थां गतो यथा 2.4.465ab
तस्या मेधातपोजत्वात्पौनःपुन्येन तच्छ्रुतेः 1.5.341cd
तस्यारं छिद्रमेतत्स्याच्छान्दसी वर्णनिह्नुतिः 4.3.1352cd

तस्यारादुपकारित्वात्सहायत्वाय कल्प्यते SV 214cd
तस्यालोकनहेतुः स्यादग्निर्देवस्य सर्वदा 3.9.35cd
तस्यावच्छित्तये वृत्तिर्दुःखभूत्यैव जायते 2.4.349cd
तस्यावाक्यार्थरूपस्य पदमेतत्प्रचक्षते 1.4.1003ab
तस्या वा नाम गृह्णीयान्मन्त्रमुच्चारयन्पतिः 6.4.107cd
तस्या विक्षेपसंहारौ शाकल्यः पर्यपृच्छत 3.9.7ab
तस्या विपरिलोपोऽत्र न कथं चन युज्यते 4.3.1424cd
तस्या विपरिलोपोऽयं हेत्वभावान्न युज्यते 4.3.1421cd
तस्या विवेको व्याख्यातो यथोक्तवचसात्मनः 4.3.1090ab
तस्याविंशतिवाक्येन विरोधादेव कारणात् 1.4.1741cd
तस्या विशेषनिष्ठत्वान्मृषात्वं नोपपद्यते 5.16.31ef
तस्या वेदिरुपस्थः स्याद्दूर्वोरुपरि दर्शनम् 6.4.8cd
तस्याश्च क्रियमाणत्वाज्जन्मनाशाभिसंगतिः 3.4.150ab
तस्याश्चाप्याहुतेः सोमो राजा संभवतीति च 6.2.87ab
तस्यासाधारणात्मोत्थविज्ञानविषयत्वतः 1.4.279ab
तस्यास्य कर्मकाण्डेन संबन्ध इति भाष्यकृत् SV 313cd
तस्यास्य कर्मकाण्डेन संबन्ध इति यः पुरा SV 1092ab
तस्यास्य दर्शनोपायः कः स्यादित्यभिचोदिते 4.4.648ab
तस्यास्य धर्मरूपस्य कार्यकारणतां मिथः 1.4.1623ab
तस्येच्छाद्यभिसंबन्धः केन मानेन गम्यते 4.4.471cd
तस्येति वर्ण्यतेऽथेदं विधिना येन तच्छृणु 4.3.832cd
तस्येहैव रागुच्छेदात्तद्धेत्वज्ञानहानतः 2.4.205cd
तस्यैकमपि चैतन्यं बहुधा प्रविभज्यते 3.5.45ab
तस्यैतस्य यथोक्तस्य कृत्स्नप्राणोपसंहृतेः 4.4.74ab
तस्यै द्वौ स्तनावित्युक्त्या कथ्यन्ते च स्तनास्तथा 5.10.4cd
तस्यैव कर्मकाण्डस्य प्रामाण्यमवसीयताम् 2.1.536cd
तस्यैव ज्ञानमात्रस्य ग्राह्यग्राहकलक्षणम् 4.3.475ab
तस्यैव तद्वदेवेत्साक्षान्नान्यदेहाश्रितस्य तत् 4.3.202cd
तस्यैव नामोपनिषद्ब्रह्मणो भण्यते द्वयोः 5.7.2ab
तस्यैव परिणामित्वात्प्रमेयेन च संगतेः 4.4.762cd
तस्यैव प्रथमं वृत्तिनिरोध उपजायते 4.4.67cd
तस्यैव ब्रह्मणोऽथान्यदुपासनमिहोच्यते 5.10.1ab

तस्यैव सत्यनाम्नोऽथ तदुपासाप्रसिद्धये 5.7.1cd
तस्यैव हृदयाख्यस्य ब्रह्मणोऽन्यदुपासनम् 5.4.1ab
तस्यैवान्नपतेर्जाया येयं सव्येऽक्षिण संस्थिता 4.2.44ab
तस्यैवाव्यभिचारित्वात्सर्वेषु व्यभिचारिषु 1.4.1376ab
तस्यैवैतानि रूपाणि कस्मान्नेत्यभिधीयताम् 2.3.150cd
तस्योतप्रोतभावोऽयं ब्रह्मलोकेषु भण्यते 3.6.18ab
तस्योत्क्रामन्ति न प्राणा आसते नापि तत्र ते 4.4.286cd
तस्योत्तरत्रासद्भावाद्ध्रौव्यं च स्यात्तथा सति 4.3.605cd
तस्योपदर्शितस्याथ निषेधः क्रियते नञा 2.3.183cd
तस्योपनिषदित्युक्तं तद्व्याख्यात्राधुनोच्यते 2.2.2ab
ता एता देवताः सप्तदश ज्ञानक्रियात्मिकाः 1.3.257ab
ता एतास्तेजसो मात्राः समस्ताश्चाभिमुख्यतः 4.4.43ab
ता एवेन्द्रियवृत्तीः स्वाश्चैतन्यखचिता यदा 2.1.337ab
तां प्रकुर्वीत विज्ञाय स्वात्मानं न त्वनात्मनः 4.4.867cd
तां मलोद्वाससं पत्नीमाहुस्तत्कर्मकारिणः 6.4.28cd
तां योगमिति मन्यन्ते स्थिरामिन्द्रियधारणाम् 4.4.1255ab
तांस्ते प्रेत्याभिगच्छन्ति येऽविद्वांसोऽबुधो जनाः 4.4.608ab
तां स्त्रियं मैथुनेनाथ मनुः समभवत्तदा 1.4.118ab
तां हैतामिति वाक्येन सावित्रीं प्रतिदर्श्यताम् 5.16.43ab
ताः सत्यमिति तेनाह सत्यं ब्रह्मातिविस्तृतेः 5.5.8cd
ताः सर्वाः संपरित्यज्य निमेषादौ व्यवस्थितः 4.4.1242cd
ताच्छीलिकोकञ्श्रवणात्तच्छीलत्वं निवार्यते 1.5.45cd
तात्पर्यं प्रोक्षणाद्युक्तेर्न स्वतन्त्रेऽधिकारवत् SV 580cd
तात्स्थ्याद्धृदयशब्देन बुद्धिरत्राभिधीयते 2.1.239ab
तादर्थ्ये कारणाभावान्नैतदप्युपपद्यते 4.3.613cd
तादात्म्यभावनायां तु पुंसां संभावनापि न 1.4.955ab
तादात्म्यमनयोस्तस्मान्नीलोत्पलविलक्षणम् SV 904cd
तादात्म्यमेव सर्वस्य कार्यकारणवस्तुनः 4.4.293ab
तादात्म्यव्यतिरेकाभ्यां तमस्तज्जं च नात्मनः 4.3.1516ab
तादात्म्येऽपि न चेज्ज्ञातो मानात्कोऽतिशयो मतः 1.2.23cd
तादृक्क्षयः सुषुप्तेऽपि नैवास्माभिर्निवार्यते 3.2.77cd
तादृक्पुत्रार्थिनः कर्म त्वेषामित्यादिनोच्यते 6.3.2cd

तादृक्पुत्रोऽत्र वक्तव्य इत्यारब्धोत्तरा श्रुतिः 1.5.274cd
तादृक्प्रतिग्रहस्येह न क्वचित्संभवो यतः 5.16.53cd
तादृक्प्रवेशो नेशस्य स्वातन्त्र्यादुपपद्यते 1.4.543ab
तादृक्फलं प्रकल्प्यं स्याद्यथा न्याय्यं तथास्त्विह 3.3.104cd
तादृक्षं संपदो न स्यान्न च दुःख्यात्मबोधतः 1.4.1264ab
तादृक्संप्रतिपत्त्यर्थं न चासतीति भण्यते SV 1051cd
तादृक्स्वप्नसुषुप्तं स्यात्सुषुप्तं च त्रिधोच्यते 4.3.1058cd
तादृगेव विशेषोऽत्र न मनागपि गम्यते 1.4.780cd
तादृग्यत्रास्ति तन्मानं नास्ति यत्र न तन्मितिः 1.4.906ab
तादृग्लब्धोऽप्यलब्धः स्यादविद्यामात्रहेतुतः 1.4.1017ab
तादृङ्नोपास्य एवेति प्राहुरागमवेदिनः 2.5.75cd
तानि भूतान्यविद्येति प्राहुस्त्रय्यन्तनिष्ठिताः 2.4.418cd
तानि रूपाणि भण्यन्ते मृत्योस्तस्य परात्मनः 4.3.455cd
तानि वा इति निन्दित्वा न्यासो ब्रह्मेति शासनात् 4.4.1085cd
तानुद्दिश्य ततोऽद्यापि जुह्वति प्र च जुह्वति 1.5.40cd
तानुद्दिश्य विचारोऽयं प्रारब्धो गुरुभिः स्फुटः 1.4.1165cd
तानेवोद्दिश्य तेनेदं विशेषणमिहेरितम् 4.4.409cd
तान्यप्यस्यापजह्रुस्ते ब्रह्मविद्वेषहेतुतः 3.9.131cd
तान्येव तु निषिद्धानि कर्माणीह शमादिभिः 4.4.1245cd
तान्येवैतानि भूतानीत्येवं यद्वत्प्रजायते 4.3.135ab
तापाय पुण्यमप्याहुः परिणामादिसंगतेः 4.4.1173ab
ता भावना उपादाय प्रत्यङ् स्वप्ने रिरंसया 4.3.909ab
ताभिः प्रत्यवसृप्यात्मा वृत्तीर्नाडीभिरानयन् 2.1.339ab
ताभिरेवोपसंहृत्य प्राज्ञो याति सुषुप्तताम् 2.1.330cd
ताभ्यां च भावनोद्भूतिर्निर्देशोऽतो यथोदितः 4.4.123cd
ताभ्यां चाप्यनुमासिद्धिरेवमन्योऽन्यसंश्रयः 4.3.776cd
ताभ्यां तत्प्रत्यगात्मानं कथं पश्येश्चितिं स्वतः 3.4.160cd
ताभ्यां विना कुतोऽज्ञायि त्वेवंरूपमितीर्यताम् 1.4.251cd
ताभ्यां विना प्रमेयोऽर्थो नितरां न प्रसिध्यति 4.3.1667cd
ताभ्यां विलक्षणस्त्वात्मा स्वप्ने योऽयं प्रपञ्चितः 4.3.1149ab
ताभ्यां सर्वमिदं गच्छद्यथाकर्म यथाश्रुतम् 6.2.42ab
तामपान्य प्रयत्नेन प्राण्यान्मन्त्रेण कारयेत् 6.4.47cd

तामप्यत्र न कुर्वीत किमु वक्तव्यमन्यतः 1.5.214cd
तामवस्थां तिरश्चक्र आयियासुस्ततोऽपराम् 4.3.1067cd
तामसं कठिनं चोर्वी शरीरं वाच उच्यते 1.5.171ab
तामादायैति देहं स्वं हंस आत्मामृतोऽव्ययः 4.3.941cd
तामेतामनतिप्रश्न्यामतिप्रश्नेन साहसात् 3.6.25ab
तामेतामेक आचार्या उपनीताय यत्नतः 5.16.44ab
तामेव परिषदं तस्मादाजगाम त्वरान्वितः 6.2.22cd
तामेवायं पुनर्योनिं स्वप्न आत्मा प्रपद्यते 4.3.993cd
ताम्रं नौदुम्बरं ग्राह्यमिध्मैस्तस्य विरोधतः 6.3.13ab
तारतम्यं यथा कार्ये कारकाणामसंभवात् 4.4.815cd
तारतम्यादुपायानां शुद्धिस्तरतमा धियः 4.3.1853ab
तार्किकैः सह संधिं च चिकीर्षन्ति यथाबलम् 2.3.115cd
तावताप्यमृताहं स्यां किं वा नेत्युच्यतां यथा 2.4.49cd
तावतावसितेर्विद्या स्वार्थैवेति विनिश्चयः 1.4.1450cd
तावतैव कृतार्थत्वात्किमन्यत्प्रार्थ्यते श्रुतेः 1.4.1111cd
तावतैव कृतार्थत्वाद्विधेर्नित्यस्य कर्मणः 3.3.83ab
तावतैव कृतार्थत्वाद्व्यर्थं ध्यानादिचेष्टितम् 1.4.898cd
तावतैव कृतार्थत्वान्न कार्यमवशिष्यते 4.4.924cd
तावतो व्यवधानत्वाद्बुभुत्सा च न युज्यते 1.4.466cd
तावत्तावत्प्ररूढत्वं दुःखस्याप्यभिजायते 2.1.358cd
तावत्तावद्धियः स्वास्थ्यं तावत्तावत्सुखोन्नतिः 4.3.1854cd
तावत्तावद्धियोऽस्वास्थ्यं दुःखोद्भूतिस्तथा तथा 4.3.1855cd
तावत्प्रज्ञां प्रकुर्वीत यावद्ध्वस्ता निरन्वया 4.4.885ab
तावत्सर्वं जयत्याशु प्रथमोपासितत: फलम् 5.16.10cd
तावत्सर्वमवाप्नोति यथोक्तोपासनान्नरः 5.16.13cd
तावथर्वाब्रवीदिन्द्रश्छिन्द्यान्मे ब्रुवतः शिरः 2.5.99cd
तावदेव चिरं तस्येत्यपवादः श्रुतीरितः 1.4.1549cd
तावदेव निरोद्धव्यं हृदि यावत्क्षयं गतम् 4.4.890ab
तावदेव हतान्धयस्य तदन्यानवशेषतः 5.1.25cd
तावदेव हि तत्कर्म नाज्ञातद्रव्यदैवतम् SV 360cd
तावदेवास्तु तद्वस्तु स्वप्नभूमिगवस्तुवत् 4.3.533cd
तावद्यावदमी सर्वे विशेषाः स्युः क्षयं गताः 4.4.732ef

तावन्त एव सोऽसुः स्याज्जगत्यस्मिंश्चराचरे 3.9.9ab
तावन्तं लोकमाप्नोति यावन्तं वाजपेयतः 6.4.12cd
तावन्नावसितुं शक्यं भवितव्यमिहाग्निना 4.3.728ab
तावन्मात्रपरत्वेन वेदान्तानामुपक्षयात् 2.3.137cd
तावन्मात्रप्रधानत्वात्प्रमाणफलमुच्यते 4.4.754ab
तावन्मात्रप्रमाणत्वात्तादृगेवास्तु तन्मितेः 1.4.900cd
तावन्मात्रावसायित्वं सम्यग्बोधादतस्तयोः 3.4.57cd
तावन्मात्रावसायित्वाद्द्वैतं नासावपीक्षते 4.4.666cd
तावन्मात्रैकनिष्ठत्वादात्मज्ञानं सदास्पदम् 1.4.1371cd
तावन्मात्रैकयाथात्म्यं ब्रह्मेत्युक्तं प्रतीयताम् 2.4.262cd
तावन्मात्रैकयाथात्म्यप्रत्यगात्मत्वकारणात् 1.4.318ab
तावन्मात्रैकयाथात्म्यात्तया व्याप्तैव जायते 3.4.96cd
तावन्मात्रैकयाथात्म्याद्बुद्ध्यादे रज्जुसर्पवत् 1.4.975cd
तावन्मात्रोऽधिकार्यत्र नाग्निहोत्राधिकारिवत् 1.4.1085cd
तावन्मात्रोक्तितो नासौ प्रश्नार्थोऽवधृतो भवेत् 3.5.32cd
ता वा अस्य हिता नाम नाड्यः सूक्ष्मा हृदि स्थिताः 4.3.1214ab
तावांनपि न पर्याप्तो निरोधो मुक्तये कथम् 1.4.1536cd
तासां निरोधोऽसंभाव्यो जन्मन्येकत्र मानवैः SV 459cd
तास्वन्नरसपूर्णासु स आत्माविद्ययात्मनः 4.3.1216ab
तितिक्षुवचनेनात्र दुरुक्तादेस्तथैव च 4.4.1244cd
तित्तिरादिसमुत्पाते वेपथुर्जायते भयात् 1.2.187cd
तित्यक्षा जायते पुंसो नित्येष्वपि च कर्मसु 4.4.1214cd
तित्यक्षितं च संत्यक्तं पितुस्तदनुशासनम् 4.1.33cd
तिथ्यादिलक्षणश्चान्यस्ताभ्यां मुक्तिरिहोच्यते 3.1.31cd
तिरस्कृत्यासुरं दैवं भावं यामोऽधुना वयम् 1.3.123cd
तिरोहितार्थतामाह नात्रेत्यादिवचः श्रुतिः 1.3.363cd
तिरोहितार्थरूपत्वान्मन्त्राणां न नृधीगतिः 1.3.353ab
तिर्यञ्चोऽप्यत एवेह कामयन्ते सुखं तथा SV 1015ab
तिष्ठन्पृथिव्यां योऽत्र स्यात्सोऽन्तर्यामीति गृह्यताम् 3.7.26ab
तिष्ठासेदथ बाल्येन कृत्स्नानात्मधियो ह्नुतिः 3.5.175cd
तिष्ठासेदिति चात्रापि प्रत्यक्षः श्रूयते विधिः 3.5.166ab
तिष्ठासेदिति संबन्धः सर्वत्र विधिना भवेत् 3.5.177cd

तिसृणामेषणानां स्यात्प्रजामित्युपलक्षणम् 4.4.1097cd
तिसृभिरिति संख्यार्थप्रश्ननिर्णयमब्रवीत् 3.1.51ab
तिस्रो रात्रीर्न कांस्येन पानं कुर्यात्तथाशनम् 6.4.66cd
तिस्रः पुरोनुवाक्याद्या ऋचः पूर्वमुदीरिताः 3.1.57ab
तीरे तस्यासते सप्त वायवः करणाश्रयाः 2.2.27ab
तीर्णबुद्धिर्हि तद्धर्मांस्तस्मादेषोऽतिवर्तते 4.3.1373cd
तीर्णो हीति तथा चैतदुत्तरत्राभिधास्यते 2.1.342ab
तीर्त्वात्मविद्यया विद्वानमृतत्वं समश्नुते 1.4.1717cd
तीर्थेन विद्या देयेति नातीर्थेनेति चागमः 6.2.66ab
तीव्रदुःखोद्भवो बुद्धौ संस्कारो यावदेव तु 2.4.76ab
तीव्रानर्थफलायेति ब्रह्मविद्याधिकारतः 1.4.5cd
तुरीयं पदमादित्यो लोकद्वारं च येन सः 5.17.2ab
तुरीवेमशलाकादेः स्वकार्येऽन्योऽन्यसंहतेः 1.5.231ab
तुल्यत्वाद्भूतमात्राणां स्वप्नजाग्रदवस्थयोः 4.3.1122ab
तुल्यशक्तिमतां नापि मिथोऽपेक्षास्ति कुत्रचित् 1.4.229cd
तुल्याभिधानधर्मत्वाल्लता सोमोऽपि गृह्यते 2.1.57ab
तुल्यो देवादिसंबन्धो ब्रह्मणो मशकादिभिः 1.4.1442cd
तुषतण्डुलनिर्मोके प्रत्यक्षे ह्यवघातजे 3.3.98ab
तुषाग्रमात्रमपि हि मृत्युः सर्वमिदं ततः 4.3.456cd
तृणाग्रस्था जलूकेह प्राप्य तस्मात्तृणान्तरम् 4.4.134ab
तृतीया याज्ञवल्क्यार्थं तिस्रोऽप्युक्तीरितीरयेत् 3.3.142cd
तृतीयेयं न कर्त्रादौ प्रतीचि तदसंभवात् 4.4.571cd
तृप्तः स्वप्नेऽथ संबुद्धः क्षुत्परीतः प्रबुध्यते 4.3.1010ab
तृप्ता मोदामहे येन क्षरन्तीति क्रियापदम् 6.3.46ab
तृप्तिशक्तिरिहापि स्यात्प्राणान्नाद्यात्मनोर्युतौ 5.14.9cd
तृष्णया प्रहितो बालः सोऽकामयत मानवः 1.4.1823cd
तृष्णया साधयन्प्रीतिं न प्रीतिलवमिच्छति SV 303cd
तृष्णाक्षयसुखस्यैते नार्हतः षोडशीं कलाम् 4.3.1884cd
तेऽनुवित्त्वेति च तथा त्रयीत्यागे वचः स्फुटम् 4.4.966cd
तेऽपि रक्षन्ति यत्नेन न च सामान्यमानुषम् 1.4.1808cd
तेऽपि साधारणाः प्राणा देहेऽसाधारणास्तु ते 2.1.416ab
तेऽपि सामान्यमात्रं चेद्विशेषा भवतो मताः 4.3.1650ab

तेजआद्यभिसंबन्धः कारणं खिल्यरूपिणः 2.4.409ab
तेजः सर्वशरीरस्य निर्मातृ स्यादसंशयः 2.3.70cd
तेजःशब्देन संशुद्धं सत्त्वमेवाभिधीयते 4.4.578ab
तेजसस्तु तृतीयांशश्चतुर्थोऽपां तथा भुवः 2.4.337ab
तेजस्तच्चाप्यनेकात्मविभिन्नार्थावभासनात् 2.2.26cd
तेजस्त्रयाणां वायुस्तु द्वयोरेकात्मकं नभः 2.4.334cd
तेजःसंबन्धमासाद्य यथाम्भः खिल्यतामगात् 2.4.417ab
तेजःसामान्यमात्रं स्यात्तदधिष्ठातृदेवता 3.7.46ab
तेजोऽतो भौतिकं सर्वमन्यत्र परमात्मनः 4.4.41ab
तेजोबन्नादिभूतानां तुल्या सत्कारणात्मता 1.4.1662cd
तेजोभूयस्तया तीक्ष्णो लघुर्वायुप्रधानतः 2.4.359ab
तेजोमात्रादिवचसा स एवात्राभिधीयते 4.4.35cd
तेजोमात्रा यथादेशं समये मृतिकर्मणः 4.4.20cd
तेजोवयवसंबन्धसमुत्थं विनिवर्तते 2.4.408cd
तेजोविकृतिहेतुत्वात्तेजोमात्राश्च ताः स्मृताः 4.4.24cd
तेजोवियोगात्काठिन्यं ध्वस्तौ भवति तद्घनम् 2.4.406cd
तेजो विरोधिनीं प्राप्य प्रकृतिं विजहात्यथ 2.4.406ab
ते तूपसंहृताः सर्वेऽसंसारित्वमतो दृशेः 2.1.261cd
ते तेषु ब्रह्मलोकेषु दीप्यमानाः पराः समाः 6.2.141ab
तेन तेन विना शक्तमतस्तत्तदचीक्लृपत् 1.4.1602cd
तेन तेन विशेषेण कारणं प्रथते सदा 1.4.200cd
तेन तेन विशेषेण देवतैव यतो भवेत् 1.5.176cd
तेन तेन विशेषेण प्रत्यगर्थः प्रतीयते 1.4.1395cd
तेन तेन स्वरूपेण प्रत्यगात्मैव कारणम् 2.3.63cd
तेन तेन स्वरूपेण भावना व्यवतिष्ठते 1.3.875cd
तेन तेनात्मकार्येण स्वात्माभासतमोवधिः 1.4.16ab
तेन तेनेदृगेवात्मा नातिशीतिर्मनागपि 3.5.206cd
तेन निःशेषवेदोक्तकारिणोऽत्राधिकारिता SV 285ab
तेन निःसारतां बुद्ध्वा कर्मणां वेदतत्त्ववित् SV 88ab
तेन पारिक्षितान्खेन चित्यात्मत्वमुपागतान् 3.3.156ab
तेनागमस्य तत्र स्यादज्ञातत्वविघातिनः SV 1007ab
तेनानन्वागत इतिप्रतिज्ञातार्थसिद्धये 4.3.1001ab

तेनानन्वागत इति प्राक्कृतेनैव कर्मणा 4.3.1002cd
तेनानुच्छिन्नसंस्कार आत्मायं प्राक्प्रबोधतः 2.1.222cd
तेनानुभवसिद्धानां लोकेऽज्ञानविघातिनः SV 1003ab
तेनानेन पथा धीराः प्रत्यग्ध्वान्तच्छिदा सदा 4.4.552ab
तेनान्यं सन्तमप्यर्थं द्वेषान्न प्रतिपद्यते 4.4.825ab
तेनाप्तवाक्यं मायोगे मानादर्थेऽपि निष्ठितम् SV 708cd
तेनासदृश आदेशो नन्वयुक्तोऽयमीर्यते 2.3.236cd
तेनास्य कर्मसंबन्धो न मानेनोपपद्यते SV 433cd
तेनेदं सदृशं वस्तु त्विति चापि न युक्तिमान् 4.3.681ab
तेनैता देवताः सर्वास्तृप्यन्त्यन्नेन सर्वदा 1.3.252ab
तेनैति ब्रह्मवित्तस्मान्नान्यः पन्था इति श्रुतेः 4.4.575cd
तेनैव कर्मणा मुक्तिं प्राप्स्यामः शास्वतीं वयम् 1.4.1665ab
तेनैव ज्ञात्मनाशेषं तद्ध्वान्तं ध्वान्तजं तथा 4.2.89ab
तेनैव धर्मता तस्याः कार्ष्ण्यादेरिव मीयते 4.3.123cd
तेनैव हेतुना कर्मकाण्डस्यापि प्रमाणता SV 561cd
तेनैव हेतुना कर्मकाण्डस्यापि प्रसज्यते SV 562cd
तेनैवाण्वादि निःशेषं तस्य सर्वविरोधतः 3.8.101cd
तेनोपमार्थसंसिद्धेर्यथा स्वप्नेन्द्रजालयोः 2.4.462cd
ते प्राणाः स्वगुणैरुक्तैर्वसिष्ठत्वादिलक्षणैः 6.1.16ab
तेभ्यो निर्धारणार्थाय सप्तमीयं प्रयुज्यते 4.3.325ab
तेभ्यो व्युत्थितचित्तानां संन्यासस्त्वात्मकामिनाम् 2.4.29cd
ते य एतद्यथाजातं ज्ञानं पञ्चाग्निसंश्रयम् 6.2.119ab
ते य एवं विदुरिति यदि वा गृहिणां ग्रहः 6.2.125ab
ते यथा कर्मणोपात्ता राज्ञः प्रागेव चागमात् 4.3.1964ab
ते वा एते इति तथा परिणामोऽखिलं जगत् 1.5.59ab
तेषां च ज्ञानसंयोगे प्रधानगुणभेदतः 3.3.46ab
तेषां चाप्यप्रमाणत्वं प्रापदद्वैतवादिनः 5.1.62cd
तेषां चेत्स्यात्स्वसंवेद्यं निर्देश्यं तद्घटादिवत् 3.8.70ab
तेषां दुःशकमत्यन्तमबुद्धार्थावबोधनम् 1.4.243ef
तेषां प्रत्यक्षतः सिद्धेरतः शुद्ध्यादिमानसुः 1.3.46cd
तेषां प्रत्यक्षमानेन बाधो लिङ्गधियो भवेत् 2.1.611cd
तेषां फलत्वादुक्तेभ्यः साधनेभ्योऽन्यता यतः 1.5.46cd

तेषां मुक्तिफलत्वं तु न श्रुतेर्नापि चान्यतः 3.3.50cd
तेषां मुक्तिफलत्वे हि न मानं विद्यते यतः 3.3.51cd
तेषां विप्रतिषेधार्थं ज्योतिरित्यभिधीयते 4.3.336cd
तेषामथैतमध्वानमावर्तन्ते यथागतम् 6.2.153cd
तेषामन्तर्बहिर्व्याप्तिः पृथिव्यैवेह लक्ष्यते 3.6.6cd
तेषामन्ते विनाशित्वात्प्रदीपादिविनाशिवत् 4.3.577cd
तेषामपि कुतो भेदो वस्त्वैक्याद्धर्म्यभेदतः SV 973cd
तेषामपि गुणे मानं नीलवन्न त्ववस्तुनि SV 960cd
तेषामपि निषेधार्थं कर्तव्यातो विचारणा 3.9.174cd
तेषामेव तदप्यस्तु तदानर्थक्यचोदनात् SV 274cd
तेषामेव विशुद्ध्यर्थं विचारः क्रियतेऽधुना 3.1.16cd
तेषामेवाधिदैवेऽथ व्याख्या प्रस्तूयतेऽधुना 1.5.168cd
तेषु प्रत्यन्तदेशेषु तन्निवासिषु चासुरान् 1.3.222ab
तेषु यत्नविधेयत्वात्सफलं स्याद्विशेषणम् 4.4.437cd
तेषु लब्धास्पदं नाम परस्मिन्नुपचर्यते 2.3.245cd
तेषु व्युह्यैव लिङ्गात्मा यतोऽलं स्यात्स्वकर्मणे 4.3.1940cd
तेषु शास्त्रैकदीपेषु साध्यसाधनवर्त्मसु 2.1.586ab
तेष्वप्यस्तमितेष्वस्य पुंसो वाग्ज्योतिरिष्यताम् 4.3.50ab
तेष्वसत्स्वथ पाङ्क्तत्वमुच्यतेऽध्यात्मकर्मणः 1.4.1841cd
तेष्वेव चित्स्वभावः सन्साक्षितां प्रतिपद्यते 1.4.345cd
तैरप्यज्ञातता चेत्स्यात्कातिशीर्तिर्मितेर्भवेत् 1.4.295cd
तैरभिव्यक्तिशब्दार्थो वक्तव्यः कीदृगिष्यते 4.4.325ab
तैर्दत्तानप्रदायैभ्यो यो भुङ्क्ते स्तेन एव सः 1.5.31cd
तैलवर्त्यग्नयो यस्मात्प्रदीपोत्पत्तिकारणम् SV 814ab
त्यक्तद्रव्यादिसंभेददृष्ट्यैव नियतत्वतः 1.4.1731ab
त्यक्ताप्रियपरागर्थो ह्यमानित्वादिसाधनः 1.4.1062ab
त्यक्ताशेषक्रियस्यैव संसारं प्रजिहासतः SV 12ab
त्यक्ताशेषक्रियैस्तस्मात्तदुपास्यं सदात्मना 4.4.446cd
त्यक्ताशेषैषणः सोऽथ प्रत्यग्याथात्म्यनिश्चयः 2.4.4cd
त्यक्त्वा कर्माणि निःसङ्गाः कर्मणां चरितार्थतः 1.4.1072ab
त्यक्त्वा कर्माण्यतोऽसङ्गाः प्रत्यक्प्रवणबुद्धयः SV 1134ab
त्यक्त्वा कर्माण्यथैकात्म्यज्ञानं सर्वात्मनाश्रयेत् 6.2.11cd

त्यक्त्वानं मुख्यमात्मानमाश्रयेन्मृत्युवर्जितम् 1.3.233cd
त्यक्त्वान्यत्सकलं तस्मात्सम्यग्ज्ञानस्य लब्धये 1.5.91ab
त्यजतैव हि तज्ज्ञेयं त्यक्तुः प्रत्यक्परं पदम् SV 215cd
त्यजतैव हि तज्ज्ञेयं त्यक्तुः प्रत्यक्परं पदम् 1.4.411cd
त्यजतैव हि तज्ज्ञेयं त्यक्तुः प्रत्यक्परं पदम् 2.4.23cd
त्यज धर्ममधर्मं च उभे सत्यानृते त्यज 4.4.593ab
त्यज धर्ममधर्मं च उभे सत्यानृते त्यज 4.4.1261ab
त्यज धर्ममधर्मं च तथा सत्यानृते त्यज 3.5.162ab
त्यज धर्मगधर्मं चेत्येवमादि स्मृतेरपि 1.4.1054cd
त्यत्संज्ञके तु विज्ञेये वाय्वाकाशे महात्मभिः 1.6.38cd
त्यदित्याचक्षते तस्मात्प्राणं ब्रह्म परोक्षतः 3.9.30cd
त्यस्य ह्येष इति ह्युक्त्या न्यायः श्रुत्यायमुच्यते 2.3.58ab
त्यस्य ह्येष रस इति तत्सिद्धौ कारणाभिधा 2.3.51cd
त्यस्य ह्येष रस इति यथोक्तो मण्डलात्मनि 2.3.48cd
त्याग एव हि विज्ञेयं मनोवाक्कायकर्मणाम् 4.4.1088cd
त्याग एव हि सर्वेषां मोक्षसाधनमुत्तमम् SV 215ab
त्याग एव हि सर्वेषां मोक्षसाधनमुत्तमम् 1.4.411ab
त्याग एव हि सर्वेषां मोक्षसाधनमुत्तमम् 2.4.23ab
त्यागोऽतश्चोद्यते श्रुत्या नित्यानामपि कर्मणाम् 4.4.1230cd
त्यागोऽतिसाहसं मन्ये ननु यागादिकर्मणाम् SV 309cd
त्रय आवसथा इति तथा च श्रुतिशासनम् 4.3.1168ab
त्रय इत्यादिकोक्तिस्तु नियमार्थेति निश्चयः 1.5.162cd
त्रय एव यतो लोकाः साध्याः पुत्रादिसाधनैः 1.5.224ab
त्रयं वा इदमित्युक्तं वाङ्मनःप्राणभेदवत् 4.4.382cd
त्रयं वा इदमित्येवं प्रतिज्ञार्थमिदं वचः 1.6.11ab
त्रयं वा इदमित्येवं रूपं नाम च कर्म च 2.1.13ab
त्रयं सदेकमेव स्यादेकं सत्तद्यथा त्रयम् 1.6.47ab
त्रयमेतत्सदा ग्राह्यं न कार्यं कारणं विना 3.8.31cd
त्रयस्त्रिंशच्च ये देवाः स्युस्तेऽध्यात्मादिभूमिगाः 6.2.84ab
त्रयस्त्रिंशत्प्रभृत्येषां षडादिषु यथाक्रमम् 3.9.10ab
त्रयस्यापि च संक्षेपो लिङ्गदेहात्मसंहतिः 2.1.13cd
त्रया इत्यादिको ग्रन्थः स्पष्टार्थोऽतो न यत्यते 5.2.3cd

त्रयाणामपि चान्यत्र ज्ञानकर्मादिचित्रतः 2.3.164cd
त्रयाणामपि वर्णानां तत्पाठः फलवान्भवेत् 3.1.49cd
त्रयाणामपि वर्णानां श्रुतौ संन्यासदर्शनात् 1.4.1651ab
त्रयाणामपि संगानाच्छास्त्राचार्यात्मनां स्थिरम् 2.4.219cd
त्रयाणामप्यतस्तानि वाग्वाकाशौ प्रयुञ्जते 1.4.366cd
त्रयाणामविशेषेण संन्यासः श्रूयते श्रुतौ 3.5.89ab
त्रयीयं धयते सर्वं स्वाहाकारादिभिः स्तनैः 5.10.3ab
त्रयी वाक्त्वां श्रोत्रमार्गेण श्रेयसे प्रविशत्वियम् 6.4.120ab
त्रयो देवास्ततोऽग्न्याद्याः कृत्स्नान्तर्भावकारणात् 3.9.21cd
त्र्यन्तस्य ग्रहोऽत्र स्यात्साक्षाज्ज्ञाने तु तद्ग्रहः 4.4.1037cd
त्र्यन्तेषूपपद्यन्ते तत्सृष्ट्वेत्यादिकानि च 1.4.620cd
त्र्यैव ब्राह्मणो विद्वानात्मनैवाद्वयं परम् 6.5.13ab
त्रायते तस्य गायत्री बटोः प्राणान्न संशयः 5.16.41cd
त्रायते हेति युक्त्युक्तिः क्षत्रत्वस्य प्रसिद्धये 5.15.7cd
त्रिकं त्रिकं तथोच्चार्य ह्युत्तरेष्वपि योजयेत् 6.3.47cd
त्रिकमुच्चार्य भूः स्वाहेत्याहुतिं प्रक्षिपेन्मुखे 6.3.47ab
त्रिकाललक्षणार्थं चेदस्तीति यदि भण्यते 4.3.613ab
त्रिगुणं सत्प्रधानस्थं पुरुषार्थेन हेतुना 2.3.89ab
त्रिदण्डिनः समाख्यायास्तेष्वेवातिप्रसिद्धितः 4.4.1084cd
त्रिधा जग्धं भवत्यन्नं परिणामविशेषतः 1.3.253ab
त्रिधा त्रिधा वा क्लृप्तेः स्यादेकैकस्येत्यदोषता 4.3.1054ab
त्रिधा त्रिधा व्यवच्छिन्न एवं सर्वत्र लक्षयेत् 1.4.681cd
त्रिधा विकल्पो विज्ञेयो विमुक्तिफलसिद्धये 3.3.46cd
त्रिरुक्तेरुपयोगोऽयं विभागेनोपवर्ण्यते 3.3.141cd
त्रिलोकी च त्रिवेदी च प्राणादित्रयमेव च 5.16.36ab
त्रिलोकीसाधनत्यागान्नापि संन्यासिनो ग्रहः 6.2.127ab
त्रिविधत्वात्सुषुप्तस्य सर्वं रत्वादि युज्यते 4.3.1060ab
त्रिविधस्य सदर्थस्य निशब्दोऽपि विशेषणम् SV 4cd
त्रिविधेनाधिपत्येन स जगत्पाति सर्वदा 4.4.992cd
त्रिषु लोकेषु यावत्स्यात्पुंभोगायेह साधनम् 5.16.10ab
त्रिष्वाश्रमेषु को न्वर्थो भवेत्परमभीप्सतः 1.4.1588cd
त्रिष्वाश्रमेषु को न्वर्थो भवेत्परमभीप्सतः 2.4.34cd

त्रिष्वेव त्वविनाभावादिति यद्धर्मकीर्तिना 4.3.753ab
त्रिष्वेव त्वविनाभावादिति योक्ता प्रयत्नतः 4.3.788ab
त्रिष्वेव त्वविनाभावाद्द्वद्रं तैरपि कीर्तितम् 4.3.742cd
त्रिष्वेव पवमानेषु यथा वागादिभिः पुरा 1.3.364cd
त्रीण्यन्नानि फलं कर्तुश्चत्वार्यन्नानि यानि तु 1.5.14ab
त्रीण्येव कारणानीति निष्फलावधृतिर्भवेत् 1.2.84ab
त्रेधा व्यभजदात्मानमित्येतद्वा प्रदर्श्यते 1.2.171ab
त्रैगुण्यात्सर्वभावानां मोहदुःखसुखात्मता 1.4.1036ab
त्रैलोक्यसंख्यासामान्यात्स्यात्सर्वप्राणभृज्जयः 3.1.52ab
त्रैलोक्यात्मकदेहात्मा नापश्यदपरं पृथक् 1.4.41ab
त्रैलोक्यात्मशरीर्येष विश्वरूपः प्रजापतिः 2.1.14ab
त्रैलोक्याभिहितिरियमष्टाक्षरसमत्वतः 5.16.7ab
त्रैविद्यलक्षणः सोऽपि तृतीयं नाप्नुयात्पदम् 5.16.61cd
त्रैविध्यं लक्ष्यते यस्माद्बुद्ध्यादिप्राणभूमिषु 2.1.215ab
त्र्यन्नात्मकमिदं विश्वं नातोऽभिव्यक्तिरिष्यते 1.5.333cd
त्र्यन्नात्मदेवतायास्तु तस्मादेवं विधीयते 1.5.390cd
त्र्यन्नात्मभावसंप्राप्तेर्जीवतैव कृतत्वतः 1.5.304ab
त्वं चाहं चैव संभूय योनौ रेतो दधावहै 6.4.95cd
त्वं तु सर्वात्मनात्मानं कृत्स्नं मामाप्तुमिच्छसि 2.4.69cd
त्वं त्वज्ञो मूढ एवेति भव कामं यथेच्छसि 4.4.363ab
त्वं न उद्गाय उद्गानं त्वत्प्रधानं भवत्विदम् 1.3.129ab
त्वं ब्रह्मेति गुरोर्वाक्यात्तन्निविष्टपदार्थयोः 1.4.1387ab
त्वं ब्रह्मेति तु वाक्यार्थः श्रुत्येदानीं विभाव्यते 1.5.295cd
त्वं ब्रह्मेति हताशेषक्लेशो मोहप्रहाणतः SV 889cd
त्वं ब्रह्मेतीह वाक्यार्थो ह्ययमत्र विवक्षितः 1.5.292ab
त्वं ब्रह्मेत्यादिभिर्वाक्यैः सोऽपि प्रत्याह बोधितः 1.5.287cd
त्वं ब्रह्मेत्यादिवाक्यानां नातोऽन्योऽर्थो विवक्षितः 1.5.298cd
त्वगादयोऽपि सन्त्यास्ये यतोऽतस्तद्विशेषणम् 1.3.203ab
त्वगादिज्ञानशक्तीनां बुद्धिः सामान्यमुच्यते 2.4.367ab
त्वगारम्भकसामान्यं त्वग्गिरातोऽत्र गृह्यते 2.4.355ab
त्वग्गोचराणां स्पर्शानां त्वगेवैकायनं परम् 2.4.332cd
त्वचोपस्पृष्टिमात्रेण स्पर्शमात्रं प्रपद्यते 1.5.126ab

त्वत्कर्तृकं तदस्त्वत्र पितुरेवं विवक्षितम् 1.5.293cd
त्वत्पक्ष एव दृष्टान्तो यथा नास्ति तथोच्यते 1.6.55cd
त्वत्पक्षेऽप्ययग्रहो दोषस्तुल्यश्चेदिति चोद्यते 2.1.123ab
त्वत्पक्षे बहु कल्प्यं स्यात्सर्वं मानविरोधि च SV 182ab
त्वत्पण्डितेषु सर्वेषु पृच्छ मां यदि शङ्कसे 6.2.28cd
त्वत्संप्रदानतः पूर्वं विद्येयं हि कदा चन 6.2.71ab
त्वदभ्युपगतेर्भेदः स्यात्प्रमाणप्रमेययोः 4.3.557cd
त्वदभ्युपगमादेव तदभ्युपगतं मया 4.3.471ab
त्वदभ्युपगमार्थाय यत्नोऽयं क्रियते मया 4.3.259ab
त्वदशेषप्रवृत्तीनां निरोधश्च प्रसज्यते 4.3.245ab
त्वदुक्तं नैतदेवं स्यादवक्तव्यत्वहेतुतः SV 73ab
त्वदुक्तात्प्रश्नगणतो न वेद्म्येकमपीरितम् 6.2.43ab
त्वद्दर्शनार्थिने मह्यं पूषन्द्वारमपावृणु 5.17.4ab
त्वद्वसिष्ठतयैवाहं वाग्वसिष्ठेत्युदाहरत् 6.1.29ab
त्वमेकशफमित्युक्तं शफैका या त्वदात्मिका 6.3.29cd
त्वमेव राजन्ब्रह्मेति क्षत्रे तद्यश आत्मनः 1.4.1605cd
त्वयैवात्मार्थमागीते त्वय्येवान्नमतोऽखिलम् 1.3.249ab
त्वयोक्तं न विवेदाहं नानुशिष्टिरिहास्ति मे 6.2.32ab
त्वां वारयति यत्नेन साधुब्राह्मणसंसदि 3.9.61cd
त्वाष्ट्रमेव हि सर्वत्र तेजो रूपादिलक्षणम् 1.6.20ab
दंशाश्च मशकाश्चैव दन्दशूकाः सपन्नगाः 6.2.159cd
दक्षिणस्य पथो व्याख्या यथावदनुवर्णिता 6.2.156ab
दक्षिणाक्षिग्रहस्तस्माद्वोक्तृत्वप्रतिपत्तये 4.2.38cd
दक्षिणा दक्षिणे प्राणाः प्रत्यञ्चश्चापि पश्चिमाः 4.2.87ab
दक्षिणेऽक्षणि लिङ्गस्य विशेषः कश्चिदिष्यते 2.3.81cd
दक्षिणेऽक्षन्निति वचः श्रुतेर्यत्नादिहेष्यते 2.3.82cd
दक्षिणेऽक्षन्पुमानिति लिङ्गात्मा परिगृह्यते 2.3.149ab
दक्षिणेऽक्षणीन्धनामायं पुमान्भोक्तेति यं विदुः 4.2.39ab
दक्षिणोत्तरमार्गोक्तिस्तथा सति विरुध्यते 1.4.1243ab
दक्षिणोदगधोगत्या प्रत्यगज्ञानमूढधीः SV 1110ab
दक्षिणोदगधोमार्गा विहितप्रतिषिद्धयोः 6.2.5ab
दग्धः सद्यो ममारैव ब्रह्मविद्विड्ज्वरान्वितः 3.9.119cd

दग्धक्रोधनिदानः सन्याज्ञवल्क्योऽपि शत्रुताम् 3.9.128ab
दग्धमोहान्धकारस्य प्रत्यग्बोधाग्निना मुनेः 3.9.162ab
दग्धात्मतमसः पुंसो नैषणापेक्षितेष्यते 4.4.1107cd
दग्धाशेषान्तरायस्य विराजोऽपि महत्तमः 1.4.74ab
दग्धृत्वादिस्वभावोऽग्नेः शक्तिश्चेद्भवतोच्यते 4.3.257ab
दण्डसर्पादिवद्रज्ज्वां स्वतोऽपूर्वादिमान्यतः 2.4.229cd
दण्डापूपिकनीत्यैव करणानामभोक्तृता 2.1.135ab
दद्याच्छापभयात्सा चेदनुलोमं तदाचरेत् 6.4.34cd
दधाति भास्वद्ब्रह्माख्यं यस्मिन्सर्वं प्रतिष्ठितम् 1.4.1606ab
दधीचोऽश्व्यं शिरश्छित्वा निकृत्यास्य शिरोऽश्विनौ 2.5.110cd
दधीत गर्भमित्येवं यामिच्छेत्पतिरङ्गनाम् 6.4.47ab
दध्ना च मधुना पिष्टं सम्यगालोड्य पात्रगम् 6.3.17ab
दध्नेन्द्रियादिवज्ज्ञेयो विधिर्गुणसमाश्रयः 1.3.196cd
दध्यङ्ङाथर्वणोऽश्विभ्यां यदुवाचात्मबोधनम् 2.5.106cd
दध्यङ् ह वा आभ्यामिति श्रूयते ब्राह्मणोक्तितः 2.5.105cd
दमादिविधिशेषोऽयमर्थवादोऽभ्युपेयताम् 5.2.3ab
दंपती घृतवन्तं तमश्नीयातामथौदनम् 6.4.72ab
दर्पणाभिहता दृष्टिः पर्यावृत्य स्वमाननम् 1.4.618ab
दर्पादिदर्शनान्नूनं वेत्त्यकृत्स्नात्मदर्शनम् 2.1.34ab
दर्पोत्सेकसमावेशान्नानुशिष्टोऽयमादरात् 6.2.26ab
दर्शनं क्रियमाणं हि कर्माश्रित्य प्रसिध्यति 1.4.923ab
दर्शनं तदपेक्ष्यायमनुशब्दः प्रयुज्यते 1.4.38cd
दर्शनं ब्रह्मचर्यादेस्तथा प्राव्राज्यशासनात् SV 91cd
दर्शनं शुक्लपीतादेर्जायते कर्मणो वशात् 4.3.1232cd
दर्शनस्पर्शनाभ्यां स्याद्यथैकार्थग्रहस्तथा 4.3.1713ab
दर्शनस्य विधानार्थं तस्य प्राचीति कीर्त्यते 1.2.166cd
दर्शनस्य विधेयत्वात्तत्संबन्धोपलक्षितः SV 762ab
दर्शनस्य स्तुतिरियं स य इत्यादिनोच्यते 5.16.53ab
दर्शनस्याविधेयत्वात्तदुपायो विधीयते 2.4.213ab
दर्शनस्यास्य तेनात एकवाक्यत्वमिष्यते 3.1.17ab
दर्शनाज्ज्ञप्तिमात्रं स्यादर्थस्तेषां प्रसिद्धितः 4.3.1769cd
दर्शनात्परिणामस्य पक्ता सर्वत्र पावकः 6.2.19cd

दर्शनादर्शनोक्तिभ्यामविभागात्मको दृशिः 4.3.1492ab
दर्शनादस्तु सा कामं दर्शनाधीनसिद्धितः 4.3.727ab
दर्शनादिक्रियां कुर्वन्सर्वदाव्यभिचारतः 4.3.147ab
दर्शनादिक्रियाकारि देहश्चेदभ्युपेयते 4.3.148ab
दर्शनादिक्रियाणां यदस्तित्वं तन्न वास्तवम् 4.3.1623ab
दर्शनादिक्रियावांश्चेद्देह एवाभ्युपेयते 4.3.262ab
दर्शनाद्यभिनिर्वृत्तो यस्त्वेवं हयसाधनः 1.2.220ab
दर्शनाद्विधिसंसिद्धेर्विधेर्दर्शनसिद्धितः SV 656cd
दर्शनानि विचित्राणि कल्पयन्ति यथारुचि 4.4.561cd
दर्शश्च पौर्णमासश्च देवान्ने ते यतः श्रुते 1.5.44ab
दर्शादिवत्फलैकत्वात्तच्चानिष्टं प्रसज्यते 3.3.49cd
दर्शाहृदेवता चेह सिनीवालीति भण्यते 6.4.101ab
दवीयसाभिसंबन्धस्तच्छब्दस्योच्यते कुतः 1.4.1127cd
दश तानि सहस्त्राणि शतानि प्राणिभेदतः 2.5.131cd
दशमस्त्वमसीत्यस्माद्यथैवं प्रत्यगात्मनि SV 208cd
दशमोऽस्मीतिवाक्योत्थसम्यग्ज्ञानानलार्चिषा 1.4.602ab
दशावरा पर्षदिति ह्यपेक्षन्ते च सद्धियः 4.3.31cd
दशेति नियमार्थं स्यान्न ततोऽन्यनिषेधने 6.3.15ab
दहतीह तथा द्रष्टा नाप्राप्तं दृश्यमीक्षते 4.3.1565cd
दहनौष्ण्यादिवद्वह्नेर्विभिन्नाः स्युः परस्परम् 4.3.1637ab
दाक्षायणादावावृत्तेर्यत्रापि फलमुच्यते SV 805ab
दातृप्रतिग्रहीत्रोश्च क्रियात्यक्तव्ययोस्तथा 3.8.142ab
दानादिकर्मणः साक्षात्पश्यन्तः फलसंगतिम् 3.8.144ab
दानादिफलसंप्राप्तिः सेव्याद्भवितुमर्हति 3.8.150ab
दान्तोऽश्वो गौर्गजो वापि प्रयोगस्तत्र वीक्ष्यते 4.4.1205cd
दान्तो दाता दयालुश्च सबाह्याभ्यन्तरः शुचिः 5.2.2ab
दान्तो भूत्वा ततः शान्तस्ततश्चोपरतो भवेत् 4.4.1203ab
दाम प्रतनुतां याति यदा कर्मक्षयात्तदा 2.2.21ab
दारपुत्रधनादीनि देहबाह्यानि यानि च SV 113ab
दारु कृत्स्नमभिव्याप्य यथाग्निर्दारुणि स्थितः 1.4.640cd
दार्ष्टान्तिकत्वेन यतः सुषुप्तोऽत्र विवक्षितः 2.1.356ab
दार्ष्टान्तिकार्थासंभित्तेरेकेनैव कृतार्थतः 2.4.286ab

दार्ष्टान्तिकोऽर्थः प्राज्ञस्य दृष्टान्तस्यावशेषतः 4.3.1900ef
दार्ष्टान्तिकोऽर्थः सर्पस्य दृष्टान्तस्याथ उच्यते 4.4.512cd
दार्ष्टान्तिकोक्तावात्मैव यतः साक्षादिह श्रुतः 2.5.78cd
दाहकस्य न दाहोऽस्ति वह्नेर्दाह्येन वस्तुना 4.4.916cd
दाहकस्य न बह्नस्ति दाह्ययोगाभिवृद्धितः 5.16.81ab
दाहच्छेदादयो यद्वददाह्याच्छेद्यतन्विनः 4.4.13ab
दाहपाकप्रकाशादिभेदेऽप्यग्नेरभिन्नता SV 957ab
दाह्यं दग्ध्वा यथा वह्निर्दाह्यनाशमनु स्वयम् 4.4.724ab
दाह्याभावाद्यथा वह्निः स्वात्मन्येवोपशाम्यति 4.3.1201ab
दिक्षु द्वितीयोऽनपगः सद्वितीयः सदैव सः 2.1.77ab
दिग्देशकालशून्यस्य प्रवेशो बिलसर्पवत् 1.4.621ab
दिग्भेदक्लृप्तिवद्व्योम्नि भेदोऽयं तद्वदात्मनि 2.1.410cd
दिग्विभागादिवद्व्योम प्राग्यानं च रवौ तथा 1.4.469ab
दिग्विभागाधिकारेण यथोक्ता एव देवताः 3.9.67ab
दिग्विभागोऽविभागेऽपि व्योम्नि यद्वत्प्रकल्पितः 1.4.990ab
दिग्विभागोऽविभागेऽपि व्योम्नि यद्वत्प्रकल्पितः 4.3.1744ab
दिङ्मोहाकुलविज्ञानो नष्टमार्ग इवाध्वगः 2.1.267cd
दिदृक्षितपरिच्छिन्नपराग्रूपाद्यपेक्षया 3.4.159ab
दिवो यदूर्ध्वं वस्तु स्यात्सद्वासद्वा विशेषितम् 3.8.4ab
दिव्यो ह्यमूर्तः पुरुषः सबाह्याभ्यन्तरो ह्यजः 2.1.484ab
दिव्यो ह्यमूर्तः पुरुषो नेति नेतीति चासकृत् 1.4.539ab
दिशश्च हृदये सर्वाः समाने हृदयादिकम् 3.9.110ab
दिशां यद्वत्प्रधानस्त्वं मनुष्याणां तथा ह्यहम् 6.3.58ab
दिशामन्त इह ग्राह्यो मध्यदेशोपलक्षितः 1.3.219ab
दिष्ट्या त्वं वर्धसे भद्र जातः पुत्रस्तवर्धिमान् SV 576ab
दीपकुम्भादिको बुद्धैर्व्यवहारप्रसिद्धये 4.3.541cd
दीपस्य घटवद्यस्माद्भिन्नविज्ञानगम्यता 4.3.508ab
दीपादिवदसंभाव्या भवतोऽर्थक्रिया यतः 4.3.622ab
दीपादेरपि तेनैव क्षणिकत्वाद्यसंभवः 4.3.651cd
दीपादेरपि नैवासावस्ति तेनैव हेतुना 4.3.650cd
दीपेनान्यो मथा चान्यस्तथा चक्रादिना परः 1.2.98ab
दीपोऽयमात्मनात्मानं व्यनक्तीति न तच्छुभम् 4.3.509ab

दीपो व्यभिचरत्यत्र तच्चाप्यनुभवाश्रयात् 4.3.504cd
दीप्तिर्नादोऽधःशयनमाज्यमांसपयोम्भसाम् 3.1.54ab
दुःखत्वाच्च न यागस्य ह्युपायोऽतोऽत्र बोध्यते 4.4.939cd
दुःखस्यात्मनि संयोगजत्वाभ्युपगमेऽपि च 1.4.587ab
दुःखस्यापि तनुत्वं स्यात्तावत्तावत्सुखात्मनः 2.1.359cd
दुःखहेतुविनिर्मुक्तावतिघ्नीमेत्यतः स्वतः 2.1.362cd
दुःखात्मकत्वात्सर्वेषां शिखिविन्यस्तहस्तवत् 4.4.1197ab
दुःखात्मके मनो धत्ते यागादौ चोदनावशात् SV 1040cd
दुःखात्मकेषु नित्येषु समीक्षापूर्वकारिणः 3.3.78ab
दुःखात्मनोर्मिथोयोगे नानुमानप्रमाणता 1.4.585cd
दुःखादिभावना ध्वस्ता कथं तद्भावना नुदेत् SV 460cd
दुःखादिवच्च नैवात्मा चितेः स्वार्थैकरूपतः 2.4.204cd
दुःखाद्यात्मकमेवेदं विज्ञानं चेत्त्वयोच्यते 4.3.705ab
दुःखापनयनार्थित्वप्रवृत्तेर्दर्शनादपि 1.4.1240ab
दुःखाभावः सदेहस्य नैवास्तीति श्रुतेर्मतम् 4.4.1285ab
दुःखाभावः सदेहस्य नैवास्तीति श्रुतेर्वचः 4.3.816ab
दुःखार्जितधनत्यागिनुतिश्च जगतीक्ष्यते 3.8.141ab
दुःखित्वं नात्मनि ज्ञेयं यत्र त्वस्येति निह्नुतेः 1.4.571cd
दुःखित्वमपि संप्राप्तं कुम्भीपाकादिदेहिषु 3.9.202cd
दुःखिनः साक्षितायुक्ता साक्षिणो दुःखिता तथा 1.4.560cd
दुःखी गौरो द्विजश्चेति शरीरोत्थानतः परः 2.4.428cd
दुःखी यदि भवेदात्मा कः साक्षी दुःखिनो भवेत् 1.4.560ab
दुःख्यस्मीत्यपि चेद्ध्वस्ता कोटिकल्पोपबृंहिता 1.4.1538ab
दुन्दुभिध्वनिरित्येतत्कुतो लब्धं विशेषणम् 2.4.278ab
दुन्दुभिध्वनिरेवैकः सर्वत्राव्यभिचारवान् 2.4.276cd
दुन्दुभिध्वनिसामान्यव्यतिरेकेण तेन ते 2.4.277ab
दुन्दुभेर्ग्रहणेनेति लब्धमेतद्विशेषणम् 2.4.278cd
दुन्दुभेस्तु रवा एत इत्येवं ग्रहणे सति 2.4.279ab
दुन्दुभ्यद्युक्तदृष्टान्तन्यायमार्गेण यत्नतः 2.4.395cd
दुन्दुभ्यन्वितशब्दस्य सर्वत्राव्यभिचारतः 2.4.275ab
दुन्दुभ्याद्यैश्च दृष्टान्तैर्हेतुभिश्च समर्थ्यते 2.1.502ab
दुर्गन्धो जायते गन्धः पापकर्मप्रबोधतः 2.4.360cd

दुर्निवारेह साप्नोति योक्ता दोषपरंपरा 4.4.591cd
दुर्बलत्वादविद्याया आत्मत्वाद्बोधरूपिणः 1.4.860ab
दुर्बलानां विरुद्धानां बलवद्भिरपाक्रिया 1.4.254ab
दुर्वारत्वात्प्रसङ्गस्य ह्यनवस्था प्रसज्यते 3.4.139cd
दुःशकोत्तरमित्येवं प्रश्नं मत्वान्वपृच्छत 3.2.26ab
दुःसंभाव्यात आत्मायमात्मनैवानुभूयते 1.4.1408cd
दुःसंभाव्या हि पूर्वा दिङ्मुक्त्वाशां पश्चिमां जनैः 2.1.77cd
दुहिता पण्डितेत्यत्र स्त्रीणामुचितकर्मसु 6.4.74ab
दूरतोऽमुष्य लोकस्य स्यादसाविति गौरियम् 6.2.75ab
दूरमेवंविदः पाप्मा कथमध्यवसीयते 1.3.213ab
दूरसूक्ष्मादिदृष्टौ स्यान्न रूपे श्रोत्रवृत्तिता 2.4.174cd
दूरान्तिकादिभिन्नेषु कल्पिताकल्पितेष्वपि SV 351cd
दूरे स्थितं प्रपश्यामि यन्न दृष्टमिदं तथा 4.3.704ab
दूषिता न परिस्पन्दो दूरं मृत्युरसोस्ततः 1.3.217cd
दृक्शक्तिः पुरुषे तत्र या रूपाद्यनुरोधिनी 4.3.1547cd
दृगादिशक्तिभेदानां चक्षूरूपादिभेदतः 4.3.1780ab
दृगादिशक्त्यनेकत्वेऽप्येकमेव परं विदुः 1.6.48ab
दृङ्मात्राविक्रियात्मत्व एकत्वाकारकत्वतः 4.3.1487cd
दृढपूर्वश्रुतत्वाच्च प्रमादाच्चापि लौकिकात् 4.4.826ab
दृशौ स्यात्समवनयः सर्पादीनां यथा स्रजि 3.2.30cd
दृश्यं चेन्मनसैवैतद्द्रष्टृत्वादिप्रभेदतः 4.4.658ab
दृश्यतेऽन्तःस्थतोयानां बहिष्ठः परिपाकतः 1.4.533ab
दृश्यते त्वग्र्यया बुद्ध्या मनसैवेति यद्वचः 2.5.85ab
दृश्यते नाश्यमानं हि न चास्यावृत्तिरीक्ष्यते SV 1089cd
दृश्यते मनसैवासौ नातोऽन्येनेह केनचित् 4.4.714cd
दृश्यत्वाद्घटवद्देहः प्राणादेः करणत्वतः 3.4.71ab
दृश्यमन्यदविद्योत्थं पश्येत्स्वप्ने यथा तथा 4.3.1791cd
दृश्यार्थवदभिन्नोऽयं द्रष्टृदर्शनसाक्ष्यपि 4.3.92ab
दृश्यार्थासंभवाद्यद्वत्पश्यन्नपि न पश्यति 4.3.1478ab
दृष्टं कष्टज्वरेऽप्येवं विशेषेणोपदिश्यते SV 766cd
दृष्टं फलमदृष्टं तु ह्युक्थस्यैकात्म्यमश्नुते 5.15.3cd
दृष्टं मृषापि श्रवणं न तु दृष्टिर्मृषेक्ष्यते 5.16.31cd

दृष्टं विशेषणं लोके यथेहापि तथेक्ष्यताम् 6.2.3cd
दृष्टं सर्वत्र लोकेऽस्मिन्न तु सिंहशृगालयोः 1.2.60cd
दृष्टं हि कर्मणः कार्यमुत्पत्त्यादिचतुष्टयम् 3.3.25cd
दृष्टः काण्डरुहोऽपीह वृक्षस्तद्वच्च नेष्यते 3.9.140ab
दृष्टत्वात्परिपाट्या स्यात्तस्माद्वृत्तिरिति स्थितम् 4.3.1135cd
दृष्टमैक्यं न भिन्नानां भिन्नजातौ तथेति चेत् 2.4.300cd
दृष्टसंसारतत्त्वश्च वैराग्यं संसृतेर्व्रजेत् 1.4.9cd
दृष्टस्यानुपपन्नत्वं किमाश्रित्याभिधीयते 1.4.1234cd
दृष्टस्यैव स्मृतौ न स्यात्स्वप्ने चार्थस्य दर्शनम् 4.3.262cd
दृष्टादृष्टप्रवृत्त्योश्च न विशेषोऽस्ति कश्चन SV 418ab
दृष्टादृष्टार्थरूपं यत्तच्च कर्मेति गृह्यते 4.4.115cd
दृष्टादृष्टार्थसंबन्धिप्रीत्युत्कर्षाविशेषतः SV 299ab
दृष्टानन्दाभिलाषं स न मन्दीकर्तुमप्यलम् SV 348cd
दृष्टा नराणां निःशेषकुतूहलैर्निराक्रिया SV 588cd
दृष्टान्तः कश्चिदप्यस्ति जगत्यस्मिंश्चराचरे 4.3.1779cd
दृष्टान्तः संप्रसादो वा स्वप्नजाग्रदवस्थयोः 4.3.1060cd
दृष्टान्तत्रितयं तावत्स्थितिकाल उदाहृतम् 2.4.296ab
दृष्टान्तत्वेन राज्ञासौ सर्वोऽपीह विवक्षितः 4.3.1898cd
दृष्टान्तत्वेन स्वापस्य सैव साक्षाद्विवक्ष्यते 2.1.355cd
दृष्टान्तमात्रनास्तित्वं दोषोऽस्मास्विह चोद्यते 4.3.1760ab
दृष्टान्तश्च कुमारादि तथा च घटतेऽञ्जसा 2.1.245ab
दृष्टान्तश्च न नो नास्ति मण्यादेरिह संभवात् 4.3.1758ab
दृष्टान्तस्य सुषुप्तेश्च नार्थं दार्ष्टान्तिकं जगौ 4.3.1900ab
दृष्टान्तानामिहोक्तिः स्याद्भूयसां भिन्नरूपिणाम् 4.3.1936cd
दृष्टान्ताभ्यामिमां वृत्तिं व्याचष्टे प्रत्यगात्मनः 1.4.636ab
दृष्टान्तार्थेन संबन्ध एवमेवेति भण्यते 4.3.1914cd
दृष्टान्तेन बहूनां तु किमर्थोक्तिरितीर्यते 2.4.286cd
दृष्टान्तोऽस्त्येव नः स्पष्टस्त्वन्मुखेनैव तद्ग्रहात् 4.3.1760cd
दृष्टान्तोऽस्त्येव नो भूयान्न चेन्न भवतोऽप्यसौ 4.3.538cd
दृष्टान्तो भवतः कः स्यात्कामितार्थप्रसिद्धये 4.3.537cd
दृष्टा पुष्पेष्विति वचो यच्चापि समुदाहृतम् 4.3.707cd
दृष्टार्थतो वा विद्याया मनुष्यग्रहणं कृतम् 1.4.1085ab

दृष्टार्थत्वाच्च तद्बुद्धेः पाठान्नादृष्टकल्पना SV 341cd
दृष्टिं तत्रापि चाध्यस्य परिहारं प्रचक्षते 4.3.1050cd
दृष्टिकर्तृत्वमाचष्टे तृजन्तेन तथात्मनः 3.4.170ab
दृष्टिभेदमकृत्वैव दृष्टेरित्यादिकां श्रुतिम् 3.4.167ab
दृष्टिमात्रं स्वतः सिद्धं विशेषणफलं भवेत् 3.4.18cd
दृष्टिमात्रस्वभावाच्च नात्मा दर्शनमर्हति 4.3.104cd
दृष्टिमात्रात्मयाथात्म्यात्कार्यकारणवस्तुनः 2.4.443ab
दृष्टिमात्रात्मवस्तुत्वात्कार्यकारणवस्तुनः 1.4.1415cd
दृष्टिमात्राद्वयत्वं च तर्केण महतात्मनः 4.3.7cd
दृष्टिमात्रैकरूपत्वान्न तथात्मानमीक्षते 1.4.734cd
दृष्टिरित्यपि भावः स्यात्समाप्तिर्या क्रियात्मनः 4.3.1626ab
दृष्टिरेकैव सर्वत्र सर्वानात्मविलक्षणा 3.7.60ab
दृष्टिरेव तु यो द्रष्टेत्याह दृष्टिविशेषणम् 1.4.735cd
दृष्टिरेव तु सा द्रष्टा न तु कारकलक्षणः 4.3.1435ab
दृष्टिर्दृष्ट्यादिवाच्येह विनाशादिनिषेधतः 4.3.1635cd
दृष्टृभेदः प्रसक्तोऽतो नान्योऽतोऽस्तीति भण्यते 3.7.57cd
दृष्टेः कर्तारमात्मानं न पश्येः क्रियमाणया 3.4.168ab
दृष्टे चानुपपन्नत्वं किंबलादभिधीयते SV 548cd
दृष्टेनाप्रतिरूपेण कार्यगेणानुमीयते 1.3.151ab
दृष्टेरपरिलोपश्चेदथ कस्मान्न पश्यति 4.3.1603ab
दृष्टेरिति च षष्ठीयं क्रियमाणत्वहेतुतः 3.4.169ab
दृष्टेर्जडस्वभावायाः परार्थायाः स्वतश्चितिम् 3.4.158ab
दृष्टेर्द्रष्टारमित्यत्र यः साक्षी प्रागुदाहृतः 3.7.53ab
दृष्टेर्द्रष्टुश्च लोपोऽत्र प्रत्यग्दृष्ट्येकसाक्षिकः 4.3.1433cd
दृष्टेर्द्रष्टेति विज्ञानान्नात्र विप्रतिषिद्धता 1.4.1394ab
दृष्टोऽपवादो लोकेऽस्मिन्नुत्सर्गविषये सति 3.8.76ab
दृष्टो दीपप्रकाशार्थं न हि दीपान्तराहृतिः 4.3.501cd
दृष्टो वा यदि वादृष्टो वाग्ब्रह्मातः प्रतीयताम् 4.1.14cd
दृष्टौ नाभावशङ्कातः सर्वसिद्धेस्तदन्वयात् 4.3.1437cd
दृष्ट्यन्तरस्य द्रष्टुश्च न च द्रष्ट्रन्तरं तथा 3.4.180cd
दृष्ट्यन्तरेण संव्याप्तिर्नातो दृष्टेः कथं चन 3.4.181cd
दृष्ट्यात्मकं वा किं वस्तु द्रष्टेत्यत्र विवक्ष्यते 4.3.1580cd

दृष्ट्यादिजन्मनाशादिसाक्ष्यभेदात्मकं स्वतः 4.3.1732cd
दृष्ट्यादिभिन्नचेष्टास्ता भिन्नदेशादिलक्षणाः 4.3.1774ab
दृष्ट्यादिभेदसिद्ध्यर्थं नेदं वचनमिष्यते 4.3.1751ab
दृष्ट्यादिवचसां लोके प्रवृत्तेर्ज्ञान एव च 4.3.1769ab
दृष्ट्यादिशक्तिभेदोऽयं मा प्रसाङ्क्षीदितीर्यते 4.3.1633cd
दृष्ट्यादिशब्दैस्तस्माच्च सलिलादिवचोऽर्थवत् 4.3.1634cd
दृष्ट्या पश्येः स्वमात्मानं न कथं चन कर्तृतः 3.4.175cd
दृष्ट्या रूपानुपातिन्या न क्रिया कर्तृकर्मिका 3.4.168cd
दृष्ट्या विरुद्धदिक्स्थस्य प्रतीचो दर्शनं कुतः 4.3.1727cd
दृष्ट्या संबध्यते द्रष्टा द्रष्टृत्वस्य तदाश्रयात् 4.3.1475cd
दृष्ट्वानुभवतस्तत्त्वमात्मानात्मपदार्थयोः 2.4.91ab
दृष्ट्वापि यत्समाख्यातुं प्रबुद्धो नैव शक्नुयात् 4.3.1058ab
दृष्ट्वा श्रुतिः शिरस्ताडमनुक्रोशति दुःखिता 4.3.952cd
दृष्ट्वेहां श्रोतृगां सोऽपि न सम्यगभिमन्यते SV 736ab
दृष्ट्वैवात्मा न कृत्वेति प्रत्यङ् तस्मान्न कारकः 4.3.985cd
दृष्ट्वैवेत्येवशब्देन कारकत्वं निवार्यते 4.3.982ab
देदीप्यमाना विज्ञप्तिर्विशेषात्मावतिष्ठते 4.3.1394cd
देवता आस्रवत्येतद्व्याप्नोत्येतद्यथोदितम् 4.2.56cd
देवतां च ततो यान्ति देवलोकाभिमानिनीम् 6.2.139ab
देवताकरणो देव एष एवोच्यते विराट् 1.4.511cd
देवताग्रहणात्तस्माद्देवतैवार्चिरुच्यते 6.2.134cd
देवताज्ञाकरत्वेन ब्रह्मविद्या विरुध्यते 1.4.1695cd
देवताज्ञाकरत्वेन ब्रह्मविद्या विहन्यते 1.4.1729cd
देवताज्ञाकरत्वेनेत्युक्तं यत्प्रणिधानतः 1.4.1721cd
देवता तु ह्यधिष्ठात्री धर्मोऽस्मीत्यभिमानिनी 1.4.1631ab
देवतातो यथाध्यात्ममधिभूतं तथैव सा 4.2.72cd
देवतात्मनिषेधार्थपरत्वात्तद्ग्रहोऽर्थवान् 2.1.131cd
देवतात्मानमेत्याशु सदा तद्भावभावितः 1.3.182cd
देवतादिपरिज्ञानं दैवं पश्वादि मानुषम् 4.4.1121cd
देवतादिपरिज्ञानं मन्त्रवद्वित्तमुच्यते 3.5.114cd
देवतादिशरीराद्यैर्देवतादीन्नियच्छति 3.7.36cd
देवता देवतात्मानं तर्पयन्तीह ताः सदा 4.2.55cd

देवता देवतामेति लिङ्गैक्यं करणं तथा 4.4.60cd
देवताद्रव्यकर्त्रादि ननु वस्त्वस्तु नाद्वयम् SV 185ab
देवताद्रव्ययाथात्म्यज्ञानं कर्माङ्गतां गतम् SV 360ab
देवताध्यानवत्कल्प्यं फलमैकात्म्यवेदनम् SV 784cd
देवतानां तथान्यासां नाड्यो ज्ञेयाः सहस्रशः 4.2.54cd
देवतानामभिः काश्यो गत्वा सुप्तं यथोदितैः 2.1.98ab
देवतान्नरसाणुत्वज्ञानाय च पुनर्ग्रहः 4.3.1219ab
देवताप्रतिषेधार्थं बोध्यते चन्द्रनामभिः 2.1.132cd
देवताभोगशङ्का च विद्यते नेह काचन 4.3.431ab
देवताभ्योऽन्यदेवातो ज्योतिरात्मेति गम्यताम् 4.3.432cd
देवतामनिलं यातु वायुर्योऽयं शरीरगः 5.17.12ab
देवतायतने चैव प्रतिष्ठोपनिषत्तथा 4.1.12ab
देवतायाः समाख्यातो विभागो वर्णसंश्रयः 1.4.1637ab
देवताया गतिस्तस्माद्वायुर्ज्यायानिहैकलः 3.3.166cd
देवतालिङ्गकर्मादि सर्वमत्रैव संश्रितम् 3.7.13cd
देवतावर्त्मना नाहं गन्तव्यं वेद्मि किं चन 4.2.31cd
देवतावाप्तिमात्रं हि त्वत्तः प्राक्श्रुतवानहम् 4.2.32ab
देवताविषयप्राणबुद्धितद्वृत्तितः परः 4.3.330ab
देवताविषयो भेदः स कथं विनिवार्यते 2.1.136cd
देवतासमुदायस्य भेदः संक्षेपलक्षणः 3.9.34cd
देवतासूपसंहृत्य विराज्यपि च देवताः 4.2.78cd
देवता सैव न प्राण इत्याशङ्क्येदमुच्यते 1.3.298cd
देवतास्तित्वपक्षेऽपि किमस्तित्वादि नेष्यते 2.1.25ab
देवतास्थानकरणत्रयं प्राणगिरोच्यते 3.7.47ab
देवतास्य स्त्रियो ज्ञेयाः कामः स्त्रीतो हि जायते 3.9.50cd
देवतेन्द्रियसंबन्धं तत्तत्तदभिधीयते 2.3.8cd
देवतैकात्म्यमेवेह दैवज्ञानक्रियाफलम् 1.3.24ab
देवतोपासनस्येह प्रकृतत्वात्तथा गतेः 6.2.130ab
देवतोपासनाद्येतज्ज्ञानोत्पत्त्यै विवक्षितम् 4.2.12cd
देवत्वं प्रापयत्प्राणः कथमित्येतदुच्यते 1.3.228cd
देवप्राप्तिं श्रुतिः प्राह भावनाबलसंश्रयात् 1.4.775cd
देवभावः किमर्थेयं तद्वैतदिति हि श्रुतिः 1.3.387cd

देवभावः किमुद्गातुर्यजमानस्य वाथ किम् 1.3.378cd
देवभावेन विज्ञानं संस्करोत्येव तद्धियम् 1.3.389ab
देवमानुषतिर्यक्षु कर्तुः शास्त्रैर्निदर्शितम् SV 377cd
देवयाजिसकाशाच्च विशेषश्चात्मयाजिनः 3.3.127ab
देवयानं च यत्कृत्वा पितृयाणं च लभ्यते 6.2.161cd
देवयानः समासेन पन्था यत्नात्प्रपञ्चितः 6.2.146ab
देवलोकः फलं यस्माद्देवस्यापि न तत्पदम् 1.4.1032cd
देवलोकगिरा तेऽत्र भण्यन्ते सूक्ष्ममूर्तयः 4.3.1859cd
देवलोकफलं ज्ञानमेषणैवेति गम्यते 4.4.1127cd
देवलोकादिसंपत्स्याद्दीप्तिमत्त्वादिसंभवात् 3.1.54cd
देवलोकाप्तिसंबन्धाद्देवताविषयैव सा 1.5.253ab
देवसंख्यां स संपृष्टो निविदैव प्रपेदिवान् 3.9.8ab
देवस्य द्योतनवतो हृद्यं यच्चिन्तयेमहि 6.3.48ab
देवा एवाभवन्दैत्यकृत्स्नपाप्मविनाशतः 1.3.178cd
देवादयः स्वतन्त्रत्वात्फलप्राप्तिविघातयोः 1.4.1477ab
देवादयोऽपि गृहिणा तद्वदेव स्वकर्मभिः 1.4.1786ab
देवादिक्रिमिपर्यन्तं बिभर्ति जगदव्ययम् 1.5.3ab
देवादिज्ञानहीनेन येऽथ यज्ञेन सद्द्विजाः 6.2.147ab
देवादिभिरुपात्तोऽयमित्येतद्गम्यते कुतः 1.4.1794ab
देवादिविषयोद्भूतवासनास्य यदा तदा 4.3.1271ab
देवादीनां तथाविद्वान्पशुः स्यादुपकारकृत् 1.4.1571cd
देवादीनां विशेषोऽत्र गृहस्थस्यात्मदेहयोः 1.4.1801cd
देवादीनामतो यो यो यथोक्तेनैव वर्त्मना 1.4.1437ab
देवादीनि वराणि त्वं सर्वैर्भोगैः प्रपुष्यसि 6.4.125ab
देवाद्यैश्वर्यविषयव्यतिक्रान्तत्वहेतुतः 1.4.1464ab
देवानप्येति सोऽग्न्यादीञ्शरीरत्यागतः परम् 4.1.27cd
देवा निविदि यावन्तो वैश्वदेवस्य संश्रिताः 3.9.8cd
देवान्तरेण सोऽगायदयास्यः प्राणविग्रहः 1.3.326cd
देवान्विराडपि ब्रह्मा ससर्जेत्यनुषज्यते 5.5.9cd
देवाभ्युदय उद्गानं देवेभ्योऽर्थाय वागियम् 1.3.137ab
देवावाप्तौ भवेच्छङ्का मनुष्यस्य तदाप्तिवत् 1.3.373cd
देवाश्च पितरश्चैव मनुष्याणामधीनताम् 3.8.159ab

देवासुरत्वं प्राणानां विरुद्धोपाधिकारणात् 1.3.20cd
देवासुरादिभेदेन जातिरूपक्रियागुणैः 1.3.268ab
देवास्त्वग्न्यादयो ज्ञेया वेदाश्चैव प्रसिद्धितः 3.7.4cd
देवेभ्योऽन्ने यतः प्रत्ते हुतप्रहुतलक्षणे 1.5.40ab
देवेश्वरादयः के स्युर्विघ्नं वा कस्य कुर्वते 1.4.1504cd
देवोपासनतः पूर्वं नाभूद्देव उपासकः 4.1.26cd
देवो भूत्वेति जीवन्संभावनोपचयान्नरः 4.1.24ab
देवो भूत्वेति देवांश्च सदा तद्भावभावितः 1.4.775ab
देवो भूत्वेति देवान्हि प्रधानफलकीर्तनम् 4.1.23ab
देवो भूत्वेति वचसा तत्कस्मादिह पृच्छ्यते 4.2.10cd
देवो भूत्वेह देवोऽसौ भावनोपचयाद्भवेत् 1.3.184ab
देवो भूत्वैति विबुधान्भावनोपचयान्नरः 1.4.957ab
देवो राजेव चास्मीति मोहादेवं क्रियाफलम् 4.3.1277cd
देवो राजेव चास्मीति स्वप्नकर्मवशाद्विभोः 4.3.1271ef
देवो राजेव यत्स्वप्ने दर्शनं प्रत्यगात्मनः 4.3.1276ab
देशकालनिमित्तादिव्यपेक्षं वस्तु यद्भवेत् 1.4.1332ab
देशकालनिमित्तादिव्यपेक्षं वस्तु यद्भवेत् 3.4.134ab
देशकालवयोजातिरूपशक्त्यादिभेदतः 4.3.223ab
देशकालादिगावस्थाभेदेनैवाखिलं यतः 4.3.572ab
देशकालादिसंभेदादसाधारणतत्त्वयोः 3.4.98ab
देशकालादिहीनस्य ह्यनवच्छिन्नवस्तुनः 4.3.1265ab
देशकालाद्यनियमात्पुमिच्छानामनन्तता 3.3.111ab
देशकालाद्यभिन्नत्वादेकात्मत्वाच्च संविदः 4.3.1685cd
देशकालाद्यसंबन्धाद्देशादेर्मोहकार्यतः 1.4.1452ab
देशकालाद्यसंभेदात्क्रमेणोत्क्रमणं कथम् 4.4.88cd
देशकालानवच्छिन्नसुखाद्यर्थित्वदर्शनात् SV 290cd
देशतः कालतो रूपाद्वस्त्ववस्थादितोऽपि च 1.4.659ab
देशादिमच्छरीरेण न संबन्धस्तमो विना 4.4.518cd
देशाद्यत्यन्तसंभिन्नतद्विलक्षणभास्वर- 4.3.34cd
देशान्तरगतिः पुंसो नापि नाशोऽस्य युक्तिमान् 2.1.204cd
देशान्तराद्यसंबन्धान्मोहाद्यव्यवधानतः 4.3.105ab
देशान्तरोपगमनं गुणवदद्रव्यवर्जनात् 2.3.132cd

देशाभेदादभिन्नौ तावेष सोम इति श्रुतेः 6.2.96cd
देशे काले च पात्रे च दानं श्रद्धादिपूर्वकम् 4.4.1053ab
देहं देहं प्रविष्टः संस्तद्देहाकारतामगात् 2.5.126cd
देहं रसादिना बद्ध्वा सूक्ष्मांशेन शिशुं तथा 2.2.20ab
देहं विना कथमगाद्गतिसाधनवर्जितः 2.1.299cd
देहं संपद्यमानोऽजस्तदात्मा जायते खवत् 4.3.812ab
देहकर्मक्षये देहपातश्चास्य यदा तदा 4.3.819ab
देहग्रहणहेतुत्वं येषां नः श्रुतिरब्रवीत् 3.8.30cd
देहजात्यादिमानस्य वृद्धिहान्यादिसंगतेः 4.4.1186cd
देहद्वयविमोकेऽपि नैव मुक्तः पुमानिति 3.2.41cd
देहपातव्यपेक्षातो न स्यादूर्ध्वश्रुतेरिह 4.4.560cd
देहपातव्यपेक्षा स्याद्यत्र कारणसंगतिः 4.4.558ab
देहप्रवेशनिर्याणहेतोर्देहाद्गृहादिवत् 4.3.950ab
देहस्तस्य कथं मृत्युर्जीवस्येहोपपद्यते 3.2.34ab
देहस्थितेरवसितिर्मृतिशब्देन भण्यते 4.4.1331ab
देहस्य मृत्युर्विच्छेदो वियोगो देहलिङ्गयोः 3.5.65cd
देहस्य व्यवहारार्थं देहव्यवहृतिस्तथा 4.3.871cd
देहस्य सर्वदैवास्य जीवतश्चित्स्वभावतः 4.4.935ab
देहस्यान्तर्गतः प्राणः स्थूणावद्देहभृत्सदा 2.1.158ab
देहस्यैव मृतेर्नैवं जीवो न म्रियते सदा 3.2.32cd
देहहृद्वागवत्रोऽन्योऽन्यप्रतिष्ठाः संहतत्वतः 3.9.92ab
देहहेत्वन्तराभावाद्द्वयोऽपि विफलैव धीः 1.4.1752ab
देहाच्च देहधर्मेभ्यो विधर्मात्मावभुक्ततः 2.1.159cd
देहात्प्रत्यक्षनिष्पत्तौ न च प्रत्यक्षमिष्यते 2.1.143ab
देहात्मभावविलयः स्वर्गकामपदे यथा SV 379ab
देहात्स्याद्भिन्नजातीयं वस्तु देहावभासि यत् 4.3.229ab
देहादस्मात्परिभ्रष्टः कर्मप्राधान्यसंश्रयात् 3.2.164cd
देहादावात्मबुद्धिर्नो न कदाचिद्विहन्यते 1.4.1377ab
देहादिनाशे तुल्येऽपि तत्रैकेषां पुनर्भवः 3.3.1cd
देहादिभिन्नजातीयो भोक्ता यस्य च वादिनः 2.1.150cd
देहादिवज्जरामेति तस्मादात्माजरः स्मृतः 4.4.1328cd
देहादिवेन्द्रियेभ्योऽपि व्युत्थापनचिकीर्षया 4.3.324ab

देहादिव्यतिरिक्तोऽत आत्मा सिद्धो यथोदितः 4.3.261ab
देहादिष्वभिमानोऽस्य कादाचित्कः सहेतुकः 2.1.201ab
देहादिसंहतावस्यामात्मेति ह्यभिधाधियौ 4.3.277ab
देहादिसाधनास्तस्माद्द्वयमात्मान एव हि 2.1.601ab
देहादेर्यदि नामेदं ज्योतिरर्थान्तरं मतम् 4.3.140ab
देहादेर्व्याप्तिश्चेत्स्याज्जडादित्यादिहेतुतः 4.3.370ab
देहाद्देहान्तरं गच्छन्केनचित्प्रतिहन्यते 4.2.64cd
देहाद्देहान्तरप्राप्तौ तथैवेति विनिर्दिशेत् 4.3.1950ab
देहाद्भिन्नस्य विज्ञातुरिष्टं चेन्निष्फलः श्रमः 2.1.25cd
देहाद्भिन्नोऽधिकार्यत्र स्वर्गभोग्यवगम्यते SV 379cd
देहाद्यध्यक्षतां हित्वा यदायं वर्तते तदा 2.1.246ab
देहाद्यनभिसंबन्धात्प्रवृत्तिः स्यात्क्रियास्विह SV 1050cd
देहाद्यनात्मदृक्तद्वत्तत्क्रियां वीक्षतेऽपि न 3.3.64cd
देहाद्यात्यन्तिकी हानिरन्येषां यत्र कारणे 3.3.2ab
देहाद्युपाधिसंबन्धं सिद्धं मान्तरसंश्रयात् 2.1.473ab
देहान्तः प्रत्यगात्मायं पञ्चधा गम्यते मितेः 3.4.121ab
देहान्तरं करिष्यन्ति प्रत्यभिज्ञा यदीष्यते 4.3.134cd
देहान्तरगृहीत्यर्थं प्राणिनां मरणं यतः 4.3.1952ab
देहान्तरग्रहाभावात्प्राणोत्क्रान्तेरसंभवः 3.2.27cd
देहान्तरविनिर्माणं जाग्रच्चैतन्यवद्ध्रुवम् 4.3.130ab
देहान्तरस्थान्प्राणांश्च नियुङ्क्ते सा ततोऽधिका 6.1.10cd
देहान्तरादमुं देहं पूर्वमागाद्यतस्ततः 4.3.1947ab
देहान्तराभिसंबन्धी नत्वात्मास्तीत्यजानतः SV 105ab
देहान्तराभिसंबन्धो भावित्वान्नाक्षगोचरः SV 1055ab
देहान्तरेष्वपि तथा ह्यन्योऽन्यव्यभिचारतः 1.4.305ab
देहान्तात्कर्तुरन्यो यो बुद्ध्यन्ताद्बोद्धुरेव च 1.4.1378ab
देहान्तो दृष्टिकारी यो द्रष्टा धर्मादिहेतुमान् 4.3.1433ab
देहाभावे ह्यभावोऽस्याश्चितेः स्यात्किंप्रमाणकः 4.3.243cd
देहाभावो हि मोक्षोऽयं करणानि न सन्त्यतः 3.9.186cd
देहारम्भे न शुद्धस्य कर्मणः शक्तिरिष्यते 3.2.158ab
देहारम्भे पुनर्देवा यथास्वं कुर्वते क्रियाम् 4.3.1138cd
देहावयवदुःखादेः प्रात्यक्ष्यान्नात्मदुःखिता 1.4.568cd

देहावयवसंघातजातिसंस्थानतत्क्रिया– 4.3.34ab
देहावस्थान्तरावेशे प्रमाणं वाच्यमात्मनः SV 1052cd
देहाश्रयादृते कामाः सन्ति नान्यत्र कुत्रचित् 4.3.1021ab
देहिनः प्राणवत्साक्षात्संवृत्ता नामरूपिणः 2.3.94cd
देहिनो जन्मबीजं सा तदुच्छेदाद्विमुच्यते 4.4.400cd
देहि प्रश्नात्मिकां वाचं यां मत्सूनोरभाषथाः 6.2.59cd
देहेऽपि तस्य सद्भावान्नापेक्षा स्यात्तदा रवौ 4.3.227cd
देहेऽभिव्यज्यते यस्मादात्मा कर्म ततो भवेत् 1.4.1850cd
देहे न प्रत्यभिज्ञा स्याज्जाते स्मर्तरि युज्यते 4.3.223cd
देहेन्द्रियमनोधीभ्यो विविच्यात्मानमेकलम् 2.1.183ab
देहेन्द्रियमनोधीभ्यो ह्यन्वयव्यतिरेकतः 4.4.1277ab
देहेन्द्रियमनोधीषु चैतन्याभासरूपकम् 1.4.1001cd
देहेन्द्रियमनोबुद्धिक्षेत्रज्ञेषु पृथक्पृथक् 2.1.600ab
देहेन्द्रियमनोबुद्धिधर्मानिषोऽत्यवर्तत 3.5.208ab
देहेन्द्रियमनोबुद्धिप्राणादेर्नियतेक्ष्यते 3.4.74ab
देहेन्द्रियमनोबुद्धिभावाभावादिसाक्षिणम् 1.4.63ab
देहेन्द्रियमनोबुद्धिवेदनाव्यतिरेकतः 3.4.4ab
देहेन्द्रियमनोबुद्धिव्यतिरेकप्रसिद्धये 4.3.294ab
देहेन्द्रियमनोबुद्धिसंघातो वायुभिः सह 4.3.344cd
देहेन्द्रियमनोबुद्धिसर्वव्यापारभासिनः 1.4.767ab
देहेन्द्रियगनोबुद्धीः सुखादींश्च घटादिवत् 4.3.191ab
देहेन्द्रियाद्यवस्थाभिरतो धीः सर्वमेव तु 1.5.117cd
देहेन्द्रियाद्युपादानत्यागसंतानलक्षणः 4.3.404ab
देहैकदेश एवास्य देवतानुग्रहस्ततः 4.3.290ab
देहैकदेशगं दुःखं विशिनष्टि स्वदेशगाम् 2.4.348cd
दैत्यास्तन्नाशतो देवा देवा एवाभवन्सदा 1.3.176cd
दैवं च मानुषं वित्तं कर्मणो यत्प्रयोजकम् 4.4.1121ab
दैवं वरं न संदातुं प्रत्याख्यातुं च तं द्विजम् 6.2.65ab
दैवं विराजं सूत्रं च मृतः सन्प्रतिपद्यते 1.4.1151cd
दैवगोचर एवैष न तु मानुषगोचरः SV 74cd
दैवभावाप्तितो दैवं ज्ञानं वित्तमिहोच्यते 1.4.1849ab
दैवमानुषताप्यस्य साधनत्वोपचारतः 1.4.1847cd

दैवमानुषवित्तेन संपन्नोऽहमथोत्तरम् 1.4.1826ab
दैवमेकेऽपरे कालं स्वभाव इति चापरे 1.4.1487cd
दैववर्णविभागस्य मनुष्येष्वपि भण्यते 1.4.1635ab
दैववागादिसंपत्तिर्मृतस्य त्र्यन्नदर्शिनः 1.5.363ab
दैववागादिसंपत्तिस्तथा त्र्यन्नात्मदर्शिनः 3.2.73cd
दैवसाधनसंपन्नः पुत्र एवावतिष्ठते 1.5.319ab
दैवाधिष्ठित एवायं कर्मकालवशानुगः 3.2.144ab
दैवीर्भूमीर्नयामैनमिति देवचिकीर्षितम् 1.3.27cd
दैवी विद्या हि वित्तं स्याद्वित्ताच्च व्युत्थितिर्यतः 6.2.127cd
दैवी ह्येषा गुणमयी मम माया दुरत्यया 2.1.270ab
दैवी ह्येषा गुणमयी मम मायेति च स्मृतिः 1.4.383ab
दैवेभ्य एनमाच्छिद्य कामक्रोधादिसाधनाः 1.3.28ab
दैवेष्वयं वरः सिद्धो मानुषाणां वरं वृणु 6.2.60cd
दैव्यां वाचि यदुद्दिष्टं तुल्यव्याख्यानहेतुतः 1.5.178cd
दैव्यासुरीभ्यामन्योऽन्यमस्पर्धन्त विरोधतः 1.3.29cd
दोषवद्गुणवत्त्वेन विकल्पोऽनेकधा पुनः 1.4.88ab
दोषहेतावपि तथा कालादिनियमस्तथा 1.3.107ab
दोषाः सर्वेऽपि चायान्ति प्रत्यगात्मानमेकलम् 2.3.126cd
दोषान्तरप्रसङ्गार्थं परिहारः कृतस्ततः 4.4.1234ab
दोषान्तरमिह प्राप्तं तत्तावत्प्रविचार्यते 1.4.555cd
दोषोऽतः सांप्रतं भाष्यग्रन्थं व्याचक्ष्महे स्फुटम् 1.4.1311cd
दोषोऽयमपि नैव स्याज्ज्ञानोपाये यथोदिते SV 227cd
दोषोक्तिमात्रतस्तर्हि न पक्षः सिद्धिमश्नुते 4.3.692cd
दौर्बल्यमेवं संप्राप्य संमोहमिव यात्यथ 4.4.8cd
द्यतेरेतद्यतो रूपमवखण्डनकर्मणः 5.9.2cd
द्यावापृथिव्योर्लोकेऽस्मिन्नान्यथेयं समीक्ष्यते 3.8.138ab
द्युलोकः पितृलोकोऽथ पिता हि द्यौर्यतो मतः 6.3.50ab
द्युलोकः सामवेदश्च मनुष्याः प्रजया सह 1.5.158ab
द्युलोकोपक्रमो ज्ञेयो यावत्पुरुषसंभवः 6.2.77cd
द्योतिकैव यतो विद्या न त्वसौ कारकं ततः 1.4.1081ab
द्यौरग्निः समिदादित्यः श्रद्धा तस्मिन्हि हूयते 6.2.88ab
द्रव्यं विशेषणान्येति तथोपात्तविशेषणम् 1.4.1421cd

द्रव्यतन्नाशयोर्यस्मान्नैवेहास्त्येककालता 4.3.610cd
द्रव्यदृष्ट्या समीक्ष्यन्ते धर्मा नीलादयो यथा 3.2.110ab
द्रव्यमेव पृथक्त्वं चेदपृथक्स्यादिदं जगत् 5.1.92cd
द्रव्यस्वरूपेऽसाध्यत्वाद्विधिः कथमिहेष्यते 1.4.796ab
द्रव्याण्योषधयश्चैव देशश्च तदनन्तरम् 6.3.7cd
द्रव्यादि चात्मनो रूपं प्रमेयं यदुदीरितम् SV 1068ab
द्रव्यादिदर्शनाधीनं फलं सर्वस्य कर्मणः 1.5.9ab
द्रव्याद्भिन्नं पृथक्त्वं चेदनवस्थैति सत्वरा 5.1.92ab
द्रव्यान्तराच्छादनाद्वा सहजस्याप्यनीक्षणम् 4.3.709ab
द्रव्येऽपि न खलु व्योम्नि वासना काचिदीक्ष्यते 2.3.106ab
द्रव्येणैवाभिसंबन्धाद्गुणानां न परस्परम् 1.6.80ab
द्रव्ये त्वक्चक्षुषोस्तद्वत्प्रसज्येताप्रमाणता SV 691cd
द्रव्ये सत्यपि लोकेऽस्मिन्व्यभिचारस्य दर्शनात् 4.3.1590cd
द्रव्यैकपरतन्त्राणां गुणानामेव युक्तिमान् 1.4.542cd
द्रव्यैर्यायाद्वियोगं वा संविदर्ते तथा धियः 4.4.930cd
द्रष्टव्य इत्यादिविधौ प्रवर्तेत जडः कथम् 3.2.119cd
द्रष्टव्यं तत्कथं साक्षान्मातृमानाद्यसंभवात् 4.4.710cd
द्रष्टव्यं नाभिधानं स्यादभिधेयमृते क्वचित् 2.4.315cd
द्रष्टव्यं मनसैवैतन्नान्या गतिरिहेष्यते 4.4.711ab
द्रष्टव्यं स्याद्विभक्तं तन्नाविभक्तं यथोदितम् 4.3.1562ef
द्रष्टव्यमात्मनस्तत्त्वमित्याहास्मद्धितैषिणी 4.4.657cd
द्रष्टव्यमात्मनैवैनं सत्यं पश्येद्यथोदितम् 2.3.250cd
द्रष्टव्यमित्यतो वक्ति त्विदं ब्रह्मेति नः श्रुतिः 2.4.261cd
द्रष्टव्यश्चेद्भवेदात्मा स्यान्नियोगस्तथात्मनि 1.4.884ab
द्रष्टव्यस्यात्मनस्तद्वदैकात्म्यं श्रुतिरब्रवीत् 1.4.1257ab
द्रष्टव्याद्यनुसारिण्या प्रत्यङ्मोहप्रसृतितः 4.3.1727ab
द्रष्टव्याद्युक्तितस्तस्मात्पश्यतीत्यभिधीयते 4.4.1274cd
द्रष्टव्यो दृष्टियोग्योऽर्थो ह्यन्योऽनन्यश्च युज्यते 4.3.1617cd
द्रष्टा कस्येत्यपेक्षायां दृष्टेरित्यभिधीयते 4.3.1625cd
द्रष्टा दृष्टिक्रियाकारी विज्ञानात्मा पुमानिह 4.3.1545ab
द्रष्टा श्रोतेति नानात्वं याति यद्वदलक्तकम् 4.3.1776cd
द्रष्टा सलिलवच्छुद्धो निःसङ्गैकाद्वयस्तथा 4.3.1811ab

द्रष्टास्ते प्रज्वलन्त्यात्र सुषुप्ते यो विवक्षितः 4.3.1557cd
द्रष्टुं तत्परमद्वैतं सर्वकामासमाप्तितः SV 343cd
द्रष्टुः प्रतीचि यत्साक्षात्प्रत्यग्दृष्ट्यावसीयते 4.3.1732ab
द्रष्टुरन्यस्य चाभावान्न तं पश्यन्ति देवताः 3.7.52cd
द्रष्टुरात्मा पृथक्चेत्स्यात्पृथगात्मेति दुर्वचः 2.4.140cd
द्रष्टुरात्मैव या दृष्टिः प्रत्यग्दृष्ट्या समीक्ष्यते 4.3.1424ab
द्रष्टुरिति तृजन्तेन कर्तृत्वमभिधीयते 4.3.1625ab
द्रष्टुर्दृष्टेः किमायातं क्रिया दृष्टिर्गुणो न तु 4.3.1588cd
द्रष्टुर्दृष्टेरिति ततो द्रष्टा नैवेह कारकम् 4.3.1432cd
द्रष्टुर्दृष्ट्यादयो धर्मा भिन्नाभिन्नात्मना स्थिताः 4.3.1637cd
द्रष्टुर्दृष्ट्या न चानाप्तोऽनात्मा कश्चित्प्रसिध्यति 1.4.1383ab
द्रष्टुर्विनाशिनस्तस्या नोच्छित्तिरुपपद्यते 4.3.1425cd
द्रष्टुर्विपरिलोपोऽत्र मनागपि न विद्यते 4.3.1549ab
द्रष्टुर्विशेषणत्वेन दृष्टेरिति परिग्रहात् 4.3.1435cd
द्रष्टुर्हि व्यापृतिर्दृष्टौ दृष्टे रूपादिकर्मणि 3.4.160ab
द्रष्टुश्चापि न नित्यत्वं क्रियोद्भूतिनिमित्ततः 4.3.1592ab
द्रष्टुस्ततोऽविनाशित्वान्नित्या नित्यस्य धर्मिणः 4.3.1556ab
द्रष्टृत्वादिविभागेन विभक्तो यस्त्वविद्यया 4.3.1533ab
द्रष्टृत्वाद्यभिसंबन्धोऽकारकस्यापि सर्वदा 4.3.312ab
द्रष्टृदर्शनदृश्यांश्च यः स्वप्ने प्रसमीक्षते 4.3.192ab
द्रष्टृदर्शनदृश्यादिभेदोऽविद्याप्रकल्पितः 4.3.1535ab
द्रष्टृदर्शनदृश्यादिवस्त्वन्यदवसीयते 4.3.1736cd
द्रष्टृदर्शनदृश्यानां प्रत्यक्तत्त्वं यतस्ततः 1.4.748ab
द्रष्टृदर्शनदृश्यानां प्रत्यग्दृष्टिसमीक्षणे 3.7.49ab
द्रष्टृदर्शनदृश्यानां प्रात्यक्ष्यान्नागमेक्षणम् 2.4.140ab
द्रष्टृदर्शनदृश्यानां संहतानां परस्परम् 3.4.82ab
द्रष्टृदर्शनदृश्यानां संबन्धोऽतो न वीक्ष्यते 4.3.1534ab
द्रष्टृदर्शनदृश्यार्थप्राप्तावाद्यविशेषणात् 3.4.16ab
द्रष्टृदर्शनदृश्यार्थसंभेदविषयस्य हि 3.4.17ab
द्रष्टृदर्शनदृश्यार्थसंभेदस्य निषेधतः 3.4.18ab
द्रष्टृदर्शनदृश्यार्था विभक्ताः स्युः परस्परम् 4.3.1620cd
द्रष्टृदर्शनभेदेऽपि न भेदोऽस्य मनागपि 4.3.92cd

द्रष्टृदृश्यादिभावश्च कथं शुद्धस्तथा सति 2.1.307cd
द्रष्टृदृष्ट्यतिरेकेण नित्या दृष्टिरतो मम 4.3.1470cd
द्रष्टृद्रष्टव्ययोर्भेदे सत्येवं धीर्विधीयते 2.4.97ab
द्रष्टृशब्दाभिलप्यस्य नित्या दृष्टिः कथं भवेत् 4.3.1462cd
द्रष्टृश्रोत्रादिरूपश्च यश्च द्रष्ट्रादिसाक्ष्यपि 1.4.614ab
द्रष्टृस्थत्वान्न कर्मस्थं द्रष्ट्रा दृश्येत बोधवत् 1.4.569cd
द्रष्ट्रधीना क्रियादृष्टिरिति चेद्भवतोच्यते 4.3.1571ab
द्रष्ट्रा च क्रियते दृष्टिर्न चासौ परिलुप्यते 4.3.1573ab
द्रष्ट्रादिनाशसाक्षित्वात्सा दृष्टिरविनश्वरी 4.3.1434cd
द्रष्ट्रादिभेदसद्भावे द्रष्टव्यत्वप्रसिद्धितः 4.4.679cd
द्रष्ट्रादिरूपतस्तावद्व्यतिरेकोऽभवत्पुरा 1.4.612ab
द्रष्ट्रादिरूपसंभेदाद्यत्पश्येज्जागरे यथा 4.3.1519cd
द्रष्ट्रादिलोपसाक्षित्वात्तस्या लोपो न युज्यते 4.3.1426cd
द्रष्ट्रादि संहतं सर्वं यस्मिंश्च सति वीक्षते 1.5.105cd
द्रष्ट्रादेरात्मनश्चोक्तं वैलक्षण्यं तथा पुरा 4.3.1491cd
द्राघीयसा स कालेन गन्धारान्प्रतिपद्यते 1.4.1552cd
द्वन्द्वप्रवाहसंपातसहिष्णुरभिधीयते 4.4.1244ab
द्वन्द्वयुक्तं जगत्यस्मिन्यावत्किंचित्समीक्ष्यते 1.4.120ab
द्वयमप्यभ्युपेतं स्यान्न ह्यसद्धन्यतेऽसता 1.2.36cd
द्वयाविविक्तो हि परो भोक्ता कर्तेति चोच्यते 2.1.218cd
द्वया हेत्येतमाद्येयं प्रचक्राम परीक्षितुम् 1.3.11cd
द्वयोरपि समानत्वाद्व्यङ्ग्यव्यञ्जकता तथा 4.3.512cd
द्वयोरवस्थयोर्यद्वत्प्रकाशतमसोरिह 5.1.69cd
द्वयोरेकक्रियावेशात्तथाप्यन्यानपेक्षता SV 683cd
द्वयोरेकस्य वा मात्वे न संबन्धादि शस्यते SV 318cd
द्वयोर्भावैकरूपत्वात्कातिशीतिर्मितेस्तयोः SV 928cd
द्वयोर्यथोक्तयोर्मध्ये कतरोऽयं समुच्चयः 1.4.1710ab
द्वात्रिंशद्गुणितस्तावान्व्याप्तो भानुगभस्तिभिः 3.3.143cd
द्वात्रिंशद्गुणितो मार्गो रथगत्या विवस्वतः 3.6.15ab
द्वात्रिंशद्भिरहोरात्रैर्यावन्तं देशमुद्व्रजन् 3.3.144ab
द्वारं न नियतं मुक्तेः प्राजापत्यं पदं भवेत् SV 350ab
द्वारं मुखं प्रतीकं वा यदि वा लिङ्गमुच्यते 3.8.105ab

द्वावप्येतौ ममात्मानौ प्राण एव प्रतिष्ठितौ 3.9.90ab
द्वासप्ततिसहस्राणि नाडीर्व्याप्यावतिष्ठते 1.3.263cd
द्वासप्ततिसहस्रैस्ते संख्याता योगचिन्तकैः 2.1.325cd
द्विकाष्ठसंततताघातमाडम्बरमिहोच्यते 5.12.4ab
द्विजातीनां खरादेस्तु त्वदुक्त्या स्यादसंशयात् SV 101cd
द्वितीयं नेक्षते कस्मादित्यत्रैवाभिधीयते 4.3.1605ab
द्वितीयदर्शनायालं रूपमासीद्यदात्मनः 4.3.1514ab
द्वितीयपदविज्ञानक्षतिरेव न सर्वतः 5.16.60cd
द्वितीयमन्त्रानूक्तिः स्यात्तमसो मेत्युदीरणम् 1.3.359cd
द्वितीयसंगतिर्यस्माल्लोकेऽशुद्धेः प्रयोजिका 1.4.485cd
द्वितीयेन मथालोड्य ह्यथाभिमृशति पाणिना 6.3.25cd
द्वितीयेनोच्यते तत्त्वं प्रत्यङ्मोहनिवृत्तये 3.5.28cd
द्वितीयो न मदन्योऽस्ति कस्माद्धेतोर्भयं मम 1.4.93cd
द्वितीयो नेति यः सोऽथ भावनाप्रतिषेधकृत् 3.2.96cd
द्वित्र्यादिबुद्धिरेकस्मिन्मिथ्यातद्रूपवस्तुनः 4.3.1680ab
द्विधर्मत्वेऽपि वस्त्वेतदेकं स्यादुत्पलादिवत् SV 964cd
द्विधा त्रिधा वा बहुधा कारणं सद्भवेदिह 4.3.1808ab
द्विधेतं द्वीतमित्याहुस्तद्भावो द्वैतमुच्यते 4.3.1807ab
द्विधैवाध्यात्मिकं वित्तं कार्यभेदात्प्रचक्षते 1.4.1847ab
द्विप्रकारो विनाशश्च द्विर्हेतूक्त्या निषिध्यते 4.3.1496cd
द्विरूपमिति निर्दिष्टं वियद्वत्कुम्भसंश्रयात् 2.3.5cd
द्विर्विनाशप्रसक्तिः स्यात्क्षणिकत्वं च हीयते 4.3.607cd
द्विवचश्च तथायुक्तं त्रैरूप्यस्येह संभवात् 2.3.142ab
द्विषंश्चाप्यद्विषञ्छत्रुरासुरादन्य इष्यते 1.3.189ef
द्विषत्सु स्वेषु च न चेदाधिपत्यं तथापि च 1.3.285ab
द्विष्टायां सत्यपि स्त्रीत्वे चेतो नैवानुरज्यते 4.3.1311cd
द्विष्ठत्वादन्वयस्यापि व्याप्यव्यापकयोर्मिथः 2.4.271ab
द्वीतं द्विधेतमेकं सत्तद्भावो द्वैतमुच्यते 2.4.457cd
द्वे एव तु यदा रूपे मूर्तामूर्ते सवासने 2.3.139ab
द्वे एवेति न संध्यत्वात्स्वप्नस्य स्थानयोर्द्वयोः 4.3.836cd
द्वेधा भिन्नं जगत्सर्वमन्नमन्नाद एव च 1.4.159ab
द्वे वाव ब्रह्मणो रूपे इति पूर्वमवादिषम् 4.4.143cd

द्वे सृती अश्रृणवं साक्षात्संबन्धिन्यौ दिवौकसाम् 6.2.41ab
द्वैतं वस्तु न चेदस्ति सर्वस्यैकात्म्यमात्रतः 2.4.459cd
द्वैतकारणबाधेन सम्यग्ज्ञातत्वसिद्धितः 4.4.661cd
द्वैतग्राहि यथा मानं न किंचिदपि विद्यते 2.1.595ab
द्वैतत्वाद्यः पुनर्धीमान्कर्मावस्थां यथोदिताम् 1.4.1704ef
द्वैतदृष्ट्यैव निःशेषद्वैतकार्यपरिक्षयात् 3.2.47ab
द्वैतभेदानिमान्सर्वानेकैकस्य न वेत्ति यः 3.2.108cd
द्वैतमाभासते व्योम्नि नीलदिङ्मण्डलत्ववत् 4.3.1332cd
द्वैतसंसर्गबाधेन पूर्णं वस्तु प्रतीयते 3.4.29cd
द्वैतस्याद्वैतयाथात्म्यात्क्लृप्तसर्पादितत्त्ववत् 1.4.1138cd
द्वैतस्यैति पुमर्थश्च नातोऽन्यत्किंचिदिष्यते 3.2.78cd
द्वैताद्वैतात्मकं ब्रह्म पर्णत्वेनाविभागतः 5.1.48cd
द्वैताद्वैतात्मकं ब्रह्म मैत्रेय्यै वर्णितं किल 5.1.30ab
द्वैताद्वैतात्मकं ब्रह्म यदाण्वभ्युपगम्यते 5.1.105ab
द्वैताद्वैतात्मकत्वं च प्रमाणान्नोपपद्यते 4.3.1621ab
द्वैताद्वैतात्मसंदृष्ट्योर्दन्तोलूखलयोरिव 3.2.50cd
द्वैताधिकारमापन्ना वैश्वरूप्यं निगच्छति 1.5.119cd
द्वैताभिधायकाञ्शब्दान्ध्यानकाले न चिन्तयेत् 4.4.738ab
द्वैतार्थस्य विशुद्धिश्च कीदृश्यत्र विवक्षिता 3.2.99ab
द्वैतावस्थामुपास्ते यस्तस्यासौ क्षीयते ध्रुवम् 1.4.1704cd
द्वैतैकत्वं श्रुताच्छब्दात्पश्यतीह यदा ह्यसौ 4.4.719ab
द्वैतैकत्वधिया नैव पूर्वया फल्गुकार्यया 1.4.1130ab
द्वैतैकत्वधिया मृत्युं कामकर्मस्वलक्षणम् 1.4.1717ab
द्वैतैकत्वमतिर्यद्वत्स्वानुरूपफलाप्तये 1.4.1131ab
द्वैतैकत्वमतीहाभिः सूत्रान्तं फलमाप्य ना SV 344ab
द्वैतैकत्वात्मकं ज्ञानं कर्म च ज्ञानसंभृतम् 1.2.176cd
द्वैतैकत्वात्मकं रूपं वैराजं कार्यमात्मनः 1.2.123ab
द्वैतैकत्वात्मकं साक्षाद्ब्रह्मविद्योदयात्पुरा 1.4.1128ab
द्वैतैकत्वात्मकब्रह्मविद्याकर्मैकसाधनः 1.4.1198ab
द्वैतैकत्वात्मविज्ञानकर्मानुष्ठायिनः पितुः 1.4.1739ab
द्वैतैकत्वात्मिकावस्था विरिञ्चाख्या परात्मनः 1.4.1702ab
द्वैधीभावाय नैवालं तथा नैव प्रमाणधीः 1.4.867cd

द्वैविध्यं चाप्यविद्याया न च युक्त्यावसीयते 2.4.199ab
द्वैविध्यादावृतेः कार्यं नेक्षते तेन संवृतम् 1.2.88ab
द्वौ पदार्थावुपन्यस्तावित्येतदतिदुर्घटम् 4.3.1577ab
द्वौ वा हेतू यथोक्तार्थौ द्वयोरपि प्रतिज्ञयोः 4.3.1506ab
धनं निसृष्टं राज्ञेह ब्रह्मिष्ठोद्देशतो यतः 3.9.102ab
धनवन्तं यथा यत्नाद्दिदृक्षन्तीह संघशः 1.3.338ab
धनार्थं ब्राह्मणा यान्ति राजानमिति युज्यते 4.1.5ab
धनी गोमान्दरिद्रो वा धनाद्यर्थात्मसंगतेः 2.4.429ab
धन्यासीदिति दृष्टश्चेन्न लक्षणविरोधतः 4.3.612ab
धर्मं बलं समाश्रित्य जेतुं लोके तथा यथा 1.4.1619cd
धर्मत्वेनाप्यहंबुद्धेर्न भेदो धर्मिणात्मना SV 1067ab
धर्मधर्म्यप्रसिद्धिश्च तदभेदेऽपि सज्यते 4.3.1652cd
धर्मधर्म्यभिसंबन्धा गृह्यन्तेऽनात्मवस्तुषु 1.4.1274ab
धर्मधर्म्यभिसंबन्धा नेक्ष्यन्ते मानतो यथा 4.3.1262ab
धर्मधर्म्यभिसंबन्धान्यथा मोहैकसंश्रयात् 4.3.419ab
धर्मधर्म्यभिसंबन्धे नागृहीतेऽनुमा यतः 2.4.172cd
धर्मधर्म्यभिसंबन्धो दृश्यत्वादद्द्रष्ट्रपेक्षया 4.3.1810cd
धर्मबुद्धिप्रभेदेऽपि धर्म्यभेदः सदेष्यते SV 965ab
धर्मयोः समवायः स्यान्न तु नीलोत्पलादिवत् 3.5.37cd
धर्मव्रतं तदेवाद्य बिभ्रत्यग्न्यादयः शुभम् 1.5.383ef
धर्मसत्यप्रयुक्तोऽयं लिङ्गपिण्डस्वलक्षणः 2.5.52ab
धर्मस्य यागादि दया दमश्च मोक्षस्य सर्वोपरमः क्रियाभ्यः 4.4.596cd
धर्मस्य वेदमूलत्वादवेदस्य न धर्मता 4.4.1150ab
धर्मस्यैव तु रूपेण देवता रूपिणी मता 1.4.1632ab
धर्मस्यैव प्रतिज्ञोक्तेर्न तु ब्रह्म प्रतीष्यते SV 241cd
धर्माख्यं कर्म च ज्ञेयं स्वाधिकारनियन्तृतः 1.4.1664cd
धर्मादन्यन्महद्भूतं न भूतं न भविष्यति 1.4.1617cd
धर्मादिकारणोद्भूतवासनाराशिसाक्षिता 4.3.450ab
धर्मादिप्रेरकोद्भूतरथस्त्रीहस्तिलक्षण- 4.3.1246ab
धर्मादिहेतुकं प्राज्ञे तद्ध्वस्तं कर्मणः क्षयात् 4.3.1510cd
धर्मादिहेतुकं येऽपि परिणामं प्रचक्षते 1.4.455ab
धर्मादिहेतुसंबन्धबहुत्वात्स्यात्समञ्जसम् 2.1.151ab

धर्मादीनां विभक्तत्वमविभक्तेऽपि धर्मिणि 4.3.1619ab
धर्मादेः फलदातृत्वं स्वभावोऽवश्यमेव तत् 4.3.253ab
धर्माधर्मनिमित्तश्चेत्किं पुनर्धर्मपातके SV 53ab
धर्माधर्मप्रयुक्तो वा देवतानुग्रहात्तथा 4.3.852ab
धर्माधर्मफलं साक्षात्प्रत्यक्षेणानुभूयते 4.3.254cd
धर्माधर्ममयो भूत्वा पुमान्सर्वमयो भवेत् 4.4.192ab
धर्माधर्मसमायोगो लोकवच्छासनात्प्रभोः 4.4.993ab
धर्माधर्मसमुत्थोऽस्य बाह्यज्योतिरनुग्रहः 4.3.289ab
धर्माधर्मांशसाम्ये च मनुष्यत्वं प्रपद्यते SV 1112ab
धर्माधर्मात्मकं कर्म संसारानर्थकारणम् 4.4.202ab
धर्माधर्मादितन्त्रोऽर्थस्तत्फलेनेह लिप्यते 4.4.1007ab
धर्माधर्मादिपाप्मानो रूपमात्मन उच्यते 4.3.1300cd
धर्माधर्माद्यपेक्षत्वादनात्माकारतां प्रति 4.4.929cd
धर्माधर्माद्यपेक्षत्वादन्यत्वाच्चान्यवस्तुनः 4.4.653ab
धर्माधर्माद्युपादानसाधना नश्वरी गतिः SV 1113ab
धर्माधर्मानपेक्षः सन्नानन्त्येनावतिष्ठते 1.3.308cd
धर्माधर्मानपेक्षत्वाच्चैतन्याभासतां प्रति 3.4.101ab
धर्माधर्मासमायोगो यस्मात्प्रत्यग्धियः फलम् 4.4.1194ab
धर्माधर्मैकसाध्यत्वाद्ब्रह्मादेः स्थावरावधेः 1.3.26ab
धर्माधर्मैकहेतुत्वात्सर्वस्य जगतस्ततः 4.4.192cd
धर्माधर्मौ च देहस्य योनिरित्यागमाश्रयात् 1.4.170cd
धर्माधर्मौ रजो ज्ञेयं रजोवत्तन्मलत्वतः 4.4.699ab
धर्मा न त्वात्मनः शास्त्रे ह्यसङ्गो हीति वारणात् 2.3.134cd
धर्मानन्वयतः प्राज्ञ इत्येवमभिचोदिते 4.3.1378cd
धर्मानपेक्षसंलब्धसत्त्वादिस्वार्थरूपकः 2.1.161cd
धर्मान्तैः संहतैर्यस्मात्कर्म सिध्यति नान्यथा 1.4.1602ab
धर्माभावात्प्रतीचश्च तद्भेदे हेतुता कुतः 2.1.607cd
धर्माभ्युपगमे दोषो ह्यनवस्था प्रसज्यते 4.3.154cd
धर्मार्थौ यत्र च स्यातां शुश्रूषा वापि तद्विधा 2.1.37ab
धर्मार्थौ यत्र न स्यातां शुश्रूषा वापि तद्विधा 2.1.36ab
धर्मा लभन्त आत्मानं पारतन्त्र्यात्मकत्वतः 4.3.1655cd
धर्मिधर्मत्वरूपस्य संबन्धस्यासमन्वयात् 4.3.1658cd

धर्मिप्रतीतिरेव स्यात्सापि चेहैककर्मिका 4.3.1684cd
धर्मिबुद्धेर्न धर्मेषु बुद्धिभेदः प्रजायते 4.3.1685ab
धर्मी च सर्वधर्माणां न परोक्षस्ततोऽश्ववत् 3.8.42cd
धर्मेण नियतात्मा सञ्जुहोत्यादिस्वकर्मभिः 1.5.2cd
धर्मैश्चतुर्भिर्मूर्ताद्यैर्भूतत्रयवदन्वितम् 2.3.59cd
धर्म्यन्तरस्य चास्तित्वे प्रतिज्ञार्थो न सिध्यति 4.3.1656ab
धर्म्यन्तराश्रितैर्धर्मैर्नान्यो धर्मी विशेष्यते 4.3.1658ab
धर्म्यसिद्धिः प्रतिज्ञायां हेतुश्चानाश्रयो भवेत् 1.2.21ab
धवादावपि तद्वृत्तेर्वृक्षात्मा शिंशपा न हि 4.3.745cd
धातुरूपानुरोधी सन्नसो रक्तादिमेत्यथ 4.3.1231ab
धातू न तु स्वतन्त्रं सन्नावदत्तेजसीत्यतः 3.6.12cd
धातूपसर्गयोरर्थस्त्वत्पक्षे न च लभ्यते 4.3.631cd
धातूपसर्गयोर्मुख्यस्तथार्थोऽप्याश्रितो भवेत् 1.5.288cd
धात्वर्थावेशतः सोऽपि प्राप्ते चास्मिन्न तु स्वतः SV 806cd
धानारुहो यथा वृक्षः साक्षादव्यवधानतः 3.9.138ab
धारणं च धृतिर्ज्ञेया बुद्धयोपात्तस्य वस्तुनः 1.5.113ab
धावतोऽविदुषो दृष्ट्वा मृगतृष्णोदकार्थिनः 4.4.1110ab
धिगङ्गाद्यभिधानैस्तु लिङ्गभूतैरिहेङ्गिताः SV 491ab
धियं तद्देशदुःखित्वाद्दुःखित्वं जायते धियः 2.4.349ab
धियं साक्षीक्षते तस्मात्प्रत्यग्ध्यानादिवर्जितः 4.3.439cd
धियः प्रचोदयेद्यो न उद्यन्प्रज्ञेन्द्रियाणि च 6.3.51ab
धिया धिया हि पुरुषः कर्मभिश्चान्नमात्मनः 1.5.85cd
धिया धियेति कार्यत्वं कृत्स्नस्य जगतः स्वयम् 1.5.331ab
धिया धियेति च तथा प्रागेतदुपपादितम् 4.3.868ab
धिया धियेति लिङ्गाच्च गृह्येते ज्ञानकर्मणी 1.5.20ab
धिया धियेति वाक्येन भोगादेव क्रियोत्थितेः 1.5.251cd
धिया समान इत्येवं यः प्रागात्मोपपादितः 4.3.461cd
धिया समानः सन्नात्मा संसरत्या विमोक्षतः 4.3.821cd
धियोऽन्तःकरणस्येह स्थानं हृदयमिष्यते 2.1.333ab
धियो नो विषये शङ्का व्यभिचारानुसारिणी 4.3.720cd
धीः पाण्डित्यगिरा साक्षादन्वयव्यतिरेकतः 3.5.179cd
धीमनश्चक्षुरादीनि भिन्नरूपाणि सर्वथा 4.3.423cd

धीमानाज्ज्ञानमेवेदमभ्युपेत्य ततोऽपरम् 4.3.539ab
धीरेव चित्स्वरूपेयं प्रथते ग्राहकात्मना 4.3.468ab
धीर्विपर्ययरूपेयं यतः शुक्लादिरूपिणी 1.5.122ab
धीविक्रियासहस्राणां साक्ष्यतोऽहमविक्रियः 1.4.561cd
धीविक्रियासहस्राणां साक्ष्यतोऽहमविक्रियः 4.3.396cd
धीस्वान्तेन्द्रियसंघाते चिदाभासैकवर्त्मना 4.3.398ab
धूमवत्परमार्थत्वमुपायत्वान्न लभ्यते SV 898ab
धूमस्याप्नोति भेदो वा द्वयोर्हेत्वोर्निवर्तते 4.3.755cd
धूमाग्न्योरिव संबन्धस्तयोर्दृष्ट इहात्मनि 4.4.191ab
धूमादिभेदभिन्नानां यथैकत्वं विभावसौ 2.4.301ab
धूमादिलिङ्गेनेहार्थो भवता कोऽनुमीयते 4.3.729cd
धूमादीन्हुतभुक्तद्वत्प्राणादीन्प्रत्यगीश्वरः 2.4.303cd
धूमाभासात्तु बाष्पादेर्यदग्निर्नावगम्यते SV 897ab
धूमार्चिर्विस्फुलिङ्गादि यथापूर्वं विभागतः 2.4.298ab
धूमोऽभ्राणीति सादृश्याद्विद्युदर्चिस्तथैव च 6.2.98cd
धृतिश्रद्धे विना न स्युः कामाद्याः कारणादृते 1.5.112ab
धेनुमित्येव तां तेन सदोपासीत भारतीम् 5.10.3cd
ध्याता ध्यानं तथा ध्येयं त्रयं स्वात्मैकसाक्षिकम् 4.3.411ab
ध्यानादिकारिसाक्षित्वान्नात्मा ध्यानादिकार्यवान् 4.3.409cd
ध्यानादि यदुपन्यस्तं निःशेषानर्थमुक्तये 4.4.779cd
ध्यानादिसंस्कृतं चेतो यदि मुक्तौ प्रणश्यति 4.4.768ab
ध्यानाशङ्कानिवृत्त्यर्थं विज्ञानेनेति भण्यते 2.4.233ab
ध्यायतीत्यादिवाक्येन प्रत्यक्कौटस्थ्यवित्तये 4.3.408cd
ध्यायतीव स कौटस्थ्यात्तथा लेलायतीव च 4.3.409ab
ध्यायतीवेति च तथा निषिद्धैव स्वतो गतिः 4.4.237cd
ध्यायतो विषयान्पुंसः सङ्गस्तेषूपजायते 4.4.227ab
ध्येयं तदोमिति सदा पक्षयोरुभयोरपि 5.1.122cd
ध्येयत्वेनेह सर्वेषां खरोष्ट्रादेरपीक्षणात् 5.1.80cd
ध्रुवान्तमन्त्राम्नायोक्त एष इत्यभिधीयते 4.4.976ab
ध्रुवायां संहतिर्नाम्नो हृद्येवं सर्वसंहतिः 3.9.76cd
ध्रुवास्य देह एवायं जीवन्स्यात्षोडशी कला 1.5.220cd
ध्वंसमात्रस्य सिद्ध्यर्थमारब्धोपनिषन्मया 1.4.599cd

ध्वंसमेति ततः संज्ञा नाविद्योत्थावशिष्यते 2.4.437cd
ध्वंसादव्यतिरेकेऽपि धियो नित्यत्वमापतेत् 1.2.19cd
ध्वंसिनोरिव सादृश्यं स्थायिनोरपि नेष्यते 1.2.67ab
ध्वस्तत्वात्तस्य सर्वस्य प्रत्यग्याथात्म्यदर्शनात् 4.4.287cd
ध्वस्तध्वान्तस्य विज्ञानादतो हेतुफलात्मनाम् 3.2.30ab
ध्वस्तराजत्वसंस्कारो वसञ्शबरसद्मनि 2.1.509cd
ध्वस्तराजाभिमानः सन्मुग्धो वनमुपेयिवान् 2.1.508ab
ध्वस्ताज्ञानतदुत्थोऽयं संविन्मात्रसतत्त्वकः 2.5.61ab
ध्वस्तातिशयनिष्ठत्वाल्लोके सातिशयात्मनः 4.3.1878ab
ध्वस्तात्ममोहतत्कार्यः स्यात्प्रबोधे यदा तदा 4.3.1272ab
ध्वस्तात्माज्ञानतत्कार्याः प्रत्यग्याथात्म्यबोधतः 3.8.68ab
ध्वस्तात्मान्ध्यस्य विदुषः सम्यग्ज्ञानोदये भवेत् 2.4.472cd
ध्वस्ताध्यात्मादिसंभेदः प्रत्यङ्मोहैकमात्रभाक् 3.2.119ab
ध्वस्तान्ध्यस्यापि सा चेत्स्यादनिर्मोक्षः प्रसज्यते 1.4.96cd
ध्वस्तापि पुनरेवैति तज्जरागादिदर्शनात् 4.4.883cd
ध्वस्ता बाधिष्यतेऽविद्या विद्यामित्यत्र का प्रमा 4.4.917cd
ध्वस्ताविद्यस्य चैकात्म्यात्कैवल्येन परायणम् 3.9.165cd
ध्वस्ताविद्यस्य तन्न स्यात्तस्यैकात्म्यस्वभावतः 1.4.1560cd
ध्वस्ताशेषतमस्कत्वात्सम्यग्ज्ञानप्रसूतितः 4.4.276ab
ध्वस्ताशेषविकारस्य ब्रह्मणोऽविद्ययात्मनः 2.4.340cd
ध्वस्तेऽज्ञाने सकार्येऽथ यद्रूपं तदिहोच्यते 4.4.1324cd
ध्वस्तेऽतो ज्ञानतोऽज्ञाने ब्रह्मास्मीति भवेत्फलम् 1.4.862cd
ध्वस्तौ ध्वस्तिरनर्थानां पुमर्थश्च समाप्यते 1.4.188cd
ध्वान्तनाशोऽथ विद्यायाः कार्यं चेदभिधीयते 1.4.1745ab
ध्वान्तमात्रनिरासेन न ततोऽन्यान्यथा मतिः 1.4.1451cd
ध्वान्तादिघस्मरे प्रत्यक्चैतन्यात्मैकनिष्ठिते 1.4.1456ab
ध्वान्तादिविषयान्तोऽर्थो जडत्वान्नात्मसिद्धिकृत् 4.3.59ab
ध्वान्तापध्वंसिरविणा न तमः सह जायते 1.4.80cd
ध्वान्तोच्छित्तौ विकर्तृत्वं कर्मणस्त्वनुवर्तते 3.2.59cd
नंष्टृतन्त्रो विनाशोऽपि गन्तृतन्त्रा गतिर्यथा 1.2.42ab
न कंचनेति कामो यः स्वप्नजाग्रदवस्थयोः 4.3.1165ab
न कंचनेति वाक्येन तयोरेव ग्रहः श्रुतेः 4.3.1169cd

न कथं चन संभाव्यमनुवादत्वकारणात् 4.3.1747cd
न कपित्थादिवत्तत्त्वं स्वतोऽनेकस्वभावकम् 4.3.1800ab
न करोति क्षतिं तद्वद्गर्भ एजतु ते सुखम् 6.4.109cd
न करोति यतः स्वप्ने क्रियामिव समीक्षते 4.3.1009ab
न कर्तृता प्रमात्रादेः साक्ष्यत्वेनैव तत्क्षयात् 3.4.111cd
न कर्म कारणं मुक्तेः क्षयिष्णुत्वसमन्वयात् 1.4.1693ab
न कर्म कारणं मुक्तेर्नाग्निर्दाहज्वरापनुत् 6.2.8ab
न कर्म कारणं मुक्तेर्नाग्निस्तापस्य भेषजम् 2.4.55cd
न कर्म कुरुते स्वप्ने कारकाणामसंभवात् 4.3.1004ab
न कर्मणा कनीयस्ता महत्त्वं चान्तरात्मनः 6.2.9ab
न कर्मणा कनीयस्ता वृद्धिर्वा नान्तरात्मनः 3.3.55ab
न कर्मणा कनीयस्ता वृद्धिर्वा नान्तरात्मनः 4.3.1835ab
न कर्मणा भवेन्मुक्तिर्नापि चाग्निरागाश्रयात् 1.4.1669ab
न कर्मणामनारम्भात्तथा च स्मृतिशासनम् 4.4.1092cd
न कर्मणामनारम्भान्नैष्कर्म्यं पुरुषोऽश्नुते 1.4.1585ab
न कर्म तत्फलं वेत्ति न च कस्यैति संगतिम् 3.2.142cd
न कर्म पूर्वस्कन्धेषु नष्टत्वादुपपद्यते 3.2.151ab
न कर्मफलमप्यत्र स्वप्ने तद्धेत्वसंभवात् 4.3.917ab
न कर्ममय एवायं पुमान्सर्वमयः कुतः 4.4.210cd
न कर्मव्यापृतिर्मुक्तावाप्त्यादीनामभावतः SV 366ab
न कर्मोपचयोऽतोऽत्र स्वप्ने जाग्रद्वदिष्यते 4.3.1042ab
न कश्चित्फलभेदोऽत्र तस्मादुभयथापि सन् 1.4.1668cd
न कश्चिदपि दोषः स्याद्वचस्यस्मिन्मनागपि SV 1045cd
न कश्चिदपि दोषोऽत्र पूर्वोऽतः प्रसज्यते 1.4.1440cd
न कश्चिदपि दोषोऽत्र यथा तदभिधीयते 5.1.36ab
न कश्चिदपि दोषोऽत्र यथैतदुपपत्स्यते 1.4.1123ab
न कश्चिदपि शब्दोऽत्र साक्षाद्ब्रह्मणि वर्तते 2.3.242cd
न कश्चिदपि संबन्धो नीरूपस्यासदात्मनः SV 946cd
न कश्चिदपि संभाव्यो यथोक्तन्यायगौरवात् 1.4.922ab
न कश्चिदुपयोगोऽत्र कामानां विद्यते स्थितौ 4.4.457ab
न कश्चिन्नियतो भावो मृत्युरित्युपदिश्यते 3.2.15ab
न कस्यांचिदवस्थायामात्मा लोकेऽप्रियो मतः 2.4.81ab

न कामयन्ते नेच्छन्ति पुत्रोत्पत्त्यादिलक्षणाः 4.4.1098ab
न कारकं न धात्वर्थो नापि यत्स्यात्क्रियाफलम् 3.9.151cd
न कारणं विना कार्यं न कार्यं कारणं विना 1.4.363ab
न कारणातिवर्त्यस्ति कार्यं जगति कुत्रचित् 1.4.483ab
न कार्यं करणं चास्य किंचिदात्मीयमिष्यते 3.7.32cd
न कार्यं कारणं चातः कटाक्षेणापि वीक्षते 4.3.1321cd
न कार्यं कारणं वास्ति प्रत्यग्वृत्तव्यपेक्षया 4.3.1531cd
न कार्यं स्यात्स्वभावो वा तयोरत्यन्तभेदतः 4.3.778cd
न कार्यकारणं वास्य यत्कर्तृत्वादिकारणम् 4.4.1002ab
न कार्यप्रलयो दृष्टो यस्मादन्यत्र कारणात् 2.4.354cd
न कार्ये कारणे वातो वस्तुतत्त्वं समीक्ष्यते 4.3.400cd
न कार्ये कारणे वापि तदभावेऽथवान्यतः 4.3.367ab
न कार्यैवात्मधीः पुंभिः कृतत्वादेव हेतुतः 4.4.933cd
न किंचिज्जान इत्येवं पृष्टो वक्ति प्रमां विना SV 993cd
न किंचित्साहसं त्वत्र प्रत्यक्षश्रुतिवाक्यतः SV 312ab
न किंचित्स्यात्परिज्ञातं नानात्मातः प्रमित्सितः 1.4.972cd
न किंचिदवशिष्टं स्यादिति यद्वत्तथेह तत् 3.2.38cd
न किंचिन्नः सुरैः प्रत्तमृणित्वं येन नो भवेत् 1.4.1561cd
न किंचिन्न जहातीति प्रसिद्धेरिदमुच्यते 3.2.37cd
न कृत्स्नमिति तद्ग्राह्यं तत्प्रमाणाद्यसंभवात् 1.4.1097ab
न केवलं क्रिया न स्यात्कर्मणां प्रत्युताक्रिया SV 364cd
न केवलं त्वाष्ट्रमेव कक्ष्यमप्यब्रवीन्मधु 2.5.114cd
न केवलं प्राण आत्मा नाम्नोऽप्यात्मेति भण्यते 1.3.295cd
न केवलमिदं ज्ञानं कर्मसाधननिस्पृहम् 4.5.25ab
न क्रिया कर्तृसंबन्धात्फलं नानिष्टरूपतः SV 623ab
न क्रियाकार्यविरहे कारणं सिध्यति क्वचित् 1.4.195ab
न क्रियात्वं फलत्वं वा नापि कारकरूपता SV 237cd
नक्षत्रलोकशब्देन ये पूर्वं प्रतिपादिताः 4.3.1859ab
नक्षत्राणि स्फुलिङ्गाः स्युस्तस्मिन्नित्यादि पूर्ववत् 6.2.103cd
न क्षयो ज्ञानकार्यस्य कृतकत्वाद्यसंभवात् 1.4.1686cd
न क्षीयते कर्म तस्य सदैकात्म्यावसानतः 1.4.1707cd
न क्षीयते कर्म तस्याद्वैतत्वादेव कारणात् 1.4.1705cd

नखाग्रावधिका यस्मात्संवित्पुंसोऽभिजायते 1.4.635ab
न गन्तव्यं पथानेन गृहाणेमं निधिं तथा SV 593cd
नगराध्वोपदेशस्य शेषत्वं प्रतिपद्यते SV 401cd
नगराप्तौ तदध्वस्थग्रामादिगुणगीरिव SV 403cd
नगराप्तौ तु माभावात्प्रयतेत पुमान्कुतः SV 405cd
न घटादेर्घटत्वादि घटाद्यभ्याससंश्रयम् 2.4.202cd
न च कर्त्राद्यनिर्मुक्तौ मुक्तिः संभाव्यतेऽन्यतः SV 57cd
न च कर्मफलत्वेन पारिशेष्यं प्रसिध्यति 3.3.113cd
न च कर्मातिरेकेण मुक्त्यभ्युदयसाधनम् SV 33cd
न च कश्चित्फले भेदो मेयमानप्रमातृषु 1.4.265cd
न च कामाश्रयत्वेऽन्यत्प्रमाणं किंचिदीक्ष्यते 4.4.466ab
न च कारणमात्रत्वं रूपमिष्टं परात्मनः 4.4.499ab
न च कारणसंसर्गो नाशोऽज्ञानस्य भण्यते 4.4.923ab
न च कार्यपरत्वेऽपि पदानां संहतिः स्थिता SV 872ab
न च कालत्रयास्पर्शवाच्यत्वं कार्यलक्षणम् SV 624ab
न च कुम्भादिवद्दृष्टिरात्मनोऽव्यतिरेकतः 3.2.104ab
न च कृत्स्नतमोहानिः सर्वज्ञानोदयो न च 4.4.869cd
न च केवलकर्मभ्यो मुक्तिर्युक्त्योपपद्यते SV 437ab
न चक्षुरादिदृष्टीनामन्तर्देहसमीक्षणम 2.1.298ab
न चक्षुषा गृह्यते नापि वाचा नान्यैर्देवैस्तपसा कर्मणा वा 4.4.1258ab
न च गोदोहनन्यायः काम्यकर्मसु युज्यते 3.3.51ab
न च चैतन्यमित्किंचिच्चैतन्याल्लभ्यते पृथक् 4.3.211cd
न च जाड्यातिरेकेण ह्यविद्या काचिदिष्यते 1.4.256ab
न च ज्ञातिष्वधिपतिः स्पर्धमानोऽनवेदिना 1.3.289cd
न च ज्ञात्रनुरोधिन्या दृष्ट्याज्ञानासमन्वितम् 1.4.1385ab
न च तत्त्वे विशेषोऽस्ति कटकादीव हेमनि SV 353cd
न च तत्प्रार्थनीयं मे भूरि यद्विद्यते मम 6.2.63ab
न च तद्भावभावित्वं व्यतिरेकाप्रसिद्धितः 4.3.243ab
न च तादृङ्मृतस्यास्ति यस्मात्तस्य पुनर्भवः 3.9.139cd
न च तार्किकयुक्त्यापि प्रतीचीहासुखात्मता 1.4.575ab
न च तेनैव तस्यैव विनाश उपपद्यते 4.3.1555ab
न च तेषु निरुद्धेषु किंचिन्नः स्यात्प्रयोजनम् 1.4.1535ab

न च त्र्यन्नात्मसंप्राप्तिः कैवल्यमिति युज्यते 1.5.341ab
न च दुःखादिधीवत्स्याज्ज्ञातस्यैवानुभूतितः 1.4.260ab
न च देहान्तरं कृत्वा राज्ञो भृत्या इवासते 4.3.1955ab
न च द्रष्टात्मनोऽन्योऽस्ति द्रष्ट्रन्तरनिषेधनात् 2.4.136ab
न च द्रष्ट्रोर्द्वयोर्लोके द्रष्टृदृश्यत्वसंगतिः 2.4.136cd
न च धर्म्यन्तरासत्त्वे प्रत्यगात्मातिरेकिणः 4.3.1655ab
न च धीजन्ममात्रेण परमात्मप्रबोधवत् 1.3.381ab
न च नानात्वकृल्लोके संयोगोऽभेदकारणात् 1.4.553ab
न च नाशस्य कालोऽस्ति क्षणमध्ये तथा बहिः 4.3.611ab
न च नास्ति पदार्थानां लोकेऽसाधारणः क्वचित् 4.3.152ab
न च निर्विषयं तत्स्यान्मेयभेदात्त्वगादिवत् 2.1.587cd
न च पापैः कनीयस्ता तस्यासाध्यत्वहेतुतः 4.4.1183cd
न च प्रत्यक्षवत्सिद्धं स्वानुभूतिसमाश्रयात् 1.4.288cd
न च प्रत्यक्षविज्ञानात्स्मृतेर्भेदं लभेमहि 1.4.465ab
न च प्रत्यग्धियं मुक्त्वा पराग्बुद्धिर्मितिर्भवेत् 1.4.488cd
न च प्रत्यग्धिया द्रष्टुं पराग्वस्त्विह शक्यते 1.4.966ab
न च प्रमाणं तत्रास्ति कल्प्यं च स्यात्फलान्तरम् 2.1.505ab
न च प्रमाणतः सिद्धिरज्ञातत्वस्य शक्यते 4.3.547ab
न च प्रमाणतास्तित्वमीदृक्तस्मान्न युज्यते SV 939cd
न च प्रमाणनास्तित्वमीदृक्तस्मान्न युज्यते 4.3.1710cd
न च प्रमाणसद्भावः सर्वस्य ज्ञानमात्रतः 4.3.659cd
न च प्रमादपाठोऽयं सर्वेषामविगानतः 3.4.184ab
न च प्रमान्तरैः साक्षादज्ञाते ब्रह्मवस्तुनि 4.4.816ab
न च प्रयोजनैकत्वलक्षणात्रैकवाक्यता SV 832ab
न च प्रवर्तकत्वेऽपि वाक्यस्याङ्गीकृते त्वया SV 601ab
न च प्राणातिरेकेण देवतान्योपपद्यते 2.1.135cd
न च प्रादुर्भवत्यस्य ज्ञानमन्यद्विशेषवत् 4.3.1569ab
न च प्रामाणिकं ज्ञानमुत्पत्त्यादौ नियुज्यते 4.4.791ab
न च बद्धस्ततोऽन्योऽस्ति यस्य नश्यति बन्धनम् 4.4.321cd
न च ब्रह्मपरिज्ञानहुताशप्लुष्टमण्वपि 1.4.1541ab
न च ब्रह्मोपदेशस्य सर्वभावातिरेकतः 1.4.1247ab
न च भावातिरेकेण भाववत्सिद्धिमश्नुते SV 929cd

न च भेदमनाश्रित्य स्वभावादि प्रसिध्यति 4.3.804ab
न च भेदस्य वस्तुत्वं वस्तुतत्त्वानपेक्षणात् SV 920cd
न च भोक्त्रन्तरं प्राणाद्गार्ग्येणेहाभ्युपेयते 2.1.119ab
न च मात्रादिसद्भावस्तस्यात्यन्तमदृष्टतः 1.4.271ab
न च मानात्प्रसिद्धिः स्यात्कूर्मलोमादिवस्तुनः 1.4.241ab
न च मानानपेक्षस्य सिद्धिरभ्युपगम्यते 1.4.1098ab
न च मानान्तरादिष्टं तयोस्तुल्यस्वभावतः 4.4.339cd
न च मानान्तरैर्मेये मानस्येष्टा विरोधिता 4.4.792ab
न च मानेन विषये बोधितेऽन्वेषणं पुनः SV 848ab
न च मिथ्यात्वधीर्भेदे जन्मनैवेह कस्यचित् 5.1.98ab
न च मिथ्याधियोऽभ्यासात्सम्यग्ज्ञानसमुद्भवः 4.4.821ab
न च मोहादिवत्प्रत्यक्तथा दर्शनमर्हति 4.3.105cd
न च यूपादिवच्छक्यं वेदेनैव समर्पणम् SV 657ab
न च रागादिसंसिद्धौ मानव्यापार ईक्ष्यते 1.4.264cd
न च वस्तुनि मानत्व उदाहरणमिष्यते SV 448ab
न च वस्तुस्वरूपं तद्बाधात्तस्य प्रमाणतः 1.4.431ab
न च वाक्याद्विपर्यस्ता यदि वा संशयात्मिका 1.3.72ab
न च विप्रतिपद्यन्ते वादिनोऽनुभवात्मनि 1.4.1398ab
न च वेदान्तवाक्योत्थज्ञानस्येहास्ति बाधकम् 2.1.551ab
न च वेदान्तसिद्धान्ते परमात्मातिरेकतः 4.4.38ab
न च वेदैकमूलत्वविरहात्स्यात्प्रमाणता 4.4.1149ab
न च वेदोक्तितो वेदः श्रद्धेयार्थ इहेष्यते 2.4.325ab
न च शक्यं प्रतिज्ञातुं जन्मारभ्यामृतेर्नृभिः SV 70cd
न च श्रुत्यावयरतत्र तेन स्यान्न समुच्चयः SV 366cd
न च संविद्द्वयाभासो नानुमेयं फलं क्वचित् SV 1063cd
न च सत्तेति सामान्यं प्रत्ययार्थासमीक्षणात् 3.8.20cd
न च सत्त्वादिमात्रेण रूप्यादिमितिसंभवः 1.4.278cd
न च संन्यसनादेव सिद्धिं समधिगच्छति 1.4.1585cd
न च संपत्तमोहन्त्री मिथ्याज्ञानात्मकत्वतः 1.4.1260cd
न च संबन्धमात्रं स्याद्यथोक्तादेव कारणात् 4.3.730cd
न च संमोहविध्वस्तौ यथावस्त्ववबोधतः 1.4.765ab
न च सापेक्षताप्यस्ति मितेर्मानत्वतः क्वचित् SV 681ab

न च सामान्यतो ज्ञानं ल्यबन्तेनाभिधीयते 4.4.794ab
न च सामान्यबुद्ध्येह भेदबुद्धिर्निवर्तते 4.3.1642ab
न च सिद्धत्वमात्रेण शङ्क्यते मान्तरं क्वचित् SV 680ab
न च सौगतसिद्धान्तस्तत्सिद्धौ मित्यभावतः 1.4.246ab
न च स्कन्धातिरेकेण स्थिरः कश्चिदपीष्यते 3.2.153ab
न च स्मृतिस्तदेवेदमित्येवमनुभूतितः 4.3.677ab
न च स्मृतेः प्रमाणत्वं क्वचित्सिद्धान्त इष्यते 4.4.959ab
न च स्वप्नविनिर्माणे देवताव्यापृतिर्भवेत् 4.3.1137ab
न च स्वरूपे भेदोऽस्ति कस्यचिद्वस्तुनः क्वचित् 4.3.1648ab
न च स्वर्गादिकार्याणां प्रयाजार्थसमानता SV 409ab
न च स्वाभाविको धर्मः कस्यचिन्नास्ति वस्तुनः 4.4.319ab
न च हेतुफलत्वं स्यादेककालीनयोस्तयोः 4.3.655ab
न चांशत्रयशून्येह भावनेष्टा परीक्षकैः SV 251cd
न चाकर्तुः फलं गौण्या वृत्त्या चेत्सुतरां न तत् SV 1053cd
न चागमस्य तात्पर्यमेवंभूतेऽस्ति वस्तुनि 1.6.53ab
न चागमस्य स्वातन्त्र्यं युक्त्युक्तेरपनुद्यते 3.1.6ab
न चाग्निहोत्रशेषत्वमुक्तदृष्टेरिहेष्यते 6.2.126ab
न चाङ्गनिर्णयोक्त्यैव निर्णयं मन्यतेऽङ्गिनः 4.3.968ab
न चाजानन्स्वसाध्यार्थं विद्वान्कश्चित्प्रवर्तते SV 305ab
न चाज्ञानातिरेकेण व्यवधानान्तरं मतम् 3.3.92ab
न चात्मकाम इत्यत्र कामाधारत्व आत्मनः 4.4.462ab
न चात्मनो निरंशस्य तथासंसारिणः स्वतः 2.1.528ab
न चात्मन्यप्रसिद्धे स्यात्संसारस्य प्रसिद्धता 2.4.141ab
न चात्मविषयं ज्ञानं वेदान्तेषु विधीयते 1.4.797ab
न चात्मानुभवादन्यो विषयः कश्चिदिष्यते SV 471ab
न चात्यन्तासतो जन्म कुर्याल्लोकेऽपि कारणम् 3.2.91ab
न चात्र चोदितः कालः संख्या वा येन निश्चयः SV 836ab
न चात्र प्रत्यभिज्ञास्ति मिथ्यापरिणतेस्तव 4.3.131ab
न चात्रानुभवो लुप्तो न जानामीति बोधनात् SV 996ab
न चानधिगतत्वस्य प्रसिद्धिः स्यात्प्रमाणतः 4.4.895ab
न चानपनयन्यागः कामिनः स्वर्गकामिताम् SV 534ab
न चानवच्छिन्नतनोर्निर्विभागात्मवस्तुनः 1.4.537ab

न चानवयवं वस्तु क्वचिदप्युपलभ्यते 1.4.589ab
न चानवस्थया सिद्धिरभिप्रेतस्य वस्तुनः 4.3.155ab
न चानवस्थेहाप्नोति सर्वमृत्युत्वकारणात् 3.2.16cd
न चानागतता मेये मिथ्याज्ञानमतो भवेत् 1.4.302cd
न चानाहितसन्मानस्वतश्चिन्मात्रविग्रहात् 4.3.174ab
न चानिवर्तकं ज्ञानं प्रत्यङ्मोहस्य युज्यते 1.4.1523ab
न चानुभूतिः प्रात्यक्ष्यमन्यतोऽपेक्षते जडात् 2.1.142cd
न चानुमानतस्तस्य सद्भावोऽप्यवधार्यते 4.3.464ab
न चानुमाने दोषोऽपि तत्र कश्चिद्विभाव्यते 4.3.716cd
न चानुष्ठेयता तस्य मनागप्युपपद्यते 1.3.84cd
न चानेकस्वभावांशवत्त्वं ज्ञानस्य संमतम् 4.3.698ab
न चान्यतम एतेषां मोक्षो युक्त्योपपद्यते 3.3.27ab
न चान्यथाङ्गता दृष्टा प्रधानानुपकारिणः SV 833cd
न चान्यदीयव्यापारे ह्यन्योऽशक्तेर्नियुज्यते 2.4.184ab
न चान्यस्मिन्विभक्त्यर्थे यथोक्तेनैव हेतुना 4.3.629ab
न चान्या व्यापृतिस्तस्य कार्यसिद्धौ त्वयेष्यते SV 647ab
न चापर उपायोऽस्ति मेयसद्भावसिद्धिकृत् 1.4.227ab
न चापि कर्मकाण्डोक्तिः स्वार्थे न कुरुते प्रमाम् 2.1.571ab
न चापि केवलं कर्म पुंसः स्यादाश्रयो यतः 3.2.147ab
न चापि चिद्विशिष्टत्वं प्रत्यक्षेणोपलभ्यते 2.1.140ab
न चापि तदभावश्च नेत्यस्थूलादिशास्त्रतः 3.9.152ab
न चापि त्रयसद्भावे मिथ्याज्ञानं जगत्यपि 1.4.446ab
न चापि न प्रवर्तन्ते पुरुषाः काम्यकर्मसु 2.1.577ab
न चापि नित्यप्राप्तत्वात्तयोरस्तीह संभवः 4.4.937ab
न चापि मानव्यापारव्यपेक्षैकात्म्यनिश्चितौ 2.1.172ab
न चापि मिथ्याविज्ञानं परिच्छेदकमिष्यते 3.2.85ab
न चापि मुख्यया वृत्त्या साध्येऽसति जगत्यपि 2.4.188ab
न चापि वाक्याद्विज्ञानं कर्तृद्वारेण गच्छति SV 334ab
न चापि वास्तवी सिद्धिः प्रमात्रादिविरोधिनी 1.4.1289ab
न चापि सर्वसामान्यविशेषार्थावबुद्धये 1.6.92ab
न चापि स्वप्रमेयेऽस्ति मानानां बोधहेतुतः 4.4.815ab
न चापीह निरंशेषु भिन्नाभिन्नत्वकल्पने 4.3.1779ab

न चापीहागमाभासोऽचोदनालक्षणत्वतः 1.3.69ab
न चाप्यतिक्रमार्थत्वं जय्य इत्यस्य युक्तिमत् 1.4.1741ab
न चाप्यनात्मना सिद्धिरज्ञातस्येह वस्तुनः 4.4.896ab
न चाप्यविद्यानाशोऽत्र संसर्गः कारणात्मनि 2.4.196ab
न चाप्यविद्यामसतीं शक्नुतः कामकर्मणी 3.2.90ab
न चाप्यसत्यता तस्मात्तेषां सत्यं परं पदम् 2.3.247cd
न चाप्यस्यार्थवादत्वं विधिना वाक्यभेदतः SV 341ab
न चाप्याख्यायिकारूपमनुग्राह्यं श्रुतौ मतम् SV 846ab
न चाप्यात्मन्यविज्ञातेऽहंबुद्धेः सिद्धता तव SV 1072ab
न चाप्युपासनपदं कृत्स्नेऽपि ब्राह्मणे श्रुतम् 2.5.77cd
न चाप्यैकात्म्यशास्त्रस्य तैर्विकल्पसमुच्चयौ SV 912ab
न चाप्रमेयमिति तच्छशशृङ्गादिवन्मतम् 4.3.108ab
न चाभावप्रमाणात्सा सति मातर्यभावमा SV 550ab
न चाभावमुखोऽनात्मा नान्वयेनाप्यतो दृशि 2.4.272cd
न चाभावावसाय्येतदभावस्यापि भाववत् 4.4.158ab
न चाभीष्टत्वकार्यत्वमभिन्नं व्यतिरेकतः SV 514ab
न चाभेदेऽस्ति संव्याप्तिरैकात्म्यादेव कारणात् 2.4.135cd
न चाभ्यासात्प्रमाणानि कुर्वन्त्यर्थावबोधनम् 1.4.1511cd
न चाभ्यासाद्यपेक्षापि स्वतोमुक्तत्वकारणात् 2.4.202ab
न चायं नेति नेतीति कारणत्वादिहोच्यते 3.8.36ab
न चार्थवादता तेषामन्याशेषत्वकारणात् 1.4.1524cd
न चार्थवादतैतस्यां जुह्वामिव फलश्रुतेः 1.3.83cd
न चार्धवैशसं युक्तं तत्त्वज्ञाने विवक्षिते 1.4.1276ab
न चावच्छेदमानित्वं विदुषोऽस्त्यासुरत्वतः 5.1.108ab
न चावयविनो वृत्तिर्निरंशैकत्वहेतुतः 2.1.408ab
न चावाच्यं भवत्पक्षे किंचिद्वस्त्वभ्युपेयते 4.3.641ab
न चाविद्यातिरेकेण कौटस्थ्यात्प्रत्यगात्मनः 4.3.1260ab
न चाविद्यातिरेकेण मुक्तेर्बन्धोऽन्य इष्यते 3.3.22ab
न चाविद्यानिरास्यत्र प्रत्यग्याथात्म्यबोधतः 2.4.187ab
न चाविद्यासमुच्छित्तिर्ज्ञानोत्पत्त्यातिरेकतः 2.4.195ab
न चाविशुद्धे द्वैतार्थे शक्यमद्वैतमीक्षितुम् 3.2.61cd
न चाविषयविज्ञानमनाकारं च भाव्यते 2.4.203ab

न चावृत्तिव्यपेक्षः सन्व्यञ्जकत्वात्तमोपनुत् 4.4.953cd
न चावृत्त्या प्रमोत्पत्तिं प्रमाणानि प्रकुर्वते 1.4.882cd
न चाश्रमान्तरं युक्तं मुनेर्व्युत्थायिनः सतः 3.5.195ab
न चाश्रौषं श्रुतेर्वाक्यात्कर्म मोक्षफलं क्वचित् 3.3.53cd
न चासत्त्वं घटस्यैवं प्रागभावो घटो न च 1.2.118ab
न चासद्विषया काचिद्बुद्धिर्जगति वीक्ष्यते 1.3.68ab
न चासावस्ति तेनान्यदात्मज्योतिः प्रतीयताम् 4.3.433cd
न चासौ बोध्यमानोऽपि प्रत्यबुध्यत नाम तत् 2.1.121ab
न चासौ लभ्यते तादृग्भविता हि विनश्वरः 4.3.630cd
न चास्ति कश्चिद्दृष्टान्तः सर्वशून्यत्ववादिनः 1.2.21cd
न चास्त्येकविषयत्वं प्रत्यक्षवचसोर्यतः SV 203ab
न चाहंप्रत्ययात्सिद्धिरात्मनः स्यात्कदा चनः SV 1057ab
न चाहंबुद्धिगम्योऽर्थो दृष्टो देहातिरेकतः 4.3.119ab
न चाहंबुद्धिनिर्ग्राह्यमिदंधीग्राह्यगोचरः 4.3.204ab
न चेच्छुक्तितमोजस्य ज्ञानस्यापि प्रमाणता 1.2.24cd
न चेज्जामि भवेद्वाक्यं पृथग्लोकैषणाग्रहात् 3.5.116cd
न चेत्करोत्युपनिषत्प्रमामित्यभिधीयते 2.1.546ab
न चेत्कारकतन्त्रोऽर्थो ज्ञातस्यानुष्ठितिः कथम् SV 1029ab
न चेत्कारकभेदोऽत्र कालभेदोऽथवेक्ष्यते 4.3.654ab
न चेत्कार्यं नियोगः स्यात्कोऽर्थो यागादिसिद्धितः SV 740ab
न चेत्कार्यो विनाशः स्यान्नाशोऽकार्येण नेष्यते 1.2.37cd
न चेत्तत्संपदा किं स्याद्येन तामनुरुध्यसे 1.4.1251cd
न चेत्तित्यक्षितं सर्वं प्रतिप्रसवगीर्भवेत् 1.5.308cd
न चेत्शक्नुतोऽविद्यां रक्षितुं कामकर्मणी 3.2.94ab
न चेत्परमतां यातः कथं परमतोच्यताम् 5.14.10ab
न चेत्प्रमाणतः सिद्धिरस्याव्याकृतरूपिणः 1.4.218cd
न चेत्समर्पितं साक्षाद्वस्तु श्रुत्या यथोदितम् 4.4.785ab
न चेत्समूहो वस्त्वस्ति एकैकत्वात्समूहिनाम् 4.3.1681ab
न चेत्संभाव्यते कर्त्रा पुमर्थः कस्यचिद्विधेः SV 1039ab
न चेदं दर्शनं गौणमग्निर्माणवको यथा 4.3.1461ab
न चेदं स्मरणाज्जातं नापि सामान्यहेतुजम् 1.4.448ab
न चेदग्नेः प्रकाशादिस्वभावोऽभ्युपगम्यते 4.4.318ab

न चेदथ परं विद्मः शास्त्राचार्यानुसारतः 4.4.625ab
न चेदनुभवव्याप्तिः सुषुप्तस्याभ्युपेयते 3.4.103ab
न चेदभावः कार्योऽर्थः सिद्धेऽर्थे मानता भवेत् SV 1031cd
न चेदर्थसजातीयं सर्वार्थग्रहणं भवेत् 2.4.365ab
न चेदात्माभिसंबन्धः संसारोऽयं समीक्ष्यते 2.4.142ab
न चेदात्मेतिधीमानात्प्रतीचोऽन्योऽर्थ ईक्ष्यते 4.3.114ab
न चेदानींतनाद्बोधाद्बोदाभावगतिर्भवेत् SV 998ab
न चेदायतनाद्युक्तमेकपाद्ब्रह्म तर्हि तत् 4.1.15ab
न चेदारब्धकार्येषु ज्ञानस्वातन्त्र्यमिष्यते 1.4.1534ab
न चेदुत्पत्तिरसतो न विनाशः सतस्तथा 4.3.608ab
न चेदृशं प्रमाणत्वं दृष्टमन्यत्र कुत्रचित् SV 858ab
न चेदेवं फलं तत्स्याद्वाक्तालुगलशोषणम् 4.4.964cd
न चेद्युक्तं फलं तस्य तदभावेऽपि चात्ययः 1.5.248cd
न चेद्वः सर्वसिद्धान्तो नश्येत्सैकतकूपवत् 1.2.78cd
न चेद्वक्ष्यसि तं मे त्वं मूर्धा ते विपतिष्यति 3.9.118ab
न चेद्वाक्योत्थविज्ञानपरिच्छेद्यं तदिष्यते 1.4.807ab
न चेद्विरुध्यतेऽथोच्चैर्विरोधः किमितीर्यते 2.1.593cd
न चेद्वीप्सा तदा वाक्यद्वयमेतद्विवक्षितम् 2.3.203ab
न चेन्द्रियाणि ते सन्ति प्रत्यक्षैकप्रमाणिनः 4.3.241ab
न चेप्सिततमत्वं स्याद्द्रष्टुर्दृष्टेरसंभवात् 3.4.180ab
न चेश्वरातिरेकेण कश्चित्स्रष्टाभ्युपेयते 2.4.321ab
न चेश्वरे स्थितिस्तस्य शास्त्रानारम्भसक्तितः 3.2.143ab
न चेह परिणामः स्यादुत्तरस्कन्धसंगतौ 3.2.151cd
न चेह राजता धर्माः कुतो ज्ञानं तदाकृति 1.4.453ab
न चेह लोकशब्देन कश्चिदन्योऽभिधीयते 1.4.1771ab
न चेह लौकिको जल्पः प्रष्टृभेदो यतो भवेत् 3.5.7cd
न चेह वास्तवं रूपं तदध्यासेन बाध्यते 1.4.252ab
न चेहावसरोऽस्त्यस्य सम्यग्ज्ञानस्य कश्चन 1.4.98ab
न चेहाविदुषोऽपि स्यादृणित्वं हेत्वसंभवात् 1.4.1561ab
न चेहोभयमप्यस्ति कुतो मिथ्येति भण्यते 1.3.57ab
न चैकत्रैकदा स्थानं विरोधाज्जन्मनाशयोः 3.2.152cd
न चैकबुद्धिबाधेन द्व्यादिधीरुपजायते 4.3.1679ab

न चैकमेव सद्वाक्यं करोति न करोति च 2.1.556ab
न चैकात्म्यपरिज्ञानमभ्यासापेक्षमिष्यते SV 438ab
न चैकात्म्यस्वभावेन कुतस्तन्मानगोचरः 1.4.218ef
न चैकात्म्याभ्युपायस्य मिथ्यात्वमिह शङ्क्यते SV 894ab
न चैतदिष्टं देवानां मर्त्यैरुपरि वर्तनम् 1.4.1581cd
न चैवं युज्यते वक्तुं द्वयोरपि मितित्वतः 4.4.817cd
न चैवं सति मानानां द्व्यर्थता स्यात्कथं चन 1.3.60ab
न चोक्तज्ञानकर्मभ्यः सा निवृत्तिः प्रसिध्यति 1.4.10cd
न चोच्छिन्नात्ममोहस्य सदैवात्मधियः स्थितेः 1.3.102ab
न चोत्पत्त्यादिमत्किंचित्तत्र साक्षात्फलं श्रुतम् 3.3.75cd
न चोत्सर्गापवादोऽपि साक्षाद्वेदग्रहश्रवात् 2.4.311cd
न चोद्गीथादिविषयज्ञानवत्कर्मसंगतिः SV 332ab
न चोपक्रमसंहारविरुद्धोक्तिः प्रशस्यते 1.4.1266cd
न चोपपद्यते मानात्तयोरेकात्मकत्वतः 4.4.342cd
न चोपास्योऽयमप्यर्थः सर्वकामादिवच्छ्रुतेः 4.4.463ab
न चोष्णत्वं सतोऽप्यग्नेः काष्ठादावुपलभ्यते 4.3.1587cd
न जडं ज्ञानरूपत्वादानन्दत्वान्न निःसुखम् 3.9.209ab
न जन्मान्तरसंस्काराद्वामदेवस्य तद्भवेत् 1.4.1443cd
न जन्यजनकं वस्तु न द्रव्यगुणकर्मभिः 3.3.103ab
न जन्यतेऽतः क्षीयेत न त्वेतन्नेह जन्यते 3.2.65cd
न जाग्रद्देशगः स्वप्नो जाग्रत्सामग्र्यभावतः 4.3.963ab
न जाग्रद्वस्तुवत्तस्याज्ज्ञानमात्रस्वरूपतः 4.3.563cd
न जातु कामः कामानामुपभोगेन शाम्यति SV 346ab
न जातो न भविष्योऽस्ति शत्रुरैकात्म्यदर्शनात् 2.1.31ab
न जाने क्व गमिष्यामि कथं वेत्यब्रवीन्नृपः 4.2.18cd
न जाने मुग्ध एवाहं भवदुक्तं मनागपि 4.4.362ab
न जायत इति स्पष्टं श्रुतिमन्त्रोक्तिसंश्रयात् 4.3.319cd
न जायतेऽज इत्यादि विज्ञानघन इत्यपि 1.4.321ab
न जायते जनिष्यन्वा तस्मादस्तीह कश्चन 3.9.144cd
न जायते जन्यते वा नापि हन्ति न हन्यते 1.4.404ab
न जायते म्रियते वा इति षड्भावविक्रिया- 2.1.483ab
न ज्ञातः कुम्भवन्नापि चित्स्थत्वात्खरशृङ्गवत् 3.8.35cd

न ज्ञानमात्रमेवेदं भवताप्यभ्युपेयते 4.3.558ab
न ज्ञेयं नापि च ज्ञाता तदभावोऽपि नेष्यते 2.1.278cd
नञ्घटाद्यर्थविज्ञानं सत्येव जगतीष्यते 1.4.177cd
नञ्घटार्थावपह्नुत्य संवित्सद्रूपमात्रया 1.4.989ab
नञ्घटार्थावपह्नुत्य संवित्सद्रूपमात्रया 4.3.1743ab
नञ्वृत्तिस्तं सदाबुद्धं लक्षयत्यपृथक्प्रमम् 2.3.229cd
न ढौकते पराचीनं प्रत्यक्त्वासङ्गतः परः 1.4.505ab
न तच्छक्तिं विना कश्चित्पुमांस्तत्र चिकीर्षति 2.4.179cd
न तत्तमोनिवृत्तिः स्यात्तदुत्थस्य च वस्तुनः 1.4.1495cd
न तत्पूर्वं तदूर्ध्वं वा तेन वा अवधारणम् 4.3.813cd
न तत्र करणापेक्षा नेतिकर्तव्यता तथा SV 248ab
न तत्र तावद्विज्ञानं तद्ग्राह्येऽस्तीह वस्तुनि 4.3.774ab
न तत्र दक्षिणा यन्ति विद्ययैव तदाप्यते 1.5.269ab
न तत्र दक्षिणा यन्ति विद्ययैव तदाप्यते 3.3.54ab
न तत्र दक्षिणा यन्ति विद्ययैव तदाप्यते 6.2.10ab
न तत्र सूर्यो भातीति तथा चाथर्वणे वचः 4.3.291ab
न तत्र सूर्यो भातीति नान्योऽतोऽस्तीति च श्रुतेः 4.4.367cd
न तत्र सूर्यो भातीतिमन्त्राम्नायो ह्यनेकशः 4.3.363cd
न तत्रेति प्रवृत्तैषा प्रत्यगात्मविशुद्धये 4.3.904cd
न तत्स्थास्न्विति मन्तव्यं पण्यस्त्रीगमनं यथा 4.4.777cd
न तथा ब्रह्मणस्तस्मात्तत्स्वयंभ्विति शब्द्यते 6.5.9cd
न तथेहाद्वयावस्था श्रुत्योत्सर्गेण यत्नतः 5.1.66ab
न तदङ्गं प्रधानं वा ज्ञानं स्यात्कर्मणः क्वचित् 4.4.1126cd
न तदर्थान्तराभावादिति पूर्वमवादिषम् 1.4.825cd
न तदश्नातिवाक्येन यतस्तद्वार्यते द्वयम् 3.8.108cd
न तदस्ति द्वितीयत्वं संविदैव समाप्तितः 4.3.1524cd
न तदस्ति यतस्तस्मात्पश्यन्नपि न पश्यति 4.3.1606cd
न तदस्ति सुखं लोके यन्न दुःखकरं भवेत् 2.4.85ab
न तदा लिङ्गविध्वस्तौ वासनात्मनि युज्यते 2.3.128cd
न तदेकत्वतो वेत्ति ब्रह्मानन्दं स्वकं तथा 3.9.190cd
न तद्वारयितुं शक्यं लोके विधिशतैरपि 2.4.177cd
न तन्नामा न तद्रूपस्तदन्यत्र च कर्मणि 1.4.678ef

न तपत्यथ तं कस्मात्तापकोऽप्यात्मवेदिनम् 4.4.1286ab
न तस्य कर्मापेक्षास्ति कर्मापेक्षा ततोऽन्यतः 4.4.1116cd
न तस्य क्रियमाणत्वं खपुष्पाकाशयोरिव 2.4.116cd
न तस्य क्रियमाणत्वं खपुष्पाकाशयोरिव 4.3.1596cd
न तस्य जीवतः कश्चिद्विशेषोऽस्ति मृतस्य वा 4.4.306ab
न तस्य प्रतिमा अस्ति यस्य नाम महद्यशः 4.4.1178ab
न तस्य मानतः सिद्धिस्तत्सिद्धेः प्राक्प्रमागमात् SV 987cd
न तस्य विषयाक्षेपं मुक्त्वान्यत्र कृतार्थता SV 729cd
न तस्येत्युत्तरोक्त्यायं यथोक्तोऽर्थः समर्थ्यते 4.4.284cd
न तादात्म्यतदुत्पत्ती मिथोऽयोगादपोहयोः 4.3.801ab
न तान्प्रति समारम्भः सिद्ध एव हि तान्प्रति 3.4.5cd
न तापयति कर्मैतन्नेति नेत्यात्मदर्शिनम् 4.4.1176cd
न तावत्किंचिदप्याप्तं सुखं दुःखविवर्जितम् SV 1105cd
न तावत्प्रक्रियेहास्ति व्रीह्यादिप्रोक्षणे यथा SV 428ab
न तावत्प्रेरणा कार्यं कार्यार्थविषया हि सा SV 622ab
न तावत्संभवेत्स्वर्गो ज्ञातोपाधिवियोगतः SV 307ab
न तावत्स्यात्समुच्छेदो द्रष्टुर्दृष्टेस्तदाश्रयात् 4.3.1550cd
न तावदधिकारोऽस्ति कैवल्यज्ञानवर्त्मनि 2.4.93cd
न तावदिह संभाव्यं प्रत्यक्षं तदसंभवात् 1.4.259ab
न तावद्दृष्टिकर्तृत्वं कौटस्थ्यादात्मवस्तुनः 4.3.1581ab
न तु चिन्मात्ररूपस्य ध्रुवानंशात्मनः स्वतः 5.1.74ab
न तु चिन्मात्ररूपस्य ह्यत्रावोचं विरुद्धताम् 5.1.78cd
न तु चैतन्यवत्साक्षात्संसारोऽस्य स्वतो मतः 4.4.147ab
न तु तच्छक्तिरित्येवं शक्तिमात्रतया स्थितौ SV 58cd
न तु तत्साक्षिणो युक्तस्तस्य रूपनिषेधतः 2.3.158cd
न तु तद्व्यतिरिक्तस्य भोक्तृता मित्यसंभवात् 2.1.138cd
न तु त्वमेतयोर्वेत्थेत्युत्क्रान्त्यादिस्वलक्षणम् 6.2.13ab
न तु देहग्रहे प्रश्नः सति गन्तरि पृच्छ्यते 3.1.40ab
न तु द्वितीयं जाग्रद्वत्पश्यत्यात्मा सुषुप्तगः 4.3.1604cd
न तु निःशेषसंसारविध्वंसिन्यात्मबोधने 3.2.22cd
न तु निःसङ्गकूटस्थप्रतीचः स्यादहंमतिः 2.4.354ab
न तु प्रवर्तकं तस्मान्नार्थवादत्वसंभवः SV 125ab

न तु प्लुष्टात्मयाथात्म्यविज्ञानतमसामसौ 1.4.1469cd
न तु ब्रह्मैव तां कुर्यात्सर्वज्ञं प्रत्यगात्मनि 1.4.1218cd
न तु मानाभ्युपगमो मितेस्तदवसानतः 1.4.1287cd
न तु मृत्युं यतः स्वप्ने मोदत्रासादि दृश्यते 4.3.971cd
न तु मृत्युमृते ज्ञानाज्जहात्यात्मा निजं तमः 4.3.820cd
न तु मोहोत्थचिद्बिम्बहेतुवृत्तव्यपेक्षया 4.3.414cd
न तु यद्वास्तवं वृत्तं पश्यतीत्यक्रियात्मनः 4.3.1000cd
न तु यादृच्छिकी सिद्धिर्वक्तव्येह विपश्चिता SV 74ab
न तु वस्त्वन्तरं तत्स्याद्यथा तदिह वर्ण्यते 1.6.8cd
न तु वागादिभावोऽस्यास्तत्र हेतुरिहोच्यते 6.1.2cd
न तु विध्वस्तनिःशेषजन्मनाशादिकारणे 4.4.40cd
न तु विध्वस्तनिःशेषप्रत्यगज्ञानतद्भव- 1.4.396ab
न तु विध्वस्तनिःशेषसंसारानर्थवर्त्मनि 1.4.1807ab
न तु विध्वस्तभेदस्य स्यादौपनिषदस्य सः SV 435cd
न तु विध्वस्तमोहानां प्रत्यङ्मात्रैकशायिनाम् 1.4.132cd
न तु विध्वस्तसकलकर्महेतुं द्विजं प्रति SV 164cd
न तु विध्वस्तसंमोहप्रत्यङ्मात्रसतत्त्वगम् 1.6.2cd
न तु वेदान्तवचसां दृष्टार्थत्वेन हेतुना SV 275ab
न तु व्यापारविरहान्नातो द्विकरता श्रुतेः SV 774cd
न तु षष्ठीसमासोऽत्र विभागस्याप्रसिद्धितः 4.3.1817cd
न तु संशयितं यस्मात्संशयात्मा विनश्यति 1.4.1277cd
न तु संन्यासिनो न्याय्या दाहासंभवहेतुतः 5.17.13cd
न तु स्वातन्त्र्यतो लभ्यः स्वातन्त्र्यासंभवादिह 4.4.100cd
न तूक्तशेषतैतस्या भिन्नोपास्तित्वकारणात् 6.1.4cd
न तूपनिषदां न्याय्यं पार्थगर्थ्यस्य संभवात् SV 273ab
न तूपासनमिति चेन्मैवमैकार्थ्यकारणात् 1.4.772cd
न त्वं पाकसमायोगात्फलवन्नाशमृच्छसि 6.3.40cd
न त्वकारणकार्येऽस्मिन्नित्यबुद्धे परात्मनि 4.3.1530cd
न त्वग्न्यपेक्षयौष्ण्यादेरभिव्यक्तस्वभावतः 4.4.312cd
न त्वनापदि विद्यार्थं तं यान्तीह द्विजोत्तमाः 4.1.5cd
न त्वन्योक्तिपरित्रासाद्याज्ञवल्क्योऽब्रवीदिदम् 3.2.137ab
न त्वन्वयादिनैवेह वस्तुतत्त्वस्य संस्थितिः 2.1.167cd

न त्वपास्तसमस्तान्ध्ये नेति नेति परात्मनि 1.3.269cd
न त्वपूर्वार्थविज्ञानं प्रतिज्ञातं यथा त्वया 2.1.46ab
न त्वभूतार्थवादित्वं पापश्लोकाश्रुतेर्यथा SV 128cd
न त्वभ्यवहृतिन्र्याय्या वेदवर्त्मनि तिष्ठताम् 6.2.152cd
न त्वयं मृत इत्यस्मात्कारणादवसीयताम् 3.9.86ab
न त्वयोगव्यवच्छेद उत्कर्षस्तादृगिष्यते 3.3.171cd
न त्वर्चिरादिवत्तस्य प्राप्तये गतिकल्पना 4.2.90cd
न त्वाक्रम्य समादत्ते कथं तदिति भण्यते 4.4.44cd
न त्वागन्तुरविद्येयमनिर्मोक्षप्रसङ्गतः 4.3.1208ab
न त्वागमैकगम्येषु तथात्वमवसीयते 1.5.345cd
न त्वाञ्जसः परस्यास्ति तेनाविद्याप्रकल्पितः 1.4.621cd
न त्वात्मगुणता तस्य कर्मणः स्यात्कदा चन 4.3.1036cd
न त्वात्मनो निरंशत्वान्मुख्यौ संभवतः क्वचित् SV 146ab
न त्वात्मलाभमात्रेण जयः स्याज्ज्ञानकर्मवत् 1.5.324ab
नत्वाभ्युदयिकानां स्यादभीष्टत्वात्क्षयस्तव SV 84cd
न त्वित्यपि तथा वाक्यं न बाह्यं चेति वक्ष्यति 4.3.1046cd
न त्विह प्रतिपत्तव्याः करणस्थानगोचराः 1.3.133cd
न दाहज्वरनुत्त्यर्थमग्निना स्याद्विषक्रिया 4.3.176cd
न दृष्टा नियता चेष्टा रथादेर्जडरूपिणः 3.4.73cd
न देशकालावस्थादावपेक्षास्त्यात्मनः स्वतः 1.4.1331ab
न देशकालावस्थादावपेक्षास्त्यात्मनः स्वतः 3.4.133ab
नद्यास्तीरे फलानीव प्रत्यक्षाद्यनपेक्षतः 1.4.869ab
न द्रष्ट्रोर्दृश्ययोर्नापि तथा दर्शनयोर्मिथः 3.7.50ab
न धीः प्रत्यक्षगम्यैवं नात्मा प्रत्यक्षगोचरः 4.3.463cd
न नः परिहृतेनार्थश्चोद्येनानेन कश्चन 1.4.418ab
न नाशो हन्ति नष्टारं गन्तारमिव तद्गतिः 1.2.18ab
न निमित्ताद्यर्थतापि पञ्चम्या उपपद्यते 2.1.368ab
न निवर्तयितुं शक्तं रागाद्याकृष्टचेतसः 2.1.582ab
न निवृत्तिं प्रवृत्तिं वा पुंसः शास्त्रं करोति तत् 2.1.583cd
न निषेधो निषेध्यार्थो लक्षणार्थपरत्वतः 2.3.215ab
ननु कर्ता पुमानेष स हि कर्तेतिवाक्यतः 4.3.1027ab
ननु कर्तृत्वभोक्तृत्वकार्यमेवात्मसंसृतिः SV 58ab

ननु कर्मणि कृत्योऽयं तयोरेवेति शासनात् SV 510ab
ननु कामवशादस्य त्वयोक्तं परिवर्तनम् 2.1.307ab
ननु कालोपबन्धोऽत्र कार्यबुद्धिविघातकृत् SV 507ab
ननु कुम्भादिवैधर्म्यं प्रदीपस्य समीक्ष्यते 4.3.506ab
ननु क्रियात एवेयं संसारोच्छित्तिरिष्यते 3.8.161ab
ननु चात्मप्रबोधेन विधिगोचरलङ्घिनः 4.4.1146ab
ननु चात्मावबोधस्य निचाय्येति फलं श्रुतम् SV 43ab
ननु चाव्यभिचार्येव संबन्धो गमको भवेत् 4.3.718ab
ननु चाशिंशपाद्यर्थविविक्तोऽर्थः प्रतीयते 4.3.789ab
ननु चास्त्येव तद्दृश्यं समस्तव्यस्तरूपतः 4.3.1610ab
ननु चोद्यानुवादोऽयं न पश्यतिगिरोच्यते 4.3.1482ab
ननु जाग्रच्छरीरादेर्मात्रोपादानमीरितम् 4.3.897ab
ननु जाग्रत्स्थलोकानां मिथ्यात्वं प्राक्प्रपञ्चितम् 2.1.288ab
ननु जाग्रदवस्थायां दृष्ट्वैवेत्युच्यते कथम् 4.3.1075ab
ननु जाग्रद्वदीक्ष्यन्ते ग्रहीतृग्रहणादयः 4.3.901ab
ननु ज्ञानस्य तद्भिन्नग्राहकग्रहणे सति 4.3.522ab
ननु ज्ञानादिगम्यत्वे ज्ञानाद्यन्तरसंश्रयात् 4.3.519ab
ननु तद्व्यतिरेकेण प्रागादित्यादिरीरितः 2.1.136ab
ननु तस्यापि विज्ञानं नोपदेशव्यपेक्षया 1.4.1192ab
ननु दानादिसंबद्धमहावाक्यानुमानतः SV 493ab
ननु दान्तशमोक्त्यैव सर्वस्यैवेह कर्मणः 4.4.1221ab
ननु दीपः स्वमात्मानं स्वात्मनैवावभासयन् 4.3.501ab
ननु दुर्वारसंसारदुःखसंदर्भहानतः SV 1008ab
ननु दूरिति हि प्राण उक्तो वागादिवत्कथम् 1.3.243cd
ननु देह इदंबुद्धिर्घटादाविव जायते 4.3.124ab
ननु देहाद्यभिन्नत्वादात्मनो मुक्तता कुतः 4.3.116ab
ननु देहासजातीयमन्तस्थातीन्द्रियत्वतः 4.3.141ab
ननु दोषः समानोऽयं विधेरन्यपदेष्वपि SV 727ab
ननु द्रष्टव्यमस्त्येव द्वैताद्वैतात्मकत्वतः 4.3.1562ab
ननु द्वैतमिवेत्येतदुपमानं कथं भवेत् 2.4.459ab
ननु धीव्यतिरेकेण धीसाक्षी नाधिगम्यते 4.3.461ab
ननु ध्वस्तस्य मिथ्यात्वसिद्धिः कथमिहेष्यते 4.3.492ab

ननु न लुप्यत इति वचनान्न विलोप्स्यति 4.3.1430ab
ननु न स्तोऽस्य लोकौ द्वौ यावात्मा संचरत्ययम् 4.3.826ab
ननु नास्त्येव बाह्योऽर्थ इति प्रत्यवतिष्ठते 4.3.531cd
ननु नास्त्येव बाह्योऽर्थो घटदीपादिलक्षणः 4.3.532ab
ननु निर्धूतशोकादि फलं यच्छ्रूयते श्रुतौ SV 200ab
ननु नैव क्रिया साक्षाद्धानवृद्धी प्रतीष्यते 4.3.1016ab
ननु पर्यङ्क आसीनो गच्छञ्शिबिकया वनम् 2.1.301ab
ननु पाषाणसर्पेण पुनरुक्तमिदं कथम् 1.4.546ab
ननु पूर्वं य उक्तोऽर्थः स एवेहापि भण्यते 3.1.3ab
ननु प्रतीचि विदिते तदन्यद्विदितं भवेत् 1.4.1009ab
ननु प्रत्यक्षमानेन साक्षाद्दुःखादिदर्शने 1.4.558ab
ननु प्रमाणविरहात्स्वतःसिद्धो यदीष्यते SV 546ab
ननु प्रवेशस्तस्येह कथं श्रुत्योपदिश्यते 1.4.529cd
ननु प्रश्नः समाप्तश्चेन्नादात्सर्वं स किं नृपः 4.4.533ab
ननु प्रश्ना यथोक्ताश्चेन्निर्णीतार्थाः पुरोक्तिभिः 4.3.1897ab
ननु प्राणादिभिः सद्भिः कथं निर्भेदतात्मनः 2.1.382ab
ननु बोधे यथा लोकास्तत्कालाव्यभिचारिणः 2.1.287ab
ननु ब्रह्म यदि ज्ञातं तावतैव कृतार्थता 1.4.1251ab
ननु ब्रह्माक्षरमिति व्यपदेशोऽत्र नामभिः 2.3.252cd
ननु ब्रह्माधिकारत्वात्कथमात्मेत्यनूद्यते 3.9.96ab
ननु भङ्गुरधात्वर्थे तृच्प्रयोगो जगत्यपि 4.3.1462ab
ननु भेदाश्रितैर्वाक्यैर्विधायकनिषेधकैः SV 911ab
ननु मानादिविरहादकृत्स्नमपि नेष्यते 1.4.1284ab
ननु मृत्योरतिक्रान्तेरुद्गीथज्ञानकर्मणोः 1.3.8ab
ननु यद्यर्थशेषोऽस्ति कस्माद्ब्रूते न पूर्ववत् 4.4.541ab
ननु युक्ता पराग्भूते प्रमातुर्व्यतिरेकतः 4.3.120ab
ननु वाङ्मनसे स्तोऽस्य तत्कुतोऽस्यासपत्नता 1.5.189cd
ननु विज्ञानमात्रेऽस्मिन्सम्यङ्मिथ्यात्वधीगतिः 4.3.487ab
ननु विप्रतिषिद्धार्थं तदात्मानमितीर्यते 1.4.1393cd
ननु विप्रतिषिद्धोक्तिर्भवतेहाभिधीयते 4.3.1428ab
ननु वेदान्तसिद्धान्ते न वस्त्वन्तरमिष्यते 2.1.163ab
ननु व्याक्रियतेत्युक्तं स्वयमेव जगत्पुरा 1.4.515ab

ननु शास्त्रोपदेशोऽयमेवं सत्यफलो भवेत् 1.4.1225ab
ननु श्रुतौ पुरोक्तानि वाक्यानि बहुशो मया SV 35ab
ननु सत्स्वपि वाक्येषु नैतदध्यवसीयते 3.9.182ab
ननु सर्वस्य वेदस्य त्वत्पक्षेऽपि न सिध्यति 4.4.1035ab
ननु सामान्यविज्ञानविशेषाज्ञानसंश्रयात् 1.4.415ab
ननु सिद्धे यथोक्तार्थे नारम्भे हेतुरीक्ष्यते SV 1093ab
ननु सुख्यहमस्मीति विज्ञानमनुभूयते 3.9.185ab
ननु सुप्तेऽपि पुंस्यस्मिन्बोधितः सन्स्वनामभिः 2.1.113ab
ननु स्तुत्यर्थतैवास्य शुद्ध्यादेरवगम्यते 1.3.43ab
ननु स्वप्नेऽपि जाग्रद्वत्प्रत्यक्षमुपलभ्यते 2.1.262ab
ननु स्वप्ने न वस्त्वस्ति विज्ञानव्यतिरेकतः 4.3.563ab
ननु स्वप्नोऽपि लोकोऽस्य कथं स्यादवधारणम् 4.3.836ab
ननूक्तं कर्मशेषत्वमात्मनो यागकर्तृता SV 102ab
ननूक्तं प्रागिदं सर्वं विशेषज्ञानमात्मनः 4.3.1389ab
ननूक्ता मधुकाण्डेऽपि दुन्दुभ्याद्युपपत्तयः 3.1.12ab
ननूक्तोपनिषद्भिर्हि गन्तव्यं प्राक्प्रबोधितम् 4.2.10ab
ननूत्पत्तिविधिर्यद्वत्कर्मबोधे व्यवस्थितः SV 755ab
ननूपलब्ध्यभावो योऽनुपलब्धिः स उच्यते 4.3.793ab
ननूपसंहृताशेषकरणत्वाददधीः पुमान् 4.4.94ab
ननूर्मिषट्कातीतत्वं दुःखित्वं चाद्वयात्मनि 3.5.33ab
न नेहार्थावबोधोऽस्ति मिथ्याज्ञानत्वकारणात् 1.4.276cd
न न्याय्यं वचनं तस्य शास्त्रमात्रव्यपाश्रयात् 1.5.34cd
न न्याय्या सेति दृष्टत्वाद्देवस्य त्वादिवाक्यवत् SV 276ef
नन्वकृत्स्नं भवेज्ज्ञानं यद्यात्मैव समीक्ष्यते 2.4.228ab
नन्वज्ञानमवस्तुत्वात्कथं संसारकारणम् 1.4.421ab
नन्वत्रापि कृतैवासौ ल्यबन्तेनाभिधीयते 4.4.798ab
नन्वत्रापि समो दोषो वाक्यस्य पुनरुक्तता 2.1.370ab
नन्वध्यात्मेऽधिभूते च परिच्छिन्नाः पुरोदिताः 1.5.196ab
नन्वनुशिष्ट एवायं पूर्वोक्तैरनुशासनैः 4.1.31ab
नन्वन्यज्ञाने नान्यस्य क्वचिदस्त्यवबुद्धता 1.4.981cd
नन्वप्रयुक्तमप्येतद्वक्त्रा वाक्यं विवक्षितम् SV 593ab
नन्वप्राप्तनिषेधोऽयं न पश्यन्तीति भण्यते 1.4.652ab

नन्वप्राप्तौ विधिर्युक्तः प्राप्तास्त्वेते दमादयः 4.4.1207ab
नन्वभ्युदयवत्साध्या मुक्तिरप्राप्तरूपतः SV 26ab
नन्वभ्युदयवन्मुक्तिं गृह्णीमो विधिलक्षणाम् SV 20ab
नन्ववाक्यप्रमाणत्वमननुष्ठानतो भवेत् 1.3.78ab
नन्वविद्यामृतेऽप्यन्यद्दृष्टमन्यविशेषणम् SV 116cd
नन्वस्थाद्यो हि यत्रेह स तस्मादन्यतो व्रजन् 2.1.366ab
नन्वस्यैव तु तत्कर्म भावनापेक्षयाखिलम् 4.3.1031ab
नन्वात्मप्राणवागादेरन्योऽन्यव्यतिमिश्रणात् 4.4.88ab
नन्विदानीं यथा तद्वन्मुक्तौ चेदविशेषता 4.4.349ab
नन्विह प्रलयः श्रुत्या विषयस्यैव भण्यते 2.4.393ab
नन्विहात्मार्थसंदृष्टावहंप्रत्ययगम्यता 1.4.769ab
नन्वेकत्वे विभागोऽत्र नास्ति कारकसंश्रयः 3.9.179ab
नन्वेवं कौशले राज्ञः किमर्थं पृष्टवान्मुनिम् 4.3.28ab
नन्वेवं चेत्स्वभावोऽस्य निर्विभागैकदृष्टिता 4.3.1788ab
नन्वेवं तर्ह्यविश्रम्भो ह्यदृष्टफलसंपदि 1.4.1474ab
नन्वेवमपि मानत्वव्याघातः स्यात्क्रियाविधेः SV 161ab
नन्वेवमपि सिद्धः स्यात्प्रवेशः सर्वकर्मसु SV 107ab
न पदार्थो न वाक्यार्थ आत्मायं वस्तुतो यतः SV 462ab
न पश्यतिगिरा रूपमात्मनस्तदिहोच्यते 4.3.1481cd
न पश्यति यथा प्राज्ञ उक्तहेत्वविशेषतः 4.3.1494ab
न पश्यतीक्षत इति विरुद्धार्थो यथोच्यते 4.3.1486cd
न पश्यतीति द्रष्टोक्तौ न तु दृष्टिविनाशतः 4.3.1564cd
न पश्यतीति न पुनर्द्रष्टव्यो हेत्वसंभवात् 4.3.1542cd
न पश्यतीति प्राप्तत्वान्नापूर्वोऽर्थोऽवबोध्यते 4.3.1578ab
न पश्यतीति मन्वीथाः सुषुप्ते यन्न तत्तथा 4.3.1413ab
न पश्यतीति यत्तूक्तं तदिदानीं प्रपञ्च्यते 4.3.1558cd
न पश्यतीति यत्तूक्तं तस्य व्याख्याधुनोच्यते 4.3.1602cd
न पश्यतीति वचनं कारकादेरसंभवात् 4.3.1417ab
न पश्यतीति वचनं न त्वर्थान्तरमुच्यते 4.3.1579cd
न पश्यतीति वचनं शृणु तच्च यथा तथा 4.3.1507cd
न पश्यतीति वाक्यस्य व्याख्यानमिदमीरितम् 4.3.1569cd
न पश्यतीति व्याख्यानं कारकादिनिषेधनम् 4.3.1488cd

न पश्यतीत्यतोऽनूद्य पश्यन्निति विधीयते 4.3.1578cd
न पश्यतीदं द्रष्टव्यमिति यत्सूत्रितं पुरा 4.3.1559ab
न पश्यत्येव नन्वत्र चक्षुरादेरसंभवात् 4.3.1414ab
न पश्यत्येष आत्मात्र स्वयंज्योतिश्च स स्वतः 4.3.1411ab
न पश्यन्ति तमित्याह ये पश्यन्ति यथोदितम् 1.4.649cd
न पश्यन्तीत्यतः प्राह बोद्धृत्वादिसमन्वयम् 1.4.1359ab
न पश्यन्तीत्यतो युक्तं नेक्षन्ते वस्तु तत्परम् 1.4.650cd
न पश्यन्तीत्यतो लिङ्गाज्ज्ञानमेव विधित्सितम् 1.4.772ab
न पश्यामीति चाप्यस्य तथैवेहात्मसाक्षिकम् 4.3.1469cd
न पश्यामीतिफलतः कारकस्य यथा तथा 4.3.1478cd
न पश्यामीत्यपि तथा नित्यदृष्ट्यैव वीक्षसे 4.3.1474cd
न पश्येः प्रत्यगात्मानं द्रष्टारं दृश्ययानया 3.4.158cd
न पश्येदात्मवत्कामं कर्मस्थं स्वप्रबोधयोः 4.3.1040cd
न पश्येयुस्त्रयासत्त्वान्न हि तच्चाक्षुषं यतः 1.4.468cd
न पाणिपादचपल इत्युक्तेर्वा निषेधतः 4.4.1212ab
न पारिशेष्यसंसिद्धिस्तथापीहोपपद्यते 3.3.114cd
न प्रकाशक्रिया काचिदस्य स्वात्मनि विद्यते 4.3.892ab
न प्रकाशक्रिया काचिदस्य स्वात्मनि विद्यते 4.3.1460ab
न प्रत्यक्षबलीयस्त्वादनुमानप्रबोधतः 2.1.573cd
न प्रत्यक्षानुमानाभ्यामतोऽर्थापत्तितोऽपि न 1.4.268ab
न प्रत्यक्षाभिसंबन्धः कुम्भप्रत्यक्षतो भवेत् 4.3.1683cd
न प्रत्यङ्मात्ररूपस्य विरोधादुष्णशीतवत् 1.4.576cd
न प्रत्येमि यतः साक्षात्प्रत्यक्षं ज्ञानतः फलम् SV 205ab
न प्रपद्येत तेनायं स्यात्सुदुःखभिषक्क्रियः 4.3.949cd
न प्रमाणं प्रमेयं वा तदभावविशेषणम् 4.3.1714ab
न प्रमाणाद्बहिर्वस्तु न मानं वस्तुनो बहिः SV 923cd
न प्रमाणान्तरैर्गम्यं पराग्घेत्वसमन्वयात् 2.3.13ab
न प्रमाणान्न चाभावात्प्रत्यभिज्ञात इष्यते 1.4.271cd
न प्रमाता प्रमाणं वा क्रियामेयफलानि वा SV 474ab
न प्रमान्तरसंसिद्धविपरीतात्मबोधनम् 2.1.495cd
न प्रयोज्यो यदा भोगः स्वाम्यर्थः कर्मणस्तदा 1.4.370ab
न प्रवर्तेत वाक्यार्थसंबोधायेति चेन्मतम् 1.4.826cd

न प्रवृत्तिनिवृत्तिभ्यां शून्यस्य वचसो यतः SV 481ab
न प्राज्ञे तु ततोऽयुक्तं दृश्यमात्रनिषेधनम् 4.3.1609ab
न प्रात्यक्ष्यं द्रष्टृदृष्टयोः स्यात्सुषुप्तप्रसिद्धिवत् 4.3.1607cd
न प्रेरकतया सा स्यात्प्रत्यक्षादेरनीक्षणात् SV 638cd
न बहिर्विक्रियां मुक्त्वा देहेऽहंवृत्तिसंभवः 2.4.351cd
न बाध्यजन्यपेक्षं हि ज्ञानं बाधकमिष्यते 2.4.258ab
न बिभेति यतस्तस्माद्भेतव्यं जनकाद्भृशम् 4.3.1896cd
न बीजादग्निसंव्याप्तादङ्कुरोद्भूतिरीक्ष्यते 1.2.43cd
न ब्रह्मता क्रियातः स्यादुत्पत्त्यादिसमन्वयात् 1.4.1114ab
न भवत्यथ जल्पन्ति स्वस्थोऽयमिति लौकिकाः 4.3.1099cd
न भावनानपेक्षोऽसौ विधिर्यस्मात्प्रवर्तते 2.4.180cd
न भावनान्तरमियं न च मानान्तरं तथा 2.4.181ab
न भावनेह संभाव्या मोहे सत्येव सा यतः 1.4.853cd
न भावयोरभिन्नत्वाद्धर्मधर्मित्वमिष्यते 4.3.1716ab
न भावयोरसंभित्तेर्धर्मधर्मित्वमिष्यते 4.3.1698ab
न भावाभावयोरेवं विरोधादितरेतरम् SV 932cd
न भावाभावयोर्योगो नापि चायमभावयोः 1.2.122ab
न भिद्यते प्रमेयोऽर्थो मानाद्येषां च वादिनाम् 1.4.243cd
न भिन्नद्रष्टृकं यस्मात्प्रतिसंधानमर्हति 4.3.268cd
न भूतं तत्पृथिव्यादि नापि भूतगुणास्तथा 3.8.96ab
न भूतकालस्पृक्प्रत्यङ्न चागामिस्पृगीक्ष्यते 1.4.301ab
न भूतमात्रोपादाने बीजमस्ति मनागपि 3.2.47cd
न भेदोऽनुपलब्धिर्वो नातो लिङ्गं कथं चन 4.3.767cd
न भेदो न च संसर्गो नाप्यभावोऽवसीयते 5.1.22ab
न भोक्तृत्वं विना मानादाशङ्का निष्प्रमाणिका 4.3.434cd
न भोक्त्री सुखदुःखादिफलानां स्यात्कदा चन 2.1.148cd
नभो मूर्तं घटोऽमर्तो विश्रब्धैः किं न साध्यते 4.3.1715cd
नभोवत्सदिदं सर्वं तत्र यत्तत्सदात्मना 4.3.1707ab
नमउक्तिमतो भक्त्या तुभ्यं बहुतमां धिया 5.17.22ab
नमस्तेऽस्तु तुरीयायेत्युक्त्या तुर्यप्रधानताम् 5.16.70ab
न मां दुष्कृतिनो मूढाः प्रपद्यन्ते नराधमाः 2.1.269ab
न मातुस्तस्य मेयत्वान्नापि मेये फलं क्वचित् SV 1065cd

न मानं किंचिदप्यस्ति ज्ञानकर्मसमुच्चिततेः 3.3.73ab
न मिथो व्यतिरेकेण शक्तिशक्यौ प्रसिध्यतः 4.3.1446ab
न मुक्तिसाधनत्वेन तस्यानधिगमाच्छ्रुतेः 1.4.849ab
न मुक्त्याशास्ति पूर्वोक्तन्यायमार्गसमाश्रयात् SV 100cd
न मुख्योपसदामत्र संभवोऽस्तीति गम्यते 6.3.12cd
न मृतस्येह रेतोऽपि विद्यते कस्यचित्क्वचित् 3.9.136cd
न मृत्यवः स्वभावोऽस्य कार्याणि करणानि च 4.3.808ab
न मृदोऽन्यत्र कुम्भादेः शरावे प्रलयो यतः 2.4.356ab
न मेये पूर्वमानेन तद्वन्मानान्तरैरपि SV 1077cd
नमोऽसाधारणज्ञातृज्ञानज्ञेयात्मबोधिने 2.5.1ab
नयतस्तदभावो वा मेयत्वेनैव तत्स्थितेः SV 941cd
न यतो युगपत्कृत्स्नवस्तुज्ञानं क्रमेण वा 1.4.689ab
न यथा श्रोत्रविज्ञानं रूपेणैति समागमम् 2.1.310ab
न युक्तं कामना मुक्तौ पुंसां नास्तीति भाषितुम् SV 290ab
न युक्तः परिणामोऽयं लौकिकस्यापि नेष्यते 4.3.397cd
न युक्तिमदिदं गीतं ह्यपवादविकल्पनम् 5.1.64ab
न युक्तोऽज्ञानविध्वंसो बलात्कल्पयितुं त्वया 3.3.100cd
न युक्तो निरपेक्षत्वाद्गमनेक्षणयोरिव 1.5.228cd
न योगोऽभावयोर्दृष्टो वन्ध्यासूनुखपुष्पयोः SV 932ab
नरकादिव निर्विण्णो यावन्नाब्रह्मणो नरः 2.4.93ab
नरप्रजापतितनावेवं देवासुरा मिथः 1.3.118ab
नरप्रवृत्तिसद्भावान्नन्नु तस्य प्रमाणता 1.4.911ab
नरलोकः सुतेनायं जय्य एवेति भण्यते 1.5.241ab
नरलोकादिकामानां सुतोत्पत्त्यादि साधनम् 2.4.29ab
नरव्यापारलिङ्गेन धूमाग्निवदसंशयम् 4.3.70cd
नरस्यातः प्रधानत्वात्पृथक्तस्या ग्रहः कृतः 4.4.121cd
न रूपमात्मनोऽस्त्यन्यच्छ्रुतिन्यायानुभूतितः 4.4.569cd
न रूप्यधीः प्रमाणं स्यात्प्रमेयासंभवादिह 4.4.903cd
नरेण परिसंख्यातुं न शक्याः कल्पकोटिभिः 4.3.1367cd
नरोऽकामयमानः स्यात्कामहेतोर्निराकृतेः 4.4.256cd
नरोक्तौ मान्तरापेक्षा तेन मान्तरसंभवः SV 699cd
नर्गादिषु सतामेव सत्सु दृष्टिसमन्वयात् 1.3.66cd

नर्तेऽविद्यां कार्यमिदं हीति हेतावतः पदम् 2.4.455cd
नर्ते धरां सुवृष्ट्यापि पद्मिनीसंभवोऽम्बरात् 3.2.91cd
नर्ते लिङ्गं शरीरस्य स्थितिः काचिदिहेष्यते 3.9.87ab
नर्ते विभागं संबन्धः प्रतीचानात्मनोऽस्ति हि 1.4.974ab
नर्ते स्याद्विक्रियां दुःखी साक्षिता का विकारिणः 1.4.561ab
नर्ते स्याद्विक्रियां दुःखी साक्षिता का विकारिणः 4.3.396ab
नर्मार्थो जक्षतिर्ज्ञेयो हर्षार्थो मोदतिस्तथा 4.3.943ab
न लभ्यते यतो नात ऐकात्म्ये स्याद्विरुद्धता 1.4.1298cd
न लोकत्रयसाध्यस्य साधनैकव्यपाश्रयात् 1.4.1830ab
न वदिष्येऽहमित्यत्र व्रते हेतुर्न वीक्ष्यते 4.3.14ab
न वदिष्ये नृपेणाहमिति बद्ध्वा व्रतं किल 4.3.9cd
नवसंख्याहतज्ञानो दशमो विभ्रमाद्यथा SV 211ab
नवसंख्येयमात्रेक्षी दशमो विभ्रमाद्यथा 1.4.600ab
नवसूज्ञीयमानेषु तं वृणीताविचारयन् 1.3.368cd
न वस्तुस्पृग्विकल्पत्वाच्छब्दालम्बनमात्रतः 4.3.775ab
न वस्तु स्पृशतस्तस्मात्प्रमाणोत्थप्रबोधतः 4.4.852cd
न वस्त्ववसरापेक्षं स्वतःसिद्धत्वकारणात् 1.3.104ab
न वा अर इति ह्युक्त्या वक्तुं समुपचक्रमे 2.4.73cd
न वा अरे पत्युरिति तदेतत्प्रेय इत्यपि SV 473ab
न वाक्यपदयोरर्थो भेदसामान्यवर्जनात् 2.3.12cd
न वा निन्दति निःशेषद्वैतहेतुविनाशतः 4.4.634ab
न वा निषेधः स्थूलादेस्तस्य प्रागेव सिद्धितः 3.8.86ab
नवान्नवतरं रूपं कल्याणतरमेव च 4.4.141ab
न वायोः क्षिप्रकारित्वाच्छ्वेतालम्भो विभूतये SV 855ab
न विकल्पः समृद्धिः स्यात्कर्मणोऽस्य समुच्चितौ 6.3.8cd
न विकारो न चारभ्यं बौद्ध कार्यमसंभवात् 4.3.656ab
न विजज्ञौ च शाकल्यस्तमात्मानं यथोदितम् 3.9.118cd
न विज्ञातात्मयाथात्म्यं प्रत्यृणित्वं भवेद्यतः 1.4.1559ab
न विज्ञानात्मनो रूपं चैतन्यादन्यदिष्यते 4.3.1221ab
न विदुस्ते भवन्तीह कीटाद्या दुःखभोगिनः 6.2.157cd
न विद्यमानमात्रेण ह्यभिव्यक्तिरपीष्यते 1.2.77ab
न विधिर्दर्शनेऽपि स्यादन्योऽन्याश्रयदोषतः SV 656ab

न विनश्यति सा दृष्टिर्द्रष्टुश्चेत्यतिसाहसम् 4.3.1428cd
न विनश्यत्यसौ कस्मादिति हेतुरिहोच्यताम् 4.3.1553ab
न विरुद्धोऽग्निरेकोऽपि तद्वत्कार्येऽपि किं न ते SV 958cd
न विशेषणमित्यस्मादमूर्तत्वादिकल्पनम् 4.4.485cd
न विशेषात्मलाभोऽस्ति खिल्यस्येव महोदधौ 2.4.416cd
न विशेषान्तरे वृत्तिर्विशेषस्यास्ति गोत्ववत् SV 734cd
न विशेषो न सामान्यं भेदतोऽभेदतोऽस्ति नः 1.6.23ab
न विशेषो न सामान्यमन्योऽन्यासंगतेर्भवेत् 1.6.82cd
न वेत्ति दशमोऽस्मीति वीक्षमाणोऽपि तान्नव SV 211cd
न वेत्ति दशमोऽस्मीति स्वीक्षमाणोऽपि तान्नव 1.4.600cd
न वेत्यैकात्म्यमस्मीति वीक्षमाणोऽप्यनात्मनः 1.4.601cd
न वेदार्थो न चापीदृक्तर्केणाप्युपपद्यते 1.6.93ab
न वेदेत्यात्मनः श्रुत्या कर्तृत्वं प्रतिषिध्यते 2.1.313ab
न वेद्मीत्यनुभूतिर्हि सर्वेषामात्मसाक्षिका 1.4.1214cd
न वै सशरीरस्येति श्रुतेरध्यवसीयते 1.4.170ab
न व्यनक्ति प्रदीपोऽपि स्वतो भास्वररूपतः 1.4.583ab
न व्यापारयितुं शक्यं वह्निं दग्धुमिवोल्मुकम् SV 150cd
न व्यापारान्तरं यस्मात्सुखार्थं किंचिदीक्ष्यते SV 583ab
न व्यापृतिरतः प्रत्यङ्ज्योतिषा स्वेन वर्तते 4.3.907cd
न व्याप्नुतस्ते तं कस्मात्कर्मणी साध्वसाधुनी 4.4.1174ab
न व्यावृत्तं विशेषेभ्यो नानुवृत्तं च गोत्ववत् 3.8.58ab
न व्यावृत्तमिदं सर्वं पराक्प्रत्ययमानगम् 5.1.9ab
न व्यावृत्तिः पटादीनामताद्रूप्यात्तथा पटे SV 979cd
न व्यावृत्त्यनुवृत्त्यादिव्यापारोऽस्ति मितेः क्वचित् 4.4.337cd
न शक्त्याधानकृच्छास्त्रं तस्याभिव्यञ्जकत्वतः 2.1.455ab
न शक्नुमो विना युक्तीरतो न श्रद्दधामहे 1.4.701cd
न शरीरं विना लिङ्गं कस्मैचित्कर्मणे क्षमम् 3.9.87cd
न शर्म लेभिरे देवाः स्वात्मत्राणासमीक्षणात् 1.3.121cd
न शुक्तौ रजतज्ञानं नेदंता रजतेऽस्ति नः 1.4.275cd
न शोको नारतिः काचिन्न कर्तृत्वं न कार्यता 2.1.278ab
न शौक्ल्ये शुक्लतापत्तिः पटादेः सा विधीयते SV 618ab
नश्यतीदं मनस्तद्वदद्वैतमद्वैतरूपताम् 4.4.724cd

नश्यत्यविद्यया सार्धं हत्वा रोगमिवौषधम् 1.4.863cd
नश्यत्युत्पद्यमानोऽर्थ इत्येतन्मुग्धभाषितम् 4.3.598ab
नश्यद्विशेषणत्वं तन्मानं याति फलात्मनि 4.4.753cd
नश्येत्स्ववेगाच्छतधा ह्याखणाश्मसमागमात् 1.3.175cd
नष्टोत्पन्नसदभावशब्दप्रत्ययभेदधीः 1.2.92ab
नष्टाश्वदग्धरथवन्न्यायं चाश्रित्य भूमिपम् 2.1.38ab
नष्टे तमसि कुम्भोऽपि स्वयमेवोपलभ्यते 1.2.99cd
नष्टे द्वैतेऽखिले न स्यात्समस्तव्यस्तदर्शनम् 3.2.101cd
नष्टेन नश्यता वापि न शाल्याद्याहृतिक्रिया 4.3.618cd
न संयोगो वियोगो वा यस्य केनचिदिष्यते 4.3.713ab
न संविदः पृथक्त्वेन नापि संविदि तद्धिया 1.4.985ab
न स जानात्यकृत्स्नत्वात्पूर्णं वस्तु यतः स्वतः 1.4.709cd
न सतो व्यतिरेकेण सतोऽन्यो भाव ईक्ष्यते 3.8.21ab
न सत्यं ग्राह्यतः स्वप्नज्ञानग्राह्यघटादिवत् 4.3.535cd
न सन्त्यश्वादयस्तद्वद्रथयोगाः सवर्त्मकाः 4.3.914cd
न संन्यासविधिर्यस्माच्छ्रुतौ क्षत्रियवैश्ययोः 3.5.88cd
न सपत्नो भवत्यस्य योऽसपत्नं विवेद हि 1.5.192ab
न स पाप्मन इत्यस्मादश्रुता न च गृह्यते 1.5.35cd
न समस्तं न च व्यस्तं नोभयं प्रत्यगात्मनि 1.4.968ab
न समुच्चय उद्गातुः कर्माभावादिहेष्यते 1.3.379ab
न संप्राप्तेत्यतो यत्नात्प्रारब्धोपरतश्रुतिः 4.4.1226cd
न संबन्धिग्रहाभावे संबन्धोऽयं प्रसिध्यति SV 948cd
न संभवत्यसौ यत्नो यौगपद्येन नीडयोः 4.3.1135ab
न संभाव्या यथा सिद्धिः प्रतीच्येवं तमोवताम् 1.4.684cd
न संभूय यतः पादास्तैलवर्त्यग्नयो यथा SV 811ab
न सम्यगिति मन्वाना गार्ग्यपृच्छदतः पुनः 3.6.3cd
न सम्यगेतद्व्याख्यानं यथा तदभिधीयते 3.5.15cd
न स वेदेत्यविद्येयं नामरूपप्रपञ्चकृत् 1.4.1569cd
न सामर्थ्यं यतस्तस्मान्न युक्ता मुक्तिकल्पना 3.3.106cd
न सामर्थ्यं यतस्तेभ्यो व्यावृत्त्यर्थं परा श्रुतिः 1.4.1026cd
न सामान्यं विशेषं वा प्रत्यग्धीरवगाहते 4.3.79ab
न सामान्यं विशेषो वा कात्स्न्र्यादात्मा ततो भवेत् 4.3.387cd

न सामान्यं विशेषो वा यथैकात्म्येऽवगम्यते 1.4.1006ab
न सामान्यविशेषाभ्यां वायोरन्यस्य वस्तुनः 3.3.170ab
न सिद्धयोर्मिथोऽपेक्षा न स्वतोऽसिद्धयोस्तथा 4.3.1594ab
न सिद्धो नापि चाभावः कारकापेक्ष ईक्ष्यते SV 1029cd
न सिध्येदावयोरुक्तं प्रयोजनमिदं ध्रुवम् 3.2.136cd
न सुषुप्तगविज्ञानं नाज्ञासिषमिति स्मृतिः 1.4.300ab
न सुषुप्तप्रसिद्धिः स्याद्दृष्टेर्लोपो भवेद्यदि 4.3.1438ab
न स्थानान्तरनिह्नुत्यै यत्तूक्तमवधारणम् 4.3.837cd
न स्मृतिर्विस्मृतिर्वेह संभाव्येतापि केनचित् 1.4.846ab
न स्यात्तथोपसंहारस्तेनेयं कल्पना मुधा 2.1.256cd
न स्यात्सांपादिकं ज्ञानमित्येतच्चापि वक्ष्यते SV 439cd
न स्यादतिशयाभावाद्ग्राहकाद्यन्तरादपि 4.3.521cd
न स्यादात्मानमेवावेदहं ब्रह्मेतिमानजा 2.3.157ab
न स्यादाद्यन्तवद्ब्रह्म ह्यपूर्वाजादिशास्त्रतः 1.4.1114cd
न स्याद्देहस्य तच्चापि देहो द्रष्टा भवेद्यदि 4.3.267cd
न स्युर्हर्षभयोद्वेगहानोपचयमृत्यवः 2.1.277cd
न स्वकारणसंसर्गस्तस्य ज्ञानादपह्नुतेः 3.2.31ab
न स्वतः काम्यनित्यत्वविवेकोऽस्तीह कर्मणः 1.3.94cd
न स्वतः परतो वातो वस्तुतः प्रत्यगात्मनि 4.3.1109cd
न स्वतः परतो वायं भेदो वस्तुन ईक्ष्यते 5.1.85ab
न स्वतोऽदर्शनात्प्राज्ञ इत्याशङ्क्यैतदीरितम् 4.3.1752cd
न स्वभावोऽथवा कार्यं प्रतिज्ञा च मृषा भवेत् 4.3.787cd
न स्वरूपं लिङादीनां प्रेरणाज्ञापकत्वतः SV 635ab
न स्वरूपेऽथवा स्वांशे मानमेयत्वसंभवः 4.3.549ab
न स्वलक्षणयोस्तद्वन्नाप्यपोहवतोस्तयोः 4.3.801cd
न हास्य क्षीयते कर्म यद्यत्कामयतेऽक्षरात् 1.4.1718ab
न हास्य क्षीयते कर्मेत्यस्माद्धयेवेति चोक्तितः 1.4.1714cd
न हास्येति गिरा नातो मुमुक्षोः फलकीर्तनम् 1.4.1052cd
न हि कर्म तमो हन्ति तमसीवोत्थितं तमः 3.3.37cd
न हि कारणतोऽन्यत्र वृत्तिः कार्यात्मनः क्वचित् 1.4.1610cd
न हि कात्स्न्र्यमभिव्यक्तेर्व्यक्तस्याकात्स्न्र्यदर्शनात् 1.4.209cd
न हि कार्यमनाश्रित्य कारणं जगतीक्ष्यते 1.2.80cd

न हि कृत्स्नमनादाय जगदेतन्मनागपि 1.3.271ab
न हि गुण्यविनाशेन तद्गुणस्य निराकृतिः 4.3.970cd
न हि च्छिन्नेन कर्णेन तद्वानस्मीति मन्यते 4.3.824ab
न हि जात्यादिसंभेदसंसिद्धौ मानता श्रुतेः 5.1.83ab
न हि तस्यानपेक्षत्वं सिद्धवस्त्ववबोधनात् SV 479ab
न हि ते परिसंख्यार्था नापि चैते नियामकाः SV 412cd
न हि दीपान्तराद्दीपो भारूपत्वं प्रपद्यते 1.4.225cd
न हि दृष्टं श्रुतं वर्ते सार्थापत्तिः प्रसिध्यति 1.4.268cd
न हि दृष्टं समुल्लङ्घ्य ततोऽन्यद्बलवन्मतम् 4.3.149cd
न हि द्रष्टुरितीत्थं च सौकर्येणावगम्यते 4.3.1544cd
न हि धीपूर्वकारी सन्निःशेषानर्थदायिनीम् 1.4.1219ab
न हि निष्कृष्य सामान्याद्विशेषः कश्चिदीक्ष्यते 1.6.14cd
न हि निष्पद्यते स्वप्ने क्रिया जागरिते यथा 4.3.1005ab
न हि पूर्णपरिज्ञानः कश्चिद्दृप्यति निर्द्वयः 2.1.17cd
न हि प्रतीचि विज्ञाते कश्चिदप्यवशिष्यते 1.4.971ab
न हि प्रत्यक्षतोऽप्राप्तं स्मर्यते वस्तु किं चन 1.6.67cd
न हि प्रत्यक्षविज्ञानादतीतत्वं समीक्ष्यते 1.4.302ab
न हि प्रमाणतो मृत्युः शक्यो दर्शयितुं ततः 4.3.458ab
न हि प्रमाणविरहादस्ति वस्त्विति वीक्ष्यते 3.8.110cd
न हि प्लुष्टाखिलाविद्यः प्रतीच्यन्यन्मनागपि 1.4.1182ab
न हि ब्रह्मातिरिक्तेऽर्थे सति संभाव्यतेऽजडैः 1.4.1285cd
न हि ब्रह्मातिरेकेण ब्रह्माविद्याकृदिष्यते 1.4.1222ab
न हि ब्राह्मणविज्ञाने किंचिदस्ति त्वयागतम् 6.2.52cd
न हि भावातिरेकेण भावाभावः प्रमाणभाक् SV 927ab
न हि भूतातिरेकेण प्रतीचः किंचिदिष्यते 2.2.5cd
न हि मानं विहायेह साध्यसाधननिश्चितौ 1.3.45ab
न हि मानमनाश्रित्य वस्त्वात्माज्ञानहानिकृत् 1.4.1100ab
न हि मानुषतो दैवः प्रार्थनीयो विजानता 6.2.61ab
न हि मेयप्रतिस्पर्धि तन्मानं मेयबोधितः 1.4.1292ab
न हि मोहैकनिष्ठेन तद्धीनं वस्तु मीयते 1.4.1359cd
न हि यो यत्र साक्षीह स तत्राज्ञ इतीर्यते 4.4.360ab
न हि रूपमनाश्रित्य विद्येते नामकर्मणी 1.6.30cd

न हि रेतो विना जन्म प्राणिनोऽत्र समीक्ष्यते 6.1.14cd
न हि लूनोत्थितेष्वेषु विना जातिसमाश्रयम् 4.3.667ab
न हि लोकातिरेकेण ब्रह्मत्वमुपपद्यते 4.3.1822ab
न हि लोकेऽस्ति नियमो घटाभिव्यक्तिहेतुकः 1.2.97ab
न हि लौकिकचक्षुर्भिर्वैलक्षण्यात्समर्थ्यते 3.3.122ab
न हि वस्तु स्वतःसिद्धमन्यत्स्यात्परमात्मनः 1.5.330ab
न हि वस्त्वनपाश्रित्य मानत्वं लभ्यते मितेः 1.4.1293ab
न हि वस्त्वनुरोध्येतज्ज्ञाताज्ञातत्वलक्षणम् 1.4.284ab
न हि वस्त्वात्मनैवात्ममोहाद्युच्छित्तये क्वचित् 1.4.998ab
न हि वाक्यसमुत्थेन ब्रह्मावाक्यार्थरूपकम् 1.4.803ab
न हि वेदान्तसिद्धान्ते ह्यज्ञातात्मातिरेकतः 4.4.179ab
न हि श्रोत्रोत्थविज्ञानं रूपवासनयाञ्ज्यते 2.3.108ab
न हि संविदनारूढः प्रमात्रादिः प्रसिध्यति 1.4.282ab
न हि संगच्छते विद्याविद्यायोगं विरोधतः 1.4.1566cd
न हि सद्व्यतिरेकेण त्वसद्वस्त्वपि सिद्ध्यति 1.4.330ab
न हि साधनसापेक्षं वस्तु स्यात्पारमार्थिकम् 1.4.1146ab
न हि सावयवं किंचिदृतेऽवयवसंयुतिम् 1.4.597ab
न हि सिद्धस्य साध्यत्वं निपुणेनापि गम्यते 1.4.796cd
न हि स्वप्नदृशो योगः स्वप्नेऽन्येनास्ति केनचित् 4.3.1376cd
न हि स्वभावो भावानां व्यावर्त्येतौष्ण्यवद्रवेः SV 56ab
न हि हृद्व्यतिरेकेण कामानामाश्रयान्तरम् 4.4.439ab
न हीति तु प्रतिज्ञोक्तिरनुमोक्त्यनुसारिणी 4.3.1501cd
न हीति हेतुवचनं प्रतिज्ञातार्थसिद्धिकृत् 4.3.1496ab
न हीति हेतुवचसी द्वे स्यातामुत्तरे तयोः 4.3.1503cd
न हीदमात्मनः स्थानं ततोऽन्यत्रापि वाश्नुते 4.4.156ab
न हीयते हीयमान आगच्छति न चैति यः 1.4.1381ab
न हीश्वरस्य कैवल्यं साधनायत्तमिष्यते 1.4.1244cd
न हीहापास्तनिद्रोऽपि सुप्तवत्स्वप्नमीक्षते 1.4.763cd
न हीहोत्कृष्टसत्त्वेषु देवादिषु परात्मनः 1.4.1461ab
न हेतोः स्यात्स्वभावत्वं क्रियात्वं च न विद्यते 4.3.769cd
न हैवालोक्यतायै नुरस्याशापीह विद्यते 1.3.376ab
न ह्यक्रियस्य संबन्धो धर्मेणास्तीतरेण वा 1.4.171cd

न ह्यग्निसाध्ये शोषादौ नियोगो घटतेऽम्भसः 2.4.184cd
न ह्यचित्कं प्रमेयं सच्चिचन्मितिंकिंचिदपीक्ष्यते 2.1.142ab
न ह्यज्ञाते यथा ज्ञाते विशेषणविशेष्यता 4.3.175ab
न ह्यदृश्यनिषेधः स्याद्घटादेरिव भूतले SV 951ab
न ह्यद्विष्टमनस्कस्य कर्मैतत्सिद्धिमश्नुते 6.4.50ab
न ह्यन्यदृष्टं वस्त्वन्यैः प्रत्यभिज्ञायते क्वचित् 1.2.61cd
न ह्यन्योऽतोऽस्ति द्रष्टेति तथा च श्रुतिशासनम् 1.4.1222cd
न ह्यन्योऽन्यातिरेकेण संहतानां क्वचित्स्थितिः 3.9.88ab
न ह्यप्रसिद्धसंबन्धी संबन्धः क्वचिदिष्यते 2.4.141cd
न ह्यभिन्नधिया गोत्वं विशेषेषु प्रतीयते 1.6.59ab
न ह्यम्भस्थेन शैत्येन शिखिनः स्याद्विशेषणम् 4.3.1703cd
न ह्यविद्यादिविरहे द्वैतधीरुपपद्यते 4.3.1806cd
न ह्यविद्यामनादाय वस्तुयाथात्म्यसंश्रयात् 1.4.56ab
न ह्यसंनिहितं बोद्धुर्वस्तु बुद्धौ करोति हि 1.4.475ab
न ह्यसौ कृत्स्नतामेति चक्षुःश्रोत्रादिसंहतः 1.4.663cd
न ह्याकारमनालिङ्ग्य ज्ञानमाकारवत्क्वचित् 1.4.453cd
न ह्यात्मज्ञानविरहात्कर्म कर्तुं न शक्यते SV 104ab
न ह्यात्मव्यतिरेकेण किंचित्कारणमिष्यते 2.3.63ab
न ह्यालभन्ते वाहीकं मुख्ये गवि सति क्वचित् 1.4.1091cd
न ह्यावृत्तिव्यपेक्षं सन्मानं जगति किं चन 4.4.776ab
न ह्यावृत्तौ प्रमाणस्य प्रमेयेऽतिशयो यतः SV 818cd
न ह्युत्सर्गेण सर्वेषां फलवत्त्वस्य संश्रवात् SV 1128ab
न ह्युपाधिषु तत्त्वस्य विशेषः कश्चिदीक्ष्यते SV 350cd
न ह्युष्णत्वं हुताशस्य परतः कुर्वते बुधाः 1.4.1104cd
न ह्येकदेशः साध्यस्य दृष्टान्तत्वाय कल्पते 4.3.238cd
नाकामितत्वाद्ग्रामादिगतेर्युक्तैव शेषता SV 402ab
नाकारकं समीक्षेत द्रष्टृदर्शनगोचरान् 3.4.161ab
नाकारकः क्रियां कर्तुमलं जगति वीक्ष्यते 1.4.1382cd
नाकारकस्य जगति क्रियया संगतिस्तथा 1.4.172ab
नाकारि कार्यं यत्पित्रा स्वाधीत्यादि प्रमादतः 1.5.320ab
नाकार्यं विद्यते तेषां वैश्वानरवराश्रयात् 1.4.700cd
नाकाशस्य विशेषोऽस्ति कुम्भद्रोण्याद्युपाधिषु SV 351ab

नाकाशे नापि तत्पुष्पे पुंव्यापारानपेक्षता SV 655cd
नाकुर्वत्कारणं दृष्टं कार्यं चाक्रियमाणकम् SV 62ab
नाकृत्वा तानि कुर्वन्ति प्रकाशं गतिवद्यतः 4.3.63cd
नाक्षादिपञ्चकं तस्य बोधकं सत्समन्वयात् SV 941ab
नाख्यातपदसद्भावात्स्यादेव पदसंहतिः 2.4.161ab
नागमादपरं मानं मुक्तावभ्युपगम्यते 3.3.32ab
नाग्निर्दहति काष्ठानि न तापयति भास्करः 2.1.547ab
नाग्निस्तस्य प्रसिद्धत्वान्नापि देशः प्रसिद्धितः 4.3.730ab
नाग्न्यादिदेवतात्मत्वतत्फलावगमाच्छ्रुतेः 1.3.9ab
नाग्रहीन्न च गृह्णाति न ग्रहीष्यति शब्दवत् 2.3.208cd
नाचेतनस्य भोक्तृत्वं कथंचिदवकल्पते 2.1.139ab
नाजस्यापरिणामस्य मरणं जगतीक्ष्यते 4.4.1332ab
नाज्ञातं किंचिदप्यस्ति नानपास्तं तमोऽप्यतः 1.4.1416ab
नाज्ञातं किंचिदप्यस्ति नानपास्तं तमोऽप्यतः 2.4.443cd
नाज्ञातत्वस्य बाधः स्याच्छुक्तिकाबाधसिद्धिवत् 4.4.907cd
नाज्ञातरज्जुजः सर्पो रज्जुमुल्लङ्घ्य वर्तते 1.4.303cd
नाज्ञातेऽनुभवादेषां कश्चिदन्यस्तथेक्ष्यते 4.3.177cd
नाज्ञासिषमहं पूर्वमित्येवं प्रमिते घटे SV 991ab
नाडीः सूक्ष्माः प्रविश्यासौ देवताः प्रीणयत्यथ 1.3.255cd
नाडीगतरसोपाधिसंसर्गात्स्फटिकादिवत् 4.3.1245cd
नाडीनां परिणाहोऽथ सम्यक्श्रुत्येह वर्ण्यते 4.2.51cd
नाडीनां स्यादुपन्यासस्ता वा अस्येतिवाक्यतः 4.3.1211cd
नाडीभिस्ता वितत्यात्मा स्वप्नान्पश्यति कामतः 2.1.329cd
नाडीव्यत्यासगमनशङ्कयैवानुशासति 4.3.948ab
नाडीस्त्यक्त्वा यतः स्वप्ने जाग्रद्भोगप्रदाः पुमान् 4.3.940ab
नाड्य आध्यात्मिकस्येव ह्यधिदैवात्मनस्तथा 4.2.76ab
नाड्यः कर्मादिहेतूत्थाः स्वप्नादिफलभुक्तये 2.1.323cd
नाड्यग्रं हृदयस्याथ प्रकर्षेण प्रकाशते 4.4.74cd
नाड्यन्तरेष्वपि तथा सर्वासां संहतत्वतः 4.2.70ab
नाड्यायत्ता यतोऽविद्याकार्यदृष्टिरतः परम् 4.3.1211ab
नाड्योऽणिम्ना समानास्ता नानान्नरससंभृताः 4.3.1215cd
नाड्योऽतिसूक्ष्माः पुंसोऽस्य व्यवहारप्रसिद्धये 4.2.52ab

नाड्योऽस्य रश्मयोऽनन्ता हृदयं मण्डलं रवेः 1.3.276ab
नातः कर्माधिकार्यत्र दृष्टार्थत्वादपेक्ष्यते 1.4.1086cd
नातः कारणरूपस्य नाप्यकारकवस्तुनः 4.3.1436cd
नातः प्रमेयता तस्य स्वतश्चावगमात्मनः 4.4.694cd
नातः शक्तेस्तदंशत्वं कथंचिदपि युज्यते SV 77cd
नातः शुक्लादिवस्त्वस्ति बुद्धिरेव क्रियावशात् 1.5.121ab
नातः संवेद्य आनन्दो ब्रह्मणीहोपपद्यते 3.9.180cd
नातः समुच्चयान्मुक्तिर्नापि स्यात्सा विकल्पतः 1.4.1696cd
नातः समुच्चयाशेह कर्तव्या सूक्ष्मदर्शिभिः 4.3.1871cd
नातः संभाव्यते कर्म मुमुक्षोश्चापलं क्वचित् 4.4.1212cd
नातः स्याद्भावनापेक्षा नापि मानान्तरं प्रति 1.4.864cd
नातः स्याद्युगपज्ज्ञानमिति चेन्न तथापि तत् 4.3.1129cd
नातत्प्रकरणान्न्याय्यमितोऽन्यत्र च तद्विधेः 1.3.35cd
नातश्चोद्यावकाशोऽत्र शमादेर्विहितत्वतः 4.4.1232cd
नातस्तन्निरपेक्षस्य प्रामाण्यं वचसो भवेत् 1.4.800cd
नातिक्रान्तभवे त्वासीद्ब्रह्मविद्या प्रजापतेः 1.4.89ab
नातिभारोऽस्ति नो बुद्धेः शास्त्रं चेत्तत्परं भवेत् 3.1.50ab
नातियत्नो भवेन्नॄणां शास्त्रवैयर्थ्यमेव च 4.4.349cd
नातिरिक्तलिङाद्यर्थव्यवधानविडम्बना SV 643cd
नातिरेकान्वयाभ्यां यद्वस्तु संभाव्यते कथम् 4.3.168ab
नातोऽनात्माभिसंबन्धः कूटस्थैकात्म्यहेतुतः 4.3.1045cd
नातोऽनुग्राहकत्वादिनियोगोऽयं समञ्जसः 4.3.233cd
नातोऽन्तर्यामिणः कल्प्यमन्यदव्याकृतं बुधैः 3.8.27ab
नातोऽन्यत्कर्मणः कार्यं नातो मुक्तौ तदिष्यते 3.3.26cd
नातोऽन्यथा शक्तिवादः प्रमाणेनावसीयते 4.3.1784cd
नातोऽन्येन प्रमाणेन प्रष्टव्या देवतागमात् 3.6.27cd
नातोऽपवादकृत्सा स्यादैकात्म्यज्ञानजन्मनः 1.3.109ab
नातोऽवतारो मानानामैकात्म्येनैव संक्षयात् SV 163ab
नातोऽवाप्तपुमर्थस्य स्वरूपावस्थितस्य तु SV 110cd
नातोऽविद्यासमुच्छित्तौ ब्रह्मयाथात्म्यबोधतः 4.4.956ab
नातोऽस्य कारकत्वं स्यात्साक्षित्वाच्च क्रियावताम् 4.3.1582cd
नातो देहादिदुःखेन दुःखित्वं प्रत्यगात्मनः 4.4.614ab

नातो धियोऽर्थवादत्वं तद्विधेर्नितरां न च SV 1121cd
नातो धीव्यतिरेकेण प्रत्यगात्मोपलभ्यते 4.3.469ab
नातो भौतिकमेतत्स्यान्नापि स्याद्देवताकृतम् 4.3.1145ab
नातो मिथ्याधियोऽभ्यासः सम्यग्ज्ञानस्य जन्मने 4.4.827ab
नातो वस्तुनि संभेदो वस्तुनोऽभेदरूपतः SV 923ab
नातो वस्त्वन्तरं ज्ञेयं तदन्यस्य निषेधतः 4.3.1729cd
नातो वस्त्वन्तरव्याप्तिं व्यावृत्तिं वाश्नुते प्रमा 4.4.663cd
नातो वाक्यान्तरं तत्स्याद्यथोक्तार्थानुवादतः 1.4.940cd
नातो विज्ञाततत्त्वस्य कर्महेतुप्रबाधनात् 4.4.1165ab
नातो विदितवेद्यस्य कथंचित्स्यादृणश्रुतिः 1.5.339cd
नातो विपरिलोपः स्याद्द्रष्टुर्दृष्टेः कदा चन 4.3.1423cd
नात्मज्ञानस्य कूटस्थवस्तुतन्त्रत्वहेतुतः SV 168cd
नात्मज्ञानाद्यतोऽज्ञानं विद्यतेऽनात्मनस्ततः 1.4.1354ab
नात्मत्वाद्व्यतिरेकोऽस्य कार्यकारणभूमितः 4.3.387ab
नात्मधर्मो विनष्टत्वात्तस्माच्चैतन्यमत्र तत् 4.3.1382cd
नात्मनः कारकत्वं स्यात्सर्वावस्थातिलङ्घिनः 4.3.1077cd
नात्मनः कारणादन्यः कश्चित्संभाव्यते श्रुतेः 3.8.25cd
नात्मनः स्युः समस्तानि कार्यकारणबाह्यतः 4.4.424cd
नात्मना वस्तुनो भेदो भेदस्यान्यव्यपाश्रयात् 4.3.1717ab
नात्मनि स्यात्स्वशब्दोऽत्र विरुद्धा स्वात्मनि क्रिया 4.3.763ab
नात्मनोऽनात्मनस्ते तु काम इत्यादिनोदिताः 4.4.419cd
नात्मनोऽन्यत्र लभ्योऽसौ नाप्यात्मा ब्रह्मणोऽन्यतः 4.4.164cd
नात्मनोऽन्यत्र संभाव्यमपूर्वादि यदीरितम् 2.5.142ab
नात्मनोऽस्य स्वतः सन्ति तत्साक्षित्वात्तु ते मृषा 4.3.435cd
नात्मनो विद्यतेऽपेक्षा वस्तुनोऽन्यसमाश्रया 1.4.435cd
नात्मन्येव तदध्यासाच्छुक्तिकारजतादिवत् 2.1.382cd
नात्मन्येवात्मशब्दस्य प्रयोगात्स्यादलौकिकः SV 861ab
नात्मयाथात्म्यविज्ञानाज्ज्ञानमन्यदनात्मनः 1.4.1354cd
नात्मयाथात्म्यसंबोधिवाक्यश्रवणमात्रतः 1.4.827ab
नात्मलाभातिरेकेण व्यञ्जकस्य मनागपि 2.4.190ab
नात्मलाभात्परो लाभः कृत्स्नेऽपि जगतीक्ष्यते 4.4.1103ab
नात्मवत्स्यात्स्वतःसिद्धमुत्पत्त्यादिश्रुतेस्तथा 1.5.332cd

नात्मवत्स्यादसंबोधस्तस्य सर्वाभिमानतः 2.1.125cd
नात्मवस्तुनिमित्तत्वात्सम्यग्बुद्धेः सदा स्थितेः 1.3.103cd
नात्मवस्त्वनुरोधेन तदबोधात्तदश्नुते 4.4.260cd
नात्मविद्यातिरेकेण पितुर्वस्त्वन्तरे यतः 4.1.32ab
नात्मवृत्तमपेक्ष्येदं नापि बाह्यस्य वस्तुनः 4.3.1325ab
नात्माज्ञानाय सा युक्ता स हि साक्षात्तदीक्षते 3.8.65cd
नात्मात्मीयत्वबुद्ध्यासौ देहादीन्समुदीक्षते 4.4.504cd
नात्मानं लभते कर्म देवेशाद्यनपेक्षि सत् 1.4.1480cd
नात्मानं लभते कर्म यतोऽसंश्रित्य साधनम् 3.7.10ab
नात्मानं लभते कर्म यतो वित्तमृते ततः 3.5.115ab
नात्मानात्मीयकार्यस्य स्यादुपादानकारणम् 3.2.88ab
नात्माभिव्यक्तये दीपो ह्यन्यमापेक्षते स्वतः 4.3.506cd
नात्मार्थं पाचयेदन्नमिति चापि स्मृतेर्वचः 1.5.31ab
नात्माविद्यामतिक्रम्य कर्मैकात्म्यानुरोधि हि 3.3.39ab
नात्माविद्याहानमात्रकारित्वादागमात्मनः 4.4.350ab
नात्मोपास्यत्वावगमाद्वाक्यशेषे भवेदिदम् 1.4.936ab
नात्यन्तमेव सर्वत्र विभागोऽयं समीक्ष्यते 4.3.1612ab
नात्यन्तानुपलब्धेषु त्वभावोऽतोऽस्य निश्चितः SV 880cd
नादग्ध्वाभ्याहितं दाह्यमग्नेरग्नित्वमिष्यते 4.4.790ab
नादातुं शक्नुयात्कश्चिद्विशेषानसिकोशवत् 2.4.267cd
नादित्यादिसजातीयमात्मज्योतिरितीष्यताम् 4.3.106ab
नादिर्न मध्यं नैवान्तो नेयत्ता विद्यते यतः 2.3.169ab
नादिर्नान्तो न मध्यं वा यस्य वित्तस्य विद्यते 2.4.62ab
नादर्षितात्मभिर्यस्मात्प्रतीचोऽन्यन्मनागपि 1.4.703ab
नादेयस्रोतसाहार्यो मत्स्यो दृष्टान्त उच्यते 4.3.1083cd
नाद्राक्षं स्वप्नमद्येति प्रतिबुद्धोऽभिभाषते 4.3.1404ab
नाद्राक्षमिति संधत्ते दृष्टवत्स्वचिदात्मना 4.3.1420cd
नाद्रियन्त इदं ज्ञानमुदङ्मार्गाप्तिसाधनम् 6.2.158ab
नाधाक्षीदात्मविद्या नः काशाविद्यापनुत्तये 1.4.74cd
नाध्येयत्वाच्च शास्त्रार्थकल्पनेयं त्वया कृता 5.1.79ab
नानन्तरफलाभावे विसंवादोऽत्र शङ्क्यते SV 537ab
नानन्तरफलो यागो दृष्टो लोकेऽपि हि क्वचित् SV 641ab

नानन्दा अपि तत्रेति ह्यतः श्रुतिरभाषत 4.3.917cd
नानन्दादन्यतो मुख्यात्पण्डितः पर्यवस्यति SV 299cd
नानन्यव्यञ्जकत्वं स्याद्यस्मात्कुम्भादिवस्तुनः 4.3.497cd
नानयोर्धर्मधर्मित्वं विरोधादितरेतरम् 4.3.1705cd
नानयोर्व्यतिरेकोऽस्ति भोक्तृभोग्यात्मनोः क्वचित् 4.2.46ab
नानवाप्तं सुखं किंचिन्नानपास्तं तथा सुखम् 4.4.215ab
नानश्वरूपे सिद्धेऽपि गव्यश्वस्य प्रसिद्धता SV 843cd
नानाकारानुपादत्ते चैतन्याकारमेव सत् 2.4.125ab
नानाकृतिरसाद्यात्म ह्यात्मनोऽलुप्तचक्षुषः 4.3.1246cd
नानाक्रियाभिसंबन्धादग्निः सोमश्च गम्यताम् 1.4.157ab
नानाज्योतींषि सिद्धानि संहतानि मिथस्तथा 4.3.424ab
नानात्मरूपमात्मायं किंचिदन्यदपेक्षते 4.3.1226cd
नानात्मवदनेकत्वं कश्चिदात्मनि वीक्षते 2.1.610cd
नानात्वदर्शनं यस्माद्द्वयादज्ञानजं मतम् 4.3.1392ab
नानात्वदृष्टिनिन्दां च मृत्योरिति तथा वचः 2.1.526ab
नानात्वदृष्टेर्मिथ्यात्वं स्वयमेवावदत्पुरा 4.4.678cd
नानात्वबुद्धये नालममितोऽर्थो यतस्ततः 4.4.660ab
नानात्वैकत्वरूपाभ्यां सा पुनः प्राणदेवता 3.9.6ab
नानात्वैकत्ववत्स्थूलं दृष्टं वस्तु यथा तथा 4.3.1644ab
नानादन्यस्य सामर्थ्यं विद्यतेऽसुरनाशने 1.3.148ab
नानादृत्यागमेनार्थमज्ञातं वेत्ति कश्चन 2.1.498cd
नानाद्रव्यसमायोगे वियोगे च घटात्मनः 2.4.144ab
नानाद्रव्यसमाहारः पृथिवीवत्परो भवेत् 2.1.474cd
नानाद्वन्द्वोपघातार्थहेतूनां बहुलत्वतः 4.3.1862ab
नानापदार्थसंसृष्टरूपं शब्दात्प्रजायते 1.4.804ab
नानाप्रकार आसङ्गो विषक्तो योऽस्य बाह्यतः 2.4.92ab
नानार्थवाचिनां लोक आश्रयाश्रयिणामिह 4.3.582ab
नानार्थसाधनैर्मार्गे यथानः सुसमाहितम् 4.3.1912ab
नानावयवसंभेदभिन्नार्थश्चेन्नगादिवत् 1.4.694ab
नानाविकल्पसद्भावात्संदेहो गमनं प्रति 4.4.126ab
नानाविधपुमर्थाप्तिरपि वक्तुः समीहिता SV 596ab
नानासंस्कारसंसर्गिप्रत्यगज्ञानमेव तत् 4.3.88ab

नानासाधनसंबन्धात्कर्तृत्वं जगतीक्ष्यते 4.3.1044ab
नानास्तीत्येवमेकत्वमस्मिञ्शास्त्रेऽभिधीयते 4.4.730cd
नानाहेतुकपातस्य फलस्य प्रतिपत्तये 4.3.1936ab
नानिवृत्तस्तथानर्थो नानवाप्तं सुखं तथा 2.4.102ab
नानिष्पन्नस्वभावोऽपि भावः कर्तव्यता यतः SV 506ab
नानुग्राह्यसजातित्वं तस्यानुग्राहकत्वतः 4.3.228cd
नानुग्राह्यसजातीयं नाप्यनुग्राहकं तथा 4.3.230ab
नानुत्पन्नं क्वचिज्ज्ञानं नेहाध्वस्तं तमोऽप्यतः 4.4.870cd
नानुत्पन्नमतो ज्ञानं नानपास्तं तथा तमः 1.4.747ab
नानुत्पन्नमतो ज्ञानं नाप्यज्ञानमबाधितम् 4.4.1281ab
नानुत्पन्नमदग्धं वा ज्ञानमज्ञानमस्त्यतः 1.4.1452cd
नानुत्पन्नमितो ज्ञानात्किंचिदप्यवशिष्यते 3.8.181ab
नानुत्पन्नस्य हेतुत्वमुदकाद्याहृतौ भवेत् 4.3.623ab
नानुत्पन्ने विधिः पुंसोऽशक्यत्वाद्वस्तुतन्त्रतः 4.4.858ab
नानुध्यायाद्बहूञ्शब्दानिति कस्मादिहोच्यते 4.4.969ab
नानुपादाय कृत्स्नानि जन्तोः काचित्क्रियेष्यते 5.16.49cd
नानुभूतिः प्रतीचीयमभेदाद्भेदमीक्षते 4.3.1678ab
नानुभूतेः प्रमाणाद्वा तदन्यद्वस्तु लभ्यते 1.4.1224cd
नानुभूत्यैव तत्सिद्धेर्ज्ञातकुम्भानुभूतिवत् 1.4.1214ab
नानुमाकौशलं तावत्प्रत्येकं तेषु विद्यते 2.1.600cd
नानुमेयत्वतोऽस्त्येव तस्यावयवसंयुतिः 1.4.596cd
नानुवादः फलोक्तिर्वा यथाव्याख्यातवेदिनः 4.3.1970cd
नानुवादस्वरूपस्य निरस्तविधिकस्य हि 1.4.794ab
नानुवृत्तं तथैवैतन्नाप्यभावैकनिष्ठितम् 5.1.9cd
नानुशिष्टस्य जगति वृत्तमीदृक्समीक्ष्यते 6.2.27cd
नानुष्ठाने विरोधोऽस्ति फलभूमार्थिनः क्वचित् SV 416ef
नानूक्तं केचिदिच्छन्ति देवाद्यार्जितसिद्धये 1.4.1796cd
नानेकजातिमद्धेतुकर्मणेऽलं ततो भवेत् 1.4.1599cd
नानेकदृष्टिविध्यर्थमेकैकोपास्तिकृत्स्नम् 1.4.690ab
नानेकस्यात्मनो न्याय्या तदसंभवहेतुतः 3.5.21cd
नानेकस्यैकता न्याय्या तथैकस्याप्यनेकता SV 171ab
नान्तरेण नियन्तारं तयोरेषा व्यवस्थितिः 3.8.136cd

नान्तरेण नियन्तारं संभाव्येत्यवसीयताम् 3.8.140cd
नान्तरोऽपि प्रयत्नः स्यान्मानान्तरगतेस्तथा SV 622cd
नान्तवद्ब्रह्मरूपत्वादिति वाक्यप्रमाणतः 3.9.209cd
नान्त्याविद्यापनुद्बुद्धिरात्मैकविषयत्वतः 1.4.1510ab
नान्त्योऽविद्यापनुद्बोध इति सर्वत्र गम्यताम् 1.4.76ab
नान्नत्रयं व्यपेक्ष्येह जन्म प्राणस्य कथ्यते 1.5.187ab
नान्यजातिविशिष्टोऽर्थः स्वतो जात्यन्तरं ततः 2.1.439ab
नान्यतः कृतकृत्यः स्यादुक्तज्ञानातिरेकतः 4.4.1306cd
नान्यत्र कारणाद्वृत्तिः कार्याणां जागरेऽपि हि 4.3.896ab
नान्यत्र क्षत्रियाद्विद्या यत्र संभाव्यते क्वचित् 4.1.6ab
नान्यत्र पर्यवस्यन्ति ज्ञानादैकात्म्यगोचरात् SV 326cd
नान्यत्रार्थाः प्रसिध्यन्ति लीयन्ते नाप्यनात्मनि SV 1001cd
नान्यत्रेहाद्वितीयार्थात्साक्षादात्मार्थसंभवः 3.5.181ab
नान्यथा युज्यते यस्मादतस्तद्धानिहोच्यते 1.4.1784cd
नान्यदज्ञानतोऽस्तित्वं द्वितीयस्यात्मनो यथा 2.3.210ab
नान्यदज्ञानतोऽस्तित्वं द्वितीयस्यात्मनो यथा 3.8.122ab
नान्यदज्ञानतोऽस्तित्वं द्वितीयस्यात्मनो यथा 4.4.301ab
नान्यदज्ञानतोऽस्तित्वं द्वितीयस्यात्मनो यथा 4.4.855ab
नान्यदुत्सहते वोढुमिति पूर्वमवादिषम् 5.1.27cd
नान्यसिद्धान्तसंसिद्धिर्लभ्यते सर्वतार्किकैः 4.3.806cd
नान्यस्मिन्प्रकृतेऽन्योऽर्थो विरहय्य विशेषणम् 1.4.1779ab
नान्याभावविशिष्टत्वं कृत्स्नाभावगतौ भवेत् SV 951cd
नान्येन कर्मणात्रार्थो नृलोकजयसिद्धये 1.5.279cd
नान्योऽन्यातिविरुद्धार्थवाक्यानां तत्र दर्शनात् 3.9.172ab
नान्योऽन्यार्थातिरेकेण सिध्येते कार्यकारणे 4.4.1312cd
नान्योऽयमात्मान्यत्राभून्नान्योऽन्यस्मात्तथैति च 2.1.380ab
नान्योऽस्ति ब्रह्मसंबोधाच्छ्रुतिस्तेनेत्यतोऽवदत् 4.4.554cd
नान्यो हेतुरविज्ञानादिन्द्रियादेरिहात्मनि 2.5.132ab
नान्यो हेतुर्यतस्तस्मान्न त्रय्यन्ते विधिः प्रमा 2.4.151cd
नान्वयं सहते प्रत्यङ्न चापि व्यतिरेकताम् 3.2.29ab
नान्वयव्यतिरेकाभ्यां नाप्यभावेन तद्गतिः 4.4.854ab
नान्वयव्यतिरेकाभ्यामैकात्म्यानुभवो भवेत् SV 787ab

नान्वयो व्यतिरेको वा कल्पितस्यानृतत्वतः 2.1.166ab
नापरिच्छिन्नबुद्धित्वात्तस्य दुःखाद्युपप्लुतिः 1.5.354ab
नापश्यदपरं किंचित्सोऽहमित्यभ्यधादथ 1.4.40cd
नापि कार्यं विलीनत्वात्स्वात्मोत्पत्तौ प्रवर्तते 2.1.398cd
नापि चात्मातिरेकेण ग्राहकोऽन्योऽवसीयते 4.4.474ab
नापि चात्मातिरेकेण वस्त्वन्यन्मानभूमिगम् SV 476ab
नापि चात्यन्तमूढेषु विशेषः कश्चिदीक्ष्यते 1.4.1461cd
नापि चारभते कार्यं पुरतः कुम्भकारवत् 4.3.658ab
नापि चाव्यतिरेकेण तै तु ब्रह्मैव निर्द्वयम् 2.3.22cd
नापि चाव्यभिचारित्वमात्मनः कर्मणेक्ष्यते SV 433ab
नापि तद्विषणायाश्च कार्यत्वात्स्यात्तथार्थता 1.3.74ab
नापि तल्लक्षितावृत्तिर्विधेया श्रुतहानतः SV 808ab
नापि देहाद्विनिष्क्रम्य पर्वतादीन्समीक्षते 2.1.299ab
नापि निःशेषवेदार्थमनुष्ठातुं क्षमो नरः SV 287ab
नापि निष्क्रियरूपं सत्कारणत्वं समश्नुते 2.1.400cd
नापि प्रीतेरियत्तायाः स्वर्गशब्दोऽस्ति वाचकः SV 304cd
नापि बालादिस्वापस्य विशेषः कश्चिदीक्ष्यते 2.1.356cd
नापि बुद्ध्यादिभिः साक्षात्तत्स्थानासंगतेर्भवेत् 2.1.341cd
नापि रूढिस्तदन्यस्मिन्नश्वकर्णादिवद्भवेत् 1.4.1269cd
नापि वाक्येन संबन्धो जुहूपर्णमयीत्ववत् SV 430ab
नापि व्यभिचरेज्ज्ञानं यदि स्मर्तव्यपृष्ठगम् 1.4.464ab
नापि श्येनादितुल्यत्वं फलदोषेण दुष्टता SV 85cd
नापि श्रोतुः प्रवृत्तिः स्याच्छब्दात्कोपाद्यवेदनात् SV 489cd
नापि सांख्यप्रमासिद्धमात्मानमवगच्छतः SV 1050ab
नापि सामान्यधीबाधो विशेषोत्थधियेष्यते 4.3.1642cd
नापि सिद्धः स्वतोऽसिद्धं नृशृङ्गवदपेक्षते 1.4.231ab
नापि स्मृतिव्यपेक्षास्ति श्रुतेः स्वातन्त्र्यकारणात् 4.4.1152ab
नापि स्वप्नानुभूतेश्च मिथ्यात्वं स्वप्नवन्मतम् 4.3.217ab
नापि स्वार्थं परार्थं वा विहन्त्युपनिषत्क्वचित् 2.1.567ab
नापि स्वार्थातिरेकेण प्रमाणफलभाग्भवेत् 2.1.141cd
नापीन्द्रियमिदं ज्ञेयं यतोऽचक्षुष्कमक्षरम् 3.8.98ab
नापुत्रस्येति निःशेषलोकाप्तौ साधनं सुतः 1.5.243ab

नापूर्वः कश्चिदत्र स्यादत एवापरोऽपि न 1.4.838cd
नापूर्ववद्विधेयत्वं न च त्यागाद्विमुक्तता 4.4.543cd
नापूर्वविधिरित्येष कदाचिदपि गृह्यते 1.4.752ab
नापूर्वविधिरेष स्यात्पक्षेप्राप्तत्वकारणात् 1.4.758ab
नापृष्ट इति नन्वेतद्विरुद्धमकरोदृषिः 2.1.33ab
नापेक्षते भवद्वाक्यं सिद्ध्यर्थं प्राक्प्रसिद्धितः 2.1.48cd
नापेक्षा कर्मकाण्डे स्यात्तत्प्रामाण्यकृतार्थतः 1.4.1565cd
नापेक्षापूरणाशक्तेः प्रयोगे समवायिता SV 864ab
नापेक्ष्यापेक्षकत्वं हि लोकेऽप्यतिशयं विना 1.4.230cd
नापोढ्री नापि कर्त्रीयं विद्यातो वस्तुनः क्वचित् 1.4.1211cd
नाप्नुयुर्हव्यकव्यार्थं यदि नाभूत्प्रशासिता 3.8.159cd
नाप्नोति ब्रह्मतां साक्षात्सत्सु संसारिवस्तुषु 2.4.16cd
नाप्यकुम्भव्युदासेन कुम्भस्य स्याद्विशेषणम् 4.3.1703ab
नाप्यध्वस्तं तथाज्ञानं कृत्स्नज्ञेयसमाप्तितः 3.8.181cd
नाप्यनीशमपूर्वं च प्रकल्प्यं फलसंगतौ 3.8.146ab
नाप्यनुष्ठेयरूपेण पारिव्राज्येन संस्तुतिः 4.4.1139ab
नाप्यनेकार्थदर्श्यस्ति सादृश्यं स्याद्यतस्तव 4.3.665cd
नाप्यन्वयं तदव्याप्तेर्नाप्यभावः सतीष्यते 3.8.16cd
नाप्यपादानतः सिध्येन्न वाधिकरणाश्रयात् 4.3.628cd
नाप्यपर्वं क्वचिद्दृष्टं तन्मानासंभवादिह 3.8.156cd
नाप्यर्थेऽतीन्द्रिये सिद्धे मानं लिङ्गाद्यपेक्षते 2.4.170ab
नाप्यविद्येति वक्तव्यं तस्या ध्वान्तैकमात्रतः 1.4.1810ab
नाप्यागन्तु तथाज्ञानं हिरुक्सिद्धेरसंभवात् 1.4.1369cd
नाप्युत्थायेह कर्मभ्यो ब्रह्म ज्ञातुं क्षमो नरः 1.4.1694cd
नाप्येकाश्रयिणां लोके धर्माणां क्वचिदीक्ष्यते 4.4.345ab
नाप्राक्षीत्तत्र यद्राजा वरदानादनन्तरम् 4.3.15ab
नाफलस्य तु मात्रैव ह्यतोऽन्यत्र वृथा श्रमः 1.4.262cd
नाबाधित्वेह बाध्यार्थं बाधको बाधकात्मताम् 1.4.1453ab
नाभावनिष्ठोऽन्यत्रापि निषेधः किमुताक्षरे 3.8.74cd
नाभावभावयोगेषु मितेर्धीः कस्यचित्तथा SV 926cd
नाभावयोर्मिथो योगोऽवस्तुत्वाभेदतस्तयोः SV 924ab
नाभावरादिवद्विश्वमध्यात्मादिभागवत् 1.4.138ab

नाभावेन निरात्मत्वाद्व्यावृत्त्या वा मितेर्भवेत् SV 922cd
नाभावोऽसौ यतोऽभावो मतो वोऽनुपलब्धितः 4.3.790cd
नाभिधानाभिधेयत्वसंगत्यातः प्रबोध्यते 4.4.690cd
नाभिध्यायेदतः शब्दाननात्मार्थावबोधिनः 4.4.962ab
नाभिनेमिद्वयस्थाने दृष्टान्तत्वेन संमते 2.5.78ab
नाभिन्नयोरतो मुक्त आत्मस्थानामभेदतः 4.4.407cd
नाभिप्रेतपुरप्राप्तिसमर्थं सुगमं शिवम् SV 131cd
नाभिव्यञ्जकसंसाध्या घटादेरिव चात्मनः 4.4.313ab
नाभिव्यनक्ति सविता खरशृङ्गं स्फुरन्नपि 4.3.162cd
नाभुक्त्वा फलमाप्नोति निर्वृतिं परमां नरः 1.5.247cd
नाभूत्तत्प्राक्समुत्पत्तेः प्राणाद्युत्पत्तिसंश्रवात् 1.2.2cd
नाभेदो मेषयोर्योगे यथा भिन्नौ तथा युतौ 1.6.60cd
नाभ्युदयस्य मुक्तेश्च साध्यासाध्ये ध्रुवाध्रुवे SV 23ab
नामज्ञस्तमुपासीनः सर्वस्यात्तादितिर्भवेत् 1.2.194cd
नामतो रूपतश्चैवं प्राणनादिषु कर्मसु 1.4.675ab
नामन्यन्त यथा तद्वद्वानप्यपराधिनः 6.2.70cd
नाममात्रावशेषं तदित्युक्तौ गम्यते यतः 3.2.38ab
नाममात्रावशेषोऽसावन्तरालेऽवतिष्ठते 3.2.42ab
नाम रूपं तथा कर्म यदेतत्त्रयमीरितम् 1.6.28ab
नाम रूपं तथा कर्म संहतं सत् त्रिदण्डवत् 1.5.152ab
नामरूपक्रियातत्त्वमेतत्सर्वं प्रतीयताम् 1.6.10cd
नामरूपक्रियात्वेन मोहकार्योपसंहृतेः 1.5.343ab
नामरूपक्रियादेहः सर्वोऽस्मीत्यभिमानवान् 1.5.273ab
नामरूपक्रियाभिन्नो देहोऽयं गृह्यते यतः 1.6.34cd
नामरूपक्रियाभेदैर्यथा पूर्वमवादिषम् 2.5.134ab
नामरूपप्रकाश्या च क्रिया प्राणात्मिका तथा 1.4.706ab
नामरूपमतस्ताभ्यां पश्यन्नपि न पश्यति 1.4.687cd
नामरूपातिरेकेण न ज्ञेयं वस्तु विद्यते 1.4.705ab
नामरूपात्मकाः प्राणाः परसत्याभिसंगतेः 2.1.424ab
नामरूपात्मसत्त्येन च्छन्नं प्राणामृतं तु तत् 1.6.36cd
नामरूपादिना येयमविद्या प्रथतेऽसती 1.2.135ab
नामरूपादिभिन्नानामैकात्म्यं तद्वदात्मनि 2.4.301cd

नामरूपादिभेदेन वर्णादिप्रविभागतः 4.4.418ab
नामरूपादिभेदेन विभक्तं यत्तमो दृशेः 4.3.1518cd
नामरूपादिमत्कार्यं यः प्रविष्टः स्वमोहजम् 4.3.1ab
नामरूपादिमद्देहसंबन्धात्तद्विधर्मकः 1.2.156ab
नामरूपादिविकृतं पराङ्मानैकगोचरः 1.4.193ab
नामरूपादिसद्भावो दोषश्चेदिह चोद्यते 3.5.38cd
नामरूपादिसंभिन्नं जगदेतत्कथं पुनः 2.4.264ab
नामरूपाद्यभिव्यक्तेः प्राक्तनः काल उच्यते 1.4.204ab
नामरूपाद्यभिव्यक्तेः प्राग्व्यक्तापह्नवेऽप्यभूत् 1.4.520ab
नामरूपाभिमानाभ्यां मर्त्याभ्याममृतः स्वयम् 1.6.45ab
नामरूपाभ्यामेवेति न समुच्चयनिश्चितौ 1.4.398ab
नामरूपे तथा कर्म प्राणा लोकादयस्तथा 2.3.180ab
नामरूपेहचित्राद्या स्वप्नमायेन्द्रजालवत् SV 1112ef
नामवद्रूपवच्चेह कारणं यावदीक्ष्यते 1.2.2ab
नामात्मना तु तन्मानं मनोरूपं च मीयते 1.5.164cd
नामात्याः शेरते यस्माद्राज्ञि स्वामिनि जाग्रति 2.1.130cd
नामात्र वाङ्मयं सर्वं रूपं सर्वं मनोमयम् 1.5.154ab
नामात्वं कर्मकाण्डस्येत्यत्र प्रतिविधीयते 5.1.82cd
नामादिजन्मनि द्रष्टेत्यादिरूपान्वयोऽप्यभूत् 1.4.612cd
नामादिलयनिष्ठत्वे ह्यभ्युपेतेऽप्रमाणके SV 399cd
नामादीनि च तत्त्वानि प्राणान्तानि तथात्मनि 2.4.295ab
नामादौ तु यतो नैवं तस्मादसदिदं वचः 1.3.65cd
नामाद्यात्मकतैतस्य प्रपञ्चस्य प्रसाध्यते 1.6.9cd
नामाद्यात्मकतैवास्य ब्रह्मादेः स्थावरावधेः 1.6.8ab
नामाद्याशावसानं च प्राणे सर्वं प्रतिष्ठितम् 2.1.229ab
नामापि गृह्यमाणं सद्रूपं भवति शौक्ल्यवत् 1.5.142ab
नामाभिव्यक्तिकृद्वाक्स्यादेवं सर्वत्र योजना 1.4.706cd
नामीषां व्यापृतिस्तत्र ह्युत्पत्त्यादिविरोधतः 4.4.774cd
नामोपक्रममाशान्तं प्राणकारणसंश्रयम् 4.4.525ab
नामोपक्रममाशान्तामरनाभिनिदर्शनात् 1.4.351ab
नाम्नः सामान्यमात्रस्य त्वसाविति समीरणम् 1.4.393ab
नाम्नश्चाप्युपसंहारो ध्रुवायां हृदि वर्णितः 3.9.78ab

नाम्नायार्थो भवेत्तर्हि नैवं वेदार्थ एव हि 1.4.807cd
नाम्नि ब्रह्मेति दृष्टं चेन्न भेदप्रतिपत्तितः 1.3.63ab
नाम्नोरेवं च संबन्ध ऐकात्म्यात्स्यात्क्रियां विना SV 906ab
नायं कर्ममयो यस्मान्न च काममयः स्वतः 4.3.1043ab
नायं गुणविधिर्ज्ञेयस्तत्फलस्याश्रुतत्वतः 1.3.211cd
नायं धर्म इति ज्ञेयो योऽयं सृष्टाविहेरितः 1.4.1630ab
नायमन्योऽथवानन्यः प्रत्यगज्ञानजत्वतः 2.4.229ab
नायःशलाकाकल्पानां विशेषणविशेष्यता 1.4.1422ab
नारण्यस्था न च ग्राम्या अपेक्षन्तेऽत्र विद्यया 6.2.123ab
नारायणः परोऽव्यक्तादण्डमव्यक्तसंभवम् 3.7.40ab
नारायणाय विश्वाय देवानां परमात्मने 3.7.41cd
नार्तवानि प्रसूयन्ते योग्यहेतौ च तज्जनिः 4.3.1599cd
नार्थवादान्तरापेक्षा ह्यर्थवादस्य युज्यते 4.4.1134ab
नार्थस्पृग्भावना चेत्स्याद्ब्रह्मधीजन्मने न सा 1.4.883ab
नार्थानधिगतत्वं च प्रमाणेभ्यः प्रसिध्यति 4.3.171ab
नालं विमुक्तये काम्यं यदि नाम तथापि तु SV 1106ab
नालं विरोधात्पुरुषः पराञ्चीत्यागमोक्तितः 1.6.5cd
नालं साध्यान्तरायेह किम्वसाध्यार्थसिद्धये SV 1100cd
नालक्तकादेर्विकृतिर्निष्क्रियत्वादिहेष्यते 4.3.1584cd
नालमेतद्धि सर्वेषां पाप्मनां विनिवृत्तये 1.5.27cd
नावभास्यत्वतुल्यत्वाद्दीपस्यापि घटादिभिः 4.3.502ab
नावयोर्निष्प्रमाणोक्तं यतः संगच्छते सुधीः 4.3.544cd
नावशिष्यत एतस्मात्तदविद्योत्थमण्वपि 1.4.1580ab
नावश्यकार्यता चैषां सिद्धातोऽन्यत्र मानतः 1.4.1797ab
नाविकृत्य हि संयोगि गुणो द्रव्यं कदा चन 1.4.588ab
नावित्तसंगतिः शब्दो गमकोऽतोऽनुवादकः SV 742cd
नाविद्याघस्मरैकात्म्यसम्यग्दृष्ट्या समीक्ष्यते 4.3.80ab
नाविद्याघातिविज्ञानाद्द्वयध्वस्तिरभूद्विभोः 1.4.97ab
नाविद्या नापि तत्कार्यं प्रत्यक्स्थमपि ढौकते 1.4.1404cd
नाविद्या नापि तत्कार्यं यस्मादात्मसमीक्षणे 4.3.1252ef
नाविद्यामनुपादाय जाग्रत्स्वप्नसुषुप्तिषु 1.4.1384ab
नाविद्यामनुपादाय प्रतीचोऽनात्मसंगतिः 4.3.1797ab

नाविद्यामनुपादाय प्रत्यक्कारकतां व्रजेत् 1.4.1382ab
नाविद्यामन्तरेणैषां विशेषणविशेष्यता SV 121ab
नाविद्याया यतोऽस्तीह द्वैविध्यं तेन दुर्घटम् 2.4.200cd
नाविद्यारागद्वेषादिदोषदुष्टस्य तद्विधेः 1.3.93ab
नाविद्यावान्भवेदात्मा नापि तत्कार्यवांस्ततः 4.4.357cd
नाविद्यासंगतिस्तत्र तदकार्यत्वहेतुतः 1.4.1318ab
नाविद्यास्येत्यविद्यायामेवासित्वा प्रकल्प्यते SV 176ab
नाविद्याहानिकृज्ज्ञानमत्र प्रतिविधीयते 1.4.1528cd
नाविद्योपाश्रयं मुक्त्वा संभाव्यं प्रत्यगात्मनि 1.4.487cd
नाविध्वस्तं तमोऽतोऽस्ति न च ज्ञानमनुत्थितम् 2.4.101cd
नाविनश्यन्यतो वह्निर्व्यावर्त्येतौष्ण्यतः क्वचित् SV 57ab
नाविरक्तस्य निःशेषसांसारिकपुमर्थतः 6.2.6ab
नाविरतो दुश्चरितादिति चागमिकं वचः 1.4.1767ab
नाविरतो दुश्चरितान्नाशान्तो नासमाहितः SV 222ab
नाविरतो दुश्चरितान्नाशान्तो नासमाहितः 4.4.1249ab
नाविरोधात्तमो हन्ति कर्म किंचित्कदा चन 3.3.94cd
नावेदिषं सुषुप्तेऽहमिति धीः किंबलाद्भवेत् 3.4.103cd
नावेदिषमिति प्राह स्वानुभूत्यनुसारतः 1.4.289cd
नाव्याकृतं परादन्यदागमादवगम्यते 1.4.356cd
नाव्याकृतादेः संसिद्धौ परमात्मातिरेकतः 1.3.187ab
नाव्युत्थितमनाः कश्चित्प्रतीचोऽन्यत्प्रपश्यति 2.4.106ab
नाशकद्रक्षितुं नाशात्कथं ते कामकर्मणी 1.4.1749cd
नाशभेदविरुद्धार्थप्रमेये च व्यवस्थिते 1.2.68ab
नाशादि न स्वयं सिध्येद्विना नाशादिसाक्षिणा 4.3.1423ab
नाशान्तमानसो वापि प्रज्ञानेनैनमाप्नुयात् SV 222cd
नाशान्तमानसो वापि प्रज्ञानेनैनमाप्नुयात् 4.4.1249cd
नाशिनोऽपि न साक्षित्वं नाशेनाव्यतिरेकतः 1.4.378cd
नाशेऽपि तस्य नंष्टृत्वान्न नंष्टुः स्याद्विनाशिता 1.4.201cd
नाशोऽथ न किंचित्स्यात्सत्त्वं नैवमपोद्यते 1.2.47cd
नाशोत्पत्त्यादयो धर्मा हेतुमद्वस्तुनो यतः 4.3.1422ab
नाशौ यस्मादतः सिद्ध आत्मा कूटस्थदर्शनः 4.3.1500cd
नाश्रयापेक्षयैतत्स्याद्धृदीतीह विशेषणम् 4.4.438ab

नाश्रौषीद्यन्निमित्तं ज्ञस्तन्निमित्तमिदं शृणु	2.1.214cd
नासंवृतं तथा किंचित्प्रोततन्तुवदात्मना	2.5.122ab
नासंसारी परोऽन्योऽस्ति पाणिपेषप्रबोधितात्	2.1.433ab
नासंहतायाः कर्तृत्वं देवतायाः स्वतोऽपरैः	1.5.198cd
नासतो जन्मना योगः सतः सत्त्वान्न चेष्यते	1.4.626ab
नासतो जन्मना योगः सतः सत्त्वान्न चेष्यते	2.1.384ab
नासतो विद्यतेऽपेक्षा नापि कूटस्थवस्तुनः	4.3.1595ab
नासतो विद्यते भावो नाभावो विद्यते सतः	1.4.234ab
नासत्सद्व्यतिरेकेण नासता च सदन्वितम्	4.3.802ab
नासमीक्ष्य स्वसामर्थ्यं पुमान्विधिशतैरपि	2.4.178ab
नासिकाग्रे महद्दुःखं पादाङ्गुष्ठाग्र एव च	1.4.568ab
नासिद्धयोः स्वतोऽपेक्षा सिद्धयोश्चापि नेष्यते	1.4.230ab
नासौ कामोऽथवा कामी तत्संबन्धोऽथवा स्वयम्	4.4.469cd
नासौ ब्रह्मणि साफल्यं नाप्यन्यस्मिन्समश्नुते	1.4.1225cd
नासौ भूतात्मनाज्ञायि भूतज्ञानमनाश्रयम्	1.4.456cd
नासौ श्रेष्ठः पुरोगन्ता नान्नादोऽसुरवद्भवेत्	1.3.289ab
नास्ति ज्ञानमनुत्पन्नं नाप्यध्वस्तं तथा तमः	2.4.230cd
नास्ति रोगो न संतापो नास्ति कामादिसंप्लुतिः	2.1.277ab
नास्ति वस्तु यथा तद्वज्जाग्रद्बाह्यार्थवस्त्वपि	4.3.534cd
नास्ति व्याधिर्जरा नास्ति नास्ति देशपरिभ्रमः	2.1.276cd
नास्तीति तु विना मानं न सिध्येत्कुम्भवत्स्वतः	3.8.117cd
नास्तीति ब्रुवतो लज्जा धाष्टर्यादेव न जायते	4.3.540cd
नास्तीह कश्चिद्धात्वर्थो यः स्वहेतुं विनाशयेत्	1.2.42cd
नास्त्यत्र हन्ता जेता वा किंत्वज्ञानोत्थमेव तत्	4.3.1249ab
नास्त्यर्थोऽपि कथं जीवेदस्त्यर्थविरहादिह	4.3.573cd
नास्य धर्मो भवेदेतत्सुषुप्ते तददर्शनात्	4.3.1382ab
नास्य स्वापः प्रबोधो वा कुतः स्वप्नस्य संभवः	2.1.264ab
नास्यास्तित्वे यथा मानमेकत्वादक्षरात्मनः	3.8.124ab
नाहं तद्भगवन्वेद यत्र यास्याम्यतः परम्	4.2.31ab
नाहं ममेति वा बुद्धिस्तत्राहेरुपजायते	4.4.510ab
नाहं वेदेति च नृपो जानन्नप्यब्रवीत्कथम्	4.2.11ab
निकषोपलसंस्थेषु वेदवित्सु परीक्ष्यताम्	6.2.21ab

निकृष्टदेहसंबन्धप्रापकैरपि कर्मभिः 4.3.1364ab
निखिलेऽपि जगत्यस्मिन्प्रधानं नात्मनोऽपरः SV 473cd
निगडध्वंसवन्नापि पुंसो मोक्ष इहात्मनः 4.4.320ab
निगमायोत्तरो ग्रन्थः प्रतिज्ञाया विवक्षितः 2.5.12cd
निगीर्णं सज्जलूकादि दृष्टं देशं यथाश्रयेत् 1.4.346ab
निगृह्यमाणयोगे च प्लुतिमत्र विनिर्दिशेत् 2.1.86ab
निचिक्युस्ते विदुः साक्षादग्र्यं ब्रह्म सनातनम् 4.4.643cd
नितरां चापि विज्ञाते मृषाधीर्नास्त्यबाधिता SV 178cd
नितरामभावयोर्न स्याद्दूरतो भावाभावयोः 4.3.1716cd
नितरामभावयोर्न स्यान्न विरुद्धाविरुद्धयोः 4.3.1698cd
नित्यं चायुतसिद्धांशानुगतोऽवयवी यदि 2.1.479cd
नित्यं न भवनं यस्य यस्य वा नित्यभूतता 2.4.116ab
नित्यं न भवनं यस्य यस्य वा नित्यभूतता 4.3.1596ab
नित्यं भवितृतन्त्रत्वात्संतानस्याप्यनित्यता 4.3.631ab
नित्यं भुङ्क्ते यथैवान्नमात्मा वाग्देहबुद्धिभिः 3.2.66ab
नित्यं संनिहिते तस्मिंस्तत्स्मृत्या किं प्रयोजनम् 1.4.832cd
नित्यं ह्युपनिषत्स्वेव श्रूयते वैदिकीष्वयम् 3.9.120cd
नित्यकर्मप्रसिद्ध्यर्थमतो वित्तमिहेष्यते 3.5.116ab
नित्यकर्मफलत्वं चेन्मुक्तेरप्यभ्युपेयते 3.3.115ab
नित्यकर्मफलत्वेन मुक्तेरपि परिग्रहात् 3.3.114ab
नित्यकर्मवचःस्वेवं नातो मुक्तिविनिश्चयः SV 93cd
नित्यकर्मविधेर्यस्माच्छमादिविधिना हतिः 4.4.1226ab
नित्यकर्माद्यनुष्ठानसंशुद्धधिषणः पुमान् 2.4.2ab
नित्यकर्माभिसंबन्धो मुक्तेः स्यात्पारिशेष्यतः 3.3.108cd
नित्यकर्मैव सूत्रेषु तेन विद्वत्प्रयोज्यता 1.3.347cd
नित्यत्वं चात्मनः सिद्धं प्रत्यभिज्ञादिमानतः 5.1.74cd
नित्यत्वाद्धेतुवचनं न युक्त्यातोऽवगम्यते 1.4.1797cd
नित्यनैमित्तिकानीह कर्तृसंस्कारतो यतः SV 326ab
नित्यप्रयोगरूपोत्थविज्ञानात्तद्विनिश्चितिः 1.4.1625cd
नित्यप्राप्तं च विज्ञानं प्रतीचः संनिधेः सदा SV 370ab
नित्यप्राप्तिमिहाचष्टे विध्यर्थापनुनुत्सया 1.4.759ab
नित्यमक्षजगम्यत्वाद्दुःखस्योत्पलनीलवत् 1.4.586ab

नित्यमुक्तत्वविज्ञानं वाक्यादेवाञ्जसा भवेत् 2.4.111ab
नित्यमुक्तत्वविज्ञानं वाक्याद्भवति नान्यतः SV 206ab
नित्यमेकं विभु द्रव्यं यदि कालोऽभ्युपेयते 2.1.406ab
नित्यमेवेति चेन्नैवमन्यथात्वातिरेकतः 1.4.591cd
नित्ययज्ञगृहीत्यर्थं के च यज्ञा इतीरणम् 1.5.294cd
नित्यलब्धैकरूपस्य नालाभोऽज्ञानतोऽन्यतः 1.4.1011ab
नित्यविघ्नकृदेवैष प्राणाप्तावासुरो मतः 1.3.190ab
नित्यशक्तितत्वपक्षेऽपि युगपत्प्रभवादिकम् 2.1.403ab
नित्यशुद्धश्च बुद्धश्च यस्मादात्मा परः स्वतः 1.4.491ab
नित्यस्य कर्मणः कार्यं पारिशेष्यसमाश्रयात् 3.3.107ab
नित्यस्य सर्वकर्मभ्यो वैलक्षण्याच्च कारणात् 3.3.119ab
नित्यस्याकरणाद्यः स्यादनर्थः करणादपि 4.4.1213ab
नित्यस्याकरणे दोषस्तत्क्रियायां न यद्यपि SV 82ab
नित्यस्यानुच्छित्तिरिति चोद्यस्यापि न संभवः 1.4.359ab
नित्यस्यावाप्यतेऽसौ चेद्वद किं नित्यकर्मणा 4.4.1213cd
नित्याज्ञानसमुच्छित्तौ यतः प्रामाण्यमाश्रितम् 1.4.359cd
नित्यात्मज्योतिषा दीप्तां विशिंषन्ति सुखादयः 1.4.563cd
नित्यात्मदृष्टिश्चिन्मात्रः पश्येत्तं पृथिवी कथम् 3.7.51cd
नित्यादिकरणान्नापि काम्यादेश्चापि वर्जनात् SV 78ab
नित्यादेः फलमिष्टं चेदुपात्तदुरितक्षयः SV 83ab
नित्यानां कर्मणां कस्मात्परित्यागो विधीयते 4.4.1229cd
नित्यानां कर्मणां तस्मिन्सत्येव घटते यतः 3.3.77cd
नित्यानामपि संन्यासः कर्मणां स्यात्तदैव तु 1.5.306cd
नित्यानामफलत्वात्तु मुक्तिरेवास्तु तत्फलम् SV 1127cd
नित्यानुमितरूपस्य गृहीतिः स्यान्मनागपि 1.4.580cd
नित्यान्यपि च कर्माणि तत्संस्कारफलाश्रयात् 1.4.12ab
नित्यास्तत्राहुतीर्हुत्वा आवापस्थान आदरात् 6.4.84cd
नित्येषु शुद्धेः प्राधान्याद्भोगोऽप्यप्रतिबन्धकः SV 1131ab
नित्योऽकर्मप्रयुक्तः स न विधेयः कथं चन 1.4.889cd
नित्योऽतो नित्यया दृष्ट्या पश्यन्नेवाविलुप्तया 4.3.1557ab
नित्योऽनित्यानामिति च येन सूर्यस्तथा परः 4.3.363ab
नित्योऽस्य महिमेत्येवमुदर्केऽपि प्रवक्ष्यते 3.3.55cd

नित्यो ध्यानादिरूपो वा स स्याद्बुद्धिविशुद्धये 4.4.757cd
नित्योपात्तानि भूतानि करणानि च देहिनः 4.4.143ab
नित्योपासनसंप्राप्तिस्तज्ज्ञानानां तदन्वयात् 1.4.919cd
निदाघे शीतवद्यस्मादतोऽसम्यगिदं वचः SV 69ab
निदानबहुलाज्ञानसमुच्छित्त्यै परा श्रुतिः 1.4.1281cd
निदानस्यानिषिद्धत्वात्पूर्वोक्तैः कर्मभिः पुर SV 1094cd
निदिध्यासनवाक्येन साधनं ध्यानलक्षणम् 4.4.809cd
निदिध्यासनशब्देन ध्यानमाशङ्क्यते यतः 2.4.233cd
निदिध्यासनशब्देन सम्यग्ज्ञानं विवक्षितम् 1.4.899ab
निदिध्यासनसिद्ध्यर्थं केचिद्व्याचक्षते परम् 2.5.14ab
निदिध्यासनसिद्ध्यर्थो यत्नोऽतोऽयमनर्थकः 2.5.17ab
निदिध्यासस्व चेतोऽतो व्याचक्षाणस्य तन्मम 2.4.70cd
निदेशाय च कल्पन्ते प्राणा वा इति नान्यथा 2.3.95ab
निद्रां हत्वा यतः स्वप्नज्ञानादपि विबुध्यते 1.2.133cd
निद्रान्धः सन्यथा स्वप्ने ह्यग्निव्याघ्रादिसंगतेः 4.4.840ab
निद्रास्वप्नप्रहाणेन बोधमात्रार्थभाग्भवेत् 4.4.840cd
निधनं कारणत्वात्त्वं कारणे कार्यसंलयः 6.3.34cd
निनङ्क्षु नश्यन्नष्टं च प्रत्यभिज्ञामृते कथम् 4.3.620cd
निन्दाश्रुतेर्न काम्यानां कार्यताध्यवसीयते SV 327cd
निपुणोऽपि नरः शक्तः खिल्यरूपेण पूर्ववत् 2.4.402ab
निमित्तत्वेन सन्मानं सुषुप्तोत्थापकोक्तिवत् 3.2.115cd
निमेषादिविभक्तानां कालांशानां व्यवस्थितिः 3.8.139ab
नियच्छति क्षितिं देवीं सर्वावस्थासु सर्वदा 3.7.45cd
नियच्छति यतो गन्धे त्रयमप्येतदीश्वरः 3.7.47cd
नियतानि तथैवेह प्रत्यग्लोकाप्तिमिच्छताम् 4.4.1089cd
नियतानेकहेतुत्वान्नातो भुजिसमा क्रिया 1.3.106cd
नियतैव प्रवृत्तिश्च स्रोतसां महतामपि 3.8.140ab
नियतोपायसाध्यत्वादवाप्यपरिहार्ययोः SV 887ab
नियन्तव्यनियन्तृत्वसंबन्धस्य प्रसिद्धये 3.9.7cd
नियन्ता कारणं चेति न तु सूत्रान्तिकेऽसति 3.8.37cd
नियन्ता चाभिमन्ता च ब्राह्मणत्वस्य हव्यवाट् 1.4.1666ab
नियन्तुरपि चेन्मैवं श्रुतेर्वस्तुन्यपि ध्रुवम् 3.8.147ab

नियमं त्वपरे धीराः परिसंख्यामथापरे 1.4.751cd
नियमः परिसंख्या वा न तेनेहोपपद्यते 2.4.146cd
नियमाद्द्वन्द्वसंपातसहनं तप उच्यते 4.4.1054ab
नियमाभावतो नासावनवस्था प्रसज्यते 4.3.523ab
नियमार्थो विधिरयमिति भाष्यकृतो वचः 1.4.921ab
नियमासंभवः प्राप्तद्व्यतिरेकस्तयोर्यदि SV 60cd
नियमेन प्रयुज्यन्त इत्यत्र मितिरस्ति ते SV 575cd
नियमेन फलं तद्वत्साधनानुष्ठितेर्भवेत् SV 639cd
नियमे परिसंख्यायां सर्वानात्मासमीक्षणात् 4.4.936ab
नियमे हेत्वसद्भावान्न स्यान्नैयमिकी स्थितिः 3.2.146cd
नियमोऽस्यैवकारेण पवमानेषु कथ्यते 1.3.348cd
नियमो युक्तिमानेष कर्मिणामुपपद्यते 3.9.159cd
नियम्यं कार्यमापेक्ष्य नियन्तैष तमोवधिः 1.4.345ab
नियम्यदेवताभेदव्याससंक्षेपवर्त्मना 3.9.2cd
नियम्यमानो दैवेन क्षत्रियेण मनुष्यगः 1.4.1641ab
नियुक्तोऽपि न तत्कर्तुमलं शक्ये स हीश्वरः 1.4.878cd
नियुक्तोऽपि नियोगेन तादृङ्नैवेक्षितुं क्षमः 1.4.892cd
नियुङ्क्ते पुरुषं तस्माद्वस्तुवृत्तं सुदुर्लभम् 1.4.877cd
नियुज्यते फलप्राप्तौ यथा तदभिधीयते 5.1.110cd
नियुज्यमान एवेह विषयं साध्यमीक्ष्यते SV 530cd
नियोगं शब्दतो बुद्ध्वा योऽपि श्रोता प्रवर्तते SV 738ab
नियोगः कस्ततः पूर्वं संबन्धे हेतुरुच्यताम् SV 609cd
नियोगपक्षमाश्रित्य विध्यर्थासंभवो यथा SV 797ab
नियोगवर्त्मना चेय यथा मुक्तिर्न सिध्यति SV 461ab
नियोगस्तदसंवादाच्चित्रादौ ते विहन्यते SV 518cd
नियोगस्यात एवात्र कर्तृत्वेन नियुज्यते SV 520cd
नियोगस्यापि कार्यत्वं प्रेषणाध्येषणादिभिः SV 712ab
नियोगस्यापि मानत्वं नानपेक्ष्य प्रमामिमाम् 1.4.875cd
नियोगस्यापि संसिद्धौ स दोषो नापनुद्यते SV 717cd
नियोगात्कर्मसंबन्धे पश्चाद्यातीह कर्तृताम् SV 523cd
नियोगादिः प्रमाणार्थो नानुभूतिर्नियोगतः SV 466cd
नियोगादेव तद्बुद्धौ नियोगत्वं भवेद्यतः 1.4.894cd

नियोगानुप्रवेशेन यतो वस्त्ववबोध्यते 1.4.793cd
नियोगानुप्रवेशेन वस्तुतत्त्वावबोधनम् 1.4.891cd
नियोगार्थानुरोधेन यदि वस्त्ववबोध्यते 1.4.893cd
नियोगे लौकिके चापि हरीतक्यादिभक्षणे SV 692ab
नियोगोऽथ प्रमारूपो विधिशब्दप्रकाशितः SV 748ab
नियोगोऽपि नियोज्यस्य व्यापारः स कथं भवेत् SV 625ab
नियोगोऽपीह नायाति भिन्नकर्त्रादिगो ह्यसौ 1.4.1361cd
नियोगो न प्रतीयेत विशिष्टविषयस्तथा SV 608ab
नियोज्यतद्विषययोर्यत्र भेदोऽवसीयते 1.4.855ab
नियोज्यविषयाभेदे घटते न विधिर्यतः 2.4.97cd
नियोज्यस्य च नैश्वर्यं धीसम्यक्त्वं प्रतीष्यते 2.4.152ab
निरंशस्य न चाप्यंशकल्पनाप्युपपद्यते SV 1073ab
निरंशेषु न चाप्येवं सभागेष्विव वस्तुषु 4.3.1778ab
निरच्चकं मध्यतो मृत्युर्निर्जीवं देहवत्स्थितम् 5.5.13ab
निरधारि पुरा तस्य याथात्म्यं त्वत्र पृच्छ्यते 3.5.26cd
निरधारि पुरा ब्रह्म मधुकाण्डागमेन यत् 4.5.1ab
निरनुग्रहं निष्करणं वासनोपाधिमात्रकम् 4.3.1146ab
निरनुग्रहतैवास्य पर्यावर्तनमुच्यते 4.4.58ab
निरन्तरायतोऽशेषपुमर्थस्यात्मरूपतः SV 251ab
निरन्तरायो वाक्यार्थं वाक्यादेवावगच्छति 2.4.110ab
निरन्वयविनाशस्य निषेधोऽत्र विवक्ष्यते 4.3.1505ab
निरन्वयविनाशाय योऽलं संसाररूपिणः 1.4.1320cd
निरन्वयोऽयं नाशः स्यादेषामन्यतमोऽपि न 1.4.199cd
निरन्वयो विनाशोऽस्य हीत्युक्त्या निषिध्यते 4.3.1497ab
निरपेक्षमलं मुक्त्या इत्येतदभिधीयते 4.5.22cd
निरपेक्षात्मनैवेह सर्वस्यात्मवतो यतः 4.4.644ab
निरपेक्षा प्रमाणाप्तौ मानाप्तकरबिल्ववत् 4.4.908ef
निरमन्थतां याभ्यां तावश्विनावमृतं पुरा 6.4.104cd
निरर्थकमिदं च स्याद्दृष्टेरिति यदुच्यते 3.4.182cd
निरवर्ततेवास्यात्मा परिच्छेदाभिमानतः 1.2.160cd
निरविद्य इहाद्वैते भेदहेतोरसंभवात् 1.4.1185ab
निरविद्यं तु यद्रूपमनन्यापेक्षसिद्धिकम् 4.3.1333ab

निरविद्याद्वयत्वात्तत्साक्षाद्ब्रह्मेति शब्द्यते 3.9.156cd
निरविद्ये च विद्याया आनर्थक्यं प्रसज्यते SV 175cd
निरविद्योऽसितो भास्वदविलुप्तचिदात्मकः 3.9.98ab
निरस्तदारसंबन्धे न तु स्याद्ब्रह्मचारिणि 1.5.266cd
निरस्ताज्ञानतत्कार्यं पश्येत्तद्वदनात्मसु 1.4.728cd
निरस्ताज्ञानतत्कार्ये लब्ध आत्मन्यथात्मना 2.3.196ab
निरस्तातिशयं कर्म ज्ञानं चाप्यापि बालवत् 1.4.55ab
निरस्तातिशयज्ञानो याज्ञवल्क्यो यतो गृही 2.4.22ab
निरस्तातिशयानन्दरूपता प्रत्यगात्मनः 1.4.189ab
निरस्तातिशयानन्दो भवतीत्यस्य निर्णयः 4.3.1852cd
निरस्तावयवे व्योम्नि मिथोभिन्नप्रदेशिनाम् 1.4.684ab
निरस्ताशेषदुःखे च मोहात्तत्र विपर्ययः 4.4.257cd
निरस्ताशेषसंभेदं दृष्टिमात्रं निरञ्जनम् 4.4.305ab
निरस्ताशेषानर्थश्च तन्मोहाद्विपरीतधीः 1.4.1813cd
निरस्ताशेषानर्थाप्तकृत्स्नाह्लादसतत्त्वकः 2.1.5ab
निरस्य पूर्वपक्षोक्तीः परिहारोक्तिभिः क्रमात् 4.3.1538ab
निराकर्तुं न च ततः शक्यते येन केनचित् 4.4.229cd
निराकर्तुमभिप्रायः सुमूढस्यापि जायते 4.3.559cd
निराकार्षं सुयुक्त्युक्त्या मोक्षोऽतोऽज्ञाननिह्नुतिः 4.4.323ab
निराकृता स्वयं सद्भिर्यथा वियति कृष्णिमा 4.3.1706cd
निराचिकीर्षया शून्यवादिनोऽविषयत्वतः 4.3.807cd
निरात्मकपरार्थत्वहेतुभ्यां शुक्तिरूप्यवत् 1.4.1324cd
निरात्मका न शक्यन्ते तद्विशेषाः समीक्षितुम् 2.4.277cd
निरात्मवादः पूर्वोक्तस्तस्मान्नैवं प्रकल्पयेत् SV 64cd
निरात्मवादसक्तिश्च मोहोच्छेदे भवेदिह 2.3.131cd
निरानन्दं तथा केचित्कैवल्यं प्रतिजानते 3.9.174ab
निराशिषमनारम्भं निर्नमस्कारमस्तुतिम् 4.4.594ab
निरासङ्गः पुमानेष स्वप्नबुद्धान्तयोरपि 4.3.1074ab
निरासङ्गत्वसिद्ध्यर्थं प्रत्यगात्माख्यवस्तुनः 4.3.1082cd
निरासङ्गस्य विदुषस्तस्मान्मुक्तिं प्रतीमहे 4.3.1100ab
निरुणद्धि यथा जन्म तन्नाशमपि तत्तथा 3.2.20ab
निरुणद्ध्यात्मविज्ञानं तदानिष्टं प्रसज्यते 1.4.1532cd

निरुह्य कार्यतां नीत्वा प्रत्युह्याथात्मकारणे 3.9.113cd
निरुह्येति तथा श्रुत्या कारणात्माभिधीयते 2.4.386ab
निरूप्यमाणे नान्यादृग्यस्मात्तत्त्वं समीक्ष्यते 4.5.19cd
निरेषणात्मसंबोधाद्बाध्यैवेयमतो भवेत् 3.5.131cd
निरेषणानां नेदृग्घि संसारं प्रजिहासताम् 1.4.1023ab
निरेषणैकयाथात्म्ये न यथावस्तुकामधीः 3.5.131ab
निरोधकाले चित्तस्य वासकत्वं न युज्यते 4.3.687ab
निरोधस्तर्हि पूर्वोक्तान्मतमर्थान्तरं यदि 1.4.848ab
निर्गच्छन्प्रविशन्सर्पो निर्मोकमनुरुध्यते 4.4.509cd
निर्गमय्याण्डतः प्रादाद्वायवे सूक्ष्मरूपिणे 3.3.158cd
निर्गुणं सन्तमात्मानं रञ्जयित्वावतिष्ठते 4.4.493cd
निर्गुणोऽपि परैकांशो बहिरभ्यागतेन सः 2.3.119ab
निर्ग्रन्थिशास्त्रतुल्यत्वं स्मृतीनां वः प्रसज्यते 4.4.1151cd
निर्ज्ञातमागमात्तस्मात्पृच्छ्यते साधनान्तरम् 3.5.193cd
निर्ज्ञातविषयत्वाच्च कर्मशक्तेर्जगत्यपि 3.3.25ab
निर्ज्ञाताशेषकर्मोत्थफलफल्गुत्वबुद्धयः SV 1125cd
निर्णयाघाटविज्ञप्त्यै नाशेषप्रश्ननिर्णयात् 4.3.973cd
निर्णयार्थाय ते ब्रह्म जग्मुरिन्द्रं प्रजापतिम् 6.1.17ab
निर्णीतं प्रथमं वस्तु पश्यन्निति यदीरितम् 4.3.1602ab
निर्णीतः प्रागथेदानीमाङ्गिरसत्वविनिर्णयः 1.3.290cd
निर्णीतार्थो न तावत्स्यात्प्रश्नः साक्षादितीरितः 3.6.4cd
निर्णीतेऽप्यथ मां राजा पुनः पुनरपृच्छत 4.3.1892ab
निर्णुदेत्संशयं प्राज्ञ एवमन्योऽन्यहेतुता 1.4.1626cd
निर्णेनेक्ति स्फुटं वस्तु यथोक्तेनैव वर्त्मना 1.4.316cd
निर्दुःखित्वे परस्येष्टे तदन्यस्याप्यभावतः 1.4.598ab
निर्देशस्तु परिच्छिन्नविषयोऽत्राभिधीयते 2.3.75cd
निर्देश्यत्वानुमादोषप्रसङ्गविनिवृत्तये 3.8.66ab
निर्देष्टुं शक्यते तस्मादनिर्देश्योऽपि सन्नसौ 4.4.491cd
निर्द्वयं सद्वयं वेति नोवत्तहेतोस्तदीक्ष्यते 3.4.19cd
निर्धारणे वा षष्ठीयं ज्ञेयार्थस्यावधारणात् 1.4.977ab
निर्धारितार्थं जानीयात्स्फुटन्यायसमाश्रयात् 1.4.1735cd
निर्धूताशेषकलुषं शान्तदर्पं समीक्ष्य तम् 6.2.44ab

निर्धूताशेषदुःखौघहेतुत्वात्सुखमेव तत् 3.9.154ab
निर्धूताशेषनानात्वतद्धेतुरविभागवान् 1.4.611ab
निर्निमित्तं प्रमात्रादेः प्रत्यग्रूपमनात्मनः 1.4.1499ab
निर्निमित्तस्य कृत्स्नत्वेऽप्यस्मदादेस्तथा न किम् 1.4.1120ab
निर्निमित्तात्तथैवेशाज्जगज्जन्मस्थितिक्षयाः 1.4.369cd
निर्बीजस्य च जन्मेह नागमान्न च युक्तितः 3.9.146ab
निर्भागं सकलाभिधानमननव्यापारदूरस्थितम् SV 1c
निर्भागत्वात्प्रतीचस्तत्कया युक्त्योपपद्यते 1.4.594cd
निर्भेदकस्य कुम्भस्य भेदः केनेति भण्यताम् 4.3.1699ab
निर्ममाहंकृतित्वं तु सर्पदृष्टान्तसंश्रयम् 4.4.508cd
निर्मातव्योऽथ भोक्तव्यो यो लोकोऽभूदिहात्मनः 4.3.875ab
निर्मायेति स्वयं तद्वदात्मकर्मण्यपेक्षया 4.3.873ab
निर्माल्यवत्परित्यज्य चैतन्याभासवर्त्मना 1.4.1350ab
निर्वर्तयतु रूपाणि शोभनानि सुतस्य मे 6.4.100cd
निर्वर्त्य संस्कारमथ यत्नात्प्राग्य उदाहृतः 6.4.81cd
निर्विकल्पे कथं ते स्याद्वद भेदोऽत्र किंकृतः 4.3.487cd
निर्विकल्पो यथैकोऽर्थो नेतीत्यत्रोपसंहृतः 4.5.17cd
निर्विकारात्मनां यस्माद्वालादीनां स्व आत्मनि 2.1.351ab
निर्विद्य च तथा मौनं पदार्थद्वयसंगतिम् 3.5.189cd
निर्विभागात्मनस्तस्य प्राञ्चः प्राणाः पुरास्य ये 4.2.86ab
निर्वृत्तात्माधिकारौ तावेकैवासौ भवेदसुः 1.2.224cd
निर्व्यापाराः सर्वभावाः क्षणिकाश्चेति निश्चितेः 4.3.581ab
निर्हरन्त्यृत्विजोऽरण्यमन्ये वा मां मृतं गृहात् 5.13.3ab
निर्हेतुत्वात्प्रतीचोऽस्य तमस्वित्वस्य सर्वदा 4.4.1001ab
निर्हेतुत्वात्मसंबोधरूपित्वं वस्तुरूपतः SV 544cd
निर्हेतुनाशसंव्याप्तेर्न स्यात्कुम्भजनिर्मृदः 1.2.43ab
निर्हेतु प्रत्यगज्ञानं लक्ष्यते तेन नित्यवत् 1.4.670cd
निर्हेतुसाक्षिणो न स्युरागमापायिसाक्षितः 4.3.1422cd
निर्हेत्वविद्याक्लृप्तौ तु दोषः कश्चिन्न विद्यते SV 158cd
निर्हैतुकी स्वतः प्रीतिरात्मन्येव यतस्ततः 2.4.83ab
निवर्तते च तद्द्वेषान्न शब्दव्यापृतेर्नरः SV 592cd
निवर्तते निवृत्तं चेत्येतदप्यनुभूतितः 4.4.295cd

निवर्तते स कार्पण्यात्तज्ज्ञानाद्ध्वान्तबाधतः 3.8.168cd
निवर्तनाद्धि सर्वतो न वेत्ति दुःखमण्वपि 4.3.1885cd
निवर्तनाद्धि सर्वतो न वेत्ति दुःखमण्वपि 4.4.1262cd
निवर्तयित्वा रसनं रसेभ्यो घ्राणं च गन्धाच्छ्रवणं च शब्दात्
4.4.1265ab
निवर्तेतापि कामेभ्यस्तदुपायाप्रसिद्धितः SV 347ab
निवर्त्यत्वेन मोक्षस्य कर्मणा यन्निवर्त्यते 3.3.92cd
निवर्त्यभेदाद्भिन्नोऽर्थोऽमानित्वादेर्यथा तथा 1.4.1429ab
निवासश्च निवासी च तथा चोभयमुच्यते 1.4.523ab
निविवृत्सुं नृपो विप्रं भूयोऽपृच्छद्विमुक्तये 4.3.966cd
निविवृत्सोस्तु संसारान्मुनेस्त्यक्तैषणस्य च 3.9.161ab
निवृत्तकामं मां मत्वा विद्यां भूयो न वक्ष्यति 4.4.536cd
निवृत्तावेव निःशेषसंसारस्य तदापि तु SV 254ab
निवृत्तिः क्रियते यस्य विद्येतेनेह कर्मणा 3.3.22cd
निवृत्तिमात्रं प्राप्तं वा भवेदुक्तेन वर्त्मना 4.4.1220ab
निवृत्तिमात्रं बन्धस्य कथंचिदुपपद्यते 4.4.320cd
निवृत्तिरप्यविद्याया नावगत्यात्मनोऽपरा 4.4.855cd
निवृत्तिलक्षणे वाच्यं केनायं प्रेर्यतेऽवशः 1.4.1807cd
निवृत्तिश्च यथोक्तैव तेषामैकात्म्यलक्षणा 2.3.239ab
निवृत्तिस्तद्वत्तद्धेतोर्नावगत्यात्मनोऽपरा 4.3.1521cd
निवृत्तिस्तद्वदेवास्य नावगत्यात्मनोऽपरा 2.3.210cd
निवृत्तिस्तद्वदेवास्य नावगत्यात्मनोऽपरा 3.8.122cd
निवृत्तिस्तद्वदेवास्य नावगत्यात्मनोऽपरा 4.4.301cd
निवृत्तो द्वैतविषयाद्यप्येष तथापि तु 3.2.56ab
निवृत्त्यर्थेऽविरोधित्वादत एतत्समीरितम् 1.4.406cd
निशायां संप्रवृत्तायां संहृताक्षस्य निद्रया 2.1.282ab
निशायां संप्रवृत्तायां संहृताक्षस्य निद्रया 4.3.1065ab
निश्चयेन तदासक्तं यस्मिन्विषय आत्मना 4.4.243ab
निश्चितं फलवज्ज्ञानं यस्य स्यादिति शास्त्रतः 1.4.1277ab
निश्चितं यच्च संदिग्धं तथाविज्ञातमेव च 4.4.423ab
निश्चितं साधनं वाच्यं ज्ञानं निःश्रेयसं प्रति SV 73cd
निश्चित्याचिन्त्यमेतद्यो योगिनां निलयं परम् 2.5.72ab

निःशेषं ब्रह्मलोकान्तं संहृत्य हृदयात्मना 3.9.80ab
निःशेषकरणग्रामलयेऽप्यनुभवः स्वतः SV 994ab
निःशेषकर्मकारित्वात्तस्मादुक्तमपेशलम् SV 103cd
निःशेषकर्मकार्याणां भोगेनैव समाप्तितः 1.5.246cd
निःशेषकर्मसंन्यासं विद्यायाः साधनं श्रुतिः 3.5.108cd
निःशेषकर्मसंन्यासं स्वयमेव प्रवक्ष्यति 3.5.142cd
निःशेषकर्मसंन्यासापेक्षापि स्याद्यतो मुनिः 4.5.25cd
निःशेषकर्मसंन्यासो यतोऽतो नर्णबद्धता 2.4.27cd
निःशेषकर्मसंन्यासो वाक्यार्थज्ञानजन्मने SV 214ab
निःशेषकर्महेतूत्थफलसावद्यधीस्ततः 2.4.2cd
निःशेषकर्मोज्झितिमाह साक्षात् 3.5.148d
निःशेषकल्मषध्वंसितपसा वाविपश्चितः 6.2.148ab
निःशेषकामकर्मादेर्व्युत्थाप्यात्मानमब्रवीत् 4.4.489ab
निःशेषजनिमत्कार्यहेतोर्वा ज्ञाततत्त्विनः 4.4.622ab
निःशेषजनिमद्धेतुः काम एवावधारितः 4.4.384ab
निःशेषतस्तमोध्वस्तेः पुमर्थश्च समाप्यते 2.1.8cd
निःशेषदुःखसंबन्धहेतूच्छित्तेः प्रबोधतः 4.4.614cd
निःशेषदृष्टान्तोक्त्यर्थप्रसक्तिविनिवृत्तये 1.4.1553cd
निःशेषधीविकाराणां यस्मात्साक्षित्वमात्मनः 4.3.443ab
निःशेषध्वान्तसंबन्धव्यतिक्रान्तमिदं ततः 4.3.1355cd
निःशेषनिर्णयोक्तीच्छुः कहोलोऽप्याह पूर्ववत् 3.5.54ab
निःशेषपरिणामेऽपि पयोवत्परमात्मनः 2.1.482ab
निःशेषपुण्यमोषित्वान्निषेधार्थाय कुत्स्यते 5.16.54cd
निःशेषपुरुषार्थानां कैवल्योत्तमता यथा 2.5.97ab
निःशेषपुरुषार्थानां ज्ञेयानां चापि कृत्स्नतः 1.4.1163ab
निःशेषपुरुषार्थानां पुण्यं कर्म हि साधनम् 3.3.10ab
निःशेषपुरुषार्थाप्तिः सर्वदुःखौघनिह्नुतिः 4.4.760ab
निःशेषपुरुषार्थाप्तिः सर्वानर्थात्ययः सदा 2.1.569ab
निःशेषपुरुषार्थाप्तिकारि ब्रह्मावबोधनम् 1.4.1263cd
निःशेषपुरुषार्थाप्तिर्दुःखहानिस्तु तत्फलम् 1.4.1008ab
निःशेषपुरुषार्थाप्तिलोपकृत्कर्म वर्णितम् 6.4.63ab
निःशेषपुरुषार्थाप्तिस्तद्बुद्धेरनृतन्त्रतः 1.4.1264cd

निःशेषपुरुषार्थाप्तेर्न कार्यं शिष्यते परम् 4.4.620cd
निःशेषपुरुषार्थोऽयं समाप्तो ब्रह्मबोधतः 4.4.1305ab
निःशेषप्रत्ययाधारधर्म्यस्तित्वं प्रसाध्य हि 1.5.108ab
निःशेषप्राप्त्या चोच्छिन्नकामकर्मादिबन्धनः 1.4.1199cd
निःशेषफलसंप्राप्तेर्दर्शनादेव केवलात् 1.5.226ab
निःशेषबुद्धिवृत्तीनां ध्यानं स्यादुपलक्षणम् 4.3.410ab
निःशेषबुद्धिसाक्ष्येवं परमात्मप्रदीपकः 4.3.891ab
निःशेषभूतसाम्याद्वा साम प्राणोऽभिधीयते 1.3.304ab
निःशेषभूतात्मैकः सन्नधिदैवात्मना स्थितः 1.5.347ab
निःशेषभेदसामान्यदृष्ट्यावृत्तिरुपासनम् 1.4.695ab
निःशेषभोगभुक्तत्वात्कृत्स्नप्राप्त्या द्वयात्मनः 1.4.1711cd
निःशेषमातृतद्वृत्तिजन्मनां तद्विलक्षण- SV 542ab
निःशेषमात्मसंबोधं कुर्यादिति विधीयते 3.5.177ab
निःशेषमिथ्याविज्ञानहेत्वविद्याविनाशकृत् 4.4.554ab
निःशेषमेवं सत्यस्य रूपं व्याख्याय सांप्रतम् 2.3.171ab
निःशेषलोकधीवृत्तिसाक्षिणैवाविकारिणः 4.3.882ab
निःशेषवाङ्मनःकायप्रवृत्त्युपरमात्मिका SV 281ab
निःशेषविक्रियावर्गप्रतिषेधश्रुतेस्तथा 4.3.1110ab
निःशेषविक्रियाहेतुकालातिक्रमहेतुतः 4.4.635ab
निःशेषवेदसिद्धान्तविद्वद्भिरपि भाषितम् 2.1.386ab
निःशेषसुखसंप्राप्तेः सर्वानर्थहनुतेस्तथा SV 558ab
निःशेषानर्थसंप्राप्तिकैवल्यानाप्तिकृत्तमः 4.4.781ab
निःशेषानात्मतद्धेतुनिराकरणवर्त्मना 4.4.154ab
निःशेषानात्मदृक्तद्वदनिर्ज्ञातात्मतत्त्वकः 1.4.601ab
निःशेषानात्मबुद्धीनां नित्यप्राप्तमुपासनम् 1.4.918cd
निःशेषानात्मसंदृष्टिनिराकरणसिद्धये 1.4.1684ab
निःशेषान्नादनादात्मा प्राणान्तोऽन्नाद उच्यते 4.4.1310ab
निःशेषाह्लादसंप्राप्तिः सर्वानर्थनुतिस्तथा SV 1095ab
निःशेषोपनिषत्काण्डनैरर्थक्यप्रसङ्गतः 1.4.1752ef
निःशेषोपनिषत्सारस्तदेतदिति सांप्रतम् 2.5.136ab
निःशेषोपनिषन्मानमेकं ज्ञानमितीष्यते 1.5.303cd
निषिक्तमपि तद्रेतः प्राणवृत्त्या यथाविधि 6.4.44ab

निषिद्धं नेति नेतीति मूर्तामूर्तादि वस्तु यत् 2.4.9cd
निषिद्धकाम्यकर्मादिवर्जनं निपुणैरपि SV 71ab
निषिद्धकाम्ययोस्त्यागात्कर्मणोर्नित्यकर्मणः SV 41ab
निषिद्धमखिलं वस्तु यत्किंचिज्जगतीक्ष्यते 3.8.109ab
निषिद्धमपि तत्कार्यं तत्समाप्तिप्रयुक्तितः 4.4.1239cd
निषिद्धषड्विकारस्य श्रुत्यैव परमात्मनः 1.4.1760ab
निषिद्धस्य निषिद्धत्वात्कर्मकाण्डेऽपि कर्मणः 4.4.1209ab
निषिद्धातः परागर्थात्प्रतीचि लभते स्थितिम् 2.3.213cd
निषिद्धानिष्टसंबन्धो वाक्यादेवावगम्यते 1.3.84ab
निषिद्धाशेषभेदस्य तावदेवात्मसाक्षिकम् 1.4.1409cd
निषिद्धैश्चाप्यधोजन्म कर्मसंभारसंभृतः SV 1111cd
निषिध्यते प्रयत्नेन स्थितिर्नात्र विवक्षिता 4.4.513cd
निषिध्यते यतो योगः कुत्सितेनापि कर्मणा 4.3.1360cd
निषिध्यते सुषुप्तेऽसौ तथा स्वप्नोऽपि यस्तयोः 4.3.1165cd
निषिध्यन्तेऽत्र ताः सर्वा व्याघातायैव ता यतः 4.4.1243cd
निषिध्यन्ते न चेत्कामा यथोक्ताः प्रत्यगात्मनि 4.4.455ab
निषिध्यानात्मरूपं यत्ततोऽहंकारनिह्नुतिः 2.4.100cd
निषेद्धुं वाखिलानर्थांस्तत्फलस्यातिफल्गुतः 6.2.7cd
निषेधः क्रियतेऽशेषविकारादेरिहात्मनः 4.4.356cd
निषेधकानि वाक्यानि सन्त्यपि स्मृतिशासने 4.4.459cd
निषेधकृद्वेदवाक्यं प्रत्यग्विकृतिवारणम् 2.1.483ab
निषेधति निषेध्यार्थं यद्बलान्नञ्चिदात्मनः 2.3.190ab
निषेधति विधत्ते वा न चाप्युपनिषत्क्रियाम् 2.1.570ab
निषेधत्यात्मविज्ञाने मन्त्रवर्णोऽपि काठके 3.5.147cd
निषेधमात्रनिष्ठत्वे न चादेशो भवेत्प्रभोः 2.3.218ab
निषेधवर्त्मना तस्मादनिषेध्यात्मसाक्षिणा 2.3.207ab
निषेधविधिमात्रत्वाद्वेदार्थस्येह सर्वतः SV 34cd
निषेधविधिवत्तस्मात्प्रत्यग्याथात्म्यधीविधिः 1.3.110ab
निषेधविधिहेतूनां सर्वेषां सर्ववस्तुषु 1.6.89ab
निषेधसंस्कृतधियो निषिद्धविषये न च 1.3.85ab
निषेधात्तस्य नेतीति शून्यतैव प्रसज्यते 4.4.496cd
निषेधाद्दर्शनस्येह न नियोगोऽस्त्यतः परे 1.4.884cd

निषेधान्न पुमर्थोऽपि कश्चित्सिध्येत्समीहितः 2.3.217cd
निषेधान्नान्य इत्युक्तेर्न मुक्तिः सुतजन्मतः 1.5.268cd
निषेधाभ्यासो मा मेति ज्ञातब्रह्मप्रवादिनः 2.1.47ab
निषेधायापरोक्षाद्धीरभिन्नार्थग्रहाय तु 3.4.17cd
निषेधायेयमुक्तिः स्यात्पूर्णमित्येवमादिना 5.1.8cd
निषेधोऽमुखमित्येवं त्रयस्याप्यभिधीयते 3.8.105cd
निषेधो नान्यतः शक्यः कर्तुं वर्षशतैरपि 2.3.201cd
निषेध्यं सर्वमेवैतदनिषेध्यात्मवस्तुगम् 2.3.198ab
निषेध्यहेतौ प्रध्वस्ते निषेधोऽपि निवर्तते 2.3.196cd
निषेध्यानामशेषाणामन्योऽन्यव्यभिचारतः 2.3.187ab
निष्कम्पत्वं तथा मूले समुद्रः सर्वरूपभृत् 5.1.51cd
निष्कम्पा देवदत्तस्य वृत्तिः स्यात्परमात्मना 5.1.53ab
निष्कर्मा स्याद्विपापोऽयं विरजस्कोऽप्यकामतः 4.4.1293cd
निष्कर्मिका वा प्रज्ञेह विहितेत्यथ भण्यते 4.4.872ab
निष्कलं तत्परं ब्रह्म नेति नेत्युपदिश्यते 3.2.97cd
निष्कलं निष्क्रियं शान्तं विमलं व्योमवत्स्थितम् 2.1.484cd
निष्कामत्वेन चाकामः स आत्मज्ञो विमुच्यते 4.4.282cd
निष्कारणस्य चोद्भूतौ कार्यजन्म सदा भवेत् SV 69cd
निष्कृष्यातस्ततः प्रीतिं प्रतीच्येव निवेशयेत् 2.4.87cd
निष्कृष्यात्मन्यथात्मानं सर्वमात्मेति पश्यति 2.4.114cd
निष्कृष्याभिहितो योऽत्र स समानः स्वमोहतः 4.3.379cd
निष्क्रामति यथाकर्म सविज्ञानो भवत्यथ 4.4.93cd
निष्क्रियं कारणं चेत्स्यात्तद्वन्नित्यं फलोत्थितिः 1.4.195cd
निष्क्रियश्चेतनः साक्षी सक्रियोऽचेतनः पराङ् 3.4.102ab
निष्क्रियो वासनाराशिं स्वप्नभूमौ तथेक्षते 4.3.886cd
निष्ठां प्रतीचि गमितः उत्तरोत्तरवृद्धितः 4.3.1880cd
निष्पन्नोऽपि कुठारादिः प्रयोगविरहाद्यथा 1.4.867ab
निष्पादितनियोगस्य वेदप्रामाण्यतो यथा SV 639ab
निष्पादिताधिकारोऽपि नियोगार्हः पुनर्भवेत् SV 535cd
निष्प्रमाणं यतस्तस्मात्पृच्छ्यते सप्रमाणकम् 3.8.49cd
निष्फलं कर्म सर्वं स्यान्न चेत्कामपुरःसरम् 4.4.224ab
निष्फलं च भवेज्ज्ञानं यदि कारणसंगतिः 3.2.31cd

निष्फलः सोऽभिसंवृत्तो भिन्नाभिन्नाव्यवस्थितौ 1.6.90cd
निष्फलत्वात्स चायुक्तः प्रकृतानभिसंगतेः 2.1.24cd
निष्फलेषुवितुन्नाज्ञो नङ्क्ष्यतीत्यतिदुष्करम् 1.4.833cd
निःसङ्गस्य ससङ्गेन कूटस्थस्य निरात्मना 4.3.1179ab
निःसङ्गस्य ससङ्गेन कूटस्थस्य विकारिणा 4.3.76ab
निःसङ्गस्य ससङ्गेन कूटस्थस्य विनाशिना 2.1.305ab
निःसङ्गस्य हि संबन्धो देहेनास्य न कश्चन 4.4.613cd
निःसङ्गे भिन्नजातीये ताः कुतः प्रत्यगात्मनि 4.4.487cd
निःसंबन्धात्मसंबन्धादनात्मा त्वात्मवन्न सन् 4.3.1183cd
निःसंबोधस्य गमनं कथं देहान्तरं प्रति 4.4.97cd
निःसंबोधेऽर्थ्यते सा हि न तु बोधैकलक्षणे SV 1022cd
निःसाक्षिके न वेद्मीति न कथंचित्प्रसिध्यति 4.3.353ab
निःसाधनं च कार्याणि कथं कुर्यादनेकधा 2.1.389ab
निःसाधनो न साध्योऽस्ति नासाध्यं साधनं क्वचित् 1.4.229ab
निःसामान्यविशेषं तत्प्रत्यगात्मैकनिष्ठितम् 1.4.212cd
निःसामान्यविशेषत्वाच्चित्सामान्यं कथं भवेत् 2.5.6ab
निःसामान्यविशेषेषु नातः संप्लव इष्यते SV 1081ab
निःसामान्यानि तेनाहुः सामान्यानीति वादिनः 4.3.226cd
निःसामान्या विशेषाः स्युर्गोता तेभ्यो न चेद्विरुक् 1.6.56ab
निःस्वा स्त्री स्ववता पुंसा नियुक्ता कर्मसंपदि 2.4.43ab
निहत्य विद्ययाविद्यां यामः कार्त्स्न्यं स्वतोगतम् 1.4.1083cd
निहत्याचेष्टमापाद्य स्वात्मलिङ्गोपसंहृतेः 4.4.135cd
निहत्यानर्थमूलं स्वाविद्यां प्रत्यक्तया परम् SV 6ab
निहन्त्यविद्यां तज्जं च तस्मादुपनिषद्भवेत् SV 5cd
नीत्वा समाप्तिं कर्माणि फलवन्त्यफलानि च 1.5.262cd
नीरसं सत्तदेवाङ्गमाशु शुष्यति तत्र च 1.3.293cd
नीलं कृष्णं च वातस्य परिणामं प्रचक्षते 4.3.1238cd
नीलपीतादिविज्ञानं नीलमित्येव तद्यतः 4.3.485cd
नीलादिवदभावस्य यद्यक्षादिविशेषणम् SV 942ab
नीलादिविक्रिया युक्ता परिणामस्य न त्वसौ 4.3.393cd
नीलीकृतं नभः पश्येच्चक्षुषा नीलवस्त्रवत् 1.4.499cd
नीलोत्पलदलाभं खं द्विरेफोदरवत्तमः 1.4.333ab

नीलोत्पलदलाभं खं सामान्येतरवर्जितम् 1.4.468ab
नीलोत्पलादिवद्दृष्टं न तद्दृष्टं विरुद्धयोः 4.4.473cd
नीलोत्पलादिवन्नातः संसर्गो ब्रह्मणीष्यते 3.9.205cd
नीलोत्पलानुभववत्तदेवेदमितीक्षणम् 4.3.678ab
नीलोत्पले तु नामार्थावपहाय परस्परम् SV 528ab
नीहारादौ तथैवात्मा कार्यकारणवस्तुनि 3.5.78cd
नूनं ते नासिकाग्रेण वीक्षन्ते सूर्यमण्डलम् 1.4.1521cd
नूनं दित्सुं च शुश्रूषुं संभावयति मामपि 2.1.43cd
नूनं ममापराधोऽयं यद्भवन्तोऽपि मां प्रति 2.4.57ab
नृपः स्वदेशमध्यस्थो यथेष्टं परिवर्तते 2.1.302cd
नृपस्त्ववेति संश्लेषादादित्यस्यावधारणम् 4.3.42ab
नृपाभिप्रायवित्प्राह याज्ञवल्क्योऽपि तं नृपम् 4.3.33ab
नृपोक्त्यभिभवाल्लिङ्गाद्वञ्चितोऽस्मीति लिङ्ग्यते 6.2.48ab
नृपो नैतावतेत्याह ब्रह्मत्वासंभवं स्फुटम् 2.1.89cd
नृलोकादिफलं सर्वमेषणात्रयमादरात् 4.4.1104cd
नृविवक्षाव्यवायेन लोके शङ्का भवेदपि SV 871ab
नेक्षितृत्वेऽक्षबुद्ध्यादेः प्रत्यभिज्ञोपपद्यते 4.3.268ab
नेक्ष्यतेऽन्यतमं मानं स्वतःसिद्धं न चापि तत् 1.4.258cd
नेति नेति चतुर्थेऽसौ यथैव प्रतिपादितः 4.5.16ab
नेतिनेतिस्वरूपत्वादशरीरो भवेत्ततः 4.4.517cd
नेति नेतीति चोक्तोऽर्थो जनकं प्रति यः पुरा 4.4.429ab
नेति नेतीति तस्यैव षष्ठान्त उपसंहृतेः 2.3.154cd
नेति नेतीति तस्योक्तान्निषेधान्नेह संभवः 4.4.488cd
नेति नेतीति यश्चोक्त इहौपनिषदः पुमान् 3.9.150ab
नेति नेतीतिवद्व्याख्या सर्वापीह समीक्ष्यताम् 3.8.88cd
नेति नेतीतिशब्दाभ्यां सत्यस्य ब्रह्मणः कथम् 2.3.176ab
नेति नेतीत्यतो वीप्सा जिघृक्षितनिषेधतः 2.3.199ab
नेति नेतीत्यतो वीप्सासंभवादुक्तवस्तुनः 2.3.212ab
नेति नेतीत्यथादेशं नाकरिष्यत्तदात्मनः 2.3.153cd
नेति नेत्यात्मकात्तत्त्वात्प्रकाराणां शतैरपि 4.5.19ab
नेतिनेत्यात्मविज्ञानममृतत्वैकसाधनम् 4.5.20cd
नेति नेत्यादिभूयांसि विरुध्यन्ते वचांस्यपि 3.9.195ab

नेति नेत्यादिवाक्यानां नैरर्थक्यं च सज्यते 4.3.1659ab
नेति नेत्यादिवाक्येभ्यो दृष्टिमात्रात्मवस्तुनः 3.8.172cd
नेति नेत्यादिवाक्येभ्यो योऽर्थोऽनन्यानुभूतिगः SV 1046ab
नेति होवाच पृष्टः सन्राजा पप्रच्छ तं पुनः 6.2.35ab
नेतीति पञ्चमेऽप्येवं निर्विकल्पोऽवधारितः 4.5.16cd
नेतीति प्रथमः शब्दो मूर्तामूर्तनिषेधकृत् 3.2.96ab
नेतीति ब्रह्मणोऽन्यत्र मूर्तामूर्तव्यवस्थितौ 2.4.20ab
नेतीति वचसो व्याख्या तथा सति विरुध्यते 3.2.95cd
नेतीति शास्त्रावसितौ तथैवात्मोपसंहृतः 4.5.18ab
नेतीत्यपि निषेधोक्तिस्तथा सति विरुध्यते 2.4.12ab
नेतीत्यस्थलमित्यादिवाक्याद्योऽर्थोऽवगम्यते 2.4.171ab
नेतीत्यात्मैव संवृत्तो यतोऽतस्तं विपश्चितम् 4.4.1167ab
नेत्रबन्धविनिर्मोकादुपदेशः स्मृतिं प्रति 1.4.1550ab
नेदं यदिदमित्येवं समस्तव्यस्तता कुतः 1.4.964cd
नेदीयसी यतोऽन्येभ्यो वागेवोद्गीथकर्मणि 1.3.231ab
नेदीयो ब्रह्मणः स्थानमोमितीदं प्रतीयताम् 5.1.124ab
नेन्द्रियाणां भवेत्स्वापो यदि प्राणप्रधानता 2.1.130ab
नेन्द्रियाण्यस्य विद्यन्ते नापि तत्स्वयमिन्द्रियम् 3.8.98cd
नेन्द्रियेण ग्रहोऽस्यास्ति शब्दाद्यर्थानुपातिना 2.4.204ab
नेयं युक्ताप्रसिद्धेशे तत्कर्मफलदायिनि 3.8.141cd
नेयत्तास्तीह तत्त्वानामानन्त्यान्न क्रमस्तथा 1.4.400cd
नेश्वरेणापि निर्वक्तुं समस्तव्यस्ततात्मनः 3.2.103cd
नेह चिद्व्यतिरेकेण स्वार्थं किंचिदपीष्यते 2.1.141ab
नेह नानेति भेदानां निषेधात्क्व नु भेदधीः SV 914cd
नेह नानेति वचनादेकमेवेति चोक्तितः 3.5.39ab
नेह प्रमाणतो मेयं यस्मान्नानास्ति किं चन 4.4.659ab
नेह बुद्ध्यादिसद्भावस्तदापीतिश्रुतेर्भवेत् 4.3.1440ab
नेह सद्व्यतिरेकेण स्वमहिम्ना प्रसिध्यति 1.2.12ab
नेहाज्ञामनादाय ह्यात्मानात्मानमीक्षते 1.4.505cd
नेहातो भण्यते भूयोऽनर्थत्वाच्चाप्यनादरः 3.3.8cd
नेहान्यत्रात्मनो ब्रह्म तथात्मा ब्रह्मणोऽन्यतः SV 904ab
नेहासौ प्रकृतो यस्मादतो नासौ प्रवेशभाक् 1.4.516cd

नेहेष्टयो निषिध्यन्ते देवप्राधान्यसिद्धये	1.5.45ab
नैकधीगम्यता च स्याज्ज्ञानस्यायुगपज्जनेः	4.3.1721ab
नैकस्मान्नापि च द्वाभ्यां विरुद्धार्थोऽवसीयते	2.1.558ab
नैकात्म्यं शक्यते द्रष्टुं क्लृप्तहेतोरबाधया	3.4.166cd
नैकात्म्यवस्तुसंव्याप्तिव्यतिरेकेण किं चन	1.4.801ab
नैकानुभूतिबलतो वस्तुनो लभ्यते भिदा	4.3.1676ab
नैकान्तिकफलत्वं स्याद्रोगादिपरिहारवत्	SV 156cd
नैकीभावो न विस्तारः क्षणिकत्वेऽस्ति युक्तिमान्	4.3.632ab
नैकैकस्य क्रियासिद्धिः शिबिकोद्वाहवत्ततः	6.1.22cd
नैक्येऽभिव्यक्तिशब्दार्थः कदाचिदपि लभ्यते	4.4.334cd
नैतत्संदेह एवात्र विवेकाभावतस्तव	SV 507cd
नैतत्साधु प्रमाणानां सर्वलोकाभिधं न हि	SV 186ab
नैतत्साध्वभ्यधाय्युच्चैर्नियोगविरहादपि	SV 455ab
नैतदेवं कुतो जाग्रद्वैलक्षण्यात्मकत्वतः	4.3.902ab
नैतदेवं कुतो यस्माद्दृष्टहानं प्रसज्यते	5.1.45ab
नैतदेवं भवेन्मूर्तरसेनास्यासमत्वतः	2.3.58cd
नैतदेवं यतस्तत्र नैवं प्रत्यक्तयेष्यते	SV 117cd
नैतदेवं यतस्तत्र सत्स्वेव ज्ञानहेतुषु	4.3.1397ab
नैतदेवं यतोऽदर्शि पूर्वमेतत्स्फुटं मया	4.3.1390cd
नैतदेवं यतोऽनन्ताः सर्वे भावा यथोदिताः	1.5.197ab
नैतदेवं यतोऽशेषमानानामपि मानता	SV 162ab
नैतदेवं यतोऽशेषा न कर्मविधयः श्रुतौ	SV 384ab
नैतदेवं यतोऽस्यैव मन्त्रब्राह्मणमानतः	2.1.461ab
नैतदेवं यतो द्रष्टुः कारकस्य समीक्षणे	4.3.1415ab
नैतदेवं यतो नेह पुत्रोत्पत्त्यतिरेकतः	1.5.236ab
नैतदेवं यतो नैतत्कर्माङ्गं ज्ञानमिष्यते	SV 102cd
नैतदेवं यतो भेदज्ञानं मोहोत्थकारक-	4.3.1307ab
नैतदेवं यतो मोक्षे विज्ञानं नोपपद्यते	3.9.186ab
नैतदेवं यतो वाक्यं वस्तुनिष्ठं पुरोदितम्	1.4.1109ab
नैतदेवं सुखेप्साया जिहासायाश्च दुःखतः	SV 1094ab
नैतदेवमविज्ञाततत्त्वस्यैवेह कर्मसु	SV 108ab
नैतद्यतोऽसङ्गमिदमसङ्गो हीति वक्ष्यति	3.8.97cd

नैतन्न्यारयमसद्भावात्तत्संयोगवियोगयोः 1.4.540cd
नैतस्माज्जायते किंचिन्नायं जातः कुतश् चन 2.4.244ab
नैतादृशं ब्राह्मणस्यास्ति वित्तं यथैकता समता सत्यता च 4.4.595ab
नैतादृशं ब्राह्मणस्यास्ति वित्तं यथैकता समता सत्यता च 4.4.1264ab
नैतावतापराधेन युक्तयो मानकारणम् SV 854ab
नैतावता भवेल्लोके गौरस्पर्शस्वभाविका 4.3.751ab
नैतावतास्य सामर्थ्यं हन्यतेऽन्यस्य वा भवेत् SV 876cd
नैतावतेति ब्रह्मातः काश्यो वेत्तीति लिङ्गयते 2.1.90cd
नैनं घोषं शृणोतीति प्रत्यासन्नमृतिर्नरः 5.11.4cd
नैनं ब्रह्मविदं पाप्मा तरति व्याप्नुते स्वतः 4.4.1291cd
नैनं ब्रह्मविदं पाप्मा तरत्यज्ञं यथा तथा 4.4.1283cd
नैनं स्थानान्तरं प्राप्तं ग्रामाद्ग्रामान्तरं यथा 4.3.999ab
नैनमाध्यात्मिको मृत्युस्तन्मृत्युत्वादवाप्नुयात् 1.2.226ab
नैनेनानावृतं किंचिन्नाव्याप्तं ह्योततन्तुवत् 2.5.121cd
नैमित्तिकैरिति ततो वह्न्यौष्णादिसमानता SV 66cd
नैयोगिक्योऽपि नैव स्युर्द्रव्याभावात्प्रवृत्तयः SV 417cd
नैरपेक्ष्यं चिदात्मत्वे स्याच्चान्योऽन्यसमाश्रयः SV 1059cd
नैरर्थक्यप्रसक्तिः स्यात्सम्यग्ज्ञानस्य सर्वतः 1.4.73cd
नैरर्थक्यप्रसक्तिश्च ज्योतिष्टोमादिकर्मणः 1.5.248ab
नैराकाङ्क्ष्येण तत्सिद्धेः संबन्धोऽतो न गृह्यते SV 724ef
नैवं कर्त्रादिदेहान्ताञ्जात्यादीन्देहगांस्तथा SV 119ab
नैवं कर्त्रादिसाक्षित्वात्तच्चिदाभासतस्तथा 4.3.1076ab
नैवं कार्यत्वसारूप्यात्सालक्षण्यं भवेन्न किम् 3.3.120ab
नैवं कल्पयितुं युक्तं वेदसिद्धान्तबाधनात् 2.3.125ab
नैवं कृत्स्नाभिमानित्वादेकदेशानहंकृतेः 2.1.123cd
नैवं क्रियाभ्य एवास्या मुक्तेः सिद्धत्वहेतुतः SV 40ab
नैवं गार्ग्यीयपक्षस्य विशेषावधृतेः सदा 2.1.115ab
नैवं चित्काययोः सिद्धिश्चिच्छक्त्यविषयत्वतः 4.3.122cd
नैवं तत्फलसाक्षात्त्वाज्ज्ञानोद्भूतेरनन्तरम् 1.3.82cd
नैवं तत्रापि दोषस्य प्रसक्तेरनिवृत्तितः 4.3.153cd
नैवं तत्रापि शब्दस्य सामर्थ्यं केन वार्यते SV 752cd
नैवं तत्स्यात्स्वकार्येषु तेषां ताद्रूप्यहेतुतः 1.4.307ab

नैवं तद्धेतुतद्रूपविरोधादितरेतरम् SV 46ab
नैवं तस्य समस्तस्य प्राण एकत्वहेतुतः 2.1.137ab
नैवं तस्यापि मनसो विषयत्वेन दर्शनात् 4.3.270cd
नैवं दाता जगत्यस्मिन्न च तादृक्प्रतिग्रहः 5.16.56ab
नैवं दृष्टत्वतः सिद्धेर्दृष्टे नानुपपन्नता 4.3.492cd
नैवं न कामसंप्राप्त्या तन्नाशोऽब्दशतैरपि SV 345ab
नैवं न कार्यनाशेन कारणं नश्यति क्वचित् SV 390cd
नैवं नामादिसंभूतिपिण्डप्राणादिसंश्रय- 3.9.203ab
नैवं नाम्नोः सदा योगे षष्ठीयं शैषिकी यतः SV 526cd
नैवं नियोगनिष्ठत्वाद्वेदे तेनानपेक्षता SV 695ab
नैवं निःशेषतर्कैश्चेदविरोधोऽभ्युपेयते 1.4.574ab
नैवं पयोघृतादीनामेकदेशत्वदर्शनात् 1.2.94ab
नैवं परिहृतेस्तस्य मृद्दृष्टान्तादियुक्तिभिः 3.5.39cd
नैवं पिण्डस्थदृष्टानां घटादावपि दर्शनात् 1.2.57cd
नैवं प्रकाशकत्वात्स्यात्प्रत्यगात्माख्यवस्तुनः 4.3.1464cd
नैवं प्रत्ययमात्रत्वात्संपत्तेर्न तदिष्यते 1.4.1259cd
नैवं बुद्धेरपि तथा ह्यसद्विषयता भवेत् 1.2.72ab
नैवं ब्रह्मावबोधस्य पारार्थ्येन फलत्वतः 1.4.1252ab
नैवं ब्रह्मोपदेशार्थशास्त्रानर्थक्यसक्तितः 1.4.1246ab
नैवं भेदेन संसिद्धे सुखदुःखे कथं तयोः SV 1011ab
नैवं महेश्वरस्यैव तत्राकाशत्वसंश्रयात् 2.1.448cd
नैवं मान्तरतः सिद्धेर्नृवाक्ये तत्समञ्जसम् SV 404ab
नैवं यतः पृथिव्येव शरीरं यस्य नापरम् 3.7.31cd
नैवं यतः श्रुतिः प्राह पूर्णात्पूर्णमुदच्यते 5.1.43ab
नैवं यतः श्रुतिः साक्षात्सत्त्वमेवावदत्स्वयम् 1.2.6ab
नैवं यतोऽखिलध्वान्तकार्यध्वंसो विवक्षितः 2.1.370cd
नैवं यतोऽलोहितं तत्सर्वरूपादिवर्जितम् 3.8.94cd
नैवं यतो न कर्मभ्यो मुक्तिः संभाव्यतेऽश्रुतेः 3.8.161cd
नैवं यतो मितिप्राप्तं वचो नाशं न वारयेत् 4.3.1430cd
नैवं यथास्थितार्थानां शास्त्रस्य ज्ञापकत्वतः 2.1.492cd
नैवं यस्मादनापन्नधर्मान्तर इहोच्यते 1.4.534ab
नैवं येनैव मानेन सत्ता संविद ईक्ष्यते 4.3.123ab

नैवंरूपितया यस्मादिह श्रुत्या विवक्षितः 2.3.151ab
नैवं वाक्यात्फलं यस्मान्न किंचिदपि लभ्यते 3.3.79ab
नैवं वाङ्मनसे यस्मात्प्राणवृत्त्यैव जीवतः 1.5.190ab
नैवंविद्गुणतामेति ह्यन्नं प्रति कदा चन 1.5.93ab
नैवं वेदान्तवाक्येषु न लिप्यत इति श्रुतेः 1.4.557cd
नैवं वेदान्तसिद्धान्तादन्यसिद्धान्तशासने 4.4.910ab
नैवं शब्दार्थयोरैक्यं यदा स्याल्लोकवेदयोः SV 696ab
नैवं शुद्धिप्रमाणत्वाद्योगनिष्ठस्य काम्यता SV 1129cd
नैवं सत्यनपेक्षत्वं वचसः कार्यसंश्रयात् SV 694ab
नैवं सर्वपदार्थानां नियतादानकारणात् 1.4.1478ab
नैवं साक्षाद्यथावस्तुबोधस्यैवेह संभवात् 1.4.832ab
नैवं साधारणत्वात्स्यात्पुद्गलादेरपीष्यते 4.3.642cd
नैवं सुखादिसंभूतावर्थवत्त्वोपपत्तितः SV 579cd
नैवं सृष्ट्यादिवाक्यानां प्रत्यग्बोधैकहेतुतः 1.4.652cd
नैवं स्यात्सर्वबुद्धीनां मृषात्वे मित्यसंभवात् 1.2.73ab
नैवं स्याद्ब्रह्मबोधस्य निष्फलत्वप्रसङ्गतः 1.4.1743ab
नैवं स्वप्ने यतः पुंसः कर्तृत्वं भावनाकृतम् 4.3.1027cd
नैवकाराभिसंबन्धादेवेत्यत्र न संगतिः 1.5.256cd
नैव कार्यैकनिष्ठानि व्यवहारे वचांसि हि SV 575ab
नैव दोषो यतो येषां सूर्यः स्यादुपरि स्थितः 5.16.26ab
नैव बाल्यादिवद्यस्मात्स्वप्ने देहः प्रतीयते 4.3.131cd
नैवमज्ञानहेतुत्वानर्थार्थत्वेन तुल्यता 1.3.91ab
नैवमन्योपदेशार्थप्रतिषेधपरत्वतः 1.4.81ab
नैवमीशस्य सर्वत्र पूर्वोक्तादेव कारणात् 1.5.350cd
नैवमुत्सर्गतो यस्माच्छब्दानां लोकवेदयोः SV 667ab
नैव व्यपेक्षते व्याख्यां स्पष्टार्थत्वेन हेतुना 6.4.118ab
नैव संभाव्यते यद्वत्तथेहात्मनि वीक्ष्यताम् 5.1.23cd
नैव सिध्येद्विना हेतुं सेतुरेष इतीक्ष्यताम् 4.4.1014cd
नैव सुप्तग्रहो युक्तो न त्वसुप्तस्य युज्यते 2.1.128cd
नैव ह्यावर्तनं हेतुः प्रामाण्येऽन्येष्वनीक्षणात् SV 857cd
नैवाज्ञानं मृषाज्ञानं संशयज्ञानमीक्ष्यते 1.4.299ab
नैवातोऽपि विवेकः स्यादुत्थितः कोऽनयोर्द्वयोः 2.1.114ab

नैवात्मना स्वभावेन स्वात्मानं लभते जडः 1.4.310ab
नैवात्मप्रतिपत्त्यर्थं भारत्युच्चार्यते त्वया 4.3.246cd
नैवात्र गतिरस्तीति स्पष्टमागमशासनम् 4.2.28ab
नैवाधिगतिरित्येवमनवस्था प्रसज्यते 4.3.1666cd
नैवानात्मार्थसामान्यविशेषाणां ग्रहो भवेत् 1.4.961cd
नैवानुमिन्वते त्रासात्पृथिव्यादीन्यथा तथा 3.6.28cd
नैवान्वबुध्यत यदा चक्रे यत्नान्तरं तदा 2.1.177cd
नैवाभ्यासव्यपेक्षास्ति पुण्यपापफलाप्तये 4.4.199ab
नैवायं नियमोऽस्माकं परिसंख्या हि सा यतः 1.3.108ab
नैवाविद्याकृतैवासौ वास्तवी यदि संसृतिः SV 264ab
नैवासौ पूर्यते लोको यथा वेत्थ तथात्र किम् 6.2.34cd
नैवेह किं चनेत्याह कारणेतरनिह्नुतिम् 1.2.5cd
नैवोदास्ते तथापीनो बोधाभ्युपगमात्स्वयम् 2.1.198cd
नैवोपपद्यते कृत्स्नपुरुषार्थावसानतः 3.2.49cd
नैष दोषः परस्यापि ह्यव्यक्तजगदात्मना 1.4.517ab
नैष दोषः पुरोक्तत्वात्परिहारस्य चाञ्जसा 4.4.681ab
नैष दोषः प्रधानार्थसमाप्तेरेव कारणात् 4.4.1237ab
नैष दोषश्चतुर्णां हि भूतानां संहतिस्तनुः 4.3.128ab
नैष दोषस्तदज्ञानमिथ्याधीभ्रमहेतुतः 3.5.34ab
नैष दोषोऽतिरेकेण नात्मनो ब्रह्मता यतः 3.9.96cd
नैष दोषोऽत्र विज्ञप्तिमात्ररूपे परात्मनि 4.3.1633ab
नैष दोषोऽस्ति विज्ञानं स्यादेवानन्दगोचरम् 3.9.181ab
नैष दोषो नरज्ञानपूर्विका विनियोगधीः SV 693ab
नैष दोषो भवेदत्र प्रत्यक्षप्रमितत्वतः 4.3.149ab
नैष दोषो यतस्तत्र युक्तीनामप्रधानता 3.1.13ab
नैष दोषो यतोऽप्राक्षीद्याज्ञवल्क्यो नराधिपम् 4.2.11cd
नैष दोषो यतो दृष्ट एकस्मिन्नपि वस्तुनि 2.4.460ab
नैष दोषो यतो द्रष्टुः श्रुतिराह विशेषणम् 4.3.1432ab
नैष दोषो यतो नेह क्रमकालो विवक्ष्यते 4.4.89ab
नैष दोषो यतो नेह भेदेनेशस्य संगतिः 1.4.551ab
नैष्कर्म्यसाधनेनैव ब्राह्मणः स्याद्यथोदितः 3.5.198cd
नैष्कर्म्यसाधनेष्वेवं श्रुतयः स्मृतिभिः सह 3.5.163ab

नैष्ठिकी गतिरेषास्य गत्यन्तरसमाप्तितः 4.3.1828cd
नैसर्गिकी तु याविद्या सा सकृज्ज्ञानजन्मना 4.4.883ab
नैसर्ग्यागन्तुकी चेति ह्यविद्या द्विविधा स्मृता 4.4.881ab
नोक्तत्वात्परिहारस्य न चाहंगम्यतात्मनः 1.4.1525cd
नोक्तत्वात्परिहारस्य सूर्यादावपि दर्शनात् 4.3.1463ab
नोक्तोत्तरत्वात्साध्वेतद्भवता परिचोद्यते 2.1.540ab
नोक्तोत्तरत्वात्साध्वेतद्भवतेहाभिधीयते 4.4.435ab
नो चेत्समस्तदृष्टयैव व्यस्तदृष्टिः समाप्यते 3.2.105ab
नोत्क्रामति न चाप्यास्ते न च नश्यति रज्जुतः 4.4.289cd
नोत्क्रामन्ति न तिष्ठन्ति न च नश्यन्त्यहेतुतः 4.4.288cd
नोत्पत्त्यादि स्वतो यस्य स्वत एवास्ति यस्य तत् 4.4.1116ab
नोत्पत्त्याद्यभिसंबन्ध आत्मनोऽस्योपपद्यते 4.4.1157ab
नोत्पाद्यो वा विकार्यो वा विकारप्रतिषेधतः 3.3.117cd
नोत्सर्गविधिना यस्मान्नापवादस्य बाधनम् 4.4.1222cd
नोपमेह यतस्तासां सौक्ष्म्ये जगति विद्यते 4.2.53ab
नोपलब्ध्यन्तरायार्थध्वंसाभिव्यक्त्यपेक्षतः 4.4.311cd
नोपाध्याश्रयजनितविशेषविषयत्वतः 1.4.559ab
नोपेक्षायां प्रहाणे वा न चानेकार्थता मता SV 600cd
नोभयत्राप्यभिन्नत्वमसाधारण्यसंस्थितेः 1.6.61cd
नोवास ब्राह्मणे साध्वी साक्षादपि बृहस्पतौ 6.2.71cd
नौः स्थिता तीरजा वृक्षा द्रुतं यान्तीति निश्चितिः 4.3.441cd
नौगतस्य यथा वृक्षास्तद्वत्संसारविभ्रमः 4.3.436cd
नौगत्येकप्रयुक्तत्वान्नान्येकाग्रेक्षणोऽपि सन् 4.3.437cd
नौप्रयुक्तातिरेकेण न नौस्थस्य गतिस्थिती 4.3.440ab
नौष्ण्यात्मको मितो वह्निः क्रमशोऽक्रमशोऽथ वा SV 169ab
नौसतत्त्वापरिज्ञानाद्विपरीतप्रकल्पना 4.3.441ab
न्यायं न सहतेऽतीव यथा तदधुनोच्यते SV 938cd
न्यायः पुरोदितः सर्वो यस्मादस्ति तयोरपि 1.4.257cd
न्यायः पुरोदितो योऽत्र वासनासंश्रयं प्रति 2.3.129ab
न्यायः श्रेयोऽर्थिनां मा भूद्भ्रान्तिर्वेदान्तवस्तुनि 4.3.1646cd
न्यायः सर्वोऽपि येनातो नैतत्साधु प्रचोदितम् 2.1.292cd
न्यायः साधारणं सर्वं विशेषस्तु प्रवक्ष्यते 3.9.48cd

न्यायस्तत्राप्ययं कृत्स्नः संभवत्येव निर्णये	4.4.411cd
न्यायाक्षरानुपात्तत्वाद्यथा तदभिधीयते	3.4.176cd
न्यायाभावादयुक्तैव नाप्यविद्या तमानयेत्	4.3.1107cd
न्यायासंभवतः स्पष्टं स च न्यायो विभाव्यते	5.1.64cd
न्यायेन दूषितत्वात्तद्दूषणार्थं न यत्यते	4.4.965cd
न्यायेन वक्ष्यमाणेन भूयोऽप्येतत्प्रवक्ष्यते	SV 279ab
न्यायेनानेन पुरुषो रसशब्देन भण्यते	2.3.57cd
न्यायेनोक्तेन पूर्वेण वक्ष्यमाणेन च ध्रुवम्	4.3.962cd
न्यायैर्जगति संसिद्धैः स्वयमेव विचार्यताम्	4.3.1204ab
न्यायोक्तेरेव संसिद्धेः प्रतिज्ञातस्य वस्तुनः	2.3.52ab
न्यायो वाच्यस्ततः सर्वो व्यवहारो न सिध्यति	SV 688cd
न्याय्यां वृत्तिं समुल्लङ्घ्य तद्विरुद्धतया स्थितिः	3.5.125ab
न्याय्यान्याय्येति वा यत्नाद्युक्तिभिः प्रविभागशः	4.4.742cd
न्याय्यो नियोगस्तत्रैव यत्र बुद्धास्य कार्यताम्	SV 586ab
पक्षपातः श्रुतेर्नापि प्रामाण्यादुपपद्यते	1.4.1120cd
पक्षपातो विना हेतुं बलाकाज्ञानकृन्न किम्	1.4.473cd
पक्षमासर्तुवर्षादेः स कर्ता कर्मणोऽनिशम्	1.5.208cd
पक्षयोरनयोः श्रेयान्कः पक्ष इति चिन्त्यते	1.4.144cd
पक्षश्चायं प्रमाणेन प्रत्यक्षेण विरुध्यते	4.3.702ab
पक्षादिव्यवधानत्वात्तच्चास्माकं न तान्प्रति	4.3.248cd
पक्षासिद्धिर्हि पूर्वस्मिन्भेदान्नैक्यं तथोत्तरे	4.3.1783cd
पक्षीव वृक्षात्किं तावत्परिच्छिन्नो व्रजत्ययम्	4.4.126cd
पक्षे प्राप्तिर्विचारान्ते वक्ष्यते कारणाश्रयात्	1.4.758cd
पक्षे शुक्ले तमाप्याय्य कृष्णे तं भक्षयन्त्यथ	6.2.151ab
पक्षोऽयं बुद्धभक्तस्य यथा तदभिधीयते	4.3.782cd
पक्षो निर्वहणीयः स्यादस्माभिरपि संमतः	SV 266cd
पक्षौ वितत्य नीडं स्वमेति हि श्रमहानये	4.3.1161cd
पञ्चधेहोपदिश्यन्ते तदेतदनुवर्ण्यते	3.9.67cd
पञ्च प्राणादयो वा स्युरन्नान्तास्तच्छ्रुतत्वतः	4.4.640ab
पञ्चभिर्ब्राह्मणैः श्रुत्याकारि कृत्स्नात्मबुद्धये	2.5.91cd
पञ्चभूतसतत्त्वानां शरीरकरणात्मनाम्	2.3.3ab
पञ्चमस्तद्गुणैर्भेदस्तथा स्पर्शो समीक्ष्यताम्	2.4.337cd

पञ्चमाद्युक्तिदृष्ट्यास्य ह्येकवाक्यत्वहेतुतः 1.3.334cd
पञ्चमाध्यायशेषेण परमात्मविनिर्णयः 3.5.13ab
पञ्चमान्त उपन्यस्तं रातेर्दातुः परायणम् 4.4.1308ab
पञ्चमान्ते विनिर्णीतं जल्पन्यायेन सांप्रतम् 4.1.1cd
पञ्च मामित्यतोऽवोचद्यथा ह्यननुशासनम् 6.2.50cd
पञ्चम्या आहुतेस्तस्याः पुरुषः संभवत्ययम् 6.2.110cd
पञ्चम्यामाहुतावेवं पुंनाम्नो जन्म कीर्तितम् 6.2.118ab
पञ्च श्रोत्रादिभिः साक्षाज्ज्ञानामीति समीक्ष्यते 4.3.1770ab
पञ्चाग्निज्ञानवद्भाव्या गतिरप्यत्र सर्वदा 6.2.129ab
पञ्चाग्निविद्या यत्नेन वृद्धेनाब्राह्मणादपि 6.2.18ab
पञ्चालब्राह्मणाञ्जित्वा विद्योत्कर्षैकहेतुतः 6.2.23ab
पञ्चैव किल सूत्राणि तथापीष्टं न बाध्यते 1.4.1065cd
पटसंवेदनेऽप्येवं पटमात्रं विशेषणम् SV 982ab
पटादिकार्यनिष्पत्तौ न तेषां स्यात्समुच्चयः 1.5.230cd
पड्वीशशङ्कुदृष्टान्तात्प्राणस्यैव तु शक्तयः 2.4.381ab
पण्डितो न त्वनेवंविद्यथा त्वं पण्डितायसे 3.9.39cd
पण्डेति बुद्धिनामैतत्सा जाता यस्य मानतः 3.5.173ab
पतत्यश्वत्थपातस्तु पाकेऽप्यन्यनिमित्ततः 4.3.1937cd
पतिजायासुताद्येवं प्रत्यगज्ञानहेतुजम् 2.4.88cd
पतिशापादपुत्रा सा वशमाशु भवेत्तदा 6.4.33cd
पत्रकज्जलरेखाभिर्यथा चाध्यासवर्त्मना 4.4.1343ab
पथस्त्वं देवयानस्य पितृयाणस्य वाञ्जसा 6.2.38ab
पद्मं चारोग्यकामादि भवेत्कर्तृविशेषणम् SV 521cd
पदच्छेदेन कुशला अरत्वेत्येवमादिना 4.3.1049cd
पदनीयं तथा प्रेयः पदार्थाः पञ्च सूत्रिताः 1.4.1066cd
पदनीयमिदं यस्मादनात्मभ्यः परं पदम् 1.4.970ab
पदनीयान्तरतरप्रियमित्यादिशेषतः 1.4.936cd
पदवाक्यस्वरस्थानननादादिविषयापि वा 1.3.324cd
पदवित्स्यान्महिम्नोऽस्य महत्तज्ज्ञानतः फलम् 4.4.1188cd
पदानां संहतिर्यस्मान्न दृष्टेह क्रियां विना 1.3.78cd
पदानां सपदार्थानां वाक्याद्व्यवहृतिर्यतः SV 864cd
पदानामसमर्थत्वाद्विरोधाद्वस्तुनोर्मिथः SV 944cd

पदानामिति मा प्रापदित्यर्थेयं परा श्रुतिः 1.2.211cd
पदानीह तदर्थांश्च प्रसिद्धानेव लोकतः 1.4.184ab
पदार्थ एक एव स्याद्ब्रह्माहंपदयोः परः 1.4.1430cd
पदार्थगतिमेवं वा व्याचक्षीताविरोधतः 3.8.6ab
पदार्थत्वे च तत्सिद्धिर्लिङ्गप्रत्यक्षसंश्रयात् 1.3.79ab
पदार्थप्रतिबोधो वा वाक्यार्थज्ञानजन्मने 4.4.856ab
पदार्थमात्रसंसर्गपरता किं त्वितीर्यताम् SV 602cd
पदार्थमात्रसंसर्गे कार्यार्थविरहेऽपि ते SV 604ab
पदार्थविषयः पुंसो व्यापारो योऽनुमात्मकः 4.4.860cd
पदार्थविषयस्तर्कस्तथैवानुमितिर्भवेत् 2.4.226ab
पदार्थविषया चेयं युक्तिस्तर्कोऽभिधीयते 3.1.8ab
पदार्थसंगतेः कस्माद्विध्यधीनत्वमादृतम् SV 725ab
पदार्थाधिगतिः पूर्वं ततस्तदभिसंगतिः 3.5.169ab
पदार्थानामसंबन्धोऽनपेक्षत्वाद्भवेद्ध्रुवम् SV 607cd
पदार्थान्तरतन्त्रत्वं कस्माद्धेतोर्न कल्प्यते SV 725cd
पदार्थान्तरसद्भावमपेक्ष्यान्यस्य वस्तुनः 1.4.476ab
पदार्थान्नान्यथा कर्तुं प्रवृत्तं माननिश्चितान् 2.1.493cd
पदार्थैकत्वतो भेदो ध्वान्तध्वस्तौ निवर्तते 3.5.184cd
पद्यतेऽनेन तद्यस्मात्तेनेदं पदमुच्यते 1.4.1003cd
पप्रच्छ याज्ञवल्क्योऽत इतस्त्वं क्व गमिष्यसि 4.2.9ab
पय एवाहुतिः सर्वमित्येतच्च श्रुतेर्मितेः 1.5.56cd
पयसीदं जगन्मग्नमित्येतद्गम्यते कुतः 1.5.55ab
पयसैवाग्निहोत्रं हि जुह्वत्संवत्सरं द्विजः 1.5.63ab
पयस्यन्तर्हितं विश्वं पश्यन्नेवं पयो नरः 1.5.70ab
पयस्येव जगत्कृत्स्नमग्निहोत्रे प्रतिष्ठितम् 1.5.58cd
पयःसोमादिका आपो ह्यग्निहोत्रादिकर्मसु 5.5.2ab
पयोऽन्नमेव प्रायेण मनुष्याः पशुभिः सह 1.5.48ab
पयो द्रव्यं यथातत्त्वदर्शी चेच्छ्रद्धयान्वितः 1.5.72ab
पयोद्रव्याहुतेश्चैतत्परिणामोऽखिलं जगत् 1.5.61ab
पयोम्भोवत्सूत्ररूपं क्रियाविज्ञानशक्तिमत् 1.4.509ab
पयोम्भोवदिदं लिङ्गं नानारूपैः समन्वितम् 1.3.260ab
पर आत्मनि सर्वेऽपि संप्रतिष्ठन्त एकले 1.4.742ab

परं आरभ्यते ग्रन्थो ब्रह्मविद्यावबुद्धये 3.2.44cd
परं आहात्मनः स्वास्थ्यं श्रेयो यद्यभिवाञ्छसि SV 32ab
पर एव प्रविष्टश्चेत्प्रविष्टानामनेकतः 1.4.550ab
पर एवात्मनात्मानं प्रतिपाद्य नरं श्रुतिः 2.4.308ab
परं तत्त्वं प्रदृश्यैवं मनस्यद्वैततां गते 4.4.723ab
परं तदभिमानेद्धं तच्छब्देनाभिधीयते 1.4.1337cd
परं ब्रह्म विजिज्ञासुरुपेतोऽस्म्यहमादरात् 2.1.92ab
परं रूपं समापन्नः कर्माविद्यानिमित्तकम् 4.3.1369ab
परः कारणकार्येभ्य आत्मा पूर्णत्वकारणात् 2.4.419ab
परः कारणतामेति भावनाज्ञानकर्मभिः 1.4.342cd
परकर्मप्रवेशात्स्यादुज्ञाता न स्वकर्मणि 1.3.379cd
परतन्त्रव्यवहृतिः स्वतोजाड्यस्वभावतः 4.3.18cd
परतोऽपि च कृत्स्नत्वे ब्रह्मत्वं दुःस्थसिद्धिकम् 1.4.1113ab
परपक्षे न दृष्टान्तः कश्चिदप्युपलभ्यते 1.6.51ab
परपक्षे न दृष्टान्तः कश्चिदप्युपलभ्यते 4.3.1640cd
परप्रयुक्तं वेत्तृत्वं यदस्य प्रत्यगात्मनः 2.1.316ab
परबुद्धौ समारोप्यमवश्यं वस्तु चेद्भवेत् 4.3.640cd
परब्रह्मपरिज्ञानभावनोपचयात्परः 1.4.1200ab
परब्रह्मात्मविज्ञानजन्मनापि हि कर्मणाम् 1.5.247ab
परब्रह्मैकविज्ञानं निष्फलं वः प्रसज्यते 1.5.250cd
परमं तत्तपश्चिन्त्यं परमं लोकमीप्सता 5.13.1cd
परमं तदपि ध्येयं वानप्रस्थ्येन संमितम् 5.13.3cd
परमं तदपि ध्येयमग्न्यावेशसमत्वतः 5.13.4cd
परमत्वं तथाप्यन्ते राजसूयक्रतोः पुनः 1.4.1608ab
परमात्मन्ययुक्ता चेत्साधकत्वादिकल्पना 1.4.1278ab
परमात्मस्वभावोऽयं स्वयं श्रुत्या प्रपञ्चितः 3.5.87ab
परमात्मा ग्रहीतात्र स्वाभासाभिन्नविग्रहः 2.1.227cd
परमात्मापरिज्ञानमात्रयानाप्तनिर्द्वयः 1.4.1758ab
परमात्मापि जज्ञे खं यथा कुम्भादिजन्मभिः 2.1.417cd
परमात्मा स्वतः सिद्धेरायुरस्य परार्थतः 4.4.638cd
परमात्मैकवृत्तित्वात्कुतो जीवस्य संसृतिः 2.1.490ab
परमात्मैव गन्तव्यः परमात्मविदा ननु 4.2.15cd

परमानन्द एवातः स्वर्गशब्देन भण्यते 4.4.556ab
परमार्थं त्वसंप्राप्य निषेधो नेष्यते यतः 3.4.39cd
परमार्थं न वस्त्वस्ति यत्परायत्तसिद्धिकम् 1.4.1146cd
परमार्थमनाविश्य न मिथ्येति प्रसिध्यति 4.4.948cd
परमार्थविदां न स्युरेषणा या यथोदिताः 3.5.138cd
परमार्थसतोऽसत्त्वं किंमानमिति भण्यताम् 4.3.565cd
परमार्थसत्ययाथात्म्यनिर्देशाय प्रयत्यते 2.3.171cd
परमार्थातिरेकाद्वाभेदाद्वा परमार्थतः 1.3.49ab
परमार्थात्मकत्वे तु न किंचिद्वितथं क्वचित् 1.3.51ab
परमार्थात्मदृष्ट्येयं लौकिकी दृष्टिरात्मनः 3.4.100ab
परमार्थात्मनस्तद्वत्कल्पिताज्ञानलक्षणः 4.3.1618ab
परमार्थात्मनासत्यं पदं तदपि बोधकम् 1.4.992ab
परमार्थात्मनोऽथान्यः कश्चिदात्मेति भण्यते 4.4.497ab
परमार्थादभिन्नश्चेन्नितराममृषात्मता 1.4.1005ab
परमार्थान्निषिद्धस्य तन्मोहोत्थस्य वस्तुनः 2.3.186ab
परमार्थेन तत्रापि नैव भेदोऽस्ति कश्चन 4.3.471cd
परमेष्ठ्यादिकान्सर्वान्पारंपर्येण मानुषान् 6.5.17cd
परमोऽसाविहानन्दः सर्वानन्दातिलङ्घनात् 4.3.1879cd
परमोदारफलता त्वश्वमेधाख्यकर्मणः 3.3.9cd
परलोकप्रसिद्ध्यर्थं तस्य वा इति वाक्यतः 4.3.854cd
परलोकविनाशोऽपि विद्वद्विद्वेषकारणात् 3.9.130ab
परलोकस्य सद्भावे किं प्रमाणमितीर्यताम् 4.3.839cd
परलोकाश्रयं तादृक्तस्मात्स्वप्नसमीक्षणम् 4.3.853cd
परलोकेऽपि नाशङ्का तत्सिद्धेरागमात्सदा 4.3.828cd
परलोकेहलोकौ च तथैवायमविद्यया 4.3.822ab
परलोकेहलोकौ तु गृह्येते संध्यसिद्धये 4.3.844cd
परलोकेहलोकौ तु न तथा मानगोचरौ 4.3.827cd
परलोकोन्मुखीभूतं तमाश्रित्याक्रमं स्वकम् 4.3.849cd
परश्चेत्स प्रमेयः स्यात्कथं चानुभवः फलम् SV 824cd
परसंबन्धमेत्यात्मा कार्यकारणरूपिभिः 2.1.352ab
परस्परं व्यपाश्रित्य यथोक्तं साधनत्रयम् 4.4.589ab
परस्परविरुद्धत्वादेकदैकत्र न द्वयम् SV 239cd

परस्परविरोधाच्च नैकदैकत्र संभवः	5.1.69ab
परस्परविरोधाच्च पराक्प्रत्यक्फलात्मनाम्	4.4.1082ab
परस्परविरोधाच्च प्रकाशतमसोरिव	2.1.535ab
परस्परविरोधित्वाच्छैत्यं यद्वद्विभावसुम्	4.3.1670cd
परस्परविरोधित्वान्न सहावस्थितिस्तयोः	1.4.1764cd
परस्परविरोधित्वान्न स्यादेकत्र संगतिः	4.3.639cd
परस्परव्यपेक्षत्वाच्छक्तिशक्यस्वरूपयोः	4.3.1446cd
परस्परव्यपेक्षत्वादेवं स्यादेकवाक्यता	4.3.1196cd
परस्परात्तृभोज्यत्वसंस्कारोपनिबन्धनम्	3.2.71ab
परस्परानपेक्षत्वाद्धिमवद्विन्ध्ययोरिव	1.4.1422cd
परस्परानपेक्षत्वान्नितरामविरुद्धता	2.1.555cd
परस्परानपेक्षौ चेत्संसारीशौ स्वतः स्थितौ	2.1.456ab
परस्परानभिव्याप्तेर्नामरूपक्रियात्मनाम्	1.4.664ab
परस्पराभिसंबन्धाद्विशिष्टार्थावबोधिता	SV 754cd
परस्पराभिसंबन्धौ गायत्रीवर्त्मनोदितौ	5.16.12cd
परस्पराविरोधेन विशिंषन्त्यात्मसंश्रयम्	1.4.1424ab
परस्पराश्रयत्वं च प्राप्नुयाच्छक्तिवादिनः	4.3.1447cd
परस्परोपकारित्वहानात्कीदृक्समुच्चयः	SV 359cd
परस्परोपरोधेन स्वविरुद्धार्थहानतः	3.4.32cd
परस्मादन्य एवेह संसारी प्राविशज्जगत्	1.4.548ab
परस्मिंल्लयविक्षेपरहितेऽपरिणामिनि	2.4.377cd
परस्य पुरुषस्यायं तदबोधप्रकल्पनात्	4.3.936ab
परस्य ब्रह्मणः साक्षाद्याथात्म्याधिगमो यथा	5.1.111ab
परस्य ब्रह्मता यस्मादनन्यायत्तसिद्धिका	1.4.1190ab
परां प्रज्ञां प्रकुर्वीतेत्येष शास्त्रस्य संग्रहः	4.4.874cd
पराक्तयैव ज्ञातोऽपि प्रत्यग्याथात्म्यहेतुतः	1.4.976ab
पराक्त्वान्नापि कायः स्याच्छीततेव विभावसोः	4.3.213cd
पराक्त्वापेक्षया तद्वत्प्रत्यक्ता नात्मनीक्ष्यते	SV 907cd
पराक्प्रत्ययगम्येन दुःखेन स्याद्विशेषणम्	1.4.576ab
पराक्प्रमेयभूमिभ्यो व्युत्थाप्य मन आदरात्	2.1.234ab
पराक्प्रमेयमानानां प्रत्यगर्थधियोदितः	1.4.963ab
पराक्प्रवणया दृष्ट्या धीस्थो ज्ञो ज्ञानमात्मनि	1.4.298ab

पराक्प्रवृत्तेर्विरतो विद्याया विषयस्त्वयम् 2.1.15cd

पराक्ष्विव न भेदोऽत्र मात्रादेः प्रत्यगात्मनि 1.4.318cd

पराक्सर्वार्थविज्ञानं वस्तुवृत्तानुरोधतः 4.4.574cd

परागर्थप्रमेयेषु या फलत्वेन संमता SV 159cd

परागर्थानुसारिण्यो यतो धीवृत्तयस्ततः 4.3.334ab

परागर्थेषु सक्ता धीः प्रत्यगर्थानुरञ्जनात् 2.3.213ab

पराग्वस्तु विरोधित्वात्प्रत्यग्बुद्ध्या न गम्यते 1.4.959ab

पराङ्गं चात्मविज्ञानादन्यत्रेत्यवधारणात् 1.4.1254cd

पराङ्नान्वेति चात्मानं व्यतिरेकात्मकत्वतः 2.4.274cd

पराङ्मानप्रमेयाश्च नात्मानः स्तम्भकुम्भवत् 2.1.598cd

पराङ्मानाप्रमेयत्वमात्मनः प्रत्यबूबुधत् 4.3.301cd

पराङ्मुख उपस्पृष्टः पाणेः स्पर्शोऽयमीदृशः 1.5.125ab

पराङ्मुखं निदध्यात्तमात्माकृत्स्नत्वदर्शिनम् 2.4.249cd

पराङ्मुखीकृतः शुद्ध्या तैस्तैः सांसारिकैः फलैः 4.4.1196cd

पराचः कामानित्येवं कामानित्यपरं तथा 1.3.97ab

पराञ्चि खानीति तथा पराक्प्रवणसाधनम् 3.5.147ab

पराञ्चि खानीत्यादीनि श्रौतानि च वचांसि नः 4.4.1085ab

पराञ्चि खानीत्येतच्च साटोपमभिधीयते 1.4.489ab

पराञ्चीति च मन्त्रोक्तिः साक्षादात्मेति च श्रुतिः 4.3.301ab

पराञ्चीति तथा शास्त्रं न दृष्टेरिति च स्फुटम् 4.3.1728cd

पराञ्चीत्यपवादाच्च न पिण्डादीक्षणं श्रुतेः 1.4.698ab

पराञ्चीत्यपि हेतूक्तेर्नातः पिण्डादिकृत्स्नधीः 1.4.959cd

पराञ्चो ये रवेर्लोकास्तेषामपि परिग्रहः 5.16.27ab

पराञ्च्येव तु सर्वाणि प्रत्यक्षादीनि नात्मनि 1.4.564ab

परात्मज्ञानवत्तस्मात्तस्योपासनमुच्यते 1.5.217cd

परात्मदर्शनस्यापि तद्भावः स्यात्तथा फलम् 1.4.1154cd

परात्मनः कल्पयितुं नातो युक्ता कथं चन 2.1.499cd

परात्मनः परिच्छिन्नोऽविद्ययोषररूपया 3.2.42cd

परात्मनः प्रवेशोऽपि न्याय्यं संगच्छते न च 1.4.516ab

परात्मनः स्वतोऽविद्या बहिष्ठे कामकर्मणी 3.2.89ab

परात्मनः स्वशब्देन विशेषणसमन्वयात् 1.4.1771cd

परात्मनि तु संबोधो नित्यः स्याच्छशिशीतवत् 1.4.1158ab

परात्मनो महद्दुःखं जीवसंचरणेऽप्यतः 2.1.491cd
परात्मभेदक्लृप्तौ च संत्यागो वः प्रसज्यते 4.4.347ab
पराधीनमृतेर्जन्तोर्मुक्तिः स्यात्पाक्षिकी यतः 1.4.1726cd
परानन्दाभिलाषोऽपि तथा चेत्किं निषिध्यते SV 1018cd
परानन्दावबोधार्थं प्रवृत्तैषा परा श्रुतिः 4.3.1844cd
परापरत्वभेदेन द्वे विद्ये समुदीरिते 3.2.117ab
पराभिप्रायानियमान्नैव स्यान्मोक्षनिश्चितिः SV 158ab
परामर्शः सशब्देन पूर्वोक्तस्य प्रसिद्धितः 4.4.975ab
परामृश्य स इत्येवमव्याकृतसतत्त्वकम् 1.4.496ab
परायणमवष्टम्भ आत्मनः स्यात्तथाविधम् 3.9.38cd
परायत्तप्रबोधोऽपि शक्तो वक्तुं यतस्ततः 3.8.45cd
परायत्तप्रबोधो ना ह्यपात्रोत्थाद्रवेरिव 2.1.126cd
परायत्तात्मलाभत्वं नियोगस्येह कार्यता SV 713ab
परार्थतैव सर्वत्र ज्ञानस्येहोपलक्ष्यते SV 198ab
परार्थमपि सत्कस्मादनपेक्षं न सिद्ध्यये 1.3.389cd
परार्थसंहतानात्मभोग्यकर्त्रादिबोधिना SV 152ab
परार्था भावना यस्मात्स्वार्थं ज्योतिश्चिदात्मनः 4.3.880ab
परार्था सा मतिर्ज्ञेया बाह्यकर्मण्यपाश्रया 1.4.1161cd
परिकल्पिततादोष एवमत्र प्रसज्यते 5.1.35ab
परिच्छिनत्ति किं व्योम नीलज्ञानं मनागपि 3.2.85cd
परिच्छिनत्ति बोद्धारं बोद्धाप्याभासमात्मनः 2.4.351ab
परिच्छिन्नस्य लोकेऽपि प्रवेश उपपद्यते 1.4.548cd
परिच्छिन्नस्य संव्याप्तिर्व्याख्याता पूर्वमेव तु 3.3.136ab
परिच्छिन्नापरिच्छिन्नं तच्च कर्म स्वभावतः 3.3.135ab
परिच्छिन्नेन सर्वत्र प्रतिमानं जगत्यपि 5.16.63ab
परिच्छेत्री विनिर्मात्री विद्या लोकान्तरस्य हि 4.4.125ab
परिच्छेत्री न चाविद्या तमोरूपा हि सा यतः 3.2.84ab
परिच्छेदं हि यत्कार्यं तदेव विनिवर्तते 3.2.59ab
परिच्छेदकृदज्ञानं सासङ्गं मृत्युसंज्ञितम् 3.1.19ab
परिच्छेदप्रसङ्गश्चेन्मैवं यस्मादिदं जगत् 2.5.121ab
परिच्छेदफलत्वं हि मानत्वं तच्च भिद्यते SV 821ab
परिच्छेदेन निर्मातृज्ञानं च प्रत्यगात्मनः 4.3.1192cd

परिणामं व्रजत्तस्मादेतावदिति भण्यते 1.3.248cd
परिणामं व्रजत्येतत्स्थूलमध्यमसूक्ष्मतः 2.2.16cd
परिणामः पदार्थानां क्रिमिसर्पादिलक्षणः 1.4.533cd
परिणामनिषेधः स्यादविनाशिगिरात्मनः 4.5.13ab
परिणामात्मको मृत्युरमरोक्त्या निवारितः 4.4.1333ab
परिणामान्तरप्राप्तिस्तस्यापीति न युज्यते 4.3.394cd
परिणामोऽस्य येनान्त्यः श्रुत्येह प्रतिषिध्यते 4.4.1330ab
परिणामो हि पाकेन पाकश्च न विनाग्निना 6.2.19ab
परिणामो हि मोहादेश्चिदाभासः सदेष्यते 4.3.394ab
परिणामो ह्यपां सोमः शीतांशुस्तेन सोऽम्मयः 6.2.92ab
परिणाम्यात्मनोऽप्येवं कूटस्थावगतेरिव 4.3.397ab
परित्यजति सर्वाणि कृत्स्नसंसारदोषदृक् 1.4.12cd
परिपूरणाय सृष्टेस्तु ह्यग्निसर्गः पुरोदितः 1.4.1596ab
परिमाणमहाभूतप्राणनामान्वयादयः 3.8.72ab
परिमोषिणो यतोऽस्थीनि धनशङ्काप्रचोदिताः 3.9.131ab
परिलोपो हि कार्याणां लोके सिद्धः स्वकारणे 4.3.1436ab
परिवर्तन्ति संसारे कर्मवायुसमीरिताः 6.2.155cd
परिव्राट्श्रमणो ज्ञेयस्तापसाश्रमसंनिधेः 4.3.1365cd
परिशिष्टस्य कल्प्यस्य सेव्ये दृष्टत्वकारणात् 3.8.158cd
परिशिष्टानपि प्रश्नानुत्क्रम्य व्याकरोदसौ 3.2.138ab
परिश्रान्तः सुषुप्ताख्यं नीडं धावत्यथात्मनः 4.3.1102cd
परिष्वक्तः पुमान्प्राज्ञे प्राज्ञेनात्मायमात्मना 4.3.1317cd
परिष्वक्तगिरा चात्र व्यामिश्रीभाव उच्यते 4.3.1313ab
परिष्वक्तस्तु नैवं स वेद बाह्यं न चान्तरम् 4.3.1315cd
परिष्वङ्गाद्यथा पूर्वं वेद बाह्यान्तरं स्फुटम् 4.3.1315ab
परिस्पन्दः प्रकाशश्च ज्ञानशक्तिषु विद्यते 2.4.379ab
परिस्पन्दश्च सर्वत्र प्राण इन्द्रस्तथोच्यते 5.16.35cd
परिस्पन्दात्मिका वृत्तिः श्रोत्रादिष्वपि विद्यते 1.3.216ab
परिहारवचः श्रौतं न च वस्त्वनुरोधतः 2.1.390cd
परिहारान्तरं तस्मान्न वाच्यं तत्प्रसिद्धितः 1.4.1308cd
परिहारोऽस्य चोद्यस्य कहोलब्राह्मणेऽखिलः 4.4.1147ab
परिहार्यं तथानिष्टं कण्टकादि जिहासति SV 886ab

परीक्षणाय प्रक्षिप्तः कुर्यादात्मा तथैव च 4.3.346cd
परीक्षमाणास्ते त्राणं यथोक्ताख्यानवर्त्मना 1.3.169ab
परीक्ष्य चक्षुषा यस्माल्लभते गोधनादिकम् 1.4.1848ab
परीक्ष्य यो न गृह्णाति गृह्णाति च विपर्ययात् 4.4.825cd
परीक्ष्य लोकानित्यादि तथा चाथर्वणे वचः 3.5.156ab
परीक्ष्य लोकानित्यादि तथा नैगमिकं वचः 1.4.1054ab
परीक्ष्य लोकान्कर्मचितान्ब्राह्मणो निर्वेदमायान्नास्त्यकृतः कृतेन SV 25ab
परीक्ष्यैतत्परिग्राह्यं न तु निर्युक्तिकं बुधैः 1.5.227cd
परीक्ष्यैतद्द्वयं ग्राह्यं स्वयमेव परीक्षकैः 2.1.255cd
परीत्यादिगिरा चात्र देशसंस्कार उच्यते 6.3.18ab
परैव देवता वेदो यच्च किंचिच्चराचरम् 6.5.11cd
परोऽविवेको भूतानामात्माविद्येति कथ्यते 1.4.381cd
परोक्षं भावनारूपं तेनादोमयतेष्यते 4.4.189cd
परोक्षद्वयहानेन ह्यात्मा ब्रह्मेति बोध्यते 4.4.163cd
परोक्षनामग्रहणं तेन देवस्य रोचते 4.2.42cd
परोक्षनामग्रहणप्रिया देवा यतस्ततः 4.2.40cd
परोक्षनामग्रहणे प्रीयन्ते देवता यतः 4.2.41ab
परोक्षमपि सद्वस्तु यत्साक्ष्यात्मस्वरूपतः SV 792ab
परोक्षमिव तद्भाति तिमिरोद्भूतचन्द्रवत् 4.4.851cd
परोक्षवृत्तिर्युक्तिश्च कथं ते मितिवर्धने SV 826cd
परोक्षवृत्त्या च तथा वस्तु बोधयति स्वतः 4.4.801cd
परोक्षवृत्त्या शब्दो हि वदन्स्वार्थं स्वभावतः SV 777ab
परोपाधिनिमित्ताः स्युर्दुर्बलत्वादयस्तथा 4.4.13cd
परोपाधिनिमित्तैव कौटस्थ्यात्प्रत्यगात्मनः 1.5.315cd
पर्जन्योऽग्निरिति ज्ञेयः समित्संवत्सरः स्मृतः 6.2.97cd
पर्णज्ञानमृते यद्वज्जुहूर्लातुं न शक्यते SV 104cd
पर्यङ्कशयिताद्राज्ञः प्रत्यक्षादिप्रमाणकात् 2.1.294ab
पर्यपृच्छदतो राजा शान्तदर्पं द्विजं पुनः 6.2.37cd
पर्यपृच्छद्यथाशक्ति मुक्त्वा दिग्ज्ञानमात्रकम् 3.9.58cd
पर्यायेण यतश्चोभौ लोकौ हन्त्येकलः स्वतः 4.3.934ab
पर्यायेण समानः सँल्लोकौ यस्माद्व्रजत्ययम् 4.3.430ab
पर्युदासेऽपि क्लृप्तानां न पृथक्त्वेन संस्थितिः 3.8.75ab

पर्यैति लोकं द्विस्तावत्पृथिवी पूर्वमानतः 3.3.146cd
पलाण्डादावकरणादन्या धीर्जायते श्रुतेः 1.3.85cd
पल्वलास्त्विह वेशान्ताः प्रसिद्धार्थं तथोत्तरम् 4.3.919ab
पवमानेषु सोद्गात्री याजमानं यथाविधि 1.3.139ab
पशवः पय एवाग्रे भुञ्जते नापरं ततः 1.5.50ab
पशवोऽपि हि जानन्ति भेदमक्षादिमानतः 5.1.97cd
पशुलोकत्ववाक्याच्च पारतन्त्र्याच्च कर्मिणः 1.4.1471cd
पशुवद्देवताः पाति स जुहोत्यादिकर्मभिः 1.4.1593cd
पशुश्चाप्याज्यमेवैतत्करोतीत्यपि चागमः 1.5.57cd
पशुष्वपि तथा जातं वत्सं कश्चित्प्रपृच्छति 1.5.52cd
पशुसाधनको यस्माद्यज्ञस्तस्मात्पशुः स्मृतः 3.9.19cd
पशूनिच्छन्किमागास्त्वं प्रश्नान्वा सूक्ष्मनिर्णयान् 4.1.4ab
पश्चात्प्रमेयनिष्ठैव प्रमेयार्थानुरोधिनी 2.4.224cd
पश्चादापन्नतद्भावो देहमेतं विमुञ्चति 4.4.77cd
पश्चाद्विषयसिद्ध्यर्थं कारकादि च यच्छ्रुतम् SV 532cd
पश्यंश्चक्षुस्तथा द्रष्टा शृण्वञ्श्रोत्रं तथैव च 1.4.681ab
पश्यञ्शृण्वन्निति तथा ज्ञानशक्त्युद्भवः कृतः 1.4.704cd
पश्यता प्राणिनामेवं कर्ममूलामिमां गतिम् 4.4.81cd
पश्यन्कुम्भादिकं वस्तु देहान्तो ग्राहको यथा 4.3.1475ab
पश्यन्तोऽपि न पश्यन्ति विरुद्धं कथमुच्यते 1.4.654ab
पश्यन्द्रष्टुरिति वचः कूटस्थ उपपद्यते 4.3.1441cd
पश्यन्द्रष्टुरिति ह्येवं नैवं कर्त्राद्यसंभवात् 4.3.1439cd
पश्यन्न पश्यतीत्यत्र तस्मादेकोऽर्थ उच्यते 4.3.1489ab
पश्यन्न पश्यतीत्यत्र न तथात्मनि युज्यते 4.3.1487ab
पश्यन्न पश्यतीत्येतत्स्वतन्त्रं चागमं वचः 4.3.1501ab
पश्यन्न पश्यतीत्येवं पदार्थद्वयमीरितम् 4.3.1543cd
पश्यन्नपि यतः प्राज्ञः कौटस्थ्यान्न प्रपश्यति 2.1.313cd
पश्यन्नित्यस्य वा व्याख्या कारकत्वनिवृत्तये 4.3.1579ab
पश्यन्नेव यदि ह्यास्ते कथं तदुपपद्यते 4.3.1559cd
पश्यन्नेवायमत्रात्मा सुषुप्ते व्यवतिष्ठते 4.3.1568ab
पश्यन्नेवायमत्रास्त इति चेत्कथमुच्यते 4.3.1507ab
पश्यन्नेवायमत्रास्त इत्येतच्चेत्कुतो भवेत् 4.3.1418ab

पश्यन्नेवायमत्रास्ते द्रष्टव्यासंभवात्सदा 4.3.1564ab
पश्यन्नेवायमत्रास्ते पूर्वहेतुसमाश्रयात् 4.3.1560cd
पश्यन्नेवायमत्रास्ते सान्वयानन्वयौ ध्रुवः 4.3.1500ab
पश्यन्नेवायमात्मास्ते तद्दृष्टेश्चोद्यहेतुतः 4.3.1473cd
पश्यन्नेवायमात्मेति यथोक्तन्यायसंश्रयात् 4.3.1604ab
पश्यन्नेवाविलुप्ताक्ष आत्मायं वर्तते यतः 4.3.1413cd
पश्यन्नेवास्त इत्यस्याः प्रतिज्ञोक्तेः प्रसिद्धये 4.3.1504ab
पश्यन्नेवेति चेदेतद्वस्तुयाथात्म्यमुच्यते 4.3.1570ab
पश्यन्प्रतिपेद इति प्रयोगादवसीयते 1.4.1448ab
पश्यामीति यथाद्राक्षीरात्मदृष्ट्यैव जागरे 4.3.1474ab
पश्यामीत्ययथार्थत्वान्मिथ्याधिरेव सा मता 1.4.651cd
पश्यामीत्यस्य साक्षित्वं प्रतीचो गम्यते यथा 4.3.1469ab
पश्येदात्मानमित्यत्र नियोज्यो विषयाद्बिरुक् 1.4.1298ab
पश्येदात्मानमित्यादि वाक्यं यत्स्याद्विधायकम् 1.4.876ab
पश्येदिति प्रयत्नश्चेत्फलं स्याद्दर्शनं तदा SV 764ab
पश्येदिति हि धात्वर्थः केवलो विषयः श्रुतः SV 807cd
पश्येदित्यभिसंबन्धः पश्यतीत्यथवा भवेत् 4.4.1273cd
पश्येन्मन्त्रेण तत्तोयगानेनैवानुमन्त्रयेत् 6.4.26cd
पश्वादावेवमेव स्यात्संदिग्धेऽपि विनिश्चयः SV 768ab
पश्वादींश्च कुमारेण ह्यात्मनाजीजनज्जगत् 1.2.192cd
पाकजः परिणामोऽयमेवं पञ्चभिरग्निभिः 6.2.111cd
पाकयज्ञविधानेन संस्कृत्याज्यं यथाविधि 6.3.20ab
पाक्षिकी तावदत्रास्तामैकात्म्यार्थावलेहिनः 1.4.770ab
पाक्षिकीति ततोऽप्राप्तेर्भवेन्नैयमिको विधिः 1.4.769cd
पाक्षिक्युपासनप्राप्तिर्नित्या वेति च लिङ्गतः 1.4.760ab
पाङ्क्तं यथा तद्भवति तथैतदभिधीयते 1.4.1842cd
पाङ्क्तं हि प्रकृतं कर्म वेदेति ज्ञानमेव च 1.5.21ab
पाङ्क्तकर्मात्मको यज्ञो यज्ञकार्यमिदं जगत् 1.4.1853ab
पाङ्क्तत्वसिद्धये यावन्नोच्येते वित्तकर्मणी 1.5.206cd
पाङ्क्तस्य कर्मणः कार्यं न तावदवगम्यते 1.5.206ab
पाङ्क्तस्य कर्मणः कार्यं नोक्तं वित्तं च कर्म च 1.5.205cd
पाङ्क्तो यज्ञस्ततः सद्भिः सर्वदा समुदाहृतः 1.4.1851cd

पाणिनापिष्य बहुशः सुप्तं काश्योऽप्यबोधयत् 2.1.178ab
पाणिना मैवमित्युक्त्या तं पिता प्रत्यषेधयत् 5.14.7ab
पाणिपेषप्रबुद्धस्य नाम संसारिणो यदि 2.1.427ab
पाणिपेषादिको ग्रन्थः शुद्धिस्तत्र विवक्ष्यते 2.1.290cd
पाणिपेषोत्थितस्यैव यद्यादेशो भवेदयम् 2.3.155cd
पाणिपेषोत्थितेनायं कर्त्रा भोक्त्रा सहात्मना 2.3.114ab
पाणिपेषोत्थितोऽन्यश्चेन्नेतीति च ततोऽपरः 2.3.156ab
पाणी प्रक्षाल्य यत्नेन सामर्थ्यादेव गम्यते 6.4.88ab
पाण्डित्यबाल्ययोर्निष्ठां मुनित्वं प्रागवादिषम् 4.4.1069ab
पाण्डित्यमथ निर्विद्य बाल्यं परिसमापयेत् 3.5.168cd
पाण्डित्यादि पुरोक्तं यत्तस्येयमुपसंहृतिः 4.4.1271ab
पातनादेव निर्वृत्तेः पतिपत्न्यौ जगत्यपि 1.4.115ab
पानं सलवणस्यैवं लिङ्गात्मानुविधायिता 4.4.47cd
पानाय मम पुत्रस्य स्त्रीस्तने संनिवेशय 6.4.126ab
पापं तु सर्वदा हेयं दुःखेभ्यस्त्रस्यता भृशम् 4.4.204cd
पापकारी च पापश्च स्थाण्वादावभिजायते 4.4.197ab
पापस्य कर्मणः कार्यमन्यत्रापि मितं यतः 3.3.8ab
पापस्याकरणादेव नैति पापं कदा चन 1.5.360cd
पापानिर्मोकहेतूक्तिर्मिश्रमित्यभिधीयते 1.5.38ab
पापीयो मन्यते लोको वसिष्ठो वः समीक्ष्यताम् 6.1.20cd
पाप्मदाहारतिभीतिमर्त्यत्वादिश्रुतेर्मितेः 1.4.147ab
पाप्मनः कर्मकार्याणि विजहात्यमृतोऽव्ययः 4.3.819cd
पाप्मनोऽधर्मकार्याणि तथानन्दांश्च धर्मजान् 4.3.851ab
पाप्मनो नैव स द्रष्टा व्यावर्तत इहातुरः 1.5.25cd
पाप्मनो विजहातीति तथा चैव पुरोदितम् 4.3.1299cd
पाप्मनो विजहातीति पदार्थाः सत्रितास्त्रयः 4.3.831cd
पाप्मशब्देन चात्र स्याद्धर्माधर्मपरिग्रहः 4.3.1299ab
पाप्मशब्देन धर्मोऽपि देहोपादानहेतुतः 4.4.1284ab
पाप्मादिदोषसंपर्कः कारणस्थोऽनुमीयते 1.3.149cd
पाप्मादिप्रकृतादानत्यागाभ्यामनिशं यथा 4.3.821ab
पाप्मानं हन्ति तेनातो जहाति च न संशयः 5.7.3cd
पाप्मानो देवतां तद्वद्देवतात्मस्वभावतः 1.5.361cd

पाप्मेति देहसंबन्धहेतुमात्रमिहोच्यते 4.3.814ab
पाप्मेति हेतुरधुना तत्र श्रुत्याभिधीयते 4.4.1286cd
पाप्मोपस्पृष्टमुभयं शिष्टास्तद्वर्जयन्त्यतः 1.3.223cd
पारतन्त्र्यमृते दृष्टा प्रवृत्तिर्नेदृशी क्वचित् 1.4.1811cd
पारतन्त्र्यस्वभावाच्च न चाप्राप्तसमाश्रयः 4.3.1671ab
पारतन्त्र्यान्न चापेक्षा स्वतन्त्रस्य स्वतः क्वचित् 4.4.1153cd
पारमार्थ्यं क्वचिच्छास्त्रं क्वचिच्चाप्यनृतात्मताम् 5.1.47ab
पारंपर्येण बुद्ध्यादौ स्थूलीभावं निगच्छति 4.3.1092cd
पारार्थ्याचेतनत्वाभ्यां मर्त्यत्वाच्चापि कारणात् 1.3.134ab
पारार्थ्यात्स्वार्थविरहे षष्ठगोचरवद्भवेत् 3.4.120cd
पारार्थ्येनैव सद्यच्च तत्परस्माद्बहिरुङ्न सत् 1.4.433cd
पारार्थ्येनैव सद्यच्च तत्परस्माद्बहिरुङ्न सत् 4.3.1725cd
पारिक्षिताः क्व तेऽभूवन्नित्युक्तिस्त्रिरिहोदिता 3.3.141ab
पारिक्षितानथादाय वायुः स्वात्मसमाश्रयान् 3.3.161ab
पारिव्राज्यं न तद्युक्तमननुष्ठेयरूपतः 4.4.1144cd
पारिव्राज्येऽधिकारोऽस्तीत्ययमर्थोऽवगम्यते 4.4.1080cd
पारिव्राज्येन किं कार्यमिति चेदुच्यते शृणु 4.4.1156ab
पारिशेष्यनयद्वारा मुक्तेः कर्मफलात्मता 3.3.109cd
पारिशेष्यनयो न स्यात्सर्वज्ञस्याप्यनन्ततः 3.3.113ab
पारिशेष्याददतोऽसिद्धिः स्याद्विवक्षितवस्तुनः 2.3.220ab
पारिशेष्याददथाजग्मुर्मध्यमं प्राणमादरात् 1.3.164cd
पारिशेष्यादिह ज्ञानं वेदान्ते तत्प्रसिद्धितः SV 39cd
पारिहार्यादिगं हेम्नि प्रमाणं मेयनिष्ठितम् 4.3.214ab
पारोक्ष्यप्रतिषेधार्थं ब्रह्मात्मैवेति भण्यते 2.5.143ab
पार्थगर्थ्यमतः सिद्धमपास्तविधिलक्षणम् SV 280ab
पार्थिवं च रजो लोको ह्लादकृन्मधुमांस्तथा 6.3.49cd
पार्थिवानि शरीराणि सर्वेषां देहिनां यतः 2.5.20ab
पार्थिवाप्यांशयोस्तेजःपरिक्लेदात्तथाधमः 2.4.360ab
पार्थिवाप्यौ समाश्रित्य तेजोऽभिव्यज्यते यतः 3.6.12ab
पार्थिवैः पार्थिवस्याग्नेरुपकारो यथेन्धनैः 4.3.234ab
पाशद्वयाभिसंबन्धादन्नं दामेति शब्द्यते 2.2.20cd
पिङ्गलं तत्परं ब्रह्म वह्निज्वालेव शाश्वतम् 4.4.563ab

पिङ्गलं पित्तबाहुल्याद्धरितो मन्दपित्तकः 4.3.1239ab
पिण्डनाशेऽपि नैवास्य नाशः संसारिणो यतः 4.4.31ab
पिण्डप्राणविभागेन ह्यध्यात्मे चाधिदैवते 2.3.83ab
पिण्डप्राणादिधर्मेभ्यो वैधर्म्यावधृतौ यतः 4.3.40cd
पिण्डश्च सर्वगस्तद्वज्ज्ञोत्वाभेदात्प्रसज्यते 1.6.83cd
पिण्डसृष्टौ प्रवृत्तायां नाकस्माज्ज्ञानगीः शुभा 1.4.98cd
पिण्डस्तावदिहात्मैको द्वितीयो लिङ्गसंज्ञितः 4.3.286ab
पिण्डस्य मरणे नैतन्म्रियतेऽतोऽमृतं मतम् 1.6.37cd
पिण्डात्माहमितीक्षाणः पिण्डमेव प्रपद्यते 1.4.1151ab
पिण्डादिना विनापीदं मृदादेः केवलादपि 1.2.50ab
पिण्डादिव्यतिरेकेण कारणानुपलब्धितः 1.2.53ab
पिण्डादिव्यतिरेकेण पिण्डादाविव चेत्प्रमा 1.2.55ab
पिण्डादिव्यतिरेकेण यदि मानं भवेत्ततः 1.2.54ab
पिण्डादिष्वेव प्रात्यक्ष्याद् घटादीनां लयादियम् 2.4.374ab
पिण्डान्तस्तावदात्मैको लिङ्गान्तस्तु तथा परः 3.4.63ab
पिण्डीकृत्येन्द्रियग्रामं बुद्धावारोप्य निश्चलम् 4.4.1247ab
पिण्डोऽणुत्वं यदाभ्येति जरयाभ्यर्दितस्तदा 4.3.1926ab
पितरं संविशन्त्युक्ताः सदा तद्भावभावितम् 1.5.325cd
पितरश्चात एवैनमनुशासति सत्सुतम् 1.5.301ab
पिता तु तत्फलात्मैव न तु साधनरूपभृत् 1.5.319cd
पिता पुत्रेण कुर्वाण आस्ते तत्फलभुक्स्वयम् 1.5.318cd
पितुः सामिकृतं कार्यं पूरयन्वर्तते सुतः 1.5.321cd
पितुरित्यपि नाशङ्क्या कार्या यस्मात्स एव तु 1.5.322cd
पितुर्लोक्यो यथा पुत्रः कर्मणेहोपजायते 6.3.2ab
पितृगन्धर्वदेवादौ साधुसाधनसंपदा 4.4.196cd
पितृदेवलोकसंप्राप्तिः श्रुतेहान्यैश्च साधनैः 1.5.280cd
पितृपुत्रादिसंबन्धो नातोऽस्तीह सुषुप्तगे 4.3.1358cd
पितृमात्रादिसंबन्धं सुषुप्ते सोऽतिवर्तते 4.3.1369cd
पितृलोकाच्च ते चन्द्रं यान्त्यन्नं तद्दिवौकसाम् 6.2.149ef
पितृलोकाद्यसंप्राप्तेस्तत्रातिक्रमगीर्वृथा 1.5.242cd
पितृलोको जितो यैः स्यात्पितृयज्ञादिकर्मभिः 4.3.1856ab
पितृव्रतोपरोधोऽत्र नातः कश्चन विद्यते 4.1.31cd

पितॄणां चापि मर्त्यानां मार्गौ तावधिकारतः 6.2.41cd
पितॄणामेक आनन्दस्तेन तुल्यप्रमाणतः 4.3.1850cd
पित्ताख्यं वा भवेत्तेजस्तदंशाश्चक्षुरादयः 4.4.26ab
पित्रादियोग्यं पित्र्यादि ह्युत्तमाधममध्यमम् 4.4.145ab
पित्रेति जातसंदेहः पर्यपृच्छदंदतो नृपः 6.2.26cd
पित्र्यादिलोकेष्वात्मायं यथाकर्म यथाश्रुतम् 4.4.146ab
पिष्टपेषणवत्सर्वं पूर्वपक्षोक्तिदूषणम् 3.2.46cd
पीड्यते स्त्र्यादिसंपर्कसुखविच्छेदतो यथा SV 1021cd
पीतं वस्त्रं यथा तद्वल्लिङ्गमाभाति साक्षिणः 2.3.161ab
पीतरक्तादिभी रूपैः कर्मकार्यैः प्रयुज्यते 4.4.491ab
पीताध्यात्मादिकज्योतिर्जाग्रच्छब्दादिवर्जितः 4.3.883ab
पीत्वा जन्ममृतिप्रवाहविधुरा मोक्षं ययुर्मोक्षिणः 6.5.23c
पुंविशेषणता तस्माद्भोगी कामी न कारकः SV 524cd
पुंव्यापारः सदक्षोत्थप्रमाणप्रमितः स्फुटः 4.3.68ef
पुंव्यापारप्रसिद्ध्याथ सिद्धं स्वार्थकरं मतम् SV 628ab
पुंव्यापारव्यपेक्षायां स्वसिद्धौ कार्यमुच्यते SV 616cd
पुंव्यापारस्य गन्धोऽपि न तत्रास्तीति निश्चयः 1.3.88cd
पुंव्यापारस्य संबन्धो देहादिव्यतिरेकिणा 4.3.278ab
पुंव्यापारानधीनत्वान्नेह संभाव्यते विधिः 1.4.753ab
पुंव्यापारोद्भवत्वं नः श्रुत्यापि प्रतिपादितम् 1.3.184cd
पुंव्युत्पत्तिप्रधानत्वादन्वयादेरदोषता 2.1.167ab
पुंसः कर्मक्षये स्वांशान्संहरन्ति यथायथम् 3.2.126ab
पुंसः किल ततोऽभ्येत्य भावनाप्नोति देहिनम् 4.3.1089cd
पुंसः संसरणं पूर्वं सूत्रितं यत्समासतः 4.4.4ab
पुंसः सर्वमयत्वस्य हेतुः संसारकारणम् 4 4.201cd
पुंसस्तत्र स्वतन्त्रत्वाद्विद्याच्छास्त्रं प्रवर्तकम् 4.4.755cd
पुंसस्तु प्रतिबोधेन भोक्तृतैवावसीयते 2.1.181cd
पुंसां पुमर्थसिद्ध्यर्थं प्रक्रान्तमभिधीयते 4.3.275cd
पुंसा हस्तादिनर्क्षेण मन्थमानीय सिद्धये 6.3.20cd
पुंसोऽक्षितित्वं यो वेद तस्येदं फलमुच्यते 1.5.92ab
पुंसोऽभिधावतस्तूर्णं देहदेशैः समाहतः 2.1.75ab
पुंसोऽभ्युदयदुःखाप्तौ कार्यं वर्ज्यं च तत्ततः 4.4.203cd

पुंसोऽस्य ज्ञस्वभावत्वे करणेष्वपि सत्सु च 2.1.196ab
पुंसो देहग्रहे भूयो देहस्थानेषु देवताः 3.2.127ab
पुंसो भोगप्रसिद्ध्यर्थं वैचित्र्यं धीर्निगच्छति 1.5.117ab
पुंसो या विषयादित्सा स काम इति भण्यते 4.4.228ab
पुंसो रूपमुपक्षीणं मूर्तामूर्तसमाश्रयम् 2.3.101cd
पुंसो वैराग्यहेतुत्वादुपकार्येव तन्मतम् SV 1106cd
पुंस्कामविषयाणां तु नेयत्तेहोपपद्यते 3.3.110ab
पुंस्प्रबोधप्रसिद्ध्यर्थं सृष्टिव्याजोऽयमुच्यते 2.1.385ab
पुंस्प्रयत्नादिलब्धात्मव्यभिचारिरवात्मसु 2.4.275cd
पुंस्प्रवृत्तिरियं लिङ्गं यथोक्तज्योतिषो भवेत् 4.3.66ab
पुंस्प्रवृत्तिस्तु दृष्टेयं लोडादेरेव नान्यतः SV 494cd
पुंस्प्रवृत्तेः फलं कार्यं विध्यर्थश्चापि कारणम् SV 746ab
पुंस्वभावानुरोधेन युक्तिर्वेदेऽभिधीयते 3.1.11ab
पुण्डरीकं यथा शुक्लं सौम्यमाह्लादकृत्तथा 2.3.165cd
पुण्य इत्यादिवचसा कर्मप्राधान्यवाञ्छया 4.4.208ab
पुण्यं वा यदि वा पापं न कर्मेहास्ति तादृशम् 4.4.1177ab
पुण्यः पुण्येन भवति पापः पापेन कर्मणा 1.4.1237ab
पुण्यः पुण्येन भवति पापः पापेन कर्मणा 1.4.1489ab
पुण्यः पुण्येन भवति पापः पापेन कर्मणा 3.2.165ab
पुण्यकर्मप्रयुक्तः सञ्जन्तोरासङ्गकृत्तथा 2.4.361cd
पुण्यकृज्जायते यस्माच्छुद्धधीरिह मानवः 4.4.577ab
पुण्यकृत्तैजसत्वाभ्यां ज्ञानेनाहुः समुच्चयम् 4.4.586cd
पुण्यकृत्तैजसश्चेति भवेद्ब्रह्मविदुत्तमः 4.4.576cd
पुण्यकृत्पुण्यकर्मा यो योगी तैजस उच्यते 4.4.587ab
पुण्यपापफलं चेह पुण्यपापगिरोच्यते 4.3.982cd
पुण्यपापफलं चेह पुण्यपापाभिधं मतम् 4.3.986ab
पुण्यपापाभिसंबन्धः स्वप्ने हृदयसंगतेः 4.3.1374ab
पुण्यमेव कृतं यस्मात्पुण्यमेवामुमेत्यतः 1.5.360ab
पुण्यलोका भवन्तीति तथा च श्रुतितः स्फुटम् 1.5.249cd
पुण्यसाधनताशङ्का मुक्तेरपि यतस्ततः 3.3.11cd
पुण्यापुण्यप्रयुक्तः सन्ग्रहातिग्रहबन्धनः 3.4.2ab
पुण्यापुण्यमय इति प्राक्चैतदुपवर्णितम् 4.4.233cd

पुण्यापुण्ये हि निखिलसंबन्धस्येह कारणम् 4.3.1368ab
पुत्तिकादिशरीरेण समः प्राणस्तदाश्रयात् 1.3.305cd
पुत्रकर्मापरज्ञाननृपित्रमरलोकतः 1.5.275ab
पुत्रकर्मापरज्ञानसाधनान्यपरे जगुः 1.5.335ab
पुत्रकर्मार्थमात्रत्वान्न पृथक्साधनान्तरम् 1.5.276ab
पुत्रजन्मादिवार्ताभिः प्राप्नुवन्ति सुखान्तरम् SV 1013cd
पुत्रजन्मोक्तिमात्रेण पुरुषार्थावसानतः SV 583cd
पुत्रपौत्रादिसंभिन्नं कुटुम्बं यत्प्रपश्यसि 1.4.1821cd
पुत्रमन्थेन संस्कारः स्त्रीणामेवेह वर्णितः 6.5.8ab
पुत्रश्चेदनुशिष्टः स्याल्लोकस्तेनैव जीयते 1.5.279ab
पुत्रस्यैवावधृतय एवकारो भवेदयम् 1.5.280ab
पुत्रात्प्रेय इदं तत्त्वं वित्तात्प्रियतरं तथा 1.4.1029ab
पुत्रादिकामत्यागोऽपि स्यादसाधारणोऽर्थवान् 4.4.1081cd
पुत्रादिगणसंतानस्थैर्यमेव सदा भवेत् 2.1.78cd
पुत्रादि प्रियमात्मेति द्वयोर्विवदमानयोः 1.4.1046cd
पुत्रादिभ्यस्तथा प्रेयानिति वक्ष्यति सादरम् 1.4.7ab
पुत्रादिसाधनानां च तत्त्यागस्य च वर्त्मनः 4.4.1082cd
पुत्रादिसाधनानां स्यादुत्पत्त्यादिसमन्वयात् 1.5.223ab
पुत्रादीनां स्वसाध्यार्थविनियोगोपसंहृतेः 1.5.337cd
पुत्राद्यप्राप्तिरूपं च दुःखं तत्र न कल्प्यते SV 1014ab
पुत्राधिकारनुत्यर्थमथशब्दः प्रयुज्यते 1.5.324cd
पुत्रानुमन्त्रणस्यार्थं व्याचष्टे स्वयमेव नः 1.5.290ab
पुत्राभिमानजे त्वस्मिन्न देहांशविशिष्टता 2.4.352cd
पुत्रेणैव शरीरेण कुर्वन्नास्ते नवं नवम् 1.5.322ef
पुत्रेणैवेत्यतो वक्ति नित्याधिकृतिसिद्धये 1.5.323ab
पुत्रेणैवेत्यतो वक्ति साधनान्तरनिह्नुतिम् 1.5.234ab
पुत्रे न्यस्तात्मभारस्य मरणात्परतः फलम् 1.4.1739cd
पुत्रे सत्येव सा यस्मान्नास्त्यसौ ब्रह्मचारिणः 1.5.265cd
पुत्रैषणातोऽभिन्नैव ज्ञेया वित्तैषणात्मनः 3.5.133cd
पुत्रैषणेति सेहोक्ता यदि वातोऽन्यथैषणा 4.4.1119cd
पुत्रोत्पत्तिं समुद्दिश्य दारान्परिजिघृक्षति 3.5.111ab
पुत्रोत्पत्तिं समुद्दिश्य ह्येषणा दारसंग्रहः 4.4.1119ab

पुत्रोत्पत्त्यादिसाध्येषु प्रवृत्तान्वीक्ष्य यत्नतः 4.4.1112cd
पुत्रोत्पत्त्येह तत्प्राप्तौ सात्र पुत्रैषणोच्यते 4.4.1120cd
पुत्रो वित्तं च लोकेऽपि प्रसिद्धं प्रियरूपतः 1.4.1029cd
पुनः पुनरपूर्वं वा देहारम्भाय कल्पते 4.4.138cd
पुनः प्रसक्तं नानात्वं मैवं यस्मान्निषिध्यते 4.4.658cd
पुनः स्वप्नसमारम्भो गतत्वात्किमितीर्यते 4.3.1064cd
पुनरुक्तं न च न्याय्यमेकप्रवचनस्थयोः 3.1.3cd
पुनरुक्तं न च न्याय्यमेकप्रवचने क्वचित् 3.5.7ab
पुनर्मामैतु तद्रेतो विज्ञानं तेज उच्यते 6.4.22cd
पुनश्छिन्नेऽथ शिरसि तेनेन्द्रेणाश्विनावपि 2.5.103ab
पुंदीप्तेर्वाङ्निमित्तत्वादर्चिर्वाक्तेन भण्यते 6.2.105cd
पुमर्थं प्रतिपाद्यापि प्रकृत्यैव श्रुतिः पुनः SV 853ab
पुमर्थं साधयद्दृष्टमनिर्ज्ञाताङ्गभावकम् SV 451cd
पुमर्थः कामशब्दार्थो नान्योऽर्थः काम्यते यतः 4.3.1337ab
पुमर्थकारिता बुद्धेर्नियोगादेव लभ्यते 1.4.800ab
पुमर्थत्वेन चास्येष्टं प्रामाण्यं वेदवादिभिः SV 918cd
पुमर्थमभिसंधाय यागादावथ चेष्टते SV 1041ab
पुमर्थसाधनेऽन्यस्मिन्न चासौ विनियुज्यते 1.4.1248ab
पुमर्थस्याधिकं शास्त्रात्किंचिदत्र तु नार्थ्यते SV 293cd
पुमर्थस्यानवसितेरैकात्म्याप्रसिद्धितः 1.4.1828cd
पुमर्थस्यैव मेयत्वं मातृत्वाद्यनपेक्षिणः SV 231cd
पुमर्थावसितेः शास्त्रं कृतार्थं विनिवर्तते 3.2.48ab
पुमर्थे निष्ठितं शास्त्रमिति सिद्धं समीहितम् SV 910cd
पुमर्थो लभ्यते नैवेत्यसावपि समाश्रितः SV 786cd
पुमाञ्जनिष्यमाणो वा संसारस्य प्रवाहतः 3.9.143cd
पुमाञ्शक्नोति तत्कर्तुं तस्मादेतद्विधीयते 2.4.122cd
पुमानलं विवेकाय न तु वाक्यार्थवित्तये 4.4.857cd
पुमानिष्टस्य संप्राप्तिमनिष्टस्य च वर्जनम् SV 884ab
पुमान्काममय एव कर्मादेः स्यात्प्रयोजकः 4.4.234ab
पुमान्किंज्योतिरेवायं तमस्यन्धेऽभिधीयताम् 4.3.53cd
पुमान्व्यवहरत्यात्मज्योतिषैवेति लिङ्गतः 4.3.855cd
पुमान्संवत्सरोऽग्निश्च नाड्यहोरात्रयाजुषैः 1.5.68ab

पुमान्सुप्तोत्थितोऽप्येवं प्रमात्रादिलयं स्वतः SV 997ab
पुमायुषापि येन स्यादात्मज्ञानेऽधिकारिता SV 287cd
पुमाशयवशाच्चेयं फलक्लृप्तिस्त्वयोच्यते 3.3.81ab
पुमासनादिलिङ्गेन रवीन्दूदाहृतेस्तथा 4.4.430cd
पुंबुद्धिपर्वकत्वेन यतः सापेक्षतोच्यते SV 694cd
पुंबुद्धिविषयो ह्यर्थो मानान्तरमपेक्षते SV 679ab
पुंभोगसमये कर्म प्रयुङ्क्ते सा पुनर्नवम् 4.3.1255cd
पुंमत्यूहोत्थिताशङ्कानिवृत्त्यर्थं यथोदितम् 2.6.2ab
पुरश्चक्रे द्विपदः पुरः पुरुष आविशत् 2.1.462ab
पुरश्चक्रे शरीराणि द्विपदः पक्षिमानुषान् 2.5.117ab
पुराणं यदि तद्व्योम यदि वा वायुरं भवेत् 5.1.122ab
पुराणः शाश्वतोऽचिन्त्यः सर्वभूतानुकम्पया 4.4.1288cd
पुराणः शाश्वतो विष्णुः प्रपन्नाय किरीटिने 1.4.135cd
पुराणः शाश्वतो विष्णुः प्रपन्नाय किरीटिने 2.1.268cd
पुराणमिति निर्वक्ति कारणप्रतिपत्तये 5.1.116cd
पुरा देवात्मतां योऽगात्प्लुष्टास्तेनेतरे जिताः 1.4.47cd
पुरापि चात्मसंबोधाद्ब्रह्मैवायं स्वतो ह्यभूत् 1.4.1160ab
पुरापि चैतदुदितं यथा वेदान्तबाधनम् 2.3.125cd
पुराप्यसकृदात्मायं स्थानात्स्थानान्तरं गतः 4.3.988ab
पुरा यदभवन्मोहात्स्वप्नजाग्रदवस्थयोः 4.3.1508ab
पुरीतत्प्रमुखं देहं वृत्त्या सामान्यरूपया 4.4.51ab
पुरीतदभिधानेन हृद्वेष्टनमिहोच्यते 2.1.328ab
पुरुष एवेदं सर्वमात्मैवेदमिति श्रुतिः 1.4.1224ab
पुरुषं तं मनुं विद्धि यस्येयं मानवी प्रजा 1.4.117cd
पुरुषः परमात्मायमयमस्मीतिवाक्यतः 4.4.610cd
पुरुषद्वेषिणीं भार्यां पतिश्चेदभिकामयेत् 6.4.36ab
पुरुषविध इत्युक्त्या ह्यूर्ध्वं चैवं प्रवक्ष्यते 1.4.33ef
पुरुषाः सर्व एवामी पुनर्दिक्षूपसंहृताः 3.9.109cd
पुरुषादिनिमित्तस्तु जायते यत्र संशयः 4.3.739ab
पुरुषादिप्रकारांस्तान्प्रत्यक्तत्त्वानलक्षयत् 1.4.33cd
पुरुषा न प्रवर्तेरन्न चेत्तेभ्यः फलं भवेत् 3.3.78cd
पुरुषार्थं समापित्सुः स एष इति चावदत् 3.9.94cd

पुरुषार्थत्वसामान्यात्स्वर्गादिपुरुषार्थवत् 3.3.11ab
पुरुषार्थस्य चाप्तत्वात्किमर्थं विधिशासनम् 4.4.819cd
पुरुषार्थस्य संसिद्धेर्विद्या नैष्फल्यमापतेत् SV 396cd
पुरुषार्थात्मकं वस्तु कूटस्थं तत्स्वतो यतः 4.3.715ab
पुरुषार्थाभिसंबन्धादतो विधिरिहाश्रितः 1.3.195cd
पुरुषार्थाभिसंबन्धाद्विरागित्वं यथाश्रितम् SV 1018ab
पुरुषार्थाय यन्नालं लब्धात्मापि कुठारवत् 3.5.112ab
पुरुषार्थावसायित्वाद्वेदाधीतिविधेरिति SV 557cd
पुरुषार्थावसायित्वान्नाप्यूर्ध्वमनपेक्षतः SV 895cd
पुरुषार्थेऽसति फले विधानं नोपपद्यते 3.3.77ab
पुरुषार्थोऽखिलानर्थप्रध्वस्तिः प्रत्यगात्मनः 2.1.4ab
पुरुषार्थोपदेष्टृत्वाद्यद्वत्कार्ये प्रमाणता SV 883ab
पुरुषेणेह जन्यन्ते तस्मात्स पुरुषोऽक्षितिः 3.2.67cd
पुरुषे ये दश प्राणा इन्द्रियाणि सहात्मना 3.9.14ab
पुरुषोऽग्निरिति ध्येयो व्यात्तं तस्य समित्स्मृता 6.2.104cd
पुरुषोऽजं स्वमात्मानं तदापीतो भवत्ययम् 4.3.859cd
पुरुषोऽयं भवेदात्मा पूर्णत्वाद्वाद्वयात्मनः 4.3.937cd
पुरुषोऽयं भवेदात्मा यतः शेते स पूरुषु 2.5.120ab
पुरुषोऽयं स्वतः सिद्धो यथोक्तेनैव वर्त्मना 4.3.1062cd
पुरुषोऽयमथ श्यामो डित्थ इत्यर्थभिन्नता SV 820cd
पुरुषोऽस्मीत्युपास्त्यर्थं पुरुषार्थोऽयमुच्यते 1.4.52ab
पुरुषो वा इति गिरा हेतुरुक्तोऽक्षये परः 1.5.77cd
पुरुषो वा इति ह्युक्त्या तथास्मादिति वाक्यतः 3.2.63cd
पुरेवानागतं भूयो नैष्यतीत्यत्र का प्रमा 1.4.361cd
पुरैवाव्यभिचारस्य संसिद्धेः किं ततोऽपरम् 4.3.754cd
पुरोक्तार्थवती चैवं सति सर्वा भवेद्ध्रुवम् 3.5.81cd
पुरो नवशरीराणि प्राविशज्जलचन्द्रवत् 2.5.118cd
पुरोनुवाक्याद्युक्त्या तु संख्येयार्थविनिर्णयम् 3.1.51cd
पुरो भुक्तशरीरात्स पक्षी लिङ्गमिहोच्यते 2.5.118ab
पुष्पगन्धः पुटस्थोऽपि पुष्पस्यैव यथा तथा 4.3.1033ab
पुष्पादिवासनानां हि वस्त्रादिष्वेव संगतिः 2.3.105ab
पुष्यासं स्वे गृहेऽत्राहं मनुष्याणां प्रकामतः 6.4.116ab

पूतोऽसंसर्गिधर्मत्वादजरोऽपरिणामवान् 5.16.83ab
पूरणान्निखिलस्यास्य कार्यकारणवस्तुनः 4.3.937ab
पूरयन्पुरुषः प्रत्यक्सर्पादीन्नशना यथा 2.1.192cd
पूर्णं च सर्वतोऽव्यापि सर्वत्रानवखण्डितम् 6.3.27cd
पूर्णं तदक्षरं ज्ञेयं साक्षादित्यादिलक्षणम् 3.8.100cd
पूर्णं निःश्रेयसं तस्मात्तदपूर्णमविद्यया SV 268ab
पूर्णत्वाख्याजहद्वृत्त्या समुद्रोर्मिवदीक्ष्यताम् 5.1.50cd
पूर्णत्वात्पुरुषः सोऽयं ब्रह्मैकं पुरुषस्ततः 2.5.122cd
पूर्णत्वात्पुरुषो ज्योतिरात्मैवैकोऽभिधीयते 4.3.368cd
पूर्णत्वेनाजहद्वृत्त्या त्रिष्वप्यध्वसु वर्तते 5.1.48ab
पूर्णब्रह्मपरिज्ञानाव्यतिरेकत्वहेतुतः 5.1.40ab
पूर्णमित्यादिवाक्यस्य षष्ठान्त्यवचसा सह 5.1.29ab
पूर्णस्य पूर्णमादाय पूर्णमेवावशिष्यते 5.1.16cd
पूर्णस्यानात्मना योगो वास्तवो नोपपद्यते 4.3.76cd
पूर्णाज्ञानैकहेतुत्वाद्रज्जुसर्पादिदृष्टिवत् 3.2.107cd
पूर्णात्कारणतः पूर्णं द्वैतमेतदुदच्यते 5.1.43cd
पूर्णात्मनि तदा दृष्टे कः कस्मै किं प्रदित्सति 4.2.113cd
पूर्णादित्यादिवचनान्महाप्रलय आत्मनि 5.1.49cd
पूर्णेनाभेदतः कार्यं पूर्णं स्यान्न मृषा श्रुतेः 5.1.41ab
पूर्वं कृत्वाथ तत्कर्म पश्चाद्ब्रह्मात्मनेक्षते 1.4.1723ab
पूर्वं ज्ञानसमुत्पत्तेर्नानैवेति ह्यभून्मतिः 4.4.672ab
पूर्वं तु भवतो न्याय्यं तदभावे ह्यसाधकम् SV 649cd
पूर्वं दृष्ट्वापि चेत्तिष्ठेद्यावदागामिदर्शनम् 4.3.674ab
पूर्वं पदार्थान्व्याख्याय पश्चाद्वाक्यार्थमब्रवीत् 1.3.354ab
पूर्वं प्रमाणसंबन्धाद्व्यङ्ग्यव्यञ्जकसंगतेः 4.3.1575cd
पूर्वं यदि विदित्वेति तदा द्वेधा प्रकल्पनम् 3.5.103cd
पूर्वं यद्धृदयस्याग्रद्योतनेन प्रकाशितम् 4.4.95cd
पूर्वं वस्त्विति विज्ञानं प्राण्ययं मानुषस्तथा SV 820ab
पूर्वकर्मोपभोगो यः पुरुषाणां शुभाशुभः 3.2.68ab
पूर्वकाण्डैकदेशत्वात्खिलकाण्डं न वंशभाक् 6.5.2ab
पूर्वजन्मनि यद्वृत्तं वर्तमानप्रजापतेः 1.3.13ab
पूर्वजन्माभिनिर्वृत्तप्रयोगापेक्षयोच्यते 1.2.200ab

पूर्वजन्माभिनिर्वृत्तां यथैवावन्ति देवताम् 1.5.352ab
पूर्वजन्मोत्थसंस्काराद्भयमाविरभूदिह 1.4.91cd
पूर्वत्र विद्यासंभेदाद्भिन्नौ वंशाविहोदितौ 6.5.2cd
पूर्वत्रानुक्तकार्याणामुपास्तीनामिदं फलम् 5.12.6cd
पूर्वत्राभूद्यथा साक्षादिति प्रत्युक्तितो मतिः 3.5.102cd
पूर्वदिगात्मभूतं मां त्वं विद्धयादित्यदेवतम् 3.9.71ab
पूर्वदृष्टे पुनः सोऽयमिति बुद्धिर्न युज्यते 4.3.662ab
पूर्वदेहस्थमात्मानं संहरत्यात्मनात्मनि 4.4.136ef
पूर्वदेहात्तथैवात्मा याति देहान्तरं पुनः 4.3.1948cd
पूर्वदेहेऽभिषङ्गोऽभूदपविद्धतनोरपि 1.2.205ab
पूर्वधीव्यतिरेकेण तत्कालीना परा यथा 4.3.463ab
पूर्वपक्षनिदानच्छित्काश्यः सिद्धान्तवाद्यपि 2.1.27cd
पूर्वपक्षितयाशेषदुःखहेतूपशान्तये 2.1.27ab
पूर्वपक्षेऽथ सिद्धान्तः खल्वाहुरिति भण्यते 4.4.209cd
पूर्वपूर्वप्रहाणेन तन्निष्ठा वियदात्मना 1.4.639cd
पूर्वपूर्वप्रहाणेन यान्त्यस्तं केवलाद्वये 2.4.295cd
पूर्वपूर्वस्य हेतुत्वमथशब्दैरिहोच्यते 1.4.1824cd
पूर्वपूर्वातिरेकेण नोत्तरार्थोऽनुभूयते 1.4.986cd
पूर्वपूर्वातिरेकेण नोत्तरोऽर्थोऽनुभूयते 2.4.281cd
पूर्वपूर्वातिरेकेण नोत्तरोऽर्थोऽनुभूयते 4.3.1740cd
पूर्वपूर्वोपभोगेभ्यो यावद्यावन्निवर्तते 4.3.1867ab
पूर्वप्रज्ञात उद्भूतिर्विद्यायाः कर्मणो यतः 4.4.123ab
पूर्वभूमेर्मुच्यमान उत्तरां कां गमिष्यसि 4.2.12ab
पूर्वमर्थान्तरे न्यस्ता कालान्तरगता मतिः 4.4.824cd
पूर्वमाविशति प्राणो देहं पश्चाच्च मुञ्चति 6.1.8cd
पूर्वमेव तथास्माभिर्युक्तिभिः संप्रसाधितम् SV 873cd
पूर्वयोरवधित्वेन तदुपन्यास इष्यते 2.4.217cd
पूर्वयोर्मन्त्रयोर्योऽर्थो विस्तरेणोदितः पुनः 1.3.362ab
पूर्ववच्चोत्तरत्रापि सर्वत्रैव त्रिधा त्रिधा 3.9.52cd
पूर्ववत्त्वनुकूलं त्वमिदानीमपि भाषसे 2.4.66cd
पूर्ववद्देहसंबन्धः किमिवेह न जायते 4.4.502cd
पूर्ववन्न तु तत्तादृग्देहाद्भिन्ना ततश्चितिः 4.3.203cd

पूर्ववाक्ये यथा व्याख्या कृता कृत्स्ना तथैव सा 4.3.1622ab
पूर्ववालैरिमे वालाः सदृशा इति जायते 4.3.668cd
पूर्वशक्तिनिरासेन शक्त्यन्तरसमुद्भवः 3.3.30ab
पूर्वस्थानवियोगेन स्थानान्तरसमागमः 1.4.537cd
पूर्वस्मिन्प्रतिषिद्धेऽन्यः सामर्थ्यादेव ढौकते 3.8.92cd
पूर्वाज्ञातत्वविषयो भूयोऽप्यनुभवो यतः SV 991cd
पूर्वानन्देभ्य एतेषामानन्दोऽतो महान्मतः 4.3.1861cd
पूर्वाभ्यामन्य एवायं तृतीयश्चेत्समुच्चयः 1.4.1736ab
पूर्वेऽतिक्रान्तकालीना विद्वांसो ज्ञाततत्त्वकाः 4.4.1097ab
पूर्वेण निश्चिते चेत्स्यान्नोत्तरस्य प्रमाणता SV 1080ab
पूर्वे समुद्रे यः पन्था न स गच्छति पश्चिमम् 4.4.1083ab
पूर्वैश्चतुर्भिरध्यायैर्यद्धीः कैवल्यसिद्धये 5.1.3cd
पूर्वैश्चतुर्भिरध्यायैस्तथा श्रुत्योदितोऽञ्जसा 5.1.111cd
पूर्वैश्चतुर्भिरध्यायैस्त्वाष्ट्रं कक्ष्यं च यन्मधु 6.5.3ab
पूर्वोऽनधिगते वृत्तः प्रत्यययोऽधिगते परः SV 1079cd
पूर्वोक्तस्यानुवादोऽयं सोऽयास्येत्याद्युपक्रमः 1.3.291ab
पूर्वोक्तस्यैव दार्ढ्यार्थं प्रश्नोऽयं पृच्छ्यते पुनः 3.8.44cd
पूर्वोक्तानां परिच्छेदो ह्यविद्याकामकर्मभिः 1.4.513cd
पूर्वोक्तेन प्रमाणेन संगतेर्मेय उच्यते 4.4.751cd
पूर्वोक्तेनैव न्यायेन नातस्तद्विधिशेषता SV 273cd
पूर्वोक्तेनैव न्यायेन नैव कल्प्यो विधिस्ततः SV 670cd
पूर्वोक्तेनैव न्यायेन वक्तव्यं नावशिष्यते 1.4.1547ab
पूर्वोक्तैकात्म्यतात्पर्याद्भेदस्यासौ न युज्यते SV 357cd
पूर्वोक्त्यैवोत्तरेषां च दोषाणां परिहारतः 1.4.1308ab
पूर्वोत्तरनिषेध्यानां सामर्थ्यादेव च क्रमः 3.8.92ab
पूर्वोत्तरविरोधोऽयं तदा नैवेह ढौकते 4.3.280cd
पूर्वोत्तरोक्तवचसोर्व्याहतिर्वः प्रसज्यते 1.4.1715ab
पूर्वोपचितसंस्कारहेतुभ्यः साभिजायते 4.4.119ab
पूर्वोपलम्भसंस्कारसमुत्थस्मृतिविभ्रमात् 3.4.145ab
पूर्वो भागः समस्तोऽपि वेदान्तार्थावबुद्धये 4.4.973ab
पृक्तावयवयोः प्रीत्या स्त्रीपुंसोरपरस्परम् 4.3.1313cd
पृच्छन्त्या मूर्धपातस्ते स्यादेव स्वापराधतः 3.6.25cd

पृच्छाम्यतोऽमृतत्वस्य साधनं स्यात्कथं धनम् 2.4.48cd
पृथक्त्वं चापृथक्त्वं च गुणो येषां च वादिनाम् 4.3.1668ab
पृथक्त्वस्य न चेदन्यत्पृथक्त्वान्तरमिष्यते 4.3.1672cd
पृथक्त्वेन भवन्तीयं कथं स्याच्चिद्विशेषिता 4.3.208cd
पृथक्त्वे वापृथक्त्वे वा नैव तस्य मृषात्मता 4.4.947ab
पृथक्त्वे वापृथक्त्वे वा भूतेभ्यो देवतात्मनः 4.3.1147ab
पृथक्त्वे स्वमहिम्नैव तस्य सिद्धेः परात्मवत् 4.4.947cd
पृथक्प्रसिद्धयोः केयं हिमवद्विन्ध्ययोरिव 2.1.399cd
पृथगेवाधिकारोऽतो यथोक्तज्ञानकर्मणोः SV 434cd
पृथग्गुणस्ततोऽन्येभ्यः पृथक्त्वे वा पृथग्गुणात् 4.3.1669ab
पृथग्गुणाच्च व्युत्थाप्य द्रव्यादेः किं स्वलक्षणम् 4.3.1674ab
पृथग्वा फलनिर्देशाद्यो ह वा इति पञ्चधा 6.1.6ab
पृथिवीं पार्थिवं चांशं शरीरं साधिदैवतम् 2.5.41ab
पृथिवी देवता तर्हि त्वदुक्तार्थसमन्वयात् 3.7.28ab
पृथिवी यं न वेदेति यदुक्तं तस्य निर्णयः 3.7.48ab
पृथिवी शरीरमित्युक्तेः शरीरित्वं प्रजापतेः 1.5.342cd
पृथिवी शारीर इत्येवं खण्डशो यः पुरोदितः 2.5.54ab
पृथिव्यंशस्य बाहुल्यात्कर्कशः स्पर्श उच्यते 2.4.338cd
पृथिव्यग्निस्वरूपेण क्वचिद्भागात्मना भवेत् 1.5.177cd
पृथिव्यनन्तरं साक्षात्समुद्रः श्रूयते श्रुतौ 3.3.149ab
पृथिव्यपि च यं देवं न वेद स्वात्मनि स्थितम् 3.7.30ab
पृथिव्यबग्निभूतानि सत्संज्ञान्यत्र लक्षयेत् 1.6.38ab
पृथिव्या अपि कार्यत्वान्मधु तेऽपि भवन्त्यतः 2.5.19cd
पृथिव्यां चापि तन्मुख्यं यदुक्तं मूर्तलक्षणम् 2.3.78ab
पृथिव्या तानि सृष्टानि पृथिव्यन्वयदर्शनात् 2.5.20cd
पृथिव्यादिमयोऽप्यात्मा यस्मादूध्र्वं प्रवक्ष्यते 4.3.322cd
पृथिव्यादिषु यः पूर्वं व्याख्यातोऽन्तरबाह्यतः 2.5.35ab
पृथिव्यादीनि भूतानि तदंशाश्च समीरिताः 2.5.43ab
पृथिव्यादीह सामान्यं विशेषः पिण्डमात्रकम् 2.5.45cd
पृथिव्यादेश्च द्रष्टृत्वं तथान्तर्यामिणः श्रुतम् 3.7.57ab
पृथिव्याद्यक्षरान्तश्च प्रश्नो वाचक्नवस्तथा 1.4.36ab
पृथिव्याद्यध्यवस्यायं स्वयंज्योतिरनुग्रहात् 4.3.19ab

पृथिव्याद्या अनात्मान इति चार्थवणे वचः 1.4.742cd
पृथिव्याद्यास्तथैवेमा अक्षरस्य प्रशासने 3.8.131cd
पृथिव्याप्यात्मभोगार्थं सृष्टाः सर्वेऽपि जन्तवः 2.5.19ab
पृथिव्यायतनं यस्य तत्स्थोऽग्निर्लोक एव च 3.9.35ab
पृथिव्या हि समिद्धोऽयं समित्तेन क्षितिर्मता 6.2.101cd
पृथिव्येवाहमित्येवं योऽभिमानी व्यवस्थितः 3.9.41ab
पृथिव्यै चैनमित्यादि तद्व्याचष्टे यथा तथा 1.5.326ab
पृथिव्यै चैनमित्यादि त्र्यन्नात्मावाप्तिलक्षणम् 1.4.1740ab
पृथिव्यै चैनमित्याद्या स्वयं निर्वक्ति नः श्रुतिः 1.5.340cd
पृथुष्टुकेति सैवोक्ता पृथुस्तुतिरसौ यतः 6.4.101cd
पृथूदकादितीर्थेषु तथा च मरणं स्मृतौ 4.4.1061ab
पृष्टं भूयोऽपि चापृच्छदुक्तधीदृढनिश्चितौ 3.8.45ab
पृष्टं यद्याज्ञवल्क्येन न विदुर्ब्राह्मणाश्च यत् 3.9.148ab
पृष्टं वस्तु सुनिर्णीतं मयेतिप्रकृतोक्तितः 4.3.966ab
पृष्टेनापि न विज्ञातं भवता तदिदं मया 2.1.213ab
पृष्टोऽध्यर्ध इति प्राह सोपहासमृषिः सुधीः 3.9.24cd
पृष्टो जरद्गवं यान्तमद्राक्षीस्त्वमितीतरः 1.5.102ab
पृष्ठतोऽपि नरः स्पृष्टो मनसैव प्रपद्यते 1.5.124cd
पेशस्कारी यथा मात्रामुपादायेह पेशसः 4.4.140ab
पेषणापेषणकृतवेदनायां भवेद्विदा 2.1.151cd
पौतिमाष्यादिको ग्रन्थः श्रुत्याथ प्रतिपाद्यते 2.6.3cd
पौनरुक्त्यभयाच्चात्र यद्यर्थान्तरकल्पनम् SV 847ab
पौरुषायासमात्रोत्थमज्ञानं रजतादिवत् 1.4.890cd
पौरुषेयवचःस्वेव युक्तेः प्राधान्यमिष्यते 3.1.9ab
पौर्वदैहिकमेवातो वयस्याद्येऽभिवीक्षते 4.3.841cd
पौर्वापर्यं यथायोगं क्त्वान्तयोः पदयोर्द्वयोः 3.5.103ab
पौर्वापर्यं समीक्ष्यात्मा निष्क्रियः केवलोऽद्वयः 4.3.1152cd
पौल्कसः पुल्कसो ज्ञेयः स्वार्थ एव च तद्धितः 4.3.1363cd
प्रकर्षगुणसंबन्धाः प्रमुदो मुद एव तु 4.3.918cd
प्रकारदर्शनायैव तेनोदाहृतिरिष्यते 2.3.170cd
प्रकारान्तरनिर्देशो तदासेति च तद्वचः 5.4.2cd
प्रकाशकत्वात्सर्वासां धिष्ण्याश्चाप्यग्नयो मताः 6.4.24ab

प्रकाशकत्वाद्वागग्निरेवमेकः प्रजापतिः 1.3.265cd
प्रकाशनपरो ज्ञेयः सिद्धसाध्यात्मवस्तुनः SV 556cd
प्रकाशयिता सविता व्याप्तृ वापि वियत्तथा 4.3.1463cd
प्रकाशवद्घटं चर्ते कुतस्तत्तमसो ह्नुतिः 1.2.104cd
प्रकाशवृत्तिर्या ज्ञस्य सा हृद्धर्मानुगा सती 2.1.252ab
प्रकाशस्यैव सर्वस्य शब्दत्वप्रतिपत्तये 1.5.136ab
प्रकाशिकैव चात्यन्तं वाग्रूपस्येति निश्चितिः 1.5.140cd
प्रकाशैकस्वभावे हि साक्षादेव प्रतिष्ठितम् 5.16.32cd
प्रकाशोऽपि च यः कश्चिदभिव्यञ्जक इष्यते 4.4.421ab
प्रकाश्यमानमात्मानं वेदानुवचनेन तु 4.4.1032ab
प्रकाश्यमाने मानेन बुभुत्सापि न युज्यते 4.4.1039ab
प्रकाश्यमेव चात्यन्तं मनो रूपं यथा तथा 1.5.140ab
प्रकाश्यमेव रूपं स्यात्प्रकाशो वाक्तथैव च 1.5.141ab
प्रकाश्यार्थाभिसंबन्धे कर्तृत्वं सवितुर्यथा 4.3.1457ab
प्रकृतज्योतिःसंबन्धो ज्योतिरित्यभिधीयते 4.3.337cd
प्रकृतत्वात्तथा दृष्टेर्लोकनं लोक उच्यते 4.3.1816cd
प्रकृतस्यात्मकात्स्न्र्यस्य वैशब्दः स्मृतये मतः 1.4.1282cd
प्रकृतात्मपरामर्शः सशब्देन विवक्ष्यते 4.4.6ab
प्रकृतात्माभिधानं वा स इत्येतत्पदं भवेत् 2.5.38ab
प्रकृतापूर्वसंबन्धं बोधयेदिति युज्यते SV 429cd
प्रकृतापूर्वसंबन्धलक्षणापरतः स्थितेः SV 428cd
प्रकृतायां त्रिसंख्यायां सर्वशब्दप्रयोगतः 6.4.76ab
प्रकृताया विभक्तेश्च विभक्त्यन्तरसंश्रयात् 3.2.123cd
प्रकृतार्थावलेहित्वात्सर्वनाम्ना स उच्यते 1.4.495cd
प्रकृतार्थोपरोधाच्च मुख्यब्रह्मार्थलाभतः 1.4.1283ab
प्रकृतिं यान्ति भूतानि निग्रहः किं करिष्यति 1.2.202cd
प्रकृतैकात्म्यविद्याया व्युत्थानायाथगीरियम् 1.4.1566ab
प्रकृत्यर्थातिरेकेण प्रत्ययार्थो न गम्यते 4.3.1688ab
प्रकृत्यर्थेऽथवायं स्यान्मतुब्यद्वा ततोऽन्यतः 4.3.1783ab
प्रकृष्टफलसंप्राप्तेः स्मृतिमात्रैकहेतुतः 5.17.17cd
प्रकृष्टाभ्युदयार्थानि क्रममुक्तिकराणि च 5.1.5ab
प्रक्रियां रचयित्वाहुर्वेदान्तार्थाविपश्चितः 2.3.90cd

प्रक्रियानियमो नापि पुंव्युत्पत्तिप्रधानतः 1.4.401ab
प्रक्रियानुचितं वस्तु सुसाध्वपि समीरितम् 1.4.99ab
प्रक्रियान्नत्रयस्यापि विभागः प्रकृतस्तथा 1.5.203cd
प्रक्रियाफलसंयोगो नातो बोधेऽस्य वीक्ष्यते 4.3.1009cd
प्रक्षेपोऽग्नौ हुतं विद्यात्तत्पूर्वं बलिकर्म च 1.5.39ab
प्रक्षेपोत्तरकालं ताः सर्वमानातिवर्तिना 5.5.4ab
प्रचोदयतु नो देवः श्रेयसे सर्वदात्मनः 6.3.51cd
प्रजया किं करिष्याम आक्षेपो ब्रह्मवेदनात् 6.2.128ab
प्रजया किं करिष्याम इत्येवं च प्रवक्ष्यति 1.5.339ab
प्रजया किं करिष्यामः कनीयःफलया वयम् 4.4.1100ab
प्रजादिना करिष्यामः किं तत्फलवितृष्णवः 2.4.30cd
प्रजापतिः परं ब्रह्म कारणं तदपत्यतः 5.17.8ab
प्रजापतित्वं पितरि तस्मादेतदिहोच्यते 3.9.57cd
प्रजापतिरिति ज्ञेयं हृदयं तेन हेतुना 5.3.4cd
प्रजापतिरिवैतस्यां सृष्टौ स्यात्सर्गकृन्नरः 1.4.164ab
प्रजापतिर्विराडत्र योऽण्डस्यान्तर्व्यवस्थितः 3.6.17ab
प्रजापतेराविरभूत्कुत एकत्वदर्शनम् 1.4.71ab
प्रजासु साक्षाद्यः पाप्मा यश्च तत्कारणाश्रयः 1.3.153cd
प्रज्ञां कुर्यादसंसर्गिब्रह्मयाथात्म्यबोधिनीम् 4.4.807cd
प्रज्ञां कुर्वीत यदिह तत्तमेव यथोदितम् 4.4.867ab
प्रज्ञां कुर्वीत विज्ञायेत्येवमादीनि यत्नतः 1.4.808cd
प्रज्ञां कुर्वीतेति विधिः किमर्थ इति भण्यताम् 4.4.784cd
प्रज्ञातः करणं तस्या भूयः कस्माद्विधीयते 4.4.798cd
प्रज्ञाद्युपनिषत्कान्यो ध्यानाद्देवो भवेदिह 4.1.11cd
प्रज्ञानं ब्रह्म चेत्येवं ज्ञानमात्रात्मतात्मनः 4.3.1757cd
प्रज्ञानघनताप्यस्य न बुद्धिप्रज्ञयोच्यते 2.4.390ab
प्रज्ञानव्यतिरेकेण यथैव स्थितिसर्गयोः 2.4.327ab
प्रज्ञानानि च सर्वाणि देव विद्वान्क्रियास्तथा 5.17.20cd
प्रज्ञाफलं जायतेऽथ यदपूर्वादिलक्षणम् 4.4.837cd
प्रज्ञा मेधा स्मृतिः स्थैर्यं ज्ञानादाववसीयते 1.4.78ab
प्रज्ञायाश्च समाप्तत्वादविद्याया निराकृतेः 4.4.819ab
प्रज्ञा वा परमात्मेह प्रज्ञानमितिवाक्यतः 4.4.873ab

प्रज्ञेत्यादिकया वाचा ह्यात्मप्रत्यय उच्यते 4.4.842cd
प्रज्ञेयं किं ततो भिन्ना प्रतिष्ठायतने यथा 4.1.18ab
प्रणिधायात्मनि दृष्टिं प्रत्यग्बोधैकरञ्जिताम् 3.4.50ab
प्रतिकूलं विमुक्तेश्च क्रियमाणमसंशयम् SV 261cd
प्रतिकूलत्वतो विद्वान्यतः कर्मसु नेहते SV 137cd
प्रतिक्षणविनाशीनि द्रव्याणीत्यवगम्यताम् 4.3.577ab
प्रतिग्रहस्य निन्दा वा विद्वन्मानात्प्रसक्तितः 5.16.54ab
प्रतिज्ञातार्थसिद्ध्यर्थं हेतूनुक्त्वा पृथग्विधान् 2.5.13ab
प्रतिज्ञातार्थसिद्ध्यर्थहेत्वर्थं तद्विशेषणम् 4.4.435cd
प्रतिज्ञातार्थहानाप्तेर्नैवमप्युपपद्यते 3.3.86cd
प्रतिज्ञातमशक्या स्यात्तथा शून्यत्वमापतेत् 4.3.571cd
प्रतिज्ञातो वरस्तावद्भवताप्रार्थितोऽपि सन् 6.2.58cd
प्रतिज्ञापदयोश्चात्र विरोधः स्यात्परस्परम् 4.3.597cd
प्रतिज्ञामात्रतः सिद्धेर्वृथा स्याद्धेतुकीर्तनम् 4.3.737cd
प्रतिज्ञाय पुरा साक्षाद्ब्रह्माहं दर्शयामि ते 3.4.75ab
प्रतिज्ञायाथवैकात्म्यं हेतूनुक्त्वोक्तसिद्धये 2.5.12ab
प्रतिज्ञायापि संबन्धं कस्मात्तन्नोक्तवान्स्फुटम् SV 313ef
प्रतिज्ञायाह युक्तिं च तज्जलानिति सादरात् 4.4.445cd
प्रतिज्ञार्थस्य संत्यागो न युक्तः शाक्यभिक्षुभिः 4.3.788cd
प्रतिज्ञार्थस्य सिद्ध्यर्थं न पश्यन्तीति भण्यते 1.4.660ab
प्रतिज्ञावचसी द्वे वा पश्यन्नित्यादिनोदिते 4.3.1503ab
प्रतिज्ञाहेतुदृष्टान्तभेदस्तावत्परस्परम् 4.3.701ab
प्रतिज्ञाहेतुदृष्टान्ता भिन्नाभिन्नत्ववादिनः 4.3.1759ab
प्रतिज्ञाहेतुदृष्टान्तैर्ज्ञानं तेनापि दूष्यते 1.2.22cd
प्रतिदेहं लयोत्पत्तिश्रुतेर्ह्यात्मनि शङ्क्यते 2.5.10ab
प्रतिदेहं विभिन्ना च त्वसाधारणकारणात् 3.4.95cd
प्रतिद्रव्यफलं कृत्स्ना खण्डादौ गोत्ववत्स्थिता 1.3.279cd
प्रतिन्यायगिरा चास्य यथावत्सोऽभिधीयते 4.3.995ab
प्रतिपक्षमविद्याया अहमेवेदमित्यतः 4.3.1392cd
प्रतिपत्तिः पुरा शाब्दी यावन्न मनुते श्रुतम् 2.4.220ab
प्रतिपत्तिक्रिया वा स्यादातुरन्यासदर्शनात् 1.5.285cd
प्रतिपत्तिरसंख्येयवस्तुनः स्याद्यथा तथा 4.4.1339cd

प्रतिपत्तिविधिस्तावन्नात्मा द्रष्टव्य इत्ययम् SV 654ab
प्रतिपत्तुं क्वचिच्छक्यं प्रकृतिप्रत्ययार्थयोः 4.3.1782cd
प्रतिपत्तुं वयं तादृक्शक्नुमो नाञ्जसा परम् 1.4.951cd
प्रतिपत्तुं स्वतः सिद्धोऽशक्यो विधिगिरा तथा 2.4.156cd
प्रतिपद्वचनस्यार्थं यत्कृत्वेत्यादराच्छ्रुतिः 6.2.39ab
प्रतिपन्नात्मयाथात्म्यः प्रसंख्यानादि नेक्षते SV 785ab
प्रतिपन्ने विधेयार्थे प्रवृत्तिः फलमिष्यते SV 662ab
प्रतिपाद्यात्मनात्मानं नामरूपादिसाधनः 6.5.12ab
प्रति प्रत्याहितत्वाच्च प्रत्याधानं शिरो विदुः 2.2.13ab
प्रतिप्रसूयते कस्मान्नाग्निहोत्रादिकं तथा 1.5.311cd
प्रतिप्राणि च वैचित्र्याद्देशकालादिहेतुतः 3.3.112ab
प्रतिप्राणिपरिच्छेदो ज्ञानकर्मानुरोधतः 1.3.308ab
प्रतिप्राणि ममेदं स्यादभिलाषश्च दृश्यते 1.5.30ab
प्रतिबिम्बप्रवेशोऽयं तत्र न त्विह युज्यते 1.4.541cd
प्रतिबिम्बोदयः कार्यं प्रतिरूपं यतस्ततः 2.1.68ab
प्रतिभागं समाप्तत्वात्पूर्वोक्तस्येह वस्तुनः 4.2.72ab
प्रतिमावद्धि नामादौ ज्ञाते ब्रह्मेति धीरियम् 1.3.63cd
प्रतियोनि यथास्थानमाद्रवत्येष जन्मने 4.3.1951cd
प्रतियोनि यथास्थानमित्यत्रापि तथैव तत् 4.3.1950cd
प्रतियोनिरवेणैव यथास्थानमिहोच्यते 4.3.995cd
प्रतिरूप उपास्योऽप्सु फलमप्यस्य तादृशम् 2.1.68cd
प्रतिलोमं चिकीर्षन्ति कोऽन्यः स्याद्धितकृन्मम 2.4.57cd
प्रतिलोममवस्तीर्य कर्मणः प्रतिलोमतः 6.4.54ab
प्रतिलोममिदं वृत्तं धर्मशास्त्रैर्निषिद्धतः 2.1.93cd
प्रतिवक्तुं न शक्तः स्यान्न चेत्प्राक्शिक्षितो भवेत् 1.5.289cd
प्रतिवक्त्येष इति तं याज्ञवल्क्योऽप्युदारधीः 3.4.50cd
प्रतिवाक्यं बहूक्तिश्च षण्णामेकत्वसिद्धये 4.1.25cd
प्रतिवादिधियो यत्नाद्भुज्युनाख्यायिकोच्यते 3.3.138cd
प्रतिवाद्यादिकं वस्तु तस्य दूष्यत्वकारणात् 4.3.558cd
प्रतिवाद्यादिदूष्यस्य न स्वांशांशित्वसंगतौ 4.3.559ab
प्रतिशाखं तथान्यानि ज्ञानोपायप्रसिद्धये 4.4.1259ab
प्रतिशुश्राव सोऽप्युक्तो भो३ इत्युक्त्या गुरुं यथा 6.2.25cd

प्रतिश्रवणवेलायां श्रोत्रे यः संनिधीयते 3.9.53ab
प्रतिश्रुति विगीतिश्च प्रक्रियाणां समीक्ष्यते 1.4.401cd
प्रतिश्रुत्यादिरूपत्वात्प्रतिरूपस्ततोऽस्तु सः 2.1.70cd
प्रतिषिद्धं तथा काम्यं चापलं नित्यमेव च 4.4.1208ab
प्रतिषेधविधेर्यद्वदुभयोरविशेषतः 1.3.111cd
प्रतिष्ठां कल्पयानीति यस्यां पुंस्त्वं प्रपद्यते 6.4.1cd
प्रतिष्ठां तादृशीमीशः प्रजापतिरचीक्लृपत् 6.4.2cd
प्रतिष्ठितमिहाध्यात्म एवमुक्तेन वर्त्मना 5.16.36cd
प्रतिष्ठितौ तावध्यात्मे चक्षुष्यादित्य एव च 5.6.3cd
प्रतिष्ठितौ तावन्योऽन्यं कथमित्युच्यते यथा 5.6.4ab
प्रतिसंख्यानिरोधोऽत्र सर्वं सुस्थं भवेत्ततः 4.3.578cd
प्रतिसंधानकृत्तर्हि मनः संस्कारसंश्रयात् 4.3.270ab
प्रतिसाध्यं सुतादीनि यथा लोकत्रयार्थिनाम् 4.4.1089ab
प्रतिस्पर्धी न सोऽलं स्याद्वरणाय कथं चन 1.3.288cd
प्रतीक्षन्ते प्रयत्नेन ब्रह्मैतीत्यभिकाङ्क्षया 4.3.1966cd
प्रतीच ईदृशी वृत्तिः स्वपितीत्यभिधीयते 4.3.882cd
प्रतीच उपपन्नस्तु स समान इतीर्यते 4.3.426cd
प्रतीचश्च निरंशत्वान्न दीपेन सधर्मता 1.4.584ab
प्रतीचस्तद्व्युदासार्थं स्वं लोकमिति शब्द्यते 1.4.1672cd
प्रतीचा तस्य जग्धत्वात्क्वानात्मा सिध्यतामयम् 1.4.731cd
प्रतीचा व्यतिरेकी सन्नानात्मा ह्येति संगतिम् 1.4.973cd
प्रतीचि कल्पितोऽनात्मा प्रतीचि व्यभिचारितः 4.3.1455cd
प्रतीचि कामसंबन्धो न तथेति निषिध्यते 4.4.458cd
प्रतीचि चेद्भवेद्दुःखं व्यापि चैतन्यवद्भवेत् 1.4.569ab
प्रतीचि जायते ज्ञानं वाक्यादज्ञानहानिकृत् 4.3.1282cd
प्रतीचि ज्ञानमात्राच्चेत्तदन्यत्प्रार्थ्यते कथम् 2.4.89cd
प्रतीचि निर्निमित्तैव सर्वावस्थास्वपीष्यते 1.4.1035ab
प्रतीचि प्रतिपत्तिः स्यात्प्रत्यगज्ञानबाधया SV 213cd
प्रतीचि भूयोऽविद्यायाः संभवोऽस्ति प्रमाणतः 4.4.956cd
प्रतीचि साक्षाद्विज्ञाते ज्ञेयं सर्वं समाप्यते 2.1.8ab
प्रतीचोऽकारकत्वं नः सर्वत्र प्रतिपाद्यते 2.1.314cd
प्रतीचोऽनर्थ इत्यस्माद्भीतोऽत्यर्थं मुमुक्षति 2.1.3cd

प्रतीचोऽनवशेषेण कार्यकारणसंगतिः 4.3.386ab

प्रतीचोऽर्थस्य ज्ञेयत्वादनवस्था च नेष्यते 1.4.1309ab

प्रतीचोऽलमृते कार्यं कारणं न हि कारणम् 1.4.1747cd

प्रतीचोऽव्यतिरेकेण तदन्यद्वस्तु सिध्यति 1.4.731ab

प्रतीचोऽव्यभिचारोऽतस्तत्राध्यस्तं निषिध्यते 2.3.187cd

प्रतीचोऽसङ्ग्याथात्म्यान्मोहादेश्चाप्यवस्तुतः 3.5.83ab

प्रतीचोऽस्त्यभिसंबन्धो ह्यशनायादिलक्षणैः 3.5.77cd

प्रतीचो गृह्यते मानादतोऽयं तत्स्वभावकः 2.1.208cd

प्रतीचो दर्शनं स्वप्ने मूढस्येहोपजायते 4.3.1251ab

प्रतीचो दर्शनं स्वप्ने श्रुत्या मिथ्येति वर्ण्यते 4.3.1237cd

प्रतीचो देहसंबन्धो नात्माज्ञानादृते तथा 4.4.516cd

प्रतीचो न तदत्रास्ति रूपं यत्कारकात्मकम् 4.3.1508cd

प्रतीचो ब्रह्मणात्तत्वान्न मोक्षो नापि संसृतिः 2.4.15cd

प्रतीचो ब्रह्मवत्प्रत्यग्ब्रह्मणोऽपि विशेषणम् 1.4.1270cd

प्रतीचो भोगसिद्ध्यर्थं देवतैति मृषात्मिकाम् 4.3.1217cd

प्रतीचो वस्तुनस्तावद्वस्तुवृत्तं यथोदितम् 1.4.736ab

प्रतीचो वास्तवं वृत्तं विरुद्धमभिधीयते 2.4.410cd

प्रतीचो व्यतिरेकेण तथैवाव्यतिरेकतः 4.4.322ab

प्रतीचो ह्यनधिगतान्नान्योऽनधिगतो यतः 1.4.977cd

प्रतीच्यथात्मशब्दस्य मुख्यार्थो ब्रह्मणीर्यते 2.4.36cd

प्रतीच्यनन्य एकस्मिन्नविद्यापिहितेक्षणः 1.4.1567ab

प्रतीच्यवसरोऽस्तीह वाङ्मनःकायकर्मणाम् 1.3.102cd

प्रतीच्यविद्ययाध्यस्तमहमैतद्विशेष्यते 4.3.1280cd

प्रतीच्यविद्यां विसृजेद्यान्यत्रापि न काम्यते 1.4.1219cd

प्रतीच्यव्यभिचार्येकं तदन्ये व्यभिचारिणः 2.4 125cd

प्रतीच्यानन्दविषयं न प्रत्यक्षं विरोध्यतः 3.9.185cd

प्रतीच्येकतनुग्राह्ये तदन्यत्र तथेक्ष्यते 1.4.1496cd

प्रतीच्येवं तदज्ञानक्लृप्तानामेकतेष्यते 1.4.946cd

प्रतीच्येव प्रवृत्तं तत्सदसीति वचोऽञ्जसा 1.4.564cd

प्रतीच्येव यतश्चाभूदागाच्च प्रत्यगात्मनः 2.1.203ab

प्रतीच्येव यतोऽज्ञानमतस्तत्तत्त्वविद्यया 1.4.1342ab

प्रतीच्येव यदेहात्मा प्रत्यगात्मानमीक्षते 1.4.64ab

प्रतीच्येव समाप्तं यदक्रियाकारकात्मकम् 4.3.1481ab
प्रतीतिः स्यान्न वाक्यार्थे स्यादुक्तेऽर्थ्यर्थतापि च SV 605cd
प्रतीतेर्माफलत्वाच्च कथं मेयैकनिष्ठता SV 470ab
प्रतीन्द्रियं दश दश निर्गता विषयोन्मुखाः 2.1.323ab
प्रतीयमान एवातः पुरुषार्थः प्रसिद्धितः SV 450cd
प्रतीयाच्चतुरो वेदान्सर्वशब्दार्थवित्तये 6.4.76cd
प्रत्यंशावसितेस्तस्य तदापि परमात्मनः 2.1.480cd
प्रत्यक्कूटस्थ आत्मानं पश्यन्नास्ते फलात्मना 2.3.227cd
प्रत्यक्कूटस्थनिष्ठत्वात्तद्बाध्यं कारणेतरत् 1.4.306cd
प्रत्यक्कूटस्थरूपेण तथा सर्वनिषेधकृत् 3.8.103cd
प्रत्यक्कैवल्यसंसिद्धौ ज्ञानादेव तमोहतेः 3.3.73cd
प्रत्यक्चित्पूर्णतां मुक्त्वा शून्यतां न च ताः सदा 4.4.931cd
प्रत्यक्चिदवभासश्च कारणानुगमोऽपरः 2.1.216ab
प्रत्यक्चिदवभासान्तः कर्ता क्षेत्रज्ञ उच्यते 2.1.225cd
प्रत्यक्चिदाकृतिर्बुद्धौ मेयार्थाकृतिवत्स्थिता 4.3.299ab
प्रत्यक्चिदाकृतिस्तत्र सर्वदा धर्मधर्मिणोः 4.4.651ab
प्रत्यक्चिदाभ आगत्य ध्रियते प्रत्यगात्मने 4.3.1173cd
प्रत्यक्चिदाभाविद्यातो ह्यविचारितसिद्धिका 4.3.1111ab
प्रत्यक्चिदुपरक्तायां बुद्धौ धर्मादिहेतुकः 3.4.152ab
प्रत्यक्चिद्देशभेदेन न हि शुक्लादिवस्तुनः 1.5.120ab
प्रत्यक्चैतन्यमात्रत्वान्न तु निद्रेह युज्यते 2.1.245cd
प्रत्यक्चैतन्यसंदीप्तः सर्वांश्चेष्टाः प्रपद्यते 4.3.52cd
प्रत्यक्चैतन्यसंबन्धो नित्यो नित्यात्मसाक्षिकः 2.4.145cd
प्रत्यक्चैतन्यसृत्यैवं विन्देत्तत्परमं पदम् 1.4.1000cd
प्रत्यक्तत्त्वतमोध्वंसव्यतिरेकेण मुक्तये 2.1.522ab
प्रत्यक्तत्त्वधियः सूतेः किमन्यद्विधिनेष्यते 1.4.827cd
प्रत्यक्तत्त्वधिया हत्वा तावुपैत्यात्ममात्रताम् 1.4.721cd
प्रत्यक्तत्त्वधियो वास्ति स्वतोबुद्धैकतात्मनः 1.4.1462ab
प्रत्यक्तत्त्वपरिज्ञानजन्मैव ध्वंसहेतुताम् 3.2.78ab
प्रत्यक्तत्त्वपरिज्ञानसमुत्पत्तौ समाप्तितः 1.4.1163cd
प्रत्यक्तत्त्वापरिज्ञानादात्मनो हरयस्तथा 2.5.130cd
प्रत्यक्तत्त्वे विनिर्ज्ञाते नेति नेतीतिवाक्यतः 2.3.209ab

प्रत्यक्तत्त्वैकसंबोधे तद्वाक्योपक्षयत्वतः 2.1.570cd
प्रत्यक्तत्वं तमोमात्रव्यवधानादिहोच्यते 1.4.1175ab
प्रत्यक्तमोजयाथात्म्यमात्राभिजनहेतुतः 2.4.257ab
प्रत्यक्तमोवसाय्येव पराग्ज्ञानमशेषतः 2.1.272ab
प्रत्यक्तया तदैकात्म्यं स्वयमेव प्रतीयताम् 3.8.57cd
प्रत्यक्तयात्मसंबन्धान्मोहादेश्चिन्निभात्मता 1.4.1319ab
प्रत्यक्तयानात्मनोऽतः प्रत्यगात्मेति भण्यते 1.4.739cd
प्रत्यक्तया यः प्रथते चतुष्टयविलक्षणः 2.5.33ab
प्रत्यक्तया यः प्रथते ज्योतिरात्मा स ईक्ष्यताम् 4.3.330cd
प्रत्यक्तया यः प्रथते स्वयंज्योतिःस्वभावकः 1.4.716ab
प्रत्यक्तया यदाभाति ह्यागमापायिसाक्षितः 1.4.1001ab
प्रत्यक्तया विभिन्नस्य चैतन्यस्य विशेषणम् 4.3.213ab
प्रत्यक्तया श्रुतेर्वाक्यात्तमेवोक्तविशेषणम् 4.4.704ab
प्रत्यक्तयास्य साक्षात्त्वादक्रियाकारकत्वतः 4.4.153ab
प्रत्यक्तयैव संबन्धादात्मनोऽनात्मवस्तुना 1.4.1441ab
प्रत्यक्तयैवावसितेः प्रतीचोऽन्यस्य वस्तुनः 3.4.59ab
प्रत्यक्तां मदिति प्राह त्वन्यन्नास्तीति चैकताम् 1.4.66ab
प्रत्यक्तान्यानपेक्षा हि तदन्यत्तदपेक्षया 1.4.1042ab
प्रत्यक्ता ब्रह्मणो यस्माद्ब्रह्मता चात्मनः स्वतः 1.4.67ab
प्रत्यक्ता लभ्यते साक्षान्महानात्मेत्यतोऽत्र गीः 4.4.847cd
प्रत्यक्त्वं ब्रह्मणस्तत्त्वं ब्रह्मत्वं चात्मनस्तथा 4.4.163ab
प्रत्यक्त्वं ब्रह्मणस्तद्वद्वचसैव प्रबोध्यते 4.4.1323cd
प्रत्यक्त्वमद्वितीयत्वं बोधवन्नान्यबन्धनम् SV 908ab
प्रत्यक्त्वेन य आभाति प्रत्यग्बुद्धिप्रमाणकः 2.4.262ab
प्रत्यक्प्रज्ञोत्थिताभाससंबन्धात्प्राज्ञ उच्यते 2.1.390cd
प्रत्यक्प्रत्यय एवैकः सर्वत्राव्यभिचारवान् 1.4.305cd
प्रत्यक्प्रत्यय एवैकः सर्वत्राव्यभिचारवान् 4.3.198cd
प्रत्यक्प्रत्यय एवैकः सर्वत्राव्यभिचारवान् 4.3.305cd
प्रत्यक्प्रधानया दृष्ट्या पश्येदात्मानमद्वयम् 1.4.1386cd
प्रत्यक्प्रमेयपूर्वैवं सर्वासां नो यतो धियाम् 1.4.1513cd
प्रत्यक्प्रवणया दृष्ट्या जाग्रत्स्वप्नसुषुप्तिषु 1.4.299cd
प्रत्यक्प्रवणया दृष्ट्या पश्यात्मानं त्वमञ्जसा 2.1.234cd

प्रत्यक्प्रवणया दृष्ट्या संसारो नात्मनीक्ष्यते 1.4.572cd
प्रत्यक्प्रवणया बुद्ध्या वीक्ष्यतां यदि शक्यते 1.4.968cd
प्रत्यक्ष आत्मनि यथा तथान्यत्रापि लिङ्ग्यते 4.4.190cd
प्रत्यक्षं च तदेवेदमित्येतद्वस्तुकर्मकम् 4.3.670ab
प्रत्यक्षं च यथासन्नं परोक्षाद्वस्तुनो मतम् SV 188ab
प्रत्यक्षं तद्विरुद्धं त्यदप्रत्यक्षं तथोच्यते 2.3.26cd
प्रत्यक्षं तस्य का शक्तिः स्वार्थायां चिति वर्तितुम् 4.3.209cd
प्रत्यक्षं नाधिकारानुप्रवेशं प्रतिपद्यते SV 760cd
प्रत्यक्षं नापि चेशस्य केनचित्प्रतिहन्यते 1.2.110ab
प्रत्यक्षं फलरूपेण स एष इति दर्श्यते 1.2.220cd
प्रत्यक्षं मानमेवेदमिति यस्मात्प्रसिध्यति 4.3.189ab
प्रत्यक्षं वर्तते यत्र तत्फलं तत्र नेक्ष्यते 4.3.196ab
प्रत्यक्षकर्तृता तत्र यत आत्मन ईक्ष्यते 4.3.1075cd
प्रत्यक्षकार्यवत्तस्य लौकिकत्वं प्रसज्यते SV 739cd
प्रत्यक्षकुम्भवत्साक्षात्सुषुप्तेऽनन्यबोधगम् 1.4.297ab
प्रत्यक्षगम्यकार्येण नियोगस्यानुमेयतः SV 739ab
प्रत्यक्षगम्यधर्मश्चेद्व्यावृत्तिर्भवतोच्यते 4.3.1684ab
प्रत्यक्षगोचरं देवं लोकं चातिप्रमादिनम् 4.3.952ab
प्रत्यक्षगोचरे साध्याभावश्चेत्प्रतिपाद्यते 4.3.724ab
प्रत्यक्षग्राह्य एषोऽर्थो न तदन्यप्रमाणकः 2.4.163ab
प्रत्यक्षतममप्येनं वितमस्कं स्वयंस्थितम् 4.3.953ab
प्रत्यक्षतोऽनुमानाद्वा यो धीसाक्षीति भण्यते 4.3.469cd
प्रत्यक्षतो हि दृष्टोऽयं द्वैताख्यो विषयः स्फुटः 5.1.45cd
प्रत्यक्षत्वं पृथक्त्वस्य गुणत्वाद्यैरपीष्यते SV 960ab
प्रत्यक्षत्वान्न तन्मानं नात्मा स्वार्थजडत्वतः SV 1071cd
प्रत्यक्षदृक्स्वयंज्योतिस्तदात्मेत्यभ्युपेयताम् 4.3.189cd
प्रत्यक्षनामग्रहणं परिहृत्य परोक्षतः 4.2.40ab
प्रत्यक्षनामग्रहणं प्रद्विषन्ति जगत्यपि 4.2.43ab
प्रत्यक्षबाधसिद्ध्यर्थं न न्याय्योक्तिपरंपरा 1.4.558cd
प्रत्यक्षबुद्धिर्देहेऽस्मिञ्जायते कृष्णसर्पवत् 4.3.118cd
प्रत्यक्षमन्तरेणापि भवेद्दुःखविशेषणः 1.4.579ab
प्रत्यक्षमागमापायि विद्यात्पूर्णमिदं तथा 5.1.19cd

प्रत्यक्षमात्मना लोके द्रष्टाद्यर्थावभासनम् 4.3.1465ab
प्रत्यक्षमानगम्यत्वं विषाणस्यावधारितम् 4.3.109ab
प्रत्यक्षमानग्राह्यत्वात्फलतीरार्थसंगतेः 2.4.162cd
प्रत्यक्षमानसिद्ध्यर्थं तस्मात्प्रत्यक्षवादिना 4.3.183ab
प्रत्यक्षमाविरुद्धत्वं तथा चोक्तेः प्रसज्यते 3.4.185cd
प्रत्यक्षमेव सत्सिद्धं सदन्यस्याप्रसिद्धितः 1.2.10cd
प्रत्यक्षवत्प्रमाणत्वं नापि प्रत्यक्षतो गतिः 4.3.478cd
प्रत्यक्षवदयं धर्मस्तस्मादेवाभिधीयते 2.5.46cd
प्रत्यक्षवद्बोधयितुं किमु प्रत्यङ्निरञ्जनम् 3.8.62cd
प्रत्यक्षवेदवचनप्रामाण्याद्याश्रयत्वतः SV 436ab
प्रत्यक्षवेदवचनविरुद्धं तेषु यद्वचः 2.4.320ab
प्रत्यक्षश्रुतिमूलोऽयं सर्वाश्रमसमुच्चयः 3.5.151cd
प्रत्यक्षश्रुतिविध्यन्तविहितानामकारणात् SV 309ab
प्रत्यक्षस्यानुवृत्तिं च व्यावृत्तिं तद्विदां च सः 4.4.667ab
प्रत्यक्षस्यार्थसंवादादनुमित्यविरोधतः 4.3.480ab
प्रत्यक्षा एव विद्यन्ते संन्यासप्रतिपादिकाः 2.4.35cd
प्रत्यक्षात्तदसंसिद्धेर्विरोधस्तेऽनुमाश्रिते: 4.3.257cd
प्रत्यक्षात्तदद्वयं सत्स्यान्नो चेदस्तु ध्रुवो घटः 1.2.46cd
प्रत्यक्षादनुमानाच्च तथा चैवागमादपि 4.3.528ab
प्रत्यक्षादिर्निवृत्तिश्चेत्तस्याः किं रूपमुच्यताम् SV 977ab
प्रत्यक्षादि प्रमाणं स्यान्न स्वतो नापि चान्यतः SV 990cd
प्रत्यक्षादिप्रमाणेन नामीषामात्मनि ग्रहः 1.4.1274cd
प्रत्यक्षादिप्रमेयेति शक्या वक्तुं विपश्चिता SV 598cd
प्रत्यक्षादिफलं ज्ञानं कथं तस्य प्रमेयता 1.4.261ab
प्रत्यक्षादिविरोधः स्यादनिर्मोक्षस्तथैव च SV 141ab
प्रत्यक्षादिविरोधश्च कार्यपक्षेऽपि तु स्थितः SV 850ab
प्रत्यक्षादिविरोधोऽपि नातश्चोद्यः कथं चन 4.4.960cd
प्रत्यक्षादीनि मानानि भेदग्राहीणि सर्वदा 5.1.62ab
प्रत्यक्षाद्यतिवर्तित्वाद्युक्त्यपेक्षा न विद्यते 3.1.10ab
प्रत्यक्षाद्यनवष्टब्धमैकात्म्यं बाधवर्जितम् 4.3.115cd
प्रत्यक्षाद्यनवष्टब्धे तस्यामात्वं यतः स्थितम् 5.1.83cd
प्रत्यक्षाद्यप्रमेयत्वादैकात्म्याख्यस्य वस्तुनः 2.4.164cd

प्रत्यक्षाद्यभिधानेन सर्वमानोपलक्षणम् SV 569ab
प्रत्यक्षाद्यवसेयं यत्पूर्णं तदपि पूर्ववत् 5.1.14cd
प्रत्यक्षाद्युपलब्धौ यौ बुद्धौ संस्कार आहितः 4.3.85ab
प्रत्यक्षानवताराच्च नानुमानेन मीयते 2.4.172ab
प्रत्यक्षानुमयोर्नापि विरुद्धाव्यभिचारिता 4.3.614cd
प्रत्यक्षापाश्रयान्नित्यं नानपेक्षं तदक्षवत् 1.2.59cd
प्रत्यक्षाप्रमितं कस्माद्बोक्तृत्वं तस्य कल्प्यते 4.3.273cd
प्रत्यक्षाभावमानाभ्यां नानुभूतिरिहास्ति नः 4.3.1713cd
प्रत्यक्षाभावसंसिद्धौ किं प्रमाणमितीर्यताम् 4.3.250cd
प्रत्यक्षाभावसंसिद्धौ किं प्रमाणमितीर्यताम् 4.3.1695cd
प्रत्यक्षाभासतासिद्धेस्तेन नोक्तिविरोधिता 1.4.559cd
प्रत्यक्षार्थवदेवैषा मिथ्याधीरनुभूयते 1.4.260cd
प्रत्यक्षार्थस्यैष इति न विद्मः को विवक्षितः 3.4.51cd
प्रत्यक्षाविषयत्वं च प्रतीचः प्रागवादिषम् 1.4.577ab
प्रत्यक्षासन्ननिष्ठत्वादेतच्छब्दस्य कुम्भवत् 3.8.61ab
प्रत्यक्षेण घटे बुद्धे का युक्तिः कार्यमेव वा SV 849ab
प्रत्यक्षेण न तावत्सा तस्य सद्वस्तुमानतः 4.3.784ab
प्रत्यक्षेण विरुद्धत्वं न तावदुपपद्यते 4.3.157ab
प्रत्यक्षेण विरुद्धत्वादैकात्म्यं चापि न श्रुतेः 4.3.116cd
प्रत्यक्षेण विरुद्धार्थं त्वदीयं वचनं भवेत् 2.1.546cd
प्रत्यक्षेण विरोधाच्च न क्षणस्य विनाशिता 4.3.614ab
प्रत्यक्षेण विरोधे हि लिङ्गमाभासतां व्रजेत् 4.3.672ab
प्रत्यक्षेणानुपात्तत्वान्न स्मृतिस्तदितीक्षणम् 1.6.67ab
प्रत्यक्षेणापि नाभावः क्वचिज्जगति मीयते 4.3.1694ab
प्रत्यक्षेणेक्ष्यते नित्यमात्मनात्मा त्वकारकः 4.3.304cd
प्रत्यक्षेणैव दृष्टोऽयं देहो नातस्ततोऽपरः 4.3.147cd
प्रत्यक्षेणैव मानेन त्वयमित्यभिधीयते 4.3.300cd
प्रत्यक्षेणैव मानेन विमुखीकरणं कृतम् 4.3.187cd
प्रत्यक्षेणैव सं पश्येत्कथमित्यभिधीयताम् 4.4.667cd
प्रत्यक्षेणैव सिद्धत्वादनुमैवं वृथा भवेत् 4.3.724cd
प्रत्यक्षैकप्रमाणेन देहे चिद्धर्मकेऽञ्जसा 4.3.146ab
प्रत्यक्षैकप्रमाणोऽर्थो लौकिकोऽपि न शक्यते 3.8.62ab

प्रत्यक्षोऽर्थोऽयमित्येवं मिथ्यात्वं तस्य चोदितम् SV 187cd
प्रत्यक्षो गम्यते मात्रा प्रतीचोऽत्यन्तभेदतः 4.3.184cd
प्रत्यक्षोपनिषद्वाक्यविहितायास्ततोऽपि तु SV 310ab
प्रत्यक्षो बाध्यते नायमनुमानेन केनचित् 4.3.671cd
प्रत्यक्संवित्तिवस्तुस्थः प्रमाणविरहादयम् 3.8.35ab
प्रत्यक्संवित्त्वविज्ञाता तथैवेहानुभूयते 4.4.906ab
प्रत्यक्संवित्प्रमाणत्वं परलोकेहलोकयोः 4.3.829ab
प्रत्यक्समीक्षते नित्यं नातो द्रष्टृ भवेन्मनः 4.3.272cd
प्रत्यक्संबोधविध्वस्तप्रत्यङ्मोहः परात्मनः 1.4.1171ab
प्रत्यक्साक्ष्यतिरेकेण नाभावोऽपि प्रसिध्यति 3.4.123ab
प्रत्यक्स्वभाव एवास्य जाग्रत्स्वप्नसुषुप्तयः 2.1.264cd
प्रत्यगज्ञानजानेकविविधोपाधिसंगतेः 1.4.150ab
प्रत्यगज्ञानतत्कार्यैरसंस्पृष्टः स्वभावतः 4.3.1406cd
प्रत्यगज्ञानतस्तस्मात्तन्मयत्वमिवेक्ष्यते 4.3.1043cd
प्रत्यगज्ञानमात्रैकनीडत्वान्नान्यरूपता 1.4.671ab
प्रत्यगज्ञानमात्रोत्थं ग्राहकाद्यत्र भण्यते 2.4.467cd
प्रत्यगज्ञानमात्रोत्था जगत्सृष्ट्यादयस्ततः 1.4.625cd
प्रत्यगज्ञानमेवेह तदन्यद्वस्तुकारणम् 2.4.201ab
प्रत्यगज्ञानमेवैकं भीतिहेतुर्भवेद्यदि 1.4.69ab
प्रत्यगज्ञानविध्वंसिज्ञानाभ्यासोऽपि नेष्यते 4.4.775ab
प्रत्यगज्ञानविध्वंसे सामर्थ्यान्नित्यकर्मणः 3.3.100ab
प्रत्यगज्ञानविध्वस्तौ रज्ज्वज्ञानहताविव 1.3.315ab
प्रत्यगज्ञानसंभूतकामोत्थं साधनात्मकम् 3.5.114ab
प्रत्यगज्ञानसंभूतनानात्वोत्थप्रबोधतः 4.4.841ab
प्रत्यगज्ञानहेतुः स्यात्तदुच्छित्तौ न सा ततः 4.4.269cd
प्रत्यगज्ञानहेतुत्वात्तज्जस्यानन्त्यमुच्यते 1.3.304cd
प्रत्यगज्ञानहेतुत्वात्तदन्यस्येह वस्तुनः 1.4.978cd
प्रत्यगज्ञानहेतूत्थदुःखित्वमतिविभ्रम- 1.4.599ab
प्रत्यगज्ञानहेतूत्थमात्मैवं मायया जगत् 1.4.633cd
प्रत्यगज्ञानहेतूत्थशास्त्राचार्यादिसाधनः 1.4.604ab
प्रत्यगज्ञानहेतूत्थस्तद्बोधादेव तद्धतिः 1.3.52cd
प्रत्यगज्ञानहेतूत्था भावनेयं न तु स्वतः 2.4.193ab

प्रत्यगज्ञानहेतुत्थो यत्रानात्मा प्रसिध्यति 4.4.691ab
प्रत्यगत्ति यतोऽतोऽसावात्मेत्युक्तो मनीषिभिः 1.4.743cd
प्रत्यगर्थमनालिङ्ग्य न पराग्वर्ति किं चन 1.4.928ab
प्रत्यगर्थमनालिङ्ग्य न पराग्वर्ति जायते 1.4.1396ab
प्रत्यगर्थोऽविभागात्मा नातः संगच्छते द्वयम् 1.4.974cd
प्रत्यगात्मतमोध्वस्तौ नासावन्यदपेक्षते 4.3.16cd
प्रत्यगात्मनि तद्यस्मात्सम्यग्ज्ञानान्न भिद्यते 1.4.1501cd
प्रत्यगात्मनि तु ज्ञाते श्रुत्युक्तेनैव वर्त्मना 4.4.870ab
प्रत्यगात्मनि विज्ञाते नाज्ञातमवशिष्यते 1.4.1007ab
प्रत्यगात्मनि विश्वस्य ततोऽनात्मनि तद्वशात् 1.4.1400ab
प्रत्यगात्मन्यविद्येति त्वविद्यापरिकल्पना 2.1.272cd
प्रत्यगात्मविवक्षैव तत्र ज्ञेयाभिधानतः 1.4.526cd
प्रत्यगात्मस्वभावत्वात्सुखविज्ञानयोरतः 4.4.329cd
प्रत्यगात्मातिरेकेण प्राज्ञोऽन्यश्चेद्विवक्ष्यते 4.4.488ab
प्रत्यगात्मातिरेकेण यस्माच्चान्यन्न पश्यति 4.4.612ab
प्रत्यगात्मात्मकं भास्वत्प्रज्ञानघनतत्त्वकम् 2.5.135cd
प्रत्यगात्मापि तद् ब्रह्म परोक्षमभवन्मृषा 2.4.434cd
प्रत्यगात्माप्यसंदृष्टो मुक्त्या नैवोपतिष्ठते 1.4.1695ab
प्रत्यगात्मावसानेषु पूर्वपूर्वप्रहाणतः 2.4.294cd
प्रत्यगात्मा स्वयंज्योतिः साध्यते तच्च नानुमा 4.3.145cd
प्रत्यगाह्लादकारित्वादप्रियोऽपि प्रियो मतः 2.4.79cd
प्रत्यगेकस्वयंज्योतिःस्थिरासंहतनिष्क्रिय- 4.3.37ab
प्रत्यगैकात्म्यतोऽन्यत्र यथोक्तां धुरमुद्वहेत् 4.3.174cd
प्रत्यगैकात्म्यसंबोधात्तद्धर्मैर्लक्ष्यते कथम् 3.5.208cd
प्रत्यग्ज्ञानविरुद्धत्वान्मनोवाक्कायकर्मणाम् 4.4.1086cd
प्रत्यग्ज्ञानशिखिध्वस्ते मिथ्याज्ञाने सहेतुके 4.4.517ab
प्रत्यग्ज्ञानसमुत्पत्तौ विनियोगः प्रदर्शितः 3.2.79cd
प्रत्यग्ज्ञानस्य नैवातः कर्मणा स्यात्समुच्चयः 3.9.122ab
प्रत्यग्ज्ञानस्य लभ्येत न त्वसौ लभ्यते तथा 1.4.799cd
प्रत्यग्ज्ञानस्वभावेन कार्यकारणसंहतिः 2.1.232cd
प्रत्यग्ज्ञानाय नैवालमतस्तानि विरोधतः 4.4.1087cd
प्रत्यग्ज्ञाने निरुध्यन्ते चित्ततद्वृत्तयो यतः 1.4.850cd

प्रत्यग्ज्ञानोदयेऽतः स्यान्निवृत्तिः सर्वकर्मणाम् 3.5.121cd
प्रत्यग्ज्ञानोद्भवे तस्मात्समाप्तिः सर्वकर्मणाम् 1.3.101cd
प्रत्यग्दृशं विमोक्षाय संसाराय पराग्दृशाम् 1.4.27cd
प्रत्यग्दृष्टेर्हि विषयः स्यादात्मेत्यनुभूतितः 1.4.696ab
प्रत्यग्दृष्ट्यनुविधाहंप्रत्ययैकप्रमाणकः 1.4.37ab
प्रत्यग्दृष्ट्यव्यवहितेः प्रात्यक्ष्यादात्मवस्तुनः 4.3.1814ab
प्रत्यग्दृष्ट्या तदज्ञानतज्जं नैवेक्षते स्वतः 1.4.65ab
प्रत्यग्दृष्ट्या विरुद्धत्वान्न परागर्थदर्शनम् 1.4.698cd
प्रत्यग्दृष्ट्येक्षतेऽन्यस्य तदविद्यैकहेतुतः 1.4.1182cd
प्रत्यग्दृष्ट्येक्षितुं शक्यं वस्तु स्वप्नदृशा यथा 1.4.703cd
प्रत्यग्दृष्ट्यैव तद्ब्रह्म दृश्यते न पराग्धिया 4.3.1734cd
प्रत्यग्धियः समारोहमन्वात्मारूढवद्यतः 4.3.1918cd
प्रत्यग्धीगोचरो नो चेदनात्मासौ घटादिवत् 2.4.134ab
प्रत्यग्धीमात्रगम्योऽर्थो यस्मादात्मेति निश्चितः 2.4.133cd
प्रत्यग्धीमात्रतः प्रत्यङ्ङद्वयत्वविशेषणः 4.3.1183ab
प्रत्यग्ध्वान्तं चिदाभासं स्वकार्यनियमात्मकम् 3.7.43ab
प्रत्यग्ध्वान्तमतो ज्ञानं स्वात्मलब्ध्यैव हन्ति तत् 1.4.866cd
प्रत्यग्ध्वान्तसमुच्छेदि ज्ञानमैकात्म्यनिष्ठितम् 2.5.2ab
प्रत्यग्बुद्धिः प्रमात्रादौ सर्वत्रैवोपजायते 1.4.1394cd
प्रत्यग्बुद्धिस्त्वहंभागे नानयोर्धर्मधर्मिता 4.3.124cd
प्रत्यग्बोधातिरेकेण साधनान्तरनिस्पृहाः SV 1125ab
प्रत्यग्बोधातिरेकेण साधनान्तरनिह्नुतौ 1.4.1438ab
प्रत्यग्बोधात्परं नान्यन्मुक्तेरस्तीह साधनम् 1.4.849cd
प्रत्यग्बोधानिरस्तोऽर्थः प्रत्यग्वन्न हि सिध्यति 2.4.272ab
प्रत्यग्बोधैकयाथात्म्यवस्तुमात्रोपरोधतः 3.4.127cd
प्रत्यग्बोधोऽप्रमः सिद्ध आगमापायिमातृवत् 4.4.943ab
प्रत्यग्ब्रह्मत्वसिद्ध्यर्था सर्वैवोपनिषत्त्वियम् 2.3.137ab
प्रत्यग्भूतः परार्थेभ्यो योऽनन्यानुभवं प्रति 1.4.22ab
प्रत्यग्याथात्म्यजिज्ञासोः कथं सा विषयो भवेत् 2.4.193cd
प्रत्यग्याथात्म्यदृक्सिद्धिहेतुत्वाच्च भवेदिदम् 1.4.623ab
प्रत्यग्याथात्म्यदृष्ट्या तन्निपुणोऽपि न वीक्षते 1.4.488ab
प्रत्यग्याथात्म्यदृष्ट्यात्मा कारणं स्वतमोवधि 3.5.79ab

प्रत्यग्याथात्म्यधीमात्रात्परलोकाप्तिरिष्यते 1.4.1644cd
प्रत्यग्याथात्म्यधीरेव प्रत्यगज्ञानहानिकृत् SV 18ab
प्रत्यग्याथात्म्यनिर्णीतौ तार्किकोक्तात्मवस्तुवत् 1.4.852cd
प्रत्यग्याथात्म्यबोधस्य कुतोऽमूढः प्रवर्तते 1.4.819cd
प्रत्यग्याथात्म्यबोधस्य व्युत्पत्तेर्गुरुशास्त्रतः 4.4.656cd
प्रत्यग्याथात्म्यबोधार्थं रूपं मायामयं विभोः 2.5.128ab
प्रत्यग्याथात्म्यमात्रत्वात्तन्मोहाद्यप्यशेषतः 4.4.295ab
प्रत्यग्याथात्म्यमोहस्य कार्येयत्तेह भण्यते 3.3.6ab
प्रत्यग्याथात्म्यमोहस्य महिमैष त्वयोदितः 3.9.111ab
प्रत्यग्याथात्म्यमोहोत्था विरिञ्चोपक्रमा मृषा 2.4.430ab
प्रत्यग्याथात्म्यमोहोत्थौ तन्नाशे नश्यतस्ततः 2.4.242cd
प्रत्यग्याथात्म्यविज्ञानं न बाध्यं बाधकं यतः 3.5.46cd
प्रत्यग्याथात्म्यविज्ञानं नानवस्थाप्यतो भवेत् 3.2.20cd
प्रत्यग्याथात्म्यविज्ञानं नान्यत्किंचिदपेक्षते 4.5.23cd
प्रत्यग्याथात्म्यविज्ञानं मृत्युरज्ञानरूपिणः 3.2.19ab
प्रत्यग्याथात्म्यविज्ञानं यदत्रेत्यभिधीयते 4.4.389ab
प्रत्यग्याथात्म्यविज्ञानजन्मनेऽतः श्रुतिः स्वयम् 2.4.38ab
प्रत्यग्याथात्म्यविज्ञानजन्मने श्रुतिवाक्यतः 4.4.1218ef
प्रत्यग्याथात्म्यविज्ञानजन्मनो नातिरेकभाक् 1.4.1555ab
प्रत्यग्याथात्म्यविज्ञाननिष्ठता मुनिता यतः 4.4.1073ab
प्रत्यग्याथात्म्यविज्ञानभास्करोदयहेतवे SV 1135cd
प्रत्यग्याथात्म्यविज्ञानभास्वद्भास्करदीधिति- 2.4.471ab
प्रत्यग्याथात्म्यविज्ञानमात्रमेव समाश्रयेत् 4.4.1252cd
प्रत्यग्याथात्म्यविज्ञानमात्रव्युत्पत्तिसिद्धये 1.4.1434ab
प्रत्यग्याथात्म्यविज्ञानविरहादन्यसाधनः 1.4.54ab
प्रत्यग्याथात्म्यविज्ञानशिखिप्लुष्टमहत्तमाः 1.4.62ab
प्रत्यग्याथात्म्यविज्ञानसमाप्त्यापेक्षितत्ववतः 4.4.1238ab
प्रत्यग्याथात्म्यविज्ञानसाधनत्वप्रसिद्धये 3.5.143ab
प्रत्यग्याथात्म्यविज्ञानस्वभावश्चेत्समर्थ्यते 3.5.91ab
प्रत्यग्याथात्म्यविज्ञानात्तत्तमो नात्मबाधतः 3.4.49ab
प्रत्यग्याथात्म्यविज्ञानादन्योऽन्यव्यभिचारतः 2.3.221cd
प्रत्यग्याथात्म्यविज्ञानाद्वस्तुवृत्तानुरोधतः 2.4.331ab

प्रत्यग्याथात्म्यविज्ञानान्निर्वान्तीत्येष निश्चयः 1.4.1769cd
प्रत्यग्याथात्म्यविद्याग्निसंप्लुष्टाशेषतत्तमः 1.4.1181ab
प्रत्यग्याथात्म्यविद्यैव निःशेषपुरुषार्थकृत् 1.4.57ab
प्रत्यग्याथात्म्यव्याख्यानमात्रेणैव विना विधिम् 1.4.826ab
प्रत्यग्याथात्म्यसंबुद्धौ न सत्तन्नासदुच्यते 1.4.178cd
प्रत्यग्याथात्म्यसंबोधमात्रत्वादेव हेतुतः 2.5.17cd
प्रत्यग्याथात्म्यसंबोधात्तदन्यत्रैव या मतिः 1.4.1161ab
प्रत्यग्याथात्म्यसंबोधात्सर्वं तेन कृतं भवेत् 4.4.620ab
प्रत्यग्याथात्म्यसंबोधान्नान्यो हेतुः समीक्ष्यते 1.4.1320ab
प्रत्यग्याथात्म्यसंमोहः क्रियाकारकरूपवान् 3.3.13ab
प्रत्यग्याथात्म्यसंमोहध्वंसमात्रात्प्रबोधतः 4.4.783cd
प्रत्यग्याथात्म्यसंमोहमृते सत्त्वं न कुत्रचित् 1.4.178ab
प्रत्यग्याथात्म्यसंमोहान्न त्वसौ परमार्थतः 1.4.643cd
प्रत्यग्रूपस्य संसिद्धौ प्रतीचोऽन्यन्न कारणम् 2.4.283ab
प्रत्यग्रूपस्य स्थास्नुत्वाज्ज्ञातुर्मोहेन चान्वयात् 1.4.380ab
प्रत्यग्रूपातिरेकेण नान्यद्रूपमनात्मनः 1.4.1325ab
प्रत्यग्रूपात्परं रूपं न वस्तूत्प्रेक्ष्यते मितेः 4.3.1724cd
प्रत्यग्रूपात्पृथग्रूपं संभाव्यं केनचित्क्वचित् 4.3.365cd
प्रत्यग्रूपावबोधस्य भावाभावात्मवस्तुषु 3.4.25ab
प्रत्यग्वस्तु न वेत्तीति भवतेहाभिधीयते 4.3.1383cd
प्रत्यग्वस्तु पराग्बुद्धिगम्यैरिच्छादिभिः कथम् 4.4.472ab
प्रत्यग्वस्तुप्रमेयस्य तावतैव कृतार्थतः 4.3.1722cd
प्रत्यग्वस्तु यतः सिद्धमसामान्यविशेषवत् 4.4.794cd
प्रत्यग्वस्तूपरोधेन नानार्थो नावशिष्यते 3.4.24cd
प्रत्यग्वस्त्वतिरेकेण नान्यदात्मा तदेक्ष्यते 3.4.56cd
प्रत्यग्वस्त्वद्वयमपि तदबोधोपघाततः 4.4.850ab
प्रत्यग्वस्त्वात्मकत्वेऽपि चित्रमज्ञानचेष्टितम् 1.4.1356cd
प्रत्यग्विज्ञप्तिमात्रेण समाप्तिं जगदात्मनः 2.5.65ab
प्रत्यग्विज्ञानतो ध्वस्तेस्तत्प्राप्तिर्नान्यसाधना 1.4.1449cd
प्रत्यग्विद्यैव तेन स्यादुदारफलसाधनम् 2.5.95cd
प्रत्यग्विरोधतस्तद्वन्न किंचिन्नापि निह्नुतम् 3.8.179cd
प्रत्यग्विविदिषान्यत्र कर्मणां श्रूयते फलम् 1.5.244cd

प्रत्यग्विविदिषामात्रहेतुत्वान्न मृतेर्भयम् 4.4.1059ab
प्रत्यग्विविदिषासिद्धयै वेदानुवचनादयः SV 14ab
प्रत्यङ्ङकारकस्तस्माल्लिप्यते न क्रियाफलैः 4.3.1011cd
प्रत्यङ्ङभिहितो यत्नात्तद्गिरा सोऽत्र युज्यते 3.8.60cd
प्रत्यङ्ङविद्यया यां यामवस्थामभिमन्यते 4.3.447ab
प्रत्यङ्मात्रतयैवातोऽनात्मात्मनि विलीयते 3.4.61ab
प्रत्यङ्मात्रदृशः पुंसो न न्याय्यः स्यात्समुच्चयः 1.4.1685ab
प्रत्यङ्मात्रदृशि ह्यस्मिञ्जाग्रत्स्वप्नसुषुप्तिषु 2.3.191ab
प्रत्यङ्मात्रप्रमाणं स्यात्परागेवैति चित्रताम् 1.4.26cd
प्रत्यङ्मात्रफलत्वेन साक्षित्वेन च सर्वदा 4.4.943cd
प्रत्यङ्मात्रस्य ब्रह्मोक्तेः समस्तव्यस्तता कुतः 1.4.967cd
प्रत्यङ्मात्रस्वभावत्वाद्ब्रह्मणोऽव्यवधानता 3.4.37cd
प्रत्यङ्मात्रावशेषत्वात्कुतः षष्ठ्यर्थसंभवः 3.5.83cd
प्रत्यङ्मात्रावशेषत्वात्स्यामपूर्वादिमानहम् 3.4.49cd
प्रत्यङ्मात्रावसायित्वं प्रत्यग्दृष्टेर्यतस्ततः 4.3.1804ab
प्रत्यङ्मात्रेक्षणादात्ममोहतज्जनिराकृतेः 1.4.1411ab
प्रत्यङ्मात्रेक्षणादात्ममोहतज्जनिराकृतेः 2.4.441ab
प्रत्यङ्मात्रैकतां मुक्त्वा तदविद्यामृते न हि 4.4.955ab
प्रत्यङ्मात्रैकदृष्टित्वाद्धियां वाचामगोचरः SV 1086cd
प्रत्यङ्मात्रैकधीगम्यं रूपं वास्तवमात्मनः 2.3.11cd
प्रत्यङ्मात्रैकनिष्ठत्वान्न भावाभावयोः स्थितिः 4.4.292cd
प्रत्यङ्मात्रैकयाथात्म्यं चतुर्धोक्तस्य बोध्यते 2.5.34cd
प्रत्यङ्मात्रैकयाथात्म्यं न दोषो जामिता ततः 2.1.371cd
प्रत्यङ्मात्रैकयाथात्म्यं श्रूयते सोपपत्तिकम् 2.4.103cd
प्रत्यङ्मात्रैकयाथात्म्यात्कार्यकारणवस्तुनः 2.4.231ab
प्रत्यङ्मात्रैकयाथात्म्यात्कुतस्तद्व्यतिरेकतः 1.4.658cd
प्रत्यङ्मात्रैकयाथात्म्यात्क्षेत्रक्षेत्रज्ञवस्तुनः 1.4.1687ab
प्रत्यङ्मात्रैकयाथात्म्यादविद्यादेरिहात्मनि 4.4.766cd
प्रत्यङ्मात्रैकयाथात्म्यादश्रुतत्वान्न चार्थतः 4.4.158cd
प्रत्यङ्मात्रैकयाथात्म्यादात्माविद्यातदुत्थयोः 3.4.57ab
प्रत्यङ्मात्रैकयाथात्म्याद्रूपं संभाव्यतेऽण्वपि 4.3.367cd
प्रत्यङ्मात्रैकरूपत्वादात्मा नानात्मतां स्वतः 2.4.273ab

प्रत्यङ्मात्रैकरूपेण तदबोधनिराकृतेः 2.3.177cd
प्रत्यङ्मात्रैकसाक्षित्वात्तमस्तत्प्रत्यगात्मनि 1.4.1341cd
प्रत्यङ्मानैकमेयत्वं वेदान्तेष्वात्मवस्तुनः 1.4.489cd
प्रत्यङ्मानैकमेयोऽतो भोक्ता भोग्यं ततोऽपरम् 2.1.176ab
प्रत्यङ्मोहजबुद्ध्यादिजडरूपप्रधानतः 3.4.112ab
प्रत्यङ्मोहजवस्तूनां प्रतीच्यवगते तथा 1.4.749cd
प्रत्यङ्मोहतदुत्थस्य प्रत्यग्याथात्म्यबोधतः 2.3.235ab
प्रत्यङ्मोहमरुद्बुद्धिचक्षुर्देहादिरूपिणाम् 1.4.504ab
प्रत्यङ्मोहस्य नातः स्याज्ज्ञानकर्मसमुच्चयः 3.3.24cd
प्रत्यङ्मोहस्य यत्कार्यमधुना तत्प्रपञ्च्यते 4.3.1241cd
प्रत्यङ्मोहाभिनहनध्वंसश्चाप्यन्यथामतेः 1.4.1555cd
प्रत्यङ्मोहैकनिष्ठं सच्चिदाभत्वात्तदात्मनि 4.3.910cd
प्रत्यङ्मोहैकमात्रोत्थं ध्यानलेलायनादिकम् 4.3.417ab
प्रत्यङ्मोहैकहेतुत्वात्सर्वानर्थमृषामतेः 1.4.418cd
प्रत्यङ्मोहैकहेतुत्वाद्वाङ्मनःकायकर्मणाम् 1.3.110cd
प्रत्यङ्मोहोद्भवानात्मप्राधान्येन तमोन्वयात् 2.4.113ab
प्रत्यज्ज्ञायि प्रतिज्ञेयं हीयेतासौ न संशयः 4.3.753cd
प्रत्यञ्चं मदिति प्राह तद्दृष्ट्या नेक्षते द्वयम् 1.4.63cd
प्रत्यबुध्यत तद्ब्रह्म स स तदभवत्परम् 1.4.1437cd
प्रत्यबुध्यत यो यस्तदिति चोर्ध्वं प्रवक्ष्यति 1.4.1086ab
प्रत्यभिज्ञात्मकं ज्ञानं संज्ञानमिति भण्यते 4.4.95ab
प्रत्यभिज्ञानतस्तत्र ध्रौव्यं चेदात्मनो मतम् 4.3.133ab
प्रत्यभिज्ञानतोऽभेदः खण्डमुण्डस्थगोत्वयोः 1.6.65ab
प्रत्यभिज्ञानतो नैवं पूर्वदृष्टस्य वस्तुनः 4.3.1401cd
प्रत्यभिज्ञाबलाद्वापि नाभावेऽस्त्युभयं हि तत् 4.3.1712cd
प्रत्यभिज्ञामृते तस्य प्रतिज्ञार्थो न सिध्यति 1.2.64cd
प्रत्यभिज्ञामृते नायं प्रतिज्ञार्थः प्रसिध्यति 4.3.599cd
प्रत्यभिज्ञाय तदिदमज्ञातं वस्त्ववैति हि 1.4.460cd
प्रत्यभिज्ञायते साक्षाद्दृष्टपूर्वो यथा तथा 1.4.270cd
प्रत्यभिज्ञायमानेऽर्थे तदेवेदमिति ध्रुवे 1.2.58ab
प्रत्यभिज्ञा स एवाहमिति तद्वद्भवेन्न किम् 4.3.135cd
प्रत्ययः करणार्थः स्यात्क्रियायां भावसाधनः 2.1.185cd

प्रत्ययश्च यथारूपो मानसोऽस्योपजायते 4.4.716ab
प्रत्ययोऽव्यभिचार्येकश्चैतन्यप्रतिबिम्बितः 1.4.1397cd
प्रत्यर्थिनि च शब्देऽस्मिन्नाभावोऽनुपलब्धितः SV 538ab
प्रत्यर्थिनि पुमर्थे तत्सुधीभिर्गृह्यते कथम् SV 1037cd
प्रत्यर्थिनि श्रुतेर्वाक्ये सत्यैकात्म्यावबोधिनि 3.9.182cd
प्रत्यर्थिनि स्थितेऽनात्मधियां स्यात्सत्यता कुतः 1.4.1456cd
प्रत्यर्थिनि हि प्रत्यक्षे तद्विरुद्धः कुतोऽमितेः 1.2.68cd
प्रत्यर्थि मेयविषये मानस्येहास्ति किं चन 4.4.787cd
प्रत्यवायाद्यभावश्च फलं नित्यस्य कर्मणः 3.3.82ab
प्रत्याख्यातः स चेत्तेन क्वानात्मा सिद्ध्यतामयम् 1.4.944cd
प्रत्याख्यातः स चेत्तेन क्वानात्मा सिध्यतां ततः 1.4.1363cd
प्रत्याख्यातस्वभावोऽपि सिध्यतीवाग्रहो दृशौ 1.4.1405cd
प्रत्याख्यातात्मनैवेयं प्रत्यगात्मानमेकलम् 4.3.1180ab
प्रत्याख्यातुं समर्थः को ब्रुवन्तं ब्राह्मणं नृपः 6.2.72cd
प्रत्याख्यातैव साविद्या सकार्या सर्वदात्मना 4.3.1176ab
प्रत्याख्यातोपदेशः सन्संवादेन पुनः पुनः 2.1.82ab
प्रत्याख्याय न चात्मानमनात्मा व्यतिरिच्यते 4.4.160ab
प्रत्याचष्टे तु नाविद्या निरात्मत्वाच्चिदात्मनः 4.3.1176cd
प्रत्याचष्टे श्रुतिरतः सर्वं नेतीति चात्मनि 4.4.161ab
प्रत्याधानसमूढस्य शिशोस्तस्यैव काश्चन 2.2.22ab
प्रत्याय्यैवं परात्मानं मुनिराह नराधिपम् 4.2.92ab
प्रत्याह पृष्टः स्वां जायां नामृतत्वं धनादिति 2.4.51ab
प्रत्याहैष त आत्मेति याज्ञवल्क्योऽपि पूर्ववत् 3.5.53ab
प्रत्युक्तिर्गार्गि वायावित्येवमेवोत्तरेष्वपि 3.6.11ab
प्रत्युक्तिश्च तवात्मेति भिन्नार्थे वचसी कथम् 3.5.17cd
प्रत्युक्तेरेष त इति प्रश्नयोरुभयोरपि 3.5.16ab
प्रत्युक्तौ न निमित्तादि यदि साक्षात्समीक्ष्यते 2.1.369ab
प्रत्युच्चार्याथ गार्ग्योक्तमाकाशे प्राब्रवीदृषिः 3.8.13ab
प्रत्युत्थानाभिवादाभ्यां पुनस्तान्प्रतिपद्यते 4.4.1224ab
प्रत्यूषसि ततो भक्त्या ह्यादित्यमुपतिष्ठते 6.3.56ab
प्रत्येकं नीलपीतादिग्रहणे चित्रता कुतः SV 954ab
प्रत्येकं प्रमितेर्वृद्धिरित्येतत्स्यात्तदा मृषा SV 812cd

प्रत्येकं प्राणिनां ह्येतद्ब्रह्मचक्रमवस्थितम् 2.5.73ab

प्रत्येकं भिन्नसाध्यं हि पुत्रकर्मादिसाधनम् 1.5.233ab

प्रत्येकं शक्तिमत्त्वोक्तिर्वीत्यादिवचसोच्यते 5.14.10cd

प्रत्येकं शक्त्यभावेऽपि चैतन्यं मदशक्तिवत् 4.3.117cd

प्रत्येकमुच्यतेऽत्रैतद्वाक्येष्वेतेषु वस्तुनः 4.3.1627cd

प्रत्येनसोऽत्र ते ज्ञेया भिन्नास्ते स्वाधिकारतः 4.3.1962cd

प्रथतेऽनेकरूपाभं तज्ज्ञानं ज्ञातृकर्तृकम् 3.4.107cd

प्रथतेऽपास्तनिःशेषक्रियाकारकवस्तुनि 3.3.13cd

प्रथतेऽविकृतात्मैकनित्यदृष्टेः परात्मनः 1.4.280ab

प्रथते पुरतोऽविद्यामात्रतत्त्वं विनश्वरम् 4.3.1246ef

प्रथते भेदवज्ज्ञानं न क्वचिद्वस्तुसंश्रयात् 4.3.484cd

प्रथते यः स्वयं साक्षादज्ञातत्वादिभूमिषु 1.4.292ab

प्रथते वैश्वरूपेण यतोऽविद्यैव सर्वथा 1.4.207ab

प्रथते स इहात्मेति जगत्यस्मिन्निगद्यते 1.4.22cd

प्रथमश्चेत्त्वयैवोक्तं क्षीयेते कामकर्मणी 1.4.1711ab

प्रथमश्रवणे यत्र न शब्दार्थावधारणम् SV 875ab

प्रथमा संस्कृतिरिति मन्त्रवर्णोऽपि दृश्यते 2.3.71ab

प्रथमे हेतुवचसि परिणामस्तथोत्तरे 4.3.1505cd

प्रथमोऽथ द्वितीयो वा न न्यायोऽस्त्युभयोरपि 1.4.1710cd

प्रथमोत्तमे त्वमृतमक्षरे सस्वरत्वतः 5.5.12cd

प्रदीपवद्विनष्टोऽयमिति चेदभिधीयते 4.3.1401ab

प्रदीपवन्न भूतेभ्यो जात्यन्तरमतो भवेत् 4,4.28cd

प्रदीपवीक्षणे नैव प्रदीपान्तरमार्गणम् 4.3.525cd

प्रदीपादेरभिव्यङ्ग्यं नैव कार्यं घटादिकम् 4.4.315cd

प्रदीपासंनिधौ यद्वत्कुम्भस्य प्रसमीक्ष्यते 4.3.510ab

प्रद्योतेन यथोक्तेन प्रद्योतितपथा कृत– 4.4.80ab

प्रधानं करणं बुद्धिर्द्वारमात्रं ततोऽपरम् 4.3.317cd

प्रधानं तर्हि मां वित्त भवन्तश्चापराधिनः 6.1.27cd

प्रधानगुणभावश्च क्वचित्कस्यचिदिष्यते 1.4.1482cd

प्रधानगुणभावेन गुणानां भूरिरूपता 2.4.362cd

प्रधानगुणभावेन सर्वत्रैते व्यवस्थिते 4.2.46cd

प्रधानगुणभावोऽपि विरोधान्न तयोर्भवेत् 1.4.1121cd

प्रधानगुणवृत्त्योक्तौ सूक्ष्मस्थूलविभागतः 4.4.184cd
प्रधानचोदनैवास्य चोदनातोऽवगम्यते 4.4.1240ab
प्रधानत्वं च विद्यायास्तमेतमिति दर्शितम् SV 86cd
प्रधानफलसंबन्धो यत्र तु स्याच्छ्रुतेर्मुखात् 1.3.197ab
प्रधानभूतः सन्भुङ्क्ते सर्वदान्नं स कामतः 1.5.93cd
प्रधानवदतो नेदं लोकस्तुतिपरं भवेत् 4.4.1138ef
प्रधानवादः प्राप्नोति यदि देहात्मनोः पृथक् 4.4.514ab
प्रधानवादमाशङ्क्य यस्माद्भूयोऽपि भण्यते 1.4.480ab
प्रधानाहुतयस्तिस्त्रो याः स्युरग्न्यादिपर्विकाः 6.4.85ab
प्रध्वंसात्तस्य चार्थस्य नातोऽर्थस्पर्शिनी स्मृतिः 1.4.465cd
प्रध्वंसादात्ममोहस्य तथैकात्म्यं समश्नुते 4.4.841cd
प्रध्वस्ततत्त्वतमसः कुतः स्यात्कारणादृते 1.4.1543cd
प्रध्वस्तत्वात्कुतः शङ्का तन्मूलासंभवाद्भवेत् 1.3.377cd
प्रध्वस्तत्वादविद्याया ब्रह्मात्मज्ञानवह्निना 1.4.1580cd
प्रध्वस्तभेद ऐकात्म्ये नोपासनविधिर्यतः 2.5.88cd
प्रध्वस्तभेदहेतुत्वात्कारणादेरसंभवात् 4.4.642ab
प्रध्वस्ताज्ञानतज्जः सन्परां निर्वृतिमागतः 4.4.1320cd
प्रध्वस्तायामविद्यायां पूर्णमेवावशिष्यते SV 269cd
प्रध्वस्ताशेषभेदेऽपि मयि भिन्नधियस्तथा 1.4.990cd
प्रध्वस्ताशेषभेदेऽपि मयि भिन्नधियस्तथा 4.3.1744cd
प्रध्वस्तिः कर्मभिः कर्तुं शक्या तेषाममानतः SV 1102cd
प्रध्वस्तैकात्म्यसंमोहो नेति नेत्यात्मविद्यया 4.4.1159ab
प्रध्वस्यात्मायमत्येति तदुत्थं वस्तुवृत्ततः 3.5.74cd
प्रपञ्चनाशनेनाथ नाश्यते भेदकारणम् SV 390ab
प्रपञ्चविलयेनैव सर्वानर्थप्रहाणतः SV 396ab
प्रपञ्चाभिनिवेशित्वहेतौ तुल्येऽपि चानयोः SV 419ab
प्रपञ्चो वर्तमानस्तु कार्यत्वान्नश्यति स्वतः SV 394cd
प्रपद्यते विवेकेन यथा कुम्भादिवीक्षणे 4.3.1608cd
प्रपश्यति तदानात्मा न पृथग्व्यवशिष्यते 4.4.1278cd
प्रपूर्वीं पीवरीमन्यां याहि विश्वावसो द्रुतम् 6.4.91cd
प्रपूर्व्यामिति नार्यत्र भण्यते तरुणी किल 6.4.91ab
प्रपूर्व्यामिति लिङ्गाच्च तरुण्यां सत्पतिः सदा 6.4.92ab

प्रबन्धशतसंपातैः संचरत्येष न स्वतः 4.3.404cd
प्रबन्धेनार्चिषो धर्मा धर्मिण्यग्नौ व्यवस्थिते 4.3.621ab
प्रबोधनाडीस्त्यक्त्वात्मा स्वप्ननाडीरयं गतः 4.3.947ab
प्रबोधयन्ति विध्वस्तनिखिलद्वैतगोचरम् SV 709cd
प्रबोधवत्सुषुप्तेऽस्मिन्निति प्रतिविधीयते 4.3.1603cd
प्रबोधोत्पत्तिहेतूनां दृष्टो बोधादिकार्यकृत् 1.4.85cd
प्रभूतशब्दाभिध्यानं नालं मोक्षार्थसिद्धये 4.4.964ab
प्रमां तत्प्रतिषेधं च कुर्वत्क्वचिदिहेष्यते 2.1.556cd
प्रमाणं बोधकं सर्वं तच्च सिद्धस्य वस्तुनः 4.3.1575ab
प्रमाणं भवता वाच्यं भेदाभेदत्वसिद्धये 4.3.544ab
प्रमाणं मेयविषयं तत्फलं मातृसंश्रयम् 4.3.194ab
प्रमाणं यदि विज्ञानं मेया नीलादिरूपता 4.3.550ab
प्रमाणकार्ये निर्वृत्ते नान्यत्किंचिदपेक्षते 1.4.1295cd
प्रमाणगोचराणां च स्वतः सिद्धेर्न निह्नुतिः 2.3.194cd
प्रमाणगोचरातीतं तत्त्वं स्यान्निर्दिदिक्षितम् 2.3.176cd
प्रमाणज्ञाः प्रशंसन्ति यच्च तच्च सतीश्वरे 3.8.144cd
प्रमाणतोऽपि संप्राप्तं यदि वस्त्वतिशङ्क्यते 4.4.814ab
प्रमाणतोऽप्रमाणाद्वा सर्वं विद्येति भण्यते 4.4.112cd
प्रमाणत्वं पुमर्थश्च स एव विदुषां मतः SV 1007cd
प्रमाणत्वाप्रमाणत्वे नान्यथा ते प्रसिध्यतः 2.1.543cd
प्रमाणदृष्टियोग्यत्वात्प्रमात्राद्यात्मवस्तुनः 4.3.1490cd
प्रमाणनिरपेक्षं सद्वस्त्वलं स्वप्रसिद्धये 1.4.998cd
प्रमाणफलकारूढं स्वतमो हन्ति नान्यथा 4.3.182ab
प्रमाणफलयोर्भेदस्तथा मानप्रमेययोः 4.3.188ab
प्रमाणबलतः प्राप्तमपि भूरि न वार्यते 3.3.80ab
प्रमाणभूमावैकात्म्यं विरोधान्न प्रतीयते 1.4.997ab
प्रमाणभूमौ स्थित्वैतदुक्तं सर्वं प्रसिध्यति 3.4.125cd
प्रमाणमप्रमाणं च प्रमाभासं च यद्भवेत् 2.4.124ab
प्रमाणमप्रमाणं च प्रमाभासस्तथैव च 1.4.874ab
प्रमाणमप्रमाणं च प्रमाभासस्तथैव च 2.1.552ab
प्रमाणमप्रमाणं वा मेयसंगत्यसंगतेः 2.4.132cd
प्रमाणमस्ति यत्प्राणाद्भवानेवं प्रभाषते SV 186cd

प्रमाणयोग्यतैवोक्ता न त्वैकात्म्यमितात्मता 1.4.219cd
प्रमाणरूपावष्टम्भात्प्रमा पूर्वं प्रजायते 2.4.224ab
प्रमाणलक्षणाभावान्न च बाधोऽप्रमाणतः 4.4.959cd
प्रमाणलब्धसद्भावो निष्फलोऽपि न वार्यते 4.4.458ab
प्रमाणवन्त्यदृष्टानि कल्प्यानि सुबहून्यपि 2.5.76ab
प्रमाणवन्त्यदृष्टानि कल्प्यानि सुबहून्यपि 4.4.461ab
प्रमाणवर्त्मनायातमिदं मोहापनुत्तये 3.4.129ab
प्रमाणवादिभिर्दृष्टमनन्यायत्तसिद्धिकम् 1.4.593cd
प्रमाणविरहात्सिद्धा सेयमन्धपरंपरा 4.3.686ab
प्रमाणविरहात्सिद्धिरेतच्च स्वानुभूतितः 1.4.1290cd
प्रमाणवृत्तमुक्त्वैतन्मनसैवेतिवाक्यतः 4.4.709cd
प्रमाणव्यतिरेकेण नाप्यसत्त्वं प्रसिध्यति 4.3.163ab
प्रमाणव्यतिरेकेण प्रमेयोऽर्थो भवन्भवेत् 1.2.79ab
प्रमाणव्यवहारोऽयं सर्वेषामपि वादिनाम् 1.4.1402ab
प्रमाणव्यापृतिफलप्रसिद्धिश्च प्रमातरि 4.3.297ab
प्रमाणव्यापृतिर्यापि भवतेहोपवर्णिता 4.4.745ab
प्रमाणव्यापृतेः पूर्वमेवं मेयोऽत्र लभ्यते 4.4.909ab
प्रमाणव्यापृतेरूर्ध्वं ज्ञाताज्ञातद्वयं मिथः 4.3.178ab
प्रमाणव्यापृतेर्ज्ञातोऽज्ञातोऽज्ञातत्वहानिकृत् 1.2.105ab
प्रमाणव्यापृतेर्यस्मान्मेयस्य व्यापृतेस्तथा 4.4.837ab
प्रमाणव्यापृतेस्तूर्ध्वं वासनाधानकारणात् 3.4.143ab
प्रमाणसंप्लवोऽप्युक्तो दूरादेव निवर्तितः SV 1076ab
प्रमाणस्य च तत्सर्वमक्षरे प्रतिषिध्यते 3.8.90cd
प्रमाणस्य ततोऽन्यस्मिन्न तन्मानत्वमर्हति 4.3.1723ab
प्रमाणस्य न तन्न्याय्यं सिद्धार्थव्यञ्जकत्वतः 2.4.189cd
प्रमाणहेतोः केन स्यादज्ञातत्वमितीर्यताम् 4.3.159cd
प्रमाणाच्च न तत्सिद्धिस्तस्य मानविरोधतः 4.3.548ab
प्रमाणाच्चानधिगतौ तन्निवृत्तिः कुतो भवेत् 4.3.176ab
प्रमाणादेः प्रसिद्धिः स्यान्मेयस्यापि प्रमाणतः 4.3.296cd
प्रमाणादेव यत्प्राप्तं कथं तदतिशङ्क्यते 4.4.813ab
प्रमाणादेव शास्त्रात्सा न मेयात्कार्यतो भवेत् SV 851cd
प्रमाणाधिगतौ सत्यां पुंसो मेयानुरोधतः 1.3.76ab

प्रमाणानभिसंबद्धं प्रमाणाच्चेति साहसम् 1.4.220cd
प्रमाणानां प्रमाणत्वं न क्वचिद्वः प्रसिध्यति 1.4.1306cd
प्रमाणानां प्रमाणत्वं न स्वरूपप्रमेयता 4.4.339ab
प्रमाणानां प्रमाणत्वं नोभयत्रापि लभ्यते 4.3.160cd
प्रमाणानां प्रमेयः स्यात्सर्वमेतद्विचार्यते 1.4.222cd
प्रमाणानां प्रवृत्तिः स्यादन्यथा नोपपद्यते 4.4.217cd
प्रमाणानामभावस्य गमकः को भविष्यति SV 940cd
प्रमाणानामभावस्य गमकः को भविष्यति 4.3.1711cd
प्रमाणानि च शास्त्राणि तत्प्रामाण्यं न चान्यतः 1.4.413ab
प्रमाणान्तरगम्यत्वाल्लौकिकत्वं तदापतेत् SV 1028cd
प्रमाणान्तरगम्येऽर्थे विवक्षा च व्यवस्थिता SV 722cd
प्रमाणान्तरसंवादात्पुंसां विश्वासधीर्यतः 1.4.1444cd
प्रमाणान्यन्तरेणापि देहादिश्चेत्प्रसिध्यति 4.3.161ab
प्रमाणाभिजनादेव यथाभूतार्थता धियः 1.3.74cd
प्रमाणायत्तमेतावत्स्वप्रमेयावभासनम् SV 716ab
प्रमाणावगतेस्तत्र किं चिन्त्यमिति चेन्मतम् 3.9.171cd
प्रमाणासंभवश्च स्यादात्मभेदप्रकल्पने 4.4.348cd
प्रमाणासंभवात्तस्मात्सा न कल्प्या विपश्चिता 4.4.460cd
प्रमाणासंभवात्तस्मादसमीचीनमुच्यते 3.2.76cd
प्रमाणासंभवान्मैवं वोचो लौकिकवस्तुवत् 3.3.31cd
प्रमाणैरपि संबन्धः प्रत्यक्षप्रमुखैः क्वचित् 4.4.664cd
प्रमाणैर्गृह्यते प्रीतिर्व्यभिचारिण्यनात्मसु 1.4.1039ab
प्रमाणोत्पत्तिरन्वेष्या प्रत्यग्ध्वान्तापनुत्तये 4.3.180cd
प्रमातत्फलयोर्भित्तेर्नेह चोद्यस्य संभवः 4.4.695ab
प्रमातरि च मेये स्यात्फलं कस्येति भण्यताम् SV 1065ab
प्रमाता च प्रमाणं च प्रमेयोऽथ क्रियाफले 2.3.182ab
प्रमाता च प्रमाणं च प्रमेयो निश्चितिस्तथा 1.4.870ab
प्रमातात्मा न मानांशो यद्ययं व्यावहारिकः SV 824ab
प्रमातुं तदृतेऽनात्मा ह्यन्धकारप्रनृत्तवत् 4.3.1291cd
प्रमातृक्रियया व्याप्तिर्द्रष्टव्य इति भण्यते 2.4.130cd
प्रमातृतन्त्रा सा चेत्स्यात्प्राप्ता लोकाग्निबुद्धिवत् 2.4.120cd
प्रमातृत्वादिका सर्वा प्रथते विषयात्मना 4.3.885ab

प्रमातृत्वादिना यावत्किंचिदत्र विवक्षितम् 2.3.197ab
प्रमातृत्वादिसंबन्धो नासदात्मकवस्तुनि 1.4.177ab
प्रमातृदृष्टिरेकात्र शब्दाद्यर्थावलेहिनी 3.4.94ab
प्रमातृपरिणामत्वात्प्रमासिद्धिः प्रमातरि 3.4.138ab
प्रमातृमानतन्मेयेष्वागमापायिषु त्रिषु SV 1000ab
प्रमातृमानाभावोऽपि भवता प्रतिपाद्यते 4.3.251ab
प्रमातृमेयभेदोऽत्र न तावद्गम्यते मितेः 2.4.133ab
प्रमातृस्थं न कामादि तद्वदेयात्प्रमेयताम् 4.4.475cd
प्रमात्रतिशयेनैव कारणं स्यात्प्रमात्रपि 3.4.140ab
प्रमात्र बोधिकैवातो न प्रवृत्तिः प्रमाणतः 4.4.940cd
प्रमात्रव्यवधानेन संविदैव न वृत्तिभिः 3.4.138cd
प्रमात्रादित्रयं यस्मात्संविन्मात्रवपुर्भृतः SV 791ab
प्रमात्रादिनिषेधेन श्रुत्याव्याकृतमुच्यते 1.4.210ab
प्रमात्रादिपदार्थस्तु धर्माधर्मादिहेतुकः 3.4.92cd
प्रमात्रादिप्रवृत्तेः प्राक्सदानस्तमितोदिता 3.4.83ab
प्रमात्रादिविभागेन मानं मेयं समश्नुते 4.4.838ab
प्रमात्रादिविभागेन यज्ज्ञानं प्रथते क्वचित् 1.4.1355ab
प्रमात्रादिविविक्तार्थमनुभूयोत्थितस्ततः 1.4.289ab
प्रमात्रादिव्यपेक्षेयं लौकिकी दृष्टिरात्मनः 3.4.99ab
प्रमात्रादीह यत्किंचित्प्रत्यगज्ञानहेतुजम् 1.4.477ab
प्रमात्रादेरभावे च नाप्यभावः प्रमेष्यते 1.4.267ab
प्रमात्रादेरभावोऽतो यः सिद्धः स्वात्मबोधतः 2.3.229ab
प्रमात्रादेरभावोऽपि प्रत्यग्बोधाश्रयात्तथा 2.3.223cd
प्रमात्रादेरुपादानमैकात्म्यप्रतिबन्धकम् 4.4.682ab
प्रमात्रादेस्तदज्ञाननिवृत्तौ विनिवृत्तितः 4.4.302cd
प्रमात्राद्यतिरेकेण ह्यसंविदितरूपकम् 1.4.339ab
प्रमात्राद्यतिरेकोऽपि वस्तुनो बोधरूपिणः 3.4.88ab
प्रमात्राद्यनभिव्याप्तं वस्तु पूर्वं समीक्ष्य हि 4.3.1420ab
प्रमात्राद्यभिसंबन्धो यथानुभवसिद्धिकः 3.4.91ab
प्रमात्राद्युत्थितेः पूर्वं कारकं दुर्लभं मितेः 1.4.322ab
प्रमात्राद्युत्थितेः पूर्वं चिदन्यानन्वयात्तमो- 1.4.290ab
प्रमात्राद्युत्थितेरग्रे ब्रह्मैवासीद्यथोदितम् 1.4.1333ab

प्रमादिनो बहिश्चित्ताः पिशुनाः कलहोत्सुकाः 1.4.1584ab
प्रमाननुविधानाच्च न स्मृतिर्बाधिकापरा 1.4.844ab
प्रमान्तरविरुद्धं च मातुं नोत्सहते श्रुतिः 4.3.1749ab
प्रमान्तरविरुद्धत्वान्नेन्द्रेणाप्यधिगम्यते 2.1.496cd
प्रमान्तरविरुद्धार्थमिमं ग्रन्थं यथोदितम् 1.4.1692cd
प्रमान्तरविरोधेन न प्रमेहास्ति काचन 4.3.479cd
प्रमान्तरानधिगता ब्रह्मता प्रत्यगात्मनः 4.4.1323ab
प्रमान्तरानधिगते मानानां मानतेष्यते 4.3.1748ab
प्रमान्तरानपेक्षोऽपि स्वयमात्मा प्रकाशते SV 444cd
प्रमान्तराविरोधेन य आत्मेत्युपपद्यते 4.3.114cd
प्रमान्तरेण चेज्ज्ञातं ब्रह्मासंसर्गरूपकम् 4.4.818ab
प्रमान्तरैरविज्ञातं प्रमेयं वस्तु भण्यते 1.4.360ab
प्रमान्तरोपलब्धोऽतः काममस्तु तयोर्भिदा 4.3.466cd
प्रमाफलं त्वप्रमेयं यतो नातो विरुद्धता 4.4.683cd
प्रमाफलाभिसंबन्धः किंमान इति कथ्यताम् 1.4.263cd
प्रमामेवेह कुर्वन्ति प्रामाण्यं यान्ति नान्यथा SV 563cd
प्रमायुकत्वं मर्त्यत्वात्प्राणादेर्न तु वार्यते 1.4.1051cd
प्रमायोगो हि भोक्तृत्वं प्रमा चैवात्मनः सदा SV 143cd
प्रमाविरोधि यद्वाक्यं तत्तत्कार्यसमाश्रयम् 1.3.152cd
प्रमितेश्च प्रमेयस्य वृद्धौ वृद्धिः स्वतो न हि SV 827ab
प्रमित्सिते प्रतीच्यस्मान्न दोषो नापि बाधकम् 1.4.1502cd
प्रमुक्तिरात्मनो नास्ति तैरसंसर्गतः सदा 4.4.406cd
प्रमुच्यतेऽथ तद्धानाच्छुद्धो ब्रह्म समश्नुते 4.4.404ef
प्रमुच्यन्ते विनश्यन्ति तेषामज्ञानहेतुतः 4.4.376cd
प्रमेयं यत्पुरा पृष्टं तद्ब्रह्म किमवेदिति 1.4.1352ab
प्रमेयकर्तृकैवासौ यथावस्त्ववबोधिनी 2.4.183cd
प्रमेयत्वं तथाज्ञाते न तु ज्ञाते फलात्मता 4.4.686cd
प्रमेयत्वानुभूतेश्च न विज्ञानांशता तथा 4.3.699ab
प्रमेयभेदभिन्नत्वं ज्ञानामिव भेदकम् 2.4.200ab
प्रमेयमयतां कामं प्रमातैव व्रजत्वयम् 4.4.762ab
प्रमेयविषयं मानं वस्तुनश्च प्रमेयता SV 920ab
प्रमेयादित्रयं यस्मात्परस्परविलक्षणम् SV 1084ab

प्रमेयाधिगमं कुर्वत्प्रमाणमफलं यदि 1.4.1229ab
प्रमेयार्थविवक्षायां शब्दः स्यात्कर्मसाधनः 2.1.186ab
प्रमेया सैव वेदान्तेष्वनुभूतिरिहात्मनः SV 230cd
प्रमेयेऽपि तथैवैतत्पूर्वं मेयप्रधानकम् 4.4.749cd
प्रमेये च क्रियायां च प्रमाणेऽथ प्रमातरि 1.4.328ab
प्रमेयोपाश्रयादेव यतः प्रामाण्यमुच्यते 1.4.1135cd
प्रमैवोत्पद्यते नेति वक्तुमेतन्न शक्यते 2.1.572cd
प्रमोपजायते तावदहं ब्रह्मेत्यलौकिकी 2.4.167ab
प्रयच्छति यतो नातः प्रयोगान्तरमीक्ष्यते 1.5.73cd
प्रयत्नानन्तरः शब्दोऽनित्यः कुम्भादिवद्भवेत् 2.4.304cd
प्रयत्नायौगपद्येन स्वप्नजाग्रद्द्वयाद्धिरुक् 4.3.1133cd
प्रयद्भिरसकृद्भूतैर्महद्भिर्बहुभिः सदा 6.2.34ab
प्रयुक्तः स्यादतो वेद ओंकार इति गम्यताम् 5.1.130cd
प्रयुक्ताः कर्मणा पुंसां वर्तन्ते भोगसिद्धये 3.9.92cd
प्रयुङ्क्ते योग्यतस्तस्यास्तदलब्धवारतिः प्रभोः 1.4.111cd
प्रयुञ्जते हि घ्राणादींस्ततस्ते स्युरतिग्रहाः 3.2.12cd
प्रयोक्त्रव्यक्तयोस्तस्माद्रसः क्षेत्रज्ञ उच्यते 2.3.50cd
प्रयोक्त्री भावना तत्र कर्मं त्वस्य विकारकृत् 4.3.1195ab
प्रयोक्त्री भावनैवात्मकर्तृभोक्तृत्वयोर्मृषा 4.3.1256cd
प्रयोगमपि विद्येयं नोपरुध्यति दात्रवत् 4.3.17cd
प्रयोगरूपेणैवातो वेष्टितं कर्म तिष्ठति 3.8.33ab
प्रयोगलक्षणो योऽयं श्रुतिस्मृत्युदितो मतः 1.4.1624ab
प्रयोगविधिशेषत्वात्तन्मूला एव नाशयात् SV 504ab
प्रयोगसमवायित्वं पूर्वेष्वन्नेषु वर्णितम् 1.5.96ab
प्रयोगसमवायित्वात्तानि स्युः कर्मसाधनम् 1.5.14cd
प्रयोगसमवायित्वात्पूर्वेषां कर्मणां सताम् 1.5.97ab
प्रयोगसमवाय्येव द्रव्यकर्त्रादिसाधनम् 3.1.28ab
प्रयोगात्मा पृथक्तादृङ्नेह कश्चिदपीक्ष्यते 1.4.811cd
प्रयोगात्सुविनिश्चेयो न्यायाद्वात्यन्तनिश्चितात् 4.3.323cd
प्रयोगानुगमे चैतद्दर्शनं येन चोद्यते 1.3.369ab
प्रयोगापेक्षमेवास्ते कर्म बुद्ध्यादिसंक्षये 4.3.1037ab
प्रयोगावसितेनैवं जरिणोऽधिकृतिर्न च 1.5.305cd

प्रयोगावसितेस्तूर्ध्वं कालः प्राक्च प्रयोगतः 3.1.29ab
प्रयोगेऽपि च संशीतौ वाक्यार्थज्ञानसंश्रयात् 1.4.1626ab
प्रयोगे दक्षिणायां च समानोऽयं परिक्रमः 3.3.48ab
प्रयोजकं प्रयोज्याच्च प्रधानमिति निश्चितम् 4.4.207cd
प्रयोजकत्वेऽविद्येयं यदि नामेह न श्रुता 4.4.218ab
प्रयोजकत्वे कर्मादेः कामप्राधान्यमीरितम् 4.4.213ab
प्रयोजकप्रयोज्यत्वं कर्मसाधनयोर्भवेत् 1.4.367ab
प्रयोजकप्रयोज्यत्वं यतोऽमीषां विवक्षितम् 4.4.89cd
प्रयोजकप्रयोज्यत्वे ज्ञानादीनां प्रयोजकम् 4.4.211cd
प्रयोजकमतेरेष विध्यर्थोऽत्रावगम्यते 1.4.1058cd
प्रयोजकात्मकाः कामा निष्क्रान्ता यस्य बुद्धितः 4.4.268ab
प्रयोजकादि निःशेषं म्रियमाणाद्विपश्चितः 3.2.35cd
प्रयोजकानां निष्ठात्वे न तु कामो विवक्षितः 4.4.213cd
प्रयोजकाभ्यां देहस्य तथैव करणस्य च 4.3.1150cd
प्रयोजकावधृतये याज्ञवल्क्येत्युवाच ह 3.2.122cd
प्रयोजनं तत्सुकरं विध्युद्देशेऽपि भाषितुम् SV 1123ab
प्रयोजनमतिर्नित्यमेवं मोक्षाश्रमी भवेत् 4.4.1263cd
प्रयोजनाभिधित्सायाः उपोद्घाते प्रवर्तते 1.4.1068cd
प्रयोज्यमितरत्सर्वं विज्ञानादि यदीरितम् 4.4.207ab
प्रयोज्यविरहात्कर्मकार्यस्यासंभवात्तथा 4.3.1199ab
प्रयोज्यस्य हि बन्धस्य प्रयोजकमिहोदितम् 3.3.134ab
प्रलयोऽज्ञानविध्वसाद्यस्त्वसौ बुद्धिपूर्वकः 2.4.331cd
प्रवक्तव्योऽतस्तद्योग्यौ प्रश्नौ द्वौ समुदाहृतौ 2.1.375cd
प्रवक्ता याज्ञवल्क्योऽत्र तं पृच्छन्त्यश्वलादयः 3.1.22ab
प्रवक्तुमुपचक्राम पुत्रवित्तैषणैकताम् 3.5.132cd
प्रवदन्ति यथा वेत्थ तथाशु प्रतिपद्यताम् 6.2.36cd
प्रवर्ग्याध्याययोरेवं त्वाष्ट्रज्ञानोपसंहृतिम् 2.5.115ab
प्रवर्तकत्वं मन्त्रस्य न प्रवर्त्यवशाद्यथा SV 1043ab
प्रवर्तकात्प्रवृत्त्यार्थे प्रत्ययो ह्यनुमीयते SV 482cd
प्रवर्तको नापरोऽतः कामादित्यवसीयते 1.4.1817cd
प्रवर्ततां चेत्पुरुषो नैवमप्युपपद्यते 3.2.144cd
प्रवर्ततेऽथ सैषेति तत्स्तुतिस्तावदुच्यते 1.4.160cd

प्रवर्ततेऽनपेक्षत्वं कुतो विधिवचःस्वतः 2.4.178cd
प्रवर्तते कथं तस्य कर्तृत्वं विनिवार्यते 4.3.1031cd
प्रवर्तते तदा कर्तुर्न प्रमादो मनागपि 1.4.1629cd
प्रवर्तते पुरेवातो ब्रह्मण्यप्ययसिद्धये 3.2.57cd
प्रवर्तते स्वतन्त्रं सदिदमित्यपि कापिलाः 2.3.89cd
प्रवर्तनां वदञ्शब्दः प्रवर्तक इतीर्यते SV 486ab
प्रवर्तमानः पुरुषः शास्त्रोद्दीपितवर्त्मना 1.4.409ab
प्रवर्तमानाः पुरुषा दृश्यन्तेऽद्यापि कामिनः 2.1.584cd
प्रवाहरूपी संसारो दीपार्चिर्वदवस्थितः 3.9.144ab
प्रविभक्तं हि तच्छब्दस्पर्शाद्यर्थावभासनात् 4.4.25cd
प्रविभक्तक्रमवती मनसा तस्य कल्प्यते 4.4.713cd
प्रविविक्ततराहारं श्रुतिः सूक्ष्मान्नसंस्थितेः 4.2.63cd
प्रविविक्ततराहारो लिङ्गात्मायं पुरोदितात् 4.2.61cd
प्रविविक्ततरोऽन्नांशस्तर्पयन्प्राणदेवताः 4.2.60ab
प्रविवेक्ता तु रूपादेः सम्यङ्नैव पुमान्भवेत् 4.4.69cd
प्रविश्य प्राणभृत्सर्वं पक्षतौ जायते पुनः 1.5.210cd
प्रविष्ट इत्यनेनात्र स्वाभासैकतमोन्वयात् 1.4.501cd
प्रविष्टवचसैकात्म्यं गुणप्राधान्यमुच्यते 1.4.504cd
प्रविष्टस्य न चेत्कात्स्न्र्यं विज्ञानात्मन इष्यते 3.5.23cd
प्रविष्टोऽकृत्स्नरूपत्वात्संसारानर्थचोदितः 1.4.1347cd
प्रवृत्तं फलदानाय यदिदं जन्म वर्तते 4.3.861ab
प्रवृत्तं विषये मानमवच्छेदफलं मतम् SV 992ab
प्रवृत्तय इहेक्ष्यन्ते वाङ्मनःकायसाधनाः 4.4.187ab
प्रवृत्तस्य णिचोक्तिः स्यात्पचन्तं पाचयेद्यथा SV 525cd
प्रवृत्तस्य ततः पुंसः करणं याग इष्यते 1.4.786ab
प्रवृत्ताख्यायिका यत्नाद्रागादीन्द्रियनिन्दया 1.3.19cd
प्रवृत्ताख्यायिका सेयं समाप्तानवशेषतः 3.3.163cd
प्रवृत्ता पुरुषार्थाय न तु भेदावबुद्धये SV 917cd
प्रवृत्तिं वा निवृत्तिं वा यदाभिप्रेत्य चेतसा SV 597ab
प्रवृत्तिः कामशब्दस्य भूयःस्वर्थेषु दृश्यते 4.4.440ab
प्रवृत्तिरप्रवृत्तिर्वा देवतैश्वर्यतः सदा 3.2.146ab
प्रवृत्तिरप्रवृत्तिर्वा मेयवस्त्वनुरोधिनी 4.4.940ab

प्रवृत्तिररतेः कार्यं मोहस्यानर्थसंप्लुतिः 3.5.64cd
प्रवृत्तिर्नियता दृष्टा लोकेऽतो न विपर्यये 4.4.62cd
प्रवृत्तिर्ब्रह्मशब्दस्य बृहद्वस्त्वेकगोचरा 5.1.114ab
प्रवृत्तिर्मुक्तये तस्माच्छ्रुत्या यत्नात्तदुच्यते 6.2.6cd
प्रवृत्तिर्येन तेनैभ्यो ज्ञात्मान्योऽभ्युपगम्यताम् 3.4.74cd
प्रवृत्तिलक्षणो योगो ज्ञानं संन्यासलक्षणम् SV 217ab
प्रवृत्तिलक्षणो योगो ज्ञानं संन्यासलक्षणम् 2.4.32ab
प्रवृत्तिलक्षणो योगो ज्ञानं संन्यासलक्षणम् 3.5.4ab
प्रवृत्तिविषयं दुष्टं दृष्ट्वातो विनिवर्तते 1.4.409cd
प्रवृत्तिविषयप्रत्यग्याथात्म्यज्ञानिनामिह 4.4.1111cd
प्रवृत्तिहेतुप्रध्वस्तेर्न प्रवृत्तौ कथं चन SV 131ab
प्रवृत्तिहेतुमात्रं च प्रवृत्त्यात्रानुमीयते SV 744ab
प्रवृत्तिहेतुर्न फलं भवतैवाभिधीयते SV 746cd
प्रवृत्तिहेतून्निःशेषांस्तन्मूलोच्छेदकत्वतः SV 7ab
प्रवृत्तेः प्रतिकूलत्वान्मुक्तिं प्रति विरोधतः SV 130ab
प्रवृत्तेश्च विधिज्ञानमेवमन्योऽन्यसंश्रयः SV 662cd
प्रवृत्तोऽपि निवर्तेत न कामोपायकर्मतः SV 422cd
प्रवृत्तौ च निवृत्तौ च यथोक्तस्याधिकारिणः 1.4.1806ab
प्रवृत्तौ चोपसंहारे तथैवोपासनश्रुतेः 1.4.777ab
प्रवृत्तौ वा निवृत्तौ वा को हेतुरिति भण्यताम् 4.4.954cd
प्रवृत्तौ वा निवृत्तौ वा गुणभावः सदेष्यते 2.1.580cd
प्रवृत्त्या कर्मणा जात्या चक्रवर्त्युचितैस्तथा 2.1.513ab
प्रवृत्त्या स्वात्मसिद्ध्यर्थं कारकं सदपेक्षते 1.4.815ab
प्रवेशः श्रूयते साक्षात्परमेशस्य सर्वतः 2.1.461cd
प्रवेशोऽप्यस्य तादृक्स्यादैकात्म्यप्रतिपत्तये 1.4.605cd
प्रवेशो ब्रह्मणोऽयुक्तः फले बीजादिवत्सदा 1.4.545cd
प्रवेशो विषयत्वेन तुल्यं चोद्यमतो द्वयोः SV 782cd
प्रवेशो व्याकृते क्लृप्तो जलपात्रार्कबिम्बवत् 1.4.608cd
प्रवेष्टुं पुरुषेणैवं न खेनैतद्विधर्मतः 1.4.530cd
प्रव्रजन्तीति च विधिरर्थवादेन संगतेः 4.4.1133cd
प्रव्रजन्तीति नाप्येतत्सकृच्छ्रुतमिहेष्यते 4.4.1138ab
प्रव्रजन्तीत्यतो नास्य स्तुतिगन्धोऽपि विद्यते 4.4.1145ef

प्रव्रजन्तीत्येष विधिरर्थवादेन चान्वयात् 4.4.1136cd
प्रव्रजेच्च परं स्थानं पारिव्राज्यमनुत्तमम् 1.4.1586cd
प्रव्रजेच्च परं स्थानं पारिव्राज्यमनुत्तमम् 3.5.152cd
प्रव्रजेयुः समस्ताभ्य एषणाभ्यो द्रुतं बुधा 4.4.1118cd
प्रव्रजेयुरतो लोकमीप्सन्तो ब्राह्मणा बुधाः 4.4.1133ab
प्रव्राजिनोऽत्र गृह्यन्ते प्रसिद्धेर्यदि वा परे 4.4.1084ab
प्रशंसैषा यथोक्तस्य विज्ञानस्येति निश्चितिः 1.5.94cd
प्रशासन इदं तस्थौ यस्यान्तर्यामिरूपिणः 3.9.95ab
प्रशासनमृते शास्तुर्न व्यवस्थेदृशी भवेत् 3.8.137cd
प्रशासने यथा राज्ञोऽभिन्नमर्यादिकाः प्रजाः 3.8.131ab
प्रशासितापि चाप्येष तदेतदभिधीयते 4.4.1012cd
प्रशास्तृ तद्भयाद्यस्मात्क्षत्रं भीतं प्रवर्तते 1.4.1616cd
प्रश्नं मा मामतः प्राक्षीरित्युक्त्वावाक्शिरा ह्यभूत् 6.2.43cd
प्रश्नं यदिदमित्येवं याज्ञवल्क्यं महाधियम् 3.6.8cd
प्रश्नप्रतिवचस्तेन ब्राह्मणः स्याद्यथोदितः 3.5.197ab
प्रश्नप्रतीकानवदत्पृष्टः पित्रा समासतः 6.2.51cd
प्रश्नयोः स्वयमेवार्थं काश्यो वक्तुं प्रचक्रमे 2.1.212cd
प्रश्नरूपमिदं वाक्यं यतः प्रत्युक्तिरुच्यते 1.5.377ab
प्रश्नशेषमथेदानीं स्वयमेव श्रुतिर्जगौ 3.3.164ab
प्रश्नस्तन्निर्णयार्थाय सर्वथेत्यादिरुत्तरः SV 1092cd
प्रश्नस्य कस्मात्तानीति श्रुत्यैवाचार्यभूतया 1.5.77ab
प्रश्नस्य क्वैष इत्यादेः किमर्थोऽयमुपक्रमः 2.1.194cd
प्रश्नस्य विषयत्वेन विज्ञानात्मोपयोगतः 3.2.128cd
प्रश्नस्येह चतुर्थस्य प्राधान्याद्विद्यते क्रमः 6.2.73cd
प्रश्नानुक्तिर्विरुद्धत्वाद्विद्यायाः कर्मभिः सह 4.3.15cd
प्रश्नार्थप्रतिकूलत्वात्प्रत्युक्तेर्नेदृगर्थता 2.1.203cd
प्रश्नार्था प्रथमोक्तिः स्यात्प्रत्युक्त्यर्था तथा परा 3.3.142ab
प्रश्नार्थेऽस्मिन्समाप्तेऽपि पूर्ववत्तं मुनिं नृपः 4.3.1887ab
प्रश्नास्ते कतमे वत्स यांस्त्वं न ज्ञातवानसि 6.2.51ab
प्रश्नेन भावितस्तुष्टः पाणिमस्याग्रहीदृषिः 3.2.133ab
प्रश्नोऽयं न तृतीयः स्यात्प्रतिज्ञातत्वतो द्वयोः 3.8.44ab
प्रश्नोऽयं साधनज्ञप्त्यै ब्राह्मणस्येह पृच्छ्यते 3.5.196ab

प्रश्नोक्तिरेकरूपा च प्रत्यभिज्ञायतेऽञ्जसा 3.5.17ab
प्रष्टव्यमेतद्गार्ग्येण शिष्यत्वान्न त्वचूचुदत् 2.1.198ab
प्रष्टुं नैवाधिकारोऽतोऽब्रह्मिष्ठस्येह विद्यते 3.9.102cd
प्रष्टृभेदाददोषश्चेन्मैवं प्रत्युक्तिभेदतः 3.5.6ab
प्रसक्तान्यपि नोच्यन्ते त्रीण्यन्नान्यत्र कारणात् 1.5.46ab
प्रसक्ते सांख्यसिद्धान्ते सर्वमात्मेति वोच्यते 2.4.20cd
प्रसंख्यानविधिर्न स्यात्सहापि मननादिभिः SV 772cd
प्रसंख्यानात्मकोऽत्रापि प्रयत्नोऽनुभवं प्रति SV 762cd
प्रसंख्याने च शास्त्रार्थे सकृदेव कृते भवेत् SV 835ab
प्रसंख्याने तदैकात्म्यतात्पर्यं कथमुच्यते SV 800cd
प्रसङ्गमुत्तरे मन्त्रे पर्वयोरिव वीक्ष्य हि 1.3.363ab
प्रसजेत्तद्विरोधश्च भिन्नाभिन्नत्ववादिनः 5.1.75ab
प्रसज्यपर्युदासाभ्यां नञर्थः कोऽत्र गृह्यते 3.8.73ab
प्रसवाधिकृतेश्चात्र सावित्रः प्रसवस्ततः 1.5.182ab
प्रसादादनु शास्त्रादेर्मनसैवेत्यतः श्रुतिः 4.4.657ab
प्रसाध्य वा प्रमाणत्वं वेदान्तानां प्रयत्नतः SV 320ab
प्रसारयति धीर्वृत्तीर्मत्स्यजालकवद्बहिः 2.1.335ab
प्रसार्यायतनस्थानि तानि धीरधितिष्ठति 2.1.335cd
प्रसिद्ध एव चेदर्थो विज्ञानालम्बनाप्तिता 4.4.325cd
प्रसिद्धं मिथुनं चात्र न कथं चन युज्यते 1.2.174cd
प्रसिद्धत्वादतो हीति व्याचष्टे श्रुतिरञ्जसा 1.5.22cd
प्रसिद्धमहिमानौ वा पुण्यकृद्योगिनाविह 4.4.585ab
प्रसिद्धमेतल्लोकेऽपि यदि रोगादिसंगतिः 4.3.1099ab
प्रसिद्धवदुपादानमराज्ञो हीति सादरम् 4.3.1041cd
प्रसिद्धातीव जगति श्रुत्यैवं तेन भण्यते 1.4.1682cd
प्रसिद्धातीव विद्वत्ता पञ्चालब्राह्मणेषु हि 6.2.22ab
प्रसिद्धिरिति तामाह तस्मादित्येवमादिना 3.7.19cd
प्रसिद्धेरिति चेन्मैवमुद्गीथो ह्यसुरेव तु 1.3.317cd
प्रसिद्धेर्गम्यते न्यायाद्यतोऽसावभिधीयते 1.5.55cd
प्रसिद्ध्यसंभवात्त्वद्य ह्युक्तं मांसौदनं प्रति 6.4.78ab
प्रसीदति परो देवः प्रतीच्येव परे पदे 4.3.987cd
प्रसूतिमात्रादेवास्या ध्वस्तिरात्यन्तिकी भवेत् 4.2.94cd

प्रसूतिरिह कामानामतोऽनेकसमाश्रयात् 4.4.398cd
प्रसृता हृदयान्नाड्यो याभिर्व्याप्तं शरीरकम् 2.1.326cd
प्रस्तब्धोऽसि स्थिरत्वाच्च वियद्वन्न विकम्पसे 6.3.28ab
प्रस्तोता प्रस्तुयाद्यत्र तदैतानि जपेदिति 1.3.349cd
प्रहुतं चेह विज्ञेयं ते देवेभ्यो ददौ पिता 1.5.39cd
प्राकृतासङ्गतो मुक्त्वा पितायं दैवसाधनैः 1.3.117ab
प्राकृतासङ्गविज्ञानकार्ये ह्यधिकृतिः स्वतः 1.3.113ab
प्राक्क्रियाया विनिष्पत्तेः कर्वद्रूपं न लभ्यते 4.3.1444ab
प्राक्चोक्तमात्मनैवायं ज्योतिषेत्यादिकं वचः 4.3.1920ab
प्राक्तथाप्यपलापोऽस्या नानुभूतेर्घटादिवत् 4.3.179cd
प्राक्तदात्मानमेवावेदिति यच्च समीरितम् 4.4.1271cd
प्राक्तनान्यपि जन्मानि सम्यग्ज्ञानं तु हन्ति नः 3.2.21cd
प्राक्प्रमाणसमुत्पत्तेर्देहादेर्विषयस्य ते 4.3.159ab
प्राक्प्रमात्रादिसंभूतेर्यत्प्रमात्रादिकारणम् 3.4.126ab
प्राक्प्रमात्रादिसंभूतेर्या तु दृष्टिरकर्तृका 4.3.1434ab
प्राक्प्रयोक्त्रभिसंसिद्धौ किं फलं यागसिद्धितः SV 1035ab
प्राक्प्रवृत्तेः प्रमाणानामज्ञातं यदिहोदितम् 1.4.1358ab
प्राक्फलोद्भवतो नष्ट्वा प्रतीचि व्यवतिष्ठते 3.8.34cd
प्रागज्ञातं तदैकात्म्यं यथैवानुभवान्मतम् 1.4.1228ab
प्रागज्ञातस्य निर्वृत्तिर्न यतो वीक्ष्यते क्वचित् SV 1027cd
प्रागपि ब्रह्मविज्ञानात्सिद्धं तादात्म्यमुच्यते 4.1.29cd
प्रागपि ब्रह्मविज्ञानाद्ब्रह्मैवाभूद्यथा तथा 4.1.26ab
प्रागप्यनात्मसंपातात्प्रतीचैवाप्तमेयकम् 1.4.835ab
प्रागप्यनात्मसंबन्धाज्जन्मनैवात्मकर्मकम् 1.4.929ab
प्रागप्यवोचं बहुश इममर्थं यथोदितम् 4.4.551ab
प्रागप्युक्तं तदत्रापि संधेयं वस्तुसिद्धये 5.1.94cd
प्रागप्यैकात्म्यविज्ञानादविचारितसिद्धिका 4.2.93cd
प्रागभावादयोऽभावाः सन्तः स्युरतिरेकिणः 1.2.114ab
प्रागभावो घटस्येति घट एवोच्यते यदि 1.2.117ab
प्रागात्मक्रतुसंक्रान्तेरभूद्यादृक्क्रतुः पिता 1.5.314ab
प्रागात्मज्ञानसंभूतेः संन्यासो ज्ञानसाधनम् 4.4.544ab
प्रागात्मबोधात्पिण्डादौ यात्मेत्यासीन्मतिर्दृढा 1.4.1179ab

प्रागुक्तं तत्र यन्नोक्तं तदेवेहोच्यतेऽधुना 4.4.2cd
प्रागुपासितवान्यत्नादुपास्यं तेन तत्ततः 6.4.4cd
प्रागूर्ध्वं च तदन्येषु प्राणासंभवहेतुतः 1.4.678cd
प्रागूर्ध्वं तदभिव्यक्तेर्विशेषस्यासमीक्षणात् 4.3.509cd
प्रागेवानात्मसंबन्धादुत्पत्तावेव लब्धतः 4.3.1722ab
प्रागेवास्माभिरुक्तोऽसौ यथावदुपपत्तिभिः 3.9.204cd
प्राग्ज्ञानाज्ज्ञानकाले च मानं मेयोऽप्यपेक्षते 1.4.1295ab
प्राग्दाराद्यभिसंबन्धादेकाक्ययेव पुमानभूत् 1.4.1818ab
प्राग्दारोद्वहनात्कृत्स्नं कुटुम्बं यत्प्रपश्यसि 1.4.1820ab
प्राग्बाधकागमात्सिद्धिर्लौकिकस्यापि वस्तुनः SV 1005ab
प्राग्यथोक्तात्मनोर्योगात्प्राणोऽभूदन्तरिक्षगः 1.5.185cd
प्राग्यथोक्तात्मविज्ञानसाधनस्येह चाश्रवात् 4.4.539cd
प्राग्वा मेयाभिसंबन्धान्मितेर्बोधात्मता भवेत् 4.3.170cd
प्राङ्मानादभ्युपेयोऽर्थो योऽज्ञातत्वादिसिद्धिकृत् 4.3.183cd
प्राङ्मृतेर्मुक्त्यसंसिद्धेरबीजत्वाच्च संसृतेः 1.4.1535cd
प्राचीक्लृपदथेदानीं सृष्टिस्तस्य विवक्ष्यते 1.2.152cd
प्राची दिगेव संवृत्तास्तदवच्छेदहानतः 4.2.86cd
प्राच्यां किंदेवतोऽसीति विदग्धस्तमपृच्छत 3.9.70cd
प्राच्यां रूपोपसंहारो दिक्त्रये कर्मसंहृतिः 3.9.76ab
प्राजापत्यं पदं भुक्त्वा तदैकात्म्यं प्रपद्यते SV 344cd
प्राजापत्यं पदं यो यो ह्यधिकारी परीप्सति 1.3.12ab
प्राजापत्यत्वहेतोश्चाप्यश्वनामाङ्कितत्वतः 1.1.1cd
प्राजापत्यमपूर्वं यत्सर्वभूतप्रयोजकम् 2.5.49ab
प्राजापत्या इहोच्यन्ते वागाद्युक्तेश्च लिङ्गतः 1.3.16cd
प्राजापत्योऽसि तेन त्वं गीयसे विपुलश्रुतैः 5.17.8cd
प्राज्ञ आत्मापि तादात्म्यात्तन्मयत्वं निगच्छति 4.4.716cd
प्राज्ञः कारणबद्धस्तु द्वौ तु तुर्ये न सिध्यतः 1.4.712cd
प्राज्ञस्याभ्यन्तरं रूपं तन्माहारजनादिकम् 4.4.397ab
प्राज्ञादात्मन एतस्मात्प्रमुच्यन्तेऽखिला यदा 4.4.393ab
प्राज्ञावस्थात्मकाद्यस्मादुत्पत्तिः श्रूयते श्रुतौ 2.1.433cd
प्राज्ञेऽपि च तथैवायं यद्वै तदितिवाक्यतः 4.3.1907cd
प्राज्ञेऽपीयं तथैवास्ते कूटस्थैकात्म्यलक्षणा 4.3.1754ab

प्राज्ञेनाधिष्ठितं गच्छेद्रथिना स्वार्थरूपिणा 4.3.1918ab
प्राज्ञेनेहात्मना तस्मादन्वारूढोऽभिधीयते 4.3.1919ab
प्राज्ञोऽनन्वागतस्ताभ्यां कर्महेत्वसमन्वयात् 4.3.1368cd
प्राञ्चं कृत्वाथ तं शिश्नं यथैवाभिषवोपलम् 6.4.6ab
प्राण आङ्गिरसः प्रोक्तस्तद्विद्भिस्तद्गुणाश्रयात् 1.3.207cd
प्राण आत्मेत्युपासीनो यथोक्तं फलमश्नुते 1.3.286ab
प्राण एकस्तु जागर्ति भोक्ता यो गार्ग्यसंमतः 2.1.107ab
प्राण एव क्रियाशक्तिसामान्यं तद्वदुच्यते 2.4.367cd
प्राण एव ततः साम युक्तो वागुपसर्जनः 1.3.303cd
प्राण एव प्रतिष्ठैवं सदा स्यान्नामरूपयोः 1.6.31ab
प्राणं ब्रह्म त्यदित्याहुः पारोक्ष्येण महाधियः 3.9.31cd
प्राणः करणसंघातश्छन्नः संवेष्टितः सदा 1.6.45cd
प्राणः प्रजेति तां चेष्टां प्राहुर्वेदविदो जनाः 1.4.1846cd
प्राणकर्मणि तेनैतदेकमेव व्रतं चरेत् 1.5.386ab
प्राणद्वारक एवैषामुपकारो न तु स्वतः 1.3.242cd
प्राणनादिकृतां मध्य एकैकं यः समीक्षते 1.4.709ab
प्राणनादिक्रियाः कुर्वन्प्राण इत्यभिधीयते 1.4.665cd
प्राणनाद्यनुमानेन ग्राहयित्वा धियः परम् 3.4.66ab
प्राणनानन्तरं यस्मात्क्रियाशक्तेः समुद्भवः 1.4.679ab
प्राणन्नेवेत्यवधृतेस्तदर्थान्तररूपतः 1.4.676ab
प्राणन्वदन्निति द्वाभ्यां क्रियाशक्तिसमुद्भवः 1.4.704ab
प्राणन्वदन्नित्युक्तानि नामरूपाणि यानि तु 1.4.685ab
प्राणपिण्डात्मकः काल आ महाप्रलयात्स्थितः 1.5.209ef
प्राणपिण्डादिकार्याणां समुद्रः परमेश्वरः 1.2.8ab
प्राणप्रधानया वाचा ह्ययास्योऽगायदित्यतः 1.3.325cd
प्राणप्राणोऽपि सन्मोहात्प्राणनादि प्रपद्यते 4.4.172cd
प्राणप्राधान्यसिद्ध्यर्थं श्रुत्याख्यायिकच्छद्मना 6.1.23ab
प्राणबन्धनं सोम्येति सर्वकारणमुच्यते 1.4.353cd
प्राणबन्धनवाक्याच्च सूक्तमेतद्यथोदितम् 2.1.229cd
प्राणभूतादिजन्मैव जन्मात्मन इहोच्यते 1.4.355ab
प्राणभृद्धिंसनं यत्नात्किन्त्वनारब्धपीडनम् 1.5.213cd
प्राणभृद्धिंसनस्येह नान्यदस्य प्रयोजनम् 1.5.215cd

प्राणभृन्निखिलं तस्माद्धिंसां तस्यां परित्यजेत् 1.5.211cd
प्राणमात्रविनाशे स्याद्भूयो जन्म प्रयोजकात् 3.2.36ab
प्राणरूपाभिधानाभ्यां ख्याता वागादयो यथा 1.5.374ab
प्राणलोकादिरप्येवमनात्मा प्राग्विभागतः 2.4.299ab
प्राणवाग्द्वयतोऽन्येन देवेनासौ प्रयत्नवान् 1.3.328cd
प्राणवित्संज्ञया ख्यातिं याति विद्वत्कुलं तथा 1.5.374cd
प्राणविद्या पृथङ्मन्थान्मन्थस्तु महिमार्थिनः 6.1.6cd
प्राणविद्विद्विषः सर्वे नालं भार्येभ्य एव च 1.3.287cd
प्राणव्यूहस्य संसिद्धिः कथमस्येति शङ्क्यते 4.3.1954ab
प्राणव्यूहाय चैवायमाद्रवत्यन्यदेहतः 4.3.1953ab
प्राणव्रतं चेदारब्धं चिकीर्षेत्तत्समापनम् 1.5.389cd
प्राणव्रतविधानार्थं परो ग्रन्थोऽवतार्यते 1.5.364cd
प्राणशब्दः पुरा प्रोक्तो वृत्तिमात्राभिधायकः 1.5.151ab
प्राणशब्देन चाप्यत्र कारणात्माभिधीयते 4.2.83ab
प्राणशब्देन लिङ्गात्मा भण्यते करणात्मकः 1.6.37ab
प्राणश्चेन्द्रोऽत्र विज्ञेयः स एव प्रार्थ्यते ततः 6.4.112cd
प्राणसंशयमापन्नस्तस्माच्चैवावसीयते 2.5.112ab
प्राणसंस्पर्धिनो यद्वद्विनेशुरसुरास्तथा 1.3.287ab
प्राणस्तु मध्य आस्यस्य तस्मादन्तर्विशेषणम् 1.3.204cd
प्राणस्य किमु वक्तव्यं कृत्स्नाध्यात्मेन्द्रियग्रहः 1.3.156cd
प्राणस्य तत्र संवर्गाद्वागाद्यध्यात्मदैवयोः 1.2.141cd
प्राणस्य तद्गुणानां च तथार्थत्वं प्रतीयताम् 2.1.162cd
प्राणस्य तु समाप्तत्वात्समस्तव्यस्तवस्तुषु 2.1.125ab
प्राणस्य तेन रोगात् प्रथमेत्यभिधीयते 1.3.231cd
प्राणस्यातोऽद्वितीयत्वं ततश्चेन्द्रत्वमेव च 1.5.191cd
प्राणस्यार्थेन्द्रियाणां तु शब्दाद्यर्थावलेहिनी 1.3.216cd
प्राणस्याभोक्तृतासिद्धिः स्वनामाग्रहणादपि 2.1.132ab
प्राणस्येन्दोस्तथा चापां त्र्यन्नात्माविष्कृतौ यतः 2.1.110ab
प्राणस्येव पराभूतो द्विषन्पाप्मासुरोऽखिलः 1.3.189ab
प्राणस्यैव यतो वृत्ती उक्ते वाङ्मनसे अपि 1.5.191ab
प्राणस्यैव व्रतं धार्यमतो नान्यस्य कस्यचित् 1.5.369cd
प्राणस्यैव स विज्ञेयस्तेषां त्वर्थप्रकाशनम् 1.5.371cd

प्राणस्यैवाधिदैवेऽपि प्रसवोऽयमिहोच्यते 1.5.186cd
प्राणस्वभावसंपत्तेः प्राणवद्देवता अपि 1.3.178ab
प्राणस्वरूपापत्तिश्च यतोपासाफलं श्रुतम् 1.3.40ab
प्राणस्वान्ततनूधर्मा अशनायादिलक्षणाः 3.5.93ab
प्राणा एव विलीयन्ते किं वान्यदपि कृत्स्नतः 3.2.35ab
प्राणाः किमात्मकास्तेषां कथं सत्यत्वमिष्यते 2.3.2ab
प्राणाः श्रोत्रादयोऽत्र स्युर्दश सप्त च ये मता 2.1.414ab
प्राणाः सहेतवः सर्वे तदैवास्ता निरन्वयाः 3.2.28cd
प्राणाग्नय इति स्पष्टं तथानस्तमितश्रुतेः 2.1.108ab
प्राणाग्नयः पुरा बुद्धेः सुप्तेष्वन्येषु जाग्रति 1.4.674ab
प्राणात्मक इति ज्ञेयो हन्तास्यैवेति च श्रुतेः 2.4.380cd
प्राणात्मत्वाच्च बुद्ध्यादेः पिण्डान्तस्याप्यनात्मता 3.4.70cd
प्राणात्मत्वाभिमानी सन्यतः प्राणः प्रसूयते 4.4.172ab
प्राणात्मना करोत्येष पश्यत्यग्न्यात्मना तथा 1.3.264cd
प्राणात्मना तदज्ञातं ब्रह्म कारणमुच्यते 1.5.164ab
प्राणात्मनि श्रुतिश्चाह कस्मिन्निति च सादरा 2.4.383cd
प्राणात्मनैव वागादिव्रतान्यपि चरेत्सदा 1.5.388ab
प्राणात्मभाव एवोक्त आनन्तर्यार्थमेव तु 6.1.3cd
प्राणात्मभावाद्धत्वागो वैराजं रूपमाप्तवान् 1.3.179cd
प्राणात्मवेदिनस्तेषां प्रयोगोऽत्रोपवर्ण्यते 6.1.5cd
प्राणात्मा एक एवास्ते प्रज्ञानघनविग्रहः 4.2.85cd
प्राणात्मात्वैव सोऽवश्यमुपासनबलाद्भवेत् 1.2.196ab
प्राणात्मानं यथोक्तेन पादेनापाद्य यत्नतः 5.16.16ab
प्राणात्मैव भवत्याशु सदा तद्भावभावितः 5.16.16cd
प्राणादयोऽत आत्मैव द्रष्टव्यः सर्वदर्शनात् 1.4.750cd
प्राणादिकार्यकरणैः स्वतोऽसंहत एकलः 3.4.72ab
प्राणादिजन्मना जज्ञे विस्फुलिङ्गैर्यथा शिखी 2.1.417ab
प्राणादित्यादिना भानोरुदयास्तमयौ कथम् 1.5.377cd
प्राणादित्यौ हि गायत्रीसक्तावुक्तेन वर्त्मना 5.16.37ab
प्राणादिमयतां यात्वा तद्वृत्तीनामबोधतः 4.4.180ab
प्राणादिवदतः कार्त्स्न्यं न तेषां युक्तिमद्भवेत् 1.4.953cd
प्राणादिशुक्रमादाय कृत्वा तद्भावनामयम् 4.3.932ab

प्राणादि सर्वमेवेदं पञ्चभूतसतत्त्वकम् 2.2.5ab
प्राणादीनां यतो जन्म वक्ष्यते प्रत्यगात्मनः 2.1.242ab
प्राणादेः प्रत्यगात्मानं बुबोधयिषुरञ्जसा 3.4.65cd
प्राणादेरात्मवत्ता स्यात्प्राणस्य प्राणमित्यतः 4.4.644cd
प्राणाद्यकृत्स्नतासिद्ध्यै व्यभिचारः प्रदर्श्यते 1.4.676cd
प्राणाद्यनात्मजातं यद्रूपं नाम च कर्म च 2.1.164cd
प्राणाद्युद्भूतितो नान्या क्षेत्रज्ञोद्भूतिरिष्यते 2.1.418ab
प्राणाधिकरणे पूर्वे शोकमोहौ मनोगतौ 3.5.66ab
प्राणानां देवतानां च पुरुषस्य च संकरात् 2.1.101ab
प्राणानां प्रथमः प्राणः स ह्यत्तान्नं हि तस्य तत् 6.1.15cd
प्राणानात्मा तथादाय स्वप्नान्पश्यति कामतः 2.1.303cd
प्राणानामपि सत्यत्वं भूतसत्याभिसंगतेः 2.3.93ab
प्राणान्गयान्यतस्तत्रे गायत्रीयमतो मता 5.16.38cd
प्राणान्तात्करणाच्चान्यः प्रत्यग्दृष्ट्या य ईक्ष्यते 1.4.1378cd
प्राणान्स्वशक्तिभिः साकं मनोऽप्यात्मनि लीयते 2.1.249cd
प्राणापानव्यानरूपा अध्यात्मं ताः प्रचक्षते 3.1.58cd
प्राणापानात्मकं यस्माद्व्रतं प्राणैककर्तृकम् 1.5.387ab
प्राणायेति ततो वक्ति जन्मन्यसति नो मृतिः 4.3.1952cd
प्राणारूढमेवैतद्धन्त्यविद्याद्यशेषतः 1.4.315ab
प्राणा वागादयः सर्वे तं समायन्ति कृत्स्नतः 4.4.16cd
प्राणा वै सत्यमित्यस्या व्याख्योपनिषदः कृता 2.1.423cd
प्राणा वै सत्यमित्युक्ते के प्राणा इति यत्नतः 2.2.6ab
प्राणिकर्मानुरोधेन प्लुष्यादिपरिमाणता 4.4.130ab
प्राणिधर्माद्यपेक्षं चेदुष्णत्वादि हविर्भुजः 4.3.153ab
प्राणिनो न च सम्यग्धीस्तेषां ब्रह्मणि जायते 4.4.822cd
प्राणिव्यवहृतिः सर्वा प्रत्यगात्माभिमानतः 4.3.372cd
प्राणेन प्राणितीत्युक्तो दृष्टेर्द्रष्टेति चोदितः 3.5.178ab
प्राणेन बोद्धृरूपत्वाद्बाह्यं दग्ध्वा यथा दहेत् 2.1.120cd
प्राणेन मध्यमेनान्नं जग्धं वागादितर्पणम् 2.2.7ab
प्राणेन रक्षन्निति च तथोदर्के प्रवक्ष्यते 2.1.107cd
प्राणेन ह्यवरं रक्षन्मरणाद्देहकं परः 4.3.939ab
प्राणेनैव तु तत्सर्वं लोकोऽन्नं ह्यत्ति सर्वदा 1.3.240cd

प्राणेभ्यः प्राब्रवीद्ब्रह्म पक्षपातभयात्किल 6.1.18cd
प्राणे म्लोचन्ति वायौ च वागाद्यग्न्यादयो यतः 1.5.369ab
प्राणेषु योऽर्थोऽनुगतः स आत्मेत्यवधार्यताम् 4.3.325cd
प्राणेष्वात्मीयरूपेषु प्रत्यक्त्वेनावभाति यः 4.3.326ab
प्राणेष्विति श्रुतिर्वक्ति प्राणाः पञ्चदशोदिताः 4.3.324cd
प्राणे सति यजुस्तस्मात्फलोक्तिः पूर्ववत्तथा 5.15.5cd
प्राणे सति रमन्ते हि लोके दृष्टानि सर्वदा 5.14.13ab
प्राणैकात्म्याश्रयाद्यस्मादात्मलाभः सदा तयोः 1.6.31cd
प्राणैकालिङ्गनात्प्राणा यथा तन्नामरूपिणः 1.5.370ab
प्राणोऽनूत्क्रामति ततः प्राणं प्राणास्तथा परे 4.4.87cd
प्राणोऽपाने तथापानो व्यानात्मनि विलीयते 2.4.388ab
प्राणोऽपाने स च व्यान उदाने व्यान आश्रितः 3.9.90cd
प्राणोऽभवद्यथाध्यात्मे प्रजा वाक्स्वान्तयोस्तथा 1.5.186ab
प्राणोऽभोक्ता ततः सिद्धः स्वनामाप्रतिबोधनात् 2.1.121cd
प्राणोऽयमनिरुक्तो हि कस्तं निर्वक्तुमर्हति 3.6.29ab
प्राणोत्क्रान्तिनिषेधोक्तिर्यत आत्मावबोधतः 4.3.454ab
प्राणोत्क्रान्तेः प्रयोक्त्री सा वागाद्युत्क्रमणस्य च 4.4.90cd
प्राणो देवोऽत एवैकस्तस्यैव महिमा परः 3.9.29cd
प्राणो नाम मरुद्वृत्तिरपानस्त्वधुनोच्यते 1.5.145cd
प्राणोपनिषदश्चोक्ताः प्राणाश्चापि समासतः 2.3.1ab
प्राणो बुद्धिर्मनश्चक्षुःश्रोत्राद्यज्ञस्य जायते 4.4.176cd
प्राणो ब्रह्मेति चाप्यन्ये तच्च ग्राह्यं पुरेव न 5.14.3ab
प्राणो ब्रह्मेति वचसा तदात्मनि निषिध्यते 4.4.525cd
प्राणो वृत्तिविशेषेण बहिर्वत्कुरुते ध्वनिम् 2.1.75cd
प्राणो हिरण्यगर्भात्मा यावत्तदभिमानिता 1.3.181cd
प्राणो ह्येतानि सर्वाणि भवतीति च लिङ्गतः 6.1.32cd
प्राणो ह्येष सर्वभूतैरिति चाथर्वणे वचः 1.4.353ab
प्राण्यप्राणि जगत्सर्वं तस्मिन्नेव प्रतिष्ठितम् 1.5.54cd
प्राण्यादपान्याच्च ततो नित्यमा मरणाद्बुधः 1.5.387cd
प्राण्यादपान्यात्प्राणात्मा ह्युक्त्यादिष्वपि कर्मसु 1.5.385ab
प्राण्यादौ रेचकं कृत्वापानयेत्तदनन्तरम् 6.4.43ab
प्रातर्देशावसानत्वादग्निहोत्रादिकर्मणः 1.5.306ab

प्रातिलोम्यार्थ एवातः प्रतिशब्दोऽयमिष्यते 4.3.990ab
प्रातिलोम्येन तु ज्ञेयो ह्यनर्थः स्यात्तथा सति 2.1.69cd
प्रातिलोम्येन यत्स्थानं व्युत्थानमिति तद्विदुः 4.4.1131cd
प्रात्यक्ष्यं च यथैतेषां तथा पूर्वमवादिषम् 4.3.1491ab
प्रात्यक्ष्यं न च तस्यास्ति शास्त्रमात्रप्रमाणतः 1.5.29ab
प्रात्यक्ष्याच्च प्रमोत्पत्तेर्ज्योतिष्टोमादिवाक्यतः 2.1.572ab
प्रात्यक्ष्यात्सोऽयमित्येवं प्रत्यक्साक्ष्यभिधीयते 2.5.33cd
प्रात्यक्ष्यादस्य लोकस्य नास्त्याशङ्कास्ति तां प्रति 4.3.828ab
प्रात्यन्तिकजनोद्देशः पापीयोजनसंश्रयात् 1.3.221cd
प्राथम्यं चात्र दुर्लक्ष्यं बीजतत्कार्ययोरिव SV 741ab
प्रादात्सहस्रमेवास्मै शुश्रूषालिङ्गवित्तये 4.4.537cd
प्रादुरासीन्मतिः साध्वी दैतेयभयनाशिनी 1.3.122cd
प्रादुर्भावे तथासत्याः क्रियायाश्च क्रियात्मता 4.3.1572cd
प्राधान्यं याज्ञवल्कीये युक्तीनामभिधीयते 3.1.13cd
प्राधान्याच्चैव गृह्यन्ते न त्वन्यद्विनिवार्यते 5.5.3cd
प्राधान्यायेह कल्पन्ते भोक्तुरेव प्रधानतः SV 474cd
प्राधान्येन तदन्येषां न तथा लक्ष्यते सदा 1.3.331cd
प्राधान्येनेह कर्मैव तदन्यत्तूपसर्जनम् 3.3.134cd
प्रापिता तद्विशेषेऽसौ निर्भागत्वान्निषेधभाक् 5.1.66cd
प्रापितोऽस्त्यभयं पूर्वं यत्प्रतिज्ञातवानहम् 4.4.1301cd
प्राप्तं मार्गं समुत्सृज्य तद्विरुद्धेन वर्त्मना SV 132cd
प्राप्तं वेदानुवचनं तदन्यस्याप्रकाशनात् 4.4.1032ef
प्राप्तजारोऽपि मे शत्रुस्तथैवाशु विदीर्यताम् 6.4.52cd
प्राप्तवल्लोकनुत्यर्थमर्थवादव्यपेक्षि च 4.4.1138cd
प्राप्तस्य ज्योतिषा तस्य पुत्रेणातिक्रमो जयः 1.5.239ab
प्राप्तस्य परमं स्वास्थ्यं वद किं स्यात्प्रजादिभिः 4.4.1109ab
प्राप्तस्य भिन्नरूपस्य शून्यतातः प्रसज्यते 1.6.69cd
प्राप्तानामेव तेषां तु साधनत्वं विधीयते 4.4.1218cd
प्राप्ताय लोकभोगार्थं वायुस्तस्मै विगच्छति 5.12.3ab
प्राप्तार्थो यो विधिः सोऽन्यनिवृत्तिफल इष्यते SV 413cd
प्राप्ताशेषपुमर्थश्च ब्राह्मणोऽत्राभिधीयते 3.8.170cd
प्राप्ताशेषपुमर्थोऽयं स्वत एवेह मानवः 1.4.1813ab

प्राप्तोऽद्रष्टा तथाश्रोता स्मृतिस्वप्नादिभूमिषु 4.3.82cd
प्राप्तोऽभ्युदयमोक्षार्थसाधनव्यापृताविह 1.4.1474cd
प्राप्तोऽसीति च निर्देशाज्ज्ञानमेवात्मनो गतिः 4.2.95ab
प्राप्तोऽसीति मुनेरुक्तेः परिहारो न युज्यते 4.2.103cd
प्राप्तोऽसीति यतो ज्ञानजन्ममात्रं प्रवक्ष्यति 4.2.35cd
प्राप्तोऽस्यभयमित्येवं भयहेतुविनाशतः 4.2.92cd
प्राप्त्यतिक्रमसंभित्तेर्विषयप्रविभागतः 1.5.235ab
प्राप्नुयां सुमहद्वित्तमिति यः कामयेत ह 6.3.4ab
प्राप्नोति चेन्न तत्प्राप्तिः स नेति वचसः श्रुतेः 4.4.993cd
प्राप्नोति लिङ्गमाहारः स तस्येत्यभिधीयते 4.2.60cd
प्राप्नोति सर्वकार्यस्य न च तद्वर्तते तथा 2.1.403cd
प्राप्नोत्यत्रमसौ क्षत्रमत्रात्तृकमनीश्वरम् 5.15.9ab
प्राप्यस्य सर्वस्यावाप्तेस्तथा हेयस्य हानतः 4.4.913ab
प्राप्याथ पितरं रोषात्साभ्यसूयं निराह सः 6.2.46ab
प्रामाणिकी हि तत्सिद्धिरतो नासौ विरुध्यते 2.1.171cd
प्रामाणिकोऽभिसंबन्धो यस्मात्प्राणस्य गम्यते 1.3.44ab
प्रामाणिक्युभयत्रापि प्राप्तिर्यस्मादिहेक्ष्यते 1.3.42cd
प्रामाण्यं कर्मकाण्डस्य यस्मिन्विषय इष्यते 1.4.1564ab
प्रामाण्यं चास्य यत्रेष्टं श्रुतेस्तत्रास्त्वनेन किम् SV 750cd
प्रामाण्यं न स्वतस्तस्मात्कार्ये वेदस्य मानता SV 540cd
प्रामाण्यं नान्यथा तस्य प्रामाण्यमुपपद्यते 2.4.319cd
प्रामाण्यं वा निषेद्धव्यमत्र प्रतिविधीयते SV 541cd
प्रामाण्यं वेदवाक्यानां न च मानान्तराश्रयात् 2.4.326ab
प्रामाण्यमविरुद्धं स्यादैकात्म्यज्ञानजन्मने 1.4.408cd
प्रामाण्यमेतत्पृष्ठेन कस्मान्नास्त्यभिधाश्रुतेः 1.4.875ab
प्रामाण्यवत्प्रसङ्गः स्यादप्रमात्वेऽपि ते ध्रुवम् 1.2.25cd
प्रामाण्यस्य पुरोक्तत्वात्तत्सिद्धेश्चानुमानतः 3.8.147cd
प्रामाण्यहेतुसद्भावान्नाप्रामाण्यमिहेष्यते 1.4.905ab
प्रामाण्यहेतुसद्भावान्नैतत्साध्वभिधीयते 1.4.912ab
प्रामाण्याद्वेदवचसस्तज्जं मिथ्या भवेत्कथम् 4.4.877cd
प्रामाण्यायैव तेनादौ सर्वोऽपीत्यादि भण्यते SV 315cd
प्रामाण्ये त्वतिशीतिस्तु न काचिदपि दृश्यते 2.4.166cd

प्रामाण्ये नापि बाध्यत्वं तेषां तेन कथं चन SV 912cd
प्रामाण्योच्छेद एव स्याच्छ्रुतेरेवं समर्थने 5.1.46cd
प्रायत्यार्थमपां पाने दृष्टेः प्रकरणादिह 6.1.39cd
प्रायश्चित्ती भवेन्नैव तत्पराधीनवृत्तितः SV 1042cd
प्रायस्ताभ्यां न कामाय यष्टव्यमिति गम्यते 1.5.44cd
प्रायार्थत्वं प्रतीचोऽतस्तदभिन्नग्रहाद्भवेत् 2.1.190cd
प्रायार्थे च मयड्ज्ञेयो विकारादेर्निषेधनात् 4.4.177ab
प्रायेण वीक्षते स्वप्ने वासनाः कर्मणो वशात् 4.3.842cd
प्रारब्धात्मफलं नो चेत्कर्म ज्ञानं निवर्तयेत् 1.4.1533ab
प्रारब्धेयं प्रयत्नेन वेदान्तोपनिषत्परा SV 17cd
प्रारब्धेयं प्रयत्नेन वेदान्तोपनिषत्परा SV 1116cd
प्रार्थनाशेति विज्ञेया पराकाशा प्रतीक्षणम् 6.4.60ab
प्रार्थनीयः पुरा कालो विशुद्धिश्चात्मनस्ततः 6.3.7ab
प्रार्थयत्योमिति गिरा मुमूर्षुस्तत्परीप्सया 5.17.15cd
प्रार्थ्यते व्यभिचारो हि जाताशङ्के न गोचरे 4.3.719cd
प्रावर्तन्त ततो भीताः कर्मस्वज्ञाततत्त्वकाः 3.5.144cd
प्राह मानुषवित्ताढ्यं दैववित्तसमन्वितम् 2.1.38cd
प्राहात्मपक्षवाद्यत्र सिद्धं नो यत्समीहितम् 4.3.1130ab
प्राहास्य विद्यमानस्य विक्रियामात्रमेव तु 3.2.74cd
प्राहेममेव बहुशः प्राणिनां हितकाम्यया 3.7.39cd
प्रियमित्यादौ दृष्टत्वादप्रियोपासनं गुणात् 1.4.933cd
प्रियया कामयन्त्या च परिष्वक्तः पुमानिह 4.3.1312cd
प्रियात्मानमुपासीत शक्रवद्ब्रह्मचर्यवान् 1.4.1062cd
प्रियोऽप्यप्रियतां याति यस्य संगतिकारणात् 2.4.90cd
प्रियोऽप्रियश्च जायादिर्यथानात्मा मुहुर्मुहुः 2.4.81cd
प्रीणयन्नुपचिन्वंश्च दामान्नमिति भण्यते 2.2.19cd
प्रीतिरग्न्युष्णवत्तस्मादात्मा प्रेयाननात्मनः 1.4.1035cd
प्रीतिर्या काचिदिष्टा चेत्स्वर्गशब्देन भण्यते SV 305cd
प्रीतिसाधनहेतुत्वात्प्राणादौ प्रीतिरिष्यते 1.4.1033ab
प्रीतेः श्रुतः प्रकर्षोऽपि स्वर्गस्वाराज्यभेदतः SV 304ab
प्रीत्युत्कर्षोऽपि लोकेऽस्मिन्दृष्टः स किं न काम्यते SV 298cd
प्रेतीभूतोऽसि नूनं त्वं प्रेतवद्भाषसे यतः 3.9.83ab

प्रेत्य संज्ञेह नास्तीति श्रुतिरेव निषेधति 3.9.193ab
प्रेम्णोपमन्त्रिताप्यस्मै पत्ये दद्यान्न चेदसौ 6.4.31ab
प्रेयोगिरात्मनो यस्मान्निष्ठानन्दस्य भण्यते 1.4.1028cd
प्रेरकाभावतो वेदे तद्व्यापारोऽपि नेरणा SV 636cd
प्रेरणापीह नैव स्यादज्ञातज्ञापनात्पृथक् SV 634ab
प्रेहि तत्र गमिष्यावस्तद्विद्यालब्धिसिद्धये 6.2.54ab
प्रैषादयो न शब्दार्था न चानेकार्थता मता SV 502cd
प्रैषादिभ्यो यथैवेयं भिन्ना कर्तव्यतेक्ष्यते SV 505ab
प्रैषादिष्वपि कृत्यानां तथा च स्मरणं मनेः SV 511ab
प्रैष्यन्निति च कालोऽस्य कर्मणोऽत्र विधीयते 1.5.286ab
प्रोक्तवैफल्यमाशङ्क्य ह्याहाधिपतितां फलम् 1.3.285cd
प्रोक्षितं सर्वदेवत्यं प्राजापत्यं तुरंगमम् 1.2.217cd
प्लवा ह्येते परीक्ष्येति तथा तद्य इहेति च SV 308ab
प्लवा ह्येते परीक्ष्येति तथा तद्य इहेति च SV 327ab
प्लुष्ट्वात्मदशमाज्ञानं दशमोऽस्मीति वीक्षते 1.4.602cd
प्लुष्ट्वेहात्मतमस्तज्जं तथैकात्म्यं प्रपद्यते 1.4.603cd
प्लुष्यादिना समोऽतोऽयं श्रुतावप्यभिधीयते 1.6.41cd
फट्कारेणैव जुहुयाच्छरभृष्टीर्यथोदिताः 6.4.57cd
फलं कथं नु न भवेद्विश्वजिन्न्याय ईर्यताम् 3.3.84cd
फलं च घटते नेह युक्तिभिः शाक्यपुङ्गवे 4.3.711cd
फलं च ज्ञानयुक्तानां कर्मणामेतदिष्यते 3.2.5ab
फलं च न विधेयं स्यादतो नेदं विधीयते 2.4.123cd
फलं चैतत्त्वयैवोक्तं प्रथमायाः समुच्चिते 1.4.1756ab
फलं तत्रैव संताने कार्पासे रक्तता यथा 4.3.689cd
फलं तत्संपरित्यज्य कस्माल्लक्षणया स्तुतिम् SV 202ab
फलं तदेव तस्य स्यात्सर्ववाक्येषु निर्णयः 2.1.60cd
फलं तादृग्विधं दातुमेकीभवति सात्मनः 4.3.1190cd
फलं तुल्यं तयोर्युक्तं कर्मिणो विदुषस्तथा SV 1120cd
फलं त्वयैव व्याख्यातं द्वितीयस्याः समुच्चिते 1.4.1716ab
फलं नित्यस्य नापीह दुरितक्षयमात्रकम् SV 96ab
फलं पश्चाद्यथोक्तस्येत्येष व्याख्याक्रमः श्रुतेः 1.3.354cd
फलं प्रकाशनं ज्ञानं तत्कर्तृत्वं च वस्तुनः 4.3.1627ab

फलं प्रबोधे यद्धुक्तं तच्छेषो भावनोच्यते 4.3.1254cd
फलं प्रवर्तकं प्रापन्न नियोगस्तथा सति SV 1041cd
फलं यद्गुणकं यत्र तद्गुणं स्यादुपासनम् 2.1.73ab
फलं युक्तं प्रवृत्त्यङ्गमर्थवादो भवेदतः 1.4.1023cd
फलं रूपोपलब्धिश्च कर्तुर्दृष्टव्यवसानजम् 3.4.172cd
फलं वदनमात्रं तु वाच एव न दैविकम् 1.3.142cd
फलं स्यात्प्राणसायुज्यं सर्वं तस्य हि भोजनम् 6.1.34cd
फलं स्यादात्मबोधस्य यथा कर्मफलं तथा 1.4.801cd
फलके चाधिषवणे यथासंख्येन निर्दिशेत् 6.4.10ab
फलतोऽवगतेरेव न तथेहात्मदर्शने 1.4.836cd
फलतोऽवाप्तकामोऽसौ परानन्दस्वभावतः 4.4.271cd
फलदातृत्वसामर्थ्ये दानं चाभ्यधिकं तथा 3.8.157cd
फलदानेऽनुलोमत्वान्नामी स्युर्विघ्नकारिणः 1.4.1481ab
फलप्राप्तावहेतुत्वं शास्त्रन्यायावधारणात् 1.4.1490ef
फलभते तु विज्ञाने नाधिकारो निरूप्यते SV 228cd
फलभेदः क्रियाभेदात्तत्र भिन्नार्थता तयोः 1.4.1014cd
फलभोगावसानेऽथ किमसौ प्रतिपद्यते 4.4.246ab
फलमण्वपि संभाव्यं ज्ञानस्याकारकत्वतः 1.4.1261cd
फलमात्रमयं तत्र भुङ्क्ते स्वाभासवर्त्मना 4.3.1004cd
फलमित्यतिशङ्क्याह पुण्य इत्यादिकं वचः 4.4.198cd
फलमुद्गाय शेषेषु ह्युदगायदथात्मने 1.3.139cd
फलवत्कर्मणां क्वापि किंचित्सामान्यसंश्रयात् 3.1.47ab
फलवत्कर्म तत्रैव ततोऽन्यत्राफलं भवेत् 4.4.1117cd
फलवत्त्वं समाचष्टे नित्यानामपि कर्मणाम् SV 97cd
फलवत्त्वे हि नित्यानां काम्यत्वमिति चेन्मतम् SV 1129ab
फलवन्निश्चितज्ञानजनकस्य किमागतम् 1.4.909cd
फलवन्निश्चितज्ञानजन्म प्रामाण्यकारणम् 1.4.905cd
फलवन्निश्चितज्ञानजन्म साक्षात्समीक्ष्यते 1.4.907ab
फलवादोऽर्थवादः स्यादस्यैव तु विधेः परः 4.4.1189cd
फलश्रुतेरभावो हि साध्यः स्यादफलः कथम् SV 385cd
फलसंपद एवैता नात्र कर्म विवक्ष्यते 3.1.53cd
फलसंभोगमात्रं च यस्मात्स्वप्ने समीक्ष्यते 4.3.1008ab

फलसाधनशक्तिश्चेद्विध्यायत्ता भविष्यति	SV 752ab
फलस्य विध्यधीनत्वादुपेक्षाफलतान्यथा	SV 671cd
फलस्य संश्रवान्नातो मृत्युप्राप्तिस्तयोः फलम्	1.3.8cd
फलहेतुनिषेधाच्च न युक्तं सर्वथा वचः	4.3.648ab
फलहेतुप्रबन्धेनेत्येवं सुस्थमिदं भवेत्	4.3.626cd
फलहेत्वोर्मिथोऽत्यन्तं सर्वदाव्यतिरेकतः	1.5.90ab
फलातिशीतिरभ्यासाज्जायते पुण्यपापयोः	4.4.200ab
फलात्मकः स एवैष पार्थिवोऽग्निः प्रदर्श्यते	1.2.223ab
फलात्मकानामन्नानां प्रसङ्ग इदमीरितम्	4.4.416cd
फलात्मनैव तन्मानं न तु मात्रादिरूपतः	4.4.685ab
फलानां साधनानां च भेदाभावे प्रसज्यते	4.3.556ab
फलानुत्पत्तितस्तस्मान्न कार्येणापि संगतिः	SV 647cd
फलानुमानतस्तत्र न फलं ह्यनुपासितम्	2.1.73cd
फलान्तरश्रुतेः साक्षात्तद्यथाम्रस्मृतेस्तथा	SV 96cd
फलान्तराय तद्दृष्टिर्न च स्यादग्निदृष्टिवत्	1.4.1112cd
फलान्तरारम्भविधिर्नातः स्यादक्रियात्मनः	4.3.1008cd
फलाप्तिकल्पनासिद्धावपन्यायोऽन्यथा भवेत्	3.8.153cd
फलाप्त्यैव तमोध्वंसादमृतं मेत्यतोऽवदत्	1.3.361cd
फलाभिधित्सयेदानीं देवसृष्टिविदः श्रुतिः	1.4.160ab
फलाभिसंधिमात्रे तु निन्दायामेव युज्यते	SV 328cd
फलाभिसंधिरहितं विद्येतं कर्म मुक्तये	3.3.14cd
फलाय स्यादविज्ञात इत्येतदधुनोच्यते	4.4.1307cd
फलार्था चेल्लये न स्यान्नोभयं वाक्यभेदतः	SV 395cd
फलार्थिवन्न च ज्ञानं क्रियाङ्गत्वेन चोदितम्	SV 106cd
फलार्थैषणयैकत्वप्रसिद्ध्यर्थमतः श्रुतिः	3.5.132ab
फलावधित्वात्सर्वेषामुपायानां जगत्यपि	4.4.761cd
फलावस्थस्य च सतः कुतो रागादिसंप्लुतिः	1.4.1540cd
फलाश्रयस्य चाभावान्निर्वाणादि स्वलक्षणम्	4.3.711ab
फलाश्रितोऽसौ भावोऽत्र दृष्टिशब्देन भण्यते	4.3.1626cd
फलेऽन्यस्मिन्ननिर्दिष्टे वाक्यशेषगतं फलम्	6.1.7ab
फलेनास्याभिसंबन्धान्निष्कामं नित्यमुच्यते	3.3.85cd
फले बीजवदित्युक्तं नैष दोषो भवेत्कुतः	1.4.546cd

फलोक्तिरद इत्येतदुपासितुरहं तथा 5.16.71cd
फलोक्तेः पर्णमय्यां तु युज्यते कर्मशेषतः SV 125cd
फलोक्तेरर्थवादत्वं द्रव्यसंस्कारकर्मसु SV 44ab
फलोत्पत्तिर्ममाप्येवं तथा सति भविष्यति SV 648cd
फलोद्देशेन या चेष्टा सैव लोकैषणा यतः 4.4.1128cd
बन्धकीप्रीतिवन्मुख्या नैवानात्मसु युज्यते 1.4.1033cd
बन्धमोक्षादिरूपोऽयमात्मनीति विनिश्चयः 4.4.368cd
बन्धहेत्वपि मोक्षाय विरुद्धफलकृद्यथा 3.3.15ab
बन्धाय विषयासक्तं मुक्त्यै निर्विषयं यदा 4.4.889cd
बन्धः कारणमात्मोक्तौ मृत्युरत्र स एव तु 1.2.8cd
बन्धो बन्धनहेतुश्च मोक्षस्तद्धेतुरेव च 4.3.1904ab
बम्भ्रमीत्यनिशं दुःखी पुमान्कर्मपुरःसरः SV 1110cd
बर्हिर्देवसदनं दामीत्यादौ च यथा तथा SV 333ef
बर्हिस्तज्जानि लोमानि चर्माधिषवणे तथा 6.4.9ab
बलवत्क्षत्रतस्तस्मान्नान्यद्भूतमिहेष्यते 1.4.1603cd
बलवत्प्रक्रियातो हि वाक्यं सामान्यमात्रगम् 1.3.227cd
बलावष्टम्भ एतस्मिन्प्राणो देहेऽवतिष्ठते 2.2.14cd
बलीयसापि राज्ञेह स्पर्धमानोऽबलोऽपि सन् 1.4.1621ab
बलीयानन्तरङ्गत्वाद्बहिरङ्गं प्रबाधते 4.3.1673cd
बलीयानन्तरङ्गत्वाद्बहिरङ्गं प्रबाधते 5.1.91cd
बले प्राणे प्रतिष्ठा च चक्षुषोऽपि प्रदर्श्यते 5.16.33cd
बहिः कुलायादित्युक्तं पाप्मनो विजहाति च 4.3.1020cd
बहिः समीक्ष्यते राजा स्वप्नदृग्भिर्वनं गतः 2.1.294cd
बहिरङ्गं तु कर्म स्याद्बाह्यद्रव्याश्रयत्वतः SV 367cd
बहिरन्तःक्रियातोऽन्या न क्रिया विद्यते यतः 4.4.1222ab
बहिरन्तर्विभागोऽस्य कार्यकारणता तथा 2.5.80ab
बहिर्गतासु नाडीषु विषक्ता हृदयादधि 4.2.67cd
बहिर्देहं चरित्वाथ पुनरैति यथागतम् 4.3.939cd
बहिष्करणचेष्टाया निवृत्तौ दान्त उच्यते 4.4.1205ab
बहिष्कुलायवचनादेतच्चाध्यवसीयते 4.3.1144cd
बहुत्वजन्मनाशादि यात्यविद्योत्थसंगतेः 4.3.1631cd
बहुद्रष्टृनिषेधार्थं नान्यदित्याद्युदीरणम् 3.8.176ab

बहुनात्र किमुक्तेन यदेवायं समीक्षते 4.3.1268ab
बहुप्रकारसिद्ध्यर्थं वाशब्दव्याहृतिस्त्विह 4.3.1938ab
बहु भिक्षाटनाद्यस्ति तत्कस्मान्न निषिध्यते 4.4.1235cd
बहुशश्च प्रयोगोऽतो वायुरं खं प्रतीयताम् 5.1.121cd
बहुशोऽसङ्गवचसा निःसङ्गत्वं ब्रुवाणया SV 204ab
बहुष्वेकं यदाभाति प्रत्यक्षं कारणं तु तत् 1.2.56cd
बहुसाधनसाध्यत्वात्क्रियाणामितिहेतुतः 2.1.605ab
बहुहेतुर्मृतिर्यस्मात्प्राणिनां जगतीक्ष्यते 4.3.1938cd
बहूक्त्यैव तु सर्वेषां सिद्धं पूर्वमुपासनम् 1.5.365ab
बहूनामपि संमोहो लिङ्गादिषु समीक्ष्यते 4.3.30ab
बहूनामेकयोगित्वादेकत्वं किं न चोद्यते 1.4.552cd
बहूनित्यनुवादः स्यात्तद्बहुत्वस्य सिद्धितः 4.4.962cd
बहूपकारकृद्यद्वद्गवादिर्लौकिकः पशुः 1.4.1571ab
बहोरनन्तापर्यन्तदैववित्तस्य लोभतः 6.2.64ab
बह्वेतदिति विज्ञेयं प्रयोजनबहुत्वतः 6.4.19ab
बाढं पित्रानुशिष्टोऽस्मि किं न पश्यसि मज्जयम् 6.2.28ab
बाढमस्त्येव तद्दृश्यं न त्वत्यन्तविभागवत् 4.3.1611ab
बाढमेवं भवेदेतदाशङ्काकारणं न चेत् 4.3.734ab
बाधकानामपि सतां प्रत्यग्याथात्म्यरूपतः 2.1.551cd
बाधतेऽव्यभिचारित्वाद्व्यभिचारि तमोन्वयम् 2.4.256cd
बाधितत्वादतोऽवोचदिति ब्रह्मेति मोहनुत् 2.3.235cd
बाधितस्यैव तत्सूतेस्तदप्युक्ते न दूषणम् 4.4.957cd
बाधित्वाज्ञानसंसारौ यात्यपूर्वादिरूपताम् 3.5.79cd
बाधित्वा स्वमसंबोधं हित्वा व्याधत्वमात्मनः 2.1.514cd
बाधोऽतोऽसाध्वभिहितं समस्तव्यस्ततां प्रति 1.4.963cd
बाध्य एवात्मसंमोहो न त्वसौ बाधको यतः 3.5.46ab
बाध्यं तमो मितेः कृत्स्नं तज्जं चाप्यतिदुर्बलम् 1.4.845ab
बाध्यज्ञानस्य हेतुः स्यान्नातोऽन्यद्बाध्यकारणम् 1.3.56cd
बाध्यत्वेनैव माबुद्धेर्निष्ठिताभूदनात्मधीः 1.4.844cd
बाध्यबाधकभावाच्च पञ्चास्योरणयोरिव 3.3.59ab
बाध्यबाधकभावाच्च प्रत्यङ्मोहप्रबोधयोः 1.4.821ab
बाध्यबाधकभावेन काममस्तु समुच्चितिः 3.3.60ab

बाध्यबाधकभावोऽयं न तयोर्युज्यते ततः	3.3.96cd
बाध्यबाधकभावोऽयं विरोधाद्घटते तयोः	3.3.95cd
बाध्यबाधकयोरेवं ज्ञातयोरुक्तवर्त्मना	4.3.1282ab
बाध्यबाधकयोर्यस्मात्संबन्धः सकृदेव तु	4.4.958ab
बाध्यबाधकयोर्योगः स्वशक्त्यनपहारतः	1.4.255ab
बाध्यबाधकरूपं च न व्येतीति प्रकाशयन्	3.5.48cd
बाध्यस्य बाधनादेव प्रमाणस्य प्रमाणता	4.4.789ab
बाध्याविद्या कथं विद्यां बाधिकां बाधते वद	4.4.916ab
बालः प्रवर्तते तत्र ज्ञायते प्रेरणार्थता	SV 495cd
बालमौढ्यमदान्धत्वनिवृत्त्यर्थं तथोच्यते	2.1.348cd
बालस्य निर्विवेकत्वात्सविवेकः क्षितीश्वरः	2.1.349ab
बालाकेर्बोधयिष्यामीत्यतः सुप्तमगान्नृपः	2.1.97cd
बालादित्रयमप्येतदेको दृष्टान्त इष्यते	2.1.348ab
बालोन्मत्तोक्तिवच्चाहं वक्तुं दूषणमादरात्	2.4.312ab
बाल्यं चैव यथायोगमन्वयव्यतिरेकतः	3.5.170cd
बाल्यशब्दाभिधेया स्यात्तां समापय्य शुद्धधीः	3.5.176ab
बाल्ये दृढो यथा तद्वन्नैवं पक्वरसस्य सः	4.3.1933cd
बाष्पवन्नापि मिथ्यात्वादनुपायत्वमिष्यते	SV 899ab
बाहुल्यादिति विज्ञेयो यथोक्तगुणसंश्रयात्	2.4.340ab
बाह्यं कर्मास्य बुद्ध्यादिप्रयोगाश्रितमेव हि	4.3.1089ab
बाह्यज्योतिरभावेऽतो वाङ्मनःकायहेतुके	4.3.293ab
बाह्यदृष्ट्याद्युपाधिस्था प्रत्यगात्मैकलक्षणा	4.3.1635ab
बाह्यमेयप्रधानत्वे सत्यसाधारणार्थधीः	3.4.141cd
बाह्यवागाविचेष्टा च या चान्तःकरणाश्रया	1.4.1850ab
बाह्यवादेऽपि मिथ्यात्वं ज्ञानबाधेन जायते	4.3.493ab
बाह्यवित्तेन संबन्धमुक्त्वाथान्तर्धनात्मना	1.3.339ab
बाह्यस्य कर्मणस्तावदात्माद्यैः पाङ्क्ततोदिता	1.4.1841ab
बाह्यस्याप्यग्रहो बाधान्न तु स्थिरतया मतः	4.3.491cd
बाह्या तावदियं वृत्तिर्व्याख्याता प्रत्यगात्मनः	4.4.14ab
बाह्यादित्यादिज्योतिर्भिः पुमान्संदीपितेन्द्रियः	4.3.52ab
बाह्यादित्यादिविरहे करणव्यापृतिं विना	4.3.263ab
बाह्याद्देहात्तथैवान्तर्लिङ्गं स्वाप्नं प्रपद्यते	4.3.1949ab

बाह्याध्यात्मिकभेदेन कर्मैतदुभयात्मकम् 1.4.1842ab
बाह्यानामान्तराणां च कार्यकारणता मिथः 4.4.269ab
बाह्यानिति तथा चोक्तिर्विशेषाणां तु केवलम् 2.4.289ab
बाह्यान्तःप्रविभागोऽयं किमाश्रित्य प्रकल्प्यते 4.3.1105cd
बाह्यान्तर्ज्योतिषोर्मध्ये देहो बुद्ध्यादिसंहतः 4.3.287ab
बाह्यार्थदर्शने हेतुः कौटस्थ्यान्न तदक्षरम् 4.3.1527cd
बाह्यार्थबद्धधिषणः प्रत्यग्याथात्म्यवित्तये 1.6.5ab
बाह्यार्थभासनेऽप्यस्य सूर्यादेरिव कर्तृता 4.3.1458ab
बाह्यार्थवादिदोषोक्तिस्तत्र तावदिहोच्यते 4.3.495cd
बाह्यार्थवादिनि ध्वस्ते तद्वद्विज्ञानवाद्यथ 4.3.531ab
बाह्यार्थेऽपहृते चैवं प्रदीपादेरसंभवात् 4.3.537ab
बाह्येष्वर्थेष्वनात्मत्वात्पुनः शङ्का भवेदपि SV 901ab
बाह्यैराध्यात्मिकैरेवं साधनैरन्वितः पुमान् 4.3.1846cd
बाह्योऽस्य धर्मः सौस्वर्यं सौवर्ण्यं त्वान्तरं धनम् 1.3.340ab
बाह्योपरक्तबुद्धीनां भोगश्चिदवसानता 1.4.1791cd
बिभर्ति वासनैवास्य क्रियाकारकरूपताम् 4.3.1007cd
बिभित्सन्ति स्वतोऽभिन्नां देवतां मूढदृष्टयः 1.4.130cd
बिभित्सायै यथा वेगाल्लोष्टः क्षिप्तोऽश्मनोऽन्तिकात् 1.3.175ab
बिम्बात्मना प्रवेशस्य ननु दूषणमीरितम् 1.4.609ab
बिलानि सुषयश्चैता जाग्रद्वत्प्रत्ययोद्भवाः 2.1.322ab
बिले त्यक्तेऽहिना यद्वत्स्वनिर्मोके न पूर्ववत् 4.4.509ab
बीजं कार्यस्य सर्वस्य प्राज्ञश्चेति निरुच्यते 4.2.83cd
बीजप्रध्वंसकृज्ज्ञानफलवज्जन्मकारिता 1.4.913cd
बीजमेवाङ्कुरादीनां यथा कारणमिष्यते 2.4.323ab
बीजवत्स्यात्प्रवेशश्चेन्नैवमप्युपपद्यते 1.4.544ab
बीजस्थस्याङ्कुरस्येह जन्माश्रित्य यथैव गाम् 4.4.401ab
बीजाद्वनस्पतेर्जन्म मूलाच्चेहोपलभ्यते 3.9.135ab
बुद्धतत्त्वस्य लोकोऽयं जडोन्मत्तपिशाचवत् 1.4.1173ab
बुद्धतत्त्वोऽपि लोकस्य जडोन्मत्तपिशाचवत् 1.4.1173cd
बुद्धवाक्यादिवत्तादृक्त्याज्यं श्रुतिविरोधतः 2.4.320cd
बुद्धात्मनोऽपि सा बाह्यपदार्थज्ञानविभ्रमात् 2.1.236ab
बुद्धान्तादेर्यथा तद्वन्नातः स्यात्पुनरुक्तता 4.3.1064ef

बुद्धिः कारणसंस्थैव कृत्स्नव्यवहृतिक्षमा 4.3.299cd
बुद्धिजागरणे यद्वज्जागर्मीत्यभिमन्यते 4.3.448ab
बुद्धितत्कारणोपाधी क्षेत्रज्ञेश्वरसंज्ञकौ 1.4.614cd
बुद्धितद्वृत्तयश्चैवं तप्तायोविस्फुलिङ्गवत् 1.4.834cd
बुद्धितद्वृत्तिभावोऽयमभावश्चाप्यनन्यमात् SV 545ab
बुद्धितद्वृत्तिसाक्षित्वाद्बुद्धितत्प्रत्ययैरजः 3.4.155ab
बुद्धिपूर्वस्तु विलयः सम्यग्ज्ञानैकपूर्वकः 2.4.397cd
बुद्धियोगकृतोऽतोऽयं विज्ञानमय उच्यते 4.3.312cd
बुद्धिरध्यवसानाय साक्षी क्षेत्रज्ञ उच्यते 1.4.682cd
बुद्धिरुत्पद्यतेऽस्माकं यथाभूतार्थबोधिनः 1.3.72cd
बुद्धिवन्नाप्रमाणत्वं वेदस्येहोपपद्यते 2.4.306cd
बुद्धिविज्ञानसंपृक्तो यस्मादेष प्रमीयते 4.3.311ab
बुद्धिशुद्धौ च नित्यादिकर्मभ्यो नान्यदिष्यते 1.3.99cd
बुद्धिश्च न विचेष्टेत तामाहुः परमां गतिम् 4.4.1254cd
बुद्धिसाक्षी तृतीयः स्याद्योऽयं संदिह्यते तथा 3.4.63cd
बुद्धिस्थश्चलतीवात्मा ध्यायतीव च कल्प्यते 4.3.436ab
बुद्धिस्वापेऽपि तत्साक्ष्यात्स्वप्नो भूत्वेति मोहधीः 4.3.448cd
बुद्धीन्द्रियशरीरादावात्मत्वं प्रतिपेदिवान् 2.1.517cd
बुद्धीन्द्रियाणि पञ्चैव तथा कर्मेन्द्रियाण्यपि 1.3.258ab
बुद्धीन्द्रियादिसंसर्गादभिव्यक्तिः समीक्ष्यते 4.3.1119cd
बुद्धेः प्रद्योततेऽथाग्रं हृदयस्य यियासतः 4.4.75cd
बुद्धेः संस्कारकत्वेन यथा तदभिधीयते 4.4.972cd
बुद्धेः सामान्यवृत्त्येह व्याप्तिरादेहसंक्षयात् 2.4.346ab
बुद्धेः सेयमहंवृत्तिर्दुःखावच्छेदिनी सती 2.4.350cd
बुद्धेरन्तः प्रतीचोऽन्यो नार्थः संभाव्यते यतः 2.1.241ab
बुद्धेर्विषयविज्ञानसामान्यमपि चात्मनि 2.4.377ab
बुद्धेश्च मनसश्चैक्यं विवक्षित्वोपसंहृतिः 1.5.115ab
बुद्धोऽपि रागाद्युच्छित्तौ यतते नात्मनिह्नुतौ 1.4.410cd
बुद्ध्यन्तः पर एवात्मा विज्ञानात्मेति भण्यते 3.7.54ab
बुद्ध्यन्तस्यास्य मूढस्य सुखशब्दादिदर्शिनः 4.3.1532ab
बुद्ध्यन्ताद्व्यतिरिक्तोऽस्ति साक्षी प्रश्नस्य गोचरः 3.5.27ab
बुद्ध्यागमापायसाक्षी नियन्तैवोच्यते परः 3.7.54cd

बुद्धयात्मनोऽभिनिर्वृत्तिर्व्यवसायात्मनस्ततः 1.4.510ab
बुद्धयादिकरणोत्थाया व्यावृत्त्यर्थं विशेषणम् 4.3.878ab
बुद्धयादिकर्तृसाक्षित्वात्कर्तृत्वाद्यात्मनो भवेत् 4.3.927cd
बुद्धयादिकारकस्थस्य भावना कर्मणो गुणः 4.3.1033cd
बुद्धयादिकारणं नित्यमात्माविद्येति भण्यते 4.3.348cd
बुद्धयादिकार्यगैर्धर्मैः प्रतिबिम्बवदीक्ष्यते 1.4.619cd
बुद्धयादिकार्यविषया व्यापिव्याप्यत्वमेतयोः 1.4.628cd
बुद्धयादिकार्यसंस्थस्य कूटस्थासङ्गरूपिणः 4.3.384ab
बुद्धयादिकार्यसंहारे प्रत्यक्चैतन्यरूपिणः 4.3.1174ab
बुद्धयादिदेहपर्यन्तं प्रत्यगज्ञानहेतुकम् 4.3.347ab
बुद्धयादिभिस्तथात्मानं भ्रान्तोऽध्यारोप्य चेष्टते 3.3.66cd
बुद्धयादिर्जडरूपत्वात्स्वमहिम्ना न सिध्यति 4.4.945ab
बुद्धयादिर्विषयान्तोऽर्थो यत्साक्षिक इवेक्ष्यते 4.3.331cd
बुद्धयादिविषयान्तो हि प्रत्यक्चैतन्यबिम्बितः 4.3.36cd
बुद्धयादिव्यतिरिक्तत्वमात्मनोऽस्यावसीयताम् 4.3.950cd
बुद्धयादिव्यतिरिक्तोऽयं न चेदात्मा भवेत्तदा 4.3.428ab
बुद्धयादिव्यतिरेकोऽयं नैवं सत्युपपद्यते 4.3.426ab
बुद्धयादिषु परार्थेषु ह्यागमापायिवस्तुषु 4.3.341ab
बुद्धयादिष्वपि सूक्ष्मेषु यत्सूक्ष्मतममुच्यते 4.3.348ab
बुद्धयादिस्मृतिरूपेण प्रथते कर्मणो वशात् 4.3.88cd
बुद्धयादेः कृत्स्नकार्यस्य पुंस्कर्मोद्भूतिहेतुतः 2.1.217ab
बुद्धयादेः प्रविलीनत्वाद्देहादेश्च जडत्वतः 3.4.104ab
बुद्धयादेरभिसंबन्धो जन्मनैव चिदात्मना 3.4.93ab
बुद्धयादेर्विषयान्तस्य नित्यमेतदतो जगत् 1.4.1326cd
बुद्धयादेर्विषयान्तस्य निरस्तस्यात्मनो बहिः 1.4.729ab
बुद्धयादेर्विषयान्तस्य प्रतीचोऽन्यस्य वस्तुनः 4.4.928ab
बुद्धयादेर्विषयान्तस्य सिद्धिः स्यात्साक्षिणस्ततः 4.3.356cd
बुद्धयादेर्व्यतिरिक्तत्वं स्वयंज्योतिष्ट्वमागमात् 4.3.945ab
बुद्धयादेश्च समुत्पत्तौ धर्माद्येवात्र कारणम् 4.3.1529ab
बुद्धयाद्यर्थाभिसंबन्धपक्षतैवावसीयते 4.3.1036ab
बुद्धयाद्यव्यतिरेके हि न स्याद्धीवृत्तिसाक्षिता 4.3.442cd
बुद्धयाद्युत्क्षेपसंहारौ तस्मात्कर्मनिबन्धनौ 2.1.217cd

बुद्ध्याद्युपाध्यवच्छेदान्मात्रेति व्यपदिश्यते 4.3.1842cd
बुद्ध्युपात्तस्य रूपादेर्विज्ञातृत्वं न चात्मनः 4.3.1583ab
बुद्ध्युपात्तस्य रूपादेर्विज्ञानं च ततः परम् 4.3.1545cd
बुद्ध्युपाधिव्यवच्छेदाद्व्रीह्यादिपरिमाणता 5.8.4ab
बुद्ध्युपाध्यनुरोधेन प्रतीचः प्रभवाप्ययौ 2.1.338ab
बुद्ध्युपाध्यविविक्तश्च विज्ञानमय उच्यते 4.3.310cd
बुद्ध्वा क्लृप्तैः प्रतीक्षन्त उग्राः सूतादयो जनाः 4.3.1960cd
बुद्ध्वाथान्यत्तदभवत्तदन्यत्किमबुध्यत 1.4.1119ab
बुध्यते योऽनुमानेन शब्दबुद्धं न वेत्ति सः SV 743ab
बुबोधयिषितं भोक्तुरस्मद्गोचरवर्तिनः 2.1.207cd
बुभुक्षादिनिषेधोऽयं तथाप्यात्मन उच्यते 3.5.130ab
बुभुक्षाद्येकदेहस्थनिषेधादनिषेधतः 3.6.5ab
बुभुत्सामात्र एवामी वेदानुवचनादयः 4.4.1024ab
बुभुत्सासाधनेष्वेषु वेदानुवचनादिषु 4.4.1026ab
बुभुत्सितस्य कृत्स्नस्य वीप्सैवातो निषेधनी 2.3.199cd
बुभुत्सोच्छेदिनीं प्रज्ञां सर्वाज्ञाननिरासतः 4.4.705ab
बुभुत्सोच्छेदिनैवास्य सदसीत्यादिना दृढा SV 213ab
बृहत्त्वादग्रन्थतोऽर्थाच्च बृहदारण्यकं मतम् SV 9cd
बृहद्विचारे सम्यक्च प्रागप्येतद्विचारितम् 3.5.35ab
बृहन्निति ततश्चन्द्रः प्रमाणेनाभिधीयते 2.1.54ef
बृहन्नित्यादिभिः प्राणो बोध्यमानोऽपि यत्नतः 2.1.177ab
बृहन्नित्येवमादीनि सन्तु चेहोपलक्षणम् 2.1.111ab
बृहस्पतिसवे यद्वत्क्षत्रियो न प्रवर्तते 3.3.63ab
बृहस्पत्यादिभिर्धर्मैरसोरन्यदुपासनम् 1.3.297ab
बृहस्पत्यादिभिर्धर्मैरुपास्यानमनो भवेत् 1.3.322ab
बैजिकं गार्भिकं चैनो द्विजानामपमृज्यते 4.4.1048cd
बोद्धारमपि चापेक्ष्य न संज्ञा प्रत्यगात्मनि 2.4.483ab
बोद्धुः कर्तुश्च पुंसोऽस्य प्रवृत्तिर्येह काचन 4.3.56ab
बोद्धुः कर्तुश्च संबन्धो ज्ञानेन क्रियया यथा 4.3.412ab
बोद्धृतज्ज्ञानविषयैर्न बोद्धा गृह्यते यतः 2.4.483cd
बोद्धेत्यादिसमुत्थानं भण्यते परमात्मनः 2.4.427cd
बोधकं यत्प्रमेयस्य तत्प्रमाणमिहेष्यते 4.3.1710ab

बोधकं यदबुद्धस्य तन्मानमिति हि स्थितिः SV 939ab
बोधमात्रातिरेकेण नान्योऽर्थोऽज्ञानसिद्धिकृत् 4.4.898ab
बोधमात्रैकयाथात्म्यान्नायं संमोहभाग्यतः 4.4.9cd
बोधयित्वापि चैकात्म्यं नान्तरा पर्यवस्यति SV 776ab
बोधाच्च ध्वस्तसंमोहः स्मृतिं नैव व्यपेक्षते 1.4.842cd
बोधात्मकत्वं च मितेः किमासीन्मेयसंगतेः 4.3.170ab
बोधात्मवत्स्वतःसिद्धप्रत्यक्सिद्ध्यैव सिध्यति 4.4.945cd
बोधादेव प्रसिध्यन्ति कालावस्थादयो यतः SV 999ab
बोधानुभववत्तस्या बाधको नेक्ष्यते यतः 4.3.217cd
बोधानुभवसंवित्तिवित्तयो ह्यात्मवाचिनः SV 1057cd
बोधाबोधौ चितेर्न स्तः कूटस्थज्ञप्तिमात्रतः 2.1.126ab
बोधाबोधौ यतो दृष्टौ स्वानुभूत्यनुसारतः SV 548ab
बोधावस्थां तिरोनीय देहाद्याश्रयलक्षणाम् 2.1.283ab
बोधाविशेषादथवा भेद एव न विद्यते 2.4.302ab
बोधेऽविद्यासहायत्वमिह त्वात्मैव निर्द्वयः 4.3.1278cd
बोधेऽस्मिञ्शब्दतो जाते न प्रवर्त्योऽफलत्वतः SV 663ab
बोधे न शक्यते कर्तुं विवेको भोक्तृभोज्ययोः 2.1.101cd
बोधे साधारणा येऽस्य स्वप्ने तेऽनन्यद्रष्टृकाः 2.1.285cd
बोधे हस्त्यादिकं स्वप्ने तदेवाविद्ययात्मनि 4.3.1269ab
बोधोऽप्यकारको यस्माद्धन्त्यज्ञानमिहात्मनि 4.4.953ab
बोध्ये हि लौकिकेऽपेक्षा परतोऽवगतौ तथा 1.4.868cd
बौद्धराद्धान्तसक्तिः स्यात्स्वार्थस्य क्षणिकत्वतः 1.4.244cd
बौद्धविज्ञानविक्षेपसंहारकथनाय तु 4.3.1218ab
बौद्धेऽथ स यदा तत्त्वं परं समनुपश्यति 4.4.721ab
ब्रवाण्युपास्यं तत्तेऽहं सर्वापध्वस्तिकारणम् 2.1.32cd
ब्रह्मक्षत्रादिरूपाणि यतोऽतीत्यासृजत्प्रभुः 1.4.1615ab
ब्रह्मचर्यं च वत्स्याव आवां तत्र नृपे गतौ 6.2.54cd
ब्रह्मचर्यं समापय्य गृही तस्माद्भवेद्द्विजः 3.5.149ab
ब्रह्मचर्यं समाप्येतिप्रत्यक्षश्रुतिमूलतः 4.4.1148ab
ब्रह्मचर्यादेवेत्यादिवाक्यानि शतशः श्रुतौ 1.5.267ab
ब्रह्मचर्याद्गृहाच्चैव वनाच्चापि विधीयते 2.4.27ab
ब्रह्मचर्यान्तवाक्येन ब्रह्मचारिपरिग्रहः 4.4.1064ab

ब्रह्मचर्याश्रमादेव प्रव्रजेदिति भूरिशः 3.5.203ab
ब्रह्मचर्याश्रमादेव यदि वा प्रव्रजेद्द्विजः 3.5.154ab
ब्रह्मजातिः परादध्यादसम्यग्दर्शिनं नरम् 2.4.250cd
ब्रह्म जिज्ञासवो विप्रा आहुर्यद्गुरुसंनिधौ 1.4.1069cd
ब्रह्मज्ञानस्य वा वंशो यत्नाच्छ्रुत्यायमुच्यते 2.6.2cd
ब्रह्मज्ञानात्तदन्यत्र परार्थं ज्ञानमिष्यते 1.4.1253cd
ब्रह्मज्ञानेऽधिकारी स्यात्कथं नामेति भण्यते 1.6.3cd
ब्रह्मज्ञानैकनिष्ठः सन्पुण्यकृत्तैजसश्च सन् 4.4.588ab
ब्रह्मज्ञानोदये यस्माज्जन्मबन्धो व्यपेयते 4.4.390ab
ब्रह्मणः प्रागुपन्यस्तोऽसाध्वीयं कल्पना कथम् 5.1.77cd
ब्रह्मणः स्थानमायान्ति यद्वा स्वाश्रमकर्मभिः 6.2.137ab
ब्रह्मणश्चेद्भवस्तस्या अनिर्मोक्षः प्रसज्यते 4.4.920ab
ब्रह्मणस्त्वप्रसिद्धत्वात्क्रियतेऽसूत्रकः पटः 1.4.895cd
ब्रह्मणा चेत्कृता विद्या निष्फलेयं प्रसज्यते 1.4.1134ab
ब्रह्मणा मनसा सृष्टो मानसः पुरुषस्ततः 6.2.140ab
ब्रह्मणैवानुवित्तोऽयं तेन पन्था गुरूक्तितः 4.4.568cd
ब्रह्मणैवेति च ज्ञेया इत्थंभूतार्थलक्षणा 4.4.571ab
ब्रह्मणोऽनात्मतारूपमब्रह्मत्वं तथात्मनः SV 903ab
ब्रह्मणोऽन्यद्यतो वस्तु ब्रह्मैव परमार्थतः 1.4.1153ab
ब्रह्मणोऽप्यात्मनो मोहादब्रह्मत्वं न वस्तुतः 3.4.47ab
ब्रह्मणोऽब्रह्मता तद्वद्विद्यानर्थक्यसांशते SV 174cd
ब्रह्मणोऽविद्यया योऽपि स्यादवच्छेद आत्मनः 2.4.185ab
ब्रह्मणोऽव्यतिरेके च तद्वच्चासति दुःखिनि 2.1 431ab
ब्रह्मणोऽस्य कथं नास्ति द्रष्टव्यमिति भण्यताम् 4.3.1562cd
ब्रह्मणो न त्वनर्थित्वात्तथा चाप्रकृतत्वतः 1.4.1195cd
ब्रह्मणो नान्यतः प्रत्यक्साक्षात्त्वाद्ब्रह्मवस्तुनः 1.4.1271cd
ब्रह्मणो मान्तरासिद्धेः शून्यतैव प्रसज्यते 2.3.215cd
ब्रह्मणो याद्वयावस्था सैव तावदिहोदिता 5.1.38ab
ब्रह्मणो वोपदेशः स्यादथवाब्रह्मणो भवेत् 3.4.8ab
ब्रह्मणो व्यतिरेकेण प्रत्यक्ता नान्यतस्तथा 4.3.1822cd
ब्रह्मण्यवस्थितस्यापि त्वक्षयत्वं श्रुतिर्जगौ 3.2.75cd
ब्रह्मण्यविदिते बोधान्नाविद्येत्युपपद्यते SV 178ab

ब्रह्मण्यविद्यासंसिद्ध्यै स्मर्तव्यं तदिहाखिलम् 1.4.1215cd
ब्रह्मण्यस्तमितेऽत्यर्थं जगत्यस्मिन्नशेषतः 2.1.396ab
ब्रह्मण्यानन्दः संवेद्यो लौकिकानन्दवद्यदि 3.9.170ab
ब्रह्मण्यानन्दशब्दोऽयं प्रयुक्तः सुखवाचकः 3.9.166ab
ब्रह्मण्येव समध्यस्तं शुक्तिकारजतादिवत् 1.4.1280cd
ब्रह्मता न मदन्यत्र कौटस्थ्यान्मम नाशिषु 1.4.1271ab
ब्रह्मता नात्मनोऽन्यत्र नात्मता ब्रह्मणोऽन्यतः 1.4.1013ab
ब्रह्मता नात्मनोऽन्यत्र नात्मता ब्रह्मणोऽन्यतः 1.4.1390ab
ब्रह्म तुभ्यं ब्रवाणीतिवाङ्मात्रव्यापृतावहम् 2.1.40ab
ब्रह्म तेऽहं ब्रवाणीति गार्ग्यः काश्यमभाषत 2.1.30cd
ब्रह्म तेऽहं ब्रवाणीति प्रकृत्य ब्रह्मबोधनम् 2.1.449ab
ब्रह्म तेऽहं ब्रवाणीति प्रतिज्ञाय ततो नृपः 2.1.434ab
ब्रह्म तेऽहं ब्रवाणीति प्रारभ्यापूर्णवाक्यतः 2.4.1cd
ब्रह्मत्वं किं स्वतस्तस्य किं वा तत्परतो मतम् 1.4.1103cd
ब्रह्मत्वं नानयोर्यस्मादेकैकस्य न युक्तिमत् 5.14.4ab
ब्रह्मत्वं नान्यतोऽज्ञायि वाक्यं तत्प्रतिपत्तिकृत् 4.3.1114cd
ब्रह्मत्वं ब्रह्मणो न स्याद्द्वितीये सति वस्तुनि 2.4.13cd
ब्रह्मत्वमन्यो वेदेति तदैकत्वं विरुध्यते 3.9.192cd
ब्रह्मत्वस्य स्वतः सिद्धेर्ब्रह्मणि स्यादनर्थकः 3.4.8cd
ब्रह्मत्वादाप्ततद्भावो नित्यमेव न साधनात् 1.4.1205cd
ब्रह्मदत्तश्चकारोच्चैः शपथं वादिनः प्रति 1.3.325ef
ब्रह्मदत्ताभिसंबन्धादनित्यत्वं प्रसज्यते 1.3.332cd
ब्रह्मदृष्ट्या त्वविद्येयं न कथं चन युज्यते SV 176cd
ब्रह्म नैवेह वस्त्वस्ति दृष्टिरेवेति चेन्मतम् 1.3.66ab
ब्रह्मप्रज्ञां प्रकुर्वीत विशेषणसमाश्रयात् 4.4.845cd
ब्रह्मप्रतीचोरैकात्म्यात्तद्दूरीकृत्य गर्जति 1.4.65cd
ब्रह्म प्रत्यक्तया विद्मः कथंचित्कल्मषक्षयात् 4.4.624cd
ब्रह्मप्राप्त्यन्तरायस्य प्रत्यक्संमोहमात्रतः 1.4.1449ab
ब्रह्मबुद्ध्या भविष्यामः कृत्स्नं ब्रह्मेति तद्विदः 1.4.1132ab
ब्रह्म ब्रवाणीत्यात्थ त्वमेतावद्ब्रह्म तच्च ते 2.1.86cd
ब्रह्मभाविरवं श्रुत्वा ये तु व्याचक्षतेऽन्यथा 1.4.1165ab
ब्रह्मभावी ततो नेशः किंतु तद्व्यतिरेकभाक् 1.4.1245ab

ब्रह्मभावीति न पुनर्वस्तुतत्त्वव्यपेक्षया 1.4.1175cd
ब्रह्मभावी नरोऽतोऽत्र ब्रह्मशब्देन भण्यते 1.4.1200cd
ब्रह्मभावोऽत्र नित्यः स्यात्कारणाद्यनपेक्षतः 1.4.1155ab
ब्रह्मभूयाय भवति परिव्राडिति च श्रुतिः SV 225cd
ब्रह्म मूर्तादि नेत्युक्तौ मूर्तादेर्न निषेधगीः 2.3.218cd
ब्रह्म मे वक्ष्यतीत्यर्थं निषिद्धं नृपसर्पणम् 2.1.94cd
ब्रह्म यस्मात्परं नास्ति न च वस्त्वन्तरं यतः 2.1.32ab
ब्रह्मयाथात्म्यविज्ञानसाधनत्वं विनागमात् 2.4.7ab
ब्रह्म रूपि तृतीयं च तदा वावेति युज्यते 2.3.139cd
ब्रह्मलोकनिरासार्थं वचः स्यात्सविशेषणम् 1.4.1778cd
ब्रह्मलोकपरिप्राप्तौ मूर्ध्न आत्मा निगच्छति 4.4.84cd
ब्रह्मलोकमिमं साक्षाद्धे सम्राड्ब्रह्मविद्यया 4.4.1301ab
ब्रह्मलोकान्तवाक्येन तस्य स्यादुपसंहृतिः 4.3.1886cd
ब्रह्मलोकान्स नयति सोऽप्यभ्येत्याथ वैद्युतान् 6.2.140cd
ब्रह्मवन्मानमस्तीह तथा निर्मोक्षतापतेत् 1.3.187cd
ब्रह्म वा इत्युपक्रम्य मोहकार्यं विवक्षितम् 4.4.415cd
ब्रह्म वा इदमित्यत्र न्यायेनैकात्म्ययायिना 2.4.109cd
ब्रह्म वा इदमित्यादि कस्मान्नारभ्यतेऽधुना SV 1117cd
ब्रह्म वा इदमित्यादि मधुकाण्डे यदीरितम् 5.1.17ab
ब्रह्म वा इदमित्यादिर्नातो दोषोऽत्र कश्चन 1.4.1351cd
ब्रह्म वा इदमित्यादिर्ब्रह्मैवेति तथा श्रुतिः SV 29ab
ब्रह्म वा इदमित्युक्तेः प्रागपि ज्ञानजन्मतः 3.3 18ab
ब्रह्म वा इदमित्येवं तथा ब्रह्मैव सन्निति 4.1.29ab
ब्रह्म वा इदमित्येवं सूत्रितं वस्तु यत्पुरा 4.4.298ab
ब्रह्म विज्ञापयिष्यामि यज्ज्ञाने सर्वविद्भवेत् 2.1.95cd
ब्रह्मवित्त्वे च को हेतुरित्याशङ्क्याह नः श्रुतिः 4.4.576ab
ब्रह्मवित्त्वे च पारार्थ्यं देवादीन्प्रति हीयते 1.4.1472ab
ब्रह्मवित्त्वे तु राज्ञोऽस्य मितिं नोपलभामहे 4.2.20ab
ब्रह्मवित्स्तूयते ताभ्यां ब्रह्मविद्याप्रवृत्तये 4.4.585cd
ब्रह्म विद्धि तदेव त्वं न तु तद्यदुपासते 3.4.163cd
ब्रह्म विद्धि तदेव त्वं न त्विदं यदुपासते 1.4.885cd
ब्रह्म विद्धि तदेव त्वं न त्विदं यदुपासते 3.4.164cd

ब्रह्म विद्धि तदेव त्वं न त्विदं यदुपासते 4.3.1730cd
ब्रह्म विद्धि तदेवेति ब्रह्मता च समर्पिता 1.4.887cd
ब्रह्मविद्भिरतो यत्नात्प्रमाणमिह संश्रितम् 1.4.315cd
ब्रह्मविद्या किमर्थेयं नान्यन्मुक्तेः फलं ततः 3.1.26cd
ब्रह्मविद्यात आरब्धा ब्रह्माविद्यानिवृत्तये 1.4.1758cd
ब्रह्मविद्या ततो नास्या मुक्तौ स्यात्साधनं परम् 2.5.96cd
ब्रह्मविद्यातिरेकेण तत्प्राप्तौ नापरा क्रिया 2.5.82cd
ब्रह्मविद्याधिकारत्वादित्येतदधुनोच्यते 4.2.3cd
ब्रह्म विद्याधिकारित्वं द्वैविध्यात्प्रतिपद्यते 1.4.1335cd
ब्रह्मविद्याधिकारेऽस्मिन्यावत्किंचिदुपासनम् 2.1.421ab
ब्रह्मविद्याप्लवेनेमं संसाराब्धिं तितीर्षवः 1.4.1072cd
ब्रह्मविद्याफलप्राप्तौ विघ्नं कुर्वन्ति देवताः 1.4.1470ab
ब्रह्मविद्यामृते नान्यद्भयहेतुविनाशकृत् 1.4.68ab
ब्रह्मविद्या समाप्तेयं ससंन्यासाद्भयात्मिका 4.4.1304ab
ब्रह्मविद्याहतध्वान्ते तस्मिन्ब्रह्मणि निष्ठिते 2.5.59ab
ब्रह्मविद्याहुताशेन विनाशोऽस्याप्यकर्तृता 1.4.1802ab
ब्रह्मविद्येति तां साक्षाच्छ्रेमुषीं प्रतिजानते 1.4.1077cd
ब्रह्मविद्येति सर्वाप्तावसाधारणकारणम् 1.4.1137cd
ब्रह्मविद्येति सिद्धः स्याद्व्यपदेशो न चान्यथा 1.4.1272cd
ब्रह्मविद्यैव कृत्स्नाप्तौ यस्मात्साधनमुच्यते 1.4.1080ab
ब्रह्मविद्योत्थितिफलं तत्सर्वमिति निर्दिशेत् 2.1.421cd
ब्रह्मविद्योदयाद्यस्मादभूदब्रह्म पुरापि तत् 1.4.1134cd
ब्रह्मविद्योपदेशस्य कैमर्थक्यं प्रसज्यते 2.1.431cd
ब्रह्मविद्योपदेशस्य विषयश्चावधार्यते 1.4.1167ab
ब्रह्म वेदेति च तथा नैवं तस्यार्थवादतः SV 43cd
ब्रह्म वेदेत्येवमादौ क्लृप्ताः सृष्ट्यादयस्ततः 1.4.624cd
ब्रह्मशब्दाभिधेयश्च संसार्येव तदा भवेत् 2.1.428ab
ब्रह्मश्रुतेश्च मुख्योऽर्थः प्रतीचोऽन्यत्र दुर्लभः 1.4.1299ab
ब्रह्म संसर्गरूपं चेद्वाक्यादध्यवसीयते 1.4.900ab
ब्रह्म संसर्गरूपं वा यदि वातोऽन्यथा श्रुतेः 4.4.813cd
ब्रह्मसंपदतः शास्त्रं तादर्थ्यादर्थवद्भवेत् 1.4.1250cd
ब्रह्माकर्त्रपि संबोधात्प्रागभूत्तदसंसृति 1.4.1227ab

ब्रह्माकाशः प्रतिष्ठा च नामोपनिषदुच्यते 4.1.10cd
ब्रह्माकाशः प्रतिष्ठा स्यात्प्रज्ञास्योपनिषत्तथा 4.1.17cd
ब्रह्माकाशात्परो नान्य आकाश इह गृह्यते 2.1.243cd
ब्रह्माकृत्स्नं मतं तच्चेदुक्तदोषानिराकृतेः 1.4.1090ab
ब्रह्माज्ञानं यतो हेतुरेषणानां न वस्तुतः 3.5.138ab
ब्रह्माज्ञानसमुत्थत्वान्मिथ्याज्ञानत्वकारणात् 1.4.1093cd
ब्रह्माण्डसंपुटस्तस्मात्परेणाभ्येति सर्वतः 3.3.148cd
ब्रह्माण्डाद्बहिरन्तश्च समष्टिव्यष्टिरूपिणः 3.3.137ab
ब्रह्मातिरेकतो नान्यद्यतो वस्त्ववशिष्यते 2.3.173cd
ब्रह्मात्मतत्त्वव्युत्पत्तिमात्रेणाप्यधिकारिता SV 283ab
ब्रह्मात्मनि समाप्तत्वाद्गतिः का परमात्मनि 4.2.23cd
ब्रह्मात्मनि समाप्तस्य न तदन्यार्थशेषता 1.4.1685cd
ब्रह्मात्मनोरभिन्नत्वं वस्तुतो यद्यपीक्ष्यते 4.4.573ab
ब्रह्मात्मनोरसंसर्गस्तद्विरुद्धार्थयोरिव 3.5.184ab
ब्रह्मात्मनोश्च संसर्गो मा प्रापत्कृष्णसर्पवत् 4.4.526ab
ब्रह्मात्मलक्षणासाध्वी तेनेयं कल्पना कृता 1.4.1762cd
ब्रह्मात्मवस्त्विति ज्ञेयमिति श्रौतं वचः स्फुटम् 4.3.1624cd
ब्रह्मात्मशब्दयोस्तद्वदेकाधिकरणश्रुतेः 2.1.465ab
ब्रह्मात्मात्मानमेवावेदहं ब्रह्मेति च श्रुतेः 4.3.1734ab
ब्रह्मात्मानमुपासीत ब्रह्मतत्त्वाविचक्षणः 4.4.449ab
ब्रह्मात्मार्थप्रसिद्धौ च लोपगन्मानप्रवेशिता SV 860cd
ब्रह्मात्मैकत्वशंसीनि वाक्यान्यपि तथा सति 2.1.459ab
ब्रह्मात्मैकस्वभावेन साक्षादिति विशेष्यते 3.4.44ab
ब्रह्मात्मैवेत्यतो वक्ति श्रुतिरैकात्म्यसिद्धये 2.5.142cd
ब्रह्मादावित्यनेनापि जनिमत्सर्वमुच्यते 1.4.502ab
ब्रह्मादिमध्यपातित्वं ततश्चास्य प्रसज्यते 2.4.134cd
ब्रह्मादि सर्वमात्मेति प्रतिज्ञाय श्रुतिर्यथा 2.1.501cd
ब्रह्मादि सर्वमात्मेति संपन्नातोऽत्र युज्यते 1.4.1257cd
ब्रह्मादिस्तम्बपर्यन्तं कार्यं प्राविशदुच्यते 1.4.494cd
ब्रह्मादिस्तम्बपर्यन्तं देहेष्विति तथोच्यते 1.4.503ab
ब्रह्मादिस्थावरान्तेषु भूतेषु प्राविशत्परः 2.1.469cd
ब्रह्मादीनां शरीराणि श्वसूकरशरीरवत् 4.3.815ab

ब्रह्मादीनि च भूतानि ग्रथितान्यक्षसूत्रवत् 3.7.5ab
ब्रह्माद्या स्थावरान्तैवं प्रत्यगज्ञानहेतुजा SV 1112cd
ब्रह्मानधिगतं चेदं वाक्यादन्यैः प्रमान्तरैः 4.4.812ab
ब्रह्मानन्दमथान्यः सन्वेद मुक्तो घटादिवत् 3.9.192ab
ब्रह्मानुपाधि पूर्वत्र व्याख्यातं यत्नतोऽधुना 5.3.1ab
ब्रह्मान्यदन्यदेवददात्मन्वीत्यन्तमादरात् 2.1.82cd
ब्रह्मापि तत्स्वतः साक्षात्तदबोधैकहेतुतः 1.4.1334ab
ब्रह्मापियन्ति निर्द्वन्द्वा आप्तमेव तमोह्नुतेः 4.4.552cd
ब्रह्मापि संस्तथैवात्मा सद्वितीयतयेक्ष्यते SV 909cd
ब्रह्माप्येतीत्यतो वाक्यमुपचारसमाश्रयात् 4.4.372ab
ब्रह्मार्थोऽपि महत्त्वेन प्रसिद्धो व्यवहारतः SV 861cd
ब्रह्मार्पणमिति वचो यथोक्तेनैव वर्त्मना 1.4.1735ab
ब्रह्मावाप्त्यै तु तत्त्याग ईप्सन्तीतिश्रुतेर्बलात् SV 14cd
ब्रह्माविद्यावदिष्टं चेन्ननु दोषो महानयम् SV 175ab
ब्रह्माविद्यासमुत्थानात्कार्यकारणलक्षणात् 2.4.8ab
ब्रह्मा विश्वसृजो धर्म इति कर्मफलात्मता 1.4.148ab
ब्रह्मा विश्वसृजो धर्म इत्यादिवचनान्मनोः 1.4.1763cd
ब्रह्मा विश्वसृजोवाक्याद्देवसाष्टर्यातिरेकतः 3.3.131ab
ब्रह्मासंसर्गि तद्यस्मादसामान्यविशेषवत् 4.4.800ab
ब्रह्मासंसर्गि साक्षाच्च शब्दः शक्नोति बोधितुम् 4.4.802cd
ब्रह्मासंसृष्टरूपत्वात्तेनातो नावगम्यते 1.4.805cd
ब्रह्मासृजद्यतः क्षत्रमात्मनोऽप्यतिवीर्यवत् 1.4.1603ab
ब्रह्मास्तु तर्हि तत्कृत्स्नमुक्तदोषासमन्वयात् 1.4.1096ab
ब्रह्मास्मीति धियो जन्मसमकाला विमुक्तता 2.1.541ab
ब्रह्मास्मीति न तावद्धीर्जायते सान्तरायतः 4.4.863cd
ब्रह्मास्मीतिपरिज्ञानध्वस्तध्वान्तत्वकारणात् 2.5.63ab
ब्रह्मास्मीति परिज्ञानात्प्रत्यगज्ञानहानतः 4.4.375cd
ब्रह्मास्मीति प्रकुर्वीत बुभुत्सोच्छेदिनीं दृढाम् 4.4.835cd
ब्रह्मास्मीति यदैवैतमात्मानं देवमञ्जसा 4.4.630ab
ब्रह्मास्मीति हि तद्ध्वंसान्न क्वचिद्भेदधीर्यतः 1.4.436cd
ब्रह्मास्मीत्यपि संबोधस्तथैवानुभवाश्रयात् 1.4.1228cd
ब्रह्मास्मीत्यविनिर्ज्ञाते कथं ब्रह्मणि सा भवेत् 1.4.1249cd

ब्रह्मास्मीत्यागमाद्बोधः सुषुप्तोदाहृतेर्मतः 4.3.1900cd
ब्रह्माहमर्थयोर्ज्ञेयस्तयोरैकार्थ्यहेतुतः 1.4.1429cd
ब्रह्माहंपदयोरर्थौ यौ तयोः संगतिर्मिथः 1.4.1417ab
ब्रह्मेति चात्मयाथात्म्यं लक्ष्यते नाभिधीयते 4.3.1820cd
ब्रह्मेति जातिनिर्देशः क्षत्रसंनिधिकारणात् 2.4.250ab
ब्रह्मेति जातिरेवात्र ग्राह्या न तु पराक्षरम् 1.4.1659ab
ब्रह्मेति ध्वस्तसंभेदं यन्नेतीति पुरोदितम् 2.5.40ab
ब्रह्मेति प्राक्प्रतिज्ञाय यथावदुपदर्शितम् 2.2.1cd
ब्रह्मेति बोध्यते साक्षात्तत्तमोध्वस्तिवर्त्मना 4.3.1733cd
ब्रह्मेतिब्रह्मशब्देन कृत्स्नं वस्त्वभिधीयते 1.4.1282ab
ब्रह्मेति ब्रह्मशब्देन तदेवात्राभिधीयते 1.4.1313ab
ब्रह्मेति ब्रह्मशब्देन द्वैतैकत्वात्मकं किल 1.4.1189ab
ब्रह्मेति ब्रह्मशब्दोऽयं मुख्यब्रह्मार्थवाचकः 1.4.1169ab
ब्रह्मेति मुख्यवृत्त्येह वस्तु श्रुत्याभिधीयते 4.3.1815cd
ब्रह्मेति वास्तवं वृत्तं तावदस्यावबोध्यते 2.5.138ab
ब्रह्मेति श्रावितो राज्ञा ब्रह्मा प्रत्याह तं नृपम् 1.4.1605ab
ब्रह्मेतीह विशेष्यार्थः खमित्यपि विशेषणम् 5.1.113ab
ब्रह्मेत्यादिपदार्थोऽयमुक्तस्तावत्समासतः 1.5.295ab
ब्रह्मेत्याहात्मनस्तत्त्वं ब्रह्म त्वभयमेव हि 4.4.1336cd
ब्रह्मेदंमात्रश्रवणात्कुतोऽग्र इति भण्यते 1.4.1316cd
ब्रह्मेह परमात्मोक्तो लोका भरादयस्तथा 3.7.4ab
ब्रह्मैककारणो राजा तस्माद्ब्रह्मैव संश्रितः 1.4.1610ef
ब्रह्मैकजात्यवच्छिन्नं यस्मादग्रे व्यवर्तत 1.4.1599ab
ब्रह्मैकत्वविरोधो नः कथं भिन्नार्थबुद्धिभिः 2.1.592ab
ब्रह्मैकदेशभूतस्य विज्ञानात्मन एव ते 2.3.140ab
ब्रह्मैतदुभयं जग्ध्वा पूर्णमेवावशिष्यते 1.5.166cd
ब्रह्मैव चान्ततः क्षत्रमुपनिश्रयतीत्यतः 1.4.1609ab
ब्रह्मैव चेदविद्याया जन्मनः कारणं मतम् 3.2.92ab
ब्रह्मैव तदुपाधीहेदंशब्देनाभिधीयते 1.4.1176cd
ब्रह्मैव तद्वदात्मापि सद्वितीयवदीक्ष्यते 1.4.1391cd
ब्रह्मैव तेज एवेति ह्युभयत्रावधारणम् 4.4.528ab
ब्रह्मैव प्रोच्यते साक्षात्प्रत्यगात्मविशेषणम् 4.4.1321cd

ब्रह्मैव ब्राह्मणः साक्षादुपचारात्परायणम् 3.9.163cd
ब्रह्मैव भवतीत्यादितदापत्तिवचांस्यपि 1.4.1258cd
ब्रह्मैव रूप्यते ताभ्यां ब्रह्मत्वं न हि रूपवत् 2.3.6cd
ब्रह्मैव सन्तो विज्ञानात्प्रागतो ब्रह्मबोधतः 4.4.629ab
ब्रह्मैव सन्नवाप्नोति ब्रह्मेति वचनं स्फुटम् 4.2.26ab
ब्रह्मैव सन्निति तथा प्रागपीदं श्रुतीरितम् 4.4.560ab
ब्रह्मैव सन्स्वतो यत्र ब्रह्माप्येति तमोह्नुतेः 4.4.774ab
ब्रह्मैव सन्स्वतो यस्माद्ब्रह्माप्येत्यवबोधतः 4.3.1833ab
ब्रह्मैवात्मानमेवेति प्रत्यबुध्यत वाक्यतः 1.4.1181cd
ब्रह्मैवात्मा स्वतोऽबोधादब्रह्मैव प्रकाशते 4.4.1322ab
ब्रह्मैवात्मेति च तथा संसारित्वनिवृत्तये 2.5.143cd
ब्रह्मैवापि स्वतो मोहान्न तत्संभावयत्यपि 1.4.1172cd
ब्रह्मैवाप्येति ब्रह्मैव प्रागप्यासीद्यतोऽद्वयम् 1.3.185ab
ब्रह्मैवाविकृतं यस्मात्पूर्वयोर्विकृतिं पुनः 1.4.1642ab
ब्रह्मैवेति तु शब्देन तद्विशेषणमुच्यते 4.4.523cd
ब्रह्मैवेदं तथात्मैव पुरुषश्चेति चागमः 1.5.334ab
ब्रह्मैवेदं यथा सर्वं विद्यया तदबोधजम् 1.4.1144ab
ब्रह्मैवेदं विश्वमिति साक्षादाम्नायशासनम् 1.4.1661ab
ब्रह्मैवैकः स आत्मोक्तो ह्यध्यायेषु चतुर्ष्वपि 4.5.15ab
ब्रह्मैवैतीह सन्ब्रह्म तस्मान्मोहनिराकृतौ 4.4.300cd
ब्रह्मैषा सर्वसंव्याप्तेरात्मेत्येतामुपास्महे 2.1.59ab
ब्रह्मोपदेशविषयः श्रुत्यैवोत्थाप्यते जडः 1.6.44cd
ब्रह्मोपमर्दनात्पापः प्रागपि क्रूरकर्मकृत् 1.4.1612ab
ब्रह्मोपास्तिर्भवेदेवं कर्म चानुष्ठितं भवेत् 1.4.1706ab
ब्राह्मणं न ह्यनाश्रित्य राजसूयादिहेतुकः 1.4.1655ab
ब्राह्मणः स्वमहिम्नैव पुरुषार्थं समश्नुते 1.4.1656cd
ब्राह्मणग्रहणं चात्र द्विजानामुपलक्षणम् 4.4.1029ab
ब्राह्मणग्रहणेनातः कृतकृत्य इहोच्यते 4.4.1187cd
ब्राह्मणज्ञानतोऽन्यत्र विद्यां पप्रच्छ भूमिपः 6.2.52ab
ब्राह्मणत्वात्मलाभोऽपि यः स्यात्क्षत्रियवैश्ययोः 1.4.1654ab
ब्राह्मणत्वादिविज्ञानमग्निहोत्रादिकर्मणाम् SV 363ab
ब्राह्मणत्वानहंमानी विप्रो वा क्षत्रकर्मणि 3.3.63cd

ब्राह्मणत्वाभिसंबन्धः प्राधान्यं तेन पूर्वयोः 1.4.1655cd
ब्राह्मणस्य च गायत्री कारणं तेन सा वरा 5.16.4cd
ब्राह्मणस्य पुरानुक्तेस्तदुक्त्यर्था परा श्रुतिः 1.4.1634cd
ब्राह्मणस्य प्रधानत्वाद्युक्तं तदुपलक्षणम् 1.4.1653cd
ब्राह्मणस्यैव संन्यास इति श्रुत्या विरुध्यते 1.4.1651cd
ब्राह्मणा जातिमात्रेण स्त्रीभिर्हृतशुभागमाः 6.4.18ab
ब्राह्मणानामतो युक्तं फलपर्यवसायिनाम् 3.8.67cd
ब्राह्मणास्तदभिध्यानाद्विदन्ति ब्रह्म निर्भयम् 5.1.127cd
ब्राह्मणास्तद्वदन्तीति स्वापराधनिषेधगीः 3.8.65ab
ब्राह्मणेन तदेवाभूदब्रह्मैवाविकृतात्मना 1.4.1638cd
ब्राह्मणैर्घातयिष्यामि मां जिघांसन्तमाश्विमम् 3.9.65ab
ब्राह्मणोक्तार्थदार्ढ्याय श्लोको मन्त्रोऽनुकीर्त्यते 1.5.376ab
ब्राह्मणोक्तिबलात्तस्मात्कामितोऽर्थो न सिध्यति 1.4.1652cd
ब्राह्मण्यं गौणमन्यत्र पूर्वभूमिषु नाञ्जसा 3.5.191cd
ब्राह्ममानाः समा ग्राह्या ब्रह्मलोकेषु तच्छ्रुतेः 6.2.141cd
ब्रुवाणं तं प्रति ब्रूयादिति श्रुत्यनुशासनम् 1.4.1047cd
ब्रूत कर्मणि को हेतुः सर्वानन्यत्वदर्शिनः 5.1.106cd
ब्रूतातो जगतो मूलं यतो भूयोऽभिजायते 3.9.146cd
ब्रूह्यतोऽश्व्येन शिरसा मधुविद्यां विमुक्तये 2.5.101cd
भगवत्पादभाष्येऽस्मिन्नन्यदीयोऽपि वर्ण्यते 1.4.1124cd
भगवत्संगतेर्नान्यः पुरुषार्थोऽमृतत्वतः 2.4.48ab
भगवन्ननुशाधीति यथेहाभिमतं तव 4.2.4cd
भगवन्सत्यरूपेण मद्धर्मोऽपि भवांस्तथा 5.17.10cd
भण्यतेऽतोऽप्रमाणत्वं शुक्तिकारजतादिवत् 1.4.482cd
भण्यते न परं ब्रह्म तस्य विद्यानपेक्षतः 1.4.1189cd
भण्यते वचसोक्तस्य निरिन्द्रियपरःसरम् 6.4.62cd
भयं त्वेकान्ततोऽविद्याकार्यमाहुर्विपश्चितः 4.3.1253ab
भयप्रध्वंसिनं हेतुमीक्षांचक्रेऽथ जातभीः 1.4.92ab
भयहेतुरविद्यैव सा च दुःस्थितसिद्धिका 4.2.93ab
भयहेतोरविद्यायाः सर्वज्ञत्वादसंभवात् 4.3.1894cd
भयहेतोर्निरासेन स ब्रह्माभयमश्नुते 4.4.1337cd
भयाहेतु यथातत्त्वदर्शनं कृतवान्विभुः 1.4.59cd

भरणात्सर्वकार्याणां प्राणो ब्रह्मेति भण्यते 3.9.30ab
भर्ता च संनिविष्टानां श्रेष्ठश्च गुणतो भवेत् 1.3.283ab
भर्ता श्रेष्ठः पुरो गन्ता ह्यन्नादोऽधिपतिस्तथा 1.3.246cd
भर्तृप्रपञ्चप्रस्थानमेवमेतद्यथोदितम् 1.4.1164ab
भर्तृप्रपञ्चभाष्यस्य प्रचारोऽयं प्रदर्शितः 1.4.1188ab
भल्लातकाङ्कवद्वस्त्रे न हि लोके स्फुरन्नपि SV 54ab
भवतैवाभ्युपेतव्यौ भिन्नाभिन्नत्वसिद्धये 4.3.1762cd
भवत्पक्षेऽपि तुल्यं चेन्नाविद्यामात्रहेतुतः 4.3.714ab
भवत्यतीव संशुद्धं प्रसन्नं व्यवतिष्ठते 4.3.1393cd
भवत्यत्ता स सर्वस्य नान्नं भवति कस्यचित् 6.1.35ab
भवत्येवात्र जिज्ञासोरज्ञस्यापि मुमुक्षतः SV 283cd
भवत्संन्यासवन्नूनमस्मद्धितकरं धनम् 2.4.46cd
भवद्भिक्षाटनादौ स्यादिति चेन्नैतदेव तु 1.3.107cd
भवद्भिरपि चैवैतदभ्युपेयं प्रयत्नतः SV 595ab
भवद्व्याख्यात एवार्थो न चास्य वचसो ध्रुवम् 4.4.831ab
भवद्व्याख्यानतोऽस्माभिरुक्ता दोषपरंपरा 4.4.832ab
भवानप्यहमेवेति यदा साक्षाद्विनिश्चयः 4.2.111ab
भवामो ब्रह्म नानाप्तं दशमो दशमं यथा 4.4.629cd
भवितारमपेक्ष्यैव भावः सिध्येन्न सोऽन्यथा 4.3.630ab
भविष्यच्च यदागामि नातीतं नापि वर्तते 3.8.7ab
भविष्यति न भाव्यर्थो वर्तमाननिषेधवत् 1.2.112cd
भविष्यत्कालसंबन्धि फलं चेह न नाकवत् 1.4.841ab
भविष्यद्देहसंबन्धी वाक्यादात्मा न चेन्मितः SV 1049ab
भविष्यद्वृत्तिमाश्रित्य यजमानः प्रजापतिः 1.3.14ab
भविष्यद्वृत्त्या लोकेऽपि प्रयोगो दृश्यते यथा 1.4.1201ab
भविष्यल्लोकसंबन्धी येषामागमतो मतः 3.4.5ab
भवेदिदानीं लोकस्य तथा कालान्तरेऽप्यभूत् 2.4.173cd
भवेदुपनिषन्नामा लाङ्गलं जीवनं यथा SV 8cd
भवेद्द्विकर्मसंयोगात्सप्तमी चाष्टमी च वाक् 2.2.29cd
भवेन्निःसाक्षिकैवेयमन्धकारप्रनृत्तवत् 4.3.370cd
भवेयं त्वत्प्रसादाद्वोः स्फीतः पुंभोगसाधनैः 6.3.58cd
भवेल्लोकजिदेवेह कर्मशून्यमपि ध्रुवम् 1.3.375cd

भस्मसात्करणादुक्तो विषासहिरितीश्वरैः 2.1.66cd
भस्मान्तमिति लिङ्गाच्च कर्मिणः स्यादुपस्थितिः 5.17.13ab
भाः प्रकाशोऽमलं ज्योतिः सा सत्यमविनाशतः 5.8.3ab
भाक्तं प्रियं परित्यज्य मुख्यं प्रियमुपाश्रयेत् 2.4.83cd
भाक्तैवानात्मसु प्रीतिर्यस्मात्तस्मादनात्मनः 1.4.1045ab
भागभागिविभागेन नाभिनेम्यरवत्तथा 1.4.950ab
भागभाग्यभिसंबन्धः ख्यातो बीजफलात्मनोः 1.4.547ab
भागवत्त्वं च संसिद्धं वाक्यवाक्यार्थयोरतः SV 869cd
भागान्तरप्रवेशेन भागत्यागेन च स्फुटम् SV 866ab
भागान्यथात्वादद्रव्यस्य नानित्यत्वं क्वचिन्मितम् 1.4.594ab
भागेषु निष्कलत्वैक्यनिःसामान्यत्वकारणात् 2.1.408cd
भाज्योतिरनुरोधेन सामर्थ्यादेव कारणात् 4.3.879cd
भानुचन्द्रमसोस्तेजो जलदैरभिभूयते 2.1.61ab
भानुनेवोदपात्रादेरारोहो नात्मनः स्वतः 4.3.1919cd
भानुप्रकाशवच्छब्दो नित्योऽयं न तु कृत्रिमः 2.4.307cd
भानुप्रकाशसंव्याप्तो विराजो विस्तृतिस्त्वियम् 3.3.152cd
भानुप्रकाशसंबन्धे भानोर्नान्यदपेक्षते 3.8.118cd
भानुमण्डलतो यस्माद्द्विगुणं चन्द्रमण्डलम् 2.1.54cd
भानुवद्बोधकं दृष्टं नातोऽनुष्ठेयतो मितिः 1.3.77cd
भानुस्यन्दनगत्याध्वा मितो यावानहर्निशम् 3.3.143ab
भानुदयं प्रपश्यामश्चोरदृग्रोगिदिग्दृशाम् 1.4.1037cd
भानौ तमोवत्तेनेदृग्ब्रह्म नैवोपपद्यते 1.4.1105cd
भान्वनुग्रहवत्पुंस आसनादिप्रसिद्धये 4.3.100cd
भान्वादिज्योतिषा तावद्व्यवहर्तुरनुग्रहः 4.3.284ab
भान्वादिज्योतिषा सोऽयं सम्यक्संदीपितेक्षणः 4.3.288ab
भान्वादिबाह्यज्योतिर्भिः संकीर्णः प्रागभूदयम् 4.3.895ab
भान्वादिवदतो बुद्धिं स्वाभासैकसहायवान् 4.3.89ab
भान्वादिवदतो राजा भूयः पप्रच्छ तं गुरुम् 4.3.71cd
भान्वादिष्वपि सर्वेषु तदेव प्राग्विवक्षितम् 4.3.65cd
भान्वादिसर्वज्योतिर्भ्यो विविक्तोऽयं पुमानिति 4.3.856ab
भान्वादेरिव कर्तृत्वं कर्त्राद्यर्थावभासनात् 4.3.927ab
भान्वाद्यनुग्रहाद्बोध आत्मनश्चक्षुरादिषु 4.3.871ab

भान्वाद्यनुग्रहाभावे तस्मादेष पुमानिह 4.3.82ab
भान्वाद्युद्दीपिताक्षः सन्प्रमात्रादिः प्रसिध्यति 4.3.57ab
भारमुत्सहते वोढुं योऽन्यो यामस्तमाश्रयम् 1.3.168cd
भार्याद्यनुज्ञापूर्वो हि संन्यासो विहितः श्रुतौ 2.4.39ab
भावकप्रत्यगात्मत्वादाकृतेश्च निषेधतः 2.4.203cd
भावनांशत्रयं यस्मादुपासनविधावपि 1.4.783ab
भावनाकर्मविद्यानामेवमुक्तेन वर्त्मना 4.4.193cd
भावनाकारकेक्षित्वादात्मैकः कारकायते 4.3.876cd
भावनागोचरं ज्ञानं बाह्यवस्त्ववलम्बनम् 3.4.147cd
भावना च तयोरेतत्त्रयं रेतोऽभिधीयते 1.2.176ef
भावनाजं फलं यत्स्याद्यच्च स्यात्कर्मणः फलम् 4.4.777ab
भावनाज्ञानकर्मभ्यो जन्मैषां तेन नान्यतः 1.4.1149cd
भावनाज्ञानकर्माणि तथा यान्ति तमस्विनम् 1.4.346cd
भावनाज्ञानकर्माणि साधनानीति यद्यपि 1.4.1145ab
भावनाज्ञानकर्मादि कार्योत्पत्तेः प्रयोजकम् 1.4.364ab
भावनाज्ञानकर्मादिसमुदायः प्रयोजकः 2.3.114cd
भावनाज्ञानसंतानसंरूढामविचालिनीम् 4.4.737cd
भावनाज्ञानसंतानैः प्रज्ञाकरणमुच्यते 4.4.708ab
भावनातो न चान्यत्र विधिरभ्युपगम्यते SV 252ab
भावनादिविशेषेषु यच्छान्तेष्ववशिष्यते 3.2.97ab
भावनानां विनिष्पत्तौ बोधे स्वप्नेऽथ भण्यते 4.3.1247cd
भावना बहुरूपासौ बहुरूपत्वमात्मनः 4.4.494ab
भावनारञ्जितज्ञानो भवतीति न निर्द्वयः 4.3.1266cd
भावनारञ्जितमतिसाक्षित्वादात्मवस्तुनः 4.3.1267ab
भावनारूपविज्ञानमभिव्यक्तं यदा हृदि 2.1.254ab
भावनार्थस्य नैवेह भाव्यर्थत्वात्तथार्थता 1.3.73cd
भावनावर्त्मनैकात्म्ये विध्यर्थासंभवो यथा SV 796ab
भावनाविग्रहो भूत्वा तत्र स्वप्नरिरंसया 4.3.1068ab
भावनाश्रयवद्भाति प्रत्यङ्जडधियामतः 4.3.1267cd
भावना स्वार्थरूपस्य प्रतीचोऽलुप्तचक्षुषः 4.3.885cd
भावनेयं यतः कर्मगुण एव सती सदा 4.3.1032cd
भावनैव विजृम्भन्ती स्थूलत्वमुपगच्छति 4.4.492ab

भावनोत्कर्षतोऽतोऽयं विचारस्तं प्रतीष्यते 1.3.322cd
भावनोपचयाद्देवो भूत्वा विद्वानिहैव तु 4.1.27ab
भावनोपचयाद्भूत्वा परिच्छेदं स्वमासुरम् 1.3.182ab
भावनोपचयान्नापि मुक्तिः स्याद्भङ्गुरत्वतः 1.4.1537cd
भावनोपचयाभावादेकैकस्मिंस्तथा सति 1.4.956cd
भावनोपचितं चेतो न च कैवल्यकारणम् 2.4.205ab
भावस्याभाव इत्यत्र षष्ठ्यर्थः कतमो मतः SV 946ab
भावात्मनाप्यतो भावो व्यवहाराय कल्पते SV 927cd
भावान्तरमभावश्चेत्सिद्धं वस्तु ततः स्वतः SV 952cd
भावान्तरमभावोऽपि निरूपाख्यः स नेष्यते SV 978cd
भावाभावग्रहो नापि सिध्येत्प्रत्यक्षमानतः 4.3.249ab
भावाभावत्वमज्ञानादतद्भूत्येव कल्पितम् 1.4.233cd
भावाभावद्वयध्वंसि ब्रह्म वेद्यं च तद्विदः 3.5.210cd
भावाभावपृथक्तापि यद्यभिन्ना ततोऽपृथक् SV 963ab
भावाभावविभागश्च स ब्रह्मास्मीति बोध्यते SV 1082cd
भावाभावविभिन्ना चेत्पृथक्ता न परस्परम् SV 963cd
भावाभावस्त्वभावोऽपि प्रसिद्धं जगति द्वयम् 4.3.793cd
भावाभावाख्यपदयोः सामर्थ्ये चेत्समासता SV 945ab
भावाभावातिरेकित्वादभ्युपेतं त्वयोच्यते 3.8.111cd
भावाभावात्मकस्यास्य कार्यकारणवस्तुनः 4.4.638ab
भावाभावात्मना स्थानं न निषेध्यस्य वस्तुनः 2.4.105ab
भावाभावात्मिका सिद्धिर्येयं सर्वाप्यनात्मनः 2.3.226ab
भावाभावादिमद्विश्वं सर्वमेतत्प्रसिध्यति 1.4.273cd
भावाभावादिरूपाय व्यवहाराय कल्पते SV 985cd
भावाभावार्थसाक्षित्वाद्भावाभावात्मिकैव सा 4.3.1756ab
भावाभावावभावेन प्रत्यक्षेणेव नेक्षते 4.4.665cd
भावाभावोऽपि किं चातः शृण्वतो यद्भविष्यति 4.3.797ab
भावाभावौ त्वविद्यादेर्विशेषः केवलस्त्विह 4.3.1754cd
भावाभावौ न वस्त्वेति प्रत्याख्यातं यदात्मना 1.4.334cd
भावाभावौ न वस्त्वेति प्रत्याख्यातं यदात्मना 3.4.114cd
भावाभावौ प्रमात्रादेस्तत्प्रसादात्प्रसिध्यतः 4.3.295cd
भावाभावौ प्रमात्रादेस्तद्विलक्षणरूपभृत् 4.3.272ab

भावाभावौ सतो न स्तः सत्त्वादेवासतः कुतः 4.3.1705ab
भावार्थविषयं कार्यं प्रसंख्याने कथं भवेत् SV 803ab
भावार्थस्य च साध्यत्वमिति तेनापि युज्यते SV 531cd
भावार्थाः कर्मशब्दा ये प्रतीयेत क्रिया ततः SV 243ab
भावितैः करणैश्चायं बहुसंसारयोनिषु 1.4.1587ab
भावितैः करणैश्चायं बहुसंसारयोनिषु 2.4.33ab
भावितैः करणैश्चायं बहुसंसारयोनिषु 4.4.1060ab
भाविनोऽर्थस्य विज्ञानं प्रत्यभिज्ञानमुच्यते 4.4.96ab
भाविनो जन्मनो रूपं स्वप्ने प्रायेण पश्यति 4.3.843cd
भावि यज्जन्म यच्चेदं प्रत्यक्षमनुभूयते 4.3.835ab
भाविलोकात्मिका यास्य प्रत्यक्चैतन्यबिम्बिता 4.4.78ab
भाविवृत्त्या स गौणस्तु प्रागतो ब्राह्मणो भवेत् 4.4.1296cd
भावैरर्थक्रिया सर्वा यथा दीपादिभिस्तथा 4.3.619cd
भावो वा यदि वाभावो ज्ञानवन्माननिश्चितः 4.3.540ab
भावो वा स्यादभावो वा सोऽस्त्येवेति विनिश्चितिः 4.3.566cd
भाव्यतेऽसन्नपीहार्थस्तस्यान्यत्र प्रसिद्धितः 1.4.895ab
भाव्युच्छेत्तुमशक्यस्ते भूतोऽप्युपरतः स्वतः SV 394ab
भाष्यकृद्भिः कृतो यत्नः स आविष्क्रियतेऽधुना 1.4.754cd
भाष्यस्य वार्तिकोक्त्यैवमध्यायः सप्तमो गतः 5.17.23cd
भाष्योपात्तमतो ब्रूमो नानुपात्तं कथं चन 3.2.46ab
भास्वज्ज्ञानं भवेत्तेजो रसः प्राणो विवक्षितः 1.2.154ab
भास्वत्स्वार्थं चिदेकस्थमदः पूर्णमिहोच्यते 5.1.18cd
भास्वद्धीसंश्रयं ज्ञानं भाःशब्देन तदुच्यते 4.3.877cd
भास्वराभास्वरत्वं च प्रत्यक्षेणैव वीक्ष्यते 4.3.150ab
भिक्षया लक्ष्यते चर्या ह्यकिंचन्यैकसंश्रया 3.5.127ab
भिक्षां दातुमलं तद्वज्ज्ञेयं स्वार्थपरार्थयोः 1.4.578cd
भिक्षाचर्यं चरन्तीति विध्यर्थः क्रियते महान् 3.5.165cd
भिक्षाटनादिना नर्ते प्रधानं हि समाप्यते 4.4.1240cd
भिक्षाटनाद्यनुष्ठानं तादर्थ्यान्न निषिध्यते 4.4.1237cd
भिद्यते हृदयग्रन्थिर्ब्रह्माप्येतीति च श्रुतेः 1.3.83ab
भिद्यते हृदयग्रन्थिश्छिद्यन्ते सर्वसंशयाः SV 296ab
भिद्यते हृदयग्रन्थिश्छिद्यन्ते सर्वसंशयाः 3.2.80ab

भिनत्ति सर्वमर्यादां नान्वयाद्यप्यपेक्षते 1.2.182cd
भिन्नं चेत्कारणात्कार्यं कार्यकारणता तयोः 2.1.399ab
भिन्नं बोधात्तमोध्वस्तौ नेतीत्यात्मावशिष्यते 5.1.21cd
भिन्नं ब्रह्मापरिज्ञानात्संसारित्वं तथात्मनः 2.5.144ab
भिन्नं वा स्यान्न वा भिन्नं सामान्यं चेद्विशेषतः 4.3.1651ab
भिन्नः शरीरतः सिद्धः प्रमाता प्रत्यभिज्ञया 4.3.222cd
भिन्नग्राहकसंवेद्यं घटदीपादि सद्ध्रुवम् 4.3.560ab
भिन्नत्वात्संगतिर्न स्याद्विशेषणविशेष्ययोः 4.3.1720cd
भिन्नदेशस्थितिस्त्वत्र वास्तवी नोपपद्यते 2.3.239cd
भिन्नदेशेषु तेष्वेकस्तथा चावयवी कथम् 2.1.409cd
भिन्नद्रव्यसमूहस्य मुख्यैकत्वं न युज्यते 2.1.478ab
भिन्नप्रकरणं ज्ञानं काङ्क्षितं न च कर्मणा SV 372ab
भिन्नप्रमेयतायां च श्रोत्रादीनां यथा तथा 2.1.555ab
भिन्नमातृप्रमाणादौ कार्यकारणवस्तुनि 1.4.1330ab
भिन्नमात्रादिविज्ञाने सापेक्षैव विनिश्चितिः 2.4.223ab
भिन्नमानप्रमात्रादौ कार्यकारणवस्तुनि 3.4.132ab
भिन्नरूपाणि कर्माणि बहुकारकसंश्रयात् SV 375cd
भिन्नसामान्ययोस्तद्वत्तदसाधारणात्मनः 1.4.630cd
भिन्नस्यौपगवापत्यप्रत्ययार्थस्य गम्यते SV 118cd
भिन्नहेतुनिषेधार्थं स्वयंभु ब्रह्म शब्द्यते 2.6.4cd
भिन्नाः कैरनुमीयन्त इति पृष्टो वदेद्यदि 2.1.597ab
भिन्नात्मनोस्तयोर्दोषो ब्रह्मत्वप्रतिपादिकाः 2.1.430ab
भिन्नाधिकरणज्ञानान्नैवमप्यभिदा तयोः 1.6.66ab
भिन्नाधिकारितालिङ्गं कर्मविज्ञानकाण्डयोः SV 223cd
भिन्नानुभूतितो नापि मिथस्तासामसंगतेः 4.3.1676cd
भिन्नाभिन्नं न वो वस्तु येन मानाविरोधिता SV 914ab
भिन्नाभिन्नं विरुद्धत्वान्नैकमानस्य गोचरः SV 955cd
भिन्नाभिन्नत्वगीर्यापि सापि दुःस्थितसिद्धिका 1.4.1273ab
भिन्नाभिन्नत्वपक्षोऽपि विरोधान्न च युज्यते 4.3.635ab
भिन्नाभिन्नत्ववचसा न चैकार्थोऽपि भण्यते 4.3.1764ab
भिन्नाभिन्नत्ववाचेह तत्कृतं खातपूरितम् 4.3.1767ab
भिन्नाभिन्नत्ववादेऽपि ब्रह्माभिन्नात्मना भवेत् 1.4.1286ab

भिन्नाभिन्नत्ववादेऽस्मिन्यो भिन्नो भवतोच्यते 4.3.1761ab
भिन्नाभिन्नप्रसिद्ध्यर्थं न चेयं श्रुतिरिष्यते 4.3.1750cd
भिन्नाभिन्नविकल्पार्हं त्वत्प्रत्यक्षं च नेष्यते 4.3.703cd
भिन्नाभिन्नात्मकं तस्मात्सर्वं वस्त्विति निश्चयः 1.6.51cd
भिन्नाभिन्नात्मकं ब्रह्म नामरूपादिवज्जगुः 1.6.46cd
भिन्नाभिन्नात्मकं वस्तु स्थापयन्त्यविशेषतः 4.3.1645cd
भिन्नाभिन्नात्मतां नैति द्वैरूप्यासंभवात्तयोः 1.6.63cd
भिन्नाभिन्नात्मतापक्षहानिरेवं प्रसज्यते 1.6.70cd
भिन्नाभिन्नात्मता यद्वत्स्थूलेष्वर्थेषु दृश्यते 1.6.50ab
भिन्नाभिन्नात्मता शक्या कर्तुं साक्षादपीश्वरैः 4.3.1778cd
भिन्नाभिन्नेक्षणं सर्वं यथोक्तन्यायवर्त्मना 1.6.93cd
भिन्नाभेदादभिन्नस्य भेदः स्यात्पिण्डवद्ध्रुवम् 1.6.83ab
भिन्नार्थत्वावबोधित्वाद्वाक्ययोर्न विरुद्धता 2.1.561cd
भिन्नार्थप्रतिषेधत्वादभिन्नवचसस्तव 4.3.1764cd
भिन्नार्थयोर्न संबन्धो ह्यन्योऽन्यार्थानपेक्षतः SV 317ab
भिन्नार्थानभिसंबन्धात्प्रतीच्येवास्य धीरभूत् 1.4.41cd
भिन्नाविव समीक्ष्येते देवतैकैव सा सती 5.6.2cd
भिन्ने भिन्नेऽपि मेये धीर्नानुवादोऽन्यबोद्धरि SV 743cd
भिन्नोऽर्थो भेदशब्दार्थान्न तथाभेदशब्दतः 4.3.1765cd
भिन्नौ च धर्मभेदेन तस्मादुभयथा श्रुतिः 6.2.97ab
भिन्नौ जातिगुणौ द्रव्यात्स्वानुभूत्यनुरोधतः 1.6.72ab
भीतं प्रत्यविशिष्टोऽसौ वास्तवत्वादनादृतः 1.4.1174cd
भुक्तत्वादविवक्षेह व्यतिक्रान्तस्य जन्मनः 4.3.844ab
भुक्तदेहादिदं लिङ्गमुत्क्रान्तं भोगसंक्षयात् 4.3.1915ab
भुक्त्वातिलङ्घनं तावद्विनापि सुतजन्मना 1.5.246ab
भुक्त्वा भोगानथ श्रान्तः पक्षौ संहृत्य चात्मनि 4.3.1171cd
भुङ्क्ते गत्वा च यत्तत्र देहारम्भे च कारणम् 4.4.109cd
भुज्यमानान्यपि ततो न क्षीयन्ते प्रबन्धतः 1.5.86ab
भुञ्जते पय एवाग्रे क्रमेणान्यत्तृणादि हि 1.5.49ab
भुञ्जते पय एवाग्रे तेषामन्नमतोऽस्तु तत् 1.5.48cd
भुवः स्वाहेति मन्थस्य द्वितीयामाहुतिं क्षिपेत् 6.3.50cd
भुवो हि स्पर्शवत्त्वस्य लोकेऽस्मिन्सुप्रसिद्धितः 4.3.751cd

भूतं भवद्भविष्यं च साध्यं साधनमेव च 2.1.11cd
भूतं यत्समतिक्रान्तं भवद्यदधुनातनम् 3.8.6cd
भूतकालोपलब्धोऽर्थः स्मृतेश्चेद्गोचरो मतः 1.4.456ab
भूतजन्मनि यद्भुक्तं कर्म तद्भावनाञ्जितः 4.3.841ab
भूतत्रयं पृथिव्यादि देहेऽपि परिगृह्यते 2.3.69ab
भूतत्रयस्य मर्तस्य रसो मण्डलमभ्यधाः 2.3.59ab
भूतद्वयममर्तं च वायुश्चाकाशमेव च 2.3.27cd
भूतद्वयरसो ज्ञेयो मण्डले चेतनः पुमान् 2.3.51ab
भूतपञ्चकमेवेदं साधारण्याद्भवेत्सदा 1.3.259cd
भूतपापैरसंकीर्णो दैवं सुखमुपाश्नुते 1.5.347cd
भूतपालस्ततो देवः कार्याणां कारणत्वतः 4.4.1009cd
भूतभौतिकमात्राः स्युः सर्वावानुच्यते ततः 4.3.864cd
भूतमात्राः प्रदीपस्य संतानेनार्चिषो यथा 3.2.70cd
भूतमात्रावदित्येवं समानं चोद्यमावयोः 4.3.1126cd
भूतमात्राविशेषत्वात्ताभ्यामात्मा न चेत्पृथक् 4.3.1087cd
भूतमात्राविशेषत्वादुभयोरपि लोकयोः 4.3.428cd
भूतराशेरगाल्लिङ्गं कर्मराशिः सकाशतः 2.3.121ab
भूतसंयोगतः प्राप्तं न च तत्पाञ्चभौतिकम् 2.3.110ab
भूतादिव्यक्तितो व्यक्तिरग्रजस्यापि नान्यथा 5.5.8ab
भूताधिपतिशब्देन ब्रह्मा वात्राभिधीयते 4.4.1011ab
भूतानां च पृथिव्याश्च मिथःकार्यत्वहेतुतः 2.5.21ab
भूतानां परिणामोऽयं यथाकर्म यथाश्रुतम् 2.1.416cd
भूतानि क्षीयमाणानि कर्मणा परमात्मनः 3.2.67ab
भूतानि चैव सर्वाणि वायुना ग्रथितान्यतः 3.7.17cd
भूतानि जनिमन्त्येष यतः पालयतीश्वरः 4.4.1009ab
भूतानि रमिति प्रोक्तस्तस्मात्प्राणोऽपि सूरिभिः 5.14.13cd
भूतानि वा रजोवाचा भण्यन्तेऽत्राखिलानि तु 5.16.22cd
भूतान्वयस्य चासत्त्वान्नापि लिङ्गात्प्रसिध्यति 4.3.215cd
भूतापीतिं मनुः साक्षाद्दर्शयत्यविनश्वरीम् 3.3.131cd
भूतार्थवादस्तद्धानादर्थवादस्त्रिधा मतः SV 567cd
भूताहिंसाविधिर्यस्मान्नाग्नीषोमीयमारभित् 4.4.1223ab
भूतेभ्यश्च चिदुत्पत्तिर्न प्रत्यक्षप्रमाणिका 4.3.215ab

भूतेभ्यो नापरं वस्तु यस्मादात्मन ईक्ष्यते 4.4.34ab
भूतेषु देवतादेस्तदश्रुतं गृह्यते कथम् 2.5.79cd
भूतेहानुविधायित्वात्क्षेत्रज्ञस्य तमस्विनः 1.3.126ab
भूत्वाप इति लिङ्गाच्च आपः श्रद्धाभिधास्ततः 6.2.90cd
भूत्वाभवंस्तथाभूत्वा भवंश्चेहातथात्मना 4.3.332ab
भूत्वा समाहित इति समाधानं विधास्यते 4.4.1231ab
भूत्वेत्यस्याभिसंबन्धः सर्वैः शान्तादिभिः पदैः 4.4.1270ab
भूमा तत्सुखमित्येवं छान्दोग्योपनिषद्वचः 3.9.169ab
भूमिरित्यादिवाक्येन त्रिलोक्यष्टाक्षरोच्यते 5.16.5ab
भूमिशय्या पयःपानं ब्रह्मचर्यं च वाग्यमः 6.3.11ab
भूमिष्ठे मधुनि प्राप्ते को विद्वान्पर्वतं व्रजेत् 4.4.1143ab
भूमौ यथाहितं लोहं भूमित्वमुपगच्छति 4.4.726ab
भूम्नश्च लक्षणं चक्रे यत्र नान्यदिति स्वयम् 2.4.99ab
भूम्न्येव तु परा निष्ठानन्दस्येति श्रुतेर्वचः 2.1.361cd
भूयःफला यतो विद्या पूर्वाभ्यां तेन सादराः 1.5.257ab
भूयसां चाप्युपन्यासो बाह्यानां ज्योतिषामिह 4.3.46ab
भूयस्त्वात्तेजसश्चोष्णः सुकुमारस्तथा मरुत् 2.4.339cd
भूयांसोऽतोऽसुरा देवाः कनीयांसोऽतियत्नजाः 1.3.25cd
भूयान्स साधुना नेति ज्ञानस्य फलमुच्यते 4.4.979ab
भूयोऽधिकारभेदेन वागादीनां तथा भिदा 1.3.21cd
भूयोऽपि परिहारोक्तौ भवेत् पिष्टस्य पेषणम् 4.4.681cd
भूयोऽपि भुञ्जते गेहे ब्राह्मणा इति दर्शनात् 4.3.584ab
भूयोऽपि लभते संज्ञां लीनं सत्कारणात्मनि 2.4.478ab
भूयोऽपि सा मृतेरूर्ध्वं नेष्यतीत्यत्र का प्रमा 4.4.914cd
भूयोऽपीह प्रवक्ष्यामः प्रसङ्गान्नातिविस्तरात् 3.3.57cd
भूयोऽप्यस्यैव दार्ढ्यार्थं पूर्वपक्षाय यत्यते 1.4.1236ab
भूयोऽप्राक्षीन्मुनिं विद्वान्याथात्म्यार्थावबुद्धये 3.5.31cd
भूयोऽमृतेन तद्ग्रस्तं मृतं चापि स्वतो यतः 5.5.13cd
भूयोऽसह्यमहादुःखनीडदेहप्रवेशन- 4.4.615ab
भूयो दुःखं किमन्यत्स्यान्नित्यानुष्ठानहानितः 1.4.13cd
भूयो बलेन ते देवा आसुरेण निराश्रयाः 1.3.30ab
भूयो यजेयेति वचः सदा तद्भावभावनात् 1.2.200cd

भूयोल्पीयःफलत्वं चेत्तुल्यसाधनयोर्न तत् 1.3.311ab

भूरि कर्म करिष्यामि तत्फलानन्त्यसिद्धये 1.4.1679ab

भूरिकल्याणदातृत्वात्सुदत्र इति भण्यते 6.4.124ab

भूरिकारकसाध्या च क्रिया लोकेऽपि दृश्यते 3.9.179cd

भूरिक्रियावांस्तु नरस्तथानेकेश्वरोऽवशः 1.4.1574ab

भूरिजात्यभिसंबन्धो जन्यकर्मवशात्स्त्रियाः 1.4.119ab

भूरि दूषणमत्रोक्तं श्रुत्या च स्वयमेव च 3.2.63ab

भूरिदोषोपदुष्टत्वात्परिसंख्याविधेरिति 6.3.15cd

भूरिनानाप्रभेदेन प्रत्यात्मं व्यवतिष्ठते 1.3.312cd

भूरिभेदान्न शक्यन्ते वक्तुं रूपाण्यशेषतः 4.4.193ef

भूरिशब्दानुचिन्तायास्तन्निषेधप्रसिद्धये 4.4.963cd

भूरिसाधनसाध्यत्वात्क्रियाणां नो विभिन्नता 2.1.601cd

भूरिसाधनसाध्यत्वात्क्रियाणामिति चेद्भवेत् 2.1.602ab

भूरिसाधनसापेक्षा सुखदुःखफलप्रदा 3.4.94cd

भूरिसामान्यविज्ञानाच्छौक्ल्यमेव करोति किम् 1.4.472ab

भूर्यर्थता प्रकाशादेः प्रत्यक्षादेव कारणात् 1.5.345ab

भूर्लोकं जानतर्ग्वेदं देवा माता च वागियम् 1.5.156ab

भूर्लोकादिषु सर्वेषु मनोवाक्प्राणलक्षणम् 1.5.160ab

भूर्लोकाद्यात्मकं सोऽश्वमात्मानं निरवग्रहम् 1.2.214cd

भेदं न लभते मेये मेयादन्यत्र न प्रमा 5.1.88cd

भेदं पश्यन्यदि मृतो बद्ध एव भवेन्नरः 1.4.1727ab

भेदः किमाश्रयस्तस्य विरोधान्न द्वयाश्रयः 5.1.90cd

भेदः पुत्रादिभावे तु जन्यत्वं वस्तुकल्पितम् SV 956ef

भेदः प्रमान्तरैः सिद्धो न त्वागमसमाश्रयात् 5.1.97ab

भेदः स एवायमिति कालरूपादिभेदतः 4.3.663ab

भेदकारणविध्वस्तौ भेदधीर्विनिवर्तते 4.3.1322cd

भेदग्राहि न नो मानं कृत्स्नेऽपि जगतीक्ष्यते 4.3.1647ab

भेदग्राहि न नो मानं घटादावपि विद्यते 1.4.137ab

भेदग्राहि न नो मानं लौकिकं वैदिकं च यत् 5.1.84ab

भेदग्राहि न नो मानमितोऽन्यत्रापि विद्यते 4.4.336ab

भेददर्शनमेवात उपास्त इति भण्यते 1.4.1568cd

भेददृष्टेर्बलीयस्त्वात्तस्याः स्वाभाविकत्वतः 1.4.1728ab

भेददृष्ट्यपवादाच्च मृत्योरिति विनिन्दनात् 5.1.81cd
भेदधीविषयो यश्च तस्मात्सद्धीर्निवर्तते 4.3.1686cd
भेदभेदवतोर्भित्तावनवस्था प्रसज्यते 4.3.1652ab
भेदमेकात्मतां यातावित्ति षष्ठी न संमता SV 528cd
भेदसंसर्गनाशार्थो नात उक्तेरिहेष्यते 1.4.1431ab
भेदसंसर्गहानार्थमेवंयत्नामपि श्रुतिम् 4.3.1809ab
भेदसंसर्गहीनत्वात्पदवाक्यार्थतात्मनः 1.4.1408ab
भेदसंसर्गहीनोऽर्थः स्वमहिम्नि व्यवस्थितः 3.5.190cd
भेदसंसर्गहीनोऽर्थस्तद्धेतुध्वंसवर्त्मना 3.5.100ab
भेदस्पृङ्नाक्षजाद्येवं न तेनैकात्म्यबाधनम् SV 919cd
भेदस्य चापुमर्थत्वात्तादर्थ्ये स्यादमानता SV 918ab
भेदस्य विलयो वेदे गम्यते कस्यचित्क्वचित् SV 378cd
भेदस्यातोऽन्यतः प्राप्तेर्न श्रुत्या तत्र यत्यते 4.3.1751cd
भेदस्यैवं च मिथ्यात्वं प्रत्यक्षेण विरुध्यते 4.3.482cd
भेदहेतुतमोघातिप्रत्यग्याथात्म्यशेमुषी- 3.4.33cd
भेदाः सामान्यतां यान्ति सामान्यं भेदतां यदि 1.6.77ab
भेदादधिकृतेरेषामग्न्यादीनामनेकधा 1.4.126ab
भेदादुत्तमसौख्यस्य साधनं चोत्तमा भवेत् 4.3.1873cd
भेदाभेदात्मकं सर्वं वस्तु दृष्टं यतस्ततः 4.3.1640ab
भेदाभेदात्मकत्वाच्चेदेकस्यापीह वस्तुनः SV 170ab
भेदाभेदाश्रयत्वेन ह्यैकात्म्यज्ञानकर्मणोः SV 359ab
भेदाभेदौ न च स्यातां विरोधाद्युगपत्क्वचित् SV 913cd
भेदाशङ्कापनुत्त्यर्थं स उ लोक इतीर्यते 4.4.623cd
भेदेऽसति गतिः केयं गन्तृगन्तव्ययोर्भवेत् 1.4.1242cd
भेदेन व्यपदेशार्हा सर्वमेवं समञ्जसम् 5.1.56cd
भेदे वा यदि वाभेदे संसृतेर्ब्रह्मणा सह SV 174ab
भेदे विशेष एव स्यात्सामान्यं खण्डमुण्डवत् 4.3.1651cd
भेदेषु चोपयुक्तं तन्नोत्वं यद्वा पृथक्स्थितम् 1.6.62ab
भेदोऽतस्तन्निवृत्त्यर्थं मधुत्वेनैकतोच्यते 2.5.10cd
भेदोऽयं लक्ष्यते मोहाद्रवेः स्वोत्थैर्जलैरिव 4.3.1638cd
भेदो वर्णेषु सर्वेषु ब्रह्मक्षत्रादिलक्षणः 1.4.126cd
भेरीं च दुन्दुभिं विद्यात्तेनोर्ध्वं यात्युपासकः 5.12.4cd

भेर्याघातग्रहाद्वापि तद्विशेषग्रहो भवेत् 2.4.280ab
भोक्तरीह यदाभाति तत्प्रमाणफलं स्मृतम् 3.4.109cd
भोक्तव्यं तन्मयेदानीं मरणात्समनन्तरम् 4.4.1169cd
भोक्तारं दर्शयित्वाथ राजा गार्ग्यमपृच्छत 2.1.183cd
भोक्तारश्चापि ये तेषां तेऽपि श्रुत्योपवर्णिताः 1.5.96cd
भोक्तुः स्वरूपविज्ञप्त्या इह नाडीपरिग्रहः 4.3.1220ab
भोक्तृत्वं नाम धर्मः स्याच्चक्षुषो दर्शनं यथा 4.3.425cd
भोक्तृत्वमपि तस्येह चैतन्याभासवर्त्मना 4.3.1583cd
भोक्तृत्वमेव पुंसोऽस्ति भोज्यत्वं न मनागपि 2.1.102ab
भोक्तृत्वे सत्यपि तथा प्राणेऽप्यप्रतिबोधनम् 2.1.127cd
भोक्तृप्रयुक्तं कर्तृत्वं कर्त्रा कर्म प्रयुज्यते 2.1.220ab
भोक्तृभोक्तव्ययोस्तत्त्वं वक्तुं युक्तमतोऽञ्जसा 2.1.205cd
भोक्तृभोग्यविवेकेन श्रुत्यैकात्म्यं प्रबोध्यते 2.1.169cd
भोक्तृभोग्याभिसंबन्धश्चेतनाचेतनात्मनोः 2.5.23cd
भोक्तृभोग्याभिसंबन्धस्तन्निमित्तोऽयमात्मनः 2.4.350ab
भोक्तृसंयोगतस्तद्वद्भोक्तृत्वं देवतात्मनः 2.1.182cd
भोक्तेह गम्यते लोके न त्वनात्ममितिप्रमः 2.1.168cd
भोक्तैव भोत्स्यते शब्दं न त्वभोक्ता परो जडः 2.1.113cd
भोक्त्रर्थ एव नान्योऽतः प्रधानं भोक्तुरिष्यते SV 472cd
भोक्त्री कर्त्री च सर्वत्र तस्य भोज्यमतोऽपरम् 2.1.58cd
भोगं भङ्गुरमीक्षन्ते बुद्धिशुद्ध्यनुरोधतः SV 1131cd
भोगक्षयेण काम्यानां निषिद्धानां च कर्मणाम् 3.2.81ab
भोगदस्यैव भोगेन सृज्यमानत्वहेतुतः 1.5.81ab
भोगमात्रप्रसिद्ध्यर्थं चैतन्याभासमात्रतः 4.3.1226ab
भोगमोक्षाभिसंबन्धी यं प्रत्येतत्प्रवर्तते 3.2.153cd
भोगसाधनभावश्च भक्षयन्तीति भण्यते 6.2.152ab
भोगे न च क्षयं याति तदेव वसु दीयताम् 2.4.62cd
भोगेन प्रक्षयाद्भोक्तुस्तद्वशीकारिकर्मणः 5.6.7cd
भोगेनेहापचीयन्ते प्रचीयन्ते च कर्मभिः 4.3.866cd
भोग्यता प्रथमान्तेन पृथिव्यादेरिहोच्यते 2.5.22ab
भोग्यत्वं चास्य देहस्य प्रत्यक्षैकप्रमाणकम् 4.3.273ab
भोग्यत्वात्सा विराडुक्ता तद्भोक्ता दक्षिणाक्षिगः 4.2.44cd

भोग्यभोक्तृत्वसंबन्धस्तस्मात्सिद्धः परस्परम् 2.5.21cd
भोग्यानां व्यभिचारेऽपि भोक्तैकोऽव्यभिचारवान् 2.1.176cd
भोजनादिनिरोधेन न च तस्याः प्रमेक्ष्यते 1.4.1516cd
भोजनादिनिरोधेन संततिश्चेत्समर्थ्यते 1.4.1515ab
भोजनादौ न च सति ज्ञानसंततिरिष्यते 1.4.1512cd
भोजनेऽभिहिते पुंसो ह्यर्थात्तृप्तिः प्रतीयते 1.4.1834cd
भोज्यत्वेन जगत्कृत्स्नं कर्मविद्यादिसाधनैः 1.4.1467ab
भौतिकत्वेन चेज्ज्योतिर्देहानुग्राहकं मतम् 4.3.227ab
भौतिकस्तु प्रकाशोऽयं भौतिकार्थप्रकाशनात् 4.4.28ab
भौतिकस्यैव कुम्भादेर्भौतिकैरेव वीक्ष्यते 4.3.139ab
भौतिकाकाशविषयो न कथं चन युज्यते 2.1.453cd
भौतिकान्येव तानीति प्रत्यङ् तेभ्यो विलक्षणः 4.4.42cd
भ्रमत्सु तद्वज्जीवेषु प्राप्नुतः परमात्मनः 2.1.488cd
भ्रमसि प्राणभूतस्त्वं न ह्येकत्रावतिष्ठसे 6.3.26cd
भ्रमसीत्यादिना मन्थं स्मरंस्तद्देवतां हृदा 6.3.26ab
भ्रमोऽयमग्निव्यापारादुष्णादेर्जन्मकल्पना 4.4.317cd
भ्रातृव्यास्ते सहोत्पत्तेः प्रत्यग्दृष्टयपहारतः 2.2.10cd
भ्रान्तिः पूर्वेषु कार्येषु लयोऽयमिति मोहतः 2.4.374cd
भ्रूणघ्नसहचारित्वाच्चाण्डालो ब्राह्मणीसुतः 4.3.1361cd
भ्रूणहत्याश्वमेधाभ्यां न परं पापपुण्ययोः 3.3.7ab
मकरी ननु दृष्टान्तो भिन्नाभिन्नत्वसिद्धिकृत् 5.1.77ab
मणेरेव विकारोऽयं यालक्तादिसरूपता 4.3.1584ab
मणेर्नीलादिवद्भेदो दृष्ट्यादिप्रत्यगात्मनः 4.3.1758cd
मण्डलात्मनि चाधारे लिङ्गात्मैवावसीयताम् 2.3.64ab
मण्डलायतने यत्तु कारणं संश्रितं विभोः 2.3.45ab
मण्यादीनां प्रवृत्तिर्हि पुंसां तैरपि दृश्यते 4.3.49cd
मतं कार्यानभिव्यक्तिर्निमित्तासंभवाद्यदि SV 65ab
मतं गुणिविनाशेन तद्गुणोऽपि विनङ्क्ष्यति 4.3.1551ab
मतं चेदस्वभावोऽसौ यो नैकार्थप्रवृत्तिमान् 4.3.745ab
मतं चेन्न फलत्वेन मोक्षो नित्योऽभ्युपेयते 3.3.86ab
मतं चेन्नैतदेवं स्याद्युगपद्वृत्त्यसंभवात् 1.4.582cd
मतं जक्षणवन्मुक्तौ सर्वात्मत्वात्परात्मनः 3.9.202ab

मतं जन्मान्तराभ्याससंस्कारोत्थमिदं यदि 1.4.73ab
मतं तद्भाजमानं स्याज्ज्ञानं यत्प्रागुदीरितम् 1.3.384ab
मतं तार्किकसमयविरोधश्चेत्प्रसज्यते 1.4.573ab
मतं त्र्यन्नात्मसंप्राप्तेरूर्ध्वं भोगस्य भुक्तितः 1.4.1742ab
मतं दुःखिन एवासौ संपदर्थं विधीयते 1.4.1249ab
मतं न जायमानोऽस्ति जातत्वादेव कारणात् 3.9.143ab
मतं नालं प्ररोहाय ये कामाः प्रत्यगात्मनि 4.4.456ab
मतं पुमर्थसिद्ध्यर्थं ज्ञानस्य विधिरिष्यते SV 671ab
मतं प्रवेशश्रवणादस्तु सावयवः परः 1.4.538ab
मतं प्राणसजातीया धीरेवात्मेति चेन्न तत् 4.3.327ab
मतं मूर्तेतरे रूपे ब्रह्मणोऽभिमते सदा 2.3.143ab
मतं यथा मृतौ देवास्त्यक्त्वा स्वं स्वमनुग्रहम् 4.3.1138ab
मतं वा किं मनोमात्रं देहाद्देहान्तरं व्रजेत् 4.4.127ef
मतं वाक्योत्थविज्ञानमात्राच्चेन्न निराकृतिः 1.4.822ab
मतं वाक्योत्थविज्ञानस्मृतिसंतानता यदि 1.4.831ab
मतं विद्यारसाकृष्टो विद्यां भूयोऽपि चेन्नृपः 4.4.534ab
मतं विषयसंसिद्ध्या कार्यमित्यभिधीयते SV 1034ab
मतं संततिमात्रत्वे निश्चितिः स्यात्तथापि च 1.4.1518ab
मतमज्ञानमेवैतत्कर्म नाशयतीति चेत् 3.3.94ab
मतमन्ते विनाशश्चेत्कोऽयमन्तस्त्वयोच्यते 4.3.603ab
मतमव्यतिरेकेण रातोऽसत्सत्तदिष्यताम् 1.2.13ab
मतमुत्पद्यते नासौ नापि साक्षाद्विनश्यति 4.3.601ab
मतिसंवाददोषेण काश्येनोत्सारिते रवौ 2.1.53ab
मतोऽवबोधोऽनित्यश्चेत्कादाचित्कं तदार्थवत् 2.1.200cd
मत्तः शरीरात्क्वान्यत्र मय्येवातः प्रतिष्ठितम् 3.9.84ab
मत्तो यन्नान्यदस्तीति ह्यथ कस्माद्बिभेम्यहम् 1.4.92cd
मत्वर्थानुपपत्तेश्च क्षणिकत्वाद्यसंभवः 4.3.610ab
मत्वास्तमित इत्येवं मुहुर्विप्रमचूचुदत् 4.3.42cd
मत्स्यदृष्टान्तवचस एतावत्फलमिष्यते 4.3.1148ab
मत्स्याभिसंगतिर्यद्वत्पर्यायेणेह कूलयोः 4.3.1125ab
मदभ्युपगमो यद्वद्भवतोऽपि तथा यदि 4.3.258ab
मधुकाण्डागमार्थस्य यथावत्प्रतिपत्तये 6.5.4ab

मधुकाण्डार्थसर्वस्वं वाक्येन प्रतिपाद्यते 2.4.37cd
मधु नक्तमथो रात्रिर्मधुरा दुःखहानिकृत् 6.3.48cd
मधुब्राह्मणमारब्धमियमित्याद्यथोत्तरम् 2.5.9cd
मधुब्राह्मणमेतत्तद्यत्प्रागुक्तमभूत्स्फुटम् 2.5.106ab
मधुब्राह्मणमेतत्तु न युक्तं प्रतिभाति नः 2.5.14cd
मधुब्राह्मणविद्यायामिदमेव प्रवक्ष्यते 1.4.1792ab
मधुविद्याप्रसङ्गेन विस्पष्टमभिधास्यते 1.5.12cd
मधु सर्वाणि भूतानि यथा पूर्वमवादिषम् 2.5.27cd
मध्यदेशावधिस्तस्माद्दिगन्त इति गृह्यते 1.3.221ab
मध्यमोऽयं तृतीयस्तु ताभ्यां राशिः प्रयोजकः 2.3.113cd
मध्ये जडस्वभावोऽयं ज्योतिषोर्वर्तते पुमान् 4.3.36ab
मध्ये वयसि कार्कश्यात्कारणानामिहार्जिताः 4.3.842ab
मध्ये वाक्यच्छिदोऽभावादितिशब्दस्य पूर्ववत् 3.9.104cd
मनआदित्रयं कार्यं तादर्थ्येनोत्तरा श्रुतिः 1.5.97cd
मनआदेरशेषस्य प्रत्यगज्ञानहेतुतः 4.4.765ab
मन आयतनं तत्र वागादीनां हि वृत्तयः 6.1.13ab
मन एव ततो ज्ञेयं शरीरेन्द्रियसंहतिः 1.5.116cd
मन एव मनुष्याणां कारणं बन्धमोक्षयोः 4.4.889ab
मन एवेत्यतः प्राज्ञाः सर्वरूपं प्रचक्षते 1.5.122cd
मनःकरणसंबन्धाद्देहेऽप्यस्योपजायते 4.3.361ab
मनःप्रधानः संघात आत्मचैतन्यबिम्बितः 4.3.285ab
मनः साधारणं दृष्टं सर्वज्ञानैकहेतुतः 4.4.650cd
मननात्मकमेवास्य कर्म नान्यद्यतस्ततः 4.4.1072ab
मननाद्यर्थवत्त्वाय पश्येदिति विधीयते SV 763cd
मनश्च ज्योतिर्विज्ञानं संकल्पादिस्वलक्षणम् 3.9.36ab
मनसश्चन्द्रभावो हि सर्वत्र श्रूयते स्फुटः 1.5.180ab
मनसा ज्ञाननिर्देशस्त्रयी वागिति भण्यते 1.2.172ab
मनसा तस्य संयोगे ततः स्वच्छैव धीर्भवेत् 2.4.344cd
मनसानुप्रविश्येदं क्रमेणैकात्म्यमुत्तमम् 4.4.734ab
मनसा मनुते यत्र येन चाहुर्मनो मतम् 3.4.164ab
मनसा शक्यते द्रष्टुं तत्तथैव प्रमान्वयात् 4.4.744cd
मनसैकादशात्रैतान्रुद्रानित्याचचक्षिरे 3.9.14cd

मनसैव यतोऽशेषकरणस्वार्थधीभवः 1.5.127ab
मनसैव यतो द्रष्टा गवादीह प्रपश्यति 1.5.107cd
मनसैवानुद्रष्टव्यमिति यद्भवतेरितम् 4.4.743ab
मनसैवेक्षते यस्मात्सर्वानिन्द्रियगोचरान् 4.3.83ab
मनसैवेत्यतः प्राह श्रुतिर्ब्रह्मावबोधने 4.4.648cd
मनसैवेत्युपक्रम्य सा त्विदानीं विचार्यते 4.4.742ab
मनसोऽग्रहणं तस्य न दृष्टेरिति वारणात् 3.4.14cd
मनसोऽस्तित्वसिद्ध्यर्थं श्रुत्योपन्यस्यतेऽनुमा 1.5.99ab
मनसो ग्रहणं चात्र बुद्धिवृत्त्युपलक्षणम् 4.4.174ab
मनसो वा निरोधेऽसौ न तु वस्त्ववबोधने SV 443ab
मनस्तन्मयतामेति तद्भावेनानुरञ्जितम् 4.4.727cd
मनस्तावत्सुनिर्णीतं शरीरं चेन्द्रियाणि च 1.5.128ab
मनस्यस्मिन्निलीने तु यत्सुखं स्वात्मसाक्षिकम् 4.4.725ab
मनःसंबन्धतश्चैवमिन्द्रियेष्वभिजायते 4.3.360cd
मनुते नो न जानातीत्येवमाहुस्तथा जनाः 4.4.71cd
मनुते मनसा यन्न येनाहुस्तन्मनो मतम् 4.3.1730ab
मनुते यन्न मनसा मतं येन मनः सदा 1.4.885ab
मनुते यन्न मनसा मनो येन मतं सदा 1.5.254ab
मनुनाप्यात्मयाजीति यदुक्तं परदर्शने 3.3.128ab
मनुर्देवान्मनुष्यांश्च स्थास्नु कृत्स्नं चरिष्णु च 1.2.139cd
मनुष्यगोचरोऽपीति नाख्यातासंभवात्तथा SV 75cd
मनुष्यजातेर्ग्रहणं सर्वजात्युपलक्षणम् 2.5.53ab
मनुष्यलोकपित्रमरलोकेभ्यः स्युर्निवृत्तये 1.5.335cd
मनुष्यलोकसंप्राप्तिं समुद्दिश्यास्य यैषणा 4.4.1120ab
मनुष्याः प्रकृताः पूर्वं ते च निःश्रेयसार्थिनः 1.4.1195ab
मनुष्याणां स यः कश्चित्संसिद्धोऽवयवैर्दृढैः 4.3.1845ab
मनुष्याणां हि निःशेषत्रय्यर्थेऽधिकृतिर्यतः 1.4.1084cd
मनुष्याधिकृतेर्वेति क्रियते पूर्वपक्षिणा 1.4.1194cd
मनुष्यानन्दतः सोऽयं गुणितः स्याच्छताधिकः 4.3.1857cd
मनुष्या यदमन्यन्त साध्वेवातस्तदीरितम् 1.4.1440ab
मनोऽक्षरे धृतं तद्वदक्षरत्वं निगच्छति 4.4.726cd
मनोऽधियज्ञं ब्रह्मैव ब्रह्मा चन्द्रोऽधिदैवतम् 3.1.41ab

मनोऽध्यात्मं यदस्याभूद्ब्रह्मा चैवाधियज्ञगः 3.1.37ab
मनोऽन्तःपाति निखिलं रूपं यद्वद्विवक्ष्यते 1.5.135ab
मनोः सशतरूपस्य पिण्डसृष्टिरिहोदिता 1.4.121ab
मनोतिरेकतोऽपेक्षा नैवातः साधनान्तरे 4.4.649cd
मनोद्वारोपसंक्रान्ता भावना यात्मनि स्थिता 4.4.400ab
मनोबुद्ध्योरभेदेन व्यवहारश्रुताविह 4.4.717ab
मनोबुद्ध्योरिति ज्ञेयमन्यथा तदसंभवात् 2.4.366cd
मनोभिमानतोऽज्ञानात्पुरुषोऽयं मनोमयः 5.8.2ab
मनोभिष्वङ्गवशगः कर्मणैति यतः सह 4.4.241ab
मनोमयादिविषयः क्रतुः पुंसो विधीयते 4.4.450ab
मनोमयोऽयमिति च तस्यैव ब्रह्मणोऽपरम् 5.8.1ab
मनोराज्यसमं मन्ये सर्वमेतत्त्वयोदितम् SV 204cd
मनोरूपं विजिज्ञास्यं प्राणस्याज्ञातमेव तु 1.5.159cd
मनोवाक्कर्मभिस्तस्माद्भक्त्या तस्मै नमः सदा 2.6.5cd
मनोवाक्तनुचेष्टाभिर्महान्तं यत्नमाचरेत् 1.5.91cd
मनोवागादिविज्ञानविग्रहः करणाख्यया 2.1.251ab
मनो वाचं तथा प्राणमात्मार्थे तानि चाकरोत् 1.5.98cd
मनोविनाशमन्वेष विज्ञानात्मा विलीयते 4.4.729ab
मनोविषयसामान्ये तस्यापि प्रलयो धियः 2.4.376ab
मनोश्चैवं ससर्जेदमापिपीलिकमात्मनः 1.4.119cd
मन्डलीकुरुते भानुस्तावांल्लोकरवेरितः 3.3.144cd
मन्तव्यो हेतुभिः सूक्ष्मैरुक्तदृष्टान्तबोधितैः 2.5.4ab
मन्त्रतः पाणिनाथैनां त्रीन्वारानन्नुलोमतः 6.4.99ab
मन्त्रद्वयेन कृत्वाथ कक्ष्यज्ञानोपसंहृतिः 2.5.115cd
मन्त्रद्वयेन ज्येष्ठादौ होमः कार्यो विजानता 6.3.24ab
मन्त्रप्रयोगे सर्वेषां संनिधौ तत्प्रकाशितम् 1.3.168ab
मन्त्रब्राह्मणयोर्वेदनामधेयत्वकारणात् 2.4.316ab
मन्त्रब्राह्मणरूपिण्याथेदानीं विनियुज्यते 4.4.1200ab
मन्त्रवत्तेन तच्छास्त्रं स्यादनर्थकमेव तु 1.4.1248cd
मन्त्राज्जगादाथात्रार्थे ब्राह्मणोक्तेरनन्तरम् 4.3.929cd
मन्त्राम्नायसमाप्त्यर्थं यदि वेतिसमीरणम् 4.4.967cd
मन्त्राम्नायोऽप्युपन्यस्तो यथेह न विरुध्यते 3.2.116ab

मन्त्रार्थं स्वयमेवातो व्याचष्टे श्रुतिरञ्जसा 1.3.353cd
मन्त्रार्थवादनाम्नां च कार्यार्थानुप्रवेशतः SV 540ab
मन्त्रार्थे यत्नमाहाथ ह्यमृतं मामिति श्रुतिः 1.3.359ab
मन्त्रेण प्राशनं चापामेकेषां शाखिनां मतम् 6.1.38cd
मन्त्रेण स तृतीयेन संक्षेपेणाभिधीयते 1.3.362cd
मन्त्रेणाथैष सोष्यन्तीमद्भिरभ्युक्षयेच्छनैः 6.4.108ab
मन्त्रेणाप्यात्मनो रूपं तदेतदिति वर्ण्यते 4.4.1179cd
मन्त्रे द्वित्वाविशिष्टत्वाद्धुतप्रहुतलक्षणे 1.5.43ab
मन्त्रोऽपि चैकात्म्यविनिश्चयाय 3.5.148c
मन्त्रोऽप्याहेममेवार्थं रूपं रूपमिति स्फुटम् 1.4.653ab
मन्त्रोक्तेरिव लोडादेः प्रवृत्तिरिति चेन्मतम् SV 1042ab
मन्त्रोक्त्यनन्तरं तस्या विजिहीथामितीरयेत् 6.4.96cd
मन्त्रोक्त्या ब्राह्मणोक्त्या च पुंसां श्रेयोभिवाञ्छिनाम् 4.4.968cd
मन्थं शुष्केऽपि यः स्थाणौ निषिञ्चेदुक्तसंस्कृतम् 6.3.61ab
मन्थकर्मणि ये मन्त्राः पञ्च ज्येष्ठादयः श्रुताः 6.1.5ab
मन्य आत्मानमेवातः कार्यकारणवज्जगत् 4.4.641cd
मन्यतिश्चाभिपर्वोऽयं हिंसार्थः स्यात्प्रसिद्धितः 1.2.189ab
मन्यन्त इत्यनेनैव यच्छब्दो याति संगतिम् 1.4.1075cd
मन्यन्त उभयत्रापि श्रुतिमानाविशेषतः 1.4.1087cd
मन्यामहे वरीयांसं गुणवद्भ्यो गुणाधिकम् 6.3.39cd
मन्वादि जन्मनः पूर्वमात्मैवेदमभूज्जगत् 1.4.24cd
मन्वादि सृष्टेस्तत्पूर्वमात्मैवाभूदिदं जगत् 1.4.30cd
मन्वानोऽविद्ययात्मैति तन्मयत्वं न तु स्वतः 4.4.182cd
मम तवेत्यवच्छेदव्यवहारश्च त्रुट्यति 4.3.696ab
मम तावदिदं बुद्धौ भवद्भ्यो यन्न रोचते 1.4.572ab
मम शास्त्रप्रमाणत्वात्पश्चादपि भवेत्फलम् SV 649ab
मम स्वभूते योषाग्नौ समिद्धे यौवनादिना 6.4.56ab
ममात्मनामनेकेषां संभवादप्रबोधतः 3.4.62ab
ममाप्यस्त्येव तत्सर्वं यद्यद्दित्ससि मानुषम् 6.2.62ab
ममाहमितिहेतूत्थं स्वामित्वं चाप्यबोधजम् 4.3.1264cd
ममेव भवतोऽपीदं न च किंचिदसंगतम् 4.2.112ab
मयण्नातो विकारे स्यात्प्रायार्थस्त्वत्र युज्यते 4.3.320cd

मया ज्ञानातिरेकेण तन्मानासंभवादिह 4.3.542cd
मयाध्यक्षेण प्रकृतिः सूयते सचराचरम् 1.4.327ab
मयायमनुयातव्यः कर्ता चायं ममाभवत् 3.2.148ab
मयि तेजोऽस्तु विज्ञानमिति रेतोऽभिधीयते 6.4.27ab
मयि प्रव्रजिते तस्माद्युवयोर्नार्थसंगतिः 2.4.43cd
मयि प्राणानिति ग्रन्थः स्वयमेवावगम्यताम् 6.4.118cd
मयोभूरन्नभृतोऽयं सर्वप्राणिभृदुच्यते 6.4.122cd
मय्यग्नौ शिशुवन्मोहात्प्रविशन्तं न कश्चन 3.9.61ab
मरणेऽपि न विश्वासो हिक्किकावशवर्तिनः 1.4.1520ab
मरिष्यतोऽन्यदेहार्थं पूर्वप्रज्ञेति तां विदुः 4.4.120cd
मरिष्यतोऽस्य या वृत्तिरान्तरी साधुनोच्यते 4.4.15ab
मर्त्यं मरणधर्मि स्याद्ध्विनश्वरलक्षणम् 2.3.24ab
मर्त्यः स्विन्मृत्युना वृक्णः कस्मान्मूलात्प्ररोहति 3.9.142cd
मर्त्यजन्म तथा साक्षाद्यतस्तदभिधीयताम् 3.9.138cd
मर्त्यत्वान्न तु गृह्यन्ते करणस्थानगोचराः 1.3.23cd
मर्त्यस्य जन्ममूलं यत्तद्ब्रूत ब्राह्मणा मम 3.9.135cd
मर्त्याच्छतगुणेनात उत्तरोत्तरवृद्धितः 3.9.206ab
मर्त्यो वा यजमानः सन्नस्राक्षीदमृतान्सुरान् 1.4.163ab
मर्मकृन्तनसंभूतवेदनार्दितमानसम् 4.3.1921ab
मर्मसूत्कृत्यमानेषु मुच्यमानेषु संधिषु 4.3.1923ab
मलं प्रकल्प्य तत्स्वास्थ्यं शुद्धिं व्याचक्षतेऽपरे 4.3.475cd
मलवत्संवृतं रूपं यस्मात्तस्यापि कल्पितम् 4.3.477cd
मलवद्वाससं प्राहुः श्रियं श्रीहेतुतः स्त्रियम् 6.4.29cd
मशकेभविराड्देहैः समः प्राणो यथोदितः 1.3.306ab
मस्करीन्द्रप्रणीतस्य भवनामभृतो यतेः 5.17.23ab
महता च यतोऽश्विभ्यामायासेनार्जिता पुरा 2.5.96ab
महतातिप्रयत्नेन ह्युदर्केऽपि प्रवक्ष्यते 1.4.203cd
महती शक्तिरित्यत्र युक्तमाशङ्कितुं फले 1.4.1476cd
महतेह प्रयत्नेन यतः प्राक्प्रतिपादितम् 4.3.1400ab
महत्तत्परिमाणेन यक्षं पूज्यतमत्वतः 5.4.4ab
महत्ता न विना वित्तं कर्मातो वित्तसिद्धये 6.3.5cd
महत्ता यद्वदाकाशे घटाकाशव्यपेक्षया SV 907ab

महत्त्वमात्मनोऽत्यर्थं यो वा कामयते गृही 6.3.5ab
महत्सत्यमतो ब्रह्म यक्षत्वं तूपवर्ण्यते 5.5.10cd
महदित्यभिधानं स्यात्कौटस्थ्यार्थं च भूतगीः 2.4.411cd
महन्नो भयमायातमिति बुबुधिरेऽसुराः 1.3.145ab
महानज इति वचस्तद्विशेषणसिद्धये 4.4.976cd
महानर्थफलायैव न मोक्षायेति निश्चितिः 1.4.4cd
महानित्यभिधानेन सत्यज्ञानादिलक्षणम् 4.4.1321ab
महानुभावसंपर्कः कस्य नोन्नतिकारणम् 2.4.47ab
महान्तं विभुमात्मानं मत्वा धीरो न शोचति 1.2.158cd
महाप्रतिग्रहेणापि नैवंविद्दोषमृच्छति 5.16.52cd
महाभूतादिधृत्यन्तं क्षेत्रमेवेति चाब्रवीत् 4.4.365ab
महामत्स्याख्यदृष्टान्तः स्वप्नजाग्रदवस्थयोः 4.3.1116ab
महामत्स्यादिवाक्यस्य स यथोक्तस्तथोच्यते 4.3.1088cd
महामीमांसका धीरा अत्र प्रतिविधीयते 4.4.891cd
महायज्ञैश्च यज्ञैश्च ब्राह्मीयं क्रियते तनुः 4.4.580cd
महायज्ञैश्च यज्ञैश्च ब्राह्मीयं क्रियते तनुः 4.4.1049cd
महाराजादयो नास्य स्वप्नानुभवगोचराः 2.1.293ab
महावाक्यप्रयोगेऽपि पदार्थप्रविवेचने SV 494ab
महासत्ता वियज्ज्ञेयं कृत्स्नार्वागभूमिसंप्लुतेः 1.4.644ab
महासामान्य एकत्र भयसां स्याद्यथा तथा 2.4.292cd
महासामान्य एकस्मिन्विशेषाणामशेषतः 2.4.287ab
महासामान्यदृष्टान्तो दौन्दुभो रत्र उच्यते 2.4.288ab
महासामान्यवत्प्रत्यक्सर्वानात्माप्ययः स्वतः 2.4.296cd
महि महत्त्वं जानीम आमोऽसि त्वं तथा प्रभो 6.3.40ab
महिमाख्यौ तयोरेतदहर्वा इति दर्शनम् 1.1.7ef
महिमानं श्रुतेर्वेत्ति फलं चेत्स्यात्ततोऽपि किम् 4.4.1191cd
महिमानो यदामी स्युरविद्याया न वस्तुनः 1.4.1503ab
महिमा ब्राह्मणस्योक्तो नेतीत्याद्युक्तिभिः पुरा 4.4.1182cd
महिमा विद्यमानोऽपि तदविद्यासमुद्भव- 4.4.1186ab
महिमाविष्कृतः श्रुत्या विद्यायुक्तस्य संभ्रमात् 3.3.172cd
महिमैवंविधो यस्माद्ब्राह्मणस्यात आदरात् 4.4.1188ab
महिम्नोऽस्यैव वा साक्षाद्वाक्यार्थप्रतिबुद्धये 4.4.1190ab

मह्यं प्रतिवचो वाच्यं दोषस्तु स्यात्ततोऽन्यथा 3.4.77cd
मां प्रत्येवैतीह यथासाधारण्येन भास्करम् 3.7.59ab
मां मुक्त्वासंभवो यस्माद्ब्रह्मार्थस्यात उच्यते 4.4.549ab
मांसं कृष्णमृगच्छागविषयं त्वद्य कुर्वते 6.4.78cd
मांसपेशी समा तन्वी सावरेति निगद्यते 6.4.112ab
मां स्पृष्टो मामनुप्राप्त एष पन्था यथोदितः 4.4.549cd
माक्रियाफलयोगोऽयं यतो मातरि भोक्तरि SV 470cd
मागोचरातिवर्तित्वाददृष्टं स्यात्तदक्षरम् 3.8.173cd
मागोचरातिवर्तित्वादसाधारणदृष्टितः 3.7.52ab
माङर्थस्तु तथाभेदे व्याख्येयः प्रतिषेधकृत् 1.3.226cd
मा ज्ञासिष्ट कथं नाम नामतत्त्वं बहिर्जनः 4.2.42ab
माणवकस्योपनयनसमये वेदवादिनाम् 5.16.42ab
माण्डूकेयश्रुतिवच्च इति स्पष्टमधीयते 3.8.26cd
माता मातरि मानं च मानान्मेयं प्रसिध्यति 3.4.124cd
मातारं मेयसंबद्धं जाग्रद्भूमौ यथेक्षते 4.3.886ab
मातारमपि नाप्नोति यत्प्रमेयैकनिष्ठितम् 4.3.209ab
मातीत्य प्रश्नविषयं गार्गि प्राक्षीः कथं चन 3.6.22ab
मातृजस्यासृजो हेतुरमृतं सोऽत्र भण्यते 3.9.45cd
मातृतन्त्रे तथैवायं न विधिः प्रत्यगीक्षणे 2.4.143cd
मातृत्वकञ्चुको यद्वदात्मानात्मानमीक्षते 1.4.734ab
मातृधर्माः प्रसिध्यन्ति विशिंषन्तः स्वसंविदम् SV 984cd
मातृमात्राश्रयं तत्स्यान्न स्वतःसिद्धिनिष्ठितम् 3.4.148cd
मातृमानक्रियामेयविभागैर्न विभज्यते 1.4.716cd
मातृमानक्रियामेयव्यवहारस्य संभवः 4.4.279cd
मातृमानप्रभेदेऽपि प्रतिदेहं न भिद्यते 3.4.54ab
मातृमानप्रमेयाणां गुणवद्दोषवत्त्वतः 1.4.88cd
मातृमानप्रमेयाणां प्रत्यक्त्वादात्मवस्तुनः 4.4.694ab
मातृमानप्रमेयात्मा कर्तृसाधनकार्यवान् 4.3.38ab
मातृमानप्रमेयादिसामग्री वासनात्मिका 4.3.884ab
मातृमानप्रमेयादेरन्योऽन्यव्यभिचारतः 4.3.1737ab
मातृमानप्रमेयादौ तत्सिद्धेर्विधिना विना SV 673cd
मातृमानप्रमेयार्थांश्चागमापायिनः सदा 4.4.467ab

मातृमानादयश्चापि कुतस्तैरस्य विक्रिया SV 999cd
मातृमानाप्रसिद्धिश्च तदन्यापोहनादृते 4.3.1667ab
मातृमानिति हेतूक्तिः सम्यग्वक्तृत्वसिद्धये 4.1.13ab
मा ते मूर्धा व्यपप्तेति त्वामहं वारयाम्यतः 3.6.22cd
मातोऽनधिगतत्वस्य सिद्धिः स्यादथवान्यतः SV 685ab
मात्रन्तरे व्यपेक्षायां मातुर्मानान्तरे मितेः 3.4.139ab
मात्रादानं यदकरोदात्मा स्वप्नरिरंसया 4.3.977ab
मात्रादानस्य या यस्य योनिरासीत्पुरात्मनः 4.3.993ab
मात्रादिकारणध्वस्तेः पराङ्मानप्रबाधतः 4.4.960ab
मात्रादिजन्मनः प्राक्च नानुभूत्यतिरेकतः 4.3.1736ab
मात्रादित्रयहानेऽपि हानसाक्षितयेक्ष्यते SV 795ab
मात्रादिबोधकं मानं प्रत्यगात्मनि साक्षिणि SV 150ab
मात्रादिलक्षणा यत्र सामग्री वस्तुनीष्यते 3.8.107ab
मात्रादिविक्रियाग्रामसाक्षिणी साविनश्वरी 4.3.1753cd
मात्रादिव्यभिचारेऽपि संविदव्यभिचारिणी 2.4.126ab
मात्रादिव्यवधानेन यथान्यत्र मितेः फलम् 1.4.836ab
मात्रादिसव्यपेक्ष सद्यत्र ज्ञानं प्रजायते SV 720ab
मात्रादिसिद्धिदस्यैष स्वतःसिद्धेर्न सर्वदा 4.3.110cd
मात्राद्यप्रविभक्तं सदद्वैतं ब्रह्म शाश्वतम् 4.4.710ab
मात्राद्यभावसंसिद्धिः कथं मात्रादिपूर्विका SV 550cd
मात्रालक्षणमादानं कृत्वा स्वप्नस्य सर्जनम् 4.4.107ab
मात्रासंसर्ग एवास्य तथा चैव प्रवक्ष्यते 4.4.32ab
मात्रासंसर्गजस्त्वेष यो विनाशादिधर्मवान् 4.5.14ab
मात्रेण रूपं वीक्षन्ते नापेक्षन्ते ततोऽपरम् 1.4.86cd
मात्रेति मानमिच्छन्ति मेयोऽर्थस्तेन गीयते 3.8.106ab
मात्रोपादानरूपेण स्वेन भासा पुराब्रवीत् 4.4.79ab
मात्वमक्षादयो यान्ति नाज्ञातज्ञाततोऽन्यथा SV 1003cd
मानं किं नानपेक्षं स्यात्पुमर्थश्च स्वरूपतः SV 678cd
मानं नालं निराकर्तुं वस्तु यन्मान्तरैर्मितम् SV 244cd
मानं प्रवर्तते तस्मान्नैतदध्यवसीयते 3.9.183cd
मानं बाधकमेवात्र बाध्येन न हि हन्यते 4.4.788cd
मानं बाधकमेवासीत्स्मृतिरप्यनयोस्तथा 1.4.845cd

मानं विधिमुखं मुक्त्वा न व्यावृत्त्येकवर्त्मना 4.3.1662ab
मानं हि व्यञ्जकं लोके सिद्धे तच्च स्वकारणात् SV 555ab
मानकार्यं फलं चेत्स्यान्न स्यात्तन्मातृमानयोः 1.4.266ab
मानतां न जहात्येव जगत्याप्तवचो यथा SV 706cd
मानपादोपजीवित्वं स्वभावोऽनात्मवस्तुनः 4.3.110ab
मानप्रसादात्सिद्धं सत्स्पर्धते मितिबाधितैः 1.4.1292cd
मानभूमेश्च व्युत्थाप्य तथा विदितभूमितः 1.4.967ab
मानमेयत्वयो रूपं यस्मान्नैवेह गम्यते 4.3.554ab
मानमेयत्वसंसिद्धिर्नातस्तत्रोपपद्यते 4.3.554cd
मानमेयत्वसंबन्धो मिथोयोग्यत्वतस्तथा 4.4.345cd
मानमेयातिवर्तित्वात्स्वतः सिद्धेश्च वस्तुनः 4.4.466cd
मानमेव तदा तत्स्यान्नातोऽन्यन्मानलक्षणम् SV 682cd
मानलक्षणसद्भावाज्ज्योतिष्टोमादिवाक्यवत् SV 574cd
मानव्यापारकाले स्याद्ग्राह्यमेयोपसर्जनम् 3.4.142ab
मानव्यापारतः पूर्वं सिद्धामेवावबोधयत् 4.3.166ab
मानव्यापारतश्चेत्स्यान्मेयानधिगतिस्तदा 4.3.172ab
मानव्यापारविरहात्प्रथनं वा दृगात्मनः SV 463cd
मानव्याप्तिक्षमं चेत्स्यादज्ञातत्वं घटादिवत् SV 687ab
मानस्य व्यञ्जकत्वात्तु मेयतत्त्वानुरोधिता 4.4.829cd
मानस्य हि फलं यत्र न तन्मानस्य गोचरः 4.3.195ab
मानस्येव क्रिया तद्वदात्मार्थोपासनेष्वपि 1.4.782cd
मानस्येव क्रिया यस्मादविशिष्टोभयोरपि 1.4.781cd
मानस्वभावमाश्रित्य सर्वोऽपीत्याद्युदीरणम् SV 554ab
मानहेत्वतिवर्तित्वान्नेह मात्रादिसंभवः 1.4.215cd
मानांशो यस्य मेयः स्यान्मेयांशो वा भवेत्प्रमा 4.3.553ab
मानाघातासहिष्णुत्वमसाधारणमिष्यते SV 181cd
मानातराभ्युपगमाद्भवतश्च तथा सति 4.3.256ab
मानातिरेकासंसिद्धेर्मेय एव तथा न किम् 1.4.225ab
मानात्मकेऽपि मेयेऽर्थे यद्यबुद्धत्वमिष्यते 1.4.248ab
मानादज्ञातता चेत्स्यान्न सा तत्फलमिष्यते SV 989cd
मानादज्ञाततासिद्धौ स्यादन्योऽन्यसमाश्रयः SV 570cd
मानादनुभवः सिद्धो जडः स्याद्धटवन्न चेत् SV 1059ab

मानादवगतं तच्चेन्मैवमव्यतिरेकतः 1.4.250cd
मानादव्यतिरेके हि मानमेयौ न सिध्यतः 1.2.79cd
मानादियत्नानर्थक्यप्रसक्तिः स्यात्तथा सति 1.4.1098cd
मानादेव स विज्ञात इत्येतत्स्यात्कुतोऽमितेः 1.4.224cd
मानाद्यनभ्युपेतौ हि न किंचिद्वस्तु सिध्यति 1.4.1101ab
मानाद्यपेक्षा सिद्धस्य नानुन्मत्तेन चोद्यते 1.4.1288cd
मानानपेक्षसिद्धिस्तु कस्मान्मानमपेक्षते 4.4.693cd
मानानि मानसंबन्धादज्ञातत्वं च नश्यति 1.2.101cd
मानान्तरप्रवेशेन सापेक्षत्वं प्रसज्यते SV 517cd
मानान्तरप्रसिद्धत्वात्प्रामाण्यं लभ्यते श्रुतेः 4.4.462cd
मानान्तरप्रसिद्धार्थवादित्वादनुवादकम् SV 730ab
मानान्तरमिताः सन्तस्ते हि पुंसां प्रवर्तकाः SV 490cd
मानान्तरविरुद्धं च न च मानं सदिष्यते 2.1.497ab
मानान्तरविरोधाच्च नैतासां मानतेष्यते 2.1.538cd
मानान्तरविरोधेन न हि मानं प्रवर्तते 2.1.455cd
मानान्तरविरोधेन न हि लोकेऽपि किं चन 3.9.183ab
मानान्तरविरोधोऽपि तथा च सति नेष्यते 2.1.559cd
मानान्तरव्यपेक्षत्वाद्विहन्येतार्थनिश्चितौ SV 707cd
मानान्तराच्च कः कुर्याददृष्टार्थाः क्रियाः सुधीः SV 1049cd
मानान्तराच्च नैवास्ति मान्तराविषयत्वतः 2.1.562cd
मानान्तराच्च यत्प्राप्तं मानत्वं तत्र च श्रुतेः 4.3.1747ab
मानान्तरानधिगतं मेयं तावन्निरूपितम् 1.4.384ab
मानान्तरानधिगतं सिद्धं वस्त्ववबोधयत् SV 678ab
मानान्तरानधिगतोक्त्यर्थाधिगम एव नः 1.4.854ab
मानान्तरानपेक्ष चेन्मानं मेयं प्रबोधयेत् SV 682ab
मानान्तरानपेक्षः सन्नाक्षेपकतया प्रमा SV 748cd
मानान्तरापरिज्ञाते प्रमेयार्थे प्रमां स्फुटाम् 4.4.811ab
मानान्तरासंभवेन प्रसज्येतानपेक्षता SV 692cd
मानान्तरेण तत्सिद्धेर्नात्र व्याप्रियते वचः SV 443cd
मानान्तरेण विज्ञातो नाज्ञातः शून्यताप्तितः SV 921cd
मानान्तरेण संवादो यदि चेदनुवादिता 2.1.554ab
मानान्तरेण संप्राप्तां साध्यसाधनसंगतिम् SV 324ab

मानान्तरेणागमतो मा प्राक्षीरित्यतो वचः 3.6.29cd
मानान्तरेणासंव्याप्ते मेये स्यान्मानता यतः 2.1.497cd
मानान्तरैर्विरोधश्चेन्मानस्याभ्युपगम्यते 4.4.793ab
मानान्तरोत्थविज्ञानप्राप्तावेव नियुज्यते 1.4.894ab
मानान्मानफलस्यैव पुमर्थत्वसमन्वयात् SV 469cd
मानापेक्षा न भूयः स्यात्फलाप्तेस्तत्कृतार्थतः 5.1.103cd
मानापेक्ष्येव यो भावः स एवामानतो न सन् 4.4.693ab
मानाभावं किमद्राक्षीर्येनैवमभिधीयते 3.8.112cd
मानाभावस्य मानत्वं मेयाभावस्य मेयता SV 938ab
मानाभावान्न चेदिष्टा संततिर्येह कल्पिता 4.3.692ab
मानाभावे च तन्नेति व्यतिरेकः कुतोऽन्वयम् 3.8.112ab
मानाभावे ह्यसौ मानमानन्तर्यं त्वचोदितम् SV 538cd
मानाभिधानयोर्यावान्कश्चिद्विषय इष्यते 2.3.179ab
मानाभिधानविषयो यावन्नात्मानमात्मनि 2.3.195ab
मानाभेदाच्च मेयस्य नाज्ञातार्थः प्रसिध्यति 1.2.23ab
मानाविरोधात्केनैषां शुद्ध्यादीनां मृषार्थता 1.3.47cd
मानित्वादिनिषेधः स्याद्यथैकाक्रियरूपतः 3.8.103ab
मानुषस्तूचितो दातुमादातुं मानुषाद्वरः 6.2.61cd
मानुषानन्दमारभ्य ह्युत्तरोत्तरवृद्धितः 4.4.272ab
मानुष्यकेण भोगेन संपन्नानां नृणामिह 4.3.1848ab
मानेन नाश्यतेऽज्ञानं ज्ञापकं हि न कारकम् SV 1054cd
मानेन विषयासिद्धौ तद्विदृक्षावियोगतः SV 772ab
मानेनानभिसंबन्धान्नेयं षष्ठेन्द्रियार्थवत् 4.4.908ab
मानेनेह कथं कुर्यादन्योऽन्याश्रयकारणात् 4.3.1664cd
मानेभ्यस्तत्फलासूतेरन्धकारप्रनृत्तवत् 1.4.227cd
मानैश्चेदविरोधः स्यात्कुतोऽज्ञातत्वनिह्नुतिः 4.3.548cd
मा नोऽपराधिनो मंस्थास्तव पूर्वे पितामहाः 6.2.70ab
मान्तरं नागमादन्यद्यदैकात्म्यावबोधकृत् SV 569cd
मान्तरानवबुद्धं हि बोधयन्मानमुच्यते SV 681cd
मान्तरानुप्रवेशित्वं कार्यस्य तु न शङ्क्यते SV 485ab
मान्तरेणापि संबद्धमर्थं वाक्यं प्रबोधयत् SV 706ab
मान्तरैरवबुद्धेऽपि ज्ञातेऽप्यज्ञाततोऽन्यतः SV 1078cd

माफलं न च मेयस्थं क्रियाफलवदिष्यते 1.4.261cd
माफलस्य तु मेयत्वे प्राप्नोतीहानवस्थितिः 1.4.263ab
मा बिभर्गर्भमित्येवमथ यां कामयेत सः 6.4.41ab
माभावस्याप्यभावेऽस्मिन्संसिद्धेरनुभूतितः 4.3.796ab
मा भूत्कामादिधर्मित्वमात्मनीति प्रयत्यते 1.5.101cd
मा भूत्सर्वस्वहानिर्नो ब्रह्मयाथात्म्यविद्यया 1.4.1803cd
मा भूदग्न्याद्यभावेऽपि कदाचिद्धूमसंभवः 4.3.725cd
मा भूद्दुःखं ममेत्येवं जाड्यात्कामयतेऽनिशम् 4.4.259cd
मा भूद्व्याकृतधीः पुंसां नामरूपात्मवस्तुनि 1.4.208ab
मा भरभ्यवदान्यस्त्वं दाता भूत्वेह नः प्रति 6.2.64cd
मा भैषीरिति चोक्तेऽपि न नियोगः प्रतीयते SV 585ab
मामियं कामयेतेति कुर्यात्तस्या इमं विधिम् 6.4.36cd
मामृतेऽन्नं न वः शक्तं पोष्टुं क्षणमपि क्वचित् 1.3.251ab
मामृते जीवितुं यूयं यद्यशक्ताः स्थ सर्वदा 6.1.27ab
मामेयमात्रसद्भावात्तेभ्योऽत्यन्तनिवृत्तितः 3.8.116ab
मामेयसंगतिफलभित्त्यभ्युपगमस्त्वया 4.3.545ab
मामेव ये प्रपद्यन्ते मायामेतां तरन्ति ते 2.1.270cd
माययापहृतज्ञाना आसुरं भावमाश्रिताः 2.1.269cd
मायां तु प्रकृतिं विद्यान्मायिनं तु महेश्वरम् 1.4.382cd
माया तस्याः परं सौक्ष्म्यं मृत्युनैवेति भण्यते 1.2.135cd
मायाभिः प्रत्यगज्ञानैर्यदि वानृतबुद्धिभिः 2.5.127ab
मायामात्रमिदं सर्वं जगत्स्थावरजङ्गमम् 2.1.266ab
मायिनस्तस्य पश्यन्ति न तं पश्यति कश्चन 4.3.944cd
मायेन्द्रजालसदृशं व्यामोहास्पदमात्मनः 2.3.86cd
मायोगेऽपि न मानत्वमनाप्तवचसः क्वचित् SV 708ab
मार्गान्तरोपदेशाद्वा वेदेऽप्येवं प्रतीयताम् SV 382cd
माला गङ्गेव शंभुं पदममलमजं वैष्णवं सानुयाता 6.5.22d
मा वोचोऽतो यतो वेद्मि विनापि वचनात्तव 2.1.46cd
माव्यापारसमाप्तत्वान्न भूयस्तदपेक्षिता SV 442ab
मा शङ्किष्ठास्ततो मां त्वं नोक्तं सर्वं ममेति हि 6.2.53cd
मा समृद्ध्यथवा सोऽस्मै तं वाहं प्राप्नुयामिति 5.16.72cd
मासाभिमानिनो देवा आदित्यास्तेन ते स्मृताः 3.9.16cd

मासेभ्यः पितृलोकं हि पितरो यत्र शेरते 6.2.149cd
माहात्म्यमेतच्छब्दस्य यदविद्यां निरस्यति 1.4.859ab
माहारजनमित्यत्र हारिद्रं रूपमुच्यते 2.3.160ab
माहारजनमित्यादि रूपं चेत्साक्षिणो भवेत् 2.3.153ab
माहारजनमित्यादिर्न त्वियत्ता विवक्षिता 2.3.170ab
माहारजनमित्यादिवाक्येनात्मविशुद्धये 4.4.396cd
मितिप्रवृत्तिहेतुत्वात्तथाप्यत्राश्रितैव सा 4.4.218cd
मितेः स्वरूपलाभाय न तु मेयोपलब्धये SV 811cd
मिते तत्र न पूर्वस्मिन्सिद्धेऽप्यर्थेऽनुवादता SV 677cd
मितेरनेवंधर्मत्वान्नाभावे व्यापृतिर्मितेः 4.3.1663cd
मितेर्मेये समाप्तत्वान्मिथ्यात्वं न मितेर्भवेत् 1.3.57cd
मितेश्चासंभवाच्छून्यं सर्वथा नोपपद्यते 3.2.154cd
मित्युत्पत्तावनुत्पत्तिर्विरोधाद्बाध्यते यतः 1.4.437ab
मिथः कृत्स्नेऽपि जगति तदन्यद्व्यभिचारि तु 2.4.126cd
मिथः क्षणानां संबन्धः शृङ्खलाकटकादिवत् 4.3.694ab
मिथः संकीर्णवृत्तिस्थं देह आत्मेति चोच्यते 1.5.152cd
मिथः सास्नादयो भिन्ना गोत्वाभिन्नास्तथापि ते 1.6.49cd
मिथश्चासंगतेस्तेषामतो दोषान्न मुच्यते 4.3.691cd
मिथस्तयोरपेक्षा का यत उक्तं प्रसिध्यति 4.3.550cd
मिथःसंकीर्णधर्मोक्तौ यथायोगं व्यवस्थितिः 3.5.10cd
मिथुनद्वारिका यास्य सृष्टिः सैवाधुनोच्यते 1.4.113ab
मिथुनारतिमोहादेः प्रत्यग्याथात्म्यवेदिनः 1.4.100ab
मिथोऽपास्तव्यपेक्षं हि नामरूपादिमज्जगत् 1.4.26ab
मिथोऽविभिन्नयोर्नासौ नापि सैकात्म्य इष्यते 1.4.630ab
मिथोऽसंगतितो व्याप्तिर्हिमवद्विन्ध्ययोरिव 1.4.629cd
मिथो जिगीषतां पुंसां ज्ञानकर्मादिसाधनैः 1.4.47ab
मिथो न व्यतिरेकेण सिध्येते कार्यकारणे 4.3.1600cd
मिथो नाडीशतानद्धं तयोः प्रावरणं तथा 4.2.49ab
मिथो भिन्नं यदाहुस्त एकैकं देवमध्वरे 1.4.136ab
मिथोभिन्नपदार्थानां नामरूपक्रियात्मभिः 2.4.293ab
मिथो भिन्ना न सन्तीह भिन्नाभिन्नत्वमात्रतः 4.3.1759cd
मिथो वाक्यमतो नेदृग्वक्तव्यं मानिना ततः 4.4.361cd

मिथो विभक्ता एकत्र क्षुरधाने यथा क्षुराः 1.4.637ab
मिथो विभागसंसिद्धिर्धर्माणां नात्मसंश्रयात् 4.3.1810ab
मिथोविभिन्नरूपत्वात्सादृश्यं चेह दुर्घटम् 4.3.679ab
मिथोविरुद्धवादित्वाद्द्वयोरागमयोरपि 1.4.149ab
मिथो विरोधतः सिद्धावधुना तत्र चोद्यते SV 19cd
मिथो विरोधतो नातः संगतिर्ज्ञानकर्मणोः 3.3.70cd
मिथोविरोधसिद्ध्यर्थं कर्मज्ञानाधिकारिणोः SV 11ab
मिथ्याज्ञानं कथं वस्तु न हि मिथ्येति वस्तु सत् 1.4.425ab
मिथ्याज्ञानं तमः कुर्वदीदृगेव करोति तत् 2.4.426cd
मिथ्याज्ञानग्रहायासावविद्या प्रत्यगात्मनः 4.3.1091cd
मिथ्याज्ञानमतोऽनात्मा ह्यात्माज्ञानसमुत्थितेः 1.4.1383cd
मिथ्याज्ञानमनात्माभं मोह इत्यपदिश्यते 3.5.62cd
मिथ्याज्ञानमृते नान्यत्कार्यं किंचिदपोष्यते 4.3.1108ab
मिथ्याज्ञानस्य कार्यत्वात्किं तत्कारणमुच्यताम् 1.4.427ab
मिथ्याज्ञानस्य वस्तुत्वं येनैव स्यात्सदात्मना 1.4.442ab
मिथ्याज्ञानस्य वस्तुत्वात्तदेवास्त्विह कारणम् 1.4.421cd
मिथ्याज्ञानातिरेकेण नान्यदज्ञानमिष्यते 1.4.420ab
मिथ्याज्ञानादिसंसिद्धौ क उपाय इतीर्यताम् 1.4.277ab
मिथ्याज्ञानादिसंसिद्धौ न चाभावोऽपि शङ्क्यते 1.4.269cd
मिथ्याज्ञानादिहेतुत्वं काम्यानामिव चेन्मतम् 1.3.92cd
मिथ्याज्ञानाधिपत्वेन भूयस्त्वं तमसो भवेत् 4.4.605cd
मिथ्याज्ञानापनुत्त्यर्थमात्मैवेत्यब्रवीच्छ्रुतिः 1.4.697cd
मिथ्याज्ञानाभ्यासहेतुः संस्कारो न तु जन्मने 4.4.823cd
मिथ्याज्ञाने जनस्तुष्टः स्वप्नमायेन्द्रजालवत् 1.4.648cd
मिथ्या तद्वस्तु चेत्युक्तिर्महतामेव शोभते 1.4.425cd
मिथ्यात्मकत्वात्सर्वस्य नैतदेवं कुतो यतः 2.1.289cd
मिथ्यात्वकारणं प्राह यदेवेति श्रुतिः स्वयम् 4.3.1251cd
मिथ्यात्वप्रतिपत्त्यर्थं स्वप्नस्य क्रियते स्फुटम् 2.1.281cd
मिथ्यादर्शनजा ये तु माहारजनपूर्वकाः 4.4.408ab
मिथ्यादर्शनदोषित्वान्मिथ्यादर्शनकारणम् 4.4.671ab
मिथ्याधियोऽपि बाध्यत्वमज्ञानैकसमन्वयात् 1.4.438ab
मिथ्याधीमात्रहेतुत्वात्प्रेरकत्वं न युक्तिमत् 1.4.1810cd

मिथ्याध्यासैश्च तत्कार्यैरप्रमेयं प्रमीयते 2.3.10cd
मिथ्याभावनमात्राधेर्निरस्तविकृतेरिह 4.3.1237ab
मिथ्याभावो न नास्तीति वक्तुं कश्चिदपि क्षमः 2.4.463cd
मिथ्याभिमानतो देहं यदात्मेत्यभिमन्यते 4.3.811cd
मिथ्याभिमानात्संपत्तिरविद्योत्थासु भूमिषु 1.4.1184ab
मिथ्याभिवादिनः साक्षाद्विपातयतु सत्वरः 1.3.329cd
मिथ्यामिथ्याविकल्पो हि स्थायित्वे वस्तुनो भवेत् 4.3.490ab
मिथ्यासंशयविज्ञानमनात्मानं प्रतीष्यते 1.4.1501ab
मिथ्येति गम्यते श्रौतान्मृत्योरिति च निन्दनात् 4.4.675cd
मिथ्येति ग्राहयच्छास्त्रमनर्थार्थं यतो भवेत् 1.3.62cd
मिथ्येतिप्रत्ययोत्पत्तिस्तथा कारणदोषतः 1.3.56ab
मिथ्येव भाति सत्योऽपीत्यपि लोकेऽभिधीयते 2.4.463ab
मिनोति नात्मनोऽभावमुपलब्धिस्तथैव च 4.3.795cd
मीमांसान्यायवत्त्वाभ्यां धर्ममीमांसनोक्तिवत् SV 246ab
मीयते चेत्प्रमाणेन नाप्रमेयं तदिष्यते 4.4.680cd
मीयन्ते विषया याभिर्मात्रास्ताश्चक्षुरादयः 4.4.24ab
मीयन्ते सर्वमात्मेति प्रत्यक्षेण विरुध्यते 2.1.589cd
मुक्तं चातः स्वतस्तत्त्वं मुक्तमित्युपचर्यते 4.4.303ab
मुक्तं चातः स्वतो वस्तु किमन्यत्कार्यमिष्यते 4.4.530cd
मुक्तत्वं च सितत्वं च परस्परविरुद्धयोः 3.5.37ab
मुक्तये भावनार्थं वा तथा चोर्ध्वं प्रवक्ष्यते SV 438cd
मुक्तश्चातोऽवसेयोऽसौ सद्वेदान्तोक्तिमानिना 1.4.491cd
मुक्तस्य च मुमुक्षोश्च सर्वत्यागव्यपेक्षतः 4.4.542cd
मुक्तामुक्तत्वरूपोऽयं न विशेषोऽस्ति वस्तुनि 4.4.351ab
मुक्तावनुयियासि त्वं मदैकात्म्यपरीप्सया 2.4.68cd
मुक्तिं कामयमानोऽन्यत्कटाक्षेणापि वीक्षते SV 1024cd
मुक्तिं सर्वाणि कर्माणि यदि संभूय कुर्वते 3.3.52cd
मुक्तिप्रवेशोपायोऽयं यथोक्तेनेह वर्त्मना 4.4.731ab
मुक्तिभागिति चेहोक्तः संन्यासेन समुच्चयः 2.4.21cd
मुक्तिर्विलक्षणैतेभ्यस्तेनेहानर्थको विधिः SV 236cd
मुक्ते मेये सदा मुक्तिर्बन्धो वा स्याद्विपर्यये 3.2.87cd
मुक्तेरर्वाक्पुमर्थोऽन्यो नेह कश्चित्समीक्ष्यते SV 558cd

मुक्तेरर्वाक्षु काम्येषु मुमुक्षुत्वाद्विरक्ततः 4.4.1210ab
मुक्तेर्बिभ्यत इत्यादि तथा च श्रुतिशासनम् 1.4.14ab
मुक्तेर्हि बिभ्यतो देवा मोहेनापिदधुर्नरान् 4.4.1250ab
मुक्तेश्च कर्मकार्यत्वे विशेषो भवतोच्यताम् 3.3.88ab
मुक्तेश्च कर्महेतुत्वादनित्यत्वं प्रसज्यते 4.4.308cd
मुक्तेश्च बिभ्यतो देवा मोहेनापिदधुर्नरान् SV 218ab
मुक्तेश्च बिभ्यतो देवा मोहेनापिदधुर्नरान् 2.4.24ab
मुक्तेश्च बिभ्यतो देवा मोहेनापिदधुर्नरान् 3.5.144ab
मुक्तेश्च साधनत्वेन कर्म नैव श्रुतं श्रुतौ 3.3.36cd
मुक्तेष्वादिवदित्यादि यच्च किंचित्समीरितम् 1.4.932ab
मुक्तोऽपि न च संसारी तयोरेकत्वहेतुतः 3.9.191ab
मुक्तो वेत्ति परानन्दमिति तस्माद्वचो मृषा 3.9.191cd
मुक्तौ काम्यफलेऽभीष्टे सकृत्करण एव च SV 307cd
मुक्तौ च कर्मसाध्यायां किमेकैकं विमुक्तिदम् 3.3.43ab
मुक्तौ चेन्न भवेत्स्वर्गो वाक्यभेदान्न च द्वये SV 408cd
मुक्तौ तद्व्यज्यत इति विशेषवचनं मृषा 4.4.330ab
मुक्तौ तद्व्यज्यते ज्ञानं सुखं चेति यदीरितम् 4.4.327cd
मुक्तौ तमोतिरेकेण नान्तरायोऽन्य इष्यते 4.4.559ab
मुक्तौ विभागविज्ञानमेकत्वादेव कारणात् 3.9.193cd
मुक्त्यन्तरायसंमोहविध्वंस्यैकात्म्यबोधतः 1.4.825ab
मुक्त्यभ्युदययोस्तस्मान्न सम्यग्भवतोदितम् SV 46cd
मुक्त्यर्थी न हि काम्यादि वर्जयेदिति चोदना SV 76ab
मुक्त्येकसाधनं ज्ञानं दातुं शक्यमिदं मया 2.4.64cd
मुक्त्वान्यो नास्ति संबन्धो दाह्यदाहकयोरिव 4.4.915cd
मुक्त्वैकं प्रत्यगात्मानं न तत्रास्ति त्रयं यतः 1.4.461cd
मुक्त्वैकात्म्यस्य चाज्ञानं नान्तरायान्तरं यतः 2.4.150ab
मुक्त्वैव देहसंबन्धं स्वप्नोऽयं प्रत्यगात्मनः 4.3.1144ab
मुखविज्ञानविरहादनर्थफलकीर्तनम् 5.16.78ab
मुखसंचारिणाप्राणो यः प्राणेनानितीक्षिता 3.4.68ab
मुख्यं ब्रह्म न चेदस्ति गौणं स्यात्तद्विना कुतः 1.4.1092ab
मुख्यकर्तृत्वपक्षेऽपि ह्यनिर्मोक्षः प्रसज्यते SV 1054ab
मुख्यप्राणस्य योत्क्रान्तिः प्रयोक्त्री सैव नापरा 4.4.91ab

मुख्यमग्निं विना गौणं न लोकोऽप्यवगच्छति 1.4.1092cd
मुख्यमैकार्थ्यमेवं स्याद्ब्रह्मलोकपदार्थयोः 4.3.1821cd
मुख्यवृत्तिग्रहायातो व्यापिलक्षणसिद्धये 2.3.80ab
मुख्यवृत्त्या समर्थं स्यात्तत्रैवामूर्तलक्षणम् 2.3.77cd
मुख्यस्य संभवे यस्मादुपचारो न युज्यते 4.3.585ab
मुख्यस्यानुपसंहारान्न तद्वाचक इष्यते 2.1.259cd
मुख्यां वृत्तिं समाश्रित्य तथोदर्केऽपि वक्ष्यते 1.4.403cd
मुख्यार्थं संपरित्यज्य पुंसि ब्रह्मेति कल्पनम् 1.4.1208cd
मुख्यार्थता वा प्रागुक्ता ब्रह्मेत्यस्य सदादृशि 2.4.36ab
मुख्यार्थलाभतश्चापि तस्य च प्रकृतत्वतः 1.4.1096cd
मुख्यार्थो ब्रह्मशब्दः स्यान्न त्वदुक्तेऽतथात्वतः 2.1.88cd
मुख्यार्थो ब्रह्मशब्दोऽयमेवं सत्युपपद्यते 1.4.1076cd
मुख्योऽन्यस्मिन्सति यतो ब्रह्मार्थो नावसीयते 2.3.240cd
मुच्यते मृत्युतो विद्वानिति नैगमिकं वचः 1.4.839cd
मुच्यन्ते न निवर्तन्ते यथा धूमादिमार्गगाः 6.2.144cd
मुच्यमानोऽथ यत्र त्वं गमिष्यसि नराधिप 4.2.33cd
मुञ्जेषीकावदुत्कृष्य पश्येदात्मानमात्मनि 4.4.1277cd
मुण्डोऽपरिग्रहश्चेति प्रत्यक्षश्रुतिवाक्यतः 3.5.158ab
मुण्डोऽपरिग्रहोऽसङ्गो बहिरन्तःशुचिः सदा SV 225ab
मुनित्वं न्यासिनो युक्तं मौनाच्चाप्यस्य सर्वदा 4.4.1072cd
मुनित्वं प्रत्यगज्ञानहेतुकर्मापवर्जनात् 4.4.1075cd
मुनिभावं ततो गत्वा ब्रह्मैव ब्राह्मणो भवेत् 3.5.176cd
मुमुक्षति न तावत्तं राजा प्रश्नार्थशेषतः 4.3.1899cd
मुमुक्षवः प्रवर्तेरन्कथं नामात्मवेदने SV 1126ab
मुमुक्षुं तत्त्ववित्साक्षात्संसारव्युत्थितैषणम् 2.1.519cd
मुमुक्षुं विनियुञ्जन्ति सदात्मज्ञानजन्मने 3.5.163cd
मुमुक्षुः प्रापितः स्वास्थ्यं परमैकात्म्यलक्षणम् 4.4.1161cd
मुमुक्षुत्वस्य तद्धेतोः कर्मकार्यं न तत्ततः 1.4.1115cd
मुमुक्षुपुरुषार्थस्य मोहमात्रान्तरायतः 1.4.809ab
मुमुक्षुरस्ति नास्तीति परो ग्रन्थोऽवतार्यते 3.4.3cd
मुमुक्षोरधिकारोऽतो निवृत्तौ सर्वकर्मणाम् SV 130cd
मुमुक्षोर्गतिमार्गस्य देशभेदोपदेशतः 1.4.1242ab

मुमुक्षोर्लक्षणं तादृक्श्रद्दधाना यदब्रुवन् 3.5.211cd
मुमुक्षोस्तदनिष्टत्वादिह निःशेष उच्यते 4.4.1284cd
मुमुक्षववस्थां संप्राप्त एवं पूर्वोक्तसाधनैः 4.4.1199cd
मुमूर्षतोऽत्र यद्दुःखं स्मर्यतां तन्मुमुक्षुभिः 4.3.1923cd
मुमूर्षुश्च पिता पुत्रमथाहूयानुमन्त्रयेत् 1.5.287ab
मुषितात्मपरिज्ञानः प्रज्ञां कुर्यात्कथं जडः 4.4.918cd
मूढाज्ञयोस्तु यः साक्षी नासौ मुग्धोऽज्ञ एव वा 4.4.363cd
मूढात्मनामपि ह्येतन्न विसंवादमृच्छति 1.4.1500cd
मूढोऽस्मीत्यपि साक्षाच्च मोहोऽयमनुभूयते 3.8.40cd
मूढोत्पत्तेः पुरा मोहः प्रत्यग्वस्त्वनुरोध्यभूत् 3.8.41ab
मूर्छादाविव संमोहमिहाप्यात्मा निगच्छति 4.4.9ab
मूर्तं मर्त्यं स्थितं सच्च क्षित्यबग्नित्रयं विदुः 2.3.28ab
मूर्तं मर्त्यं स्थितं सच्च पृथिव्यप्तेजसामिदम् 4.4.485ab
मूर्तं संस्थानवद्धयेतत्तथा मर्त्यं विनाशवत् 2.3.36ab
मूर्तत्वादेव मर्त्यं तन्मर्त्यत्वादेव तत्स्थितम् 2.3.29ab
मूर्तमेव च तद्रूपं ब्रह्मणोऽमूर्तमेव च 2.3.17cd
मूर्तशब्देन यत्प्राणद्व्द्वयोर्मनश्चापरं च यत् 2.3.69cd
मूर्तस्य च तथा पृथ्वी मध्ये संकीर्णता तयोः 2.3.178cd
मूर्तादीनामनिर्देश्यादितिर्मत्तो निवर्तते 2.3.189cd
मूर्तामूर्तं हि सत्याह्वं प्राणाः सत्यास्तदात्मतः 2.3.244ab
मूर्तामूर्तत्वहीनस्य प्रतीचो विक्रिया कुतः SV 143ab
मूर्तामूर्तरसे भानौ त्रिपादेषा प्रतिष्ठिता 5.16.28cd
मूर्तामूर्तविभागेऽस्य विभागो विनिवर्तते 2.3.111ab
मूर्तामूर्तविभागोऽयं यदि नामेह भण्यते 2.3.72ab
मूर्तामूर्तविभागोऽयमध्यात्ममधुनोच्यते 2.3.68cd
मूर्तामूर्तव्यवहृतिस्तथा तत्रापि दृश्यते 2.3.79cd
मूर्तामूर्तस्वभावस्य सत्यस्याविष्कृतेरथ 2.3.173ab
मूर्तामूर्तात्मकं सत्यं प्राणादेः कार्यरूपिणः 2.3.246ab
मूर्तामूर्तात्मकं सत्यं ब्रह्म पूर्वं प्रपञ्चितम् 5.4.3cd
मूर्तामूर्तात्मको राशिरेको बाह्यः किलेष्यते 2.3.112cd
मूर्तामूर्तात्मनोरुक्तो विभागो ब्रह्मरूपयोः 2.3.83cd
मूर्तामूर्तादयो यद्वत्पदार्था माननिश्चिताः 2.1.494ab

मूर्तामूर्तादिभावाच्च क्षीयमाणा हि सैव तु 4.4.493ab
मूर्तामूर्तादिराशिस्तु प्रयोज्यः साधनं तथा 2.3.115ab
मूर्तामूर्तादिसंबन्धाद्वासना लिङ्गमाश्रिताः 2.3.85ab
मूर्तामूर्ताद्यपह्नुत्या ह्यात्मनस्तत्त्वमब्रवीत् 4.3.1045ab
मूर्तामूर्ताविष्करणं गुणाविष्कृतिरिष्यते 2.4.335cd
मूर्तामूर्ते च द्वे रूपे तृतीयं वासना यतः 2.3.142cd
मूर्तो वा यदि वामूर्तः सच्च त्यच्चेति भण्यते 2.3.92cd
मूर्ध्नि प्रत्याहितं प्राणमृषयः प्राणसंज्ञकाः 2.2.24ab
मूलं च जगतो वाच्यमत आख्यानतोऽपि च 3.9.133ab
मूलं च जायमानस्य प्रधानं तेन भण्यते 4.4.124cd
मूलकारण एवैषां सर्वेषां विलयो भवेत् 2.4.373ab
मूलध्वस्तौ हतं तच्चेन्मिथ्याधीः किं करोति नः 1.4.438cd
मूलात्मैव त्रिधात्मानमभिनत्स प्रजापतिः 1.2.165ab
मूलाद्बीजाच्च वृक्षस्य साक्षाद्यद्वत्समुद्भवः 3.9.141ab
मृगतोये प्रवृत्तस्य तृडार्तस्योषरेक्षणात् 1.3.87ab
मृगाम्बुधीवन्मिथ्यात्वं स्यादेवं तदिदंधियोः 1.2.71ab
मृतः शेते स आध्मातो जीवतैतद्विरुध्यते 1.4.1755cd
मृतकल्पमिमं देहं स्वचित्तावेशयन्निव 2.1.155ab
मृतमेनं तथा मन्ये नेदृक्चिह्नं मृतिं विना 3.7.21cd
मृतस्य बीजस्थानीयं न च किंचिदिहेक्ष्यते 3.9.137cd
मृतानां जीवनं तद्वद्वृद्धानां यौवनं कुतः 2.1.297cd
मृता सत्यहिना न्यस्ता वल्मीकान्तर्बिलाश्रये 4.4.506cd
मृतास्ते धूममायान्ति धूमाद्रात्रिं तमस्विनः 6.2.148cd
मृतिजन्मप्रबन्धेन संसरत्या विमोक्षतः 4.3.822cd
मृतिरात्ममतिस्तस्य हेतुहेतूपमर्दनात् 4.4.390cd
मृतेरुच्छिद्यते लोकः साधनोच्छित्तिहेतुतः 1.5.322ab
मृतोऽस्मीत्यपि संवित्तिश्चैतन्यापगमे कुतः 4.3.216ab
मृतौ चाविकलस्यैव दर्शनादेरसंभवात् 4.3.267ab
मृतौ सहैव चानेन प्रकर्षोऽत्रात ईक्ष्यते 4.3.1946cd
मृत्युं साक्षादवाप्नोति ज्ञानयुक्तेन कर्मणा 1.3.6ab
मृत्युः स्वाभाविकं ज्ञानं शास्त्रीयं संभवस्तथा 1.4.1766ab
मृत्युकालात्पुरा नास्य व्याधिरप्युपसर्पति 2.1.79cd

मृत्युजन्मप्रबन्धेन जाग्रत्स्वप्नाख्यलोकवत् 4.3.826cd
मृत्युना कारणेनेदं कार्यं सर्वं समावृतम् 1.2.7ab
मृत्युना श्रमरूपेण ग्रस्ता वागादयो यतः 1.5.367ab
मृत्युनैवेत्युपक्रम्य तथा च श्रुतिरब्रवीत् 3.5.72ab
मृत्युमत्यवहत्प्राणः सामान्योक्तेर्विशेषतः 1.3.230ab
मृत्युरूपमिदं सर्वं कार्यं च करणानि च 4.3.1148cd
मृत्युरूपात्ययश्चैवं प्रतीचः पूर्ववाक्यतः 4.3.964cd
मृत्युरूपावधृतये परं ब्राह्मणमुच्यते 3.2.1cd
मृत्युर्जनिमतः साक्षात्तत्र कार्याप्ययत्वतः 1.2.9cd
मृत्युर्दूरं यथा प्राणात्तदात्मत्वात्तथासुरः 1.3.218ab
मृत्युर्वै तम इत्याह श्रुतिरप्यात्मनिह्नवात् 4.3.452cd
मृत्युर्वै तम इत्युक्तं तच्च बोधान्निराकृतम् 4.4.676cd
मृत्युर्वै तम इत्येवमाप एवेदमित्यपि 1.2.136ab
मृत्युर्हिरण्यगर्भः स्यात्स्वकार्यप्रलयत्वतः 4.4.670ab
मृत्युश्च देवता तस्य तमसैव मृतिर्यतः 3.9.54cd
मृत्युस्तत्फलविज्ञप्त्यै परो ग्रन्थोऽवतार्यते 3.2.23cd
मृत्योः प्रयोजकं यत्स्याद्ग्रहातिग्रहरूपिणः 3.2.40ab
मृत्योः स मृत्युमाप्नोति योऽत्र नानेव पश्यति 4.4.669cd
मृत्योः स मृत्युमित्येवं तद्दृष्टिरपि कुत्स्यते 1.4.690cd
मृत्योरपि सतो मृत्युरस्त्येवेति मयोच्यते 3.2.16ab
मृत्योर्मुक्त्यतिमुक्ती द्वे पूर्वस्मिन्ब्राह्मणे गते 3.2.1ab
मृत्योर्मृत्युमसावेति यो नानेवेह वीक्षते 4.4.671cd
मृत्योर्मृत्यवपरिज्ञानादज्ञस्य मरणं तमः 1.4.1674ab
मृत्स्नवन्तं वा सनियमं तदप्यत्यन्तशुद्धिकृत् 4.4.1058cd
मृत्स्नेभके यथेभत्वं शिशुरध्यस्य वल्गति 3.3.65ab
मृदात्मनोपसंश्लिष्टं कार्यं कारणतामितम् 1.2.89ab
मृदादि कारणं लब्धं न मानं स्यान्मृदा विना 1.2.54cd
मृदाद्येव ततो ग्राह्यं कारणं ह्यन्वयान्मृदः 1.2.51ab
मृदापत्तिर्घटस्येव विकारस्यात्मनो ध्रुवम् SV 257ab
मृदुकण्टकवत्तद्धीर्नालं वेद्धुं स्वगोचरान् 2.1.345cd
मृदेव कारणं यस्मात्पिण्डादेरवगम्यते 1.2.44cd
मृदो जातस्य कुम्भस्य न लयो वीरणादिषु 1.5.381cd

मृद्वद्व्योम घटीकुर्यान्मरुद्वाग्नेश्च शीतताम् SV 55ab
मृल्लोहविस्फुलिङ्गाद्यैः सृष्टिर्या चोदितान्यथा 2.1.387ab
मृषा तत्रैव स मिथो व्यभिचाराद्ध्रुवं भवेत् 4.3.1677cd
मृषात्वात्सर्वबुद्धीनां न क्वचिन्निश्चितिर्भवेत् 1.2.65cd
मृषात्वाद्वेदजातस्य सर्गस्थित्याद्यसंभवात् 5.1.32ab
मेधया तपसेत्यादि तथा च प्रागुदाहृतम् 2.3.57ab
मेधातपोगिरा नान्ये ग्राह्ये तदफलत्वतः 1.5.20cd
मेधातपोतिरेकेण नान्यतस्यात्साधनं यतः 1.5.22ab
मेधावी पण्डितोऽतोऽयं ब्रह्मस्वादानकारणात् 4.3.1896ab
मेध्यमित्यादिकं कामं सोऽकामयत कामुकः 1.2.206cd
मेयं वस्तु ततोऽज्ञानं प्रत्यक्षं सप्रमातृकम् 1.4.281cd
मेयं सिद्धमिहैवैतन्न वेदादन्यतः क्वचित् 1.4.339cd
मेयकार्त्स्न्याविरोधित्वान्न मितेः शङ्क्यते भिदा 1.4.1291ab
मेयतो जडतात्रापि संविच्चेन्न प्रमाणजा SV 1066cd
मेयत्वं लभते नान्यद्यच्च त्यक्तक्षितिद्वयम् 3.4.117cd
मेयप्रबोधनं मुक्त्वा न मितेः सत्यतान्यतः 1.4.431cd
मेयप्रमामृते कार्यं मानानां नान्यदिष्यते 1.4.278ab
मेयमात्रावसायित्वात्सर्वमानस्य सर्वदा 4.4.336cd
मेयमानत्वसंभित्तौ न पश्यामोऽत्र साधनम् 1.4.223ab
मेयमानप्रमातॄणां प्रात्यक्ष्यं प्रागपीरितम् 3.4.186ab
मेयमानप्रमातॄणां व्यभिचारेऽपि चात्मनः 4.3.1419ab
मेयमानप्रमात्रादिविभागस्तत्र नेक्ष्यते 3.4.127ab
मेयमानादिसंभित्तिर्यदि नामेह लभ्यते 1.4.1094ab
मेयमानाभिसंबन्धान्मानमेयार्थसंकरात् 4.4.753ab
मेयमानाभिसंबन्धो यथेह प्रतिपादितः 4.4.752ab
मेयमानैकतोऽभावादज्ञातत्वस्य तत्क्षणे 1.4.246cd
मेययाथात्म्यतो जाता प्रज्ञेतीहाभिधीयते 4.4.834cd
मेययाथात्म्यसंलेहि मानं मानत्वमश्नुते 5.1.88ab
मेयरूपानुरोधित्वं मिथ्यासंशययोर्यदि 1.4.439ab
मेयवस्त्वनुरोधित्वात्परिच्छेदकता धियः 3.2.86cd
मेयव्यापारतः पश्चात्प्राप्तज्ञानानुरञ्जनात् 4.4.750ab
मेयव्याप्तिश्च मानानां नान्यव्यावृत्तिवर्त्मना 4.4.661ab

मेयसिद्धिर्यतस्तस्मान्न मानं तत्र विद्यते 4.4.910cd
मेयस्य तेन माव्याप्तिः प्रज्ञामित्यभिधीयते 4.4.836cd
मेयस्य मानसंबन्धे प्रमेय इति गीरियम् 4.4.683ab
मेयस्वरूपावसितेर्नान्या मानस्य मानता 1.4.1291cd
मेयाज्ञातत्वबाधेन कुर्वन्मानमितीर्यते 4.4.811cd
मेयादींस्तदभावं च संशयानृतनिश्चयान् 4.3.190ab
मेयान्तराभ्युपगमे न ह्यैकात्म्यं प्रसिध्यति 4.3.1485cd
मेयाभावः प्रमाणानां यद्यभावेन गम्यते SV 940ab
मेयाभावः प्रमाणानां यद्यभावेन गम्यते 4.3.1711ab
मेयाभावस्य मानत्वमविशेषात्प्रसज्यते SV 943cd
मेयाभावादिति प्राप्तावत्र प्रतिविधीयते 4.3.731cd
मेयाभिसंगतं तच्च मेयाभत्वं प्रपद्यते 1.2.103cd
मेयाभिसंगतेः पूर्वं ज्ञानं ज्ञातृसमाश्रयम् 3.4.146ab
मेयार्थानभिसंबन्धान्न यथावस्तुधीरियम् 1.4.274ab
मेयार्थापह्नुतिश्च स्यान्नाज्ञातमिति जल्पतः 1.4.242cd
मेयासंस्पर्शिदृष्टित्वान्न पश्यन्तीति भण्यते 1.4.654cd
मेयासाधारणात्मोत्थज्ञानस्यैव प्रमाणतः 1.4.1297ab
मेयासाधारणात्मोत्थरूपवान्निश्चयो यथा 3.4.141ab
मेयेनाप्तौ तु तद्ध्वस्तिर्मेययाथात्म्यमात्रतः 4.4.838cd
मेयेनैव समाप्तत्वात्ततोऽन्या व्यापृतिर्न च 4.4.663ab
मेयैकात्म्यानुरोधित्वं तथाप्यतिशयो धियः 3.3.38cd
मेयोऽनधिगतः सिद्धो ह्यभ्युपेयोऽवबुद्धवत् 4.3.173cd
मेयोऽनधिगतस्तावत्स्वानुभूत्यैकसिद्धिकः 4.3.1735cd
मेयोपसर्जना बुद्धिः स्मृत्या साक्षात्प्रतीयते 3.4.143cd
मेर्वादिज्ञानवच्चेत्स्यान्निष्फलत्वादमानता 1.3.82ab
मेलनस्यापि कार्यत्वात्कथं तत्स्यात्त्रयं विना 1.2.85cd
मेषयोर्मल्लयोर्यद्वन्न भावाभावयोस्तथा SV 931cd
मैत्रेयीत्यादिको ग्रन्थस्तस्मादारभ्यते परः 2.4.18cd
मैत्रेयीब्राह्मणं श्रुत्या तथा च न्यायविद्वचः 4.5.3cd
मैत्रेयीब्राह्मणे चैतद्व्याख्यातं वाक्यमादरात् 4.3.1794ab
मैथुनं तु विशेषेण ह्युक्तानर्थजिहासया 6.4.64cd
मैथुनोपनिषत्तत्त्वमेतद्ध स्माह भावितः 6.4.16cd

मैवं कर्मफलव्यक्तेरानन्त्यादुपपद्यते 3.3.109ab
मैवं दृष्टार्थविषये यत्कर्मास्यावशेषितम् 4.4.1268ab
मैवं न वक्त्रभिप्रायाच्छब्दार्थत्वं प्रकल्पते SV 594ab
मैवं नैकान्तिको हेतुश्चक्षुरादीन्द्रियैः स्फुटम् 4.3.142ab
मैवं पदार्थसंसर्गरूपस्यैवातथात्मके 4.4.799ab
मैवं पश्याम्यहं कुम्भं न पश्यामीति दर्शनात् 4.3.1468ab
मैवं प्रक्रमसंहारपर्यालोचनया पुरा SV 284ab
मैवं प्रैषादिवद्यस्मादुपाधित्वादवाच्यता SV 510cd
मैवं बाधात्तु मिथ्यात्वसिद्धिः स्यान्मृगतोयवत् 4.3.491ab
मैवं भिन्नैकवाक्यत्वे प्रागस्माभिः समर्थिते SV 286ab
मैवं भेदे तथाभेदे दोषः स्याच्छक्तिकार्ययोः SV 59cd
मैवं मनुष्यलोकस्य यतस्तत्राप्तिरिष्यते 1.5.238cd
मैवं मानान्तराप्राप्तसम्यगैकात्म्यबोधतः 2.4.148ab
मैवं मानान्तरावेशाल्लोके प्रैषाद्युपाधिकम् SV 519ab
मैवं मिथ्यानुभूतित्वाच्छुक्तिकारजतादिवत् 4.3.1675cd
मैवं मृषात्वात्स्वप्नोत्थसुखदुःखादिलक्षण– 2.1.263ab
मैवं विविदिषामात्रहेतोरेव परिग्रहात् 4.4.1036ab
मैवं साध्यापि नो मुक्तिर्न त्वभ्युदयवद्यतः SV 26cd
मैवं स्वतोऽवबुद्धत्वात्कुतोऽज्ञानेन संगतिः 2.1.308ab
मैवमप्रतिपन्नत्वादननुभूत्यैव वस्तुनः SV 547ab
मोक्षं यान्तं नरं सर्वे मुञ्चन्ति सहजापि 2.4.67ab
मोक्षप्रकरणान्नित्यः क्रियोत्थोऽतो न गृह्यते 4.4.556cd
मोक्षमार्गे यथोक्तेऽस्मिन्नविद्योपप्लुताशयाः 4.4.561ab
मोक्षस्य पुरुषार्थस्य वचोऽतो निष्फलं भवेत् SV 458cd
मोक्षात्फलान्तरैर्योगः काम्यानां स्याच्छ्रुतत्वतः 3.3.108ab
मोक्षाय यत्नः फलवांस्तदा स्यान्न विपर्यये 3.3.19cd
मोक्षे पुंसोऽधिकारः स्यान्न कामापहतात्मनः 1.3.96cd
मोक्षे भयश्रुतेर्नार्थस्तत्र को मोह इत्यतः 1.4.90cd
मोक्षो दार्ष्टान्तिकस्तस्य दृष्टान्तस्येह वर्ण्यते 4.4.254cd
मोघमन्नमिति तथा मन्त्रे ताच्छील्यनिन्दनम् 1.5.26cd
मोदत्रासादिको मृत्युः स्वभावो न यथात्मनः 4.3.972ab
मोहं चात्येति वैचित्यं विषयापह्नुतिं धियः 3.5.61cd

मोहं भित्त्वात्मसंबोधाद्ययुः कैवल्यमुत्तमम् 3.5.145cd
मोहकामादिदुष्टस्य नित्यं कर्म विधीयते 1.3.94ab
मोहतत्कार्यनीडं यत्कूटस्थाभासरूपकम् 1.4.374ab
मोहतत्कार्यनीडो यस्तस्याज्ञानसमन्वयात् 2.4.434ab
मोहध्वस्तौ प्रतीचोऽन्यो नातोऽर्थोऽत्रावशिष्यते 3.5.187cd
मोहमात्रप्रयुक्तत्वान्न सामान्यात्स्मृतेश्च तत् 1.4.446cd
मोहमात्रव्यवहितमाप्तुमिच्छन्त आदरात् 4.4.1076cd
मोहमात्रान्तरायत्वाज्ज्ञानमात्रमपेक्षते 2.4.31cd
मोहमात्रान्तरायत्वात्कादाचित्कं हि दर्शनम् 1.4.1156cd
मोहमात्रान्तरायत्वात्तत्कर्मालं न मुक्तये 1.4.1677cd
मोहमात्रान्तरायत्वात्पुरुषार्थस्य नापरम् 2.1.6ab
मोहमात्रान्तरायायां मुक्तावस्तु यथोदितम् SV 252cd
मोहमात्रेन तत्प्राप्तेः सामर्थ्यात्स्यान्न शब्दतः 1.4.1425cd
मोहमात्रैकहेतूनि तस्मात्कर्माण्यशेषतः 2.4.25ab
मोहव्यवहितं वा यत्प्राप्तं तद्ब्रह्मबोधतः 4.3.1303cd
मोहादेव ततः शास्त्रं तदुच्छित्तौ प्रवर्तते 1.2.130cd
मोहाध्यस्तात्मव्याधत्वान्मोहध्वंसातिरेकतः 2.1.516ab
मोहाध्वस्तेर्न चाशेषः पुरुषार्थः समाप्यते 3.2.58cd
मोहापनुत्तये प्राह प्रपन्नाय किरीटिने 3.5.48ab
मोहाल्लिङ्गात्मनोत्क्रान्तः श्रुतकर्मानुरूपतः 4.3.811ab
मोहासङ्गास्पदो मृत्युर्ग्रहातिग्रहलक्षणः 3.2.3cd
मोहोच्छित्तिर्यथावस्तुसम्यग्ज्ञानप्रसूतितः 3.8.48ab
मोहोत्थदेहबुद्ध्यादिसंगतेरिवगीरियम् 4.4.11cd
मोहोत्थाः पृथगात्मानः साधनायत्तसिद्धिकाः 1.4.1147ab
मोहोत्थाशेषकार्येभ्यो विशुद्धिं श्रुतिरब्रवीत् 2.1.364cd
मोहोत्थाहमितिज्ञानाद्द्वयारत्यादिमद्भवेत् 1.4.28cd
मोहोत्थोपाधिसंबन्धादभिन्नोऽपि स्वतो दृशिः 4.3.1776ab
मौढीं प्रसिद्धिमुल्लङ्घ्य गार्ग्योऽयं मामुपागतः 2.1.43ab
मौढ्यं जाड्यमविद्या स्यान्नित्यबुद्धात्मवस्तुनः 4.3.457ab
म्रियते स यदैवंवित्पुत्रसंक्रामितक्रतुः 1.5.313ab
म्रियमाणो न शक्नोति पुत्रं जनयितुं क्वचित् 4.3.624cd
म्लोचन्त्यपि च श्राम्यन्ति तेन भग्नव्रताः स्मृताः 1.5.367cd

य आत्मा प्रस्तुतोऽविद्वान्स यदेदं शरीरकम् 4.4.7ab
य आत्मेत्यादिभिर्वाक्यैरन्वयव्यतिरेकतः 2.1.520ab
य उक्तस्तस्य संस्थित्या तस्थुरिन्द्रान्तदेवताः 3.6.15cd
य एते पार्थिवा भावा लोष्टकुम्भादयो मताः 3.6.6ab
य एते सर्वभूतेषु वर्तन्तेऽम्भःप्रवाहवत् 3.5.93cd
य एवं वेदेति विधिः फलोक्तेरर्थवादतः 1.3.191cd
य एव जायते कर्ता स एवायं विनश्यति 4.3.600ab
य एवमभिधानज्ञ उपासीतादितिं सदा 1.2.196cd
य एष तपतीत्यत्र मण्डलं परिगृह्यते 2.3.39ab
य एष दक्षिणः पन्थाः पितृलोकः स उच्यते 4.3.1857ab
यं घनोदमिति प्राहुः पुराणज्ञा विपश्चितः 3.3.148ab
यं तं विविदिषन्त्युच्चैर्यथोक्तैः साधनैः परम् 4.4.1068ab
यं प्राप्य न निवर्तन्ते निर्वाणं परमं गताः 2.5.72cd
यं यं वापि स्मरन्भावं त्यजत्यन्ते कलेवरम् 4.4.102ab
यः कश्चिदेतं व्याख्यातं वेदोपास्ते दिवानिशम् 5.4.5ab
यः कश्चेत्यविशेषोक्तिर्नादवर्णपदोक्तिभिः 1.5.129ab
यः पृथिव्यभिमान्यत्र सर्वस्यैव परायणम् 3.9.37cd
यः पृथिव्यामिति तथा नेति नेतीति चागमः 2.1.445cd
यः पृथिव्यामितीशोऽसावन्तर्यामी जगद्गुरुः 1.4.377ab
यः पृष्टः स पराग्वृत्तिप्रमामेयातिलङ्घितः 4.3.300ab
यः प्राणेनेति वचसा न लिङ्गादुक्तबोधनम् 3.4.67cd
यः प्राणे भोग इति न पूर्ववद्वर्ण्यतेऽत्र किम् 1.3.171ab
यः स एतांस्त्वया पृष्टांश्चतुरोऽप्यष्टकानिह 3.9.113ab
यः स एव यथोक्तेभ्यः परमः स्यादनन्ततः 4.3.1882cd
यः स एव स्वयंज्योतिर्ज्योतिःशब्देन भण्यते 4.3.881cd
यः सर्वज्ञः सर्वविद्योऽशनायादिविवर्जितः 2.1.445ab
यः सर्वान्तर इत्युक्तस्तन्निर्णयविवक्षया 3.6.1ab
यः स्त्रीपुंसपरिमाणोऽभूत्स एवातो द्विधाकृतः 1.4.114cd
यः स्यात्कामग्रहग्रस्तो वित्तापत्योद्भवं प्रति 6.3.3ab
यः स्वकारणसंसर्गः कार्याणामत्ययो भवेत् 3.5.69ab
यः स्वतो नागमापायी तद्विरुद्धेषु सर्वदा 4.4.468ab
यच्च कामसुखं लोके यच्च दिव्यं महत्सुखम् 4.3.1884ab

यच्च किंचिदविज्ञातं प्राणोऽसावाधिभौतिकः 1.5.158cd
यच्च दीपप्रकाशादिक्रियावदिति चोदितम् 4.3.649ab
यच्च न ज्ञाप्यते वेदे वस्त्वत्येतदचूचुदः SV 194ab
यच्चानधीतं तस्योक्तौ ब्रह्मेत्यत्रैकता भवेत् 1.5.291cd
यच्चाप्नोति यदादत्ते यच्चात्ति विषयानिह 1.4.737ab
यच्चाप्यक्षैरनैकान्त्यं हेतोरभिहितं पुरा 4.3.237ab
यच्चाप्यहरहर्वेदमनुब्रूते प्रयत्नवान् 1.4.1798ab
यच्चाप्युक्तं श्रुतिस्मृत्योः क्रियाया इव सिद्धितः SV 191ab
यच्चाप्यैकात्म्यविज्ञानं तदज्ञानैकघस्मरम् SV 362ab
यच्चाभयं वेदयस इति प्रत्यूचिवान्नृपः 4.2.98ab
यच्चाभाणि विना कार्यं नाधिकारो निरूप्यते SV 227ab
यच्चामृतं स्वभार्यायै याज्ञवल्क्येन भाषितम् 2.5.39cd
यच्चास्य वास्तवं रूपं यच्चाविद्योत्थमात्मनः 4.4.148ab
यच्चास्य संततो भावस्तस्मादात्मेति कथ्यते 1.4.737cd
यच्चास्यासति कर्तव्ये नाधिकारो निरूप्यते SV 31ab
यच्चैतत्कृष्णसर्पादिदृष्टान्ताद्भवतोदितम् 4.3.200ab
यच्चैतदात्मज्योतिष्ट्वं व्यतिरिक्ततयोदितम् 4.3.136ab
यच्चोक्तं न पुमर्थोऽस्ति वस्तुमात्रावबोधनात् SV 196ab
यच्चोक्तमनुमीयन्ते प्रतिदेहं पृथग्विधाः 2.1.596ab
यच्चोत्पत्त्यादिमद्वस्तु तत्तुच्छं स्वप्नवस्तुवत् 4.4.1102ab
यच्चोत्पित्सु परं जन्म धृतं तदपि वायुना 3.7.14cd
यच्छेद्वाङ्मनसी प्राज्ञस्तद्यच्छेज्ज्ञान आत्मनि 4.4.1256ab
यच्छोचन्ति प्रजाः सर्वा दुःखैराध्यात्मिकादिभिः 1.5.358ab
यजते योऽश्वमेधेन यश्चैवं वेद तं क्रतुम् SV 1120ab
यजमानश्रुतेरत्र पर्वोद्गीथैकवाक्यतः 3.1.43ab
यजमानस्य कर्मास्ति ज्ञानं तूद्गातृसंश्रयम् 1.3.383ab
यजमानस्य मुक्तिः स्यादतिमुक्तिस्तथैव च 3.1.24cd
यजमानस्य येयं वाग्घोता चैतद्द्वयं यदा 3.1.23ab
यजमानोऽपि तादात्म्यात्तथैव भवति ध्रुवम् 1.3.280cd
यजमानो जपस्तत्र ज्ञानं नेत्यवसीयताम् 3.1.43cd
यजुर्ब्रह्मेति श्रवणादन्ते साम्नो ग्रहादपि 1.3.300ab
यजुश्च प्राण एवेति सदोपासीत यत्नतः 5.15.4ab

यजेति लिङ्गान्निन्दैषा कर्मिणामेव गम्यते 1.4.132ab
यजेतेतिविधिज्ञानं न विध्यन्तरमीक्षते SV 661ab
यजेतेत्यादिसामान्याद्विद्यर्थोऽतो विचार्यते 1.4.756cd
यजेय भूयोऽपीत्येवमकामयत भावितः 1.2.199ab
यजेयमश्वमेधेन भूयोऽपीत्यभ्यमन्यत 1.2.214ab
यज्जातीयैः प्रमाणैस्तु यज्जातीयार्थदर्शनम् 2.4.173ab
यज्ज्ञातमपि कात्स्न्र्येन तत्तदन्यच्च नाञ्जसा 1.4.958ab
यज्ञदानतपःकर्म न त्याज्यं कार्यमेव तत् 4.4.1045ab
यज्ञदानतपांसीह गृहस्थ इव तापसे 6.2.122ab
यज्ञदानादिभिस्तस्य साहचर्येण हेतुना 4.4.1040cd
यज्ञादिलक्षणं तावत्पारंपर्येण साधनम् 3.5.193ab
यज्ञाद्याहितसंस्कारा अपास्ताशेषसाधनाः 1.4.1071ab
यज्ञारम्भे तदा मध्ये गीयमानेऽथ सामनि 6.3.30cd
यज्ञेन कर्मणास्राक्षीज्जगदेतच्चराचरम् 1.3.275cd
यज्ञेन भूयसा यक्ष्य इत्येवं स प्रजापतिः 1.2.198ab
यज्ञो दानं तपश्चेति स्मृतेरपि वचः स्फुटम् 4.4.1042cd
यज्ञो दानं तपश्चैव पावनानि मनीषिणाम् 4.4.1045cd
यत आत्मतयैवैतैर्विशिनष्ट्यविशेषणम् SV 120ab
यत आदाविदं वृत्तमन्नागानमनात्मनि 1.3.239ab
यत आधारगो ह्येष नामरूपादिलक्षणः 2.3.98cd
यत आहवनीयोऽग्निर्द्युलोकात्मतया स्थितः 6.2.76cd
यत उक्तं चिकीर्षुः सन्ननुशिष्टश्च तादृशः 1.5.299ab
यत उत्क्रान्तिरुक्तेयं विशिष्ट्फलसंगतेः 4.4.1ab
यत एवमतः कर्मकामदोषविवर्जितः 4.3.1062ab
यत एवमतः पश्यन्नित्यस्यैवोत्तरं वचः 4.3.1488ab
यत एवमतः पश्येदात्मन्यात्मानमद्वयम् 2.1.9ab
यत एवमतः पुंभिः स्वातन्त्र्यार्थं प्रयत्नतः 4.4.104ab
यत एवमतः प्रत्यक्प्रत्ययेनोपदिश्यते 4.3.306ab
यत एवमतः प्रत्यग्याथात्म्यप्रतिपत्तये SV 1116ab
यत एवमतः प्रत्यग्याथात्म्यानवबोधतः 3.5.68ab
यत एवमतः प्राणाः सम्यग्ज्ञानस्य जन्मनि 4.4.288ab
यत एवमतः प्राणो गृहादिवदिहेष्यते 2.1.159ab

यत एवमतः प्राह तल्लिङ्गं स्थूलदेहतः 4.2.63ab
यत एवमतः प्राह नेह तद्वस्तु विद्यते 4.3.1525ab
यत एवमतः प्राहाथैष एवेति नः श्रुतिः 4.3.1876cd
यत एवमतः सर्वे कालदैवेश्वरादयः 3.2.149ab
यत एवमतः सिद्धं दर्शनं प्रत्यगात्मनः 2.4.485ab
यत एवमतः सिद्धा देहादिभ्योऽन्यतात्मनः 4.3.823ab
यत एवमतः स्वप्ने नाशङ्का देवताः प्रति 4.3.1143ab
यत एवमतस्तस्मात्सत्यं रक्ष्यं प्रयत्नतः 2.5.104cd
यत एवमतस्तानि नाडीभिः कर्मणो वशात् 2.1.334ab
यत एवमतस्तुभ्यं वक्ष्याम्यमृतसाधनम् 2.4.70ab
यत एवमतोऽन्वीक्ष्य मर्तामर्तादिवर्त्मना 2.3.249ab
यत एवमतोऽपास्तरागद्वेषादिधीमलः 1.4.607ab
यत एवमतोऽप्राक्षीद्याज्ञवल्क्यं नराधिपः 4.3.20ab
यत एवमतोऽभेदो ज्ञानलाभार्थयोरिह 1.4.1013cd
यत एवमतोऽयुक्ता पुनरुक्तार्थकल्पना 4.4.540ab
यत एवमतोऽवश्यं प्रमाणव्यापृतेः पुरा 4.3.173ab
यत एवमतोऽविद्याकार्योऽनर्थोऽखिलो भवेत् 1.4.1596cd
यत एवमतोऽविद्यासमुच्छित्ताविदं जगत् 2.4.477ab
यत एवमतोऽशेषज्ञानशक्तिलयात्परम् 2.4.387ab
यत एवमतोऽसाधु भवतैतद्दाहृतम् 4.3.513ab
यत एवमतो ग्राह्यं शुक्तिकाज्ञानमेव तु 1.4.470ab
यत एवमतो ज्ञप्तिमात्रमेवाभिधीयते 4.3.1634ab
यत एवमतो ज्ञेयो वायुरेव न चापरः 3.3.167ab
यत एवमतो दृष्टिर्नित्यैवात्मन इष्यताम् 4.3.1472ab
यत एवमतो देवाः सर्वेऽपि स्युः प्रजापतिः 1.4.140ab
यत एवमतो नात्र विधिः कल्प्यः कथं चन SV 235ab
यत एवमतो नास्ति विशेषोऽत्र मनागपि 4.4.368ab
यत एवमतो नास्य नाशान्ता विक्रियात्मनः 3.9.98cd
यत एवमतो नेशो भयान्स्यात्साधुकर्मणा 4.4.999ab
यत एवमतो नेह कश्चिद्विप्रतिपद्यते 3.8.126ab
यत एवमतो न्याय्यं कर्मैवास्य समाश्रयः 3.2.155ab
यत एवमतो ब्रूहि कतमोऽत्र विवक्षितः 3.4.64ab

यत एवमतो यत्नादुपास्यं हृदयं सदा 5.3.5cd
यत एवमतो यावत्किंचित्कार्यान्तरायकम् 4.3.1303ab
यत एवमतो यावदात्मा द्रष्टा न नश्यति 4.3.1550ab
यत एवमतो युक्तं देवादेर्भृशमप्रियम् 1.4.1575cd
यत एवमतो यो नः प्रत्यक्संमोहहानिकृत् 1.4.1527ab
यत एवमतो लोके कुमारं जातमग्रतः 1.5.51ab
यत एवमतो वस्तु मुक्तमेव विमुच्यते 4.4.296ab
यत एवमतो वाचं परं ब्रह्मेति चिन्तयेत् 4.1.20ab
यत एवमतो विद्वान्कामहेतूपमर्दनात् 4.4.263ab
यत एवमयं लोकः परश्चायं च सर्वतः 3.7.17ab
यत एवमविद्योत्थं प्राणाद्यस्यातदात्मनः 1.4.687ab
यत एवमसंतोषात्पक्षान्तरसमाश्रयः 1.4.1194ab
यत एवमिदं दृष्टमन्वयव्यतिरेकतः 1.3.294ab
यत एवमिदं वस्तु अतिच्छन्दादिलक्षणम् 4.3.1355ab
यत एव समुत्पत्तिस्तत्रैव प्रलयोऽपि च 1.5.381ab
यतः कर्म तमोहेतुस्तस्मादेव मुमुक्षुभिः 4.4.1251ab
यतः कर्मसहायोऽयमेकाक्येवेह गच्छति 4.3.1955cd
यतः काममयो भूत्वा प्राप सर्वमयात्मताम् 4.4.211ab
यतः पदार्थसंबोधान्नेति नेत्यादिलक्षणम् 4.4.1191ab
यतः प्रजापतिः पूर्वमेतस्मिन्दर्शने स्थितः 1.3.275ab
यतः प्रत्यभिजानाति सुषुप्तादुत्थितस्ततः 4.3.1402ab
यतः प्रवृत्तिर्भूतानां येन सर्वमिदं ततम् 3.8.152ab
यतः प्रागकरोत्कर्म तत्कार्येऽपि तथा ततः 1.3.272cd
यतः प्रागपि तद्बोधात्सर्वो जन्तुः स्वभावतः 1.4.1205ab
यतः प्राणादिभावोऽयं प्राणादीनां तमेव ये 4.4.643ab
यतः प्राप्तमतः श्रुत्या साधनत्वं विधीयते 4.4.1219cd
यतः शास्त्रेण तेनायं विभागः क्रियते मया 2.4.45cd
यतः संयोगिनिर्मुक्तौ वस्तु शुद्धमिहेष्यते 4.3.706ab
यतः सति क्रियाभेदे किं पूर्वमिति चोदना 1.2.102ab
यतः समीक्षितुं शक्यस्तेनासौ रज्जुसर्पवत् 2.4.268cd
यतः सर्वविशेषाणामविद्यैवास्ति कारणम् 4.4.306cd
यतः सिद्धायते सोऽर्थो ज्ञेयः सिद्धः स्वतः सदा SV 545cd

यतः सूत्रपदे द्वित्वमविशेषेण चोदितम् 1.5.41ab
यतः स्पर्शादिनाप्येषां प्रवृत्तिर्दृश्यते नृणाम् 4.3.51cd
यतः स्वकार्यनिर्देशः स्वान्तस्य स्पर्शनेन्द्रिये 1.5.116ab
यतश्चोदेति सूर्योऽसौ यत्र चास्तं निगच्छति 1.5.376cd
यतस्ततोऽज आत्मायं वसुदान इहोच्यते 4.4.1313cd
यतस्ततोऽतिरेकेण मोक्षोऽनित्यो भवेद्ध्रुवम् 3.3.23cd
यतस्ततो न साध्यं तज्ज्ञानकर्मादिसाधनैः 1.4.1333cd
यतस्तत्प्रतिषेधार्थमनण्विति जगाद ताम् 3.8.71cd
यतस्तदपकर्षेण विज्ञानात्मोपसंहृतिः 4.4.45cd
यतस्तदवरोधार्थं तस्मात्सर्वविशेषणम् 4.4.378ef
यतस्तद्धनवत्तस्मात्स्वरार्थं यत्नमाचरेत् 1.3.337cd
यतिथ्यामिति यः प्रश्नः स पुंजन्मोक्तितो गतः 6.2.160ab
यतोऽकरोद्विराडेवं तस्मादेवेह याज्ञिकाः 1.2.217ab
यतोऽकामादयोऽप्यत्र ह्युक्ता एवार्थतो मताः 1.5.112cd
यतोऽज्ञातत्वसंसिद्धिर्ज्ञातत्वस्यापि चाञ्जसा 1.4.287ab
यतोऽत आत्मनि ज्ञाते कृतकृत्यत्वहेतुतः 4.4.760cd
यतोऽत आत्मरूपार्थमात्मेत्येवं विशेष्यते 3.4.21cd
यतोऽत आत्मवस्त्वेव कार्यकारणवज्जगत् 4.4.155cd
यतोऽत उत्तरो ग्रन्थः सम्यग्व्याख्यायतेऽधुना 3.3.133cd
यतोऽत एकवाक्यत्वे ब्रह्मात्माख्यपदार्थयोः 3.4.29ab
यतोऽतः कर्मणां कार्यं नेह संभाव्यतेऽण्वपि 4.4.1157cd
यतोऽतः कर्मदृष्ट्या तं द्रष्टारं नानुपश्यति 3.4.170cd
यतोऽतः कर्म मन्थाख्यं तादर्थ्येनाभिधीयते 6.3.1cd
यतोऽतः कर्मशुद्धात्मा भवादस्माद्विरज्यते 2.4.72cd
यतोऽतः कारणध्वस्तौ बुद्ध्याद्येत्यात्मकारणम् 4.3.1529cd
यतोऽतः कार्यतां तस्या नेश्वरोऽपि प्रसाधयेत् 1.4.336cd
यतोऽतः कार्यतां तस्या नेश्वरोऽपि प्रसाधयेत् 3.4.116cd
यतोऽतः पाक्षिकी प्राप्तिर्नेहास्त्यैकात्म्यदर्शने 2.4.146ab
यतोऽतः पुनरित्येवं संप्रसादाप्तितोऽभिधा 4.3.988cd
यतोऽतः प्रत्यग्याथात्म्यभास्वद्विज्ञानभास्कर- 4.2.94ab
यतोऽतः प्राणसंबन्धात्पूर्वं व्याख्या प्रपञ्च्यते 2.2.3cd
यतोऽतः सर्वतो नृणामिति भाष्यकृदब्रवीत् SV 1025cd

यतोऽतः सर्वमात्मैव प्राब्रवीच्छ्रुतिरञ्जसा 2.4.105cd
यतोऽतः सूत्रितं नेदं सूत्रकृद्भिर्यथोदितम् 6.3.9cd
यतोऽतः सूत्रिता नेयं सूत्रकृद्भिरनित्यतः 1.5.284cd
यतोऽतः स्त्रीप्रधानोऽयं पुत्राणां वंश उच्यते 6.5.8cd
यतोऽतः स्वार्थदेशः स स्वार्थश्चानन्यसिद्धिकः 1.4.310cd
यतोऽतत्त्वविदां कामो न कदाचिन्निवर्तते 2.1.577cd
यतोऽतश्चिन्निभेनैव व्याप्तिः स्यात्कारणात्मना 2.1.340cd
यतोऽतश्चोदयामोऽत्र यथा विप्रतिषिद्धता 1.4.1088cd
यतोऽतस्तत्त्वसंबोधाद्ब्रह्म ब्रह्म प्रपद्यते 1.4.1160cd
यतोऽतस्तत्परिज्ञाने नात्माज्ञानमपेक्षते 4.3.1456cd
यतोऽतस्तत्प्रबोधेऽस्मिन्न प्रमात्राद्यपेक्षते 4.4.682cd
यतोऽतस्तत्स्वसंवेद्यं गार्ग्यक्षरमिदं ध्रुवम् 3.8.69cd
यतोऽतस्तदनूद्याह ह्यात्मैवेति श्रुतिः स्फुटम् 1.3.54cd
यतोऽतस्तन्निषेधार्थं निषिद्धं सन्निषिध्यते 3.8.83cd
यतोऽतस्तन्निषेधार्थं सर्वान्तर इतीरणम् 3.4.23ab
यतोऽतस्तार्किकोक्तीस्ता नैवापेक्षामहे वयम् 4.4.482cd
यतोऽतस्तीर्थसृत्यैव मत्तो विद्यां त्वमाप्नुहि 6.2.66cd
यतोऽतस्ते न जानाति नावो नौस्थस्तटस्थवत् 4.3.440cd
यतोऽतिसूक्ष्मो लिङ्गात्मा नातोऽयं स्थूलदेहवत् 4.2.64ab
यतोऽतिसृष्टिस्तेनेयं यैषेहाग्न्यादिरीरिता 1.4.162cd
यतोऽतोऽकुर्वदेवेह स्यात्सर्वत्रैव कारकम् 4.3.1444cd
यतोऽतोऽङ्गिरसं त्यक्त्वा दूरित्येवाभिधीयते 1.3.210cd
यतोऽतोऽज्ञानविध्वस्तौ मुक्तः सन्ना विमुच्यते 4.4.559cd
यतोऽतोऽतिशयवता गम्यतेऽनतिशयं सुखम् 4.3.1878cd
यतोऽतोऽद्वयसिद्ध्यर्थं ब्रह्मेत्येतद्विशेष्यते 3.4.20ab
यतोऽतोऽनात्मयोगोऽस्य न मानादवसीयते 4.3.113cd
यतोऽतोऽन्धं तम इति विशिनष्टि श्रुतिस्तमः 4.4.599cd
यतोऽतोऽपरमप्येतद्ब्रह्मोक्त्यर्थं विनियुज्यते SV 475cd
यतोऽतोऽविद्यातज्जानां बाधितत्वात्प्रबोधतः 1.4.1454ab
यतोऽतोऽविद्यानाशार्थं प्रपञ्चविलयोऽफलः SV 391cd
यतोऽतोऽसङ्ग एवायं पुरुषः स्वप्नभग्मिगः 4.3.1020ab
यतोऽतो गतिरप्युक्ता नान्यथा तदुदीरणम् 6.2.129cd

यतोऽतो गार्ग्याभिमतो न भोक्तेत्यवगम्यते 2.1.99cd
यतोऽतो दृष्ट एतस्मिन्प्रत्यगात्मनि केवले 2.4.230ab
यतोऽतो देहमरणं प्रात्यक्ष्यादुपपद्यते 3.2.34cd
यतोऽतो न तृतीयेयं कर्त्रादाविह युज्यते 4.4.572cd
यतोऽतो न स्वभावादेर्हेतुत्वमुपपद्यते 4.3.762cd
यतोऽतो नागमादेव तादृशेऽर्थे विनिश्चितिः 2.4.163cd
यतोऽतो नात्मधीः कार्या नापि तत्संततिस्तथा 4.4.932ab
यतोऽतो नानुमानेन प्रत्यक्षस्यास्ति बाधनम् 4.3.672cd
यतोऽतो नेयता कार्त्स्न्यं देवताध्यात्मयोर्भवेत् 2.3.73cd
यतोऽतो नोपचारेण कर्मणो मुक्तिकार्यता 3.3.91cd
यतोऽतो नोपनिषदामन्यार्थत्वं कथं चन 2.1.542cd
यतोऽतो ब्रह्मणैवायं पन्था ज्ञातः प्रमाणतः 4.4.570ab
यतोऽतो ब्रह्म यक्षं च सत्यं प्रथमजं विदुः 5.5.11cd
यतोऽतो मोक्षमुद्दिश्य याज्ञवल्क्यमपृच्छत 4.3.968cd
यतोऽतो मोहविध्वस्तौ द्रष्ट्राद्यात्मनि नेक्ष्यते 4.3.1535cd
यतोऽतो यद्यपि क्षत्रं ब्राह्मण्यं प्रतिपद्यते 1.4.1607ab
यतोऽतो लोकबुद्ध्यैव देवादीनामितीर्यते 1.4.1442ab
यतोऽतो वातपित्तादीन्धातून्सोऽप्यनुरुध्यते 4.3.1230cd
यतोऽतो वितरः पन्थाः प्रत्यग्बोधोऽभिधीयते 4.4.548cd
यतोऽत्यर्थं प्रवृत्ता वाग्घटबोधे प्रदीपवत् 1.5.132ab
यतोऽत्र न क्रिया तस्मादवबद्धे श्रुतिः स्वयम् 4.3.985ab
यतोऽत्राप्रविभक्तेन स्वेन बोधेन तिष्ठति 4.3.1398cd
यतोऽनन्वागतं रूपं सुषुप्तेऽस्यात्मनः स्वतः 4.3.1371ab
यतोऽनवयवेनैव रज्जुसर्पादिवत्तथा 2.4.236ab
यतोऽनवसितं वाक्यं पुमर्थानवसानतः 3.2.57ab
यतोऽनियतकालीनफला वैधी क्रियेष्यते SV 414cd
यतोऽनुभवतोऽविद्या ब्रह्मास्मीत्यनुभूतिवत् SV 177ab
यतोऽनुभूयते तस्मात्कारणत्वं परात्मनः 3.4.122cd
यतोऽनुभूयते साक्षान्नानर्थक्यं भवेत्ततः 2.1.541cd
यतोऽन्तरतमः प्रत्यक्तस्मादेवावगम्यते 1.4.1042cd
यतोऽन्तरायस्तद्धानौ तेन तत्र नियुज्यते 2.4.108cd
यतोऽपहतपाप्मादि युक्तं स्यात्तद्विशेषणम् 4.3.186cd

यतोऽपर्वस्य संसिद्धौ प्रमाणं नोपपद्यते 3.8.146cd
यतोऽबिभेदविद्यावानतोऽसावस्मदादिवत् 1.4.55cd
यतोऽबिभेद्विराट्पूर्वमेकाक्यस्मीति मूढवत् 1.4.58ab
यतोऽबोधस्य विध्वस्तौ पुंसः स्यात्कृतकृत्यता 4.4.220cd
यतोऽभग्नव्रतस्तस्मात्तस्यैव व्रतमाश्रयेत् 1.5.368cd
यतोऽभाणि मया पूर्वं नेहातः पुनरुच्यते 4.4.1147cd
यतोऽभावेऽप्यसंवित्तिश्चैतन्यस्येह दृश्यते 4.3.1384cd
यतोऽयमेव हरयो यावत्संख्या तदाश्रया 2.5.132cd
यतोऽरतिग्रहग्रस्तधिषणोऽभूत्प्रजापतिः 1.4.106ab
यतोऽवगतिरेवात्र प्रमात्रादिविशेषणा 4.3.298ab
यतोऽवगम्यते तस्मान्निर्भीतिः सुखमास्यताम् 1.4.575cd
यतोऽवगम्यते तेन ज्ञानं कर्म न ढौकते SV 129cd
यतोऽवगम्यते नातोऽकारके शक्तिरात्मनि 4.3.1781cd
यतोऽवसादयेद्विद्या तस्मादुपनिषन्मता SV 7cd
यतोऽविद्यात्मकान्येव रूपाण्येतान्यतो दृशेः 4.4.424ab
यतोऽविद्यान्वयेऽशेषसंसारानर्थसंगतिः 4.4.169ab
यतोऽविद्येव तद्धेतुस्तदुच्छित्तावतो न सन् 2.4.420ab
यतोऽविद्येव प्रथते कार्यकारणरूपिणी 3.9.111cd
यतोऽविद्येव सर्वेयं मनोवाक्प्राणलक्षणा 1.5.165ab
यतोऽविरक्तः संसारान्नात्मज्ञानाय कल्पते 1.4.6ab
यतोऽशेषतमोहन्त्री प्रज्ञा सैवात इष्यते 4.4.808cd
यतोऽश्वयदतोऽश्वोऽसुः संवृत्तः स प्रजापतिः 1.2.207cd
यतोऽसंतोषतस्तस्मात्कृता व्याख्योत्तरा शुभा 4.3.14cd
यतोऽसपत्नस्तेनायमिन्द्र इत्यभिधीयते 1.5.189ab
यतोऽसमाप्तमेवेदं दर्शनं ते विवक्षितम् 3.9.42cd
यतोऽसाधनसाध्यं तं प्रत्यगात्मानमात्मना 3.5.118ab
यतोऽसाविममेवाथ द्विधात्मानमपातयत् 1.4.113cd
यतोऽसिद्धानि सिध्यन्ति भावाभावौ यदाश्रयौ SV 1083ab
यतोऽसिद्धिरतः प्रत्यङ्निरस्ताखिलविक्रियः 1.4.337cd
यतोऽस्य न पुरा बोधात्कर्मादेः कार्यमण्वपि 2.1.208ab
यतोऽस्य संततो भावस्तस्माच्चात्मेति शब्द्यते 1.4.745cd
यतो जनिमतावश्यं विनष्टव्यं तदन्ततः 4.3.592ab

यतो जिहासितान्येव तस्माद्धर्मेऽपि पाप्मगीः 4.3.815cd
यतो दारार्थ उद्योगस्ततः पुत्रैषणोच्यते 3.5.111cd
यतो द्रष्टर्यसंभाव्यं कृत्स्नं प्रश्नविशेषणम् 3.4.177cd
यतो धनाभिलाषोऽयं कृतदारस्य सार्थकः 3.5.133ab
यतो धीव्यतिरेकार्थं हृदीति श्रुतिरभ्यधात् 4.3.327cd
यतो नङ्क्ष्यति स क्षिप्रं नश्यंश्चासुखकृत्प्रियः 1.4.1048cd
यतो न पश्यतीत्येतदनूद्यान्यद्विभाव्यते 4.3.1577cd
यतो न लभते मेयं शुक्तौ रजतधीरतः 4.4.903ab
यतो निहन्ति तेन स्यात्साफल्यं यत्नशास्त्रयोः 4.4.352cd
यतो बिभ्यति भूतानि परोत्कर्षगतान्यपि 3.5.94cd
यतो बिभ्यति भूतानि संसारानर्थलक्षणात् 1.4.385cd
यतो ब्रह्मैव सन्नेष प्रथते मोहतोऽन्यथा 4.4.300ab
यतो भूयो न तद्व्याख्या क्रियतेऽत्र ततोऽधुना 4.3.1794cd
यतो मनुष्यलोकोऽयं विशिष्टसुतसाधनः 1.5.283ab
यतो मानं न हीहास्ति नानात्वप्रतिपत्तये 4.4.668ab
यतो मानानि सिध्यन्ति जाग्रदादित्रयं तथा SV 1082ab
यतो मानान्तरमितं सिद्धं वस्त्वति भण्यते SV 479cd
यतो मिथ्यावबोधोऽयमतस्तदपनुत्तये 1.4.649ab
यतो मूलमनर्थानामात्माज्ञानं जगत्यपि 1.4.168cd
यतो यतो निवर्तते ततस्ततो विमुच्यते 4.3.1885ab
यतो यतो निवर्तते ततस्ततो विमुच्यते 4.4.1262ab
यतो यथोक्तं तत्सिद्धौ तस्मादेतद्विधीयते 3.5.167cd
यतो यो लभते सिद्धिं तस्यासावेव देवता 3.9.44ab
यतो वस्त्वनुरोध्येतन्न ज्ञातृवशवर्त्यतः SV 373ab
यतो वस्त्वन्तरं नान्यदात्मनो विद्यते परम् 4.1.34ab
यतो वा इत्यतो वाक्यान्न तदन्यत्तपो भवेत् 1.4.1061ab
यतो वागाद्युपास्त्यत्र तस्मात्सर्वं विवक्षितम् 4.1.22ab
यतो वाचोऽभिधानानि प्रयुक्तान्युपलब्धये 1.4.857ab
यतो वाचो निवर्तन्त इति च श्रुतिशासनम् 1.4.718cd
यतो वाचो निवर्तन्त इति श्रुत्यैव दर्शितम् SV 781ab
यतो वाचो निवर्तन्ते अप्राप्य मनसा सह 4.4.633ab
यतो वाचो निवर्तन्ते नेति नेतीति चापरम् 4.3.1731ab

यतो वाचो निवर्तन्ते नेति नेत्यादिकं तथा 1.4.939ab
यतो विघ्नकृतामात्मा प्रत्यग्याथात्म्यविद्भवेत् 1.4.1506ab
यतो विज्ञाततत्त्वानां भीतिर्नास्ति कुतश् चन 4.3.1253cd
यतो विज्ञानमानी सन्सर्वं वस्त्ववगच्छति 2.1.189ab
यतो विध्वंसने तस्या नात्मनोऽन्योऽवशिष्यते 4.3.1797cd
यतो विन्यदधात्प्राणस्तस्मात्तद्वर्जयेद्द्वयम् 1.3.222cd
यतो विप्रतिपद्यन्ते त्वन्तर्यामिणि वादिनः 3.8.127ab
यतो वीक्षामहे तस्माज्ज्ञानस्याज्ञानबाधनम् 4.4.880cd
यतो वैदिकपक्षस्य नातः कल्प्यात्मनो भिदा 4.4.347cd
यतो व्याख्यातमखिलं मूर्तामूर्तादिवस्त्वतः 2.3.172ab
यतो हन्ति ततो नासावभ्यासं प्रति वीक्षते 2.4.432cd
यत्कर्तुं वाप्यकर्तुं वाप्यन्यथा कर्तुमेव वा 5.1.68ab
यत्कर्तुमन्यथा कर्तुमकर्तुं वापि शक्यते 3.9.125ab
यत्कर्म कुरुते चायं शुभं वा यदि वाशुभम् 4.4.232ab
यत्कल्याणं वदत्येषा ह्यात्मने तदचीक्लृपत् 1.3.140cd
यत्कल्याणमिति च्छिद्राद्विदुः सुरचिकीर्षितम् 1.3.146ab
यत्किंचित्कामतः कुर्यादकृतार्थोऽथवा पतेत् SV 837cd
यत्किंचिदिह विज्ञातं तद्वाग्रूपं प्रचक्षते 1.5.159ab
यत्किंचेत्युपसंहारं लक्षणोक्त्या ततोऽकरोत् 1.5.161cd
यत्किंचेदं जगत्यस्मिन्नार्द्रं वस्तूपलक्ष्यते 1.4.155cd
यत्कृत्स्नं ब्रह्म पूर्वोक्तं तदेवेदमविद्यया 2.1.84ab
यत्तत्तयोः समानत्वं रज्जुसर्पादिवन्मतम् 4.3.390ab
यत्तत्त्वं गम्यते प्रत्यक्तदेवानात्मवस्तुनः 2.4.255cd
यत्तत्त्वकं स्याद्यद्वस्तु न तत्तदतिवर्तते 1.4.303ab
यत्तदस्ति मनस्तत्स्यात्प्रसिद्ध्या चास्ति तन्मनः 1.5.106ab
यत्तदस्यात्मनो मोहादद्रष्टृत्वमुपचर्यते 4.3.888cd
यत्तद्ब्रह्म खमित्युक्तं तदोंशब्दाभिधानकम् 5.1.117ab
यत्तद्विज्ञानमात्मीयं तद्विकृत्यावतिष्ठते 4.3.1091ab
यत्तु चोदितमित्येव क्रियते कर्म निष्फलम् 4.4.1129ab
यत्तु तच्छङ्क्यते कस्मादात्मा प्राज्ञे न पश्यति 4.3.1407ab
यत्तु तेषां परं सत्यं तदिदानीं निरूप्यते 2.3.1cd
यत्तु स्वात्माश्रयं कर्म ह्यनारब्धफलं भवेत् 1.4.1531ab

यत्तूक्तं ज्ञाततत्त्वानामपि रागादिदर्शनात् 1.4.1528ab
यत्तूक्तं वेदभागत्वाद्भिन्नवस्त्ववबोधिनः 5.1.82ab
यत्तूदगयनापेक्षा भीष्मस्य श्रूयते स्मृतौ 6.2.133ab
यत्त्वचोदि त्वयापीयमभ्युपेयार्थवादता SV 126ab
यत्त्वपारमनन्तं च वास्तवं ज्ञानमात्मनः 2.4.450ab
यत्त्वसाधारणं तस्य कार्यत्वमिति भण्यते SV 714ab
यत्त्वात्मलाभमात्रेण पुरुषार्थसमाप्तिकृत् 3.5.113ab
यत्नतो न्यायतः किंचित्पश्यामो वेदचक्षुषा SV 34ab
यत्नाच्छ्रुतिरतो वक्ति त्विहान्नं प्रतिष्ठति 1.3.245cd
यत्नात्प्राह श्रुतिस्तस्माद्यन्ताव्याकृतमुच्यते 3.8.29cd
यत्नादप्रमयं तत्त्वं द्रष्टव्यं तद्विपश्चिता 4.4.734cd
यत्नादासञ्जनीयोऽयं पितेत्यसुरनिश्चयः 1.3.116cd
यत्नाधेयं यतो दैवं ज्यायांसः स्युस्ततोऽसुराः 1.3.22cd
यत्नायत्नसमुत्थाभ्यां वृत्तिभ्यां देवदानवाः 1.3.29ab
यत्नेन वक्ष्यते न्यायात्पूर्वपक्षनिरासतः SV 573cd
यत्नेनोपार्जितं तच्चेत्क्रीत्वा वा मांसमाहरेत् 6.4.79ab
यत्नो न तु घटोत्पत्तौ नैवमप्युपपद्यते 1.2.96cd
यत्पण्डितस्य कर्म स्यात्तत्पाण्डित्यं प्रचक्षते 3.5.174ab
यत्पश्येदिति कर्त्रुक्तिर्द्रष्टात्राशङ्क्यते यतः 4.3.1526ab
यत्पश्येद्गोचरापन्नं सुखशब्दादिलक्षणम् 4.3.1525cd
यत्पिपृच्छिषितं गार्ग्या समष्टिव्यष्टिलक्षणम् 3.7.1ab
यत्प्रज्ञोदधियुक्तिशब्दनखजश्रद्धैकसन्नेत्रक- 6.5.23a
यत्प्रसादात्तमःसिद्धिस्तत्स्वसाक्ष्यप्यपह्नुते 1.4.1357ab
यत्प्रसादादविद्यादि सिध्यतीव दिवानिशम् 4.3.74ab
यत्प्रागाविष्कृतिस्तस्य मन्त्राभ्यां क्रियतेऽञ्जसा 2.5.98cd
यत्र कात्स्न्र्येन वृत्तिः स्याद्रज्जुसर्पादिवद्द्वयोः 1.4.632ab
यत्र क्व चैति तत्रासौ प्रतिष्ठां लभते शुभाम् 1.2.168cd
यत्र त्वस्यात्मनोऽज्ञस्य शास्त्राचार्यप्रसादतः 2.4.470ab
यत्र त्वस्येति वचनं न दृष्टेरिति चापरम् 3.9.173ab
यत्र त्वस्येति विध्वस्त आत्माज्ञाने प्रबोधतः 4.3.1309ab
यत्र त्वस्येति श्रुत्यैव सर्वमेतत्स्फुटीकृतम् 1.4.1505ab
यत्र त्वस्येत्यतः प्राह ध्वस्तात्मतमसि श्रुतिः 4.4.278ab

यत्र त्वात्मेति धीरस्य जायतेऽनात्मधीरिव 4.3.1452ab
यत्र त्वात्मैव मेयः स्यात्तत्र मेयातिरेकतः 4.4.692ab
यत्र नान्यदिति तथा चात्मैवेत्युपसंहृतेः 4.3.1793cd
यत्र नाशादिमद्वस्तु प्राधान्येन विवक्ष्यते 1.4.525ab
यत्र यत्र विधिर्दृष्टस्तत्र तत्रात्मकर्मकः 3.2.113ab
यत्र यत्रात्मभावेन श्रुत्या ब्रह्मावबोध्यते SV 248cd
यत्र यस्यामवस्थायां स्वपितीत्यभिधीयते 4.3.859ab
यत्र वा अन्यदित्यादि तथा च श्रुतिशासनम् 1.4.1560ab
यत्र वा अन्यदित्युक्तेरविद्याविषयं तु तत् 1.4.571ab
यत्र वा अन्यदित्येवं भेदज्ञानमभाषत 4.3.1308ab
यत्र वा अन्यदित्येवं यत्र त्वस्येति चापरम् 2.1.211ab
यत्र वा अन्यदित्येवं यत्र त्वस्येतिवाक्यतः 3.9.164ab
यत्र वा अन्यदित्येवं श्रुतिश्चापि जगौ तथा 1.4.1184cd
यत्र वा अन्यदित्येवं सत्येवाज्ञान आह हि 4.4.277ab
यत्र वा इति वाक्येन ध्वस्ताविद्ये विपश्चिति 2.4.469cd
यत्र सुप्तो न कमिति जाग्रत्स्वप्ननिषेधकृत् 4.3.1163cd
यत्र हि द्वैतमित्युक्तेर्यत्र त्वस्येति चेरणात् 4.3.1805ab
यत्र हि द्वैतमित्युक्त्या यत्र त्वस्येति चादरात् 5.1.30cd
यत्र हि द्वैतमित्येवं तथा च श्रुतिशासनम् 4.4.997cd
यत्र हि द्वैतमित्येवं यत्र त्वस्येति च श्रुतिः 4.4.678ab
यत्राज्ञातात्मतत्त्वात्माविद्यासंवीतशेमुषिः 2.4.453ab
यत्राज्ञातात्मयाथात्म्यस्तत्तमोपिहितेक्षणः 2.4.454ab
यत्रात्मनोऽस्य संबन्धोऽनात्मनेह विवक्ष्यते 4.3.1451ab
यत्राध्यासो यदध्यस्तं भेदसिद्धौ तयोर्मृषा 1.4.416ab
यत्रापि च प्रतीयेते हानादाने वचःश्रवात् SV 590ab
यत्रापि चान्धकारादिदोषात्क्रमविनिश्चयः SV 819ab
यत्राप्यतिशयो दृष्टः स स्वार्थानतिलङ्घनात् 2.4.174ab
यत्राप्यभीष्टं मानत्वं तत्राप्येत्यप्रमाणता 1.4.910cd
यत्रास्याविदुषः पुंसो मृतस्यायुष्परिक्षयात् 3.2.124ab
यत्रैतानि समस्तानि निष्ठां यान्ति परात्मनि 4.3.1879ab
यत्रैष एतत्सुप्तोऽभूत्स्वनामामन्त्रणध्वनिम् 2.1.214ab
यत्रोपास्यबहुत्वं स्यात्फलं तत्र प्रजास्वपि 2.1.72ab

यत्संसर्गं पुरा चक्रुरविद्यंस्तदिहोच्यते 1.3.162ab
यत्संबन्धादचित्कोऽपि जीवतीत्यभिधीयते 3.2.33cd
यत्साक्षाच्चापरोक्षाच्च ब्रह्मणः स्तो विशेषणे 3.4.36ab
यत्साक्षाच्चापरोक्षाच्च ब्रह्मात्मेति विशेषितम् 3.8.57ab
यत्साक्षादपरोक्षाभ्यां ब्रह्म वेह विशिष्यते 3.4.26ab
यत्साक्षादितिवाक्योत्थप्रत्यग्याथात्म्यलेहिना 1.4.761ab
यत्साक्षादित्युपक्रम्य य आत्मेत्युपसंहृतेः 4.2.22ab
यत्साक्षिकं द्वयं सिध्येत्स आत्मेत्यभ्युपेयताम् 4.3.194cd
यत्साक्षिकी तमःसिद्धिस्तत्कार्यस्य च लक्ष्यते 4.2.88ab
यत्साक्षिकौ यथोक्तस्य भावाभावौ प्रसिध्यतः 4.4.151ab
यत्सांनिध्यात्प्रसिध्यन्ति तत्सिद्धौ किमपेक्ष्यते 1.4.870cd
यत्सुखं साधनाधीनं दुःखमेव तदुच्यते 4.3.1851ab
यत्स्यात्स्वाभाविकं ज्ञानं यच्च कर्म स्वभावजम् 1.3.355ab
यत्स्यात्स्वाभाविकं यस्य तदुदाहरणं भवेत् 4.4.318cd
यत्स्रष्टृ ब्रह्म पूर्वोक्तं स्वात्ममोहैकवर्त्मना 1.4.1312ab
यथा कटं करोतीति कर्ममात्रावबोधनम् SV 512ab
यथाकथंचिच्छब्दार्थो यदि नामाभ्युपेयते 1.4.1102ab
यथाकथंचिदित्येतदतो नैवाभ्युपेयते 1.4.1299cd
यथा करोति तद्वाच्यं प्राणोपनिषदश्च याः 2.2.7cd
यथाकर्म गतिः स्थानं परिच्छेदोऽथ विस्तृतिः 4.4.130ef
यथा कर्म तथेशावि कर्मापेक्ष्यैव सिध्यति 1.4.1481cd
यथाकर्म यथाज्ञानं कुरुते रचनान्तरम् 4.4.144cd
यथाकर्म यथाज्ञानमुपादत्ते शरीरकम् 1.6.41ab
यथा कश्चित्तथैव त्व प्रतिज्ञाय परात्मनः 3.4.76ab
यथा काममये तद्वन्मन्त्रं श्लोकमुदाहरत् 4.4.375ab
यथा काम्याग्निहोत्रादौ साध्यसाधनसंगतिम् 2.1.576ab
यथा कार्यानपेक्षस्य प्रामाण्यं वचसः स्फुटम् 1.4.755ab
यथाक्रमो यथोपायो विद्याकर्मादिलक्षणः 4.3.849ab
यथा गवात्मना साक्षाद्गां विन्देद्गोपदानुगः 1.4.1000ab
यथाग्निगर्भा पृथिवी द्यौरिन्द्रेणेव भानुना 6.4.106ab
यथाग्निहोत्रयाथात्म्यविज्ञानव्यतिरेकतः 1.4.811ab
यथा ग्रामादिशब्दानां तथेहाप्यवसीयताम् 1.4.522cd

यथा घटस्तथैवात्मा नानात्मप्रत्ययप्रमः 4.3.210cd
यथा च कर्मणा मुक्तिर्न कथं चन युज्यते 3.8.162ab
यथा च कार्ये तात्पर्यं कार्यं चापि न विद्यते SV 873ab
यथाचारी च लोकेऽस्मिंस्तथारूपो भवत्यसौ 4.4.194cd
यथा चास्य विरुद्धत्वं तथोदर्के प्रवक्ष्यते SV 172ab
यथा चेदमसंबद्धं न युक्त्यक्षरसंश्रयम् 4.3.1567ab
यथा जन्मादिकर्तृत्वाद्बीजं नैव विनश्यति 1.4.201ab
यथा जाग्रत्कृतं कर्म कर्तारमनुगच्छति 4.3.1048ab
यथा जाग्रदवस्थायां भोक्ता प्राणः पुराभवत् 2.1.109ab
यथा जात्यमणेः शुद्धा ज्वलन्ती निश्चला शिखा 4.3.890ab
यथा जात्यमणेः शुभ्रा ज्वलन्ती निश्चला शिखा 4.3.1459ab
यथा जिगमिषुः पान्थो रथं वा नावमेव वा 4.2.5ab
यथा ज्ञातैवमेवात्मा देवताद्यात्मकार्यगः 3.7.36ab
यथा ज्ञानप्रकाशाभ्यां संप्लुतावेव नान्यथा 4.3.96ab
यथा तण्डुलनिष्पत्तिरवघाताद्यपेक्षया 1.4.924ab
यथातत्त्वं तु योऽज्ञातं वस्तु साक्षात्प्रपद्यते 4.4.1317ab
यथा तत्त्वमसीत्यादिवाक्योत्थज्ञानवह्निना 1.4.603ab
यथा तत्प्रतिपत्त्यर्थं स यथेत्युत्तरा श्रुतिः 4.4.221cd
यथा तत्र तथेहापि शास्त्रेणैव समर्प्यते 1.4.787ab
यथा तथा च वक्ष्यामः स्पष्टेन न्यायवर्त्मना SV 465cd
यथा तथातियत्नेन तत्रैवैतत्प्रवक्ष्यते 1.4.903cd
यथा तथानभिव्यक्तिः सर्वेषामपि वादिनाम् SV 147cd
यथा तथा पराश्चात्र श्रुतयः सन्ति कोटिशः 3.5.109cd
यथा तथा प्रवक्ष्याम उदर्केऽप्युपपत्तिभिः 1.3.55cd
यथा तथायं ब्रह्मैव ब्रह्मासंबोधमात्रतः 2.1.517ab
यथा तथायमप्यात्मा जाग्रत्स्वप्नौ परिभ्रमन् 4.3.1162ab
यथा तथासकृत्पर्वमवोचाम पदे पदे 4.2.110cd
यथा तथेहापूर्वादिवस्तूक्तेरेव गम्यते 1.3.71cd
यथा तथोत्तरत्रापि युक्तिभिश्चाभिधास्यते 1.3.316cd
यथा तदुक्तं श्रुत्येह मन्त्रोऽप्यत्र निगद्यते 4.4.234cd
यथा तदुच्यमानं त्वं यथावच्छ्रोतुमर्हसि 2.1.549cd
यथा तु परलोकस्य तथाथेत्यभिधीयते 4.3.845cd

यथात्मवादिवाक्यार्थश्रुतये न प्रवर्तते 1.4.830ab
यथात्मसाक्षिका तद्वन्न वेद्मीत्यात्मसाक्षिकम् 4.4.358cd
यथात्मा संहतिं प्रापद्व्याकृतः करणादिभिः 1.4.1021cd
यथा त्रयं तथा सर्वं सत्तया किं न कारणम् 1.2.84cd
यथा त्वज्ञस्य पारार्थ्यं तथेदानीं प्रपञ्च्यते 1.4.1782cd
यथादर्शतलप्रख्ये पश्यत्यात्मानमात्मनि 4.4.579cd
यथादर्शतलप्रख्ये पश्यत्यात्मानमात्मनि 4.4.1044cd
यथादर्शनमेवासौ फलमाप्नोति मानवः 2.4.259cd
यथादानं कृतं पूर्वं मात्राणां स्वप्नसर्जने 4.3.994ab
यथा दुन्दुभिशब्दत्वसामान्यादुत्थितान्पृथक् 2.4.267ab
यथादृष्टानुरोध्येव दृष्टान्तैर्वस्तु बोध्यते 2.1.494cd
यथाधिकारं सर्वत्र परो जगति सर्वथा 1.3.270cd
यथाधिगम्यते तद्वत्साक्षादित्यादिलक्षणः 3.5.99cd
यथाधुना निश्चिनुमः प्रागप्येतदभूत्तथा 1.4.519cd
यथानपाकृतर्णस्य मोक्षेच्छा वार्यते तथा 1.5.261ab
यथा न रजते मानं शुक्तावपि तथैव सा 4.4.904ab
यथा निर्ज्ञातभेदे हि विष्णुधीरुपलात्मनि 1.3.64ab
यथा निषेधवाक्येभ्यो नान्याकरणतो मतिः 1.3.86ab
यथानुभूतशक्तीह बीजं वृक्षस्य दृश्यते 3.9.139ab
यथान्तरतमः प्रत्यक्तथोदर्के प्रवक्ष्यते 1.4.1041ab
यथान्यत्र तथेहापि कस्मान्नाध्यवसीयते 1.4.773cd
यथान्यत्र तथेहापि कस्मान्नाभ्युपगम्यते 1.5.270cd
यथान्यत्र तथेहापि वेदान्तेष्वभ्युपेयताम् SV 1081cd
यथान्यायप्रतिन्यायौ यथा तत्रोदितौ पुरा 4.3.1949cd
यथा पुष्करिणीं वायुश्चालयन्नपि सर्वतः 6.4.109ab
यथा प्रकाशयत्येक इति चाप्यैश्वरी स्मृतिः 4.3.291cd
यथा प्रकाशयत्येकः कृत्स्नं लोकमिमं रविः 4.3.87ab
यथा प्रकाशयत्येकः कृत्स्नं लोकमिमं रविः 4.3.345ab
यथा प्रकाशयत्येकः कृत्स्नं लोकमिमं रविः 4.4.366ab
यथा प्रकाशयत्येकरूप एव तथा धियः 4.3.1773cd
यथाप्रतिज्ञं प्रत्युक्तिमवोचामासकृत्तव 3.4.78ab
यथाप्रतिज्ञमेवातो यथा पृष्टं तथैव तत् 3.4.77ab

यथा प्रयोगमुल्लङ्घ्य व्याख्यातुं शक्नुयात्सुधीः	1.4.1627ab
यथाप्रश्नं प्रतिवचो न सम्यगुदितं पुरा	3.5.29ab
यथाप्रश्नमियं तावत्प्रत्युक्तिर्नोपपद्यते	3.4.177ab
यथा प्रसिद्धो जगति तथैवेहापि गम्यताम्	2.4.461cd
यथाप्रार्थितमागाय याजमानं फलं परम्	1.3.364ab
यथा बाध्यमबाधित्वा नैवं बाधकता मितेः	4.4.790cd
यथा भवति वेदस्य तथाथ प्रतिपाद्यते	4.4.973cd
यथा भवति साक्षाच्च तथेदमभिधीयते	4.3.858cd
यथाभिलषितार्थोऽयं यया संभाव्यते स्फुटः	2.1.506cd
यथा भुक्त्वैति नगरं भुज्येतिक्रिययोर्नरः	1.4.535ab
यथाभूतार्थबोधित्वमेवमेव मितेर्भवेत्	1.3.60cd
यथाभूत्वा तथा भावः क्रियायास्तत्त्वमुच्यते	4.3.1589cd
यथामं भिदुरं पात्रमप्सु सद्यो विलीयते	6.4.52ab
यथा मनुरिदं सृष्टमहमस्मीत्यबुध्यत	1.4.124ab
यथा मात्रादिसत्तेयं प्रत्यक्संवित्तिसिद्धिका	2.3.223ab
यथा मूका विना वाचा यथान्धाश्चक्षुषा विना	6.1.24ab
यथायमुक्तो दृष्टान्तः पुरुषोऽप्येवमेव हि	4.3.1939ab
यथा येन मृताः सत्यो हेतुनानेन च प्रजाः	6.2.33ab
यथायोगं यथाश्रद्धं तद्बुभुत्साप्रसिद्धये	4.4.1027ab
यथायोगमयं नाडीर्गाढं सुप्तः प्रबोधितः	4.3.949ab
यथा रत्वाद्यसंभाव्यं संप्रसादे तथैव च	4.3.1061ab
यथा राजानमायान्तं सद्मपानादिसाधनैः	4.3.1960ab
यथारुचि प्रवर्तन्ते पुरुषा न तु शास्त्रतः	2.1.586cd
यथा रूपे तथा ज्ञेया शब्दादिष्वपि कल्पना	4.4.564cd
यथार्थितं सत्पुरुष इति सत्पुरुषव्रतम्	2.1.199cd
यथार्थे प्रतिशब्दोऽयं निश्चयार्थे निरित्ययम्	4.3.991ab
यथालक्षणया कर्म कृतं भावनयात्मना	4.3.1190ab
यथा लोके तथेहापि साक्षी सम्यक्प्रपश्यति	4.4.364cd
यथावकाशदात्रिति भण्यते निष्क्रियं वियत्	4.3.1442ab
यथावदनुशिष्टस्य नाभिभूतिर्यतोऽन्यतः	6.2.48cd
यथावस्तुदृशोऽप्येवं यथा रज्ज्वादिदर्शिनः	4.4.1315cd
यथावस्तुधियः सूतेः प्राङ्नित्यं तेन तन्मतम्	1.4.17cd

यथावस्तुधिया हित्वा निर्ममो निरहंकृतः 4.4.503cd
यथावस्तु यदा बोधो वेदान्तोक्तिश्रुतेर्भवेत् 2.4.431ab
यथावस्तुस्मृतिं मुक्त्वा स्मृतिर्नान्यावशिष्यते 1.4.843cd
यथावस्तु हि या बुद्धिः सम्यग्ज्ञानं तदेव नः 1.4.890ab
यथावस्त्वनुरोधित्वमज्ञानस्यापि चेन्मतम् 3.2.87ab
यथावस्त्वपरिज्ञानं कामस्यापि प्रयोजकम् 4.4.214ab
यथावस्त्वपरिज्ञानाद्धीति हेतावतः पदम् 4.3.928cd
यथावस्त्वप्रमोत्थं च चित्रं सर्वज्ञचेष्टितम् 4.4.820cd
यथावस्त्वभिसंबन्धान्निवर्तेते सहेतुके 4.4.853ab
यथावस्त्वात्मविज्ञानं मोहमात्राश्रयाः क्रियाः SV 369ab
यथावस्त्वीक्ष्यमाणं तु यथावस्त्वेव वीक्ष्यते 3.5.40cd
यथावस्त्वेव तस्यापि फलं स्यादिति भण्यते 4.4.1317cd
यथावस्त्वेव धीस्तत्र नात्राविद्याद्यपेक्षते 4.3.1452cd
यथा वागादयस्तद्वदधिदैवेऽपि योजयेत् 1.5.372ab
यथा वागादयस्तद्वद्विजज्ञुः प्राणमात्मनि 1.3.201cd
यथा वागादयो विद्वास्तद्वज्ज्ञेयास्त्वगादयः 1.3.159cd
यथा विधेयासारूप्यान्नैकात्म्यं स्याद्विधेस्तथा 2.4.176cd
यथा विप्रतिपद्यन्ते भिन्नवर्त्मप्रभेदतः 6.2.30cd
यथा विशुद्धमाकाशं तिमिरोपप्लुतो जनः 3.5.43ab
यथा विशुद्धमाकाशं सति वासति वा मले 3.5.78ab
यथा विशेषाः सामान्यं तथा व्यावर्तते ततः 4.3.1649cd
यथा व्याख्यातबाह्यार्थप्रधानोऽसंहतोऽप्रमः 1.4.1328ab
यथाव्याख्यातमैकात्म्यमहमित्यभिधीयते 4.3.1279cd
यथाशक्त्युदगायत्त यो भोगो वाङ्निबन्धनः 1.3.137cd
यथाशास्त्रं तथोल्लङ्घ्य कर्तुं शक्नोत्यथापरः 1.4.1627cd
यथाशास्त्रं यथायोगं वर्णदोषविवर्जितम् 1.3.141ab
यथाश्रुतार्थवादित्वान्न त्वभूतार्थवादता SV 127cd
यथा श्रुतौ मनस्येव प्रत्ययः सोऽवतिष्ठते 4.4.718ab
यथा श्रेयांसं हिंसित्वा पापीयान्स्यात्तथैव सः 1.4.1613cd
यथा श्रोत्रधिया रूपं रूपहेत्वसमन्वयात् 2.3.208ab
यथा संकल्पितश्चार्थ उभयोर्ज्ञानयोगयोः 4.4.729cd
यथा संचरणी नाडी प्रोक्तेयं देवतात्मनोः 4.2.54ab

यथा सति तथा विद्यात्प्रतीच्यनन्यमानके 2.4.291cd
यथासत्सति संवित्तौ सदप्येवं प्रतीयताम् 4.3.803ab
यथा सद्व्यतिरेकेण न किंचिद्वस्तु सिद्ध्यति 1.4.329ab
यथासंभवमायोज्यमेकैकस्मिंस्त्रयं त्रयम् 1.5.160cd
यथा संभाव्यते नेदृक्प्रत्युक्तौ किंचिदीक्ष्यते 3.5.30cd
यथा सर्वत्र नैवं स्याद्ग्राह्यग्राहकसंगतौ 4.3.524cd
यथा सर्वात्तृवक्त्रान्तस्थस्य प्रत्यक्षता तथा 1.5.29cd
यथासिद्धमितिहासपुराणाद्यपि गृह्यते 2.4.317ab
यथासिद्धानुवादेन पूर्वं नो ह्यभ्यधात्स्फुटम् 1.4.183ab
यथासिद्धान्युपादाय कामद्वेषवशानुगः 2.1.574ab
यथा सिद्धिस्तथा व्याख्या कार्येहोक्तेरतोऽञ्जसा 2.3.220cd
यथा सिन्धोर्महामत्स्य उभे कूले मिथः पृथक् 4.3.1084ab
यथा सैन्धवखिल्योऽस्तः स्वयोनावुदधाविह 2.4.400cd
यथास्ति तव विज्ञानमेवं कुम्भाद्यपीष्यताम् 4.3.574cd
यथास्थितात्मयाथात्म्यज्ञानजन्मातिरेकतः 1.4.1495ab
यथास्थितात्मयाथात्म्यसम्यग्ज्ञानेन बाध्यते 2.1.379cd
यथास्थितात्मवस्तूत्थज्ञानं मुक्त्वा तमोह्नुतौ 2.4.151ab
यथास्मांस्त्वं विजानासि तथैव त्वां वयं सदा 6.3.39ab
यथास्य नाड्यः पुंसः स्युरध्यात्मं सर्वतो गताः 4.2.73cd
यथास्याङ्गानि लक्ष्यन्ते विस्रस्तानि न पूर्ववत् 3.7.21ab
यथास्वं यान्त्यथ प्राणा देहादुच्छिन्नबन्धनाः 2.2.21cd
यथास्वं स्थानमायान्ति ता मृतिस्वापयोर्यतः 4.3.1137cd
यथा स्वप्नविनिर्माणं सिध्येत्स्वप्नदृशं प्रति 4.4.946cd
यथा हि कश्चित्प्रागासीच्चक्रवर्तिसुतो युवा 2.1.507ab
यथा हेत्युच्यते श्रुत्या साधनाभिन्नमात्मनः 1.4.1008cd
यथेतमेत्याथासीनः पश्चादग्नेः समाहितः 6.3.59ab
यथेति माहारजनं वासनोपचयात्मकम् 2.3.103cd
यथेयं देवता सर्वास्तथान्या अपि देवताः 4.2.68ab
यथेह कार्यकरणैः पुण्यकर्मोद्भवैर्नृणाम् 1.4.77cd
यथेह घटविज्ञाने घटाकारोऽनुभूयते 1.4.294ab
यथेह न तथा किंचिदुपादानं समीक्ष्यते 4.4.107cd
यथेह प्रयियासन्तमुग्रसूतादयो जनाः 4.3.1974ab

यथेह वस्तुनः साक्षात्तथा पर्वमवादिषम् 4.3.1621cd
यथेहासंहतान्येव भान्वादीनि प्रकुर्वते 4.3.62ab
यथैकबुद्धिनिर्ग्राह्यं द्रव्येणेह विशेषणम् 4.3.122ab
यथैतदुक्तमाचार्यैः कुर्याद्विद्वान्न तत्तथा 5.16.46ab
यथैता दर्शनावस्थाः कार्यमासां तथाविधम् 1.4.1150ab
यथैता यौगपद्येन वृत्तीरूर्मिभिरात्मनः 5.1.52ab
यथैधांसि समिद्धोऽग्निर्भस्मसात्कुरुतेऽर्जुन 1.4.1548ab
यथैधांसि समिद्धोऽग्निर्भस्मसात्कुरुतेऽर्जुन 4.4.1289ab
यथैवं कार्यतायोगान्नियोगेऽप्यनुमा न किम् SV 711cd
यथैवं तस्य लाभोऽपि तज्ज्ञानान्नान्यतो भवेत् 1.4.1011cd
यथैवं धिषणैकत्वे ध्यानलेलायने धियः 4.3.438ab
यथैवं नामरूपादिप्रपञ्चोपायहेतुतः 1.4.996ab
यथैवं नासतोऽप्येवं भेदो नैवावसीयते 5.1.89cd
यथैवं मोहजं द्वैतं नष्टे मोहेऽपि सांप्रतम् 4.3.1745cd
यथैवं श्रुतितोऽशेषवाङ्मनःकायसाधन- 4.4.1111ab
यथैवं संविदर्तेऽसन्नैति संभावनामपि 1.4.331ab
यथैवं सर्वभूतानि भोक्त्रा कर्मादिकारणैः 4.3.1965ab
यथैवं सर्वमानानि प्रत्यङ्मानातिरेकतः 4.4.905ab
यथैव तत्तनुत्वं च यावद्यावदिहात्मनः 2.1.359ab
यथैव नगराध्वस्थग्रामगत्युपदेशनम् SV 401ab
यथैव पारिहार्यादि हैमैकद्रव्यनिष्ठितम् 4.3.125ab
यथैव पार्थिवा भावाः पृथिव्यैवं धरित्र्यपि 3.6.7ab
यथैव पुरुषोऽन्नानां भोक्तात्यन्तं तथैव सः 1.5.87ab
यथैव पूर्वं संसारः काममलोऽनुवर्णितः 4.4.392ab
यथैव बाह्यनयनप्रकाशार्थाभिसंगतेः 4.3.1118cd
यथैवमवगच्छन्ति प्रध्वस्ताशेषकल्पनम् 4.4.1342ab
यथैवमवशिष्टेन तद्विशेषणहेतुतः 4.3.824cd
यथैवमात्मनोऽज्ञस्य तत्त्वमस्यादिवाक्यतः SV 234ab
यथैवमात्मनो भेदो ज्योतिष्ट्वाद्भास्यभेदतः 4.3.1777cd
यथैवमेवमात्मेदं शरीरं कर्मणः क्षयात् 4.4.135ab
यथैवमेवेहापि स्याद्य इहाचार्यवान्नरः 1.4.1553ab
यथैव विश्वजिद्यागपदे स्वार्थानुपालनम् SV 788ab

यथैवाहवनीयाग्नेः प्रसिद्धं समिदादिकम् 6.2.114ab
यथोक्त एव व्याख्याने युक्तेयं स्यात्फलश्रुतिः 3.2.22ab
यथोक्तं विदितं वेदे तथा स्मृतिवचःसु च 1.4.1804cd
यथोक्तः स्यादयं दोषो न तु तन्नेह जन्यते 1.5.78cd
यथोक्तकर्मणैतेन स्यातां तावेव दंपती 6.4.73cd
यथोक्तकर्मभिस्तेन जगत्तद्वदुपार्जितम् 1.5.4cd
यथोक्तकल्पनायां हि न युक्ता तेन कल्पना 2.3.133cd
यथोक्तकारणात्सर्वं प्रतीच्येव निवेशयेत् 2.4.92cd
यथोक्तकारिणं विप्रं नयन्ति परमां गतिम् 4.4.1066cd
यथोक्तगुणकं देवि स्वस्तनं सर्वकामदम् 6.4.126cd
यथोक्तगुणकं विद्वानुपासीत प्रजापतिम् 1.5.219ab
यथोक्तगुणवैफल्यं पुर एता न चेद्भवेत् 1.3.283cd
यथोक्तचक्रविन्यासो न श्रुतोऽक्षरपर्वकः 2.5.77ab
यथोक्तज्ञानकर्मभ्यां मनोर्जन्म ततोऽपि च 1.4.19cd
यथोक्तज्ञानतो ध्वस्तितरार्तश्रुत्यात उच्यते 3.5.213cd
यथोक्तज्ञानवत्तायामिदं कर्म विधित्स्यते 1.3.346ab
यथोक्तज्योतिर्विरहे नासौ दृष्टा कदा चन 4.3.56cd
यथोक्तज्योतिषः सिद्धावादित्यज्योतिरित्ययम् 4.3.33cd
यथोक्तज्योतिषि ततो न स्युश्चेष्टा यथोदिताः 4.3.54cd
यथोक्ततत्त्वकान्येव रज्ज्वां तत्क्लृप्तवस्तुवत् 1.4.1143ab
यथोक्ततत्त्वे नाविद्यामृते स्याद्द्वयसंगतिः 1.4.486ab
यथोक्तदर्शनस्तुल्यै दर्शनान्तरकुत्सनम् 1.5.62ab
यथोक्तदर्शनात्तस्मात्सर्वाप्त्या मृत्युजिद्भवेत् 1.5.74cd
यथोक्तदर्शनाप्तार्थो नान्यदस्तीति भावितः 2.1.29cd
यथोक्तदोषदुष्टत्वान्नात्ययो बोधतोऽन्यतः 3.3.132cd
यथोक्तदोषसंबन्धो नैवं सति भविष्यति 2.1.472ab
यथोक्तदोषाभावाच्च ब्रह्म कृत्स्नमिहास्त्वतः 1.4.1283cd
यथोक्तन्यायतः सिद्धो न तु कर्मसु कर्हिचित् SV 165cd
यथोक्तन्यायतस्तद्वदुत्पत्तावपि शक्यते 2.4.297cd
यथोक्तन्यायतो दुःखं न सार्धं देवतात्मना 1.5.359ab
यथोक्तन्यायमार्गेण स्वभावादि ततः कुतः 4.3.805cd
यथोक्तपरिमाणेन ध्यानकर्मविवक्षया 3.3.151ab

यथोक्तपुत्रप्रसवे यदि वा क्षिप्रकारिणौ 6.4.73ab
यथोक्तपुरुषार्थस्य यद्यप्याप्तस्वभावता SV 1101ab
यथोक्तफलसिद्धयर्थमारब्धोपनिषद्यदि SV 1117ab
यथोक्तबोधविरहादस्यानर्थपरंपरा 4.4.167ab
यथोक्तब्रह्मविद्याया इत आरभ्य भण्यते 2.5.93ab
यथोक्तमहिमः कस्मात्संवृत्तः पुरुषो विराट् 1.4.46ab
यथोक्तलक्षणस्येह मुख्यवृत्त्योक्तभूमिषु 2.3.74cd
यथोक्तलक्षणौ ये तु पन्थानावुत्तरेतरौ 6.2.157ab
यथोक्तवर्त्मना ह्यापः प्राप्ताः पुंस्परिणामताम् 6.2.111ab
यथोक्तवस्तुनः कस्मादित्येतत्प्रतिपाद्यते 1.6.6cd
यथोक्तवस्तुनो मैवं तस्यानत्यन्तभेदतः 4.3.1610cd
यथोक्तवस्तुवेद्येतत्फलमाप्नोत्यभीप्सितम् 1.4.1024cd
यथोक्तवस्तुसिद्धयर्थं दृष्टान्तोऽयमिहोच्यते 2.4.400ab
यथोक्तविद्याबोधित्वादग्रन्थोऽपि तदभेदतः SV 8ab
यथोक्तविषये तेषां साधनत्वं न मानतः 4.4.1219ab
यथोक्तशक्तिविक्षेपो मनोबुद्धिपुरःसरः 2.4.369ab
यथोक्तसूत्रव्याख्यायां प्रयोजनविवक्षया 1.4.1166ab
यथोक्तसूत्रसद्भावे प्रसिद्धिर्गौतमेदृशी 3.7.23cd
यथोक्तसृष्टिविद्यः स्यात्तस्यैतत्फलमीरितम् 1.4.164cd
यथोक्तस्याविसंवादं तत्तथैवेति च श्रुतिः 1.4.1049ab
यथोक्तहेतुवशगः स्वभावप्रहितोऽप्यसुः 1.2.186ab
यथोक्ताग्निमुखज्ञानाद्यदीत्यादिगिराधुना 5.16.79cd
यथोक्तात्मानभिज्ञो योऽविद्याकार्याभिमानवान् 1.4.1593ab
यथोक्तादन्यथैवेमं व्याख्यानाद्यत्नतो बुधाः 4.4.391ab
यथोक्तादात्मनोऽन्यद्यत्कार्यकारणरूपकम् 3.4.187ab
यथोक्तानां च सूत्राणामा शास्त्रस्य समामपनात् 1.4.1067ab
यथोक्ता नानुशिष्टिश्चेत्कीदृक्तदनुशासनम् 4.2.2ab
यथोक्तानामसद्भावात्प्रायार्थः प्रत्यगात्मनि 2.1.186cd
यथोक्तानुभवारूढो बुद्धयन्तोऽपि प्रसिध्यति 3.4.124ab
यथोक्तायां हि गायत्र्यां कृत्स्नं जगदुपाहितम् 5.16.47ab
यथोक्ता येन सर्वेऽपि प्रयुक्ताः स्वात्मकर्मभिः 2.5.44ab
यथोक्तार्थचिकीर्षुः संस्तन्मयस्तत्क्रतुः स्वतः 1.5.297ab

यथोक्तार्थप्रसिद्धत्वाद्वैशब्दोऽत्र प्रयुज्यते 4.3.1477ab
यथोक्तार्थप्रसिद्ध्यर्थं वचांसि सुबहून्यपि 1.4.620ab
यथोक्तार्थप्रसिद्ध्यर्थं श्रुतिराख्यायिकात्मिका 1.3.11ab
यथोक्तार्थमुपासीनं प्रति प्रववृतेऽधुना 1.3.281cd
यथोक्तार्थोपसंहार उत्तरार्थविवक्षया 1.4.1634ab
यथोक्तावगमत्वं तु न कथंचिन्निवार्यते 1.4.1310cd
यथोक्तावस्थयोर्मा भून्मृषात्वं ब्रह्मणः सदा 5.1.39cd
यथोक्ताश्रमवासार्थं सामर्थ्यान्नियमो भवेत् 3.5.150ab
यथोक्तेन प्रकारेण न मनागपि गम्यते 4.3.1746cd
यथोक्तेन विचारेण विधित्रयनिषेधनम् 1.4.914ab
यथोक्तैकात्म्यसंदृष्टावतः कात्स्न्यं ममात्मनः 1.4.747cd
यथोक्तोपनिषद्भिस्त्वं संस्कृतात्मासि भावितः 4.2.6ab
यथोक्तोपासनफलं वक्ष्यामीत्युत्तरं वचः 1.4.50ab
यथोक्तोपासनफलमुक्तब्रह्मात्मरूपता 5.10.7ab
यथोक्तोपासनादेव कैवल्यं चेद्विवक्ष्यते 3.1.26ab
यथोक्तोपासनाभ्यासभावितस्य क्रियाकृतः 5.17.1ab
यथोक्तोपासनाभ्यासाद्विराडेव भवेदसौ 5.16.9cd
यथोच्छिन्नात्ममोहस्य निह्नोतुरपि निह्नुतिः 1.4.312ab
यथोदकप्रवाहस्य सेतुर्विधरणस्तथा 4.4.1015ab
यथोदितं कर्म सत्यां कुर्यात्सत्पुत्रजन्मने 6.4.92cd
यथोदितमिदं ज्ञानं सहकार्यन्यसाधन- 4.5.22ab
यथोदितमिदं योज्यं मनःप्राणात्मनोरपि 1.5.178ab
यथोदितार्थ एतस्मिन्दृष्टान्तोऽप्यधुनोच्यते 4.3.1082ab
यथोपपद्यते सर्वं शृणु तच्चापि भण्यते 4.3.1560ab
यथोपासनमेवास्य फलं भवति नान्यथा 2.1.52cd
यथोषरात्मको दोषः पृथिव्या एव जज्ञिवान् 2.3.123ab
यदग्निनाभवद्ब्रह्म देवेष्वविकृतं नृषु 1.4.1638ab
यदजीजनत्फलं कर्ता स्वकर्मज्ञानसाधनः 1.5.13ab
यदज्ञानाज्जगत्यस्मिंस्तीव्रानर्थपरंपरा 3.8.160ab
यदज्ञानात्प्रवृत्तिर्या तज्ज्ञानात्सा कुतो भवेत् 1.3.101ab
यदज्ञानात्प्रवृत्तिर्या तज्ज्ञानात्सा कुतो भवेत् 3.5.121ab
यदज्ञानात्प्रवृत्तिर्या तज्ज्ञानात्सा कुतो भवेत् 4.4.1113ab

यदज्ञानात्प्रवृत्तिर्या तज्ज्ञाने सति सा कुतः 1.4.763ab
यदत्र किंचिद्वक्तव्यं तस्य प्रागेव चोक्तितः 4.4.978ab
यदत्र चोद्ये वक्तव्यं तत्पुरैवासकृद्ध्ह 3.5.41ab
यदद्य मेऽपतद्रेत ओषधीरसरच्च यत् 6.4.21ab
यदनन्तरमेवेहा स कामः क्रतुरुच्यते 4.4.230cd
यदनभ्युदितं वाचा मनुते मनसा न यत् 2.1.525ab
यदनेकार्थबोधित्वमेकस्य वचसः सतः 2.1.563cd
यदनेनान्नमत्तीति तस्मादेत इतीरणात् 1.5.190cd
यदन्तरतमत्वं प्रागुक्तं तत्परमात्मनि 3.5.11ab
यदभ्यधायि प्राक्श्रुत्या तदेवानूद्य पूर्ववत् 3.9.1cd
यदभ्यस्तं पुरास्याभूदहमेवेदमित्यदः 1.4.38ab
यदभ्युपगमादेव तत्सिद्धिर्वार्यते कुतः 4.3.156cd
यदर्थं सर्वशास्त्राणां प्रवृत्तिरतिविस्तरा 1.4.405ab
यदर्थमतियत्नेन महिमानस्य कीर्तितः 1.3.345ab
यदर्थस्तु प्रयासोऽयं तत्कर्माथ प्रपञ्च्यते 6.4.65cd
यदर्थोपनिषत्कृत्स्ना वृत्तिस्तस्या भविष्यति 1.4.1063cd
यदव्यवहितं द्रष्टुर्व्यवधानेन केनचित् 3.4.37ab
यदसाधारणं यस्य रूपं तत्तस्य भण्यते 4.3.644cd
यदस्ति तन्न जानाति यन्नेहास्ति तदीक्षते 2.4.251ab
यदा कामाः प्रमुच्यन्त इत्युक्त्यैव कृतार्थता 4.4.377ab
यदा चैवं स्थितः पक्षस्तदा दोषोऽयमागमत् 2.1.466ab
यदा तदा ध्वनेर्न स्यादज्ञातार्थावबोधने SV 619cd
यदा तु कल्पितं द्वैतमद्वैतं परमार्थतः 5.1.59ab
यदा तूपचितं कर्म पर्यवस्यति भोगतः 6.2.153ab
यदात्मकमिदं लिङ्गं यत्सप्तदशमुच्यते 3.7.15cd
यदात्मके नामरूपे इत्यज्ञानात्मता तयोः 1.4.482ab
यदा त्वविद्ययाध्यस्तं संसारित्वं न वस्तुतः SV 265ab
यदा न लीयते चित्तं न च विक्षिप्यते पुनः 4.4.888ab
यदानुभवकामस्य कार्यं साध्यं प्रतीयते SV 800ab
यदा पञ्चावतिष्ठन्ते ज्ञानानि मनसा सह 4.4.27ab
यदा पञ्चावतिष्ठन्ते ज्ञानानि मनसा सह 4.4.1254ab
यदापि मातरि फलं तदापि विधिनात्र किम् SV 673ab

यदापि मानयोग्यत्वं सत्त्वं तच्च प्रतीयते SV 705ab
यदापि वस्तुवृत्तेन नगरावाप्तिसाधनम् SV 406ab
यदारभत इत्युक्तं तच्चाप्यस्तु स्वगोचरे 3.3.125cd
यदालोचनमात्रं स्याद्रूपादौ चक्षुरादिभिः 4.4.69ab
यदावगम्यते नान्यत्प्रवृत्तेः कारणान्तरम् SV 498ab
यदा वै पुरुषः शेते प्राणमप्येति वाक्तदा 1.5.378ab
यदा सर्वेऽखिलाः कामाः काम्यैश्च विषयैः सह 4.4.376ab
यदा सर्वे प्रमुच्यन्त इत्येवं बहुशः श्रुतौ 1.4.1719cd
यदा सर्वे प्रमुच्यन्ते कामा येऽस्य हृदि श्रिताः SV 355ab
यदासाधारणाविद्या प्रत्यगात्मैकगोचरा 4.4.892ab
यदि कारणसंस्थं सत्तन्निमित्तं च कारणम् 1.2.90ab
यदि चेत्कारकत्वं स्यान्नो चेद्भ्रान्तिरियं भवेत् 2.1.210cd
यदि तद्वस्तुयाथात्म्यं शास्त्रं न प्रतिपादयेत् SV 841ab
यदि तद्व्यतिरेकेण तदा वक्तव्यमेव ते 4.3.799ab
यदि तावत्स्वतस्तत्स्याद्ब्रह्मविद्या निरर्थिका 1.4.1104ab
यदि ते तत्तमो यान्ति को दोष इति चोदिते 4.4.606ab
यदितोऽनप्रधानाया वाचो ह्यन्येन केनचित् 1.3.326ab
यदित्यनेन निर्देशो विशेष्यस्य विवक्षितः 3.4.11ab
यदित्यादिपदानां च सामानाधिकरण्यतः 3.4.13ab
यदिदं कर्मणोऽशेषसाधनं मृत्युनाप्लुतम् 3.1.18ab
यदिदं कर्मिणः प्राहुः कर्मभूमावमेधसः 1.4.131ab
यदिदं प्राणिभिर्नित्यमद्यतेऽहरहस्तृषा 1.5.24ab
यदिदंशब्दधीगम्यं सम्यग्ज्ञानोदयात्पुरा 1.4.1315ab
यदिदंशब्दनिर्दिष्टं पूर्णाविद्यैकहेतुजम् 1.4.1187ab
यदि नाम तथाप्यैक्यं तयोरनुभवाश्रयात् 4.3.663cd
यदि नाम न मानानि व्याप्रियन्ते विनिश्चितेः 4.3.179ab
यदि नाम सदा स्पर्शो वाय्वादावपि वर्तते 4.3.750ab
यदि नामावसितार्थो फलं दत्त्वेह भावना 4.3.1255ab
यदि नामास्ति संभेदः साक्षात्कल्पितसर्पयोः 1.4.1174ab
यदि प्रत्यक्षगम्योऽर्थो व्यावृत्तेस्तत्पृथक्त्वतः 4.3.1683ab
यदि ब्रह्मानुगं ब्रह्म स्यादनर्थात्मकं तदा 2.4.10cd
यदि भोक्ता भवेत्प्राणो जाग्रद्वच्छब्दमागतम् 2.1.112ab

यदि मानातिरिक्तार्थोऽमितः संभाव्यते तदा 4.3.164ab
यदि मालक्षणाप्तस्य साध्याभावादि भण्यते 4.3.723ab
यदि वस्तु स्वतो मुक्तं परतो बद्धमिष्यते 3.3.19ab
यदि वाक्षरयाथात्म्यं स्थूलादेरिह भण्यते 3.8.79ab
यदि वाग्नेरिदं नाम तस्य प्रकरणित्वतः 1.2.149ab
यदि वाज्ञानतस्तस्य विकारो जगदिष्यते 4.3.321ab
यदि वा तत्फलस्यैव किंचित्सामान्यवर्त्मना 3.1.48ab
यदि वा द्रष्टरि प्राप्ते साक्षादिति विशेषणात् 3.4.15ab
यदि वा द्विविधो मोक्षो जीवत्येव शरीरके 4.2.102ab
यदि वा परभागोऽस्या गन्धस्यानेकभेदतः 2.4.358ab
यदि वाभावविषया न ह्यभावो निषिध्यते 2.3.204cd
यदि वा भिन्नवाक्यत्वात्कर्मविज्ञानकाण्डयोः 4.4.971ab
यदि वा मनसि व्यक्तेर्मनसा वोपलभ्यते 5.8.2cd
यदि वायं त्रयस्त्रिंशद्द्वासप्ततिरथापि वा 1.3.266cd
यदि वा याज्ञवल्क्योक्तिरेवमेवेति यद्वचः 3.3.164cd
यदि वा लिङ्ग्यते तेन मनो लिङ्गमिहात्मनः 4.4.242cd
यदि वा विद्यते भेदः कंचनेति च लिङ्गतः 4.3.1167cd
यदि वा शोकवद्वस्तु शोकशब्देन भण्यते 4.3.1347ab
यदि वास्तु तृतीयेयमित्थंभूतार्थवाचिनी 2.1.232ab
यदि वा स्वप्न एवास्तु रत्वादि यदुदीरितम् 4.3.1053ab
यदि वा स्वयमेवैत्य देहाभेदत्वहेतुतः 4.4.8ab
यदि वैकविशेष्येण विशेषणतया युतिः 3.4.30ab
यदि वोक्तात्मयाथात्म्यबोधेनैवाद्वयात्मिकाम् 4.4.845ab
यदि व्याक्षेपकारित्वान्नित्यं कर्म निषिध्यते 4.4.1235ab
यदि संघातमात्रस्य भोक्तृत्वमिह कल्प्यते 2.1.149ab
यदि स्थानान्तरं प्राप्तमन्वियात्स्वप्नजा क्रिया 4.3.1006ab
यदि ह्यन्यत्ततो द्रष्टुर्दृश्यं तत्स्याद्विभागवत् 4.3.1563ab
यदीममभिहिंसिष्ये कनीयोऽन्नं भवेद्ध्रुवम् 1.2.189cd
यदु किंचेति विस्पष्टं प्रजादुःखनिषेधकृत् 1.5.357cd
यदुक्तं विरहेऽशेषसूर्यादिज्योतिषामयम् 4.3.855ab
यदुद्दिश्य प्रवृत्तैषा व्याख्या सर्वान्तरं प्रति 3.8.2ab
यदुपाधिनिषेधोक्त्या नेतीति ब्रह्मणः स्फुटम् 2.3.4ab

यदृच्छां संततिं शून्यं विनाशं वेति भण्यताम् 3.2.132cd
यदेकं तन्न नानेति नाना नैकमिति प्रमा 1.6.76ab
यदेतदिति तत्साक्षाद्यथावत्प्रतिपद्यताम् 3.8.61cd
यदेतद्धृदयमिति तथा चागमशासनम् 4.3.372ab
यदेवं वर्तनं श्रुत्या स्वपितीति तदुच्यते 4.3.893ab
यदेवं सति कर्तव्यं तत्क्षिप्रमनुशाधि माम् 2.4.41cd
यदेव कारणं मानैरिह साक्षाद्विनिश्चितम् 1.2.45ab
यदेव नित्यमज्ञानं मिथ्याज्ञानं तदेव तु 1.4.386ab
यदेव भगवान्वेद तेन संविभजस्व माम् 2.4.60cd
यदेव विद्ययेत्यादि श्रुतेरपि वचस्तथा 3.3.126ab
यदेवाकृत्रिमं रूपं तदेवास्यावशिष्यते 2.4.408ab
यदेवेहेति च तथा मन्त्रोऽप्युच्चैर्जगाद नः 5.1.26ab
यदैकस्य प्रधानत्वं तदान्यस्याप्रधानता 1.4.1485ab
यदैवं पूर्वमेव स्यात्तदा हेतुवचः स्फुटम् 4.3.1002ab
यदैव सम्यग्विज्ञानं जातमस्यागमोक्तितः 3.2.28ab
यदैवाहर्जुहोतीत्थं हन्ति मृत्युं तदैव सः 1.5.72cd
यदैषां स्थानसंबन्धविमोक्षः स्यात्तदैव तु 4.4.18cd
यदोद्भवति शास्त्रोत्था दैवी वृत्तिस्तदासुरी 1.3.119ab
यदोपलक्षणार्थं स्याद्ब्राह्मणग्रहणं तदा 3.5.89cd
यदोर्ध्वोच्छ्वासितैवास्य पुरुषस्य भवत्यथ 4.3.1975ab
यद्दुस्तरं यद्दुरापं यद्दुर्गं यच्च दुष्करम् 4.4.1056ab
यद्दृष्टं साध्यसिध्यै तु कर्मानुगुणमेव तत् SV 363cd
यद्धि किंचेति सर्वार्थमेवेत्यत्रावधारणम् 1.3.240ab
यद्धि प्रकरणे यस्य तत्तदङ्गं प्रचक्षते 4.4.1125cd
यद्धि यद्व्यतिरेकेण वस्तु नेहोपलभ्यते 4.3.533ab
यद्धि यस्माद्विभक्तं स्यात्तदेव स्यात्ततः कथम् 4.3.1614ab
यद्धि यस्य स्वतो रूपं न तत्प्राप्तावपेक्षते 1.4.764ab
यद्धि यस्याविरोधेन स्वभावमनुवर्तते 3.3.68ab
यद्धेतुकं प्रमाणत्वं वेदान्तानां समर्थ्यते SV 561ab
यद्धेतुकमिदं रूपं साविद्यानर्थकारिणी 4.3.1207ab
यद्ध्यायतीह मनसा वाचा वक्ति तदेव हि 1.4.1844cd
यद्बुभुत्सापि दुष्प्रापा वद तत्तत्त्वबोधनम् 4.4.1023ab

यद्ब्रह्म ते ब्रवाणीति ह्यपृष्टः काश्यमब्रवीत् 2.1.33cd
यद्भागस्यागमाद्योऽर्थभागः स्यादधिकः क्वचित् SV 867ab
यद्भावेऽपि न यन्मानं तदभावेऽपि तत्कथम् 4.3.251cd
यद्यकृत्स्नोऽपरिज्ञानाज्ज्ञानात्कात्स्न्यं समश्नुते 1.4.1777ab
यद्यतो नातिरेकेण तत्तदेवेति निश्चितिः 5.1.41cd
यद्यत्कामयते कामी कर्मभूमाववस्थितः 1.4.1689ab
यद्यत्कामयते चास्मादविद्याकामकर्मणाम् 3.2.75ab
यद्यत्प्राप्तं जगत्यस्मिंस्तत्तत्सर्वं निषिध्यते 2.3.202ab
यद्यथोक्तं परं ब्रह्म मनुष्या विद्युरञ्जसा 1.4.1578cd
यद्यद्देहसजातीयं ज्योतिर्दृष्टं तदिन्द्रियैः 4.3.141cd
यद्यद्धि कुरुते किंचित्तत्तत्कामस्य चेष्टितम् 1.4.1816cd
यद्यद्धि कुरुते किंचित्तत्तत्कामस्य चेष्टितम् 2.1.578cd
यद्यद्धि कुरुते जन्तुस्तत्तत्कामस्य चेष्टितम् 4.4.223cd
यद्यद्धि रूप्यते किंचिच्छब्दस्पर्शादिकं धिया 1.6.19ab
यद्यद्ध्यायति मनसा तत्तद्वाचा प्रभाषते 5.10.6cd
यद्यद्वैतं परं ब्रह्म तत्र स्यात्परमार्थतः 5.1.31ab
यद्यनिर्ज्ञातसंबन्धोऽप्यर्थं शब्दः प्रबोधयेत् SV 497ab
यद्यपीदं जगत्कृत्स्नं गृह्यते संहतत्वतः 1.3.157ab
यद्यपीमौ जगत्यस्मिन्नात्मज्ञानपुरःसरौ 4.4.654ab
यद्यपीष्टं तथापीदं नात्ममोहापनोदकृत् 1.4.1099cd
यद्यपीह परो हेतुः काम एव तयोरपि 4.4.222cd
यद्यपुत्र इति वचः संभवे सति युक्तिमत् 1.5.266ab
यद्यप्यत्राभिमानोऽस्ति निष्क्रियाकारकात्मनि 1.4.651ab
यद्यप्येवं तथापीह धर्माधर्मात्मकं बुधाः 4.4.206ab
यद्यप्येवमिदं वस्तु यथोक्तमहिमं परम् 4.3.374ab
यद्यप्येषां स्वविषये प्राधान्यं कस्यचित्क्वचित् 1.4.1490ab
यद्यप्यैकात्म्यधीः साक्षाच्छ्रुतिस्मृत्योर्न चोद्यते SV 193ab
यद्यर्थं कारकाधीनं दृष्ट्वा तत्कारणानुमा SV 1028ab
यद्यविद्या भवेत्कार्यमस्त्वेतद्यदिहोदितम् 1.4.1220ab
यद्यविद्यैकहेतु स्यात्संसारित्वं तदात्मनः 4.4.171ab
यद्यसन्नपि धर्मः स्यान्नैपुण्याद्भवतः क्वचित् 4.3.1715ab
यद्यस्त्यनुजिघृक्षैवं करुणा वा मयीष्यते 2.4.60ab

यद्यात्मायं स्वयंज्योतिः कामकर्मादिवत्कथम् 4.3.1381ab
यद्यात्मोपासनाप्राप्तिः क्वचित्संभाव्यतेऽञ्जसा 1.4.927ab
यद्यानन्दात्मकं ब्रह्म नित्यमात्मानमात्मना 3.9.188ab
यद्यावरणभङ्गाय यत्नः स्याद्घटवित्तये 1.2.106ab
यद्युत्पन्नानि नश्यन्ति स्यात्तदा सिद्धसाध्यता 4.3.591ab
यद्येतद्देहतोऽन्यत्र हृदयं स्यादवस्थितम् 3.9.85ab
यद्येवं तर्हि संत्याज्यं ज्योतिषेति वचः श्रुतम् 1.5.238ab
यद्येवमन्वयोऽप्यत्र नैव प्राप्नोति तत्कथम् 4.3.726ab
यद्येवमप्रमाणत्वमस्तूपनिषदां तदा 2.1.538ab
यद्वस्तु तदलं स्वात्मसंवित्त्यै निरपेक्षतः 2.4.452cd
यद्वस्तु स्वात्मनैवास्ति तत्परार्थं न बोधकृत् 1.4.433ab
यद्वस्तु स्वात्मनैवास्ति तत्परार्थं न बोधवत् 4.3.1725ab
यद्वस्त्वनुभवप्राप्तं तच्चेन्नास्तीति भण्यते 4.3.568ab
यद्वाचानभ्युदितं मनुते मनसा न यत् 2.5.83ab
यद्वा तत्रैव तात्पर्यं यत्रोपच्छन्द्य नीयते SV 405ab
यद्वानवगतोऽतोऽन्यः संभाव्यो नात्मनस्ततः SV 560ab
यद्वानात्माभिसंबन्धात्पूर्वमैकात्म्यनिष्ठिता 2.5.87ab
यद्वानुमानमेवात्र शब्दात्पर्वं हि युज्यते SV 742ab
यद्वान्तरयते शोकमानन्दैकस्वभावतः 4.3.1351cd
यद्वाभिधानमों विद्यात्तस्यैव परमात्मनः 5.1.125ab
यद्वा मृषात्वसिद्ध्यर्थं नाड्युपन्यास इष्यते 4.3.1212ab
यद्वा विराजमुद्दिश्य संकल्पमकरोन्मनः 1.2.144ab
यद्वा विविदिषार्थत्वं काम्यानामपि कर्मणाम् 4.4.1052ab
यद्वा विविदिषार्थत्वं सर्वेषामपि कर्मणाम् SV 322ab
यद्वाशरीरशब्देन तच्छ्रुतौ लिङ्गनिह्नुतिः 4.4.522ab
यद्विज्ञानात्परित्यज्य निःशेषं वित्तसाधनम् 2.4.61ab
यद्विद्यैकहेतु स्यादब्रह्मत्वं न तु स्वतः 1.4.1207ab
यद्वै चतुर्थमित्यादिवचसा यत्नतः श्रुतिः 5.16.20cd
यद्वै तदिति तच्चापि स्पष्टमध्वं प्रवक्ष्यते 1.4.1317cd
यद्वै तदिति यत्नेन श्रुत्येह क्रियतेऽञ्जसा 4.3.1412cd
यद्वै तदिति वचस इतोऽन्यार्थपरत्वतः 4.3.1750ef
यद्वै तदित्युपक्रम्य प्रत्यग्वस्तुविशुद्धये 4.3.1385cd

यद्वै तदित्युपक्रम्य व्याख्यातं वस्तु विस्तरात् 4.3.1795ab
यद्वै न पश्यतीत्येवमात्मानमतिशङ्कसे 4.3.1541ab
यन्तरि व्योम्नि तदपि दुर्वाच्यमतिसूक्ष्मतः 3.8.51cd
यन्तृत्वहेतुविध्वस्तावेष संपद्यतेऽक्षरम् 3.8.43ab
यन्न रसयतीत्यत्र विजानन्वा इतीर्यते 4.3.1632ab
यन्न संभावितं पर्वं वस्तुप्राधान्यहेतुतः 6.2.1ab
यन्निमित्तं च साक्षित्वं कारणत्वं तथात्मनः 4.3.350ab
यन्निमित्तं प्रमाणानि प्रामाण्यमिह बिभ्रति 2.4.391ab
यन्निमित्ता प्रवृत्तिः स्यात्सा कथं तन्निवर्तिका SV 422ab
यन्निषेधमुखेनेदं नेति नेतीति भण्यते 2.3.15ab
यन्मदन्यदिति चोक्तेः परस्य प्रकृतत्वतः 1.4.528ab
यन्मनुष्या वयं तत्र विरोधमनुयुञ्जमहे 1.4.1078cd
यन्मन्यन्तेऽथ तद्ब्रह्म किमवेदिति पृच्छ्यते 1.4.1132cd
यन्मन्यन्ते नरास्तत्र विरुद्धमिव लक्ष्यते 1.4.1088ab
यन्मर्त्यसाधनं साध्यं मर्त्यं तदपि जायते 3.1.20ab
यमद्राक्षं पुरा कुम्भं तमेवाद्य स्पृशाम्यहम् 4.3.269ab
यमनस्तत्प्रबोधस्थं न ततोऽन्यं कदा चन 4.3.958cd
यमपेक्ष्येश्वरत्वं स्यात्तत्तावत्प्रतिषेधति 4.4.982ab
यमप्रमीयमाणानि नानात्मानं प्रमिण्वते SV 551ab
यमान्पतत्यकुर्वाणो नियमान्केवलान्भजन् 4.4.1217cd
यमान्सेवेत सततं न नित्यं नियमान्बुधः 4.4.1217ab
यमासङ्गमिह स्वप्ने कामं त्वमनुपश्यसि 4.3.1018ab
यया यया भवेत्पुंसां व्युत्पत्तिः प्रत्यगात्मनि 1.4.402ab
यशः प्रकाशरूपेण वीर्यं तद्बलहेतुतः 1.2.203cd
यशसा च सुदीप्तेन विद्वांस्तपति विद्विषः 5.16.24cd
यशोवीर्यैकहेतुत्वात्प्राणा यश इहेष्यताम् 1.2.203ab
यश्च पर्वमुपन्यस्तो दृष्टान्तो भेदसिद्धये 4.3.470ab
यश्चात्मैव भवेत्प्रत्यक्सर्वान्तरतमस्तथा 3.4.42ab
यश्चापि प्राणवित्स्पर्धी स्पर्धामनु स मृत्युवत् 1.5.375ab
यश्चायमध्यात्ममिति योऽयं मद्देहकृन्मतः 2.5.48ab
यश्चायमात्मेत्यत्रोक्तो विज्ञानात्मेति यं विदुः 2.5.57cd
यश्चायमिति वाक्येन तथासाधारणाभिधा 2.5.47cd

यश्चोर्ध्वं वक्ष्यते तस्मात्परस्तादेतदुच्यते 1.4.206cd
यस्तु जन्मान्तराभ्यासात्क्षपिताशेषकामनः SV 89ab
यस्तु त्यक्तुं न शक्नोति रागादिप्रबलत्वतः 3.5.123ab
यस्तु धीपूर्वको ध्वंसस्तदर्थेयं परा श्रुतिः 2.4.399cd
यस्तु बाहुबलोन्मत्तः स्वां योनिं ब्राह्मणं नृपः 1.4.1611ab
यस्तु वेदोदितोपायक्षपिताशेषकल्मषः 4.4.568ab
यस्तु सूक्ष्मो रसोऽन्नस्य भागोऽमृतमितीर्यते 2.2.18ab
यस्ते प्रियतयाभीष्टः सोऽचिराद्दुःखकृद्भवेत् 1.4.1048ab
यस्ते स्तन इति गिरा शस्यतेऽत्र सरस्वती 6.4.120cd
यस्त्वक्षरपरिज्ञानान्मृत्युमृत्युः प्रमीयते 3.8.169ab
यस्त्वणीयान्रसः सूक्ष्मः स ऊर्गमृतमुच्यते 1.3.255ab
यस्त्वात्मरतिरेव स्यादात्मतृप्तश्च मानवः 1.4.133ab
यस्त्वेषणानिवृत्तः स्यान्नेति नेत्यात्मविद्यया 4.4.1166ab
यस्मात्कस्माच्चिदङ्गाद्धि प्राण उत्क्रामतीह नुः 1.3.293ab
यस्मात्कारणमुल्लङ्घ्य कार्यं नान्यत्र वर्तते 1.2.167ab
यस्मात्क्षरमतीतोऽहमक्षरादपि चोत्तमः 2.4.246ab
यस्मात्तच्छ्रुतवाक्यस्य स्वयमेवोपजायते SV 660cd
यस्मात्तदेषु निहितं तस्मात्ते वसवः स्मृताः 3.9.13cd
यस्मात्परं नापरमस्ति किंचिद्- 2.5.123a
यस्मात्पूर्णमिदं साक्षात्तादात्म्यं तेन वर्ण्यते 5.1.10cd
यस्मात्प्रसिद्धं नास्त्यन्यत्प्रसिद्धं यन्न कस्यचित् 3.8.59ab
यस्मात्स एष एवंविदुज्ञातातोऽन एव सः 1.3.366cd
यस्मात्सर्वाणि भूतानि सर्वदोपकरोत्ययम् 1.4.1800ab
यस्मात्सुषुप्त आत्मायं नात्मानं नाप्यनात्मनः 4.3.1306ab
यस्मादगात्कष्टतरं नोपवादादतः परम् 3.9.129cd
यस्मादज्ञानतो मर्त्योऽतोऽमृतोऽज्ञानहानतः 4.4.388cd
यस्मादनृतमेवेदं यत्किंचिदिह वीक्ष्यते 4.3.1011ab
यस्मादपरतन्त्रोऽयं वेदात्मा ब्रह्म भण्यते 2.6.5ab
यस्मादर्थे तु विज्ञेया यच्छब्दाः सर्व एव तु 1.4.738ab
यस्मादवदतो लोके पुरुषार्थो न कश्चन 4.1.14ab
यस्मादविद्ययैवात्मा प्राणक्षेत्रज्ञरूपभाक् 2.1.419ab
यस्मादसति कार्येऽसौ शक्तिरेव न सिध्यति SV 99ab

यस्मादस्ति ततो मुक्तौ नात्मनो गतिरिष्यते 4.2.29cd
यस्मादात्मानमेवातः प्रज्ञां विज्ञाय कुर्विति 4.4.868cd
यस्मादात्मा परं तत्त्वं पदनीयमतो भवेत् 1.4.979cd
यस्मादादिमतां नाशः सर्वैरेवाभ्युपेयते 4.3.591cd
यस्मादिहानुमीयन्ते तस्माल्लिङ्गविरोधिता 2.1.590cd
यस्मादीश्वर उद्गाता कामावाप्तावतः शुभम् 1.3.367cd
यस्मादुद्रिच्यमानं हि द्वैतं नैवातिरिच्यते 5.1.44ab
यस्मादेतत्स्वतो बुद्धं स्वतः शुद्धमतोऽद्वयम् 4.4.302ab
यस्मादेतत्स्वतो बुद्धमतः शुद्धमसंगतेः 4.4.530ab
यस्मादेवंस्वभावैषाविद्या नैसर्गिकी ततः 4.4.884ab
यस्मादेवमतः प्राह तद्वा अस्येति नः श्रुतिः 4.3.1329ab
यस्मादेवमतः प्राह न बाह्यमिति नः श्रुतिः 4.3.1323ab
यस्मादेवमतः प्रेतो देवताविरहेऽपि ना 3.2.164ab
यस्मादेवमतोऽजोऽसावकार्याकारणत्वतः 4.4.702ab
यस्मादेवमतोऽद्वैतोऽविद्यातत्कार्यलङ्घनात् 4.3.1806ab
यस्मादेवमतोऽशेषसंसारानर्थकल्पना- 1.4.1281ab
यस्मादेवमतो गार्ग्यमेतावद्धीतिवादिनम् 2.1.89ab
यस्मादेवमतो हित्वा प्राणादीनप्रियात्मनः 1.4.1050ab
यस्मादेवमयं तस्माद्विदिते परमात्मनि 4.4.1162ab
यस्मादेवंफलं ज्ञानमेवंविद्यत्नतस्ततः 4.4.1192cd
यस्मादेष स्वतो बुद्धो निरविद्यः स्वतस्ततः 3.5.76ab
यस्माद्द्रष्टुर्हि या दृष्टिर्यया द्रष्टा प्रसिध्यति 4.3.1421ab
यस्माद्धिरण्यगर्भस्य कर्म वाय्वन्तरिक्षयोः 2.3.50ab
यस्माद्यस्मादुपादाय मात्राः स्वप्ने चकार सः 4.3.996ab
यस्माद्राजास्य सर्वस्य मां च देवः स सर्वदा 6.3.41cd
यस्माद्विधीयते तस्मात्तत्त्यागी पतितो भवेत् 4.4.1228cd
यस्मान्नाणीयो न ज्यायोऽस्ति कश्चित् 2.5.123b
यस्मिंश्चाविद्ययाध्यासः संसारानर्थलक्षणः 1.4.414ab
यस्मिञ्ज्ञातेऽखिलं ज्ञातं कृतमाप्तं च कामितम् 4.1.33ab
यस्मिञ्ज्ञाते भवेज्ज्ञातं जगदेतच्चराचरम् 2.4.392ab
यस्मिन्दृष्टेऽप्यदृष्टोऽर्थः स तदन्यश्च शिष्यते 1.4.662ab
यस्मिन्नविद्ययेत्येवं ननु कारणमीरितम् 1.4.479cd

यस्मिन्नात्मनि विध्वस्तव्याकृताव्याकृतात्मके 2.5.58ab
यस्मिन्नेव तु विज्ञान आहिता कर्मवासना 4.3.689ab
यस्मिन्नेव परा सक्तिस्तस्मिन्नेव निरादरम् 2.4.74ab
यस्मिन्पञ्चजनाः पञ्च वियदन्ताः प्रतिष्ठिताः 4.4.639cd
यस्मिन्प्राप्ते यद्भवति तत्तस्मात्स्यात्कथं पुरा 1.4.1557ab
यस्मिन्व इति वाक्येन वसिष्ठत्वस्य लक्षणम् 6.1.18ab
यस्मिन्विशुद्ध इति च सत्त्वशुद्धौ ध्रुवा स्मृतिः 4.4.1043ab
यस्मिन्विशुद्ध इत्येवं सत्त्वशुद्धौ ध्रुवा स्मृतिः 4.4.584ab
यस्मिन्सत्येव यत्कार्यं न भवेदेव चासति 1.4.462ab
यस्मिन्सत्येव यत्सत्स्यात्तस्मिंस्त्वसति तन्न सत् 3.5.85cd
यस्मै प्राह स आचार्यस्तस्य प्राणानवत्यसौ 5.16.40cd
यस्य त्वष्टास्ववस्थासु प्रत्यक्त्वं सममिष्यते 1.4.1043ab
यस्य मध्ये कपाले ते यच्च भूतादिलक्षणम् 3.8.5cd
यस्य मन्थविधिज्ञस्य जाया चेदार्तवं व्रजेत् 6.4.66ab
यस्य संबन्धमाश्रित्य ह्यप्रियोऽपि प्रियायते 2.4.90ab
यस्य साधनभावः स्यात्प्रवृत्तौ सर्वकर्मणाम् 4.4.1123ab
यस्य सिद्धिर्मृषा तत्स्याद्रज्जुसर्पद्विचन्द्रवत् 1.4.476cd
यस्यां जाग्रति भूतानि सा निशा पश्यतो मुनेः 3.5.49cd
यस्यां प्रजननं पुंसा स्त्रियामभ्यन्तरीकृतम् 6.4.8ab
यस्याधिकारसंबन्धः स आत्मा न विधीयते SV 759cd
यस्यानुभवसिद्ध्यैव सिद्धिः स्याद्घटसिद्धिवत् SV 1058ab
यस्यानुशासनं तस्य स्वयंभोः प्रतिपत्तये 2.6.3ab
यस्याप्रसिद्धिर्नाज्ञानात्प्रसिद्धिर्नापि मानतः SV 467ab
यस्यावहादयो भेदाः सागरस्योर्मयो यथा 3.7.16ab
यस्यैता वृत्तयः प्रोक्ता वृत्तिमान्सोऽन उच्यते 1.5.150ab
यां काण्वोपनिषच्छलेन सकलाम्नायार्थसंशोधिनीम् SV 2a
याः काश्चिज्जीवता शक्यास्त्यक्तुं तित्यक्षता क्रियाः 4.4.1242ab
याग आसेचनाधिक्याद्धोमाख्यः स्यात्स एव तु 1.4.1795cd
यागः कार्याभिसंबन्धोऽप्यनुत्पाद्य फलं न ते SV 646ab
यागदानादिकं कर्म रूपं लोकपुरःसरम् 4.5.9cd
यागसिद्धेः पुरासिद्धेः कथं चोदनया मितम् SV 1034cd
यागसिद्ध्यापि तत्सिद्धौ प्रयोज्यत्वं कुतो यजेः SV 1035cd

यागादिः स च नो कार्यं स्वतःकार्यैकरूपतः SV 617ab
यागादिकर्मणस्तस्मादसमीचीनमुच्यते 1.4.1731cd
यागादिकार्यं देवादेर्देहलिङ्गद्वयादृते 1.4.1784ab
यागादिविषयासिद्ध्या न चासौ न प्रसिध्यति SV 718ab
यागाद्यनुष्ठितेरस्य घटादेरिव चेन्मतः SV 1036ab
यागेनापाद्य संसिध्यन्विषयस्यैति साध्यताम् SV 536cd
याजमानं यथा कर्म ह्याश्रित्य फलवद्भवेत् 1.3.386ab
याजमानमिदं ज्ञानं स्वादेः प्राग्यत्समीरितम् 1.3.334ab
या जातिर्ब्राह्मणत्वाख्या साग्निरेवेति निश्चितिः 1.4.1639ab
याजुष्मत्योऽपि तावत्य इष्टकाः स्युः प्रजापतेः 1.5.66ab
याज्ञवल्कीय एतस्मिन्काण्डे जल्पोक्तिवर्त्मना 3.1.15cd
याज्ञवल्कीयकाण्डस्य ह्युपपत्तिप्रधानतः 3.1.4cd
याज्ञवल्कीयकाण्डेन तद्युक्त्याथोपपादितम् 4.5.1cd
याज्ञवल्कीयमेतस्मान्मधुकाण्डादनन्तरम् 3.1.2ab
याज्ञवल्क्यं स्थितं भूयो विदग्धः पर्यपृच्छत 3.9.80cd
याज्ञवल्क्यस्य शिष्यत्वे ग्रन्थच्छायापि नेष्यते 4.1.7ab
याज्ञवल्क्यात्मिका भूत्वा ह्यतिनिर्बन्धकारिणम् 3.9.101cd
याज्ञवल्क्यादिरूपेण श्रुतिरेवाथवा स्वयम् 4.3.32ab
याज्ञवल्क्यार्तभागौ तावुत्क्रम्य च जजल्पतुः 3.2.139cd
याज्ञवल्क्येह यो विद्याद्वेदिता स्यात्स एव तु 3.9.39ab
याज्ञवल्क्योऽथ जनकं योगक्षेमार्थमभ्यगात् 4.3.9ab
याज्ञवल्क्योऽपि तं प्राह यः प्राणेनेति लिङ्गतः 3.4.65ab
याज्ञवल्क्योऽपि राज्ञैवं पृष्टः सन्पूर्ववत्तदा 4.3.1888ab
या तमर्हति पूर्वोक्ता सातिप्रश्न्येह देवता 3.6.24ab
या तस्या जन्मनः काले फलं श्रुत्याधुनोच्यते 4.4.1282cd
याति क्षेत्रज्ञतामीशः कूटस्थोऽपि ह्यविद्यया 1.2.137cd
याति देहान्तरं तद्वत्कर्मविद्यादिसंभृतम् 4.3.1915cd
याति बुद्ध्यादिकं स्थानं पुमान्हंसाभिधो ध्रुवः 4.3.933cd
याति मात्राः समादाय कर्मवायुसमीरितः 4.3.997cd
यातु तत्र भवानेव नाहं तं गन्तुमुत्सहे 6.2.55ab
यातेष्वस्तं दृशैवास्ते भासयंश्चित्तचेष्टितम् 4.3.112cd
या त्वश्वमेधगत्युक्तिः सोपलक्षणसिद्धये 1.3.3ab

याथात्म्यज्ञानतो नान्यत्पुरुषार्थाय कल्पते SV 888cd
याथात्म्यदर्शनायैव सृष्ट्यादि प्रत्यपीपदत् 1.4.627cd
याथात्म्यप्रतिपत्त्यर्थमुत्थितस्य प्रचक्षते 2.1.195cd
याथात्म्यावगमेऽशक्ता धूमोऽग्नाविव सापि च SV 778ab
यादृक्कर्मविधे रूपामात्मध्यानविधेरपि 1.4.780ab
यादृक्तद्गम्यते मानात्तत्तादृङ्नेति गीः कुतः 1.4.901ab
यादृक्साधनमस्येह परलोकाप्तये चितम् 4.3.848ab
यादृगर्थोऽस्य वचस उत्तरेष्वपि तादृशः 6.3.62ab
यादृगस्य द्वये तत्त्वमात्मनैवानुभूयते 1.4.1409ab
यादृगस्य द्वये रूपमात्मनैवावगम्यते 5.1.25ab
या निशा सर्वभूतानां तस्यां जागर्ति संयमी 3.5.49ab
या निशा सर्वभूतानामित्यवोचत्स्वयं हरिः 1.4.313cd
यानि ह्येवेति हेतूक्तिः प्रतिज्ञातार्थसिद्धये 4.3.956cd
यान्ति मुक्त्यानुगुण्यं चेद्विधयो वार्त्तमेव तत् SV 421cd
यामवोचत्स्वभार्यायै याज्ञवल्क्योऽतिविस्तरात् 2.5.92cd
यामस्मद्गुरुरेव वेदशिरसामैकात्म्यतात्पर्यतः 6.5.24a
या महाप्रलयात्सृष्टिः सा विरिञ्चस्य वक्ष्यते 1.4.20ab
यायादनागतत्वं च तस्यैक्याभागवत्त्वतः 2.1.405cd
यावच्च सम्यग्विज्ञानवह्निनासौ न दह्यते SV 1105ab
यावज्जीवश्रुतिप्राप्तेर्न चेत्तत्त्याग इष्यते 1.5.305ab
यावतीत्युपमोक्तेह श्रुत्याविष्क्रियतेऽनया 3.3.155cd
यावतीयं त्रयी विद्या तावन्तमपि गृह्णतः 5.16.60ab
यावत्कार्यगतं किंचिद्भावनादि समीक्ष्यते 1.4.343ab
यावत्किंचिज्जगत्यस्मिन्नाहुत्येह व्यपेक्ष्यते 5.5.5ab
यावत्किंचिज्जगत्यस्मिन्भेदकं वस्तु लक्ष्यते SV 936ab
यावत्किंचिज्जगत्यस्मिन्रूपं मेयत्वमागतम् 4.4.420ab
यावत्किंचित्फलं नादः सर्वानर्थनिवृत्तये 1.4.54cd
यावत्किंचिदविद्यायाः कार्यं वैराग्यकारणम् 2.4.6ab
यावत्किंचिदविद्योत्थमिदमा तदनूद्यते 4.3.1279ab
यावत्किंचिद्विजानाति शाकल्यः सर्वमेव तत् 3.9.58ab
यावत्किंचिन्मितेः प्राप्तं न तन्मिथ्या मितत्वतः 1.3.62ab
यावत्तावन्न विद्याया अधिकारी भवेन्नरः 2.4.71cd

यावत्त्वागमतः साक्षान्न वेत्त्यात्मानमद्वयम् 2.1.173ab
यावत्येषा च वागुक्ता तस्या इत्येवमादिना 1.5.175ab
यावत्यो भावनाः पुंसामपि तावत्य एव तु 4.4.187cd
यावत्स्वप्नेऽस्ति वक्तव्यं प्राक्तदुक्तमशेषतः 4.3.1070ab
यावदब्दं मुमोचाश्वं स्वच्छन्दं मुक्तबन्धनम् 1.2.215ab
यावदेते यथोद्दिष्टा आप्ताः स्युः कामपूर्वकाः 1.4.1839ab
यावदेवमयं वेद प्राणितीत्यादिकर्तृकम् 1.4.710ab
यावदैकात्म्यसंमोहपट्टको नापनीयते 1.4.1554cd
यावद्द्रव्यानुरोधित्वं नावश्यं गुणकर्मणोः 4.3.1590ab
यावद्धि जनिमत्किंचिन्नामादिप्रविभागवत् 3.8.15ab
यावद्यथोक्तं विज्ञानमाविर्भवति भास्वरम् 2.4.218cd
यावद्यावत्प्ररूढत्वं रागादेर्जायते शिशोः 2.1.358ab
यावद्यावद्घनीभावो बुद्धेः पापादिसंगतेः 4.3.1855ab
यावद्यावन्मलो व्येति बुद्धेर्धर्मादिसंचयात् 4.3.1854ab
यावद्रुधिरसंव्याप्तिः शरीरे तावदेव तु 2.4.345cd
यावन्त इत्युपक्रम्य मन्त्रैराज्यं यथाक्रमम् 6.3.22ab
यावन्तस्तत्र निर्देश्यास्तेऽर्थाः सर्वे निवर्तिताः 2.3.238cd
यावन्नेक्षामहे तावन्नाप्रमाणमितीर्यते 4.3.736ab
यावन्मत्कर्तृकं किंचिन्मानेन प्रतिपाद्यते 1.5.293ab
यावानात्मनि वेदात्मा प्रतीच्यात्मानमात्मना 1.4.728ab
यावान्प्रकाशो जगति स सर्वोऽग्निरिहोच्यते 5.16.35ab
यावान्बाह्यो विकारः स्यात्क्षेत्रज्ञपरिवेष्टनः 2.3.91ab
यावाल्ल्युंडर्थस्तेनायं तदविद्यैकहेतुतः 4.3.315ab
या विद्धा देवतास्तासां प्रक्रियासंहतिः पृथक् 1.3.162cd
या वृत्तिः सोच्यते साक्षाद्दृष्टान्तोक्त्या प्रयत्नतः 4.3.1930cd
यास्ता एवात्र विज्ञेयाः स्तोत्रिया अपि नापराः 3.1.57cd
या स्वलिङ्गाजहद्वृत्त्या तदीशस्य प्रशासनम् 3.8.139cd
यियासति सुधीः कश्चिद्यथा भ्रान्तोऽध्वगस्तथा SV 132ef
यियासुः परलोकं तु कर्मविद्यादिसंवृतः 4.3.843ab
यियासोः परलोकाय कर्मैवाश्रयमूचतुः 3.2.159cd
युक्त एवायमादेशो न यतो विद्यते परः 2.3.237ab
युक्तः फलानुषङ्गोऽस्य वासोलाभो विधिर्यदि 6.1.37cd

युक्तमाह भवानस्माननुरूपं चिकीर्षति 2.4.41ab
युक्तमेतद्व्यवसितं यद्वित्तं न प्रदित्सति 2.4.46ab
युक्तयोऽतोऽभिधीयन्ते पूर्वपक्षादिसंश्रयाः 3.1.15ab
युक्ताः शब्दास्तदैते स्युर्ब्रह्मण्यानन्दवाचकाः 3.9.170cd
युक्ता कल्पयितुं मुक्तिरन्यस्यासंभवो यतः 3.3.107cd
युक्ताशङ्का यतो मर्त्या देवान्प्रत्यृणिनः श्रुतेः 1.4.1471ab
युक्ता ह्यस्येति वचसा मिथ्याज्ञानैकहेतुतः 2.5.129cd
युक्तितोऽपि तथा ज्ञेयमिति चेहोपसंहृतिः 4.5.6cd
युक्तैवाविष्कृतिर्नित्यं तेषां कार्यात्मकत्वतः SV 145cd
युक्तोऽध्यात्मैकरूपस्य बाधः शास्त्राभिमानतः 1.3.215cd
युक्त्यक्षरबहिष्ठत्वान्न विद्वांस उपासते 4.3.1566cd
युक्त्या कल्पयितुं शक्यं श्रुतिवाक्यविरोधतः 1.4.1738cd
युक्त्यागमौ हि संभूय करस्थामलकादिवत् 3.1.14ab
युक्त्यादि मान्तरं नो चेन्मानांशत्वेन तत्स्थितेः SV 810ab
युक्त्या निरूप्यमाणस्य ह्यात्मा तत्त्वमनात्मनः 1.4.944ab
युक्त्या निरूप्यमाणस्य ह्यात्मा तत्त्वमनात्मनः 1.4.1363ab
युक्त्या नैवोपपद्यन्ते जगत्सृष्ट्यादयो यतः 1.4.625ab
युगपत्सापि बौद्धस्य न कथं चन युज्यते 4.3.583ab
युगपत्स्याद्द्वयोर्भोगो जाग्रत्स्वप्नकुलाययोः 4.3.1087ab
युगपन्न हि विज्ञानं जायते घटमेषयोः 4.3.1721cd
युज्यन्ते सर्वभूतानि संहन्यन्ते परस्परम् 5.15.5ab
युतसिद्धनिवृत्त्यर्थं सहजोक्त्याभिधीयते 1.4.532ab
युतिं साधारणात्मा हि यात्यसाधारणात्मभिः 1.4.1406ab
युवा साधुयुवेत्येवं तैत्तिरीयश्रुतीरणात् 4.3.1854ab
युष्मदस्मद्विभागाभ्यां यावद्वस्त्विह मीयते 1.4.1395ab
ये तद्विदुरिति श्रुत्या स्पष्टार्थप्रतिपत्तये 4.4.628cd
ये तु व्याचक्षते मोक्षे नित्यानन्दैकगोचरा 4.4.324ab
ये त्वतः कल्पयन्तीममन्यथैव महाधियः 4.4.369ab
येन कर्मविशेषेण समानायां मृतौ प्रजाः 6.2.31ab
येन चक्षुरिदं दृष्टं चक्षुषा यन्न पश्यति 3.4.163ab
येन त्वस्य विशेषेण विज्ञानात्मत्वमिष्यते 2.3.102ab
येन पुष्यसि वार्याणि सर्वाणीह सरस्वति 6.4.124cd

येन भोगेन वाग्देवांश्चक्षुरादीनहर्निशम् 1.3.138ab
येन रूपं रसं गन्धं शब्दान्स्पर्शांश्च मैथुनान् 4.3.1771ab
येन लोकेऽस्त्यतोऽपेक्षा वेदे तु स्याद्विपर्ययः SV 693cd
येनाक्रामत्यमुं लोकं सोऽस्याक्रम इहोच्यते 4.3.847cd
येनातोऽज्ञानतः सिद्धिं स्वतःसिद्धोऽप्यपेक्षते 1.4.232cd
येनात्मा स्यादहंबुद्धेरनुमेया हि सा स्थिता SV 1072cd
येनानवाप्तज्ञानोऽपि भवेदीदृश एव ना 3.5.197cd
येनान्यस्तेन संसारी कर्माधिकृत इष्यते 2.1.471ab
येनान्वितोऽयं संसारी सुषुप्ते कर्मणः क्षयात् 1.4.507ab
येनार्थस्यासमाप्तत्वात्क्रियेताध्याहृतिः पदे SV 659cd
येनाश्रुतं श्रुतमिति कस्मिनन्न्विति तथा परम् 1.4.960cd
येनाश्रुतं श्रुतमिति कस्मिनन्न्विति तथा वचः 3.2.106ab
येनासावविलुप्ताक्षस्तत्पारोक्ष्यं कथं भवेत् SV 795cd
येनास्याशङ्क्यते नाशस्तेनास्याप्रविभागतः 4.3.1554ab
येनेदृगेव चिह्नेन ब्राह्मणस्तेन लक्ष्यताम् 3.5.207cd
येनेदृगेव तेनेति तस्मादाह श्रुतिः स्फुटम् 3.5.211ab
येनेह विधृतौ नित्यं सोऽन्तर्यामीति गम्यताम् 3.8.134cd
येनैव वर्त्मना यातः पुनस्तेनैव वर्त्मना 4.3.997ab
ये यथा मां प्रपद्यन्ते तांस्तथैव भजाम्यहम् 4.4.1316ab
येषां तान्प्रति चोद्यं स्यान्न त्वज्ञातात्मवादिनाम् 1.4.420cd
येषां नो ह्ययमात्मेति कार्यलोकनिवृत्तये 1.4.1773cd
येषामनधिकारोऽत्र ह्यश्वमेधक्रतौ भवेत् SV 1118ab
येषामपि हि सामान्यभेदवद्वस्तु गृह्यते SV 973ab
यैकावशिष्यते तस्य कला पक्षक्षये तथा 1.5.210ab
यैव ज्ञानविकाशेषु साक्षिता सैव नान्यथा 1.4.683ab
योऽकाम वाक्येन ह्ययमेवार्थ उच्यते 1.4.1776ab
योऽकाम इति तद्वच्च श्रुतिः कामनिषेधनी 1.3.97cd
योऽकाम इति वचनं पूर्वप्रत्युक्तिरुच्यते 4.4.264cd
योऽकाम इत्यादिगिरा यो वेदात्मानमागमात् 4.4.285cd
योऽक्रियाकारकं साक्षादक्रियाकारकात्मकः 4.4.304ab
योऽञ्जसा दर्शितस्तस्य विशुद्ध्यै वोत्तरं वचः 4.3.378cd
योऽत्यक्रामदनानात्वो भेदसंसर्गवर्जितः 3.9.115ab

योऽनन्यार्थो यदर्थं च सर्वं योऽनन्यदृक्सदा SV 1083cd
योऽनस्तमित एकोऽत्र वागाद्यस्तमयेऽमृतः 2.1.116ab
योऽनुक्रमेणेति तथा श्रुतौ स्पष्टमिदं वचः 1.5.264ab
योऽनुभूतिविरोध्यर्थः स कथं स्थाप्यते बलात् 1.6.76cd
योऽन्यथा संगतिं ब्रूते चर्मवद्वेष्टयेत्स खम् 1.4.255cd
योऽन्यथा सन्तमात्मानमन्यथा प्रतिपद्यते 2.4.253cd
योऽन्यामित्यादिवाक्येन तत्कार्यमपि सूत्रितम् 1.4.1591cd
योऽपि प्रत्यक्षतोऽभावं वादी कश्चित्समीक्षते 4.4.666ab
योऽप्यन्यदर्शी सोऽप्यत्र नास्ति तद्धेत्वसंभवात् 4.3.1513cd
योऽप्यविद्यादिसंबन्धः सोऽप्यविद्याप्रकल्पितः 4.3.95ab
योऽबादिपरिपाट्यैवं विराजमसृजत्स्वयम् 1.2.169ab
योऽयं दक्षिणेऽक्षन्निति शास्त्रदृष्टत्वकारणात् 2.3.81ab
योऽयं पवत इत्युक्तिरध्यर्धस्य विनिर्णये 3.9.23ab
योऽयं मृत्युरिह प्रोक्तो मृत्युस्तस्यापि चापरः 3.2.13ab
योऽयं संसारभमिष्ठो व्याख्यातोऽज्ञाततत्त्वकः 4.4.299ab
योऽयमन्तरितीत्युक्त्या तद्विशेषणमुच्यते 5.11.2cd
योऽयमित्यादिना यद्वा यथोक्तस्यात्मवस्तुनः 4.3.337ab
योऽयमित्युच्यते प्रत्यग्ज्योतिषो भानुवद्वचः 4.3.294cd
योऽशनायापिपासादीन्धर्मान्सर्वान्विरोधतः 3.5.55ab
योऽशनायेति चात्रोक्तौ संभाव्यं तदशेषतः 3.5.101cd
योऽसावतीन्द्रियोऽग्राह्यः सूक्ष्मोऽव्यक्तः सनातनः 1.4.51ab
योऽसावविद्यया देही संसारी वाप्यभूत्परा 2.5.60ab
योऽसावविद्योत्सङ्गस्थः प्राक्प्रविष्ट इतीरितः 1.4.1177ab
योऽसावादित्यगो देवः सोऽहमस्मीतिबुद्धिगः 5.17.11ab
योगक्षेमफलार्थाय गमनं न निषिध्यते 2.1.94ab
योगक्षेमसमानत्वादविध्यर्थपदान्तरैः SV 728cd
योगयुक्तो विशुद्धात्मा विजितात्मा जितेन्द्रियः 4.4.1047ab
योगस्य च समस्तस्य प्रत्यग्विज्ञानजन्मने 4.4.1070ab
योगस्य भेदनिष्ठत्वान्न च भेदः पुरोक्तितः 4.3.804cd
योगादिसाधनाभ्यासः कर्तव्यः पुण्यसंचयः 4.4.104cd
योगारूढस्य तस्यैव शमः कारणमुच्यते 3.5.124cd
योगारूढस्य तस्यैव शमः कारणमुच्यते 4.4.1093cd

योगावस्थां परामेतामाहुर्योगविदो जनाः 4.4.725cd
योगिदेवादिदेहेषु जक्षणाद्युपपत्स्यते 3.9.201ab
योगिनः कर्म कुर्वन्ति सङ्गं त्यक्त्वात्मशुद्धये 4.4.580ef
योगिनः कर्म कुर्वन्ति सङ्गं त्यक्त्वात्मशुद्धये 4.4.1046cd
योगिनां मन एव स्यादस्माकं सर्व एव तु 1.4.87cd
योगिप्रत्यक्षगम्योऽयं न तत्प्रत्यक्त्वहेतुतः 2.4.171cd
योगिप्रत्यक्षमानं वा तयोरविषयत्वतः 2.4.170cd
योगिप्रत्यक्षमानादेर्न चेदैकात्म्यमेयता 2.4.175ab
योगी वा तैजसोऽत्र स्यात्प्रत्यग्दृष्टौ समर्थतः 4.4.581ab
योगे नातिशयैकत्वात्तयोश्चाप्येकरूपतः 5.1.86cd
योगैश्वर्यात्समा सिद्धिः कालादेरीश्वराद्यतः 1.3.311cd
योगोऽयं वस्तुनोर्दृष्टः पृथक्सिद्धौ परस्परम् SV 931ab
योगो वा समवायो वा नाभावक्षितिदेशयोः SV 933cd
योग्यं संनिहितं चेदं साकाङ्क्षं च समीक्ष्यते 4.4.806ab
योग्यः प्रत्यङ्ङिति ज्ञेयः पूर्वप्रश्नार्थसंग्रहः 3.5.27cd
योग्यकालावबोधार्थमासांचक्र इतीरणम् 4.1.3ab
योग्यतैवामपात्रस्य भिदुरत्वसमन्वयात् 6.4.51cd
योग्यत्वहेतुतस्तर्हि सास्त्येवास्यादिका श्रुतौ SV 701cd
योग्यायोग्यव्यपेक्षेयं मानव्यवहृतौ भवेत् 1.4.500ab
योग्येन्द्रियस्य या यस्य ततोऽन्यत्रापि लक्षिता 2.4.370ab
यो देवतां समुद्दिश्य द्रव्यत्यागः स उच्यते 1.4.1795ab
योद्यमादिक्रियाहेतुस्तथाभ्युदयकर्मकृत् 1.5.148ab
यो न वेदात्मयाथात्म्यं वेद जात्यादिमत्तया 2.4.254ab
योनिशब्दाभिलप्यं स्याज्जाग्रद्देहसमाश्रयम् 4.3.992cd
यो मामेवमसंमूढो जानाति पुरुषोत्तमम् 2.4.247ab
यो यतो लभते सत्तां निरुणद्धि स तं कथम् 1.2.17cd
यो यतो लिप्सते नासावकिंचित्को ह्यनर्थिने 1.4.578ab
यो यतो लिप्सते सिद्धिं स तं हन्ति कथं वद 1.2.18cd
यो योन्यन्तर्गतो देशः समिद्धश्चर्म निर्दिशेत् 6.4.11ab
यो वा एतदिति स्पष्टं श्रुतिरप्याह यत्नतः 3.8.167ab
यो वेदाग्निमुखामेतां गायत्रीमग्निरेव सः 5.16.80ab
यो वै भूमेति वचनाद्योऽशनायेति चात्मनि 4.4.215cd

योो वै स धर्म इत्युक्त्या वक्तुं प्रववृते श्रुतिः 1.4.1623cd
योषाग्निवच्चेच्छास्त्रं स्याद्दृष्टिमात्रविधायकम् 1.4.1107ab
योषिज्जग्धस्य योऽन्नस्य रसः स्यात्परिणामजः 3.9.45ab
योषित्समागमेच्छेह काम इत्यभिधीयते 3.9.49ab
योषिदग्निरिति ज्ञेया उपस्थश्च समित्तथा 6.2.107cd
योषिदग्न्यादिदृष्टौ हि नैव मन्तव्यताविधिः 2.4.215cd
योषिद्विदलवद्गाति पुंसः शक्त्यादिभागवत् 1.4.115cd
यो ह वा इति प्रश्नोक्तिस्तस्यायमिति निर्णयः 2.2.8ab
यो ह वै ज्येष्ठमित्युक्त्या विद्वत्ता या पुरोदिता 6.3.10ab
यो ह वै शिशुमित्यादि भविता ब्राह्मणद्वयम् 2.1.425cd
यौगिकी चाभिधा ज्ञेया क्रियायोगस्य संभवात् 1.3.351cd
रक्तत्वादिप्रसिद्ध्यर्थं विक्रियां न प्रपद्यते 4.3.1585ab
रक्तद्विष्टमनो हेतुः शब्दाद्यर्थे प्रियाप्रिये 2.4.78cd
रक्तपीतादिरूपत्वं मन्यते स्वप्नमध्यगः 4.3.1216cd
रक्तादिभेदतो भेदः प्रकाशस्य प्रकाश्यतः 4.3.1777ab
रक्ताम्बराणां सिद्धान्तस्तथाभ्युपगमात्स्वयम् 4.3.686cd
रक्षन्ति ननु देवास्तं न विशिष्टाधिकारिणम् 1.4.1808ab
रचना च पदार्थानां विवक्षापूर्विकैव तु SV 722ab
रचयन्ति तथासाध्वीं प्रक्रियां न्यायवर्जिताम् 2.3.112ab
रजतं विद्यते किंचिद्विज्ञातं चात्मवस्तुवत् 4.3.167cd
रजतं शुक्तिकेत्यादिव्यपदेशोऽप्रसिद्धितः 1.4.452cd
रजताद्यन्यथाज्ञानकारणं युक्तिगौरवात् 1.4.470cd
रजताद्यन्यथाज्ञानप्रतिषेधादृतेऽपि हि 1.4.467cd
रजसः क्वचिदुद्रेकस्तमसः क्वचिदिष्यते 2.3.163ab
रजस्तमोऽतिवर्तित्वात्सत्त्वसंशुद्धिहेतुतः 4.4.1211ab
रजस्तमोऽनुविद्धेन यतो न ब्रह्म गम्यते 2.5.86ab
रजस्तमोजरागादिदोषानाक्षिप्तशेमुषिः 4.4.1199ab
रजोधूमतुषाराभ्रनीहाराद्यन्वितं वियत् 4.3.1261ab
रज्जुः सर्पादिनेवात्मा विनाविद्यां न जायते 4.4.1325ab
रज्जुकुम्भादिवन्नैक्यं विशेषस्य समीक्षणात् 4.3.500cd
रज्जुखण्डाद्यविद्योत्थसर्पादिविनिवृत्तिवत् 4.4.354cd
रज्जुज्ञानसमुत्पत्तौ रज्ज्वा नान्योऽवशिष्यते 4.4.290cd

रज्जुज्ञानाद्धि सर्पादिप्रपञ्चविलयो यतः SV 392ab
रज्जुज्ञानेऽहिधीध्वस्तौ कृतमप्यनुशोचति SV 365cd
रज्जुत्वाहित्वयोर्यद्वदेकस्मिन्नपि वस्तुनि 3.5.36ab
रज्जुबुद्धिवदेव स्युस्तद्धीश्चाप्यहिबुद्धिवत् 1.6.88cd
रज्जुयाथात्म्यविज्ञानात्सर्पवत्कारणात्मनः 2.3.201ab
रज्जुवत्तदविज्ञानात्सर्पदण्डादिनेक्ष्यते 1.4.1316ab
रज्जुसर्पधिया लोके न रज्जुरिति धीवृतिः 1.4.252cd
रज्जुसर्पादिवत्तत्तन्नैति संभावनामपि 4.3.1738cd
रज्जुसर्पादिवत्तस्मान्नोभयत्रापि दोषता 3.8.75cd
रज्जुसर्पादिवन्नातः प्रतीचः शिष्यते पराक् 1.4.942cd
रज्जुसर्पो यथा रज्ज्वा सात्मकः प्राग्विवेकतः 1.4.443ab
रज्जुसर्पो यथा लोकेऽज्ञातरज्जुसतत्त्वकः 4.4.289ab
रज्ज्वज्ञानमनादाय न सर्पादीक्षणं यथा 4.3.1454ab
रज्ज्वां सर्पादि किंचिच्च त्यक्तमेव जिहासति SV 886cd
रज्ज्वां सर्पादिवज्जातं नामरूपक्रियात्मकम् 2.1.1cd
रज्ज्वां सर्पादिवन्नैवं प्रत्यगात्मनि सेक्ष्यते 1.4.1039cd
रज्ज्वाः सर्पादिको यद्वन्न तथा दोष इष्यते 4.3.321cd
रज्ज्वात्मना तथापीयमवस्त्वेवात्र बाध्यते 1.4.426cd
रज्ज्वादितत्त्वविज्ञानं कुर्वतः स्वेन तेजसा SV 830cd
रञ्जनं काम आसङ्गः सर्वानर्थकृदात्मनः 5.16.21cd
रत्नस्य पयसोऽत्यर्थं रत्नाधारश्च यः स्तनः 6.4.123ab
रथवाहाश्च सूताः स्यू रथवाहनकोविदाः 4.3.1963ab
रथा दार्वाद्यसद्भावान्न सन्ति स्वप्नदर्शने 4.3.914ab
रथादिवासनानीडचित्तवृत्तिसमुद्भव- 4.3.922ab
रथादिवासनीनाडधीवृत्त्युद्भवकारणम् 4.3.926ab
रथादीन्सृजतेऽथात्र जाग्रत्कर्मादिहेतुकान् 4.3.915ab
रथादेरसतस्तस्माद्द्रष्टैवात्मा न कारकः 4.3.924cd
रथादेरसतो यद्वत्स्वप्ने निर्माणमीक्ष्यते 4.3.1024ab
रथेन्द्रियादिवत्तस्मात्कामोऽप्यत्र समीक्ष्यताम् 4.3.1025ab
रमन्ते प्राणभूते च फलमेतदुपासितुः 5.14.15cd
रविबिम्बादिवत्तर्हि प्रवेशोऽस्तु परात्मनः 1.4.540ab
रविहृन्मध्यगं यायात्ततो रश्मिभिरावृतः 4.2.81ab

रवीन्द्वादिपदार्थेभ्यो ह्यनुमानैकवर्त्मना 4.3.44ab
रश्मयश्च दिशश्चैता आदित्यसमिदाश्रयाः 6.2.82ef
रश्मयो न समायान्ति विज्ञानपुरुषं प्रति 5.6.7ab
रश्मींस्त्वं पर्यावर्तयादिति चावर्तनात्मकः 1.4.774ab
रश्मीनपनुदाशेषांस्तेजः संयच्छ संहर 5.17.9ab
रस आम्रं धारयितुं नैवेहोत्सहतेऽबलः 4.3.1934cd
रसरूपरवेष्वेवं यथोक्तं प्रतिपादयेत् 2.4.362ab
रसवर्जं रसोऽप्यस्य परं दृष्ट्वा निवर्तते 4.4.386cd
रसवर्णानुरोधेन रक्तपीतादिरूपताम् 4.3.1217ab
रसाच्छोणितनिष्पत्तिः शोणिताद्बीजसंश्रयात् 3.9.46ab
रसाच्छोणितमित्यादिक्रमाच्छुक्रतया मम 6.4.39cd
रसादिः प्रविविक्तः स्यात्पुरीषादिव्यपेक्षया 4.2.62ab
रसादिग्रहणे शक्तिर्लोके दृष्टा न चक्षुषः 3.3.123ab
रसादिधातुभिर्देहस्ततोऽनुपचयादयम् 4.3.1929ab
रसादेरपि सूक्ष्मोऽयमाहारो लिङ्गतृप्तिकृत् 4.2.62cd
रसोऽपि चायं जग्धान्नपरिणाममपेक्षते 4.3.1230ab
रहस्यं युवयोः कर्म तद्वदाविष्करोम्यहम् 2.5.109cd
रागद्वेषक्रिया तत्र स्यात्फलान्तरसिद्धये 1.5.82cd
रागद्वेषवियुक्तैस्तु विषयानिति चाह हि 4.4.1057cd
रागद्वेषादिनाक्षिप्तस्ततो भूयः प्रवर्तते 2.1.211cd
रागद्वेषौ न तौ मुक्त्वा जगत्यन्यत्प्रवर्तकम् 1.4.173cd
रागद्वेषौ यतो दृष्टौ नैवर्ते साध्वसाधुनी 1.4.175cd
रागादयः सन्तु कामं न तद्भावोऽपराध्यति 1.4.1539cd
रागादयो नियोगस्य सिद्ध्यै विषयसाधनाः SV 491cd
रागादिः प्रेरणाकारी प्रेरणाज्ञापको ध्वनिः SV 487cd
रागादिकारणं चेत्स्यात्कार्यं सत्कारणं कथम् 1.4.428ab
रागादिदर्शनं यच्च ज्ञानिनोऽपीह चोद्यते 4.4.957ab
रागादिपूर्वकं कर्म जायते फलवद्यतः 1.5.83ab
रागादिप्रत्ययोद्भूतिरिषुचक्रादिवेगवत् 1.4.1529cd
रागादिरहितं तत्तु निष्फलं सुप्तवागिव 1.5.83cd
रागादिहेतुनाशार्थं कार्यं कर्मैव तेन तु 3.5.123cd
रागादेर्नापि चाभावो भावात्तदनुभूतितः 1.4.265ab

रागाद्यर्थस्य चासिद्धौ कर्तृवृत्तिर्न रागतः SV 488cd
रागाद्याकृष्टचेतस्त्वान्न चेच्छक्नोत्यशेषतः 4.4.1091ab
रागाद्याक्षिप्तदृष्टार्थप्रवृत्तिप्रतिषेधतः SV 411ab
रागाद्युत्थप्रवृत्तीनां कात्स्न्र्येन च विरोधतः SV 417ab
रागाद्युत्थप्रवृत्तीनां निषेधेषु लयोऽञ्जसा SV 381ab
रागो रज इति ज्ञेयः प्रवृत्तेः कारणं तु यत् 5.16.21ab
राजतात्मकपात्राभ्यां गृह्येते तत्र यौ ग्रहौ 1.1.7cd
राजपुत्रत्वसंप्राप्तौ नान्यत्किंचिदपेक्षते 2.1.516cd
राजसं तामसं रूपमितो ह्यन्यत्र वक्ष्यते 6.2.116ab
राजसूनोः स्मृतिप्राप्तौ व्याधभावो निवर्तते SV 233cd
राजादिषु प्रसिद्धश्च नियोगः साध्यगोचरः SV 531ab
राजानं च तथेशानं करोत्वधिपतिं च माम् 6.3.42ab
राजानं नेति होवाच नाहं वेद्मि त्वयोदितम् 6.2.37ab
राजानमपि जेष्यामीत्याजगाम नृपं ततः 6.2.23cd
राजानमभिसंयान्ति प्राणास्तद्वन्मृतौ नरम् 4.3.1974cd
राजापि तमुवाचाथ दैवेष्विति परं वचः 6.2.60ab
राजायं नः समायातीत्यासते यत्नमास्थिताः 4.3.1964ef
राजा वातिसुखी लोके प्ररूढेन्द्रियवानपि 2.1.346cd
राजेति राजनाद्भास्वदविलुप्तात्मदर्शनात् 2.5.63cd
राजेव सचिवैः सार्धं स भोक्तेहेति गम्यताम् 2.1.154cd
राजैव पूर्वं पप्रच्छेत्येतस्माद्गम्यते शुभा 4.3.13ab
राज्ञस्तु तदविज्ञानान्नाहं वेदेति युज्यते 4.2.14ab
राज्ञा बलेनाल्पबलो बलीयांसं कुटुम्बिनम् 1.4.1620ab
राज्याभिषेकमाप्नोति प्राप्य सिंहासनं पितुः 2.1.515ab
रातेर्धनस्य दातुस्तद्ब्रह्मेदं स्यात्परायणम् 3.9.158cd
रात्रिमाहुः क्षितिच्छायामङ्गाराश्चन्द्रमास्तथा 6.2.102cd
रात्रेरपरपक्षं च दक्षिणायनदेवताम् 6.2.149ab
रात्रौ यस्मात्स एतस्यां प्रविश्यास्ते प्रजापतिः 1.5.211ab
राधको वीक्षते बुद्धिं साक्षी तद्वदसंहतः 1.4.562cd
रामरावणयोर्युद्धं रामरावणयोरिव 2.4.461ab
रामो राजा बभूवेति न ह्येतावत्प्रबोधतः SV 197ab
राये कर्मफलायेति रयिः कर्मफलं यतः 5.17.20ab

राशित्रितयपक्षे च नाप्यर्थोऽत्र समञ्जसः 2.3.138ab
राहुवच्चन्द्रसंपृक्तः प्रत्यग्ज्ञानमयस्ततः 4.3.311cd
रुद्रा इत्यभिधीयन्ते प्राणा एकादशोदिताः 3.9.15cd
रुद्राद्या मध्यमं यत्नात्सततं पर्युपासते 2.2.24cd
रूढ्या वृत्तिः खशब्दस्य वायुरे व्योम्नि लक्ष्यते 5.1.121ab
रूढ्या वृत्तिर्मांसखण्डे तात्स्थ्याद्विज्ञानवाचकम् 4.4.395cd
रूपं गुणोऽस्य संसार इति वैशेषिकादयः 2.3.88cd
रूपं च बोधयत्तद्वन्नामपक्षेऽवतिष्ठते 1.5.142cd
रूपं द्रव्यात्मनो नान्यद्रसादेस्तद्विभिद्यते SV 1067cd
रूपं पूर्वमिह त्वस्य ध्वस्ताविद्यमथोच्यते 4.3.1296cd
रूपं पूर्वमुपन्यस्तं तस्य साक्षाच्चिकीर्षया 4.3.1209cd
रूपं प्रकल्प्य सत्यस्य भण्यते तदुपासनम् 5.6.1cd
रूपं रूपं च सर्वाणि त्वं स्त्री त्वं च पुमानसि 2.1.462cd
रूपं रूपं प्रति ह्येष प्रतिरूपो बभूव ह 2.5.126ab
रूपं वस्त्वपरिज्ञानसमुत्थं ज्ञातृसंश्रयम् 1.4.284cd
रूपं व्याक्रियते यत्तु तन्नामेत्युपदिश्यते 1.4.707cd
रूपं संभाव्यतेऽह्यादेरेवमात्मस्वरूपतः 4.3.366cd
रूपभास्करसत्येषु त्रिधैषोऽपि व्यवस्थितः 3.9.52ab
रूपभ्रंशो हि भवति यतो गर्भस्य धारणे 6.4.41cd
रूपमेव प्रतिष्ठा स्यात्सर्वदा नामकर्मणोः 1.6.30ab
रूपराशिरशेषेण भूम्याद्युक्त्योपसंहृतः 5.16.11ab
रूपस्यैवावभासित्वान्न चेत्स्याच्छ्रोत्ररूपवत् 2.4.364cd
रूपाणां प्रविभागश्च त्वष्टृपाकनिबन्धनः 1.5.184cd
रूपाणामिति संबन्धाद्रूपात्मत्वात्तथैव च 1.6.18cd
रूपाणि मृत्योस्तेन स्युः कार्याणि करणानि च 4.3.458cd
रूपाणि विलिखत्साक्षान्निर्वाणं संप्रलीयते 4.4.722cd
रूपाण्येवायमात्मात्र मृत्योः स्वप्नेऽतिवर्तते 4.3.971ab
रूपात्मकं यथा चक्षू रूपस्यैव प्रकाशकम् 1.5.137ab
रूपादिज्ञानसंभूतौ तद्धेतूनामनेकधा 1.4.84ab
रूपादिदर्शनान्तस्थ आगमापायसाक्ष्यसौ 3.7.51ab
रूपादिपञ्चकं यस्मात्तद्द्वारेणाश्रितं हृदि 3.9.79cd
रूपादिविषयाभासा लौकिकी दृष्टिरुच्यते 3.4.149cd

रूपादिविषयासङ्गः करणैश्चक्षुरादिभिः 4.3.1096ab
रूपाद्यक्षजगम्यैश्च सामानाधिकरण्यतः 1.4.586cd
रूपानधिगतत्वं नो न श्रोत्रादेः प्रमाणतः 4.3.171cd
रूपान्तरेभ्यः सर्वेभ्यस्तद्धि सत्यात्मकं यतः 1.4.1622cd
रूपाभिधेयसंबन्धमरूपाशब्दमक्षरम् 2.3.253cd
रूपाभिव्यक्तिरेवं स्यादविद्याध्वस्तिरात्मनः 1.4.1494cd
रूपायतनदेवस्य प्रतिबिम्बोदयाश्रयः 3.9.55ab
रूपारब्धमिदं चक्षू रूपाणामेव तद्ग्रहात् 3.9.73ab
रूपे इति तदा युक्तं कल्पनानुगुणं वचः 2.3.140cd
रूपे इति तदावक्ष्यच्छ्रौती चेत्कल्पना भवेत् 2.3.141cd
रूपे वा ब्रह्मणो विद्यान्मूर्तामूर्ते सवासने 2.3.6ab
रूप्यते यैरसौ मृत्युः कार्याणि करणानि च 4.3.455ab
रूप्याध्यारोपणं तस्माद्दाहारि गरीयसा 1.4.1217cd
रूप्याभङ्गानवेलायां शुक्तिकाधीर्न बाधते 1.4.1498ab
रेतःक्षेपफलं चाह पुंसे पुत्राय लब्धये 6.4.96ab
रेतः स्कन्दति यत्सुप्तौ जाग्रतो वापि कामिनः 6.4.19cd
रेतसस्तत्ससर्जेश उत्पन्नस्थितयेऽशनम् 1.4.155ef
रेतसोऽन्नरसस्यैव यत्रान्नाहुतिरीक्ष्यते 6.4.14ab
रेतःस्वयोनावुदक आत्मानं चेत्प्रमादतः 6.4.26ab
रेतो जुह्वति तत्राग्नौ देवाश्चेन्द्रियरूपिणः 6.2.110ab
रेतो मूलं न वो वाच्यं जीवतस्तद्धि जायते 3.9.136ab
रोगादिवदनर्थत्वात्कर्त्रादिः प्रजिहासितः SV 139cd
रोचिष्णूपनिषत्कान्तमादर्शाक्षादिबुद्धिषु 2.1.71ab
रोदयन्तो द्रवन्त्येते रुदन्ति च यतस्ततः 3.9.15ab
रौहिणस्योदयस्यातो न स्वभावाद्यपेक्षते 4.3.762ab
लक्षणं गौणमेव स्यादन्त्ययोर्मध्यभूमिषु 2.3.79ab
लक्षणं तत्र संपूर्णमन्त्यकारणकार्ययोः 2.3.76cd
लक्षणं न प्रयत्नस्य लक्षणं चेत्कथं फलम् SV 764cd
लक्षणं ह्यशनायेति प्राणमृत्युप्रबुद्धये 3.5.72cd
लक्षणेनैव संसिद्ध आधिभौतिकसंग्रहे 1.5.162ab
लक्षणे वर्तमानस्य कालस्य श्रवणं यतः 4.3.612cd
लक्षणै राजपुत्रत्वं यथा कश्चित्प्रबोधयेत् 2.1.513cd

लक्षणोक्तेर्य आत्मेति सोऽन्वेष्टव्य इति श्रुतेः 1.4.1061cd
लक्षयेन्नाञ्जसा वक्ति परं ब्रह्म कथं चन 2.3.254ab
लक्ष्यतेऽविद्यया तद्वान्नज्जुः सर्पादिभिर्यथा 1.4.675cd
लक्ष्यते नामभिः साक्षी साक्षान्न त्वभिधीयते 3.4.156cd
लक्ष्यलक्षणगत्यातो यथोक्तार्थं प्रपद्यते 3.4.34cd
लक्ष्यलक्षणता तस्मात्प्रतीच्यध्यवसीयते 1.4.1427cd
लक्ष्यलक्षणसंबन्धः पदार्थप्रत्यगात्मनाम् 3.5.185cd
लक्ष्यलक्षणसंबन्धो ब्रह्मलोकाभिधानयोः 4.3.1820ab
लघीयोऽतीव यत्तस्मात्कर्मधारय एव सः 4.4.1300cd
लडादिश्रवणात्तस्या अप्रतीतिर्लिङादिवत् SV 506cd
लब्धत्र्यन्नात्मकफलो भावनाज्ञानकर्मभिः 1.5.272ab
लब्धमात्मात्मकं वस्तु प्रतीचोऽनन्यमानतः 2.3.231cd
लब्धमात्रस्मृतिः सोऽथ राजास्मीत्यवबोधतः 2.1.514ab
लब्धात्मकस्य कुड्यादि प्राक्सृतेः कारणावृतिः 1.2.88cd
लब्धात्मलाभो दीपोऽर्थं स्वयमेव प्रकाशयेत् SV 814cd
लब्धृलब्धव्ययोर्भेदो यत्राविद्योत्थभूमिषु 1.4.1014ab
लब्धेऽपि प्रव्रजन्तीति विधावन्यत्र किं श्रमः 4.4.1143cd
लब्धे त्रैलोक्यराज्ये ना भिक्षामाद्रियते तु कः SV 371cd
लब्धे हि भूतलेऽलब्धो घटस्तत्र निषिध्यते SV 921ab
लब्धैकात्म्यस्मृतेर्व्यैति सर्वाविद्या सकार्यका SV 234cd
लब्धैकात्म्येन नैवेयं निवृत्तिः काम्यते श्रुतेः 1.4.1232cd
लभते तमृते यस्मान्नेयात्संभावनामपि 4.3.371cd
लभते न द्वितीयत्वमन्यत्वासंभवात्तमः 4.3.1523cd
लभते निर्वृतिं नैव ज्ञानादेव हि सा यतः 1.4.1671cd
लभते प्रत्यगात्मानं न नञ्तावन्निवर्तते 2.3.195cd
लभते मेययाथात्म्यहेतुमात्रव्यपेक्षतः 1.4.1453cd
लभते मेयसंबन्धं तत्सद्वस्तुपलम्भतः 4.3.1662cd
लभते व्यतिरेकं चेत्परमार्थात्ततोऽपरम् 1.3.50ab
लभ्यतेऽत्र यतस्तस्मात्तमेवेत्यभिधीयते 4.4.846cd
लभ्यते लौकिकोऽपीह किमङ्गागमसंश्रयः SV 21ab
लभ्यते विषयः कश्चित्तद्धीस्तस्मात्तमोपनुत् SV 16cd
लयनिष्ठे प्रमाणे नो वस्तुगोचरभेदतः SV 393ab

लयेनैव समाप्तत्वात्कालकर्मादिकारणम् 2.1.402ab
लवणाब्धि यथा तद्वल्लवणावयवैरिह 4.3.1843cd
लाभाय सनये क्रूरं चक्रथुर्यद्रहस्यगौ 2.5.108cd
लावकः पाचको वेति कारकस्य सतो यतः 4.3.1772ab
लिङर्थे युज्यमानस्य कर्मत्वं न च कामिनः SV 529ab
लिङादयो न कोपादेः स्मर्यन्ते प्रतिपादकाः SV 490ab
लिङादिः प्रेरणावाची कुतः कार्यमितीर्यताम् SV 633ab
लिङादिर्यागमप्येवं वक्ष्यतीत्यविशिष्टता SV 642cd
लिङादिश्रवणात्पुंसः कार्यं यत्प्रसमीक्ष्यते SV 1038ab
लिङ्गं च न्यायरहितं प्रामाण्याय न कल्पते 1.4.1652ab
लिङ्गं च सर्वतो गच्छन्न क्वचित्प्रतिहन्यते 4.4.86ab
लिङ्गं चाप्यतिसूक्ष्मं तन्नाडीमध्यगतिक्षमम् 4.3.1225ab
लिङ्गं मनःप्रधानत्वाल्लिङ्गं मन इहोच्यते 4.4.242ab
लिङ्गकार्यानभिव्यक्तेर्नालं कार्याय देवताः 4.3.1140cd
लिङ्गतश्चावसेयत्वान्न संभाव्यो विधिस्ततः 1.4.767cd
लिङ्गदेहानुरोधी सँल्लिङ्गे कर्त्रादिविक्रियाम् 4.3.1227cd
लिङ्गदेहाविमावेवं पञ्चभूतमयावुभौ 4.4.[illegible]4ab
लिङ्गमाभासतामेति प्रत्यक्षार्थविरुद्धमित् 1.2.58cd
लिङ्गमेव ततो रूपमात्माविद्यैकहेतुकम् 4.3.1224ab
लिङ्गलिङ्ग्यभिसंबन्धदुर्ज्ञेयत्वात्सुसूक्ष्मतः 4.3.29cd
लिङ्गलिङ्ग्यभिसंबन्धो यस्मादेवं मितस्ततः 4.3.69ab
लिङ्गसादृश्यविरहान्नानुमा नोपमा तथा SV 1055cd
लिङ्गस्य चाप्रमाणत्वात्कुतः प्रत्यक्षमानिता 2.1.143cd
लिङ्गस्य मात्वसंसिद्धौ दूषणं दूषणं भवेत् 4.3.239ab
लिङ्गस्य रूपं वक्ष्यामो वासनामयमात्मनः 2.3.84cd
लिङ्गस्य विक्रिया यापि सा रसानुविधायिनी 4.3.1228ab
लिङ्गस्याव्यभिचारार्थं बुद्धिवाक्कायकर्मणः 4.3.46cd
लिङ्गस्येहाप्रमाणत्वे निश्चेष्टं स्याज्जगत्तथा 4.3.245cd
लिङ्गांशश्चाक्षुषो व्यूढो लिङ्गैक्यं प्रतिपद्यते 4.4.64cd
लिङ्गात्तावदिदं ज्ञानं जातं बाधकवर्जितम् 4.3.733ab
लिङ्गात्मकानां भूतानां निर्देशोऽविद्यया सह 4.4.30ab
लिङ्गात्मा पुरुषो ज्ञेयस्तस्यैवेहाङ्गसंगतेः 4.3.1939cd

लिङ्गात्मेह यशो वीर्यमुभयं हि तदुद्भवम् 1.2.204cd
लिङ्गात्सामान्यतो ज्ञाते विशेषेणाप्यनीक्षिते 4.3.71ab
लिङ्गादात्मानमागात्स लिङ्गसंबन्धकारणात् 2.3.121cd
लिङ्गादात्मानमायान्ति गन्धो गन्धपुटं यथा 2.3.118cd
लिङ्गादिकार्यभेदेन साविद्या भिद्यते सदा 4.3.1244ab
लिङ्गादेव ततस्तस्य ध्वंसेऽनर्थो निवर्तते SV 457cd
लिङ्गाद्व्याख्योत्तरा पूर्वा न साध्वीत्यप्रमाणतः 4.3.13cd
लिङ्गानस इतो देहाद्देहमन्यं निगच्छतः 4.4.110ab
लिङ्गान्तरस्य चाभावान्नापि लिङ्गात्प्रसिध्यति 4.3.784cd
लिङ्गापेक्षानुमेयेऽर्थे नरापेक्षा नरोचिते 2.4.222cd
लिङ्गासक्तिवशादात्मा सक्त इत्यभिधीयते 4.4.240ab
लिङ्गाहारादप्यणीयान्यतः प्राज्ञात्मनस्ततः 4.2.66ab
लिङ्गेनापि तत्सिद्धौ त्वदुक्त्यैव विरुद्धता 4.3.244cd
लिङ्गेनोद्दालकः सूत्रं तदपृच्छदथागमात् 3.7.1cd
लिङ्प्रत्ययश्रुतेरत्र भ्रान्तिः समुपजायते 1.4.756ab
लीयतेऽहनि रात्रौ च व्यज्यतेऽहँल्लिकस्ततः 3.9.83cd
लेट्[illegible]पूर्वस्य संसिद्धं शब्लुकीत्यवधारणात् 6.3.37cd
लेपनादि च कर्तव्यं कृतपूर्वेऽपि तद्विधेः 6.3.19ab
लेलायनं क्रियाणां च सर्वासामुपलक्षणम् 4.3.410cd
लोक आहवनीयोऽग्निरसाविति विचिन्तयेत् 6.2.80ab
लोकं पश्यन्स्वहृदयान्निष्क्रामति यथायथम् 4.4.82cd
लोकं प्रजापतिं ब्रह्म प्रैत्यसौ भावनाबलात् 5.12.5ab
लोकं प्रत्युत्थितं यावदग्निहोत्राहुतीहयोः 6.2.14cd
लोकं यतस्ततोऽनन्तमेत्यनन्तात्मभावनात् 1.5.202cd
लोकं यथोक्तदृष्टिः सन्यजमानः फलं स्वयम् 3.1.56cd
लोकः सर्वो विजानाति जानीयात्केन तं वद 2.4.480cd
लोकः स्याद्वाजपेयेन यजमानस्य मानतः 6.4.12ab
लोककालात्मको देवो विराट्संज्ञः प्रजापतिः 1.5.207ab
लोकतः सिद्धमादाय पशुव्रीह्यादिसाधनम् SV 323ab
लोकत्रयफलं यस्मादुत्पत्त्याद्यात्मकं मतम् 1.4.1831ab
लोकत्रयस्य संप्राप्तिर्विद्ययैवेति चेन्मतम् 1.5.232ab
लोकत्रयासंगृहीतेरेतावानिति दुर्घटम् 1.4.1829cd

लोकत्वस्य विधेयत्वाद्यज्जुहोतीत्यनूद्यते 1.4.1796ab
लोकदृष्टक्रियाधर्मसामर्थ्यत्यागलक्षणः 3.8.154ab
लोकपालोऽपि चाप्येष तथाकार्यस्य दर्शनात् 4.4.1012ab
लोकप्रसिद्धन्यायार्थैरंशांशित्वादिकल्पना 2.1.499ab
लोकप्रसिद्धिबाधः स्यात्स चापि स्यादनर्थकः 1.6.77cd
लोकप्रसिद्धिमाचष्ट एकीत्यादि मुमूर्षति 4.4.63cd
लोकप्रसिद्धिमुल्लङ्घ्य यतोऽन्यार्थ्योऽन्यथाग्रहः 2.4.317cd
लोकमात्माक्रियः स्वस्थश्चाकशीत्यभिपश्यति 4.3.932cd
लोकमात्मानमेवेममुपासीतात्मविद्यया 1.4.1701ab
लोकवत्तन्निषेधार्थमपरोक्षादितीर्यते 3.4.16cd
लोकवन्ननु वेदेऽपि कार्यमात्रं न गम्यते SV 516ab
लोकव्यावृत्तिमार्गेण श्रुतिस्तेषां निषेधकृत् 1.5.336cd
लोकशब्दस्य मुख्योऽर्थ आत्मैवेह यतस्ततः 4.3.1834ab
लोकशब्देन संप्राप्तं कर्मकार्यमपेक्ष्य हि 1.4.1649ab
लोकसंचरणाद्यस्य तत्साक्षित्वान्न तु स्वतः 4.3.445cd
लोकसिद्धमतो भेदमादायेष्टार्थसिद्धये 5.1.100ab
लोकसिद्धौ तु योषाग्नी तद्दृष्टिः सुकरेष्यते 1.4.1110cd
लोकस्य ग्रहणं तस्मान्न कर्मसमवायिनः 1.4.1772cd
लोकस्यापूरणे हेतुः समाप्तावुदितः स्फुटः 6.2.162cd
लोकाः कर्मफलानीति तेषां मिथ्यात्वमुच्यते 2.1.286ab
लोकाञ्जयति स सर्वाञ्शत्रुश्चास्य जितो भवेत् 5.4.5cd
लोकाञ्जयन्ति दानेन सद्देशादिमता तथा 6.2.147cd
लोकात्परं निरालोकः सर्वप्राणिविवर्जितः 3.3.146ab
लोकानां रचना यैषा क्षित्यादीनां व्यवस्थिता 4.4.1013ab
लोकानां श्रेष्ठ इति च न चेदाप्तिर्विवक्षिता 1.5.258ab
लोकानां सर्वशब्देन तेषामेव ग्रहो भवेत् 5.16.26cd
लोकानामवसानानि पर्यपृच्छाम तं यदा 3.3.139ab
लोकानुद्दिश्य यः कामस्तत्साधनसमाश्रयः 3.5.117ab
लोकान्तरगतौ हेतुर्लोकारम्भे च भण्यताम् 4.4.108cd
लोकान्तरोपसंक्रान्तिस्तथैतदभिधीयते 4.4.73cd
लोकायतविचारेऽपि प्रत्यक्षैकप्रमाणतः 4.3.529ab
लोकायतस्य बौद्धस्य कणभोज्याक्षपादयोः 4.3.187ab

लोकालोकगिरेर्भागः सर्वप्राणिविवर्जितः 3.3.147ab
लोकालोकादिकार्याणां परिमाणवचस्ततः 3.3.151cd
लोकावच्छेदतोऽमीषां भेदोऽध्यात्मादिलक्षणः 2.1.414cd
लोकेऽनधिष्ठितस्येह केनचिच्चेतनावता 3.4.73ab
लोकेऽनिर्ज्ञाततत्त्वस्य मिथ्याधीरुपजायते 1.4.1543ab
लोकेऽपि चानभिप्रेतात्पथः साक्षान्निवारणम् SV 382ab
लोकेऽपि यस्य यः साक्षी सम्यग्दर्श्येव तस्य सः 4.4.364ab
लोकेऽपि व्याधिसंतापविच्छित्तौ सुखितेक्ष्यते SV 1009ab
लोकेऽपि हि विचार्यार्थमथ संविदते जनाः 1.3.201ab
लोकेऽपीदं सुप्रसिद्धमाङ्गनाबालपण्डितम् 1.2.191ab
लोकेऽस्मिन्द्विविधा निष्ठा पुरा प्रोक्ता मयानघ 3.5.200ab
लोके दर्शनसंबद्धं प्रसंख्यानं समीक्षितम् SV 765ab
लोके दृष्टं विनाविद्यां मोहाद्दृष्टं तु सर्वतः SV 115ab
लोके मान्तरसंसिद्धसंसर्गा रचनाबलात् SV 721cd
लोके मान्तरसिद्धोऽर्थः कार्यायैवाभिधीयते SV 480cd
लोकेष्विति श्रुतिर्वक्ति विरोधस्तन्निबन्धनः 1.3.115cd
लोके सिद्धा च दीपादेर्भिन्नग्राहकगम्यता 4.3.517cd
लोकैषणाग्रहेणैव वित्तान्तर्भावसिद्धितः 4.4.1128ab
लोकैषणेति तामाहुः काम्यकर्मार्थमुद्यमम् 3.5.117cd
लोकैषणेति तामाहुरेषणार्थविदो जनाः 4.4.1130cd
लोकोऽपि दृष्टिमात्रत्वात्प्रत्यङ्मात्रं निरुच्यते 4.4.1298cd
लोकोऽयमग्निर्विज्ञेयः पृथिवी समिदुच्यते 6.2.101ab
लोकोऽस्य मीयते येन ब्रह्मविद्याप्रकाशितः 4.4.1177cd
लोकोक्त्यैव हि यज्ञानां तत्फलत्वादग्रहे सति 1.5.294ab
लोकोद्देशेन या चेष्टा वाङ्मनःकायसाधना 4.4.1130ab
लोको भोज्यः पशुर्ज्ञेयो देवादेरुपकारकः 1.4.1793cd
लोचनस्थाञ्जनादीनां न दृष्टिपथतेष्यते 2.1.353cd
लोडादेरेव श्रवणाद्यत्र रागाद्यसंभवः SV 495ab
लोडाद्यर्थो व्रजेत्युक्तो याति स्वार्थं विना यतः SV 492cd
लोमत्वङ्मांससंघातः कार्यं तस्यायमेव तु 3.9.41cd
लोष्टादेरिव नैव स्यान्नाज्ञासिषमितीक्षणम् 3.4.104cd
लौकिकत्वं कथं तस्य सर्वमेयातिलङ्घिनः SV 1046cd

लौकिकत्वप्रसिद्ध्यर्थं नियोगस्य घटादिवत् SV 1047cd
लौकिका एव शब्दार्था न्यायेनोक्ताः श्रुतौ यतः SV 870cd
लौकिकी नश्वरी सापि दुःखसंस्कारजा तथा 3.9.207cd
लौकिकेनापि तत्सिद्धेर्नास्ति मानमलौकिके SV 744cd
लौकिकेष्वपि कार्येषु तन्नैव विनिवार्यते SV 714cd
लौकिकोऽपि न संसर्गो विध्यायत्तः स्थितो यतः SV 751cd
लौकिको वैदिकः सर्वो व्यवहारश्च वक्ष्यते 1.3.125ab
लौकिको वैदिकः सर्वो व्यवहारो जगत्यपि SV 472ab
ल्यबन्तोक्तेन सांनिध्यान्न ततोऽन्यदपेक्ष्यते 4.4.805cd
वक्तव्यं च कथं त्वेते दृष्टेनैवोपकारिणः SV 410ab
वक्तव्यं तत्र किं मानमदृष्टौ न त्रिरूपता 4.3.779cd
वक्तव्यस्तन्निरासार्थमित्यर्था स्यात्परा श्रुतिः 1.4.1812cd
वक्तव्या तत्र विद्येति निषेधादेव लिङ्ग्यते 2.1.37cd
वक्तीति वाग्भवेदात्मा ह्युच्यते वाग्भवेद्ध्वनिः 1.4.680ab
वक्तुं किमागतोऽसीति नृपः पप्रच्छ तं मुनिम् 4.1.4cd
वक्तुं तदत्र वक्तव्यं खिलकाण्डाधिकारतः 6.2.1cd
वक्तुं प्रष्टुं च बालाकिर्न यतो जज्ञिवांस्ततः 2.1.212ab
वक्तुकामो हि संबन्धमेवं यत्नादचीक्लृपत् 5.1.29cd
वक्तृतन्त्रे हि शब्दार्थे न विश्वासः श्रुतेर्भवेत् SV 595cd
वक्तृत्वात्तृत्वभेदेन वाग्द्विधैकैव भिद्यते 2.2.28ab
वक्त्यभावं भवान्यत्र तत्र वस्तुनि का कथा 4.3.641cd
वक्त्रं वक्त्रेण संधाय स्पृष्ट्वोपस्थं जपेदथ 6.4.38cd
वक्ष्यतेऽकामयमानश्च तथाकुर्वन्विमुच्यते 2.1.579cd
वक्ष्यते सर्वसौख्याप्तिस्तस्मिन्दृष्टे परात्मनि 1.4.1690cd
वक्ष्यत्येतच्च यत्नेन लोकसिद्धोपपत्तिभिः SV 209cd
वक्ष्यन्ते विस्तरेणातः परो ग्रन्थोऽवतार्यते 1.4.1594cd
वक्ष्यमाण उपोद्घातो ब्रह्मविद्या ततः परम् 1.4.1126ab
वक्ष्यमाणबुभुत्साया विषयत्वप्रसिद्धये 4.4.1004cd
वक्ष्यमाणमतस्तस्य दृष्टान्तोऽयमिहोच्यते 4.3.1156cd
वक्ष्यमाणवचो वस्तु तच्छब्देनाभिधीयते 1.4.1069ab
वक्ष्यमाणासु सर्वासु दिक्षु प्रत्येकशः क्रमात् 3.9.75cd
वक्ष्यमाणेन मन्त्रेण जायामभ्युक्षयेन्मुहुः 6.4.89cd

वक्ष्यमाणेन मन्त्रेण ह्युपासीत रविं सदा 6.3.56cd
वक्ष्यमाणेन रूपेण वेद विद्यादतस्तथा 1.2.212cd
वचनं प्रागुपन्यस्तं तदेवात्रापि हेतवे 4.3.1498cd
वचनस्याप्रमाणत्वं कारकत्वात्प्रसज्यते 4.3.1574cd
वचनात्स्यात्तदापत्तिः संपत्तेरिति चेन्मतम् 1.4.1259ab
वचनादिति चेन्नैवं तदुक्तेरर्थवादतः 1.4.1562ab
वचनानि व्रज ग्राममित्यादीनि यथा तथा SV 577cd
वचसस्त्वतिरेकेण किं मानं तद्धुरं वहेत् SV 719cd
वचसामक्रियार्थानां वाक्यभेदप्रकल्पना SV 37ab
वचसामक्रियार्थानामानर्थक्याय तद्वचः SV 272cd
वचसो बुद्धबोधित्वादप्रामाण्यं प्रसज्यते SV 546cd
वचांस्येवं सुबहुशो लक्ष्यन्ते शास्त्रभूमिषु 1.4.1489cd
वचोऽन्वाख्यायकं ग्राह्यं न ज्ञानादिविधायकम् 3.9.199cd
वचोऽर्थप्रतिबोधस्य पदार्थाज्ञानमेव तु 2.4.108ab
वचो निगमनं तत्स्याद्वाक्यस्यावयवोक्तिभाक् 4.5.4cd
वचो नैव प्रमाणं स्यात्तस्य मान्तरसंगतेः SV 674cd
वचो भेदनिषेधं चेन्न कुर्याद्भेदवाक्यवत् 1.6.70ab
वज्रादेरविभागश्चेत्तस्यासंयोगपूर्वतः 1.4.596ab
वद तस्य कुतो हेतोः कामादेः स्यात्समुत्थितिः 4.4.276cd
वदनादावभिष्वङ्ग आत्मसंभावनादभूत् 1.3.145ef
वदनादिस्वसामान्यविषयेषु तथा लयः 2.4.378ab
वदन्ति ब्राह्मणास्तेऽतस्त्यक्तसर्वैषणास्पदम् 3.8.68cd
वदन्वागित्यतः प्राह क्रमयोगानुरोधतः 1.4.679cd
वद प्रमाणैः को न्वर्थो न हि सिद्धस्य साधनम् 4.3.161cd
वनसिंहवदेवैतद्द्वयमन्योऽन्यसंश्रयम् 3.9.86cd
वनस्पतिस्तथा चन्द्रः सूर्यस्तु मधुरोऽस्तु नः 6.3.52ab
वन्दे नन्दितविश्वमव्ययमजं भक्त्या तमेकं विभुम् SV 1d
वयं चान्नमृते स्थातुं नालं क्षणमपीश्वर 1.3.249cd
वयं तु कृतकृत्यत्वादशक्ताश्च मुमूर्षवः 5.17.21cd
वयं तु वरहीनत्वाच्चर्मवद्वेष्टितुं वियत् 1.4.701ab
वरं कामं प्रयच्छामो यः कामो वाञ्छितस्त्वया 6.2.57cd
वरिष्ठब्रह्महा चेह भ्रूणहेत्यभिधीयते 4.3.1362cd

वरुणो देवता तस्य वरुणाद्धि स जायते 3.9.56cd
वर्जनीयास्ततस्ताः स्युर्नोपास्याः श्रेय ईप्सुभिः 1.3.163cd
वर्ज्यतेऽतः प्रयत्नेन तद्विद्भिरधुनातनैः 1.3.221ef
वर्णतामेति येनातः प्राण एव बृहस्पतिः 1.3.299cd
वर्णनिष्पादनं वाचा तथाद्यरसवेदनम् 2.2.29ab
वर्णस्वरादिक्रमवद्वाक्यरूपानुरञ्जितम् 4.4.747ab
वर्णाञ्जानन्त्यकारादीन्पत्रादिभ्यो विलक्षणान् 4.4.1343cd
वर्णादिग्रहणोपायो नापीहाक्षादि बाध्यते SV 915ab
वर्णान्तरगतापेक्षा नाग्निब्राह्मणयोस्तथा 1.4.1656ab
वर्णाश्रमादिसर्गोऽयं कर्मार्थो ब्रह्मणः स्मृतः 1.4.1664ab
वर्णाश्रमादिहेतूनां व्यवस्थानामसंकरः 4.4.1014ab
वर्णाश्रमादिहेतूनां सर्वेषामपि कर्मणाम् 4.3.1366ab
वर्णाश्रमाभिमानी सन्नतत्त्वज्ञः पराङ्मतिः 1.4.1781ab
वर्णोच्चारणसामर्थ्यं ममैवास्तु तदीदृशम् 1.3.141cd
वर्तते तामसे रूपे दैव्येवं द्विविधा हि वाक् 1.5.172cd
वर्तते पयसैवासावद्यापीत्यवसीयते 1.5.54ab
वर्तते यस्तमुल्लङ्घ्य सोऽतिप्रश्नोऽनुमोच्यते 3.6.23cd
वर्तते वाङ्मनःकायक्रियाकारी सुखादिमान् 4.3.287cd
वर्तमानस्य चैकत्वात्संतानो नोपपद्यते 4.3.633ab
वर्तमानात्मगं ज्ञानमतीतार्थं स्पृशेत्कथम् 1.4.459cd
वर्तमाने जगत्काल इति तावत्सुनिश्चितम् 3.8.9cd
वर्तमानोऽपि देहादौ लोकदृष्टिव्यपेक्षया 4.4.504ab
वल्मीकाश्रयणं तस्याः प्रत्यस्तेत्यभिधीयते 4.4.507cd
वव्रुर्देवा यथा वाणीं विद्वाः सर्वे तथासुरैः 1.3.154cd
वशित्वशक्तिसंबन्धान्मैवं यस्मात्पुनर्वचः 4.4.990ab
वशीकृत्येश्वरादीनि कारणानि स्वतन्त्रवत् 3.2.162ab
वषट्करिष्यंस्तां ध्यायेदिति यद्वद्विधीयते 1.4.782ab
वसत्यामन्त्रयांचक्र उष्यतामिति पार्थिवः 6.2.44cd
वसु कर्मफलं चाहुः कर्मणः साधनं वसु 3.9.13ab
वसुत्वमष्टधा भिन्ना बिभर्ति जनिमत्स्थितौ 3.9.12cd
वसुनो धनस्य लब्धा च तस्य वृष्ट्यादिहेतुनः 6.4.123cd
वसूनप्यथ संपृष्टः सोऽग्न्यादीन्प्राब्रवीद्वसून् 3.9.11cd

वसूपकरणं प्रोक्तं तद्ददातीश्वरत्वतः 4.4.1313ab
वस्तुकार्यार्थतात्पर्यभेदान्नापीह सा भवेत् SV 831cd
वस्तुग्राहितयाक्षादेरैकार्थ्येऽभिन्नमानता SV 822cd
वस्तुतः शीततामेति कर्तृतन्त्रं तथा भवेत् SV 169cd
वस्तुतत्त्वबलादेव तत्तमोऽव्यवधानतः SV 1005cd
वस्तुतत्त्वविवक्षेह मन्तव्य इतिशासनात् 2.4.215ab
वस्तुतत्त्वानपेक्षत्वात्कार्यमात्रप्रधानता SV 840ab
वस्तुतत्त्वावसायोऽतो वाक्यादेव प्रमाणतः 4.3.401cd
वस्तुतन्त्रं तु सद्यत्र विज्ञानं जायते बलात् 4.4.756ab
वस्तुतन्त्रं न हि ज्ञानं कर्तृतन्त्रं क्रिया यथा 3.9.124ab
वस्तुतन्त्रं न हि ज्ञानं नृतन्त्रं लोकवह्निवत् 1.4.1522ab
वस्तुतन्त्रं हि नो मानं कर्तृतन्त्रं विकल्पते 5.1.67cd
वस्तुतन्त्रत्वतो बुद्धेर्न चेदेवं मृषा मतिः SV 171cd
वस्तुतन्त्रा भवेद्विद्या कर्तृतन्त्रैव च क्रिया 4.4.261ab
वस्तुतन्त्रे न युक्तोऽसौ स्वयं चैव पुमर्थतः SV 229cd
वस्तुतस्त्वेक एवात्मामानित्वादिर्यथा तथा 4.4.527cd
वस्तुत्वात्सास्त्वभावस्य वस्तु नो चेत्कुतो भिदा 4.3.1708cd
वस्तुत्वान्न तमो हन्ति तथापि प्रमितिं विना 4.3.181cd
वस्तुनः प्रतिपत्तिः स्याज्जन्मादिध्वंसवर्त्मना 4.4.1340cd
वस्तुनः शक्तिकृन्नापि वचनं ज्ञापकत्वतः 1.4.1262ab
वस्तुनः सदसत्त्वाय ह्यभिव्यक्त्येकहेतुतः 1.2.87ab
वस्तुनः स्यान्मृषात्मत्वं नैवमप्युपपद्यते 1.3.49cd
वस्तुनिष्ठत्वतोऽदोषः कर्तर्यपि विवक्षिते 1.4.1136ab
वस्तुनिष्ठैव मा यस्मान्न तदज्ञानजाश्रया 1.3.59ab
वस्तुनोऽतिशयः कश्चिदभाववचसोच्यते 1.2.16ab
वस्तुनोऽन्यत्र मानानां व्यापृतिर्न हि युज्यते SV 180ab
वस्तुनोऽप्यनृतन्त्रत्वात्षोडशिग्रहणादिवत् 4.4.444ab
वस्तुनोऽवगतिर्नापि लयाद्भवति कुत्रचित् SV 386ab
वस्तुनो भेदरूपत्वे वस्त्वभावः प्रसज्यते SV 954cd
वस्तुन्यनिश्चिते वार्ता सार्थवादेऽपि दृश्यते SV 844cd
वस्तुन्युक्तेर्न चेन्मात्वं कर्मकाण्डेऽपि तद्भवेत् SV 1048cd
वस्तु बुद्धौ वद ध्यानव्यापारात्किमपेक्षते 4.4.780cd

वस्तुमात्रानुरोधित्वात्सम्यग्ज्ञानस्य दुष्करम् 1.4.891ab
वस्तुमात्रावसायित्वं संबन्धे प्राक्प्रपञ्चितम् 2.1.542ab
वस्तुमात्रावसायित्वात्तद्वचांसि न कानिचित् SV 589ab
वस्तु मान्तरयोग्यं चेद्विधौ सत्यपि तत्तथा SV 676ab
वस्तु मेयाभिसंबद्धं मानं तद्वत्तमोपनुत् 4.3.182cd
वस्तु यल्लक्ष्यते किंचिज्जगत्यस्मिंश्चराचरे 3.3.169ab
वस्तुयाथात्म्यवृत्तेन तमोऽपह्नूयते सदा 2.4.197cd
वस्तु वस्त्वन्तरं भिन्द्याद्योगाद्यद्वा विभागतः 5.1.86ab
वस्तु वस्त्वन्तरत्वेन न च विक्रियतेऽञ्जसा 2.3.146ab
वस्तुवृत्तं न पर्याप्तं तदज्ञानापनुत्तये 1.4.484ab
वस्तुवृत्तं न सामान्यं न विशेषस्तथैव च 1.6.64ab
वस्तुवृत्तं यतोऽद्वैतं नानात्वं मोहहेतुजम् 4.4.673ab
वस्तुवृत्तं समालोक्य कुतः सृष्ट्यादिसंभवः 2.1.411cd
वस्तुवृत्तमतोऽपेक्ष्य नाविद्येति निरूप्यते SV 179cd
वस्तुवृत्तमपेक्ष्यैतन्न स्वतः परतस्तमः 1.4.340ab
वस्तुवृत्तमपेक्ष्यैतन्नासीदस्ति भविष्यति 1.4.1301cd
वस्तुवृत्तमिदं तावत्प्रागपि ज्ञानसंगतेः 5.1.15cd
वस्तुवृत्तातिवर्त्यैष व्यापारः सार्वलौकिकः 3.4.145cd
वस्तुवृत्तात्मसंबोधध्वस्तसंसारकारणः 2.4.5ab
वस्तुवृत्तानभिज्ञानाद्भेदः स्वप्नेन्द्रजालवत् 3.5.24cd
वस्तुवृत्तानुरोधेन कथं तत्राप्रमा वचः SV 551cd
वस्तुवृत्तानुरोधेन नातो भेदोऽस्ति कुत्रचित् 3.5.24ab
वस्तुवृत्तानुरोध्येव यत्तु ज्ञानं भवेदिह 3.9.126ab
वस्तुवृत्तेन निःशेषान्कार्यकारणलक्षणान् 3.9.114cd
वस्तुवृत्तेन नैवालं शास्त्रानारम्भसक्तितः 3.4.129cd
वस्तुवृत्तेन प्रध्वस्तनिःशेषाज्ञानमात्मानः 4.3.339ab
वस्तुवृत्तेन संव्याप्तिर्न युक्त्येहोपपद्यते 1.4.631cd
वस्तु सिद्धं जगत्यस्मिंस्तदपह्नूयते कथम् 4.3.572cd
वस्तुस्थित्या न सत्यत्वमिति पूर्वमवादिषम् 1.2.134cd
वस्तुस्वरूपमुज्झित्वा मेयं नास्त्यपरं मितेः 4.3.1647cd
वस्तुस्वरूपमुज्झित्वा नान्यत्र व्यापृतिर्मितेः 4.3.1700ab
वस्तुस्वरूपसंस्पर्शिचक्षुरादिभ्य उत्थितम् SV 919ab

वस्तुस्वरूपान्वाख्याने न च कश्चित्प्रवर्तते 1.4.779ab
वस्तूक्तं दृष्टिशब्देन न क्रिया नापि कारकम् 4.3.1479cd
वस्तूत्पत्त्यादिमद्यस्मात्साधनानि व्यपेक्षते 4.4.1101cd
वस्तूनीह प्रमीयन्ते व्यावृत्तानि परस्परम् SV 173ab
वस्तूल्लेखी ह्यनुभवो नीलरक्तोत्पलादिवत् 4.3.677cd
वस्त्राभरणभोगाद्यैरात्मनो वशमानयेत् 6.4.31cd
वस्त्वज्ञातं समुद्दिश्य तत्प्रमित्सन्ति मानिनः 1.4.286ab
वस्त्वज्ञानैकनिष्ठत्वान्मिथ्याधीर्न हि वस्तुनि 1.4.650ab
वस्त्वधीना भवेद्विद्या कर्त्रधीना क्रिया तथा 3.3.62ab
वस्त्वधीना यतो विद्या कर्त्रधीना क्रियाखिला 3.4.136ab
वस्त्वन्तरं न च मतः क्षेत्रज्ञः परमात्मनः 2.3.147ab
वस्त्वन्तरं न संभाव्यं प्रलयेऽपि तथोच्यते 2.4.327cd
वस्त्वन्तरमभावश्चेदन्यदन्यद्भवेत्कथम् SV 947ab
वस्त्वन्तरसमायोगाद्विषादेर्दृश्यते यतः 3.3.31ab
वस्त्वन्तरस्य सद्भाव ऐकात्म्यं बाधते यतः 4.3.1106cd
वस्त्वन्तरस्य सद्भावः सिद्धे कात्स्न्र्ये विरुध्यते 1.4.1288ab
वस्त्वन्तरस्य सद्भावमभावं च प्रयत्नतः 4.4.322cd
वस्त्वन्तराच्चेद्व्यावृत्तिरिष्यते ह्यन्यवस्तुनः 4.3.1708ab
वस्त्वन्तराभ्युपगमः प्रत्यक्कात्स्न्र्यविघातकृत् 1.4.1287ab
वस्त्वन्तराभ्युपगमाज्ज्ञानतो ज्ञानवत्त्वया 4.3.538ab
वस्त्वसाधारणं रूपं मोहादेर्न प्रमीयते 1.4.430cd
वस्त्वसिद्धेस्ततः कार्यप्राधान्यादर्थवादता SV 841cd
वस्त्वात्मना न चेत्सिध्येत्कुतः सिध्येदनात्मना 1.4.732cd
वस्त्वात्मनाविरोधश्चेद्वस्त्वेव विषयस्ततः SV 956ab
वस्त्वात्मनैव चेत्तर्हि मत्पक्षः साध्यते त्वया 4.3.1699cd
वस्त्वेकं मानविषयमभावस्ते तदा कुतः SV 976cd
वस्त्वेवं चेदिहाभीष्टं किमर्थं साध्यतेऽपरम् 1.2.26cd
वस्त्वेव तत्ततोऽन्या चेदपृथग्वस्तु तर्हि ते SV 962cd
वस्त्वेव दृष्टिरत्रातो न क्रिया नापि कारकम् 4.3.1601ab
वस्त्वेव मेयं गोत्वादि शाबलेयादिवत्स्फुटम् SV 966cd
वस्त्वैकात्म्यप्रसिद्ध्यर्थं प्राधान्यातियत्नतः 1.4.1792cd
वहन्त्यम्भो यथा नद्यो नाड्यः कर्मफलं तथा 2.1.324ab

वाक्चक्षुःशब्दतो यद्वद्गृह्यते विषयस्तयोः 1.6.25ab
वाक्च जायेति विज्ञेया तदधीनत्वकारणात् 1.4.1844ab
वाक्च शब्दात्मिका तद्वच्छब्दस्यैवास्तु दीपिका 1.5.137cd
वाक्च शब्दोऽत्र विज्ञेयो ज्योतिष्कार्यसमन्वयात् 4.3.50cd
वाक्च सा सर्वभूतानां श्रोत्रं त्वग्रसनं मनः 1.5.349ab
वाक्पूर्वं चिन्तयित्वा तां तदर्थे धारयेन्मनः 4.4.740cd
वाक्प्रतिष्ठमुपासीत यदि वान्नप्रतिष्ठितम् 1.3.344cd
वाक्प्रस्रवणहेतुत्वाद्धेन्वा वत्सो मनो भवेत् 5.10.6ab
वाक्यं चातीन्द्रियार्थेषु प्रमाणमिति निश्चितम् 1.4.806ab
वाक्यद्वयं चेदथवा सिद्धसाध्यार्थभेदतः 2.1.566ab
वाक्यप्रवृत्तेस्तुल्यत्वान्न युक्तोऽत्रान्यथाग्रहः 2.3.61ab
वाक्यभेदप्रसङ्गत्वान्नैवमप्युपपद्यते 1.4.1733cd
वाक्यमानोद्भवं ज्ञानमयथावस्त्विवतीर्यते 4.4.820ab
वाक्यमाहात्म्यसंभूतं शाब्दं विज्ञानमुच्यते 4.4.834ab
वाक्यमेकीभवतीति निराशास्तस्य जीविते 4.4.66cd
वाक्ययोर्गम्यते यस्माद्विधिर्नातो विवक्षितः SV 668cd
वाक्यवाक्यार्थयोगश्चेद्वाच्यवाचकलक्षणः SV 733cd
वाक्यवाक्यार्थयोर्भेदे पदार्थानां निमित्तता SV 866cd
वाक्यश्रवणकाले तत्सर्वाज्ञानतमोपनुत् 4.4.878ab
वाक्यस्य च प्रमाणत्वं नाप्यभावैकगोचरम् SV 1031ab
वाक्यातिरेकि तन्मानं नान्यत्किंचित्त्वयेष्यते 1.4.897cd
वाक्यात्सार्वमसंसर्गमात्मानं परिपश्यति 4.4.1279cd
वाक्यादेव ततोऽसङ्गः सर्वमात्मेति वीक्षते 4.4.1202ab
वाक्याद्ब्रह्माभिसंबन्धात्तदन्यस्य तथाश्रवात् 3.4.36cd
वाक्यान्तरासंभवतस्तदा केन विरुद्धता 2.1.565cd
वाक्यार्थः कल्प्यते कस्माद्विरुद्धो यः प्रमान्तरैः 4.4.875cd
वाक्यार्थज्ञानकाले यः पदार्थो नैव विद्यते 1.4.888ab
वाक्यार्थप्रतिपत्तिस्तु वाक्यादेवाभिजायते 2.4.226cd
वाक्यार्थप्रतिपत्त्यैव प्रत्यगज्ञाननिह्नुतिः 4.3.1112cd
वाक्यार्थप्रतिबोधस्य पदार्थाज्ञानमेव तु 4.4.861ab
वाक्यार्थस्तु तदायत्तो नेत्यन्येभ्यो विशिष्टता SV 499cd
वाक्यार्थस्त्वागमादेव निरपेक्षमतो वचः 3.1.8cd

वाक्यार्थस्य च विज्ञानं पदार्थस्मृतिपूर्वकम् 2.4.111cd
वाक्यार्थस्यापि विज्ञानं पदार्थस्मृतिपूर्वकम् SV 206cd
वाक्यार्थाभाससंजातभ्रान्त्युच्छित्त्यै प्रयत्नतः 1.4.1236cd
वाक्यार्थायैव वाक्यं हि सर्वदैव प्रयुज्यते SV 865ab
वाक्यार्थोऽतीन्द्रियो वेदे वाक्यात्केन निवार्यते SV 862cd
वाक्येनावेदितं कृत्स्नं यदि साक्षात्प्रबोध्यते 4.4.780ab
वाक्येनैवाभिसंबन्धस्तत्र तस्येति वर्णितम् SV 432ab
वाक्येषु प्रतिपत्तव्या प्रत्युक्तिप्रश्नयोर्गतिः 3.6.11cd
वाक्योत्थसम्यग्विज्ञानप्रध्वस्ततमसो यतेः 1.4.1392ab
वाक्स्वान्तयोः स्वरूपोक्तिर्वृथैव स्यात्पुरोदिता 1.5.366ab
वागग्न्याद्यात्मसंपातात्संवर्गोऽसीति भण्यते 6.3.35ab
वागग्न्याद्युपसंहारं वक्ति नान्येन कारणात् 2.1.228cd
वागध्यात्मेऽधिभूते च तावत्येषाधिदैविकी 1.5.176ab
वागनुष्टुब्यतः साक्षाद्वाक्च साक्षात्सरस्वती 5.16.45ab
वागभिमानिनी चेह वाक्शब्देनाग्निरुच्यते 1.3.130cd
वागभिव्याहृतिश्चेयं लिङ्गाप्रामाण्यवादिनः 2.1.145ab
वागभिव्याहृतिश्चेयमपि ते न प्रसिध्यति 4.3.246ab
वागादयस्तावदुक्ताः संक्षेपेणाधिभौतिकाः 1.5.168ab
वागादयस्त्विह कथमनन्ता इत्युदीरणम् 1.5.196cd
वागादयोऽभिसंविष्टा जीवनार्थमनं यथा 1.3.282ab
वागादयो ग्रहा ज्ञाताश्चतुष्ट्वं चाविवक्षितम् 3.2.9ab
वागादिकरणानीति नालं पुंभोगसिद्धये 3.2.129cd
वागादिगणधारित्वाद्धर्मं वायुव्रतं विदुः 1.5.382ab
वागादिज्ञानमादाय हृत्खे शेते य उत्थितः 2.1.248cd
वागादिदेवताद्वारा भूयस्तस्यैव वित्तये 4.1.2ab
वागादिनिन्दया मुख्यप्राणोपासा न चेदिह 1.3.38cd
वागादिप्रकृतौ प्राणशब्दो घ्राणेऽवगम्यते 2.1.259ab
वागादिभ्यो विभागार्थं विशेषणमसोरिदम् 1.3.166cd
वागादिव्यापृतः कर्ता शब्दादिगुणलाञ्छितः 4.3.184ab
वागादिशब्दैरुच्यन्ते त एवात्र न पौरुषाः 3.2.125cd
वागादिसाध्यसंदृष्टेः स्वप्नो बोधसमो यदि 2.1.274ab
वागादीनां न पातोऽस्य नापि चोत्थानमीक्ष्यते 6.1.25cd

वागादीनामिव यतो नासोर्भोगो विशिष्यते 1.3.171cd
वागादीनामिह ग्राह्यं प्राणानां विषयाञ्जनम् 2.1.226cd
वागादीनि तदैवैनं स्वपितीति प्रचक्षते 2.1.257cd
वागादीन्द्रियसंघातो यजमानो यथा पुरा 1.3.179ab
वागादेरिव नासङ्गो यतः प्राणस्य विद्यते 2.2.9cd
वागाद्यग्न्यावाप्त्यैवं पाप्मनोऽपास्य सर्वतः 1.3.232ab
वागाद्यनुग्रहः सिद्धस्त्वग्न्यादेः कर्म केवलम् 1.5.373ab
वागाद्यादानमत्र स्याद्बुद्बुदानां यथाम्भसा 2.1.230cd
वागाद्यासङ्गवत्तन्मां पाप्मा मा प्रापदासुरः 1.5.388cd
वागाद्युपाधिसंबन्धे संसारित्वमिवेक्ष्यते 2.1.261ab
वागाद्यैः पञ्चभिर्युक्तं विराजं साधिभौतिकम् 1.3.234ab
वागित्यत्र त्रयी ग्राह्या न स्थानकरणादयः 5.10.2ab
वागित्यनेन शब्देन नादमात्रं विवक्ष्यते 1.6.12ab
वागीश्वरत्वादिन्द्रो वा यदि वा वर्णदेवता 1.3.324ab
वागेव प्रत्ययादौ स्यादित्येतद्गम्यते कुतः 1.5.131ab
वागेव स इति ज्ञेयः कुतो यस्मादियं सदा 1.5.130ab
वागेवायतनं तस्य वागेव करणं भवेत् 4.1.17ab
वागेवायतनमिति याज्ञवल्क्योऽप्युवाच तम् 4.1.16cd
वाग्घि संपद्यते श्रोत्रादश्रुतं न हि भाषते 6.1.12ab
वाग्जायादिप्रवृत्तीनां यजमानवदेव तत् 1.4.1843cd
वाग्देवताग्निरत्र स्यात्तथायतनमिन्द्रियम् 4.1.10ab
वाग्धेनूपाधियोगेन फलाय महतेऽधुना 5.10.1cd
वाग्वागिति हि त्रिर्ब्रूयात्त्रयी वागिति भण्यते 6.4.119cd
वाग्व्यापृततमा दृष्टा यत उद्गीथकर्मणि 1.3.298ab
वाङ्मनःकायकर्मभ्यस्तत्साध्यकटुकत्वतः 1.4.11ab
वाङ्मनःकायकर्मभ्योऽतः प्रव्रजनशीलिनः 4.4.1079ab
वाङ्मनःकायकर्माणि सर्वदैव प्रपद्यते 4.3.58cd
वाङ्मनःकायचेष्टा स्याद्यापि तत्साधनोपगा SV 1098cd
वाङ्मनःकायसाध्यं च शास्त्रतो यदि वान्यतः 4.4.115ab
वाङ्मनःकायसाध्यानामारम्भः सर्वकर्मणाम् 4.4.1165cd
वाङ्मनःकायसाध्यानामुपायानां प्रबुद्धये 4.4.105cd
वाङ्मनःकायसाध्यायाः प्रवृत्तेः काममूलता 4.4.221ab

वाङ्मनःकायसाध्याया व्यापृतेः स्यादसंभवः 4.4.761ab
वाङ्मनःप्राणकोशांस्त्रीन्विराडन्नमयः स्वयम् 1.4.34ab
वाङ्मनःप्राणरूपाणां त्र्यन्नात्मन्यपि संभवात् 3.2.8ab
वाङ्मनःप्राणरूपाणि तानि हीति श्रुतिर्जगौ 4.4.423cd
वाङ्मयोऽथ प्राणमयस्तथैव च मनोमयः 1.5.153cd
वाङ्मात्रेण प्रतिज्ञातं कर्मणा नोपपादितम् 6.4.61ab
वाङ्मात्रेणापि सक्रोधो हिनस्तीह प्रमादतः 1.4.1611cd
वाचं ते ग्लापयन्त्येतां येयमेकत्ववाचिनी 4.4.738cd
वाचं संश्रुत्य वाक्यस्थां चिनुते भावनामयीम् 1.5.329ab
वाचं संभावयामासुरियं ह्युद्गीथकर्मणि 1.3.128ab
वाचः प्राणस्य च यत उद्गीथे व्यापृतिः स्फुटा 1.3.331ab
वाचकत्वेऽपि वाक्यस्य संसृष्टार्थाभिधानतः SV 868cd
वाचक्नव्यक्षरान्तेन ग्रन्थेन प्रत्यगात्मनः 1.4.1041cd
वाचा प्रकाश्यमाने ते प्रयुज्येते यतः सदा 1.6.32cd
वाचारम्भणशास्त्राच्च विकारानृततोच्यते 1.6.21cd
वाचा सर्वाधिदैविक्या लोकादेरप्यनन्तता 1.5.197cd
वाचा सर्वाधिदैविक्या संव्याप्ता साविभागतः 1.5.170cd
वाचैव ह्यवरान्पूर्व उपयन्ति यतस्ततः 6.2.67cd
वाचो विग्लापनमिति श्रुत्या निन्दाभिधीयते 4.4.963ab
वाच्यं वा यदि वावाच्यं कस्मादित्यभिधीयताम् 4.3.640ab
वाच्यवाचकसंबन्धनियमे तस्य हेतुता 2.4.216cd
वाच्या दोषा यथायोगं संतानार्थानुरोधतः 4.3.636cd
वाजपेयाभिसंपत्स्यान्मैथुनाख्यक्रतोरतः 6.4.14cd
वाजपेये क्रतावन्नकामस्य स विधीयते 6.4.13cd
वाजिशाखासु सर्वासु ह्यासुरायणपूर्वकाः 6.5.15ab
वादन्यायेन तद्भूयः षष्ठे सम्यक्प्रपञ्चितम् 4.5.2cd
वादन्यायेन तस्यैव प्रतिपत्त्यर्थमञ्जसा 4.3.4ab
वादिनामविसंवादस्तथाज्ञानेऽप्यसंशयः 1.4.1365cd
वादिभिर्युक्तिभिः शक्यं क्वचित्साधयितुं सदा 1.4.1325cd
वादिविप्रतिपत्तेश्च केचिदिच्छन्ति वादिनः 3.9.176ab
वानप्रस्थाश्रमादूर्ध्वं प्रव्रजेदविचारयन् 3.5.151ab
वानस्पत्यमतो ग्राह्यं कर्मण्यौदुम्बरं श्रुतौ 6.3.13cd

वामदेवस्य मैत्रेय्या गार्ग्याश्चैव समज्जसम् SV 91ab
वायवः पञ्च बुद्धिश्च मनः सप्तदशं विदुः 1.3.258cd
वायुं मुक्त्वा बहिर्यस्मान्नान्यस्या विद्यतेऽबहिः 3.3.166ab
वायुः पुष्करिणीं यद्वत्समिङ्गयति चालयेत् 6.4.108cd
वायुकर्माभिमानी सन्पुमान्वायुः स उच्यते 3.7.12cd
वायुदेशं तथा तेजो वियद्देशोऽनिलोऽखिलः 4.2.24cd
वायुना विधृतं तस्य रूपं यद्वार्तमानिकम् 3.8.11cd
वायुनैव धृतं यस्माल्लिङ्गदेहादिकं ततः 3.7.20ab
वायुनैव धृताङ्गानीत्यत्र लोकेऽपि विद्यते 3.7.19ab
वायुनैव यथाङ्गानि संदृब्धानि यदा तदा 3.7.22ab
वायुनैवोपसंहारः प्राणोद्गात्रोरयं कृतः 3.1.36cd
वायुमेव स गन्धर्वः प्रशशंसातिविस्मितः 3.3.165cd
वायुरं खमिति प्राह तदालम्बनसिद्धये 5.1.119cd
वायुरित्यादिकं ग्राह्यमुपलक्षणमेव तु 5.17.14ab
वायुरेव ततोऽपूर्वमभिव्यक्ततनुर्मतः 3.3.160ab
वायुर्दिशां यथा गर्भो दृष्टः श्लथनकर्मकृत् 6.4.106cd
वायुर्वा देवता कृत्स्ना तदन्यस्य तदात्मनः 3.9.25ab
वायुवेष्टनमेतच्च यदपूर्वमिहोदितम् 3.3.159cd
वायोरपि समुत्क्रान्तिः प्रत्यक्षान्नावसीयते 4.3.218ab
वायोरिव प्रवृत्तिः स्यात्तथा चैवोपसंहृतिः 1.4.369ab
वायोर्वृष्टिमवाप्याथ वृष्टेश्च पृथिवीं ततः 6.2.154cd
वाय्वग्निर्वद्विकारो न प्रागभावाद्यसंभवात् SV 144ab
वाय्वन्तरिक्षयोर्यस्माद्रसस्तेन पुमांस्तयोः 2.3.56cd
वाय्वाकाशप्रनाड्यैवं तेजसः संभवस्ततः 2.3.55ab
वाय्वाकाशरसत्वेन तत्रामूर्तान्वयो यतः 2.3.46cd
वाय्वाकाशरसो ह्येष इति हेतुः प्रदर्श्यते 2.3.48ab
वाय्वाकाशौ समाश्रित्य पूर्वेषां साधनात्मता 1.4.366ab
वाय्वात्मना परिच्छिन्नं तदास्ते कारणात्मनि 3.7.9cd
वाय्वात्मनि समाप्तत्वात्करणानामशेषतः 1.3.307ab
वाय्वात्मा गमयामास समष्टिव्यष्टितात्पये 3.3.162cd
वाय्वाश्रितमतः कर्म स्वरूपं प्रतिपद्यते 3.7.10cd
वारिणो मत्स्यसंचारे छिद्रसंग्रथने यथा 2.1.488ab

वारितत्वादुपरतश्रुत्यान्यत्किं विधीयते 4.4.1221cd
वारिपथ्यदनोपेतं सर्वानर्थविवर्जितम् SV 132ab
वावशब्दं चशब्देन प्रत्याहृत्याभिधीयते 2.3.17ab
वासनाकामकर्माणि लिङ्गस्थान्येव नात्मनि 2.3.118ab
वासनाकामकर्मादेः कुतोऽस्यान्तररूपता 4.4.490cd
वासनाकारतां गच्छेच्चैतन्यं चेत्कपालवत् 2.3.107ab
वासनाद्यभिसंबन्ध इतीयं गीरनर्थिका 2.3.144cd
वासनानां च सर्वामाश्रयो यस्तु कथ्यते 3.7.16cd
वासनानामपि यतो न विशेषो मनागपि 2.3.145ab
वासनानामपि युतौ सैव यस्मादपेक्ष्यते SV 464cd
वासनानामभावेऽपि सुषुप्त्यादौ न मुक्तता SV 463ab
वासनानिष्फलत्वं स्याच्चैतन्यादपृथक्स्थितेः 2.3.107cd
वासनानुगतं लिङ्गं मृद्वन्मृद्विक्रियात्मसु 2.3.152ab
वासनाबलतः स्पष्टं बहिर्वद्यन्मतौ स्थितम् 3.4.147ab
वासना भूरिरूपास्ता लिङ्गस्था लिङ्गसाक्षिणः 2.3.159ab
वासनामय एवातो भुङ्क्ते स्वप्ने क्रियाफलम् 4.3.1376ab
वासनामात्रया त्वत्र सापि प्राज्ञे निवर्तते 4.3.1374cd
वासनामात्रहेतुत्वादात्मनोऽनर्थसंगतेः SV 446ab
वासनामात्रहेतुश्च स्वप्ने कर्मेन्द्रियाश्रयः 2.1.260ab
वासनारूपकान्पश्यन्प्राणान्प्राणिति वायुना 3.4.69cd
वासनालक्षणः कामः स्वप्नसर्गाय जायते 4.3.1191cd
वासनालक्षणे साक्षात्स्वयंज्योतिःस्वभावकः 4.3.899cd
वासनाविष्टविज्ञानो हननाद्यभिमन्यते 4.3.1249cd
वासनैकाधिकरणश्चिदाभासोऽभिधीयते 4.3.1266ab
वासनैवात्मनः प्रोक्ता प्रद्योतवचसा स्फुटम् 4.4.78cd
वासनोपाधिरात्मैकः स्वयंज्योतिरितीर्यते 4.3.883cd
वासुदेवः सर्वमिति प्रत्यक्षश्रुतिपूर्वकम् 1.4.236ab
वास्तवं वृत्तमापेक्ष्य न त्वियं सृष्टिरात्मनः 2.1.383cd
वास्तवं वृत्तमापेक्ष्य पश्यन्वै तदितीर्यते 4.3.1417cd
वास्तवं वृत्तमाश्रित्य प्रतीचः प्राक्प्रबोधतः 2.4.412ab
वास्तवं वृत्तमीदृङ्नः सिद्धं ह्यनुभवाश्रयम् 4.3.1288cd
वास्तवं स्यात्तदा रूपमज्ञातं च सदा भवेत् SV 687cd

वास्तवस्त्वभिसंबन्धो नोपपत्त्यात्मनो यतः 4.3.95cd
वास्तवेनैव वृत्तेन ज्ञेयकार्यसमाप्तितः 4.3.1302ab
वास्तवोऽवास्तवो वा न व्यतिरेको न चान्वयः 2.3.21cd
वास्तव्या अपि संसिद्धेः स्वमहिम्नैव नेष्यते 1.4.1290ab
वास्तव्या अपि संसिद्धेर्न सिद्धिः स्यात्प्रमां विना 1.4.1293cd
वास्तव्येव तु संसिद्धिरनुभूतेर्यतस्ततः 4.4.907ab
वास्यदेशातिरेकेण वासनाया न चेष्यते 2.3.132ab
वास्येऽर्थे वासनाः सर्वाः सजातीये च ता यतः 4.4.487ab
विकर्तृ कर्म वोढ्री च पूर्वप्रज्ञेह पर्वयोः 4.4.125cd
विकर्तृत्वेन कर्मात्र नामरूपात्मनोर्भवेत् 1.6.29ab
विकल्प एष भतानामविद्यारात्रिशायिनाम् 2.1.265cd
विकल्पकं तथैव स्याद्विभागस्तेन दुष्करः 4.3.488cd
विकल्पतो वा तत्सिद्धिर्ब्रह्मसंसारिणोर्भवेत् 1.4.1275cd
विकल्पश्चेन्न मिथ्यात्वान्न चान्या गतिरस्ति वः 4.3.489cd
विकल्पश्रवणान्मैवं कर्मणा विद्ययाथवा SV 1119cd
विकल्पहेत्वविद्यायाः प्रत्यग्याथात्म्यनिष्ठितः 2.1.279cd
विकल्पानुपपत्तेश्च षोडशिग्रहणादिवत् 5.1.67ab
विकल्पासंश्रवाद्विद्वानश्नुतेऽतः फलद्वयम् 1.3.310ab
विकल्पासंभवश्चात्र वस्तुवृत्तत्वकारणात् 3.9.175ab
विकल्पेनैव व्याख्यात एकद्वित्रिसमुच्चयः 3.5.155ab
विकल्पोऽत्र न युक्तः स्यादेवमुक्तेन वर्त्मना 4.4.452ab
विकल्पोऽप्यत्र नैवास्ति न हि वस्तु विकल्पते 4,4.444cd
विकल्पो दृश्यते लोके तथेहापीति निश्चितिः 1.4.84cd
विकारकल्पनैतेन न्यायेनात्मन्यपाकृता 4.3.1780cd
विकाररूपापन्नः सन्विज्ञानात्मत्वलक्षणः 2.1.469ab
विकारिणः प्रकाशस्य नीलरक्तादिसंगतेः 4.3.393ab
विकारेऽवयवे चैव तदा पूर्वोक्त एव तु SV 266ab
विकारे सांख्यसिद्धान्त आरम्भेऽत्यन्तभिन्नता 4.3.656cd
विकारोऽत्यन्तनिर्भिन्नो यदा तु स्याद्विकारिणः SV 262ab
विकीर्णं बोधदेशीयं समन्तात्प्रथते दृशेः 4.3.1188cd
विकृत्य परमात्मांशं विज्ञानात्मनि तिष्ठति 2.3.122cd
विक्रियामाप्नुवन्नापि नित्यं ध्वंसिगुणाश्रयम् 1.4.589cd

विक्रियावदपि द्रव्यं तत्प्रत्ययसमन्वयात् 1.4.591ab
विक्षिप्तत्वैकसामान्यात्स्फुलिङ्गाः स्तनयित्नवः 6.2.99cd
विक्षेपलयहीनस्तु स्वतः कुम्भखवत्परः 2.1.338cd
विगीता च विरुद्धा च दृष्टार्था दृष्टकारणा 3.5.159ab
विघ्नं कुर्वन्ति नो देवा विद्योत्थफलसंगतौ 1.4.1492ab
विघ्नकार्येऽपि चाप्येते नानपेक्ष्य प्रकुर्वते 1.4.1483ab
विघ्नन्ति स्वार्थमित्युक्तं यच्च तच्चापि पेलवम् 2.1.549ab
विचक्षुः प्रागपि घटं स एवैक्षिष्ट चक्षुषा 4.3.266cd
विचार्यमाणं तन्नास्ति व्योम्नि कार्ष्ण्यमिवात्मनि 2.3.193cd
विचार्यमाणे यत्नेन त्वधिकारे यथाश्रुति SV 311ab
विचार्यमाणोऽनुभवो रूप्यशुक्त्यनुभूतिवत् 2.4.132ab
विजातीयसजातीयवस्त्वन्तरनिषेधतः 3.8.176cd
विजातीयैरतो ज्योतिर्भूतजातीयमिष्यताम् 4.3.138cd
विजातीयोपकारश्चेद्भवता नाभ्युपेयते 4.3.232ab
विजानाति तदा सर्वमात्मैवेति प्रपश्यति 4.4.865cd
विजानाति मयट्तस्मात्प्रायार्थोऽत्रावसीयते 4.3.314cd
विजानातीति कर्तृस्थे परस्मिन्भावसाधनः 2.1.251cd
विजिगीतो जगत्यस्मिन्नत्यर्थं यो विशब्दितः 6.4.75ab
विजिज्ञापयिषुर्गार्ग्यमिममर्थमतो नृपः 2.1.280ab
विजिज्ञासस्व तद्ब्रह्म तपसैवेति च श्रुतिः 4.4.1055ab
विजिहीतेरिदं रूपं ण्यन्तस्य गतिकर्मणः 6.4.98ab
विज्ञातपूर्वकुम्भस्य पुनः कुम्भान्तरेक्षणे 4.3.673ab
विज्ञातयोरिदं वाक्यमहमेवेदमित्यतः 4.3.1281cd
विज्ञातस्य सतत्त्वस्य तादात्म्यप्रतिपादनम् 4.4.707cd
विज्ञातादन्यदेवैतदविज्ञातात्तथा पृथक् 1.5.166ab
विज्ञातादिविदं भोगैर्वागाद्या देवता नरम् 1.5.167ab
विज्ञातादिस्वरूपेण तमवन्ति पृथक्पृथक् 1.5.167cd
विज्ञातारमरे केन न दृष्टेरिति च स्फुटम् 1.4.565ab
विज्ञातारमरे केन विजानीयादिति श्रुतेः 1.4.1393ab
विज्ञाताशेषतत्त्वो वा ब्राह्मणः कृतकृत्यतः 2.1.347ab
विज्ञाताशेषवेदान्तसर्वस्वं ब्रह्मणि स्थितम् 1.4.1070ab
विज्ञानं केवलं शुद्धं स्वात्मन्येवावतिष्ठते 4.4.723cd

विज्ञानं जायते यस्मादात्मोपास्तिः सदा ततः 1.4.928cd
विज्ञानं तेन तत्पूर्वं सर्वमन्यत्प्रतीयते 1.4.1396cd
विज्ञानं तेनावाक्यार्थरूपं नैव च गम्यते 1.4.804cd
विज्ञानं न तथापीदमविद्यापक्षभागिति 4.3.1391cd
विज्ञानं निखिलं यस्मान्नित्यप्राप्तिरतो भवेत् 1.4.929cd
विज्ञानं निश्चितं धीः स्याद्भयं भीरभिधीयते 1.5.114ab
विज्ञानं पौरुषं शुद्धं तेनासङ्गेन दूषितम् 4.3.1097ab
विज्ञानं प्रस्तुतं तस्मिन्संदेहो नः प्रजायते 4.3.1117ab
विज्ञानं भौतिकं तावद्भूतसंसर्गजन्मनः 4.3.1118ab
विज्ञानं यल्ल्यबन्तोक्तं तदेवात्र तु साधनम् 4.4.806cd
विज्ञानं विपरीतार्थदर्शनं चेह भण्यते 4.3.1193cd
विज्ञानं संशयज्ञानं मिथ्याज्ञानमथापि वा 4.4.112ab
विज्ञानकर्मणोस्त्रेधा यद्युच्येत समुच्चयः SV 357ab
विज्ञानकर्माभिव्यङ्ग्या द्वैतत्वात्सा क्षयात्मिका 1.4.1702cd
विज्ञानकारणत्वेऽपि ह्यभ्युपेतेऽन्तरात्मनः 1.4.919ab
विज्ञानघन इत्युक्तेर्विषयोऽयमथोच्यते 2.4.469ab
विज्ञानघन एवायं विज्ञानात्मा तथैव च 4.5.11cd
विज्ञानघनमानन्दमैकात्म्यं व्यवतिष्ठते 2.4.473cd
विज्ञानजन्म युगपत्तदा प्राप्नोति ते ध्रुवम् 4.3.1122cd
विज्ञानपुरुषः सोऽयमधिदैवादिवासनः 4.3.1227ab
विज्ञानपुरुषस्यास्य या यथोक्ता पुरोक्तिभिः 4.3.1828ab
विज्ञानपुरुषस्येदं स्वभावादेव सर्वदा 5.16.48ab
विज्ञानपुरुषाणां हि सर्वेषामेकरूपता 4.3.1222ab
विज्ञानपुरुषान्तस्य ब्रह्मणः परमात्मनः 2.3.20ab
विज्ञानमपि तद्भिन्नजातिचिद्ग्राह्यमिष्यताम् 4.3.514ab
विज्ञानमय इत्यत्र वाक्ये प्रायार्थतेष्यते 4.3.322ab
विज्ञानमय इत्यस्माद्व्यपदेशान्निवर्तते 4.3.309ab
विज्ञानमय इत्युक्तिस्तदवच्छित्तये यतः 4.3.308cd
विज्ञानमय इत्युक्त्वा पृथिव्यादिमयोक्तितः 2.1.191ab
विज्ञानमय इत्येवं तस्मादात्माभिधीयते 4.3.316ab
विज्ञानमयता तस्मात्प्रतीचोऽबोधकारणात् 2.1.189cd
विज्ञानमयतामेति स्रक्सर्पमयतामिव 4.4.173cd

विज्ञानमात्रं यस्यापि जगदेतच्चराचरम् 1.2.22ab
विज्ञानमात्रमथवा वस्तु स्यात्पारमार्थिकम् 4.3.473ab
विज्ञानमानन्दमितिशब्दप्रामाण्यकारणात् 3.9.181cd
विज्ञानमानन्दमिति ह्यात्मैवेति श्रुतेस्तथा SV 231ab
विज्ञानमिति चैतन्यं कूटस्थमभिधीयते 3.9.151ab
विज्ञानमित्यनेनात्र बुद्धिरेवाभिधीयते 4.3.310ab
विज्ञानलक्षणं तेजोऽतैजसकमिति वार्यते 3.8.99ab
विज्ञानवादिनो बौद्धास्तथा नैयायिकादयः 2.3.87cd
विज्ञानव्यतिरेकेण घटो नास्तीति जल्पतः 4.3.573ab
विज्ञानव्यतिरेकेण तस्य मानासमीक्षणात् 4.3.532cd
विज्ञानव्यतिरेकेण नातो विज्ञानवादिना 4.3.562ab
विज्ञानव्यतिरेकेण नीलादिविषयो यदि 4.3.566ab
विज्ञानव्यतिरेकेण प्रतिवाद्यादिवस्तुनः 4.3.557ab
विज्ञानस्य क्रियात्वाच्च न सिद्धिः कारकैर्विना 3.9.180ab
विज्ञानातिशयं सिध्येन्मानं निश्चयवत्तथा 3.4.140cd
विज्ञानात्मन एताः स्युर्गतयो विक्रियां प्रति 2.1.474ab
विज्ञानात्मनि चोक्तापि परमात्मानमेष्यति 3.5.12cd
विज्ञानात्मन्युपक्रान्ते ब्रह्मेति यदिहोच्यते 4.3.1967ab
विज्ञानात्मभिरारब्धं बंभ्रमीत्यखिलं जगत् 3.2.71cd
विज्ञानात्ममुखेनाथ यदि वा परमात्मनः 2.3.141ab
विज्ञानात्मविकारस्य कारणैक्यं विमुक्तता SV 259ab
विज्ञानात्मा तु कर्तात्र स्वातन्त्र्यात्सर्वकर्मसु 3.4.172ab
विज्ञानात्मादिसंभेद इति केचित्प्रचक्षते 2.1.531cd
विज्ञानात्मादिसंभेदस्तद्विरुद्धः किमुच्यते 2.1.530cd
विज्ञानात्मान इत्येष भेदहेतुनिवर्तनात् 2.3.98ab
विज्ञानात्मा न तु तथा सर्वेशत्वात्परो भवेत् 4.4.1007cd
विज्ञानात्मा परिष्वक्तः प्राज्ञेनैव परात्मना 4.3.1322ab
विज्ञानात्मा पिता तावन्न मनो न प्रजापतिः 1.5.15ab
विज्ञानात्मापि महतः परमात्मस्वभावकात् 2.1.470ab
विज्ञानात्मा हि यः कश्चित्कर्मणा येन केनचित् 3.2.72ab
विज्ञानात्मेति कणभुक्चित्तमेवं समाश्रिताः 2.3.120cd
विज्ञानात्मेति यं प्राहुः परिणामः स आत्मनः 2.1.475cd

विज्ञानात्मैकनीडाया भावनायाः प्रधानता 4.4.91cd
विज्ञानादिमयत्वं स्यान्न स्वतः प्रत्यगात्मनः 4.4.763cd
विज्ञानाद्यभिसंबन्धो यथा तदधुनोच्यते 4.4.167cd
विज्ञानानन्दयोश्चैक्यादसंयोगविभागतः 3.9.196ab
विज्ञानानुविधायी हि विकारः कर्मणो यतः 4.3.1193ab
विज्ञानालम्बनत्वं नो न कदाचित्प्रपद्यते 1.2.75cd
विज्ञानालम्बनप्राप्तिः किं सतो वाथवासतः 4.4.326ab
विज्ञानालोकसंपृक्तं मेयं वस्त्वखिलं यतः 4.3.314ab
विज्ञानाव्यतिरेकित्वादसिद्धादेस्तथैव च 1.2.25ab
विज्ञानाव्यतिरेकी चेदभावः स्यात्सहेतुकः 1.2.19ab
विज्ञानेन तथा प्रत्यङ्ङात्माकारेण गृह्यते 4.3.302cd
विज्ञानेन परिच्छेत्तुं शक्यते कर्मवत्क्वचित् 1.4.803cd
विज्ञानेन विदित्वेति श्रूयतेऽस्यैककर्तृता 4.4.1137ab
विज्ञानेन विशिष्टं वा यस्मान्मेयं प्रपद्यते 2.1.190ab
विज्ञानेनाथ विज्ञानमादायेत्यपि चावदत् 4.4.32cd
विज्ञानेनेत्यथ कथं निदिध्यासनमुच्यते 2.4.232cd
विज्ञानेनैव हत्वान्यत्पूर्णत्वेनैति चित्स्वतः 2.3.190cd
विज्ञानैकघनोक्त्या च निःसंज्ञवचसा तथा 2.4.446ab
विज्ञानैकघनोक्त्याहं कृत्स्नैकात्म्यं तवाब्रुवम् 2.4.448ab
विज्ञानोत्पत्तिहेतुत्वं ध्यानादेः प्रागवादिषम् 2.4.234ab
विज्ञायते मयैवासौ भवतापि प्रमान्तरात् 6.2.62cd
विज्ञाय प्रज्ञामित्यस्य न चार्थोऽयं विवक्षितः 1.4.903ab
विज्ञाय वस्त्वसंसर्गि प्रज्ञां कुर्वीत यत्नतः 4.4.797cd
विज्ञायापि परं तत्त्वं कुर्यात्प्रज्ञां पुनः पुनः 4.4.884cd
विज्ञायेति ल्यबन्तेन प्रमाणव्याप्तिरुच्यते 4.4.836ab
विज्ञायेति वचः श्रौतमिदं व्याचक्षतेऽन्यथा 4.4.796cd
विज्ञायेत्युच्यते श्रुत्या पुंसस्तत्र स्वतन्त्रतः 4.4.856cd
विज्ञायेह तमात्मानं प्रज्ञां कुर्वीत सद्द्विजः 4.4.873cd
विज्ञायेह तमेवातः प्रज्ञां कुर्वीत सद्द्विजः 4.4.871ab
विट्क्षत्रयोर्व्यवहितं प्राधान्यं तेन पूर्वयोः 1.4.1658cd
विड्वराहादिदेहेन न ह्यैन्द्रं भुज्यते फलम् SV 1130cd
वितमस्कं स आत्मज्ञस्ततोऽन्ये मूढचेतसः 4.4.305cd

वितमस्कात्मना योगे स्वप्नजाग्रत्क्रियाक्षये 4.3.1318cd
वितर्कयन्तस्ते प्राणा उक्त्वैवं प्रत्यगात्मसु 1.3.200ab
वितृषोऽशेषतद्दोषध्वस्तश्रेयः परीप्सवः 1.4.1073cd
वित्तं चेन्नामृतत्वाय कस्माद्दित्सति तद्भवान् 2.4.52ab
वित्तं द्विविधमप्यत्र वित्तशब्देन गृह्यते 1.4.1032ab
वित्तं विना न सिद्धिः स्याद्दृष्टादृष्टार्थकर्मणः 6.3.1ab
वित्तद्वयेन संपन्नो यतोऽधिक्रियते नरः 2.1.39ab
वित्तमेव कला मे स्युः कल्पयित्वा ध्रुवां स्वयम् 1.5.218ab
वित्तमेव कलास्तस्य तद्वान्युपचयौ क्रिया 1.5.220ab
वित्तश्रुत्या न तद्ग्राह्यं तस्य कर्मविरोधतः 4.4.1122cd
वित्ताच्चेदमृतत्वं स्यात्तत्तित्यक्षा न युज्यते 2.4.59ab
वित्ताच्चेन्नामृतत्वं स्याद्वद तेन ममापि किम् 2.4.59cd
वित्तात्पुत्रः प्रियः पुत्रात्पिण्डः पिण्डात्तथेन्द्रियम् 1.4.1031ab
वित्तैषणेति तां ब्रूमो जामित्वविनिवृत्सया 4.4.1129cd
वित्तैषणेयं कर्मार्थी न लोकार्थेति निश्चितिः 3.5.115cd
वित्तो बुद्ध्यादिसाक्षीशः प्रतिबुद्धस्तथैकलः 4.4.616cd
विदधन्नानृतत्वादि कामानां वक्ति कुत्रचित् 2.1.576cd
विदधन्मानतां जह्यात्परस्परविरोधतः 5.1.47cd
विदधाति ह्यपां पानमपूर्वं शास्त्रलक्षणम् 6.1.36cd
विदितादन्यदेवैतत्तथैवाविदितादधि 4.3.1624ab
विदिताविदिताभ्यां तदन्यदेवेति च श्रुतिः 3.9.173cd
विदिताविदिताभ्यां नो व्युत्थाप्य ब्रह्म चाब्रवीत् 4.3.1729ab
विदित्वा कथमित्यस्य प्रत्युक्त्यर्था परा श्रुतिः 3.5.107ab
विदित्वा निर्वृतिं याति कार्यकारणयोः पराम् 6.5.13cd
विदुरर्चिः समायान्ति बहूक्तेश्च द्विजातयः 6.2.119cd
विदुषां श्रेयसेऽतोऽध्वा न क्वचित्प्रतिहन्यते 3.1.50cd
विदुषैव तु कर्तव्या संप्रत्तिर्नाविपश्चिता 1.5.284ab
विदुषोऽप्यासुरत्वे स्यान्निष्फलं ब्रह्मदर्शनम् 5.1.108cd
विदुषोऽस्तीत्यतः प्राह स य इत्यादिना श्रुतिः 5.16.57cd
विदेहदेवतः क्वायं भवत्येष पुमानिति 3.2.130ab
विदेहादि तदा विश्वं त्वत्तः कस्येति कथ्यताम् 4.2.111cd
विदेहो वीतसंदेहो नेति नेत्येव बोधितः 3.3.64ab

विद्धि सर्वान्तरं ब्रह्म साक्षादित्यादिलक्षणम् 3.8.87cd
विद्यमानां विनष्टां तु कर्तुं ते शक्नुतः कथम् 3.2.94cd
विद्यमानापि विध्वस्तती्व्रानर्थपरंपरा 1.4.1746cd
विद्यमाना पुनः कामं कर्म चापि प्रवर्तयेत् 1.4.1748ab
विद्यमानाप्यविद्येयं विद्यां चेन्नावधीत्पुरा 4.4.917ab
विद्यमानार्थसंबन्धात्प्रत्यक्षस्येह सर्वतः 4.3.249cd
विद्यया देवलोकाप्तिः श्रुतत्वादेव कारणात् 1.5.256ab
विद्ययापि न चेत्कार्यं कर्मभिः स्यात्कथं नु तत् 4.4.1160cd
विद्यया वीक्षते चार्थानविद्योत्थापितानिह 4.3.1197cd
विद्ययैव तमोहानादकार्ये कर्म किंफलम् 3.3.72cd
विद्ययैवाप्नुमः कात्स्न्र्यमित्यादि यदुदीरितम् 1.4.1122cd
विद्यां चेत्यादिमन्त्रोऽपि न समुच्चयबोधकः 1.4.1764ab
विद्या कर्म च संस्काराः प्रत्यगज्ञानतत्त्वकाः 3.8.30ab
विद्याकर्मसमूहेन येनायं परमात्मनः 4.4.404ab
विद्याकालैव कृत्स्नाप्तिरिति तन्मोहहानतः 1.4.1448cd
विद्यागुप्तिश्च बहुशः श्रुतावपि समीक्ष्यते 3.2.134cd
विद्याजन्मैकहेतुत्वाल्लोकवत्स्यात्समञ्जसम् 1.4.83cd
विद्याजन्मैकहेतूनां वैफल्यं चेन्न तद्यतः 1.4.82cd
विद्यात्ममोहतत्कार्यविरोधाच्च परस्परम् SV 139ab
विद्यादेतद्समासेन लक्षणं रूपसंज्ञयोः 1.5.141cd
विद्याधिकार उक्तत्वादर्थवन्तीति निश्चितिः 3.5.82cd
विद्याधिकारजीवित्वान्न स्वतन्त्रफलं भवेत् 2.1.422cd
विद्या न तु निरस्तान्यप्रत्यङ्मात्रैकगोचरा 1.5.253cd
विद्यापि विपरीतस्य प्रविभक्तस्य वस्तुनः 4.3.1200ab
विद्याप्रकरणत्वाच्च नेहोद्गीथो विधीयते 1.3.36ab
विद्याप्रकरणे चोर्ध्वमात्मनैव विशेषणात् 1.4.1773ab
विद्याप्रकरणे तस्य त्वाम्नायः किमितीर्यताम् SV 1123cd
विद्याफलं न तन्न्याय्यमिवशब्देन संगतेः 4.3.1276cd
विद्याफलस्य प्रात्यक्ष्यादितिहेतुसमाश्रयात् SV 199cd
विद्याफलस्य संप्राप्तेः प्रागपि ब्रह्मबोधतः 1.4.1743cd
विद्याभिव्यञ्जिकैवेयं स्वतः सिद्धस्य वस्तुनः 3.3.20ab
विद्यामृतेऽपि तच्चेत्स्याद्ध्रुवं विद्या निरर्थिका 1.4.1744cd

विद्यामेव प्रशंसन्ति न तथा पुत्रकर्मणी 1.5.257cd
विद्यायां चेन्न मोक्षोऽभूत्कस्याशा नो वृथा भवेत् 1.4.90ab
विद्यायाः पृच्छ्यते कर्ता कर्म वेह विवक्षितम् 1.4.1133cd
विद्यायाः संप्रदानादिविध्यर्थाख्यायिकात्र च 4.3.8cd
विद्यार्थोऽयं समारम्भो युज्यते नान्यथा सति 4.4.171cd
विद्या लोके तथेहापि तद्ध्वंसिन्येव गृह्यताम् 1.4.1212cd
विद्यावत्सह कार्येण ह्यविद्यापीह सूत्रिता 1.4.1592ab
विद्याविद्ये इहोच्येते तमोवस्त्ववसानतः 3.2.117cd
विद्याविधानं विज्ञाते पिष्टपेषणवद्यतः 1.4.1216cd
विद्याविधानाच्चाविद्या ब्रह्मण्यस्तीति गम्यताम् 1.4.1216ab
विद्याविनयसंपन्न इति च स्मृतिशासनम् 1.4.1661cd
विद्युत्तत्राप्यतितरां तेजस्वी तेन विद्युति 2.1.61cd
विद्युद्देहस्य तस्यैव ब्रह्मणोऽन्यदुपासनम् 5.9.1ab
विद्युद्ब्रह्मेति युक्तं तद्विद्युद्धि स्याद्विदानतः 5.9.2ab
विद्युद्यथा तथास्मत्तः पाप्मानं तदुपासितुः 5.9.3cd
विद्युद्वत्प्रथते रूपं किल तस्य महात्मनः 2.3.167cd
विद्येतस्य तु तस्यैव फलं ध्रौव्यं भवेदिति 3.3.29cd
विद्येति सेह विज्ञेया नैकात्म्यप्रसमीक्षणम् 4.4.603cd
विद्येयं यत्नतो वत्स द्रढिम्ने मच्छ्रुतस्य च 6.2.21cd
विद्योत्पत्तिप्रधानत्वात्सृष्टिर्वा न विवक्ष्यते 1.2.146ab
विद्वत्सभा च समितिस्तद्योग्यः समितिंगमः 6.4.75cd
विद्वद्भिस्त उपेक्ष्याः स्युर्बालोन्मत्तसमा जनाः 4.4.371cd
विद्वांसं प्रति नेशाना यदि देवादयो मताः 1.4.1563ab
विद्वान्परिहरेत्तत्र मृतिहेतुं प्रयत्नतः 4.4.1062cd
विद्वान्य एवमित्युक्त्या साध्यसाधनसंगतिः 4.1.23cd
विद्वान्नूपान्तरं पश्येद्यत्र हीति तथा श्रुतिः 4.4.955cd
विद्वान्संप्रतिगृह्णीयात्कथंचित्कामसंप्लुतेः 5.16.58cd
विधयस्तत्क्रियाणां स्युस्तद्विपर्ययहेतवः SV 349cd
विधयस्तु कथं रागं निरुन्धन्तीति भण्यताम् SV 412ab
विधायकपदाभावादसंगानं परस्परम् 1.2.211ab
विधावसति वाक्यस्य यच्चावोचोऽप्रमाणताम् SV 195ab
विधिं त्वयानिच्छतापि ह्यभ्युपेयार्थवादता SV 45cd

विधिं प्रति प्रधानत्वं स्वीकृत्याभ्येति मानताम् SV 779cd

विधिं विना श्रुतैकात्म्यस्तदर्थानुभवादृते SV 783ab

विधिः श्रुतः श्रुतौ स्पष्टस्ततश्च फलसंगतिः 1.4.774cd

विधिः सर्वप्रकारोऽपि न त्वबुद्धार्थबोधनम् 4.4.938cd

विधितः प्रतिषेधाच्च साधनापेक्षता भवेत् SV 887cd

विधितन्त्रस्य कार्यत्वान्नाज्ञाने प्रभविष्णुता 2.4.150cd

विधित्सन्तीह संन्यासं मैत्रेयीति प्रवर्तते 2.4.38cd

विधित्सितं चेत्तादृक्षं कल्पकोट्यापि दुःशकम् 1.4.695cd

विधित्सिताथ तन्निन्दा स्तुतिश्चानस्य किंफला 1.3.39ab

विधिद्वारेण तस्यैव निर्देशार्थं परा श्रुतिः 3.9.132cd

विधिना केन किं चात्मा समाश्रित्य प्रपश्यति 4.3.846cd

विधिना त्वेकवाक्यत्वादिति यच्चापि चोदितम् SV 274ab

विधिनास्यापि चाक्षेपाद्विधितन्त्रत्वमिष्यते 4.4.1270cd

विधिनिन्दासमावेशो नैवमप्युपपद्यते SV 328ab

विधिनिष्ठेऽपि शास्त्रे स्यादसिद्धेर्वस्तुनो मितेः SV 784ab

विधिनैवैकवाक्यत्वं यतो मन्त्रार्थवादयोः SV 564ab

विधिनैवैकवाक्यत्वमर्थवादस्य युज्यते 4.4.1134cd

विधिप्रशस्तज्ञानाभ्यां कुरुध्वं पुंस्प्रवर्तनम् 1.4.784cd

विधिमार्गेऽधिकारस्य परीक्षा वर्तते यतः SV 228ab

विधिराकर्षणे तावत्तेजोमात्राश्रयो गतः 4.4.54ab

विधिरागवशात्केचित्तान्प्रतीदमथोच्यते SV 757cd

विधिरेवानपेक्षत्वात्सापेक्ष्यान्नाभिधाश्रुतिः 2.4.147cd

विधिर्गुणार्थस्तस्यापि व्यापारविषयत्वतः SV 448cd

विधिर्भवति सामर्थ्याज्ज्ञाते ह्यर्थेऽनुवादता 1.4.856cd

विधिर्यतोऽभ्युपगमान्नियमोक्तिरियं ततः 1.4.922cd

विधिर्यतो नियोगोऽपि नैव स्यादनृतन्त्रतः 1.4.854cd

विधिलक्षणसिद्ध्यर्थं सन्ति वाक्यानि च श्रुतौ SV 21cd

विधिवर्त्मानुगामित्वान्नार्थस्पृक्सास्वतन्त्रतः 1.4.879cd

विधिवाक्यमृते तद्वद्विध्यर्थश्रवणेऽपि न 1.4.830cd

विधिशास्त्रस्य नैवातो वेदान्ता बाधकाः सदा 2.1.587ab

विधिशून्यस्य वाक्यस्य न प्रामाण्यं किलेष्यते 1.4.793ab

विधिशेषतया तेषामेकवाक्यत्वसंभवे SV 36cd

विधिशेषत्वमुज्झित्वा नार्थवादो यतोऽन्यतः 4.4.1135cd
विधिशेषार्थवादत्वान्नेदं ज्ञाननिरूपणम् 1.3.34ab
विधिशेषोऽपि यद्यर्थमर्थवादः समर्पयेत् SV 568ab
विधिश्रुतेः प्रवर्तेत न तु प्लुष्टतदन्वयः 1.4.816cd
विधिष्वपि लयस्तासां कार्यान्तरनियोगतः SV 381cd
विधिस्वातन्त्र्यपक्षे हि किलैकात्म्यं न सिध्यति SV 770ab
विधीनां चापि सर्वेषां निषेधवचसां तथा SV 399ab
विधीयते तथा नाम्नि ब्रह्मबुद्धिर्विधीयते 1.3.64cd
विधीयते यतो नातः समस्तव्यस्तदर्शनम् 1.4.691cd
विधीयते सहोपायं वेदान्तोक्तिप्रबोधतः 1.4.802cd
विधूताशेषसंबन्धमनन्यानुभवात्मकम् 1.4.211ab
विधूयानात्मनोऽशेषांस्तत्प्रत्यग्रूपमैक्षत 1.4.1180cd
विधृतिः पूर्वयोः प्राणो मधुकाण्डे यथोदितः 5.16.15cd
विधेरन्यपदं यस्मान्नाक्षेपोऽतः प्रतीयते SV 730cd
विधेरपीह मानत्वं नोक्तन्यायातिरेकतः 2.4.168cd
विधेरिवानपेक्षत्वं वेदान्तेष्वभिधाश्रुतेः 2.4.153ab
विधेर्दौर्बल्यसिद्ध्यर्थमतो भाष्यकृदुक्तवान् 1.4.931cd
विधेर्विध्यन्तरेऽभीष्टे कृत्स्नोऽर्थोऽप्यविवक्षितः SV 670ab
विधेर्हि तत्र साफल्यं यत्र वाक्योत्थबोधतः 1.4.810ab
विध्यन्तरस्येति ततो यथोक्तोऽर्थोऽवसीयताम् 1.4.829cd
विध्यन्तरेऽनवस्था स्यान्न चायं कर्मणि स्थितेः SV 661cd
विध्यभावे हि संसर्गः श्रोतुरस्त्यविधावपि SV 751ef
विध्यर्थशेषभावश्च ततश्चार्थान्तरोक्तिता SV 566ab
विध्यर्थसंगतावेव सापि नैव ततोऽन्यतः SV 565cd
विध्यर्थस्य पुरा प्राप्तेः काण्वानामनुवादतः 4.4.1274ab
विध्यर्थाङ्गीकृतौ त्वेतदनपेक्षं प्रमाणताम् SV 675ab
विध्यर्थाधीनसंसर्गाः पदार्था वैदिकोक्तिषु SV 721ab
विध्यर्थो ह्यपि बाल्यादिस्तथोर्ध्वमपि दृश्यते 3.5.105cd
विध्यशेषत्वतो नापि चार्थवादत्वमिष्यते 3.4.184cd
विध्युक्तीनां क्रियार्थत्वं सिद्धं हेतुतयोच्यते SV 271cd
विध्युक्तेस्तदसंसिद्धौ निष्फलत्वं प्रसज्यते SV 718cd
विध्युद्देशतया यद्वदुपयोगस्तथैव च 1.4.789cd

विध्युद्देशात्तु तत्सिद्धेः शैघ्र्यं तूक्तं प्रवृत्तये SV 855cd
विध्वंसमेत्यपचयात्कोष्ठागारादिवद्ध्रुवम् 1.4.1681cd
विनंष्टुं नात्मनः शीलं घटादेरिव युज्यते 4.3.1552cd
विनश्वरी सहेतुश्च जलक्षीरादिसंगतिः 4.3.61cd
विनष्टिं महतीं चेयाद्योऽवेद्यात्माविचक्षणः 4.4.626ab
विनष्टिर्महती चेह विनाशादिप्रसूतितः 4.4.627ab
विनष्टो वा कुतो भूयो देहमागादितीर्यताम् 2.1.197cd
विनापि प्रक्रियां तेन कर्मोपस्थापयेद्ध्रुवम् SV 431cd
विनाप्यैकात्म्यसंबोधात्कर्मणैवोक्तवर्त्मना SV 42cd
विनाशः क्रियते यत्र व्यतिरेकोऽथवान्वयः 4.4.767ab
विनाशको यतो मृत्युर्विनाश्यान्प्रति भण्यते 3.2.15cd
विनाशक्रियया व्याप्तमुत्पन्नं चेद्विनश्यति 4.3.626ab
विनाशतः स्वतस्तस्य कीदृशी फलसंगतिः 4.3.713cd
विनाशशक्त्यभावोक्तेर्न प्रतिज्ञैकदेशता 4.3.1502cd
विनाशस्यापि कार्यत्वात्सोऽपि सत्कारणो मम 1.2.37ab
विनाशिफलवत्त्वं चेत्केवलस्यैव कर्मणः 3.3.29ab
विनाशोऽतिशयः कश्चिद्यदि पिण्डादिवन्मतः 1.2.46ab
विनियुक्ता यतस्तस्मान्नैते तज्ज्ञानसिद्धये 4.4.1024cd
विनियोगप्रयत्नाच्च कर्मविज्ञानकाण्डयोः 4.4.1022ab
विनियोगो यथोक्तोऽयं वर्णानां प्रविभागशः 1.4.1635cd
विनियोजकहेत्वेतत्तयोर्वाक्यैकवाक्यतः SV 278cd
विनेशुर्विष्वग्गतयो लोष्टः क्षिप्तो यथाश्मनि 1.3.177cd
विपन्नकारकग्रामं ज्ञानं कर्म न ढौकते 3.3.69cd
विपरीतग्रहाय स्यादन्यथेति विनिश्चितिः 4.3.1195cd
विपरीतस्ततो यस्तु वाक्यादेव च गम्यते 1.4.889ab
विपरीतस्वभावोऽत आत्मलाभः स्वतः सदा 1.4.1018ab
विपरीतागतिः स्वप्ने प्रतिस्थानं तथैत्यजः 4.3.990cd
विपरीतार्थतायास्तु न हेतुर्जगतीक्ष्यते 1.3.58cd
विपर्ययेण येऽप्याहुर्यथोक्तज्ञानकर्मणोः SV 427ab
विपर्ययेणानर्थाय तदेतत्प्रतिपाद्यते 5.16.76cd
विपर्ययोऽधृतिस्तस्या ह्रीर्लज्जेत्यभिधीयते 1.5.113cd
विपाकाः कर्मणोर्वाच्यास्तद्वैराग्यप्रसिद्धये 6.2.5cd

विप्रकृष्टयाद्यभावोक्त्या भयः कस्मात्स आश्रितः 1.4.609cd
विप्रहाटकहार्यत्र स्तेनशब्देन भण्यते 4.3.1361ab
विभक्तं यत्तमोऽस्तीव नाविभक्तं मनागपि 4.3.1517ab
विभक्तमविभक्तं वा वस्तु वस्त्वन्तराश्रयात् 4.3.1613ab
विभज्य कारणादुच्चैर्नीत्वा कार्यात्मतां मुहुः 3.9.114ab
विभज्यमानस्य सतः परस्मादात्मनोऽद्वयात् 2.3.102cd
विभज्यमानोऽन्येभ्यो हि विशेषोऽपि प्रसिध्यति 1.4.1407ab
विभाग आसुरो वेधस्तेन तेष्वनुमीयते 1.3.158cd
विभागं करवाणीति भार्या तेनाभ्यचोद्यत 2.4.44cd
विभागं लभते ज्ञानाज्ज्ञानवत्स्वप्नवस्तु चेत् 4.3.564ab
विभागमसहन्तीव मदतिस्नेहकारणात् 2.4.68ab
विभागहेतोरुच्छित्तेः सर्वमात्मैव शिष्यते 1.4.1392cd
विभागहेत्वसद्भावाज्जाग्रद्वन्नोपलभ्यते 4.3.1379cd
विभागान्नापरं वस्तु ह्यविभक्तगिरा ततः 4.3.1615cd
विभागेऽपि न भेदः स्यात्तयोरेकात्मना स्थितेः 5.1.87ab
विभाव्यते सुविस्पष्टं वादन्यायेन यत्नतः 4.3.8ab
विभिन्नकार्यकर्त्रीणां शक्तीनां यद्वदाश्रयः SV 958ab
विभिन्नद्रष्टृदृष्टयाप्तिर्घटादेरिव नात्मनः 2.4.135ab
विभिन्ननामरूपाणां सरितां सागरो यथा 2.4.328ab
विभिन्नासंहतज्योतिरनुग्रहपुरःसरः 4.3.68cd
विभिन्नोऽनुभवादेव ज्ञातुर्ज्ञानात्स गोचरः 3.4.108cd
विभिन्नो बहिराभाति जातिरूपक्रियादिमान् 3.4.108ab
विभीषिका इमाः सर्वा वेदवर्त्मानुगामिनाम् 4.3.494cd
विभीषिकानिषेधार्थमत्र प्रतिविधीयते 4.3.495ab
विभुत्वाद्देवतानां च भोगः स्यादैककालिकः 4.3.433ab
विभ्वी सर्वगतानन्ता समाप्ता च प्रतिक्रियम् 1.3.279ab
विमुक्तिफलसंबन्धे न मानं विद्यते ततः 3.3.83cd
विमुच्यमान इत्युक्तेरर्चिराद्युक्तितस्तथा SV 330ab
विमुच्यमानः क्वेतस्त्वं गमिष्यसि वदाशु मे 4.2.30cd
विमृद्य रचनां पूर्वां कुरुते रचनान्तरम् 4.4.140cd
विमोक्षायेह नैवालमन्यदात्मावबोधतः 4.4.542ab
विमोक्षायैव मे ब्रूहीत्यदोषोऽयं कुतो यतः 4.4.541cd

वियच्छब्दगुणं यद्वत्प्रत्यक्चेन्नैवमिष्यते 1.4.579cd
वियतोऽजन्मनो जन्म यथा कुम्भादिजन्मना 1.4.355cd
वियतो मूर्ततैवं स्याद्भिन्नाभिन्नत्वमात्मनः 4.3.1812cd
वियत्येवं न वीक्ष्यन्ते प्रत्यग्दृष्ट्या यथोदिताः 4.3.1262cd
वियत्संपूर्णतां नर्ते घटो नानाविधैर्युतिम् 4.4.930ab
वियत्संपूर्णता नित्या वियत्सक्तेरवर्जनात् 2.4.144cd
वियत्संपूर्णतोत्पत्तौ कुम्भस्येव दृशा धियाम् SV 543cd
वियदादि च नः कार्यं तदप्येवं प्रतीयताम् 1.2.33cd
वियद्वस्तुस्वभावानुरोधादेव न कारकात् SV 543ab
वियद्वेदकलस्तस्मादीश्वरोऽभ्युपगम्यताम् 1.4.554cd
वियुक्तं देवताभिः सत्कर्मसंभारसंभृतम् 4.3.1916ab
वियुक्तस्यात्मनश्चेत्स्याद्विस्फुलिङ्गादिवद्गतिः 2.1.487ab
वियोगं वा यथा गच्छेच्चैतन्यैद्वास्तथा धियः 1.4.837cd
विरक्त आग्रजात्सोऽयं तत्सावद्यसमीक्षणात् 2.4.3ab
विरक्त आग्रजाल्लोकान्मोक्षादर्वाक्षु भूमिषु 4.4.1195cd
विरक्तः कर्मभूमिभ्यो ज्ञानं प्रति नियुज्यते 3.5.156cd
विरक्तः सर्वसंसारान्निविवृत्सुः स्वतस्ततः 1.4.1343ab
विरक्तस्य तु जिज्ञासोर्मानान्नान्यव्यपेक्षणम् SV 90ab
विरक्ता अपि संसारान्नैकात्म्यं ये विदुर्नराः 4.4.600cd
विरक्ताः सर्वसंसाराज्जिज्ञासन्ते परं पदम् SV 1132cd
विरक्ताः सर्वसंसारादाग्रजाद्बुद्धिशुद्धितः 4.4.1078ab
विरक्तिहेतुतः कर्म प्रतिषिद्धं यथा तथा SV 1107cd
विरजः शुद्ध इत्यर्थ आकाशात्परतः स्थितः 4.4.736ab
विरहय्य न वेदान्तान्वेदेऽन्येन कथं चन 4.4.1033ab
विरहे भावनायाश्च न विधेस्तत्र मानता 2.4.158ab
विराजं चोपसंहृत्य प्राणविज्ञानविग्रहे 4.2.79ab
विराजमसृजद्ब्रह्मा सोऽसृजत्पुरुषं विराट् 1.4.117ab
विराजैवात्मना हत्वा पापं भवति सोऽचिरात् 1.3.180cd
विराजो देवदेवस्य तदिदानीमिहोच्यते 2.3.45cd
विराजो रश्मयो ज्ञेयाः प्रत्यंशावसितास्तथा 4.2.76cd
विराट्प्रजापतिर्ज्ञेयस्त्रैलोक्यात्मकदेहभृत् 4.3.1875ab
विराडपि ततो जातस्त्रैलोक्यात्मकदेहवान् 1.4.19ab

विराडात्मनि देहे च बुद्धावित्यादि पूर्ववत् 2.1.80ab
विराडैच्छदृतेऽविद्यां नेच्छेशस्योपपद्यते 1.4.108cd
विराड्गृहीतिरत्र स्यात्साधारकरणग्रहात् 4.1.20cd
विराड्ढिरण्यगर्भश्च सर्वजातिश्वमन्वितः 2.5.52cd
विराड्ढिरण्यगर्भश्चेत्ययमात्मेति तद्वचः 2.5.54cd
विराड्देहावनद्धोऽसुरध्यात्माद्याधिगः खवत् 1.2.159ab
विराड्ब्रह्माथ ससृजे मनुं देवं प्रजापतिम् 1.2.139ab
विराड्भावेनातितरां चण्डप्रचलितोर्मिवत् 5.1.54ab
विरिञ्च एव तु परो मन्त्रब्राह्मणवाक्यतः 1.4.145ab
विरिञ्चस्य त्रिकालत्वादासीदस्ति भविष्यति 1.4.1193cd
विरुद्धं कर्मभिः किं वा यदुत्पत्त्यादिवर्जितम् 3.3.102cd
विरुद्धत्वाद्विशेष्यं स्यात्तमसा दिनकृद्यथा 4.4.472cd
विरुद्धधर्मकत्वं तु मिथो नाज्ञानकर्मणोः 3.3.96ab
विरुद्धधर्मसंबन्धो न प्रतीच्यस्त्यधर्मिणि 1.4.1273cd
विरुद्धमानभावेऽपि न हि वस्तु विकल्प्यते SV 913ab
विरुद्धयोरसंसर्गो यथैवमविरुद्धयोः 4.4.985ab
विरुद्धयोश्च क्रिययोरिष्टत्वादेककर्तरि 4.3.595ab
विरुद्धरूपयोरेवं निर्द्वयद्वयरूपतः 1.4.497ab
विरुद्धरूपौ प्रत्यक्षाद्गम्येते भोज्यभोजकौ 4.3.274cd
विरुद्धवस्तुसंसृष्टिं ब्रूतेऽज्ञानैककारणम् 1.4.493cd
विरुद्धागमविषयप्रविवेकप्रसङ्गतः 3.5.35cd
विरुद्धानेककार्याणां युगपज्जन्म नेष्यते 1.2.52ab
विरुद्धानेककार्याणामेकस्मादेव कारणात् 1.4.325ab
विरुद्धार्थत्ववचसां स्यादेकत्रापि संभवः 1.4.150cd
विरुद्धार्थनिवृत्त्यात्र मुनिरित्यभिधीयते 3.5.183cd
विरुद्धार्थह्नुतिः पश्चात्ततो वाक्यार्थबोधनम् 3.5.169cd
विरुद्धार्थावभासोऽयं जायमानः समीक्ष्यते 2.1.557cd
विरुद्धाव्यभिचारित्वं न च प्रत्यक्षलिङ्गयोः 1.2.59ab
विरुद्धाव्यभिचारित्वं समानबलयोर्यतः 1.2.60ab
विरुद्धैरेव दृष्टा सा तदैकात्म्ये कथं भवेत् 1.4.254cd
विरुध्यतेऽक्रियारूपं मानित्वादिक्रियात्मकैः 4.4.849ab
विरुध्यतेऽफलोक्त्यैवमारभ्यं स्याद्यतः फलम् 3.3.87cd

विरुध्यते प्रमाणं सन्न चान्यार्थत्वमिष्यते 4.4.441cd
विरूपं प्रस्तुताद्रूपादन्याद्यं भण्यते कुतः 4.3.1632cd
विरोध एव तेन स्यादेकाधिकरणत्वतः 1.4.1109cd
विरोधः कोऽनयोरत्र मिथोऽर्थासंस्पृशोः सतोः 1.4.1108cd
विरोधः सर्वशास्त्राणां स्वाभिधेयव्यपेक्षया 1.4.406ab
विरोधः स्यात्प्रमाणानामित्येतदभिधीयताम् 2.1.553cd
विरोधाच्च स्वतन्त्रं तद्गुणभूतं न कस्यचित् SV 372cd
विरोधात्तद्विरुद्धोऽर्थः प्रत्ययेनेक्ष्यते कथम् SV 152cd
विरोधात्संभवोऽस्तीह प्रकाशतमसोरिव SV 167cd
विरोधात्सुखरूपस्य न दुःखेन समागमः 3.5.129cd
विरोधादन्वयो नास्य खण्डादौ गोत्ववत्तथा 3.4.60ab
विरोधादेशतोऽकार्यकारणत्वात्परात्मनः 4.3.1516cd
विरोधाद्भावयोर्यद्वदेकत्वान्नाप्यभावयोः 1.2.115cd
विरोधाद्युगपन्नापि विधानप्रतिषेधनम् SV 949cd
विरोधान्न हि शीतत्वमुष्णस्याग्नेर्विशेषणम् 4.3.204cd
विरोधित्वाच्च नान्योऽन्यं संबन्धस्तापशीतवत् 1.2.14cd
विरोधिना जडत्वेन व्याप्तेः किमु परस्य तत् 4.3.205cd
विरोधिना यथा तद्वन्नेह स्थूलाद्यपाक्रिया 3.8.102cd
विरोधिव्यभिचारित्वात्तदन्यस्य च वस्तुनः 4.3.1723cd
विरोधे गुणवादः स्यादनुवादोऽवधारिते SV 567ab
विरोधोऽत्यर्थमेवातस्तत्त्यक्तं ज्ञानशालिना 4.5.28cd
विरोधो न तु मानानां सदैकार्थसमागमे 2.1.554cd
विरोध्यन्तरविध्वंसो दृष्टो लोके विरोधिना 3.3.93ab
विलक्षणानामपि सतां सामान्यं संहतात्मनाम् 4.3.424cd
विलक्षणोऽतो विज्ञेयः पृथिवीदेवतात्मनः 3.7.33cd
विलयः स्यात्कथं नाम व्यावृत्तान्वयरूपिणाम् 2.4.287cd
विलीनस्याद्व्य उद्धृत्य ग्रहणाय न कश्चन 2.4.401cd
विवक्षवोऽभिधावन्ति तमुद्दिश्य जिघृक्षवः 2.1.42cd
विवक्षातश्च शब्दानां प्रयोगो जगतीक्ष्यते 1.4.522ab
विवक्षाया न कार्यत्वं शब्दार्थविषया हि सा SV 500cd
विवक्षावसितिर्गार्गी तथा सत्युपपद्यते 2.1.81cd
विवक्षितं चेदैकात्म्यं सर्वोपनिषदां भवेत् 2.1.530ab

विवक्षितत्वादाक्षिप्तनियन्त्राद्यभिधीयते 1.4.517cd
विवक्षितत्वादैक्यस्य मनोबुद्ध्योरतः श्रुतिः 1.5.181ab
विवक्षिता भाष्यकृतो नित्यप्राप्तिरितीक्ष्यते 1.4.760cd
विवक्षितार्थविज्ञप्त्यै त आत्मेति ततोऽवदत् 3.4.52ab
विवक्षितार्थविज्ञानप्रसिद्धिः स्यात्कथं न्विति 4.3.1959cd
विवक्षितेह विज्ञेयामृतमित्यादिलक्षणा 3.9.44cd
विवक्षितोऽर्थो यत्नेन तद्वैराग्यविधित्सया 1.4.5ef
विवक्ष्यते स्थितिरिह न्यषेधि बहुशः स च 4.4.514cd
विवादगोचरापन्नं भास्वरत्वाद्रवीन्दुवत् 4.3.229cd
विवादगोचरापन्नं सत्कारणमिदं भवेत् 1.2.32ab
विवादगोचरापन्ना प्रमाणमनमेष्यताम् 4.3.247ab
विवादगोचरापन्ना यन्तृपूर्वा जगत्स्थितिः 3.8.132ab
विविक्तः कामकर्मादेः स्वयंज्योतिश्च शब्दितः 4.4.980cd
विविक्ततैवं यत्नेन निर्णीता प्रत्यगात्मनः 4.3.1080cd
विविक्तदेशसेवादाविच्छायां किं न रागिता SV 1019cd
विविच्यते ब्रह्मणश्चेन्मैवं दोषस्तथापि हि 2.4.13ab
विविच्य येन विज्ञातः स स्याद्विश्वकृदीश्वरः 4.4.619cd
विविच्य योऽनुगृह्णाति शब्दादींश्च जडान्पृथक् 4.3.190cd
विविच्यातः स्वमात्मानं प्रत्यभिज्ञानतस्तथा SV 441cd
विविदिषन्तीतिगिरा संबन्धः प्रतिसाधनम् 4.4.1030ab
विविधं त्वमेव भवसि यतोऽतो विभुरुच्यते 6.3.32cd
विविधास्यैव सा सृष्टिरिति हेतुसमीरणम् 1.4.139ab
विविधुस्तानथोद्गातृंस्ते विद्वास्तत्यजुः क्रियाः 1.3.147cd
विविनक्ति फलं चापि येषामित्येवमादिना 4.4.1137cd
विविनक्त्यनुमानेन तदा वाक्यार्थधीर्भवेत् 4.4.864cd
विवृतिश्छान्दसी ज्ञेया लक्षणासंभवादिह 4.3.1298ab
विवेकतोऽननुभवो वराहोरगवत्तयोः 4.3.389cd
विवेकमात्रसिद्ध्यर्थो भोक्तृभोग्यपदार्थयोः 2.1.290ab
विवेकिनो न युक्तेयं प्रवृत्तिः पारलौकिकी SV 105cd
विव्यत्सोद्देशमात्रेण प्राणो हन्ता सुरद्विषाम् 1.3.174ab
विशन्ति सर्वभूतानि ह्यन्नभूते प्रजापतौ 5.14.15ab
विशन्त्यज्ञास्तु ते सन्तस्ततो भूयः परं तमः 4.4.605ab

विशिनष्टि ततः प्राणमास्यान्तर्बिलचारिणम् 1.3.203cd
विशिनष्टि स्वमात्मानं प्रतीचीनमनात्मभिः 2.1.518cd
विशिनष्ट्यात्मनः स्वापं यत्र सुप्तगिरा स्फुटम् 4.3.1164cd
विशिष्टः स विधिर्ज्ञेयो यथाग्नेयादयस्तथा 1.3.197cd
विशिष्टः ससृजे विष्णुस्तेजोबन्नादि मायया 1.4.16cd
विशिष्टदेवतावाप्तिर्वागादीनां प्रपञ्च्यते 1.3.230cd
विशिष्टफलसंगत्या इहोक्तिः सत्यवद्भवेत् 1.5.216cd
विशिष्टफलसंबन्धो न तथापि प्रतीयते 1.5.222cd
विशिष्टमभिधित्स्वाह शास्त्रं पूर्ववदेव च 1.3.297cd
विशिष्टाकृतिदेशेहाकालधर्मं प्रतीयते 1.4.451ab
विशिष्टापत्यहेतुत्वाज्जपेदेवं तथोत्तरे 6.4.27cd
विशिष्टार्थावगत्यर्थं प्रयुज्यन्तेऽपराण्यपि SV 727cd
विशिष्टार्थावबोधित्वान्नीलरक्तोत्पलादिवत् 3.4.12cd
विशिष्टार्थैकनिष्ठत्वं स्वतो न विधिहेतुतः SV 667cd
विशिष्टाह्वानसिद्ध्यर्थमृषीणामुत्तरा श्रुतिः 2.2.30ab
विशिष्टेनाविशिष्टस्य क्लृप्तेनाकल्पितात्मनः 1.4.1441cd
विशिष्टेहानुभूतिश्च सर्वमानफलं यतः 2.4.123ab
विशिष्टोपास्तिरेवेयं प्रधानफलकीर्तनात् 1.3.211ab
विशिष्यते न धर्माणां मिथः संगतिरिष्यते 2.3.18cd
विशीर्णकरणग्रामो बुद्धिभावनया युतः 2.1.250ab
विशीर्यते ततः कार्यं कृत्स्नं च कारणं तथा 1.4.1712ab
विशुद्धिं व्यतिरेकं च स्वप्नजाग्रदवस्थयोः 2.1.312ab
विशेत्पर्णमयीत्वादि प्रकृत्युपनयात्क्रतुम् SV 335cd
विशेष आत्मनः कश्चिद्दिति चेन्नैवमिष्यते 4.4.353cd
विशेष इति नैवं स्याद्ध्यायतीवेति वारणात् 4.4.355cd
विशेष उच्यतां कोऽत्र समस्तव्यस्तरूपयोः 4.3.1657cd
विशेषः कश्चिदित्येवं न प्रवृत्तिर्विधेर्भवेत् SV 619ef
विशेषकार्यं प्राणोऽसुस्तस्यापीहाधिदेवता 3.9.55cd
विशेषकार्यवाहिभ्यः स्रोतोभ्यः स्वप्नभूमिगः 4.4.50ab
विशेषज्ञानमेवास्य स्वभावो वाभ्युपेयते 4.3.1789ab
विशेषज्ञानलाभोऽस्य लिङ्गात्मानुविधानतः 4.4.45ab
विशेषज्ञानसंबन्धः कर्मणैवास्य हेतुना 4.4.100ab

विशेषणं नियोज्यस्य भवन्ननुभवः फलम् SV 802ab
विशेषणं यथोक्तं तत्कारके दृष्टिकारिणि 3.4.178cd
विशेषणं विशेष्याच्चेद्विशेष्यान्तरवत्पृथक् 4.3.1720ab
विशेषणं सर्व इति किमर्थमभिधीयते 4.4.377cd
विशेषणं स्वयमिति देहपातेऽस्य भण्यते 4.3.869cd
विशेषणं स्वरूपं वा नान्योऽन्यस्य स्वतो यतः SV 114cd
विशेषणतयानन्दशब्दोऽन्यत्रापि दृश्यते 3.9.167ab
विशेषणत्वं स्वार्थोऽपि सत्कार्ये कारणे गतः 4.4.1276ab
विशेषणप्रभेदेऽपि विशेष्योऽर्थो न भिद्यते 4.3.1719ab
विशेषणमतोऽन्याय्यमत्यन्तमिति भण्यते 4.3.1612cd
विशेषणमतो वाच्याः पन्थानः कर्महेतवः 6.2.4cd
विशेषणयुतिः शाब्दी तद्विरुद्धनिराकृतिः 1.4.1425ab
विशेषणविरोधित्वान्महत्त्वं कुम्भगं यथा 4.4.982cd
विशेषणविशेष्यत्वं व्यभिचारे सतीष्यते 3.4.183cd
विशेषणविशेष्यत्वं श्रुत्यैवेहावसीयते 3.4.13cd
विशेषणविशेष्यत्वमीशितव्येशयोरिह 4.4.981cd
विशेषणविशेष्यत्वसंबन्धोऽथ पदार्थयोः 3.5.183ab
विशेषणविशेष्यत्वे मिथो ब्रह्मात्मनोरतः 3.4.46ab
विशेषणविशेष्यत्वे संगतिश्चेद्भवेत्तयोः 4.3.207ab
विशेषणविशेष्याणां साकल्येनैव संगतिः 1.4.1420ab
विशेषणविशेष्यार्थं सर्वस्येति तथा वचः 4.4.977cd
विशेषणश्रवात्क्लृप्तिर्नैतयोस्तद्विरुद्धयोः 4.4.486cd
विशेषणस्य श्रवणाद्धृदीत्यात्मनि चेन्मतम् 4.4.434ab
विशेषणस्य सर्वस्य साक्षादित्यादिकस्य च 3.6.2ab
विशेषणा चिदेवैका स्वानुभूत्यैव गम्यते 1.4.290cd
विशेषणादन्तरिति व्यावर्त्यन्ते पराक्त्वतः 4.3.334cd
विशेषणानां संप्राप्तिर्नाञ्जसी प्रत्यगात्मनि 1.4.1426cd
विशेषणानां संबन्धो नातः स्यात्प्रत्यगात्मनः 4.4.500cd
विशेषणानां संबन्धो यतो न प्रत्यगात्मनि 1.4.1427ab
विशेषणानां संबन्धो विशेष्येण विशेषणैः 1.4.1419ab
विशेषणानि येनातस्तद्विरुद्धं न ढौकते 1.4.1424cd
विशेषणानि सर्वाणि विशिंषन्त्युत्पलादिवत् 3.4.31cd

विशेषणेन तद्व्याप्तेस्तदभावः कुतो मितेः SV 942cd
विशेषदर्शनासूतेरसंबोधस्तदात्मनः 4.3.1394ab
विशेषदर्शने यस्मादविद्यैवास्य कारणम् 4.3.1792ab
विशेषदृष्ट्यभिव्यक्तिर्यदाश्रित्य प्रसिध्यति 4.3.1606ab
विशेषनाम्ना संयोज्य देवदत्तादिनोच्यते 1.4.393cd
विशेषप्रतिषेधे च क्रम आश्रीयते ध्रुवम् 3.8.91ab
विशेषबुद्ध्यभिव्यक्तिर्जाग्रद्भूमाविवेष्यते 4.3.1561cd
विशेषमात्रनिष्ठत्वाद्भिन्नाभिन्नं किमुच्यते 1.6.59cd
विशेषवन्न चाप्यस्य विज्ञानमिह जायते 4.3.1543ab
विशेषविरहात्तर्हि सामान्यमपि दुःस्थितम् 4.3.1650cd
विशेषश्चेदपेक्ष्यः स्याद्यो देहेऽस्मिन्न विद्यते 4.3.228ab
विशेषसंज्ञा नास्त्यस्य पूर्णप्रज्ञप्तिमात्रतः 2.4.421cd
विशेषसंज्ञा यास्याभूद्विज्ञानात्मादिलक्षणा 2.4.449ab
विशेषस्याग्रहात्तद्वद्गृह्यते नेदमित्यपि 3.8.36cd
विशेषाणामनन्तत्वात्समस्तं ब्रह्म सोऽवदत् 2.1.83ab
विशेषात्मनिषेधाय तथा सामान्यरूपिणः 1.6.54ab
विशेषाननुसृप्यात्मा यात्वा हृदयमाश्रयम् 4.4.50cd
विशेषाभावतो नैवं तस्यानतिशयत्वतः 4.3.609cd
विशेषावगतिर्नाम्नः क्रमाच्चेति व्यवस्थितम् SV 339cd
विशेषावस्था प्रागुक्ता सामान्यं त्वधुनोच्यते 3.3.4cd
विशेषेऽनुगमाभाव इत्यादि यदुदीरितम् 4.3.239cd
विशेषेऽनुगमाभावः सामान्ये सिद्धसाध्यता 4.3.144ab
विशेषेऽसत्यसाध्वेतद्भवतोदाहृतं वचः 4.3.507ef
विशेषेभ्योऽविशेषेभ्यो युक्तं प्रत्यवसर्पणम् 4.4.52cd
विशेषैरन्वयो नापि सामान्यान्वयवत्क्वचित् 2.4.269ab
विशेषैरन्वयो नो चेदिभाखुव्यक्तिवन्मिथः 2.4.270ab
विशेषोऽबाह्यशब्देन ततो वाक्यार्थरूपकम् 2.5.141cd
विशेषोऽस्ति प्रवृत्तेश्चेत्तात्पर्यं वचसोऽपि च SV 579ab
विशेषो न स्वतस्तच्च नामरूपादि शोधितम् 2.3.99ab
विशेषो वाञ्छितश्चेत्स्यात्पुत्रपश्वाद्युपाधितः SV 306cd
विशेष्यमपि नाप्नोति धर्मान्तरविशेषितम् 4.3.206ab
विशेष्यमात्रनिष्ठत्वादन्यत्र स्यात्कथं नु तत् 4.3.206cd

विशेष्यस्यापि संबन्धः स्वातन्त्र्यपारतन्त्र्यतः 1.4.1419cd
विशेष्यार्थैकतन्त्रत्वाद्धर्माणां न परस्परम् 2.3.19ab
विश्वं सदेव यस्येष्टं तस्याभावः कुतो मितेः SV 929ab
विश्वकृत्त्वं भवेदेवं हीतिहेतुपरिग्रहात् 4.4.622cd
विश्वजिद्वन्न सामर्थ्यं तत्र संभाव्यतेऽण्वपि 3.3.76ab
विश्वंभरोऽग्निर्विज्ञेयो विश्वस्य भरणादिह 1.4.640ab
विश्वरूपं यशो ज्ञेयं शब्दाद्यर्थावभासकम् 2.2.26ab
विश्वरूपसमुत्पत्तिरेकरूपात्कथं भवेत् 2.1.389cd
विश्वाभिव्यक्तितः पूर्वं ब्रह्मैवानामरूपकम् 2.1.394cd
विश्वावस्वभिधानेन गन्धर्वोऽत्र प्रबोध्यते 6.4.90cd
विश्वासोऽतोऽत्र विदुषा न कार्यः स्वप्नलाभवत् 1.4.1836ab
विश्वेदेवान्मनोवृत्तीः संपाद्यानन्त्यसाम्यतः 3.1.55cd
विश्वेश्वरोऽपि प्राहैतत्प्रपन्नाय किरीटिने 1.4.233ab
विश्वो हि स्थूलभुङ्नित्यं तैजसः प्रविविक्तभुक् 1.4.744ab
विषदध्यादिवत्तस्मान्नैतत्सूक्तं भवेद्वचः 3.3.32cd
विषदध्यादिवदिति तथोदाहृतिरुच्यते 3.3.15cd
विषमस्थं यतः सर्वं प्राणव्यापत्तिकारणम् 4.3.456ab
विषयं कर्मणा सार्धं तमेवैतीति संगतिः 4.4.243cd
विषयः प्रत्यगात्मा च स्वाभासेन विशेद्धियम् 4.3.94ab
विषयः सत्प्रसंख्यानमनुभूतेर्न साधनम् SV 802cd
विषयः स नियोगस्य नात्मज्ञाने त्वभेदतः 1.4.855cd
विषयज्ञानजन्मैवमात्मनो भूतसंगतेः 4.3.1119ab
विषयत्वं समापेदेऽविकल्पोऽपि स्वतः परः 4.3.402cd
विषयत्वाच्च पुंबुद्धेर्न दीपस्योभयात्मता 1.4.583cd
विषयत्वाविशेषेऽपि कुतोऽसङ्गत्वतश्चितेः 2.3.108cd
विषयत्वेन नाक्षेपो भावार्थो विषयो मतः SV 633cd
विषयत्वोपपत्तेश्च प्रत्यङ्मोहतदुत्थयोः 4.4.357ab
विषयप्रविभागश्च विरुद्धवचसां मिथः 3.9.204ab
विषयस्पर्शजानन्दाः साधनानुविधानतः 4.3.1837ab
विषयस्य लयोक्त्यान्तःकरणप्रलयोक्तता 2.4.394cd
विषयस्यापि कार्यत्वं स्वत एव भवेत्तथा SV 614ab
विषयांस्तत्स्मृतींस्त्यक्त्वा तिष्ठेच्चिदनुरोधतः 4.4.1247cd

विषयाकृष्टधीर्यस्मान्न क्षमः प्रत्यगीक्षणे 4.4.581cd
विषयान्तरसंबद्धं मनो दृष्टं घटादिवत् 1.5.103ab
विषयान्तैर्भवेद्भ्रान्तिः सामानाधिकरण्यतः 4.3.392cd
विषयापहृतेर्नो चेद्वेदान्तोक्त्या प्रमोत्थितिः 2.1.573ab
विषयाभावतस्तस्य प्रामाण्यं दुर्लभं यतः 4.3.157cd
विषयाभिलाषः कामः स्यान्न विशेषेऽस्ति कारणम् 1.5.110ab
विषयाभ्यासजास्वास्थ्यनुत्त्यर्थमिति चेन्मतम् SV 51ab
विषया विनिवर्तन्ते निराहारस्य देहिनः 4.4.386ab
विषयित्वमथैकस्य विषयत्वं च दीपवत् 1.4.582ab
विषयेऽवधृते यस्मादुपदेशोऽर्थवान्भवेत् 3.4.7cd
विषयेन्द्रियसंबन्धजो हि पाप्मासुरो यतः 1.3.214ab
विषयेन्द्रियसंबन्धविरहात्तदसंभवः 1.4.259cd
विषयेन्द्रियसंबन्धाद्यत्तु दुःखं सुखायते 3.9.155ab
विषयेन्द्रियादि यद्वस्तु नाविद्याव्यतिरेकि तत् 4.3.1106ab
विषये यदि कार्यत्वं कार्यावगमपर्वकम् SV 611cd
विषयेष्वनभिष्वङ्गाच्छिश्रुः प्राणोऽभिधीयते 2.2.9ab
विषयोऽकार्यरूपत्वात्स्वसिद्ध्यै यद्यपेक्षते SV 614cd
विषयोऽध्येषणाया हि चेतनावान्यतो मतः 1.3.131ab
विषयो न मृषाबुद्धिः परमार्थं विना यतः 1.3.61cd
विषयो ब्रह्मविद्याया योग्यः क इति चिन्त्यते 3.4.7ab
विषयौ द्वावुपन्यस्तौ विद्याविद्यात्मनोरिह 2.1.372ab
विषायतेऽमृतमपि यथा पथ्यं मुमूर्षतः 3.9.64ab
विष्टम्भकं पृथिव्यादेः सूक्ष्ममाकाशवत्स्थितम् 3.7.15ab
विसंवादनिरासेन सद्भावश्चात्मनः पुनः 4.3.6ab
विसंवादस्त्वभूत्तेषामुद्दिश्योद्गीथदेवताम् 1.3.327cd
विसंवादोऽपि नाशङ्क्यो नियोगार्थे यथा तथा SV 640ab
विस्तरस्तस्य वक्तव्य इत्यर्थो वा परा श्रुतिः 4.4.4cd
विस्तारितकुटुम्बं तं कस्मैचित्कश्चिदन्तिके 1.4.1819ab
विस्फारिताक्षः प्रत्यग्धीर्मानान्निर्वात्यथात्मनि 2.3.192cd
विस्फारिताक्षो जानाति शब्दाद्येव न तत्परम् 1.4.713ab
विस्फुलिङ्गा इति ज्ञेयं तस्य विक्षेपसंस्थितेः 6.2.106cd
विस्फुलिङ्गा इति ज्ञेयास्तस्मिन्नग्नौ यथोदिते 6.2.83cd

विस्फुलिङ्गाः सुखलवाः क्षणिकत्वैकहेतुतः 6.2.109cd
विस्फुलिङ्गाद्युपन्यासः क्षेत्रज्ञपरमात्मनोः 2.1.500ab
विस्फुलिङ्गा यथा चाग्नेर्जायन्तेऽग्निस्वभावकाः 2.1.393ab
विहन्त्युपनिषत्स्वार्थमिति निर्लज्जगीरियम् 2.1.568cd
विहापयति मन्त्रेण ऊरू पत्न्याः प्रयत्नतः 6.4.97ab
विहाय नातः प्रकृतं युक्तोऽप्रकृतसंग्रहः 1.5.21cd
विहायारूयायिकारूपं स्वेनैव वचसा श्रुतिः 3.9.94ab
विहायैतच्छरीरं वा गतो देशान्तरं पुमान् 2.1.197ab
विहितं प्रतिषिद्धं च कर्म मूलं तयोरपि 1.4.171ab
वीक्षते केवलं शुद्धं तत्त्वं ब्रह्म सनातनम् 4.4.721ef
वीक्षते योऽविलुप्ताक्षः स आत्मानन्यमानगः 4.4.467cd
वीक्ष्यतेऽतः पृथग्भावात्फलाच्च प्राक्प्रतीतितः SV 509cd
वीक्ष्यापन्नस्य तस्यैवं सामर्थ्यं ज्ञानकर्मणोः 1.4.1700ab
वीति तेन सदा प्राणो रमित्येवमिहोच्यते 5.14.12cd
वीप्सा व्याहन्यतेऽतश्च क्षणिकोक्तिर्न युज्यते 4.3.586ef
वीयाय न परज्ञानादतोऽरतिरपीष्यते 1.4.94cd
वीरश्चोक्थात्मवित्पुत्र उपासीनस्य जायते 5.15.3ab
वीरादिरससंयुक्तो दुन्दुभ्याघात उच्यते 2.4.280cd
वीर्यं वज्रोऽशनिरिति स्तनयित्नुरिहोच्यते 3.9.19ab
वीर्यवत्कर्महेतुत्वं व्याप्य देहे च वर्तनम् 1.5.147ab
वीर्यवद्दक्षिणं लोकेऽप्यङ्गं दृष्टं यतस्ततः 2.3.82ab
वृक्ष इव स्तब्धो दिवि तिष्ठत्येक- 2.5.123c
वृक्षव्यक्तिषु सर्वत्र रूपमस्ति किलेदृशम् 4.3.770cd
वृक्षोऽयं शिंशपेत्यत्र त्ववृक्षार्थविविक्तकम् 4.3.770ab
वृक्षोऽयं शिंशपेयं च भवेद्व्यवहृतिस्ततः 4.3.772ab
वृत्तयोऽतो निवृत्त्यर्थमन्तरित्युपदिश्यते 4.3.329cd
वृत्तिं च लभते कार्यं न स्वकारणतोऽन्यतः 4.3.1531ab
वृत्तिं सज्जनशंकरीं सुविमलां नानानयोद्द्योतिताम् 6.5.24b
वृत्तिः सा त्वपरिक्षीणा मनोवृत्तिरियं भवेत् 4.4.732cd
वृत्तिः स्यादुत्तरो ग्रन्थस्तत्र तेषां समन्वयात् 1.4.1067cd
वृत्तिक्षेपादसुरयमायुषश्च तदाश्रितेः 2.1.76ab
वृत्तिभिः संविभजय स्वान्संन्यसेदिति चोद्यते 2.4.45ab

वृत्तिस्तस्यैव सा ज्ञेया न स्वभावविपर्ययः 2.4.370cd
वृत्ती द्वे प्राप्नुतेऽतद्वान्स्वप्नजाग्रदवस्थयोः 1.4.642cd
वृत्तीनां प्राणपूर्वत्वाद्व्यपदेशाच्च तत्कृतात् 6.1.15ab
वृत्त्यानन्त्यान्मनोऽनन्तं शब्दादीनामनन्ततः 3.1.55ab
वृत्त्येह मुख्ययेत्येवं शक्यो वक्तुं जगत्यपि 2.3.146cd
वृथैवेमा ह्यविद्यैव सर्वाः संपादयिष्यति SV 267ef
वृथोपायपरीक्षा स्यादुत्तीर्णस्य प्लवे यथा SV 900cd
वृद्धिहानी यतो दृष्टे कर्मसाध्यस्य वस्तुनः 4.4.1184ab
वृन्तादेवाम्रपातोऽत्र वृन्तेनोदुम्बरं सह 4.3.1937ab
वृन्तेनाम्रस्य संबन्धो रसस्यापरिपाकतः 4.3.1933ab
वृन्ते निबध्यते येन रसेनापरिपाकतः 4.3.1932ab
वृषदंशादयो रात्रौ नेत्रगोचरसंगति- 1.4.86ab
वृषलो वृषली वैनां नोपहन्यात्कदा चन 6.4.67cd
वृष्टेरागमनं यद्वत्स्तनयित्नुः प्रबोधयेत् 2.5.109ab
वृष्टेश्च संभवस्तस्माल्लोकेऽस्मिन्सापि हूयते 6.2.100cd
वेत्ति नैकलमात्मानं प्रत्यङ्मोहाप्रबोधतः SV 212cd
वेत्ति ब्रह्म सुखमिति न तु ज्ञानघनात्मनि 3.9.197cd
वेत्ति यस्तत्त्वतो वाक्यात्तस्यैवेह कृतार्थता 2.1.271cd
वेत्थ प्रतिपदं किं वा न वेत्सीत्यभिधीयताम् 6.2.38cd
वेत्थेह ता यथा भय आवर्तन्ते प्रजा इति 6.2.32cd
वेद बाह्यं जगत्सर्वं स्वं चात्मानं तमस्विनम् 4.3.1316cd
वेदब्रह्मण आरभ्य सर्वेषामपि शाखिनाम् 6.5.20ab
वेदविद्भिर्महाप्राज्ञैः पुरुषैर्विनियुज्यते 3.7.42cd
वेदव्यासोऽपि च मुनिर्जगादेमं यथोदितम् 4.4.385ab
वेदशब्दानुरोध्यत्र तर्कोऽपि विनियुज्यते 2.4.216ab
वेदशास्त्रस्य कृत्स्नस्य तथा पूर्वमवादिषम् 1.4.412cd
वेदशास्त्रानपेक्षत्वं स्मृतिशास्त्रस्य चेन्मतम् 4.4.1151ab
वेदस्य ग्रहणं यद्वन्न स्यादध्ययनादृते 1.4.1678ab
वेदस्य सिद्धे प्रामाण्ये ह्यज्ञातार्थावबोधतः SV 890ab
वेदस्यैकार्थ्यतात्पर्यमेकवाक्यतयोदितम् SV 284cd
वेदात्तदेव साध्यत्वात्कार्यं नान्यत्ततः पृथक् SV 632cd
वेदात्मना कथं नाम परं ब्रह्म प्रपत्स्यते 6.5.14cd

वेदात्मनो रवेरेवं संप्रदायोऽयमागतः 6.5.17ab
वेदात्मापि तथा चाह प्रपन्नाय किरीटिने 4.3.1078ab
वेदाधीतिविधेस्तस्माद्विधिरत्र निरर्थकः SV 669cd
वेदानुवचनस्येह न तु तत्त्वावबोधिनः 4.4.1037ab
वेदानुवचनादीनां विनियोगोक्तियत्नतः SV 223ab
वेदानुवचनादीनामैकात्म्यज्ञानजन्मने SV 321ab
वेदानुवचनोक्त्यात्र नित्यं कर्मोपदिश्यते 4.4.1040ab
वेदानुवचनोक्त्यात्र वेदाध्ययनमन्वहम् 4.4.1028ab
वेदानुवचनोक्त्या वा कर्मकाण्डपरिग्रहः 4.4.1031ab
वेदान्तज्ञानतश्चेत्स्यात्स्वार्थोऽतोऽन्यः क इष्यते 2.1.569cd
वेदान्तवचसां स्वार्थे प्रामाण्यं न विहन्यते SV 574ab
वेदान्तवाक्यजं ज्ञानं यथावस्त्वेव मोहनुत् 4.4.877ab
वेदान्तविज्ञानसुनिश्चितार्थाः 3.5.148a
वेदान्तश्रवणं यत्नादुपायस्तर्क एव च 2.4.213cd
वेदान्तश्रवणादीनां न त्यागोऽतोऽत्र भण्यते 4.4.1238cd
वेदान्तश्रवणाद्यस्ति बहु व्याक्षेपकारि च 4.4.1236ab
वेदान्तानां तथारम्भो निष्फलः संप्रसज्यते 2.1.533cd
वेदान्तानां तथैकात्म्यश्रुतिबाधः स्फुटो भवेत् SV 898cd
वेदान्तानां प्रमाणत्वं नाक्षवद्वस्तुनीष्यते SV 445cd
वेदान्तानामतस्तस्मान्नान्यमर्थं प्रकल्पयेत् SV 160cd
वेदान्तानामतो वाच्यं कार्यार्थानुप्रवेशनम् SV 541ab
वेदान्तानाममानत्वं येन वा हेतुनोच्यते SV 562ab
वेदान्तार्थं यथायातमनूद्य श्रुतिरादरात् 4.4.974ab
वेदान्तार्थापवादाय नालं सातत्प्रमाणतः SV 244ab
वेदान्तार्थावबोधोऽपि तेनैवेह समापितः 1.4.798cd
वेदान्तेषु च सर्वेषु प्रत्यगात्मैव चोद्यते 2.1.437ab
वेदान्तेष्वत आनन्दो विचार्योऽयं प्रयत्नतः 3.9.167cd
वेदान्तेष्वप्यनाश्वासस्तथा च प्रसजेद्ध्रुवम् SV 161cd
वेदान्तैः कर्मकाण्डस्य परस्परविरोधतः 4.4.971cd
वेदान्तोक्तेः प्रमाणत्वे सति संबन्ध उच्यते SV 315ab
वेदामात्वप्रसक्तौ वा सर्वमात्मेतिवाक्यतः 2.4.309ab
वेदामात्वापनुत्त्यर्थं स यथेत्यागमः परः 2.4.309cd

वेदा यज्ञाश्च लोकाश्च नातोऽन्योऽर्थोऽवशिष्यते 1.5.296cd
वेदाहमिति मन्त्रश्च ज्ञानान्मार्गान्तरापनुत् 3.3.54cd
वेदाहमितिमन्त्रोक्तेस्तमेवेत्यवधारणात् 1.5.268ab
वेदेऽनुष्ठानतात्पर्यान्न लयो गम्यते क्वचित् SV 385ab
वेदेऽपि किं तथा तत्स्यान्न वातस्तद्विधीयते SV 765cd
वेदे तु वक्त्रभावत्वादभिप्रायाद्यसंभवः SV 404cd
वेदे तु सकलाक्षादिप्रमाणागोचरत्वतः SV 522ab
वेदेत्युपासनार्थत्वमस्याप्यभ्युपगम्यते 1.4.777cd
वेदे त्वपौरुषेयत्वात्साक्षात्स्वार्थे प्रमाणता SV 871cd
वेदे प्रैषास्तु ये दृष्टा अग्नीदग्नीनितीदृशाः SV 504cd
वेदे यतो न हेत्वादि लोकवत्स्याद्विवक्षितम् 2.5.7cd
वेदैनेन यतो वेद्यं ब्रह्म वेदस्ततो मतः 5.1.126cd
वेदोऽपि शुद्धमात्मानं सुखं मुख्यं प्रदर्शयन् SV 1016ab
वेदोऽयमिति चोक्तिः स्याद्यथोक्तोपासनं प्रति 5.1.128ab
वेदोऽसाविति विज्ञेयस्त्रय्यास्तत्र समाप्तितः 5.1.129cd
वेदोऽसीत्यत एवास्य नाम जातस्य कुर्वते 6.5.14ab
वेदोक्तं निखिलं पुंसः सत्त्वशुद्धिफलं स्मृतम् 1.4.8ab
वेदो हि सर्व एवायमैकात्म्यज्ञानसिद्धये SV 325ab
वेद्मीति यद्बलादात्थ न वेद्मीत्यपि यद्बलात् 3.4.80ab
वेद्यत्वेन न तद्भिन्नं पश्येदित्यभिधीयते 2.1.437cd
वेद्यानुरोधतो यस्मात्तद्विदो न्यायलक्षणम् 3.5.210ab
वेश्मतो ग्रामतो वासौ तत एव व्रजेद्ध्रुवम् 2.1.366cd
वेश्मतो बहिरात्मानं द्रक्ष्यतीति न तद्यतः 2.1.301cd
वैचित्र्याद्भावनादेर्वा त्रिविधं फलमुच्यते 1.3.310cd
वैदिकं साधनं ज्ञेयं ज्ञानकर्मस्वभावकम् 1.4.165cd
वैदिकं साधनं ज्ञेयं ज्ञानकर्मात्मकं पुरा 1.4,4ab
वैदिकं साधनं सर्वमविद्योत्थत्वकारणात् 1.4.5ab
वैदिकत्वादुपायेऽपि नृतन्त्रे व्यभिचारिता SV 640cd
वैदिकत्वेऽपि युक्तीनामागमार्थप्रबोधतः SV 817ab
वैदिकश्च प्रयासोऽयं सर्वः स्यात्तुषकण्डनम् 2.4.12cd
वैदूर्यवच्च हरितं केचिदाहुर्विपश्चितः 4.4.563cd
वैद्युतस्य तथैवाद्भिरुपकारः समीक्ष्यते 4.3.234cd

वैधर्म्येण च दृष्टान्तः प्रतिज्ञातार्थसिद्धये 4.3.578ab
वैनाशिकेन सत्त्वेन त्वयाभ्युपगमात्तयोः 4.3.655cd
वैयर्थ्यं कर्मकाण्डस्य निर्मूलत्वात्प्रसज्यते 4.4.936cd
वैयर्थ्यं च प्रयोगस्य व्यवहाराक्षमत्वतः SV 603cd
वैराग्यहेतावप्यस्मिन्नक्तो धर्मादिहेतुतः 2.4.72ab
वैराग्यहेतून्संसारे तस्माद्यत्नादियं श्रुतिः 2.4.73ab
वैराग्यातिशयार्थत्वाद्गौणं चेन्नाशनं मतम् 1.4.1754ab
वैराजं पदमेत्येवं यजमानः सुभावितः 1.3.232cd
वैराजं स्थानमासाद्य क्ष्मादिदेशविभागवान् 1.4.511ab
वैराजपदलिप्सुभ्यस्तेनासौ पुरुषाभिधः 1.4.49cd
वैराजपदसंप्रेप्सोर्यजमानमहाजनात् 1.4.48ab
वैरूप्यलक्षणो दोषः सत्येवं वः प्रसज्यते 2.3.61cd
वैलक्षण्यं निमित्ताच्चेन्न नैमित्तिकतुल्यतः 3.3.121ab
वैलक्षण्यमतः सिद्धं विकारिभ्योऽस्य साक्षिणः 4.3.443cd
वैलक्षण्यमुपास्तीनां भण्यते ब्रह्मबोधतः 4.1.24cd
वैलक्षण्यान्न युक्तेऽयं तुल्यसाधनता तयोः SV 23cd
वैविक्त्यान्न च मानादेरनन्यानुभवात्मनि 2.3.230ab
वैशब्दः स्मरणाय स्यादग्निस्तत्परिणामतः 6.2.76ab
वैशब्दः स्मृतये तस्य मृतिजन्मादिधर्मिणः 4.4.975cd
वैशब्दोऽवधृतौ ज्ञेयो ब्रह्मैव न तदन्यथा 1.4.1314ab
वैशारद्यं तथैव स्याद्विराजोऽपि महाधियः 1.4.78cd
वैश्वदेवं हि नामैतद्यदन्नमुपसाध्यते 1.5.27ab
वैश्वानरगिरास्याग्नेः सामान्येनाभिधानतः 5.11.2ab
वैश्वानरवरात्केचिदेवं व्याचक्षते स्फुटम् 2.5.74ab
वैश्वानरवरादत्र केचिदाहुर्महाधियः 3.2.41ab
वैश्वानरवरादेव न तु न्यायानुसारतः 4.3.1187cd
वैश्वानरात्तदात्मानं प्राप्तस्य हृदि तैजसम् 4.2.82ab
वैषम्यप्रतिपत्त्यर्थं प्रश्नस्य त्रासजन्मने 3.3.138ab
वैष्णवी खल्वियं मायेत्यपि लोकेऽपि गीयते 1.4.383cd
व्यक्तं ससाधनं कर्म ब्रह्मंभावेन पश्यतः 1.4.1707ab
व्यक्ततायाः क्षयो यस्तु कारणात्मतया श्रुतः 3.2.77ab
व्यक्तधर्मनिवृत्तिर्या कारणात्मतयेष्यते 4.3.590ab

व्यक्तयोऽन्त्या विशेषाः स्युस्तदसाधारणत्वतः 1.4.644cd
व्यक्तसूत्रात्मविद्यायाः परोऽप्येष समुच्चयः 1.4.1709cd
व्यक्तां स्वयमेवैति निमित्तं नास्त्यसंहृतम् 1.4.387cd
व्यक्तावस्थाथवैतेषां निषिद्धा कारणात्मनि 3.8.84ab
व्यक्ताव्यक्तविभागोऽयं सिद्ध्येदात्मन्यतद्वति 1.4.723ab
व्यक्तिभ्यो गोत्ववद्दृष्टं ब्रह्मत्वेऽस्य किमागतम् SV 856cd
व्यक्तिर्नियतकालैव जगतोऽव्यक्तरूपिणः 1.4.368ab
व्यक्तिश्चेयं सतो युक्ता नासतो घटते यतः 3.8.10cd
व्यक्तीभूतं प्रयुङ्क्ते क्ष्माबग्न्यन्तं साधनत्रयम् 1.4.365cd
व्यक्तौ च हेतुकार्याभ्यां कथं तर्हीक्ष्यतां परम् 1.4.711cd
व्यङ्ग्यत्वं घटवत्तावदवश्यम्भावि गम्यताम् 4.3.505cd
व्यङ्ग्यव्यञ्जकयोर्भेदस्तत्संबन्धात्पुरा यतः 4.3.466ab
व्यङ्ग्यव्यञ्जकयोर्यत्तु सादृश्यभ्रमकारणात् 4.3.465ab
व्यङ्ग्यव्यञ्जकवद्भेदः साक्षिसाक्ष्यार्थयोरिति 4.3.470cd
व्यङ्ग्यव्यञ्जकसंबन्धः प्रदीपघटयोरिव 4.4.333ab
व्यङ्ग्ये तु कार्ये वेदस्य सिद्धेऽर्थे मानता भवेत् SV 1030cd
व्यङ्ग्येष्वतिशयो दृष्टस्तिष्ठतो नु गतिर्यथा 4.3.64cd
व्यङ्ग्येष्वर्थेषु नावृत्त्या व्यञ्जको हन्ति तत्तमः 2.4.433ab
व्यङ्ग्याप्यपुनरुक्तत्वं न्यायमार्गसमाश्रयात् 3.5.14cd
व्यज्यते सर्वमेवेदं सत्त्वात्सर्वस्य वस्तुनः 4.4.331cd
व्यञ्जकं विरहय्यान्यत्साधनं कारकात्मकम् SV 1103ab
व्यञ्जकत्वाच्च मानानां सिद्धवस्तुप्रयोज्यता 3.9.184ab
व्यञ्जकत्वात्प्रमाणानां मेयाभिव्यक्तितोऽपरम् 1.4.424ab
व्यञ्जकत्वाविशेषत्वाद्रविचन्द्रप्रदीपवत् 4.3.514cd
व्यञ्जकस्य समायोगो वस्तुनो वस्तुनैव हि SV 922ab
व्यञ्जकस्य स्वभावोऽयं न प्रयोगमपेक्षते 2.4.433cd
व्यञ्जकानां हि सर्वेषां न स्वरूपातिरेकतः 4.3.64ab
व्यतिरिक्तत्वशुद्धत्वस्वयंज्योतिष्ट्वनित्यता 4.3.6cd
व्यतिरिक्तसुखार्था च न प्रवृत्तिर्विरागिणाम् SV 1009cd
व्यतिरिक्तस्य तस्यैवमुक्ताध्यात्मादिभेदतः 4.4.431ab
व्यतिरिक्तस्य मेयस्य स्यादात्मैवात्मनोऽनुमा 4.3.765cd
व्यतिरिक्तस्य विज्ञातुर्विज्ञानेऽस्ति प्रयोजनम् 4.3.1120cd

व्यतिरिक्तात्मविज्ञानव्यङ्ग्यत्वं घटवन्न सः 4.3.504ab
व्यतिरिक्तो न चेज्ज्ञाता भूतेभ्योऽभ्युपगम्यते 4.3.1121cd
व्यतिरेकं सतो नेदं लभतेऽनात्मकत्ववतः 3.8.16ab
व्यतिरेकतया कश्चिद्विशिनष्टीह मानवः SV 119cd
व्यतिरेकमतो मुक्त्वा मिथो व्याप्तिर्न सिध्यति 2.4.271cd
व्यतिरेकश्चितेः सिद्धो भूतेभ्यो जाग्रतोऽप्यतः 4.3.129cd
व्यतिरेकस्य सिद्धत्वादादेशोक्तेः पुरैव हि 2.3.214ab
व्यतिरेकस्वभावत्वान्नापि चात्मनि सिध्यति 4.4.160cd
व्यतिरेकादनुष्ठेयः पदार्थः कश्चिदिष्यते 1.4.810cd
व्यतिरेकान्वयाभ्यां वै कार्यं वस्त्वभिलप्यते 3.4.40ab
व्यतिरेकेण कर्त्रादेः सिद्धेर्नात्मत्वमस्त्यतः 3.4.110cd
व्यतिरेकेण तत्सिद्धेर्नापि चात्मानमन्वियात् 4.4.949cd
व्यतिरेके सदेवासदसद्वा तत्किमुच्यते 1.2.11cd
व्यतिरेकैकरूपस्य व्यतिरेको न लभ्यते 3.4.59cd
व्यतिरेकोऽपि नैकात्म्ययाथात्म्यादुपपद्यते 3.4.60cd
व्यतिरेकोऽप्यपह्नुत्या कार्यस्येह प्रसिध्यति 2.1.170cd
व्यतिरेको द्वयाप्राप्तेरसङ्गोऽयं पुमानपि 4.3.1086cd
व्यतिरेको न संसिध्येदात्मत्वं स्यात्तदात्मनः 4.3.1653cd
व्यतीतानेकजन्मोत्थवासनानामनन्ततः SV 459ab
व्यत्ययेनावबोद्धव्या प्रथमार्थे च सप्तमी 1.1.8ab
व्यनक्ति नात्मनात्मानं प्रदीपो घटवत्सदा 4.3.507ab
व्यपदिश्यमानमैकात्म्यं सत्यस्यात्मानमद्वयम् 2.3.250ab
व्यपदेशः पदार्थानां क्षणिकत्वात्स्वभावतः 4.3.681cd
व्यपदेशः स्वभावेन व्यपदेष्टुर्विनष्टतः 4.3.682cd
व्यपदेशक्षणाभावात्पूर्वदृष्टयैव संक्षयात् 4.3.683ab
व्यपदेशाद्घटेनैषामन्योऽन्याभाववद्ध्रुवम् 1.2.114cd
व्यपदेशाय नामैतन्न स्वं नामास्य विद्यते 2.3.252ab
व्यपदेशो विना योगमतीतानागतार्थयोः 4.3.684ab
व्यपास्तानर्थसंदर्भमात्मानमवगच्छतः SV 829ab
व्यपास्ताशेषसंसर्गकल्पनं ब्रह्म निर्भयम् SV 781cd
व्यपेततमसस्तत्त्वमागमापायसाक्षिणः 1.4.1412ab
व्यपेततमसस्तत्त्वमागमापायसाक्षिणः 2.4.442ab

व्यपेतसद्यशोवीर्यममेध्यं मेध्यतामगात् 1.2.208ab
व्यभिचारं न तद्याति पुरुषेच्छावशात्क्वचित् 3.9.126cd
व्यभिचारः स्रगादीनां प्रतीच्येवमनात्मनाम् 1.4.673cd
व्यभिचारस्वभावोक्ता प्रत्यगात्मैकसाक्षिका 4.3.1286cd
व्यभिचारहेत्वसद्भावादग्नेर्हेतुत्वमेत्यसौ 4.3.757cd
व्यभिचाराच्छराच्छृङ्गाच्छरस्योत्पत्तिरीक्ष्यते 4.3.756cd
व्यभिचारादकृत्स्नत्वं स्यादनात्मैकरूपिणाम् 1.4.664cd
व्यभिचारिणीष्वनात्मोत्थबुद्धिषु प्रत्यगात्मनि 2.1.235cd
व्यभिचारि ततोऽन्यद्यद्वस्त्वतोऽद्वैतमेव सत् 4.3.1691cd
व्यभिचारित्वसंसिद्धिहेतुरैकात्म्यनिष्ठिता 4.3.1287cd
व्यभिचारि न यत्रास्ति प्रमाणं सर्ववादिनाम् 1.4.1375ab
व्यभिचारिमतिष्वेवं बुद्धिरव्यभिचारिणी 4.3.1287ab
व्यभिचारिषु बोधेषु यो बोधोऽव्यभिचारवान् 2.4.266ab
व्यभिचारिषु सर्वेषु प्रत्यगात्मैकसाक्षिषु 4.3.198ab
व्यभिचारोऽपि चेन्नाग्नि ततो युक्तिरपोर्यते 2.1.258cd
व्यभिचारोऽस्य संसिद्धस्तद्विरुद्धात्मसाक्षिकः 1.4.659cd
व्यभिचारो न यस्यास्ति सर्वेषु व्यभिचारिषु 4.4.152ab
व्यभिचारो मिथो यद्वत्प्रमात्रादेः स्वसाक्षिकः 3.4.55ab
व्यर्थं देहाद्युपादानमस्य प्राप्नोत्यसंशयम् 2.1.300cd
व्यर्थताथ विशेषश्चेत्संप्राप्ता भिन्नमानता SV 815cd
व्यर्थतान्यार्थते नेह यथा तत्प्राक्प्रपञ्चितम् 2.1.540cd
व्यर्थोपनिषदारब्धिर्यदि भेदो भवेत्तयोः 3.5.22ab
व्यवधानं तमो यस्माद्घटोऽयमिति संविदः 1.2.104ab
व्यवधानं न चेहास्ति तद्भावाभावसाक्षितः 1.4.871cd
व्यवधानमात्राभावेन ब्रह्माप्येतीति शब्द्यते 4.4.307cd
व्यवधानान्तरं तस्मादन्यदप्यापतेत्तदा 1.2.107ab
व्यवधानान्तराभावात्किमर्थं नोपलभ्यते 1.2.90cd
व्यवधानापनुज्ज्ञानं न कर्माज्ञानहानिकृत् 3.3.91ab
व्यवस्थितत्वाल्लोकस्य राजपूर्वा स्थितिर्यथा 3.8.132cd
व्यवहर्तुमशक्तोऽयं देहो मृत्पिण्डवत्स्वयम् 4.3.18ab
व्यवहारः प्रतीचोऽस्य स समानाद्यतो वचः 4.3.377cd
व्यवहारः प्रमात्रादेः स्वप्नमायेन्द्रजालवत् 3.4.130cd

व्यवहारः श्रुतेर्ज्ञातः परमार्थैकवादिनः SV 652cd
व्यवहारपथं प्राप्ता स्वतःसिद्धात्मसाक्षिका 4.3.1293cd
व्यवहारस्य लोपोऽतः सर्वस्य स्यादसंशयः 1.4.1545cd
व्यवहारस्य संसिद्धेर्व्यर्थो कार्यप्रकल्पना SV 604cd
व्यवहाराः प्रतीयन्ते सत्तत्त्वं तेष्ववस्थितम् SV 967cd
व्यवहाराय कल्पन्ते भ्रान्तो भेदः सदैव तु SV 972cd
व्यवहाराय पर्याप्तो न त्वव्यक्तात्मना यतः 1.4.392cd
व्यवहारेषु वृद्धानां संबन्धस्तत्र गृह्यते SV 865cd
व्यष्टिः समष्टिरित्येवमण्डादन्तर्बहिश्च सः 3.3.167cd
व्यष्टितामेति तद्धीनः समष्टित्वेन तिष्ठति 1.2.159cd
व्यस्ता अपि तदात्मानो धर्माः स्युश्चेत्समस्तवत् 4.3.1657ab
व्यस्तात्मनासमस्तोऽपि कुर्यात्प्लुषिधियं गिरिः 1.6.86cd
व्यस्तानां पूर्वमुद्देशः समस्तानां त्विहोदितः 2.1.81ab
व्यस्तानि स्थानसंबन्धात्करणानि यतस्ततः 4.3.1945ab
व्यस्ताभेदात्समस्तोऽर्थो व्यस्तवन्न मनागपि 1.6.85ab
व्यस्ताभेदेऽपि चेत्कुर्यात्समस्तधिषणां बलात् 1.6.86ab
व्याकुर्वन्निति वाक्येन स्वतो ज्ञोऽपि तमोन्वयात् 1.4.494ab
व्याकृतं तदशेषेण श्रुत्या व्याख्यायि यत्पुरा 1.4.166cd
व्याकृतं नामरूपाभ्यां यद्यपीदं श्रुतौ श्रुतम् SV 1114ab
व्याकृताव्याकृतं कृत्स्नमात्मतामेति बोधतः 2.4.477cd
व्याकृताव्याकृतं विश्वं प्रत्यक्प्रत्ययमात्रकम् 1.4.28ab
व्याकृताव्याकृतात्मत्वनिराकरणसिद्धये 1.4.719ab
व्याकृताव्याकृतात्मभ्यां यो भिन्नोऽज्ञानहेतुतः 1.4.721ab
व्याकृताव्याकृतावस्थे जगतोऽस्य स्वभावतः 1.4.606ab
व्याकृतिर्योदिता पूर्वं तदज्ञानविजृम्भितम् 4.4.417cd
व्याख्यातं तदशेषेण वंशस्तत्र तदर्थभाक् 6.5.3cd
व्याख्यातं यत्नतः पूर्वमात्मज्ञानप्रसिद्धये 5.1.7cd
व्याख्याततत्वात्पदार्थानां चतुर्थेऽध्याय एव तु 4.5.7ab
व्याख्यातमेवं मानानां प्राक्सूतेरनुभूतितः 4.3.1289cd
व्याख्याता या पुरा यत्नाद्गायत्री जगदात्मिका 5.16.28ab
व्याख्यातायामविद्यायां तदुच्छित्तावथाधुना 2.1.19ab
व्याख्या तुल्यैव पूर्वेण वाक्येनोत्तरवाक्ययोः 5.16.14ab

व्याख्या तुल्यैव विज्ञेया सर्ववाक्येषु पूर्ववत् 2.1.59cd
व्याख्यातोऽप्यन्यथा त्वन्ये दृष्टान्तं व्याचचक्षिरे 4.3.1116cd
व्याख्यातो नियमोऽन्योऽन्यं फलसाधनसंगतेः 1.5.275cd
व्याख्यातो यः स वक्तव्यस्तदर्थः प्रश्न उत्तरः 3.6.20cd
व्याख्यातो योऽयमत्रात्मा स विज्ञानानुरोधतः 4.4.1307ab
व्याख्याथ पितृयाणस्य सम्यगारभ्यतेऽधुना 6.2.146cd
व्याख्यानमिदमेवात्र विदोषं दोषवत्परम् 1.5.281ab
व्याख्यानमेतत्सुधियां श्रद्दधाना उपासते 4.3.1566ab
व्याख्यानमेतदेवेति नातोऽन्यदवशिष्यते 4.3.1536cd
व्याख्यानमेतन्महतां न साधु प्रतिभाति नः 3.4.176ab
व्याख्यानादन्यथा चक्रुर्व्याख्यां वेदार्थनिश्चिताः 4.4.876cd
व्याख्यानाय तु वीत्यस्य त्वन्नं वै वीति भण्यते 5.14.11ab
व्याख्यानायाथ तस्यैव यज्ञेनेत्यादिरुच्यते 4.4.1031cd
व्याख्याने प्रस्तुते त्वस्मिन्नविद्यायाः समन्ततः 1.5.163ab
व्याख्यामधीयते धीरा न्यायागमबहिष्कृताम् 4.4.412cd
व्याख्यायते न दोषः स्यात्तत्र मानस्य संभवात् 4.4.590cd
व्याख्यायन्तेऽथ ते प्राणास्तथोपनिषदश्च याः 2.2.6cd
व्याख्या व्यरोधि तेनेयं दृष्टेरित्यत्र या कृता 3.4.186cd
व्याख्येयः सोऽपरेणापि राज्ञामाज्ञां विना क्वचित् 4.4.831cd
व्याख्येह संप्रवृत्तेयमश्वमेधकृतां पथः 3.3.150ab
व्याघातान्न प्रवृत्तिः स्यान्निषेधेऽथ विधौ तथा 5.1.107cd
व्याचक्षतेऽन्यथा चेदं वाक्यमेतद्यथोदितम् 4.3.1014cd
व्याचक्षतेऽन्यथैवेमं दृष्टान्तं केचिदात्मनः 2.5.67ab
व्याचक्षते परं ग्रन्थमेवंसंबन्धपूर्वकम् 1.4.1668ab
व्याचक्षते बलात्केचित्समस्तव्यस्तदर्शनम् 1.4.693cd
व्याचक्षते महात्मानः संप्रदायबलात्किल 1.4.950cd
व्याचक्षते महात्मानो यथा तदभिधीयते 1.4.792cd
व्याचक्षते हि व्याख्यानात्तच्चापीह विभाव्यते 4.3.1537cd
व्याचक्षाणो यतः स्वप्नं ज्ञानमात्रं प्रभाषते 4.3.1022ab
व्याचख्युर्मयटं ये तु विकारार्थे महाधियः 4.3.318ab
व्याचख्यौ गौतमः साक्षाद्गन्धर्वाल्लब्धवानिति 3.7.3cd
व्याचष्टेऽतः प्रयत्नेन ब्रह्मलोकगिरा स्वयम् 4.4.1297cd

व्याचष्टे कामसंभूतं पुत्रपौत्रादिविस्तरम् 1.4.1819cd
व्याचष्टे देवयानादिप्रतिपत्तौ क्रियैव सा 6.2.39cd
व्याचष्टे स्वयमेवार्थं तुर्यादिपदसंहतेः 5.16.20ab
व्याचिख्यासुरथेदानीं सूत्रार्थाञ्श्रुतिरञ्जसा 1.4.1068ab
व्याजहार फलावस्थो ह्यहमित्यात्मवाचकम् 1.4.42cd
व्याजह्रुरमरास्तस्मात्प्राण आयास्यसंज्ञितः 1.3.206cd
व्यात्ते मुखे हि तद्दीप्तिर्धूमः प्राणो मुखोत्थितेः 6.2.105ab
व्याधिग्रहग्रहाविष्टोऽसह्यं दुःखं समश्नुते 5.13.2ab
व्याधियोगोपघातादेरुन्मत्तः समपद्यत 2.1.507cd
व्याधैः परिगृहीतश्च व्याधोऽस्मीत्यभिमन्यते 2.1.508cd
व्याध्याद्युपप्लुतो यस्माद्वक्ति निर्विण्णमानसः 1.4.1034ab
व्यानवृत्तिरियं प्रोक्ता ह्युदानाख्यापि कीर्त्यते 1.5.147cd
व्यानोऽप्युदानमप्येति ह्युदानोऽपि समानगः 2.4.388cd
व्यापारः कर्तृतन्त्रः स्यात्तनुवाग्बुद्धिसाधनः 4.4.755ab
व्यापारः कर्तृतन्त्रो हि तमेतमितिशास्त्रतः 4.4.757ab
व्यापारो नास्त्यतः स्वप्ने देवतानां मनागपि 4.3.1132cd
व्यापित्वादात्मनोऽप्येवं युगपज्ज्ञातृतेति चेत् 4.3.1126ab
व्यापित्वाद्देवतानां स्यात्स्वप्नजाग्रदवस्थयोः 4.3.1128cd
व्यापित्वेऽप्यस्य यत्नो य आत्मनः कर्तृतां प्रति 4.3.1134cd
व्यापीनि तेषां सूक्ष्माणि शरीराणि महात्मनाम् 4.3.1861ab
व्याप्तं विश्वमनन्धकारमभवद्यस्य स्म शिष्यैरिदम् 6.5.25b
व्याप्तिः क्रियागुणाभ्यां या सा वीप्सेत्यभिधीयते 4.3.582cd
व्याप्तिः प्रवेशशब्देन भण्यते कारणात्मनः 1.4.628ab
व्याप्तिर्न घटते साक्षाद्धिमवद्विन्ध्ययोरिव 3.4.98cd
व्याप्तिर्मुख्यास्तु तत्रैव तथात्मानात्मनोरपि 1.4.632cd
व्याप्तिर्विशेषरूपेण व्यष्टिरित्यभिधीयते 3.3.168ab
व्याप्तिर्हिरण्यगर्भस्य बन्धज्ञानाय भण्यते 3.3.137cd
व्याप्तिस्तत्रैव मुख्या स्याद्रज्जुसर्पादिवस्तुवत् 3.4.97cd
व्याप्नुवन्त्यविभागेन भ्रान्तिं नो जनयेद्यथा 1.4.618cd
व्याप्नोति निष्क्रियः सर्वान्भानुर्दश दिशो यथा 2.1.336cd
व्याप्नोत्यनवशेषेण सर्पादीन्स्रगिवाखिलान् 1.4.739ab
व्याप्यव्यापकसंबन्धो न चाप्यक्षरवस्तुनि 3.8.108ab

व्याप्यव्यापितयान्योऽन्यं सर्वतःपरिमण्डलाः 3.6.16cd
व्याप्येव लक्षणं युक्तमन्यथा तदलक्षणम् 2.3.75ab
व्यामिश्रं यदि वा शुद्धं गोत्वं भेदेषु गम्यते 1.6.61ab
व्यावर्ततेऽस्वरूपं चेत्स्वरूपाद्वस्तु मानतः 4.3.1661ab
व्यावर्तते स्वभावश्चेदित्येतदतिदुर्घटम् 4.3.252ab
व्यावर्त्यभेदात्तद्भित्तेरेकं वस्तु द्विरुच्यते 1.4.1012cd
व्यावर्त्यभेदादाभाति भेदो ब्रह्मात्मशब्दयोः 4.4.527ab
व्यावर्त्यार्थातिरेकेण नात्मब्रह्मपदार्थयोः 4.4.848ab
व्यावर्त्येष्वपि तत्सक्तेर्न चापि लभतेऽवधिम् 4.4.661cd
व्याविद्धसत्यराशेः स्याद्विज्ञानात्मन एव तु 2.3.96ab
व्याविद्धाशेषसंसारो विमुक्तो ना विमुच्यते 2.4.5cd
व्यावृत्तं न विशेषश्चेत्यहो विद्याविचेष्टितम् 1.6.57cd
व्यावृत्तं यदि भिन्नेभ्यस्त्वयाभिन्नगिरोच्यते 1.6.57ab
व्यावृत्तः शुक्लपीतादेरन्धकारोऽनुभूयते 3.8.39ab
व्यावृत्तश्च प्रमात्रादेः सिद्धः साक्षी सुषुप्तगः 3.4.102cd
व्यावृत्तसर्वबाह्यार्थप्रीतेस्तन्मुक्तिकामिनः 1.4.1052ab
व्यावृत्ताशेषमात्रादेरनन्यानुभवात्मना 3.9.210cd
व्यावृत्तिरनुवृत्तिर्वा सर्वस्यैवास्य वस्तुनः 4.3.1701ab
व्यावृत्तिविधिरूपाभ्यां सुषुप्तिरनुभूयते 3.8.38cd
व्यावृत्तेः स्यादवाक्यार्थः साक्षान्नस्तत्त्वमर्थयोः 3.5.186cd
व्यावृत्तेरन्यतोभावमात्रायाः केनचित्क्वचित् 2.1.594cd
व्यावृत्तेर्धर्मधर्मित्वं न तयोरुष्णशीतवत् 4.3.1697cd
व्यावृत्तेर्न तु भिन्नेषु ब्रह्मता स्याद्घटादिवत् 1.4.1286cd
व्यावृत्तेश्चाप्यवस्तुत्वान्न सद्वस्तूपलम्भनैः 4.4.664ab
व्यावृत्तोऽयमिति ज्ञानं किं कुम्भे किं ततोऽन्यतः 4.3.1702ab
व्यावृत्त्यनुगमाभावात्सर्वं तदभवत्ततः 1.4.1414cd
व्यावृत्त्यनुगमौ यस्माद्द्वितीये सति वस्तुनि 1.4.1415ab
व्यावृत्त्यर्थानि नैतानि पुत्रादीनि यथा तथा 1.5.340ab
व्युत्तिष्ठन्त्येषणाभ्यस्ते तद्विरुद्धात्मकत्वतः 3.5.119cd
व्युत्थानं तद्बलादेव न तु यत्स्याज्ज्वरादिवत् 3.5.113cd
व्युत्थानं यस्य यस्य स्यात्स स व्युत्थातुमर्हति 3.5.91cd
व्युत्थानमिति तामाहुर्व्युत्थानज्ञा महाधियः 3.5.125cd

व्युत्थानशब्दो लोकेऽपि प्रसिद्धोऽत्र तथैव सः 3.5.126cd
व्युत्थानसाधना विद्येत्ययमर्थो भवेत्तदा 3.5.106cd
व्युत्थानहेत्वसद्भावात्तदाकर्ता सुषुप्सति 2.1.219cd
व्युत्थाने चोदनापेक्षा नाधिकारोपमर्दतः 3.5.104cd
व्युत्थापितमनूद्याह सर्वमात्मेति नः श्रुतिः 2.4.104cd
व्युत्थाप्य निखिलां प्रीतिं प्रतीच्येव निवेशयेत् 1.4.1045cd
व्युत्थाप्य नेति नेतीति परं ब्रह्म प्रदर्शितम् 2.4.8cd
व्युत्थाप्य ब्रह्मणो द्वैतं तदनूद्य श्रुतिः पुनः 4.3.1660ab
व्युत्थाप्यानात्मनः पश्येत्प्रविश्यात्मानमात्मना 4.4.1201ef
व्युत्थाय कर्मणः कृत्स्नान्मोक्षाशंसेति चेन्मतम् 1.4.1723cd
व्युत्थाय कारणात्कार्यात्तत्तत्त्वज्ञानवर्त्मना 1.4.722ab
व्युत्थाय न सतो यस्माद्वस्तु संभावनामपि 4.3.1692ab
व्युत्थाय ब्राह्मणा यत्नाद्भिक्षाचर्यं चरन्ति हि 3.5.87ef
व्युत्थाय स्वप्रधानः सन्स्वप्नमायां समीक्षते 4.3.860cd
व्युत्थायाख्यायिकातो नः श्रुतिरेवेदमब्रवीत् 4.3.1827ab
व्युत्थायाख्यायिकारूपाच्छ्रुतिः स्ववपुषाधुना 1.3.150ab
व्युत्थायातो यथोक्ताभ्य एषणाभ्यो निरेषणः 3.5.168ab
व्युत्थायाथ विदित्वेति पौर्वापर्यं यदेष्यते 3.5.106ab
व्युत्थायानर्थनिःसारसाधनान्यनुमार्गति 1.4.11cd
व्युत्थायैवैषणाभ्योऽतः प्रत्यग्ज्ञानं समाश्रयेत् 1.4.1836cd
व्युत्थितस्याखिलाद्बोज्यान्नाममात्रावशेषिणः 1.4.1757cd
व्युत्थितस्यैव कर्मभ्यो मुक्त्यभ्युपगमत्वतः 1.4.1724cd
व्युत्थितात्मापि चात्मानं पश्यन्नेवान्यदीक्षते 2.4.106cd
व्युत्थिता हि सतो भेदाः प्रत्यक्षागमलिङ्गतः 4.3.1690ab
व्युत्पत्तिफलमाश्रित्य तमोऽसंभव उच्यते 1.4.1304ab
व्युत्पत्तिरियमेवात्र तात्पर्यस्य समीक्षणात् 2.1.193ab
व्युत्पत्तेः प्राक्तमस्त्वित्वं तत्साक्षित्वेऽपि गम्यते 1.4.1304cd
व्युत्पत्तेः प्रागविज्ञातं तथैवानुभवाश्रयात् 1.4.1303cd
व्युत्पत्तेः प्रागविज्ञातः सर्वाज्ञानादिसाक्ष्यपि SV 1090cd
व्युत्पत्तेः साधुलोकस्य न कश्चिदपि दित्सति 2.1.146cd
व्युत्पत्त्या न च संबन्धः क्रियते ह्यर्थशब्दयोः SV 877ab
व्युत्पाद्यते यदा साक्षाद्यथोक्तन्यायवर्त्मना 2.4.128ab

व्यूह्यात्मानं जगत्त्वेन स्वात्मन्येव समूहति 2.4.385cd
व्येति यस्मात्ततोऽशेषं देवानां स जयः स्मृतः 1.3.119cd
व्येव त्वेति प्रतिज्ञाया अर्थवत्त्वं तथा भवेत् 2.3.155ab
व्येव त्वेति प्रतिज्ञार्थो नापि चाविष्कृतो भवेत् 2.3.219cd
व्येव त्वेति प्रतिज्ञेयं तदा स्यात्सफलोदिता 2.3.211cd
व्योमकार्ष्ण्यादिवत्तज्जं संभावयति न स्वतः 1.4.298cd
व्योमतत्पुष्पयोर्न स्यात्सिद्धात्यन्ताप्रसिद्धयोः SV 629cd
व्योमवद्व्यापि सद्ब्रह्म सर्वतोऽनवखण्डितम् 5.1.37cd
व्रजत्येष यथा रज्जुरज्ञाता सर्परूपताम् 4.4.764cd
व्रजेच्छाकटिकेनेह देशान्तरमधिष्ठितम् 4.3.1913ab
व्रजो मार्गो हि गर्भस्य सार्गलोऽयं कृतः पुरा 6.4.110cd
व्रणं पूर्वकृतं दृष्ट्वा देहः किं नोच्यते ध्रुवः 4.3.132cd
व्रतस्थां नोपहन्यात्तामभीप्सितफलाप्तये 6.4.68cd
व्रीहिपात्रादिवन्नापि मोक्षः संस्कार्य इष्यते 3.3.118ab
व्रीहिशब्दस्य हि व्रीहिस्वरूपे तु निरर्थकम् SV 429ab
व्रीह्यादिविषयं यद्वद्यत्नेनापि निरूपितम् SV 760ab
शक्तयः करणान्यत्र गृह्यन्ते कारणात्मना 2.1.227ab
शक्तयः सन्ति भूयस्यस्तयोरपि मतं यदि 4.3.1786ab
शक्तस्तद्विषयं ज्ञानं कर्तुं वाक्यार्थवित्तये 4.4.859cd
शक्तितत्कार्ययोर्यस्माद्व्यतिरेको न विद्यते SV 60ab
शक्तिमत्कारकं चेत्स्यात्स्यात्कार्यं शक्तिवत्सदा 4.3.1445ab
शक्तिमात्रात्मना स्थानं कार्याणां यत्स्वकारणे 2.4.398ab
शक्तिरूपेण संबन्धो निमित्तानामपीष्यते SV 66ab
शक्तिशक्तिमतोरैक्यं तयोर्भेदात्र युक्तितः 4.3.1782ab
शक्तिशक्तिमतोरैक्याद्द्वैतमिति भण्यते 1.6.48cd
शक्तिस्वरूपहाने च शक्तिमद्रूपनिह्नुतिः SV 63cd
शक्तीनां नियमः शक्याच्छक्यानां चापि शक्तितः 4.3.1447ab
शक्तेरनभिधेयत्वात्तद्व्यापारोऽपि नेष्यते SV 636ab
शक्तेरिति न तद्युक्तं शक्तितद्धेतुसंभवात् SV 65cd
शक्त्यवस्थं यतो वस्तुहेत्वपेक्ष्यैति विक्रियाम् 4.3.1595cd
शक्त्यवस्थानि वस्तूनि योग्यहेतोरसंभवात् 4.3.1599ab
शक्त्यवस्थानिषेधोऽयं क्रियते त्वक्षरात्मनि 3.8.84cd

शक्त्यात्मनाप्यवस्थानं कारणात्मनि युज्यते 4.4.498ab
शक्त्युत्पत्त्यभ्युपेतौ च कारणं स्यादशक्तिमत् 2.1.404ab
शक्नुवन्ति न कर्माणि सर्वकामसमापनम् 6.2.7ab
शक्यं फलान्तरं वक्तुं येनासावर्थवान्भवेत् 1.4.1247cd
शक्यं वैश्वानरवरात्प्रवक्तुं न तु मानतः 1.4.490cd
शक्यते न निषेद्धुं च प्रत्यक्षाद्याश्रितत्वतः 2.3.217ab
शक्यते नाभिधानेन ह्यसद्वस्तु निरुच्यते 1.2.15cd
शक्यते प्रतिनिर्देष्टुं प्रमाणागोचरत्वतः 3.4.79cd
शक्यानामपि सद्भावः शक्तिवत्सर्वदा यतः 4.3.1445cd
शक्या सुनिपुणेनापि कर्तुं तद्व्याप्तिः कुतः 1.4.955cd
शक्यो विधायिनोऽन्येषां पदानां वक्तुमन्वयः SV 601cd
शङ्कमानात्मनो नाशं मैत्रेयी पतिमादरात् 2.4.445cd
शङ्क्यतेऽपि न वेदे तु कार्यं वाच्यमिति स्थितम् SV 503cd
शङ्क्यमानस्य मानस्य तुल्या सापेक्षता यतः SV 680cd
शतकृत्वो मनुष्याणामानन्दो गुणितस्तु यः 4.3.1850ab
शतह्रदादर्शाद्यर्था बहवस्ते प्रसिद्धितः 2.1.72cd
शताधिकोऽयमानन्दः पूर्वस्मादुत्तरः क्रमात् 4.3.1858cd
शतानि दश चैकं च चत्वारिंशत्तथाष्ट च SV 1136ab
शतानि सप्त संख्याताः प्रयोगार्धाश्च विंशतिः 1.5.65cd
शतायुरेव भवति म्रियते नापमृत्युना 2.1.76cd
शतृतृजन्तवचसा तथात्मा भण्यते ध्रुवः 4.3.1442cd
शतृतृजन्तश्रवणाद्दृष्टिश्चेत्स्यात्सकर्तृका 4.3.1439ab
शत्रुणा कामितो योऽर्थो मा प्रापत्तमसाविति 5.16.72ab
शत्रुनामगृहीत्यर्थमसाविति पदं त्विह 5.16.71ab
शपथस्यापि मानत्वमस्मादेव तु कारणात् 1.3.330cd
शप्स्यामि त्वामिति ह्युक्त्वा वशं तामानयेत्पतिः 6.4.34ab
शब्दज्ञानातिवर्तित्वख्यापनायेतिशब्दनम् 1.4.938cd
शब्दप्रधानं विज्ञानं प्रमातृव्याप्तौ पुरा 4.4.746ab
शब्दप्रवृत्तिहेतूनां प्रत्यगात्मन्यसंभवात् 2.3.194ab
शब्दप्रवृत्तिहेतूनां प्रत्यगात्मन्यसंभवात् 4.4.690ab
शब्दप्रवृत्तिहेतूनां साक्षाद्ब्रह्मण्यसंभवात् 2.3.254cd
शब्दप्रवृत्तिहेतूनामैकात्म्येन समाप्तितः 2.3.241ab

शब्दप्रवृत्तेः सिद्धे च न नियोगस्य संभवः SV 447cd
शब्दमात्रप्रमोत्थं तु न मानं वस्त्वसंश्रयात् 4.2.107cd
शब्दमात्रादसंसिद्धेरनपेक्षत्वहानतः SV 854cd
शब्दमात्रानुसारेण वेदे तात्पर्यधीर्यतः SV 407cd
शब्दयोः सामयोस्तस्मात्प्राणः सामाभिधीयते 1.3.302cd
शब्दवृत्तमथेदानीं यथावदभिधीयते 1.4.736cd
शब्दशक्तिवशात्तद्वत्क्रियादेरपि वीक्ष्यताम् SV 505cd
शब्दशक्तेरचिन्त्यत्वादात्मत्वाद्बोधरूपिणः 4.4.698ab
शब्दशक्तेरचिन्त्यत्वाद्विभ्रमस्तं मोहहानतः 1.4.860cd
शब्दश्च गम्यते स्पष्टस्तदार्थः प्रविविच्यते SV 498cd
शब्दसामर्थ्यतो यस्मात्तादर्थ्यं नान्यहेतुकम् SV 594cd
शब्दसामर्थ्यनियमो लोकादेवावगम्यते SV 480ab
शब्दस्यार्थेन संबन्ध आदिमत्ता न शङ्क्यते SV 874cd
शब्दस्याल्पीयसोऽत्यागे तत्र तावदिहोच्यते 4.4.970ab
शब्दस्यैवात्मनो जन्म चतुर्थे प्रतिपादितम् 4.5.8ab
शब्दस्वभाव एवैष संसृष्टार्थावबोधनम् 1.4.805ab
शब्दाः सन्तः कथं तेऽर्था ह्यर्हन्ति भवितुं क्वचित् 4.3.775cd
शब्दाच्च ज्ञायतेऽज्ञातसंबन्धादिति चित्रता SV 496cd
शब्दात्प्रवर्तनाबुद्धौ रागादिर्न च शङ्क्यते SV 487ab
शब्दादवाप्तमभयं न तु साक्षाच्चकार तत् 4.2.100cd
शब्दादात्मनि संसिद्धे पूर्वोक्तन्यायतो न त्र SV 1056ab
शब्दादिखचितं साक्षात्स्मृतिस्वप्नगतं मनः 4.3.271ab
शब्दादिगुणहीनत्वात्प्रत्यक्त्वासंहतत्वतः 4.3.104ab
शब्दादिग्राहिणी वृत्तिः स्वैरासङ्गात्मपाप्मभिः 1.3.217ab
शब्दादिप्रकृतीन्येव कार्याणि करणानि च 4.4.1087ab
शब्दादिबडिशाकृष्टचेतसः प्रत्यगीक्षणे 1.4.1026ab
शब्दादिबाह्यसंबन्धे विभागे च तथा धियः 2.4.145ab
शब्दादिभिर्हि घ्राणादेर्नोपकारः समीक्ष्यते 4.3.138ab
शब्दादिभोगसिद्ध्यर्थं श्रोत्राद्या ज्ञानशक्तयः 2.4.368ab
शब्दादीनिह लोकेऽतो दृष्ट्यादेर्ज्ञानवाच्यता 4.3.1770cd
शब्दादेव तु तज्ज्ञानादवृक्षार्थमतिर्भवेत् 4.3.789cd
शब्दादेव हि कार्यार्थप्रतिपत्तिर्न लोकतः SV 485cd

शब्दाद्यगोचरोऽर्थोऽतो लक्षणापाश्रयाच्छ्रुतौ	SV 704ab
शब्दाद्यदि तदेवेदमायातं पूर्वदूषणम्	SV 665ab
शब्दाद्यनात्मविज्ञानभावाभावौ स्वभावतः	4.4.654cd
शब्दाद्यन्नवहाः सूक्ष्माः श्रोत्रादिकरणाश्रयाः	4.2.55ab
शब्दाद्यर्थोपलब्धारः कर्तारश्च पृथक्पृथक्	2.1.590ab
शब्दाद्यर्थोपलब्धारः कर्तारश्चापि कर्मणाम्	2.1.596cd
शब्दाद्याकारतां यान्ति संशयाद्यात्मतां तथा	4.4.931ab
शब्दाद्याकारता तस्मात्कादाचित्की धियो भवेत्	4.4.653cd
शब्दानुमानयोर्नातः शब्दप्रथमतेष्यते	SV 741cd
शब्दानुरोधतस्तावदीदृगत्रोपजायते	2.4.131ab
शब्दान्नानाविधान्कुर्वद्गुरुभारप्रपीडनात्	4.3.1912cd
शब्दान्निद्रामपास्याथ यथावस्त्ववबोध्यते	4.4.696cd
शब्दाभिन्नं पुरा ज्ञानं शब्दरूपानुरञ्जितम्	4.4.748ab
शब्दार्थत्वे हि सर्वेषामादानायैव धीर्भवेत्	SV 600ab
शब्दार्थश्चाकृतिर्यस्मान्नातो नाम विनश्यति	3.2.39ab
शब्दार्थापोहयोर्लिङ्गं ज्ञेया गमकगम्यता	4.3.773ab
शब्दार्थारोपणेनैव सविकल्पधियो जनिः	4.3.772cd
शब्दार्थोपाधयो ह्येते पुरुषाशयपातिनः	SV 502ab
शब्देन ज्ञाप्यते यद्वत्तथैव यदि युक्तिभिः	SV 815ab
शब्दोऽयं बहुधा भिन्नो नामैव परमात्मजम्	4.5.9ab
शब्दोऽस्ति न प्रियः कश्चिदप्रियो वा स्वतस्तथा	2.4.78ab
शब्दोच्चारणशक्तं हि ननु वागिन्द्रियं मतम्	1.5.133ab
शब्दो लिङादिशून्योऽपि ह्यविज्ञातार्थबोधकः	1.4.856ab
शमादिमान्यथातत्त्वमथात्मानं समीक्षते	4.4.758cd
शमादिसाधनो भूत्वा महिम्नः पदविद्भवेत्	4.4.1193ab
शमादिसाधनो विद्यादन्वयव्यतिरेकतः	4.4.1201cd
शमादीन्येव विद्यायाः साधनानि यतस्ततः	4.4.1071ab
शमाद्यङ्गान्वितः सर्वमात्मेतिस्तुतिभूषणः	SV 763ab
शमाद्युत्पत्तये नान्यद्बुद्धिशुद्धेरपेक्ष्यते	1.3.99ab
शर आसीदिति गिरा शक्त्यवस्था विवक्ष्यते	1.2.150ab
शरदि व्योमवन्नीलमित्याहुरपरे जनाः	4.4.562cd
शरबर्हिः प्रयत्नेन विद्वान्नोषसमन्वितः	6.4.54cd

शरीरं जायते साक्षाद्येन शारीर उच्यते 3.9.46cd
शरीरं नेमिवच्चैतद्देवताद्यरवज्जगत् 2.5.69ab
शरीरं पाप्मनां कार्यं धर्माधर्मात्मनामिदम् 4.3.818ab
शरीरं भस्मसाद्यातु मर्त्यत्वं ह्येतदाश्रितम् 5.17.12cd
शरीरं यः समुत्तस्थौ स भोक्तेत्यवसीयताम् 2.1.156cd
शरीरं व्याहृतिमयं कल्प्यतेऽक्षिरविस्थयोः 5.7.1ab
शरीरकार्यसंस्थंस्य वर्ण्यतेऽध्यात्मरूपकम् 1.5.95cd
शरीरग्रहणाशक्तेरव्यूढकरणत्वतः 4.3.1954cd
शरीरज्वरमन्वेष संज्वरेद्ब्रह्म सन्कथम् 4.4.613ab
शरीरत्वाविशेषत्वात्प्रतिवादिशरीरवत् 2.1.608cd
शरीरत्वाविशेषत्वात्प्रतिवादिशरीरवत् 3.5.19cd
शरीरदेशसंस्थत्वान्न तु प्रत्यङ्ङसंहतेः 4.3.1917cd
शरीरपातः कस्मान्नेत्येतच्चाप्यपहस्तितम् 1.4.1546cd
शरीरमस्याधानं स्याच्छरीरेऽवस्थितो यतः 2.2.11ab
शरीरमिति वाक्येन जायमानविशेषणम् 4.3.810ab
शरीरमेतद्वैराजं देवताकरणं महत् 3.3.144ef
शरीरविषयस्तस्मादात्मेत्यत्राभिधीयते 1.6.26cd
शरीरस्थोऽपि कौन्तेय न करोति न लिप्यते 4.3.1079cd
शरीराद्देशभेदेन भासन्तेऽर्था घटादयः 4.3.702cd
शरीरान्तमिदं रूपं साधिभूताधिदैवतम् 4.3.1280ab
शरीरारम्भकस्यैवं मुक्तिः सिद्धान्तरात्मनः SV 42ab
शरीराश्रयिणं प्राणं यतो वागादयः श्रिताः 2.2.12ab
शरीरेऽभ्याहितः प्राणो मूर्ध्नि प्रत्याहितस्तथा 2.2.8cd
शरीरेन्द्रियकामादेरसतस्तद्वदेव तु 4.3.1024cd
शरीरेन्द्रियबुद्ध्यादेः प्रत्येकं स्यादनेकता 2.1.604cd
शरीरेन्द्रियसंघात आत्मत्वेन गतां धियम् 1.4.563ab
शल्यविद्धमृतौ कस्य फलं स्यादिति कथ्यताम् 4.3.712cd
शल्यविद्धस्य तच्छल्यनिष्कर्षोत्थं सुखं फलम् 4.3.712ab
शशयः सशयो ज्ञेयः शयश्च फलमुच्यते 6.4.121cd
शशशृङ्गादिकल्पस्य घटस्य स न युज्यते 1.2.120cd
शश्वद्वै रेतस इति तथा च श्रुतिशासनम् 2.3.71cd
शाकल्यस्यापि संयात उपवादैकदोषतः 3.9.128cd

शान्तत्ववर्तुलत्वाभ्यां विस्फुलिङ्गसमत्वतः 6.2.103ab
शान्तत्वाच्च दिशोऽङ्गाराः समिद्धि परिणामतः 6.2.82ab
शान्ताः संन्यासिनो यान्ति तस्मै मोक्षात्मने नमः 1.4.1770cd
शान्ताः संन्यासिनो यान्ति तस्मै मोक्षात्मने नमः 4.4.592cd
शान्तिवर्तुलतोऽङ्गाराः पर्जन्यशिखिनोऽशनिः 6.2.99ab
शान्तेषु सर्वज्योतिःषु पूर्वोक्तेष्वस्य देहिनः 4.3.72ab
शान्तोऽथ विशदो व्यापी स्याद् व्योम्नोऽथ प्रधानतः 2.4.359cd
शान्तो दान्त इति तथा सर्वत्यागपुरःसरम् SV 216ab
शान्तो भिक्षुस्तपस्वीति तत्प्रयोगसमीक्षणात् 4.4.1206cd
शाब्दमात्रपरिज्ञाने राज्ञो युक्तं प्रभाषितुम् 4.2.106cd
शाब्दविज्ञानमात्रेण नाचार्यत्वे नियुज्यते 4.2.105ab
शाब्दविज्ञानमानेन प्रज्ञामैकात्म्यलक्षणाम् 4.4.835ab
शाब्दी वा प्रतिपत्तिः स्याद्व्युत्थानादेः प्रयोजिका 3.5.105ab
शारीरः पार्थिवेंऽशेऽत्र देवोऽध्यात्माभिमानवान् 3.9.40cd
शारीरप्रमुखास्तद्वदष्टौ ज्ञेया यथोदिताः 3.9.109ab
शारीरवचसा चात्र लिङ्गमेवाभिधीयते 4.3.1917ab
शालग्रामो हरेर्यद्वत्सर्वानर्थापहारिणः 5.1.124cd
शाल्याद्युद्वहनादि स्यादुत्पित्सोर्वा जनिस्तथा 4.3.617ab
शाश्वतीश्च समा नित्या अस्मिंल्लोके वसत्यसौ 5.12.6ab
शास्तर्यसति तत्कर्मफलवैचित्र्यवेदिनि 3.8.145ab
शास्त्रं त्वादित्यवत्साक्षात्प्रकाशयति तान्सदा 2.1.585cd
शास्त्रं मुख्यार्थमेव स्याद्विध्यर्थं यदि कल्प्यते 6.1.37ab
शास्त्रं विरक्तचित्तान्वा न प्रवर्तयितुं क्षमम् 2.1.582cd
शास्त्रं सापेक्षमेवं स्यात्स्वतः प्रामाण्यवर्जनात् SV 809cd
शास्त्रन्यायादितोऽन्योऽपि पक्षोऽथ प्रतिपाद्यते 2.1.444cd
शास्त्रमात्रनिमित्तत्वान्नित्यानां नैवमिष्यते 1.3.92ab
शास्त्रमावर्त्यमानं हि स्वभावं नैव मुञ्चति SV 826ab
शास्त्रस्वभावजज्ञानकर्मसंस्कारहेतुतः 1.3.20ab
शास्त्राचार्यप्रसादात्तु क्षपिताशेषपाप्मनः 4.4.616ab
शास्त्राचार्यमतिर्वात्र विज्ञायेत्यभिधीयते 4.4.842ab
शास्त्राचार्यव्यपेक्षत्वात्परतन्त्रैव तन्मतिः 4.4.843ab
शास्त्राचार्यात्मतो निष्ठां नीत्वात्मप्रत्ययं यतिः 3.5.175ab

शास्त्राचार्यादयो यद्वन्मोहोत्थत्वान्न वस्तुतः 1.4.605ab
शास्त्राचार्यादितद्धेतोरसत्त्वात्तदसंभवः 1.4.71cd
शास्त्राचार्यादिना नर्ते ज्ञातुं वस्त्विह शक्यते 2.5.128cd
शास्त्राचार्यानुभवनैर्हेतुभिश्च समर्थितः 2.5.16ab
शास्त्राचार्योक्तितः पश्चादनुवित्तो मयैव च 4.4.550ab
शास्त्राच्च वस्तुनोऽलाभात्कार्यं किंविषयं भवेत् SV 840cd
शास्त्राच्छ्रवणमात्रेण कार्याच्चानुभवो यदि SV 844ab
शास्त्रात्कथं च तत्सिद्धिर्याथात्म्यानवबोधकात् SV 843ab
शास्त्राद्यारम्भानर्थक्यदोषश्चापि प्रसज्यते 1.4.1106ab
शास्त्रानारम्भदोषोऽपि नैवास्मान्प्रति ढौकते 1.4.1305cd
शास्त्रान्तरेष्वपि तथा नातः स्वातन्त्र्यखण्डनम् 3.1.7cd
शास्त्रारम्भो वृथैव स्यात्स्वप्ने को नापराध्यति 4.3.1006cd
शास्त्रार्थं स्मारितः सोऽथ राज्ञोपैमीत्यथोचिवान् 6.2.67ab
शास्त्रार्थः सूत्रितस्तावदात्मेत्येवेति यत्नतः 1.4.1590ab
शास्त्रार्थस्तत्प्रयोगश्च यदा त्वन्योऽन्यसंश्रयात् 1.4.1629ab
शास्त्रार्थस्य समाप्तेश्च मुक्तिः स्यात्तावता मितेः 1.4.1539ab
शास्त्रार्थानिश्चयो दोषः स चानिष्टः प्रसज्यते 1.4.1517cd
शास्त्रीयलौकिकज्ञानाविशेषग्रहसिद्धये 1.5.18ab
शास्त्रीयेणेतरत्तीर्त्वा विद्ययामृतमश्नुते 1.4.1766cd
शास्त्रीयो लौकिकश्चातो विरोधोऽत्र न शङ्क्यते 3.5.50cd
शास्त्रेऽस्मिन्वस्तुनिष्ठेऽपि प्रसंख्यानविधिं विना SV 786ab
शास्त्रेणानभिधाने तु नियोगेऽपि न युज्यते SV 782ab
शास्त्रेणोक्ता शरीरेऽस्मिन्वृत्तिः प्राणस्य जीवनम् 6.1.8ab
शास्त्रेणोत्सर्गतः प्राप्ता तीर्थे सापोद्यते यथा 5.1.65cd
शास्त्रैकमानतो ब्रह्म द्रष्टव्यं प्रत्यगात्मना 4.4.674cd
शास्त्रैकहेतुर्देवः स्यात्तयोः स्पर्धा विरोधतः 1.3.112cd
शास्त्रोक्तज्ञानयुक्तानां कर्मणां ज्ञानतस्तथा 1.3.1ab
शास्त्रोपदिष्टमैकात्म्यं शक्तो योगेन वीक्षितुम् 4.4.588cd
शास्त्रोपदेशानर्थक्यं तत्कर्तुश्चापि मूढता 4.3.556cd
शास्त्रोपालम्भतो नैवं शास्त्रीयेयं प्रकल्पना 1.4.1278cd
शिंशपानुपलब्धिश्चेदन्यव्यावृत्तिरूपतः 4.3.791ab
शिंशपा वृक्ष एवेति ह्यविनाभावकारणात् 4.3.746ab

शिरोदेशविशेषु प्रति प्रति स आहितः 2.2.13cd
शिष्टस्येह प्रवेश्यत्वात्पर एवाविशेदतः 1.4.521cd
शिष्टानां देवतांशानां यथास्वं प्रतिपत्तये 5.17.14cd
शीतमल्पं सुखं ग्रीष्मे तापोऽल्पः शिशिरे सुखम् 2.4.77ab
शीतवद्वा भवेच्छीतः शैत्यस्यानपहारतः 2.1.560ab
शीतश्च पिच्छिलश्चापां बाहुल्यात्स्पर्श इष्यते 2.4.339ab
शीतोष्णज्ञानवत्तस्मान्नेष्यते ज्ञानसंततिः 1.4.1514cd
शीतोष्णयोरिव कथं परस्परविरोधिनोः 3.2.102ab
शीतोष्णयोरिव तयोर्वैलक्षण्यात्परस्परम् 4.4.346ef
शीर्षण्यप्राणसंस्था ये शब्दाद्यासङ्गलक्षणाः 2.2.10ab
शीलं स्थितिर्दण्डनिधानमार्जवं ततस्ततश्चोपरमः क्रियाभ्यः 4.4.595cd
शीलं स्थितिर्दण्डनिधानमार्जवं ततस्ततश्चोपरमः क्रियाभ्यः 4.4.1264cd
शुक्तिकां मानतां याति नासिद्धं रजतादिकम् 4.3.166cd
शुक्तिकाज्ञानतो नर्ते वस्त्वीदृक्साध्यतेऽन्यतः 1.4.451cd
शुक्तिकाज्ञानसंभूतौ न स्वभ्यस्तापि रूप्यधीः 1.4.883cd
शुक्तिकानुविधायित्वान्नेदं स्मर्तव्यसंश्रयम् 1.4.454ab
शुक्तिकेयमिति ह्युक्ते यथार्थं प्रतिपद्यते 1.4.467ab
शुक्तिमृत्स्फटिकाद्येवं ज्ञानं किं नाभ्युपेयते 1.4.463cd
शुक्तेरिव त्वविज्ञातज्ञातत्वस्य ततोऽन्यतः 4.4.902cd
शुक्तौ रजतविज्ञानाच्छुक्तिवन्नामितं यतः 4.3.167ab
शुक्रं निषिक्तं यत्रेदं पुरुषत्वं निगच्छति 6.4.2ab
शुक्रप्रवहया नाड्या हृदयाच्चाभिजायसे 6.4.40ab
शुक्रस्नाय्वस्थिमज्जानो भवन्ति पितृतो यतः 3.9.57ab
शुक्राहुतिं यतोऽहौषीरेष तेऽत्र व्यतिक्रमः 6.4.56cd
शुक्लं कृष्णमणु स्थूलमिति धीः कर्मणो वशात् 1.5.119ab
शुक्लं ब्रह्मातिसंशुद्धमिति केचिद्विनिश्चिताः 4.4.562ab
शुक्लं स्यात्कफभूयस्त्वे वातपित्तसमागमात् 4.3.1238ab
शुक्लकृष्णादिभेदेऽपि गोपिण्डो न हि भिद्यते 4.3.1719cd
शुक्लस्य गृह्यमाणत्वात्पुरोदेशावलम्बिनः 1.4.448cd
शुक्लां गामानयेत्युक्ते कांचिद्गोकर्मिकां क्रियाम् SV 1026ab
शुक्लादिरूपतामेति पुरुषार्थप्रसिद्धये 1.5.121cd
शुक्लादीन्यत्र रूपाणि भास्वराण्युत्तरत्र तु 3.9.51ab

शुक्लाद्याकृतिनाडीस्थमात्मा पश्यत्यविद्यया	4.3.1242cd
शुक्लो गौरितिवन्मानं वस्तुन्येव न भेदगम्	SV 961cd
शुक्लो गौरोऽत्र विज्ञेयः शुक्लो वा बलदेववत्	6.4.70ab
शुद्धचेतस्तया तस्माद्विद्याद्ब्रह्मान्तरात्मनि	2.5.86cd
शुद्धदोषोद्भवत्वाच्च न तु कर्मैवमिष्यते	1.3.105cd
शुद्धधीः प्रव्रजेत्पश्चाद्विरक्तः कर्मणां फलात्	1.5.263ab
शुद्धबुद्धादिकं रूपमात्मनः संप्रदर्श्यते	4.3.1158cd
शुद्धश्चातोऽद्वितीयत्वात्प्रत्यङ्मुक्तः स्वतस्ततः	3.5.76cd
शुद्धसत्त्वोऽथ तद्ब्रह्म साक्षादात्मनि पश्यति	4.4.577cd
शुद्धिकृत्स्याद्धियः पुंसो बहिर्वेद्यपि शास्त्रतः	4.4.1053cd
शुद्धे वस्तुनि सिद्धे च कारकव्यापृतिस्तथा	SV 166cd
शुद्धेस्तरतमत्वाच्च सुखं तरतमं भवेत्	4.3.1853cd
शुद्ध्यशुद्ध्युक्तितश्चेह प्राणोपासा विवक्षिता	1.3.38ab
शुद्ध्यादिगुणवत्ता तु न मानादुपपद्यते	1.3.41cd
शुभं वा यदि वा पापं श्रुतकर्मानुरूपतः	4.3.1957cd
शुभकर्माभिसंबन्धः केवलो नास्य वार्यते	4.3.1360ab
शुभाशुभं यदद्राक्षीत्तत्साक्षादनुगच्छति	4.3.999cd
शुभाशुभक्रियैवेह पश्यतीत्यभिधीयते	4.3.1000ab
शुभौषध्युपयोगाच्च स्वस्थधीः समजायत	2.1.510ab
शुश्रूषति तदर्थं च सहस्रं मुनये ददौ	4.4.534cd
शुश्रूषालिङ्गमेतत्स्यान्न त्वियं गुरुदक्षिणा	4.4.535ab
शुश्रूषुं जनकं सर्वे जना दित्सन्तमेव च	2.1.42ab
शूद्रेण जातो विज्ञेयः प्रातिलोम्योपलक्षणः	4.3.1362ab
शून्यत्वमपि नैव स्यादेतस्मादेव कारणात्	4.3.660ab
शून्यस्यापि हि शून्यत्वं तत्साक्षिणि सतीक्ष्यते	3.4.119ab
शृङ्गग्राहिकया श्रुत्या ब्रह्मतापोदिता स्फुटम्	1.4.886ab
शृणु सर्वं तदज्ञानसमुत्थस्य निषेधतः	2.3.177ab
शृण्वती भवति श्रोत्रमिति व्यासोऽप्यभाषत	1.5.118cd
शृण्वेकाग्रमनाः सर्वं यदेवं सति वस्तु तत्	2.1.544cd
शेते शरीरं सूक्ष्मं च स्थूलं चैकात्म्यधीह्नुतम्	4.4.511cd
शेरते करणान्यस्य सह भोक्त्रात्मनात्मनि	2.1.106cd
शेषभक्षं न कुर्वन्ति प्रधानार्थानुरोधतः	4.4.1241ab

शेषशेषितिरोभावे सुषुप्तिरिह भण्यते 2.1.318cd
शेषामवोचदश्विभ्यामृतायन्नात्मनो वचः 2.5.104ab
शैत्यं हुताशवत्तस्माच्छोकान्तरमिदं भवेत् 4.3.1351ef
शैशिरोऽग्निर्भवेच्छीतस्तथोष्णः पार्थिवो भवेत् 2.1.561ab
शोकमोहाद्यतीतत्वं प्रकाशात्मकता तथा 3.5.12ab
शोकमोहावतः स्यातां सूत्रकार्योपलक्षणम् 3.5.80ab
शोकश्च यस्तयोर्बीजं तमप्येषोऽतिवर्तते 3.5.60cd
शोकस्य प्रत्यगात्मा वा शोकान्तरगिरोच्यते 4.3.1349ab
शोकहेतोरपि प्रत्यङ्ङात्मा स्याच्छोकवान्कथम् 4.3.1349cd
शोकादासङ्गबीजाद्धि जज्ञाते ते यथोदिते 3.5.57ab
शोकादेर्जनकं यद्वा तच्छोकान्तं भवेत्तमः 4.3.1352ab
शोकाभिधानास्तत्रापि कामा एवोदिताः पुरा 4.4.411ab
शोकायोग्यः शुचा हीनोऽशोकशब्देन भण्यते 4.3.1351ab
शोकार्हवत्पदार्थेभ्यो जात्यन्तरमिदं यतः 4.3.1348ab
शोकोऽत्रारतिमात्रं स्याच्चेतसो यानवस्थितिः 3.5.61ab
शोषमित्वा मृतिं याति द्विष्यान्नातोऽनवेदिनम् 1.5.375cd
श्मशानाग्नेस्तथैवैतत्सर्वं ज्ञेयं न कल्प्यते 6.2.114cd
श्येनः शशादो विज्ञेयो बृहत्कायश्च रोहितः 4.3.1160ab
श्येनः श्रान्तो यथाकाशे भक्ष्यहेतोः परिभ्रमन् 4.3.1161ab
श्येनवत्परमं स्थानमात्माभ्येति सुषुप्तताम् 2.1.332cd
श्येनादिविधिबाधः स्यादहिंसाविधिना यथा SV 163cd
श्रद्दधानास्तपस्यन्तः सत्यं ब्रह्म समाहिताः 6.2.136ab
श्रद्धाचारादिविध्यर्था यदि वाख्यायिका त्वियम् 2.1.29ab
श्रद्धातात्पर्यशुश्रूषाप्रणिपातादि साधनम् 1.4.82ab
श्रद्धानाशकवाक्यं तु सर्वार्थमिति गम्यते 4.4.1065ab
श्रद्धामात्रबलेन वार्तिकमिदं तस्याः समासात्कृतम् 6.5.24d
श्रद्धालुं वित्तसंपन्नं श्रेयोऽर्थिनमुपेत्य तु 2.1.30ab
श्रद्धालुरधिकारी यो जिज्ञासुर्विनयान्वितः 2.1.35ab
श्रद्धावित्तोऽयमित्युक्तः संन्यासी सर्वकर्मणाम् 4.4.1269cd
श्रद्धाहुतेर्हि सोमस्य संभवः शास्त्र उच्यते 6.2.92cd
श्रद्धैव वित्तमस्येति नान्यदस्य यतस्ततः 4.4.1269ab
श्रपणाय चरोर्भर्ता व्रीहींस्तामवघातयेत् 6.4.69cd

श्रमहेतुरतस्तापस्तप्तस्येत्यभिशब्द्यते 1.2.153cd
श्रयणाद्धारणाच्चापः श्रद्धाह्वाः कारणात्मिकाः 6.2.90ab
श्रयतेः श्रद्दधातेर्वा श्रद्धेत्याहुर्विपश्चितः 6.2.89ab
श्रवणं मननं तद्वत्तथा शमदमादि यत् 2.4.122ab
श्रवणप्रतिपत्ती च व्यर्थे स्यातां तथाद्वये 5.1.33ab
श्रवणादि कथं कुर्याद्ब्रह्मविद्योपलब्धये 1.4.1753cd
श्रवणादिक्रिया तावत्कर्तव्येह प्रयत्नतः 2.4.218ab
श्रवणादेर्न च प्राप्तिर्गुणान्न च फलं श्रुतम् SV 807ab
श्रान्तस्तच्छ्रमहानार्थं ब्रह्मनीडं प्रपद्यते 4.3.1162cd
श्रान्तस्येति तु देहस्य कर्मायोग्यत्वमुच्यते 1.2.153ab
श्रावितोऽध्वर्युणा च त्वमग्नीधा च तथोत्तरम् 6.3.31cd
श्रिता अतिग्रहाः कामा इन्द्रियाणां प्रवर्तकाः 4.4.384cd
श्रीमद्भर्तृप्रपञ्चस्य श्लोकव्याख्येयमीरिता 4.4.741ab
श्रीयशोभ्यां यथैवायं तपत्येवमुपासकः 5.16.23cd
श्रुत आगमतो योऽर्थस्तर्केणापि समर्थितः 2.5.15ab
श्रुतं चैकविभक्तित्वं युक्तं नाश्रुतकल्पना 4.3.1818ab
श्रुतं श्रुतौ हि गायत्र्यास्तदुपास्तिर्वरा ततः 5.16.3cd
श्रुतं साध्यं समुल्लङ्घ्य नातोऽन्यत्कामजं फलम् 1.5.244ab
श्रुतः प्रजापतिः पूर्वं कोऽसाविति न गम्यते 5.3.2ab
श्रुतकर्मानुरूपेण चक्षुराद्यनुरूपतः 4.3.1951ab
श्रुतकर्मानुरोधेन वृत्तिहान्युद्भवौ क्वचित् 4.4.128cd
श्रुतमेकविभक्तित्वं विभक्त्यन्तरकल्पनात् 4.4.1300ab
श्रुतयः स्मृतयश्चैवमस्मिन्नर्थे सहस्रशः 2.4.35ab
श्रुतयः स्मृतयश्चोच्चैः शुद्धन्यायसमाश्रयात् 3.5.204ab
श्रुतयः स्मृतिवादाश्च कर्मप्राधान्यमेव तु 1.4.1488ab
श्रुतादपि न चेद्वाक्याज्जायेत फलवन्मतिः SV 205cd
श्रुतादर्थान्न चान्योऽर्थो यथोक्तवचसां यतः 2.3.136ab
श्रुतान्मतात्तथोक्ताद्वा प्रमाणं दृष्टिरात्मनः 6.1.11ab
श्रुतार्थहानिरेवं स्यादश्रुतस्य च कल्पना 1.4.1209ab
श्रुतार्थापत्तिरप्यत्र नाभावो मानभावतः SV 1056cd
श्रुतावेव च दृष्टत्वात्स्वरः शातपथो जपे 1.3.350cd
श्रुतिः प्रतिवचः प्राह दोषमूलनिरासकृत् 1.4.1168cd

श्रुतिः प्रववृते सेयं नैवेहेतीह यत्नतः 1.2.140cd
श्रुतिः प्रवृत्तातस्तावत्प्रमेयोऽर्थोऽत्र चिन्त्यते 1.4.185cd
श्रुतिः प्रवृत्ता निर्वक्तुं यावदव्याकृतं परा 1.2.143cd
श्रुतिः समर्थयामास वाचेति शपथक्रियाम् 1.3.330ab
श्रुतिः स्वेनैव वचसा साक्षादित्यादिलक्षणम् 3.9.100ab
श्रुतितो न्यायतः स्पष्टं नात्मनोऽन्योऽस्ति वेदिता 4.4.551cd
श्रुतितो युक्तितश्चापि स्वयमेव प्रवक्ष्यति 1.4.481ab
श्रुतितो लिङ्गतः साक्षात्कार्यकारणसंगतिः 3.4.122ab
श्रुतिन्यायविरुद्धत्वात्प्रकृतं त्वधुनोच्यते 5.1.109cd
श्रुतिन्यायविरोधाच्च कल्पनेयमशोभना 5.1.70ab
श्रुतिन्यायादिसंसिद्धेर्नातो विघ्नकृतः सुराः 1.4.1479cd
श्रुतिमन्त्रस्ततो ह्यर्थ आदेयत्वं निगच्छति 2.5.94cd
श्रुतिमन्त्रोपदिष्टोऽर्थो यस्मादाद्रियते ततः 2.5.116cd
श्रुतिमानार्पितं चैतन्नावज्ञेयं विपश्चिता 4.3.1728ab
श्रुतिराहवनीयादेर्व्याचष्टे विस्तृतिं स्फुटाम् 6.2.79cd
श्रुतिर्गार्ग्यात्मना सेयं पूर्वपक्षमभाषत 2.1.22ef
श्रुतिलिङ्गादिको न्यायः शब्दशक्तिविवेककृत् 2.4.214ab
श्रुतिस्तत्तत्त्वबोधार्थं ब्रह्मेत्याह ततो नरम् 4.3.1968cd
श्रुतिस्तदेव चाचष्टे वस्तु ब्रह्मैव सन्निति 4.4.297cd
श्रुतिस्तिरोहितार्थत्वान्मन्त्राणामित्यतोऽवदत् 1.5.290cd
श्रुतिस्था या हि वाक्तस्याः पञ्चमीयं परा भवेत् 1.5.328ab
श्रुतिस्मृतिसदाचारसंस्कृताशयवज्जनम् 1.3.220ab
श्रुतिस्मृतिसदाचारान्प्रति यः सततोद्यतः 2.1.70ab
श्रुतिस्मृत्युक्तिकोपः स्यात्स चानिष्टः प्रसज्यते 2.1.482cd
श्रुतेऽपि स्वर्गतात्पर्ये कल्पना चेल्लयेऽर्थतः SV 425ab
श्रुतेरनुभवः साक्षाद्यथावस्तु न वेति वा 2.4.131cd
श्रुतेरेतेभ्य इति हि तथा स्पष्टं वचः श्रुतम् 2.1.418cd
श्रुतेरैकात्म्यसंवित्तौ चरितार्थत्वतो मितेः SV 900ab
श्रुतेर्ज्ञातात्मवृत्तान्तोऽननुभूतमपि स्वकम् SV 773ab
श्रुतेर्विलयतात्पर्ये फलमाकस्मिकं भवेत् SV 395ab
श्रुतेस्तदनपेक्षत्वान्नापेक्ष्यं कणभुङ्मतम् 4.4.464cd
श्रुतोऽप्यनर्थकोऽत्र स्याद्विध्यर्थासंभवत्वतः SV 30cd

श्रुतो स्मृतौ वा न्यायाद्वा दृश्यतेऽपि प्रमान्तरात् 4.4.439cd
श्रुतौ न युक्ता व्याजोक्तिरप्रमाणनरोक्तिवत् 4.4.538cd
श्रुतौ यद्यपि नैतस्यां श्रूयते गतिचोदना 4.2.17ab
श्रुतौ श्रुतेर्न संपत्स्यात्संपद्येष न हि क्रमः 1.4.1255cd
श्रुतौ स्मृतौ च विहितं कर्मैव श्रूयते यतः SV 33ab
श्रुतौ स्मृतौ वा लोके वा सिद्धश्चेदस्तु नान्यथा 1.4.1736cd
श्रुतौ स्मृतौ वा संभाव्यं ताभ्यां नान्यस्य मानता 1.4.852ab
श्रुत्यक्षरानुरोधेन दूषणं दूषितात्मनाम् 1.4.702cd
श्रुत्यक्षरानुसारेण तथानुभववर्त्मना 1.4.1188cd
श्रुत्यक्षरानुसारेण नायमर्थोऽत्र लभ्यते 4.2.19cd
श्रुत्यन्तरविरोधश्च प्रत्यग्दृष्टौ प्रसज्यते 1.4.1117cd
श्रुत्यन्तरविरोधश्च संसारी चेदिहोच्यते 2.1.450ab
श्रुत्यन्तरे श्रुतं साक्षादाकाशाद्वानवत्परम् 2.1.451cd
श्रुत्यन्तरेषु तद्वच्च सन्ति वाक्यान्यनेकशः 3.5.143cd
श्रुत्यर्थमुररीकृत्य लोकानुग्रहकाम्यया 4.4.385cd
श्रुत्याकारि कुतो भीतिर्ध्वस्ताज्ञानतदुद्भवे 1.4.70cd
श्रुत्याकारि यतस्तादृक्कथं ब्रह्मेत्युपास्यते 2.5.84cd
श्रुत्या क्रियाभिसंबन्धो व्यवच्छिद्यैव साधनम् SV 645ab
श्रुत्या गार्ग्याद्युपन्यासशिष्याचार्यस्वरूपया 2.1.20ab
श्रुत्याङ्गिरस्त्वसिद्ध्यर्थमुच्यते न्यायपूर्वकम् 1.3.291cd
श्रुत्या जाबालशाखायां तथा चानधिकारिणाम् 2.4.28ab
श्रुत्यातस्ते विकल्प्येते श्रौते स्मार्ते हि तुल्यवत् 1.5.43cd
श्रुत्यात्मकाम इत्येवमात्मैवामी न ते पृथक् 4.4.273cd
श्रुत्यादिमानप्रमितप्रत्यग्याथात्म्यनिष्ठितम् SV 123ab
श्रुत्यादिमानप्रमितयाथात्म्यज्ञानतत्फलः SV 137ab
श्रुत्यादिसाधनं साक्षात्सर्वमात्मेत्युदीरितम् 2.4.485cd
श्रुत्या नवतरं रूपं कल्याणतरमेव च 4.4.142cd
श्रुत्या निषिध्यते साक्षात्प्रत्यक्कौटस्थ्यसिद्धये 4.4.1334cd
श्रुत्या निषिध्यते साक्षाद्देहहेतोर्निषेधतः 2.1.381cd
श्रुत्यानूद्याखिलं वस्तु तस्याथ प्रतिपत्तये 4.4.1018cd
श्रुत्या नैकात्म्यविज्ञानं विनियुक्तं श्रुतौ क्वचित् SV 333ab
श्रुत्यान्तरतरोक्त्येह तद्धेतुश्चात्मतोच्यते 1.4.1040cd

श्रुत्या प्रदर्शितं साक्षात्करविन्यस्तबिल्ववत् 4.3.1304cd
श्रुत्याशेषतमोघातिप्रत्यग्ज्ञानस्य जन्मने 4.4.1200cd
श्रुत्या सिद्धान्तसिद्ध्यर्थं काश्यरूपं प्रकल्पितम् 2.1.24ab
श्रुत्या स्वतन्त्रया तन्नो ब्रह्माविष्क्रियते परम् 3.9.148cd
श्रुत्युक्तार्थस्य वा स्थेम्ने मन्त्रोदाहृतिरिष्यते 1.4.1444ab
श्रुत्युक्तोऽतो विरुद्धोऽर्थो निर्ह्रीकैरिह वर्ण्यते 4.3.1811cd
श्रुत्युक्तोऽत्र परिव्राट्स्यादैकात्म्यज्ञानजन्मने 3.5.157cd
श्रुत्येह ग्रहणं ज्ञेयं तद्बुभुत्साप्रसिद्धये 4.4.1063cd
श्रुत्येह दृष्टोऽतिशयः कश्चित्स्याद्दक्षिणेऽक्षणि 4.2.37cd
श्रुत्येह भण्यतेऽस्मभ्यं नित्यस्वाध्यायलक्षणम् 4.4.1028cd
श्रुत्येहोच्चैः प्रत्यपादि तत्त्वमस्यादिरूपया 4.3.1236cd
श्रुत्येहोत्थाप्यतेऽशेषवेदान्तार्थावबुद्धये 2.1.28ab
श्रुत्यैतत्स्वयमेवोक्तं कर्म न क्षीयते यथा 3.2.73ab
श्रुत्यैव तस्य चोक्तत्वात्तमेतमिति यत्नतः SV 319ab
श्रुत्यैव परिहारोक्तेः स्वप्नादिस्थानसंचरात् SV 203cd
श्रुत्यैव स्पष्टमाख्यातं नातोऽभिव्यक्तीरिष्यते 1.5.331cd
श्रुत्योदगयनाद्युक्त्या कर्मसिद्ध्यै प्रयत्नतः 6.3.6cd
श्रुत्योदाहारि नः साक्षात्सदैकात्म्यावबुद्धये SV 937cd
श्रुत्योपस्थाप्यते गार्ग्यो ब्रह्मविद्याभिधित्सया 2.1.16cd
श्रुत्वा मत्वाथ तं साक्षादात्मानं प्रतिपद्यते 2.4.220cd
श्रूयतेऽतः परात्मैव जगतः कारणं परम् 2.1.395cd
श्रूयते फलसंबन्धो यासूपासासु तास्विह 1.3.196ab
श्रूयते मन्दपालादि तथा चात्र निदर्शनम् 1.5.243cd
श्रूयते मुक्तये साक्षान्न भयं स्यादतो मृतेः 4.4.1061cd
श्रूयते स्पष्टवचनं देहादेर्नाशनं कुतः 1.4.1740cd
श्रूयन्ते तु ऋणवचो विरोधात्स्यादपस्मृतिः 1.5.267cd
श्रूयन्ते न्यायदृब्धानि तस्मात्तान्यादराच्छ्रयेत् 1.4.1589cd
श्रेयः संभाव्यते विद्यानिष्फलत्वप्रसङ्गः SV 78cd
श्रेयांसि बहुविघ्नानीत्याशङ्क्यैतदथोच्यते 1.4.1462cd
श्रेयांसोऽमुकमिश्रास्त इत्युक्तिं कामयन्ति च 4.2.43cd
श्रेयानस्म्यहमेवेति विवदन्तः परस्परम् 6.1.16cd
श्रेयोरूपप्रसिद्ध्यर्थं क्षत्रस्येत्यवगम्यते 1.4.1601cd

श्रेयोरूपप्रसिद्ध्यर्थं प्रसिद्धिरुपवर्ण्यते 1.4.1618ab
श्रेयोरूपस्ततो धर्मः सर्वानप्यनुशास्त्यसौ 1.4.1615cd
श्रेयोर्थिनां मनुष्याणामुपास्यप्रतिपत्तये 1.3.170ab
श्रेष्ठता वक्ष्यमाणेन ग्रन्थेनास्य विभाव्यते 6.1.9cd
श्रोतव्य इत्यतः प्राह वेदान्ताविरुरुत्सया 2.4.212cd
श्रोतव्यः श्रुतिवाक्येभ्य इत्यत्राशङ्क्यते यतः 2.4.304ab
श्रोता स्प्रष्टेतिरूपः स्यात्तथैवेन्द्रियवृत्तिभिः 2.4.428ab
श्रोतृस्थकार्यलिङ्गत्वात्कथं शब्दैकगोचरः SV 736cd
श्रोत्रत्वगादिनाडिस्थं शब्दाद्यालोचनादिभिः 1.4.646ab
श्रोत्रत्वगादिनाड्यश्च प्रोच्यन्तेऽत्राङ्गसंज्ञया 4.3.1940ab
श्रोत्रादिकरणग्राह्यं सर्वं तद्रूपमुच्यते 1.5.139ab
श्रोत्रादिकरणानीव नातो गोचरसंकरः 4.3.1750ab
श्रोत्रादिकरणान्यत्र मात्रादानस्य कारणम् 4.3.992ab
श्रोत्रादिकरणार्थोऽयं श्लोकस्तस्मादुदाहृतः 2.2.25cd
श्रोत्रादिकरणैर्यद्यत्प्रथते तत्तदुच्यते 1.4.707ab
श्रोत्रादिकरणोपेतं यतोऽन्तःकरणं दृशेः 4.3.1527ab
श्रोत्रादिनाडीमध्यस्थ आत्माव्याप्य तनुं स्थितः 1.4.642ab
श्रोत्रादिभिर्यतो भिन्ना मिथः शब्दादयस्त्वमी 2.1.589ab
श्रोत्रादिमयताप्यस्य व्याख्येया प्रत्यगात्मनः 4.4.181cd
श्रोत्रादिवत्प्रमाणानामसाधारणमेयता 1.3.48ab
श्रोत्रादिव्यापृतो माता दुःखादिगुणवान्पराङ् 4.3.185ab
श्रोत्रादेर्गुणभूतत्वात्प्रधानं प्रति सर्वदा 2.1.129ab
श्रोत्रियं ब्रह्मनिष्ठं च गुरुं यायादिति श्रुतेः 4.2.105cd
श्रोत्रियावृजिनत्वे द्वे तुल्ये एवाविरिञ्चितः 4.3.1866ab
श्रोत्रियोऽधीतवेदः स्याज्ज्ञातवेदार्थ एव यः 4.3.1863ab
श्रोत्रेण क्रियते तस्य शब्दस्यालोचितस्य तु 4.4.712cd
श्रौतं वाक्यमिदं न्याय्यं न तु सर्वोक्तिभासने 4.4.1034cd
श्रौतं स्मार्तं च यत्किंचित्पुण्यं कर्म त्वया कृतम् 6.4.59ab
श्रौतमिष्टं विजानीयात्स्मार्तं सुकृतमित्यपि 6.4.58cd
श्रौतस्मार्तविभागेन तत एतद्विकल्पितम् 1.5.41cd
श्रौतानन्तादहंमानात्परिच्छिन्नो विरुध्यते 1.3.214cd
श्रौतानि शतशः सन्ति दृगमेयत्वसिद्धये 3.4.165cd

श्रौतैर्वा यदि वा स्मार्तैर्यदि वोभयकर्मभिः 3.3.45cd
श्रौत्यानया प्रसिद्ध्या तु कार्यलिङ्गैश्च कारणम् 1.4.107ab
श्लोकं व्याचक्षतेऽयुक्त्या हुतभुग्वरसंश्रयात् 4.4.391cd
श्लोकग्रन्थिप्रबद्धाविषयमितिफला प्रेमसत्सूत्रसत्रा 6.5.22c
श्लोका अपि भवन्त्यत्र ब्राह्मणोक्तविनिश्चितौ 4.4.545cd
श्लोकांश्च गौडपादादेर्यथोक्तार्थस्य साक्षिणः 4.4.886ab
श्लोकाः संबन्धभाष्येऽस्मिन्संख्याताः संख्ययाखिलाः SV 1136cd
श्लोकेन तद्वन्मोक्षोऽपि निष्कामस्योपवर्ण्यते 4.4.392cd
श्वेतकेतुमथाप्राक्षीत्पञ्च प्रश्नान्क्रमान्नृपः 6.2.29cd
श्वेतकेतुरिति ग्रन्थः पर आरभ्यतेऽधुना 6.2.17cd
श्वेतोऽसौ धावतीत्यादेरनेकोक्तित्वकारणात् 1.5.346ab
षट्संख्यामेव संयान्ति षडग्न्याद्यास्ततः स्मृताः 3.9.20cd
षट्स्वप्येतेषु विज्ञेयमेतदेव चतुष्टयम् 4.1.12cd
षड्भावविक्रियं वस्तु ध्येयं वक्ति न हि श्रुतिः 5.1.79cd
षड्भावविक्रियाणां च निषेधश्चेतनात्मनः 2.3.109ab
षड्भावविक्रियाभावादसङ्गाच्चाप्यनात्मना 4.4.763ab
षड्भावविक्रियामेति निर्विकारेण भास्वता 4.3.343cd
षड्भावविक्रियामेति व्याप्तैवाकाशकुम्भवत् 3.4.100cd
षड्विकारनिषेधाच्च प्रायार्थत्वं समञ्जसम् 2.1.191cd
षड्विधं परिणामार्थमग्निहोत्राहुतीहयोः 6.2.13cd
षण्मासशेषप्रोद्भूता वासना यास्य देहिनः 4.4.120ab
षण्मासांश्च ततो यान्ति ह्युत्तरायणलक्षणान् 6.2.138cd
षष्ट्युत्तराणि त्रीण्येव शतानीति विनिश्चितम् 1.5.64cd
षष्ठ आरभ्यतेऽध्यायो वादन्यायेन यत्नतः 4.1.2cd
षष्ठगोचरवत्सर्वं कार्यकारणवज्जगत् 2.4.472ab
षष्ठगोचरवन्नेदमज्ञातत्वं समीक्ष्यते 1.4.288ab
षष्ठादौ सूक्ष्मनाडीनां तद्द्वारात्मावबुद्धये 4.3.1219cd
षष्ठीं च न क्रियाषष्ठ्योर्विना भेदात्प्रवर्तनम् SV 906cd
षष्ठीयं कर्मणि न्याय्या द्वयाभावविवक्षया 2.1.317cd
षष्ठेऽपि जनकाख्यानप्रारम्भे तद्वदीरितः 4.5.17ab
षष्ठे क्रमादुपन्यस्तं जाग्रदादिचतुष्टयम् 4.3.4cd
षष्ठे तु वक्ष्यतेऽध्याये विज्ञानात्मविनिर्णयः 3.5.13cd

षष्ठ्यर्थहेतुविध्वंसाद्यथावस्त्ववबोधतः 4.4.505ab
षष्ठ्यर्थासंभवोऽतः स्याद्द्वितीयासंभवात्सतः 2.4.291ab
षष्ठ्यादिकल्पनासाध्वी तस्मादत्रेति भण्यते 4.3.1819ab
षष्ठ्युक्तेरेव संसिद्धा मूर्तादेर्ब्रह्मणोऽन्यता 2.3.216ab
स आत्मा तत्परं ज्योतिः शिरसीदं वचः श्रुतेः 1.4.717cd
स आत्मानुभवात्सिद्ध आ देहादा परात्मनः 3.5.178cd
स आत्मा पुण्यपापोत्थं फलं नानाप्रभेदकम् 4.3.998ab
स आत्मा प्रकृतस्त्वेताश्चक्षुःश्रोत्रादिलक्षणाः 4.4.20ab
स आत्मा यः स्वयंज्योतिरनुमानेन दर्शितः 4.3.446cd
स आत्मेत्यभिसंबन्धान्नापि सत्ता सतोच्यते SV 703cd
स आनन्दः परो ज्ञेयः सुखदुःखविवर्जितः 4.3.1066ab
स इदं सर्वमात्मैव भवत्यज्ञानहानतः 1.4.1460cd
स एव च जगत्कारी सत्यज्ञानादिलक्षणः 2.1.447ab
स एव तदभूद्यस्मान्नातोऽभिजनकारणम् 1.4.1459cd
स एव त्राता सर्वस्य ह्यत्रं क्षत्रमतो भवेत् 5.15.9cd
स एव धर्मः सत्यं स्याद्यद्व्यवस्थाप्रयोजकम् 2.5.50cd
स एव नोऽस्तु दृष्टान्तो नातोऽन्यः प्रार्थ्यते मया 4.3.1761cd
स एव पञ्चमेऽप्युक्तः साक्षाज्जल्पैकवर्त्मना 4.3.3cd
स एव प्रादिसंबन्धाद्विशेषार्थो भवेदसुः 1.5.144cd
स एव बुद्ध्यतिशयः श्रोत्रादेरपि कारणम् 4.4.175cd
स एव ब्रह्मलोकान्तान्वेदेत्येषोऽस्य संग्रहः 3.7.7cd
स एव ब्राह्मणो नान्यो जगत्यध्यवसीयताम् 3.8.169cd
स एव स इति ह्युक्तिः कार्यकारणसंस्थयोः 1.3.153ab
स एवात्मेति विज्ञेयस्तेषु सर्वेष्वनात्मसु 4.3.326cd
स एवायमिति ज्ञेयो यो द्रष्टव्यतयोदितः 2.5.39ab
स एवार्थस्तु निष्णातो निदिध्यासनमुच्यते 2.5.15cd
स एष इति निर्देशः कथं स्यात्कृष्णसर्पवत् 1.4.497cd
स एष इत्यत्र वाक्ये नैवाकस्मिकशब्दनम् 1.4.104cd
स एष इत्यनेनापि सुविरुद्धात्मतां ब्रुवन् 1.4.493ab
स एष इत्युपन्यस्तो विज्ञानात्मा हि यः पुरा 2.1.21cd
स एष ईश्वरः साक्षादिति श्रुत्या प्रदर्शितः 4.4.981ab
स एष कर्मजो बुद्धेः प्रकाशो जायते मृतौ 4.4.76ab

स एष ज्ञः परो देवः सविज्ञानो भवत्यथ 4.4.98cd
स एष देवो यः पृष्टो वद भूयोऽप्यहल्लिक 3.9.42ab
स एष द्वैतदृष्टयात्र कर्मपक्षो निराकृतः 3.2.52ab
स एष नेति नेतीति मधुकाण्डेऽपि वर्णितः 3.9.95cd
स एष नेति नेतीति य आत्मेत्यादिना तथा 1.4.1238ef
स एष नेति नेत्यात्मा यस्मात्प्रागपि वर्णितः 4.4.1158cd
स एष नेति नेत्यात्मेत्यथैतस्मात्पुरोदितात् 4.4.1279ab
स एष नेति नेत्याद्यः प्रश्नो वायं समीक्ष्यताम् 3.9.104ab
स एष पर उत्कर्षो विद्यायाः संप्रदर्शितः 4.3.1284ab
स एष परमात्मैव स्वात्ममोहसहायवान् 1.3.264ab
स एष परमोऽप्यात्मा कामाविद्याद्युपप्लवात् 1.4.32ab
स एष परिणामः स्यात्तेजोबन्नाद्युपक्रमः 2.4.341ab
स एष पशुतामेति देवादीनां स्वकर्मभिः 1.4.1570cd
स एष पुरुषो यत्र तत्प्रयोक्तृक्रियाक्षये 4.4.57ab
स एष वायुः सूत्रात्मा देवः सर्वाश्रयः प्रभुः 3.7.13ab
स एषोऽभ्यन्तरो देवः सर्वकारणकारणः 3.7.45ab
संयच्छति प्रतीच्यात्मा स्वपितीति तदोच्यते 2.1.337cd
संयमात्सर्वयाम्यानां यमोऽसि परमेश्वरः 5.17.7ab
संयुक्तयोर्वियोगोऽपि न तयोरीक्ष्यते क्वचित् 3.8.137ab
संयोगः समवायो वा तादात्म्यं वेह संगतिः SV 925cd
संयोगपूर्वता तस्य लिङ्ग्यते मेषयोरिव 4.3.708cd
संयोगपूर्वतो नैवं तद्विभागावसानतः 1.4.595cd
संयोगश्च वियोगश्च यस्य येनेह वीक्ष्यते 1.4.541ab
संयोगश्चेद्वियोगोऽपि समवायेऽनवस्थितिः SV 971ab
संयोगा विप्रयोगान्ता मरणान्तं च जीवितम् 2.4.84cd
संयोगे च वियोगे च विशेषस्य समीक्षणात् 4.3.499cd
संयोगोत्थो वियोगोत्थो यश्चापि प्रत्ययात्मकः 1.5.129cd
संयोज्य क्रिययातस्तं व्याचष्टे श्रुतिरञ्जसा 1.3.318cd
संलयायेति यच्छुद्धं रूपं स्यात्प्रत्यगात्मनः 4.3.1173ab
संवत्सरः स्वावयवैरहोभिः परिवर्तते 4.4.636cd
संवत्सरमवाप्नोति स्वनाडीसंख्यया नरः 1.5.67cd
संवत्सराग्नेश्चित्यस्य पुंसो नाड्यस्तथैव च 1.5.66cd

संवत्सरात्मसंपत्त्या कालात्मानं समश्नुते 1.5.69ab
संवत्सरावधिं कालं सकृदाहुतिसाधने 1.5.71cd
संवत्सराश्च तावन्तस्ते प्रजापतयोऽग्नयः 4.2.71cd
संवत्सरे प्रयोगाणामग्निहोत्रे हि संख्यया 1.5.64ab
संवत्सरे समिद्धे हि पर्जन्यस्य समेधनात् 6.2.98ab
संवदिष्ये नृपेणाहमिति वा तं जगाम सः 4.3.10ab
संवर्गात्मातिवर्तित्वात्तत्कार्यातिगतिस्ततः 3.5.71cd
संविज्ज्ञानविशेषस्य तथा सति न किं चन 4.3.1120ab
संवित्तन्मोहचिद्बिम्बैः प्रात्यक्ष्यं कर्तृरूपिणः 3.4.105cd
संवित्तन्मोहधीवृत्तिशरीरादिविशेषणम् 3.4.109ab
संवित्तावदशेषेभ्यः प्रमाणेभ्योऽवसीयते 1.4.984cd
संवित्तिभावयोर्भेदो यथैवं तदभावयोः 4.3.767ab
संवित्तिस्तदसंबोधहेतूत्थानात्मजन्मना 3.4.115cd
संवित्तेरप्यसंबोधात्स्यात्तन्मानव्यपेक्षिता 1.4.296cd
संवित्प्रमाणसत्त्वेन विना वस्तु न लौकिकम् 1.4.593ab
संवित्सैवेह मेयोऽर्थो वेदान्तोक्तिप्रमाणतः SV 159ef
संविदं भिद्यते मेयात्प्रत्येकं भेदधीर्न तु SV 983cd
संविदा ज्ञाततासिद्धिर्मितेरपि न मात्मना 1.4.285cd
संविदेका स्वतःसिद्धा प्रत्यग्रूपैकलक्षणा SV 985ab
संविदेव सुखं यस्मादाप्तकाममिदं ततः 4.3.1340cd
संविदैव समाप्तत्वात्तमोजस्य पुरोत्थितेः 4.3.1523ab
संविदो व्यतिरेकेण वस्तु यद्यत्प्रसाध्यते 4.3.1738ab
संविद्क्लेशादिभेदेन वस्तु चेत्साध्यतेऽन्यतः 4.3.1739ab
संविद्रूपे प्रमेये च संविदन्या फलं भवेत् SV 1063ab
संविद्विशिष्टा संवित्स्यान्न चासावात्मनीक्ष्यते SV 1064cd
संविन्मात्रैकयाथात्म्यात्प्रमात्रादेरनात्मनः 1.4.282cd
संवृतं प्रतिषिद्धं तद्यदनात्मेव लक्ष्यते 2.5.124cd
संवृतः परमेशोऽपि त्रैलोक्यात्माग्निरुच्यते 1.2.157cd
संवृत्तः पुरुषाकार इत्यनुक्रोशतीव नः 1.4.32cd
संवेद्यानन्दकं तावद्ब्रह्मेतीहावसीयताम् 3.9.178ab
संवेद्यानन्दरूपं तद्वाक्याच्चेत्परिनिश्चितम् 3.9.171ab
संवेद्ये च सुखे लोक आनन्दाख्या प्रयुज्यते 3.9.166cd

संवेद्योऽयं किमानन्दः किं वा नेति विचार्यते 3.9.169cd
संव्याप्य तद्वदखिलं देहमात्मा व्यवस्थितः 1.4.641ab
संशयस्तु भवत्येव पक्षासिद्धिस्तु तावता SV 72ab
संशयो निश्चयश्चायमित्येतच्चानुभूतितः 4.3.515cd
संशयो हि तथा श्रोतुः स्यादनिश्चितवाक्यतः 1.4.1276cd
संशुद्धधिषणोऽत्यर्थं वैदिकैरेव साधनैः 4.4.1196ab
संशोध्य तदिदं सर्वं विज्ञानात्मा प्रदर्श्यते 2.3.99cd
संश्रयादेव न पुनर्मोहाभावे तदिष्यते 4.3.1307cd
संश्रित्य पूर्व एवार्थ इह साक्षाद्विभाव्यते 4.3.5cd
संश्लिष्टयोरपि तयोरन्यत्वमिति निश्चयः 4.3.499ab
संसक्तजायापुंमानो यावांस्तावान्बभूव ह 1.4.109cd
संसरत्यन्यथाज्ञानात्सम्यग्ज्ञानाद्विमुच्यते 2.4.260cd
संसरत्यप्रबुद्धः सन्परलोकेहलोकगः 4.4.252cd
संसर्गः प्रविवेको वा भिन्नयोर्वस्तुनोर्यतः 4.4.407ab
संसर्गः स्यात्पदार्थानां सुस्थमेवं विधिं विना SV 753cd
संसर्गकल्पनाशून्यमप्यैकात्म्यं प्रबोधयेत् SV 780ab
संसर्गधर्मता नापि भेदेनानुपलम्भनात् SV 970ab
संसर्गप्रतिषेधार्थं मा भून्नीलोत्पलादिवत् 4.4.528cd
संसर्गप्रविवेकौ स्तो यतस्तैरात्मनः सदा 4.4.409ab
संसर्गरूपं वाक्योत्थं ज्ञानं नीलोत्पलादिवत् 4.4.800cd
संसर्गलक्षणो वापि ब्रह्मात्माभेदतो भवेत् SV 902cd
संसर्गश्चेत्पदार्थानां विनापि विधिना भवेत् SV 726ab
संसारकारणं तस्मादात्माज्ञानाविरोधि यत् 4.4.114ab
संसारकारणध्वंसि यत्तु ज्ञानं परात्मगम् 4.4.113ab
संसारकारणध्वंसि यत्तु ज्ञानं विमुक्तिदम् 4.4.1122ab
संसारकारणाविद्याध्वंसकृज्ज्ञानलब्धये SV 17ab
संसारदर्शनाभ्यासात्तन्मुक्तिं ये प्रचक्षते 1.4.700ab
संसारदुःखसंस्कारस्मृतिभिः प्रेर्यमाणधीः 2.4.3cd
संसारनाशोऽविद्याया नाशान्न व्यतिरिच्यते 2.4.195cd
संसारपुरुषार्थेभ्यो यतो नाव्युत्थितात्मने 2.4.64ab
संसारफल एवेति प्रवृत्त्यङ्गतयोच्यते SV 1124cd
संसारफलता काममस्तु काम्यस्य कर्मणः SV 1127ab

संसारफलतैवातः पुत्रादेर्गम्यते श्रुतेः 1.5.338ab
संसारभूमावासीनं संसार्यस्मीत्यवस्थितम् 2.1.519ab
संसारभूमिवर्तित्वान्न चात्मा कारणाश्रयः 3.2.141cd
संसारभूमौ पुंसः स्यात्कालादेस्तत्प्रधानतः 3.2.155cd
संसारमिथ्याविज्ञानमभ्यस्यन्त्येव सर्वदा 4.4.822ab
संसारमोक्षणायाशु नित्यं कर्म न चेदलम् 4.4.1215ab
संसारवस्तुनः सोऽयमात्मेत्यत्राभिधीयते 4.4.151cd
संसारवह्निजं दुःखं संभावयति ना परम् 1.4.13ab
संसारविषयैवाप्तिर्मुक्तौ सा न मनागपि 3.3.12cd
संसारव्याविवृत्सुभ्य इत्युक्तिं भाष्यकृज्जगौ SV 11cd
संसारस्याधिकारोऽयमा श्लोकोदाहृतेर्मतः 4.4.3ab
संसारस्येत्यतो वक्ति श्रुतिस्तस्य मृषार्थताम् 2.1.263cd
संसारहेतुनिबिडध्वान्तोच्चिच्छित्सयादरात् 4.3.1078cd
संसारहेतोर्मृत्योः स्यान्नापीहास्त्यनवस्थितिः 3.2.19cd
संसारहेत्वसंबन्धः सर्वो ब्रह्मेति भण्यते 3.7.55cd
संसारहेत्विवतिवचः स्फुटन्यायोपबृंहितम् SV 15cd
संसाराख्यमहाव्याधेः किं मूलमिति चिन्त्यते 1.4.186ab
संसाराच्चेद्विरक्तासि गृहाणानुत्तमामृतम् 2.4.65cd
संसारादविरक्तस्य मुक्तीच्छा नेह कस्यचित् 1.5.89cd
संसाराद्बन्धनान्मोक्षः कर्तव्यो ज्ञानहेतुतः 3.2.6cd
संसारानर्थनाशो हि विद्यायाः प्रार्थ्यते फलम् 1.4.1744ab
संसारानर्थनिष्पत्तौ सर्वेषामविशिष्टता 4.4.205ab
संसारानर्थबीजस्य प्रध्वंसादात्मबोधतः 4.4.283ab
संसारानर्थसंप्राप्तिहेतोर्विध्वस्तयेऽधुना 3.5.2ab
संसारानर्थसंबन्धविज्ञानाय तमस्विनः 4.4.6cd
संसारानर्थसंबन्धहेतोरात्मप्रमाणतः 4.3.1182cd
संसारानर्थहानाख्यं प्रत्यक्षमनुभूयते 2.1.548cd
संसारानर्थहेतुत्वज्ञानायैव च कर्मणाम् 4.4.1051ab
संसारानर्थहेतुत्वमविद्यायाश्च वर्णितम् 1.4.1591ab
संसारानलसंतप्तस्तद्विरुद्धं परीप्सति 1.4.1343cd
संसारानवतारः स्यान्मानवैफल्यमेव च 1.4.999ab
संसारानुपपत्तिश्च कूटस्थात्मैकदेशतः 2.1.486ab

संसारान्मुच्यमानानां तथा संसरतामिह 3.3.1ab
संसारावस्थ एवायं द्वैतत्वाद्ब्रह्मभेदतः 3.2.56cd
संसारासंभवं साक्षादेकत्वमनुपश्यतः 1.4.820cd
संसारिणं समुद्दिश्य श्रुतिरेतदुदाहरत् 1.4.1237cd
संसारिणि यदुक्तं तत्तदा तत्र भविष्यति 2.1.429cd
संसारिणोऽप्यसामर्थ्याज्जगज्जन्मादिकर्मसु 2.1.442ab
संसारिणो न चेदत्ति संसार्येव प्रसज्यते 2.4.16ab
संसारिणो ननूत्पत्तिरेवमेवेति कीर्तिता 2.1.448ab
संसारिणो न संभाव्यमस्मदादेर्यथा तथा 2.1.454cd
संसारितात्मनः क्लृप्ता कृष्णिमेव नभस्तले 3.5.34cd
संसारिता परस्यैवं दोषः स्याद्दुर्निवारणः 2.1.481cd
संसारिताविशिष्टैव मोक्षादर्वाक्षु भूमिषु 1.4.1763ab
संसारित्वं परस्येति तदनन्यत्वकारणात् 2.1.466cd
संसारित्वं परिच्छिद्य प्रापितः स यदाखिलः 4.4.404cd
संसारित्वं परिच्छिन्नो विज्ञानात्मत्वमश्नुते 3.2.55cd
संसारित्वं प्रसक्तं चेन्न क्षुदाद्यत्ययश्रुतेः 1.4.556cd
संसारित्वं यतो नातः स्वतः संसारितात्मनः 4.3.405cd
संसारित्वमविद्यातो मुमुक्षुत्वं ततो भवेत् 1.4.1336cd
संसारित्वात्प्रविष्टानां परस्य तदभेदतः 1.4.556ab
संसारिब्रह्मणोः कस्य नामैतदिति भण्यताम् 2.1.426cd
संसारिविद्ययैवास्य पुरुषार्थसमाप्तितः 1.4.1246cd
संसारी प्रक्रमाच्चेह नान्यः संभाव्यते ततः 2.1.436ab
संसारी यो यथोक्तेन ग्रन्थेन प्रतिपादितः 4.4.149ab
संसारे कियती व्याप्तिरभिव्यक्तस्य कर्मणः 3.3.5ab
संसारे चापि जग्धेऽस्मिन्ब्रह्मणा निखिले सति 2.4.17ab
संसारेण तथैवात्मा कौटस्थ्यान्नैति संगतिम् 2.1.310cd
संसारे प्रथते योऽर्थ आत्मनानन्यमानगः 4.4.150cd
संसारोऽनर्थ इत्येष प्रत्यङ्मोहैकहेतुकः 3.5.94ab
संसारोऽयमतो मोहसमुच्छित्तौ विमुक्तता 4.3.1823cd
संसार्यपि स्वतोऽयं चेन्नेदृग्दृष्टेरसंभवात् 2.1.438cd
संसार्यस्मीति चेद्ध्वस्ता कोटिकल्पोपबृंहिता 4.4.778ab
संसार्यात्मनि दृष्टेऽपि न च किंचित्प्रयोजनम् 2.4.138ab

संसार्येव स विज्ञेयः श्रुतिमन्त्रस्मृतीरणात्	1.4.146cd
संसार्येवाभिधीयेत यथोक्तन्यायगौरवात्	1.4.1245cd
संसार्येवेह स इति तथान्येऽपि प्रचक्षते	1.4.144ab
संसृत्यनर्थस्य यतो निदानं सैव नापरम्	1.4.168ab
संस्कारकं तु कर्म स्याज्ज्ञानात्त्वज्ञाननिह्नुतिः	SV 368cd
संस्कारकत्वात्तस्यैव न तदन्यदिहेष्यते	1.5.312cd
संस्कारमात्रकारित्वं सर्वेषामपि कर्मणाम्	SV 301ab
संस्कारमात्रशेषास्ते सुषुप्ते यान्ति संक्षयम्	4.4.378cd
संस्कारापचयाद्ध्वंसस्तथा तासां न संशयः	1.4.1152cd
संस्काराय च यच्छास्त्रमात्मज्ञानोपकारकम्	SV 915cd
संस्कारोपचयाद्यद्वद्देवो भूत्वैति देवताम्	1.4.1152ab
संस्कारो वाथवाप्यन्यः सर्वस्याज्ञानमूलतः	4.4.379cd
संस्कार्यत्वात्पशोरेवं दृष्टीरङ्गेषु योजयेत्	1.1.3ab
संस्कृते भूप्रदेशेऽथ ह्यग्निं संस्थापयेद्गृही	6.3.18cd
संस्तुतोऽत्रैति संस्तावो हृद्याकाश इहोच्यते	4.2.47cd
संस्थानवदथेदानीमध्यात्मे चाधिदैवते	5.6.1ab
संस्थानानुपमर्देन यद्वा केशोषरादिवत्	2.1.476cd
संस्थेम्नेऽस्यैव चार्थस्य पूर्वपक्षोक्तिपूर्वकः	1.4.754ab
संहतं च प्रतीचोऽन्यज्जगदेतच्चराचरम्	3.9.88cd
संहतत्वात्तथा प्राणोऽसंहतात्मोपभोगकृत्	2.1.160cd
राहतानां क्रियासिद्धेः करणानां पृथक्पृथक्	6.1.22ab
संहतिश्चक्षुरादीनां श्लोकशब्देन भण्यते	1.4.1021ab
संहतोक्तविशेषाणां भूतानां कारणात्मता	2.4.336ab
संहतो गम्यतेऽनात्मा प्रत्यक्षेण यथा सदा	2.4.285ab
संहत्यनुपपत्तिश्च पदानामभिधाश्रुतौ	2.4.160ab
संहत्यपक्षोपमया श्रुत्येह प्रतिपाद्यते	4.3.1172cd
संहन्यते शरीरेण यथा वायुस्तथैव सः	2.1.158cd
संहरत्यात्मनात्मानं पूर्वस्मात्तत्र सा क्रमात्	4.4.134cd
संहृतात्मप्रभेदा हि सैवैका प्राणदेवता	3.9.12ab
संहृताशेषकरणो भावनाकर्महेतुतः	4.4.99ab
संहृतिः प्रातिलोम्येन व्यूहस्त्वागणनाक्षयात्	3.9.10cd
संहृत्य स्थूलमाधारं भूतानां च क्षितेस्तथा	2.5.25ab

सकलत्वे परस्योक्ताः संसारित्वादिलक्षणाः 2.3.126ab
सकारणमिदं सर्वमाकाशान्तं यथोदितम् 3.9.93ab
सकारणस्य देहस्य त्यागो हेतुर्विवक्षितः 4.4.515cd
सकारणस्य मात्रादेः प्रत्यग्दृष्टयतिरेकतः 4.4.839ab
सकार्ये तमसि ध्वस्त आत्मैवैकोऽवशिष्यते 1.4.1342cd
स कूटस्थात्मनापीतो रज्ज्वा सर्पो यथा तथा 4.3.1533cd
सकृच्छ्रुतं वचोऽशक्तं विधातुं द्वयमञ्जसा 1.5.344cd
सकृज्जातं न चेद्धन्ति ज्ञानमेव न तद्भवेत् 2.4.208cd
सकृत्करण एव स्यात्कार्यस्याभेदतस्तव SV 650cd
सकृत्प्रवृत्त्या मृद्नाति क्रियाकारकरूपभृत् 3.3.71ab
सकृदप्यनुतिष्ठन्ना प्राप्नोत्येव फलं तयोः 4.4.199cd
सकृदात्मप्रसूत्यैव निरुणद्ध्यखिलं भवम् 1.4.1451ab
सकृदात्मप्रसूत्यैव बोधस्याज्ञानहानतः 4.4.775cd
सकृदेव च मायोगान्नोर्ध्वं तच्चोदनेष्यते 1.4.1454cd
सकृद्द्वयःप्रयोगाद्वा यावज्जीवप्रयोगतः 3.3.44ab
सकृद्विद्युद्यथात्यन्तं घनध्वान्तापनोदकृत् 2.3.166ab
सकृद्विभातं चिन्मात्रं ज्योतिरित्युपदिश्यते 4.3.338cd
सकृद्विभातमैकात्म्यं वितमस्कमभेदकम् 3.4.84cd
सकृद्विभातो ह्येवैष रवौ रात्र्यहनी यथा 1.4.846cd
सकृन्निवृत्तेर्बाध्यस्य किं कार्यमवशिष्यते 1.4.1455cd
सकृन्मृत्वासुदेहेन मुच्यते सर्वबन्धनात् 1.2.226cd
सक्तः सन्कर्मणा सार्धमेत्यात्मा कर्मणः फलम् 4.4.240cd
स खलूत्पन्नविज्ञानस्तन्मयः संस्तथा व्रजेत् 4.4.720ab
सगुणात्पौर्णमासादेः फलं तत्रापि नो गुणात् SV 805cd
संकल्पाध्यवसायाभ्यां तयोर्भेदोऽपि च द्विधा 2.4.369cd
संकीर्णत्वादशक्यः स्यात्प्रबोधे भोक्तृभोज्ययोः 2.1.103ab
संकीर्णत्वान्मिथस्तेषां दुःशकं तद्विवेचनम् 2.1.104cd
संकीर्णमिव मात्राभिश्चित्राभिरुपलक्षयेत् 3.5.43cd
संकीर्यमाणेवाभाति तमसोपहतात्मनाम् 2.1.236cd
संक्रामितात्मभारस्य त्वं ब्रह्मेति वचोऽर्थवत् 1.5.307ab
संक्रामितात्मभारोऽपि नाग्निहोत्रं परित्यजेत् 1.5.302ab
संक्षिप्य चाप्युपन्यस्तमध्यायान्ते च तत्पुनः 2.1.12ab

संख्याप्राधान्यमध्यर्धे विदग्धे न विवक्षितम् 3.9.27ab
संख्येयत्वं न रेखायाः संख्यात्वं वाञ्जसेष्यते 4.4.1341ab
संगतावविरोधी चेन्न संबन्धिनिवृत्तिकृत् SV 948ab
संगतिः पुरुषस्यास्य निर्हेतुः प्रत्यगात्मना 4.3.60cd
संगतिर्निरविद्यस्य नाविद्याहेतुजैर्मलैः 1.4.213cd
संगतिर्भौतिकैर्न स्यात्तस्य दुःखादिभिः कथम् 1.5.353cd
सङ्गत्यागो ह्यसंभाव्यो विनैकात्म्यावबोधनात् 1.2.205cd
सङ्गात्संजायते काम इति सर्वज्ञशास्त्रतः 4.4.227cd
संघात एव भोक्तास्तु तस्य प्रत्यक्षसंगतेः 2.1.138ab
संघातस्य विशरणं जीवतश्चेति दुःस्थितम् 1.4.1759cd
संघातस्याविशिष्टत्वान्नातिशीतिर्भवेत्सदा 2.1.149cd
स च काममयो देवः कामभावनयाञ्जितः 3.9.50ab
स च तां नाग्रहीद्दत्तां पिता म इति हेतुगीः 4.1.30cd
स च पृष्टो यथाप्रश्नं प्रत्युत्तरमभाषत 4.3.27cd
स चापि मधु सर्वेषां भूतानां तानि तस्य च 2.5.27ab
स चापि मधु सर्वेषां सर्वभूतानि तस्य च 2.5.30cd
स चैवं शक्यते वक्तुं लोकालोकादिमानतः 3.3.150cd
सच्च त्यच्चादिकां भित्तिं मोहात्प्रापदिति श्रुतिः 1.4.445cd
सच्च त्यच्चेति तत्सत्यं पञ्चभूतात्मकं विदुः 1.6.39ab
सजनात्तावथोत्क्रम्य मिथस्तत्र यदूचतुः 3.2.140ab
सजनादिति नातः स्यादन्योक्तिभयकारणम् 3.2.138cd
सजने प्रश्न एतस्मिन्ख्याप्यमाने त्वयोदिते 3.2.136ab
सजाति नास्ति सामान्यमनवस्था तथा सति 4.3.226ab
सजातीयगिरा चात्र भवता किं विवक्षितम् 4.3.225ab
सजातीयनिषेधो वा ह्येकशब्देन भण्यते 4.3.1801ab
सजातीयप्रयुक्तं यद्बुद्ध्यन्तं रूपमात्मनः 4.3.1510ab
सजातीयाद्विनिष्क्रान्तावनुत्क्रान्ततराविमौ 3.5.201cd
सजातीयासजातीयद्वितीयार्थानभिप्लुतम् 3.4.22ab
सजातीयासजातीयनियमोऽतो न युज्यते 4.3.236ab
सजातीयासजातीयैर्देहोपकृतिरिष्यते 4.3.231ab
सजातीयेषु नियता दृश्यते नान्यजातिषु 2.3.105cd
संचक्रुर्गुरवोऽनुवृत्तगुरवो वृत्तिं सतां शान्तये SV 2b

संचेत्यते यथा दीपो विज्ञानमपि तत्तथा 4.3.515ab
संजातसंशयो राजा याज्ञवल्क्यमपृच्छत 4.3.279cd
संजीवनं तदन्येषां प्राणानां भवतीश्वरात् 5.16.37cd
संज्ञानाशेन चाविद्याहेतूत्थापह्नुतिं तथा 2.4.448cd
संज्ञा प्रेत्यात्मनो नास्तीत्येतच्छ्रुत्वा त्वचूचुदत् 2.4.445ab
संज्ञेयं किमु विध्वस्तसंसारानर्थकारणे 2.4.482ab
संज्ञेयं प्रथते मोहान्न त्वसौ वस्तुनिश्चितौ 2.4.484cd
सततं सर्वभूतानां तिष्ठत्येष पुरीतति 4.3.1066cd
स तथोद्भूतविज्ञान आत्मा देहान्निगच्छति 4.4.96cd
सतश्च ग्रहणं विद्याच्चतुर्णामुपलक्षणम् 2.3.40cd
सतश्च तस्य कामादिरूपाण्यपि च वक्ष्यति 1.5.99cd
स तादृक्क्रतुबिम्बोऽस्य संक्रान्तः स्वसुते पितुः 1.5.314cd
स तावत्परिमाणोऽभूद्योगेन परमेश्वरः 1.4.110cd
सता सोम्येति सन्नाम्ना ब्रह्म तत्र विवक्षितम् 2.1.450cd
सति कर्मणि वैचित्र्यं भूतानामुपपद्यते 3.2.157ab
सति चासति चैवं स्यात्तत्प्रयोजकमीरितम् 3.3.2cd
सति ज्ञाने तदुभयं तत्तु नैवोपपद्यते 1.4.1697ab
सति धर्मिणि धर्माणां चिन्तेयमुपपद्यते 4.3.464cd
सति नासदभावोऽपि ह्युक्तं तादात्म्यमागमात् 4.3.802cd
सति यस्य प्रमाणत्वे प्रामाण्यं स्यादद्वयोरपि 2.1.536ab
सति व्यभिचरत्येव तदन्यद्वस्तु मोहजम् 4.3.1689ab
सति स्याच्चेदनाशङ्का स्त्रीपुंदृष्टान्तनिर्णयात् 4.3.1396cd
स तु विषयसंपर्कः कस्माद्भवति कारणात् SV 51cd
सतैव सर्ववस्तूनि बिभ्रत्यात्मानमात्मना 4.3.1687ab
सतोऽभिव्यञ्जकं मानं स्वभावोऽयं मितेर्भवेत् 2.4.456ab
सतो न व्यतिरेकेण भेदो नापि सदन्वयात् 5.1.89ab
सतोरेव यतो योगः सिद्धं कार्यमतः सदा 1.2.122cd
सतो हि व्यञ्जकं मानं न तु तत्कुम्भकारवत् 3.2.86ab
सत्कर्मभिस्तु तं देवं जगतः कारणं परम् 2.1.458ab
सत्कार्यवादिनो यस्मादभिव्यक्तिः प्रशस्यते 4.4.331ab
सत्कृत्य च यथाशास्त्रं राजाथ तमुवाच ह 6.2.57ab
सत्तत्त्वं सर्वभावानां तत्र तावन्न भेदधीः 4.3.1686ab

सत्तत्त्वकमिदं सर्वमिति संसाध्य यत्नतः 1.2.29ab
सत्तत्त्वव्यतिरेकेण नान्या जनिमतो गतिः 3.8.17cd
सत्तत्त्वापेक्षयाभेदो भावानां नाभ्युपेयते SV 352ab
सत्तातोऽपि न भेदः स्याद्द्रव्यत्वादेः कुतोऽन्यतः SV 968ab
सत्तामात्रेण किं कार्यं समवाय्यादिकारणम् 1.2.81ab
सत्तामात्रेण चेत्कुर्यात्कारणत्रितयं तदा 1.2.82ab
सत्तामात्रोपकारीणि धनानि धनिनां न हि 2.4.50ab
सत्ता येनात्मना कस्मिन्नोता प्रोतेति भण्यताम् 3.8.12cd
सत्तावगुण्ठिताश्चैते सर्वे भावाः सदैव हि SV 972ab
सत्ता वानन्तरगिरा ब्रह्मणः प्रतिषिध्यते 2.5.141ab
सत्ता संभाव्यतेऽन्यत्र प्रत्यग्वद्ग्राह्यवस्तुनः 1.5.120cd
सत्तेत्यत्र ततः स्वार्थस्तद्धितोऽत्र भवन्भवेत् 4.3.1688cd
सत्त्वं तेजोऽत्र विज्ञेयं तदेव करणात्मना 4.4.25ab
सत्त्वं वा यदि वासत्त्वं कार्यकारणवस्तुनः 3.8.125ab
सत्त्वं वा यदि वासत्त्वं नातो मेये प्रमाणतः 4.3.165cd
सत्त्वपूर्वमिदं कार्यं तमोन्तस्थघटादिवत् 1.2.74cd
सत्त्ववन्नापि चाभेदे मानमेयौ प्रसिध्यतः 4.3.163cd
सत्त्वस्यापि तथोत्कर्षः कुतश्चिदुपजायते 2.3.163cd
सत्त्वाद्विनिष्ठितार्थश्च सत्स्रोतोन्तरनिष्ठितः 4.3.657ab
सत्पदेनाभिधीयेते मन्त्रेऽस्मिन्प्राग्यथोदिते 1.3.356cd
सत्परिच्छेदकैर्नापि प्रत्यक्षाद्यैर्ग्रहो भवेत् 2.1.594ab
सत्य आत्मनि कूटस्थ आश्रिता इति भण्यते 4.3.1263cd
सत्यं ज्ञानमनन्तं च विज्ञानघनमित्यपि 4.3.1757ab
सत्यं ब्रह्मासृजन्नापः कारणत्वादपां ततः 5.5.6cd
सत्यं वस्तु कथं भिन्द्यात्पुंव्यपेक्षाविनिर्मितः SV 956cd
सत्यकामादिशब्देन यदप्यन्यत्र भाषितम् 4.3.1338ab
सत्यज्ञानादिरूपस्य प्रत्यगात्मन एव च 1.4.237ab
सत्यतात्र ह्युपायानामुपेये किं तयेष्यते 1.4.993cd
सत्यत्वमिव मानेन मिथ्यात्वमपि वस्तुनः 4.3.1235cd
सत्यत्वेऽपि तथैकत्वान्नानेकत्वं तथापि च 4.3.1681cd
सत्यन्तरङ्गे विज्ञाने बहिरङ्गं न सिध्यति SV 368ab
सत्यपि ब्रह्मवेदित्वे नासंत्यक्तैषणो यतिः 2.4.21ab

सत्यभूतैकहेतुत्वान्मिथ्यात्वं तस्य किंकृतम् 4.3.220cd
सत्यभूयं भवेदेव नैनमित्यादियुक्तिगीः 5.5.14cd
सत्यमन्यत्र तद्ग्राह्यं तस्य तत्रैव योग्यतः 1.5.134ab
सत्यमित्यभिधीयन्ते तेषां सत्यं परं पदम् 2.1.424cd
सत्यमेतन्मनो मुक्त्वा न तस्यास्त्यन्यतो गतिः 4.4.743cd
सत्यमेवं तथापीदं मात्रादानं परात्मनः 4.3.898ab
सत्यमेवं तथाप्यत्र प्रष्टव्यमवशिष्यते 4.3.794ab
सत्यमेवं तथाप्येष नृपः पप्रच्छ तं मुनिम् 4.3.29ab
सत्यमेवं भवेदेतद्यद्यात्माप्यन्य इष्यते 1.4.982ab
सत्यमेवं शमादीनां प्राप्तत्वान्नेष्यते विधिः 4.4.1218ab
सत्यमेव तदासेति यदुक्तं हृदयात्मना 5.4.3ab
सत्यवादित्वसिद्ध्यर्थं शंतनोस्तदपीक्ष्यताम् 6.2.133cd
सत्यशब्दाभिधेयार्थं तया द्वारा परं पदम् 2.3.249cd
सत्यसंकल्पहेतोः स स्त्रीसक्त इव चाभवत् 1.4.112cd
सत्यस्य परमार्थस्य द्वारमाच्छादितं रवेः 5.17.3cd
सत्यस्य सत्यमिति तन्नान्यथा व्यपदेशभाक् 2.3.251cd
सत्यस्य सत्यमिति या ब्रह्मोपनिषदुच्यते 2.1.423ab
सत्या अवितथा धर्मा यस्य मानव्यपाश्रयात् 5.17.5ab
सत्यादप्यनुपायत्वाद्घटान्नाग्निर्हि गम्यते SV 896cd
सत्यानृतविभागोऽयं तथाप्यनृतवस्तुनि 4.3.1234ab
सत्यानृते इति तथा सर्वसंन्यासपूर्वकम् SV 221ab
सत्यानृते सुखदुःखे वेदाँल्लोकद्वयं तथा 3.5.161ab
सत्यामपि च सामग्र्यां वन्ध्यापुत्राद्यसत्त्वतः 1.2.75ab
सत्यामपि त्वविद्यायां प्रमाणानुगमात्पुरा 4.3.1288ab
सत्यामेव यतस्तस्यां संसारानर्थविभ्रमः 1.4.1289cd
सत्यासत्यविभागोऽयमविभागात्मवस्तुनि 1.3.52ab
सत्यास्त इम इत्यादि स्तुतिर्वा स्याद्विधित्सिते 4.4.453cd
सत्येन लभ्यस्तपसा ह्येष आत्मा सम्यग्ज्ञानेन ब्रह्मचर्येण नित्यम् 4.4.1257cd
सत्येन्द्रियविकारत्वात्तच्चापि न निराश्रयम् 4.3.1012cd
सत्येव नश्वरस्यास्य स्वतः किं साधनैर्वद 3.2.93cd
सत्येव प्रत्यगज्ञाने तस्याज्ञानसमन्वयात् 4.3.1308cd

सत्येव साक्षिणि यतो भावाभावौ प्रसिध्यतः 4.3.1427ab
सत्योपाधिविशिष्टस्य तद्वै तदिति भण्यते 5.4.1cd
सत्यो वा यदि वा मिथ्या स्वप्नदेहोऽभ्युपेयते 4.3.221ab
स त्वं जानंश्चतुष्पान्मे ब्रह्म व्याख्यातुमर्हसि 4.1.16ab
स त्वमङ्गकषायोऽसि दिग्धविद्धां मृगीमिव 6.4.40cd
स त्वयेहाभिनिर्दिष्टो दिशस्तस्यापि देवता 3.9.53cd
सत्सिद्धिमेव संभाव्य सिद्धाः स्मेत्यभिमन्वते 4.3.1693ab
सत्सु प्रत्यक्षविधिषु यथोक्तेष्वफलः श्रमः 3.5.165ab
सत्स्वप्यन्येषु भूतेषु भूयस्त्वादाप एव तु 5.5.3ab
सत्स्वश्वादिषु कालादिदृष्टीरङ्गेषु योजयेत् 1.1.4ab
सदतो जनिमत्तत्त्वं सर्पादे रशना यथा 3.8.17ab
सदन्यबुद्धिगम्यस्य श्रुतिस्तस्मादनेकशः 3.8.22ab
सदप्यन्यदुदास्ते किं स्वाश्रयग्रहणं प्रति 1.4.472cd
सदप्यभावरूपं वा तद्वदव्यरितेकतः 1.4.331cd
सदप्यात्मादिकं सर्वं दर्शनादावकारणम् 1.5.107ab
सदसत्त्वादिसंभेदशून्यत्वादात्मवस्तुनः 4.3.1623cd
सदसत्सदसच्चेति समस्तव्यस्तमेव च 2.3.181cd
सदसीति क्रियानिष्ठं प्रत्यक्षाद्यर्थनिष्ठितम् 1.4.1108ab
सदा कार्यं न जायेत कारणासंभवात्सदा SV 68cd
सदात्मतैवं सर्वस्य नाभावात्मकता सतः SV 934ab
सदात्मनोपलब्धिस्तु न कदा चन हीयते 1.2.91cd
सदा त्वाहं प्रपश्यामि सत्यधर्मान्वयाद्यथा 5.17.10ab
सदानश्वरदृष्टित्वं प्रतीचो गम्यते स्फुटम् 4.3.1468cd
सदानुदितानस्तमितभास्वद्विज्ञानमात्रतः 1.4.1213ab
सदानुदितालुप्तैकज्ञप्तिमात्रसतत्त्वकम् 1.4.1099ab
सदानुदितालुप्तैकज्ञानमूर्तिरिति त्वया 1.4.1302ab
सदानुमिन्वते सांख्यास्तथा चान्येऽपि वादिनः 1.4.107cd
सदापहतपाप्मेति भयहेतोश्च लङ्घनात् 4.3.1301ab
सदा प्राप्तात्मविद्यापि नातो विधिरिहेष्यते 1.4.766cd
सदाहीनाननुदितभास्वदेकदृगात्मनः 4.3.1515cd
सदिति व्यक्तरूपं यद्गृह्यमाणविशेषणम् 2.3.26ab
सदित्यादिपदैरात्मा साक्षान्नः प्रतिपाद्यते SV 704cd

सदृशार्थं विनैवेयं क्लृप्ता सादृश्यधीर्यदि 1.2.70cd
सदेकत्वमशेषेषु वस्तुष्वव्यभिचारि हि 4.3.1691ab
सदेवताकं पूर्वोक्तं समर्थमिति चेन्मतम् 3.2.145ab
सदेव वस्त्वभिव्यक्तं तथाव्यक्तं च लक्ष्यते 1.2.77cd
सदेव व्यज्यते सर्वमिति नैवापनुद्यते 1.2.100cd
सदेवसप्रतिष्ठादिशरीरं प्रतिजज्ञिवान् 3.9.69ab
सदेवाः सप्रतिष्ठाश्च दिशो वेदेत्यथाब्रवीत् 3.9.68cd
सदेवाः सप्रतिष्ठैता दिशोऽहमितिवादिनम् 3.9.70ab
सदेवागमतः सर्वं प्रत्यक्षाच्च सदीक्ष्यते 1.2.30ab
सदेवेति तथा स्पष्टं छान्दोग्योपनिषद्वचः 3.8.18cd
सदेवेत्यादिकं शास्त्रं बाधितं स्यात्तथा सति 1.5.330cd
सदेवेत्यादिना चास्य तथा सत्यविरुद्धता 4.3.1803ab
सदेवेत्यादिभिर्वाक्यैः कारणं ब्रह्म गीयते 1.4.375cd
सदेवेत्यादिवाक्येभ्यः कृत्स्नं वस्तु यतोऽद्वयम् 1.4.655ab
सदेवेत्यादिवाक्येभ्यः प्रमा स्फुटतरा भवेत् SV 208ab
सदेवेदमतः सर्वमुद्भूतिस्थितिहानिषु 3.8.18ab
सदेवेदमिति स्पष्टं सन्मूला इति चापरम् SV 937ab
सदेशितव्यकार्यार्थसाक्ष्यार्थेनास्य संगतेः 4.3.354cd
सदैकानुदितालुप्तप्रत्यग्दृष्टिसतत्त्वकम् 3.4.188cd
सदैवाव्यभिचारित्वाद्दृष्टिद्रष्ट्रोः परस्परम् 3.4.183ab
सदोत्पत्तेरनुत्पाद्योऽनाप्यश्चापि तथात्मनः 4.4.1114ab
सदोत्पन्नात्मनि मितिरुत्पाद्याकारणादिधीः 2.4.438ab
सद्देवभावहेतुत्वाच्छास्त्रीये ज्ञानकर्मणी 1.3.356ab
सद्धीगम्याद्धिरुग्वस्तु न मानेनावसीयते 2.4.290cd
सद्बीजं सत्प्रतिष्ठं च सदायतनमेव च 1.2.10ab
सद्भावं प्रागवोचाम प्रत्यक्षैकप्रमाणतः 4.3.527cd
सद्भावश्चोपलब्धिश्च स्वार्थप्रत्यक्चिदाश्रयात् 2.3.189ab
सद्भावेऽपि च भान्वादेः पारार्थ्याद्देहवन्न तत् 4.3.369ab
सद्यः पुमर्थसंसिद्धेः कार्यसिद्धिर्न वीक्ष्यते SV 587cd
सद्रूपत्वापरित्यागादवान्तरनिबन्धनाः SV 967ab
सद्वितीयपरोक्षत्वे यतोऽज्ञानैकहेतुके 4.4.852ab
स धर्म इति विज्ञेयः सत्यं शास्त्रार्थलक्षणम् 1.4.1624cd

सधीरिति श्रुतेरत्र हृदीति प्रकृतत्वतः 4.3.381cd
स न वेत्ति यथा बाह्यं सुखाविष्टो न चान्तरम् 4.3.1314cd
सनालं पद्मकोशाभं पञ्चच्छिद्रमधोमुखम् 2.1.320cd
सनिमित्तं प्राग्रूपमात्मनो मोहहेतुतः 1.4.1499cd
स निश्चयो वः किं शब्दादथान्यस्मादितीर्यताम् SV 664cd
संततावुपसन्ध्यां त्वं पश्वादेर्मे करिष्यसि 6.4.117cd
संततौ चानवस्थानान्नाश्रयत्वं प्रमाणतः 3.2.150cd
संतत्यन्तरवद्यद्वा विज्ञानान्तरवत्तथा 4.3.561ab
संतत्या जायमानैस्तैरिति यद्व्याहृतं पुरा 4.3.648cd
संतत्यारम्भकधियामियत्तानवधारणात् 1.4.1517ab
संतत्योत्पद्यमानैश्चेत्फलहेत्वात्मभिर्भवेत् 4.3.619ab
संतनोतीति संतानः कर्ता चेदभिधीयते 4.3.627cd
संतर्प्यातः स्वमात्मानमन्नेनास्मानपीश्वर 1.3.250ab
संतानस्याव्यवच्छित्तौ सर्वदैव प्रसज्यते 4.3.646ab
संतानानुपपत्तेश्च नैवमप्युपपद्यते 4.3.627ab
संतानिनस्तु संस्कारा विद्यन्ते परमार्थतः 4.3.691ab
संतानिनां स्वसंतानाद्भिन्नाभिन्नत्वकल्पने 4.3.636ab
संतानिभ्यश्च संतानोऽभिन्नो भिन्नोऽथवा द्विधा 4.3.633cd
संतानिव्यतिरेकेण यस्मान्नैव स विद्यते 4.3.690cd
संतानो यदि धात्वर्थो भावश्चेदभिधीयते 4.3.629cd
सन्त्यात्मनि न चेत्कामास्तदेवं फलवद्वचः 4.4.454ab
सन्त्येवात्मपरिज्ञानसाधनानां प्रसिद्धये 4.4.1260ab
संदिग्धनिश्चयाद्येवं ज्ञानधर्मो विशेषयन् SV 983ab
संदिह्यमानः सर्वत्र पदार्थोऽन्यत्र निश्चितात् 4.3.323ab
संदेहनिर्णयादन्यत्स्वभावादि यदुच्यते 4.3.741ab
संदेहस्तेन देहोऽयं संदेघश्छान्दसत्वतः 4.4.617cd
संदेहे गहनेऽत्रात्मा प्रविष्टो जलसूर्यवत् 4.4.619ab
संधत्तां सोऽश्वशिरसा युवाभ्यां मध्वथाब्रवीत् 2.5.111ab
संधत्तेऽनुभवेनैव न तदन्येन केनचित् 4.3.178cd
संध्यं तृतीयमित्युक्तिः पूरणप्रत्ययश्रुतेः 4.3.837ab
संध्यस्वप्नविधिस्तावदेवं समुपवर्णितः 4.3.854ab
संनिकृष्टार्थसंसृष्टस्वार्थमात्राभिधानतः SV 881ab

संनिधौ च विशेषो न प्रदीपे तद्वदीक्ष्यते 4.3.510cd
संनिध्यसंनिधानेषु घटादीनामविक्रिया 4.3.890cd
संनिध्यसंनिधानेषु धीवृत्तीनामविक्रियः 4.3.891cd
संनिध्यसंनिधानेषु प्रकाश्यानामविक्रिया 4.3.1459cd
संनिपत्य न च ज्ञानं कर्माज्ञानं निरस्यति 3.3.58ab
सन्नेव नाशोऽपीष्टश्चेत्सत्सता न विरुध्यते 1.2.49ab
सन्नेवाभावरूपोऽपि त्विष्टः शून्यत्ववादिनाम् 1.4.592cd
संन्यस्ताशेषकर्मा सन्बोध्यतेऽजातशत्रुणा 1.5.272cd
संन्यस्य सर्वकर्माणि प्रत्यक्प्रवणधीर्नरः 4.4.1252ab
संन्यस्य सर्वकर्माणि सर्वदोषानपानुदन् 1.5.310ab
संन्यस्यात्मानमन्विच्छेदित्यदुष्टं स्मृतेर्वचः 3.5.161cd
संन्यस्यैकात्म्यसंबोधाद्धित्वा मोहं विशुद्धधीः 2.4.25cd
संन्यास एव ताभ्यां च विशेषेणातिवर्तते 3.5.202ab
संन्यासं साधनं वक्ति वाङ्मनःकायकर्मणाम् 3.5.146cd
संन्यासः श्रूयते स्पष्टः पुत्रैश्वर्ये सुखं वसेत् 1.5.309cd
संन्यासमेव ब्रुवते मुक्तये सर्वकर्मणाम् 3.5.203cd
संन्यासमेवोपक्रम्य संप्रत्तिः श्रूयते श्रुतौ 1.5.270ab
संन्यासयोगाद्यतयः शुद्धसत्त्वाः 3.5.148b
संन्याससाधनं ज्ञानं निर्वक्त्यत्रापि च श्रुतिः 3.5.109ab
संन्याससाधनं प्रोक्तममृतत्वैकसाधनम् 2.5.2cd
संन्यासस्य न विज्ञातं तच्छास्त्रेणेह बोध्यते 2.4.7cd
संन्यासस्य विधानाच्च कार्योऽतोऽसौ मुमुक्षुभिः 2.4.28cd
संन्यासाद्ब्रह्मणः स्थानं तथा च स्मृतिशासनम् 6.2.137cd
संन्यासिनोऽपि दृश्यन्ते देवसंदूषिताशयाः 1.4.1584cd
संन्यासैकसहायात्मयाथात्म्यज्ञानमुच्यते 3.5.2cd
संन्यासोऽपि तथैवायं नैव कार्यतया मतः 4.4.1145cd
सन्मार्गप्रतिपत्त्यर्थं राजोवाच स्वशास्त्रतः 6.2.24cd
स पुत्रेणैवेति वचस्तथा च श्रूयते स्फुटम् 1.4.1825cd
सप्तमावसितावुक्तं मार्गप्रार्थनमग्नितः 6.2.2ab
सप्तमी चाष्टमी चेति सैवैका प्रोच्यते ततः 2.2.28cd
सप्तम्यन्तपदच्छेदात्कथं चेदिति भण्यते SV 316cd
सप्तम्यन्तेन तत्प्रत्यङ्लिङ्गात्मातोऽभिधीयते 2.5.56cd

सप्तान्नप्रविभागेन तद्विभज्य प्रदर्श्यते 1.5.13cd
सप्रकाशं गवाश्वं च न च पश्यति चेतनः 1.5.104cd
सप्रपञ्चं यथावच्च सर्वमुक्तमशेषतः 2.1.363cd
स प्रमेयः स्वयंज्योतिः प्राक्प्रसिद्धेः प्रमातृतः 1.4.292cd
सप्रयोगगणः सर्वः सौक्ष्म्येण परमेण तु 3.8.34ab
सप्रयोजकतन्नाशे मुक्तिरस्योपपद्यते 3.2.36cd
स ब्रह्म त्यदिति तथा श्रुतिरप्याह तत्स्फुटम् 3.9.4cd
स ब्राह्मण इति गिरा यः श्रुत्या प्रतिपादितः 4.4.1185ab
स ब्राह्मण इति स्पष्टं श्रुतिरन्ते च वक्ष्यति 3.5.92cd
सभागविक्रियानित्यत्वादिदोषः प्रसज्यते 1.4.587cd
सभागसंततिः सा हि नाविच्छेदमृते यतः 4.3.646cd
सभावनं सहेत्वेवं ध्यानं सर्वमपार्थकम् 4.4.768cd
सभावनमतः कर्म प्रतीचः प्रविविच्यते 4.3.1038cd
स भूरिगत्युपचयाद्ग्रामाद्ग्रामान्तरं व्रजेत् 1.4.1551cd
समं तद्वर्त्मनैवास्य संबन्धग्रहणं यतः SV 712cd
समं त्रयं त्रिषु भवेत्रैगुण्यं चेद्रवौ मतम् 1.4.1038ab
समग्राशेषचार्वङ्गो राद्धो भोगक्षमः पुमान् 4.3.1845cd
समञ्जसं न क्लृप्तं स्यात्संभवेऽप्यविरोधिनः 1.4.1268cd
समदृष्टिप्रशंसैषा यदि वा भूतपर्वतः 3.3.128ef
समधत्तां शिरस्तस्य विद्यां स्वशिरसाथ सः 2.5.103cd
समधत्तां शिरोऽश्वस्य तेन विद्यामुवाच सः 2.5.102cd
समन्ताद्द्विगुणोऽब्धिश्च संवेष्ट्य पृथिवीं स्थितः 3.3.153cd
समन्वालोचयच्छंभुः सिसृक्षुर्विविधं जगत् 1.2.173cd
समर्थनं कल्पनार्थस्त्वष्टावयवशस्तथा 6.4.100ab
समर्थमन्यत्पश्यामः क्रियाकारकरूपकम् 1.4.765cd
समर्था सैव ते यस्मादुद्बोद्धुं ज्ञानकर्मणी 4.4.121ab
समर्पयेयुर्विषयमित्येतदपि नेष्यते 1.4.824cd
समर्पितं चेच्छब्देन बुद्धौ वस्तु यथोदितम् 4.4.784ab
समर्पितत्वं प्राणादेः श्रूयते प्रत्यगात्मनि 2.5.79ab
समवायाच्च संबन्धे नैकरूप्यं विभिन्नयोः SV 969ab
समवायेन संबन्धे को हेतुरिति नेष्यते SV 970cd
समवेतं हि यद्यत्र चैतन्यं स्याच्छरीरके 4.3.202ab

समष्टिव्यष्टिभावेन कर्मणः सर्वदेष्यते 3.7.11cd
समष्टिव्यष्टिभावेन वायुः सर्वाश्रयः पुरा 3.6.20ab
समष्टिव्यष्टिभेदं वा व्यपेक्ष्य बहुवागियम् 6.2.142cd
समष्टिव्यष्टिरूपं यो वायुमात्मेति संश्रितः 3.3.173ab
समस्तकार्यदोषोक्तिप्रसङ्गान्मित्यभावतः SV 634cd
समस्तमृत्योस्तमसः सम्यगात्मावबोधनम् 3.2.23ab
समस्तव्यस्ततां केचिद्ब्रह्मणः प्रतिजानते 3.8.83ab
समस्तव्यस्ततां तस्मान्मानान्तरमितत्वतः 1.4.692ab
समस्तव्यस्तता तस्मान्नैवेह श्रुतिमानतः 2.4.241ab
समस्तव्यस्ततादृष्टावेवमादि सुदुर्घटम् 1.4.962ab
समस्तव्यस्ततादृष्टिरेकधैवेतिवाक्यतः 4.4.675ab
समस्तव्यस्ततापक्षस्तदा कुप्यति कल्पितः 1.6.91cd
समस्तव्यस्ततामेवं सति व्याचक्षतेऽत्र ये 4.3.1184ab
समस्तव्यस्तता यस्मान्नेह प्रत्यग्धियेक्ष्यते 1.4.1183cd
समस्तव्यस्ततारूप आत्मैवैक इतीरितः 4.3.1656cd
समस्तव्यस्ततारूपं यो वक्तीहात्मनः श्रुतेः 2.4.464ab
समस्तव्यस्तताव्याख्या तस्मादन्धपरंपरा 4.3.1187ab
समस्तव्यस्तताशङ्कामुच्छेत्तुं चोत्तरं वचः 4.3.1343ab
समस्तव्यस्ततैवं च न मानादुपपद्यते 1.4.966cd
समस्तव्यस्ततैवेह प्रत्यगज्ञानभूमिका 1.3.269ab
समस्तव्यस्तभतस्य ब्रह्मण्यवसितात्मनः 5.1.106ab
समस्तव्यस्तमैकात्म्यं येषां चापास्तभेदकम् 1.4.417ab
समस्तव्यस्तरूपत्वं यदि स्याद्ब्रह्मणः श्रुतेः 4.3.1659cd
समस्तव्यस्तरूपाभ्यां लोकेऽपि व्याकृतिर्यतः 1.4.398cd
समस्तव्यस्तसंदृष्टौ न किंचिदपि दृश्यते 3.2.107ab
समस्तव्यस्तसंदृष्टौ नाद्वैताद्द्वैतता पृथक् 3.2.100ab
समस्ताकारवज्ज्ञानं कुर्यात्प्रत्यक्षबाधतः 1.6.85cd
समस्तादिप्रतिज्ञार्थसिद्धये ब्रह्मवादिनः 2.5.67cd
समस्तैरिन्द्रियैर्हीनः संप्रसन्नो निराकुलः 4.3.1403ab
समस्योपासनं वाच्यमित्यर्थो ग्रन्थ उत्तरः 1.2.210cd
समांशपरिणामे तु सुरभिर्जायते शुभः 2.4.361ab
समाख्यानुपपत्तिश्च ब्रह्मणोऽन्यस्य वेदनात् 1.4.1269ab

समाख्यासंश्रयात्तस्मादभूत्प्राक्प्रत्यगात्मनि 2.1.258ab
समादित्सति निःशेषं ज्ञानं राजातिपण्डितः 4.3.1893cd
समान उपसंहृत्य जगत्कारणरूपके 4.4.426ab
समान एकः सन्नात्मा स्वात्माविद्यातदुद्भवैः 4.3.380ab
समान एव सँल्लोकौ प्राप्तप्राप्तव्यलक्षणौ 4.3.403ab
समानः कारणात्मा वा यत्र सर्वोपसंहृतिः 4.3.399ab
समानः सन्नुभौ लोकौ स्वप्नबुद्धान्तसंज्ञितौ 4.3.427ab
समानकर्तृकत्वोक्तेर्विभागोक्तेः फलस्य च 4.4.1136ab
समानयोने रूपस्य वाक्प्रमातोऽवबोधिका 1.5.130cd
समानलोकतानेन सालोक्यमिति शब्द्यते 1.3.309cd
समानविषयत्वेऽपि नाद्याविद्यां निहन्ति चेत् 1.4.1519ab
समानशब्दौ तेनेमौ स्यातां भिन्नार्थवाचकौ 3.5.8ab
समाना वंशर्षयोऽमी ह्या समाप्तेरितीक्ष्यताम् 6.5.15cd
समाने च तथोदानः सूत्रात्मनि समाश्रितः 3.9.91ab
समापनीयं निःशेषं समासव्यासवर्जिते 3.9.106cd
समापय्यात्मविज्ञानं भूयोऽप्याख्यानरूपकम् 3.9.100cd
समाप्तं याज्ञवल्कीयं काण्डमैकात्म्यनिष्ठितम् 5.1.1ab
समाप्तः सप्तमोऽध्यायः प्राप्तावसर उच्यते 6.1.1ab
समाप्ता ब्रह्मविद्येयं कैवल्यावाप्तयेऽखिला 2.5.92ab
समाप्ताशेषविज्ञेयपुरुषार्थस्तथा परः 2.1.18ab
सगाप्ताशेषविद्यं हि समावर्त्य पिता सुतम् 6.2.20ab
समाप्ताशेषविद्योऽसीत्येवमाहोत्ससर्ज च 6.2.20cd
समाप्तिं न समायाति प्रधानं यदसंभवे 4.4.1239ab
समाप्तिः कर्मणो नापि लोकत्रयफलादृते 1.4.1832ab
समाप्तेरधिकाराणामप्रवृत्तिः प्रसज्यते 1.6.89cd
समाप्तो मधुकाण्डार्थो याज्ञवल्कीयकाण्डगः 3.1.1ab
समाप्तौ ब्राह्मणस्योक्तेरयमर्थोऽवसीयते 6.5.5cd
समाप्य तत्फलं कृत्स्नं जातकौतूहलाः परे 1.4.1128cd
समाप्यामौनमखिलं बाल्यपाण्डित्यलक्षणम् 3.5.189ab
समाशङ्कितनिःशेषदोषानाघ्रातं स्फुटम् 1.4.1168ab
समासव्यासतस्तद्वत्पञ्च भूतान्यविद्यया 4.4.183ab
समासव्यासतस्तस्माद्यथोक्तज्ञानकर्मभिः 1.5.11ab

समासव्यासरूपेण शाकल्यो यदपृच्छत 3.9.105ab
समासेनाभिधानं स्याद्यदि वा शोककार्यतः 3.5.63cd
समासेनैव निर्दिष्टे कारणत्वाविशेषतः 4.4.122ab
समासोऽत्र परिग्राह्यो निषादस्थपतिर्यथा 4.4.1299cd
समाहरति वृत्तीर्यो हृद्देशे कीलवत्स्थितः 1.5.149ab
समाहारोऽथवा भेदो नेदित्येतत्पदं भवेत् 1.3.224ab
समाहितोक्त्याथेदानीं तन्निरोधो विधीयते 4.4.1246cd
समित्यस्याभिसंबन्धादेनेनेत्येवमुच्यते 4.3.10cd
समित्यैकात्म्यमात्रेण प्राणानां स्थितिरुच्यते 4.4.291cd
समिद्धमादिभी रूपैर्लोकयते लोकगीरपि 6.2.75cd
समिन्धनात्समिद्धान् रश्मयो धूम इत्यपि 6.2.81ab
समिन्निर्गमसामान्यादर्चिरहस्तथैव च 6.2.81cd
समीक्ष्यते हिरुङ्नापि तेनासावात्मतत्त्वकः 1.4.980cd
समुच्चयः कुतो द्रव्यगुणवज्ज्ञानकर्मणोः SV 358cd
समुच्चयनिवृत्त्यर्थं न्यायश्चापि पुरोदितः 4.3.1871ab
समुच्चयनिषेधश्च युक्तिभिर्वक्ष्यते स्फुटम् 1.4.1121ab
समुच्चयप्रसिद्धिः स्यात्तयोर्भिन्नाश्रयत्वतः 1.3.382cd
समुच्चयविवक्षात्र न मनागपि युज्यते 4.3.1870ab
समुच्चयश्चाप्यसकृत्पुरैव सुनिराकृतः 3.3.57ab
समुच्चयस्ततोऽन्योऽयमव्यक्तब्रह्मविद्यया 1.4.1709ab
समुच्चयस्तयोरेवं रविशार्वरयोरिव 3.3.61cd
समुच्चयाच्चेदुभयोरुद्गातृयजमानयोः 1.3.387ab
समुच्चयात्तु तत्प्राप्तावागमादेव निश्चितिः 1.3.374cd
समुच्चये चशब्दाश्च तथा सर्वत्र योजयेत् 1.4.738cd
समुच्चयोऽतस्तस्यापि भिन्नाधिष्ठानतो न च 1.3.383cd
समुच्चयोऽयमस्माभिर्यथाभाणि तथा यदि 4.4.590ab
समुच्चयो न तस्य स्यान्नाङ्गेनाङ्गिसमुच्चयः SV 361cd
समुच्चितिरयुक्तेयं तदाप्येकत्वहेतुतः 1.5.231cd
समुच्चितिर्न चैकस्य रुद्रेणापि समर्थ्यते 1.5.229cd
समुच्चिते सजातीयैरुत्तरैस्ते विशेषणैः 2.3.16cd
समुच्चीयेत तज्ज्ञानं न तु कर्मविरोधि यत् 3.3.101cd
समुद्र ईश्वरो ज्ञेयो योनिः कारणमुच्यते 1.1.9ab

समुद्र एव ह्यस्येति विराट्कारणमब्रवीत् 1.2.123cd
समुद्रतरुगोपिण्डदृष्टान्तैः परमात्मनः 1.4.693ab
समुद्रवन्नृत्यति च प्रत्यवस्थं विभुः स्थितः 5.1.57cd
समुद्रादेरिव तदा नावक्ष्यच्छ्रुतिरादरात् 2.1.524cd
समुद्रो द्विगुणो भूमेः परस्तादवतिष्ठते 3.3.147cd
समूलबीजं चेद्वृक्षमावृहेयुस्तदोभयम् 3.9.142ab
समूहस्योभयत्वेऽपि स्मृतेरप्यप्रमाणतः 4.3.1680cd
स मृत्युर्मृत्युशब्देन फलभूतोऽत्र भण्यते 1.3.2cd
समेति मध्ये भोगाय रोदस्योः कर्मणो जगत् 6.2.42cd
समेति स्वप्नबुद्धान्तौ यथायं स्ववशस्तथा 4.3.1902cd
समे निम्नोन्नतानीव चित्रकर्मविदो जनाः 1.4.1628cd
संपच्च परमैषैव मोहोत्थास्त्वन्यसंपदः 4.3.1831ab
संपत्तिमर्हतां संपदल्पीयःकर्मसूच्यते 3.1.47cd
संपत्परं भवेच्छास्त्रं वस्तुतात्पर्यवर्जनात् SV 845cd
संपदां चार्थवादत्वं तेन वेदान्तगोचरे SV 288ab
संपदा चेत्फलप्राप्तिरश्वमेधादिकर्मणाम् 3.1.49ab
संपदैते समाः सर्वे तस्मात्संवत्सरश्रुतिः 1.5.68cd
संपदैवाहुतीर्विद्वान्संपाद्याग्नेस्तथेष्टकाः 1.5.67ab
संपद्यतेऽथ तत्साक्षादात्मत्वेन पुमानयम् 4.4.232cd
संपद्यमान एवात्मा जायते म्रियते यतः 4.3.813ab
रांपन्नोऽतिशयेनातः संपन्नतम उच्यते 4.3.1848cd
संपर्कजनितभ्रान्तिदुःखित्वाध्यस्तहेतुतः 3.9.203cd
संपादनं भवेत्संपदग्निहोत्रादिकर्मणि 3.1.48cd
संपूर्णस्वात्मकार्योऽयं पिता दैवात्मना स्थितः 1.5.321ab
संपूर्यावस्थितो देहं शाकल्यप्रश्ननिष्ठितः 1.5.150cd
संप्रत्तिरिति नामैतदात्मसंस्कारकर्मणः 1.5.285ab
संप्रत्तिलिङ्गात्संन्यासविधिरत्र विवक्षितः 1.5.303ab
संप्रदायविदस्त्वत्र नानात्वैकत्ववादिनः 1.6.46ab
संप्रदायविदस्त्वन्ये यथावच्छास्त्रचक्षुषा 1.4.792ab
संप्रधार्य मनो वाचा मन्त्रलौकिकरूपया 1.4.1845ab
संप्रसाद इदं सर्वमात्मनैवावशिष्यते 4.3.1284cd
संप्रसादमिमं प्राहुः सुषुप्तं तद्विदो जनाः 4.3.976cd

संप्रसादस्य दृष्टान्तः श्येनेनाथाधुनोच्यते 4.3.1159cd

संप्रसादे किमङ्गायं यत्र किंचिन्न वीक्ष्यते 4.3.1074cd

संप्रसादे तु बाह्यस्य वस्तुनोऽसंभवादिदम् 4.3.1198ab

संप्रसादे प्रसन्नश्च तथासङ्गोऽपि वीक्ष्यते 4.3.1155cd

संप्लुष्टनिखिलाविद्ये तत्र कः केन किं वद 2.4.471cd

संप्लुष्टाविद्याबहुलतमसां कर्मनिह्नुतिम् 1.4.134cd

संबध्यते स्वतोऽसङ्ग आत्मत्वादेव कारणात् 4.3.1177cd

संबन्ध एव बहुशो विचारेषु च कीर्तिताः 2.1.534cd

संबन्धं कर्मकाण्डेन पश्चात्सम्यक्प्रवक्ष्यते SV 320cd

संबन्धं कुर्वते केचिदन्यथैव महाधियः 4.3.1088ab

संबन्धं मन्यते योऽपि शाब्दबोधानुसारिणीम् SV 735ab

संबन्धं लभते साक्षात्तथानात्मापि चात्मना 4.4.944cd

संबन्धं वक्तुकामेयं प्रचक्रामोत्तरा श्रुतिः 1.3.339cd

संबन्धकरणाशक्तेस्तत्कर्तुश्चास्मृतेरपि SV 878ab

संबन्धकर्तर्यसति न च सादृश्यसंश्रयात् 1.2.66cd

संबन्धजत्वात्तस्यातः कस्येत्यत्राभिधीयते 2.1.316cd

संबन्धमात्राभिव्यक्तेर्व्यञ्जकत्वात्प्रदीपवत् 1.4.1512ab

संबन्धश्च क्रियात्मत्वान्न सिध्येत्कारकं विना 1.2.116cd

संबन्धहेतोरुच्छित्तेरात्मसंबन्धवर्जितम् 4.4.511ab

संबन्धाग्रहणादात्मा ब्रह्मेति कथमुच्यते SV 859cd

संबन्धानुपपत्तिश्च तदिदंज्ञानयोर्ध्रुवम् 1.2.66ab

संबन्धाभावतस्तस्य मानमेयौ न सिध्यतः 4.3.553cd

संबन्धाभावतस्तेषां क्षणानामपरस्परम् 4.3.696cd

संबन्धावगमो नापि शब्दाद्भूतार्थवाचिनः SV 482ab

संबन्धिविरहेऽसिद्धौ षष्ठ्यर्थत्वं न सिध्यति SV 949ab

संबन्धे सति पाप्मायं स्वफलेनानुतापयेत् 4.4.1290ab

संबन्धोत्तरकाले तु तत्स्मृत्योरेव संगतिः 4.4.958cd

संबन्धो न भवेदन्यैः साधनाद्यभिधायिभिः SV 606cd

संबन्धो वायुरेवेति सावधारणवाक्यतः 3.3.170cd

संबिभत्सत्यनात्मत्वादात्मा तन्नानुमन्यते 4.3.1178cd

संबोधनीय एवासौ सुप्तो राजेव बन्दिभिः SV 240cd

संबोध्यमानोऽपि तथा सुप्तो नैवोदबुध्यत 2.1.99ab

संभवत्येव शीतोऽग्निः प्रमाणान्तरगोचरः 2.1.559ab
संभवन्तीति सर्वत्र संबन्धोऽत्रानुषज्यते 6.2.131cd
संभवस्तद्विरुद्धस्य कुतोऽकृत्स्नस्य वस्तुनः 1.4.655cd
संभवाच्चार्थशेषस्य सर्वसंन्यासरूपिणः 4.4.539ab
संभवाद्विप्रकृष्टयादेरदुष्टो दूषितः पुरा 1.4.610ab
संभवेऽन्यतमस्यापि सर्वेषां संभवो यतः 2.3.34ab
संभवे व्यभिचारे च तच्च स्यात्फलवत्सति 4.4.483cd
संभवे व्यभिचारे च विशेषणविशेष्ययोः 6.2.3ab
संभवोऽस्तीतिविध्यर्थस्तिष्ठासेदिति भण्यते 3.5.182cd
संभारः कोऽस्य गत्यर्थो देहारम्भे च कथ्यताम् 4.4.110cd
संभावनाद्वितीयत्वाद्ब्रह्मण्येवात्मसंस्थितेः 3.4.28cd
संभावनीया निःशेषसूक्ष्मवस्तुष्वपीदृशी 4.3.1643cd
संभावयति मिथ्यैव नभो नीलं यथा तथा 4.3.1269cd
संभावयति संबोधान्नान्यद्वस्त्वन्तरं यथा 1.4.1171cd
संभावयत्यकृत्स्नत्वं प्रत्यगात्मनि मूढधीः 1.4.1206cd
संभावयन्ति द्रष्टारस्तथाज्ञास्तदबोधजैः 3.7.59cd
संभावयन्ति मानानि सर्वाण्यैकात्म्यवस्तुनि 2.1.588cd
संभावयन्प्रतीच्यात्मा तन्मयत्वं निगच्छति 4.4.186cd
संभावयन्प्रमाणत्वं युक्तिं स्वीकृत्य वर्तते SV 777cd
संभावितं न यत्पूर्वं कर्मविज्ञानकाण्डयोः 5.1.2ab
संभावितं न यत्पूर्वं कृत्स्नेऽस्मिन्ब्राह्मणेऽपि तत् 6.5.1ab
संभावितात्मकर्तृत्वो ब्राह्मण्याद्यधिकारवान् 1.4.816ab
संभावितानुशिष्टयर्थं तं राजोपससाद ह 4.2.2cd
संभाव्यं नानपेक्षत्वं नियोगविरहात्क्वचित् SV 447ab
संभाव्यतेऽतो विज्ञेयो यजेतेत्यादिवद्विधिः 1.4.783cd
संभाव्यतेऽनपेक्षत्वं नियोगविरहादपि SV 465ab
संभाव्यतेऽपरं रूपमज्ञातत्वापनोदकृत् 2.4.190cd
संभाव्यते क्षयस्तस्य न कुतश्चिदनन्ततः 5.16.65ab
संभाव्यते चेदक्षादि ह्यैकात्म्यार्थे फलादिवत् 2.4.177ab
संभाव्यते जगत्यस्मिन्बोधमात्रपुरःसरम् 4.4.899ab
संभाव्यते तदज्ञानकार्यमात्रस्तमस्विभिः 3.7.58cd
संभाव्यते न नाशोऽस्य नंष्टुर्नाशाविभागतः 4.3.1554cd

संभाव्यते न यत्तत्र यजमानस्य मानतः 3.1.44ab
संभाव्यते पुमर्थोऽतो विध्यर्थविरहात्क्वचित् SV 197cd
संभाव्यते प्रसङ्गोऽत आदित्योपस्थितेरिह 5.17.2cd
संभाव्यते ब्रह्मधियः सर्वान्त्यत्वैकहेतुतः 1.4.1541cd
संभाव्यते ब्रह्मविद्भिर्यत्तदर्थबुभुत्सवः 1.4.1129cd
संभाव्यते यतोऽत्रैव साक्षादित्यादिलक्षणम् 3.5.53cd
संभाव्यते यथा चैतत्तथोदर्के प्रवक्ष्यते SV 476cd
संभाव्यते यथा मूढैरात्मैवं कर्तृतादिभिः 4.3.1261cd
संभाव्यते सर्वभूतैर्यतः सा ब्रह्मविद्यया 1.4.1130cd
संभाव्यमानसिद्धेर्हि यागादेः कार्यता मता SV 629ab
संभाव्यमिति नः प्राह तत एवेति च श्रुतिः 1.4.68cd
संभाव्यो देवभावोऽस्य देवो भूत्वेति च श्रुतेः 1.3.381cd
संभाव्यो नियमविधिरतो नात्मन्यभेदतः 1.4.930cd
संभूतिवचसापीयमविद्यैवाभिधीयते 4.4.601ab
संभूय कार्यं कुर्याच्चेत्कारणत्रितयं तदा 1.2.85ab
संभूय कार्यभूतानि भूतयोनिं यतो विभुम् 1.2.124ab
संभूय देवते तस्माद्ब्रह्मत्वं संनिगच्छतः 5.14.4cd
संभूय परमत्वं कः स्वतोऽशक्तिरवाप्नुयात् 5.14.7cd
संभूय परमत्वं हि फलोक्तिः सैव योदिता 5.14.14cd
संभूय पादाः सर्वेऽपि ह्यैकात्म्यं बोधयन्ति नः SV 810cd
संभूय फलकारित्वं क्रियाकारकसंगतेः SV 813ab
संभूय यदि सर्वाणि फलमेकं प्रतन्वते SV 812ab
संभेदोऽयं क्रियाभिः स्यान्नातोऽकारकतान्वितः 4.3.1772cd
संमितः संख्यया पादैः पाङ्क्तस्य च्छन्दसो यतः 1.4.1851ab
संमूढबुद्धिसाक्षित्वात्संमूढ इव भात्यतः 4.4.9ef
संमोहहेतुकं कार्यं संमोहात्मकमिष्यते 4.4.10ab
सम्यक्कल्पयितुं शक्यः कल्पनातो न युज्यते 2.3.136cd
सम्यक्तज्ज्ञानमेवातस्तदन्यत्र मृषा मतिः 4.1.34cd
सम्यक्तत्त्वपरिज्ञानं पुरुषार्थस्य कारणम् 2.1.4cd
सम्यक्त्वप्रतिपत्त्यर्थं तथैव स्यात्परं वचः 4.1.13cd
सम्यक्पक्तिस्ततोऽन्नस्य मन्दाग्नेर्नोपजायते 4.3.1928cd
सम्यक्संशुद्धधिषणः संसारं वेत्ति तत्त्वतः 1.4.9ab

सम्यगापूर्यते व्योम शुक्तिसंपुटवद्ध्रुवम् 1.4.116cd

सम्यगुक्तं तदखिलमिह स्मर्तव्यमादृतैः 3.5.41cd

सम्यगुक्तमिदं सूत्रं याज्ञवल्क्य यथा तथा 3.7.24ab

सम्यग्ज्ञातात्मयाथात्म्यो यदायं म्रियते पुमान् 3.2.24ab

सम्यग्ज्ञातोऽपि नैवार्थो द्वैतबोधकृदिष्यते 4.4.661ab

सम्यग्ज्ञातोपदेशार्थः स्वयं च प्रतिभानवान् 1.4.1552ab

सम्यग्ज्ञानं यतस्तस्मात्पूर्णं तज्ज्ञेयमुच्यते 5.1.11cd

सम्यग्ज्ञानं यदाश्रित्य तन्मोहोऽपि तदाश्रयः 2.4.209ab

सम्यग्ज्ञानप्रदीपेन प्रत्यक्प्रवणबुद्धयः 4.4.1077cd

सम्यग्ज्ञानप्रसिद्ध्यर्थमतः प्रश्नोऽयमुत्तरः 3.8.48cd

सम्यग्ज्ञानप्रसूतेश्च विघातायैव जायते 4.4.823ab

सम्यग्ज्ञानविरुद्धा धीर्न चैकात्म्यं विजानतः 1.4.1542ab

सम्यग्ज्ञानशिखिप्लुष्टं कुतोऽज्ञानं पुनर्भवेत् 1.3.105ab

सम्यग्ज्ञानशिखिप्लुष्टमोहतत्कार्यरूपिणः 1.4.1455ab

सम्यग्ज्ञानसमुत्पत्तावत्रैव ब्रह्म सोऽश्नुते 4.4.389cd

सम्यग्ज्ञानसमुत्पत्तिसमनन्तरमेव च 1.4.1546ab

सम्यग्ज्ञानसमुत्पत्तौ कर्मकार्यसमाप्तितः 1.4.1565ab

सम्यग्ज्ञानसमुत्पत्तौ मेयस्याकारकत्वतः 4.4.941cd

सम्यग्ज्ञानसमुत्पत्तौ हेतुत्वं तु निगच्छति 1.2.133ab

सम्यग्ज्ञानस्य बाध्योऽर्थस्तस्मान्मृत्युरितीर्यते 4.3.454cd

सम्यग्ज्ञानाख्यदानस्य तदन्या संसृतिर्यतः 4.2.97cd

सम्यग्ज्ञानाग्निना नित्यं दह्यमानं प्रजायते 3.5.51cd

सम्यग्ज्ञानाग्निनिर्दग्धे प्रत्यङ्मोहे सबान्धवे 1.4.843ab

सम्यग्ज्ञानाग्निसंप्लुष्टप्रत्यक्तत्त्वमहातमाः 2.1.521ab

सम्यग्ज्ञानातिरेकेण न चान्येनास्ति निह्नुतिः 3.3.24ab

सम्यग्ज्ञानातिरेकेण न त्वन्यन्मुक्तिसाधनम् 1.4.851cd

सम्यग्ज्ञानात्तमोध्वस्तावीश्वराणामपीश्वरः 1.4.1465cd

सम्यग्ज्ञानात्तयोर्भेदो गम्यतां केन हेतुना 1.4.439cd

सम्यग्ज्ञानादतस्तस्यां ध्वस्तायामात्ममात्रता 4.3.1796cd

सम्यग्ज्ञानादृते नास्ति तद्धेतूच्छित्तिकारणम् 1.5.90cd

सम्यग्ज्ञानान्न मुक्तिः स्यान्न ज्ञानं वस्तुनुत्क्वचित् 1.4.238cd

सम्यग्ज्ञानेऽपि चास्त्येतत्त्रयं यद्भवतेरितम् 1.4.460ab

सम्यग्ज्ञानेऽपि चेत्सा स्यादविश्रम्भः प्रसज्यते 1.4.1544ab
सम्यग्ज्ञानेऽपि तुल्यत्वादनाश्वासस्तथा सति 1.4.455cd
सम्यग्ज्ञाने कुतः कर्म कर्महेतूपमर्दनात् SV 369cd
सम्यग्ज्ञानोदयात्सर्वं वर्जितं यज्जिहासितम् 4.4.782cd
सम्यग्धियः सकृत्सूतेः किं कार्यमवशिष्यते 4.4.913cd
सम्यग्धीतोऽथ तत्सिद्धिर्न तस्या मेयसंगतेः 1.4.277cd
सम्यग्धीध्वस्तमोहस्य सा कृत्स्ना विनिवर्तते 2.4.449cd
सम्यग्धीमुदिताशेषध्वान्तस्य च न पूर्ववत् SV 136ab
सम्यग्धीर्जायते यद्वत्तथा तत्त्वमसीत्यतः 1.3.81cd
सम्यग्धीर्निखिलध्वान्तघातिनी मुक्तिदायिनी 2.3.157cd
सम्यग्निर्ज्ञातसिद्धान्तो यतो वेत्ति बलाबलम् 1.4.757cd
सम्यग्बोधाग्निना ध्वस्तौ विकल्पो नावशिष्यते 2.1.279ef
सम्यग्विज्ञाततत्त्वत्वात्कृतार्थोऽप्यखिलं स्वयम् 4.5.26ab
सम्यग्विज्ञानविध्वस्तावविद्यायाः कुतोऽरतिः 1.4.96ab
सम्यङ्निरस्तं तत्पूर्वं वियोगाच्चापि लिङ्गतः 4.3.708ab
सम्यङ्निरूपणे चैषामविद्याकार्यतैव हि SV 154cd
सम्यङ्निश्चयसिद्ध्यर्थं पक्षयोरुभयोरपि 3.9.177cd
सम्यङ्मारकतदृष्टान्तदर्शनेनात्मवस्तुनः 4.3.373cd
सम्यङ्मिथ्याधियोर्यस्माद्विशेषो नोपलभ्यते 1.4.1545ab
सम्यञ्चि सर्वभूतानि प्राणे सति यतस्ततः 5.15.6cd
स य आत्मानमित्युक्त्या प्राप्तदोषनिराक्रिया 1.4.1051ab
स य एतं यथोद्दिष्टमुपास्तेऽहर्निशं नरः 2.1.52ab
स य एतदुपास्तेऽन्नमसाधारणरूपतः 1.5.25ab
स यः कश्चिदिमाँल्लोकान्पूर्णान्पुंभोगसाधनैः 5.16.58ab
स यत्तत्रेत्यसङ्गोक्तेर्नेदमप्युत्तरं भवेत् 4.3.1050ab
स यत्रेति ह्यतः पूर्वं पूर्वपक्षत्वहेतुतः 4.3.955ab
स यत्रेत्यत आरभ्य पुंसः संसारवर्णनम् 4.4.3cd
स यत्रेत्यादिकामाह परामुक्तिपरंपराम् 2.1.280cd
स यथाकाम इत्यादि तथा चोर्ध्वं प्रवक्ष्यते 4.3.1017cd
स यथाकाम इत्यादिरेषोऽर्थश्च सविस्तरः 2.1.579ab
स यथाकाम इत्युक्त्वा क्रत्वादेः प्रसवं श्रुतिः 1.4.174ab
स यथाध्यात्मिके देहे प्राणस्तद्वत्प्रजापतेः 1.5.188ab

स यद्यतोऽतो जातिस्तं परादध्याज्जडं नरम् 2.4.254cd
स याज्ञवल्क्यः शाकल्यं सापराधत्वसिद्धये 3.9.103cd
स योऽत इत्युपक्रम्य ह्युपासनगिरैव तु 1.4.776ab
स यो वाच्यसुरैः क्षिप्तः पाप्मा कार्ये स दृश्यते 1.3.152ab
स यो हैतानिति ततो नेदं पूर्वमपेक्षते 1.5.365cd
स रसो बन्धनं ज्ञेयो वृन्तं वा बन्धनं मतम् 4.3.1932cd
सराजके समाजेऽयं विचारः क्रियते महान् 3.1.22cd
सरित्तीरे फलानीति युक्तापेक्षाभिधाश्रुतेः 2.4.162ab
सर्गक्रमं स वेदोक्तं ज्ञानेनालोचयत्प्रभुः 1.2.172cd
सर्गनाशौ तदैकस्मिन्काले प्रसजतो ध्रुवम् 4.3.593cd
सर्गस्थितिलयानां स्यादन्वाख्यानं मृषैव तु 5.1.32cd
सर्गस्य जननादादौ देवत्वं ये प्रपेदिरे 4.3.1860ab
सर्पधारादिभिर्भावैस्तद्वदात्मा विकल्पितः 2.1.2cd
सर्पनिर्मोकवत्कृत्स्नमात्माविद्यैकहेतुजम् 4.4.503ab
सर्पात्मना गृहीतायां न दण्डादीक्ष्यते स्रजि 1.4.1496ab
सर्पादयो यथा रज्ज्वा विकाराः स्युरबोधतः 4.4.178ab
सर्पादिवस्तुबोधेऽपि प्रवृत्तिर्वीक्ष्यते यतः SV 745cd
सर्पादिवस्तुवत्तस्मात्सत्सत्यमितरन्मृषा 4.3.1689cd
सर्पादीनां प्रवेशः स्यादुपलादौ मतं यदि 1.4.531cd
सर्पादेरिव कार्ष्ण्यादिर्देहधर्मस्ततश्चितिः 4.3.119cd
सर्पादेरिव रज्ज्वादिस्तत्त्वमस्ति परं पदम् 2.1.266cd
सर्पादौ धर्मसंबन्धप्रमा नात्मन्यभेदतः 4.3.120cd
सर्पाद्यभाववद्रज्जुमोहमात्रनिवृत्तितः 4.4.323cd
सर्पाभासलयेऽपीयं रज्जुस्तमसि नेक्ष्यते SV 392cd
सर्पिष्मन्तमथाश्नीयात्कामितार्थानुरोधतः 6.4.86cd
सर्व एकमिति ह्युक्तेरिहाप्यैकात्म्यदर्शनम् 1.4.691ab
सर्व एकीभवन्तीति न पृथक्त्वेन संस्थितः 3.9.189cd
सर्व एव न संसिध्येद्व्यवहारश्च लौकिकः 1.2.83cd
सर्व एव समाः प्राणा इत्युक्तेः साम्यनिश्चितौ 1.5.362ab
सर्वं कर्माखिलं पार्थ ज्ञाने परिसमाप्यते 4.4.1164cd
सर्वं कर्माखिलमिति स्मृतेरपि शुभं वचः 1.4.1776cd
सर्वं कुर्युरनाश्वासस्तस्मात्प्राप्नोति कर्मसु 1.4.1477cd

सर्वं कृत्स्नं भविष्यामो मन्यन्ते ब्रह्मविद्यया 1.4.1078ab
सर्वं चाप्यप्रमाणं स्याद्यदुक्तं भेदलक्षणम् 3.3.52ab
सर्वं चाप्यभवद्यस्माज्ज्ञानं ज्ञेयं च भण्यते 1.4.1352cd
सर्वं चेद्विनिवृत्तं स्यात्किमन्यदवशिष्यते 3.2.53ab
सर्वं तत्तपसा साध्यं तपो हि दुरतिक्रमम् 4.4.1056cd
सर्वं तन्मन एवेति श्रुत्या साक्षात्स्फुटीकृतम् 4.4.420cd
सर्वं तरति पाप्मानं सर्पादीन्रशना यथा 4.4.1292cd
सर्वं पापं तपत्येष भस्मसात्कुरुतेऽग्निवत् 4.4.1287cd
सर्वं बिभर्त्यसक्तं सदसक्तमिति च स्मृतेः 1.4.181cd
सर्वं ब्रह्माभवद्यस्माद्विज्ञानात्तदिहोच्यते 1.4.1137ab
सर्वं मिथोऽनपेक्षं सत्स्वात्ममात्रविवक्षया 4.3.1724ab
सर्वं वस्त्वभिवाञ्छन्ति तत्तु युक्त्या न युज्यते 5.1.63cd
सर्वं सदेव चेदिष्टमुपलभ्येत ते सदा 1.2.76ab
सर्वं सदेव यस्येष्टमथवासदिदं जगत् 5.1.90ab
सर्वं समभवत्कृत्स्नं यद्याथात्म्यावबोधतः 2.5.40cd
सर्वं संभक्ष्य तत्पापं शुद्धः पापवियोगतः 5.16.82cd
सर्वं सर्वक्रियाः कुर्यादेकापूर्वप्रयुक्तितः 1.3.274cd
सर्वं सर्वमपेक्ष्यैव संहतत्वात्प्रसिध्यति 1.4.1482ab
सर्वं सर्वस्य कार्यं स्यात्सर्वं सर्वस्य कारणम् 1.4.1790ab
सर्वं सर्वस्य लिङ्गं स्यात्तच्चानिष्टं प्रसज्यते 4.3.151cd
सर्वं स्यात्कारणत्वादि तदाभासैकवर्त्मना 4.3.384cd
सर्वं स्वहेतुमुन्मूल्य जायतेऽङ्कुरकुम्भवत् 1.2.34cd
सर्वं हि खल्विदं ब्रह्मेत्येवं तत्रापि च श्रुतिः 4.4.445ab
सर्वं हि मन एवेति श्रुतिराह वचस्ततः 1.5.127cd
सर्वं हि मानं लोकेऽस्मिन्वस्त्वभिव्यक्तिसाधनम् 3.8.113ab
सर्वः कृत्स्नस्तथा पूर्णः शब्दाः पर्यायवाचकाः 1.4.1435cd
सर्वः कृत्स्नोऽहमस्मीति तदैतदुपपद्यते 4.3.1274cd
सर्वः कृत्स्नो भवेदात्मा मनोवाचामगोचरः 4.3.1283cd
सर्वः श्रौतो यतस्तस्मात्स एवेहाभिधीयते 1.3.15cd
सर्वः संन्यस्तकर्मैव ज्ञानात्कैवल्यमश्नुते 2.4.26cd
सर्वः सर्वमुपादाय सर्वत्रातः प्रवर्तते 1.3.273cd
सर्वः सर्वस्य कर्ता च कार्यं चापि यथा तथा 1.5.12ab

सर्वः सर्वस्य कार्यं स्यात्सर्वः सर्वस्य भोजकः 2.5.29ab
सर्वः सर्वस्य भोक्तैव चित्प्राधान्यविवक्षया 1.4.1791ab
सर्वकर्मत्यजं प्राह श्रुतिर्विद्याधिकारिणम् SV 13cd
सर्वकर्मनिरासेऽतो ह्यधिकारो विवेकिनः SV 165ab
सर्वकर्मनिरासेन तस्मादात्मधियो जनिः SV 220cd
सर्वकर्मनिरासेन ब्राह्मण्यं लभते ततः 3.5.204cd
सर्वकर्मनिवृत्तिर्हि जीवतोऽत्र विधीयते 1.5.271ab
सर्वकर्मपरित्यागः साधनं परमं मतम् 4.4.1090ab
सर्वकर्मपरित्यागात्संत्यक्ताशेषसाधनः 3.5.157ab
सर्वकर्मपरित्यागो ज्ञानाप्त्यै तस्य साधनम् 3.5.141cd
सर्वकर्मफलप्राप्तिरीश्वरादेव नान्यतः 3.8.151ab
सर्वकर्मफलानां च तथान्तर्भावसंभवात् 4.4.1163ab
सर्वकर्ममुचां यस्मान्न तत्साधारणं ततः 4.4.1069cd
सर्वकर्मसमुच्छेदि ज्ञानं वेदान्तमानजम् SV 123cd
सर्वकर्मस्वतोऽवादीद्दालकिः काश्यमन्तिकात् 2.1.39cd
सर्वकर्माण्यतस्त्यक्त्वा प्रत्यक्प्रवणबुद्धयः 3.5.145ab
सर्वकर्मातिगं ब्रह्म प्रत्यङ्मात्रसतत्त्वकम् 4.4.1179ab
सर्वकर्माधिकाराणां निषेधं प्रत्यपीपदत् 1.4.135ab
सर्वकर्माधिकाराणां निषेधायात्मधीभवः 1.3.109cd
सर्वकामादिवचनं प्रमाणमिति चेन्मतम् 4.4.442cd
सर्वकामाशनेनाथ कृत्स्नकामलयाध्वना SV 421ab
सर्वकारकतामेवं क्रियातत्फलतामपि 1.2.128cd
सर्वकारणविध्वस्तौ नान्यद्बोधादपेक्ष्यते 4.4.558cd
सर्वकार्यविनाशेऽपि यद्बीजमवशिष्यते 4.3.350cd
सर्वकार्योपसंहारी प्राण एकोऽवतिष्ठते 2.4.387cd
सर्वकालानुवर्त्येव लोके नित्यमितीर्यते 1.4.358cd
सर्वक्लेशोपशान्त्यात्मज्ञानं चापि समाश्रयेत् SV 347cd
सर्वगाणामपि यथा भूतानां परिणामतः 1.4.531ab
सर्वगोचरभासित्वात्तादात्म्ये तच्च युज्यते 3.9.74cd
सर्वग्रप्राणधर्मत्वादशनायापिपासयोः 3.5.63ab
सर्वग्रासि तदैकात्म्यमागादिह पुनर्बलात् 2.1.537cd
सर्वचेष्टानिरोधोऽस्य पुंसः प्राप्तस्तदासति 4.3.54ab

सर्वजात्यादिमत्त्वे च परस्परविरोधतः 5.1.107ab
सर्वज्ञः सर्वकृच्चासौ निरस्ताशेषसंसृतिः 3.8.170ab
सर्वज्ञः सर्वशक्तिश्च सर्वात्मा सर्वगो ध्रुवः 1.4.376ab
सर्वज्ञः सर्वशक्तिश्च सर्वात्मा सर्वगो ध्रुवः 3.7.44ab
सर्वज्ञत्वान्मुनेर्नाभूत्प्रश्नार्थाज्ञानतो भयम् 4.3.1889ab
सर्वज्ञानां यतो वंशास्त्रयोऽप्येते यथोदिताः 6.5.7ab
सर्वज्ञेऽनुपपन्नं स्यात्कर्मज्ञानफलप्रदे 3.8.145cd
सर्वज्ञेयपुमर्थानां प्रत्यग्ज्ञाने समाप्तितः 1.4.970cd
सर्वज्ञेयसमाप्तेश्च कुर्याद्वाक्यार्थबोधतः 4.4.705cd
सर्वज्ञेयस्य तद्व्याप्तेर्ब्रह्मापि हृदयं भवेत् 5.3.5ab
सर्वज्योतिरभावेऽपि तादृगेवानुमीयते 4.3.69cd
सर्वज्योतिरुपरतौ भूरिव्यापारकारणम् 4.3.73ab
सर्वज्योतिरुपरमे किंज्योतिरिति चोदिते 4.3.77ab
सर्वतस्तु विरक्तो यः कर्मभिः शुद्धधीर्नरः 5.1.101ab
सर्वतःस्थिरमर्यादं जगदेतद्विवर्तते 3.8.130cd
सर्वतीर्थदृशां तावत्सामान्यं मानलक्षणम् 4.3.158ab
सर्वतीर्थदृशां सिद्धिः स्वाभिप्रेतस्य वस्तुनः 4.3.156ab
सर्वतोऽपरिपन्थित्वात्सर्वैश्चाप्यनुकूलतः 6.3.29ab
सर्वत्र गम्यते वेदे नानुभतेः कथं चन SV 449cd
सर्वत्र दर्शनाच्छास्त्रे पर्णमय्यां फलोक्तिवत् SV 44cd
सर्वत्र प्रतिपत्तव्या नान्यत्र प्रलयो यतः 2.4.357ab
सर्वत्र प्रतिपत्तव्या यत्रोपासा विवक्षिता 1.3.135cd
सर्वत्र यौगपद्यं स्याद्विभुत्वाद्देवतात्मनः 4.3.1131ab
सर्वत्र वेदशास्त्रेऽस्मिन्मृत्युभावः फलं श्रुतम् 1.3.1cd
सर्वत्राप्रतिघात्येव प्रत्यगज्ञो महेश्वरः 1.3.313cd
सर्वत्राव्यभिचारित्वात्तथा स्वप्नादिभूमिषु 4.3.66cd
सर्वत्राव्यभिचारित्वादात्मा सर्वान्तरो भवेत् 3.4.25cd
सर्वत्राव्याहताज्ञश्च विधेयप्रकृतित्वतः 2.1.346ab
सर्वत्रासिद्धिरूपत्वान्मिथ्याज्ञानमिदं मतम् 1.4.441cd
सर्वत्रैकार्थता दृष्टा वेदोपासनशब्दयोः 1.4.773ab
सर्वत्रैव हि विज्ञानं संस्कारत्वेन गम्यते 1.4.1254ab
सर्वथा नैव घटते ज्ञानकर्मसमुच्चयः 3.3.72ab

सर्वथापि तु यत्किंचिद्वाचो गोचरतां गतम् 3.8.90ab
सर्वथा फलवज्ज्ञानं जातत्वान्न तदन्यथा 4.3.735ab
सर्वथा यदनेनोक्तं तच्छ्रद्धेयं बुभूषता 2.4.307ab
सर्वदा तस्य तादृक्त्वात्पुमर्थः सर्वदा भवेत् SV 627cd
सर्वदातिशयाभावाद्बोधाच्चाव्यतिरेकतः 4.3.549cd
सर्वदा विषयीभूतं गन्धर्वनगरादिवत् 4.3.898cd
सर्वदाव्यभिचार्येकं व्यभिचार्यर्थबुद्धिषु 2.4.255ab
सर्वदृष्टान्तसारूप्यप्रसक्तौ तन्निषेधकृत् 1.4.1549ab
सर्वदेहसमत्वं स्यात् प्राणिकर्मानुरूपतः 1.3.307cd
सर्वदैव तु तत्प्राप्तेस्तथा नान्योऽपि कश्चन 1.4.752cd
सर्वदैवात्मनो रूपं निरस्ताशेषभेदकम् 4.3.1324cd
सर्वदैवाहुतीर्विद्वाञ्जुहोत्यश्नन्नपः पिबन् 6.4.17ab
सर्वदैवैकरूपत्वाद्बानोर्नापूर्वकारिता 4.3.1458cd
सर्वधीविक्रियासाक्षिण्येवं सिद्धे स्वतो दृशौ 1.4.320ab
सर्वधीवृत्तिसाक्षित्वात्तादात्म्याच्चाप्यनात्मनः 4.3.316cd
सर्वनाम्नामतो नाद उक्थमित्यभिधीयते 1.6.13cd
सर्वनाशो भवेदेवं सर्वाप्रामाण्यहेतुतः 5.1.60cd
सर्वपुंसामिति तथा पूर्वमेव प्रपञ्चितम् SV 1023cd
सर्वप्रत्यक्तमः सोऽयमात्मा सर्वान्तरावधिः 3.4.68cd
सर्वप्रत्यक्तमस्तद्वद्बोधो वाक्योत्थ आत्मनि SV 188cd
सर्वप्रमाणकोपश्च सर्वं स्यादधरोत्तरम् 2.1.440cd
सर्वप्रमाणभाक्तद्वत्प्रमाणाभासभागपि 1.4.1328cd
सर्वप्रमाणभूतोऽभूदज्ञाता सत्रिणां पुरा 1.3.327ab
सर्वप्रमाणविषयलिङ्गिनोऽकार्यकारण- 4.4.1340ab
सर्वप्रमाणशेषत्वं युक्तीनामुपवर्णितम् 3.1.7ab
सर्वप्रयोगबीजात्मध्वान्तोच्छेदित्वहेतुतः 1.4.1162cd
सर्वप्राणभृतां बुद्धिरित्यर्थो वचसो भवेत् 2.5.87cd
सर्वप्राणभृतां यस्मात् त्रिष्ववैवैतेषु संभवः 3.1.52cd
सर्वप्राणभृदन्नस्य तस्माद्ग्रहणमिष्यते 1.5.37ab
सर्वप्राणिभिराद्यस्य तच्चानिष्टं प्रसज्यते 1.5.33cd
सर्वप्राण्यंशमिश्रत्वं ततोऽस्मिन्नवसीयते 1.5.30cd
सर्वप्राण्युपकारित्वात्प्रासादस्थप्रदीपवत् 3.8.133cd

सर्वप्राप्यार्थसंप्राप्तेः सर्वहेयनिराकृतेः 4.4.1103cd
सर्वभावविकाराणां जन्म मूलं यतस्ततः 4.4.1326ab
सर्वभूतमयोऽचिन्त्यः स एव स्वयमुद्बभौ 1.4.51cd
सर्वभूतसमुत्पत्तेस्तथा सर्वेश्वरत्वतः 5.3.4ab
सर्वभूतस्थमात्मानं सर्वभूतानि चात्मनि 4.4.582ab
सर्वभूतात्मकत्वं स्याद्यथा सर्वात्मनस्तथा 2.5.24cd
सर्वभूतात्मकत्वात्तु सर्वार्थग्रहणं तयोः 2.4.366ab
सर्वभूतात्मतापत्तिर्यद्येवंविद इष्यते 1.5.353ab
सर्वभूतात्मभूतस्य सर्वैकात्म्यं प्रपश्यतः 4.4.1108ab
सर्वभूतात्मभूतात्मा कुर्वन्नपि न लिप्यते 4.4.1047cd
सर्वभूतात्मभूतोऽसौ सर्वानन्यत्वदर्शनः 1.5.348ab
सर्वभेदात्मरूपत्वात्कः सन्स्यादात्मना विना 1.4.1399cd
सर्वमज्ञातमेव स्याद्यस्मिन्नज्ञात आत्मनि 1.4.943ab
सर्वमज्ञातमेव स्याद्यस्मिन्नज्ञात आत्मनि 1.4.1362ab
सर्वमत्ति यतः सृष्टं तस्माददितिरुच्यते 1.2.194ab
सर्वमन्यानपेक्षं सत्स्वात्ममात्रतयेक्षितम् 4.3.1326ab
सर्वमन्यानपेक्षं सदीक्ष्यमाणं स्वमात्रया 1.4.434ab
सर्वमस्म्यहमेवेदमिति स्वप्नेऽभिमन्यते 4.3.1272cd
सर्वमस्य वशे यस्माद्वशी सर्वस्य तेन सः 4.4.989ab
सर्वमात्मानमेवेति श्रुतेरपि वचस्तथा 4.4.871ef
सर्वमात्मेति च तथा व्यतिरेकं निषेधति 4.4.161cd
सर्वमात्मेति चेत्कुर्यात्प्रमेयविषयां प्रमाम् 2.1.568ab
सर्वमात्मेति नेतीति तथा सत्युपपद्यते 2.1.412cd
सर्वमात्मेति या बुद्धिः सा प्रमेयबलाद्भवेत् 2.4.120ab
सर्वमात्मेति वाक्यस्य न च वस्तुन्यसंभवः SV 659ab
सर्वमात्मेति संदृष्टे न प्रवृत्तिरहेतुतः 1.4.920cd
सर्वमात्मेतिसम्यग्धीजन्मनैवाखिलं तमः 2.4.437ab
सर्वमात्मेत्यतः पश्येदात्मानात्मविभागवित् 2.4.211ab
सर्वमात्मेत्यतो वाक्यात्प्रत्यङ्मात्रैकरूपताम् 4.4.951ab
सर्वमात्मैव ब्रह्मैव तथा च श्रुतिशासनम् 4.2.28cd
सर्वमात्राद्यभावार्थसाक्षित्वान्न तथात्मनः 3.4.55cd
सर्वमानप्रसक्तौ च सर्वमानफलाश्रयात् 2.4.212ab

सर्वमानातिवर्त्यात्मप्रतिपत्तौ ततः श्रुतिः 3.2.115ab
सर्वमानातिवर्त्यात्मा वाक्यादेवावगम्यते 2.4.227cd
सर्वमानातिवर्त्यैकमुक्तं प्रत्यक्चिदात्मकम् 3.8.52ab
सर्वमानाभ्युपगमान्न किंचिन्नोऽस्ति दुःस्थितम् 4.3.258cd
सर्वमानाभ्युपगमान्नानवस्था ततो बलात् 4.3.260cd
सर्वमानाविरोधेन वाक्यार्थो गम्यते यथा 4.4.833ab
सर्वमानैः प्रसिद्धत्वादतो व्युत्थाप्यते ततः 1.4.647cd
सर्वमुक्तं भवेद्यस्मादतः सोऽर्थोऽधुनोच्यते 4.3.1901cd
सर्वमृध्नोति यत्प्राणे तेनेति श्रुतिहृद्गतम् 3.9.27cd
सर्वमेतदयत्नेन तत एव विनिःसृतम् 4.5.10ab
सर्वमेतद्वृथैव स्यान्न चेद्दीप्ताग्निमान्भवेत् 1.3.284ab
सर्वमेयातिवर्त्यात्मयाथात्म्यप्रतिबोधतः 4.4.219cd
सर्वमेव यतो ज्ञानं परार्थं फलवन्मतम् 1.4.1252cd
सर्वमेवात्मसात्कृत्वा तत्तत्कार्यं करोति हि 1.5.199cd
सर्वमेवाहमस्मीति यद्यपीदं विशेषवत् 4.3.1391ab
सर्वरूपात्मकः सूर्यश्चक्षुष्येव प्रतिष्ठितः 3.9.72ab
सर्वरूपेषु चक्षुश्च रूपाणि हृदये तथा 3.9.72cd
सर्वलोकप्रसिद्धत्वादद्वयस्याप्यसिद्धितः SV 185cd
सर्वलोकविरुद्धत्वान्मानैश्चापि विरुध्यते 4.3.598cd
सर्वलोकव्यवस्थानां सेतुः स परमेश्वरः 4.4.1015cd
सर्वलोकेष्विदं वाक्यमत्यये दुर्घटं भवेत् 1.5.258cd
सर्वलोकैकबीजेन गर्भ्यण्डेन बभूव ह 1.2.178ab
सर्ववादाविरोधी च नातो विधिरिहेष्यते SV 267ab
सर्ववादिविरोधेऽपि यत्सिद्धान्तबलाश्रयम् 1.4.1372ab
सर्ववादिविरोधेऽपि संवादोऽनुभवे यथा 1.4.1365ab
सर्ववेदान्तबाधश्च कामाद्याश्रयता यदि 4.4.481ab
सर्ववेदान्तवाक्यानामेतावन्मात्रनिष्ठतः 1.4.1524ab
सर्ववेदान्तवाक्येषु ब्रह्मैकत्वं विधीयते 2.1.503ab
सर्ववेदान्तविषयमन्यथा तद्विरुध्यते SV 247ab
सर्वव्यापी रसो ह्येष शश्वत्तपति यो रविः 2.3.38ab
सर्वशक्तिरियं शक्तिर्या सदित्यभिधीयते 3.8.20ab
सर्वशास्त्रसमारम्भस्तदर्थोऽयं महानिह 4.4.105ab

सर्वशून्यस्य मोक्षत्वादनावृत्तिश्च सेत्स्यति 4.3.481cd
सर्वशोकातिगः स्वस्थः स्तिमितः स्वात्मनि स्थितः 4.3.1103cd
सर्वसंशयहेतोश्च प्रत्यङ्मोहस्य नाशतः 4.4.1294ab
सर्वसंसारदुःखौघव्यतीतेयं परात्मनः 2.1.343ab
सर्वसंसारभावोऽस्य न यथा लक्षणं तथा 3.5.209ab
सर्वसंहारकाले च निरोधोऽभूदशेषतः 1.4.1536ab
सर्वसङ्गव्यतीतोऽयं भवतीत्यभिधीयते 4.3.1370cd
सर्वसंन्यासनिष्ठा च ब्रह्मविद्या समीरिता 4.5.29cd
सर्वसाधनसाध्यं च सुखं यच्चाप्यभीप्सितम् 1.4.1688ab
सर्वसाधारणं कर्म यदभिव्यक्तमिष्यते 3.7.9ab
सर्वसाधारणः सोऽयं प्राकृतः प्रलयो मतः 2.4.389cd
सर्वसामर्थ्यहीनस्य जायते तापकारणम् 4.4.1170ef
सर्वस्य कर्मणोऽत्यन्तमात्माकर्ता विलक्षणः 4.3.912ab
सर्वस्य कर्मणोऽप्येष कारकस्य च तत्कृतः 4.4.1008ab
सर्वस्य जगतो यस्मादीश एवेह कारणम् 1.1.9cd
सर्वस्य जगतो हेतू पुण्यापुण्ये समीरिते 4.4.222ab
सर्वस्य ज्ञानमात्रत्वात्तदन्यासंभवत्वतः 4.3.474cd
सर्वस्य ज्ञानमात्रत्वान्ननु नाभ्युपगम्यते 4.3.542ab
सर्वस्य परिणामस्य हानोपादानमात्रतः 4.4.1329ab
सर्वस्य प्रत्यगात्मत्वात्कूटस्थैकचिदात्मनः 4.3.413ab
सर्वस्य सदपेक्षत्वात्सत्तु नान्यदपेक्षते 1.2.12cd
सर्वस्याक्षरमात्रत्वान्न किंचिन्नोपसंहृतम् 3.8.179ab
सर्वस्यानुपपन्नत्वं सिद्धं दृष्टबलाश्रयात् 1.4.1234ab
सर्वस्यानुपलब्धेस्तु मैवं वोचो यतः श्रुतिः 1.2.5ab
सर्वस्याप्यवनादों स्यादवतेरों यतस्ततः 5.17.16ab
सर्वस्येति फलोक्तिः स्यादुक्तोपासनकर्मणः 2.2.31ab
सर्वस्येशान एवेति सर्वस्येष्टे सदैव सः 4.4.990cd
सर्वस्यैकात्म्ययाथात्म्यान्न चाब्रह्मेह लभ्यते 3.4.10ab
सर्वस्यैव ततः सिद्धेः कथं सिध्येत्तदन्यतः 2.3.232cd
सर्वस्यैव स्वतोऽभित्तेस्तदन्यस्याप्यभेदतः 5.1.85cd
सर्वस्यैवात्मभूतत्वाद्गन्तव्यं न स पश्यति 4.2.9cd
सर्वस्यैवात्मयाथात्म्यादात्मा पुरुष उच्यते 4.3.364cd

सर्वस्यैवासुभोगत्वात्किं कुतोऽत्र विशिष्यते 1.3.172cd
सर्वस्यैष वशीत्यादि तथापि प्रागवादिषम् 6.5.11ab
सर्वस्यैष वशीत्युक्त्वा यतस्तस्यैव वेद्यताम् 3.8.29ab
सर्वस्वं चेदहं दद्यामिहैव च तदा मुनिः 4.4.536ab
सर्वस्वतुल्ये नृपशौ ब्रह्मधीपरिमोषिणा 1.4.1577ab
सर्वहेतोस्त्वविद्याया ध्वस्तायाः स्यात्कुतो भवः 4.4.919cd
सर्वाकाङ्क्षैकहेतोश्च प्रत्यग्विज्ञानहानतः 1.4.853ab
सर्वाज्ञानसमुच्छित्तेः सर्वज्ञानोदयस्तथा 4.4.759cd
सर्वाज्ञानापनुत्तेश्च ज्ञेयकार्यसमाप्तितः 4.4.912cd
सर्वाण्यनभिधायैव निवर्तन्तेऽवबोध्य च 1.4.857cd
सर्वाण्युपासनान्येवं ब्रह्मविद्याभिसंगतेः 3.5.82ab
रार्वात्तृत्वेन सिद्धेऽर्थे सर्वान्नोक्तिः किमीर्यते 1.2.195ab
सर्वात्मकत्वं संयात आत्माविद्यावशादतः 4.3.398cd
सर्वात्मकत्वसंप्राप्तावसाधारणवस्तुनः 4.3.1766ab
सर्वात्मकत्वाज्ञायत्र्या अग्नेरपि परिग्रहः 5.16.77ab
सर्वात्मकत्वाद्विदुषः सर्वतःपाणिपादवत् 3.9.200cd
सर्वात्मकत्वाद्विदुषः स्याद्विमुक्तिस्तुतीरणम् 3.9.201cd
सर्वात्मकर्मसंन्यासात्प्राप्ते नैष्कर्म्यरूपके 1.5.364ab
सर्वात्मकार्यनिचयपुत्रसंक्रामितत्ववतः 1.5.308ab
सर्वात्मत्वनिषेधार्थं प्रमाभावस्त्वयाश्रितः 4.3.1766cd
सर्वात्मत्वात्तथैकत्वाद्द्रष्टुर्नाशो न विद्यते 4.3.1553cd
सर्वात्मनाप्यसौ कुर्वन्कुर्यात्तस्करकन्दुवत् 1.4.881cd
सर्वात्मभावं विद्यायाः फलमुक्त्वा च नः श्रुतिः 4.4.413ab
सर्वात्मभावः सर्वेषां सिद्धः प्रागपि बोधतः 1.4.1082cd
सर्वात्मविद्ययाविद्यां हत्वा ब्रह्माभवत्पुमान् 1.4.1159cd
सर्वाद्यान्नगृहीतौ तु हेतुर्गमक इष्यते 1.5.36ab
सर्वाधिकारप्रध्वंसान्न कृत्स्नात्मावबोधिनः 2.1.580ab
सर्वाधिकारहेत्वग्निब्रह्मज्ञानस्य जन्मनि 1.4.1579ab
सर्वानन्दातिवर्तित्वादानन्दः परमो मतः 4.3.1838cd
सर्वानन्दातिशायित्वात्तथा चैवं प्रवक्ष्यते 4.3.1836cd
सर्वानन्दैकहेतुत्वाद्ब्रह्माप्तौ प्राप्तमेव तत् 1.4.1688cd
सर्वानर्थनिरासार्थमेतावानेव चादृतैः 4.4.1305cd

सर्वानर्थनिवृत्तिश्च सर्वाह्लादाप्तिरेव च 2.4.89ab
सर्वानर्थविनिर्मुक्तेरुपपन्नात्ममुक्तता SV 59ab
सर्वानर्थस्य नष्टत्वात्किमन्यत्स्यात्तमोह्नुतेः 1.4.1745cd
सर्वानर्थाभिसंबन्धे ह्यविद्यैवास्य कारणम् SV 464ab
सर्वानर्थैकबीजस्य प्रत्यगज्ञानरूपिणः 4.4.529ab
सर्वानर्थैकमूलस्य प्रत्यङ्मोहस्य हानये 3.5.130cd
सर्वानात्मनिषेधेन बोध आत्मन्यथैकले 3.4.39ab
सर्वान्तरगृहीतिस्तु तत्पूर्वोक्तोपलक्षणम् 3.4.52cd
सर्वान्तरगृहीत्या च प्रत्यगर्थस्य संगतिः 3.4.26cd
सर्वान्तरतमात्मानमुपासीत प्रियं सदा 1.4.1050cd
सर्वान्तरत्वं नान्यस्य युज्यतेऽनात्मनो यतः 3.8.23cd
सर्वान्तरविनिर्णीतौ निर्णयः स्यात्कथं न्विति 3.6.2cd
सर्वान्तराधिकाराद्धि तथोभयनिषेधतः 3.8.96cd
सर्वान्तरावसानस्य साक्षादित्यादिकस्य च 3.5.20ab
सर्वान्तर्यामिणः शौरेर्नोपेक्ष्यं तद्व्वादृशैः 2.4.248cd
सर्वान्धकारहन्त्रीव विद्युत्तं श्रीः सदाश्रयेत् 2.3.168cd
सर्वान्नभक्षणादग्निर्मृत्युस्तावदसावपि 3.2.17ab
सर्वान्प्रत्यविशिष्टत्वात्फलं तन्न समुच्चितेः 1.4.1750cd
सर्वान्प्रत्यविशिष्टत्वादेवंविदमितीरणम् 4.3.1970ab
सर्वापत्तिरियं युक्ता देवादीनां महात्मनाम् 1.4.1458ab
सर्वापत्तेरनित्यत्वदोषासक्तेर्न तत्तथा 1.4.1203ab
सर्वाब्रह्मनिषेधेन तदर्थो वेह निश्चितः 2.4.19ab
सर्वाभक्ष्यप्रसक्तिः स्याद्यदि कर्म विधित्स्यते 6.1.39ef
सर्वाभावोऽपि नैव स्याल्लक्षणं ब्रह्मवेदिनः 3.5.209cd
सर्वाभिमानहेतुं च चिदाभासं पुराब्रवम् 4.3.373ab
सर्वाभेदाच्च सर्वस्य रज्ज्वां सर्पादिबुद्धयः 1.6.88ab
सर्वार्थं यदि वाद्यं स्यात्साक्षादिति विशेषणम् 3.4.35ab
सर्वार्थकरणं सातो दीपो ध्वान्ते यथा तथा 4.3.313cd
सर्वार्थग्रहणं तस्मात्पुरोऽवस्थितदीपवत् 4.3.317ab
सर्वार्थव्यभिचारेऽपि संविदव्यभिचारिणी 1.3.68cd
सर्वार्थस्य हि पापाय यतोऽसाधारणीक्रिया 1.5.38cd
सर्वार्थैव समुद्दिष्टा नाग्रजन्मैकगोचरा 1.4.1196cd

सर्वावतोऽस्य देहस्य स्वप्नभोगप्रसिद्धये 4.3.865ab
सर्वावस्थासु संबन्धः संबन्धोऽतोऽस्य मोहतः 4.3.1359cd
सर्वावस्थास्वयं नित्य आत्मा नैव विनश्यति 4.3.1402cd
सर्वावानिति तेनायमात्मा देहान्त उच्यते 4.3.862cd
सर्वाविद्यापनिह्नुत्या विद्यया प्रतिपद्यते 1.4.1339cd
सर्वाश्रमाणां तर्हीदं सामान्येनाभिधीयते 1.3.388ab
सर्वाश्रमैरमी कार्या वेदानुवचनादयः 4.4.1027cd
सर्वाश्रयत्वात्संवित्तेस्तथात्मन्यप्रवृत्तितः SV 571cd
सर्वासङ्गविनिर्मुक्तो मोक्षमात्रप्रयोजनः 2.4.94ab
सर्वासङ्गविनिर्मोकाद्वासनामात्रशेषतः 4.3.1042cd
सर्वासु तेन लोकेऽस्मिन्पुरुषोऽयमितीर्यते 2.5.120cd
सर्वासूपनिषत्स्वेवं कारणं नान्यदात्मनः 2.1.395ab
सर्वासूपनिषत्स्वेवं प्रमात्रादेरनात्मनः 2.4.103ab
सर्वास्वेव हितास्वासु सर्वा अध्यात्मदेवताः 4.2.57ab
सर्वाहुतिषु संसृष्टा बाहुल्यादप्परिग्रहः 5.5.2cd
सर्वेऽपि क्रमशस्त्वेते सेव्यमाना यथाविधि 4.4.1066ab
सर्वेऽपि महिमानोऽमी क्षणप्रध्वंसिनो मताः 4.4.1181cd
सर्वेऽप्येते यथादृष्टि ह्येकैकस्य तमस्विनः 1.4.1148ab
सर्वे कार्पण्ययुक्ताः स्युर्यदि न स्यात्तदक्षरम् 3.8.166ab
सर्वेच्छानां समाप्तत्वादात्मकामप्रबोधतः 4.4.611ab
सर्वेणैव विकल्पेन यथोक्तेनावतिष्ठते 1.3.270ab
सर्वेन्द्रियपरिस्पन्दो व्यज्यते नः शरीरके 1.6.26ab
सर्वेन्द्रियवियोगेऽपि सुखिदुःखित्वमात्मनः 2.1.262cd
सर्वेन्द्रियाणां लीनत्वाद्व्यापारो न प्रबोधवत् 2.1.260cd
सर्वेन्द्रियाणामथवा प्राण आत्मेति कथ्यते 1.3.205ab
सर्वेन्द्रियाणामात्मैव प्राणो सर्गो लयस्तथा 1.5.373cd
सर्वेन्द्रियेषु यावान् स्यात्परिस्पन्दः क्रियात्मसु 1.5.371ab
सर्वे पक्षा विरुध्यन्ते त्याज्यास्तेऽतः प्रयत्नतः 2.1.485cd
सर्वे भावाः स्रजा यद्वद्भोगी सिद्धायतेऽन्यतः 4.3.1693cd
सर्वे भावाः स्वयं सन्तो व्यावृत्तिः किंसमाश्रया 4.3.1706ab
सर्वेश्वरेशिता तावत्पूर्वश्रुत्योपवर्णिता 1.4.1782ab
सर्वेषां दृष्टता चेत्स्यान्न विधानाददृष्टता SV 85ab

सर्वेषां प्रतिषेधः स्यान्निषेधादात्मजन्मनः 4.4.1326cd
सर्वेषां प्रत्यगात्मत्वात्पक्षपातोऽपि नेष्यते 1.4.1660ab
सर्वेषां प्राणिनामेतत्स्वत इष्टं प्रयोजनम् SV 1095cd
सर्वेषां सर्वविज्ञानात्सर्वज्ञत्वं भवेद्ध्रुवम् 1.4.458cd
सर्वेषामपि कामानामाश्रयो हृदयं यतः 4.4.436ab
सर्वेषामपि च नृणामधिकारोऽनिवारितः SV 1025ab
सर्वेषामपि चोद्यानामेवं सति न संभवः 3.8.88ab
सर्वेषामपि तेनेदं समानं लक्षणं भवेत् 2.3.100ab
सर्वेषामपि नूनं त्वं हन्तव्यत्वेन संमतः 3.9.62ab
सर्वेषामपि भिन्नानां तथाभेदत्वहेतुतः 4.4.933ab
सर्वेषामपि भूतानां कार्यकारणसंगतेः 2.5.24ab
सर्वेषामपि मानानां प्रमाणं परमं श्रुतिः 4.4.219ab
सर्वेषामभ्युपेतोऽर्थः कुतोऽसाविति चिन्त्यते 1.4.221cd
सर्वेषामविशिष्टातः स यत्रेत्युच्यतेऽधुना 4.4.1cd
सर्वेषामान्तरो योऽर्थो नाना स कथमुच्यते 3.4.23cd
सर्वेषु संहृतेष्वेवं करणेषु सवायुषु 4.4.75ab
सर्वेष्वपि च दृष्टेषु द्वैतभेदेषु केनचित् 3.2.109ab
सर्वेष्वेतेषु शान्तेषु ज्योतिःषूक्तेषु कर्मणे 4.3.53ab
सर्वेष्वेषु प्रदेशेषु भूतमात्राग्रहः श्रुतौ 4.4.33cd
सर्वैः सर्वस्य चाभेदाद्व्यवहारोऽपि नश्यति 4.3.1767cd
सर्वैकत्वं परं ब्रह्म परमात्मेति यं विदुः 1.4.1139ab
सर्वैकत्वावबोधोऽयं ब्रह्मविद्यागिरोच्यते 1.4.1138ab
सर्वैकत्वे विभागो वाविभागो वा न युज्यते 4.3.1613cd
सर्वैकात्म्यमिदं यस्मादात्मनो रूपमीदृशम् 4.3.1334ab
सर्वैर्मानुष्यकैर्भोगैः संपन्नो न तु दैविकैः 4.3.1848ab
सर्वैषणानिवृत्त्यैव तज्ज्ञानं समवाप्नुयात् 3.5.122cd
सर्वोऽनुभव एवायमतः सर्वानुभूः परः 2.5.145ab
सर्वोऽपि वेद इत्यादि यथोक्तपरिहारकृत् SV 553ab
सर्वोऽपीति वचः प्राह तथा चोर्ध्वं प्रवक्ष्यते SV 560cd
सर्वोऽपीति वचः सिद्धिः सर्वा ह्यात्मैकसंविदः SV 559cd
सर्वोऽप्यनुभवात्सिद्धां बालोऽप्यज्ञाततां स्वतः SV 993ab
सर्वोऽप्येष तदा यत्नः फलवान्स्यान्न चान्यथा 2.1.28cd

सर्वोऽप्येष परिस्पन्दो बुद्धीन्द्रियसमाश्रयः 2.4.380ab
सर्वोऽप्येष विकल्पश्च पुनरेकैकशस्तथा 1.3.267cd
सर्वोऽस्मीति हि विद्येयमविद्यातोऽन्यदर्शनम् 4.3.1294ab
सर्वोच्छित्त्यात्मसाक्षित्वादुच्छित्तेश्चाप्यसंभवात् 4.3.1499ab
सर्वोपनिषदां चात्मज्ञानं कैवल्यसाधनम् SV 280cd
सर्वोपनिषदामाह मुक्तिमात्रं प्रयोजनम् SV 10cd
सर्वोपनिषदामेष संक्षिप्तोऽर्थ इहोदितः 4.4.1338ab
सर्वोपसंहृतेरत्र यागादेरपि भण्यते 4.5.8cd
सर्वोपसंहृद्धृदयं ब्रूहि क्वैतत्प्रतिष्ठितम् 3.9.81ab
सर्वोपाधिविनिर्मुक्तौ नैव शक्यः स ईक्षितुम् 4.3.900ab
सर्वोपाध्युपसंहारिगायत्र्युपाधिकं प्रभोः 5.16.2ab
सर्वोपाया निवर्तन्त उपेयावसितौ यतः 3.5.140ab
सर्वोपायोऽनुपायः स्यादुपेयावसितौ यतः 2.4.310cd
सर्वोपास्त्यङ्गभूतानि वक्तव्यानीति यत्यते 5.1.6cd
सलिलादिगिरा तस्य क्रियतेऽत्रोपसंहृतिः 4.3.1795cd
सलिलादिगिरा योऽर्थः प्रत्यज्ञायि पुराखिलः 4.3.1886ab
सलिलोक्त्या विजातीयसंबन्धो हि निवारितः 4.3.1801cd
स वा इति गिरा सोऽत्र स्मार्यते ब्रह्मसंगतौ 4.4.1319cd
स वा इतिवचोऽर्थस्य व्याख्यातत्वान्न यत्यते 4.4.986cd
स वा इति ह्युपक्रम्य नैनेनेत्यादिनिर्णयात् 2.1.193cd
स वा इत्यादिकं ज्ञेयं न तु नाशादिशङ्कया 4.3.1909cd
स वा इत्यादिको ग्रन्थः सदृष्टान्तोऽभिधीयते 2.5.62cd
स वा इत्यादिनाचष्टे सर्वैकात्म्यावबुद्धये 2.5.119cd
स वा इत्यादिना तस्य निर्णयः क्रियतेऽधुना 4.4.148cd
स वा इत्यादिनाथास्य फलमुक्तस्य कर्मणः 6.4.62ab
स वा इत्यादिनोक्तार्थं प्रवक्तुमुपचक्रमे 4.4.974cd
स वा इत्यादिवाक्येन सारार्थस्य जिघृक्षया 4.4.1318cd
स वा एष पुरोक्तेन यो वाक्येन प्रकाशितः 4.4.1320ab
स वायुरिति पाठे स्याद्व्याख्या माध्यंदिने त्वियम् 3.1.42cd
स विज्ञानमनःप्राणचक्षुःश्रोत्रादि मोहजम् 4.4.182ab
सविज्ञानो यथा स्वप्ने तथोत्क्रान्तावपीष्यते 4.4.99cd
सवितुस्तद्वरेण्यं स्याद्भर्गमन्त्रं महात्मनः 6.3.44ab

सवित्रैवाभिसंबन्धो मनसस्तेन शस्यते 1.5.182cd
सविस्तरः प्रवक्तव्यस्तदुक्त्यर्था परा श्रुतिः 4.3.1904cd
सविस्तरः स वक्तव्य इत्यर्थेयं परा श्रुतिः 4.3.1903cd
स वै शरीरी प्रथमः स वै पुरुष उच्यते 1.2.162ab
स वै शरीरी प्रथमः स वै पुरुष उच्यते 1.4.21ab
सव्येनाक्ष्णा न पश्यामि यथा सामर्थ्यतस्तथा 4.4.434cd
सशब्ददर्शनं यादृक्प्रागभ्यस्तं तथैव सः 1.4.42ab
सशब्देन परामर्शः परस्येह भवेदतः 1.4.528cd
सशल्यदेहशायीनि भूतान्येव तथाविधम् 4.3.134ab
सश्रद्धस्यापि सत्यस्य यद्यप्यन्यत्र संभवः 6.2.124ab
स संवत्सरोऽभवदिति परिमाणोऽयमुच्यते 1.2.181ab
ससंन्यासं विनिश्चेयमिति शास्त्रस्य संग्रहः 4.5.21ab
ससंन्यासात्मविद्या या मधुकाण्डागमोदिता 4.5.5ab
स समान इति ज्ञेयः सर्वकार्योपसंहृतिः 1.5.149cd
ससमानोक्तिसंबन्धमन्यथान्ये प्रकुर्वते 4.3.423ab
ससंभ्रमः स चोत्थाय तस्मा आसनमाहरत् 6.2.56ab
स सर्वविद्भजति मां सर्वभावेन भारत 2.4.247cd
स सर्वोऽत्रानुसंधेयः पूर्वपक्षापनुत्तये 2.3.129cd
ससाधनमिदं कर्म ब्रह्मभावेन पश्यतः 1.4.1722ab
ससाधनमिदं कर्म ब्रह्मैवेति समीक्षणम् 1.4.1732ab
स स्वयंज्योतिरात्मैव बाह्यज्योतिर्विवर्जितः 4.3.858ab
सहकर्त्री भवेच्छक्तिरिति न्यायाद्भवेद्यदि SV 75ab
सहजं सर्वभूतानां वृत्तमासुरमिष्यते 1.3.22ab
सहतेऽनात्मतां नात्मानात्मा तद्विरहे कुतः 1.4.732ab
सहते नापि चानात्मा स्वार्थादन्यत्र सिध्यति 2.4.273cd
सह प्रमातृज्ञानेन वागादेरुपसंहृतिः 2.1.231cd
सह भावनया बुद्धेः श्रुतत्वादुपसंहृतेः 2.1.256ab
सहसिद्धगिरस्तस्मान्नैष दोषः प्रसज्यते 1.4.81cd
सहस्रतमभागेन केशस्य परिणाहतः 4.3.1215ab
सहस्रदशभागर्द्ध्या सुखानन्त्यं परात्मनः 1.4.1690ab
सहस्रदशभागेन निष्ठानन्दस्य भण्यते 2.1.360cd
सहस्रदशमांशोक्त्या परानन्दो निरूपितः 4.4.272cd

सहस्रदानं तूक्तस्य स्वयंज्योतिष्ट्ववस्तुनः 4.3.973ab
सहस्रभेदवत्साक्षादिदमा जगदुच्यते 1.4.193cd
सहस्रभेदसंभिन्नकेशैकांशसमा हिताः 4.2.52cd
सहस्रमेव तु प्रादादेकदेशोक्तिवत्कथम् 4.4.533cd
सहस्रसंख्यया शश्वद्बहोर्नाम सहस्रगीः 6.4.116cd
सहस्रादिर्यथा भेदः प्राणस्यैकस्य शब्द्यते 1.3.21ab
सहाध्यात्माधिदैवं हि साधिभूतमिदं जगत् 2.5.28ab
सहार्थे वा तृतीयेयं विज्ञानेनेति या श्रुता 2.1.231ab
सहावस्थानताभावात्प्रवृत्तेः स्यादसंभवः 1.4.821cd
स हि कर्तेति तस्यैव वचनं स्यात्पुनःश्रुतिः 4.3.1030cd
स हि तस्मिन्यतः शक्तो लोकाग्न्यादिविधौ यथा 4.4.450cd
स हि धीहाप्रबन्धेन सर्वदान्नं करोत्यतः 1.5.79cd
स हि सर्वस्य कर्तेति तस्मादेवाभिधीयते 4.4.621ab
स हीतिहेतुनिर्देश उक्तसिद्ध्यर्थमिष्यते 4.3.446ab
स हीदमन्नं कुरुते तत्तत्कालप्रसूतया 1.5.85ab
स हृद्देशं समागम्य नाडीमध्यसमाश्रयः 2.2.18cd
सहेतुकस्य वृत्तिः स्यान्नित्यबोधावबोधिनि 2.3.230cd
सहेतुकावभिहितौ बन्धमोक्षौ प्रयत्नतः 4.4.968ab
सहेतुरस्य संसारः परलोकेहलोकयोः 4.3.1903ab
सहैव कर्मशक्त्यातो ज्ञानशक्तिर्विलीयते 2.4.383ab
सहैव सिद्धं चेज्ज्ञानं भीतिहेतोरसंभवः 1.4.80ab
सहैवायतनैः सर्वैः प्राधान्यं मनसस्ततः 1.5.109cd
सहोपलब्धिसंस्कारवशाद्भूमादिदर्शनात् 4.3.732ab
सहोपलम्भमात्रेण न यतः पितृसूनुवत् 4.3.718cd
सहोपलम्भमात्रेण सा तु सर्वत्र जायते 4.3.720ab
सहोपलम्भसंस्कारात्पुनर्धीर्येकदर्शनात् 4.3.717ab
स होपायनकीर्त्यैव ब्रह्मचर्यमुवास ह 6.2.68ab
सांसारिकपुमर्थेभ्यो विरक्ताः शुद्धबुद्धयः 1.4.1071cd
सांसारिकसुखस्यास्य दुःखत्वादुक्तहेतुतः 2.4.87ab
साकाङ्क्षत्वादिह ज्ञेयो निराकाङ्क्षत्वसिद्धये 4.4.1030cd
साक्षाज्ज्ञातात्मतत्त्वानां प्रत्यक्षतममेव तत् 4.3.1881cd
साक्षाज्ज्ञानातिरेकेण नालमन्यद्विमुक्तये 4.2.110ab

साक्षात्करणसिद्ध्यर्थमतो राजाब्रवीन्मुनिम् 4.2.101ab
साक्षात्कुर्वत्स्वमात्मानं यदालम्बनतां व्रजेत् 3.4.144ab
साक्षात्कृतात्मभावोऽयमेवंलक्षणवस्तुनि 2.1.16ab
साक्षात्कृतिश्च संतत्या संततिश्च न विद्यते 1.3.380cd
साक्षात्कृतैकतत्त्वस्याप्यैकात्म्यप्रलयं प्रति 4.2.108ab
साक्षात्तु वस्तुविज्ञाने श्रुत्या यत्र नियुज्यते 4.4.1062ab
साक्षात्त्वं तदसंपाद्य लिङ्गेनावेदयस्यमुम् 3.4.76cd
साक्षात्त्वाद्वस्तुनो मात्रेर्बुभुत्सा प्राक्प्रमायुतेः 4.4.1039cd
साक्षात्पश्याम्यहं कुम्भं न पश्यामीति लोकतः 4.3.1467ab
साक्षात्प्रमाफलं न्याय्यं प्रत्यगात्मैकसाक्षिकम् 4.3.298cd
साक्षात्स्वयंभूर्वेदात्मा संसारानर्थशान्तये 4.4.365cd
साक्षादनन्तदेहोऽयमिति ध्यायन्विमुच्यते 3.1.33cd
साक्षादनभिधानेऽपि न द्वितीया प्रसज्यते SV 513cd
साक्षादनुशशासैनमित्युक्तिः स्याच्छ्रुतेरियम् 4.4.1302cd
साक्षादवति तं भोगमुदगायदशेषतः 1.3.138cd
साक्षादविद्याप्रध्वस्तौ पारंपर्यात्तु युज्यते 3.3.42cd
साक्षादव्यवधानेन तत्प्रसिद्धिरथोच्यते 4.3.857cd
साक्षादसति संबन्धे पारंपर्यं न तु क्वचित् SV 644ab
साक्षादात्मप्रसिद्धौ च नाभ्यासस्तत्फलस्थितेः 2.4.207ab
साक्षादात्मावबोधेन प्रत्यग्ध्वान्तच्छिदा न चेत् SV 460ab
साक्षादात्मेति तं पश्य प्रत्यग्दृष्ट्यैकमात्मनि 4.3.333cd
साक्षादात्मेव चाभाति तस्मिन्पारोक्ष्यधीः कथम् SV 792cd
साक्षादात्मोत्सृजन्वायुं तस्मिन्प्राणनकर्मणि 1.4.667ab
साक्षाददिश्यते येन तादृगादेश उच्यते 2.3.206cd
साक्षादित्यभिधानेन प्रत्यक्षोऽर्थोऽभिधीयते 3.4.14ab
साक्षादित्यव्यवहितमगौणमपरोक्षतः 3.4.27ab
साक्षादित्यादिकं यस्मान्न मनागपि युज्यते 3.4.178ab
साक्षादित्यादिकं सर्वं तद्विशेषणमुच्यते 3.4.12ab
साक्षादित्यादिकं सर्वं संभाव्यं स्याद्विशेषणम् 3.4.58cd
साक्षादित्यादिकं सर्वमुषस्तप्रश्नगोचरः 3.5.101ab
साक्षादित्यादिकः प्रश्नो यदेवेतिपुरःसरः 3.5.52cd
साक्षादित्यादिकानां स्यान्मिथोऽन्योऽन्यानपेक्षतः 3.4.30cd

साक्षादित्यादिनाज्ञासीद्विरुद्धं साध्यसाधनैः 3.5.118cd
साक्षादित्यादिना पृष्टं साक्षादित्यादिलक्षणम् 3.5.30ab
साक्षादित्यादिना प्रोक्तस्तथा सर्वान्तरश्च यः 3.9.149ab
साक्षादित्यादिभिः प्रत्यक्प्रत्यग्दृष्ट्या यदेक्ष्यते 3.4.56ab
साक्षादित्यादिमानात्मा निर्धार्येदंतयान्यतः 3.4.64cd
साक्षादित्यादि याथात्म्यं भूयोऽप्यात्मन उच्यते 3.9.2ab
साक्षादित्यादिरूपत्वान्नापि स्यात्तदपह्नुतिः 3.8.53ed
साक्षादित्यादिरूपोऽथ ब्रह्म ब्राह्मण उच्यते 3.5.190ef
साक्षादित्यादिवाक्येन योऽशनायादिना तथा 3.8.60ab
साक्षादेवं च संबन्धः साध्यसाधनयोर्भवेत् SV 643ab
साक्षाद्दर्शनसिद्ध्यर्थमन्यत्रापि विधीयते 4.4.809ab
साक्षाद्धस्तिनि दृष्टेऽपि न हि हस्तिपदानुमा SV 426ab
साक्षाद्ब्रह्मत्वसिद्ध्यर्थमादेशोऽयमथोच्यते 2.3.214cd
साक्षाद्ब्रह्मविदप्येष नात्माप्तौ गतिविन्नृपः 4.2.15ab
साक्षाद्ब्रह्माथवाब्रह्म यदि वोभयरूपकम् 1.4.1167cd
साक्षाद्ब्रह्मावबोधस्य प्रतिज्ञातत्वकारणात् 2.1.205ab
साक्षाद्वस्त्वेकनिष्ठत्वाद्यथेयं शुक्तिकामतिः 1.4.464cd
साक्षाद्विहितमप्येवं तादर्थ्यात्कर्म नो मतम् 4.4.1241cd
साक्षान्निर्देशनुत्त्यर्थं कारणत्वावबुद्धये 3.9.31ab
साक्षान्मानप्रसिद्धेषु प्रतिषिद्धेतरग्रहः 2.3.205ab
साक्षिणः प्राणशब्देन विशेष्यस्याभिधेष्यते 4.4.523ab
साक्षिणः सद्वितीयत्वं ब्रह्मणश्च परोक्षताम् 4.4.524ab
साक्षिणो विषयीभूतं विभक्तं कार्यरूपतः 4.3.1522cd
साक्षितत्त्वापरिज्ञानात्तद्विरुद्धार्थकल्पनम् 4.3.444ab
साक्षित्वमात्मनो नित्यं वस्तुस्वाभाव्यमुच्यते 3.4.82cd
साक्षित्वेनात्मनः सिद्धिर्मात्रादिव्यतिरेकतः 3.4.111ab
साक्षित्वेनोपलभ्यत्वात्साक्ष्यबुद्ध्यादिसंश्रयात् 2.1.188ab
साक्षिबुद्धिशरीरान्तेष्वात्मबुद्धिसमन्वयात् 4.3.281cd
साक्षिमात्रादिकस्तस्मात्पौरुषोऽयमितीर्यते 4.3.936cd
साक्षिरूपं स्वतःसिद्धं तेनैष्वव्यभिचारतः 1.4.669ab
साक्षिवस्तुनि नैव स्यात्केवलानुभवात्मनि SV 151cd
साक्षिसाक्ष्यादिमिथ्याधीस्तत्त्वज्ञानान्निवर्तते 4.3.444cd

साक्षिसाक्ष्याभिसंबन्धः प्रमात्रादौ यथा तथा SV 151ab
साक्षी चेता जगद्बीजमन्तर्यामीति च श्रुतौ 4.3.383cd
साक्षी बाह्यार्थवद्यस्मात्त आत्मेत्युच्यते ततः 3.4.54cd
साक्षी स्वात्मातिरेकेण न पश्येन्नौस्थवत्पृथक् 4.3.438cd
साक्षेपं प्रागुपन्यस्तं तस्यायं निर्णयः कृतः 2.5.90cd
साक्षेपमाहुः श्रेयांसं गुरुं प्राप्य निरेषणाः 1.4.1074ab
साक्ष्यमातृप्रमारूपं मानभूमौ यथेक्ष्यते 4.3.177ab
साक्ष्यसंबन्धतः साक्षी न स्वतः साक्षितात्मनः SV 1086ab
साक्ष्यसाक्ष्यपि संसिध्येत्स्वार्थत्वान्न तु शून्यता 3.4.120ab
साक्ष्यात्मा भावनारूपकामस्य स्वप्नसद्मनि 4.3.1039cd
साक्ष्यार्थानभिसंबन्धात्तस्मिन्सत्यपि नाचितेः 3.4.89cd
साक्ष्यार्थो दृष्टियोग्यः स्यादन्यो मात्रादिरात्मनः 4.3.1620ab
सांख्यमुक्तिनिवृत्त्यर्थमथवास्तूत्तरा श्रुतिः 1.4.1028ab
सांख्यराद्धान्तपुंवत्तत्प्राप्तं नानात्वदर्शनात् 3.4.22cd
सांख्यराद्धान्तवत्किंचित्प्रत्यगात्मैकवस्तुनः 2.1.163cd
सांख्यराद्धान्तवन्नातश्चोद्यं मत्तोऽन्यतः कृतम् 4.3.1484cd
सांख्यादयस्तथेशस्य ह्यभावं बहुयुक्तिभिः 2.1.441ab
सांख्यानामिव सिद्धान्ते लभ्यते कारणान्तरम् 4.4.179cd
सा चात्मोत्पत्तितो नान्यद्ध्वान्तध्वस्तावपेक्षते SV 18cd
सा चैकैवाविभागत्वात्कार्यकारणभेदतः 5.1.56ab
सांजीवीपुत्रतस्त्वर्वाक्प्रतिशाखं पृथकपृथक् 6.5.21ab
सांजीवीसूनुपर्यन्तो वंश एको न भिद्यते 6.5.20cd
सा तत्त्वमसंप्राप्य सिद्धा स्रगहिबोधवत् 1.4.1179cd
सा त्रिरात्रान्त आप्लुत्याहतवासाः शुचिः सती 6.4.69ab
सादृश्यक्षणिकत्वे द्वे त्वदिष्टे न प्रसिध्यतः 4.3.676cd
सादृश्यतस्त्वभिन्नोऽयमिति भ्रान्तिरियं मता 4.3.467ab
सादृश्यधिषणां चेह न कश्चित्कर्तुमर्हति 4.3.685cd
सादृश्यधीप्रसिद्ध्यर्थमित्यभ्युपगमेऽपि च 4.3.674cd
सादृश्यप्रत्ययो युक्तो न त्वसौ क्षणिकात्मसु 4.3.673cd
सादृश्यव्यपदेशादि सर्वं सुस्थं भवेत्ततः 4.3.694cd
सादृश्यात्प्रत्यभिज्ञानं कृत्तकेशनखादिवत् 4.3.664ab
सादृश्यादन्वयभ्रान्तिस्तन्निवृत्तावपीति चेत् 1.2.57ab

सादृश्यान्न च केशादौ स एवायमितीक्षणम् 4.3.666ab
सादृश्यासंभवश्चापि सर्वस्य क्षणिकत्वतः 4.3.665ab
सादृश्यासंभवाच्चेह नोपमानस्य संभवः 1.4.269ab
साद्गुण्यविगुणत्वाभ्यां सा स्यात्कर्मण एव च 1.4.1491cd
साधनं किंचिदापेक्ष्यं स्वर्गे यागादिवत्क्वचित् 2.4.187cd
साधनं च तदुत्पत्तौ संन्यासोऽतोऽत्र भण्यते 3.5.3cd
साधनं चाधिकारी च कर्मविज्ञानकाण्डयोः SV 19ab
साधनं तदपीहोक्तं ज्ञानकर्मस्वलक्षणम् 6.2.162ab
साधनं दूषणं सर्वं न तन्निह्नुतिरिष्यते 1.4.1372cd
साधनं दूषणं सर्वं यस्य पादव्यपाश्रयात् 1.4.1373ab
साधनं ब्रह्मविद्येव ब्रह्मज्ञानस्य जन्मने 4.4.1106cd
साधनं स्वाधिकारस्य भवतीह कथं चन SV 534cd
साधनत्वं यतस्तुल्यं श्रोत्रियावृजिनत्वयोः 4.3.1872ab
साधनत्वं समानं स्यात्त्रयाणामिह यद्यपि 4.3.1869ab
साधनत्वाविशेषत्वात्पुत्रवित्तैषणात्मनोः 3.5.134ab
साधनत्वेन कर्तात्र दृष्टाववसितिं गतः 3.4.173ab
साधनत्वेन शान्त्यादेः सम्यग्ज्ञानस्य जन्मने 4.4.1232ab
साधनात्तमसो मां त्वं ज्योतिः साध्यं नयामृतम् 1.3.361ab
साधनादित्रयाद्बाह्यं पुरुषार्थबहिष्कृतम् SV 621ab
साधनादिव्यपेक्षैव सुखसंवित्तिरिष्यते 3.9.207ab
साधनानां फलान्तत्वात्संन्यासः किं निवार्यते 1.5.304cd
साधनानामपि तथा तद्विद्योत्तमसाधनम् 2.5.97cd
साधनानामसामग्र्यात्सामग्र्याच्चेह कर्तरि 4.3.1486ab
साधनानामिहैकात्म्ये तथा च प्रागवादिषम् 3.5.205cd
साधनानीष्टलाभार्थमनिष्टार्थापनुत्तये 2.1.575ab
साधनानुमितं साध्यं मुक्तिः केनात उच्यते 3.1.20cd
साधनान्तरजय्योऽयं लोकोऽतश्चोदितं न सत् 1.5.236cd
साधनान्तरविषया तज्ज्ञानव्यतिरेकतः 4.4.341cd
साधनान्तरसंभाव्यं यावत्संभाव्यते फलम् 1.4.1775ab
साधनान्येव मनसो बुद्धिकर्मेन्द्रियाण्यपि 1.5.109ab
साधनायत्तलब्धात्मा न लोकेऽस्त्यविनश्वरः 1.4.1203cd
साधनायासतः प्राक्च ब्रह्मैवासीदितीरितम् 1.4.1300cd

साधनेनैतदैकात्म्यं येन येन चिकीर्ष्यते 3.5.206ab
साधनेहानुबन्धस्य वेदे कार्यस्य बोधनात् SV 516cd
साधनैकसजातित्वादानन्तर्यमकारणम् 1.5.47cd
साधनोक्त्यैव तत्साध्यं यदि नामावसीयते 1.5.222ab
साधयित्वा स्वयंज्योतिः सुषुप्ते युक्तिभिः स्फुटम् 4.3.1539ab
साधयेद्व्यापृतं वेदं तथापीष्टं न सिध्यति 1.2.81cd
साधर्म्यमुच्यते श्रुत्या तद्वनस्पतिमर्त्ययोः 3.9.134cd
साधर्म्ये सति वैधर्म्यं शक्यं प्रष्टुं यतस्ततः 3.9.134ab
साधारणः पृथिव्यादिकारी धर्मोऽभिधीयते 2.5.47ab
साधारणत्वात्सर्वासां कार्यस्य करणस्य च 4.2.68cd
साधारणमिदं युक्तं सर्वभूतस्थितेस्ततः 1.5.24cd
साधारणविशेषात्मफलमारभते द्विधा 1.5.7cd
साधारणविशेषात्मा यदपूर्वं तदुच्यते 2.5.48cd
साधारणविशेषाभ्यां धर्मवत्तदपि द्विधा 2.5.51ab
साधारणविशेषार्थव्यवस्थाकारणत्वतः 2.5.51cd
साधारणस्य यो वायुर्विशिष्टस्य च धारकः 3.7.11ab
साधारणात्मनः स्रष्टा नातः क्षेत्रज्ञतोऽपरः 1.5.16cd
साधारणात्मनो योंऽशो भोक्तृकर्मवशीकृतः 4.4.55ab
साधारणादिसंभेदभिन्नं तेन क्रियाफलम् 1.5.9cd
साधारणानि वस्तूनि तथासाधारणान्यपि 1.5.5cd
साधारणानि वस्तूनि तथासाधारणान्यपि 5.16.49ab
साधारणोऽयं विलयः समानान्तोऽभिधीयते 2.4.384ab
साधारण्यं तयोर्मानात्समस्तव्यस्तयोः कुतः 1.6.87cd
साधारण्यविशेषाभ्यां कर्मणश्च व्यवस्थितिः 3.3.4ab
साधितं च प्रयत्नेन स्वयंज्योतिष्ट्वमात्मनः 4.3.1380cd
साधिभूताधिदैवं च नामरूपक्रियात्मकः 1.3.235ab
साधिभूताधिदैवस्य जगतः सर्गकारणम् 3.2.72cd
साधुकारी पुमान्यः स्यात्साधुरेव भवत्यसौ 4.4.196ab
साधुभृत्यपरीवारः सर्वदोपासको भवेत् 2.1.78ab
साध्यं च लोकतः सिद्धमुत्पत्त्यादिचतुष्टयम् 2.4.189ab
साध्यं लोकत्रयमतस्त्रयो वावेति च श्रुतिः 1.5.223cd
साध्यं हि सर्वदा कार्यमन्यत्तस्य प्रसिद्धये SV 801cd

साध्यत्वं नान्यथा दृष्टमसतो यदि वा सतः 4.3.1707cd
साध्यत्वेऽपि हि सिद्धस्य किंत्वसाध्यस्य वस्तुनः 3.5.139cd
साध्यमानं प्रसंख्यानं यागवत्साधयेत्फलम् SV 823ab
साध्यसाधनतां तस्मादज्ञानैकव्यपाश्रयाम् 1.2.129ab
साध्यसाधनताज्ञानं नियोगादेव नान्यतः SV 522cd
साध्यसाधनबुद्धिर्नो वचनात्पारलौकिकी 3.3.53ab
साध्यसाधनभावत्वादेककालानवस्थितेः 3.3.58cd
साध्यसाधनरूपाभ्यस्तस्मादुक्तार्थवेदिनः 3.5.119ab
साध्यसाधनरूपाभ्यां विरुद्धं प्रत्यगीक्षणम् 3.5.167ab
साध्यसाधनरूपे द्वे एषणे काम उच्यते 1.4.1835ab
साध्यसाधनरूपे हि द्वे एवात्रैषणे यतः 1.4.1827cd
साध्यसाधनवत्कृत्स्नकार्यरूपविवक्षया 1.2.140ab
साध्यसाधनसंबन्ध आगमैकप्रमाणकः 3.3.36ab
साध्यसाधनसंबन्धमात्रैकविषयत्वतः 5.1.99cd
साध्यसाधनसंबन्धविज्ञानं नान्यतः श्रुतेः 3.2.114ab
साध्यसाधनसंबन्धविधाने सत्यसंभवः 4.4.1233ab
साध्यसाधनसंबन्धविषयत्वं पुमर्थतः SV 520ab
साध्यसाधनसंबन्धानिष्टानिष्टफलोदयान् 2.1.585ab
साध्यसाधनसंबन्धे तस्यापीष्टा प्रमाणता 5.1.96cd
साध्यसाधनसंबन्धे शास्त्रापेक्षैव नापरा 2.4.222ab
साध्यसाधनसंबन्धो न शक्योऽभिधया यथा 2.4.156ab
साध्यस्य कर्मणस्त्यागात्सामर्थ्यादेव सिद्धतः 4.4.1267ab
साध्यस्य साधनादानमतः साध्यानुरोधतः 3.5.136cd
साध्यादप्यासुराद्वैतसाध्यापिरतिमुक्तिता 3.1.25cd
साध्यानां साधनैकत्वादसाध्यासाधनात्मता 4.3.555cd
साध्याभावे कथं हेतोरभाव इति कथ्यताम् 4.3.722ab
साध्याभावेन तद्धेतोरभावपरिमार्गणम् 4.3.721cd
साध्यार्थेन समानत्वात्तदप्युक्तमशोभनम् 4.3.649cd
साध्यावृत्त्यात्मकं ज्ञानं कर्मैवावस्तुतन्त्रतः 3.3.34ab
साध्येऽर्थे साधनापेक्षा सिद्धे तन्न व्यपेक्षते SV 798cd
साध्ये हि साधनापेक्षा सिद्धेऽसौ विनिवर्तते 5.1.104ab
साध्यैषणाप्रयुक्तत्वात्पुत्रवित्तैषणात्मनः 3.5.135ab

साध्वसाध्विति चाध्यासौ मूलं विद्यात् तयोरपि 1.4.175ab
साध्वसाध्विति वा ज्ञानं ज्ञातमेयस्य जायते 1.4.176cd
साध्वादि भयोऽभ्यासात्स्यात्ताच्छील्यप्रत्ययश्रुतेः 4.4.198ab
साध्वाद्यनभिसंबन्धे यदि वा हेतुरुच्यते 4.4.1006ab
साध्वेतदिति संभाव्य सजनादुत्ससर्पतुः 3.2.139ab
साध्वेवातः प्रयत्नेन कर्म कार्यं विपश्चिता 4.4.81ab
सानुमा संभवस्तत्र व्यभिचारस्य चेन्न हि 4.3.717cd
सापराधं स्वमात्मानं राजा परिहरन्नथ 6.2.69ab
सापराधत्वतो मुक्तिः संदिग्धैव प्रसज्यते SV 101ab
सापि कामं भवत्वेव न दोषस्तत्र भण्यते 4.4.745cd
सापि तन्मात्रनिष्ठत्वान्नैव भेदस्पृगिष्यते SV 974cd
सापीहान्तरसंबुद्धमेयमात्रव्यपाश्रयात् SV 549cd
सा पृथिव्यभवच्चेति विराजो जन्मशब्दनम् 1.2.150cd
सापेक्षत्वं च लोके स्याद्विनियोगप्रधानतः SV 695cd
सापेक्षत्वादमानं चेदभिधा लोकवर्त्मना 2.4.159ab
सापेक्षस्येह वचसः प्रामाण्यमुपपद्यते 1.4.794cd
साप्येषैव च विज्ञेया व्याख्याता या प्रयत्नतः 5.16.40ab
साफल्यं कर्मणस्तत्र तदभिव्यक्तिकृद्धि तत् 2.4.118cd
सामग्र्यभावान्नैवेह कर्तृत्वादि विवक्ष्यते 4.3.894ab
सामग्र्यां घटवत्सत्यां सर्वं सद्वादिनो ध्रुवम् 1.2.76cd
सामग्र्या स यया पूर्वमद्राक्षीच्छिखरं गिरेः 4.3.264ab
सामञ्जस्येन गच्छन्ति न च श्रुत्यक्षराण्यपि 2.3.133ab
सामन्तो व्युत्थितो राज्ञा विरोधेन व्यवस्थितौ 3.5.126ab
सामर्थ्यं यस्य यत्रैव दृष्टं तत्रैव तस्य तत् 3.3.124ab
सामर्थ्यस्याग्रहात्तस्मान्न विरुद्धा प्रकल्प्यते 3.3.123cd
सामर्थ्याच्च ततोऽस्यैव प्रत्यग्याथात्म्यवेदिनः 4.4.1075ab
सामर्थ्याच्च मनोऽप्यत्र विज्ञेयमुपसंहृतम् 3.9.79ab
सामर्थ्यात्कल्प्यते कार्यं प्राणानां नाशनं पितुः 1.4.1742cd
सामर्थ्यात्तद्विनिष्पत्तिर्नाग्निहोत्रादिकर्मणः 3.3.99ab
सामर्थ्यात्स्वविरुद्धानां न विशेष्येऽस्ति संभवः 1.4.1423cd
सामर्थ्यादपि संप्राप्तो न चेदक्षरपूर्वकः 2.5.75ab
सामर्थ्यादेक एवार्थो भूयो भूयोऽभिधीयते 4.3.1616cd

सामर्थ्यादेव नान्यस्मात्कारणादिति निश्चयः 3.8.91cd
सामर्थ्याद्विस्तरस्तस्या आध्यायान्तादिहोच्यते 1.4.1592cd
सामस्त्येनाददानः सन्न्त्सद्मन्युपसर्पति 4.4.43cd
सामानाधिकरण्यं च तद्वेदमिति युक्तिमत् 1.4.35cd
सामानाधिकरण्यं च विशेषणविशेष्यता 3.5.185ab
सामानाधिकरण्यं च विशेषणविशेष्यता 4.3.1819cd
सामानाधिकरण्यस्य तथैवेहोपचारतः 1.4.567ab
सामानाधिकरण्यस्य तदिदंपदयोः श्रुतेः 1.4.194ab
सामानाधिकरण्यस्य विभिन्नार्थव्यपाश्रयात् 1.6.68ab
सामानाधिकरण्यादेर्घटेतरखयोरिव 3.5.186ab
सामानाधिकरण्यादेर्नेह तत्पुनरुच्यते 4.4.978cd
सामानाधिकरण्यादेर्वाक्यादैकात्म्यमुच्यते 5.1.20cd
सामानाधिकरण्यार्थमस्मीत्येतत्पदं भवेत् 1.4.1416cd
सामानाधिकरण्येन तथा ब्रह्मात्मशब्दयोः 1.4.1255ab
सामानाधिकरण्योक्तिर्व्यक्तस्याव्यक्तसिद्धये 1.4.209ab
सामानाधिकरण्योक्तिस्तस्माद्ब्रह्मात्मशब्दयोः 3.4.45cd
सामानाधिकरण्योक्तेर्ब्रह्मात्मार्थाभिधायिनोः 3.4.43ab
सामानाधिकरण्योक्तेर्विशेषणविशेष्यतः 3.4.34ab
सामानाधिकरण्योक्तेस्तद्वृत्तिः कृष्णसर्पवत् 5.1.113cd
सामान्यं च विशेषश्च द्रव्यतन्त्रौ मतौ यदि 1.6.78ab
सामान्यं वा विशेषो वा कोऽनयोरभिधीयताम् 1.6.62cd
सामान्यं वा विशेषो वा चिदसंबोधहेतुतः 2.4.282cd
सामान्यं वा विशेषो वा न यतोऽत्रावशिष्यते 4.4.53cd
सामान्यं वा विशेषो वा नातः स्याद्व्राजती स्मृतिः 1.4.474cd
सामान्यज्ञानग्रहणं मेधयेत्यभिधित्सितम् 1.5.18cd
सामान्यनररक्षायां तस्मादेतदनुत्तरम् 1.4.1809cd
सामान्यप्रज्ञया देहं संव्याप्यान्तर्बहिः श्रमात् 2.1.332ab
सामान्यभेदरूपाणां विशेषाणामशेषतः 2.4.292ab
सामान्यभेदैकात्म्याख्यतदनन्यप्रमात्मना 1.4.396cd
सामान्यभोज्यविषयस्त्वन्नशब्दो यतस्ततः 1.3.238ab
सामान्यमथवा व्यक्तिर्यदि सामान्यमुच्यते 4.3.225cd
सामान्यमात्रप्रत्युक्तेर्न यथापृष्टवस्तुधीः 3.5.102ab

सामान्यमात्रवाचित्वात्खशब्दस्य विशेषणम् 5.1.116ab
सामान्यमात्रविज्ञानाद्विशेषस्याप्रतीतितः 3.4.11cd
सामान्यमात्रवृत्तिं स सुषुप्ते प्रतिपद्यते 1.4.643ab
सामान्यमेतत्सर्वेषां विशेषाणां समं हि तैः 1.6.22cd
सामान्यरूपतामेति स्वकार्यैः कारणं तथा 1.4.357cd
सामान्यवचसोपात्तेर्न विशेषपरिग्रहः 6.2.123cd
सामान्यविषयश्चायं निषेधो नानविद्वतः 1.3.227ab
सामान्यवृत्त्या प्राणोऽयं तस्मादाधानमुच्यते 2.2.11cd
सामान्यव्यक्तिभेदेन ह्येकानेका च सोच्यते 1.5.173cd
सामान्यस्य विशेषत्वाद्विशेषा एव केवलाः 1.6.58cd
सामान्यस्याविशेषत्वान्नातः सामान्यधीग्रहः 2.4.269cd
सामान्यात्मविशेषत्वं तदुपाधिरगात्परः 1.4.645cd
सामान्यात्मविशेषाभ्यामित्येतद्बुज्युनोच्यते 3.3.5cd
सामान्यादिति विज्ञेयं वाजपेयफलार्थिनाम् 6.4.14ef
सामान्याद्यविशेषेऽपि नियमोऽप्येवमिष्यताम् 1.4.471cd
सामान्यानि विशेषाश्च तन्मध्यपतितानि च 1.4.645ab
सामान्यानि विशेषाश्च व्यावर्तन्ते परस्परम् 1.4.953ab
सामान्यानीह खण्डादौ तेनान्योऽन्यविरुद्धता 1.6.75cd
सामान्यान्तरनिर्मुक्तं तथासाधारणैरपि 1.4.447ab
सामान्याम्मयदेहस्य विशिष्टाः कार्यमस्य ताः 3.9.56ab
सामान्येऽभिन्नधीर्यस्माद्भिन्नेष्वेव तु भिन्नधीः 1.6.66cd
सामान्येतरतो भिन्नं द्रव्यं चेद्द्रवतो मतम् 1.6.81ab
सामान्येतररूपत्वात्साध्यस्याग्न्यादिरूपिणः 4.3.240ab
सामान्येतररूपस्य दुन्दुभ्याघात इष्यते 2.4.288cd
सामान्येन ग्रहात्तस्याः पञ्चाग्निरितिलिङ्गतः 6.2.126cd
सामान्येन विशेषेण वायुरेव तदीक्ष्यते 3.3.169cd
सामान्येन समष्टिश्च वायुरेव द्विधा स्थितः 3.3.168cd
सामान्येन समस्तं तद्विशेषैर्व्यस्तमेव च 1.4.948ab
सामान्येनेक्षमाणस्य विशेषेण च वस्त्विदम् 4.4.795ab
सामान्येनौषधं यद्वज्ज्वरनाशोपलक्षितम् SV 766ab
सामान्योक्तावास्य इति तद्विशेषणमुच्यते 1.3.202ab
सामान्योक्तेर्विशेषार्थमेष इत्यादि भण्यते 5.3.2cd

सामापि प्राण एवेति कथं तदिति भण्यते 5.15.6ab
सामिप्रमापितस्यापि रात्रौ तस्यां विवर्जयेत् 1.5.213ab
सामुद्रमम्भः खिल्यत्वं याति भानुविपाकतः 2.4.404ab
सामुद्ररूपान्नान्येन ग्रहीतुं कश्चन क्षमः 2.4.402cd
सामोभयं समुदितं गुणप्राधान्यरूपतः 1.3.301cd
साम्न आप्नोति सायुज्यमैकात्म्यं प्राणरूपताम् 1.3.309ab
साम्यं केन प्रकारेणेत्यनन्ता इत्यतोऽवदत् 1.5.195ab
सा यथा प्रसजेन्नेह व्याख्येयं तत्तथा वचः 4.4.832cd
सारस्त्रयाणां भूतानां रसो मण्डलमुच्यते 2.3.44ab
सारेण यदि नामेयं पूर्णा स्याद्वसुना मही 2.4.49ab
सार्ष्टिसालोक्यसायुज्यव्यपेक्षा बहुगीरियम् 6.2.142ab
सालक्षण्येऽपि च सति बुद्धेरेव विलक्षणः 4.3.425ab
सावशेषात्मनोऽकृत्स्नान्निःशेषात्मतया यतः 1.4.740ab
सावित्रः पुरुषस्तस्य चक्षुः सत्यं च देवता 3.9.51cd
सावित्रीं मधुमतीश्चैव तिस्त्रोऽपि व्याहृतीस्तथा 6.3.53cd
सावित्रीं याममूं प्राह बटवे मन्त्रलक्षणाम् 5.16.39cd
साविद्यः प्रत्यगात्मा यो वियद्योनिरुदाहृतः 3.9.157ab
साविद्या सति बाह्येऽर्थे द्रष्टव्येऽलं न चासति 4.3.1194ab
सा विध्वस्तात्ममोहस्याप्यरतिः संबभूव ह 1.4.105cd
साश्रयैः करणैर्हीनो ग्रस्ताध्यात्माधिदैवतः 4.2.85ab
सासङ्गत्वं समाशङ्क्य प्रवृत्तैषा यतः श्रुतिः 4.3.1003ab
सासङ्गश्च समृत्युश्च सकार्यकरणस्तथा 4.3.1154ab
सा सैव प्रक्रियेह स्यात्साध्वी सा चानवस्थिता 1.4.402cd
सास्नादयो मिथो भिन्ना न चान्योऽन्यविरोधिनः 4.3.1641cd
सास्नादिषु यथा गोत्वमभेदेन व्यवस्थिम् 1.6.49ab
सा स्वतः परतो वास्येत्येतदत्राधुनोच्यते 4.3.1207cd
सा हि देहान्तरप्राप्तावात्मनो मार्गदर्शिनी 4.4.92ab
सा हैषेति श्रुतिरतो यथोक्तार्थावबुद्धये 5.16.38ab
सिद्ध आत्मा पृथङ्मातुर्नो चेन्माता न सिध्यति SV 1075cd
सिद्धं कारणमेवं स्यान्न मा मेयं विना यतः 1.2.55cd
सिद्धं चेत्कारणात्सिद्धमुपमर्दं विनैव तु 1.2.39ab
सिद्धं चेद्दर्शयेद्वेदः प्रसिद्धं दर्शनं तथा SV 658ab

सिद्धः कुतश्चिन्मानात्स्यादनुवादस्तथा सति 1.4.694cd
सिद्धत्वहेतुको योऽपि दोष ऐकात्म्य उच्यते SV 717ab
सिद्धवस्त्ववबोधित्वं विधेरपि तदा भवेत् SV 740cd
सिद्धसाध्यत्वतो नैवं तथा चोक्तोत्तरत्वतः 3.8.111ab
सिद्धसाध्यत्वमथवा नङ्क्ष्यतीति मतं यदि 4.3.615ab
सिद्धसाध्यत्वमेवं स्यादिष्टैव क्षणसंगतिः 4.3.587cd
सिद्धसाध्यप्रमेयत्वभेदो यदि परं तयोः 2.4.166ab
सिद्धसाध्यादिभेदेन स्वशब्देनाभिधीयते SV 619ab
सिद्धस्य व्यञ्जकं मानं न तु तत्कारकं यतः 4.3.1431ab
सिद्धस्य व्यञ्जकं मानं न मानं कारकं क्वचित् SV 1033ab
सिद्धातोऽसौ न साध्या स्यादग्निहोत्रादिकार्यवत् 1.4.1433cd
सिद्धान्तस्य स्थितत्वाच्च यथावदुपपत्तिभिः 4.3.1400cd
सिद्धान्तहानिरेवं च कल्पनायां ध्रुवं भवेत् 2.3.147cd
सिद्धान्तो दुःस्थितोऽत्यर्थं तदा वः प्राप्नुयाद्ध्रुवम् 1.4.574cd
सिद्धान्तोपक्रमः पूर्वं पूर्वपक्षः प्रदर्श्यते 1.4.757ab
सिद्धान्वागादिदृष्टान्तान्पुरस्कृत्यात उच्यते 1.3.160ab
सिद्धायतेऽखिलोऽनात्मा स्वतःसिद्धात्मसंश्रयात् 2.3.224cd
सिद्धायतेऽप्रसिद्धं सत्तत्सिद्धौ किमपेक्षते SV 791cd
सिद्धायते तीर्थदृशां कुतः स्यात्तस्य निह्नुतिः 1.4.1373cd
सिद्धायते प्रतीचीयं प्राक्सम्यग्ज्ञानजन्मनः 4.3.1111cd
सिद्धायते यतोऽतः स्यादविचारितसिद्धिकम् : 1.4.332cd
सिद्धासंकीर्यमाणेह साप्यस्यैवानुशासनात् 4.4.1013cd
सिद्धा सादृश्यधीरेवं क्षणिकत्वं तु नश्यति 4.3.675ab
सिद्धिर्विविदिषायाः स्याद्वेदानुवचनादिभिः 4.4.1041ab
सिद्धिर्विषयसिद्धौ चेन्नैवं स्यात्कर्मणा न हि SV 626ab
सिद्धेऽनवगते यस्मात्पुरस्ताद्व्याप्तिर्मितेः SV 570ab
सिद्धेऽर्थे द्योतको दीपो न तु कार्ये यतस्ततः 1.4.1082ab
सिद्धेऽसति विशिष्टे न विषये कार्यमिष्यते SV 610ab
सिद्धेऽसिद्धेऽथ वैकात्म्ये विधिर्नैवोपपद्यते SV 655ab
सिद्धे पुमर्थे विलयकल्पना निष्प्रयोजना SV 397cd
सिद्धे वस्तुनि वेदस्य मानत्वं तेन भण्यते SV 314cd
सिद्धेष्वतीन्द्रियोऽप्यर्थो वाक्यादेवावगम्यते SV 863cd

सिद्धे सामान्यतो लिङ्गात्संबन्धे कर्मभिस्ततः	SV 339ab
सिद्धे ह्यनेकवाक्यत्वे कल्प्या भिन्नाधिकारिता	SV 285cd
सिद्धोऽङ्गानां रसः प्राणः प्राणोऽङ्गानां रसः कथम्	1.3.292ab
सिद्धो निषेधः प्रागेव सर्वस्यानात्मवस्तुनः	2.3.221ab
सिद्धो यस्मादतस्तस्मिन्वाक्यं स्यादनुवादकम्	4.3.1113cd
सिद्ध्यसिद्ध्योः प्रमात्रादेस्तत्सिद्धौ किमपेक्षते	4.4.688cd
सिद्ध्येद्दर्शननिष्पत्तिस्तद्वदात्माद्यपेक्षया	1.4.924cd
सिध्यतीह ततोऽस्तित्वं स्वत एवाक्षरात्मनः	3.8.120cd
सिध्यत्येवं भवत्पक्षो दोषोऽपि स्यादनीप्सितः	4.3.786cd
सिन्धोरायातः स यतस्तस्मात्सैन्धव उच्यते	2.4.404cd
सिसृक्षितत्वान्मनसस्तथा त्र्यन्नात्मनः प्रभोः	1.5.16ab
सुॠॠषुप्ते योऽवशिष्टोऽत्र कौटस्थ्यान्नान्यदश्यर्सौ,	4.3.1513ab
सुखं मे स्यादिति सदा नरः कामयतेऽबुधः	4.4.258cd
सुखदुःखादिसंवित्तिः फलं पूर्वस्य कर्मणः	1.5.82ab
सुखदुःखादिसंस्कारसंस्कृतोऽयं जडः पुमान्	2.1.211ab
सुखदुःखादिसंदृष्टेर्न चाप्यस्तीह संशयः	SV 81cd
सुखदुःखादिसंबद्धं यथा दण्डेन दण्डिनम्	1.4.562ab
सुखदुःखादिहेतूनामुत्तमाधममध्यतः	2.1.152ab
सुखयन्तस्तदा प्राणाः संयान्त्युत्क्रान्तिवेदिनम्	4.3.1975cd
सुखविज्ञानयोश्चापि किमभेदोऽथवा भिदा	4.4.334ab
सुखसंविद्धि काम्योऽर्थो बाह्यसाधनसाधनः	4.3.1340ab
सुखादिफलदं कर्मेत्यस्मिन्पक्षे व्यवस्थिते	1.4.1479ab
सुखादिफलभोगाय स्वप्नः क्षुद्रस्य कर्मणः	4.3.1192ab
सुखादिव्यक्तितः पूर्वं यस्य संसारिता मता	4.4.346ab
सुखाद्यनुगमात्तस्य व्यतिरेकः सुदुर्लभः	4.3.395cd
सुखाद्युत्पत्तिहेतूनि दृश्यन्तेऽकार्यवन्त्यपि	SV 577ab
सुखावबुद्धये हेति निपातोऽत्र प्रयुज्यते	1.4.192cd
सुखावबोधतश्चैव स्वयमेव प्रतीयताम्	6.3.62ef
सुखावबोधसिद्ध्यर्थं श्रोतुरर्थे विवक्षिते	4.3.1911cd
सुखावबोधसिद्ध्यर्थमियमाख्यायिकोदिता	2.1.20cd
सुखिदुःखित्वमोहादिदर्शनान्नेति चेन्मतम्	1.4.557ab
सुखिदुःखित्वसाक्षित्वं दुःस्थितं स्यात्तथा सति	4.3.395ab

सुखी गौरो धनी गोमान्बाह्यमेयसमाश्रयात् 3.4.125ab
सुखी दुःखी च देहान्तः प्रत्यगज्ञानहेतुतः 4.3.1528cd
सुखीभवनमस्यार्थान्नोपदेशव्यपेक्षया SV 578cd
सुखेन दर्शनं तावदैहिकस्येह जन्मनः 4.3.845ab
सुख्येधीति न चानेन प्रवृत्तिरुपदिश्यते SV 578ab
सुतजन्मादिभिश्चेत्स्यात्सर्वकर्मफलात्ययः 1.5.250ab
सुतादिना न तर्ह्यर्थो नापि स्यात्पाङ्क्तकर्मणा 1.5.226cd
सुतेनातिक्रमोऽप्राप्तेः प्राप्तो निर्विषयस्ततः 1.5.237cd
सुदूरमपि गत्वेह ह्यतिशीतिरपीष्यते 3.3.124cd
सुपथा नय नो वह्ने सुपथेति विशेषणात् 5.17.19ab
सुपथेति ततो युक्तं संभवे भूयसां पथाम् 6.2.4ab
सुपथेति श्रुतं तत्र श्रुत्या मार्गविशेषणम् 6.2.2cd
सुप्तं न बोधयेद्गाढमिति तद्दोषदर्शिनः 4.3.948cd
सुप्तं न बोधयेद्गाढमिति वादो हि लौकिकः 4.3.946ab
सुप्तं पुरुषमभ्येत्य पाणिना बोधयन्स्वयम् 2.1.434cd
सुप्तः प्रबुद्ध इत्येवं स्वप्नं पश्यति चेति यः 2.1.265ab
सुप्तः स्वप्नान्न जानाति यः स आत्मेति भण्यते 4.3.1403cd
सुप्तस्तिसृष्ववस्थासु सामान्येन यतस्ततः 4.3.1164ab
सुप्तासुप्तत्वसंभेदविशेषन्यायसंभवात् 2.1.128ab
सुप्तेऽस्मिन्करणग्रामे योऽसुप्तोऽलुप्तदृष्टितः 3.4.69ab
सुप्तोऽपि कर्म कुरुते नरः स्वप्ने प्रबोधवत् 4.3.1057ab
सुप्रसिद्धं यदस्माकं त्वच्छासनमृतेऽपि तत् 2.1.48ab
सुप्रसिद्धे जगत्यस्मिन्नायोषिद्बालपण्डितम् 4.3.277cd
सुरद्विषां सुराणां तु शास्त्रोत्थज्ञानदीपितः 1.3.113cd
सुविस्पष्टार्थतो भाष्यं टीकां नैव व्यपेक्षते 3.2.121ab
सुव्याख्येयत्वतः शेषः स्वयमेवावगम्यताम् 6.4.70cd
सुषुप्त इव तेनासन्मात्रादानमिदं कृतम् 4.3.900cd
सुषुप्त इव निद्राया दुर्बलत्वाच्च बाध्यते 1.4.859cd
सुषुप्तजाग्रन्मूढः स्याच्छान्तोऽसौ स्वप्न उच्यते 4.3.1059ab
सुषुप्तनरवच्छ्रुत्या बोध्योऽतोऽयं न कार्यते SV 29cd
सुषुप्तप्रलयावस्थप्राणात्माक्षरमुच्यते 3.9.4ab
सुषुप्तस्थस्तथा धीस्थात्कर्तृभोक्तृत्वलक्षणात् 1.4.613cd

सुषुप्तस्थानगं रूपं तदेतत्प्राक्प्रदर्शितम् 4.3.1395ab
सुषुप्ताख्यं ततस्तस्मात्प्राणाद्युत्पत्तिमब्रवीत् 2.1.435cd
सुषुप्ताज्जाग्रदापत्तिर्यथा तदधुनोच्यते 2.1.365cd
सुषुप्तादात्मनस्तद्वत्प्राणादीनां समुद्भवः 2.1.393cd
सुषुप्तादुत्थितो राज्ञः स्वयमेव यथा तथा 1.4.388ab
सुषुप्तादेश्च संसिद्धिर्मात्रादिविरहेऽपि या SV 549ab
सुषुप्तेऽतो न धात्वर्थः प्रत्ययार्थश्च नेष्यते 4.3.1440cd
सुषुप्तेऽत्र पिता चेति सर्वसंबन्धवारणम् 2.1.342cd
सुषुप्तेऽप्यतिमूढस्य सर्वसंसारनिह्नुतिः 3.5.212ab
सुषुप्तेऽस्य स्वभावत्वाज्जह्याच्चैतन्यमित्यतः 4.3.1381cd
सुषुप्ते चानुभूतिस्तु तयोरव्यभिचारिणी 4.3.193cd
सुषुप्ते तत्परित्यागः कस्मादित्यभिधीयते 4.3.1789cd
सुषुप्ते न तदस्तीह प्रयुक्तं यत्स्वगोचरैः 4.3.1509cd
सुषुप्ते नन्वसंबोधाद्द्रत्वादि कथमुच्यते 4.3.1046ab
सुषुप्ते ब्रह्मणोऽन्यस्य नावकाशोऽस्ति दुःखिनः 2.1.452cd
सुषुप्ते मातृपूर्वत्वात्सर्वमाव्यापृतेरिह 1.4.267cd
सुषुप्ते स्वपितीत्युक्तेस्तदेतदभिधीयते 2.1.247cd
सुषुप्तोदाहृतिर्येयं तया समुपलक्ष्यते 2.1.394ab
सुषुप्तौ न शरीरेण संगतिः प्रत्यगात्मनः 2.1.341ab
सुषुप्सुः कर्मणां ध्वस्तौ विहत्येत्युच्यते ततः 4.3.870cd
सुषुप्सुर्मनसैवात्मा मनस्येव समूहति 2.1.249ab
सुसंस्कृतधियः पुंसो यथोक्तैः कर्मभिः समम् 3.3.130ab
सुसूक्ष्ममपि सद्वस्तु शक्तौ ज्ञापयितुं यतः 3.1.14cd
सूक्तादिज्ञापनार्थाय ह्यहं मनुरितीरणम् 1.4.1446ab
सूक्ष्मं हि तदतीवोक्तं सर्वसत्त्वसमाश्रयम् 3.7.8cd
सूक्ष्मताव्यापिते ज्ञेये भूम्यादेरुत्तरोत्तरम् 2.4.294ab
सूक्ष्मताव्यापिते ज्ञेये भूम्यादेरुत्तरोत्तरम् 3.6.13ab
सूक्ष्मताव्यापिते ज्ञेये भूम्यादेर्यावदक्षरम् 1.4.639ab
सूक्ष्मदेहनिषेधोक्त्या स्थूलस्यापि निषेधतः 4.4.521ab
सूक्ष्मधर्मविवेकार्थमत एवाब्रवीन्मनुः 4.3.31ab
सूक्ष्मस्थूलशरीराभ्यां चिदाभाभ्यामविद्यया 1.2.157ab
सूक्ष्मापराधसंदृष्टेरतियत्नवतामपि SV 71cd

सूक्ष्मेष्वपि तथा विद्यादनुमानबलाद्बुधः 1.6.50cd
सूक्ष्मो देहोऽत्र लिङ्गं स्याल्लिलङ्गनात्प्रत्यगात्मनः 4.4.236ab
सूतिराम्रेडनं तस्मात्सिद्धमात्मधियः सदा 1.4.1513ef
सूत्रं तावत्सदुर्ज्ञानमाकाशस्तु ततोऽप्यति 3.8.50ab
सूत्रं प्राणोऽङ्गिराः सत्यमृक्सामेत्यन उच्यते 1.3.235cd
सूत्रं विराड्देवता च यावत्किंचिच्च वस्त्विह 1.4.1143cd
सूत्रादप्यन्तरतमस्त्वन्तर्याम्यधुनोच्यते 3.7.25ab
सूत्रादयस्तृणान्ताः स्युरन्योऽन्यव्यभिचारिणः 1.4.1147cd
सूत्रादयोऽनुभूयन्ते यथाकर्म यथाश्रुतम् 1.4.1148cd
सूत्रादिकार्यमार्गेण यन्तृत्वं कारणात्मनः 3.9.1ab
सूत्रादिक्षितिपर्यन्तमर्वाग्यन्तुरचेतनम् 3.8.49ab
सूत्रादिदर्शनानां स्यात्सूत्राद्येव यथा फलम् 1.4.1154ab
सूत्रादिस्थाणपर्यन्तं जगत्सृष्ट्वात्ममायया 1.4.514ab
सूत्रादेः कर्मणः कार्यं किम्यन्तस्याभिजायते 1.5.8cd
सूत्राद्यवच्छेदवशात्सर्वमेतन्नियच्छति 3.9.5cd
सूत्राद्यागमसंप्राप्तिं सोऽथाख्यानैकवर्त्मना 3.7.3ab
सूत्रान्तं वस्तु निर्देश्यमनिर्देश्ये प्रवेशितम् 3.8.51ab
सूत्रान्तजगतो व्यक्तेः प्राक्तनः काल उच्यते 1.4.1317ab
सूत्रान्तर्यामिरूपेण यो वेदैतान्पुरोदितान् 3.7.7ab
सूत्रेण ध्रियमाणानि सदैवेशयतानि च 3.7.5cd
सूत्रेण ध्रियमाणेयं महाभूतशरीरिणी 3.7.29ab
सूत्रेण विधृतं चान्तर्यामिणा संयतं तथा 3.7.6ab
सूत्रे तावदिदं सर्वमोतं च प्रोतमेव च 3.8.9ab
सूर्याचन्द्रमसावीशौ मर्यादां नातिगच्छतः 3.8.134ab
सूर्याचन्द्रमसावेव विज्ञेयावश्विनाविह 6.4.102cd
सूर्याचन्द्रमसौ तज्जकार्याभिज्ञपुरःसरौ 3.8.133ab
सूर्यादिकरणं देवं ब्रह्मास्राक्षीज्जगद्गुरुम् 5.5.9ab
सूर्ये समिधि दीप्तायां श्रद्धां जुह्वति देवताः 6.2.88cd
सृष्टानामथ भूतानामग्न्यादिप्रमुखा इमाः 1.4.125ab
सृष्टावन्यपरायां तु न चोद्यस्यास्ति संभवः 2.1.388ab
सृष्टिनामा मनुर्जात एतस्मादेव कारणात् 1.4.123cd
सृष्टिप्रस्ताव एतस्मिन्प्राणादेर्जन्म सूत्रितम् 2.2.3ab

सृष्टिमेतां समुद्दिश्य तन्मनोऽकुरुतेति या 1.2.143ab
सृष्टेषु न परः साक्षात्प्राविशत्परमेश्वरः 2.1.468cd
सृष्ट्यादिवचसां नैव युक्तार्थान्तरकल्पना 2.1.504cd
सृष्ट्यादिश्रुतयस्तस्मान्न तु तत्प्रत्ययाय ताः 2.1.527cd
सृष्ट्यालोचनहेत्वेतत्सृष्टावाविरभूद्विभोः 1.2.177ab
सृष्ट्वा जगत्सृष्टिमनु तदेव प्राविशच्छ्रुतेः 1.4.549cd
सृष्ट्वाथाधः प्रदेशे तामुपास्ते ग्राम्यधर्मतः 6.4.3cd
सृष्ट्वाद्यं घस्मरः पुत्रं तमभिव्याददात्क्षुधा 1.2.182ab
सृष्ट्वापि चतुरो वर्णान्व्यवस्थाकारणं विना 1.4.1614ab
सृष्ट्वेदं सकलं विश्वं पश्चात्तत्प्राविशद्विभुः 1.4.536ab
सेतिकर्तव्यताकेयं साङ्गा निःश्रेयसे नृणाम् 4.4.1304cd
सेतिकर्तव्यताकोऽथ विधिस्तस्याग्रमुच्यते 4.4.1271ef
सेति वाचोऽभिधानं स्यादमः प्राणाभिधा तथा 1.3.301ab
सेनापराजितेत्यस्मात्सपत्नानां पराजयः 2.1.65cd
सेन्द्रियस्यास्य देहस्य पुरुषोक्त्या परिग्रहात् 4.3.238ab
सेयमित्यादिकं वाक्यं छान्दोग्योपनिषद्यपि 2.1.464cd
सेवायाश्च क्रियात्मत्वाद्दानयागादि च क्रिया 3.8.149cd
सेवासांग्रहणीहावत्तुल्यकार्यतया न च SV 414ab
सेव्यात्क्रियाफलप्राप्तिर्दृष्टेयं न त्वपूर्वतः 3.8.156ab
सेव्यात्सेवाफलप्राप्तिदर्शनान्न त्वपूर्वतः 3.8.149ab
सैन्धवादिरसव्याप्ते पीयमाने यथोदके 4.4.47ab
सैवातः प्रतिपत्तव्या सर्वासु ध्यानभूमिषु 1.3.133ab
सैवातोऽनुपलब्ध्युक्त्या भवद्भिरुपवर्ण्यते 4.3.796cd
सैवात्मा विदुषः साक्षादात्मा स्यादजरोऽमरः 1.2.225cd
सैवेह दृष्टिविध्यर्थं श्रुत्या व्याख्यायतेऽञ्जसा 6.2.78cd
सैवेह सृज्यते धात्रा नियमार्थप्रसिद्धये 1.4.1631cd
सैषाविद्या परिच्छेत्री ययायं परमात्मनः 3.2.55ab
सोऽकाम इति संभाव्यः कृत्स्नकर्मनिराकृतेः 4.4.265cd
सोऽकामयत इत्यादिः परो ग्रन्थोऽवतार्यते 1.2.197cd
सोऽकामयत इत्येवं पुराप्युक्तं तमस्विनः 3.5.120cd
सोऽकामयत जायेति साधनान्येव नः श्रुतिः 1.5.221ab
सोऽतिग्रहग्रहाविष्टो विपरीतार्थनिश्चयः 1.4.1822cd

सोऽनन्तमेव वागादिलोकमाप्नोति मानवः 1.5.201cd
सोऽनुवीक्ष्यात्ममोहोत्थदृष्ट्याविद्योत्थरूपकम् 1.4.37cd
सोऽन्तर्यामीति मन्तव्यो न त्वियं देवता क्षितिः 3.7.30cd
सोऽन्नमत्ति प्रतीकेन वृत्त्यान्नं मुख्ययात्ति सः 1.5.92cd
सोऽन्य एव सदाव्यक्तनित्यज्ञानसुखात्मनः 4.4.346cd
सोऽपहन्ति पुनर्मृत्युं मृत्युमात्मानमेत्यसौ 3.3.173cd
सोऽपि ज्ञानेन संयुक्तो हयमेधो महाक्रतुः SV 1124ab
सोऽप्यस्य देवतातन्त्रो देवताश्चान्नसंश्रयाः 4.2.58cd
सोऽभ्यादानस्य कर्तात्र लिङ्गं योऽस्मीति मन्यते 4.4.48ab
सोऽयं सप्तदशग्रामो भोक्तुः करणलक्षणः 1.3.257cd
सोऽयं सांसारिकैरर्थैः प्रत्यक्तत्त्वाप्रबोधतः 2.1.518ab
सोऽयं साक्षात्परं ब्रह्म विद्यया वर्ततेऽधुना 2.5.60cd
सोऽयं सैन्धवखिल्योऽस्तो यथैवेह महोदधौ 2.4.405cd
सोऽयमुक्तस्तथोत्कर्षः परः पुण्यस्य चोदितः 3.4.3ab
सोऽयमैकात्म्यगर्भः सन्मोहः सर्वस्य कारकः 3.8.42ab
सोऽयास्याङ्गिरसः प्रोक्तस्तत्रायास्यो यथा तथा 1.3.290ab
सोऽरत्यतिग्रहाविष्टस्तदपध्वस्तये विराट् 1.4.109ab
सोऽरोदीत्यादिवाक्यानां कार्यविशात्प्रमाणता SV 893ab
सोऽरोदीदिति वाक्येभ्यो निश्चितं फलवच्च किम् 1.4.908ab
सोऽस्य कर्मक्षयादक्षणः पराङावर्तते हृदि 4.4.59cd
सोऽहं सहस्रमित्याह तस्मादेव च कारणात् 4.4.532cd
सोऽहमित्यादिकं वाक्यं गुरुमाह त्वरान्वितः 4.4.1303cd
सोत्प्रासमिव चाहातो बाढमित्येवमादिना 1.4.1230ab
सोपाख्यत्वान्न तद्द्व्यापि क्वचिदेकांशवत्स्थितेः 2.3.30ab
सोपाधिकस्य तस्यैव व्यवहारानुपातिनः 5.1.4ab
सोपाधिकस्य तस्यैव ह्युपास्तिर्वक्ष्यते स्फुटा 5.3.1cd
सोपानपङ्क्तिगत्येव हर्म्यपृष्ठाधिरोहणम् SV 400cd
सोपायो विहितोऽस्त्येव प्रतिपत्तिविधिं विना SV 761cd
सोपासनानि पाङ्क्तस्य वक्तव्यमवशिष्यते 1.5.204cd
सोम एवेति तं विद्याद्यद्यग्निरपि हूयते 1.4.158ab
सोम एवेत्यवधृतेरग्नीषोमव्यवस्थितिः 1.4.156cd
सोमं जुह्वति तत्राग्नौ देवाश्चात्रोदिताः पुरा 6.2.100ab

सोमचन्द्रमसोरेवं भेदः शास्त्रेण दर्शितः 6.2.93cd
सोमचन्द्रमसोस्तस्माद्भेदः समवगम्यते 6.2.96ab
सोमस्तु मण्डले श्वेतो वर्धते ह्रसते च यः 6.2.94cd
सोमाग्नीन्द्रादिका यापि साप्युक्तवदपेक्ष्य सः 1.4.121cd
सोमाभिषवरूपत्वक्लृप्तये ऽथाधुनोच्यते 6.4.5ab
सोमोऽप्यग्निरिति ज्ञेयो यदि तत्रापि हूयते 1.4.158cd
सोमो राजेत्यतो वक्ति तदुपासाविधित्सया 2.1.56cd
सोमो वृष्टयादिभावेन प्रभुः प्रभवसीत्यतः 6.3.33ab
सौकर्यप्रतिपत्तेश्च भूयोविषयतस्तथा 1.5.47ab
सौक्ष्म्यस्य तारतम्येन स्थितस्य विषयावधि 4.3.362ab
सौगतं दर्शनं पथ्यं दोषवत्त्वन्यदर्शनम् 4.3.480cd
सौगताद्युक्तिवत्तस्मान्न कामाश्रयतात्मनः 4.4.465cd
सौभाग्यं पुनरग्निः स्युः परिशिष्टाश्च देवताः 6.4.23ab
सौषुप्तं स्थानमाप्तस्य रूपं कामादिवर्जितम् 4.4.253cd
सौषुप्ती न हि बोधस्य कालभेदेन भिन्नता SV 998cd
स्तनंधयो यथा बालो रागद्वेषविवर्जितः 2.1.344ab
स्तनयित्नुरिह ज्ञेयस्तथा यज्ञः प्रजापतिः 3.9.18cd
स्तनौ भ्रुवौ वा निमृजेन्मध्ये च स्तनयोस्तदा 6.4.25cd
स्तुतित्वादर्थवादोऽयं नातोऽन्योऽर्थोऽवसीयते 5.1.128cd
स्तुत्यर्थं ब्रह्मविद्याया ब्रह्मविद्वंश उच्यते 2.6.1ab
स्तुत्यर्थत्वं यतोऽस्येह भवता परिकल्प्यते 4.4.1141cd
स्तुत्यानया च वेदोक्तक्रियाज्ञानस्तुतिर्भवेत् 1.4.3ab
स्तैनेदं पूर्णं पुरुषेण सर्वम् 2.5.123d
स्तैमित्यमात्मनश्चेत्स्यात्तद्वस्त्वेवास्मदीहितम् SV 977cd
स्तोत्रेणास्याभिसंबन्धाद्व्यक्तिमात्रं न तु क्वचित् 1.3.130ab
स्तोत्रेषु परिशिष्टेषु वागागायदथात्मने 1.3.140ab
स्त्रियं ससर्ज तद्योग्यां मधुकाण्डे यथोदिताम् 6.4.3ab
स्त्रीणां च सुकृतं वृङ्क्ते सर्वमावर्जयेच्छुभम् 6.4.15ab
स्त्रीणां यदुचितं वाक्यं प्रतिलोमं न भाषसे 2.4.66ab
स्त्रीपुंदृष्टान्तवचनं यद्वै तदिति चापरम् 3.9.194ab
स्त्रीपुंदृष्टान्तवचसा तदेतत्प्रतिपाद्यते 4.3.1310cd
स्त्रीपुंदृष्टान्तवाक्येन परिहारश्च दर्शितः 4.3.1379ab

स्त्रीपुमांसौ परिष्वक्तौ यावन्मानौ बभूवतुः 1.4.110ab
स्त्रीलक्षणे प्रवेश्यान्तरात्मीयं पुंस्त्वलक्षणम् 6.4.38ab
स्त्र्याकाङ्क्षो हि तु भागोऽयं पुमाकाशस्ततः स्त्रिया 1.4.116ab
स्थवीयान्मध्यमोऽणीयानित्येवं कालतोऽग्नितः 1.3.253cd
स्थवीयान्यात्यधोभागो रसादिक्रमशोऽपरः 1.3.254ab
स्थाणुं चोरधियालाय भीतो यद्वत्पलायते 3.3.66ab
स्थाणुं संभावयत्यज्ञो न तु दृष्टं तमो विना SV 116ab
स्थाणोः सतत्त्वविज्ञानं यथा नाङ्गं पलायने 3.3.67ab
स्थाण्वज्ञानमनादाय न चोरादीक्षणं यथा 1.4.506ab
स्थानं निर्माय संध्याख्यं विपाकानुभयानयम् 4.3.850ab
स्थानकं वाञ्छतः शास्त्रात्प्रसंख्यानं विधीयते SV 773cd
स्थानमात्राच्च तौ भिन्नौ वस्तुतो नावयोर्भिदा 5.17.11cd
स्थानानि सुरमर्त्यादिजुष्टान्यस्य भवन्त्युत 2.1.321cd
स्थानेष्वव्यूढकरणो नालं स्यात्कर्मणे यतः 4.3.1953cd
स्थापयेत्कृतरक्षं सच्छुचौ देशे प्रयत्नतः 6.3.17cd
स्थालीपाकविधानेन संस्कृत्याज्यं तथैव तु 6.4.82cd
स्थालीपाके क्रिया या सा चावृदित्यभिधीयते 6.4.82ab
स्थास्नुत्वाद्ब्रह्मणो नित्यं किरणानां रवेरिव 4.4.920cd
स्थास्नुष्वपि महद्दुःखं कण्टकादिषु देहिनाम् 2.1.491ab
स्थास्नौ प्रत्यक्चिदाकारे बाह्यहेतुनिबन्धनः 3.4.153ab
स्थास्न्वनुभवमात्रत्वात्कार्यकारणवस्तुनः 2.4.192ab
स्थितत्वाच्चापि तन्मर्त्यं मर्त्यत्वान्मूर्तमेव च 2.3.30cd
स्थितत्वादिन्द्रियग्राह्यं निर्धार्येदंतया पृथक् 2.3.29cd
स्थितस्य स्थानयोः साक्षाद्यद्ग्रहात्तत्प्रसीदति 5.7.2cd
स्थिता जगदिदं व्याप्य प्राणिकर्मवशादियम् 3.9.6cd
स्थितास्तत्पूर्विकाश्चैव ध्यायतः साधनं हि तत् 6.1.13cd
स्थितिकाले यथैकात्म्यं शक्यते ज्ञातुमञ्जसा 2.4.297ab
स्थितिमात्रं ह्यसोरन्नं यद्वासङ्गो न शङ्क्यते 1.3.246ab
स्थितिमात्राभिसंबन्धान्नायं दोष इहेष्यते 1.3.244ab
स्थितेऽप्येवं प्रमाणार्थे केचिद्व्याचक्षतेऽन्यथा 1.4.1692ab
स्थितेरङ्गारवच्चक्षुरङ्गाराः श्रोत्रमेव च 6.2.106ab
स्थित्यपाये प्रयाणं च श्रुत्याभेदि क्रमस्ततः 6.2.74cd

स्थित्युत्क्रान्तिविनाशानां रज्जुस्तत्त्वं यतस्ततः 4.4.290ab
स्थित्युत्क्रान्त्योर्हि यो हेतुरात्माविद्यादिलक्षणः 4.4.287ab
स्थित्वाग्नौ ब्राह्मणे चेह लोकमीप्सन्ति कर्मिणः 1.4.1643cd
स्थिरस्य धर्मिणः सेह तिरोभावगिरोच्यते 4.3.590cd
स्थिरस्य वस्तुनोऽवश्यं निमेषक्षणलक्षणैः 4.3.588ab
स्थिरस्यैव हि मिथ्यात्वं न चेदं राजशासनम् 4.3.493cd
स्थूलं ह्युपचिनोतीमं कुड्यं मृत्स्नेव सर्वदा 1.3.254cd
स्थूलदेहपरिच्छिन्नः स एवाद्यः प्रजापतिः 1.2.161ab
स्थूलदेहोपचित्यर्थो मध्यमोंऽशः प्रकीर्तितः 2.2.17cd
स्थूलसूक्ष्मशरीराभ्यां केवलश्चेतनोऽक्रियः 4.3.1149cd
स्थूलसूक्ष्मात्मना सर्वास्तारतम्येन संस्थिताः 3.6.16ab
स्थूलस्यामृत इत्युक्त्या निषिद्धत्वान्न निह्नुतिः 4.4.522cd
स्थूलांशः पृथिवीमेति पुरीषं मूत्रमेव च 2.2.17ab
स्थूलादिपरिमाणं हि द्रव्यमात्रव्यपाश्रयम् 3.8.89ab
स्थूलादिमेयमामातृनिषेधफलगं स्वभम् 3.8.87ab
स्थूलादिविक्रियाषट्कप्रतिषेधश्रुतेर्न च 1.4.545ab
स्थूलादिहेतोर्दाहो वा ध्वान्तस्य प्रत्यगात्मनि 3.8.80ab
स्थूलादीनां च सर्वेषां प्रतीचि प्रतिषेधतः 4.4.500ab
स्थूलादेरपवादोऽयं निर्द्वये घटते कथम् 3.8.76cd
स्थूलाद्यनभिसंबन्धे कार्यकारणरूपिणाम् 2.4.293cd
स्थूलाद्यनेकधर्माणां निषेधायासकारणात् 3.8.114ab
स्थूलाद्यशेषापह्नुत्या चाक्षरे प्रत्यगात्मनि 1.4.965ab
स्थूलान्यनुमया युक्तं प्रष्टुं तत्त्वानि कामतः 3.6.26ab
स्थूलापह्नुतिरत्र स्याद्वस्तु यत्पारमार्थिकम् 3.8.74ab
स्थूलापह्नुतिरेकत्र पर्युदासे तदन्यता 3.8.73cd
स्थूलीभूता बहिः सेयं प्रकाशत्वाय कल्पते 4.3.1093ab
स्थूलेषु यद्वत्सामान्यविशेषात्मकता तथा 4.3.1643ab
स्थैर्यस्तम्भमुमुक्षुदुःखितकृपायत्नोत्थबोधामृतम् 6.5.23b
स्नेहोपरोधादेवैतां पत्नीं मे वशमानय 6.4.40ef
स्पर्शनादिविशेषं तु मनसैव प्रपद्यते 1.5.126cd
स्पर्शनाद्यात्मनात्यन्तं परं काठिन्यमागतः 2.4.341cd
स्पर्शभेदपरिज्ञानं ततोऽभिव्यज्यते दृशेः 2.4.342cd

स्पर्शशब्देन विषयस्त्वग्ग्राह्योऽत्राभिधीयते 2.4.333ab
स्पर्शात्तनुं रूपगुणाच्च चक्षुस्ततः परं पश्यति स्वं स्वभावम् 4.4.1265cd
स्पर्शादिज्ञानभेदानां त्वगाद्येकायनं तथा 2.4.329ab
स्पर्शादिभेदविज्ञानं स्यादचेतनमेव तु 2.4.343ab
स्पर्शादिमात्रासु लयस्तासामपि लयस्तथा 2.4.375cd
स्पर्शादिवत्परार्थत्वात्स्वार्थं तन्न तु साक्षिवत् 2.4.343cd
स्पर्शादिविषयाणां वागिह स्यादुपलक्षणम् 4.3.51ab
स्पष्टं च वक्ष्यतेऽथोर्ध्वमेतेभ्य इति हि श्रुतिः 4.4.29ab
स्पष्टं व्याख्याय तच्छ्रुत्या ह्युपसंह्रियतेऽधुना 4.4.298cd
स्पष्टता सर्वभावानां जाग्रत्काले हि लक्ष्यते 2.1.100cd
स्पष्टभ्रान्तितिरोहितात्ममतयो यं भागशो मन्वते SV 1b
स्पष्टानि सन्ति वाक्यानि यथोक्तार्थप्रसिद्धये 4.4.1266cd
स्पष्टार्थमुत्तरं भाष्यं न व्याख्यानमपेक्षते 3.3.133ab
स्पष्टेन न्यायमार्गेण वक्ष्यामोऽवसरे तथा SV 461cd
स्फुटन्यायोक्तिभिस्तच्च यत्नात्परिहरिष्यति SV 195cd
स्फुटार्थं गौडपादीयं वचोऽर्थेऽत्रैव गीयते 1.4.389cd
स्फुरतापि सतो नान्यदभिधातुं घटादिवत् 1.2.15ab
स्मरणादिविभागेन ज्ञातर्येकत्र यत्पृथक् 3.4.107ab
स्मर्तव्यं स्मर तेनाद्य मरणे प्रत्युपस्थिते 5.17.18ab
स्मार्तमाचमनं त्वन्ते प्रायत्यार्थमिहोच्यते 6.3.55ab
स्मार्तमाचमनं शुद्ध्यै पाणिप्रक्षालनोक्तितः 6.4.88cd
स्मार्तान्नानन्तरोक्तत्वात्स्मार्तत्वं स्याद्द्वयोस्तयोः 1.5.42ab
स्मृतयोऽपीममेवार्थं तत्र तत्र प्रचक्षते 3.5.199cd
स्मृतावपि निषिद्धेयं हिंसा पर्वसु कर्मिणाम् 1.5.216ab
स्मृतिः सा न यथावस्तु तेनासावप्रमोदिता 1.4.283cd
स्मृतिज्ञानेषणादीनां संधानानुपपत्तितः 2.1.133ab
स्मृतिनिश्चितिसंशीतिरागादिर्हिरुगात्मनः 3.4.106ab
स्मृतिवाक्यानि पुंबुद्धिशुद्धिशंसीनि कर्मभिः 4.4.1050cd
स्मृतिस्त्वनुवदत्येव श्रुत्यर्थं परतन्त्रतः 4.4.1154cd
स्मृतिस्वप्नसमाधाने पुरुषस्य समीक्ष्यते 4.3.55ab
स्मृत्यर्थं न श्रुतिस्तस्मादनुवक्तीह कुत्रचित् 4.4.1154ab
स्मृत्यर्थस्यानुवादोऽयं पारतन्त्र्येऽसति श्रुतेः 4.4.1152cd

स्मृत्याप्यभाणि बहुशः कस्य संसारिरूपता 1.4.148cd
स्यात्प्रातिपदिकार्थस्य भावार्थेनेत्यसंकरः SV 527cd
स्यादकामयमानोऽत्र न त्वविद्वान्कथं चन 4.4.263cd
स्यादनैकान्तिको हेतुरन्यान्त्येष्वसमीक्षणात् 1.4.75cd
स्यादन्यतरवैकल्ये न वेत्येतदनिश्चितम् 4.3.1100cd
स्यादेतत्फलसंबन्धो नियोगविरहाद्यदि 1.4.799ab
स्यादेतदग्निरेवैनं ब्रह्मभावाय वक्ष्यति 1.4.1667ab
स्यादेव चेच्छ्रुतेर्मात्वान्न मितेर्व्यञ्जकत्ववतः 4.4.828cd
स्यादेषोऽविचिकित्सोऽतः सर्वसंशयवर्जितः 4.4.1294cd
स्याद्वा सत्साधनोत्पत्तेर्लोकवज्ज्ञानमात्मनः 1.4.77ab
स्याद्विभक्तं तदन्यच्चेत्पश्येदेव प्रबोधवत् 4.3.1611cd
स्रक्तत्त्वव्यतिरेकेण सिद्धिर्नान्यत्र कुत्रचित् 4.4.157ef
स्रक्स्थाण्वादावदृष्टत्वादुक्तदोषोऽपि चापतेत् 1.4.1100cd
स्रगज्ञानमनादाय तदुत्थैः संगतिः स्रजः 5.1.23ab
स्रगज्ञानमनादाय नाहियोगः स्रजो यथा 4.4.516ab
स्रगज्ञानसमुच्छित्तौ न तज्जस्यान्यतः स्रजः 4.3.366ab
स्रगज्ञानैकहेतूनां स्रग्धिया ज्ञातता यथा 1.4.749ab
स्रगियं न फणीत्युक्ते दृष्टा विषनिराक्रिया SV 584cd
स्रगिवाह्यादिरूपेण प्रथते भेदवन्मृषा 4.4.850cd
स्रगुक्तेरेव निःशेषसाध्वसध्वंसलाभतः SV 585cd
स्रग्याथात्म्यमहेर्यद्वत्तथास्याक्षरमात्रतः 3.8.79cd
स्रग्वत्सर्पादिकान्यद्वद्रूपं सर्वं बिभर्ति हि 1.6.23ef
स्रग्वत्सर्पादिक्लृप्तानां प्रत्यङ्मात्रैकरूपतः 3.4.24ab
स्रजस्तत्त्वापरिज्ञानाद्युक्ता दण्डादयो यथा 2.5.130ab
स्रजि दण्डादयो यद्वत्स्रगज्ञानैकहेतुकाः 2.4.88ab
स्रजि सर्पादिकः क्लृप्तो नाभिन्नो भिन्न एव वा 4.3.805ab
स्रजीव कल्पिताहिर्ना तत्रासादाकुलेन्द्रियः 1.4.60ab
स्रजीव सर्पदण्डादेः स्रगविद्योत्थवस्तुनः 4.4.157cd
स्रष्टृत्वात्स सृजत्येव खाद्यतेऽन्नं सदाद्यतः 1.2.193cd
स्रष्टृप्रवेष्ट्रोरेकत्वान्नैवमप्युपपद्यते 1.4.549ab
स्रष्टृ यज्जगतः पूर्वमात्मैवेत्यभिशब्दितम् 1.4.1598ab
स्रष्ट्रत्त्रोः कार्यभक्ष्याभ्यामन्योऽन्याव्यतिरेकतः 1.2.193ab

स्रोतोमध्ये द्वयाप्राप्तेरसङ्गोऽयं तिमिर्यथा 4.3.1085cd
स्व एवात्मा स्वभावश्चेत्तदान्यस्य ह्यसंभवात् 4.3.765ab
स्वः स्वाहेत्याहुतिक्षेपः समस्तां व्याहरेत्ततः 6.3.53ab
स्वकर्तुरुपभोगार्थं कर्माव्याकृतरूपकम् 1.4.365ab
स्वकर्तृफलदायित्वं स्वभावः कर्मणां मतः 4.4.994ab
स्वकर्मणा तमभ्यर्च्य सिद्धिं विन्दति मानवः 3.8.152cd
स्वकर्मणानुपात्तस्य न च भोगोऽत्र दृश्यते 1.5.6ab
स्वकर्मनिर्मितं लोकं येनात्मायं प्रपश्यति 4.4.76cd
स्वकर्मफलदेशेषु क्षेत्रज्ञस्य प्रसज्यते 2.1.486cd
स्वकर्मभिर्नियुक्तः संस्तथा चोत्पाद्य कर्मभिः 1.4.118cd
स्वकर्मार्जितसंभोगदायित्वेऽस्ति न कश्चन 1.4.1801ab
स्वकारणं चेदुत्साद्य कार्यं सर्वं प्रजायते 1.2.35ab
स्वकारणक्षयाद्ध्वस्तौ नात्मा पश्यन्नपीक्षते 4.3.1532cd
स्वकारणविनाशाय सिद्धं वासिद्धमेव वा 1.2.38ab
स्वकारणातिरेकेण वृत्तिः कार्यस्य नान्यतः 2.1.489cd
स्वकारणाभिसंबन्धाच्चैतन्याभासता धियः 4.3.357ab
स्वकारणाविशिष्टत्वे सलिलादिति हेतुगीः 1.4.483cd
स्वकार्यभूतां तामेव पृथिवीं मोहवर्त्मना 3.7.34ab
स्वकार्यस्याभिनिष्पत्तौ तथा स्वप्नेऽपि देवताः 4.3.1141cd
स्वकार्याण्येव संश्रित्य मृदसाधारणा यथा 1.4.357ab
स्वकार्यार्थानुगामित्वं भावनाज्ञानकर्मणाम् 2.4.206ab
स्वकार्योपक्षयादेव विधीनां च परस्परम् SV 398ab
स्वगिरानात्मनो लोकाद्विशिनष्ट्यात्मरूपकम् 1.4.1649cd
स्वगोचरसजातीयं करणं मन्यते श्रुतिः 2.4.394ab
स्वगोचरेश्वरं मानं न मानान्तरगोचरे 4.3.1749cd
स्वगोचरेषूत्सृष्टानि यदा गृह्णात्ययं स्वयम् 2.1.257ab
स्वगोचरेष्वशक्तिर्या संमोहोऽसाविहात्मनः 4.4.12cd
स्वगोचरैकसामान्ये सरितां सागरे यथा 2.4.376cd
स्वगोचरोन्मुखं ज्ञानं वागादीनामशेषतः 2.1.253ab
स्वग्राह्यार्थसजातीयमिन्द्रियं स्यात्प्रदीपवत् 2.4.364ab
स्वचिदाभासमोहेन तदुत्थानखिलान्यतः 1.4.741ab
स्वचिदाभासवन्मोहपृष्ठेनैवेति कर्तृताम् 1.4.319ab

स्वचिदाभाससंव्याप्तिः पुंभोगः सुखदुःखयोः 4.2.58ab
स्वच्छैकरूपतस्तस्य दाडिमादिफलं यथा 4.3.698cd
स्वजन्मोपचयग्लानिनाशाख्याकृतिजन्मदिग्- 2.1.161ab
स्वत आकारवत्किंचित्परतश्चापि दृश्यते 1.4.463ab
स्वत आनन्दयाथात्म्यात्कुतो दुःखेन संप्लुतिः 1.4.190ab
स्वत एवंविधं वस्तु यतोऽतस्तदबोधतः 4.4.216ab
स्वत एवंस्वभावोऽपि तदविद्यासमाश्रयात् 4.4.1003ab
स्वत एव तु तत्सिद्धेर्नातस्तदभिधीयते 1.4.1190cd
स्वत एव त्वनध्यस्ता ह्येवं केचित्प्रचक्षते 1.4.1036cd
स्वत एव न यागादेः कार्यसिद्धिस्तथा भवेत् SV 1043cd
स्वत एव प्रवृत्तत्वात्कर्तुरेवाधिकारिता SV 521ab
स्वत एव प्रवृत्तिः स्यान्न शब्दान्नार्थतस्तथा SV 620cd
स्वत एव प्रसिद्धश्चेत्प्रमेयोऽर्थस्तथापि न 1.4.228ab
स्वत एव यतः पुंसां प्रवृत्तिः स्वार्थसिद्धये 1.4.407ab
स्वत एव यतो मुक्ता मुच्यन्तेऽतस्तमोह्नुतेः 4.4.557cd
स्वत एव विमुक्तत्वाद्बन्धाभावात्स्वतस्तथा 2.1.533ab
स्वत एवाखिलसुखप्राप्ततत्त्वे स्व आत्मनि 4.4.257ab
स्वत एवात्मनः कार्त्स्न्यान्न कार्त्स्न्यं साधनाश्रयात् 1.4.1300ab
स्वत एवात्मनो ग्राह्या चैतन्यमिव सर्वदा 4.3.1639cd
स्वत एवाप्रियोऽनात्मा ह्यात्मप्रीत्यर्थसाधनात् 2.4.82ab
स्वत एवाभिसंपत्तिर्यत्र त्वस्येतिशास्त्रतः 1.4.1185cd
स्वतःकूटस्थचित्सिद्धिरैकात्म्यं चानुभूतितः 4.3.188cd
स्वतः कूटस्थतत्त्वस्य तदसंबोधतस्ततः 4.4.39ab
स्वतः कृत्स्नोऽप्यसंबोधादकृत्स्नो विपरीतधीः 1.4.1823ab
स्वतः पूर्णात्मकं ज्योतिरद्रष्टेत्यभिधीयते 4.3.1805cd
स्वतः प्रसिद्धात्संसिध्येत्तदसिद्धिः कुतो भवेत् SV 793cd
स्वतः प्राप्तमनूद्येह तमेवेति नियम्यते 4.4.866cd
स्वतः प्राप्तस्य संप्राप्तौ वाक्यान्मोहप्रहाणतः 5.1.103ab
स्वतः सर्वज्ञतैव स्यान्न वस्त्वज्ञातमस्ति हि 1.4.240cd
स्वतः सिद्धस्तदज्ञानसमुत्थस्य मृषात्मनः 2.4.237cd
स्वतः सिद्धेऽथ वा नित्यं मेयमात्रं विशिष्यते SV 555cd
स्वतः सिद्धेर्न मिथ्यात्वं तस्य स्यात्परमार्थवत् 1.4.1004cd

स्वतः सिद्धोऽथवासिद्धो देहादिस्ते भवन्भवेत् 4.3.160ab
स्वतः सिद्धौ न चेत्सिध्येत्किमन्यद्वेषजं ततः 1.4.945cd
स्वतः सेद्धुमशक्तत्वात्खमृते वायुवत्सदा 1.4.1405ab
स्वतः सेद्धुमशक्तत्वान्मोहादेरात्मसंगतिः 1.4.1321cd
स्वतन्त्र ईश्वरो यस्मान्नातो धर्मादितन्त्रता 4.4.1008cd
स्वतन्त्रयोर्मिथोऽपेक्षा नापि स्यात्परतन्त्रयोः 4.4.1153ab
स्वतन्त्रावीश्वरौ स्यातां सत्पुत्रप्रसवाय तौ 6.4.72cd
स्वतन्त्रोऽधिपतिर्ज्ञेयो मनुष्यैर्न विहन्यते 4.3.1847cd
स्वतश्च तज्जिहासायाः सिद्धत्वान्नेह कीर्त्यते 3.3.9ab
स्वतश्चेत्कल्पना व्यर्था द्रव्यस्याप्येकता स्वतः SV 971cd
स्वतश्चेत्तत्तमोवत्स्याज्ज्ञातत्वं रज्जुसर्पवत् 1.4.249cd
स्वतश्चेद्वस्तुनो भेदो वस्तु शून्यं प्रसज्यते 5.1.93ab
स्वतस्तन्मोहतश्चैव संभवस्तद्वदात्मनि 3.5.36cd
स्वतस्तस्य च संसिद्धेः कार्यता नोपपद्यते SV 260ab
स्वतस्तस्य च संप्राप्तेर्विनाप्यागमशासनम् 5.1.80ab
स्वतस्तु व्याप्तिसंहाररहितत्वात्परात्मनः 4.4.46cd
स्वतस्तु सत्यता साक्षान्नोभयोरपि विद्यते 1.4.444ab
स्वतस्त्यागं करोत्येव प्राप्तास्तेन शमादयः 4.4.1216cd
स्वतस्त्वकरणोऽदेहो निर्गुणोऽभेद एव च 3.7.37ab
स्वतस्त्वविद्याभेदोऽत्र मनागपि न विद्यते 4.3.1244cd
स्वतःसिद्धत्वतस्तस्य व्यञ्जकं नान्यदीक्ष्यते 5.1.102cd
स्वतःसिद्धस्य मोक्षस्य न साध्यमुपकारकम् SV 833ab
स्वतःसिद्धस्य विज्ञप्त्यै महदित्यादि भण्यते 2.4.412cd
स्वतःसिद्धात्ममेयोत्थरूपतैव प्रतीयते 4.3.1290cd
स्वतःसिद्धात्मवस्त्वेकमात्रोत्थानत्वकारणात् 3.3.40ab
स्वतःसिद्धात्मसंबोधव्याप्तिर्वस्त्वनुरोधतः SV 542cd
स्वतःसिद्धाद्यतः सिद्धिरज्ञातादपि चात्मनः 4.4.688ab
स्वतःसिद्धानुभतिश्च नाज्ञानाद्व्यतिरिच्यते 4.3.1484ab
स्वतःसिद्धार्थबोधित्वादभिधायास्तु मानता 2.4.158cd
स्वतःसिद्धैकलो ह्यात्मा येषां लोको ध्रुवोऽक्षयः 4.4.1100cd
स्वतःसिद्धोऽपि वस्तुत्वान्मुञ्चत्यात्मा प्रमां विना SV 1004cd
स्वतःसिद्धौ तदन्येषां श्रुतिकोपः प्रसज्यते 1.3.186ab

स्वतोऽखिलोऽप्रियोऽनात्मा प्रत्यङ्मोहैकहेतुतः 2.4.79ab
स्वतोऽतः स परं ब्रह्म तस्योपनिषदुच्यते 2.1.419cd
स्वतोऽदिग्देशकालादेः प्रत्यक्चिन्मात्रवस्तुनः 4.4.518ab
स्वतोऽनतिशयानन्दस्वाभाव्यैकात्म्यनित्यता 4.3.7ab
स्वतोऽनन्तत्वतो मानात्सर्वेशानादिरूपता 5.8.4cd
स्वतोऽनवस्थितो यत्र हेतुना स्थाप्यते बलात् SV 49ab
स्वतोऽनानात्मकेऽज्ञानाद्यन्नानात्मसमीक्षणम् 3.5.62ab
स्वतोऽनुभवतः सिद्धेरैकात्म्याख्यस्य वस्तुनः SV 439ab
स्वतोऽनुभवनिष्ठः स्यान्न चेत्षष्ठेन्द्रियार्थवत् 1.4.1402cd
स्वतोऽनेकात्मकं तत्स्यादित्याशङ्क्यैक उच्यते 4.3.1799cd
स्वतोऽपि यदि सा वस्तु रज्ज्वां सर्वादिका मतिः 1.4.426ab
स्वतोऽपृथक्त्वात्सार्वस्य पृथक्त्वमपि दुर्लभम् 4.3.1674cd
स्वतोऽब्रह्मत्वतस्तस्य नातोऽब्रह्मण इष्यते 3.4.9cd
स्वतोऽभिधानशक्तत्वान्नापि चैकात्म्यबोधने SV 834cd
स्वतोऽभिन्नस्वभावत्वान्न भेदोऽन्योऽन्यसंश्रयः 4.3.1718ab
स्वतोऽरूपं परं ब्रह्म तदविद्यादिहेतुतः 2.3.5ab
स्वतोऽलुप्तदृशा यस्मादात्मात्मानं सदेक्षते 1.4.304cd
स्वतोऽलुप्तदृशोऽस्तित्वं प्राक्साक्षात्प्रतिपादितम् 4.3.529cd
स्वतोऽवगतिसंबन्धात्तथाभावोऽवगम्यते 3.8.119ab
स्वतोऽवगमरूपेऽस्मिन्कूटस्थे कारणात्मना 2.1.244ab
स्वतोऽवबुद्धं तद्यस्मान्निरविद्यमतः सदा 1.4.213ab
स्वतोऽवबोधमात्रत्वात्कुतोऽविद्यादिसंप्लुतिः 4.3.1798ab
स्वतोऽशक्तिमतोर्लोके शक्तियोगेऽपि नेक्ष्यते 5.14.8ab
स्वतोऽसङ्गस्वभावत्वात्खचरादि वियद्यथा 1.4.1404ab
स्वतोऽसङ्गस्वभावत्वान्निरंशैकत्वतस्तथा 4.4.1002cd
स्वतोऽसंदूषितः प्रत्यङ्कामकर्मादिभिर्मलैः 4.4.432ab
स्वतोऽसिद्धेऽप्रमेये च नासतो व्यञ्जिका प्रमा 4.3.162ab
स्वतो गुणवतोरेवमन्नप्राणात्मनोर्भवेत् 5.14.14ab
स्वतो बुद्धं च शुद्धं च मुक्तं रूपमिहात्मनः 4.3.1157ab
स्वतोबुद्धं तदप्राप्य नाम्ना सह निवर्तते 1.4.858cd
स्वतो बुद्धं यतो वस्तु स्वतः शुद्धमतोऽद्वयम् 4.3.1354ab
स्वतो बुद्धं स्वतः शुद्धं स्वतो मुक्तं निरात्मिका 4.3.75ab

स्वतो बुद्धमिदं यस्मादतः शुद्धमसद्वयम् 1.4.485ab
स्वतो बुद्धे कुतोऽविद्या तामृते संसृतिः कुतः 1.4.311ab
स्वतो ब्रह्मत्ववतस्तस्य संसारित्वमविद्यया 4.3.1967cd
स्वतो माफलरूपत्वान्न माकार्यं प्रमाणतः 3.8.117ab
स्वतो मुक्तं यतस्तस्माद्ब्रह्म विद्यां तदर्हति 1.4.1336ab
स्वतो मुक्तमतः सिद्धमविद्यातज्जहानतः 4.3.1354cd
स्वतोमुक्तान्तरायस्य तमसो विद्यया हतेः SV 27ab
स्वतोमृतस्य मरणं नाविद्यातो यतोऽन्यतः 4.3.453ab
स्वतो यतोऽयं संसारी तेनाज्ञो विपरीतदृक् 2.1.5cd
स्वतो यद्वस्तुतो नास्ति तत्कुतोऽन्यव्यपेक्षया 4.3.1327cd
स्वतो वा ज्ञातताायाश्च कुतः सिद्धिरितीर्यताम् SV 685cd
स्वतो वा परतो वास्य विशेषाभावहेतुतः 4.3.507cd
स्वतो वा परतो वेदमज्ञातत्वं भवद्भवेत् 1.4.249ab
स्वतो वेदात्मनस्तस्मात्सर्वज्ञानमयो हि सः 6.5.10cd
स्वतो हि ग्राहकादीनां ग्राहकत्वादिसिद्धितः 4.3.520ab
स्वत्वेनाव्यभिचारित्वाद्व्यभिचारादनात्मनः 1.4.1650ab
स्वदेहराष्ट्रसंस्थोऽयं जाग्रद्भावनिरूपिणः 2.1.303ab
स्वदेहवद्यतो भुङ्क्त एकैकोऽनवशेषतः 1.5.5ab
स्वधर्मं च पदं जह्यात्संबन्धज्ञाननिह्नुतौ SV 732ab
स्वपक्षसिद्धयेऽप्येवं क्लिश्यतोऽपि न सिध्यति 4.3.782ab
स्वपतो न भवेत्काम इत्येतदभिधीयते 4.3.1018cd
स्वपरोभयहेतुत्वे ह्यनिर्मोक्षप्रसङ्गतः SV 154ab
स्वप्न आदाय ता मात्राः स्वाप्नीं योनिं प्रपद्यते 4.3.994cd
स्वप्न आस्ते मनोरूपं वासनामयविग्रहम् 4.3.1375cd
स्वप्न एव तु संसिद्धिरादावन्ते ह्यसंभवात् 2.1.275cd
स्वप्नं न कंचनेत्युक्त्या सर्वस्वप्ननिषेधनम् 4.3.1170ab
स्वप्नकर्मण्युपरमे ततः प्राज्ञे स्वयंप्रभः 4.3.987ab
स्वप्नकर्मसमुद्भूता वासना या हृदि स्थिताः 2.1.329ab
स्वप्नजागरितौ लोकौ यथा प्रत्यक्षमानतः 4.3.827ab
स्वप्नजाग्रत्तथारूपं स्वप्नः स्वप्नात्मकोऽत्र यः 4.3.1057cd
स्वप्नजाग्रत्प्रचारेऽस्मिन्नात्मा श्येनः पतन्निव 4.3.1102ab
स्वप्नदर्शनमेतत्स्यात्प्रत्यग्धीवस्तुसंश्रयम् 4.3.1146cd

स्वप्नदेहादिसंबन्धिप्रत्यभिज्ञाबलान्ननु 4.3.129ab
स्वप्ननिद्रायुतावाद्यौ प्राज्ञस्त्वस्वप्ननिद्रया 1.4.615ab
स्वप्नप्रपञ्चः सर्वोऽपि वासनामात्रमेव तु 4.3.1021cd
स्वप्नप्रपञ्चनिष्पत्तिर्यस्मात्तस्माद्विशेषणम् 4.3.873cd
स्वप्नप्रबोधयोर्यद्वद्दृष्टिरस्यात्मनः स्वतः 4.3.1753ab
स्वप्नबुद्धान्तयोर्वेह दृष्टान्तः संप्रदर्शितः 4.3.1159ab
स्वप्नबुद्धान्तवाक्याभ्यां मृत्योरासङ्गलक्षणात् 4.3.1080ab
स्वप्नबुद्धान्तसंचार आत्मनो यः पुरोदितः 4.3.1898ab
स्वप्नबोधात्तदा तद्वद्विविक्तोऽर्थोऽनुभूयते 3.8.40ab
स्वप्नभूमावपि तथा कर्मणोत्थापिता इमाः 4.3.867ab
स्वप्नभूमावयं रत्वा क्रीडां कृत्वात्ममायया 4.3.981ab
स्वप्नभूमावसङ्गोऽसौ संप्रसादे प्रसीदति 4.3.974cd
स्वप्नभोगप्रदा याति बहिर्नीडादतस्तदा 4.3.940cd
स्वप्नमायाप्रपञ्चस्थ आत्माप्नोतीव निष्क्रियः 4.3.942cd
स्वप्नमेति सुषुप्ताच्च स्वप्नाद्बुद्धान्तमेव च 4.3.1405ab
स्वप्नयोरभितः प्राज्ञादनन्वागतताप्यतः 4.3.1053cd
स्वप्नवन्नान्यमानत्वमित्यस्तित्वं विवक्षितम् 4.3.829cd
स्वप्नविज्ञाननिर्ग्राह्यं स्वप्नज्ञानातिरेकतः 4.3.534ab
स्वप्नविज्ञानवन्नासौ सत्यमेयव्यपाश्रया 1.2.132cd
स्वप्नवृत्तावुपादानं साधनं वा न विद्यते 4.3.924ab
स्वप्नवृत्त्या विहत्येमं जाग्रद्देहं क्रियाक्षयात् 4.3.930ab
स्वप्नसंचारवत्तस्माज्जीवसंसार इष्यते 2.1.490cd
स्वप्नसर्गे पुनस्ताः स्वमधिकारं प्रकुर्वते 4.3.1139cd
स्वप्नस्कन्नं यथा स्वप्ने तथा बोधेऽपि वीक्ष्यते 4.3.1013ab
स्वप्नस्कन्ननिमित्तं तु प्रायश्चित्तं यदुच्यते 4.3.1012ab
स्वप्नस्थानं समाश्रित्य परलोकं प्रपश्यति 4.3.846ab
स्वप्नस्य जाग्रत्स्थानत्वमथो खल्वितिवाक्यतः 4.3.956ab
स्वप्नस्य देहबुद्ध्यादेः स्वप्नवृत्तावसंभवात् 4.3.902cd
स्वप्नात्मप्रत्यभिज्ञेयं मृषार्था सापि पूर्ववत् 4.3.133cd
स्वप्नादिज्ञानदृष्टान्तात्प्रत्ययत्वादिहेतुतः 4.3.700cd
स्वप्नादियुक्तिभिश्चेत्तल्लौकिकीभिः प्रसाध्यते SV 816ab
स्वप्नादिवदनात्मार्थो मृषा स्यात्क्षणिकोऽपि वा 1.4.245cd

स्वप्नादिव्यवहारेऽस्मिञ्ज्योतिरात्मैव नापरम् 4.3.293cd
स्वप्नादौ भवतैवायं जाग्रद्वदनुभूयते 4.3.567ab
स्वप्नाद्बोधाप्तिवच्चास्माल्लोकाल्लोकान्तरं गतः 4.3.1910cd
स्वप्नाद्यथेतो बुद्धान्तं स्वप्नं बुद्धान्ततः पुनः 4.3.1948ab
स्वप्नाश्रयाणि हृन्मध्ये नीलाद्याभानि देहिनः 2.1.321ab
स्वप्नेऽतोऽयं निरासङ्गः पुमानभ्युपगम्यताम् 4.3.1025cd
स्वप्नेऽपि चक्षुरादीनामपीतिः श्रूयते श्रुतौ 4.3.1416ab
स्वप्नेऽपि स्वप्नकालस्थास्तद्वत्सन्त्विति भण्यते 2.1.287cd
स्वप्नेऽप्येतत्त्रयं नाभूद्वासनामात्रशेषतः 4.3.1512ab
स्वप्नेऽप्येष तथैवास्ते बोद्धा चेद्बुध्यतामयम् 2.1.109cd
स्वप्ने कामस्य दृष्टत्वाद्यत्र काममिति श्रुतेः 4.3.1063cd
स्वप्नेक्षणं विजानीयान्नान्यत्रेति विनिश्चयः 4.3.957cd
स्वप्ने च करणाभावः श्रुत्यैव प्रतिपादितः 4.3.1142cd
स्वप्ने जाग्रदवस्थावत्तथा चाद्यन्तवत्त्वतः 4.3.1072cd
स्वप्ने तमेव चात्मानं सुप्तोऽयमभिमन्यते 4.3.958ab
स्वप्ने तु कारकाभावान्न क्रियासिद्धिरात्मनः 4.3.984ab
स्वप्ने तु वासनाकामसंयुक्तो मृत्युवर्जितः 4.3.1155ab
स्वप्नेन निर्णयो वाच्य एतेषामित्यतोऽधुना 4.3.832ab
स्वप्ने नानाप्रपञ्चाढ्यं मिथ्याज्ञानमृते त्रयात् 1.4.469cd
स्वप्ने प्रत्यभिजानाति तानेव न ततोऽपरान् 4.3.959cd
स्वप्ने प्रबुद्धस्य सतो मृषा स्याद्वनमाश्रितः 2.1.295cd
स्वप्ने प्राणावशेषत्वात्स्थानात्करणसंहतेः 4.3.1946ab
स्वप्ने बुद्ध्याद्युपरतौ वासनामात्रशेषतः 4.3.376ab
स्वप्नेभबुद्धिर्नष्टेऽपि स्वप्न आभाति जागरे 4.3.1745ab
स्वप्ने भवत्वात्स्वप्न्येति जाग्रत्स्वापाद्विवेचनम् 2.1.281ab
स्वप्ने भाःशब्दवाच्यास्य स्वयंज्योतिष आत्मनः 4.3.884cd
स्वप्ने मृषात्वमाहैवं गमनादेः श्रुतिः स्वयम् 4.3.916cd
स्वप्ने रत्वाद्यथ मतं नैवमप्युपपद्यते 4.3.1047ab
स्वप्ने वा कामविरहाद्यथोक्तेनैव वर्त्मना 4.3.1166ab
स्वप्ने विवेको व्याख्यातः कर्मणोऽस्यात्मनोऽधुना 4.3.1094ab
स्वप्ने समीक्षते नात आत्मनोऽन्यः प्रपश्यति 4.3.265cd
स्वप्नेहलोकयोस्तावत्सत्त्वं प्रत्यक्षगोचरम् 4.3.839ab

स्वप्नो भत्वा यथात्येति मृत्यो रूपाण्यसङ्गतः 4.3.809ab
स्वप्रतिष्ठैकभान्वाख्यज्योतिषैव पुमानयम् 4.3.35ab
स्वप्रधानात्मबुद्ध्यैव तदन्यस्य प्रसिद्धितः SV 468ab
स्वप्रमेयप्रमोत्पत्त्यनुत्पत्त्येकहेतुके 2.1.543ab
स्वप्रमेयाखिलाज्ञानध्वंसिनीति समीक्ष्यते 1.4.1212ab
स्वप्रमेयार्पणं मुक्त्वा मानत्वेऽन्यन्न कारणम् 1.4.1294ab
स्वप्रमेयावबोधौ हि मानानां स्वार्थ उच्यते 2.1.550ab
स्वप्रमेये तमो हन्ति स्वसाध्ये साधनं यथा 4.4.776cd
स्वप्रमेये प्रमां साक्षात्करोत्युपनिषद्यदि 2.1.545ab
स्वप्रमेये प्रमाणं तदिति यद्वदिहोदितम् 4.4.749ab
स्वप्रमेये प्रमाणं सत्प्रवृत्तं स्वात्मलाभतः 4.4.786ab
स्वफलेऽन्यानपेक्षाणां साधनानां समुच्चयः 1.5.228ab
स्वभागानुगतो दोषो गुणो वास्य प्रसज्यते 2.1.481ab
स्वभाव आत्मनो भाव इति चेद्भवतो मतम् 4.3.764cd
स्वभावः कारकाणां च यदकृत्वेह कुर्वते 4.3.1443ab
स्वभावकार्यतासिद्धिरनुमानसमाश्रयात् 4.3.776ab
स्वभावकार्ये लिङ्गे स्तः स्वाभाव्यादि च लिङ्ग्यते 4.3.773cd
स्वभावतोऽखिलं कर्म धर्माधर्मादिलक्षणम् 1.5.7ab
स्वभावतोऽखिलं वाक्यं संसर्गात्मकमेव हि 4.4.801ab
स्वभावमतिलङ्घ्यैते तिष्ठतः शास्तृशासने 3.8.138cd
स्वभावमपि जह्याच्चेदग्निः शीतो भवेद्ध्रुवम् 2.1.440ab
स्वभाववादिनोऽपीयं कार्या नैवात्मधीस्तथा 4.4.935cd
स्वभावव्यतिरेकाभ्यां ध्वान्तसिद्धेरसंभवात् 1.4.218ab
स्वभावस्तमृते शृङ्गं स्वभावमतिवर्तते 4.3.109cd
स्वभावहानादन्योऽन्यं विशेषो बाह्य एव सः SV 352cd
स्वभावहेतुना साध्यं वद यत्ते विवक्षितम् 4.3.754ef
स्वभावादविनाभावे स्यादौष्ण्यस्याग्निलिङ्गता 4.3.743ab
स्वभावादेव तत्सिद्धेः सर्वप्राणभृतामपि 4.4.932cd
स्वभावादेव साधूनां प्रवृत्तिरुपकारिणी 2.4.56ab
स्वभावाद्विनिवृत्तोऽर्थो निःस्वभावः खपुष्पवत् SV 56cd
स्वभावानपहारेण संगतिः स्यात्ततस्तयोः 3.5.47ab
स्वभावान्नैव संसिध्येद्वस्तुनोऽव्यभिचारिता 4.3.752cd

स्वभावोऽग्न्यादिकानां हि नोष्णत्वाद्यन्यहेतुतः 4.3.152cd
स्वभावोऽथाविनाभावात्कार्ये प्राप्ता स्वभावता 4.3.743cd
स्वभावो नात्मनः कामकर्मविद्यादि बोधवत् 4.3.1408ab
स्वभावो वस्तुनस्तत्त्वं तत्त्वात्तत्त्वं न हीयते 4.3.252cd
स्वभावो वाथवा कार्यं विकल्पोऽयं मतो यतः 4.3.774cd
स्वभूमेश्चाव्यमानानां सुराणामसुरैस्तदा 1.3.122ab
स्वमहिम्ना च यत्सिद्धं तदपह्नूयते कथम् 1.4.1375cd
स्वमहिम्ना तयोर्नासावग्निब्राह्मणसंश्रयात् 1.4.1654cd
स्वमहिम्ना त्वभावोऽपि सेद्धुं नैवात्मवत्क्षमः 3.8.115ab
स्वमहिम्ना न संसिद्धयेत्स्वतोऽनवगतात्मकम् 1.4.334ab
स्वमहिम्ना न संसिध्येत्स्वतोऽनवगमात्मकम् 3.4.114ab
स्वमहिम्ना प्रसिद्धेश्च कुतोऽभावस्य संभवः 3.8.116cd
स्वमहिम्नैव चेत्सिद्धयेदुपायः परमार्थवत् 1.4.1004ab
स्वमहिम्नैव चेन्न स्याद्ग्राहकादि ततोऽन्यतः 4.3.521ab
स्वमहिम्नैव तत्सिद्धेः कथं नास्तीति भण्यते 4.3.564cd
स्वमहिम्नैव तत्सिद्धेः किमिव स्यान्मृषार्थता 1.3.50cd
स्वमहिम्नैव निष्पत्तिर्न विना साधनं यतः 3.5.136ab
स्वमहिम्नैव यः सिद्धः सर्वप्रत्यक्तमश्च यः SV 794ab
स्वमांसान्यपि खादन्ति नियोगानतिलङ्घिनः 1.4.880ab
स्वमात्रेण च यत्सिद्धं तस्यापेक्षान्यतः कुतः 4.3.1593cd
स्वमात्रेण न यत्सिद्धं तत्सिद्धं परतः कथम् 4.3.1593ab
स्वमेयतत्त्वसंबन्धलब्धरूपस्य सर्वदा 4.4.789cd
स्वमेयमात्रशूरत्वान्मितेर्नान्यत्र मानता SV 245ab
स्वमेयव्यक्तितस्तस्य न कार्यान्तरमिष्यते 4.4.791cd
स्वमेयव्यतिरेकेण मेयान्तरसमाश्रयः 4.4.337ab
स्वयं तद्व्याकृतिमगाद्यथैतर्हि तथैव तत् 1.4.397cd
स्वयं तु भवतो यस्माद्वस्तुनोऽन्येन संगतिः 4.4.319cd
स्वयं निरधिकारस्तु दैवप्राणोऽवतिष्ठते 1.5.317cd
स्वयं निर्माय सृजत इत्यकर्मापि भण्यते 4.3.920cd
स्वयं प्रबोधितेऽप्यर्थे यदि युक्त्याद्यपेक्षते SV 809ab
स्वयं प्राहेममेवार्थं कामानर्थजिहासया 4.3.1883cd
स्वयंरूपत्वतो नात्मा ह्यात्मनो व्यतिरिच्यते 4.3.1654ab

स्वयं रूपेण यो भाति स्थास्नुः स्वार्थः स भण्यते 4.3.341cd
स्वयंज्योतिः कथं तेषु सत्सु स्वप्नेऽभिधीयते 4.3.901cd
स्वयंज्योतिःप्रसङ्गेन तदुक्तं प्रागपि श्रुतौ 4.4.41cd
स्वयंज्योतिःप्रसिद्धिर्वा पूर्वमुक्तानुमानतः 4.3.857ab
स्वयंज्योतिः शरीरादेर्बुद्ध्यन्तादनुमानतः 4.3.379ab
स्वयंज्योतिः स वा एष यः पुरा प्रतिपादितः 4.3.974ab
स्वयंज्योतिरयं प्रत्यङ्सर्वसाधननिस्पृहः 4.3.887ab
स्वयंज्योतिरिति प्रोक्तो निष्क्रियोऽकारकोऽफलः 4.3.881ab
स्वयंज्योतिर्य आत्मोक्तस्तस्याविद्याक्रियोद्भवाः 4.3.833cd
स्वयंज्योतिर्विशुद्ध्यर्थं स वा इत्यादिका श्रुतिः 4.4.431cd
स्वयंज्योतिष्कमपि तं राजा पप्रच्छ मोहतः 4.3.73cd
स्वयंज्योतिष्ट्वनिर्णीतिः कृतातोऽनवशेषतः 4.3.1891cd
स्वयंज्योतिष्ट्वमस्योक्तं स्वप्ने चाकारकात्मता 4.3.964ab
स्वयंज्योतिष्ट्वमस्योक्त्वा बुद्ध्यादेश्चातिरेकताम् 4.3.929ab
स्वयंज्योतिष्ट्वमारभ्य यच्छ्रुत्योक्तमिहात्मनि 4.3.954ab
स्वयंज्योतिष्ट्वमुक्तं यदात्मनः प्राक्प्रयत्नतः 4.3.1305ab
स्वयंज्योतिष्ट्वमुदितं मुक्तेरङ्गममन्यत 4.3.967ab
स्वयंज्योतिष्ट्वशास्त्राच्च प्रत्यगात्मा प्रकाशकः 4.3.1465cd
स्वयंज्योतिष्ट्वसिद्धिश्च श्रुतिन्यायपुरःसरा 4.4.479ab
स्वयंज्योतिःस्वभावत्वान्निरुद्धस्वान्तवासनः SV 444ab
स्वयंज्योतिःस्वभावस्थस्तस्मादात्मा सुषुप्तगः 4.3.1406ab
स्वयमेव कृतार्थत्वात्कापेक्षास्यर्त्विजं प्रति 1.3.384cd
स्वयमेव तु वाक्प्रज्ञा ब्रह्मणो न तु भिद्यते 4.1.19ab
स्वयमेव फलात्मत्वात्फलं चास्मान्न भिद्यते 1.4.1401cd
स्वयमेव विहत्येति देवताप्रतिषेधकृत् 4.3.869ab
स्वयमेवानुमायेदृग्ज्योतिः किं न प्रपद्यते 4.3.28cd
स्वयमेवेश्वरः प्राह प्रपन्नाय किरीटिने 4.4.1288ab
स्वयंप्रमाणकस्तावत्साक्ष्यन्तोऽर्थो व्यवस्थितः 4.3.295ab
स्वयंमातृक एवायमात्मत्वादेव कारणात् 4.3.342cd
स्वयोनिं वाक्समप्येति वातं प्राणोऽनुगच्छति 3.2.124cd
स्वरवर्णपदोक्त्यानुपूर्वी या प्रविभागभाक् 4.4.713ab
स्वररश्मिस्रग्विणौ तौ हि प्रसिद्धौ जगति यतः 6.4.103ab

स्वरसेनैव संप्राप्तेर्तथात्मोपासनस्य च 1.4.915cd
स्वरूप आत्मनः स्थानमाहुर्निःश्रेयसं बुधाः SV 109ab
स्वरूपं यत्तदधुना वक्तव्यमवशिष्यते 2.3.96cd
स्वरूपं यद्यसाध्यं तत्स्वातन्त्र्येण प्रसिद्धितः SV 825ab
स्वरूपं वा मनोज्योतिर्यस्य देवस्य भण्यते 3.9.36cd
स्वरूपनाशदोषः स्यादेकदेशेऽपि पूर्ववत् SV 264cd
स्वरूपनिश्चयार्थाय प्रारब्धं ब्राह्मणं परम् 2.3.3cd
स्वरूपपररूपाभ्यां यदा सदसदात्मकम् SV 976ab
स्वरूपमात्रसंबोधि नात्मनोऽपि क्षयोदयौ 4.3.675cd
स्वरूपमेव तस्येति विशेषणमनर्थकम् 4.4.327ab
स्वरूपलाभः सिद्धश्चेत्स्वतो वा यदि वान्यतः SV 697ab
स्वरूपलाभतो नान्यदभिव्यक्तावपेक्षते SV 813cd
स्वरूपलाभमात्रेण यतोऽविद्यां निहन्त्यतः 4.3.17ab
स्वरूपलाभमात्रेण यत्त्वविद्यां निहन्ति नः 4.4.1126ab
स्वरूपलाभमात्रेण सम्यग्बोधोऽखिलं तमः 2.4.432ab
स्वरूपलाभमात्रेण साधनत्वं निगच्छतः 1.5.277ab
स्वरूपव्यभिचारोऽपि सुषुप्तादौ स्वसाक्षिगः 2.3.222cd
स्वरूपसाधनत्वाभ्यां त्यागस्यैवान्तरङ्गतः 4.4.543ab
स्वरूपस्य तु निर्मुक्तौ किमन्यदवशिष्यते 4.3.706cd
स्वरूपाच्चान्यतो भेदः प्रमाणाभासगोचरः 4.3.1648cd
स्वरूपानुपमर्देन स विराड्देवतात्मभिः 1.2.164ab
स्वरूपानूक्तिमात्रत्वादप्रामाण्यं मतं यदि 1.4.904ab
स्वरूपाव्यतिरेकाच्च नापि चानात्मनीक्षते 4.3.1678cd
स्वरूपेऽनुपयोगित्वान्न प्रमाणव्यपेक्षणम् SV 697cd
स्वरूपेऽवस्थितिर्मुक्तिरात्मनो भवतोच्यते SV 47ab
स्वरूपेऽस्ति भिदा काचिदमानित्वादिवस्तुवत् 4.4.848cd
स्वरूपे वेद्यवेत्तृत्वायोगाद्द्वैतप्रसङ्गतः SV 1010cd
स्वर्गं पुमर्थमुद्दिश्य सर्वप्राणभृतामियम् SV 1098ab
स्वर्गमित्यादिभिर्वाक्यैस्त्रय्यन्तेष्वपि गीयते SV 1097cd
स्वर्गलोकगतावत्र साधनं पृच्छ्यते यतः 3.1.39ab
स्वर्गशब्दाभिधश्चायं पुमर्थो यो यथोदितः SV 1097ab
स्वर्गादाविव यागादेर्विधानादेव कारणात् 4.4.1233cd

स्वर्गादावेवमेव स्यात्सापेक्षं च भवेत्तदा SV 828cd
स्वर्गादिकामिनो यद्वदग्निहोत्रविधिस्तथा 1.3.93cd
स्वर्गादिकाम्यपि यतो मुक्तिं कामयते न तु SV 1024ab
स्वर्गादिकार्यमार्गेण मन्यसे यदि कर्मणाम् SV 400ab
स्वर्गादिभ्यो विनाशादौ मोक्षे तेऽनिर्वृतिर्यतः 3.3.88cd
स्वर्गादिश्च किमंशः स्यात्प्रयाजादिस्तथा परः 1.4.786cd
स्वर्गादेरपि विभ्रष्टो नरकं स निगच्छति 1.4.1583cd
स्वर्गादेर्न तु शेषत्वं पुरुषार्थत्वहेतुतः SV 402cd
स्वर्गादौ यदि तात्पर्यं न स्यादैकात्म्यबोधने SV 408ab
स्वर्गे नैवाधिकारोऽस्ति तस्य सिद्धत्वतः स्वतः SV 1099cd
स्वर्गोऽयमेव प्रागुक्तः स्वर्गकामवचस्यपि 4.4.555ab
स्वलोकस्यार्थवादत्वान्नैवमप्युपपद्यते 1.4.1774cd
स्वल्पीयोऽभ्यासजा स्थास्न्वी भावनेत्यत्र का प्रमा 4.4.778cd
स्ववाक्यावगतात्कार्यादपेक्षन्ते फलान्तरम् SV 384cd
स्ववानेव पुरा न्यासाद्युवयोः स्वेन सांप्रतम् 2.4.44ab
स्वविकारोपसंश्लेषाद्विज्ञानात्मत्वमेत्यतः 4.5.12ab
स्वविभूतीक्षणं सृष्टौ विभोरर्चनमुच्यते 1.2.145ab
स्वविशेषानुरोधित्वं सामान्यानां मतं यदि 1.6.91ab
स्ववृत्तेः परवृत्तेश्च संपच्छ्रोत्रे प्रतिष्ठिता 6.1.12cd
स्वव्याख्यानविरोधः स्यात्तेषां चानर्थसंगतिः 4.3.318cd
स्वव्याख्यानविरोधित्वान्नैवमप्युपपद्यते 1.4.1754cd
स्वव्यापारतिरोधानं कारकाणां न च स्थितम् SV 775ab
स्वव्यापारमुखेनैव शास्त्रं स्वार्थावबोधकृत् SV 774ab
स्वव्यापारेऽनपेक्ष्यैव वस्तुवृत्तं वचो यतः 1.4.877ab
स्वव्यापारे हि विधिना नियोक्तुं शक्यते यतः 1.4.795cd
स्वव्यापारैकविषयः सर्व एव यतो विधिः 1.4.753cd
स्वशक्तिः सर्वमानानां यथा वस्त्ववबोधने 2.4.169ab
स्वशक्त्यननुरूपं चेत्कार्यं वाक्यशतैरपि 1.4.878ab
स्वशक्त्यनपहारेण दाह्यदाहकयोरिव 3.3.60cd
स्वशब्दाविह विज्ञेयावात्मीयात्मार्थवाचिनौ 4.3.879ab
स्वसंवित्तित्वमात्रे च न तमःसंभवः क्वचित् 1.4.253ab
स्वसंविदितमात्रत्वान्न त्वेवंरूपता चितेः 4.3.121cd

स्वसंज्ञयाप्यसंबोधो यथा दृष्टस्तदात्मनः 2.1.127ab
स्वसत्तयात्मनो मोहं न यतो वस्तु हन्त्यतः 1.4.1305ab
स्वसाक्षिकैव सर्वस्य न वेद्मीत्यपि या मतिः 2.4.129ab
स्वसाक्षिणं भावयन्ती न त्वसावात्मनो गुणः 4.3.1032ef
स्वसामर्थ्याद्यथा कार्यं कालास्पृष्टं प्रभाषते SV 642ab
स्वसिद्धान्तविरोधोऽपि तदभिव्यक्तिवादिनः 4.4.330cd
स्वसिद्धान्तविरोधोऽयं बलादायात्यनीप्सितः 4.3.256cd
स्वसिद्धान्तस्य च ध्वस्तिर्न च संगच्छते जनः 4.3.635cd
स्वसुवर्णप्रतिष्ठाधीरुद्गातुरिति गम्यते 1.3.335ab
स्वस्थानेभ्योऽपकृष्टानि मरणे यान्त्यथैकताम् 4.3.1945cd
स्वस्थावस्थैव यैतेषां प्रसिद्धा जगतीक्ष्यते 2.1.355ab
स्वस्थेन्द्रियमनोबुद्धेर्नैवाहमिति वीक्ष्यते 2.4.352ab
स्वस्वभावं न चोल्लङ्घ्य स्वभावान्तरसंश्रयात् 4.4.802ab
स्वस्वभावानुरोधाच्च व्याधेभ्यो व्युत्थितात्मधीः 2.1.510cd
स्वस्वभावानुरोधेन तेऽस्पर्धन्त स्ववृत्तिभिः 1.3.118cd
स्वस्वामित्वादिसंबन्धस्तथा नास्याद्वितीयतः 4.4.997ab
स्वस्वामिभोगसिद्ध्यर्थमेवं व्याकृततेष्यते 1.4.367cd
स्वहेतुमात्रया स्थानमिन्द्रियाणां न कार्यतः 2.1.340ab
स्वहेतुमात्रसंसर्गान्नायमात्यन्तिको लयः 2.4.384cd
स्वहेतुसत्तासंबन्धः संबन्धस्य सदाश्रयात् 1.2.121ab
स्वहेतुसिद्धिः कार्योऽर्थो न दृष्टः कारणं विना 1.2.20cd
स्वहेतूच्छित्तयेऽलं चेदजातमपि सद्यदि 1.2.36ab
स्वां योनिमिति हेतूक्तिः कार्यं कारणसंश्रयम् 1.4.1610ab
स्वांशिभ्यामेकतापत्तौ देवतालिङ्गभागयोः 4.4.65ab
स्वाकारकार्यकृत्सैव न कार्यं कार्यकृन्मतम् 4.3.693cd
स्वाकारमात्रनिष्पत्तेर्नालं कार्यान्तराय हि 1.4.474ab
स्वाकूतानुविधायित्वं यत्तदा करणात्मनाम् 4.4.22ab
स्वाख्याविशेषसंबन्धाग्रहणाच्चेन्न बुद्धवान् 2.1.122ab
स्वातन्त्र्यं पारतन्त्र्यं वाणिमाद्यैश्वर्यमेव वा 4.4.131ab
स्वातन्त्र्यं यत्र कर्तुः स्यात्तत्र कर्ता नियुज्यते 2.4.107ab
स्वातन्त्र्यं येषु कर्तुः स्यात्करणाकरणं प्रति 4.4.1245ab
स्वातन्त्र्यप्रतिपत्त्यर्थं महानिति विशेषणम् 4.3.1083ab

स्वातन्त्र्यात्तत्र भवता क्रियतां तद्यथेष्टकम् 3.9.125cd
स्वातन्त्र्येणापि तद्वृत्तेः सिद्धेर्भूयः पृथग्ग्रहः 4.3.1636cd
स्वातन्त्र्येणेशविषया बुभुत्साप्यतिदुर्लभा 4.4.1021ab
स्वातन्त्र्येणेह चेल्लभ्या न तु लभ्या तथाह च 4.4.101cd
स्वातन्त्र्ये सति संसारसृतौ कस्मात्प्रवर्तते 1.4.1806cd
स्वात्मकार्यसमुद्भूतिरम्बरादभ्रभूतिवत् 2.1.179cd
स्वात्मचैतन्यबिम्बेन निःसङ्गः सक्त आत्मना 4.4.236cd
स्वात्मतन्त्रे च विषये मानबोधः सदा भवेत् SV 1073cd
स्वात्मदृष्ट्यनुरोधेऽपि मौढ्यमेव प्रसज्यते 2.1.146ab
स्वात्मनः प्रतिलाभाय न त्वात्मानमपेक्षते 4.3.1038ab
स्वात्मनस्त्वेव कामाय ह्यात्मार्थत्वश्रुतेर्भवेत् 1.4.570ab
स्वात्मन्येव सदन्यत्र सर्ववस्तु प्रसिध्यति 1.4.733ab
स्वात्मन्येवाथ संशुद्धं ज्ञानमद्वैतरूपकम् 4.4.733ab
स्वात्मन्येवास्त इत्येतत्कुतश्चेत्स्वपितीत्यतः 2.1.246cd
स्वात्मभूतं हि यद्यस्य नैव तद्व्यवधीयते 4.4.328ab
स्वात्मरूपात्पृथग्रूपं न वस्तूत्प्रेक्ष्यतेऽण्वपि 1.4.434cd
स्वात्मसाक्षिकतां मुक्त्वा भावाभावात्मवस्तुनः 1.4.337ab
स्वात्मसाध्यातिरेकेण सर्वमेव हि साधनम् SV 1100ab
स्वात्मांशांशिसजातीयविविक्तफलसद्भवत् 2.1.160ab
स्वात्मानं लभते यस्मात्तां विना तदनर्थकम् 4.3.1034cd
स्वात्मानुभवतन्त्रत्वात्प्रत्याख्यातुं न शक्यते 3.8.38ab
स्वात्मापसर्पणाद्देहं निःसंबोधं करोति यः 4.3.870ab
स्वात्माभासप्रवेशो यः प्रत्यङ्मोहनिबन्धनः 1.4.508ab
स्वात्माभासाः पराचीना धीपृतीर्विषयोन्मुखाः 1.4.743ab
स्वात्मावभासतो भोक्ता कर्ता त्वज्ञानहेतुतः 2.1.218ab
स्वात्मावभास्यः कुम्भादिर्दीपादिश्चापि नान्यतः 4.3.496ab
स्वात्मावभास्यो बाह्योऽर्थ इत्येतदसमञ्जसम् 4.3.497ab
स्वात्मावयवभूताभ्यो देवताभ्यो यथायथम् 1.2.216ab
स्वात्माविद्यानुरोध्येव समासव्यासतामगात् 3.9.112ab
स्वात्माविद्यावधिः सोऽयं परः कारणमुच्यते 4.3.383ab
स्वात्माविद्यासमुत्थेऽस्मिन्नात्माविद्यासमाश्रयात् 4.4.1276cd
स्वात्माविद्यैकहेत्वेव तस्य रूपान्तरं यतः 4.3.1221cd

स्वात्मैकाज्ञानवृत्तेन ग्रसिष्णु प्रभविष्णु च 1.2.126cd
स्वात्मोत्पत्तावशक्तं तद् व्यक्तं सामर्थ्यभाग्यतः 2.1.402cd
स्वादिधर्माभिसंबन्धं प्रचक्राम प्रभाषितुम् 1.3.333cd
स्वाधिकारविनिष्पत्तौ देवता देवतागणम् 1.5.199ab
स्वाधिकारसुतावेशात्पितैवाविशतीत्यतः 1.5.317ab
स्वाधिकाराच्च्याव्यमानास्ते विदुर्देवहृद्गतम् 1.3.143cd
स्वाध्यायस्य विधिर्ब्रूते लिङाद्यात्मानमेव च 1.4.784ab
स्वाध्यायाधीतिविधिना ज्योतिष्टोमादिबोधवत् 1.4.766ab
स्वाध्यायाधीतिविधिना ज्योतिष्टोमादिबोधवत् 1.4.798ab
स्वाध्यायेन व्रतैर्होमैस्त्रैविद्येनेज्यया सुतैः 4.4.1049ab
स्वानन्दाभिमुखः स्वापे बोध्यमानोऽत एव च SV 1021ab
स्वानुभूतिबलादेव भवतापि विभाव्यते SV 466ab
स्वानुभूतिर्न वेद्मीति प्रागैकात्म्यप्रबोधतः 1.4.216cd
स्वानुभूतिविरुद्धत्वादग्निदाहादिबोधवत् 1.4.1523cd
स्वानुभूतिविरोधोऽपि ब्रह्मत्वं चेद्धवेत्स्वतः 1.4.1106cd
स्वानुभूत्यनुरोधेन योऽज्ञातार्थः पुरोदितः 1.4.495ab
स्वानुभूत्यनुरोधेन राज्ञो राजामृषा गृहे 2.1.295ab
स्वानुभूत्यनुसारेण प्रत्यङ्मात्रसतत्त्वकम् 1.4.384cd
स्वानुभूत्यनुसारेण यथोक्तोऽर्थोऽवसीयताम् 1.4.215ab
स्वानुभूत्यनुसारेण सर्वं सुस्थं भवेदतः 5.1.36cd
स्वानुभूत्यैव संसिद्धेर्नाज्ञातः खरशृङ्गवत् 1.4.296ab
स्वान्ते त्वगादयस्तद्वद्बुद्धौ च मनसस्तथा 2.4.329cd
स्वान्तोपाधिविशिष्टस्य ह्युपासनमथोच्यते 5.8.1cd
स्वापबोधाविमौ तस्य न तु तत्साक्षिणो दृशेः 4.3.905cd
स्वापराधात्तु मद्वाक्यं विरुद्धार्थं त्वमीक्षसे 2.4.447cd
स्वाप्नान्भोगांस्ततो भुङ्क्ते जाग्रद्भावनयाञ्जितः 4.3.449cd
स्वाप्नान्भोगानशेषेण भुक्त्वा स्वप्नक्रियाक्षये 2.1.330ab
स्वाभाविकं कर्म मृत्युर्विद्या शास्त्रीयमुच्यते 1.4.1765cd
स्वाभाविकः प्रपञ्चश्चेत्स निरोद्धुं न शक्यते SV 387ab
स्वाभाविकगुणध्वस्तौ रागाद्यागन्तुकात्मता 4.3.707ab
स्वाभाविकत्वं मा प्रापच्छोकादेरात्मसौख्यवत् 3.5.85ab
स्वाभाविकत्वादासुर्या भूयस्या सेनयार्दिताः 1.3.121ab

स्वाभाविकत्वाशङ्कायाः प्रतिषेधस्य सिद्धये 4.4.1327cd
स्वाभाविकात्स्वभावाच्च नित्यो नान्योऽस्ति कश्चन 4.4.309cd
स्वाभाविकासङ्गमृत्योरतिक्रान्तिः पृथक्फलम् 1.3.9cd
स्वाभाविकैकदोषोत्थो व्यवहार इहासुरः 1.3.112ab
स्वाभाविकोऽयं प्रलय इति पौराणिका जगुः 2.4.397ab
स्वाभाविक्यप्यविद्येयमनुभूत्यावभासिता SV 1088ab
स्वाभाविक्या कृतो मिथ्या शुक्त्यादौ रजतादिवत् 1.4.414cd
स्वाभासफलकारूढस्तदज्ञानजभूमिषु 1.3.53ab
स्वाभासभ्रमदोषेण तन्मयः पुरुषो मतः 2.3.85cd
स्वाभासवत्स्वयं साक्षाद्वियत्कुम्भादिगं यथा 4.3.94cd
स्वाभासवदविद्योत्थबुद्ध्यादिव्याप्तिविभ्रमात् 2.1.187ab
स्वाभासवर्त्मनैवास्ते जाग्रत्स्वप्नसुषुप्तिषु 4.3.1377ab
स्वाभासवर्त्मनैवैतत्स्वात्माज्ञानजभूमिषु 1.2.127ab
स्वाभासान्तः परोऽप्यात्मा ध्यायतीवेति वीक्ष्यते 4.3.416cd
स्वाभासान्तः स संमोहान्नामरूपात्मकोऽभवत् 1.4.1177cd
स्वाभासाविद्योपाधिः सन्साक्ष्यन्तर्यामितां व्रजेत् 1.4.151cd
स्वाभासैकसहायात्मा तदेव प्राविशद्धरिः 1.4.514cd
स्वाभासैर्बहुतामेति मनोबुद्ध्याद्युपाधिभिः 2.4.425cd
स्वाभिधेयावबोधस्य ह्या समाप्तेरियं यतः 1.5.131cd
स्वाभ्यस्तभावनातोऽस्य श्रुतकर्मानुरोधतः 4.4.176ab
स्वाभ्युपेतनयस्यैव त्यागः प्राप्नोत्यनीप्सितः SV 750ab
स्वाभ्यूह इति मा शङ्कीर्यतो मार्गद्वयेऽपि नः 6.2.40ab
स्वामिकर्मवशात्तच्च रूपं गृह्णाति दैवतम् 4.3.1225cd
स्वामिकोपप्रसादादिहृदयाकूतवेदनात् SV 489ab
स्वामिनो यदि वान्यस्य कर्म प्रत्येव च क्रिया 3.4.174ab
स्वामिन्येव यतः सर्वं समवैति क्रियाफलम् 4.3.1264ab
स्वामिमन्त्रर्त्विगग्न्यादि त्वभिपन्नं वशीकृतम् 3.1.18cd
स्वामी सन्न हि भृत्येन स्वामिनेव नियुज्यते SV 240ab
स्वाम्यर्थ एव चोत्तम्भस्तृप्तिरापूर उच्यते 1.3.256ab
स्वाराज्यमीप्सति भवांस्तदेव वसु देहि मे 2.4.61cd
स्वार्थं प्रत्येव विज्ञेयाः सदसत्त्वादिकल्पनाः 2.1.273ab
स्वार्थं प्रत्येव संसिद्धेः परार्थस्येह वस्तुनः 1.4.245ab

स्वार्थं प्रत्येव सर्वोऽपि परार्थोऽर्थः प्रसिध्यति 4.4.946ab
स्वार्थं फलमपेक्ष्यैते परार्थत्वात्तमो मते 1.3.360cd
स्वार्थं यत्प्रथते नित्यं जाग्रत्स्वप्नसुषुप्तिषु 4.3.340cd
स्वार्थं विज्ञापयिष्यामि विभज्यातः परा श्रुतिः 4.3.44cd
स्वार्थं सन्न परार्थस्य स्वातन्त्र्यात्स्याद्विशेषणम् 4.3.211ab
स्वार्थः प्रत्यक्तदर्थत्वात्सहेतोर्जगदात्मनः 2.5.64cd
स्वार्थचिन्मात्रभोक्तुश्च प्रात्यक्ष्यात्तद्विरोधिनः 4.3.434ab
स्वार्थदेशः परार्थोऽर्थः स्वप्नदर्शनवद्यतः 4.2.25ab
स्वार्थदेशः परार्थोऽर्थो विकल्पस्तेन स स्मृतः 1.4.301cd
स्वार्थमन्यानपेक्षं सच्चैतन्यं नाक्षमानगम् 4.3.242cd
स्वार्थमात्रावसायित्वं नोपास्तीनां प्रतीयते SV 330cd
स्वार्थमात्रावसायित्वे वाक्यार्थप्रत्ययः कुतः SV 603ab
स्वार्थमेव तु विज्ञानं मुक्तिमात्रफलं स्मृतम् 2.4.234cd
स्वार्थसाधनयत्नादीननपेक्ष्योत्सृजेद्यथा 2.4.303ab
स्वार्थस्तस्यां य आभाति स आत्मा बुद्धिवृत्तिदृक् 4.3.328cd
स्वार्थस्य ज्योतिषोऽभावे भावत्वायापि च क्षमम् 4.3.369cd
स्वार्थस्य प्रत्यगात्मत्वात्प्रत्यग्याथात्म्यतोऽपि च 4.4.950ab
स्वार्थस्यैवमुपायत्वमसत्यस्यात्मनीक्ष्यताम् 1.4.992cd
स्वार्थात्मज्योतिषैवातो भावाभावात्मतां जगत् 4.3.371ab
स्वार्थानन्यप्रमाणात्स्यात्प्रसिद्धिस्तमसस्तथा 1.4.272cd
स्वार्थासंत्यागमार्गेण नानासंसर्गबाधनात् 3.4.33ab
स्वार्थे च सा प्रमां कुर्वत्यमानं कथमुच्यते 2.1.571cd
स्वार्थे त्वहमद इति ह्युपस्थाने फलं भवेत् 5.16.74ab
स्वार्थेनाधिष्ठितं गच्छेत्पथि शाकटिकेन तत् 4.3.1914ab
स्वाविद्याविभवप्रसूतविपुलद्वैतप्रपञ्चाहित- SV 1a
स्वाश्रयत्वादभिन्नस्य कुतोऽस्य स्यात्पराश्रयः 1.6.73cd
स्वाश्रयेभ्यो यियासन्ति करणानि हृदीश्वरम् 4.4.18ab
स्वास्थ्यं प्रसन्नतैतस्मिन्सुषुप्ते भवतीत्यतः 4.3.976ab
स्वाहाकारादि नान्यत्र त्रय्याः संभाव्यते क्वचित् 5.10.2cd
स्वाहाकारावसानाः स्युर्मन्त्राः सर्वे यथोदिताः 6.3.23ab
स्वीकृत्यैव प्रसंख्यानं युक्तिर्वस्तुनि वर्तते SV 778cd
स्वीरणाच्छीततोयादेः सूर्यस्तेनासि घर्मदः 5.17.7cd

स्वेन भासेति च स्वप्ने सर्वकामादिवर्जितम् 4.4.478ab
स्वेनार्थेनाभिसंबन्धः सिद्धशब्दस्य यः सदा 4.4.714ab
स्वेनेति भासः प्रत्यक्चिदभिव्यक्तिकृतोऽभिदा 4.3.878cd
स्वेनैव ज्योतिषा स्वप्ने यथा तद्वदिहापि तत् 4.4.79cd
स्वेनैव ज्योतिषेत्युक्तं स्वयंज्योतिष्ट्वसिद्धये 4.4.478cd
स्वेन्द्रियादिलयः स्वापे स्वत एव न शास्त्रतः SV 388cd
स्वैः स्वैस्तानिन्द्रियासङ्गैः पाप्मभिस्त उपासृजन् 1.3.161cd
स्वोक्त्यैवापह्नुतेः कृत्स्नवस्तुनोऽतो न यत्यते 4.3.807ab
स्वोत्पत्तावेव विद्येयं हेत्वन्तरमपेक्षते 4.3.16ab
स्वोत्पत्तिव्यतिरेकेण ज्ञानकालोऽपि नेष्यते 1.4.457ab
स्वोत्सृष्टतोयधाराद्यैर्वैश्वरूप्यं रविर्यथा 1.4.354cd
स्वोपादानानरोधित्वात्केनचिन्नास्य संगतिः 4.3.415cd
स्वोपेयार्थप्रसिद्धौ च नोपायानामुपायता 2.4.311ab
हंसत्वमृषयः प्राहुरात्मनः पारदर्शिनः 4.3.938cd
हठो यदृच्छा नियतिः कारणत्वेन नाश्रिताः 3.2.150ab
हत्वाविद्यां धियैवेयात्तद्विष्णोः परमं पदम् SV 219cd
हन्तर्यसति हानोक्तिर्लक्ष्यते शिशुवक्तृका 1.2.41cd
हन्तेर्वेदं जहातेर्वाहरित्येतदिहेष्यते 5.7.3ab
हन्त्यात्मलाभमात्रेण न तदन्या तमोह्नुतिः 1.4.865cd
हरिर्ब्रह्मा पिनाकीति बहुधैकोऽपि गीयते 1.4.377cd
हरेरवयवेष्वेवं योज्याः कालादिदृष्टयः 1.1.2cd
ह वा इति प्रसिद्ध्यर्थं मुक्तिर्न ज्ञानतोऽन्यतः 1.4.1670cd
हविषा कृष्णवर्त्मेव भूय एवाभिवर्धते SV 346cd
हस्तपादादितश्छिन्नान्न मृतस्य पुनर्भवः 3.9.140cd
हस्तेनालभ्य तद्रेतः पश्चाच्चाप्यनुमन्त्रयेत् 6.4.20ab
हस्त्यृषभमिति चोक्त्या भण्यते गुरुदक्षिणा 4.1.30ab
हानिवृद्धिस्वभावेन कारणात्मैव वर्तते 3.8.64ab
हानिवृद्धिस्वभावेन वित्तं चाप्यत्र लक्ष्यते 1.5.209ab
हानिवृद्धी न तस्यातो धर्माधर्मैरसंगतेः 4.4.1001cd
हानेनाङ्गविकल्पानां नवानां संचयेन च 4.3.938ab
हिंसां न कुर्यात्तस्यापि किंत्वनारब्धहिंसनम् 1.5.212cd
हिंसाभिप्रवणं चेतः प्रायेण श्रेयसामपि 1.3.25ab

हिंसायाः प्रतिषिद्धत्वात्पशून्हन्यान्न तु स्वयम् 6.4.79cd

हिक्किकालक्षणं शब्दं मृतिकाल उपस्थिते 4.3.1921cd

हितं फलं प्रयच्छन्ति यस्मात्तस्माद्धिताः स्मृताः 2.1.327ab

हित्वा कर्माखिला व्यक्तीरविशेषात्मतां व्रजेत् 1.4.370cd

हित्वा धनं च मानं च लब्धेत्युक्तिः स्तुतिर्धियः 6.2.18cd

हित्वाध्यात्मपरिच्छेदं ततस्तं प्रतिपद्यते 1.3.234cd

हित्वाध्यात्मपरिच्छेदं दैवं बीजमतः परम् 1.3.352ab

हित्वा निद्रां प्रबुध्यन्ते यथेहापि तथात्मनि 4.4.697cd

हित्वा निद्रां प्रबुध्यन्ते सुषुप्ते बोधिताः परैः 1.4.861cd

हित्वा मोहोत्थमखिलं ब्रह्मैव ब्रह्म यात्यथ 2.1.521cd

हिमघर्माम्बुदानेन पुष्णातीदं यतो जगत् 5.17.6ab

हिमवत्प्रभृतीनां च कुतोऽन्तः संभवो हृदि 2.1.298cd

हिरण्मयस्ततो देवः स्वार्थेऽत्र मयडिष्यते 4.3.935cd

हिरण्यं ज्योतिरमृतं तन्मय्यावरणी शुभे 6.4.104ab

हिरण्यं ज्योतिरमृतं मण्डलेन तदात्मना 5.17.3ab

हिरण्यं ज्योतिर्विज्ञानं तावन्मात्रसतत्त्वकः 4.3.935ab

हिरण्यगर्भ एवात्मा यः परात्मेति गीयते 1.4.143cd

हिरण्यगर्भं यं प्राहुरुपादानं जगद्धियाम् 1.4.510cd

हिरण्यगर्भक्षेत्रज्ञं रसं केचित्प्रचक्षते 2.3.49ab

हिरण्यगर्भतत्त्वस्य जायमानस्य केशवात् 2.3.167ab

हिरण्यगर्भतां नीत्वा कृत्स्नमध्यात्मरूपकम् 1.4.1338ab

हिरण्यगर्भद्वारैव मुक्तिरित्यपि यद्वचः 1.4.1761ab

हिरण्यगर्भभेदानां भूतानां च पृथक्पृथक् 2.5.55ab

हिरण्यगर्भमात्मानं ततस्तत्कारणं बुधः 4.2.81cd

हिरण्यगर्भमिति च स्मार्तान्यपि वचांसि नः 1.4.147cd

हिरण्यगर्भं तं चापि प्राणात्मन्युपसंहरेत् 4.2.82cd

हिरण्यगर्भलिङ्गांशास्तथा पूर्वोक्तमूर्तयः 2.5.43cd

हिरण्यगर्भवत्किं वा निर्भेदस्येह भण्यते 4.3.1341cd

हिरण्यगर्भवद्यस्मात्क्रिम्यादेरपि संगतिः 1.4.1762ab

हिरण्यगर्भविज्ञानकर्मणोः प्रथमः किल 1.4.1708ab

हिरण्यगर्भे तं चापि सर्वकारण आत्मानि 4.2.79cd

हिरण्यगर्भो ब्रह्मात्र तथा ब्रह्मगिरोच्यते 4.3.1875cd

हिरण्यनिधिदृष्टान्तादिदमेव च दर्शितम् SV 295cd
हिरुक्स्थितिः कथं तस्य परमार्थात्मनाथवा 2.3.186cd
हीति हेतावतः प्राह तद्व्याख्यानाय चोत्तरः 1.3.292cd
हुतमेवं जगत्कृत्स्नं नातोऽन्यदवशिष्यते 1.5.74ab
हुतायामाहुतौ वेत्थ यतिथ्यां पुरुषाभिधाः 6.2.35cd
हुत्वा स्विष्टकृदन्तं तत्समापय्य यथोदितम् 6.4.85cd
हुत्वा हुत्वा च मन्थेऽथ संस्रवं प्रक्षिपेन्मुहुः 6.3.22cd
हृच्छब्देन च धीरेव तात्स्थ्यादत्राभिधीयते 4.3.328ab
हृत्सद्मन्युपसंहारो यथा स्यादिन्द्रियात्मनाम् 4.4.15cd
हृदयं नाम विज्ञानं मांसपेशी च भण्यते 4.4.395ab
हृदयं बुद्धिरालोकः सर्वं तेन हि पश्यति 3.9.49cd
हृदयं सत्यमित्यादिबहूपाधिसमाश्रयम् 5.16.1ab
हृदयसृतनाडीभिरित आत्मा निगच्छति 4.4.85cd
हृदयस्यैव धर्मास्ते शोककामादयो यतः 4.3.1373ab
हृदयाख्याक्षराणां च श्रुत्योपासनमुच्यते 5.3.5ef
हृदयाग्रप्रकाशेन निष्क्रान्तस्यापि देहतः 4.4.97ab
हृदयातिक्रमाद्यस्मात्तद्धर्माननतिवर्तते 4.3.1372ab
हृदयात्ता विनिष्क्रान्ता यथार्काद्रश्मयस्तथा 2.1.327cd
हृदयाद्युक्तनाडीभिः संदध्यात्सूर्यरश्मिभिः 4.2.80cd
हृदयाद्विप्रकीर्णाभिर्नाडीभिर्लिङ्गदेवताः 2.2.19ab
हृदयाश्रयणं तेषां विशेषणमिहोच्यते 4.4.399ab
हृदयाश्रयिकामेभ्य आत्मसंश्रयिणां यतः 4.4.398ab
हृदयाश्रयिणस्ते तु बाह्याः स्युर्बाह्यसंश्रयात् 4.4.397cd
हृदयाश्रयिणो येऽस्य न त्वात्मैकसमाश्रयाः 4.4.410ab
हृदयेन च संबन्धाद्दृश्यन्ते येन तेऽखिलाः 4.4.402ab
हृदयेनाभिसंबन्धाद्देवतात्र प्रजापतिः 1.3.323ab
हृदये ह्येव रूपाणि ध्यायतीवेति चापरम् 2.3.135ab
हृदयोत्पाद्यता नापि कामानामिह कीर्त्यते 4.4.428ab
हृदि नामादिसंहारं यत्र शाकल्य ऊचिवान् 5.3.3cd
हृदि येऽस्य श्रिताः कामाः प्रमुच्यन्ते त एव तु 4.4.394ab
हृदि श्रिता इति वचः कामधर्म्यब्रवीन्मनः 4.4.380ab
हृदि श्रिता इति वचस्तेषामवरुरुत्सया 4.4.384ef

हृदि श्रिता इति वचो नाश्रयान्तरवीक्षया 4.4.440ef
हृदि श्रिता इति ह्युक्तेर्न श्रुता कारणात्मता 4.4.428cd
हृदि श्रिता यतः कामाः प्रमुच्यन्तेऽखिलास्ततः 4.4.381cd
हृदि श्रिता यदा कामाः प्रमुच्यन्तेऽस्य देहिनः 4.4.403ab
हृदीत्याधारनिर्देशाद्धीस्था आत्मेति शङ्क्यते 4.3.329ab
हृद्गिरा मांसपेश्युक्ता तात्स्थ्याद्बुद्धिस्तु लक्ष्यते 5.3.3ab
हृद्यनाश्रितकामानां संभवादिष्टमेव तत् 4.4.484ab
हृद्याकाश इहात्मेति स्यादाकाशाप्ययत्वतः 3.2.128ab
हृद्याकाशात्प्रसृत्यात्मा नाडीभिः स्वप्नमश्नुते 2.1.250cd
हृद्याश्रितत्वं कामानां नन्वत्रोक्तं विशेषणम् 4.4.483ab
हृद्वियुक्तं तदा देहमद्युः श्वानो मृतं ध्रुवम् 3.9.85cd
हृल्लिङ्गप्रसृतो योंऽश उपभोगार्थमक्षिणि 4.4.59ab
हेतवोऽपि च तत्सिद्धौ श्रवणादिपुरःसराः 2.5.3ab
हेतुं व्यपेक्षते यत्नात्स्वरूपं हि न तद्भवेत् SV 48cd
हेतुतज्जाविभागेन कार्यकारणहेतुतः 1.6.21ab
हेतुतत्फलरूपेण मूर्तादेः संगतिर्मिथः 2.3.32cd
हेतुतद्वत्तया ज्ञेयामूर्तादेरपि संगतिः 2.3.33cd
हेतुतां प्रतिपद्यन्ते कर्माण्यपि विमुक्तये 4.4.972ab
हेतुत्वं लभते नापि तथैवावस्थितः क्वचित् 4.3.625ab
हेतुध्वस्तौ भवेद्ध्वस्तिरकार्याकारणेऽक्षरे 4.4.765cd
हेतुप्रतिज्ञयोः स्पष्टो विरोधः स्यात्तथा सति 4.3.602ab
हेतुमज्जनिमत्सर्वं कार्यत्वात्पटकुम्भवत् 1.2.33ab
हेतुमन्यं प्रपश्यामः कर्तृत्वादिप्रसिद्धये 4.3.1260cd
हेतुर्न तु तदस्तीति पश्येद्यद्वस्तु बोधवत् 4.3.1605cd
हेतुर्न हीतिवचनमुत्तरस्यापि चोत्तरम् 4.3.1504cd
हेतुश्चाभिहितोऽस्माभिः प्रवृत्तिर्न तु कारणम् 1.4.912cd
हेतुस्तत्रानुपायत्वमसत्यत्वं पुनर्न तु SV 897cd
हेतुस्तवाप्यनेकत्वमेकस्यापि प्रसज्यते 2.1.602cd
हेतुस्त्रय्यास्तु संत्यागे तमेतमिति वक्ष्यते 4.4.970cd
हेतुस्वरूपकार्याणां प्रकाशतमसोरिव 3.3.70ab
हेतुस्वरूपकार्याणि विरोधीनि परस्परम् 2.1.376ab

हेतुहेतुमदुक्त्यैतद्व्याख्येयं त्रयमात्मनि	3.5.84ab
हेतूक्तितः प्रतिज्ञायाः सिद्धार्थाया यदुत्तरम्	4.5.4ab
हेतूक्तिरथवातः स्यादुक्तवस्तुस्वभावतः	3.4.189ab
हेतूक्तिरविनाशित्वादित्युक्तार्थप्रसिद्धये	4.3.1502ab
हेतूक्तिरुत्तरो ग्रन्थस्तेषामित्यादिनोच्यते	1.6.11cd
हेतोः कार्यसमुत्पत्तेः सिद्धेः प्रागपि संविदः	3.4.118ab
हेतोः साधारणात्मत्वं यदानेकस्य तन्मतम्	4.3.748cd
हेतोर्निगमनं पश्चात्क्रियतेऽथोत्तरोक्तिभिः	2.5.13cd
हेत्वन्तरानपेक्षं सत्तदव्याकृतरूपकम्	1.4.387ab
हेत्वन्तरानपेक्षत्वादात्मत्वात्संनिधेः सदा	4.4.651cd
हेत्वन्तरानपेक्षस्तु प्रत्यग्ज्योतिरनुग्रहः	4.3.289cd
हेत्वन्तरासंभवोऽतो दुर्ज्ञानः संभवाद्भवेत्	SV 92cd
हेत्वन्तरेऽनुमेये च किंचित्सामान्यगन्धतः	4.3.151ab
हेत्वन्तरोपदेशो वा पदनीयत्व आत्मनः	1.4.1027ab
हेत्वर्थ इतिशब्दोऽयं बहुशब्दजिहासया	4.4.967ab
हेत्वर्थे चाथशब्दोऽयं हेत्वर्थप्रकृतत्वतः	4.4.388ab
हेत्वर्थे त्वथशब्दोऽयं हेतूक्तेः प्रकृतत्वतः	4.4.515ab
हेत्वर्थो वाथशब्दोऽयं यस्मात्संक्रामितक्रतुः	1.5.326cd
हेत्वविद्यासमुच्छित्तेर्देहं चानुविशेत्कुतः	4.4.615cd
हे दस्रावपि कक्ष्यं यत्प्रत्यग्याथात्म्यदर्शनम्	2.5.113cd
हेमन्तेऽनुपलब्धत्वाद्ग्रीष्मधर्मापनिह्नुतिः	4.3.571ab
हेमादि विस्मृतं किंचित्करस्थमपि लिप्सते	SV 885cd
हैरण्यगर्भमात्मेति बौद्धं ज्ञानं तदा भवेत्	4.4.719cd
हैरण्यगर्भे तत्त्वज्ञो वैराजे च शरीरके	1.6.43ab
होतारः परिणामेषु तथैवोत्तरभूमिषु	6.2.85cd
होतारस्तत्र तत्र स्युः कर्मज्ञानानुरोधतः	6.2.84cd
होत्रर्त्विजाग्निना वाचा मृत्योराप्तेर्विमुच्यते	3.1.21ab
ह्रस्वं नैव यतोऽह्रस्वं नापि दीर्घं यतोऽक्षरम्	3.8.93cd
ह्रासवृद्धिप्रबन्धेन यथेदं वर्तते जगत्	4.3.868cd
ह्रासवृद्ध्योर्यतः कर्ता वायुश्चन्द्रमसस्ततः	3.1.36ab
ह्रियमाणे पशौ तीव्रं दुःखं समुपजायते	1.4.1576cd

ह्रियमाणे महद्दुःखं तस्मादेषां तदप्रियम् 1.4.1578ab
ह्रीतो रोषाच्च तद्वाक्यं वसत्यर्थमुदीरितम् 6.2.45ab

****